Human Sexuality
in a World of Diversity

- Are there studies that show the effects of being raised by homosexual parents? (p. 314)
- How often do pregnant women have to go to the doctor during the pregnancy, assuming everything is going okay, and what kinds of things happen during the visits? (p. 333)
- What can caffeine do to a baby when it's inside the mom? (p. 344)
- What triggers childbirth? Why does it trigger premature births? (p. 347)
- If my druggist refuses to fill my birth control pills, can I sue? (p. 366)
- Are there negative effects from taking birth control pills for too long? (p. 370)
- Why is it taking so long for male birth control pills to be available? What are the side effects? How would they work? (p. 371)
- If I use two condoms, does it give double protection? (p. 382)
- I was watching *Grey's Anatomy* the other night, and a patient wanted to have her tubes tied without her husband knowing. Is there a law that says that spouses need to talk to each other before a procedure is done? (p. 390)
- Will having an abortion make it difficult for me to get pregnant again? (p. 399)
- Can you buy that abortion pill online or over the counter? (p. 400)
- I had an abortion. Should I tell the father—even if we are not seeing each other? (p. 403)
- What are the effects of children observing their parents in the nude/showering together/having sex? Is it different in a stepfamily situation? (p. 410)
- Will masturbating earlier make you develop sooner? (p. 412)
- How can you tell the difference between normal childhood sex play or exploration and signs of sexual abuse? (p. 413)
- How can I keep my partner interested in sex? We have been together for five years. (p. 452)
- Is there any credibility to the "seven-year itch" idea—that partners will tend to stray every seven years? (p. 456)
- Is it possible to stay in an unhappy marriage and not have it affect children in the family? (p. 459)
- I caught my grandparents having sex. Now they will not talk to me, and they act differently toward me. What can I do? (p. 463)
- How do individuals who are mentally retarded ever truly consent to sexual activity? (p. 467)
- I do not feel sexual during times when I have a lot of schoolwork. Is that normal? (p. 474)
- What does "prude" mean? Is this considered a sexual dysfunction? (p. 475)
- I was molested as a child, and the thought of sex does not interest me. What can I do about this? (p. 477)
- Do women find a man ejaculating disgusting? Is that a dysfunction? (p. 479)
- I know that Viagra helps put more blood into the penis—but how does it do that? How does it actually work? (p. 494)
- If you have a cold sore on your lips or mouth (oral herpes), can you give your partner genital herpes through oral sex? (p. 536)
- Do some infections just naturally go away? (p. 540)
- Can you get crabs if you are shaved? (p. 541)
- Isn't it true that if you get treated for an STI once, you have immunity to it? (p. 542)
- Is having sex underwater considered atypical? Can it cause infection? (p. 553)
- At what point does a sexual interest become a fetish? (p. 555)
- Do people get genital piercings for sexual pleasure? (p. 564)
- Are there cultures that allow sex with animals/pets? (p. 568)
- Do you think it's unhealthy to try to fulfill wild, way-out, socially unacceptable fantasies, such as group sex? (p. 575)
- What is the statute of limitations on pressing rape charges? (p. 583)
- Can a prostitute be raped? (p. 589)
- Isn't there a dye you can put into your drink so you know if someone has given you a date-rape drug? (p. 591)
- A friend of mine was raped at a party last semester. I took her to the hospital, but she refused to report it to the police. How can I convince her? (p. 595)
- Does being sexually abused as a child mean someone will sexually abuse their children? (p. 606)
- Isn't S&M the same thing as sexual coercion? How does one know the difference? (p. 613)
- What does the term *fluffer* mean? (p. 622)
- I worked as a dancer and sometimes had sex for money. Should I tell my present boyfriend (who I might marry), who does not know my past? (p. 623)
- Do women use male prostitutes at all? Do they use female prostitutes? (p. 629)
- How much do "porn stars" get paid? And prostitutes? How many times in a day do they need to "perform"? Does sex become just a job for them? (p. 634)
- How do you know if you are addicted to pornography? (p. 638)

Human Sexuality in a World of Diversity

SEVENTH EDITION

Spencer A. Rathus
New York University

Jeffrey S. Nevid
St. John's University

Lois Fichner-Rathus
The College of New Jersey

PEARSON

Boston • New York • San Francisco
Mexico City • Montreal • Toronto • London • Madrid • Munich • Paris
Hong Kong • Singapore • Tokyo • Cape Town • Sydney

Senior Series Editor: Stephen Frail
Editorial Assistant: Mary K. Tucker
Executive Marketing Manager: Karen Natale
Senior Production Administrator: Donna Simons
Cover Administrator: Linda Knowles
Composition Buyer: Linda Cox
Manufacturing Buyer: JoAnne Sweeney
Editorial Production Service: Publishers' Design and Production Services, Inc.
Electronic Composition: Publishers' Design and Production Services, Inc.
Interior Design: Carolyn Deacy
Photo Research: Laurie Frankenthaler
Cover Design: Suzanne Harbison

For related titles and support materials, visit our online catalog at
www.ablongman.com

ISBN-10: 0-205-53291-8
ISBN-13: 978-0-205-53291-9

Library of Congress Cataloging-in-Publication Data

Rathus, Spencer A.
    Human sexuality in a world of diversity / Spencer A. Rathus, Jeffrey S. Nevid,
Lois Fichner-Rathus.—7th ed.
        p.   cm.
    Includes bibliographical references and index.
    ISBN 0-205-53291-8 (alk. paper)
    1. Sex.   I. Nevid, Jeffrey S.   II. Fichner-Rathus, Lois, 1953–   III. Title.

HQ21.R23 2008
306.7—dc22   2007015750

Photo credits appear on page 699, which constitutes an extension of the copyright
page.

Printed in the United States of America

10 9 8 7 6 5 4 3 2   RRD-OH   11 10 09 08 07

Dedicated with love to our children Taylor Lane Rathus and Michael Zev Nevid, who were born at the time the first edition of this book was written.

Brief Contents

Contents

4 Male Sexual Anatomy and Physiology 102

15 Sexual Dysfunctions 470

16 Sexually Transmitted Infections 506

18 Sexual Coercion 578

Feature Boxes

The World of Human Sexuality

A Closer Look

Self-Assessment

Preface

There are more things in heaven and earth, Horatio,
Than are dreamt of in your philosophy.

—Shakespeare, *Hamlet*

There are indeed more kinds of people in this world, and more ways in which people experience their sexuality, than most of us might imagine. Human sexuality may be intimately related to human biology, but it is embedded within the fabric of human cultures and societies. The approach that has separated *Human Sexuality in a World of Diversity* from other human sexuality textbooks is its full embrace of the richness of human diversity.

Let us first consider what has changed in the seventh edition, including the new pedagogical package that further enhances learning and retention. Then we will consider the themes of the text, which represent continuing concerns in the realm of human sexuality. We will also discuss the features that give the book its vitality and motivational force.

What's New in the Seventh Edition

The seventh edition of *Human Sexuality in a World of Diversity* embodies many exciting changes—changes that reflect the rapid developments in the behavioral and social sciences, and in biology and medicine. In addition to what is listed in the following sections, there are literally hundreds of new references throughout the text that reflect the newest research in the field of human sexuality. No part of the text has been left untouched by change. The following are just a few examples of updates within chapters.

Chapter 1
New chapter-opening vignette on sexuality on the islands of Mangaia and Inis Beag
New "A Closer Look: Thinking Critically about Sexual Advice on the Internet: Are There Any Quick Fixes?"
New section on gay activism
New discussion, within "Sociological Perspectives," of culture wars within a larger society, as within the United States and within France
New "The World of Human Sexuality" feature ("The New Berlin Wall") about the "honor killing" of a young Muslim woman in Western Europe

New section on feminist theory
New section on queer theory

Chapter 2
New chapter-opening vignette on a humorous misunderstanding that occurred during the interviews for the classic Kinsey Reports
Revised discussion of the Kinsey continuum of heterosexuality–homosexuality
New coverage of the National Survey of Family Growth
Extended coverage of the research of Gail Wyatt
New coverage of Katherine Frank's participant–observation research when she worked as a stripper
New "The World of Human Sexuality: The Tuskegee Syphilis Study: Ethics Turned Upside Down in Research Gone Wrong"

Chapter 3
New chapter-opening vignette on female genital mutilation
Revised coverage of the G-spot in "A Closer Look: The G Spot and Female Ejaculation: Sexual Realities or Gynecological Myths?"
Updated coverage of cervical cancer, focusing on the role of human papillomavirus (HPV) and the availability of a vaccine for HPV
Updated coverage of endometrial cancer
Updated coverage of ovarian cancer
Updated coverage of the utility of mammography and the risk factors for breast cancer
Updated coverage of the controversy about hormone replacement therapy

Chapter 4
New chapter-opening vignette on Koro and other culture-bound syndromes
Updated information on andropause
Updated information on testicular cancer
Updated coverage of prostate cancer

Chapter 5
New chapter-opening vignette on pheromones secreted by certain plants and how they mimic pheromones secreted by bees
Revised "A Closer Look: The Search for a 'Magic' Love Potion: On the Threshold?"
New section titled "Attraction to—or Dislike of—Body Odors of Heterosexual Males and Females versus Gay Males and Lesbians"
Updated information on binge drinking and risky sexual behavior
Updated information on the effects of marijuana on sexual response
Updated information on the effects of ovariectomy on sexual response

Chapter 6
New chapter-opening vignette on a transsexual's letter to her parents
New discussion of Turner syndrome
Updated discussion in "Boys Who Are Reared as Girls"
New discussion of homosexual transsexuals
Revised section on outcomes of sex reassignment
New "The World of Human Sexuality: Third Gender/Third Sex," including topics such as hermaphrodites; the Hijra of south central Asia; Thai "ladyboys"; lesbian, gay, bisexual, transgender communities; and the "two spirits" of the Native Americans

New information on women entering fields in science and professions formerly dominated by men

Chapter 7

New discussion of lesbians' preferences based on waist-to-hip ratio

New research on the phase of the menstrual cycle and preference for voice quality in males

New reference to the attraction–similarity hypothesis

New neurological research on effects of romantic love on the brain ("A Closer Look: Watching New Love as It Sears the Brain")

New neurobiological research on love concerning the roles of monoamines, neuropeptides, oxytocin, vasopressin, and other substances

Chapter 8

New "A Closer Look: They Say You Can't Hurry Love . . . But How about Speed Dating?"

New research on self-disclosure in cyberspace

New research on jealousy and evolutionary theory in the section titled "Lack of Sex Differences in Responses to Affairs among Gay Males and Lesbians"

New information on satisfaction in "Relationships between Heterosexuals, Gay Males, Lesbians, Bisexuals, and Transgendered Individuals"

Chapter 9

New chapter-opening vignette on Rachel Maines's research as reported in *The Technology of Orgasm: "Hysteria," the Vibrator, and Women's Sexual Satisfaction*

Amplified history of attitudes toward masturbation and how they influenced the medical community

New cross-cultural research on foreplay

Updated information on anal intercourse

A challenging look at new research that purports to demonstrate the superiority of penile–vaginal intercourse over masturbation ("A Closer Look: The Brody Studies on the Effects of Masturbation versus Penile–Vaginal Intercourse: Time for Some Critical Thinking")

New section titled "Sexual Fantasies of Lesbian, Gay, and Bisexual (LGB) Individuals"

Chapter 10

New chapter-opening vignette about the movie *Brokeback Mountain*

Updated definitions of terms involved in sexual orientation, including *gender identity, heterosexual,* and *homosexual*

Updated discussion of classification of sexual orientation, including a possible sex difference

New research by Chivers and Bailey that would appear to support the view that women's sexual orientations are more flexible than men's

Updated information on contemporary attitudes toward gay males and lesbians, and toward gay marriage and civil unions

New section titled "Mexican American Attitudes toward Gay Males and Lesbians"

New research on the neurophysiology of sexual orientation ("A Closer Look: Pheromones and Sexual Orientation")

Updated information on the psychological and social adjustment of gay males and lesbians

New feature on gay people who enter, and many who remain in, male–female marriages ("A Closer Look: Many Couples Must Negotiate Terms of 'Brokeback' Marriages"

Chapter 11

Updated information on preimplantation genetic diagnosis for sex selection

Updated statistics on fertility and infertility

Updated information on drinking during pregnancy and risks to the fetus

Updated information on smoking during pregnancy and risks to the fetus

Updated information on C-section, including women's use of a method to time delivery of their child

New feature that stresses the connection between empowerment of women and low rates of maternal and infant mortality ("The World of Human Sexuality: Maternal and Infant Mortality around the World")

Updated information on "baby blues" and more severe postpartum-onset mood disorders

Updated information on breast-feeding versus bottle feeding

Chapter 12

New information on Seasonale, Seasonique, and Lybrel

New information on Plan B

New information on the contraceptive patch

New information on injectable contraceptives—Lunelle and Depo-Provera

New information on American's attitudes toward abortion, Roe v. Wade, and the selection of Supreme Court justices, as reported in the new "A Closer Look: The Abortion Battle: A Nation Divided?"

Updated "A Closer Look: The Battle over Partial-Birth Abortion"

Chapter 13

New chapter-opening vignette about a woman's recollections about the fantasized sex lives of her Barbie dolls

New research on "co-sleeping"

Updated information on adolescents and sex from the National Survey of Family Growth

New "The World of Human Sexuality: Teen Sex Is Common Worldwide," analyzing behavior in 30 countries and suggesting that sex education decreases the incidence of unwanted pregnancy

Chapter 14

New chapter-opening vignette on the HBO series *Big Love*

Updated statistics on singles and single-mother family groups

Updated figures on cohabitation and marriage

New feature ("A Closer Look: Is Marriage in Trouble?") that points out that fewer and fewer young people see marriage as being "very important" for people who are going to have a child together

New section on gay marriage

Updated information on homogamy in marriage

New feature ("A Closer Look: From Tinseltown to Splitsville: Just Do the Math") that is a somewhat less than serious diversion that derives a formula for predicting the duration of marriages among the "glitterati"—couples such as Brangelina, TomKat, Britney Spears and Kevin Federline, and so on

New, timely section titled "Life in Blended Families: His, Hers, Theirs, and . . ."
New coverage of the sex lives of people with multiple sclerosis

Chapter 15
Updated challenge of the concept of low sexual desire
Updated challenge of whether dyspareunia is a sexual dysfunction or whether it belongs in the American Psychiatric Association's *Diagnostic and Statistical Manual of Mental Disorders*
Updated information on the incidence of erectile disorder
New research on the possible role of low tactile sensitivity in sexual arousal disorder
New, timely section titled "A Special Warning about SSRIs and Sexual Response" that points out that many people find that they continue to have problems becoming sexually aroused even after they discontinue using selective serotonin reuptake inhibitors (SSRIs)
New feature ("A Closer Look: The Search for the Female Equivalent of Viagra") on the medicalization of sex therapy approaches for women

Chapter 16
Updated facts and figures on the incidence of sexually transmitted infections (STIs)
Updated information on the availability of vaccines for STIs
New United Nations AIDS global map of the HIV/AIDS epidemic
New feature ("A Closer Look: Is Kissing Safe?") that refers to HIV/AIDS
New coverage of Atripla, the three-in-one pill for HIV/AIDS

Chapter 17
New chapter-opening vignette on subway riders who contend with exhibitionists and mashers
Updated research on the paraphilias
New coverage of chat scatophilia
New "A Closer Look: Say Cheese, You Sleaze! Cam-Phone Gals Snap Subway Gropers"

Chapter 18
New chapter-opening vignette about Justin Berry and the Justice Department's investigation of the men who victimized him online when he was underage
New coverage of the cases of Pamela Rogers, Debra LaFave, Sandra Beth Geisel, Lisa Lynette Clark, Silvia Johnson, and Mark Foley
New "The World of Human Sexuality: Pakistan's War of Terror on Rape Victims"
New "A Closer Look: 'Rophies'—The Date Rape Drug"
New "A Closer Look: *Desperate Housewives*' Star Teri Hatcher Reveals History of Childhood Sexual Abuse"
New "A Closer Look: The Siren Song of Sex with Boys"
New section titled "Sexual Harassment with Victims from Minority Groups"

Chapter 19
New "A Closer Look: 'Prostitution' or 'Sex Work'? What's in a Name?"
New "The World of Human Sexuality: A Woman without Importance: Sex Slavery in Pakistan"
New "The World of Human Sexuality: The West Gets Wilder—A Brothel for Women"
New "A Closer Look: Porn in Your Pocket?"

New coverage of snuff films
New coverage of regulation of the adult film industry
New "The World of Human Sexuality: Feminists and Antipornography Campaigns"
Expanded coverage of addiction to online pornography (cybersex)

PQ4R—An Enhanced Pedagogical Package

The PQ4R method remains a strong pedagogcal tool in the seventh edition. The method stimulates students to engage subject matter actively by being proactive rather than reactive. PQ4R stands for *preview, question, read, reflect, review,* and *recite*—a method that is related to the work of educational psychologist Francis P. Robinson. PQ4R is more than the standard built-in study guide. It goes well beyond the isolated questions and exercises that are found in many textbooks. It is an integral part of every chapter. It flows throughout every chapter. It begins and ends every chapter, and it accompanies the student page by page.

Preview Previewing the material helps shape students' expectations. It enables them to create mental templates or "advance organizers" into which they categorize the subject matter. Each chapter of the seventh edition of *Human Sexuality in a World of Diversity* previews the subject matter with a "Truth/Fiction?" section and a chapter preview. The "Truth/Fiction?" items stimulate students to delve into the subject matter by challenging folklore and common sense (which is often common nonsense). The chapter preview outlines the material in the chapter, creating mental categories that guide students' reading.

Question Devising questions about the subject matter is another feature of the PQ4R method. Thinking about questions gives students goals: They attend class or read the text to answer those questions. Questions are placed in all primary sections of the text to help students use the PQ4R method most effectively. These questions appear in the margins and are titled "Reflect" (application-type questions, described later) and "Critical Thinking" (questions that allow students to evaluate claims, research, and current events). When students see these questions throughout the text, they can pause and use the information they have just read to answer that question. If they wish, they can also write the questions and answers in their notebooks, as recommended by Robinson. In addition, each chapter contains several new SafeZone boxes that feature common questions collected from college students around the country, reflecting their concerns or misunderstandings about human sexuality. These questions are then answered in the text.

Read The first R in the PQ4R method stands for *read.* Although students will have to read for themselves, they are not alone. The text helps them by providing:

- truth/fiction sections that stimulate students by challenging common knowledge and folklore
- previews that help them organize the material
- presentation of the subject matter in clear, stimulating prose
- a running glossary that defines key terms in the margin of the text, near to where the terms appear in the text

- development of concepts in an orderly fashion so that new concepts build on previously presented concepts

Our writing style is "personal." It speaks directly to the student and uses humor and personal anecdotes to motivate and stimulate students. The style of *Human Sexuality in a World of Diversity* is as alive as the students it embraces, and it is intended to leave readers informed, interested, and refreshed.

Review   The second R in PQ4R stands for *review*. Regular reviews of the subject matter help students learn. Therefore, a review practice test opportunity is included at the end of every chapter. The reviews contain 15 multiple-choice items that foster active learning, retention, and critical thinking.

Reflect   The third R in PQ4R stands for *reflect*. Students learn more effectively when they reflect on what they are learning. Psychologists who study learning and memory refer to reflection on subject matter as *elaborative rehearsal.* One way for students to reflect on a subject is to relate it to things they already know, whether they be academic material or events in their own lives (Willoughby et al., 1994). Reflecting makes the material meaningful and easier to remember (Woloshyn et al., 1994). It also makes it more likely that students will be able to apply the information to their own lives (Kintsch, 1994). Through effective reflection, students can embed material firmly in their memory so that rote repetition is unnecessary. Thus, "Reflect" questions appear several times throughout each chapter.

Recite   The PQ4R method recommends that students regularly recite the answers to the questions aloud. Hence, the fourth R stands for *recite*. Reciting answers aloud helps students remember them by means of repetition, by stimulating students to produce concepts and ideas they have learned, and by associating them with spoken words and gestures (Dodson & Schacter, 2001). "Recite" sections are included at the end of each chapter. They help students summarize the material, but they are active summaries. They are written in question-and-answer format and include most of the key terms found in the text.

The Themes of *Human Sexuality in a World of Diversity*

The seventh edition of *Human Sexuality in a World of Diversity* builds upon the strong themes for which it has come to be known. Four themes are woven throughout the text:

1. The rich diversity found in gender roles, sexual attitudes, and sexual behaviors and customs
2. Critical thinking
3. Making responsible sexual decisions
4. Sexual health

Theme 1: Human Diversity Colleges and universities are undertaking the mission of broadening students' perspectives so that they will appreciate and tolerate human diversity. The United States is a nation of hundreds of different ethnic and religious groups, many of which endorse culturally distinctive beliefs about appropriate gender roles for men and women, and distinctive sexual practices and customs. Diversity is even greater within the global village of the world's nearly 200 nations and those nations' own subcultures. *Human Sexuality in a World of Diversity* incorporates a multicultural, multiethnic perspective that reflects the diversity of sexual experience in our society and around the world. Our book thereby broadens students' understanding of the range of cultural differences in sexual attitudes and behavior worldwide and within our own society. In addition, the "The World of Human Sexuality" feature highlights the rich variety of human sexual customs and practices in our own society and in others around the world. Discussion of diversity encourages respect for people who hold diverse beliefs and attitudes. We also encourage students to question what is deemed appropriate for women and men in terms of social roles and sexual conduct in light of cultural traditions and standards.

Theme 2: Critical Thinking Colleges and universities in the new millennium are also encouraging students to become critical thinkers. Today's students are so inundated with information about gender and sexuality that it can be difficult to sort truth from fiction. Not only do politicians, theologians, and community leaders influence our gender- and sex-related attitudes and behaviors, but newspapers, TV programs, and other media also brim with features about gender roles and issues concerning human sexuality.

Critical thinking means being skeptical of information that is presented in print or on the Internet, or uttered by authority figures or celebrities. Critical thinking requires thoughtful analysis and probing of the claims and arguments of others in light of evidence. Moreover, it requires a willingness to challenge conventional wisdom and common knowledge that many of us take for granted. It means scrutinizing definitions of terms, evaluating the premises or assumptions that underlie arguments, and examining the logic of arguments.

Throughout this book we raise issues that demand critical thinking throughout each chapter. These issues are intended to stimulate student interest in analyzing and evaluating their beliefs and attitudes toward gender roles and sexuality in light of the accumulated scientific evidence. Moreover, this edition fosters critical thinking through a section called "Thinking Critically about Human Sexuality," in Chapter 1, and by including several "Critical Thinking" questions throughout each chapter.

Theme 3: Responsible Sexual Decision Making We also encourage students to make responsible sexual decisions. There are psychological and physical dangers in "going with the flow" or being passive about our sexuality. Of course we do not encourage students to be sexually active (such a decision is personal). On the other hand we do encourage students to make their own sexual decisions actively, on the basis of accurate information.

Decision making is deeply intertwined with our sexual experiences. For example, we need to decide

- whom to date, and how and when to become sexually intimate
- whether to practice contraception and which methods to use
- how we will protect ourselves against HIV/AIDS and other STIs

Responsible sexual decision making is based not only on acquiring accurate information, but also on carefully evaluating this information in the light of one's own moral values. We encourage students always to consider their own values, needs, and interests, rather than going along with the crowd or merely acceding to the wishes or demands of their partners. Throughout the text we provide students with the information they need to make responsible decisions about their physical health, the gender roles they will enact, sexual practices, birth control, and prevention of STIs.

Theme 4: Sexual Health   *Human Sexuality in a World of Diversity* places a strong emphasis on issues relating to sexual health, including extensive coverage of such topics as HIV/AIDS and other STIs, innovations in contraception and reproductive technologies, breast cancer, menstrual distress, sex and disabilities, and diseases that affect the reproductive tract. The text encourages students to take an active—in fact, a proactive—role in health promotion. For example, it includes exercises and features that help students examine their bodies for abnormalities, reduce the risk of HIV infection, and cope with menstrual discomfort.

Features

Like earlier editions, the seventh edition of *Human Sexuality in a World of Diversity* contains various features that stimulate student interest and enhance understanding.

New! SafeZone   What do students know about human sexuality? What are they too embarrassed to ask of professors, peers, or parents? This new feature highlights questions, collected from college students from across the country, on any human sexuality topic concerning them—big or small. We then answer their questions. Sample questions include the following:

- One of my breasts is bigger than the other. Is this normal?

- How do you tell someone the relationship is over?

- How can I keep my partner interested in sex? We've been together for five years.

SafeZone

Q *If a boy plays with dolls when he's young, won't he be gay?*

A Complicated question and complicated answer: The politically correct answer is no, suggesting that choices of toys in childhood have no implications for sexual orientation, but the truth is that studies show that they might—as long as it is the child who is doing the choosing. In other words, many gay males report that as children they were drawn to "girls' toys." But there are also layers of values implied by your question, one of which is that it's bad to be gay or bad to give a young boy dolls as toys. We don't buy into either of these assumptions. Children will choose the toys they want, and forcing toys on them won't have much of an effect, except encouraging them to set aside the ones they don't want. Labels, by the way, are also interesting. For example, is not a toy soldier a "doll"?

The World of Human Sexuality   "The World of Human Sexuality" feature highlights the rich variety of human sexual customs and practices in our own society and in those throughout the world. Viewing human sexuality in a multicultural context helps students better understand how cultural beliefs, values, and attitudes can influence the expression of sexuality. Students may come to understand that their partners, who may not share the same ethnic or religious heritage as themselves, may feel differently than they do about sexual intimacy. Students will learn about cultural differences related to gender roles, sexual orientation, sexual jealousy, and premarital and extramarital sexual patterns.

THE WORLD OF Human Sexuality

Historical and Cross-Cultural Perspectives on Menstruation

In Peru, they speak of a "visit from Uncle Pepe," whereas in Samoa, menstruation is referred to as "the boogie man." One of the more common epithets for menstruation is "the curse." The Fulani of Upper Volta in Africa use a term that translates "to see dirt." Nationalism also rises to the call, with some nations blaming "the curse" on their historical enemies. The French once dubbed menstruation "the English," and its onset, "the English are coming."

It is a common folk belief that menstruating women are contaminated. Men may thus avoid contact with menstruating women. To prevent their contaminating others, menstruating women in tribal societies have been dispatched to huts on the fringe of the village. In the traditional Navajo culture, for instance, menstruating women would be consigned to huts that were set apart from other living quarters. In many Islamic societies, the men-

and killed crops. In 77 CE, the Roman historian Pliny summed up Roman misbeliefs about menstrual blood:

Contact with it turns new wine sour, crops touched by it become barren, grafts die, seeds in gardens are dried up, the fruit of trees falls off. . . . [The] edge of steel and the gleam of ivory are dulled, hives of bees die, even bronze and iron are at once seized by rust, and a horrible smell fills the air; to taste it drives dogs mad and infects their bites with an incurable poison.

Ancient societies—and some contemporary ones—have a limited understanding of bodily processes, or else they rely on tradition more than science. Science teaches that there is no medical basis for isolating menstruating women or avoiding sex during menstruation.

We might laugh at these misconceptions as folly and reflect on

A Closer Look

THINKING CRITICALLY ABOUT SEXUAL ADVICE ON THE INTERNET: ARE THERE ANY QUICK FIXES?

www.goaskalice.columbia.edu
www.advocatesforyouth.org
www.cdc.gov
www.oxygen.com
www.healthgate.com
www.lovingyou.com
www.unet.com

shy people, anxious people, confused people, and people with sexual problems surf the Internet in the hope of finding the website that will provide the answer. How can they evaluate the merits of these websites? How can they separate the helpful wheat from the useless and sometimes harmful chaff? Unfortunately, there are no easy

ness of a new sexual cure-all as easily as they can lie about sightings of Elvis Presley or UFOs.

How can you protect yourself? How could you know, for example, whether a website advertising the truth about STIs or offering Viagra at a special price is "the real thing"? How could you know that ethical, helping professionals would never promise that they can enable people to become sexually aroused and reach orgasm every time they make love?

Try some critical thinking:

1. **First, in this instance, do "judge the book by its cover."** Does the website look well organized? Do the links within the Web pages work? A credible website will look professional and will be well maintained.

2. **Ignore websites that make extravagant claims.** If it sounds too

---

A Closer Look The "A Closer Look" feature provides in-depth discussions of scientific techniques (for example, "Physiological Measures of Sexual Arousal") and skill-building exercises ("Breast Self-Examination," "Self-Examination of the Testes").

SELF-ASSESSMENT

Would You Tell an Interviewer the Truth on a Survey about Your Sexual Behavior? The Social-Desirability Scale

Researchers into human sexuality frequently encounter the problem of social desirability in their subjects. That is, many people being interviewed tell the researcher what they think he or she wants to hear, rather than divulge the truth about their sexual attitudes and behavior. The reason is often to earn the approval of the researcher. The tendency to respond in what people believe to be the socially desirable direction distorts the accuracy of the results in the case-study and survey methods.

What about you? Would you provide an interviewer with honest answers about your sexual attitudes and behaviors, or would you misrepresent your beliefs and behaviors to earn his or her approval?

You can complete the Social-Desirability Scale devised by Crowne and Marlowe to gain insight into whether you have a tendency to produce socially desirable responses.

DIRECTIONS Read each item and decide whether it is true (T) or false (F) for you. Try to work rapidly and answer each question by circling either T or F, then turn to the scoring key in the Appendix to interpret your answers.

T F 1. Before voting I thoroughly investigate the qualifications of all the candidates.

T F 2. I never hesitate to go out of my way to help someone in trouble.

T F 13. No matter who I'm talking to, I'm always a good listener.

T F 14. I can remember "playing sick" to get out of something.

T F 15. There have been occasions when I have taken advantage of someone.

T F 16. I'm always willing to admit it when I make a mistake.

T F 17. I always try to practice what I preach.

T F 18. I don't find it particularly difficult to get along with loud-mouthed, obnoxious people.

T F 19. I sometimes try to get even rather than forgive and forget.

T F 20. When I don't know something I don't mind at all admitting it.

T F 21. I am always courteous, even to people who are disagreeable.

T F 22. At times I have really insisted on having things my own way.

T F 23. There have been occasions when I felt like smashing things.

T F 24. I would never think of letting someone else be punished for my wrongdoings.

T F 25. I never resent being asked to return a favor.

T F 26. I have never been irked when people expressed ideas very different from my own.

Self-Assessments Self-scoring questionnaires stimulate students' interest and provide self-insight by helping them satisfy their curiosity about themselves. These questionnaires also enhance the relevance of the text to students' lives. Examples include "Would You Tell an Interviewer the Truth on a Survey about Your Sexual Behavior? The Social-Desirability Scale" and "Sternberg's Triangular Love Scale" (which may help students decide whether they are "in love" and, if so, just what type of love they are in). Scoring rubrics are found in an appendix at the end of the text.

TRUTH or fiction

Which of the following statements are true, and which are fiction? Look for the Truth/Fiction icons on the pages that follow to find the answers.

1. Scientific knowledge will enable you to make the right sexual decisions. T F

2. The sexual advice on the Internet is posted by respected authorities. T F

3. In ancient Greece, a mature man would take a sexual interest in an adolescent boy, often with the blessing of the boy's parents. T F

4. Throughout most of human history, women were considered to be the property of their husbands. T F

5. The production of sex manuals originated in modern times. T F

6. The graham cracker came into being as a means for helping young men control their sexual appetites. T F

7. Female redback spiders eat their mates after they have been inseminated. T F

8. In our dr[...] sticks, an[...] genitals.

Truth or Fiction Revisited: Although science provides us with information, it cannot make sexual decisions for us. In making sexual decisions, we also consider our **values.** The Declaration of Independence endorsed the fundamental values of "life, liberty, and the pursuit of happiness"—not a bad beginning. Our religious traditions also play a prominent role in shaping our values, as we see in the following section.

Sexuality and Values

[...]ociet[...]listi[...] It embraces a wide [...] of sexual atti[...] and [...]

Truth/Fiction? and Truth/Fiction? Revisited These unique chapter-opening devices motivate students by challenging common sense, stereotypes, and folklore. "Truth/Fiction? Revisited" sections are interspersed throughout each chapter and provide feedback to students regarding the accuracy of their assumptions in light of the evidence presented in the chapter.

Running Glossary   Research shows that most students do not make use of glossaries at the end of books. Searching for the meanings of terms is a difficult task and distracts them from the subject matter. Therefore, *Human Sexuality in a World of Diversity* has a running glossary. Key terms are in bold type in the text and are defined in the margins near to where they appear. Students can readily find the meanings of key terms without breaking their concentration on the flow of the material.

Recite   Recite sections help students summarize the material they have read, which is essential when it comes time to study. These active summaries are written in question-and-answer format, and include most of the key terms found in the text.

Review   A review practice test is included at the end of every chapter to give students the opportunity to test themselves before an in-class exam. These tests contain 15 multiple-choice items that foster active learning, retention, and critical thinking.

The Supplements Package

Human Sexuality in a World of Diversity presents instructors and students with a wide range of ancillaries and teaching aids.

Instructor's Supplements

Instructor's Manual The instructor's manual is a wonderful tool for classroom preparation and management. Each chapter includes an at-a-glance grid, with detailed pedagogical information that links to other available supplements; a comprehensive chapter outline; teaching objectives that cover major concepts within the chapter; a list of key terms; lecture material and student activities; a list of video and media sources; and an updated list of Web links. In addition, the instructor's manual includes a preface, a sample syllabus, and a comprehensive list of student handouts.

Test Bank A thoroughly revised and updated test bank helps students prepare for exams with challenging questions that target key concepts. Each chapter includes more than 100 questions, including multiple choice, true/false, short answer, and essay, each with an answer justification, page reference, a difficulty rating, and type

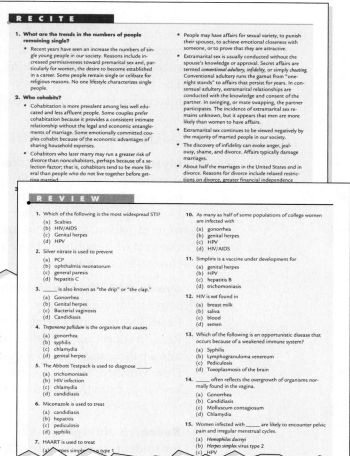

designation. This product is also available in TestGen 5.0 computerized version for ease in creating tests for the classroom.

PowerPoint™ Presentation Completely revised, the PowerPoint presentation is an exciting interactive tool for use in the classroom. Each chapter pairs key concepts with images from the textbook to reinforce student learning.

Transparencies for Human Sexuality These color acetates enhance classroom lecture and discussion. They include over 100 images from *Human Sexuality in a World of Diversity* and other sources.

VideoWorkshop for Human Sexuality *VideoWorkshop for Human Sexuality* contains 18 observational video segments specially selected to illustrate many of the theories and concepts discussed in the human sexuality course. The accompanying *Instructor's Teaching Guide* and CD-ROM and *Student Learning Guide* and CD-ROM are designed to help instructors and students make the most of this video resource, correlating it to the material in the *Human Sexuality in a World of Diversity* text and encouraging students to think critically about various aspects of human sexuality. The guide provides corresponding questions to test student understanding of the material as well as related websites to extend exploration of each topic.

Student Supplements

MyHumanSexualityKit, www.myhumansexualitykit.com A new online resource, MyHumanSexualityKit, provides a wealth of study tools for students looking to clarify and deepen their understanding of the foundations of human sexuality. Each chapter includes learning objectives, updated Web links for additional sources of information, animations and simulations, flash-card glossary terms, online practice tests with multiple-choice and true/false questions, and Allyn & Bacon's *Research Navigator* (see below).

Grade Aid Workbook with Practice Tests This is a comprehensive and interactive study guide filled with in-depth activities. Each chapter includes a "Before You Read" section, with a brief chapter summary and chapter learning objectives; "As You Read," a collection of demonstrations, activities, and exercises; "After You Read," containing three short practice quizzes and one comprehensive practice test; "When You Have Finished," with Web links for further information; and crossword puzzles using key terms from the text. An appendix includes answers to all practice tests and crossword puzzles.

Research Navigator Allyn & Bacon's new *Research Navigator* is the easiest way for students to start a research assignment or research paper. Complete with extensive help on the research process and three exclusive databases of credible and reliable source material (including EBSCO's ContentSelect Academic Journal Database, *New York Times* Search by Subject Archive, and "Best of the Web" Link Library), *Research Navigator* helps students quickly and efficiently make the most of their research time. The accompanying updated booklet contains a practical and to-the-point discussion of search engines, detailed information on evaluating online sources and citation guidelines for Web resources, Web links for human sexuality, and a complete guide to *Research Navigator*.

Study Cards for Human Sexuality Packed with useful information, Allyn & Bacon/Longman's Study Cards make studying easier, more efficient, and more enjoyable. Course information is distilled down to the basics, helping students quickly master the fundamentals, review a subject for understanding, or prepare for an exam.

Acknowledgments

We owe a great debt of gratitude to the many researchers and scholars whose contributions to the body of knowledge in the field of human sexuality are represented in these pages. Underscoring the interdisciplinary nature of the field, we have drawn on the work of scholars in such fields as psychology, sociology, medicine, anthropology, theology, and philosophy, to name a few. We are also indebted to the many researchers who have generously allowed us to quote from their work and reprint tabular material representing their findings. We also wish to thank our professional colleagues who reviewed this text at various stages in its development:

Michael Bailey, Northwestern University; Keith E. Davis, University of South Carolina; Randy D. Fisher, University of Central Florida; Kam Majer, Glendale Community College; Patricia A. Tackett, San Diego State University; Michael L. Vinson, College of Charleston; and Mark A. Yarhouse, Regent University.

In addition, the following instructors provided invaluable feedback in their reviews. Their comments have contributed substantially to this edition. Several reviewers also supplied anonymous SafeZone questions from their students, for which we are grateful:

Rebecca L. Bosek, University of Alaska, Anchorage; Nancy P. Daley, The University of Texas at Austin; Darci Dance, Linn–Benton Community College; Dale Doty, Monroe Community College; Mary E. Doyle, Arizona State University; Laura Duvall, Heartland Community College; Kathy Erickson, Pima Community College; Debra L. Golden, Grossmont College; Tawanda M. Greer, University of South Carolina; Chuck Hallock, University of Arizona; Mark L. Harmon, Reedley College–North Centers; Deborah Kindy, Sonoma State University; Amy Kolodji, Ithaca College; Holly Lewis, University of Houston–Downtown; Sonya Lott–Harrison, Community College of Philadelphia; Mary L. Meiners, San Diego Miramar College; Ramona M. Noland, Sam Houston State University; Jim Pond, Butler Community College; Rosalind Shorter, Jefferson Community College; Dana Stone, Virginia Tech; Mary Anne Watson, Metropolitan State College of Denver; Lester Wright, Western Michigan University; and Brian Zamboni, Health University of Minnesota.

Lastly, we want to thank our long-time buddy David McPatchell, Associate Professor of Psychology, Compton Community College—and his students—for providing the heart of many of this edition's personal stories, including SafeZone features. It just would not have been the same without him—and them.

Spencer A. Rathus
Jeffrey S. Nevid
Lois Fichner-Rathus

1

What Is Human Sexuality?

TRUTH? fiction

Which of the following statements are true, and which are fiction? Look for the Truth/Fiction icons on the pages that follow to find the answers.

1 Scientific knowledge will enable you to make the right sexual decisions.   T   F

2 The sexual advice on the Internet is posted by respected authorities.   T   F

3 In ancient Greece, a mature man would take a sexual interest in an adolescent boy, often with the blessing of the boy's parents.   T   F

4 Throughout most of human history, women were considered to be the property of their husbands.   T   F

5 The production of sex manuals originated in modern times.   T   F

6 The graham cracker came into being as a means for helping young men control their sexual appetites.   T   F

7 Female redback spiders eat their mates after they have been inseminated.   T   F

8 In our dreams, airplanes, bullets, snakes, sticks, and similar objects symbolize the male genitals.   T   F

Let's Google the islands off the coast of Europe and in the South Pacific—both in space and time. We go to Google Maps, find Inis Beag, click on Satellite, then click on 1955 (no, you can't really do this), and swoop in and in and in. . . .

And suddenly we find ourselves visiting two islands that are a world apart—sexually as well as geographically. Our first stop is Inis Beag, which lies in the Atlantic, off the misty coast of Ireland. Our second stop will be Mangaia, which lifts languidly out of the blue waters of the Pacific.

The distant satellite image shows Inis Beag as a green jewel, fertile and inviting. The residents of this community do not believe that it is normal for women to experience orgasm. Anthropologists reported that any woman who finds pleasure in sex—especially the intense waves of pleasure that can accompany orgasm—is viewed as deviant.

Premarital sex is all but unknown on Inis Beag. Prior to marriage, men and women socialize apart. Marriage comes late—usually in the middle 30s for men and the middle 20s for women. Mothers teach their daughters that they will have to submit to their husbands' animal cravings to obey God's injunction to "be fruitful and multiply."

But the women of Inis Beag need not be overly concerned about frequent sex, because the men of the island believe, erroneously, that sexual activity will drain their strength. Consequently, men avoid sex on the eve of sporting activity or strenuous work. Because of taboos against nudity, married couples have sex with their undergarments on. Intercourse takes place in the dark—literally as well as figuratively.

On to Mangaia. Mangaia is a pearl of an island. It lies on the other side of the world from Inis Beag—in more ways than one. From an early age, Mangaian boys and girls are encouraged to get in touch with their own sexuality through sexual play and masturbation. At about the age of 13, Mangaian boys are initiated into manhood by adults who instruct them in sexual techniques.

Mangaia. *Perhaps they didn't wear coconut shells, but a generation or so ago, sex on Mangaia was free-wheeling. In other places and at other times, sex has been seen as a necessary evil to follow God's command to "be fruitful and multiply."*

Boys practice their new techniques with girlfriends on secluded beaches or beneath the listing fronds of palms. They may visit girlfriends in huts where they sleep with their families. Parents often listen for their daughters to laugh and gasp so they will know their daughter has reached orgasm with a visiting young "sleepcrawler." Parents often pretend to be asleep so as not to interfere with courtship and impede their daughters' chances of finding a mate. Daughters may receive a nightly succession of sleepcrawlers and have multiple orgasms with each one.

Mangaians expressed concern when they learned that many Western women do not regularly experience orgasm. Orgasm is apparently universal among Mangaian women. Therefore, Mangaians could only assume that Western women suffered from some abnormality of the sex organs.

The residents of Inis Beag and Mangaia have vastly different attitudes toward sex. Their cultural settings influence their patterns of sexual behavior and the pleasure they gain—or fail to gain—from sex. Sex may be a natural function, but few natural functions have been influenced so strongly by religious and moral beliefs, cultural tradition, folklore, and superstition.

We are about to embark on the study of **human sexuality**. But why, you may wonder, do we need to study human sexuality? Isn't sex something to do rather than to talk about? Isn't sex a natural function? Don't we learn what we need to know from personal experience or from our parents or our friends?

Yes. And no. We can learn how our bodies respond to sexual stimulation—what turns us on and what turns us off—through personal experience. But personal experience teaches us little about the biology of sexual response and orgasm. Nor does experience inform us about the variations in sexual behavior that exist around the world, or in the neighborhood. Experience does not prepare us to recognize the signs of sexually transmitted infections (STIs) or to evaluate the risks of pregnancy. What many of us learned about sex from our parents can probably be summarized in a single word: "Don't." The information we received from our friends was probably riddled with exaggeration, misinformation, and even lies. Many young people today do receive accurate information through sex education courses in the schools, but they are usually taught about STIs and contraception, not about sexual techniques.

You may know more about human sexuality than your parents or grandparents did at your age, or do today. But how much do you really know? What, for example, happens inside your body when you are sexually aroused? What causes erection or vaginal lubrication? What factors determine sexual orientation? What are sexual dysfunctions and what causes them? How do our sexual responsiveness and interests change as we age? Can you contract an STI and not know it? If you have no symptoms, can you infect others?

These are just a few of the issues we will explore in this book. Much of the information we present was discovered in recent years. It is almost as new to us as it may be to you. One feature of this book, SafeZone, illustrates some of the questions and erroneous ideas many of us have about sex. In the SafeZone—where we answer real questions submitted by real students of ours and by students of other instructors—we will attempt to debunk common but erroneous ideas and explain some of the mysteries of human sexuality. An example follows.

SafeZone

Q *I am 17 years old, and the topic of sex in my family is nonexistent. How do I begin a conversation with my family?*

A Most people find it difficult to talk about sex. You'll find ideas for initiating conversations about sex with family members and other people throughout this text—conversations about contraception, STIs, and problems in relationships. In all cases, think about selecting a good time and place to talk. Consider asking permission to talk about a sensitive topic, as in "I know that talking about birth control is a no-no in this house, but I have some questions. Can we talk about them?" Or, "I could use some help. Can we talk about it?" People who care about you might just surprise you by accepting the challenge of trying to communicate about topics that can be off-limits. If you desire parental help, you might think about catching the more receptive parent when he or she is alone.

Human sexuality The ways in which we experience and express ourselves as sexual beings

Before we begin, let us define our subject.

What Is Human Sexuality?

What *is* human sexuality? This is not a trick question. Consider the meaning, or rather meanings, of the word *sex*. The word derives from Latin roots meaning "to cut or divide," signifying the division of organisms into male and female. One use of the term *sex*, then, refers to our anatomic sex, male or female. The words *sex* and *sexual* are also used to refer to anatomic structures, called *sex organs* or *sexual organs*, that play a role in reproduction or sexual pleasure. We may also speak of sex when referring to physical activities involving our sex organs for purposes of reproduction or pleasure: masturbation, hugging, kissing, sexual intercourse, and so on. Sex also relates to erotic feelings, experiences, or desires, such as sexual fantasies and thoughts, sexual urges, or feelings of sexual attraction to another person.

We usually make our usage of the term *sex* clear enough in our everyday speech. When we ask about the sex of a newborn, we are referring to anatomic sex. When we talk of "having sex," we generally mean the physical expression of erotic feelings. When we think of a "sex partner," we think of a person with whom we share a sexual experience. Many researchers reserve the word *sex* for reference to anatomic or biological categories, but prefer the word **gender** when they are referring to social or cultural categories. For example, one might say that reproductive anatomy appears to depend on the *sex* (not the *gender*) of the individual, but in so-called traditional societies, **gender roles** (not *sex roles*) are often seen as polar opposites.

Sexual behavior refers to activities that involve the body in the expression of erotic or affectionate feelings. Sexual behavior may or may not involve reproduction. *Masturbation*, for example, is performed for pleasure, not reproduction. Kissing, hugging, manual manipulation of the genitals, and oral–genital contact are all sexual behaviors that can provide sensual stimulation, even though they do not directly lead to reproduction. They may also be used as forms of foreplay, which leads to sexual intercourse (technically, **coitus**), which can lead to reproduction.

The term *human sexuality* refers to the ways in which we experience and express ourselves as sexual beings. Our awareness of ourselves as females or males is part of our sexuality, as is the capacity we have for erotic experiences and responses. Our knowledge of the gender roles in our culture also has a profound influence on us. Our sexuality is an essential part of ourselves, regardless of whether we engage in sexual intercourse or sexual fantasy, or even if we lose sensation in our genitals because of injury.

The Study of Human Sexuality

The study of human sexuality draws upon the scientific expertise of anthropologists, biologists, medical researchers, sociologists, and psychologists, to name but a few of the professional groups involved in the field. These disciplines all make contributions, because human sexuality reflects biological capabilities, psychological characteristics, and social and cultural influences. Biologists inform us about the physiological mechanisms of sexual arousal and response. Medical science teaches us about STIs and the biological bases of sexual dysfunctions. Psychologists examine how our sexual behavior and attitudes are shaped by perception, learning, thought, motivation and emotion, and personality. Sociocultural theorists examine relationships between sexual behavior and religion, race, and social class. Anthropologists focus on cross-cultural similarities and differences in sexual behavior. Scientists from many disciplines explore parallels between the sexual behavior of humans and other animals.

Gender The behavioral, cultural, or psychological traits typically associated with one sex

Gender roles Complex clusters of ways in which males and females are expected to behave within a given culture

Coitus (co-it-us or co-EET-us) Sexual intercourse

Truth or Fiction Revisited: Although science provides us with information, it cannot make sexual decisions for us. In making sexual decisions, we also consider our **values**. The Declaration of Independence endorsed the fundamental values of "life, liberty, and the pursuit of happiness"— not a bad beginning. Our religious traditions also play a prominent role in shaping our values, as we see in the following section.

Sexuality and Values

Our society is pluralistic. It embraces a wide range of sexual attitudes and values. Some readers may be liberal in their sexual views and behavior. Others may be conservative. Some are pro-choice on abortion; others, pro-life. Some approve of premarital sex for couples who know each other casually. Others hold the line at emotional commitment. Still others believe in waiting until marriage. People's sexual attitudes, experiences, and behaviors are shaped, to a large extent, by their cultural traditions and beliefs. Much of the variability in the ways in which we express our sexuality reflects cultural traditions and beliefs. They influence how, where, and with whom we become sexually involved.

But we also choose when to become sexually intimate with our partners. We decide whether we initiate sexual relations or wait for our partners to approach us. There are also decisions to be made about contraception and preventing STIs.

As noted by feminists, some of the variability in sexual behavior between males and females reflects power rather than choice (Saul, 2003). For example, throughout history and in many places, women have been considered the property of men. Even today, women are often "given away" by their fathers to their husbands.

Now let us consider the various value systems on which people draw when making sexual decisions.

Value Systems for Making Sexual Decisions

Making choices is deeply intertwined with our sexual experience. Although sex is a natural function, the ways in which we express our sexuality are matters of personal choice. We choose how, where, and with whom to become sexually involved. We face a wide array of sexual decisions: Whom should I date? When should my partner and I become sexually intimate? Should I initiate sexual relations or wait for my partner to approach me? Should my partner and I practice contraception? If so, which method? Should I use a condom to protect against STIs or insist that my partner does? Should I be tested for HIV (the virus that causes AIDS)? Should I insist that my partner be tested for HIV before we have sex?

What kinds of value systems do people have? We all have unique sets of moral values—as Americans, as members of one of America's hundreds of subcultures, as individuals. No single value system defines us all. Indeed, the world of diversity in which we live is a mosaic of different moral codes and cultural traditions and beliefs.

Value systems provide a framework for judging the moral acceptability of sexual options. We often approach sexual decisions by determining whether the choices we face are compatible with our moral values. Our value systems—our sexual standards—have many sources: parents, peers, religious training, ethnic subcultures, the larger culture, and our appraisal of all these influences. Value systems that provide a guiding framework to determine the moral acceptability of sexual choices include legalism, situational ethics, ethical relativism, hedonism, asceticism, utilitarianism, and rationalism.

Values The qualities in life that are deemed important or unimportant, right or wrong, desirable or undesirable

What Role Do Our Values Play in Making Responsible Sexual Decisions? *In making decisions about sexual behavior, people consider not only their knowledge of biology and sexuality but also their values. There are a variety of value systems, some of which based on religion and some which are not. This south central Asian couple are following ancient Hindu traditions in their marriage ceremony.*

LEGALISM   The legalistic approach formulates ethical behavior on the basis of a code of moral laws derived from an external source, such as the creed of a religion. The Bible contains many examples of the moral code of the Jewish and Christian religions. In the Book of Leviticus (20:10–17) in the Hebrew Bible we find many of the prohibitions against adultery, incest, sexual activity with people of one's own gender, and **bestiality**:

> And the man that committeth adultery with another man's wife, even he that committeth adultery with his neighbor's wife, both the adulterer and the adulteress shall surely be put to death. . . . And if a man lie with mankind, as with womankind, both of them have committed abomination: they shall surely be put to death. . . . And if a man lie with a beast, he shall surely be put to death; and ye shall slay the beast. . . . And if a man shall take his sister, . . . and see her nakedness, and she sees his nakedness: it is a shameful thing; and they shall be cut off in the sight of the children of their people. . . .

Leviticus also prohibits intercourse during menstruation.

Many religious followers today accept the moral codes of their religions as a matter of faith and commitment, not necessarily because they can logically or rationally derive them from contemporary societal needs. Some people find it reassuring to be informed by religious authorities or scripture that a certain course of action is right or wrong. Others, however, take a more liberal view. They say that the Bible was inspired by God, but that it was written or transcribed by fallible humans and is subject to various interpretations. They may also assert that the Bible reflects the social setting of the time in which it was written, not just divine inspiration. At a time of burgeoning population growth in many parts of the world, biblical injunctions to be fruitful and multiply may no longer be socially and environmentally sound. Prohibitions, such as that against coitus during menstruation, may have been based on prescientific perceptions of danger. Some people may thus view religious teachings as a general framework for decision making rather than as a set of absolute rules.

Bestiality Sexual relations between a person and an animal

SITUATIONAL ETHICS Episcopal theologian Joseph Fletcher (1966, 1967) argued that ethical decision making should be guided by genuine love for others rather than by rigid moral rules. Fletcher advocated that sexual decision making should be based on the context of the particular situation that the person faces. For this reason, his view is termed *situational ethics.* According to Fletcher, a Roman Catholic woman will have been taught that abortion is the taking of a human life. Her situation, however—her love for her existing family and her recognition of her limited resources for providing for another child—might influence her to decide in favor of an abortion.

Fletcher argues that rules for conduct should be flexible guidelines. "The situationist is prepared in any concrete case to suspend, ignore, or violate any principle if by doing so he can effect more good than by following it" (1966, p. 34).

ETHICAL RELATIVISM Ethical relativism assumes that diverse values are fundamental to human existence. Ethical relativists reject the idea that there is a single, correct moral view—about subjects as diverse as revealing clothing, masturbation, premarital sex, oral sex, anal sex, contraception, and abortion. One person may believe that premarital sex is unacceptable under any circumstances, whereas another may hold that "being in love" makes it acceptable. Still another person may believe that premarital sex is morally permissible without an emotional commitment between the partners. The ethical relativist believes that there is no objective way of justifying one set of moral values over another. In this view, the essence of human morality is to derive one's own principles and apply them according to one's own conscience. Opponents of ethical relativism argue that allowing people free rein to determine what is right or wrong may bring about social chaos and decay.

One form of ethical relativism is *cultural relativism.* From this perspective, what is right or wrong must be understood in terms of the cultural beliefs that affect sexual decision making. In some cultures, premarital sex is tolerated or even encouraged, whereas in others it is considered immoral. Cultural relativism, like ethical relativism, does not ascribe moral superiority to one cultural tradition over another.

HEDONISM The hedonist is guided by the pursuit of pleasure, not by whether a particular behavior is morally or situationally justified. "If it feels good, do it" expresses the hedonistic ethic. The hedonist believes that sexual desires, like hunger or thirst, do not invoke moral considerations.

ASCETICISM Religious celibates, such as Roman Catholic priests and Buddhist monks, choose *asceticism* (self-denial of material and sexual desires) to devote themselves to spiritual pursuits. Many ascetics in Eastern and Western religions seek to transcend physical and worldly desires.

SafeZone

Q *Is a person who takes a vow of chastity, such as a nun, no longer considered a sexual being?*

A A person who takes a vow of chastity only promises not to be a sexually *active* being. The reason usually involves dedication to values in which self-denial of sexual desires plays a key role, as in a religious tradition. But this doesn't mean that the person is no longer a sexual being. The person remains female or male, and continues to be subject to the sexual drives, sexual health issues, and cultural expectations that affect females and males.

UTILITARIANISM Ethical guidelines can be based on principles other than religious ones. The English philosopher John Stuart Mill (1806–1873) proposed an ethical system based on *utilitarianism*—the view that moral conduct is based on that which will bring about the greatest good for the greatest number. The utilitarian characterizes behavior as ethical when it does the greatest good and causes the least harm. This is not license. Utilitarians may come down hard in opposition to premarital sex and bearing children out of wedlock, for example, if they believe that these behavior patterns jeopardize a nation's health and social fabric. Mill's ethics require that we treat one another justly and honestly, because it serves the greater good for people to be true to their word and just in their dealings with others.

RATIONALISM Rationalism is the use of reason to determine a course of action. The rationalist believes that decisions should be based on intellect and reasoning, rather than emotions or strict obedience to a particular faith. The rationalist assesses the facts in a sexual situation and then logically weighs the consequences of courses of action to make a decision. The rationalist shares with the utilitarian the belief that reasoning can lead to ethical behavior. The rationalist is not bound, however, to the utilitarian code that makes choices on the basis of the greatest good for the greatest number. The utilitarian may decide, for example, to prolong an unhappy marriage because of the belief that the greater good (of the family and the community) is better served by maintaining an unhappy marriage than by dissolving it. The rationalist might decide that the personal consequences of continuing an unhappy marriage outweigh the consequences to the family or the community at large.

These ethical systems represent general frameworks of moral reasoning or pathways for judging the moral acceptability of sexual and nonsexual behavior. Although some of us may adopt one or another of these systems in their purest forms, others adopt a system of moral reasoning that involves some combination or variation of these ethical systems. Some also shift from one ethical system to another from time to time, sometimes reasoning legalistically and sometimes adopting a more flexible situational approach. Table 1.1 summarizes some of the value systems in use.

Many readers will not only be making sexual decisions, they will also be deciding what kind of value system to use when making these decisions. One tool they can use in deciding is critical thinking. The following section describes what is meant by critical thinking as it applies to issues concerning human sexuality.

REFLECT

Which value system or systems guide your ethical decision making? Is it one of those discussed in this chapter? How did you develop your system of values?

Thinking Critically about Human Sexuality

We are flooded with so much information about sex that it is difficult to separate truth from fiction. Newspapers, TV shows, popular books and magazines, and the Internet contain one feature after another about sex. Many of them contradict one another, contain half-truths, or draw unsupported conclusions.

Most of us also tend to assume that authority figures like doctors and government officials provide us with factual information and are qualified to make decisions that affect our lives. But when two doctors disagree on the need for a hysterectomy, or two officials disagree regarding whether condoms should be distributed in public schools, we wonder how both can be correct. Critical thinkers never say, "This is true because so-and-so says it is true."

TABLE 1.1

Value Systems for Making Sexual Decisions

System	Core Belief	Example
Legalism	Ethical behavior is derived from an external source, such as a religion.	The Old Testament contains prohibitions against adultery, incest, sexual activity with people of one's own sex, and bestiality.
Situational Ethics	Ethical decision making should be guided by the situation and by genuine love for others.	A woman who has been taught that abortion is the taking of a human life may find herself with limited resources and decide in favor of an abortion.
Ethical Relativism	There is no objective way of justifying one set of moral values over another.	Cohabitation is tolerated in some cultures but considered immoral in others.
Hedonism	Pursuit of pleasure is the guide.	Hedonists might argue that sexual desires, like hunger or thirst, do not involve moral considerations.
Asceticism	One denies sexual desires to devote oneself to spiritual pursuits.	Many ascetics in Western and Eastern religions seek to transcend physical and worldly desires.
Utilitarianism	Moral conduct brings about the greatest good for the greatest number.	We should be honest and just because it serves the greater good for people to be true to their word and to treat each other justly.
Rationalism	Sexual decisions should be based on intellect and reason, not blind obedience.	The rationalist might decide that the personal consequences of continuing an unhappy marriage outweigh the effects on the family or the community at large.

To help students evaluate claims, arguments, and widely held beliefs, most colleges encourage critical thinking. The core of critical thinking is skepticism—not taking things for granted. Critical thinking means being skeptical of things that are presented in print, uttered by authority figures or celebrities, or passed along by friends. Another aspect of critical thinking is thoughtful analysis and probing of claims and arguments. Critical thinking requires willingness to challenge the conventional wisdom and common knowledge that many of us take for granted. It means scrutinizing definitions of terms and evaluating the premises of arguments and their logic. It also means finding reasons to support your beliefs, rather than relying on feelings. When people think critically, they maintain open minds. They suspend their beliefs until they have obtained and evaluated the evidence.

Principles of Critical Thinking

Critical thinkers maintain a healthy skepticism. They examine definitions of terms, weigh premises, consider evidence, and decide whether arguments are valid and logical. Here are some principles of critical thinking:

1. *Be skeptical.* Politicians, religious leaders, and other authority figures attempt to convince you of their points of view. Even researchers and authors may hold certain biases. Accept no opinion as fact until you have personally weighed the evidence.
2. *Examine definitions of terms.* Some statements are true when a term is defined in one way but not in another. Consider the maxim "Love is blind." If love is defined as head-over-heels infatuation, there may be substance to the statement.

Who are the authority figures in your own life? Have others encouraged you to follow the demands of authority figures without examining them critically? How do you feel about this?

Infatuated people tend to idealize loved ones. However, if love is defined as deep caring and commitment based on a more realistic (if still somewhat slanted) appraisal of the loved one, then love is not so much blind as a bit nearsighted.

3. *Examine the assumptions or premises of arguments.* Consider the statement, "Abortion is murder." Webster's New World Dictionary defines murder as "the unlawful and malicious or premeditated killing of one human being by another." The statement is true, according to this dictionary, only if the victim is a human being (and if the act is unlawful and malicious or premeditated). Most pro-life advocates argue that embryos and fetuses are human beings. Most pro-choice advocates claim they are not. So the argument that abortion is murder rests in part on the premise that the embryo or fetus is a human being.

4. *Be cautious in drawing conclusions from evidence.* Recent research finds that teenagers who listen to rap, hip-hop, pop, and rock music with sexually explicit lyrics or lyrics that refer to women as sex objects are more likely to initiate sexual activity at early ages (Martino et al., 2006). The popular media seem obsessed with the idea that "dirty" songs instigate sex, and lots of it. However, teens who choose to dwell on these songs may differ in their values from those who do not, so that they not only spend hours with their iPods blasting sexual lyrics into their ears but they also choose to have sex at an early age. The evidence of a connection between listening to this music and having sex is open to various interpretations, which brings us to our next principle of critical thinking.

5. *Consider alternative interpretations of research evidence.* For example, teens who dwell on sexual song lyrics may also be more open to sexual activity because they are less traditional than teens who (literally) turn off these songs. This example shows that correlations between events do not necessarily reveal cause and effect.

6. *Consider the kinds of evidence upon which conclusions are based.* Some conclusions, even seemingly "scientific" conclusions, are based on anecdotes and personal endorsements. They are not founded on sound research.

7. *Do not oversimplify.* Consider the statement, "Homosexuality is inborn." There is some evidence that sexual orientation may involve inborn predispositions, such as genetic influences. However, biology is not destiny in human sexuality. Gay male, lesbian, and heterosexual sexual orientations appear to develop as the result of a complex interaction of biological and environmental factors.

8. *Do not overgeneralize.* Consider the belief that gay males are effeminate and lesbians are masculine. Yes, some gay males and lesbians fit these stereotypes; however, many do not. Overgeneralizing makes us vulnerable to accepting stereotypes.

Throughout this text, we will give you plenty of opportunities to apply these principles, but it is up to you to practice them.

CRITICAL Thinking

What kinds of intellectual and interpersonal conflicts are likely to be encountered by people who decide that they would like to become critical thinkers?

Perspectives on Human Sexuality

Human sexuality is a complex topic. No single theory or perspective can capture all its nuances. In this book we explore human sexuality from many perspectives. In this section we introduce a number of them—historical, biological, evolutionary, cross-species, sociological, psychological, and sociocultural. We draw on these perspectives in subsequent chapters.

The Historical Perspective

History places sexual attitudes and behavior in context. It informs us with respect to whether sexual behavior reflects trends that have been with us through the millennia or with respect to the customs of a particular culture and era. History shows little evidence of universal sexual trends. Attitudes and behaviors vary extensively from one time and place to another. Contemporary American society may be permissive compared with the Victorian and post-World War II eras. Yet it looks staid when compared with the sexual excesses of some ancient societies, most notably the ruling class of ancient Rome. History also shows how religion has been a major influence on sexual values and behavior. Let us trace some historical changes in attitudes toward sexuality. We begin by turning the clock back 20,000 or 30,000 years, to the days before written records were kept—that is, to prehistory.

The "Venus of Willendorf." *This tiny ancient figurine is believed to be a fertility symbol.*

PREHISTORIC SEXUALITY   From female idols to phallic worship, information about life among our Stone Age ancestors is drawn largely from cave drawings, stone artifacts, and the customs of modern-day preliterate peoples whose existence changed little throughout millennia. From such sources, historians and anthropologists infer a prehistoric division of labor. By and large, men hunted for game; women tended to remain close to home. Women nurtured children and gathered edible plants and nuts, crabs, and other marine life that wandered along the shore or swam in shallow waters.

Art produced in the Stone Age, some 20,000 years ago, suggests the worship of women's ability to bear children and perpetuate the species (Fichner–Rathus, 2007). Primitive statues and cave drawings portray women with large, pendulous breasts; rounded hips; and prominent sex organs. Most theorists regard the figurines as fertility symbols. Stone Age people may have been unaware of the male's contribution to reproduction.

As the ice sheets of the last Ice Age retreated (about 11,000 BCE) and the climate warmed, human societies turned agrarian. Hunters and gatherers became farmers and herders. Villages sprang up around fields. Men tended livestock. Women became farmers. As people grew aware of the male role in reproduction, **phallic worship** (worship of the penis) sprang into being. Knowledge of paternity is believed to have developed around 9000 BCE, as a side benefit of the herding of livestock. When people began to observe the same animals throughout the year, they also began to understand that a predictable period of time elapsed between **copulation** and the birth of new animals.

The penis became glorified in art as a plough, an ax, or a sword. **Phallic symbols** played roles in religious ceremonies in ancient Egypt. The ancient Greeks sometimes rendered phalluses as rings and sometimes as necklaces. In ancient Rome, a large phallus was carried like a float in a parade honoring Venus, the goddess of love.

The **incest taboo** may have been the first human taboo. All human societies apparently have some form of incest taboo, but societies have varied in terms of its strictness. Brother–sister marriages were permitted among the presumably divine rulers of ancient Egypt and among the royal families of the Incas and of Hawaii, even though they were generally prohibited among commoners. Father–daughter marriages were also permitted among the aristocracy and royalty of ancient Egypt. Incestuous relationships in these royal blood lines may have kept wealth and power, as well as "divinity," in the family.

THE ANCIENT HEBREWS   The ancient Hebrews viewed sex, at least sex in marriage, as a fulfilling experience intended to fulfill the divine injunction to "be fruitful and multiply." The emphasis on the procreative function of sex led to some

Phallic worship Worship of the penis as a symbol of generative power

Copulation Sexual intercourse; from the Latin *copulare,* meaning "to unite" or "to couple"

Phallic symbol An image of the penis

Incest taboo The prohibition against intercourse and reproduction among close blood relatives

A Closer Look

THINKING CRITICALLY ABOUT SEXUAL ADVICE ON THE INTERNET: ARE THERE ANY QUICK FIXES?

www.goaskalice.columbia.edu

www.advocatesforyouth.org

www.cdc.gov

www.oxygen.com

www.healthgate.com

www.lovingyou.com

www.uneet.com

http://backupmd.com/eschec.html

www.dyspareunia.org

www.aasect.org

"Go ask Alice?" "Oxygen?" "Back up MD?" These are just a few of the websites offering sexual advice that have flooded the Internet in recent years. Every day, shy people, anxious people, confused people, and people with sexual problems surf the Internet in the hope of finding the website that will provide the answer. How can they evaluate the merits of these websites? How can they separate the helpful wheat from the useless and sometimes harmful chaff?

Unfortunately, there are no easy answers. Many of us believe the things we see posted. Anecdotes about how Tyrone increased the size of his penis by 30% and how Maria learned to reach orgasm "every time" can have a powerful allure.

Be on guard. A price we pay for freedom of speech is that nearly anything can wind up posted on a website or in print. Authors can make extravagant claims with little fear of punishment. They can lie about the effectiveness of a new sexual cure-all as easily as they can lie about sightings of Elvis Presley or UFOs.

How can you protect yourself? How could you know, for example, whether a website advertising the truth about STIs or offering Viagra at a special price is "the real thing"? How could you know that ethical, helping professionals would never promise that they can enable people to become sexually aroused and reach orgasm every time they make love?

Try some critical thinking:

1. **First, in this instance, do "judge the book by its cover."** Does the website look well organized? Do the links within the Web pages work? A credible website will look professional and will be well maintained.

2. **Ignore websites that make extravagant claims.** If it sounds too good to be true, it probably is. No method helps everyone who tries it. Very few methods work overnight. The website that promises to enable you to reach orgasm in five minutes will probably attract more attention than the one that says it can take up to half an hour or more and still remain within normal limits, but extravagant claims are a clue to look elsewhere.

---

interesting social customs. For example, childlessness and the development of a repulsive abnormality, such as a boil, were grounds for divorce. Male–male and female–female sexual behavior were strongly condemned, because they threatened the perpetuation of the family. Adultery, too, was condemned—at least for a woman. Although the Hebrew Bible (called the *Old Testament* in the Christian faith) permitted **polygamy**, the vast majority of Hebrews practiced **monogamy**.

The ancient Hebrews approved of sex within marriage not simply for procreation, but also for mutual pleasure and fulfillment. They believed that sex helped strengthen marital bonds and solidify the family. Jewish law even legislated the minimum frequency of marital relations, which varied according to the man's profession and the amount of time he spent at home:

> Every day for those who have no occupation; twice a week for laborers; once a week for ass-drivers; once every thirty days for camel drivers; and once every six months for sailors. (Mishna Ketubot 5:6; Ketubot 62a–62b)

Polygamy The practice of having two or more spouses at the same time; from the Greek *poly-,* meaning "many," and *-gamos,* meaning "marriage"

Monogamy The practice of having one spouse; from the Greek *mono-,* meaning "single" or "alone"

3. **Check the credentials of the people who posted the information.** Be suspicious if the author's title is "Dr." and is placed before the name. The degree could be a phony doctorate bought through the mail. It is better if the "doctor" has a Ph.D., Psy.D., M.D., or Ed.D. *after* her or his name.

4. **Check authors' affiliations.** Helping professionals who are affiliated with colleges, universities, clinics, and hospitals may have more to offer than those who are not.

5. **Check the *evidence* reported on the website.** Unscientific websites (and books) usually make extensive use of *anecdotes*. Anecdotes are unsupported stories or case studies about fantastic results with one or a few individuals. Responsible helping professionals check the effectiveness of techniques with large numbers of people. They carefully measure the outcomes. They use cautious language. For example, they say "It appears that . . ." or "It may be that . . . ."

6. **Check the reference citations for the evidence.** Legitimate research is reported in the journals or on the websites you will find in the References section of this book. These journals report research methods

Are They Buying What's Being Sold? *Critical thinkers carefully consider the premises of arguments, weigh all the evidence, and arrive at their own conclusions. Critical thinking is important in matters of human sexuality and is of value in all areas of life.*

and outcomes that seem to be scientifically valid. If there are no links to reference citations on the website, or if the list of references looks suspicious, you should be suspicious too.

7. **Ask your instructor for advice.** Ask for advice on what to do, where to go (electronically, perhaps), whom to talk to, what to read.

8. **Check out textbooks and professional books.** Search the college bookstore for information in fields that interest you.

9. **Talk to someone in your college or university health center.**

Truth or Fiction Revisited: You cannot trust everything that is posted on the Internet. Much of the material may be written or posted by respected authorities, but check out the authorities' credentials. Be skeptical. Weigh the evidence. In general, there are few, if any, quick fixes to problems concerning sex and relationships. Do your homework.

TRUTH? fiction 2

Among the ancient Hebrews, women were to be good wives and mothers. According to the Book of Proverbs, a good wife rises before dawn to tend to her family's needs, brings home food, instructs the servants, tends the vineyards, makes the clothes, keeps the ledger, helps the needy, and works well into the night. Despite all this, a wife was considered the property of her husband and could be divorced on a whim. A wife could also be stoned to death for adultery, but she might have to share her husband with secondary wives and **concubines**. Men who consorted with the wives of other men were considered to have violated the property rights of those men and might have to pay for "damages."

In case the notion that a woman is a man's property sounds ancient to you, we must note that in many cultures it remains current. For example, in Afghanistan, some fathers have given other men their daughters as payment for gambling debts (Bearak, 2006). And Zambian judge Alfred Shilibwa recently ordered a hotel employee, Obert Siyankalanga, to pay a woman's husband $300 in compensation after he slipped his hand into the woman's blouse and fondled her breasts ("Man pays

REFLECT

Throughout much of history, women were considered to be the property of their fathers and then their husbands. Are there "remnants" of this belief in people from your own background? Explain.

Concubine A secondary wife, usually of inferior legal and social status; from the Latin *concubina*, meaning "lying with"

victim's husband," 2000). The woman, a hotel employee named Bertha Kosamu, had been ironing at the time. She explained the scars on Obert's face and head: "I clobbered him on the head with the iron." There is one contemporary ring to the story: Because Obert was Bertha's supervisor, the judge also found him guilty of sexual harassment.

THE ANCIENT GREEKS   The classical or golden age of ancient Greece lasted about 200 years, from about 500 BCE to 300 BCE. Within this relatively short span lived the philosophers Socrates, Plato, and Aristotle; the playwrights Aristophanes, Aeschylus, and Sophocles; the natural scientist Archimedes; and the lawgiver Solon. Like the Hebrews, the Greeks valued family life. But Greek men also admired the well-developed male body and enjoyed nude wrestling in the arena. Erotic encounters and off-color jokes characterized the plays of Aristophanes and other playwrights. The Greeks held that the healthy mind must dwell in a healthy body. They cultivated muscle and movement along with mind.

The Greeks viewed their gods—Zeus, god of gods; Apollo, who inspired art and music; Aphrodite, the goddess of carnal love whose name is the basis of the word *aphrodisiac;* and others—as voracious seekers of sexual variety. Not only were they believed to have sexual adventures among themselves, but they were also thought to have seduced mortals.

Three aspects of Greek sexuality are of particular interest to our study of sexual practices in the ancient world: male–male sexual behavior, **pederasty**, and prostitution. The Greeks viewed men and women as **bisexual**. Male–male sex was deemed normal and tolerated as long as it did not threaten the institution of the family.

Pederasty means love of boys. Sex between men and prepubescent boys was illegal, however. Families were generally pleased if their adolescent sons attracted so-

Pederasty Sexual love of boys; from the Greek *paidos,* meaning "boy"

Bisexual Sexually responsive to either gender; from the Latin *bi-,* meaning "two"

Many Ancient Greek Ceramics Depict Male–Male Sexual Activity. *The ancient Greeks believed that males were bisexual. In Homer's* Iliad, *brought to the silver screen as* Troy, *Achilles is spurred to battle by the killing of his lover Patroclus. The film, however, glossed over this motive by emphasizing the family relationship between the two.*

cially prominent mentors. **Truth or Fiction Revisited:** It is true that men in ancient Greece might take on an adolescent male as a lover and pupil. Pederasty did not impede the boy's future male–female functioning, because the pederast himself was usually married, and Greeks believed people equally capable of male–female and male–male sexual activity.

Prostitution—the sale of sex for money or goods—flourished at every level of society. Prostitutes ranged from refined **courtesans** to concubines, who were usually slaves. Courtesans could play musical instruments, dance, engage in witty repartee, and discuss politics. They were also skilled in the arts of love. No social stigma was attached to visiting a courtesan. At the lower rungs of society were streetwalkers and brothel prostitutes. The latter were not hard to find: A wooden or painted penis invariably stood by the door.

Women held low social status. The women of Athens had no more rights than slaves. They were subject to the authority of their male next-of-kin before marriage and to their husbands thereafter. They received no formal education and were consigned mostly to women's quarters in their homes. They were chaperoned when they ventured out of doors. A husband could divorce his wife without cause and was obligated to do so if she committed adultery. **Truth or Fiction Revisited:** Women in the ancient world were treated as property.

THE WORLD OF ANCIENT ROME   Much is made of the sexual excesses of the Roman emperors and ruling families. Julius Caesar is reputed to have been bisexual—"a man to every woman and a woman to every man." Other emperors, like Caligula, sponsored orgies at which guests engaged in sexual practices including bestiality and **sadism**. Sexual excesses were found more often among the upper classes of palace society than among average Romans, however.

Romans disapproved of male–male sexual behavior as a threat to the integrity of the Roman family. The family was viewed as the source of strength of the Roman empire. Although Roman women were more likely than their Greek counterparts to share their husbands' social lives, they still were the property of their husbands.

Western society traces the roots of many of its sexual terms to Roman culture, as indicated by their Latin roots. **Fellatio**, for example, derives from the Latin *fellare*, meaning "to suck." **Cunnilingus** derives from *cunnus*, meaning "vulva," and *lingere*, "to lick." **Fornication** derives from *fornix*, an arch or vault. The term stems from Roman streetwalkers' practice of serving their customers in the shadows of archways near public buildings such as stadiums and theaters.

THE EARLY CHRISTIANS   Christianity emerged within the Roman Empire during the centuries following the death of Jesus. Early Christian views on sexuality were largely shaped by Saint Paul and the church fathers in the first century, and by Saint Augustine in the latter part of the fourth century. Adultery and fornication were rampant among the upper classes of Rome at the time, and early Christian leaders began to associate sexuality with sin.

In replacing the pagan values of Rome, the early Christians, like the Hebrews, sought to restrict sex to marriage. They saw temptations of the flesh as distractions from spiritual devotion. Paul preached that celibacy was closer to the Christian ideal than marriage. He recognized that not everyone could achieve celibacy, however, so he said that it was "better to marry than to burn" (with passion, that is).

Christians, like the Jews before them, demanded virginity of brides. Prostitution was condemned (Allen, 2000; Laqueur, 2003). Early Christians taught that men should love their wives with restraint, not passion. The goal of procreation should govern sexual behavior—the spirit should rule the flesh. Divorce was outlawed.

TRUTH fiction 3

TRUTH fiction 4

Courtesan A prostitute, especially the mistress of a noble or wealthy man; from the Italian *courtesan,* meaning "court lady"

Sadism The practice of achieving sexual gratification through hurting or humiliating others

Fellatio A sexual activity involving oral contact with the penis

Cunnilingus A sexual activity involving oral contact with the female genitals

Fornication Sexual intercourse between people who are not married to one another; if one of the partners is married, the act may be labeled *adultery*

An Illustration from the _Kama Sutra_. _The_ Kama Sutra, _an Indian sex manual believed to have been written sometime between the third and fifth centuries_ CE, _contained graphic illustrations of sexual techniques and pratices._

Unhappiness with one's spouse might reflect sexual, thus sinful, restlessness. Dissolving a marriage might also jeopardize the social structure that supported the church. Masturbation, male–male sexual behavior, female–female sexual behavior, oral–genital contact, anal intercourse—all were viewed as abominations in the eyes of God (Laqueur, 2003; Stengers et al., 2001).

Saint Augustine (353–430 CE), a key theologian who supported the concept of original sin, associated sexual lust with the original sin of Adam and Eve in the Garden of Eden. To Augustine, lust and shame were passed down from Adam and Eve through the generations. Lust made any sexual expression, even intercourse in marriage, inherently evil. Only through celibacy, according to Augustine, could men and women attain a state of grace.

ISLAM   Islam, the dominant religion in the Middle East, was founded by the prophet Muhammad. Muhammad was born in Mecca, in what is now Saudi Arabia, in about 570 CE. The Islamic tradition treasures marriage and sexual fulfillment in marriage. Premarital intercourse invites shame and social condemnation—and, in some fundamentalist Islamic states, the death penalty.

The family is the backbone of Islamic society. Celibacy is frowned upon. Muhammad decreed that marriage represents the road to virtue. Islamic tradition permits a sexual double standard, however. Men may take as many as four wives, but women are permitted only one husband. Public social interactions between men and women are severely restricted in more conservative Islamic societies. Women are expected to keep their heads and faces veiled in public and to avoid all contact with men other than their husbands.

INDIA   Perhaps no culture has cultivated sexual pleasure as a spiritual ideal to the extent of the ancient Hindus of India. From the fifth century CE onward, temples show sculptures of gods, heavenly nymphs, and ordinary people in erotic poses. Hindu sexual practices were codified in a sex manual, the _Kama Sutra_. The _Kama Sutra_ illustrates sexual positions, some of which would challenge a contortionist. It also holds recipes for alleged aphrodisiacs. This manual is believed to have been written by the Hindu sage Vatsyayana sometime between the third and fifth centuries CE, at about the time that Christianity was ascending in the West.

In its graphic representations of sexual positions and practices, the _Kama Sutra_ reflected the Hindu belief that sex was a religious duty, not a source of shame or guilt. Hindu deities were often portrayed as engaging in same-sex as well as male–female sexual activities. In the Hindu doctrine of karma (the passage of souls from one place to another), sexual fulfillment was regarded as one way to become reincarnated at a higher level of existence. Indian society grew more restrictive toward sexuality after about 1000 CE.

THE FAR EAST   In the cultures of the Far East, sexuality was akin to spirituality. To the Taoist masters of China, who influenced Chinese culture for millennia, sex was a sacred duty—a form of worship that led toward harmony with nature and immortality.

Truth or Fiction Revisited: It is not true that the production of sex manuals originated in modern times. The Chinese culture was the first to produce a detailed sex manual, which came into use about 200 years before the birth of Jesus. The man was expected to extend intercourse as long as possible to absorb more of his wife's natural essence, or yin. Yin would enhance his own masculine essence, or yang. Moreover, he was to help bring his partner to orgasm so as to increase the flow of energy that he might absorb.

TRUTH?fiction 5

Taoists believed that it was wasteful for a man to "spill his seed." Masturbation, acceptable for women, was ruled out for men. Sexual practices such as anal intercourse and oral–genital contact (fellatio and cunnilingus) were permissible, so long as the man did not squander yang through wasteful ejaculation. Same-sex activity was not prohibited by Taoist holy writings, but some Taoists frowned on exclusive homosexuality. A parallel to Western cultures was the role accorded women in traditional Chinese society. The "good wife," like her Western counterparts, was limited to domestic roles.

CHRISTIANITY IN THE MIDDLE AGES The Middle Ages, sometimes called *medieval times,* span the millennium of Western history from about 476 to 1450 CE. The attitudes of the Roman Catholic Church toward sexuality, largely unchanged since the time of Augustine, dominated medieval thought. Yet some currents of change crept across medieval Europe in the social standing of women. The Church had long regarded all women as being tainted by the sin of Eve; but in the Eastern church of Constantinople, the cult of the Virgin Mary flourished. The ideal of womanhood was in the image of Mary: good, gracious, loving, and saintly. Imported by the Crusaders and others who returned from the East, the cult of the Virgin Mary swept European Christendom and helped elevate the status of women.

Two conflicting concepts of women came to dominate medieval thought: one, woman as Eve, the temptress; the other, woman as Mary, virtuous and pure. Contemporary Western images of women still show the schism between the good girl and the bad girl—the Madonna and the whore.

THE PROTESTANT REFORMATION During the Reformation, Martin Luther (1483–1546) and other Christian reformers such as John Calvin (1509–1564) split off from the Roman Catholic Church and formed their own sects, which led to the development of the modern Protestant denominations of Western Europe (and later, the New World). Luther disputed many Roman Catholic doctrines on sexuality. He believed that priests should be allowed to marry and rear children. To Luther, marriage was as much a part of human nature as eating or drinking. Calvin rejected the Roman church's position that sex in marriage was permissible only for procreation. He believed that sexual expression in marriage also strengthened the marriage bond and helped relieve the stresses of everyday life.

THE VICTORIAN ERA Early settlers brought to North America the religious teachings that had dominated Western thought and culture for centuries. Whatever their differences, each religion stressed the ideal of family life, and viewed sex outside of marriage as immoral or sinful. A woman's place, by and large, was in the home and in the fields. Not until 1833, when Oberlin opened its doors to women, were women permitted to attend college in the United States. (Not until 1920 did women gain the right to vote.)

The middle and latter parts of the 19th century are generally called the Victorian period, named after Queen Victoria of England. Victoria assumed the throne in 1837 and ruled until her death in 1901. Her name has become virtually synonymous with sexual **repression**. Victorian society in Europe and the United States, on the surface at least, was prim and proper (Horowitz, 2002). Sex was not discussed in polite society. Even the legs of pianos were draped with cloth for the sake of modesty. Many women viewed sex as a marital duty to be performed for procreation or to satisfy their husbands' cravings. Consider the following quotation:

> I am happy now that Charles calls on my bed chamber less frequently than of old. As it is, I now endure but two calls a week and when I hear his steps outside my door I lie down on my bed, close my eyes, open my legs and think of England. (Attributed to Alice, Lady Hillingdon, wife of the Second Baron Hillingdon)

Women were assumed not to experience sexual desires or pleasures. "I would say," observed William Acton (1814–1875), an influential English physician, in 1857, "that the majority of women (happily for society) are not much troubled with sexual feeling of any kind."

It was widely believed among medical authorities in England and the United States that sex drains the man of his natural vitality. Physicians thus recommended that intercourse be practiced infrequently, perhaps once a month or so. The Reverend Sylvester Graham (1794–1851) preached that ejaculation deprived men of the "vital fluids" they need to maintain health and vitality. Graham preached against "wasting the seed" by masturbation or frequent marital intercourse (Laqueur, 2003; Stengers et al., 2001). (How frequent was "frequent"? In Graham's view, intercourse more than once a month could dangerously deplete the man's vital energies.) **Truth or Fiction Revisited:** Graham recommended that young men control their sexual appetites by a diet of simple foods based on whole-grain flours, and invented what we now call the graham cracker to serve this purpose.

It appears, though, that the actual behavior of Victorians was not as repressed as advertised. Despite Acton's beliefs, Victorian women did experience sexual pleasure and orgasm. Consider some findings from an early sex survey conducted in 1892 by a female physician, Clelia Duel Mosher. Although her sample was small and nonrandom, 35 of the 44 women who responded admitted to desiring sexual intercourse. And 34 of them reported experiencing orgasm. Women's diaries of the time also contained accounts of passionate love affairs.

Prostitution flourished during the Victorian era. Men apparently thought that they were doing their wives a favor by looking elsewhere. Accurate statistics are hard to come by, but there may have been as many as one prostitute for every 12 men in London during the 19th century; in Vienna, perhaps one for every seven men.

Same-sex sexual behavior was considered indecent in Victorian society. The celebrated, gay Anglo-Irish novelist and playwright Oscar Wilde—author of *The Picture of Dorian Gray, An Ideal Husband,* and *The Importance of Being Earnest*—was imprisoned after being convicted of "gross indecency."

FOUNDATIONS OF THE SCIENTIFIC STUDY OF SEXUALITY Against this backdrop of sexual repression, scientists and scholars began to approach sexuality as an area of legitimate scientific study. The English physician Havelock Ellis (1859–1939) published a veritable encyclopedia of sexuality between 1897 and 1910, *Studies in the Psychology of Sex*. Ellis drew information from case histories, anthropological findings, and medical knowledge. He argued that sexual desires in women were natural and healthy. He promoted the view that many sexual problems had psychological rather than physical causes. He also argued that a gay male or lesbian sexual orientation was a natural variation within the spectrum of normal sexuality and not an aberration. As do most health professionals today, Ellis treated gay

Repression The automatic ejection of anxiety-evoking ideas from consciousness

male and lesbian sexual orientations as inborn dispositions, not as vices or character flaws.

Another influential **sexologist**, the German psychiatrist Richard von Krafft-Ebing (1840–1902) vividly described case histories of individuals with sexual deviations in his book *Psychopathia Sexualis* (1886/1978). Cases included deviations such as sadomasochism (sexual gratification through inflicting or receiving pain), bestiality (sex with animals), and necrophilia (intercourse with dead people). Krafft–Ebing viewed deviations as mental diseases that could be studied and perhaps treated by medical science.

At about the same time, a Viennese physician, Sigmund Freud (1856–1939), was developing a theory of personality that has had an enormous influence on modern culture and science. Freud believed that the sex drive was our principal motivating force.

Alfred Kinsey (1894–1956), an Indiana University zoologist, conducted the first large-scale studies of sexual behavior in the 1930s and 1940s. Kinsey had been asked to teach a course on marriage. When researching the subject matter, Kinsey found that little was known about sexual practices in American society. He thus embarked upon an ambitious research project, conducting detailed interviews with nearly 12,000 people across the United States. The results of his surveys were published in two volumes, *Sexual Behavior in the Human Male* (Kinsey et al., 1948) and *Sexual Behavior in the Human Female* (Kinsey et al., 1953). These books represent the first scientific attempts to provide a comprehensive picture of sexual behavior in the United States.

The books made for dry reading. They were filled with statistical tables rather than racy pictures or vignettes. Nevertheless, they became best-sellers, exploding on a public that had not yet learned to discuss sex openly. Their publication—especially the book on female sexuality—unleashed the dogs of criticism. Kinsey's work had some methodological flaws—especially in its selection of participants—but much of the criticism branded it immoral and obscene. *The New York Times* refused to run advertisements for the 1948 volume on male sexuality. Many newspapers refused to report the results of his survey on female sexuality. A congressional committee in the 1950s claimed that Kinsey's work undermined the moral fiber of the nation, rendering it more vulnerable to a Communist takeover. Despite all the brouhaha, Kinsey and his colleagues made sex research a scientifically respectable field of study and helped lay the groundwork for discussing sexual behavior openly.

THE SEXUAL REVOLUTION   The period of the mid 1960s to the mid 1970s is often referred to as the *sexual revolution* (Allyn, 2001; Kamen, 2002). Dramatic changes occurred in American sexual attitudes and practices during the "Swinging Sixties." Our society was on the threshold of a major social upheaval, not only in sexual behavior, but also in science, politics, fashion, music, art, and cinema. The so-called Woodstock generation, disheartened by commercialism and the Vietnam War, tuned in (to rock music on the radio), turned on (to drugs), and dropped out (of mainstream society). The heat was on between the hippies and the hardhats. Long hair became the mane of men. Bell-bottomed jeans flared out. Films became sexually explicit. Critics seriously contemplated whether the pornography "classic" *Deep Throat* had deep social implications. Hard rock music bellowed the message of rebellion and revolution.

No single event marked the onset of the sexual revolution. Social movements often gain momentum from a timely interplay of scientific, social, political, and economic forces. The war (in Vietnam), the bomb (fear of the nuclear bomb), the pill (the introduction of the birth control pill), and the mass media (especially television)

Sexologist A person who engages in the scientific study of sexual behavior

were four such forces. The pill lessened the risk of unwanted pregnancy for young people. It permitted them to engage in recreational or casual sex, rather than procreative sex. Pop psychology movements, like the Human Potential Movement of the 1960s and 1970s (the "Me Decade"), spread the message that people should get in touch with and express their genuine feelings, including their sexual feelings. "Doing your own thing" became one catchphrase. "If it feels right, go with it" became another.

The sexual revolution was tied to social permissiveness and political liberalism. In part reflecting the times, in part acting the catalyst, the media dealt openly with sex. Popular books encouraged people to explore their sexuality. Film scenes of lovemaking became so commonplace that the movie rating system was introduced to alert parents.

GAY ACTIVISM   Gay activism mushroomed during the sexual revolution. Not only did gays become more voluble in demanding equal rights, they also began gay parades in major cities. Annual parades in San Francisco and New York's Greenwich Village are among the best known of these. In the early 1980s, gay people also built social institutions to tackle the problem of AIDS, which affected gay people disproportinately to their numbers in the general population. We will learn more about AIDS and sexual orientation in Chapters 10 and 16. Here let us note that because AIDS was (and often remains) lethal, many homosexuals adopted the motto that "silence equals death." This motto encouraged many homosexuals to identify their sexual orientations publicly and to speak up to spur on medical research.

SEX RESEARCH   During the sexual revolution, sexually explicit questionnaires proliferated in popular magazines, interviewers posed sexually explicit questions by telephone and in person, and some pioneers, including William H. Masters and Virginia Johnson, observed people enaging in sexual activity in the laboratory. Shere Hite published some controversial books based on magazine surveys, but her popularity fell when it became clear that even 3,000 respondents did not represent the country, or even all readers of a magazine. Morton Hunt conducted a telephone survey financed by *Playboy* in the 1970s, and he claimed to find a populace more sexually liberal than in Kinsey's day. However, he, like Shere Hite, had a relatively low response rate. In the 1960s, Masters and Johnson were condemned by many as destroying the moral fabric of the nation—a complaint similar to those leveled earlier against Kinsey. Today, sexual research continues, with more valid methods of sampling the population and a somewhat less outraged citizenry.

RECENT TRENDS   More teenagers are sexually active today, and at younger ages (Henshaw, 2003). In addition to premarital sex, two other features of the sexual revolution have become permanent parts of our social fabric: the liberation of female sexuality and a greater willingness to discuss sex openly. Hundreds of thousands of pornography websites populate the Internet and are capable of being accessed by many children. As late as the early 1960s, men's magazines might reveal models' breasts and nudist magazines might show some more. Today, however, with multiple websites offering the opportunity to download videos of celebrities such as Pamela Anderson and Paris Hilton engaging in sexual activity, pornography has nearly reached the status of wallpaper.

In sum, all societies have some form of an incest taboo. Most societies have placed a value on procreative sex within the context of an enduring relationship, usually in the form of marriage. Marriage provides security for children, maintains or increases the population, and institutionalizes the orderly transfer of property from generation to generation. Other sexual practices—masturbation, promiscuous sex,

CRITICAL Thinking

What does history tell us about sex? Is there a universal standard for defining sexual values, or are there many standards?

male–male sexual behavior, female–female sexual behavior, prostitution, polygamy, and so on—have been condemned in some societies, tolerated by others, and encouraged by still others.

The Biological Perspective

The biological perspective focuses on the roles of **genes**, hormones, the nervous system, and other biological factors in human sexuality. Sex, after all, serves the biological function of reproduction. We are biologically endowed with structures that make sexual behavior possible—and, for most people, pleasurable.

Study of the biology of sex informs us about the mechanisms of reproduction. It informs us of the mechanisms of sexual arousal and response. Biology teaches us that erection occurs when the penis becomes engorged with blood. We learn that vaginal lubrication is the result of a "sweating" action of the vaginal walls. We learn that orgasm is a spinal reflex as well as a psychological event.

Biological researchers have made major strides in assisting infertile couples to conceive, for example, through laboratory-based methods of fertilization. Knowledge of biology has furthered our understanding of sexuality and our ability to overcome sexual problems. To what extent does biology govern sexual behavior? Is sex controlled by biological instincts? Or are psychosocial factors, such as culture, experience, and decision-making ability more important? Although the sexuality of other species is largely governed by biological processes, culture and experience play vital roles—and in some cases, the more central roles—in human sexuality. Human sexuality involves a complex interaction of biological and psychosocial factors.

Are Today's Young People More or Less Liberal in the Expression of Their Sexuality Than People in Earlier Generations? *Today the threat of HIV/AIDS hangs over every sexual encounter. While many young people today are selective in their choice of partners and take precautions to make sex safer, more teenagers are engaging in sexual activity, and at younger ages, than in previous generations.* (Models for illustrative purposes only.)

The Evolutionary Perspective

Species vary not only in their physical characteristics but also in their social behavior, including their mating behavior. Scientists look to **evolution** to help explain such variability. The English naturalist Charles Darwin (1809–1882) believed that current species of animals and plants evolved from other life forms through **natural selection**, or "survival of the fittest." In each species, individuals vary, and some are better adapted to their environments than others. Better adapted members are more likely to survive to reproduce. Therefore, they are also more likely to transmit their traits to succeeding generations. They are not necessarily the strongest or fleetest of foot, although these traits are adaptive for some species and enhance their reproductive success.

New variations in species can be introduced through random genetic changes called **mutations**. Mutations occur randomly but are subject to natural selection. Mutations that are adaptive enhance reproductive success. As more members of the species come to possess these traits, the species changes.

We know now that traits are transmitted by units of heredity that we call *genes*. Traits are determined by single genes or combinations of genes that offspring inherit from their parents. Genes are segments of **chromosomes**, which are composed of **deoxyribonucleic acid (DNA)**. Each human cell normally contains 46 chromosomes, which are arranged in 23 pairs. Each pair of chromosomes consists of 1,000 or so genes. A child normally inherits one member of each pair from each parent. Each

Genes The basic units of heredity, which consist of chromosomal segments of DNA

Evolution The development of a species to its current state, which is believed to involve adaptations to its environment

Natural selection The evolutionary process by which adaptive traits enable members of a species to survive to reproductive age and transmit these traits to future generations

Mutation A random change in the molecular structure of DNA

Chromosomes The rodlike structures that reside in the nuclei of every living cell and carry the genetic code in the form of genes

DNA Deoxyribonucleic acid; the chemical substance with molecules that make up genes and chromosomes

child inherits half of his or her genes from each parent. The particular combinations of genes that one inherits account for whether one has blue eyes or brown eyes, light or dark hair, or arms or wings.

Some scientists suggest that there is also a genetic basis to social behavior, including sexual behavior, among humans and other animals (Buss, 2005). If so, we may carry traits that helped our prehistoric ancestors survive and reproduce successfully.

Does biology govern sexual behavior? Although the sexuality of other species is largely governed by biological processes, culture and experience also play vital roles in human sexuality (Plomin & Asbury, 2005). *Human* sexuality involves a complex web of biological, psychological, and cultural factors.

THE EVOLUTIONARY PERSPECTIVE AND EROTIC PLASTICITY

Consider the concept of *erotic plasticity* (Baumeister, 2000), which addresses the fact that in response to various social and cultural forces, people show different levels of sex drive and express their sexual desires in a variety of ways. Roy Baumeister (2000) reports evidence that women show greater erotic plasticity than men do. For example, (1) individual women show greater variation than men in sexual behavior over time; (2) women seem to be more responsive than men to most specific cultural factors, such as cultural permissiveness or restraint; and (3) men's sexual behavior is more consistent with their sexual attitudes than women. Baumeister concludes that evolutionary, biological forces may be an important factor in the greater female erotic plasticity.

ALTRUISM

There is a tendency to think of adaptive traits as somehow more "worthy," "good," or "admirable" than less adaptive traits. Evolution is not a moralistic enterprise, however. A trait either does or does not enhance reproductive success. It is not in itself good or bad. It is apparently adaptive for the female of one species of insect to eat the male after mating. "Dad," then, literally nourishes his offspring during the period of gestation. In evolutionary terms, his "altruism"—his personal sacrifice—is adaptive if it increases the chances that the offspring will survive and carry his genes. In other species, it may be adaptive for fathers to "love them and leave them"—that is, to mate with as many females as possible and abruptly abandon them to "plant their seed" elsewhere.

Truth or Fiction Revisited: Shortly after inseminating a female, the male redback spider does a somersault into her mouth and becomes her postcoital meal. It turns out that females pause in their sexual activity after "taking in" their partners. Thus, their partner's sacrifice improves the chance that his own sperm will fertilize her eggs before another male can have at her.

SEX DIFFERENCES IN PREFERRED NUMBER OF SEX PARTNERS

Some **evolutionary psychologists** argue that men are naturally more promiscuous than women because they are the genetic heirs of ancestors whose reproductive success was related to the number of women they could impregnate (Buss, 2005; McBurney et al., 2005; Schmitt, 2003). Women, by contrast, can produce only a few offspring in their lifetime. Thus, the theory goes, women have to be more selective with respect to their mating partners. Women's reproductive success is enhanced by mating with the fittest males—not with any Tom, Dick, or Harry who happens by. From this perspective, the male's "roving eye" and the female's selectivity are embedded in their genes.

The Cross-Species Perspective

The study of other animal species places human behavior in a broader context. A surprising variety of sexual behaviors exists among nonhumans. There are animal examples, or **analogues**, of human male–male sexual behavior, female–female sex-

TRUTH fiction 7

REFLECT

Does the theory of evolution contradict any of your religious views? Explain.

Evolutionary psychologist A psychologist who studies the effects of evolution on behavior and mental processes

Analogue Something that is similar or comparable with something else

Human Sexuality

Influences of Sex, Ethnicity, Age, Marital Status, Level of Education, and Religion on Numbers of Sex Partners

Evolutionary theory suggests that males are more interested than females in having multiple sex partners because doing so increases their reproductive opportunities. Women, however, might be more likely to favor development of relationships that provide a protective environment in which they can successfully carry and bear children. Research does support the view that men as a group have more sex partners than women do. For example, Table 1.2 reports the results of a national survey concerning the number of sex partners reported since the age of 18 (Laumann et al., 1994). Males report having more sex partners than females. One male in three (33%) reports having 11 or more sex partners since the age of 18, compared with fewer than one woman in 10 (9.2%). However, the question remains as to *why*.

Note, too, that the numbers of sex partners increase with age into the 40s. Does this mean that older people have more of a roving eye? Not at all. As people age, they have more opportunity to accumulate life experiences, including sexual experiences. But then the numbers of partners fall off among respondents in their 50s. Many older respondents to this survey entered adulthood before the sexual revolution and were thus exposed to more conservative sexual attitudes. Thus, although age might appear to be a biological matter, it is also connected with the amount of experience one has and kinds of social influences that were prevalent during childhood and adolescence. The varied experiences of different age groups are referred to as *cohort effects*.

Although roles for biology and evolution remain steeped in controversy, it seems clearer that differences in race or ethnicity, marital status, level of education, and

religion play key roles. Consider race or ethnicity. The research findings listed in Table 1.2 show that European Americans and African Americans reported the highest numbers of sex partners. Asian Americans reported the fewest partners. However, the sample sizes of Asian Americans and Native Americans may be too small to draw accurate conclusions.

Not surprisingly, the highest percentage of virgins is found among people who have never married nor lived with a partner without being married. By contrast, married people are most likely to have had just one sex partner.

Generally speaking, education appears to be a liberalizing influence on sexual behavior. Therefore, people with some college education, or who have completed college, are likely to have more sex partners than those who attended grade school or high school only. Conservative religious experience, on the other hand, is a restraining factor. In Table 1.2, those who report no religion and liberal Protestants (e.g., Methodists, Lutherans, Presbyterians, Episcopalians, and United Church of Christ) report higher numbers of sex partners than do Catholics and conservative Protestants (e.g., members of Baptist churches, Pentecostal churches, Churches of Christ, and Assemblies of God). Latino and Latina Americans are mostly Catholic, and Catholicism tends to restrain sexual behavior.

The values, beliefs, and norms of a group influence their members' sexual behavior. We tend to share attitudes and behaviors with people from similar backgrounds. Even so, not all members of a given ethnic group act or think alike.

---

ual behavior, oral–genital contact, and oral–oral behavior (i.e., kissing). Foreplay is also well-known in the animal world. Turtles massage their mate's head with their claws. Male mice nibble at their partner's neck. Most mammals use only a rear-entry position for copulation, but some animals, such as apes, use a variety of coital positions.

Cross-species research reveals an interesting pattern. Sexual behavior among "higher" mammals, such as primates, is less directly controlled by instinct than it is among the "lower" species, such as birds, fish, or lower mammals. Experience and learning play more important roles in sexuality as we travel up the evolutionary ladder.

CRITICAL Thinking

Biological, evolutionary, and cross-species perspectives may offer some insights into what kinds of sexual behavior are "natural." If a sexual behavior pattern is judged to be natural, does that mean that it is right or good? Explain.

TABLE 1.2

Number of Sex Partners Since Age 18 as Found in the NHSLS* Study

Social Characteristics	Number of Sex Partners (%)					
	0	1	2–4	5–10	11–20	21+
By Sex						
Male	3.4	19.5	20.9	23.3	16.3	16.6
Female	2.5	31.5	36.4	20.4	6.0	3.2
Race/Ethnicity						
European American	3.0	26.2	28.9	22.0	10.9	9.1
African American	2.2	18.0	34.2	24.1	11.0	10.5
Latino and Latina American	3.2	35.6	27.1	17.4	8.2	8.5
Asian American[†]	6.2	46.2	24.6	13.8	6.2	3.1
Native American[†]	5.0	27.5	35.0	22.5	5.0	5.0
By Age						
18–24	7.8	32.1	34.1	15.4	7.8	2.8
25–29	2.2	25.3	31.3	22.2	9.9	9.0
30–34	3.1	21.3	29.3	25.2	10.8	10.3
35–39	1.7	18.9	29.7	24.9	14.0	10.8
40–44	0.7	21.9	27.6	24.2	13.7	12.0
45–49	2.0	25.7	23.8	25.1	9.6	13.9
50–54	2.4	33.9	27.8	18.0	9.0	9.0
55–59	1.3	40.0	28.3	15.2	8.3	7.0
Marital Status						
Never married (not cohabiting)	12.3	14.8	28.6	20.6	12.1	11.6
Never married (cohabiting)	0.0	24.6	37.3	15.7	9.7	12.7
Married	0.0	37.1	28.0	19.4	8.7	6.8
Level of Education						
Less than high school	4.2	26.7	36.0	18.6	8.8	5.8
High school graduate	3.4	30.2	29.1	20.0	9.8	7.4
Some college	2.1	23.9	29.4	23.3	11.9	9.3
College graduate	2.1	24.1	25.8	23.9	11.1	13.0
Advanced degree	3.5	24.6	26.3	22.8	9.6	13.2
Religion						
None	2.6	16.2	29.0	20.3	15.9	15.9
Liberal, moderate Protestant	2.3	22.8	31.2	23.0	12.4	8.3
Conservative Protestant	2.9	29.8	30.4	20.4	9.5	7.0
Catholic	3.8	27.2	29.2	22.7	8.1	9.1
Jewish[†]	0.0	24.1	13.0	29.6	16.7	16.7

SOURCE: Adapted by permission from E. O. Laumann, J. H. Gagnon, R. T. Michael, and S. Michaels (1994). *The Social Organization of Sexuality: Sexual Practices in the United States.* Chicago: University of Chicago Press, Table 5.1C, p. 179.
*These sample sizes are quite small.
[†]National Health and Social Life Survey.

Sociological Perspectives

REFLECT

What social and cultural institutions have played prominent roles in your life? Are you comfortable with, or in conflict with, any of these institutions? Explain.

Sociological perspectives, like the historical perspective, provide insight into the ways in which cultural insitutions and beliefs affect sexual behavior and people's sense of morality (Henslin, 2007). Interest in the effects of culture on sexuality was spurred by the early–twentieth century work of Margaret Mead (1901–1978) and Bronislaw Malinowski (1884–1942).

In *Sex and Temperament in Three Primitive Societies* (Mead, 1935), Mead laid the groundwork for recent psychological and sociological research challenging gender-role stereotypes. In most cultures characterized by a gender division of labor, men typically go to business or to the hunt, and—when necessary—to war. In such cultures, men are perceived as strong, active, independent, and logical. Women are viewed as passive, dependent, nurturing, and emotional. Mead concluded that these stereotypes are not inherent in our genetic heritage. Rather, they are acquired through cultural expectations and socialization. That is, men and women learn to behave in ways that are expected of them in their particular culture.

Malinowski lived on the Trobriand island of Boyawa in the South Pacific during World War I. There he gathered data on the Trobrianders and the Amphett islanders. The Amphett islanders maintained strict sexual prohibitions, whereas the Trobrianders enjoyed greater freedom. Trobrianders, for example, encouraged their children to masturbate. Adolescents were expected to have multiple sex partners until they married. Malinowski found Trobrianders to be less anxiety ridden than Amphett islanders. He attributed the difference to their sexual freedom, thus making an early plea to relax prohibitions in Western societies.

In 1951, Clellan Ford, an anthropologist, and Frank Beach, a psychologist, reviewed sexual behavior in almost 200 preliterate societies around the world. They found great variety in sexual customs and beliefs. They also found some fairly common threads. Kissing was quite common, although not universal. The Thonga of Africa did not practice kissing. Upon witnessing European visitors kissing each other, members of the tribe commented that they could not understand why Europeans "ate" each other's saliva and dirt. The frequency of sexual intercourse also varies from culture to culture, but intercourse is relatively more frequent among young people everywhere.

Societies differ in their attitudes toward childhood masturbation. Some societies, such as the Hopi tribe of the southwest United States, ignore it. Trobrianders encourage it. Other societies condemn it.

There can also be political and sexual "culture wars" within a large society, such as that of the United States (Henslin, 2007). For example, some Americans are liberal concerning sex, some are conservative, and many are in the middle—"moderate." The family and peer groups are of immense importance in forming values. Social institutions such as legislatures, religions, the media, and the medical establishment also play key roles. These institutions and groups all have their internal conflicts as well as their efforts to influence society at large. For example, France officially promotes secularism and religious tolerance, but subcultures within France, such as the Islamic subculture, tend to be more religious and conservative. In an effort to integrate Muslim girls better into the larger French society, France has outlawed the use of Muslim head scarves in public schools. And, quite naturally, there are differences of opinion within the Muslim subculture itself.

Societies differ widely in their sexual attitudes, customs, and practices. The members of all human societies share anatomic structures and physiological capacities for sexual pleasure, however. The same hormones flow through their arteries. Yet their sexual practices, and the pleasure they reap or fail to attain, may set them apart. If human sexuality were predominantly determined by biology, we might not find such diversity.

The New Berlin Wall

By Peter Schneider, The New York Times

Hatun Surucu, 23, was killed on her way to a bus stop in Berlin-Tempelhof by several shots to the head and upper body, fired at point-blank range. The investigation revealed that months before, she reported one of her brothers to the police for threatening her. . . . [T]hree of her five brothers are on trial for murder. According to the prosecutor, the oldest of them (25) acquired the weapon, the middle brother (24) lured his sister to the scene of the crime and the youngest (18) shot her. . . . Ayhan Surucu, the youngest brother, had confessed to the murder and claimed that he had done it without any help. According to Seyran Ates, a lawyer of Turkish descent, it is generally the youngest who are chosen by the family council to carry out such murders—or to claim responsibility for them. German juvenile law sets a maximum sentence of 10 years' imprisonment for murder, and the offender has the prospect of being released after serving two-thirds of the sentence.

Hatun Surucu grew up in Berlin as the daughter of Turkish Kurds. When she finished eighth grade, her parents took her out of school. Shortly after that she was taken to Turkey and married to a cousin. Later she separated from her husband and returned to Berlin, pregnant. At age 17 she gave birth to a son, Can. She moved into a women's shelter and completed the work for her middle-school certificate. By 2004 she had finished a vocational-training program to become an electrician. The young mother who had escaped her family's constraints began to enjoy herself. She put on makeup, wore her hair unbound, went dancing and adorned herself with rings, necklaces and bracelets. Then, just days before she was to receive her journeyman's diploma, her life was cut short.

Evidently, in the eyes of her brothers, Hatun Surucu's capital crime was that, living in Germany, she had begun living like a German. In a statement to the Turkish newspaper *Zaman,* one brother noted that she had stopped wearing her head scarf, that she refused to go back to her family and that she had declared her intent to "seek out her own circle of friends." It's still unclear whether anyone ordered her murdered. Often in such cases it is the father of the family who decides about the punishment. But Seyran Ates has seen in her legal practice cases in which the mother has a leading role: mothers who were forced to marry forcing the same fate on

their daughters. Necla Kelek, a Turkish–German author who has interviewed dozens of women on this topic, explained, "The mothers are looking for solidarity by demanding that their daughters submit to the same hardship and suffering." By disobeying them, the daughter calls into question her mother's life—her silent submission to the ritual of forced marriage. Meanwhile, the two elder brothers have papered their cell with pictures of their dead sister.

There is a new wall rising in the city of Berlin. To cross this wall you have to go to the city's central and northern districts—to Kreuzberg, Neukölln and Wedding—and you will find yourself in a world unknown to the majority of Berliners. Until recently, most Berliners held to the illusion that living together with some 300,000 Muslim immigrants and children of immigrants was basically working. Take Neukölln. The district is proud of the fact that it houses citizens of 165 nations. Some 40 percent of these, by far the largest group, are Turks and Kurds; the second-largest group consists of Arabs. Racially motivated attacks occur regularly in Brandenburg, the former East German state that surrounds Berlin, where foreigners are few (about 2 percent). But such attacks hardly ever happen in Neukölln. . . .

But tolerance of Muslim immigrants began to change in the aftermath of Sept. 11, 2001. Parallel to the declarations of "unconditional solidarity" with Americans by the German majority, rallies of another sort were taking place in Neukölln and Kreuzberg. Bottle rockets were set off from building courtyards: a poor man's fireworks, sporadic, sparse and joyful; two rockets here, three rockets there. Still, altogether, hundreds of rockets were shooting skyward in celebration of the attack, just as most Berliners were searching for words to express their horror. . . .

When a broader German public began concerning itself with the parallel Muslim world arising in its midst, it was primarily thanks to three female authors, three rebellious Muslim musketeers: Ates, who in addition to practicing law is the author of *The Great Journey into the Fire;* Necla Kelek (*The Foreign Bride*); and Serap Cileli (*We're Your Daughters, Not Your Honor*). About the same age, all three grew up in Germany; they speak German better than many Germans and are educated and successful. But they each had to risk much for their freedom; two of them narrowly escaped Hatun Surucu's fate. Necla Kelek was threatened by her father with a hatchet when she refused to greet him in a respectful manner when he came home. Seyran Ates was lucky to survive a shooting attack on the women's shelter that she founded in Kreuzberg. And Serap Cileli, when she was 13 years old, tried to kill herself to escape her first forced marriage; later she was taken to Turkey and married against her will, then she returned to Germany with two children from this marriage and took refuge in a women's shelter to escape her father's violence. Taking off from their own experiences, the three women describe the grim lives and sadness of Muslim women in that model Western democracy known as Germany.

Reading their books brought to mind a forgotten scene from seven years ago. Every time my daughter, who was 14 at the time, invited her schoolmates for a sleep-over, the Muslim fathers would be standing at the door at 10 P.M. to pick up their daughters. My wife, an immigrant herself, was indignant. I didn't like these fathers' dismissive, almost threatening posture, either, but I was a long way from protesting. Nor did I worry much when my daughter told me that one or another girl in her class was not taking biology or physical education and no longer going on field trips.

For a German of my generation, one of the most holy legacies of the past was the law of tolerance. We Germans in particular had no right to force our highly questionable customs onto other cultures. Later I learned from occasional newspaper reports and the accounts of friends that certain Muslim girls in Kreuzberg and Neukölln went underground or vanished without a trace. Even those reports gave me no more than a momentary discomfort in our upscale district of Charlottenburg.

But the books of the three Muslim dissidents now tell us what Germans like me didn't care to know. What they report seems almost unbelievable. They describe an everyday life of oppression, isolation, imprisonment and brutal corporal punishment for Muslim women and girls in Germany, a situation for which there is only one word: slavery.

Seyran Ates estimates that perhaps half of young Turkish women living in Germany are forced into marriage every year. In the wake of these forced marriages often

come violence and rape; the bride has no choice but to fulfill the duties of the marriage arranged by her parents and her in-laws. One side-effect of forced marriage is the psychological violation of the men involved. "Although they are the presumed beneficiaries of this custom, men are likewise forbidden to marry whom they want." A groom who chooses his own wife faces threats, too. In such cases, according to Seyran Ates and Serap Cileli, the groom as well as the bride must go underground to escape the families' revenge. . . .

Before the murder of Hatun Surucu there were enough warnings to engage the Germans in a debate about the parallel society growing in their midst. There have been 49 known "honor crimes," most involving female victims, during the past nine years—16 in Berlin alone. Such crimes are reported in the "miscellaneous" column along with other family tragedies and given a five-line treatment. Indeed, it's possible that the murder of Hatun Surucu never would have made the headlines at all but for another piece of news that stirred up the press. Just a few hundred yards from where Surucu was killed, at the Thomas Morus High School, three Muslim students soon openly declared their approval of the murder. Shortly before that, the same students had bullied a fellow pupil because her clothing was "not in keeping with the religious regulations." Volker Steffens, the school's director, decided to make the matter public in a letter to students, parents and teachers. More than anything else, it was the students' open praise of the murder that made the crime against Hatun Surucu the talk of Berlin and soon of all Germany. . . .

Politicians and religious scholars of all faiths are right in pointing out that there are many varieties of Islam, that Islamism and Islam should not be confused, that there is no line in the Koran that would justify murder. "We Western Muslim women," Seyran Ates says, "will set off the reform of traditional Islam, because we are its victims."

Peter Schneider is a writer based in Berlin.

SOURCE: "The New Berlin Wall" by Peter Schneider, *The New York Times Magazine,* December 4, 2005, p. 66. © 2005, Peter Schneider. Reprinted by permission.

Psychological Perspectives

Psychological perspectives focus on the many psychological influences—perception, learning, motivation, emotion, personality, and so on—that affect our sexual behavior and our experience of ourselves as female or male. Some psychological theorists, such as Sigmund Freud, focus on the motivational role of sex in human personality. Others focus on how our experiences and mental representations of the world affect our sexual behavior.

SIGMUND FREUD AND PSYCHOANALYTIC THEORY Sigmund Freud, a Viennese physician, formulated a grand theory of personality termed **psychoanalysis.** Freud believed that we are all born with biologically based sex drives that must be channeled through socially approved outlets if family and social life are to carry on without undue conflict.

Freud proposed that the mind operates on conscious and unconscious levels. The conscious level corresponds to our state of current awareness. The unconscious mind refers to the darker reaches of the mind that lie outside our direct awareness. The ego shields the conscious mind from awareness of our baser sexual and aggressive urges by means of **defense mechanisms** such as repression, or motivated forgetting of traumatic experiences.

Although many sexual ideas and impulses are banished to the unconscious, they continue to seek expression. One avenue of expression is the dream, through which sexual impulses may be perceived in disguised, or symbolic, form. The therapists and scholars who follow in the Freudian tradition are quite interested in analyzing dreams, and the dream objects listed in Table 1.3 are often considered sexual symbols.

Truth or Fiction Revisited: To a psychoanalyst, dreams of airplanes, bullets, snakes, sticks, and similar objects may indeed symbolize the male genitals. But this is the case according to psychoanalytic theory, and is not necessarily supported by research evidence. To his credit, Freud himself maintained skepticism about the import of dream symbols. He once remarked, "Sometimes a cigar is just a cigar."

Freud introduced us to new and controversial ideas about ourselves as sexual beings. For example, he originated the concept of **erogenous zones**—the idea that many parts of the body, not just the genitals, are responsive to sexual stimulation.

One of Freud's most controversial beliefs was that children normally harbor erotic interests. He believed that the suckling of the infant in the oral stage was an erotic act. So too was anal bodily experimentation through which children learn to experience pleasure in the control of their sphincter muscles and the processes of elimination.

He theorized that it was normal for children to progress through stages of development in which the erotic interest shifts from one erogenous zone to another, as, for example, from the mouth or oral cavity to the anal cavity. According to his theory of **psychosexual development,** children undergo five stages of development: oral, anal, phallic, latency, and genital, which are named according to the predominant erogenous zones of each stage. Each stage gives rise to certain kinds of conflicts. Moreover, inadequate or excessive gratification in any stage can lead to **fixation** in that stage and the development of traits and sexual preferences characteristic of that stage.

Freud believed that it was normal for children to develop erotic feelings toward the parent of the other gender during the phallic stage. These incestuous urges lead to conflict with the parent of the same sex. In later chapters we will see that these devel-

TRUTH fiction 8

Psychoanalysis The theory of personality originated by Sigmund Freud, which proposes that human behavior represents the outcome of clashing inner forces

Defense mechanisms In psychoanalytic theory, automatic processes that protect the ego from anxiety by disguising or ejecting unacceptable ideas and urges

Erogenous zones Parts of the body, including but not limited to the sex organs, that are responsive to sexual stimulation

Psychosexual development In psychoanalytic theory, the process by which sexual feelings shift from one erogenous zone to another

Fixation In psychoanalytic theory, arrested development, which includes attachment to objects of an earlier stage of psychosexual development

TABLE 1.3

Dream Symbols in Psychoanalytic Theory*

Symbols for Male Genital Organs

Airplanes	Fish	Neckties	Tools	Weapons
Bullets	Hands	Poles	Trains	
Feet	Hoses	Snakes	Trees	
Fire	Knives	Sticks	Umbrellas	

Symbols for Female Genital Organs

Bottles	Caves	Doors	Ovens	Ships
Boxes	Chests	Hats	Pockets	Tunnels
Cases	Closets	Jars	Pots	

Symbols for Sexual Intercourse

Climbing a ladder	Flying in an airplane
Climbing a staircase	Riding a horse
Crossing a bridge	Riding an elevator
Driving an automobile	Riding a roller coaster
Entering a room	Walking into a tunnel or down a hall

Symbols for the Breasts

Apples	Peaches

*Freud theorized that the content of dreams symbolized urges, wishes, and objects of fantasy that we would censor in the waking state.

SOURCE: From *Psychology in the New Millennium (with Info Trac), 8th edition* by Rathus. Reprinted with permission of Wadsworth, a division of Thomson Learning: www.thomsonrights.com. Fax 800 730-2215.

opments, which Freud termed the **Oedipus complex,** have implications for the assumption of gender roles and sexual orientation.

LEARNING THEORIES   To what extent does sexual behavior reflect experience? Would you hold the same sexual attitudes and do the same things if you had been reared in another culture? We think not. Even within the same society, family and personal experiences can shape unique sexual attitudes and behaviors. Although psychoanalytic theory plumbs the depths of the unconscious, learning theorists focus on environmental factors that shape behavior.

Behaviorists such as John B. Watson (1878–1958) and B. F. Skinner (1904–1990) emphasized the importance of rewards and punishments in the learning process. Skinner termed events that increase the frequency or likelihood of behavior reinforcements. Children left to explore their bodies without parental condemnation will learn what feels good and will tend to repeat it. The Trobriand child who is rewarded for masturbation and premarital coitus through parental praise and encouragement will be more likely to repeat these behaviors than the child in a more sexually restrictive culture, who is punished for the same behavior. When sexual behavior (like masturbation) feels good, but parents connect it with feelings of guilt and shame, the child is placed in conflict and may vacillate between masturbating and swearing off it. If, as young children, we are severely punished for sexual exploration, we may come to associate sexual stimulation in general with feelings of guilt or anxiety. Such early learning experiences can set the stage for sexual problems or dysfunctions in adulthood.

Oedipus complex In psychoanalytic theory, a conflict of the phallic stage in which the boy wishes to possess his mother sexually and perceives his father as a rival in love; the analogous conflict for girls is the *Electra complex*

Behaviorists Learning theorists who argue that a scientific approach to understanding behavior must refer only to observable and measurable behaviors

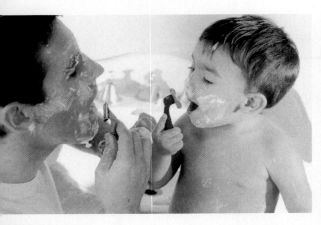

Acquisition of Gender Roles. *According to social–cognitive theory, children learn gender roles by means of reinforcement of certain behavior patterns and by observing the gender-related behaviors of their parents, peers, and other role models in media such as TV, films, and books.*

Modeling Acquiring knowledge and skills by observing others

Social–cognitive theory A cognitively oriented learning theory in which observational learning, values, and expectations play key roles in determining behavior

Feminist theory A theory that challenges acceptance of the male as the norm, traditional gender roles, and male oppression of females

COGNITIVE VIEWS Cognitive psychologists recognize the value of rewards and punishments in influencing behavior, but they emphasize the importance of cognitive activity (problem solving, decision making, expectations, and so on). They also recognize that people learn intentionally and by observing others. Observational learning, or **modeling**, refers to acquiring knowledge and skills by observing others. Observational learning involves more than direct observation of other people. It includes seeing models in films or on television, hearing about them, and reading about them. According to **social–cognitive theory**, children acquire the gender roles deemed appropriate in a society through reinforcement of gender-appropriate behavior and through observing the gender-role behavior of their parents, their peers, and other models on television, in films, in books, and so on.

In Chapter 6 we will more fully explore the nature of masculine and feminine gender roles, and why most males enact masculine roles and most females enact feminine roles. We will see that the acquisition of gender roles is likely to involve a complex interaction of psychological, biological, and social factors. But now let us turn our attention to a perspective—feminist theory—that challenges many commonly held ideas about these roles.

Feminist Theory

The Greek philosopher Aristotle is said to have described a female as a deformed male. We can only guess at the number of objectionable beliefs expressed in this description, such as seeing the male as the ideal, focusing on the differences rather than the similarities between men and women, and the implicit right of men to hold power over women.

Feminism and **feminist theory** are born of protest against ideas such as those of Aristotle's, ideas that remain with us today in many if not most parts of the world (Chesler, 2006). Definitions of feminism and of feminist theory are controversial, but it is clear enough that feminist theory focuses on the subordination of women to men, analyzing the relationships between sexism, heterosexism (prejudice or discrimination against homosexuals by heterosexuals), racism, and class oppression, and exploring means of resistance—on individual and societal levels (Butler, 1993, 2003).

Among other things, feminist theory challenges

- traditional views of men as breadwinners and women as homemakers
- traditional views of men as political policymakers, especially because those policies affect women and children
- traditional views of men as sexual "aggressors" and women as sexual "gatekeepers"
- traditional gender roles that view men as objective and rational, and women as emotional and irrational

It is of interest that some feminists even challenge the very concepts of femininity and masculinity, because their existence tends to suggest that there is some sort of biological or "actual" basis to the distinction (Squier & Littlefield, 2004; Wood, 2005). They argue, instead, that femininity and masculinity might be purely social constructions that have the effect of giving women second-class citizenship—or, in many historical eras and parts of the world, no citizenship whatsoever.

In terms of topics most relevant to this book, we will find feminists asserting that men have no right to control women's bodies—for example, that abortion is the personal choice of a woman and that women have as much right as men to decide whether to engage in sexual activity, and with whom. Feminists also argue that there are few, if any, sex differences in intelligence and specific mental abilities, such as those abilities used in math and science; that most medical research has been conducted by men for men, with men as subjects.

Although the extent and nature of sex differences remain controversial, we can note that many traditions that subjugate women are falling by the wayside, at least in developed nations. Most Western women, for example, are now in the workforce. As a result, many men now share part of the child rearing and housekeeping with female partners. In the United States, as many women as men are pursuing careers in traditionally male domains, such as business, law, and medicine (Stamback & Miriam, 2005). Many women now feel free to initiate sex and relationships.

Queer Theory

The word *queer* was initially used as an insult to describe homosexuals. After approximately two centuries, the term became gradually replaced by the word *gay* (Bhugra, 2005). However, homosexuals have reappropriated the word *queer* as a sign of pride, as shown by the title of the popular TV show *Queer Eye for the Straight Guy*. As one result of this reappropriation, a widely cited theory of the psychology and sociology of gender roles and sexual orientation is termed **queer theory** (Alexander, 2006; Valocchi, 2005).

Queer theory challenges a number of commonly held assumptions about gender and sexuality, such as the assumptions that heterosexuality is normal and superior to homosexuality (Elia et al., 2003; Gordon, 2005; Sullivan, 2003). Queer theory also challenges the assumption that people are naturally divided into heterosexuals and homosexuals (Halpern, 2003; Hird, 2004).

Queer theory argues that the concepts of heterosexuality and homosexuality are social constructs that ignore commonly experienced mismatches among people's anatomic sex, society's gender roles, and individuals' sexual desires (Schlichter, 2004). Queer theory asserts that human sexuality has always been more varied than those in power—particularly male heterosexuals—are willing to admit. They point to historical examples such as ancient Greek bisexuality and to current **homophobia** as evidence. We revisit concepts of queer theory in later chapters, particularly the chapters on gender and sexual orientation.

Multiple Perspectives on Human Sexuality

Given the complexity and range of human sexual behavior, we need to consider multiple perspectives to understand sexuality. Each perspective—historical, biological, cross-species, sociological, psychological, feminist, and queer—has something to teach us. Let us venture a few conclusions based on our overview of these perspectives. First, human sexuality appears to reflect a combination of biological, social, cultural, and psychological factors that interact in complex ways. Second, there are few universal patterns of sexual behavior, and views on what is right and wrong show great diversity. Third, although our own cultural values and beliefs may be deeply meaningful to us, they may not indicate what is normal, natural, or moral in terms of sexual behavior. The complexity of human sexuality—a complexity that causes it to

Queer theory A theory that challenges heteronormativity and heterosexism

Homophobia Although this term derives from roots meaning *fear of homosexuals,* it is usually used to refer to hatred of homosexuals

remain somewhat baffling even to scientists—adds to the wonder and richness of our sexual experience.

SafeZone

Q *If there are so many ways of looking at sex, how can you tell what is the right way of thinking about things? It makes it hard to make decisions.*

A Yes, it can be hard to make sexual decisions, but it doesn't have to be! If the decisions are informed decisions, if they are consistent with your values, and—most important—if they are *your* decisions, you can be quite comfortable with them. Do not allow yourself to be pressured by someone else; if you're pressured and you go along with the pressure, it's not *you* making the decision. This textbook will suggest things to consider when making decisions about dozens of sexual topics. But in the end, the decisions have to be *your* decisions. What is right for someone else might not be right for you. One more thing: We don't know anyone who makes the right decision about every issue all the time. Be stubborn about matters of sexual health, but if you err in a judgment about another person, know that you're not alone. We've "been there."

RECITE

1. What is the science of human sexuality about?

- Human sexuality concerns the ways in which we experience and express ourselves as sexual beings. The study of human sexuality draws upon the expertise of anthropologists, biologists, medical researchers, sociologists, psychologists, and other scientists.

2. What value systems affect sexual attitudes and decisions?

- Along with accurate knowledge about human sexuality, our values inform our sexual decisions.

- Value systems include legalism, situational ethics, ethical relativism, hedonism, asceticism, utilitarianism, and rationalism.

3. What does it mean to think critically about human sexuality?

- Critical thinking is a skeptical approach to evaluating arguments, widely held beliefs, and evidence: Critical thinkers examine definitions of terms and the premises of arguments, and use caution in drawing conclusions from evidence.

4. What are the various perspectives on human sexuality?

- The historical perspective suggests that there are few universal sexual trends. There is evidence of ancient worship of generative power. Ancient Hebrew, Greek, and Romans dwelled in male-oriented societies that viewed women as property. Repressive Victorian sexual attitudes gave way to the sexual revolution of the 1960s and 1970s.

- The biological perspective focuses on biological sexual processes such as genetic, hormonal, and neural factors. Knowledge of biology enables us to enhance our sexual health.

- Evolutionary theory suggests that social behaviors that enhance reproductive success may be subject to natural selection.

- The cross-species perspective reveals the variety of sexual behaviors among nonhumans. For example, there are animal analogues of oral sex and foreplay.

- The sociological perspective studies ways in which cultural beliefs affect sexual behavior and attitudes. All cultures apparently place some limits on sex, but some are more permissive than others.

- Psychological perspectives focus on the processes of perception, learning, motivation, emotion, and personality that affect gender and sexual behavior. Freud formulated the theory of psychoanalysis, which proposes that biologically based sex drives come into conflict with social codes. Learning theories focus on the roles of rewards and punishments. Social–cognitive theory views people as decision makers and emphasizes the role of observational learning.

- Feminist theory challenges traditional gender roles and male oppression of females.

- Queer theory challenges heteronormativity—the view that heterosexuality is normal—and points out mismatches among anatomic sex, gender roles, and sexual desires as evidence.

1. Critical thinking involves all of the following *except*

   (a) skepticism
   (b) challenging tradition
   (c) evaluating the premises of logic
   (d) blindly following authority figures

2. Stone Age art suggests that people worshiped

   (a) women's ability to bear children
   (b) a scientific approach to human sexuality
   (c) bisexuality in men
   (d) men's ability to father children

3. The taboo against _____ is likely to have been the first taboo.

   (a) masturbation
   (b) incest
   (c) oral sex
   (d) anal intercourse

4. The ancient _____ were first to produce a sex manual.

   (a) Greeks
   (b) Romans
   (c) Chinese
   (d) Indians

5. According to the text, _____ challenged the prevailing British view by arguing that sexual desires in women were natural and healthy.

   (a) Havelock Ellis
   (b) Sylvester Graham
   (c) Sigmund Freud
   (d) Richard von Krafft–Ebing

6. Which theory proposes that dispositions toward behavior that enhances reproductive success may be transmitted by genes?

   (a) Psychological
   (b) Sociological
   (c) Feminist
   (d) Evolutionary

7. A controversial Freudian belief is that

   (a) children normally harbor erotic interests
   (b) children ignore unacceptable impulses
   (c) childhood is an important time of life
   (d) children seek pain and avoid pleasure

8. Masters and Johnson are best known for using _____ in their research on human sexual response.

   (a) correlation coefficients
   (b) cross-cultural methods
   (c) the laboratory observation method
   (d) the survey

9. Of the following, the group with the highest numbers of sex partners is

   (a) Asian Americans
   (b) Males
   (c) High school graduates
   (d) 55- to 59-year-olds

10. Queer theory opposes

    (a) heterosexism
    (b) use of the word *queer*
    (c) activism
    (d) challenging prevailing views of gender and sexuality

11. According to _____ theory, children acquire the gender roles deemed appropriate in a society through reinforcement and observational learning.

    (a) evolutionary
    (b) social–cognitive
    (c) feminist
    (d) psychoanalytic

12. Martino's research finds _____ between listening to sexually explicit music lyrics and sexual initiation at an early age.

    (a) a causal relationship
    (b) no relationship
    (c) a connection or correlation
    (d) an evolutionary relationship

13. *Psychoipathia Sexualis* was written by

    (a) Havelock Ellis
    (b) Sylvester Graham
    (c) Sigmund Freud
    (d) Richard von Krafft-Ebing

14. _____ plays a relatively more important role in sexuality as we travel up the evolutionary ladder.

    (a) Learning
    (b) Motivation
    (c) The genetic code
    (d) Biology

15. According to queer theory,

    (a) there is no such thing as homosexuality
    (b) all heterosexuals are prejudiced
    (c) everybody is bisexual
    (d) popular categories of sexual orientation do not adequately describe the population

Answers 1. d; 2. a; 3. b; 4. c; 5. a; 6. d; 7. a; 8. c; 9. b; 10. a; 11. b; 12. c; 13. d; 14. a; 15. d

2

Research Methods in Human Sexuality

TRUTH fiction

Which of the following statements are true, and which are fiction? Look for the Truth/Fiction icons on the pages that follow to find the answers.

1 The science of human sexuality tells people how they ought to behave.   T   F

2 You could study the sexual behavior of millions of Americans and still not obtain an accurate picture of the sexual behavior of the general American population.   T   F

3 Case studies have been carried out on people who are dead.   T   F

4 Only a small minority of adolescents and young adults are concerned about their sexual health.   T   F

5 Some sex researchers have engaged in "swinging" with the people they have studied.   T   F

6 Masters and Johnson created an artificial penis containing photographic equipment to study the female sexual response.   T   F

7 Viagra causes risky sexual behavior.   T   F

8 People who attend church regularly tend to be more satisfied with their relationships.   T   F

9 Women who suffer sexual problems and dysfunctions after having their clitorises cut out in fundamentalist societies are likely to continue the practice with their own daughters.   T   F

10 Researchers often publish the names of participants in sex research in professional journals. T   F

Wardell B. Pomeroy, one of Alfred Kinsey's co-researchers in the 1940s, was interviewing a man about his first ejaculation. He asked, "When?" The man answered, "Fourteen." Pomeroy then asked, "How?" and was surprised to hear: "With a horse."

In his biography, *Sex the Measure of All Things: A Life of Alfred C. Kinsey,* Jonathan Gathorne-Hardy records what happened next. Pomeroy asked the man, "How often were you having intercourse with animals at 14?"

The man looked confused and said, "Well, yes, it is true I had intercourse with a pony at 14." Pomeroy, it turned out, had misheard the man's previous answer. It was "with whores," not "with a horse." So the man was stunned that Pomeroy had had the insight to ask him the horse question out of the blue (Boxer, 2000).

The question was asked during the Kinsey studies of sexual behavior in the United States—the best known surveys in the history of studying sexual behavior. The survey method typically gathers information about sexual attitudes and behaviors through questionnaires or interviews.

In this chapter we see how **sexologists**—scientists who study human sexuality—carry out research. Many of them, like Wardell Pomeroy and other members of the Kinsey team, interview respondents. Interviews and questionnaires are examples of the

Research Interview. *Interviewing is a commonly used method in surveys. Questionnaires are also used.*

survey method. However, we will see that there are many other methods, including the case study, the field study, and the experiment, to name but a few. Then we will discuss ethical issues in sex research. The core concern of ethics is that research subjects or participants should not be exposed to harm.

But let us begin by exploring the scientific method. Science is what separates research findings from opinion, superstition, folklore, and error.

SafeZone

Q *How much research is there really on sexuality? It seems hard to study. How much do we really know?*

A The short answer is: Enough to fill nearly countless encyclopedias. We know volumes about sexual anatomy and physiology, about sex hormones, about conception and pregnancy, about sex and aging, about STIs, about cancer of the sex organs, and on and on. Do we know what your partner wants? Ask him or her. There are also some areas of the science of sexuality about which we still have many questions, such as why some people find sex with violence to be more appealing than sex with respect, or why some people are so outraged or frightened by homosexuality.

A Scientific Approach to Human Sexuality

Sexologists—like other scientists—take an **empirical** approach. They base their knowledge on research evidence, rather than on intuition, faith, or superstition. Scientists' and other people's intuitions or religious beliefs may suggest topics to be studied scientifically. Yet once the topics are selected, answers are sought on the basis of the scientific method.

The Scientific Method

Critical thinking and the scientific approach share the hallmark of skepticism. As skeptics, sexologists question prevailing assumptions and theories about sexual behavior. They are willing to dispute the assertions of authority figures such as political and religious leaders—even other scientists. Sexologists also recognize that they cannot gain perfect knowledge. One era's "truths" may become another era's ancient myths and fallacies. Sexologists are involved in the continuous quest for truth, but they do not see themselves as experiencing revelations or defining final truths.

The scientific method is a systematic way of gathering scientific evidence and testing assumptions through research. It has a number of elements:

1. *Formulating a research question.* Does alcohol inspire or impair sexual response? Scientists formulate research questions on the basis of their observations of, or theories about, events or behavior. They then seek answers to such questions by conducting empirical research.

2. *Framing the research question in the form of a* **hypothesis.** Experiments are usually undertaken with a hypothesis in mind—a precise prediction about behavior that is often derived from theory. A hypothesis is tested through research. For instance, a scientist might theorize that alcohol enhances sexual responsiveness either by directly stimulating sexual response or by reducing feelings of guilt associated with sex. He or she might then hypothesize that an intervention (called, in experimental terms, a *treatment*), such as drinking alcohol in a laboratory setting, will lead to heightened sexual arousal in the presence of erotic stimuli (such as sexually explicit films).

3. *Testing the hypothesis.* Scientists then test hypotheses through carefully controlled observation and experimentation. A specific hypothesis about alcohol and sexual arousal—that alcohol either increases or decreases sexual responsiveness—might be tested by administering a certain amount of alcohol to one group of people and then comparing their level of sexual arousal after receiving specific types of sexual stimulation (such as exposure to sexually explicit films) with the level of sexual arousal of another group of people who were shown the films but not given any alcohol.

4. *Drawing conclusions.* Scientists then draw conclusions or **inferences** about the correctness of their hypotheses, based on their analyses of the results of their studies. If the results of well-designed research studies fail to bear out certain hypotheses, scientists can revise the theories that served as the frameworks for the

REFLECT

Does it seem appropriate to you to study human sexual behavior scientifically? Why or why not?

Sexologist A person who engages in the scientific study of sex

Empirical Derived from or based on observation and experimentation

Hypothesis A precise prediction about behavior that is tested through research

Inference A conclusion or opinion

Kissing Gouramis. *These fish obtain their moniker from pressing their open mouths against one another. Yet if the word* kissing *is meant to imply affection, think again. Prolonged observations of the fish suggest "kissing" is more likely to be a test of strength. Describing the behavior of the fish as "kissing" confuses inference (that is, drawing conclusions) with description. One of the challenges to scientists is to separate description from inference.*

hypotheses. Research findings often lead scientists to modify their theories, and in turn generate new hypotheses that can be tested in further research.

Goals of the Science of Human Sexuality

The goals of the science of human sexuality are congruent with those of other sciences: to describe, explain, predict, and control the events (in this case, the sexual behaviors) that are of interest. Description is a basic goal of science. Before we can understand sexual behavior, we must be able to describe it. Scientists attempt to be clear, unbiased, and precise in their descriptions of events and behavior. The scientific approach to human sexuality describes sexual behavior through techniques as varied as the field study, the survey, the individual case study, and laboratory observation.

To underscore the importance of the need for unbiased description, consider the name of a tropical fish that will be familiar to many readers: the kissing gourami. These small, flat fish—particularly males—press their open mouths against one another. Yet the term *kissing gourami* may be a misnomer if it is meant to imply affection. Prolonged observations of the fish suggest that it is more likely that kissing in gouramis is a test of strength. The error in describing the behavior of gouramis as "kissing" involves confusing inference with description. It is, in fact, an **anthropomorphism;** it involves applying human standards to explain animal behavior. One of the great challenges to scientists is the separation of description from inference.

Inference—that is, the drawing of conclusions—like description, is crucial to science. Inference allows us to move from observations or descriptions of particular events or behavior to general principles that can be woven into models and theories that help explain them, such as psychoanalytic and learning theories or models.

Researchers attempt to relate their observations to other factors, or **variables**, that can help explain them. For example, researchers may attempt to explain variations in the **frequency** of coitus by relating—or correlating—coitus with **demographic** variables such as age, religious or social background, or cultural expectations. The variables that are commonly used to explain sexual behavior include biological (age, health), psychological (anxieties, skills), and sociological (educational level, socioeconomic status, ethnicity) ones. Explanations of behavior can involve reference to many variables.

Theories provide frameworks within which scientists can explain what they observe and make predictions. Theories must allow us to make predictions. One test of the soundness of psychoanalytic and learning theories is whether they allow us to predict behavior. Sex researchers study factors that may predict various types of sexual behavior. Some researchers, for example, have examined childhood interests and behavior patterns that may predict the development of a gay male or lesbian sexual orientation. Others have explored factors, such as the age at which dating begins and the quality of the relationships between teens and their parents, that may predict the likelihood of premarital intercourse during adolescence.

The concept of "controlling" human behavior does not mean coercing people to do the bidding of others. Rather, it means drawing upon scientific knowledge to help people create their own goals and marshal their resources to meet them. Reputable

Anthropomorphism The attributing of human characteristics to an animal

Variables Quantities or qualities that vary or may vary

Frequency The number of times an action is repeated within a given period

Demographic Concerning the vital statistics (race, gender, age, religion, and so on) of human populations

scientists are held to ethical and professional standards that safeguard the rights of participants in research.

Truth or Fiction Revisited: The science of human sexuality does not tell people how they ought to behave. Rather, it furnishes information that people may use to help themselves or others make decisions. For instance, the science of human sexuality provides information that increases the chances that a couple that is having difficulty becoming pregnant will be able to conceive. At the same time, it develops and evaluates means of birth control that can be used to help couples regulate their reproductive choices. "Control" also takes the form of enabling couples to give and receive more sexual pleasure, of enhancing fetal health, and of preventing and curing STIs.

Let us now examine the ways in which sexologists study human sexuality. Sexologists must first identify whom or what they will study, which brings us to the topic of sampling.

TRUTH fiction 1

CRITICAL Thinking
Does the science of human sexuality aim to tell people how they ought to behave? Why or why not?

Populations and Samples: Representing the World of Diversity

Sexologists seek to learn about **populations.** Populations are complete groups of people or animals. Many researchers have attempted to learn about people in the United States, for example. Other researchers may identify American adults or American adolescents as their population. Still other researchers attempt to compare the sexual behavior of African Americans with that of Latino and Latina Americans and other Americans. These are termed the *populations of interest* or *target populations.* These target populations are all sizable. It would be expensive, difficult, and, in fact, all but impossible to study every individual in them.

Because of the impossibility of studying all members of a population, scientists select individuals from the population and study them. The individuals who participate in research are said to compose a **sample.** However, we cannot truly learn about the population of interest unless the sample represents that population. If we wished to study the sexual behavior of Asian Americans, our population would consist of all Asian Americans. If we used only Asian American college students as our sample, we could not **generalize** our findings to all Asian Americans in all age ranges.

Including everyone in the United States in a study of sexual behavior would be impossible. We cannot even find all people in the United States when we conduct the census each decade. Sex research would undoubtedly cause many more people to refuse to participate than would a simple counting of noses. Sampling a part of a target population makes research practical and possible.

Population A complete group of organisms or events
Sample Part of a population
Generalize To go from the particular to the general

Populations and Samples. *To what populations do you belong? College students? Returning students? What of your gender? What about your ethnic background? How do researchers obtain samples that represent populations such as these? What problems do they encounter in attempting to do so?*

Sampling Methods

Now and then magazine editors boast that they have surveyed samples of 20,000 or 30,000 readers, but size alone does not mean that a sample is representative. *Psychology Today* and *Glamour* regularly poll readers, but their readers do not represent the general population. Readers of *Psychology Today* are "biased" in that they tend to be better educated and more liberal than the population at large (*Psychology Today*, 2006). Readers of *Glamour* are "biased" in that they are also better educated than the average American, and more likely to be concerned about their appearance and optimizing their sex lives. **Truth or Fiction Revisited:** It is true that you could study the sexual behavior of millions of Americans and still not obtain an accurate picture of the sexual behavior of the general American population. Researchers need to obtain samples that represent the target population.

One way of acquiring a representative sample is through **random sampling**. A random sample is one in which every member of the target population has an equal chance of participating. In a **stratified random sample**, known subgroups of a population are represented in proportion to their numbers in the population. For instance, about 13% of the American population is African American. Researchers could therefore decide that 13% of their sample must be African American if they are to represent the population of the United States. The randomness of the sample would be preserved because the members of the subgroups would be selected randomly from their particular subgroups.

Random samples can be hard to come by, especially when it comes to asking people about their sexual attitudes or behavior. For instance, sexual research is almost invariably conducted with people who volunteer to participate. Volunteers tend to differ from people who refuse to participate (Quartaro & Spier, 2002; Zelenski et al., 2003). For example, volunteers tend to be more open about their sexuality than the general population. They may even tend to exaggerate behaviors that others might consider deviant or abnormal.

One study attempted to assess the incidence of male–male sexual behavior that placed Hong Kong men at risk for contracting HIV, the virus that causes AIDS (e.g., anal intercourse without use of condoms), by means of random telephone numbers generated by a computer (Lau et al., 2002). Eighty-five of 2,074 men contacted (4%) admitted to having sex with other men and described their sexual behavior. But how can we determine whether there were many others who had sex with men but denied doing so? How can we know whether the men who admitted to male–male sexual behavior accurately described their contacts? Another study assessed the usefulness of brief telephone interviews in a Boston neighborhood believed to have many lesbian residents (Meyer et al., 2002). There was a high (94%!) level of cooperation with the researchers, and 14% of respondents identified themselves as lesbians. But did every one of the 94% who cooperated tell the truth? And what can we conclude about the incidence of a lesbian sexual orientation in the general population from such a survey?

The problem of **volunteer bias** is a thorny one for sex researchers, because the refusal of people who have been randomly selected to participate in the survey can ruin the representativeness of the sample. Because it would be unethical to coerce people to participate in a study on sexual behavior (or any other type of study), researchers must use samples of volunteers, rather than true random samples. A low response rate to a voluntary survey is an indication that the responses do not represent the people to whom the survey was distributed.

In some cases, samples are samples of convenience. They consist of individuals who happen to be available to the researcher and who share some characteristics with the target population, perhaps religious background or sexual orientation. Still,

REFLECT

How would you define yourself? What population or populations would you represent if you were recruited for a study on human sexuality?

Random sample A sample in which every member of a population has an equal chance of participating

Stratified random sample A random sample in which known subgroups in a population are represented in proportion to their numbers in the population

Volunteer bias A slanting of research data caused by the characteristics of individuals who volunteer to participate, such as willingness to discuss intimate behavior they do not truly represent the target group. Convenience samples often consist of European American middle-class college students who volunteer for studies conducted at their schools. They may not be (and probably are not) representative of students in general.

Methods of Observation

REFLECT

Did you ever hear researchers or pollsters say they used a "scientific sample" of people? What did you think was meant by the term *scientific sample*? What does it actually mean?

After scientists have chosen those they will study, they observe them. In this section, we consider several methods of observation: the case–study method, the survey method, naturalistic observation, ethnographic observation, participant observation, and laboratory observation.

The Case–Study Method

A **case study** is a carefully drawn, in-depth biography of an individual or a small group. The focus is on understanding one or several individuals as fully as possible by unraveling the interplay of various factors in their backgrounds. In most case studies, the researcher comes to know the individual or group through interviews or other contacts conducted over a prolonged period of time. The interviewing pattern tends to build upon itself with a good deal of freedom, as opposed to the one-shot, standardized set of questions used in survey questionnaires.

Researchers also conduct case studies by interviewing people who have known the individuals or by examining public records. Sigmund Freud, for example, drew upon historical records in his case study of the Renaissance inventor and painter Leonardo da Vinci. Freud concluded that da Vinci's artistic productions represented the sublimating, or channeling, of male–male sexual impulses. **Truth or Fiction Revisited:** It is true that case studies have been carried out on people who are dead, as was the case with Freud's study of Leonardo da Vinci. Such case studies rely on historical records rather than interviews with the individuals themselves or their contemporaries.

Reports of innovative treatments for sexual dysfunctions often appear as detailed case studies. A clinician may report the background of the client in depth, describe the treatment, the apparent outcomes, and suggest factors that might have contributed to the treatment's success or failure. In writing a treatment case study, the therapist attempts to provide information that may be of help to therapists who treat clients with similar problems. Case studies or "multiple case studies" (reports concerning a few individuals) that hold promise may be subjected to controlled investigation—ideally to experimental studies involving treatment and control groups.

Despite the richness of material that may be derived from case studies, they are not as rigorous a research design as an experiment. People often have gaps in memory, especially concerning childhood events. There is also the potential of observer bias; that is, clinicians and interviewers may unintentionally guide people into saying what they expect to hear. Researchers may even inadvertently color people's reports when they jot them down—shape them subtly in ways that reflect their own views.

The Survey Method

Sexologists may **survey** respondents by interviewing or administering questionnaires to thousands of people from particular population groups to learn about their sexual behavior and attitudes. Interviews such as those used by Alfred Kinsey

Case study A carefully drawn, in-depth biography of an individual or a small group of individuals that may be obtained through interviews, questionnaires, and historical records

Survey A detailed study of a sample obtained by means such as interviews and questionnaires

and his colleagues (1948, 1953) have the advantages of face-to-face contact and of giving the interviewer the opportunity to probe—that is, to follow up on answers that seem to lead toward useful information. A skilled interviewer may be able to set a respondent at ease and establish a sense of trust or rapport that encourages self-disclosure. (Unskilled interviewing may cause respondents to conceal information.)

Questionnaires are less expensive than interviews. The major expenses in using questionnaires involve printing and distribution or posting them on a website. Questionnaires can be administered to many people simultaneously. Respondents can return them unsigned, so that they are anonymous. Anonymity may encourage the disclosure of intimate information. Questionnaires, of course, can be used only by people who can read and record their responses. Interviews can be used even with people who cannot read or write.

Some of the major surveys described in this book were conducted by Kinsey and his colleagues (1948, 1953), the University of Chicago group (Laumann et al., 1994), and the Kaiser Family Foundation and others (2003). The book also discusses surveys conducted by popular magazines such as *Glamour*. By and large, these surveys have reported the **incidence** and frequency of sexual activities among men and women; both married and single; male–female, male–male, and female–female sexual activity; and the sexual behavior of adolescents, adults, and older people.

Many of these surveys have something to contribute to our understanding of human sexuality, but none represents the American population at large. Most people consider their sexuality to be among the most intimate, private aspects of their lives. People who willingly agree to be polled on political matters may resist participation in surveys about their sexual behavior. It is thus difficult, if not impossible, for researchers to recruit a truly representative sample of the population. Even the best surveys provide, at best, an approximation of sexual attitudes, beliefs, and behaviors.

Let us review the methods of some surveys of human sexuality, beginning with those used by Kinsey and his colleagues.

THE KINSEY REPORTS   Alfred Kinsey and his colleagues (1948, 1953) interviewed 5,300 males and 5,940 females in the United States between 1938 and 1949. They posed questions about sexual experiences, including masturbation, oral sex, and intercourse before and during marriage. Kinsey obviously could not use direct observational methods, such as sending his researchers to peer through bedroom windows. Nor did he try to obtain a random sample. He believed that a high refusal rate would wreck his chances of accurately representing the general population. Instead, he used group sampling. He recruited participants from the organizations and community groups to which they belonged, such as college fraternities and sororities. He contacted representatives of groups in diverse communities and tried to persuade them to secure the cooperation of fellow group members. If he showed these individuals that they would not be subjected to embarrassment or discomfort, Kinsey hoped they would persuade other members to participate. In some cases he obtained the full participation of a group.

Still, Kinsey's samples did not represent the general population. People of color, people in rural areas, older people, poor people, and Catholics and Jews were all underrepresented (Barth et al., 2002; Sharp, 2002). It is thus unlikely that Kinsey's results accurately mirrored the U.S. population at the time. In Chapter 10 we'll see that his estimate that 37% of the male population had reached orgasm at least once through male–male sexual activity might have been high. But the relationships Kinsey uncovered, such as the positive link between level of education and participation in oral sex, are probably quite generalizable.

Incidence A measure of occurrence or the degree of occurrence of an event

In Chapter 10 we will see that Kinsey concluded that one's designation as heterosexual and homosexual can be more than a simple checkmark in one column or the other. Kinsey suggested that there is a continuum of heterosexuality–homosexuality. Although some critics argued in favor of a yes–no designation of one's sexual orientation, sexologists, including queer theorists, continue to debate the distribution of sexual orientation intensely.

Alfred Kinsey. *The "Kinsey Reports" shocked the United States of the 1950s. What kinds of surveys are there? How do researchers attempt to encourage people to participate? How do gaps in memory, volunteer bias, and social desirability distort the results of surveys?*

Kinsey did take measures to urge honest answers. Participants were assured of the confidentiality of their records. Interviewers were trained to conduct the interviews nonjudgmentally. They held a "calm and steady eye" and tone of voice. On the other hand, all of Kinsey's interviewers were men. Women respondents might have felt freer to open up to female interviewers.

Kinsey checked the reliability of his data by reexamining hundreds of subjects after 18 months or more had passed. Their reports of the incidence of sexual activities (e.g., whether they had ever engaged in premarital or extramarital coitus) were highly consistent, but reports of the frequency of sexual activities (such as the number of times one has masturbated to orgasm, or the frequency of coitus) were less consistent. People seem to find it more difficult to estimate the frequencies of their activities than to answer whether they have ever engaged in them.

Kinsey knew that consistency of responses across time did not guarantee **validity**. That is, repeat interviews did not show whether the reported behaviors actually took place as described. However, he found high consistency in the reports of 706 pairs of spouses, suggesting that their self-reports were reasonably accurate.

SafeZone

Q *I saw the movie* Kinsey; *is it really true that he had sex with people other than his wife for purposes of research?*

A We won't join the gossip about Kinsey, but we'll note that the history of legitimate sex research is tainted by the occasional stories of abuse. However, a checkered past doesn't mean we should toss the research enterprise into the wastebasket. It has saved lives and given countless people pleasure.

THE NHSLS STUDY The National Health and Social Life Survey (NHSLS) was intended to provide general sexual information about people in the United States along with specific information that might be used to predict and prevent the spread of HIV/AIDS. It was conducted by Edward O. Laumann of the University of Chicago and three colleagues—John H. Gagnon, Robert T. Michael, and Stuart Michaels—in the 1990s and was published as *The Social Organization of Sexuality: Sexual Practices in the United States* in 1994. The NHSLS was to be originally supported by government funds, but Senator Jesse Helms blocked federal financing on the grounds that it was inappropriate for the government to support sex research (Bronner, 1998). The research team therefore obtained private funding but had to trim the scope of the project.

Validity With respect to interviews, questionnaires, and tests, the degree to which an item measures what it is supposed to measure

The sample included 3,432 people. Of this number, 3,159 were drawn from English-speaking adults living in households (not dormitories, prisons, and so forth), age 18 to 59. The other 273 were purposely obtained by oversampling African American and Latino and Latina American households, so that more information could be obtained about these ethnic groups. Although the sample probably represents the overall U.S. population quite well (or at least those of age 18 to 59), there were too few Asian Americans, Native Americans, and Jews to offer much information about these groups.

The researchers identified samples of households in geographic areas—by addresses, not names. They sent a letter to each household, describing the purpose and methods of the study, and an interviewer visited each household one week later. Potential subjects were assured that the purposes of the study were important and that their identities would be kept confidential. Incentives of up to $100 were offered for cooperating. A high completion rate of close to 80% was obtained in this way.

THE NATIONAL SURVEY OF FAMILY GROWTH (NSFG) The NSFG was conducted by the Centers for Disease Control and Prevention (CDC) as another means of assessing sexual behavior "relevant to demographic and public health concerns" (Mosher et al., 2005). It involved face-to-face interviews in the homes of 12,571 people, including 4,928 men and 7,643 women age 15 to 44. The interviewees responded to questions about their sexual behavior on laptop computers to ensure their privacy and encourage honesty. There was a completion rate of 79%. All in all, the NHSLS and NSFG may be the best surveys since Kinsey's day to offer a reasonably accurate—if not perfect—snapshot of the sexual behavior of the general population of the United States.

There were some interesting findings about male–male and female–female sexual behavior. For example, 5.7% of the males had had oral sex with another male, and 3.7% had had anal sex with another male. Among females, 11% said "yes" when asked, "Have you ever had any sexual experience of any kind with another female?" In Chapter 10, we will see that smaller percentages of males and females identify themselves as homosexual or bisexual, adding more evidence that—as queer theorists suggest—there are discrepancies between sexual interests, sexual behavior, and expressed sexual orientations. Ten percent of European American women reported having 15 or more sex partners compared with 9% of African American women and 5% of Latina American women.

THE NATIONAL SURVEY OF ADOLESCENTS AND YOUNG ADULTS The Kaiser Family Foundation and others (2003) tried to obtain a nationally representative sample of 13- to 24-year-olds by selecting telephone numbers at random and conducting telephone interviews with 1,854 young people either in English or Spanish. They purposefully oversampled people in ethnic minority groups—African Americans, Latino and Latina Americans, and Asian Americans—because most studies do not generate enough information about them. Parents provided permission to interview minors (respondents younger than 18). The response rate was 55%.

Truth or Fiction Revisited: Four out of five respondents reported that they were concerned about their sexual health.

Note some of the study's findings:

- About one adolescent in three reported being pressured into sex—exceeded only by the number who reported being pressured to drink alcohol.

- Sixty percent of the sample agreed with the statement, "Waiting to have sex is a nice idea, but nobody really does."

- One adolescent in three had engaged in oral sex, often to avoid intercourse. Many adolescents and young adults underestimated the risk of contracting an STI via oral sex.

- Seventy percent of sexually active young adults and 40% of sexually active adolescents reported that they or their partner had a pregnancy test.

- Four out of five adolescents reported that adolescents tend to drink or use drugs before sex. Many adolescents and young adults reported doing more than they had planned to do under the influence of alcohol or drugs, including "bareback sex" (that is, sex without a condom).

- Many adolescents did not know the details regarding how many STIs are transmitted and their health consequences.

- About 70% of adolescents erroneously believed that other forms of contraception provide better protection against STIs than condoms do.

- Although 90% of adolescents said that using condoms is a sign of respect and caring for one's partner, about half were reluctant to discuss condoms with their partners, fearing, for example, that raising the subject would be embarrassing or suggest that one is suspicious of one's partner.

- More than three adolescents and young adults out of four said they would like to have more information about STIs.

THE PLAYBOY FOUNDATION SURVEY The Playboy Foundation commissioned a survey of sexual practices in the 1970s, which was reported in Morton Hunt's 1974 book, *Sexual Behavior in the 1970's*. The Playboy/Hunt survey sought to examine the changes in American sexual behavior between Kinsey's day and the early 1970s.

The Playboy sample was drawn randomly from phone book listings in 24 American cities. People were asked to participate in small group discussions focusing on trends in sexual practices in the United States. Hunt argued that his final sample of 2,026 participants was stratified properly with regard to the ages and races of urban residents across a diverse sample of American cities, but many groups such as rural people and inmates of prisons and mental hospitals were grossly underrepresented. However, the major flaw in the method is volunteer bias; 80% of the people contacted refused to participate. It is logical to assume that the 20% who did participate were more open and frank about sexual issues than the population at large.

MAGAZINE SURVEYS Major readership surveys have also been conducted by popular magazines, such as *Psychology Today, Glamour, Ladies' Home Journal*, and *Cosmopolitan*. Although these surveys may obtain large numbers of respondents, their sampling techniques are unscientific and biased. Each sample represents, at best, the readers of the magazine in which the questionnaire appears. Moreover, we learn only about readers who volunteer to respond to these questionnaires, which is a small percentage of the overall readership. Finally, readers of these magazines are wealthier than the public at large, and readers of *Cosmopolitan, Psychology Today*, and *Glamour* tend to be more liberal (Barney & Feenberg, 2004; *Psychology Today*, 2006). In addition, the samples only represent readers who are willing to complete the surveys.

SURVEYS OF SPECIFIC POPULATIONS The NHSLS and NSFG study were broad based. They queried men and women from different localities, socioeconomic strata, and age groups. Some researchers have focused their efforts on particular populations, such as adolescents, older people, people from particular racial/ethnic groups, and gay men and lesbians.

UCLA Researcher Gail Wyatt

In recent years, large-scale studies in the United States and other countries have been conducted to acquire information concerning sexual practices that might prove useful in the fight against AIDS. In the United States, for example, researchers from the Battelle Memorial Institute of Seattle interviewed a nationally representative sample of 3,321 men between the ages of 20 and 39 to determine the prevalence of unsafe sexual practices among young adult men (Billy et al., 1993; Tanfer et al., 1993).

In 1978 and 1981, the Indiana University Institute for Sex Research (also called the Kinsey Institute) reported the results of a survey of 979 gay people from the San Francisco area and a reference group of 477 people matched for age, race, and educational and occupational achievements (Bell & Weinberg, 1978; Bell et al., 1981). In their book, *Homosexualities,* researchers Alan Bell and Martin Weinberg (1978) recognized that their findings could not necessarily be extended to gay people who lived in other cities or sections of the country. Indeed, they acknowledged that their sample might not even represent gay people in San Francisco. It consisted of people who had "come out of the closet" to join gay rights organizations, who attended gay bars and baths, and so forth. Nevertheless, these reports have provided wide-ranging information on parent–child relationships and sexual orientation, and on the diversity of lifestyles among gay people (see Chapter 10).

Questions abound about the sexual behavior of Native Americans and African Americans. Kinsey did not survey Native Americans, and the number of Native Americans in the NHSLS study was too small to draw conclusions. Kinsey obtained some data on the sexual behavior of African Americans, but did not report it because African Americans were underrepresented in his samples. However, more recent studies by Gail Wyatt and the NHSLS group have reported some useful information. University of California at Los Angeles (UCLA) researcher Gail Wyatt and her colleagues (Wyatt, 1985, 1989; Wyatt et al., 1988a, b) examined the sexual behavior of a sample of 122 European American and 126 African American women in Los Angeles County. The women ranged in age from 18 to 36 years and were sampled randomly from telephone listings. People who agreed to participate were selected to balance the sample with respect to demographic characteristics such as age, education, number of children, and marital status. One in three prospective participants refused to cooperate. The participants were interviewed in Kinsey-style, face-to-face interviews.

One of the striking differences between Kinsey's data and Wyatt's was that African American and European American women in Wyatt's 1980s sample engaged in intercourse for the first time at earlier ages. Kinsey reported that by the age of 20, about one in five women had engaged in premarital coitus. By contrast, Wyatt reported that 98% of the people in her study (African American and European American) had done so by that age (Wyatt, 1989). When social class differences were taken into consideration, the ages of first intercourse for African American and European American women in Wyatt's sample were quite similar. Wyatt's research, of course, was limited to Los Angeles and cannot be said to represent the general U.S. population. But Kinsey's sample was also geographically skewed. Kinsey overrepresented the northeastern United States, although he included respondents from other regions.

In recent years, Gail Wyatt has turned her attention to the problem of HIV/AIDS, particularly among women. She has looked at predictors of risky sexual behavior among single and married women (Wayment et al., 2003), and at the complex relationships among childhood sexual abuse and efforts to reduce risky sexual behavior later on (Wyatt et al., 2004a, b, 2005).

LIMITATIONS OF THE SURVEY METHOD   One limitation of surveys involves the fact that they are self-reports of respondents' behaviors. But self-reports are subject to inaccuracy or bias because of factors such as faulty memory; tendencies to distort or conceal information because of embarrassment, shame, or guilt; or attempts to present a socially favorable image of oneself (Rosenbaum, 2006). People may not recall the age at which they first engaged in petting or masturbated to orgasm. People may have difficulty recalling or calculating the frequencies of certain behaviors, such as the weekly frequency of marital intercourse. Survey data may also be drawn from haphazard or nonrepresentative samples and thus may not represent the target population.

Participants in surveys of sexual behavior may feel pressured to answer questions in the direction of **social desirability.** Some respondents try to ingratiate themselves with their interviewers by offering what they believe to be socially desirable answers. Some people may not divulge sensitive information for fear of disapproval or criminal prosecution. Even though interviewers may insist that participants will remain anonymous, respondents may fear their identities could be exposed someday. You can assess your own tendency to provide socially desirable answers by taking the nearby self-assessment.

In addition, some respondents choose to exaggerate. In our culture men may tend to exaggerate their sexual exploits. Women may tend to play them down (Ferraro, 2004; Nanda & Warms, 2004). Some respondents falsify their attitudes and exaggerate the bizarreness of their behavior to draw attention to themselves or to foul up study results.

Because many people refuse to participate in surveys, samples are biased by large numbers of volunteers. Volunteers tend to be more sexually permissive and liberal minded than nonvolunteers. The results of a survey based on a volunteer sample thus may not accurately reflect the population at large.

You might think that these problems would render the survey method useless as a means of learning about human sexuality. Actually, carefully conceived and executed surveys offer many insights into sexual attitudes and practices. In many cases they are the only available means. Before Kinsey we had little information about the sexual practices of people in our society.

SafeZone

Q *How could I be part of a study on sexuality?*

A In general, responding to the typical questionnaire you find in a magazine or on a website isn't helpful to the study of sexuality. The sampling is probably biased and the "scientific" analysis of answers may not be all that scientific. Instead, you can check with your professor or a nearby medical school about useful studies that may be underway on campus or nearby. If a sexuality study comes your way, and you're satisfied that it is supported by a legitimate governmental agency or educational institution or private group, feel free to participate.

The Naturalistic Observation Method

In **naturalistic observation,** also called the *field study*, scientists directly observe the behavior of animals and humans where it happens. Anthropologists, for example, have dwelled in preliterate societies and reported on their social and sexual customs. Sociologists have observed the street life of prostitutes. Psychologists have observed patterns of nonverbal communication and body language in romantic couples.

Scientists take precautions to keep their naturalistic observations unobtrusive. They try not to influence the behavior of the individuals they study. Throughout the

Social desirability A response bias to a questionnaire or interview in which the person provides a socially acceptable response

Naturalistic observation A method in which organisms are observed in their natural environments

SELF-ASSESSMENT

Would You Tell an Interviewer the Truth on a Survey about Your Sexual Behavior? The Social-Desirability Scale

Researchers into human sexuality frequently encounter the problem of social desirability in their subjects. That is, many people being interviewed tell the researcher what they think he or she wants to hear, rather than divulge the truth about their sexual attitudes and behavior. The reason is often to earn the approval of the researcher. The tendency to respond in what people believe to be the socially desirable direction distorts the accuracy of the results in the case–study and survey methods.

What about you? Would you provide an interviewer with honest answers about your sexual attitudes and behaviors, or would you misrepresent your beliefs and behaviors to earn his or her approval?

You can complete the Social-Desirability Scale devised by Crowne and Marlowe to gain insight into whether you have a tendency to produce socially desirable responses.

DIRECTIONS   Read each item and decide whether it is true (T) or false (F) for you. Try to work rapidly and answer each question by circling either T or F, then turn to the scoring key in the Appendix to interpret your answers.

T F 1. Before voting I thoroughly investigate the qualifications of all the candidates.

T F 2. I never hesitate to go out of my way to help someone in trouble.

T F 3. It is sometimes hard for me to go on with my work if I am not encouraged.

T F 4. I have never intensely disliked anyone.

T F 5. On occasion, I have had doubts about my ability to succeed in life.

T F 6. I sometimes feel resentful when I don't get my way.

T F 7. I am always careful about my manner of dress.

T F 8. My table manners at home are as good as when I eat out in a restaurant.

T F 9. If I could get into a movie without paying and be sure I was not seen, I would probably do it.

T F 10. On a few occasions, I have given up something because I thought too little of my ability.

T F 11. I like to gossip at times.

T F 12. There have been times when I felt like rebelling against people in authority even though I knew they were right.

T F 13. No matter who I'm talking to, I'm always a good listener.

T F 14. I can remember "playing sick" to get out of something.

T F 15. There have been occasions when I have taken advantage of someone.

T F 16. I'm always willing to admit it when I make a mistake.

T F 17. I always try to practice what I preach.

T F 18. I don't find it particularly difficult to get along with loud-mouthed, obnoxious people.

T F 19. I sometimes try to get even rather than forgive and forget.

T F 20. When I don't know something I don't mind at all admitting it.

T F 21. I am always courteous, even to people who are disagreeable.

T F 22. At times I have really insisted on having things my own way.

T F 23. There have been occasions when I felt like smashing things.

T F 24. I would never think of letting someone else be punished for my wrongdoings.

T F 25. I never resent being asked to return a favor.

T F 26. I have never been irked when people expressed ideas very different from my own.

T F 27. I never make a long trip without checking the safety of my car.

T F 28. There have been times when I was quite jealous of the good fortune of others.

T F 29. I have almost never felt the urge to tell someone off.

T F 30. I am sometimes irritated by people who ask favors of me.

T F 31. I have never felt that I was punished without cause.

T F 32. I sometimes think when people have a misfortune they only got what they deserved.

T F 33. I have never deliberately said something that hurt someone's feelings.

SOURCE: D. P. Crowne and D. A. Marlowe, "A new scale of social desirability independent of pathology," *Journal of Consulting Psychology, 24* (1960): 351. Copyright 1960 by the American Psychological Association. Reprinted by permission.

years, naturalistic observers have been placed in ethical dilemmas. They have allowed sick or injured animals to die, rather than intervene, when medical assistance could have saved them. They have allowed substance abuse and illicit sexual behavior to go unreported to authorities. The ethical trade-off is that unobtrusive observation may yield data that will benefit large numbers of people—the greatest good for the greatest number.

The Ethnographic Observation Method

Ethnographic observation provides data concerning sexual behaviors and customs that occur among various ethnic groups—those that vary widely across cultures and those that are limited to one or few cultures. Anthropologists are the specialists who typically engage in ethnographic research. They have lived among societies of people in the four corners of the earth to observe and study human diversity. Margaret Mead (1935) reported on the social and sexual customs of various peoples of New Guinea. Bronislaw Malinowski (1929) studied the Trobriand islanders, among others. Even so, ethnographic observation has its limits on the study of sexual behavior. Sexual activities are most commonly performed away from the watchful gaze of others, especially visitors from other cultures. Ethnographers may thus have to rely on methods such as interviewing.

The ethnographer who studies a particular culture or subgroup within a culture tries not to alter the behavior of the members of the group by focusing attention on some facets of their behavior. Falling prey to social desirability, some people may "straighten out their act" while the ethnographer is present. Other people may try to impress the ethnographer by acting in ways that are more aggressive or sexually provocative than usual. In either case, people supply distorted information.

Katherine Frank. *Frank worked as a stripper in graduate school, both to augment her income and to learn about men who frequented strip clubs.*

The Participant Observation Method

Truth or Fiction Revisited: It is true that some sex researchers have engaged in "swinging" with the people they studied. In **participant observation**, investigators learn about people's behavior by directly interacting with them. Participant observation has been used in studies of male–male sexual behavior and mate swapping. In effect, participation has been the "price of admission" for observation. In some cases, researchers have engaged in coitus with participants during "swinging parties," which raises questions regarding what is permissible "for the sake of science."

We do not hear much anymore about "scientific swinging" with the public, but there are more current uses of participant observation. For example, as a graduate student in anthropology, Katherine Frank worked as a stripper at several clubs in a southeastern city "both as a means of earning extra cash for graduate school and as part of a feminism theory project investigating female objectification and body image" (Steinberg, 2004). In reports of her experiences, Frank (2002, 2003) notes that many men told her they attend the clubs because they "just want to relax." She writes that male customers may encounter some stigma for visiting the clubs, but not as much as the strippers do. Some men, moreover, do business in strip clubs and charge the expenses to their corporate accounts.

The Laboratory Observation Method

Rather than study individuals in their natural settings, laboratory observation brings them into the laboratory, where their behavior can be more carefully monitored. In

TRUTH**fiction 5**

Ethnographic observation Data concerning sexual behaviors and customs that occur among various ethnic groups

Participant observation A method in which observers interact with the people they study as they collect data

A Closer Look

PHYSIOLOGICAL MEASURES OF SEXUAL AROUSAL

The validity of scientific studies depends on the ability to measure the events of interest. Sexual arousal may be measured by different means, such as self-report and physiological measures. Self-report measures of sexual arousal are considered subjective. Researchers ask people to give their impressions of the level of their sexual arousal at a given time, such as by circling their response on a 10-point scale that ranges from 0 (not at all aroused) to 10 (extremely aroused). Physiological devices measure the degree of vasocongestion that builds up in the genitals during sexual arousal. (Vasocongestion—that is, congestion with blood—leads to erection in men and vaginal lubrication in women.) In men, vasocongestion is frequently measured by a **penile strain gauge**. This device is worn under the man's clothing. It is fitted around the penis and measures his erectile response by recording changes in the circumference of the penis. The device is sensitive to small changes in circumference that may not be noticed (and thus not reported) by the man.

Physiological measurement of sexual arousal in women is most often accomplished by means of a **vaginal photoplethysmograph**. The vaginal photoplethysmograph is a tampon-shaped probe with a light and a photocell in its tip. It is inserted in the vagina and it indicates the level of blood congestion by means of measuring the amount of light reflected from the vaginal walls. The more light that is ab-

REFLECT

What are your own feelings about the methods of laboratory observation used by Masters and Johnson? Why?

Penile strain gauge A device for measuring sexual arousal in men in terms of changes in the circumference of the penis

Vaginal photoplethysmograph A tamponlike probe that is inserted in the vagina; indicates the level of vasocongestion by measuring the light reflected from the vaginal walls

Vasocongestion Congestion from the flow of blood; from the Latin *vas*, meaning "vessel"

Human Sexual Response (Masters & Johnson, 1966), William Masters and Virginia Johnson were among the first to report direct laboratory observations of individuals and couples engaged in sex acts. In all, 694 people (312 men and 382 women) participated in the research. The women ranged from 18 to 78 years in age; the men, from 21 to 80 years. There were 276 married couples, 106 single women, and 36 single men. The married couples engaged in intercourse and manual and oral stimulation of the genitals. The unmarried people participated in studies that did not require intercourse, such as measurement of female sexual arousal in response to insertion of a penis-shaped probe, and male ejaculation during masturbation. Masters and Johnson performed similar laboratory observations of same-sex sexual response for their 1979 book, *Homosexuality in Perspective*.

Truth or Fiction Revisited: It is true that Masters and Johnson created an artificial penis containing photographic equipment to study the female sexual response. The transparent device enabled them to observe changes in women's internal sexual organs as they became sexually aroused. From these studies, they observed that it is useful to divide sexual response into four stages (their "sexual response cycle"): excitement, plateau, orgasm, and resolution (see Chapter 5).

Direct laboratory observation of biological processes was not invented by Masters and Johnson. However, they were confronting a society that was still unprepared to speak openly of sex, let alone to observe people engaged in sexual activity in the laboratory. Masters and Johnson were accused of immorality, voyeurism, and an assortment of other ills. Nevertheless, their methods offered the first reliable set of data on what happens to the body during sexual response. Their instruments permitted them to measure **vasocongestion** directly (blood flow to the genitals), **myotonia** (muscle tension), and other physiological responses.

One confounding factor in Masters' and Johnson's research is that people who participate in laboratory observation know they are being observed and their responses are being measured. The problem of volunteer bias, troublesome for sex sur-

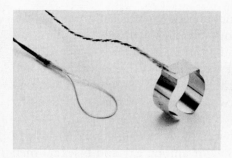 

The Penile Strain Gauge and the Vaginal Photoplethysmograph. *These devices measure vasocongestion in the genitals of men and women, providing an objective measure of their level of sexual arousal. Can you think of other aspects of sexual arousal?*

sorbed by the vaginal walls, the less that is reflected. Less reflected light indicates greater vasocongestion.

Sex researchers sometimes measure sexual arousal in response to stimuli such as erotic films or audiotaped dramatizations of erotic scenes. What happens when physiological devices give a different impression of sexual arousal than those offered by self-report? Objectively (physiologically)

measured sexual arousal does not always agree with subjective feelings of sexual arousal, as measured by self-report. For example, a person may say that he or she is relatively unaroused whereas the physiological measures suggest otherwise. Which is the truer measure of arousal, the person's subjective reports or the levels shown on the objective instruments?

Discrepancies across measures suggest that people may be sexually aroused (as measured by physiological indicators) but psychologically unprepared to recognize it or unwilling to admit it. In the real world of human relationships, sexual arousal has psychological as well as physiological aspects. The reflexes of erection and vaginal lubrication do not necessarily translate to "yes."

veys, is even thornier in laboratory observation. How many of us would assent to performing sexual activities in the laboratory while we were connected to monitoring equipment in full view of researchers? Some of the women observed by Masters and Johnson were patients of Dr. Masters who felt indebted to him and agreed to participate. Many were able to persuade their husbands to participate as well. Some were medical students and graduate students who may have been motivated by earning extra money (participants were paid for their time) as well as by scientific curiosity. Observing people engaged in sexual activities may also alter their responses. People may not respond in public as they would in private.

Researchers have since developed more sophisticated physiological methods of measuring sexual arousal and response. Masters' and Johnson's laboratory method is now used, with some variations but with less controversy, in research centers across the country.

CRITICAL Thinking

Which strikes you as the truer measure of sexual arousal: the person's subjective reports of arousal or the levels shown on objective instruments such as the penile strain gauge or vaginal photoplethysmograph? Support your answer. (Hint: Critical thinkers pay attention to definitions of terms. What does the word *truer* mean to you?)

Correlation

What are the relationships between age and frequency of sex among married couples? What is the connection between socioeconomic status and teenage pregnancy? How about listening to sexually explicit rap music and age of sexual initiation? In each case, variables are being related to one another The correlational method describes the relationship between variables in numerical terms, and as positive or negative.

A **correlation** is a statistical measure of the relationship between two variables. In correlational studies, two or more variables are related, or linked to, one another by statistical means. The strength and direction (positive or negative) of the relationship between any two variables is expressed with a statistic called a **correlation coefficient.**

Myotonia Muscle tension

Correlation A statistical measure of the relationship between two variables

Correlation coefficient A statistic that expresses the strength and direction (positive or negative) of the relationship between two variables

CRITICAL
Thinking

Would you expect that there would be a positive or negative correlation between satisfaction in a relationship and communication? Explain.

TRUTH? fiction **7**

TRUTH? fiction **8**

Research has shown relationships (correlations) between satisfaction with a relationship and a host of variables: communication skills, shared values, flexibility, frequency of social interactions with friends, and church attendance, to name a few (Figure 2.1). Although such research may give us an idea of the factors associated with satisfaction in a relationship, the researchers have not manipulated the variables of interest. For this reason we cannot say which, if any, of the factors is causally related to happiness in the relationship.

Research has also shown relationships between the use of sildenafil (Viagra) to enhance sexual response and risky sexual behavior among gay and bisexual men (Kim et al., 2002). Men who use Viagra also report a greater number of sex partners and higher levels of anal sex without using a condom. **Truth or Fiction Revisited:** There is no evidence that Viagra *causes* risky sexual behavior. It is more likely that the effort to enhance sexual response explains both the use of Viagra and risky sexual activity.

Correlations may be positive or negative. Two variables are positively correlated if one increases as the other increases. A Spanish study of 412 university students correlated sociodemographic, psychological, and interpersonal variables with sexual behavior and feelings of intimacy (Yela, 2000). It was found that commitment, feelings of intimacy, and frequency of sexual relations correlated positively with feelings of love and sexual satisfaction for both men and women. However, the researcher did not manipulate the variables. Therefore, we cannot conclude that sexual satisfaction causes high coital frequency. It could also be that frequent sexual activity contributes to greater sexual satisfaction. It is also possible that there is no causal relationship between the variables. Perhaps both coital frequency and sexual satisfaction are affected by other factors, such as communication ability, general marital satisfaction, general health, and so on (Figure 2.1). Similarly, height and weight are positively correlated but do not cause each another. Other factors that we label growth contribute to both. **Truth or Fiction Revisited:** Evidence suggests that people who attend church regularly tend to be more satisfied with their relationships. (After all, satisfaction with a relationship could motivate couples to improve their communication, rather than the other way around.)

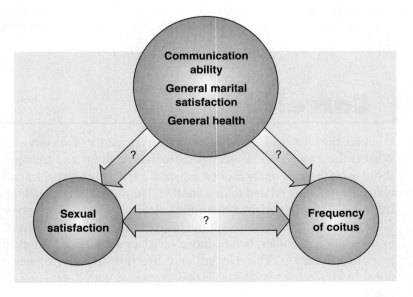

Figure 2.1 What Is the Relationship between Frequency of Intercourse and Sexual Satisfaction? *Couples in relationships who engage in more frequent sexual relations report higher levels of sexual satisfaction, but why? Because researchers have not manipulated the variables, we cannot conclude that sexual satisfaction causes high coital frequency. Nor can we say that frequent coitus causes greater sexual satisfaction. Perhaps both variables are affected by other factors, such as communication ability, health, and general satisfaction with the relationship.*

Dutch researchers found a negative correlation between anxiety disorders and the sexual functioning of 44 women (Van Minnen & Kampman, 2000). Women with anxiety disorders reported less sexual desire and a lower frequency of sexual contact with their partners than women who lacked anxiety disorders but were otherwise similar. Women with anxiety disorders were also more likely to report sexual aversions—that is, a strong distaste for sexual contact.

Although correlations do not show cause and effect, they can be used to make predictions. For example, we can predict that women who have been circumcised (had their clitorises cut out) in fundamentalist Islamic cultures will be prone to sexual problems and dysfunctions. Egyptian psychiatrist Mohammed El-Defrawi and his colleagues (2001) interviewed 250 women in Ismailia, Egypt, who had been circumcised during preadolescence. Female circumcision, discussed in Chapter 3, is carried out in some societies in the belief that it stems the expression of female sexuality, which these societies perceive as an abomination that threatens the social structure. Critics of the practice, including Dr. El-Defrawi, refer to female circumcision as genital mutilation. In any event, El-Defrawi and his colleagues found that women who had been circumcised were more likely to report painful menstruation, vaginal dryness during intercourse, lack of sexual desire, and difficulty reaching orgasm than uncircumcised women. The authors suggest that circumcision has a negative effect on women's sexual lives. It is also possible that the fundamentalist beliefs in the cultures to which these women belong lead both to female circumcision and to sexual problems and dysfunctions. **Truth or Fiction Revisited:** There is evidence that the victims of genital mutilation—the women who are circumcised—tend to internalize the beliefs of their cultures. Not only do they generally support female circumcision, they also accept the right of husbands to beat their wives (Refaat et al., 2001).

TRUTH fiction 9

The Experimental Method

The best method for studying cause and effect is the **experiment.** Experiments permit scientists to draw conclusions about cause-and-effect relationships because the experimenter directly manipulates the variables of interest and observes their effects.

In an experiment on the effects of alcohol on sexual arousal, for example, a group of participants would receive an intervention, called a treatment, such as a dose of alcohol. (In other experiments, the intervention or treatment might involve the administration of a drug, exposure to violent pornography, a program of sex education, and so forth.). They would then be carefully observed to learn whether this treatment made a difference in their behavior—in this case, their sexual arousal.

In an experiment, the variables (**treatments**) that are hypothesized to have a causal effect are manipulated or controlled by the researcher. Consider an experiment designed to determine whether alcohol stimulates sexual arousal. The design might involve giving one group of participants a certain dosage of alcohol and then measuring its effects. In such an experimental arrangement, the dosage of alcohol is considered an **independent variable,** the presence and quantity of which is manipulated by the researchers. The measured results are called **dependent variables**, because changes in their values are believed to depend on the independent variable or variables. In this experiment, measures of sexual arousal would be the dependent

Experiment A scientific method that seeks to confirm cause-and-effect relationships by manipulating independent variables and observing their effects on dependent variables

Treatment In experiments, an intervention that is administered to participants (e.g., a test, a drug, or sex education program) so that its effects may be observed

Independent variable A condition in a scientific study that is manipulated so that its effects may be observed

Dependent variables The measured results of an experiment, which are believed to be a function of the independent variables

CRITICAL Thinking

Would it be possible to run an experiment to study the effects of rape on psychological health? Why or why not?

CRITICAL Thinking

To run a true experiment on the effect of a new drug on people with HIV/AIDS, some of the people with HIV/AIDS would have to be assigned to a control group. To control for the effects of expectations, they might be told they are being given the real drug when they are really receiving "sugar pills" that look like the real thing. Can researchers justify withholding the real drug from people in the control group? What do you think?

Experimental groups Groups of study participants that receive a treatment

Control groups Groups of study participants that do not receive the experimental treatment; however, other conditions are held comparable with those in the experimental group

Selection factor A bias that may operate in research when people are allowed to determine whether they will receive a treatment

variables. Dependent variables are outcomes; they are observed and measured by the researchers, but not manipulated. Sexual arousal might be measured by means such as physiological measurement (gauging the degree of penile erection in the male, for example) or self-report (asking participants to rate their sexual arousal on a rating scale).

In a study of the effects of sex education on teenage pregnancy, sex education would be the independent variable. The incidence of teenage pregnancy would be the dependent variable. Researchers would administer the experimental treatment (sex education) and track the participants for a period of time to determine their pregnancy rates. Ideally, as we see in the next section, the incidence of pregnancy among these subjects would be compared with that among subjects who do not receive sex education but are similar to the subjects in all other respects.

Experimental and Control Groups

True experiments randomly assign subjects to **experimental groups** and **control groups**. Subjects in experimental groups receive the treatment. Subjects in control groups do not. Every effort is made to hold all other conditions constant for both groups. By using random assignment and holding other conditions constant, researchers can be reasonably confident that the independent variable (treatment), and not extraneous factors (such as the temperature of the room in which the treatment was administered or differences between subjects in the experimental and control groups), brought about the results.

Why do experimenters assign subjects to experimental or control groups at random? Consider a study conducted to determine the effects of alcohol on sexual arousal in response to sexually explicit material, such as "adult" films. If we permitted participants to choose whether they would drink alcohol, we might not know whether it was the alcohol itself that accounted for the results. Some other factor, called a **selection factor**, might discriminate between people who would or would not choose to drink alcohol. One difference might be that people who chose to drink might also have more permissive attitudes toward sexually explicit material than the others. Their permissiveness, rather than the alcohol, could affect their sexual responsiveness to these stimuli. If this were the case, experimental outcomes might reflect the effects of the selection factor rather than the alcohol.

Although scientists agree that the experimental method provides the strongest evidence of cause and effect, experimenters cannot manipulate many variables of interest directly. For example, we cannot conduct experiments to determine the effects of cohabitation on college students. We cannot assign an experimental group to cohabitation and a control group to separate living quarters. We can only compare groups that have chosen to cohabit with groups that have not. Our research may thus inform us that cohabitors who get married are more likely, eventually, to get divorced than married couples who have never cohabited, but it cannot show that these problems are *caused* by cohabiting (Chapter 14). Cohabitors and noncohabitors may differ on other factors—such as nontraditional versus traditional attitudes—that give rise to different outcomes of marriage.

Similarly, we cannot conduct experiments to determine the effects of pornography on children and adolescents. Societal prohibitions and ethical standards preclude experimenters from exposing children or adolescents to erotic materials. Researchers use other approaches, such as the correlational method, to study variables that cannot be manipulated.

Q *How do you make people feel okay in the research you have done?*

A Most sex research actually isn't so controversial or invasive that participants need to be made to feel okay. For example, most studies, even in biologically related areas, do not usually require direct observation of your genitals or your sexual activity by strangers. When studies are somewhat controversial, as in measuring your biological sexual response to pornography, a legitimate researcher will ask you for your **informed consent**. This means that you'll be told enough about the purposes and methods of the research so that you can make an intelligent decision regarding whether to participate—and are free to quit at any time. Also, your participation should be kept confidential, and the researcher should have a way that gives you confidence that your identity or responses will not be disclosed. In the rare case in which the researcher must deceive you with regard to the purposes or methods of a study, you should be "debriefed" afterward; this means that you should receive a full explanation afterward. And nobody—repeat, *nobody*—has the right to force you into research of any kind.

CRITICAL Thinking

What types of harm could occur if a researcher disclosed the identity of an individual in a sex survey and his or her sexual behavior?

Ethics in Sex Research

Sex researchers are required to protect the people being studied. This means that people will not be subjected to physical or psychological harm and will participate of their own free will. In colleges, universities, hospitals, and research institutions, ethics review committees help researchers weigh the potential harm of administering the independent variables and they review proposed studies in light of ethical guidelines. If the committee finds fault with a proposal, it may advise the researcher how to modify the research design to comply with ethical standards; it may withhold approval until the proposal has been modified. Let us consider a number of the ethical issues that have been raised concerning sex research:

- *Exposing participants to harm.* Individuals may be harmed if they are exposed to pain or placed in stressful situations. For this reason, researchers do not expose children to erotic materials to determine the effects. Nor do researchers expose human fetuses to male or female sex hormones to learn whether they create predispositions toward tomboyishness, gay male or lesbian sexual orientations, and other variables of interest.

- *Confidentiality.* **Truth or Fiction Revisited:** It is not true that researchers publish the names of participants in sex research in professional journals. Sex researchers must keep the identities and responses of participants confidential to protect them from possible harm or embarrassment.

  Researchers can do many things to ensure the **confidentiality** of participants. They can make questionnaires anonymous. Interviewers may not be given the identities of interviewees. In reports of research, enough information about participants' backgrounds can be given to make the studies useful (size of city of origin, region of country, religion, age group, race, educational level, and so on)

TRUTH **fiction 10**

Informed consent The term used by researchers to indicate that people have agreed to participate in research after receiving information about the purposes and nature of the study, and its potential risks and benefits

Confidentiality Ethics requires that sex researchers keep the identities and behaviors of participants in research confidential. Sometimes records are coded so that someone breaking into them would not be able to decipher the identity of participants. Records are also usually destroyed after all useful information has been gleaned from them

The Tuskegee Syphilis Study: Ethics Turned Upside Down in Research Gone Wrong

The Tuskegee Syphilis Study, carried out in Macon County, Alabama, from 1932 to 1972, is an example of medical research gone wrong. The United States Public Health Service, in trying to learn more about syphilis and justify treatment programs for African Americans, withheld adequate treatment from a group of poor black men who had the disease, causing needless pain and suffering for the men and their loved ones.

In the wake of the Tuskegee Syphilis Study and other studies, the federal government took a closer look at research involving human subjects and made changes to prevent the moral breaches that occurred in Tuskegee from happening again.

The Study Begins

In 1932, the Public Health Service, working with the Tuskegee Institute, began a study in Macon County, Alabama, to record the natural history of syphilis in hopes of justifying treatment programs for blacks. It was called the Tuskegee Study of Untreated Syphilis in the Negro Male.

The study involved 600 black men—399 with syphilis and 201 who did not have the disease. Researchers told the men they were being treated for "bad blood," a local term used to describe several ailments, including syphilis, anemia, and fatigue. In truth, they did not receive the proper treatment needed to cure their illness. In exchange for taking part in the study, the men received free medical exams, free meals, and burial insurance. Although originally projected to last six months, the study actually went on for 40 years.

What Went Wrong?

In July 1972, a front-page *New York Times* story about the Tuskegee Syphilis Study caused a public outcry that led the Assistant Secretary for Health and Scientific Affairs to appoint an ad hoc advisory panel to review the study. The panel had nine members from the fields of medicine, law, religion, labor, education, health administration, and public affairs.

The panel found that the men had agreed freely to be examined and treated. However, there was no evidence that researchers had informed them of the study or its real purpose. In fact, the men had been misled and had not been given all the facts required to provide informed consent.

The men were never given adequate treatment for their disease. Even when penicillin became the drug of choice for syphilis in 1947, researchers did not offer it to the subjects. The advisory panel found nothing to show that subjects were ever given the choice of quitting the

CRITICAL
Thinking

In experiments on the effects of violent pornography on aggression, men are led to believe that they are shocking women by pressing a button when they actually are not. Do you believe that this deception is justified? Can you think of a more ethical way of measuring "aggression?"

without divulging their identities. After the need for follow-up has passed and the results have been fully analyzed, the names and addresses of participants and their records can be destroyed.

- *Informed consent.* The principle of informed consent requires that people freely agree to participate after being given enough information about the procedures and purposes of the research, and its risks and benefits, to make an informed decision. After the study has begun, participants are free to withdraw at any time without penalty.

- *The use of deception.* Ethical conflicts may emerge when experiments require that participants not know all about their purposes and methods. For example, in ex-

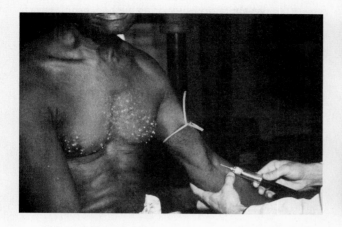

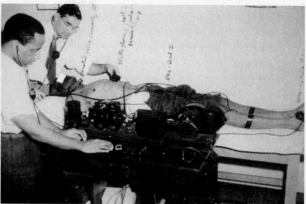

study, even when this new, highly effective treatment became widely used.

The Study Ends and Reparation Begins

The advisory panel concluded that the Tuskegee Syphilis Study was "ethically unjustified"—the knowledge gained was sparse when compared with the risks the study posed for its subjects. In October 1972, the panel advised stopping the study at once. A month later, the Assistant Secretary for Health and Scientific Affairs announced the end of the Tuskegee Syphilis Study.

In the summer of 1973, a class-action lawsuit filed by the National Association for the Advancement of Colored

People ended in a settlement that gave more than $9 million to the study participants. As part of the settlement, the U.S. government promised to give free medical and burial services to all living participants. The Tuskegee Health Benefit Program was established to provide these services. It also gave health services for wives, widows, and children who had been infected because of the study. The CDC was given responsibility for the program, where it remains today in the National Center for HIV, STD, and TB Prevention.

SOURCE: Centers for Disease Control and Prevention. (2005, May 23). The Tuskegee Syphilis Study: A Hard Lesson Learned. www.cdc.gov/nchstp/od/tuskegee/time.htm

periments on the effects of violent pornography on aggression against women, participants may be misled into believing that they are administering electric shocks to women (who are actually confederates of the experimenter), even though no shocks are actually delivered. The experimenter seeks to determine participants' willingness to hurt women after exposure to aggressive erotic films. Such studies could not be carried out if participants knew that no shocks would actually be delivered.

Research is the backbone of human sexuality as a science. This textbook focuses on scientific findings that can illuminate our understanding of sexuality, help enhance the sexual experience, prevent and treat STIs, and build more rewarding relationships.

CRITICAL Thinking

What ethical principles were violated in the Tuskegee Syphilis Study?

1. What is the scientific method?

- The scientific method is a systematic way of gathering scientific evidence and testing assumptions through empirical research. It entails formulating a research question, framing a hypothesis, testing the hypothesis, and drawing conclusions about the hypothesis.

- The goals of the science of human sexuality are to describe, explain, predict, and control sexual behaviors. People often confuse description with inference. Inferences are woven into theories, when possible.

2. How do researchers represent populations in their studies?

- A population is a complete group of people or animals that a researcher targets for study.

- A sample is a subgroup of a population that a researcher selects to study the population.

- Researchers use random sampling, when possible, to ensure that every member of a population has an equal chance of being selected. In a stratified random sample, identified subgroups within a population are selected according to their numbers in the population.

3. What methods of observation do researchers use?

- Case studies are carefully drawn biographies of individuals or small groups that focus on unraveling the interplay of various factors in individuals' backgrounds.

- Surveys typically gather information about behavior through interviews or questionnaires administered to large samples of people. Gaps in memory, use of volunteers, and the tendency of respondents to offer socially desirable responses are sources of bias in surveys.

- In naturalistic observation, scientists directly observe the behavior of animals and humans where it happens—in the "field." The scientists remain as unobtrusive as possible in an effort to avoid affecting the behavior they wish to study.

- Ethnographic research provides us with data concerning sexual behaviors and customs that occur widely across cultures and those that are limited to one or a few cultures. It is usually conducted by anthropologists.

- In participant observation, investigators learn about people's behavior by interacting with them.

- In the laboratory observation method, people engage in the behavior under study in the laboratory setting. When methods of observation influence the behavior under study, that behavior may be distorted. Masters and Johnson studied people involved in sexual activity in the laboratory to learn how their bodies respond to sexual stimulation.

4. What is the correlational method?

- Correlational research reveals the strength and direction of the relationships between variables, such as communication ability and satisfaction with a relationship. However, the relationships do not show cause and effect.

5. What are experiments?

- Experiments allow scientists to draw conclusions about cause-and-effect relationships because they directly control or manipulate the variables of interest and observe their effects. The variables manipulated are called *independent variables*; the outcome variables are termed *dependent variables*.

- Well-designed experiments randomly assign individuals to experimental and control groups to avoid the selection factor. Thus it can be assumed that different outcomes between groups represent the manipulation of the independent variables and not differences between the individuals in the experimental and control groups.

6. What kinds of ethical issues are raised concerning sex research?

- Ethical standards require that potentially harmful research may be conducted only when the expected benefits clearly outweigh the risks to participants and when the experimenter tries to minimize risks. Sex researchers keep the identities of participants confidential and obtain their informed consent to participate, but they must deceive people now and then regarding the purposes and methods of a study.

- The Tuskegee Syphilis Study was unethical because partcipants were harmed and deceived, and had never provided informed concent.

1. In a(n) _____ sample, every member of the target population has an equal chance of participating.

   (a) distribution
   (b) digitized
   (c) egalitarian
   (d) random

2. The _____ reports interviewed 5,300 males and 5,940 females in the United States between 1938 and 1949.

   (a) Playboy
   (b) Kinsey
   (c) Wyatt
   (d) Masters and Johnson

3. Wyatt compared the sexual behavior of _____ American and European American women who live in Los Angeles.

   (a) African
   (b) Asian
   (c) Latina
   (d) Native

4. Morton Hunt obtained the cooperation of _____% of the people he contacted for his survey.

   (a) 20
   (b) 40
   (c) 60
   (d) 80

5. Experimenters randomly assign subjects to experimental or _____ groups.

   (a) placebo
   (b) stratified
   (c) control
   (d) naturalistic

6. A scientific sample must be

   (a) large
   (b) representative
   (c) natural
   (d) neutral

7. Ethnographic research is usually conducted by

   (a) anthropologists
   (b) biologists
   (c) sociologists
   (d) psychologists

8. Participants did not provide informed consent in the _____ Syphilis Study.

   (a) Texarkana
   (b) Tucson
   (c) Tuskegee
   (d) Tuckahoe

9. People who agree to participate in psychological research may not represent the general population because of

   (a) obtrusive means of measurement
   (b) volunteer bias
   (c) dishonesty
   (d) level of education

10. Most researchers agree that the best means of learning about cause and effect is

    (a) the experiment
    (b) the correlational method
    (c) the survey
    (d) the case study

11. Katherine Frank engaged in

    (a) the experimental method
    (b) participant observation
    (c) the case–study method
    (d) an online survey

12. Myotonia means

    (a) muscle tension
    (b) nausea
    (c) anxiety
    (d) intoxication

13. About _____ % of the male respondents to the National Survey of Family Growth said they had had oral sex with another male.

    (a) 1
    (b) 6
    (c) 20
    (d) 37

14. Alan Bell and Martin Weinberg studied lifestyles of gays in

    (a) San Jose
    (b) San Fernando
    (c) Santa Cruz
    (d) San Francisco

15. _____ conducted a case study of Leonardo da Vinci.

    (a) Michelangelo
    (b) Alfred Kinsey
    (c) Sigmund Freud
    (d) Gail Wyatt

Answers 1. d; 2. b; 3. a; 4. a; 5. c; 6. b; 7. a; 8. c; 9. b; 10. a; 11. b; 12. a; 13. b; 14. d; 15. c

3

Female Sexual Anatomy and Physiology

TRUTH fiction?

Which of the following statements are true, and which are fiction? Look for the Truth/Fiction icons on the pages that follow to find the answers.

1 Women, not men, have a sex organ whose only known function is experiencing sexual pleasure.   T   F

2 Women urinate and engage in sexual intercourse through the same bodily opening.   T   F

3 One may determine whether a woman is a virgin by examining her hymen.   T   F

4 Women with larger breasts produce more milk while nursing.   T   F

5 Women who have had abortions are at greater risk of breast cancer.   T   F

6 The American Cancer Society recommends that women engage in a breast self-examination once a month.   T   F

7 Sexual intercourse during menstruation is harmful.   T   F

8 The ancient Romans believed that menstrual blood soured wine and killed crops.   T   F

9 At menopause, women experience debilitating hot flashes.   T   F

10 Menopause signals an end to women's sexual appetite.   T   F

Despite hundreds of years of tradition, Hajia Zuwera Kassindja would not let it happen to her 17-year-old daughter, Fauziya. Hajia's own sister had died from it. So Hajia gave her daughter the inheritance from her deceased husband, which amounted to only $3,500 and left Hajia a pauper. Fauziya used the money to buy a phony passport and flee the African country of Togo to the United States.

Upon arrival in the United States, Fauziya requested asylum from persecution. She was then imprisoned for more than a year because of her illegal entry into the country. However, the Board of Immigration Appeals finally agreed that Fauziya was fleeing persecution and she was allowed to remain in the United States.

From what had Hajia's sister died? From what was Fauziya escaping? **Clitoridectomy**, a form of female genital mutilation practiced in her home country. Some cultures in Africa and the Middle East ritually mutilate the female genitals, removing the clitoris and surrounding genital structures. Cutting out the clitoris—*clitoridectomy*—is a rite of initiation into womanhood in many Islamic cultures. It is often performed as a puberty ritual in late childhood or early adolescence (not within a few days of birth, like male circumcision). In modern-day Egypt, the vast majority of female adolescents, age 10 to

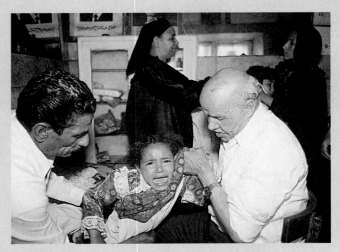

Clitoridectomy. *Some predominantly Islamic cultures in Africa and the Middle East ritually remove the clitoris as a rite of initiation into womanhood.*

19, have their clitoris removed (El-Gibaly et al., 2002).

The clitoris gives rise to feelings of sexual pleasure in women. Its destruction is an attempt to ensure the girl's chastity, because it is assumed that uncircumcised girls are consumed with sexual desires. Cairo physician Said M. Thabit says, "With circumcision we remove the external parts, so when a girl wears tight nylon underclothes she will not have any stimulation."

TRUTH?fiction 1

The French have a saying, "Vive la différence!" ("Long live the difference!"). It celebrates the differences between men and women. Given their possession of a clitoris, some might assert that women in particular have much to celebrate. **Truth or Fiction Revisited:** The historical view of women as unresponsive to sexual stimulation is ironic, because only women possess a sex organ—the clitoris—that is solely devoted to pleasurable sensations. The clitoris is the woman's most erotically charged organ; women most often masturbate through clitoral stimulation, not vaginal insertion.

This chapter explores women's sexual anatomy and physiology. We explore the female sex organs. Even generally sophisticated students may fill in some gaps in their knowledge. Most of us know what a vagina is, but how many of us realize that only the female has an organ that is exclusively dedicated to pleasure? Or that a woman's passing of urine does not involve the vagina? How many of us know that a newborn girl already has all the **ova** she will ever produce?

Chapter 4 describes the sexual anatomy and physiology of men. Despite the obvious differences, we will see that there may be more similarities in the sex or-

Clitoridectomy Surgical removal of the clitoris

Ova Egg cells; Sing., ovum

gans than you would imagine. In Chapter 6 we discuss similarities and differences between men and women in intellectual functioning, personality, and behavior. Once more we will see that women and men may be more alike than you had anticipated.

As female readers encounter the features of their sexual anatomy in their reading, they may wish to examine their own genitals with a mirror. By following the text and the illustrations, students may discover some new anatomic features. They will see that their genitals can resemble those in the illustrations yet also be unique.

External Sex Organs

When I was six years old I climbed up on the bathroom sink and looked at myself naked in the mirror. All of a sudden I realized I had three different holes. I was very excited about my discovery and ran down to the dinner table and announced it to everyone. "I have three holes!" Silence. "What are they for?" I asked. Silence even heavier than before. I sensed how uncomfortable everyone was and answered for myself. "I guess one is for pee-pee, the other for doo-doo, and the third for ca-ca." A sigh of relief; no one had to answer my question. But I got the message—I wasn't supposed to ask "such" questions, though I didn't fully realize what "such" was about at that time. (Boston Women's Health Book Collective, 2005)

Talking about one's sexual anatomy, as this six-year-old discovered, has often been met with prejudice and misunderstanding. The derivation of the word *pudenda*, which refers to the external female genitals, speaks volumes about sexism in the ancient Mediterranean world.

Even today, this cultural heritage may lead women to develop negative attitudes toward their genitals. Girls and boys are both sometimes reared to regard their genitals with shame or disgust. Both may be reprimanded for expressing normal curiosity about them. They may be reared with a "hands-off" attitude, to keep their "private parts" private, even from themselves. This is unfortunate, because knowledge of one's sexual anatomy contributes both to sexual health and to pleasure.

Taken collectively, the external sexual structures of the female are termed the **pudendum** or the vulva. **Vulva** is a Latin word that means "wrapper" or "covering." The vulva consists of the *mons veneris,* the *labia majora* and *labia minora* (major and minor lips), the *clitoris,* and the vaginal opening (Figure 3.1). Figure 3.2 shows variations in the appearance of women's genitals.

Pudendum The external sexual structures of the female; from the Latin meaning "that which makes one ashamed"; suggestive of ancient negative attitudes toward the female sexual structures

Vulva Another term for the external sexual structures of the female

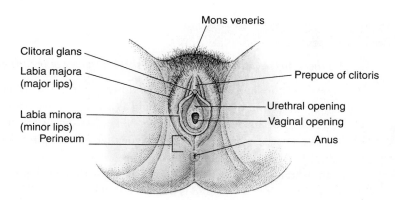

Figure shows labels: Mons veneris, Clitoral glans, Labia majora (major lips), Labia minora (minor lips), Perineum, Prepuce of clitoris, Urethral opening, Vaginal opening, Anus

Figure 3.1 External Female Sex Organs. *This figure shows the vulva with the labia opened to reveal the urethral and vaginal openings.*

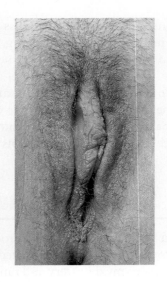

Figure 3.2 Normal Variations in the Vulva. *The features of the vulva show a great deal of variation. A woman's attitude toward her genitals is likely to reflect her general self-concept and early childhood messages rather than the appearance of her vulva per se.*

The Mons Veneris

The **mons veneris** consists of fatty tissue that covers the joint of the pubic bones in front of the body, below the abdomen and above the clitoris. At puberty the mons becomes covered with pubic hair that may be thick and curly, but varies from person to person in waviness, texture, and color. The pubic hair captures the chemical secretions that exude from the vagina during sexual arousal. Their scent may allure lovers. The mons cushions a woman's body during sexual intercourse, protecting her and her partner from the pressure against the pubic bone that stems from thrusting. There is an ample supply of nerve endings in the mons, so that caresses can produce pleasurable sensations.

The Labia Majora

The **labia majora** are large folds of skin that run downward from the mons along the sides of the vulva. In some women, the labia majora are thick and bulging. In others, they are thinner, flatter, and less noticeable. When close together, they hide the labia minora and the urethral and vaginal openings. The outer surfaces of the labia majora, by the thighs, are covered with pubic hair and darker skin than that found on the thighs or the labia minora. The inner surfaces of the labia majora are hairless and lighter in color. They are amply supplied with nerve endings that respond to stimulation and can produce sexual pleasure. The labia majora also shield the inner female genitals.

Mons veneris A mound of fatty tissue that covers the joint of the pubic bones in front of the body, below the abdomen and above the clitoris; a Latin phrase meaning "hill" or "mount of Venus," the Roman goddess of love

Labia majora Large folds of skin that run downward from the mons along the sides of the vulva; Latin for "large lips" or "major lips"

SafeZone

Q *Are there any negative consequences to shaving (partly or in full) pubic hair?*

A Unless you cut yourself seriously, your downside is probably limited to some skin irritation and then to some itching as the hair grows back. But these side effects are not absolutely predictable. "Bikini waxing" is an alternative, but this can be painful. Some feminists will argue that your concern about shaving pubic hair—or underarm hair—reflects an unhealthy need to conform to antifeminist cultural standards of beauty. Others will argue that you should do what makes you happy. It's your call and is unlikely to usher in a health crisis.

The Labia Minora

The **labia minora** are hairless, light-colored membranes located between the major lips. They surround the urethral and vaginal openings. The outer surfaces of the labia minora merge with the major lips. At the top they join at the prepuce (hood) of the clitoris. The labia minora differ in appearance from woman to woman. The labia minora of some women form protruding flower shapes that are valued greatly in some cultures, such as that of the Hottentots of Africa. (Hottentot women purposely elongate their labia minora by tugging at them.) Rich in blood vessels and nerve endings, the labia minora are highly sensitive to sexual stimulation. When stimulated they darken and swell, engorging with blood.

The Clitoris

What's the matter, papa? Please don't stall.
Don't you know I love it and want it all?
I'm wild about that thing. Just give my bell a ring.
You pressed my button. I'm wild about that thing.

—"I'm Wild about That Thing," recorded by Bessie Smith, 1929

Worldwide, the clitoris is known by many names, from *bijou* (French for "jewel") to *pokhotnik* (Russian for "lust"). The Tuamotuan people of Polynesia have 10 words for it, emblematic of their interest in female sexuality.

The word *clitoris* derives from the Greek word *kleitoris,* meaning "hill" or "slope." It receives its name from the manner in which it slopes upward in the shaft and forms a mound of spongy tissue at the glans (Figure 3.1). The body of the **clitoris**—the clitoral shaft—is about one inch long and a quarter inch wide. The clitoral shaft consists of erectile tissue that contains two spongy masses called **corpora cavernosa** ("cavernous bodies") that fill with blood (become engorged) and become erect in response to sexual stimulation. The stiffening of the clitoris is less apparent than the erection of the penis, because the clitoris does not swing free from the body. The **prepuce** (meaning "before a swelling"), or hood, covers the clitoral shaft. It is a sheath of skin formed by the upper part of the labia minora. The clitoral glans is a smooth, round knob or lump of tissue above the urethral opening. The glans is revealed by gently separating the labia minora and retracting the hood. It is highly sensitive to touch because of the rich supply of nerve endings.

The size of the clitoris varies from woman to woman. Because the clitoral glans is highly sensitive to touch, women usually prefer to be stroked or stimulated on the mons, or on the clitoral hood, rather than directly on the glans (Boston Women's Health Book Collective, 2005).

In some respects, the clitoris is the female counterpart of the penis. However, a survey of 373 Texas college students found that they had overwhelmingly been taught that the vagina was the counterpart to the penis (Ogletree & Ginsburg, 2000). Nevertheless, both organs—clitoris and penis—develop from the same embryonic tissue, which makes them similar in structure, or **homologous** (see Chapter 4). They are not fully similar in function, or **analogous,** however. Both organs receive and transmit sexual sensations, but the penis is directly involved in reproduction and excretion by serving as a conduit for sperm and urine respectively.

Cutting out the clitoral hood—clitoridectomy—is common among Muslims in the Near East and Africa. As we see in "The World of Human Sexuality" feature on the next page, it is a "rite of passage" to womanhood that leaves scars—physical and emotional.

CRITICAL Thinking

Do you believe that disapproval of clitoridectomy by Americans and other Westerners shows cultural condescension or cultural insensitivity? Why or why not?

Labia minora Hairless, light-colored membranes located between the labia majora; Latin for "small lips" or "minor lips"

Clitoris A female sex organ consisting of a shaft and glans located above the urethral opening; extremely sensitive to sexual sensations

Corpora cavernosa Masses of spongy tissue in the clitoral shaft that become engorged with blood and stiffen in response to sexual stimulation

Prepuce The fold of skin covering the glans of the clitoris (or penis)

Homologous Similar in structure; developing from the same embryonic tissue

Analogous Similar in function

Female Genital Mutilation

Approximately 130 million women and girls have undergone genital mutilation. Feminists note that female genital mutilation is an attempt by patriarchal societies to control the bodies and behavior of women (www.feminist.com, 2006). In terms of their own perceptions, of course, some groups in Egypt and in the Sudan simply perform clitoridectomies because it is a social custom that has been unchallenged in their own experience (Missailidis & Gebre-Medhin, 2000). Because women tend to adopt the values of the larger cultures in which they dwell, female genital mutilation is usually carried out by women who have undergone the process themselves (Nour, in Dreifus, 2000). Some perceive it as part of their submission to Islam. However, it is debatable whether the Koran—the Islamic bible—authorizes it (Dreifus, 2000). The typical young woman in this culture—like the typical woman in most patriarchal cultures—does not grasp that she is a victim (www.feminist.com, 2006). She assumes that clitoridectomy is part of being female. As one young woman told gynecologist Nawal M. Nour (Dreifus, 2000), the clitoridectomy hurt but was a good thing, because now she was a woman.

What effects does "circumcision" have on women? A study of 250 female patients from the Maternal and Childhood Centers of Ismailia, Egypt, found that those who were circumcised were 80% more likely to complain of painful **menstruation,** 49% more likely to complain of vaginal dryness during intercourse, 45% more likely to lack sexual desire, 49% less likely to be pleased by sex, and 61% more likely to have difficulty reaching orgasm (El-Defrawi et al., 2001).

In many locales, clitoridectomies are performed in unsanitary conditions without benefit of anesthesia. Medical complications are common, including infections, bleeding, tissue scarring, painful menstruation, and obstructed labor.

A more radical form of clitoridectomy, called *excision,* is practiced widely in the Sudan, Ethiopia, and some other African nations (Eltahawy, 2003). Excision is removal of the clitoris along with the labia minora and labia majora. Only a tiny opening is left to allow passage of urine and menstrual discharge. The sewing together of the vulva is intended to ensure chastity until marriage. Medical complications, including menstrual and urinary problems, are common—even death. After marriage, the opening is enlarged to permit intercourse. Hemorrhaging and tearing of surrounding tissues are common. Mutilation of the labia is now illegal in the Sudan, although the law continues to allow removal of the clitoris. Some African countries, including Egypt and Kenya, have outlawed clitoridectomies, although such laws are often unenforced.

More than 100 million women in Africa and the Middle East have undergone excision. Clitoridectomies remain common, even universal, in nearly 30 countries in Africa, in many countries in the Middle East, and in parts of Malaysia, Yemen, Oman, Indonesia, and the India–Pakistan subcontinent. Thousands of African immigrant girls living in European countries and the United States have also been mutilated (Dreifus, 2000).

Do not confuse male circumcision with the maiming inflicted on girls in the name of circumcision. Nour (Dreifus, 2000) depicts the male equivalent of female genital mutilation as cutting off the penis. The Pulitzer Prize–winning, African American novelist Alice Walker drew attention to the practice in her best-selling novel *Possessing the Secret of Joy* and called for its abolition in her book and film *Warrior Marks.*

The United States has outlawed ritual genital mutilation within its borders and directed American representatives to world financial institutions to deny aid to countries that have not established educational programs to bring an end to the practice. Yet calls from Westerners to ban the practice have sparked arguments that people in one culture cannot dictate the cultural traditions of another. Yet for Alice Walker, "torture is not culture." As the debate continues, some two million African girls are mutilated each year.

The Vestibule

Menstruation The cyclical bleeding that stems from the shedding of the uterine lining

The word *vestibule,* which means "entranceway," refers to the area within the labia minora that contains the openings to the vagina and the urethra. The vestibule is richly supplied with nerve endings and is very sensitive to tactile or other sexual stimulation.

The Urethral Opening

Urine passes from the female's body through the **urethral opening** (Figure 3.1), which is connected by a short tube (the urethra) to the bladder (Figure 3.3). The urethral opening lies below the clitoral glans and above the vaginal opening. The urethral opening, urethra, and bladder are unrelated to the reproductive system.

Truth or Fiction Revisited: Many males (and even some females) believe erroneously that for women urination and coitus occur through the same bodily opening. The confusion may arise from the fact that urine and semen both pass through the penis of the male or because the urethral opening lies near the vaginal opening.

The proximity of the urethral opening to the external sex organs can pose hygienic problems for sexually active women (Sheffield & Cunningham, 2005). The urinary tract, which includes the urethra, bladder, and kidneys, may become infected by bacteria from the vagina or rectum. Disease organisms may pass from the a partner's sex organs or hands to the urethral opening during sexual activity. Anal intercourse followed by vaginal intercourse may transfer disease organisms from the rectum to the bladder. For similar reasons, women should first wipe the vulva, then the anus, when using the bathroom.

Cystitis is a bladder inflammation that may stem from any of these sources. Its symptoms include burning and frequent urination (also called urinary urgency). Pus or a bloody discharge is common, and there may be discomfort above the pubic bone. These symptoms may disappear after several days, but consultation with a gynecologist is recommended, because untreated cystitis can lead to kidney infections. "Honeymoon cystitis" is caused by the tugging on the bladder and urethral wall that occurs during vaginal intercourse. It may occur upon beginning coital activity (although not necessarily on one's honeymoon) or upon resumption after lengthy abstinence. Figure 3.3 shows the close proximity of the urethra and vagina.

A few precautions may help women prevent serious inflammation of the bladder:

- Drinking two quarts of water a day to flush the bladder
- Drinking orange or cranberry juice to maintain an acidic environment that discourages growth of infectious organisms
- Decreasing use of alcohol and caffeine (from coffee, tea, or cola drinks) that may irritate the bladder

TRUTH **fiction 2**

Urethral opening The opening through which urine passes from the female's body

Cystitis An inflammation of the urinary bladder

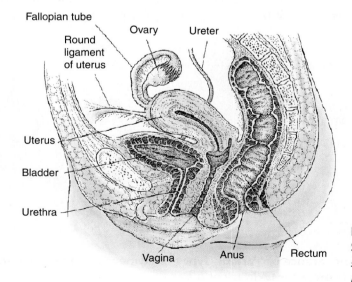

Figure 3.3 The Female Reproductive System. *This cross-section locates many of the internal sex organs that compose the female reproductive system. Note that the uterus is normally tipped forward.*

- Washing the hands prior to masturbation or self-examination
- Washing one's partner's and one's own genitals before and after intercourse
- Preventing objects that have touched the anus (fingers, penis, toilet tissue) from subsequently coming into contact with the vulva
- Urinating soon after intercourse to help wash away bacteria

The Vaginal Opening

When I was five or six, my mother told me about sex. I remember that I was confused about what my mother said, because somehow I couldn't conceptualize what the female vagina looked like. I was curious to see an actual vagina and not just how it looked diagramed in a book. (Morrison et al., 1980, p. 35)

One does not see an entire vagina, but rather the vaginal opening, or **introitus,** when one parts the labia minora. The introitus lies below and is larger than the urethral opening. Its shape resembles that of the **hymen.**

The hymen is a fold of tissue across the vaginal opening that is usually present at birth and may remain at least partly intact until a woman engages in coitus. For this reason the hymen has been called the *maidenhead.* Its presence has been taken as proof of virginity, and its absence as evidence of coitus. However, some women are born with incomplete hymens, and other women's hymens are torn accidentally, such as during horseback riding, strenuous exercise or gymnastics—or even when bicycle riding. A punctured hymen is therefore poor evidence of coital experience. A flexible hymen may also withstand many coital experiences, so its presence does not guarantee virginity.

Truth or Fiction Revisited: Contrary to myth, it is not true that one may determine whether a woman is a virgin by examination of the hymen. Some people believe incorrectly that virgins cannot insert tampons or fingers into their vaginas, but most hymens will accommodate these intrusions without great difficulty.

Figure 3.4 illustrates various vaginal openings. The first three show common shapes of hymens among women who have not had coitus and whose hymens have not otherwise ruptured. The fifth drawing shows a *parous* ("passed through") vaginal opening, typical of a woman who has delivered a baby. Now and then the hymen consists of tough fibrous tissue and is closed, or *imperforate,* as in the fourth drawing. An imperforate hymen may not be discovered until after puberty, when menstrual dis-

Introitus The vaginal opening

Hymen A fold of tissue across the vaginal opening that is usually present at birth and remains at least partly intact until a woman engages in coitus; Greek for "membrane"

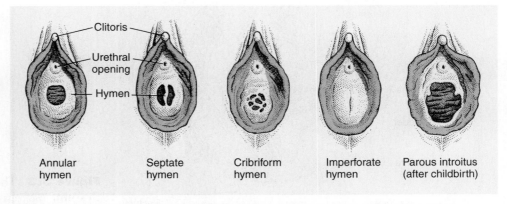

| Annular hymen | Septate hymen | Cribriform hymen | Imperforate hymen | Parous introitus (after childbirth) |

Labels: Clitoris, Urethral opening, Hymen

Figure 3.4 Appearance of Various Types of Hymens and the Introitus (right) as It Appears after Delivery of a Baby

charges begin to accumulate in the vagina. In these rare cases, a surgical incision will perforate the hymen. A woman may also have a physician surgically perforate her hymen if she would rather forgo the tearing and discomfort that may accompany her initial coital experiences. A woman may also stretch the vaginal opening over several days in preparation for intercourse by inserting a finger and gently pressing downward toward the anus. After several repetitions, she may insert two fingers and repeat the process, spreading the fingers slightly after insertion.

The hymen is found only in female horses and humans. It is not present in animal species closest to humans on the evolutionary scale, such as chimps and gorillas. The hymen remains something of a biological mystery, because it serves no apparent biological function.

The Perineum

The **perineum** incorporates the skin and underlying tissue between the vaginal opening and the anus. The perineum is rich in nerve endings. Stimulation of the area may heighten sexual arousal. Many physicians make a routine perineal incision during labor, called an episiotomy, to facilitate childbirth.

Structures That Underlie the External Sex Organs

Figure 3.5 shows what lies beneath the skin of the vulva. The *vestibular bulbs* and *Bartholin's glands* are active during sexual arousal and are found on both sides (shown on the right in Figure 3.5). Muscular rings (sphincters) that constrict bodily openings such as the vaginal and anal openings are also found on both sides.

The clitoral **crura** are wing-shaped, leglike structures that attach the clitoris to the pubic bone beneath. The crura contain the corpora cavernosa, which engorge with blood and stiffen during sexual arousal.

The **vestibular bulbs** are attached to the clitoris at the top and extend downward along the sides of the vaginal opening. Blood congests them during sexual arousal, swelling the vulva and lengthening the vagina. This swelling contributes to coital sensations for both partners.

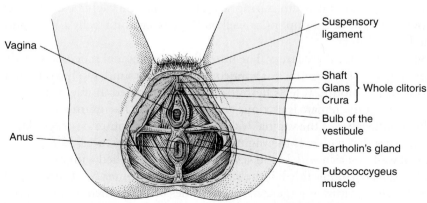

Figure 3.5 **Structures That Underlie the Female External Sex Organs.** *If we could see beneath the vulva, we would find muscle fibers that constrict the various body openings, plus the crura ("legs") of the clitoris, the vestibular bulbs, and Bartholin's glands.*

Perineum The skin and underlying tissue that lies between the vaginal opening and the anus

Crura Anatomic structures resembling legs that attach the clitoris to the pubic bone

Vestibular bulbs Cavernous structures that extend downward along the sides of the introitus and swell during sexual arousal

Bartholin's glands lie just inside the minor lips on each side of the vaginal opening. They secrete a couple of drops of lubrication just before orgasm. This lubrication is not essential for coitus. In fact, the fluid produced by Bartholin's glands has no known purpose. If the glands become infected and clogged, however, a woman may notice swelling and local irritation. It is wise to consult a gynecologist if these symptoms do not fade within a few days.

It was once believed that the source of the vaginal lubrication or "wetness" that women experience during sexual arousal was produced by Bartholin's glands. It is now known that engorgement of vaginal tissues during sexual excitement results in a form of "sweating" by the lining of the vaginal wall. During sexual arousal, the pressure from this engorgement causes moisture from the many small blood vessels that lie in the vaginal wall to be forced out and to pass through the vaginal lining, forming the basis of the lubrication. In less time than it takes to read this sentence (generally within 10 to 30 seconds), beads of vaginal lubrication or "sweat" appear along the interior lining of the vagina in response to sexual stimulation, in much the same way that rising temperatures cause water to pass through the skin as perspiration.

Pelvic floor muscles permit women to constrict the vaginal and anal openings. They contract automatically, or involuntarily, during orgasm, and their tone may contribute to coital sensations.

Internal Sex Organs

The internal sex organs of the female include the innermost parts of the vagina, the cervix, the uterus, and two ovaries, each connected to the uterus by a fallopian tube (Figures 3.3 and 3.6). These structures comprise the female reproductive system.

The Vagina

The **vagina** extends back and upward from the vaginal opening (Figure 3.3). It is usually three to five inches long at rest. Menstrual flow and babies pass from the uterus to the outer world through the vagina. During coitus, the penis is contained within the vagina.

The vagina is commonly pictured as a canal or barrel; but, when at rest, it is like a collapsed muscular tube. Its walls touch like the fingers of an empty glove. The vagina expands in length and width during sexual arousal. The vagina can also expand to allow insertion of a tampon, as well as the passage of a baby's head and shoulders during childbirth.

The vaginal walls have three layers. The inner lining, or vaginal mucosa, is made visible by opening the labia minora. It is a mucous membrane similar to the skin that lines the inside of the mouth. It feels fleshy, soft, and corrugated. It may vary from very dry (especially if the female is anxious about something, like examinations) to very wet. The middle layer of the vaginal wall is muscular. The outer or deeper layer is a fibrous covering that connects the vagina to other pelvic structures.

The vaginal walls are rich with blood vessels but poorly supplied with nerve endings. Unlike the sensitive outer third of the vaginal barrel, the inner two thirds are so insensitive to touch that minor surgery may sometimes be performed on those portions without anesthesia. The entire vaginal barrel is sensitive to pressure, however, which can be experienced as pleasurable.

The vaginal walls secrete substances that help maintain the vagina's normal acidity (pH, 4.0 to 5.0). Normally they taste salty, but their odor and taste may vary dur-

Bartholin's glands
Glands that lie just inside the minor lips and secrete fluid just before orgasm

Vagina The tubular female sex organ that contains the penis during sexual intercourse and through which a baby is born; Latin for "sheath"

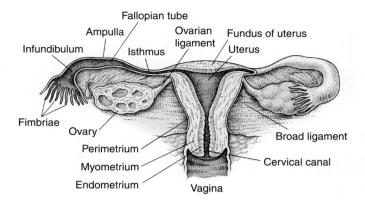

Figure 3.6 **Female Internal Reproductive Organs.** *This drawing highlights the relationship of the uterus to the fallopian tubes and ovaries. Note the layers of the uterus, the ligaments that attach the ovaries to the uterus, and the relationship of the ovaries to the fimbriae of the fallopian tubes.*

ing the menstrual cycle. The secretions may contain substances that act as sexual attractants. Women who frequently **douche** or use feminine deodorant sprays may remove or mask substances that arouse sex partners. Douching or spraying may also alter the natural chemical balance of the vagina, which can increase the risk of infections. Feminine deodorant sprays can also irritate the vagina and evoke allergic reactions. The normal, healthy vagina cleanses itself through regular chemical secretions that are evidenced by a mild white or yellowish discharge.

Vaginitis refers to any vaginal inflammation, whether it is caused by an infection, birth control pills, antibiotics that alter natural body chemistry, an allergic reaction, chemical irritation, or lowered resistance, as may be caused by fatigue or poor diet. Changes in body chemistry or lowered resistance permit microscopic organisms normally found in the vagina to multiply to infectious levels. Vaginitis may be recognized by abnormal discharge, itching, burning of the vulva, and urinary urgency. Women with vaginitis are advised to seek medical attention, but let us note some suggestions that may help prevent vaginitis:

- Wash your vulva and anus regularly with mild soap. Pat dry (taking care not to touch the vulva after dabbing the anus).
- Wear cotton panties. Nylon underwear retains heat and moisture that cause harmful bacteria to flourish.
- Avoid pants that are tight in the crotch.
- Be certain that sex partners are well washed. Condoms may also reduce the spread of infections from one's sex partner.
- Use a sterile, water-soluble jelly such as K-Y jelly if artificial lubrication is needed for intercourse. Do not use Vaseline. Birth control jellies can also be used for lubrication.
- Avoid intercourse that is painful or abrasive to the vagina.
- Avoid diets high in sugar and refined carbohydrates, because they alter the normal acidity of the vagina.
- Women who are prone to vaginal infections may find it helpful to douche occasionally with plain water, a solution of one or two tablespoons of vinegar in a quart of warm water, or a solution of baking soda and water. Douches consisting of unpasteurized, plain (unflavored) yogurt may help replenish the "good" bacteria that are normally found in the vagina and that may be destroyed by use of antibiotics. Be careful when douching, and do not douche when pregnant or when you suspect you may be pregnant. Consult your physician before deciding to douche or to apply any preparations to the vagina.
- Watch your general health. Eating poorly or getting insufficient rest will reduce your resistance to infection.

Douche Application of a jet of liquid to the vagina as a rinse

Vaginitis Vaginal inflammation

A Closer Look

THE G SPOT AND FEMALE EJACULATION: SEXUAL REALITIES OR GYNECOLOGICAL MYTHS?

The Grafenberg spot, or G spot, is theorized to be a part of the vagina—a bean-shaped area in the anterior (front) wall that may have special erotic significance. The G spot is believed to lie about one to two inches from the vaginal entrance and to consist of a soft mass of tissue that swells from the size of a dime to a half dollar when stimulated (Figure 3.7). The name derives from the gynecologist Ernest Grafenberg, who first suggested the possible erotic import of the area. The spot can be directly stimulated by the woman's or her partner's fingers or by penile thrusting in the rear entry or the female-superior positions. Some researchers suggest that stimulation of the spot produces intense erotic sensations and that, with prolonged stimulation, a distinct form of orgasm that is characterized by intense pleasure and, in some cases, a biological event formerly thought to be exclusively male: ejaculation (Perry & Whipple, 1981; Whipple & Komisaruk, 1988). These claims have been steeped in controversy. Even supporters of the existence of the G spot admit that it is difficult to locate, because it is not apparent to the eye or touch (Ladas et al., 1982). Terence Hines (2001) summarizes criticisms of the research into the G spot by noting that it is based on anecdotes and case studies with small numbers of subjects. Hines characterizes the evidence for the existence of the G spot as weak and unsupported by more rigorous anatomic and biochemical research. He dubs the G spot a "modern gynecological myth."

Research on female ejaculate is not much clearer. In a laboratory experiment, Zaviacic and his colleagues (1988a, b) found evidence of an ejaculate in 10 of 27 women studied. Some researchers believe that this fluid is urine that some women release involuntarily during orgasm. Others believe that it differs from urine (Zaviacic & Whipple, 1993). The nature of this fluid and its source remain unclear, but Zaviacic and Whipple (1993) suggest that it may represent a fluid that is released during sex by a "female prostate," a system of ducts and glands called Skene's glands, in much the

CRITICAL Thinking

Some observers of the research on human sexuality suggest that the arguments over the existence of the G spot and female ejaculation have political as well as scientific implications. How do you think that the debates might relate to larger issues concerning the study of female sexuality and male sexuality? Explain.

SafeZone

Q *I feel like I have an unpleasant odor from my vagina. Should I douche?*

A Most health care providers will recommend regular superficial washing, as when taking a shower, and then, if the issue remains in your mind, talking to your gynecologist about it. An unpleasant odor can be a sign of a health problem. If you're 18 or younger and sexually active, you need to have a gynecologist and to see her (or him) regularly. Some vaginal odor is normal. If you are attending to your personal hygiene and are not diagnosed with a health problem, a partner is as likely—or more likely—to find normal vaginal odors attractive rather than repulsive.

The Cervix

When someone first said to me two years ago, "You can feel the end of your own cervix with your finger," I was interested but flustered. I had hardly ever put my finger in my vagina at all, and felt squeamish about touching myself there, in that place "reserved" for lovers and doctors. It took me two months to get up nerve to try it, and then one afternoon, pretty nervously, I squatted down in the bathroom and put my finger in deep, back into my vagina. There it was, feeling slippery and rounded, with an indentation at

same way that semen is released by the prostate gland in men. Zaviacic and Whipple suggest that "many women who felt that they may be urinating during sex . . . [may be helped by] the knowledge that the fluid they expel may be different from urine and a normal phenomenon that occurs during sexual response" (p. 149). Some women, however, may expel urine during sex, perhaps because of urinary stress incontinence (Zaviacic & Whipple, 1993). Zaviacic and Whipple also suggest that stimulation of the G spot may cause some women to ejaculate but not others.

Contemporary sexologists seem to agree on a number of points concerning the G spot and "female ejaculation." One is that most or even all of the anterior wall of the vagina, not just one area, is richly supplied with nerve endings and may be sensitive to erotic stimulation (Alzate & Hoch, 1986; Levin, 2003a). However, it has not been adequately demonstrated that any particular zone of the anterior wall functions as a discrete sex organ; the area or areas that are exquisitely sensitive may

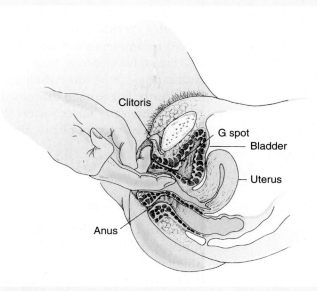

Figure 3.7 The Grafenberg Spot. *It is theorized that the G spot can be stimulated by fingers or by intercourse in the rear entry or the female-superior positions. Does stimulation of the G spot produces intense erotic sensations and a distinct form of orgasm?*

vary from woman to woman (Maaita et al., 2002). Second, many females may exude a fluid through the urethra at about the time of orgasm. However, it is not clear what such fluid might be, and it is even less clear that it might correspond in some way to male ejaculation (Alzate & Hoch, 1986; Hines, 2001). Third, many sexologists wonder why other sexologists are so "sensitive" about this issue and why it has become so politicized (Alzate & Hoch, 1986).

the center through which, I realized, my menstrual flow came. It was both very exciting and beautifully ordinary at the same time. Last week I bought a plastic speculum so I can look at my cervix. Will it take as long this time? (Boston Women's Health Book Collective, 2005)

The **cervix** is the lower end of the uterus. Its walls, like those of the vagina, produce secretions that contribute to the chemical balance of the vagina (Levin, 2005b). The opening in the middle of the cervix, or **os,** is normally about the width of a straw, although it expands to permit passage of a baby from the uterus to the vagina during childbirth. Sperm pass from the vagina to the uterus through the cervical canal.

CERVICAL CANCER   Cervical cancer is relatively uncommon in the United States, although there are about 10,000 new cases a year and 4,000 deaths (American Cancer Society, 2006). The primary cause of cervical cancer is infection with the human papilloma virus (HPV; see Chapter 16). A vaccine has been developed that makes most women immune to the form of HPV connected with cancer. A woman is best vaccinated before she becomes sexually active and may be exposed to the virus (Grady, 2005). Cervical cancer is more common among women who have had many sex partners, became sexually active at a relatively early age, and smoke (Duggirala et al., 2003). The mortality rate is higher for African American women than European American women, at least in part because it tends to be diagnosed later in African Americans (National Cancer Institute, 2006).

Cervix The lower end of the uterus; Latin for "neck"

Os The opening in the middle of the cervix; Latin for "mouth"

A **Pap test** examines a sample of cervical cells that are smeared on a slide to screen for cervical cancer and other abnormalities. The American Cancer Society (2006) recommends annual Pap tests along with a pelvic examination for women who are, or have been, sexually active or who have reached age 18. Most cases of cervical cancer can be successfully treated by surgery and **radiotherapy** if they are detected early. For women diagnosed with localized cancer, the survival rate is nearly 100% (American Cancer Society, 2006). Cervical cancer can also be prevented by removal or destruction of precancerous tissue. The overall five-year survival rate is about 70%.

The Uterus

The **uterus,** or womb (Figures 3.3 and 3.6), is the organ in which a fertilized ovum implants and develops until birth. The uterus usually slants forward (is *antroverted*), although about 10% of women have uteruses that tip backward (are *retroverted*). In most instances a retroverted uterus causes no problems, but some women with one find female–male coitus in certain positions painful. A retroverted uterus normally tips forward during pregnancy. The uterus is suspended in the pelvis by flexible ligaments. In a woman who has not given birth, it is about three inches long, three inches wide, and one inch thick near the top. The uterus expands to house a fetus during pregnancy and shrinks after pregnancy, although not to its original size.

The uppermost part of the uterus is called the **fundus** (Figure 3.6). The uterus is shaped like an inverted pear. If a ceramic model of a uterus were placed on a table, it would balance on the fundus. The central region of the uterus is called the body. The narrow lower region is the cervix, which leads downward to the vagina.

Like the vagina, the uterus has three layers (Figure 3.6). The innermost layer, or **endometrium,** is richly supplied with blood vessels and glands. Its structure varies according to a woman's age and phase of the menstrual cycle. Endometrial tissue is discharged through the cervix and vagina at menstruation. In some women, endometrial tissue may also grow in the abdominal cavity or elsewhere in the reproductive system. This condition is called **endometriosis,** and the most common symptom is menstrual pain. If untreated, it may lead to infertility.

ENDOMETRIAL CANCER Cancer of the endometrial lining is called endometrial cancer. There are about 40,000 new cases each year and 7,000 deaths from this form of cancer (American Cancer Society, 2006). Risk factors for endometrial cancer include high exposure to estrogen during early menarche, late menopause, or estrogen replacement therapy. For women who obtain hormone replacement therapy (HRT), combining estrogen with progestin lessens the risk of endometrial cancer. Not having children places the woman at risk, whereas pregnancy and hormonal contraceptives appear to lessen the risk. Endometrial cancer is symptomized by abnormal uterine staining or bleeding, especially after menopause. The most common treatment is surgery (American Cancer Society, 2006). The five-year survival rate for endometrial cancer is up to 92% if it is discovered early and limited to the endometrium. (Endometrial cancer is usually diagnosed early because women tend to report postmenopausal bleeding to their doctors quickly.) The survival rate drops when the cancer invades surrounding tissues or metastasizes.

The second layer of the uterus, the **myometrium**, is well muscled. It endows the uterus with flexibility and strength, and creates the powerful contractions that propel a fetus outward during labor. The third or outermost layer, the **perimetrium**, provides an external cover.

Pap test A test of a sample of cervical cells that screens for cervical cancer and other abnormalities; named after the originator of the technique, Dr. George Papanicolaou

Radiotherapy Treatment of a disease by x-rays or by emissions from a radioactive substance

Uterus The hollow, muscular, pear-shaped organ in which a fertilized ovum implants and develops until birth

Fundus The uppermost part of the uterus

Endometrium The innermost layer of the uterus

Endometriosis A condition caused by the growth of endometrial tissue in the abdominal cavity or elsewhere outside the uterus and characterized by menstrual pain

Myometrium The middle, well-muscled layer of the uterus

Perimetrium The outer layer of the uterus

The Fallopian Tubes

The **fallopian tubes** are about four inches in length and extend from the upper end of the uterus toward the ovaries (Figure 3.6). The part of each tube nearest the uterus is the *isthmus,* which broadens into the *ampulla* as it approaches the ovary. The outer part, or *infundibulum,* has fringelike projections called *fimbriae* that extend toward, but are not attached to, the ovary. Ova pass through the fallopian tubes on their way to the uterus. The fallopian tubes are not just passageways. They help nourish and conduct ova. The tubes are lined with tiny hairlike projections termed *cilia* ("lashes") that help propel ova through the tube at about one inch per day. Because ova must be fertilized within a day or two after they are released from the ovaries, fertilization usually occurs in the infundibulum within a couple of inches of the ovaries. The form of sterilization called tubal ligation ties off the fallopian tubes, so that ova cannot pass through them or become fertilized.

During an **ectopic pregnancy**, the fertilized ovum implants outside the uterus, most often in the fallopian tube where fertilization occurred. Ectopic pregnancies can eventually burst fallopian tubes, causing hemorrhaging and death. Ectopic pregnancies are thus terminated before the tube ruptures. They are not easily recognized, however, because their symptoms—missed menstrual period, abdominal pain, irregular bleeding—suggest many conditions. Any of these symptoms is an excellent reason for consulting a gynecologist. Women who are of advanced age, who have had pelvic inflammatory disease (PID), who have undergone tubal surgery, or who have used intrauterine devices (IUDs) are at increased risk of developing ectopic pregnancies (Boston Women's Health Book Collective, 2005).

The Ovaries

The two **ovaries** are almond-shaped organs that are each about 1.5 inches long. They lie on either side of the uterus, to which they are attached by ovarian ligaments. The ovaries produce ova (egg cells) and the female sex hormones **estrogen** and **progesterone**. Estrogen is a generic term for several hormones (such as estradiol, estriol, and estrone) that promote the changes of puberty and regulate the menstrual cycle. Estrogen also helps older women maintain cognitive functioning and feelings of psychological well-being (Ross et al., 2000). Progesterone also has multiple functions, including regulating the menstrual cycle and preparing the uterus for pregnancy by stimulating the development of the endometrium (uterine lining). Estrogen and progesterone levels vary with the phases of the menstrual cycle.

The human female is born with all the ova she will ever have (about two million), but they are immature in form. Of these, about 400,000 survive into puberty, each of which is contained in the ovary within a thin capsule, or **follicle**. During a woman's reproductive years, from puberty to menopause, only 400 or so ripened ova, typically one per month, will be released by their follicles for possible fertilization. How these ova are selected remains a mystery.

OVARIAN CANCER   Each year some 22,000 women in the United States are diagnosed with ovarian cancer, and about 16,000 die from it (American Cancer Society, 2006). Ovarian cancer most often strikes women between the ages of 40 and 70, and ranks as the fourth leading cancer killer of women, behind lung cancer, breast cancer, and colon cancer. Women most at risk are those with blood relatives who had ovarian cancer or breast cancer, especially a first-degree relative (mother, sister, or daughter). Other risk factors are high body weight and never having given birth.

Fallopian tubes Tubes that extend from the upper uterus toward the ovaries and conduct ova to the uterus; after the Italian anatomist Gabriel Fallopio

Ectopic pregnancy A pregnancy in which the fertilized ovum implants outside the uterus, usually in the fallopian tube

Ovaries Almond-shaped organs that produce ova and the hormones estrogen and progesterone

Estrogen A generic term for female sex hormones or synthetic compounds that promote the development of female sex characteristics and regulate the menstrual cycle; from the roots meaning "generating" (*-gen*) and "estrus"

Progesterone A steroid hormone secreted by the corpus luteum or prepared synthetically that stimulates proliferation of the endometrium and is involved in regulation of the menstrual cycle; from the root *pro-,* meaning "promoting," and the words *gestation, steroid,* and *one*

Follicle A capsule within an ovary that contains an ovum

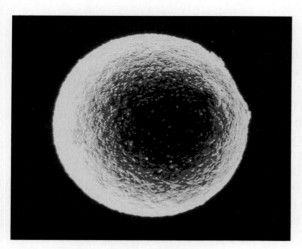

A Magnified Human Ovum (Egg Cell)

Early detection is the key to fighting ovarian cancer. When it is detected before spreading beyond the ovary, 94% of victims survive. However, the overall five-year survival rate is about 44% (American Cancer Society, 2006). Unfortunately, ovarian cancer is often "silent" in the early stages, showing no obvious signs or symptoms. The most common sign is enlargement of the abdomen, which is caused by the accumulation of fluid. Periodic, complete pelvic examinations are important. The Pap test, which is useful in detecting cervical cancer, does not reveal ovarian cancer. The American Cancer Society (2006) advises women older than the age of 40 to have a cancer-related check-up every year.

Surgery, radiation therapy, and drug therapy are treatment options. Surgery usually includes the removal of one or both ovaries, the uterus, and the fallopian tubes.

HYSTERECTOMY   One woman in three in the United States has a **hysterectomy** by the age of 60. Most women who obtain them do so between the ages of 35 and 45. The hysterectomy is the second most commonly performed operation on women in this country. (Cesarean sections are the most common.) A hysterectomy may be performed when a woman develops cancer of the uterus, ovaries, or cervix, or another disease that causes pain or excessive uterine bleeding. A **complete hysterectomy** is the surgical removal of the ovaries, fallopian tubes, cervix, and uterus. It is usually performed to reduce the risk of cancer spreading throughout the reproductive system. A **partial hysterectomy** removes the uterus but spares the ovaries and fallopian tubes so that the woman continues to ovulate and produce adequate quantities of female sex hormones. The hysterectomy can relieve symptoms associated with various gynecological disorders and improve the quality of life for many women (Kjerulff et al., 2000). However, many gynecologists believe that hysterectomy is recommended too often, before proper diagnostic steps are taken or when less radical interventions might alleviate the problem (Broder et al., 2000). We advise women whose physician advises a hysterectomy to seek a second opinion before proceeding.

The Pelvic Examination

Women are advised to have an internal (pelvic) examination at least once a year by the time they reach their late teens (or earlier if they become sexually active) and twice yearly if they are older than 35 or use birth control pills. The physician (usually a gynecologist) first examines the woman externally for irritations, swellings, abnormal vaginal discharges, and clitoral adhesions. The physician normally inserts a speculum to help inspect the cervix and vaginal walls for discharge (which can be signs of infection), discoloration, lesions, or growths. This examination is typically followed by a Pap test to detect cervical cancer. A sample of vaginal discharge may also be taken to test for the STI gonorrhea (see Chapter 16).

To take a Pap smear, the physician will hold open the vaginal walls with a plastic or metal (hopefully prewarmed!) speculum so that a sample of cells (a *smear*) may be scraped from the cervix with a wooden spatula (Figure 3.8). Women should not douche prior to Pap tests and should not schedule this test during menstruation, because douches and blood confound analysis of the smear.

The speculum exam is normally followed by a bimanual vaginal exam in which the index and middle fingers of one hand are inserted into the vagina while the lower part of the abdomen is palpated (touched) by the other hand from the outside. The

Hysterectomy Surgical removal of the uterus

Complete hysterectomy Surgical removal of the ovaries, fallopian tubes, cervix, and uterus

Partial hysterectomy Surgical removal of the uterus, but not the ovaries and fallopian tubes

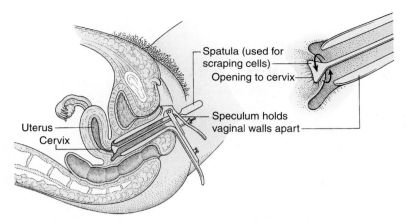

Figure 3.8 Use of the Speculum and Spatula during a Pelvic Examination. *The speculum holds the vaginal walls apart while the spatula is used to scrape cells gently from the cervix. The Pap test screens for cervical cancer and other abnormalities.*

physician uses this technique to examine the location, shape, size, and movability of the internal sex organs, searching for abnormal growths and symptoms of other problems. Palpation may be somewhat uncomfortable, but severe pain is a sign that something is wrong. A woman need not hide such discomfort from the examiner. She may only be masking a symptom (that is, depriving the physician of useful information). Physical discomfort is usually mild, however, and psychological discomfort is sometimes lessened by discussing it.

Finally, the physician should do a rectovaginal examination in which one finger is inserted into the rectum while the other is inserted into the vagina. This procedure provides additional information about the ligaments of the uterus, the ovaries, and the fallopian tubes. The procedure also helps the physician evaluate the health of the rectum.

Although it may be somewhat uncomfortable, the pelvic examination is not ordinarily painful. It is normal for a woman who has not had one, or who is visiting a new doctor, to be anxious about the exam. The doctor should be reassuring if the woman expresses concern. If the doctor is not, the woman should feel free to consult another doctor. She should not forgo the pelvic examination itself, however. It is essential for early detection of problems.

The Breasts

College women recall:

> I was very excited about my breast development. It was a big competition to see who was wearing a bra in elementary school. When I began wearing one, I also liked wearing see-through blouses so everyone would know.

> My breasts were very late in developing. This brought me a lot of grief from my male peers. I just dreaded situations like going to the beach or showering in the locker room.

> All through junior high and high school I felt unhappy about being "overendowed." I felt just too uncomfortable in sweaters—there was so much

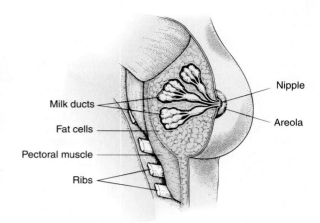

Figure 3.9 **Breast of an Adult Woman.** *This drawing reveals the structures underlying the breast, including milk ducts and fat cells.*

Secondary sex characteristics Traits that distinguish the sexes from one another but are not directly involved in reproduction

Mammary glands Milk-secreting glands

Areola The dark ring on the breast that encircles the nipple

to reveal and I was always sure that the only reason boys liked me was because of my bustline.

By the time I was 11 I needed a bra. . . . The girls in my gym class in sixth grade laughed at me because my breasts were pretty big and I still didn't have a bra. I tried to cover myself up when I dressed and undressed. On my 11th birthday my mom gave me a sailor blouse and inside was my first bra. . . . [It] was the best present I could have received. The bra made me feel a lot better about myself, but I was still unsure of my femininity for a long time. (Morrison et al., 1980, pp. 66–70)

In some cultures the breasts are viewed merely as biological instruments for feeding infants. In our culture, however, breasts have taken on such erotic significance that a woman's self-esteem may become linked to her bustline.

The breasts are **secondary sex characteristics**. That is, like the rounding of the hips, they distinguish women from men, but they are not directly involved in reproduction. Each breast contains 15 to 20 clusters of milk-producing **mammary glands** (Figure 3.9). Each gland opens at the nipple through its own duct. The mammary glands are separated by soft, fatty tissue. It is the amount of this fatty tissue, not the amount of glandular tissue, that largely determines the size of the breasts (Levin, 2006). **Truth or Fiction Revisited:** Women vary little in their amount of glandular tissue, so breast size does not determine the quantity of milk that can be produced.

The nipple, which lies in the center of the **areola**, contains smooth muscle fibers that erect the nipple when they contract. The areola, or area surrounding the nipple, darkens during pregnancy and remains darker after delivery. Oil-producing glands in the areola help lubricate the nipples during breast-feeding. Milk ducts conduct milk from the mammary glands through the nipples. Nipples are richly endowed with nerve endings, so that stimulation of the nipples heightens sexual arousal for many women. Male nipples are similar in sensitivity (Levin, 2006).

Figure 3.10 shows some of the normal variations in the size and shape of the breasts of adult women. The sensitivity of the breasts to sexual stimulation is unrelated to their size. Small breasts may have as many nerve endings as large breasts, but they will be more densely packed.

Women can prompt their partners to provide breast stimulation by informing them that their breasts are sensitive to stimulation. They can also guide a partner's hands in ways that provide the type of stimulation they desire. The breasts vary in sensitivity with the phases of the menstrual cycle, and some women appear less responsive to breast stimulation than others. However, some less sensitive women may learn to enjoy breast stimulation by focusing on breast sensations during lovemaking in a relaxed atmosphere.

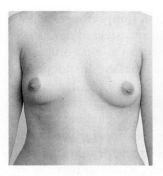 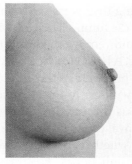 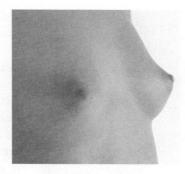

Figure 3.10 **Normal Variations in the Size and Shape of the Breasts of Adult Women.** *The size and shape of the breasts have little bearing on their ability to produce milk or on sensitivity to sexual stimulation. Breasts have become highly eroticized in our culture.*

SafeZone

Q *Is there any way to make my breasts larger without having plastic surgery?*

A You'll come across advertisements for dietary supplements that supposedly do the job, but we advise you not to take anything without discussing it with your health care provider. But think about why you are concerned about your breast size. Is it because you are succumbing to the popular idea that a sex partner will prefer a woman with large breasts? Some do, but many do not, and who you are as a person is more important than your cup size! If your partner doesn't agree with that, you need another partner, not larger breasts. In any case, small breasts are as sensitive to sexual stimulation as larger breasts, so show your partner what you want.

SafeZone

Q *One of my breasts is bigger than the other. Is this normal?*

A Sure. Unless there's a huge difference, don't worry about it. It is mostly the amount of fatty tissue in the breasts that accounts for differences in the size of the breasts among women. Moreover, breasts expand with pregnancy, and smaller breasts tend to increase more dramatically in size than larger breasts. And because production of milk depends on the amount of glandular tissue in the breasts, not fatty tissue, the size of your breasts has nothing to do with the amount of milk you can produce if you have children. On the other hand, if you have noticed a change in the size of one breast relative to the other, or in the texture of your breast tissue or in the nipple or areola, bring it to the attention of your health care provider. It could mean nothing, but it's better to be sure.

Breast Cancer

Susan contracted breast cancer in her 30s. A lump "suddenly" appeared in her **mammogram**. She and the family dwelled in fear for the next couple of weeks as tissue from the tumor was sampled, found to be malignant, and arrangements were made to remove the breast. Given the "aggressiveness" of the tumor—the rapidity with which it had grown—every physician she consulted recommended **mastectomy**

Mammogram A special type of x ray test that detects cancerous lumps in the breast

Mastectomy Surgical removal of the entire breast

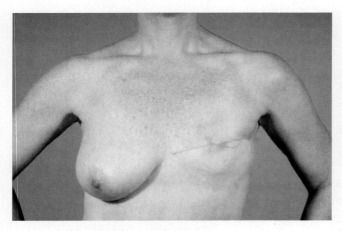

A Woman Following a Mastectomy

(removing the breast) rather than **lumpectomy** (just removing the lump). The question arose regarding whether she should remove the healthy breast as a precautionary measure. A blood test determined that she did not possess genetic mutations (the BRCA1 or BRCA2 gene) connected with early-onset breast cancer, so the healthy breast was preserved. There was additional anxiety after the removal of the breast as tissues were examined to determine whether the cancer had spread within the breast or to lymph nodes. Fortunately, it had apparently remained within a duct despite the rapidity of its growth.

Susan then dealt with the psychological issues of feeling unwhole, which were to some degree mitigated by attending a support group of women undergoing similar experiences. Reconstruction of the breast was an unexpected and lengthy process during which the muscles that normally underlie the breasts were gradually expanded to surround and support a silicone implant. A new cosmetic nipple was constructed from thigh tissue. It was decided that Susan did not need chemotherapy or radiation, but she did go on tamoxifen, a drug that decreases the body's supply of estrogen—a factor in the development of cancerous tissue in the breast. There is no evidence of remaining **malignant** tissue as she approaches the "magical" five-year postsurgical survival date.

Breast cancer strikes nearly 270,000 women in the United States each year and takes about 40,000 lives (American Cancer Society, 2006). An estimated 460 men also die of breast cancer each year. It is not cancer in the breast that kills, but rather its spread to vital body parts, such as the brain, bones, lungs, or liver.

More early cases of breast cancer are apparently being detected because of the increased use of the mammogram, a kind of x-ray that detects cancerous lumps in the breast. Advances in early detection and treatment have led to increased rates of recovery. On the other hand, some critics argue that mammography has led to the detection and treatment of some localized cancers that might never have grown. The American Cancer Society (2006) counters that the majority of these small tumors would grow. In any event, the five-year survival rate for women whose breast cancers have not spread beyond the breast is about 98%, up from nearly 80% in the 1950s (American Cancer Society, 2006). The five-year survival rate drops to about 80% if the cancer has spread to the surrounding region and to about 26% if it has spread to more distant sites.

RISK FACTORS Breast cancer is rare in women younger than the age of 25. The risk increases sharply with age. About four of five cases develop in women older than 50 years. The risk of developing breast cancer is about 1 in 229 for women age 30 to 39 years (National Cancer Institute, 2006), and it increases with each decade of life. The National Cancer Institute (2006) puts the probability that a woman will be diagnosed with breast cancer at some time at about one in seven to eight (13.2%).

Genetic factors are involved in breast cancer, in particular among women who inherit the genetic mutations associated with breast cancer (BRCA1 and BRCA2) and among women with a family history of the disease (American Cancer Society, 2006). A study of more than 100,000 female nurses showed that those with mothers or sisters who had breast cancer had nearly twice the chance of developing the disease themselves (Colditz & Rosner, 2000). Women who had both a mother and a sister with the disease had two to three times a greater risk for developing the disease. Moreover, women who inherit the BRCA1 or BRCA2 mutations have a 50% to 85% chance of developing breast

Lumpectomy Surgical removal of a lump from the breast

Malignant Lethal; causing or likely to cause death

African American Women and Breast Cancer

Overall, African Americans are more likely than European Americans to develop cancer. The case is somewhat different with breast cancer. As a group, African American women are somewhat less likely than European American women to develop breast cancer. However, when they do, they frequently do so at an earlier age (Carey et al., 2006). They tend to be diagnosed with the disease somewhat later, and they are also more likely to die from it (American Cancer Society, 2006). Some aspects of the racial differences, such as the tendency to be diagnosed later, may reflect less access to health care. On the other hand, genetic factors are also likely to be involved. It is usually estrogen that causes the proliferation of breast cancer cells, and thus some drugs, like tamoxifen, treat breast cancer by suppressing the body's supply of estrogen. However, African American women are more likely to develop tumors that are *estrogen-receptor negative*. That is, they develop rapidly even in the absence of estrogen (Carey et al., 2006). These tumors are highly aggressive—that is, they grow very rapidly—and are a major factor in the higher mortality rate for African American women (American Cancer Society, 2006).

Heavy drinking of alcohol also heightens the risk of breast cancer (American Cancer Society, 2006; Stein & Colditz, 2004) as do high amounts of fatty tissue in the body (American Cancer Society, 2006; Stein & Colditz, 2004).

Does abortion increase a woman's risk of breast cancer? Some researchers have speculated that because pregnancy decreases the risk of breast cancer, having an abor-

African American Women and Breast Cancer. *African American women are generally less likely than European American women to develop breast cancer. But, when they do, the cancer tends to be more aggressive and deadly. The racial difference may be largely genetic.*

tion will indirectly increase the risk (Malec, 2003). **Truth or Fiction Revisited:** Carefully controlled studies, however, do not find abortion to increase a woman's risk of breast cancer (American Cancer Society, 2006; Tang et al., 2000). Nor have silicone breast implants been shown to increase the risk of breast cancer either, but they can lead to the development of scar tissue and may obscure mammogram readings (American Cancer Society, 2006).

TRUTH? fiction 5

cancer (American Cancer Society, 2006), compared with one woman in eight or nine in the general population. They also have an increased risk of developing ovarian cancer.

Genes for breast cancer appear to predict not only whether women will contract the disease but also how deadly it will be. Health professionals can test the genomes of women with breast cancer to help determine how aggressively they should treat the disease by means such as chemotherapy and radiation, after the tumors have been removed surgically (American Cancer Society, 2006).

A key risk factor in breast cancer is prolonged exposure to estrogen, which stimulates breast development in young women and the proliferation of breast cancer cells as well (Colditz et al., 2004). The following all heighten the risk of breast cancer because they increase women's exposure to estrogen: early onset of menstruation (before age 14), late menopause (after age 55), delayed childbearing (after age 30), and never giving birth (American Cancer Society, 2006). Exercise, by the way, may reduce the risk of breast cancer by decreasing the amount of fatty tissue in the body. Fat is connected with higher levels of estrogen production.

DETECTION AND TREATMENT Women with breast cancer have lumps in the breast, *but most lumps are not cancerous.* Most are either **cysts** or **benign** tumors called **fibroadenomas**. Breast cancer involves lumps in the breast that are malignant.

Early detection and treatment reduce the risk of mortality. The sooner cancer is detected, the less likely it is to have spread to critical organs.

Breast cancer may be detected in various ways, including breast self-examination ("BSE"), physical examination ("clinical breast examination," or "CBE"), mammography, and ultrasound. Using mammography, tiny, highly curable cancers can be detected—and treated—before they can be felt by touch. By the time a malignant lump is large enough to be felt by touch, it already contains millions of cells and may have metastasized—splintered off to form colonies elsewhere in the body. A mammogram can detect tiny tumors before metastasis. One study found that 82% of women whose breast cancers were detected early by mammography survived for at least five years after surgery compared with 60% of those whose cancers were discovered later.

Early detection may offer another benefit. Smaller lumps are sometimes removed by lumpectomy, sparing the breast. More advanced cancers are likely to be treated by mastectomy.

Many drugs are also used to treat breast cancer, and others are in the research pipeline. For example, tamoxifen locks into the estrogen receptors of breast cancer cells, thereby blocking estrogen's stimulation of the cells to grow and proliferate. However, tamoxifen increases the risks of uterine cancer and of blood clots in the lungs, along with some other side effects. The risks of these side effects were lowest among women younger than the age of 50. The drug raloxifene has also been shown to reduce the risk of breast cancer (Cummings et al., 1999). Moreover, raloxifene does not appear to have the side effects associated with tamoxifen. (Nevertheless, Susan was prescribed tamoxifen.) Other drugs are also being studied for use against breast cancer. Ask your gynecologist for the latest research results and which drugs, if any, are right for you.

Many women who have had mastectomies have had surgical breast implants to replace the tissue that has been removed. Other women have breast implants to augment their breast size. Research suggests that breast implants probably have no effect on the probability of developing breast cancer, rheumatoid arthritis, and a number of other health problems, casting doubts on previous studies that had implicated them in the development of these problems (Spiegel, 2001; Wooster & Weber, 2003). Again, consult your gynecologist.

The American Cancer Society (2006) recommends that women have a clinical breast exam every three years when they are between 20 and 39 years of age and annually thereafter. In 1985, 20% of women had had a mammogram within the past two years, as opposed to more than 70% in 2005 (Kolata, 2005). *The New England Journal of Medicine* reported that mammography was likely to be responsible for anywhere from 28% to 65% of the increase in the breast cancer survival rate during the past two decades (Berry et al., 2005).

Truth or Fiction Revisited: The American Cancer Society no longer recommends monthly BSEs. However, the nearby "A Closer Look" feature (page 84) provides instructions for women who choose to engage in breast self-examination.

The Menstrual Cycle

Menstruation is the cyclical bleeding that stems from the shedding of the uterine lining (endometrium). Menstruation takes place when a reproductive cycle has not led to the fertilization of an ovum. The word *menstruation* derives from the Latin *mensis*, meaning "month." The menstrual cycle averages 28 days.

CRITICAL Thinking

The American Cancer Society no longer recommends that women need to conduct breast self-examinations as a means of detecting breast cancer early. Do you believe that it is a good idea for women to do breast self-exams anyway? Why or why not?

TRUTH fiction **6**

Cysts Saclike structures filled with fluid or diseased material

Benign Doing little or no harm

Fibroadenoma A benign, fibrous tumor

The cycle is regulated by the hormones estrogen and progesterone, and can be divided into four phases. The first phase, the *proliferative phase,* follows menstruation. During this phase, estrogen levels increase, causing the ripening of perhaps 10 to 20 ova (egg cells) within their follicles and the proliferation of endometrial tissue in the uterus. During the second phase of the cycle, estrogen reaches peak blood levels, and **ovulation** occurs. Normally only one ovum reaches maturity and is released by an ovary during ovulation. Then the third phase—the *secretory phase* or *luteal phase*—of the cycle begins. The luteal phase begins right after ovulation and continues through the beginning of the next cycle.

The term *luteal phase* is derived from **corpus luteum,** the name given the follicle that releases an ovum. The corpus luteum functions as an **endocrine gland** and produces large amounts of progesterone and estrogen. Progesterone causes the endometrium to thicken, so that it will be able to support an embryo if fertilization occurs. If the ovum goes unfertilized, however, estrogen and progesterone levels plummet. The drops trigger the fourth phase, the *menstrual phase,* which leads to the beginning of a new cycle.

Ovulation may not occur during every menstrual cycle. *Anovulatory* ("without ovulation") cycles are most common in the years just after **menarche.** They may become frequent again in the years prior to menopause, but they may also occur irregularly at any age.

Although the menstrual cycle averages 28 days, variations among women, and in the same woman from month to month, are common. Girls' cycles are often irregular for a few years after menarche, but later assume regular patterns. Variations from cycle to cycle tend to occur during the proliferative phase that precedes ovulation. Menstruation tends to follow ovulation reliably by about 14 days.

Hormones regulate the menstrual cycle, but psychological factors can affect the secretion of hormones. Stress can delay or halt menstruation. Many women in otherwise good health stopped menstruating during imprisonment in Nazi concentration camps during World War II (Ofer & Weitzman, 1998; Ritner & Roth, 1993).

Regulation of the Menstrual Cycle

The menstrual cycle involves finely tuned relationships between structures in the brain—the **hypothalamus** and the **pituitary gland**—and the ovaries and uterus. All these structures are parts of the endocrine system, which means that they secrete chemicals directly into the bloodstream (see Figure 3.12 page 86). The chemicals secreted by endocrine glands are called **hormones.** The ovaries and uterus are also reproductive organs.

The gonads—the ovaries in the female and the **testes** (or testicles) in the male—secrete sex hormones directly into the bloodstream. The female gonads, the ovaries, produce the sex hormones estrogen and progesterone. The male gonads, the testes, produce the male sex hormone **testosterone.** Males and females also produce relatively small amounts of the sex hormones of the other sex.

The hypothalamus is a pea-sized structure in the front part of the brain. It weighs four to five grams and lies above the pituitary gland and below (hence the prefix *hypo-,* for "under") the thalamus. Despite its small size, it is involved in regulating many states of motivation, including hunger, thirst, aggression, and sex. For example, when the rear part of a male rat's hypothalamus is stimulated by an electric probe, the rat runs through its courting and mating sequence. It nibbles at a female's ears and at the back of her neck. When she responds, they copulate. Human sexuality is not so stereotyped or mechanical—although in the cases of people who have fallen into ruts, it may seem to be.

Ovulation The release of an ovum from an ovary

Corpus luteum The follicle that has released an ovum and then produces copious amounts of progesterone and estrogen during the luteal phase of a woman's cycle

Endocrine gland A ductless gland that releases its secretions directly into the bloodstream

Menarche The first menstrual period

Hypothalamus A structure near the center of the brain that is involved in regulating body temperature, motivation, and emotion

Pituitary gland The gland that secretes growth hormone, prolactin, oxytocin, and others

Hormone A substance secreted by an endocrine gland that regulates various body functions; from the Greek *horman,* meaning "to stimulate" or "to goad"

Testes The male gonads

Testosterone The male sex hormone that fosters the development of male sex characteristics and is connected with the sex drive

A Closer Look

BREAST SELF-EXAMINATION

Mammograms and regular visits to a physician provide the best protection against breast cancer, because they may lead to early detection and treatment. However, many women find lumps themselves. It was once recommended that women conduct BSEs at least once a month, but now the American Cancer Society considers BSEs to be optional. On the other hand, BSEs may have psychological advantages for many women—empowering them to investigate their own bodies and to actively participate in their own disease prevention. Moreover, the American Cancer Society (2006) continues to recommend that women be "aware" of what is going on in their bodies. BSE would appear to be one way to cultivate awareness.

The following instructions for BSE are based on American Cancer Society guidelines (Figure 3.11). Additional material on BSE may be obtained from the American Cancer Society by calling 1-800-ACS-2345. However, women are advised to initiate BSEs with a health professional to determine their baseline "lumpiness" and to learn the proper technique.

1. *In the shower.* Examine your breasts during your bath or shower; hands glide more easily over wet skin. Keep your fingers flat and move gently over every part of each breast. Use the right hand to examine the left breast and the left hand for the right breast. Check for any lump, hard knot, or thickening.

2. *Before a mirror.* Inspect your breasts with your arms at your sides. Next, raise your arms high overhead. Look for any changes in the contour of each breast, a swelling, dimpling of skin, or changes in the nipple. Then rest your palms on your hips and press down firmly to flex your chest muscles. Your left and right breasts will not exactly match. Few women's breasts do. Regular inspection shows what is normal for you and will give you confidence in your examination.

3. *Lying down.* To examine your right breast, put a pillow or folded towel under your right shoulder. Place your right arm behind your head. This position distributes breast tissue more evenly on the chest. With your left hand, fingers flat, press gently with the finger pads (the top thirds of the fingers) of the three middle fingers in small circular motions around an imagi-

---

Prolactin A pituitary hormone that stimulates production of milk

Oxytocin A pituitary hormone that stimulates uterine contractions in labor and the ejection of milk during nursing

Gonadotropins Pituitary hormones that stimulate the gonads; Literally, "that which 'feeds' the gonads"

Follicle-stimulating hormone (FSH) A gonadotropin that stimulates development of follicles in the ovaries

The pituitary gland, which is also about the size of a pea, lies below the hypothalamus at the base of the brain. Because many pituitary secretions regulate other endocrine glands, the pituitary has also been called the *master gland*. Pituitary hormones regulate bone and muscle growth, and urine production. Two pituitary hormones are active during pregnancy and motherhood: **prolactin,** which stimulates production of milk, and **oxytocin,** which stimulates uterine contractions in labor and the ejection of milk during nursing. The pituitary gland also produces **gonadotropins** (literally, "that which 'feeds' the gonads") that stimulate the ovaries: **follicle-stimulating hormone (FSH)** and **luteinizing hormone (LH).** These hormones play key roles in regulating the menstrual cycle.

The hypothalamus receives information about bodily events through the nervous and circulatory systems. It monitors the blood levels of various hormones, including estrogen and progesterone, and releases a hormone called **gonadotropin-releasing hormone (Gn-RH),** which stimulates the pituitary to release gonadotropins. Gonadotropins, in turn, regulate the activity of the gonads. It was once thought that the pituitary gland ran the show, but it is now known that the pituitary gland is regulated by the hypothalamus.

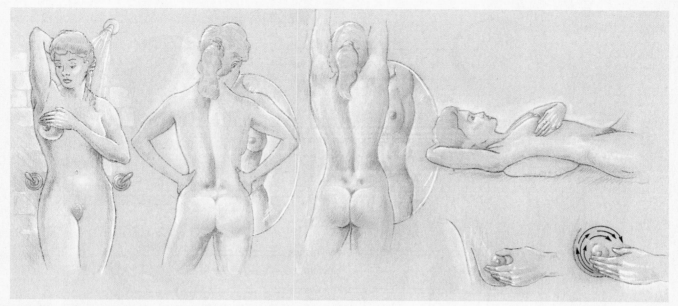

Figure 3.11 A Woman Examines Her Breast for Lumps

nary clock face. Begin at the outermost top of your right breast for 12 o'clock, then move to one o'clock, and so on around the circle back to 12. A ridge of firm tissue in the lower curve of each breast is normal. Then move in one inch, toward the nipple. Keep cir-

cling to examine *every part of your breast,* including the nipple. This requires at least three more circles. Now slowly repeat the procedure on your left breast. Place the pillow beneath your left shoulder, your left arm behind your head, and use the finger pads on your right hand.

After you examine your left breast fully, squeeze the nipple of each breast gently between your thumb and index finger. Any discharge, clear or bloody, should be reported to your doctor immediately.

Phases of the Menstrual Cycle

The menstrual cycle has four stages or phases: proliferative, ovulatory, secretory, and menstrual (Figure 3.13). It might seem logical that a new cycle begins with the first day of the menstrual flow, because this is the most clearly identifiable event of the cycle. Many women also count the days of the menstrual cycle beginning with the onset of menstruation. Biologically speaking, however, menstruation is really the culmination of the cycle. In fact, the cycle begins with the end of menstruation and the initiation of a series of biological events that lead to the maturation of an immature ovum in preparation for ovulation and possible fertilization.

THE PROLIFERATIVE PHASE The first phase, or **proliferative phase,** begins with the end of menstruation and lasts about 9 or 10 days in an average 28-day cycle (Figures 3.13 and 3.14). During this phase, the endometrium develops, or "proliferates." This phase is also known as the *preovulatory* or *follicular phase,* because certain ovarian follicles mature and the ovaries prepare for ovulation.

Luteinizing hormone (LH) A gonadotropin that helps regulate the menstrual cycle by triggering ovulation

Gonadotropin-releasing hormone (Gn-RH) A hormone secreted by the hypothalamus that stimulates the pituitary to release gonadotropins

Proliferative phase The first phase of the menstrual cycle, which begins with the end of menstruation and lasts about nine or ten days; the phase during which the endometrium proliferates

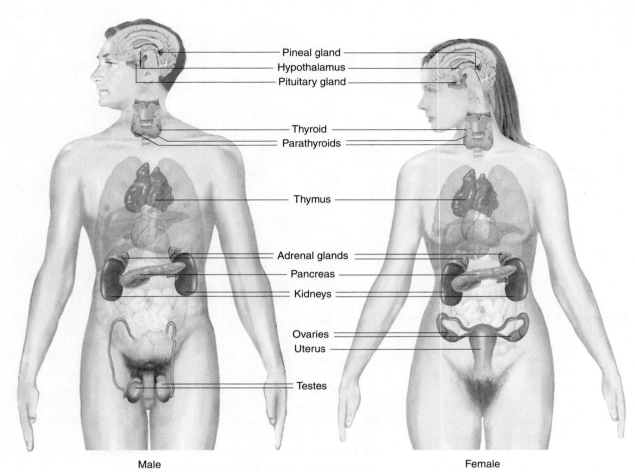

Pineal gland
Hypothalamus
Pituitary gland

Thyroid
Parathyroids

Thymus

Adrenal glands
Pancreas
Kidneys

Ovaries
Uterus

Testes

Male   Female

Figure 3.12 **Major Glands of the Endocrine System.** *The endocrine system consists of glands that secrete chemicals called* hormones *directly into the bloodstream.*

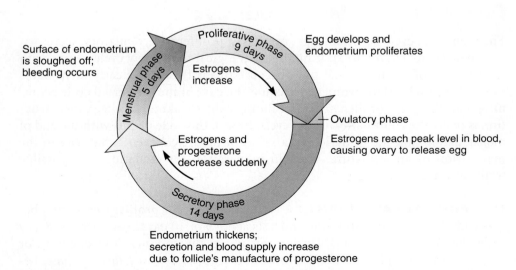

Surface of endometrium is sloughed off; bleeding occurs

Menstrual phase 5 days

Proliferative phase 9 days

Estrogens increase

Egg develops and endometrium proliferates

Ovulatory phase

Estrogens reach peak level in blood, causing ovary to release egg

Estrogens and progesterone decrease suddenly

Secretory phase 14 days

Endometrium thickens; secretion and blood supply increase due to follicle's manufacture of progesterone

Figure 3.13 **The Four Phases of the Menstrual Cycle.** *The menstrual cycle has proliferative, ovulatory, secretory (luteal), and menstrual phases.*

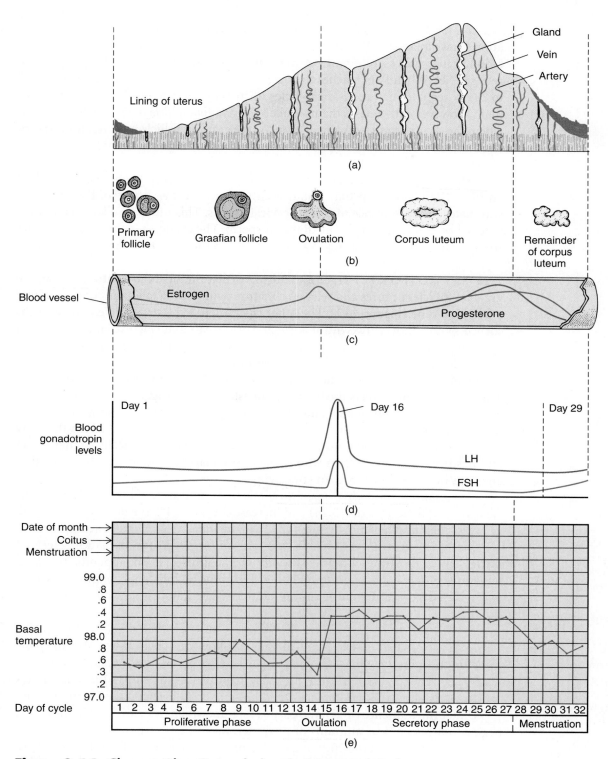

Figure 3.14 Changes That Occur during the Menstrual Cycle. *This figure shows five categories of biological change: (a) changes in the development of the uterine lining (endometrium), (b) follicular changes, (c) changes in blood levels of ovarian hormones, (d) changes in blood levels of pituitary hormones, and (e) changes in basal temperature. Note the dip in temperature connected with ovulation.*

Low levels of estrogen and progesterone are circulating in the blood as menstruation draws to an end. When the hypothalamus senses a low level of estrogen in the blood, it increases secretion of Gn-RH, which in turn triggers the pituitary gland to release FSH. When FSH reaches the ovaries, it stimulates some follicles (perhaps 10 to 20) to begin to mature. As the follicles ripen, they begin to produce estrogen. Normally, however, only one of them—called the *graafian follicle*—will reach full maturity in the days just preceding ovulation. As the graafian follicle matures, it moves toward the surface of the ovary, where it will eventually rupture and release a mature egg (Figures 3.14 and 3.15).

Estrogen causes the endometrium in the uterus to thicken to about one eighth of an inch. Glands develop that would eventually nourish an embryo. Estrogen also stimulates the appearance of a thin cervical mucus. This mucus is alkaline and provides a hospitable, nutritious medium for sperm. The chances are thus increased that sperm that enter the female reproductive system at the time of ovulation will survive.

THE OVULATORY PHASE During ovulation, or the **ovulatory phase,** the graafian follicle ruptures and releases a mature ovum *near* a fallopian tube—not *into* a fallopian tube (Figure 3.15). The other ripening follicles degenerate and are reabsorbed by the body. If two ova mature and are released during ovulation, and both are fertilized, fraternal (nonidentical) twins will develop. Identical twins occur when one fertilized ovum separates into two **zygotes.**

Ovulation is set into motion when estrogen production reaches a critical level. The hypothalamus detects the high level of estrogen and triggers the pituitary to release copious amounts of FSH and LH (Figures 3.14 and 3.15). The surge of LH triggers ovulation, which usually begins 12 to 24 hours after the level of LH in the body has reached its peak. The synthetic hormone *clomiphene* is chemically similar to LH and has been used by women who ovulate irregularly to induce reliable ovulation and thus increase the chances of conceiving.

A woman's *basal body temperature,* taken by oral or rectal thermometer, dips slightly at ovulation (Figure 3.14) and increases by about 1°F the day after ovulation. Many women use this information to help them conceive or avoid conceiving.

Some women have discomfort or cramping during ovulation, termed **mittelschmerz.** Mittelschmerz is sometimes confused with appendicitis. Mittelschmerz, however, may occur on either side of the abdomen, depending on which ovary is releasing an ovum. A ruptured appendix always causes pain on the right side.

THE SECRETORY PHASE The phase following ovulation is called the *post-ovulatory* or **secretory phase.** Some people refer to it as the *luteal phase,* which reflects the name given the ruptured (graafian) follicle—the *corpus luteum.* Figures 3.14 and 3.15 show the transformation of the graafian follicle into the corpus luteum.

Under the influence of LH, the corpus luteum, which has remained in the ovary, begins to produce large amounts of progesterone and estrogen. Levels of these hormones peak at around the 20th or 21st day of an average cycle (Figure 3.14). These hormones cause the glands in the endometrium to secrete nutrients to sustain a fertilized ovum that becomes implanted in the uterine wall.

If implantation does not occur, the hypothalamus responds to the peak levels of progesterone by signaling the pituitary to stop producing LH and FSH. This feedback process is similar to that of a thermostat in a house reacting to increasing temperatures by shutting down the furnace. The levels of LH and FSH decline rapidly, leading the corpus luteum to decompose. After its decomposition, levels of estrogen and

Ovulatory phase The second stage of the menstrual cycle, during which a follicle ruptures and releases a mature ovum

Zygote A fertilized ovum (egg cell)

Mittelschmerz Pain that occurs during ovulation; German for "middle pain," reflecting the fact that the pain occurs midway between menstrual periods

Secretory phase The third phase of the menstrual cycle, which follows ovulation; also referred to as the *luteal phase,* after the *corpus luteum,* which begins to secrete large amounts of progesterone and estrogen after ovulation

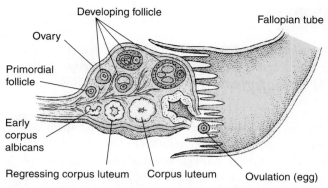

Developing follicle

Fallopian tube

Ovary

Primordial follicle

Early corpus albicans

Regressing corpus luteum   Corpus luteum   Ovulation (egg)

Figure 3.15 **Maturation and Eventual Decomposition of an Ovarian Follicle.** *Many follicles develop and produce estrogen during the proliferative phase of the menstrual cycle. Usually only one, the graafian follicle, ruptures and releases an ovum. The graafian follicle then develops into the corpus luteum, which produces copious quantities of estrogen and progesterone. When fertilization does not occur, the corpus luteum decomposes.*

progesterone fall precipitously. The corpus luteum sows the seeds of its own destruction: Its hormones signal the brain to shut down secretion of substances that maintain it.

THE MENSTRUAL PHASE   The **menstrual phase** occurs when decreasing estrogen and progesterone levels can no longer sustain the uterine lining. The lining then disintegrates and is discharged from the body, along with the menstrual flow.

The low estrogen levels of the menstrual phase signal the hypothalamus to release Gn-RH, which in turn stimulates the pituitary to secrete FSH. FSH, in turn, prompts ovarian secretion of estrogen and the onset of another proliferative phase. Thus a new cycle begins. The menstrual phase is a beginning as well as an end.

Menstrual flow contains blood from the endometrium (uterine lining), endometrial tissue, and cervical and vaginal mucus. Although the flow can appear persistent and last for five days or more, most women lose only a total of two or three ounces of blood (four to six tablespoonfuls). A typical blood donor, by contrast, donates 16 ounces of blood at a sitting. Extremely heavy or prolonged (more than a week) menstrual bleeding may reflect health problems and should be discussed with a health care provider.

Prior to 1933, women generally used external sanitary napkins or pads to absorb the menstrual flow. In that year, however, tampons were introduced. Tampons are inserted into the vagina and are left in place to absorb menstrual fluid. Women who use tampons can swim without concern while menstruating, wear more revealing or comfortable apparel, and feel less burdened.

Questions have arisen about whether tampons cause or exacerbate infections, such as *toxic shock syndrome (TSS),* which is sometimes fatal. Signs of TSS include fever, headache, sore throat, vomiting, diarrhea, muscle aches, rash, and dizziness. Peeling skin, disorientation, and a plunge in blood pressure may follow. TSS is caused by the *Staphylococcus aureus* ("staph") bacterium, which is most likely to overbreed when highly absorbent tampons are left in place for many hours. As a result, many women now use regular rather than superabsorbent tampons. Others change their tampons three or four times a day, or alternate them with sanitary napkins. Women are encouraged to consult their health care providers about TSS.

Menstrual phase The fourth phase of the menstrual cycle, during which the endometrium is sloughed off in the menstrual flow

Q *As a guy, I don't really know what girls go through day to day when they have their period. I also don't have a sister. Do they use more than one tampon a day? Do they leave the tampon in? Do all girls use tampons? I want to understand what they actually have to go through.*

A In developed nations today, many women use tampons or feminine napkins and change them several times a day. So-called superabsorbent tampons, which could be left in for much or most of a day, have gone out of fashion because of the risk of TSS. In most cases, there is probably also less blood than you would imagine. However, many females experience premenstrual or menstrual pain (especially cramping) and some irritability, which are uncomfortable, but absolutely normal. At the time of the sexual revolution, sexologists and social critics minimized premenstual syndrome (PMS) and other menstrual problems as a way of minimizing sex differences in general. Today, however, menstrual problems are accepted as widely occurring and reflective of female sexual anatomy and physiology. Today, the question is, how can we help women who encounter such difficulties, not how can we pretend they don't exist.

Sex during Menstruation

TRUTH **fiction 7**

Many couples continue to have sex during menstruation; others abstain. Some people abstain because of religious prohibitions. Others express concern about the "fuss" or the "mess" of the menstrual flow. **Truth or Fiction Revisited:** Despite traditional attitudes that associate menstruation with uncleanliness, there is no evidence that coitus during menstruation is physically harmful to either partner. Ironically, menstrual coitus may be helpful to the woman. The uterine contractions that occur during orgasm may help relieve cramping by dispelling blood congestion (Masters & Johnson, 1966). Orgasm from masturbation may have the same effect.

Women may be sexually aroused at any time during the menstrual cycle. The preponderance of the research evidence, however, points to a peak in sexual desire in women around the time of ovulation.

Human sexual patterns during the phases of the menstrual cycle reflect personal decisions and not just hormone fluctuations. Some couples may decide to increase their frequency of coitus at ovulation to optimize the chances of conceiving, or to abstain during menstruation because of cultural or religious beliefs. Some may also increase their coital activity preceding menstruation to compensate for anticipated abstinence during menses or may increase coital activity afterward to make up for deprivation. In contrast, females of other species that are bound by the estrous cycle generally respond sexually only during estrus.

Menopause, Perimenopause, and the Climacteric

Menopause The cessation of menstruation

Perimenopause The beginning of menopause, as characterized by 3 to 11 months of amenorrhea or irregular periods

Menopause, or the "change of life," is the cessation of menstruation. Menopause is a process that most commonly occurs between the ages of 46 and 50 and lasts for about two years. However, it may begin any time between the ages of 35 and 60.

Perimenopause refers to the beginning of menopause and is usually characterized by 3 to 11 months of amenorrhea (lack of menstruation) or irregular periods

Historical and Cross-Cultural Perspectives on Menstruation

In Peru, they speak of a "visit from Uncle Pepe," whereas in Samoa, menstruation is referred to as "the boogie man." One of the more common epithets for menstruation is "the curse." The Fulani of Upper Volta in Africa use a term that translates "to see dirt." Nationalism also rises to the call, with some nations blaming "the curse" on their historical enemies. The French once dubbed menstruation "the English," and its onset, "the English are coming."

It is a common folk belief that menstruating women are contaminated. Men may thus avoid contact with menstruating women. To prevent their contaminating others, menstruating women in tribal societies have been dispatched to huts on the fringe of the village. In the traditional Navajo culture, for instance, menstruating women would be consigned to huts that were set apart from other living quarters. In many Islamic societies, the menstrual flow is considered unclean, and menstruating women are not permitted to pray or enter a mosque.

Women in industrialized nations are not consigned to special huts, but throughout the history of Western culture, menstruation has been seen as unclean, contaminating, even magical. **Truth or Fiction Revisited:** The ancient Romans believed that menstrual blood soured wine and killed crops. In 77 CE, the Roman historian Pliny summed up Roman misbeliefs about menstrual blood:

Contact with it turns new wine sour, crops touched by it become barren, grafts die, seeds in gardens are dried up, the fruit of trees falls off. . . . [The] edge of steel and the gleam of ivory are dulled, hives of bees die, even bronze and iron are at once seized by rust, and a horrible smell fills the air; to taste it drives dogs mad and infects their bites with an incurable poison.

Ancient societies—and some contemporary ones—have a limited understanding of bodily processes, or else they rely on tradition more than science. Science teaches that there is no medical basis for isolating menstruating women or avoiding sex during menstruation.

We might laugh off these misconceptions as folly and ignorance, if it were not for their profound effect on women. Women who believe the myths about menstruation may see themselves as unclean and endure anxiety, depression, and lowered self-esteem. Negative cultural beliefs concerning menstruation may also exacerbate menstrual distress.

TRUTH? fiction 8

(Bastian et al., 2003; Torpy et al., 2003). Perimenopause ends with menopause. Menopause, in other words, is a specific event in a longer term process known as the **climacteric** ("critical period"). The term *climacteric* specifically refers to the gradual decline in the reproductive capacity of the ovaries. The climacteric generally lasts about 15 years, from about age 45 to 60. After age 35 or so, the menstrual cycles of many women shorten, from an average of 28 days to 25 days at age 40 and to 23 days by the mid 40s. By the end of her 40s, a woman's cycle may become erratic, with some periods close together and others absent.

During menopause, the pituitary gland continues to pour normal levels of FSH and LH into the bloodstream; but, for reasons that are not well understood, the ovaries gradually lose their capacity to respond. The ovaries no longer ripen egg cells or produce the sex hormones estrogen and progesterone.

The deficit in estrogen may lead to a number of unpleasant perimenopausal sensations, such as night sweats and hot flashes (suddenly feeling hot) and hot flushes (suddenly looking reddened) (Bastian et al., 2003; Dennerstein et al., 2000). Hot flashes and flushes may alternate with cold sweats, in which a woman feels suddenly cold and clammy. Anyone who has experienced "cold feet" or hands from anxiety or fear will understand how dramatic the shifting patterns of blood flow can be. Hot

REFLECT

Do you (or your loved ones) experience PMS or PMDD? What are you (or they) doing about it? Why?

Climacteric A long-term process, including menopause, that involves the gradual decline in the reproductive capacity of the ovaries

Not for Women Only.
Osteoporosis is usually thought of as a health problem that afflicts older women, but men make up about 2 million of the 10 million people with osteoporosis in the United States. Men are at less risk for osteoporosis because they have larger, stronger bones than women. Osteoporosis is more likely to strike men who have low testosterone levels, use medications like steroids, smoke, drink heavily, and lead sedentary lives (Anderson et al., 2002).

Osteoporosis A condition caused by estrogen deficiency and characterized by a decline in bone density, such that bones become porous and brittle; from the Greek *osteon*, meaning "bone," and the Latin *porus*, meaning "pore"

flashes and flushes stem largely from "waves" of dilation of blood vessels across the face and upper body. All these sensations reflect *vasomotor instability*. That is, there are disruptions in the body mechanisms that dilate or constrict the blood vessels to maintain an even body temperature. Additional signs of estrogen deficiency include dizziness, headaches, pains in the joints, sensations of tingling in the hands or feet, burning or itchy skin, and heart palpitations. The skin usually becomes drier. There is some loss of breast tissue and decreased vaginal lubrication during sexual arousal. Women may also encounter sleep problems, such as awakening more frequently at night and having difficulty falling back to sleep. A Chinese study found that about one perimenopausal woman in six experienced migraine headaches (Wang et al., 2003).

Long-term estrogen deficiency has been linked to brittleness and porosity of the bones—**osteoporosis.** Bones break more readily, and some women develop "dowager's hump" (Seifert–Klauss et al., 2005). Osteoporosis can be handicapping, even life-threatening. The increased brittleness of the bones increases the risk of serious fractures, especially of the hip, and many older women never recover from them (Marwick, 2000). Estrogen deficiency also has psychological effects. It can impair cognitive functioning and feelings of psychological well-being (Ross et al., 2000; Yaffe et al., 2000).

Hormone Replacement Therapy: Good Medicine or Menace?

Candace tried almost everything to manage her discomforts of perimenopause: a chiropractor, acupuncture, antianxiety pills, soy tablets, and herbal remedies. Finally, she relented and followed her doctor's recommendation that she use HRT. The doctor's attitude seemed to be that the immediate benefits, for Candace, age 51, outweighed the risks (Rabin, 2006).

Some women with severe physical symptoms, like Candace, have been helped by HRT, which typically consists of synthetic estrogen and progesterone. The hormones are used to offset the losses of their naturally occurring counterparts. HRT may help reduce the hot flushes and other symptoms brought about by hormonal deficiencies during menopause (den Tonkelaar & Oddens, 2000). There is also evidence that estrogen replacement lowers the woman's risk of osteoporosis (Grady, 2003a, b) and colon cancer (Grady, 2003b; Solomon & Dluhy, 2003).

Yet HRT is controversial. Although it has been helpful to many women, the Women's Health Initiative study of some 16,600 postmenopausal women age 50 to 79 found that exposure to a combination of estrogen and progestin appears to significantly increase the risk of breast cancer, stroke, and blot clots, and did not have a protective effect on the heart (Chlebowski et al., 2003). (Progestin is used along with estrogen, because estrogen alone exposes women to a greater risk of uterine cancer [Duenwald, 2002].) The Chlebowski study found that in addition to stimulating the growth of breast cancer, the combination of hormones also makes the tumors harder to detect, causing dangerous delays in diagnosis. During the course of the study of 8,506 women on HRT, 199 developed invasive breast cancers compared with 150 cases among the 8,102 women taking a placebo. Also, despite having yearly mammograms, 25.4% of the women who developed cancer while using HRT had cancers that had begun to metastasize compared with 16% of those taking the placebo.

Although estrogen stimulates proliferation of breast cancer cells, research suggests that women who have had hysterectomies might not be placed at increased risk of breast cancer by estrogen replacement (Stefanick et al., 2006). This is one of those

A Closer Look

MYTHS ABOUT MENOPAUSE

Menopause is certainly a major life change for most women. For many women, menopause symbolizes the many midlife issues they face, including changes in appearance, sexuality, and health. Yet exactly what types of changes do we find? Many of us harbor misleading ideas about menopause—ideas that can be harmful to women. Consider the following myths and the realities. To which myths have you fallen prey?

- *Menopause is abnormal.* Of course not. Menopause is a normal development in women's lives.

- *The medical establishment considers menopause a disease.* No longer. Menopause is described as a "deficiency syndrome" today, referring to the decline in secretion of estrogen and progesterone. Unfortunately, the term *deficiency* also has negative meanings.

- *After menopause, women need complete replacement of estrogen.* Not necessarily. Some estrogen continues to be produced by the adrenal glands, fatty tissue, and the brain (Guzick & Hoeger, 2000).

- *Menopause is accompanied by depression and anxiety.* Sometimes but not

necessarily. A number of reviews of the literature have found no consistent relationship between menopause and these psychological symptoms (Avis, 2003; Kessler, 2003). A Dutch study monitored 2,103 women age 46 to 54 for five years. During this time, the number of women who reached post-menopausal status doubled, and the percentage of women reporting depression increased from 18.5% to 23.7% (Maartens et al., 2002). The increase is unlikely to be the result of chance, but more than three out of four women in the study did not report significant levels of depression or anxiety at any time during the experience of menopause. Much of a woman's response to menopause reflects its meaning to her, not physical changes (Hunter & O'Dea, 2001). Women who adopt the commonly held belief that menopause signals the beginning of the end of life may develop a sense of hopelessness about the future, which in turn can set the stage for depression. Women whose entire lives have centered around childbearing and child rearing are more likely to experi-

ence a sense of loss. Moreover, there is a cultural bias to explain depression and other problems of middle-age women in terms of menopause, rather than to explore psychosocial factors.

- *At menopause, women experience debilitating hot flashes.* **Truth or Fiction Revisited:** Again, sometimes but not necessarily. Many women do not have hot flashes during menopause. Among those who do, the flashes are often mild. However, some women *do* have disturbing hot flashes, and we advise them to consult their gynecologists.

TRUTH? fiction 9

- *A woman who has had a hysterectomy will not undergo menopause afterward.* Actually, it depends on whether the ovaries (the major producers of estrogen) were also removed. If they were not, menopause should proceed normally.

- *Menopause signals an end to a woman's sexual appetite.* **Truth or Fiction Revisited:** It is not true that menopause signals an end to women's sexual appetite. In fact, some women feel newly sexually liberated because of the separation of sex from reproduction.

TRUTH? fiction 10

- *A woman's general level of activity is less after menopause.* Many post-menopausal women become peppier and more assertive.

studies that challenge conventional thinking and need to be replicated (repeated) to put women contemplating estrogen replacement at ease.

Levels of low-density lipoprotein (LDL; "bad cholesterol") are known to increase among menopausal women, whereas levels of high-density lipoprotein (HDL; "good cholesterol") decrease (Hall et al., 2002). A number of studies suggest that HRT increases levels of HDL and decreases levels of LDL (Herrington et al., 2000; Nieto et al., 2000; Shlipak et al., 2000). Because high levels of LDL are connected with cardiovascular disease, it was believed that HRT would reduce the risk of heart disease in postmenopausal women. Although this view was supported in research that monitored 120,000 nurses throughout the years, the women in the Hormone Replacement Therapy trial of the Women's Health Initiative apparently ran a slightly *greater* risk of heart attack and stroke (Fletcher & Colditz, 2002).

Because of these concerns, the number of women using HRT dropped by about half during the past few years (Rabin, 2006). However, more recent research from the Nurses Health Study (Grodstein et al., 2006) suggests that the women in the Women's Health Initiative trials might have been too old to profit from HRT—an average age of 64, when the average age of menopause is closer to 51. The arteries of women in their 50s are more elastic than those of women in their 60s, and estrogen might help them remain supple and reduce the buildup of plaque (Rabin, 2006). But women in their 60s generally have less flexible arteries and some plaque. Because estrogen can increase the clotting of blood, it might pose a risk to the older women, even if it helps the younger women.

What can we conclude? Research results on the benefits and dangers of HRT are mixed, and women considering HRT are well advised to explore the latest findings with their health care providers. They might also consider alternatives. Breast cancer specialist Larry Norton (cited in Duenwald, 2002) notes that progestin alone prevents or lessens hot flashes in about 70% of women. Selective serotonin reuptake inhibitors (SSRIs) like Effexor, Paxil, and Prozac are also of help (Stearns et al., 2003). Women using SSRIs to treat hot flashes usually take half the dose used to treat depression, which is their main usage, although they are also helpful with PMS, **premenstrual dysphoric disorder (PMDD)**, eating disorders, and some other problems.

Vaginal dryness can be treated with estrogens that are used locally—that is, placed in the vagina rather than the bloodstream, as hormones usually are. Creams (e.g., Estrace), suppositories (Vagifem), and a plastic ring (Estring) are available for the purpose.

Drinking milk, which is high in calcium, increases bone density in females and is likely to help prevent against osteoporosis later in life. Calcium supplements and the bisphosphonates (Actonel or Fosamax) also help maintain bone strength.

Some women use HRT to help get through the years leading up to menopause and then stop it. At this time it appears that the one thing we can predict is that health care providers are likely to have different views on the matter.

CRITICAL
Thinking

Why might a person be justified in complaining that she or he is confused about the evidence concerning the effects of HRT?

Menstrual Problems

Although menstruation is a natural biological process, 50% to 75% of women experience some discomfort prior to or during menstruation (Sommerfeld, 2000). The following Self-Assessment concerns common premenstrual symptoms. The problems we explore in this section include dysmenorrhea, mastalgia, menstrual migraine headaches, amenorrhea, PMS, and PMDD.

Dysmenorrhea

Pain or discomfort during menstruation—**dysmenorrhea**—is the most common menstrual problem. Most women at some time have at least mild menstrual pain or discomfort, so it is perfectly normal, even if annoying. Pelvic cramps are the most common manifestation of dysmenorrhea. They may be accompanied by headache, backache, nausea, or bloated feelings. Women who develop severe cases usually do so within a few years of menarche. **Primary dysmenorrhea** refers to menstrual pain or

Premenstrual dysphoric disorder (PMDD) A diagnosis used by the American Psychiatric Association to describe cases of PMS that are characterized by severe changes in mood and impairment of functioning at work, at school, or in social relationships

Dysmenorrhea Pain or discomfort during menstruation

Primary dysmenorrhea Menstrual pain or discomfort that occurs in the absence of known organic problems

discomfort in the absence of known organic pathology. Women with **secondary dysmenorrhea** have identified organic problems that are believed to cause their menstrual problems. Their pain or discomfort is caused by, or secondary to, these problems. Endometriosis, PID, and ovarian cysts are just a few of the organic disorders that can give rise to secondary dysmenorrhea. In addition, evidence is accumulating that supposed primary dysmenorrhea is often secondary to hormonal changes, although the precise causes have not been delineated. For example, menstrual cramps sometimes decrease dramatically after childbirth, as a result of the massive hormonal changes that occur with pregnancy. Women who have been pregnant report a lower incidence of menstrual pain but a higher incidence of premenstrual symptoms and menstrual discomfort.

Menstrual cramps appear to result from uterine spasms that may be brought about by the copious secretion of hormones called **prostaglandins**. Prostaglandins apparently cause muscle fibers in the uterine wall to contract, as during labor. Most contractions go unnoticed, but powerful, persistent contractions are discomfiting in themselves and may temporarily deprive the uterus of oxygen, another source of distress. Women with more intense menstrual discomfort apparently produce higher quantities of prostaglandins. Prostaglandin-inhibiting drugs, such as ibuprofen, indomethacin, and aspirin are thus often of help. Menstrual pain may also be secondary to endometriosis.

Pelvic pressure and bloating may be traced to pelvic edema (Greek for "swelling")—the congestion of fluid in the pelvic region. Fluid retention can lead to a gain of several pounds, sensations of heaviness, and **mastalgia**—a swelling of the breasts that sometimes causes premenstrual discomfort. Masters and Johnson (1966) noted that orgasm can help relieve menstrual discomfort by reducing the pelvic congestion that spawns bloating and pressure. Orgasm may also increase the menstrual flow and shorten this phase of the cycle.

Headaches frequently accompany menstrual discomfort. Most headaches (in both sexes) stem from simple muscle tension, notably in the shoulders, the back of the neck, and the scalp. Pelvic discomfort may cause muscle contractions, thus contributing to the tension that produces headaches. Women who are tense about their menstrual flow are thus candidates for muscle tension headaches. Migraine headaches may arise from changes in the blood flow in the brain, however. Migraines are typically limited to one side of the head and are often accompanied by visual difficulties.

Amenorrhea

Amenorrhea is the absence of menstruation and is a primary sign of infertility. **Primary amenorrhea** describes the absence of menstruation in a woman who has not menstruated at all by about the age of 16 or 17. **Secondary amenorrhea** describes delayed or absent menstrual periods in women who have had regular periods in the past. Amenorrhea has various causes, including abnormalities in the structures of the reproductive system, hormonal abnormalities, growths such as cysts and tumors, and psychological problems, such as stress. Amenorrhea is normal during pregnancy and after menopause. Amenorrhea is also a symptom of **anorexia nervosa,** an eating disorder characterized by an intense fear of putting on weight and a refusal to eat enough to maintain a normal body weight, which often results in extreme (and sometimes life-threatening) weight loss. Hormonal changes that accompany emaciation are believed responsible for the cessation of menstruation. Amenorrhea may also occur in women who exercise strenuously, such as competitive long-distance runners. It is unclear whether the cessation of menstruation in female

Secondary dysmenorrhea Menstrual pain or discomfort that is caused by identified organic problems

Prostaglandins Hormones that cause muscle fibers in the uterine wall to contract, as during labor

Mastalgia A swelling of the breasts that sometimes causes premenstrual discomfort

Amenorrhea The absence of menstruation

Primary amenorrhea Lack of menstruation in a woman who has never menstruated

Secondary amenorrhea Lack of menstruation in a woman who has previously menstruated

Anorexia nervosa A psychological eating disorder characterized by intense fear of putting on weight and refusal to eat enough to maintain normal body weight

athletes is the result of the effects of strenuous exercise itself, related physical factors such as low body fat, the stress of intensive training, or a combination of factors.

Premenstrual Syndrome and Premenstrual Dysphoric Disorder

The term **premenstrual syndrome (PMS)** describes the combination of biological and psychological symptoms that may affect women during the four- to six-day interval that precedes their menses each month. For many women, premenstrual symptoms persist during menstruation. PMDD is a more technical term used as a diagnostic category by the American Psychiatric Association in its *Diagnostic and Statistical Manual* (DSM). PMDD is more severe than PMS and is characterized by the symptoms shown in Table 3.1. The term is not always used precisely, and some make the mistake of confusing it with PMS (Smith et al., 2003). However, the diagnosis of PMDD requires that five or more of the symptoms listed in Table 3.1 be present most of the time during the week before the period and ending within a few days after the period begins. At least one symptom must be one of the first four. In addition, to diagnose as PMDD, the DSM requires that these symptoms must be present for most menstrual cycles during the past year and that they notably impair functioning at work or school, or in social activities and relationships.

Nearly three women in four experience some premenstrual symptoms (Sommerfeld, 2000). A study of Chinese women in Taiwan, reported in a Scandinavian journal, reported that the most common symptoms of PMS are minor psychological discomfort, muscular tension, and aches or pains (Hsiao et al., 2002). The great majority of cases involve mild to moderate levels of discomfort. Only a small minority of

TABLE 3.1

Symptoms of Premenstrual Dysphoric Disorder

1. Feelings of sadness, hopelessness, or worthlessness
2. Tension, anxious, feeling "on edge"
3. Notable changes in mood, including frequent crying
4. Persistent irritability and anger, often leading to increased interpersonal conflict
5. Lessened interest in usual activities, possibly with withdrawal from social relationships
6. Difficulty concentrating
7. Fatigue, lethargy, lack of energy
8. Notable changes in appetite, such as binge eating or craving certain foods
9. Hypersomnia (sleeping too much) or insomnia
10. Feeling overwhelmed or out of control
11. Other physical symptoms, for example, tenderness or swelling of the breasts, headaches, joint or muscle pain, feelings of bloating, weight gain

SOURCE: American Psychiatric Association. 2000. *Diagnostic and statistical manual of mental disorders. DSM-IV-TR*. 4th ed. Washington, DC: American Psychiatric Association. Reprinted by permission.

To diagnose PMDD, the DSM-IV-TR requires that symptoms must be present for most menstrual cycles during a given year. Five or more of the symptoms must be present most of the time during the week before the period and end within a few days after the period begins. At least one symptom must be one of the first four. The symptoms must notably impair functioning at work or school, or in social activities and relationships.

Premenstrual syndrome (PMS) A combination of physical and psychological symptoms (e.g., anxiety, depression, irritability, weight gain from fluid retention, and abdominal discomfort) that regularly afflicts many women during the four- to six-day interval that precedes their menses each month

women report menstrual symptoms severe enough to impair their social, academic, or occupational functioning and thus to be categorized as having PMDD. The causes of PMS and PMDD are unclear, but evidence is accumulating for a biological basis. Researchers are looking to possible relationships between menstrual problems, including PMS and PMDD, and chemical imbalances in the body. Researchers have yet to find differences in levels of estrogen or progesterone between women with PMDD and those with PMS or no symptoms (Bäckström et al., 2003). Research suggests that it is not the level of these hormones themselves that contributes to PMS and PMDD, but rather an abnormal response to the presence of these hormones (Schmidt et al., 1998). PMS and PMDD also appear to be linked with imbalances in neurotransmitters such as serotonin (Bäckström et al., 2003; Mortola, 1998). (Neurotransmitters are the chemical messengers in the nervous system.) Serotonin imbalances are also linked to changes in appetite. Women with PMS and PMDD show greater increases of appetite during the luteal phase than other women do. Another neurotransmitter, gamma-aminobutyric acid (GABA) also appears to be involved in premenstrual problems because medicines that affect the levels of GABA help many women with these problems (Bäckström et al., 2003). PMS and PMDD may well be caused by a complex interaction between ovarian hormones and neurotransmitters (Bäckström et al., 2003).

Today there are many treatment options for premenstrual disorders. These include exercise, dietary control (for example, eating several small meals a day rather than two or three large meals; limiting salt and sugar; vitamin supplements), hormone treatments (usually progesterone), and medications that reduce anxiety or increase the amount of serotonin in the nervous system. You can get in touch with whether you have PMS, and how the symptoms affect you, by completing the nearby Self-Assessment. If you have severe or disabling symptoms, you may be diagnosed with PMDD. What can women do about PMS or PMDD? Check with your gynecologist and consider the suggestions in the following section.

Exercise as a Strategy for Coping with Menstrual Discomfort. *Some women find that vigorous exercise helps relieve menstrual discomfort.*

How to Handle Menstrual Discomfort

Most women experience some menstrual discomfort. Women with persistent menstrual distress may profit from the suggestions listed in the following pages. Researchers are exploring the effectiveness of these techniques in controlled studies. You might consider trying the techniques that sound right for you—all of them, if you wish. Try them for a few months to see if you reap any benefits.

- Don't blame yourself! Menstrual problems were once erroneously attributed to women's "hysterical" nature. This is nonsense. Menstrual problems appear, in a large part, to reflect hormonal variations or chemical fluctuations in the brain during the menstrual cycle. Researchers have not yet fully identified all the causal elements and patterns, but their lack of knowledge does not mean that women who have menstrual problems are hysterical.

- Keep a menstrual calendar, so that you can track your menstrual symptoms systematically and identify patterns.

- Develop strategies for dealing with days that you experience the greatest distress—strategies that will help enhance your pleasure and minimize the stress affecting you on those days (Hunter et al., 2002). Activities that distract you from your menstrual discomfort may be helpful. Go see a movie or get into that novel you've been meaning to read.

- Consider whether you harbor self-defeating attitudes toward menstruation that might compound distress (Hunter et al., 2002). Do close relatives or friends see

CRITICAL Thinking

Critical thinkers avoid oversimplification. Explain how PMS and PMDD can have complex causes that involve both biological and psychological factors. Is there any significance in the fact that the research suggests that both medication and cognitive–behavioral therapy can be of help to women with PMS or PMDD?

REFLECT

Do people from your sociocultural background tend to hold any particular attitudes toward menstruation? What are they? Do you share these attitudes? Explain.

Do You Experience PMS or PMDD?*

PMS is a group of symptoms that may affect women for about eight days prior to and during menstruation. Research evidence suggests that most women have some of these symptoms, but that most often they are not severe enough to seriously impair daily functioning. When they do, they may qualify as PMDD. Women who have severe, even disabling, symptoms, are advised to discuss them with their gynecologists.

Do you experience PMS or PMDD? Complete the following self-assessment to gain insight into whether you do.

DIRECTIONS The following is a list of psychological and physical symptoms of PMS and PMDD. Indicate whether you encounter these symptoms and how severe they are by checking the appropriate box. Then turn to the answer key in the Appendix to assess your responses.

Symptoms of PMS	Do not have	Mild	Moderate	Severe	Disabling
Part I: Psychological symptoms of PMS					
Accident prone					
Depression					
Anxiety					
Panic					
Mood swings					
Crying spells					
Sudden anger					
Irritability					
Loss of interest in usual activities					
Difficulty concentrating					
Lack of energy					
Excessive use of alcohol					
Frustration					
Overeating or cravings for certain foods					
Insomnia or excessive sleeping					
Feelings of being out of control or overwhelmed					
Paranoia					
Part II: Physical symptoms of PMS					
Migraines					
Breast tenderness					
Joint or muscle pain					
Stiffness					
Weight gain					
Feeling bloated					
Blurred vision					
Poor motor coordination					
Exhaustion					
Dark circles under the eyes					
Runny eyes					

*Lois Fichner–Rathus and Spencer A. Rathus. All rights reserved.

menstruation as an illness, a time of "pollution," a "dirty thing?" Have you adopted any of these attitudes—if not verbally, then in ways that affect your behavior, such as by restricting your social activities during your period?

- See a gynecologist about your concerns, especially if you have severe symptoms. Severe menstrual symptoms can be secondary to medical disorders such as endometriosis and PID. Check it out.

- Ask your gynecologist about oral contraceptives that reduce the number of menstrual periods to four per year (Seasonale or Seasonique) or one per year (Lybrel). Still others shorten periods (Roan, 2006).

- Develop nutritious eating habits—and continue them throughout the entire cycle (that means always). Consider limiting intake of alcohol, caffeine, fats, salt, and sweets, especially during the days preceding menstruation. Research suggests that a low-fat, vegetarian diet reduces the duration and intensity of menstrual pain and the duration of premenstrual symptoms (Barnard et al., 2000).

- Eat several smaller meals (or nutritious snacks) throughout the day, rather than a few highly filling meals.

Seasonale. *Women who use Seasonale have just four periods per year.*

- Some women find that vigorous exercise—jogging, swimming, bicycling, fast walking, dancing, skating, even jumping rope—helps relieve premenstrual and menstrual discomfort. Evidence suggests that exercise helps to relieve and possibly prevent menstrual discomfort (Ling, 2000; Pearlstein & Steiner, 2000).

- Check with your doctor about vitamin and mineral supplements (such as calcium and magnesium). Vitamin B6 appears to have helped some women (Chavez & Spitzer, 2002).

- Ibuprofen (brand names: Medipren, Advil, Motrin, and so on) and other medicines available over the counter may be helpful for cramping. Prescription drugs such as antianxiety drugs (e.g., alprazolam) and antidepressant drugs (SSRIs) may also be of help (Bäckström et al., 2003; Hunter et al., 2002; Stearns et al., 2003). "Antidepressants" affect the levels of neurotransmitters in a way that can be helpful for women with PMS or PMDD. Their benefits do not mean that women with PMS or PMDD are "basically" depressed. Ask your doctor for a recommendation.

- Remind yourself that menstrual problems are time limited. Don't worry about getting through life or a career. Just get through the next couple of days.

In this chapter we explored female sexual anatomy and physiology. In the following chapter we turn our attention to male sexual anatomy and physiology.

1. What are the female external sex organs?

- The mons veneris is a mound of fatty tissue that covers the pubic area. The labia majora are large folds of skin that run downward from the mons along the sides of the vulva. The labia minora are hairless, light-colored membranes that surround the urethral and vaginal openings.

- The clitoris is the female sex organ that is most sensitive to sexual sensation, but it is not directly involved in reproduction.

- The vestibule contains the openings to the vagina and the urethra. Urine passes from the female's body through the urethral opening. The vaginal opening, or introitus, lies below the urethral opening. The penis, babies, and menstrual flow go through this opening.

2. What are the internal female sex organs?

- Menstrual flow and babies pass from the uterus to the outer world through the vagina. During coitus, the vagina contains the penis.

- The cervix is the lower end of the uterus. It contains an opening called the os. Cervical cancer is connected with HPV and is detectable via a Pap test. When detected early, the survival rate approaches 100%.

- The uterus is the pear-shaped organ in which a fertilized ovum implants and develops until birth. The uterine lining is called the endometrium. Risk factors for endometrial cancer include high body weight and lengthy exposure to estrogen.

- Two fallopian tubes extend from the upper end of the uterus toward the ovaries. Ova pass through the fallopian tubes on their way to the uterus and are normally fertilized within these tubes.

- The ovaries lie on either side of the uterus and produce ova and the sex hormones estrogen and progesterone. Ovarian cancer usually strikes women between the ages of 40 and 70. Women most at risk are those with first-degree blood relatives who had the disease. Other risk factors include never giving birth, breast cancer, and high body weight.

3. What are the breasts?

- The breasts are secondary sex characteristics that contain mammary glands. Women with breast cancer have lumps in the breast, but most lumps are benign. Breast cancer may be detected by clinical examination, mammography, or BSE. Risk factors include the BRCA1 or BRCA2 mutations, exposure to estrogen, and alcohol.

4. What is the menstrual cycle?

- Menstruation is the cyclical bleeding that stems from the shedding of the endometrium when a reproductive cycle has not led to the fertilization of an ovum. The cycle has four phases: proliferative, ovulatory, secretory, and menstrual. During the first phase, ova ripen within their follicles and endometrial tissue proliferates. During the second phase, ovulation occurs. During the third phase, the corpus luteum produces copious amounts of progesterone and estrogen that cause the endometrium to thicken. If the ovum goes unfertilized, a plunge in estrogen and progesterone levels triggers the fourth, or menstrual, phase.

- There is no evidence that coitus during menstruation is harmful.

- Menopause is the cessation of menstruation. Perimenopause is the beginning of menopause and is charactered by months of irregular periods or amenorrhea. The climacteric is a multiyear process marked by declining levels of estrogen and ends in menopause.

- HRT offsets loss of estrogen and progesterone and can help women with perimenopausal and postmenopausal symptoms, which include night sweats, hot flashes, hot flushes, dry skin, loss of breast tissue, and decreased vaginal lubrication. However, HRT has been linked to an increased risk of breast and endometrial cancers, and may offer no protection from heart disease.

5. What kinds of menstrual problems do women encounter?

- Dysmenorrhea—painful menstruation—is the most common menstrual problem, and pelvic cramps are the most common symptom. Amenorrhea—lack of menstruation—can be caused by problems such as abnormalities in the structures of the reproductive system, hormonal abnormalities, cysts, tumors, and stress. PMS can be characterized by depression and anxiety, irritability, difficulty concentrating, migraines, breast tenderness, and bloating. PMDD is like a severe case of PMS and is said to occur when symptoms are extreme and impair functioning in school, at work, or in relationships.

- PMS and PMDD can be alleviated to some degree. Medicines that may help include SSRIs and drugs that relieve cramping. Psychological methods include engaging in enjoyable activities and exercise.

1. HPV is connected with
   (a) cervical cancer
   (b) endometrial cancer
   (c) breast cancer
   (d) ovarian cancer

2. Urine passes through the
   (a) uterus
   (b) urethra
   (c) cervix
   (d) introitus

3. _____ is defined as the absence of menstruation.
   (a) Dysmenorrhea
   (b) Premenstrual syndrome
   (c) Premenstrual dysphoric disorder
   (d) Amenorrhea

4. Menstrual cramps are thought to be caused by
   (a) estrogen
   (b) progesterone
   (c) prostaglandins
   (d) testosterone

5. Hot flashes and flushes stem largely from waves of dilation of
   (a) the cervix
   (b) blood vessels
   (c) ovarian follicles
   (d) muscles

6. The endometrium develops during the _____ phase of the menstrual cycle.
   (a) ovulatory _2nd_
   (b) menstrual _4th_
   (c) secretory _3rd_
   (d) proliferative _1st_

7. A surge of _____ triggers ovulation.
   (a) FSH
   (b) LH
   (c) oxytocin
   (d) prolactin

8. The _____ is the only organ with the only known purpose of experiencing sexual pleasure.
   (a) cervix
   (b) vagina
   (c) breast
   (d) clitoris

9. For women who obtain HRT, combining estrogen with _____ lessens the risk of endometrial cancer.
   (a) progestin
   (b) prolactin
   (c) oxytocin
   (d) prostaglandins

10. The clitoral shaft stiffens when the _____ fills with blood.
    (a) introitus
    (b) os
    (c) corpora cavernosa
    (d) pituitary gland

11. Mittelschmerz occurs during the _____ phase of the menstrual cycle.
    (a) secretory
    (b) menstrual
    (c) proliferative
    (d) ovulatory

12. Breast cancer strikes about _____ people in the United States each year.
    (a) 270
    (b) 2,700
    (c) 27,000
    (d) 270,000

13. Skeptics concerning the G spot are most likely to argue that
    (a) the anterior vaginal wall is not sensitive to erotic stimulation
    (b) the G spot is not a discrete sex organ
    (c) no research has been done into the existence of the G spot
    (d) G spot is a silly name for a sex organ

14. When the hypothalamus senses a low level of estrogen in the blood, it increases secretion of Gn-RH, which in turn triggers the pituitary gland to release
    (a) FSH
    (b) LH
    (c) the graafian follicle
    (d) prolactin

15. Cystitis is an inflammation of the
    (a) vagina
    (b) ovaries
    (c) bladder
    (d) areola

4

Male Sexual Anatomy and Physiology

TRUTH?
fiction

Which of the following statements are true, and which are fiction? Look for the
Truth/Fiction icons on the pages that follow to find the answers.

1 The penis contains bone and muscle.   T   F

2 The father determines the baby's sex.   T   F

3 *Semen* is a synonym for *sperm*.   T   F

4 Morning erections reflect the need to urinate.   T   F

5 Men can will themselves to have erections.   T   F

6 The penis has a mind of its own.   T   F

7 Many men who are paralyzed below the waist can attain erection, engage in sexual intercourse, and ejaculate.   T   F

8 Males can have orgasms without ejaculating.   T   F

H. K. F., a 34-year-old Chinese man, felt the need to urinate while at the movies. In the bathroom, he suddenly lost feeling in his genital region and developed the fear that his penis was going to retract into his body. He went into a panic and his legs gave way. He sat on the floor, holding on to his penis to prevent it from retracting and waited a half hour, until the attack was over. He visited a health professional who assured him that his penis would not retract into his body and has not suffered another attack since.

H. K. F. had experienced Koro, otherwise known as genital retraction syndrome, a syndrome found in Malaysia, Indonesia, and China, in which men mistakenly believe that their penises will shrink and retract into their bodies (Dzokoto & Adams, 2005; Freudenmann & Schönfeldt–Lecuona, 2005). The anxiety they experience during an attack does cause the penis to shrink somewhat, but it does not retract into the body—an anatomic impossibility. Koro is most likely to occur when a man attempts to urinate in the cold, feels guilty about masturbating or visiting prostitutes, is worried about his sexual performance, or has argued with his wife.

The man will typically grab his genitals to prevent them from retracting. He may use mechanical devices like cords, chopsticks, clamps, or small weights to prevent retraction until he can find help. Koro is not all that common, but there was an epidemic of the problem, a sort of mass hysteria, that occurred among men in Singapore a few years back.

Many men who experience Koro attacks, like H. K. F., profit from anatomic information and reassurance, as given by a health professional. In a couple of recent cases, men with attacks have also been treated effectively with antidepressant medications (Kennedy & McDonough, 2002; Nakaya, 2002). The reason for the effectiveness of these medications is

Koro Syndrome. *Koro is a rare culture-bound syndrome that is found among some Chinese men. It involves the erroneous belief that one's genitals are retreating into one's body, and is involved with the roles of the concepts on yin and yang in Chinese culture.*

not quite clear. Given that these were uncontrolled case studies, it is possible that the antidepressants worked like *placebos*—that is, sugar pills—and that the patients' belief that they would work was the curative agent.

Koro is one of a number of Chinese culture-bound syndromes that are believed to reflect loss (or fear of loss) of *yang,* a form of positive male energy that is balanced in nature by *yin,* or female energy. Nevertheless, there are some cases of Koro spreading to other cultures (Kennedy & McDonough, 2002). However, as contemporary health information becomes more widely spread, we will probably have fewer rather than more cases of Koro overall.

The experience of H. K. F. informs us about the perceived importance of the size of the male genitalia in the eyes of men, and of the folklore that has grown around it. From the earliest days of civilization, male-dominated societies have exalted the male genitalia. The ancient Greeks carried oversized images of fish as **phallic symbols** in their Dionysian processions, which celebrated the wilder and more frenzied aspects of human sexuality. In the murky predawn light of Western civilization, people engaged in phallic worship. Phallic symbols became glorified in art in the form of plows, axes, and swords.

The ancient Greeks adorned themselves with phallic rings and necklaces. The ancient Romans honored Venus by outfitting a float in the shape of a large phallus and parading it through the streets. Men in Roman courts often swore to tell the truth with their hands on their genitals—as we swear to tell the truth by placing our hands on the Bible. The words *testes* and *testicles* derive from the same Latin word as "testify." The Latin *testis* means "a witness."

Even today, men with large genitals are accorded respect from male peers and sometimes adoration from admirers. Given these cultural attitudes, it is not surprising that young men (and some not-so-young men) belittle themselves if they feel that their penises do not measure up. Boys who mature late may be ridiculed by their peers. Adult men, too, may wonder whether their penises are large enough to satisfy lovers. Or they may fear that their partners' earlier lovers had larger genitals.

In this chapter we examine male sexual anatomy and physiology, and we attempt to sort out truth from fiction. As in our exploration of female sexual physiology and anatomy, we begin with the external genitalia and then move inward. Once inside, we focus on the route of sperm through the male reproductive system.

SafeZone

Q *Are men really* that *obsessed with their penises? Why?*

A Not necessarily. There are individual differences. A large penis is generally considered a plus in our culture. But males with average or somewhat smaller penises tend to become less concerned about it if their sex partner or partners are adequately aroused by them.

External Sex Organs

The external male sex organs include the penis and the scrotum (Figures 4.1 and 4.2).

The Penis

"The penis mightier than the sword."

—Unknown

"Is that a gun in your pocket or are you just glad to see me?"

—Mae West

At first glance the penis may seem rather simple and obvious in its structures, particularly when compared with women's organs. Yet, as Figure 4.1 shows, the apparent

Phallic symbols Images of the penis that are usually suggestive of generative power

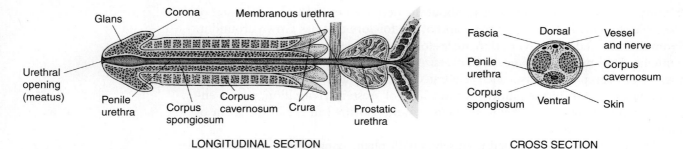

Figure 4.1 **The Penis.** *During sexual arousal, the corpora cavernosa and corpus spongiosum become congested with blood, causing the penis to enlarge and stiffen.*

LONGITUDINAL SECTION   CROSS SECTION

simplicity of the penis is misleading. Much goes on below the surface. Gender stereo-types regarding anatomy are as misleading as those regarding personality (see Chapter 6).

The penis, like the vagina, is the sex organ used in sexual intercourse. But unlike the vagina, the penis serves as a conduit for urine. Both **semen** and urine pass through the urethral opening, or urethral *meatus* (pronounced me-ATE-us and meaning "passage"). The urethra is connected to the bladder, which is unrelated to reproduction, and to those parts of the reproductive system that transport semen.

Truth or Fiction Revisited: Many mammals, including dogs, have penile bones that stiffen the penis to facilitate copulation. But despite the slang term *boner*, the human penis contains no bones. Nor, despite another slang term, *muscle*, does the penis contain muscle tissue. However, muscles at the base of the penis, like the muscles surrounding the vaginal and urethral openings in women, are involved in urination and ejaculation.

Rather than bone or muscle, the penis contains three cylinders of spongy material that run its length and swell (become "engorged") with blood during sexual

TRUTH fiction 1

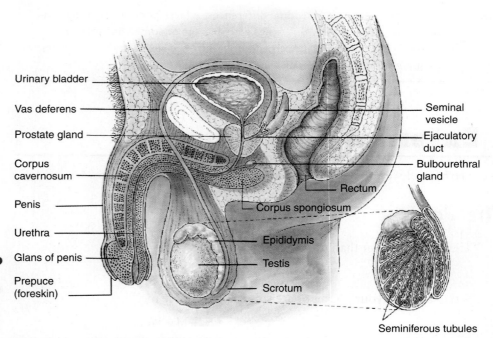

Semen The whitish fluid that constitutes the ejaculate, consisting of sperm and secretions from the seminal vesicles, prostate, and Cowper's glands

Figure 4.2 **The Male Reproductive System.** *The external male sex organs include the penis and the scrotum.*

arousal, causing erection. The larger two, the **corpora cavernosa** (Figure 4.1), lie side by side and function like the cavernous bodies in the clitoris. They fill with blood and stiffen during sexual arousal. In addition, a **corpus spongiosum** (spongy body) runs along the bottom, or ventral, surface of the penis. It contains the penile urethra that conducts urine to the urinary opening (urethral meatus) at the tip. Also at the tip, the spongy body enlarges into the glans, or head, of the penis.

The penile glans, like the clitoral glans, is highly sensitive to sexual stimulation, but direct, prolonged stimulation can become irritating. Most men prefer to masturbate by stroking the **shaft** of the penis rather than the glans. The **corona,** or coronal ridge, separates the glans from the body of the penis. It is also quite sensitive to sexual stimulation. The **frenulum,** a thin strip of tissue that connects the underside of the glans to the shaft, is also very sensitive. Most men find the top of the penis to be the least sensitive.

The base of the penis, or **root,** extends into the pelvis. It is attached to pelvic bones by leglike structures, called *crura,* similar to those that anchor the female's clitoris. The body of the penis is called the penile *shaft.* Unlike the clitoral shaft, it is free swinging. Thus, the result of engorgement, erection, is obvious.

The skin of the penis is hairless and loose, allowing expansion during erection. It is fixed to the penile shaft just behind the glans. Some of it, however, like the labia minora in the female, folds over to partially cover the glans. This covering is the prepuce, or **foreskin.** It covers part or all of the penile glans just as the clitoral prepuce (hood) covers the clitoral shaft. The prepuce consists of loose skin that freely moves over the glans. However, *smegma*—a cheeselike, foul-smelling secretion—may accumulate below the foreskin, causing it to adhere to the glans.

CIRCUMCISION   Male **circumcision** is surgical removal of the prepuce (Figure 4.3). It has a long history as a religious rite. Jews traditionally carry out male circumcision shortly after a baby is born. Circumcision is performed as a sign of the covenant between God and the people of Abraham. Muslims also have ritual circumcisions for religious reasons, although they are carried out within a few years of birth. Circumcision rates vary widely in the United States, from about 80% in the Midwest to about 40% in the West. Circumcision is uncommon elsewhere (Liptak, 2003). The rate is about 17% in Canada and 5% in England.

According to the NHSLS, of 1,410 men age 18 to 59, circumcision is most common among European American men (81%) and men whose mothers graduated from college (87%) (Laumann et al., 1997). Figure 4.4 compares the circumcision rates among various ethnic groups in the United States. The groups have some over-

Corpora cavernosa Cylinders of spongy tissue in the penis that become congested with blood and stiffen during sexual arousal

Corpus spongiosum The spongy body that runs along the bottom of the penis, contains the penile urethra, and enlarges at the tip of the penis to form the glans

Shaft The body of the penis, which expands as a result of vasocongestion

Corona The ridge that separates the glans from the body of the penis

Frenulum The sensitive strip of tissue that connects the underside of the penile glans to the shaft

Root The base of the penis, which extends into the pelvis

Foreskin The loose skin that covers the penile glans; also referred to as the *prepuce*

Circumcision Surgical removal of the foreskin of the penis

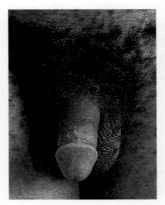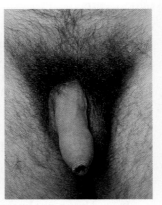

Figure 4.3 Normal Variations in the Male Genitals. *The penis and scrotum vary a good deal in appearance from one man to another. The penis in the photo on the far right is uncircumcised.*

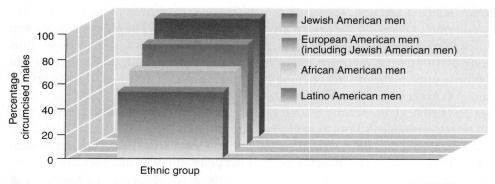

Figure 4.4 Who Is Circumcised? *Circumcision was most common among Jewish American men in the NHSLS study, for whom it is a religious rite, and among European American men in general, compared with African American men and Latino Americans. Elsewhere in the world, circumcision is relatively rare, except among Muslims, who also circumcise males for religious reasons.*

SOURCE: From "Circumcision in the U.S.: Prevalence, Prophylactic Effects and Sexual Practice", by E. O. Laumann, et al., *Journal of the American Medical Association*, 227(4/2/97)" 1052–1057. Copyright © 1997. American Medical Association. All rights reserved. Reprinted by permission.

Phimosis An abnormal condition in which the foreskin is so tight that it cannot be withdrawn from the glans

lap; the great majority of Jews, for whom circumcision is a religious rite, are also European Americans.

Circumcision became widespread in the United States because medical research suggests that it lessens the risk of infections from urinary tract infections (Wiswell, 2003, as cited in Liptak, 2003), HPV (Castellsague et al., 2002), HIV/AIDS (Bailey, 2000; Reynolds et al., 2004), and cancer of the penis. One researcher (Buve, 2000) compared the incidence of HIV infection in two African cities with high rates and two with low rates. In Yaoundé, Cameroon, and Cotonou, Benin, the prevalence of HIV among sexually active men was about 4% to 5%, and 99% of the men were circumcised. In Kisumu, Kenya, and Ndola, Zambia, where circumcision rates were much lower, the rates of HIV infection among sexually active men were about 26% to 27%. The protective effects of circumcision are likely to reflect a lower incidence of local inflammation and genital ulcers, both of which provide ports of entry for HIV, and the removal of cells in the foreskin—Langerhans cells—that are receptive to infection by HIV (Cohen, 2000; Szabo & Short, 2000).

Some negatives are that circumcision lessens sexual sensations (Liptak, 2003) and is painful if not carried out with adequate anesthesia. In 1999, the American Academy of Pediatrics issued a statement to the effect that the relatively higher risks of cancer of the penis and STIs were not sufficient to recommend that circumcision be carried out universally. Critics of circumcision also argue that it is not carried out with the informed consent of the person being operated on (who is usually only a few days old) (Liptak, 2003).

Physicians once agreed that circumcision is the treatment of choice for **phimosis,** a condition in which it is difficult to retract the foreskin from the glans. But today, only a small minority of males with phimosis are circumcised for that reason (Rickwood et al., 2000).

PENIS SIZE

IRAS: Am I not an inch of fortune better than she?

CHARMIAN: Well, if you were but an inch of fortune better than I, where would you choose it?

IRAS: Not in my husband's nose.

—William Shakespeare, *Antony and Cleopatra*

In our culture, the size of the penis is often seen as a measure of a man's masculinity and his ability to please his sex partner (Lever et al., 2006). Shakespeare and other writers inform us that men have looked down at themselves for centuries, sometimes in delight but more often in chagrin. Men who are heralded for their sexual or reproductive feats are presumed to have more prominent "testaments" to their manhood. Clinical experience with dysfunctional couples suggests that a woman is more likely to complain about her partner's communication ability or the feeling or tone of their relationship rather than the size of his penis (Zilbergeld, 1999). Nevertheless, surveys show that a minority of women are dissatisfied with the size of their partner's penises (Lever et al., 2006; Stulhofer, 2006).

An Internet survey of some 52,000 heterosexual men and women found that two-thirds of the men (66%) rated their penises as average in size (Lever et al., 2006). Twenty-two percent rated them as large, and 12% rated them as small. Self-reported penis size was correlated negatively with the amount of body fat, consistent with other studies, reported in Chapter 15, that connect male sexual functioning negatively with levels of low density ("bad") cholesterol. Most women (85%) were content with the size of their partner's penis, as compared with only 55% of the men. Forty-five percent of the men desired larger penises, and hardly any (only 0.2%) wanted smaller penises.

Penises generally range in length from three inches to a little more than four inches when flaccid, or soft (Masters & Johnson, 1966). The average erect penis ranges from five to seven inches in length. Erect penises differ less in size than flaccid (soft) penises. Penises that are small when soft tend to gain more size when they become erect.

Even when flaccid, the same penis can vary in size. Factors such as cold air or water, or emotions of fear or anxiety can cause the penis (along with the scrotum and testicles) to draw closer to the body, reducing its size. These factors sometimes trigger cases of Koro syndrome in Chinese culture, as we saw at the beginning of the chapter. The flaccid penis may also expand in warm water or when a male is relaxed.

The Scrotum

The **scrotum** is a pouch of loose skin below the base of the penis that becomes covered lightly with hair at puberty. It has two compartments that hold the testes. Each testicle is held in place by a **spermatic cord,** a structure that contains the **vas deferens,** blood vessels and nerves, and the **cremaster muscle.** The cremaster muscle raises and lowers the testicle within the scrotum in response to temperature changes and sexual stimulation. (Sexual arousal draws the testes closer to the body.)

Sperm production is optimal at slightly less than the 98.6°F that is normal for most of the body. Scrotal temperature tends to be 5 to 6°F lower than body temperature. The scrotum is loose hanging and flexible. It permits the testes and nearby structures to escape the higher body heat, especially in warm weather. In the middle layer of the scrotum is the **dartos muscle,** which, like the cremaster, contracts and relaxes reflexively in response to temperature changes. In cold weather, or when a man jumps into a body of cold water, it contracts to bring the testes closer to the body. In warm weather, it relaxes, allowing the testes to hang farther from the body. The dartos muscle also increases or decreases the surface area of the scrotum in response to temperature changes. Smoothing of the skin allows greater dissipation of heat in hot weather. Constricting the skin surface helps retain heat and wrinkles the scrotum in the cold.

The scrotum is developed from the same embryonic tissue that becomes the labia majora of the female. Thus, like the labia majora, it is quite sensitive to sexual stimulation.

Scrotum The pouch of loose skin that contains the testes

Spermatic cord The cord that suspends a testicle within the scrotum and contains the vas deferens, blood vessels, nerves, and the cremaster muscle

Vas deferens A tube that conducts sperm from the testicle to the ejaculatory duct of the penis

Cremaster muscle The muscle that raises and lowers the testicle in response to temperature changes and sexual stimulation

Dartos muscle The muscle in the middle layer of the scrotum that contracts and relaxes in response to temperature changes

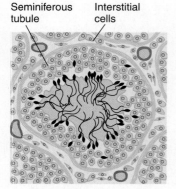

Figure 4.5 Interstitial Cells. *Testosterone is produced by the interstitial cells, which lay between the seminiferous tubules in each testis. Sperm (seen in the middle of the diagram) are produced within the seminiferous tubules.*

Seminiferous tubule   Interstitial cells

Internal Sex Organs

The male internal sex organs include the testes, the organs that manufacture sperm and testosterone; the system of tubes and ducts that conduct sperm through the male reproductive system; and the organs that help nourish and activate sperm and neutralize some of the acidity that sperm encounter in the vagina (Figure 4.2).

The Testes

The testes are the male gonads (which derives from the Greek *gone,* meaning "seed"). In slang, the testes are frequently referred to as *balls* or *nuts.* These terms are considered vulgar, but they are reasonably descriptive.

The testes serve two functions analogous to those of the ovaries. They secrete sex hormones and produce mature **germ cells**. In the case of the testes, the germ cells are **sperm** and the sex hormones are **androgens**. The most important androgen is **testosterone**.

TESTOSTERONE Testosterone is secreted by **interstitial cells**, which are also known as **Leydig's cells**. Interstitial cells lay between the seminiferous tubules and release testosterone into the bloodstream (Figure 4.5). Testosterone stimulates prenatal differentiation of male sex organs, sperm production, and development of **secondary sex characteristics**, such as a beard, a deep voice, and muscle mass.

In men, several endocrine glands, a feedback loop among the hypothalamus, pituitary gland, and testes (Figure 4.6), keep blood testosterone levels at a more or less even level, although there are slight variations with stress, time of day or month, and other factors. This contrasts with the peaks and valleys in levels of female sex hormones during the phases of the menstrual cycle.

The pituitary hormones, FSH and LH, which regulate the activity of the ovaries, also regulate the activity of the testes. FSH regulates the production of sperm. LH stimulates secretion of testosterone by interstitial cells. Low testosterone levels signal the hypothalamus to secrete the hormone LH–releasing hormone (LH–RH). Like dominoes falling in a line, LH–RH causes the pituitary gland to secrete LH, which in

Germ cell A cell from which a new organism develops

Sperm The male germ cell

Androgens Male sex hormones

Testosterone A male steroid sex hormone

Interstitial cells Cells that lay between the seminiferous tubules and secrete testosterone

Leydig's cells Another term for *interstitial cells*

Secondary sex characteristics Traits that distinguish the genders but are not directly involved in reproduction

Figure 4.6 Hormonal Control of the Testes. *Several endocrine glands—the hypothalamus, the pituitary gland, and the testes—keep blood testosterone levels at a more or less constant level. Low testosterone levels signal the hypothalamus to secrete LH–releasing hormone (LH–RH). Like dominoes falling in line, LH–RH causes the pituitary gland to secrete LH, which in turn stimulates the testes to release testosterone. FSH–RH from the hypothalamus causes the pituitary to secrete FSH, which in turn causes the testes to produce sperm cells.*

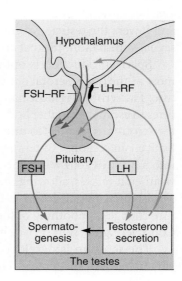

turn stimulates the testes to secrete testosterone. LH is also known as *interstitial cell stimulating hormone,* or ICSH.

When the level of testosterone in the blood system reaches a peak, the hypothalamus directs the pituitary gland *not* to secrete LH. This system for circling information around these three endocrine glands is called a *feedback loop.* This feedback loop is *negative.* That is, increases in hormone levels in one part of the system trigger another part to shut down and vice versa.

The testes usually range between 1 inch and 1.75 inches in length. They are about half as wide and deep. The left testicle usually hangs lower, because the left spermatic cord tends to be somewhat longer.

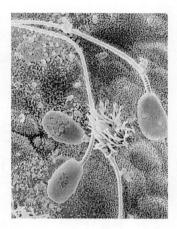
Human Sperm Cells Magnified Many Times

SPERM   Each testicle is divided into many lobes, which are filled with winding **seminiferous tubules** (Figure 4.2). Although packed into a tiny space, these tubules, placed end to end, would span the length of several football fields. Through **spermatogenesis**, these threadlike structures produce and store hundreds of billions of sperm during a lifetime.

Sperm cells develop through several stages. It takes about 72 days for the testes to manufacture a mature sperm cell. During an early stage, sperm cells are called **spermatocytes**. Each one contains 46 chromosomes, including one X and one Y sex chromosome. Each spermatocyte divides into two **spermatids,** each of which has 23 chromosomes. Half the spermatids have X sex chromosomes and the other half have Y sex chromosomes. Looking something like tadpoles when examined under a microscope, mature sperm cells, called **spermatozoa,** each have a head, a cone-shaped mid piece, and a tail. The head is about 1/50,000 of an inch long and contains the cell nucleus that houses the chromosomes. The mid piece contains structures that provide the energy that the tail needs to lash back and forth as it swims. Each sperm cell is about 1/5,000 of an inch long, one of the smallest cells in the body.

During fertilization, the 23 chromosomes from the father's sperm cell combine with the 23 chromosomes from the mother's ovum, furnishing the standard ensemble of 46 in the offspring. Among the 23 chromosomes borne by sperm cells is one sex chromosome—an X sex chromosome or a Y sex chromosome. Ova contain X sex chromosomes only. The union of an X sex chromosome and a Y sex chromosome leads to the development of male offspring. Two X sex chromosomes combine to yield female offspring.

Truth or Fiction Revisited: It is true that the father determines the baby's sex through the presence of an X or Y sex chromosome.

The testes churn out about 1,000 sperm per second or 30 *billion* per year. Mathematically speaking, 10 to 20 ejaculations hold enough sperm to populate the earth.

Researchers in Germany and at UCLA have discovered that sperm cells have the same kind of receptors that the nose uses to sense odors (Wilkinson, 2003). Sperm

TRUTH fiction **2**

Seminiferous tubules Tiny, winding, sperm-producing tubes within the lobes of the testes

Spermatogenesis The process by which sperm cells are produced and developed

Spermatocyte An early stage in the development of sperm cells, in which each parent cell has 46 chromosomes, including one X and one Y sex chromosome

Spermatids Cells formed by the division of spermatocytes; each spermatid has 23 chromosomes

Spermatozoa Mature sperm cells

SafeZone

Q *My penis curves to the right. Is this normal?*

A Sure. Penises do not tend to hang straight. As noted in the text, one testicle—usually the left testicle—tends to hang lower than the other because of the differential lengths of the spermatic cords.

A Closer Look

ANDROPAUSE: WHEN HORMONES RAGE NO MORE

Most of us are familiar enough with the phrase "raging hormones" when it comes to the alleged irritability shown by some women prior to menstruation and apparently related the fluctuations of sex hormones during the menstrual cycle. Yet men, too, could be said to be prey to "raging hormones." The male sex hormone testosterone is related to tendencies to dominate other people. There is research evidence that aggressive boys, college students, and men have higher testosterone levels than their peers (Chance et al., 2000; Dabbs et al., 1996; Giotakos et al., 2005). High levels of testosterone also appear to reduce fear of the consequences of aggression (King et al., 2005). For reasons such as these, social commentator Anna Quindlen wrote an article titled "Is Testosterone Toxic?" We will see that the answer to Quindlen's question might be "yes"—that is, testosterone might well be toxic—but not for the reasons she was writing about.

Historically speaking, more research has been done with men's health problems than women's. Yet the problems related to low levels of sex hormones in men do not even have an agreed-upon name. *Andropause* suggests a falloff in androgens (male sex hormones). *Viropause* suggests a decline in virility, which is not a scientific term and suggests a general loss of ability. *Manopause* is a widely used but unscientific knockoff of the scientific term *menopause*.

For women, menopause is a time of relatively distinct age-related declines in sex hormones and fertility. In men, the decline in the production of male sex hormones and fertility is more gradual (Tan & Culberson, 2003). It therefore is not surprising to find a man in his 70s or older fathering a child. However, many men in their 50s and 60s experience problems in achieving and maintaining erections (McElduff & Beange, 2003; Seidman, 2003), which may reflect circulatory problems or hormone deficiencies. Figure 4.7 indicates the ages at which one group of researchers found symptoms of andropause to begin.

Sexual performance is but one part of the story. Figure 4.8 shows the frequencies with which a number of symptoms of andropause occur. Between the ages of 40 and 70, the typical American male loses 12 to 20 pounds of muscle, about two inches in height, and 15% of his bone mass. (Men as well as women are at risk for osteoporosis [Tan, 2001, 2002].) The percent of fat in the body nearly doubles. There is some loss in hearing and vision. There is loss of endurance as the cardiovascular system and lungs become less capable of adapting to exertion. Figure 4.8 indicates the frequency of some symptoms among a group of more than 300 men who were diagnosed with andropause.

Some of these changes can be slowed or reversed. Exercise helps maintain muscle tone, keeps the growth of fatty tissue in check, and helps combat osteoporosis (Tan, 2002). A diet rich in calcium and vitamin D also wards off bone loss. HRT may help but is controversial.

Physicians in the United States write more than one million prescriptions for testosterone and related drugs for men each year, but the benefits are not fully proven, and the risks should make the caution lights blink (Vastag, 2003). Testosterone replacement may boost strength, energy, and the sex drive, but it also increases the risks of prostate cancer and cardiovascular disease (Tan, 2002; Vastag, 2003). In fact, in 2002, the government decided not to proceed with a study of the effects of testosterone on aging men just because of these concerns (Kolata, 2002). Dr. Richard Hodis (2002, cited in Kolata, 2002),

---

REFLECT

Considering the evidence, would you take testosterone to increase your prowess in athletics? Why or why not?

Epididymis A tube that lies against the back wall of each testicle and stores sperm

may thus find their way to an egg cell by detecting its scent. In the future we may have contraceptives that prevent fertilization by blocking these receptors from sensing the odors of egg cells.

Sperm proceed from the seminiferous tubules through a maze of ducts that converge in a tube called the **epididymis.** The epididymis lays against the back wall of the testicle and stores sperm. The epididymis, some two inches in length, consists of twisted passages that would extend 10 to 20 feet if straightened. Sperm are inactive when they enter the epididymis. They continue to mature as they make their way through the epididymis for another two to four weeks.

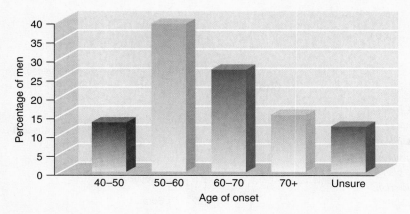

Figure 4.7 Age of Onset of Andropause. *According to one study, andropause is most likely initially to affect men in the 50- to 60-year-old age range.*

SOURCE: From "Managing the Andropause in Aging Men" by R. S. Tan in *Clinical Geriatrics,* 1999; 7(8):64. Copyright © 1997 by Multimedia Healthcare/Freedom. Reprinted by permission.

director of the National Institute on Aging, comments, "In understanding the role of testosterone replacement, we are in many ways where we were decades ago with estrogen replacement with women. It is clear that we do not know enough to inform men and their doctors on the potential advantages or risks of hormone replacement."

Perhaps research will bring us a "designer testosterone" that will target receptors that contribute to strength, sexual performance, and a psychological sense of well-being, but will not cause cancer and heart problems. Researchers are similarly searching for "designer estrogen"—forms of estrogen that will help women with perimenopausal and postmenopausal symptoms without increasing the risks of cancer and cardiac problems.

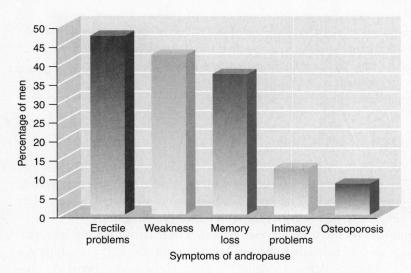

Figure 4.8 Frequency of Some Symptoms of Andropause. *Andropause is most likely to be characterized by problems in attaining and maintaining an erection, weakness, and memory problems. The researchers' label* intimacy problems *refers to increased dependence of the man of his spouse and family. As testosterone goes down, men appear to be less likely to roam.*

SOURCE: From "Managing the Andropause in Aging Men" by R. S. Tan in *Clinical Geriatrics,* 1999; 7(8):64. Copyright © 1997 by Multimedia Healthcare/Freedom. Reprinted by permission.

The Vas Deferens

Each epididymis empties into a vas deferens (also called *ductus deferens*). The vas is a thin, cylindrical tube about 16 inches long that serves as a conduit for mature sperm. In the scrotum, the vas deferens lies near the skin surface within the spermatic cord. Therefore, a **vasectomy,** an operation in which the right and left vas deferens are severed, is a convenient means of sterilization. The tube leaves the scrotum and follows a circuitous path up into the abdominal cavity. Then it loops back along the rear surface of the bladder (Figure 4.9).

Vasectomy Severing of the vas deferens, preventing sperm from reaching the ejaculatory duct

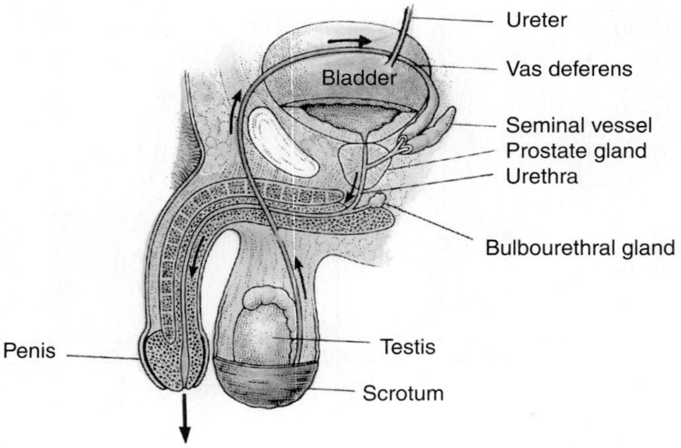

Figure 4.9 **Passage of Spermatozoa.** *Each testicle is divided into lobes that contain threadlike seminiferous tubules. Through spermatogenesis, the tubules produce and store hundreds of billions of sperm during the course of a lifetime. During ejaculation, sperm cells travel through the vas deferens, up and over the bladder, into the ejaculatory duct, and then through the urethra. Secretions from the seminal vesicles and the bulbourethral glands join with sperm to compose semen.*

SafeZone

Q *What does ejaculate taste like, and is it harmful to ingest?*

A In a word, salty. Some people like the taste, others find it unpleasant, and still others are simply indifferent to it. Some find the taste to be sexually arousing. It is not clear as to how much of the response reflects natural individual differences and how much reflects what people expect as a result of cultural reasons and tales from friends.

The substances in the ejaculate are absolutely harmless. It is vaguely conceivable (no pun intended) that the fluid of the ejaculate could go down "the wrong pipe" and cause choking, but this possibility exists with the ingestion of any fluid, even water. By the way, the ejaculate is a low-calorie food—largely protein—when ingested.

CRITICAL Thinking

Does the evidence suggest that men undergo an "andropause" that is similar to menopause? Explain.

Seminal vesicles Small glands that lay behind the bladder and secrete fluids that combine with sperm in the ejaculatory ducts

Ejaculatory duct A duct formed by the convergence of a vas deferens with a seminal vesicle through which sperm pass through the prostate gland and into the urethra

Cilia Hairlike projections from cells that beat rhythmically to produce locomotion or currents

Prostate gland The gland that lies beneath the bladder and secretes prostatic fluid, which gives semen its characteristic odor and texture

The Seminal Vesicles

The two **seminal vesicles** are small glands, each about two inches long. They lay behind the bladder and open into the **ejaculatory ducts,** where the fluids they secrete combine with sperm (Figure 4.9). The seminal vesicles were so named because they were mistakenly believed to be reservoirs for semen, rather than glands.

The fluid produced by the seminal vesicles is rich in fructose, a form of sugar, which nourishes sperm and helps them become active, or motile. Sperm motility is a major factor in male fertility. Before reaching the ejaculatory ducts, sperm are propelled along by contractions of the epididymis and vas deferens, and by **cilia** that line the walls of the vas deferens. When they become motile, they propel themselves by whipping their tails.

At the base of the bladder, each vas deferens joins a seminal vesicle to form a short ejaculatory duct that runs through the middle of the **prostate gland** (Figure 4.9). In the prostate the ejaculatory duct opens into the urethra, which carries sperm and urine out through the tip of the penis.

The Prostate Gland

The prostate gland lays beneath the bladder and approximates a chestnut in shape and size (about three quarters of an inch in diameter). It contains muscle fibers and glandular tissue that secrete prostatic fluid. Prostatic fluid is milky and alkaline. It provides the characteristic texture and odor of the seminal fluid. The alkalinity neutralizes some of the acidity of the vaginal tract, prolonging the life span of sperm as seminal fluid spreads through the female reproductive system. The prostate is continually active in mature males, but sexual arousal further stimulates secretions. Secretions are conveyed into the urethra by a sievelike duct system. There the secretions combine with sperm and fluid from the seminal vesicles.

A vasectomy prevents sperm from reaching the urethra but does not cut off fluids from the seminal vesicles or prostate gland. A man who has had a vasectomy thus emits an ejaculate that appears normal but contains no sperm.

Cowper's Glands

The two **Cowper's glands** are also known as the **bulbourethral glands,** in recognition of their shape and location. They lay below the prostate and empty their secretions into the urethra. During sexual arousal they secrete a drop or so of clear, slippery fluid that appears at the tip of the penis. The fluid may help buffer the acidity of the male's urethra and lubricate the urethral passageway, but not enough is produced to lubricate the vagina during intercourse.

Fluid from the Cowper's glands precedes the ejaculate and often contains sperm. Thus, male–female coitus may lead to pregnancy even if the penis is withdrawn before ejaculation. For this reason, people who practice the "withdrawal method" of birth control are often called "parents."

Semen

Truth or Fiction Revisited: Semen is *not* a synonym for sperm. Sperm and the fluids contributed by the seminal vesicles, the prostate gland, and Cowper's glands make up semen, or whitish seminal fluid, which is expelled through the tip of the penis during ejaculation. The seminal vesicles secrete about 70% of the fluid that constitutes the ejaculate. The remaining 30% of seminal fluid consists of sperm and fluids produced by the prostate gland and Cowper's glands. Sperm themselves account for only about 1% of the volume of semen. This is why men with vasectomies ejaculate nearly as much semen as before the operation.

Semen carries sperm through the male's reproductive system and the reproductive tract of the female. Semen contains water, mucus, sugar (fructose), acids, and bases. It activates and nourishes sperm, and the bases help shield sperm from vaginal acidity. The typical ejaculate contains between 200 and 400 million sperm and ranges between one half to one tablespoon in volume. The quantity of semen decreases with age and frequency of ejaculation.

TRUTH ? fiction 3

Cowper's glands
Structures that lay below the prostate and empty their secretions into the urethra during sexual arousal

Bulbourethral glands
Another term for Cowper's glands

Health Problems of the Urogenital System

Because the organs that comprise the urinary and reproductive systems are near each other and share some "piping," they are referred to as the urinogenital or urogenital system. A number of health problems affect the urogenital system. The type of physician who specializes in their diagnosis and treatment is called a urologist.

Urethritis

Men, like women, are subject to bladder and urethral inflammations, which are generally referred to as **urethritis.** The symptoms include frequent urination (urinary frequency), a strong need to urinate (urinary urgency), burning during urination, and a penile discharge. People with symptoms of urinary frequency and urinary urgency feel the pressing need to urinate repeatedly, even though they may have just done so and may have but another drop or two to expel. The discharge may dry on the urethral opening, in which case it may have to be peeled off or wiped away before it is possible to urinate. The urethra also may become constricted when it is inflamed, slowing or halting urination.

Preventive measures for urethritis parallel those suggested for cystitis (bladder infection): drinking more water, drinking cranberry juice (four ounces, two or three times a day), and lowering intake of alcohol and caffeine. Cranberry juice is highly acidic, and acid tends to eliminate many of the bacteria that can give rise to urethritis. Urethritis is usually treated with antibiotics.

Cancer of the Testes

Cancer of the testicles remains a relatively rare form of cancer, accounting for about 8,000 new cases annually, and about 400 men will die from it (American Cancer Society, 2006). It is the most common form of solid-tumor cancer to strike men between the ages of 20 and 34, accounting for nearly 10% of all deaths from cancer among men in that age group.

There is no evidence that testicular cancer results from sexual overactivity or masturbation. About 14% of men with testicular cancer had **cryptorchidism** as children, a condition in which one or both testicles fail to descend from the abdomen into the scrotum (American Cancer Society, 2006). Family history also increases the risk. European Americans are 5 to 10 times more likely than African Americans to develop cancer of the testes, and more than twice as likely as Asian Americans (American Cancer Society, 2006).

Although testicular cancer was generally fatal in earlier years, the prognosis today is quite favorable, especially when detected early. Treatments include surgical removal of the diseased testis, radiation, and chemotherapy. The survival rate among cases that are detected before the cancer has spread beyond the testes is about 99% (National Cancer Institute, 2006).

The surgical removal of a testicle may have profound psychological implications. Some men who have lost a testicle feel less "manly." Fears related to sexual perfor-

Urethritis An inflammation of the bladder or urethra

Cryptorchidism A condition in which one of two testicles fails to descend from the abdomen into the scrotum

mance can engender sexual dysfunctions. From a physiological standpoint, sexual functioning should remain unimpaired, because adequate testosterone is produced by the remaining testis.

The early stages of testicular cancer usually produce no symptoms, other than the mass itself. Because early detection is crucial to survival, men are advised to examine themselves monthly following puberty and to have regular medical checkups. Self-examination may also reveal evidence of STIs and other problems.

SELF-EXAMINATION OF THE TESTES   Self-examination (Figure 4.10) is best performed shortly after a warm shower or bath, when the skin of the scrotum is most relaxed. The man should exam the scrotum for evidence of pea-size lumps. Each testicle can be rolled gently between the thumb and the fingers. Lumps are generally found on the side or front of the testicle. The presence of a lump is not necessarily a sign of cancer, but it should be promptly reported to a physician for further evaluation. The American Cancer Society (2006) and the National Cancer Institute (2006) list these warning signals:

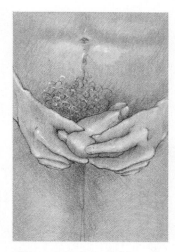

Figure 4.10 Self-Examination of the Testes

- A lump on a testicle
- Enlargement or swelling of the testicle
- Change in the consistency of a testicle
- Dull ache in the lower abdomen or groin (Pain may be absent in cancer of the testes, however.)
- Sensation of dragging and heaviness in a testicle

Less common symptoms are the following:

- Growth of breast tissue, tender or swollen breasts
- Loss of sex drive
- Premature (prior to puberty) growth of hair on the face and body

Disorders of the Prostate

The prostate gland is tiny at birth and grows rapidly at puberty. It may shrink during adulthood, but usually becomes enlarged after the age of 50.

BENIGN PROSTATIC HYPERPLASIA (BPH)   The prostate gland becomes enlarged in about half the men older than the age of 50 and in 80% of men by age 80 ("Understanding prostate," 2007). **Benign prostatic hyperplasia** (BPH) is noncancerous enlargement of the prostate gland resulting from hormonal changes associated with aging rather than other causes, such as inflammation from STIs. Because the prostate surrounds the upper part of the urethra (Figure 4.2), enlargement constricts the urethra, causing urinary frequency (including increased frequency of nocturnal urination), urinary urgency, and difficulty starting the flow of urine. Several treatments are available to relieve the pressure on the urethra and increase the flow of urine. Two types of drugs help men with BPH. The first type, 5-ARIs (5-alpha reductase inhibitors), inhibits the production of the hormone DHT (a form of testosterone), which causes enlargement of the prostate. 5-ARIs shrink the prostate, provide long-term improvement of symptoms, and reduce the risk of severe urinary retention and the need for surgery. The second type is alpha-blockers, which act by relaxing the muscles of the bladder to improve the flow of urine, providing

Benign prostatic hyperplasia Enlargement of the prostate resulting from hormonal changes of aging and symptomized by urinary frequency, urinary urgency, and difficulty starting the flow of urine

symptom relief. Part of the prostate is also sometimes surgically removed ("Understanding prostate," 2007).

PROSTATITIS   **Prostatitis** is inflammation of the prostate gland, which can be caused by various infectious agents. The chief symptoms are an ache or pain between the scrotum and anal opening, and painful ejaculation. Although aspirin and ibuprofen may relieve the pain, men with these symptoms should consult a physician. Painful ejaculation may discourage masturbation or coitus, which is ironic, because regular flushing of the prostate through ejaculation may be helpful in the treatment of prostatitis. Prostatitis is usually treated with antibiotics, most commonly ciproflaxin.

CANCER OF THE PROSTATE   Prostate cancer is a serious, life-threatening problem. About one man in six in the United States will develop prostate cancer (American Cancer Society, 2006). It is the second most common form of cancer among men, after skin cancer, and the second leading cause of cancer deaths in men, after lung cancer. There are about 230,000 new cases of prostate cancer in the United States each year, and about 90,000 deaths (American Cancer Society, 2006).

Prostate cancer involves the growth of malignant prostate tumors that can metastasize to bones and lymph nodes if not detected and treated early. African American men are about 50% more likely than European American men to develop prostate cancer (National Cancer Institute, 2006). African American men have less access to health care than European American men, so prostate cancer is diagnosed later among them and they are twice as likely to die from it (American Cancer Society, 2006).

Researchers have identified intake of animal fat as a risk factor. Men whose diets are rich in animal fats, especially fats from red meat, have a substantially higher chance of developing advanced prostate cancer than men with a low intake of animal fat. The incidence of prostate cancer also increases with age. More than 80% of cases of prostate cancer are diagnosed in men age 65 or older (National Cancer Institute, 2006). Genetic factors are also apparently involved (American Cancer Society, 2006). Moreover, testosterone spurs the development of prostate cancer as well as BPH (American Cancer Society, 2006).

The early symptoms of cancer of the prostate may mimic those of benign prostate enlargement—urinary frequency and difficulty urinating. Later symptoms include blood in the urine, pain or burning on urination, and pain in the lower back, pelvis, or upper thighs (National Cancer Institute, 2006). Most cases occur without noticeable symptoms during the early stages.

Health professionals detect and assess prostate cancer using a combination of tests. These include a PSA test, which is a blood test for *prostate-specific antigen*, recommended once a year for men age 50 and older, and beginning at a younger age for men at greater risk. African American men are advised to begin at age 45. Results less than four nanograms per milliliter are normal. More than 10 nanograms per milliliter are high; those between 4 and 10 nanograms per milliliter are borderline. PSA is a protein that helps transform a gellike substance in the prostate gland to a liquid that transports sperm during ejaculation. In the diseased or enlarged prostate, PSA seeps into the blood at higher levels, yielding higher test scores. Early detection is important because treatment is most effective before the cancer has spread. The majority of cases are discovered while they are still localized. The survival rate drops dramatically if the cancer has metastasized. Still, the overall survival rate has improved from 50% in the 1960s to more than 80% (American Cancer Society, 2006).

The American Cancer Society (2006) recommends that men receive annual digital rectal examinations (DREs) beginning at the same age as PSA tests (Figure 4.11).

CRITICAL
Thinking

If a man has a strong family history of prostate cancer, is there any point to his making an effort to watch his diet? Explain.

REFLECT

Is any man you know reluctant to undergo regular screening (digital rectal examination and PSA testing) for cancer of the prostate? What are the sources of the reluctance? What arguments might you use to convince him to undergo screening?

Prostatitis Inflammation of the prostate gland

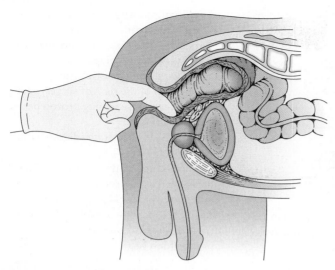

Figure 4.11 Digital Rectal Examination for Prostate Cancer

The physician inserts a finger into the rectum and feels for bumps or hard spots in the prostate gland. Unfortunately, many men are reluctant to have a rectal examination, even though it is only mildly uncomfortable and may save their lives. Some are embarrassed or reluctant to discuss urinary problems with their physicians. Some may resist the rectal examination because they associate rectal insertion with male–male sex. Some, of course, fear they may have cancer and choose to remain ignorant. Failure to have regular exams is a major contributor to the death rate from prostate cancer. Ultrasound may also be used. If cancer is suspected, a biopsy is performed, during which the doctor uses a needle to take a sample of prostate tissue and sometimes of lymph nodes in the area. If a tumor is found, pathologists "grade" two samples of tissue and rate them from 1 to 5 on the Gleason scale to provide a measure of the cancer's aggressiveness. The scores are added. Sums of 2 through 4 are considered low in aggressiveness (slow growing), 5 and 6 are intermediate, and 7 to 10 are high, with the worst prognoses. Doctors may do other tests such as bone scans, computed tomographic (CAT) scans, and magnetic resonance imaging (MRI) to determine whether the cancer has spread.

The most widely used treatment for prostate cancer is surgical removal of the prostate gland. However, the surgery may damage surrounding nerves, leading to problems in urinary and sexual functions. Surgeons attempt to spare surrounding nerves, but cannot guarantee elimination of the risk of complications. Other treatments include radiation, hormone treatment, and anticancer drugs. Hormone treatment in the form of androgen (testosterone) suppression therapy and anticancer drugs may shrink the size of the tumor and relieve pain. Men who go through surgery are more likely to have urinary incontinence (loss of control over urination) and sexual dysfunction (trouble attaining erection) than men who use radiation (Potosky et al., 2000). However, many physicians argue that surgery remains the better choice in terms of survival rates. Among older men with slow-growing prostate cancer, physicians may prefer "watchful waiting" to surgery. The men may live long enough to die from causes other than cancer. Treatment choices are explored further in the nearby "A Closer Look" feature.

A Closer Look

OPTIONS—AND DECISIONS—FOR MEN WITH PROSTATE CANCER

Mayor Rudy W. Giuliani of New York decided on a treatment for his prostate cancer, which was diagnosed in 2000, after months of private deliberation and public speculation. In mid September, the mayor, along with his doctors at Mount Sinai Medical Center, announced he had received radioactive seed implants during an outpatient procedure earlier that day. But in deciding on a treatment, Giuliani said he had great difficulty weighing his choices. Because the disease progresses at a relatively slow pace, men in the early stages can take some time to explore the expanding treatment options available to them.

Deciding on treatment can be daunting, in part because there are so many options. They include surgery, with "nerve sparing" to help reduce incontinence and impotence; external beam radiation, during which X-ray beams are directed at the prostate area; highly targeted proton radiation, during which protons are "shaped" into beams to match the shape of the tumor and to eliminate damage of surrounding tissue; cryosurgery, or freezing of the cancerous cells; radioactive seed implants, in which rice-size pellets are injected into the prostate to kill cancer cells; hormone treatments to block production of testosterone, which feeds cancer cells; combination therapies using two or more treatments; and "watchful waiting," during which patients are monitored for problems (a common practice in older patients).

Damon Harris, 50, Chose Hormones for Spreading Cancer Harris spent much of the 1970s as a singer with the Temptations. Harris had never been screened for prostate cancer, but then he noticed a lingering pain. He had a DRE, and his PSA test came back at more than 13. Within days, he was facing a cancer diagnosis. Harris began what he called "my crash course in Cancer 101. . . . I had little time to do research," he noted. As it turned out, in his case, the decision was simple. "My cancer was metastatic," he said. "I opted for the best and only treatment available, which is hormone therapy."

Harris immediately began an oral medication to neutralize testosterone and other male hormones in his system, followed by weekly injections that shut down new production of male hormones, like testosterone, needed for prostate growth. "I will be on [this medication] for the rest of my life," he declared. The most severe side effects of hormone therapy are hot flashes, weight gain, and reduced sexual desire. Harris experienced all three.

Eugene Waterman, 71, Chose Proton Beam Radiation As a doctor, Waterman, age 71, was especially aware of the risks of prostate cancer and the means of detecting it. Waterman learned that his PSA had suddenly risen to 11—very high. A biopsy indicated cancer with an aggressive Gleason score of 8. Fearful of the risks of surgery, Waterman began researching proton beam radiation therapy.

"The side effects of radiation were mild," he noted. "There was some fatigue at the end of the week and some diarrhea." He had some mild anal soreness, too, which was treated with a salve. Treatment also involved hormone therapy, an injection every three months for a year. The resulting testosterone depletion was difficult. Because the condition can lead to bone loss, he asked for a bone scan; borderline osteoporosis was found. Now he takes Fosomax twice a week.

Waterman also experienced hot flashes, 10 to 15 times a day. He suffered a complete loss of libido and sore, enlarged breasts. "But I have been off Zoladex for over a year," he said. "Testosterone levels are back to normal levels, and side effects have gone away." His sexual ability has returned with help from Viagra, but his desire is not as strong as it used to be.

Thomas Sellers, 50, Had His Prostate Removed Sellers is not only a prostate cancer survivor, but an employee of the American Cancer Society as well. As a cancer professional and an African American, Sellers knew about the need to begin annual PSA tests at age 45. A test showed that his PSA had leaped to 8.5. A biopsy confirmed cancer.

Ultimately, Sellers chose surgery, a nerve-sparing radical prostatectomy. Impotence, he said, worried him greatly, adding, "The likelihood of a cure because of early detection and the fact the cancer was still within the prostate outweighed fear of side effects." After surgery, Sellers wore a catheter for two weeks to drain urine.

Former Mayor Rudolph W. Giuliani of New York. *New York's former Mayor Rudy Giuliani decided to treat his prostate cancer with radioactive seed implants during an outpatient procedure. There are many treatments today for prostate cancer, and people with the disease must weigh the benefits and risks of each.*

He did not recover his full strength for six months. He endured short-term incontinence. "It took six months or more before I was completely dry, and nine months before I stopped wearing a pad," he noted. As for sexual activity, Sellers has some problems, despite the nerve sparing, and he is "experimenting with Viagra, with intermittent success." However, his PSA score is back to 0.

Melvin Katz, 56, Received Radiation Implants "I denied for eight months that anything was wrong with me," said Katz, a 56-year-old health care consultant. "I noticed symptoms in July and didn't do anything about it until the following March." By then, Katz's PSA had leapt to 91. A biopsy showed cancer with a Gleason score of 8. Only 48 at the time, Katz said he felt too young to have this "old man's disease."

Katz went on combination hormone therapy to halt the production of testosterone, the hormone that feeds prostate cancer. Katz chose high-dose external beam radiation five days a week for eight weeks. "It afforded me a quality of life," he explained, adding that side effects were mild. Three months after radiation, Katz stopped the hormones. His PSA went from 0 to 25 in just nine months, and he resumed hormone treatment. Then a biopsy showed lingering cancer. "I couldn't take any more external radiation, and

surgery was risky because the radiation increased the chance of bleeding," he said. His doctor suggested palladium radioactive seed implants, and Katz agreed. The procedure was done under local anesthetic and lasted about an hour. The radiation lasts for six to nine months, "and the only restriction is no little children or pregnant ladies on your lap," Katz said. Meanwhile, his PSA dropped from 25 to 0.9.

SOURCE: Adapted from "More Options, and Decisions, for Men with Prostate Cancer", by David Kirby, *The New York Times Online*, October 3, 2000. Copyright © 2000 by The New York Times Co. Reprinted by permission.

Male Sexual Functions

The male sexual functions of erection and ejaculation provide the means for sperm to travel from the male's reproductive tract to the female's. There the sperm cell and ovum unite to conceive a new human being. Of course, the natural endowment of reproduction with sensations of pleasure helps ensure that it will take place with or without knowledge of these biological facts.

Erection

Erection is caused by the engorgement of the penis with blood, such that the penis expands and stiffens. The erect penis is an efficient funnel for depositing sperm deep within the vagina.

Erection is a hydraulic event. The spongy, cavernous masses of the penis fill with blood, causing the penis to enlarge, similar to a sponge that swells as it absorbs water. Erection involves both the vascular (circulatory) system and the nervous system.

In a few moments—as quickly as 10 or 15 seconds—the penis can double in length, become firm, and shift from a funnel for passing urine to one that expels semen. Muscles close off the bladder when the male becomes sexually aroused, preventing the mixture of semen and urine.

The corpora cavernosa are surrounded by a tough, fibrous covering. Just as the rubber of a balloon resists the pressure of pumped-in air, this covering resists expansion, stiffening the penis. The corpus spongiosum, which contains the urethra, also engorges with blood during erection. It does not become hard, however, because it lacks the fibrous casing. The penile glans, which is formed by the crowning of the spongiosum at the tip of the penis, turns a dark purplish hue as it becomes engorged, but it too does not stiffen.

Erection is reversed when more blood flows out of erectile tissue than flows in, restoring the prearousal circulatory balance and shrinking the spongy masses. Loss of erection occurs when sexual stimulation ceases, or when the body returns to a (sexual) resting state after orgasm. Loss of erection can also occur in response to anxiety or perceived threats (Janssen, 2006; Janssen et al., 2006). Such loss can be abrupt, as when a man in the "throes of passion" suddenly hears a noise suggestive of an intruder. A man who fears that he will be unable to perform successfully may experience **performance anxiety**, which can prevent him from obtaining or maintaining an erection.

Men have nocturnal erections every 90 minutes or so as they sleep. They generally occur during rapid eye movement (REM) sleep. REM sleep is associated with dreaming. It is so named because the sleeper's eyes dart about rapidly under the closed eyelids during this stage.

The mechanism of nocturnal erection is physiological. That is, dreams may not have erotic content. Morning erections are actually nocturnal erections. They occur when the man awakens during REM sleep. **Truth or Fiction Revisited:** Morning erections do not reflect the need to urinate.

Spinal Reflexes and Sexual Response

Men may become sexually aroused by a range of stimuli, including tactile stimulation provided by their partners, visual stimulation (as from scanning photos of nudes on the Internet), or sexual fantasies. Regardless of the source of stimulation, the man's sexual responses—erection and ejaculation—occur by reflex.

TRUTH fiction 4

Erection Enlargement and stiffening of the penis caused by engorgement with blood

Performance anxiety Feelings of dread and foreboding experienced in connection with sexual activity (or any other activity that might be judged by another person)

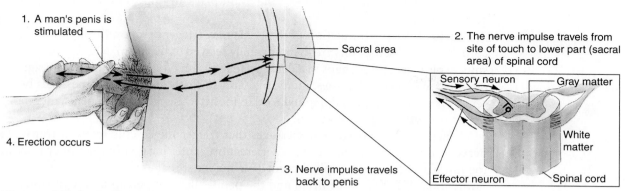

Figure 4.12 **Reflexes.** *Reflexes need not involve the brain, although messages to the brain may make us aware when reflexes are occurring. Reflexes are the product of "local government" in the spine.*

1. A man's penis is stimulated

4. Erection occurs

Sacral area

3. Nerve impulse travels back to penis

2. The nerve impulse travels from site of touch to lower part (sacral area) of spinal cord

Sensory neuron — Gray matter

White matter

Effector neuron — Spinal cord

Sexual reflexes are automatic, unlearned responses to sexual stimulation. Examples in women include vaginal lubrication and orgasm. We need not "try" to become aroused. We need only expose ourselves to sexual stimulation and allow reflexes to do the job for us.

Truth or Fiction Revisited: Men cannot will themselves to have erections. People do not control sexual reflexes voluntarily, as they might lift an arm, but they can set the stage for them to occur by seeking sexual stimulation. Efforts to control sexual responses consciously by "force of will" can backfire and make it more difficult to become aroused (e.g., to attain erection or vaginal lubrication).

The reflexes governing erection and ejaculation are controlled in the spinal cord. They are thus called spinal reflexes. Erectile responses to direct stimulation such as touching or licking involve a simple spinal reflex that does not require the direct participation of the brain (Figure 4.12). Erections can also be initiated by the brain, as when a man has sexual fantasies or catches a glimpse of an attractive person. In such cases, stimulation from the brain travels to the spinal cord, where the erectile reflex is triggered.

Tactile stimulation (touching) of the penis or nearby areas (lower abdomen, scrotum, inner thighs) causes sensory neurons to transmit nerve messages (signals) to an erection center in the lower back, in an area of the spinal cord called the **sacrum**. The sacral erection center controls reflexive erections—that is, erections occurring in response to direct stimulation of the penis and nearby areas. When direct penile stimulation occurs, messages in the form of nerve impulses are received by this erection center, which in turn sends impulses to the genitalia via nerves that serve the penis. These impulses cause arteries carrying blood to the corpora cavernosa and corpus spongiosum to dilate, so that more blood flows into them, causing erection.

The sacral erection center makes it possible for men whose spinal cords have been injured or severed above the center to achieve erections (and ejaculate) in response to direct tactile stimulation of the penis. Erection occurs even though their injuries prevent nerve signals from reaching their brains. Because of the lack of communication between the genital organs and the brain, there are no sensations, but many spinal cord–injured men report that sex remains psychologically pleasurable because they can observe the responses of their partners.

THE ROLE OF THE BRAIN If direct penile stimulation triggers erection at the spinal level, what is the role of the brain? Although it may seem that the penis

CRITICAL Thinking

Because erection and ejaculation are reflexes, how is it that people can consciously cause them to happen?

Sacrum The thick, triangular bone located near the bottom of the spinal column

sometimes has "a mind of its own," the brain plays an important role in regulating sexual responses.

Tactile (touch) stimulation of the penis may trigger erection through the spinal cord, but sexual sensations are then normally relayed to the brain, which generally results in pleasure and perhaps in a decision to focus on erotic stimulation. The sight of one's partner, erotic fantasies, memories, and so forth can result in messages being sent by the brain through the spinal cord to the arteries servicing the penis, maintaining or strengthening the erection.

When the brain originates messages that trigger the erectile reflex, it transmits nerve impulses to a second and higher erection center located in the upper back in the lumbar region of the spinal cord. This higher spinal erection center serves as a "switchboard" between the brain and the penis, allowing perceptual, cognitive, and emotional responses to make their contributions. When the nerve pathways between the brain and the upper spinal cord are blocked or severed, men cannot achieve erections in response to mental stimulation alone.

The brain can also stifle sexual response. A man who is highly anxious about his sexual abilities may be unable to achieve an erection even with intense penile stimulation. Or a man who believes that sexual pleasure is sinful or dirty may be filled with anxiety and guilt, and may be unable to achieve erection with a partner.

In some males, especially adolescents, the erectile reflex is so easily tripped that incidental rubbing of the genitals against his own undergarments, the sight of an attractive passerby, or a fleeting sexual fantasy produces erection. Spontaneous erections may occur under embarrassing circumstances, such as before classes change in middle or high school, or on a beach. In an effort to distract himself from erotic fantasies and to allow an erection to subside, many a male adolescent desperately renews his interest in his algebra or language textbook in class before the bell rings. (A well-placed towel may serve in a pinch on the beach.)

As men mature, they need more penile stimulation to achieve full erection. Partners of men in their 30s and 40s should not feel that their attractiveness has waned if their lovers no longer have instant "no-hands" erections when they disrobe. It takes men longer to obtain erection as they age, and direct stimulation becomes more important.

THE ROLE OF THE AUTONOMIC NERVOUS SYSTEM (ANS)

Stimulation that brings about an erection can originate in the brain, but erection is not a voluntary response, like raising your arm. Whatever the original or dominant source of stimulation—direct penile stimulation or sexual fantasy—erection remains an unlearned, automatic reflex.

Automatic responses, such as erection, involve the division of the nervous system called the **autonomic nervous system** (ANS). *Autonomic* means "automatic." The ANS controls automatic bodily processes such as heartbeat, pupil dilation, respiration, and digestion. In contrast, voluntary movement (like raising an arm) is under the control of the *somatic* division of the nervous system.

The ANS has two branches, the **sympathetic** and the **parasympathetic**. These branches have largely opposing effects. When they are activated at the same time, their effects become balanced out to some degree. In general, the sympathetic branch is in command during processes that involve a release of bodily energy from stored reserves, such as during running, performing some other athletic task, or being gripped by fear or anxiety. The sympathetic branch also governs the general mobilization of the body, such as by increasing the heart rate and respiration rate in response to threat.

The parasympathetic branch is most active during processes that restore reserves of energy, such as digestion. When we experience fear or anxiety, the sympathetic

Autonomic nervous system (ANS) The division of the nervous system that regulates automatic bodily processes, such as heartbeat, pupil dilation, respiration, and digestion

Sympathetic The branch of the ANS most active during emotional responses that spend energy, such as fear and anxiety; largely controls ejaculation

Parasympathetic The branch of the ANS most active during processes that restore energy, like digestion; largely controls erection

branch of the ANS quickens the heart rate. When we relax, the parasympathetic branch curbs the heart rate. The parasympathetic branch activates digestive processes, but the sympathetic branch inhibits digestive activity. Because the sympathetic branch is in command when we feel fear or anxiety, such stimuli can inhibit the activity of the parasympathetic system, possibly causing indigestion.

The divisions of the ANS play different roles in sexual arousal and response. The nerves that cause penile arteries to dilate during erection belong to the parasympathetic branch of the ANS. The parasympathetic system largely governs erection. The nerves governing ejaculation belong to the sympathetic branch, however. One implication of this division of neural responsibility is that intense fear or anxiety, which involves sympathetic nervous system activity, may inhibit erection by counteracting the activity of the parasympathetic nervous system. Because sympathetic arousal helps trigger ejaculation, anxiety or fear may also accelerate ejaculation, causing *premature ejaculation* (see Chapter 15).

The connection between emotions, sympathetic activity, and ejaculation can set up a vicious cycle. Anxiety in a sexual encounter may trigger premature ejaculation. During a subsequent sexual encounter, the man might fear recurrence of premature ejaculation. The fear may bring on the reality. He may face further sexual encounters with yet greater fear, possibly further hastening ejaculation—but possibly inhibiting erection. Methods for helping men with erectile dysfunction and premature ejaculation aim at reducing their levels of anxiety and thereby lessening sympathetic activity.

Truth or Fiction Revisited: Because erections seem spontaneous at times and often occur when men would rather not have them, it may seem to men that the penis has a mind of its own. But despite this common folk belief, the penis has no guiding intelligence. It consists of spongy masses of erectile tissue, not the lovely dense gray matter that renders your thought processes so incisive.

ERECTILE ABNORMALITIES Some men find that their erect penises are slightly curved or bent. Some degree of curvature is normal, but men with **Peyronie's disease** have excessive curvature that can make erections painful. The condition is caused by buildup of fibrous tissue in the penile shaft. Although some cases of Peyronie's disease appear to clear up on their own, most require medical attention.

Some men experience erections that persist for hours or days. This condition is called *priapism,* after Priapus of Greek myth, the son of Dionysus and Aphrodite who personified male procreative power. Priapism is often caused by leukemia, sickle cell anemia, or diseases of the spinal cord, although in some cases the cause remains unknown. Priapism occurs when the mechanisms that drain the blood that makes the penis erect are damaged and thus cannot return the blood to the circulatory system. Priapism may become a medical emergency, because erection prolonged beyond six hours can starve penile tissues of oxygen, leading to tissue deterioration. Medical intervention in the form of drugs or surgery may be required to reverse the condition.

Ejaculation

Ejaculation, like erection, is a spinal reflex. It is triggered when sexual stimulation reaches a critical point or threshold. Ejaculation generally occurs together with **orgasm**, the sudden muscle contractions that occur at the peak of sexual excitement and result in the abrupt release of sexual tension that built up during sexual arousal. Orgasm is generally pleasurable. *Ejaculation,* however, refers only to the expulsion of semen from the tip of the penis. Orgasm and ejaculation are *not* synonymous, however. For example, **paraplegics** can ejaculate if the area of the lower spinal cord that

Peyronie's disease Excessive curvature of the penis that can make erections painful

Orgasm The climax of sexual excitement

Paraplegic A person with sensory and motor paralysis of the lower half of the body

controls ejaculation is intact. They do not experience the subjective aspects of orgasm, however, because the sensations of orgasm do not reach the brain.

Truth or Fiction Revisited: Many men who are paralyzed below the waist can attain erection, engage in sexual intercourse, and ejaculate, if the spinal centers controlling erection and ejaculation remain intact.

Truth or Fiction Revisited: Prepubertal boys may also experience orgasms even though they emit no ejaculate (so-called *dry orgasms*). Boys do not begin to produce seminal fluid (and sperm) until puberty. Mature men can also experience dry orgasms. These take the form of "little orgasms" preceding a larger orgasm, or they can follow "wet orgasms" when sexual stimulation is continued but seminal fluids have not been replenished.

Ejaculation occurs in two stages (Levin, 2005a). The first phase, often called the **emission phase**, involves contractions of the prostate, seminal vesicles, and the upper part of the vas deferens (the **ampulla**). The force of these contractions propels seminal fluid into the prostatic part of the urethral tract—a small tube called the **urethral bulb**—which balloons as muscles close at either end, trapping the semen. It is at this point that the man perceives orgasm as inevitable. The man feels that nothing can prevent ejaculation.

During the second or **expulsion stage**, seminal fluid is propelled through the urethra and out of the urethral opening at the tip of the penis. During this stage, muscles at the base of the penis and elsewhere contract rhythmically, expelling semen. The second stage is generally accompanied by the sensations of orgasm.

During ejaculation, seminal fluid is released from the urethral bulb and is expelled by contractions of the pelvic muscles that surround the urethral channel and the crura of the penis. The first few contractions are the most intense and occur at 0.8-second intervals. Subsequent contractions weaken. The interval between them increases. Seminal fluid is expelled in spurts during the first few contractions. In young men, seminal fluid may be propelled 12 to 24 inches. But in some men, semen travels but a few inches or oozes from the penile opening. The force of the expulsion varies with the condition of the man's prostate, his general health, and his age. More intense orgasms tend to accompany more forceful ejaculations.

Like erection, ejaculation is regulated by two centers in the spinal cord, one in the sacral region and one in the higher lumbar region. When sexual arousal reaches the point of ejaculatory inevitability, the lumbar ejaculatory center triggers the first stage of ejaculation, seminal emission. The lower, or sacral, ejaculatory center triggers the second stage of orgasm.

Although ejaculation occurs by reflex, a man can delay ejaculation by maintaining the level of sexual stimulation below the critical threshold, or "point of no return." Men who ejaculate prematurely have been successfully treated in programs that train them to learn to recognize their "point of no return" and maintain sexual stimulation below it. (Issues concerning the definition and treatment of premature ejaculation are explored in Chapter 15 on sexual dysfunction.) Recognizing the point of no return and keeping stimulation beneath the critical level can also prolong coitus and enhance sexual pleasure for couples even when the man does not experience premature ejaculation.

RETROGRADE EJACULATION During **retrograde ejaculation**, the ejaculate empties into the bladder rather than being expelled from the body. During normal ejaculation, an external sphincter opens, allowing seminal fluid to pass out of the body. Another sphincter, this one internal, closes off the opening to the bladder, preventing the seminal fluid from backing up into the bladder. During retrograde ejac-

Emission phase The first phase of ejaculation, which involves contractions of the prostate gland, seminal vesicles, and the upper part of the vas deferens

Ampulla A sac or dilated part of a tube or canal

Urethral bulb The small tube that makes up the prostatic part of the urethral tract and that balloons out as muscles close at either end, trapping semen prior to ejaculation

Expulsion stage The second stage of ejaculation, during which muscles at the base of the penis and elsewhere contract rhythmically, forcefully expelling semen and providing pleasurable sensations

Retrograde ejaculation Ejaculation during which the ejaculate empties into the bladder

Q *Can retrograde ejaculation be fixed?*

A Yes and no. The answer depends on what you mean by "fixed." In many cases, normal ejaculation can be induced medically, typically by the use of imipramine, a drug developed in the 1950s to treat depression, that has been found to be useful in the treatment of panic attacks too. However, research suggests that retrograde ejaculation need not be directly treated to achieve pregnancy in a female partner. Many studies describe the derivation of sperm from urine, and the impregnation of women with this sperm.

ulation, the actions of these sphincters are reversed. The external sphincter remains closed, preventing the expulsion of seminal fluid, whereas the internal sphincter opens, allowing the ejaculate to empty into the bladder. The result is an apparently dry orgasm. Retrograde ejaculation may be caused by prostate surgery (much less so now than in former years), drugs such as tranquilizers, certain illnesses, and accidents. Retrograde ejaculation is usually harmless in itself, because the seminal fluid is later discharged with urine. But infertility can result and there may be changes in the sensations associated with orgasm. Persistent dry orgasms should be medically evaluated.

Male sexual functions, like female sexual functions, are complex. They involve the cooperation of the nervous system, the endocrine system, the cardiovascular system, and the musculoskeletal system. In Chapter 5 we learn more about how the female and male sex organs respond to sexual stimulation. In Chapter 6 we examine the similarities and differences between females and males with respect to sexual differentiation, behavior, and personality.

1. What are the external male sex organs?

- The external male sex organs include the penis and the scrotum, both of which are sensitive to sexual stimulation. Semen and urine pass out of the penis through the urethral opening. The penis contains cylinders that fill with blood and stiffen during sexual arousal.

- Circumcision has been carried out for religious and hygienic reasons. Research shows that circumcision makes a male less vulnerable to certain health problems; however, circumcision decreases sexual sensations, is painful, and—in infants—is carried out without the child's consent.

- The scrotum is the pouch of loose skin that contains the testes. Each testicle is held in place by a spermatic cord, which contains the vas deferens and the cremaster muscle.

2. What are the internal male sex organs?

- The internal male sex organs consist of the testes, tubes, and ducts that conduct sperm, and organs that nourish and activate sperm. The testes serve two functions, analogous to those of the ovaries. Testes secrete male sex hormones and produce germ cells—in this case, sperm. The hypothalamus, pituitary gland, and testes keep blood testosterone levels at more or less even levels through a negative feedback loop. Testosterone is produced by interstitial cells. Sperm are produced by seminiferous tubules. Sperm are stored and mature in the epididymis.

- Each epididymis empties into a vas deferens that conducts sperm over the bladder. The seminal vesicles open into the ejaculatory ducts, where their fluids nourish sperm.

- Semen is made up of sperm and the fluids contributed by the seminal vesicles, prostate gland, and Cowper's glands.

3. What health problems affect the urogential system?

- Men, like women, are subject to bladder and urethral inflammation, which is generally referred to as urethritis. Unlike women, men can experience prostatitis.

- Cancer of the testes is the most common form of solid-tumor cancer to strike young men between the ages of 20 and 34.

- Benign prostate hyperplagia (or BPH) is noncancerous enlargement of the prostate, which is caused by testosterone and is connected with aging. It can be treated by drugs that shrink the prostate or improve the flow of urine, or by partial removal of the prostate.

- Prostate cancer is the second most common form of cancer in men. Risk factors include genetics, aging, and eating animal fats. Testosterone spurs growth of prostate cancer cells. Early detection is usually by means of a DRE or blood test (PSA). Treatment options include surgery, hormone treatments, radiation, medicine, and "watchful waiting."

4. How do erection and ejaculation occur?

- The penis erects when caverns within become engorged with blood, expanding and stiffening it. Erection occurs in response to sexual stimulation but is also common during REM sleep.

- There are two erection centers in the spinal cord. Although erection is a reflex, penile sensations are relayed to the brain, where they generally result in pleasure.

- Erection and ejaculation also involve the ANS. The parasympathetic branch of the ANS largely governs erection, whereas the sympathetic branch largely controls ejaculation. Fear, which involves sympathetic activity, can inhibit erection yet trigger premature ejaculation.

- Ejaculation, like erection, is a reflex. It is triggered when sexual stimulation reaches a threshold. The emission phase of ejaculation involves contractions of the prostate, seminal vesicles, and the upper part of the vas deferens. During the expulsion stage, muscles propel semen out of the penis.

1. _____ is characterized by prolonged erection.

   (a) Phimosis
   (b) Peyronie's disease
   (c) Ejaculation
   (d) Priapism

2. During the emission stage of ejaculation, semen is pro-pelled into the

   (a) urethral bulb
   (b) prostate gland
   (c) sacrum
   (d) bladder

3. Both males and females have

   (a) sperm
   (b) semen
   (c) vas deferens
   (d) corpora cavernosa

4. Male circumcision removes the

   (a) frenulum
   (b) prepuce
   (c) glans
   (d) corona

5. _____ are circumcised for religious reasons.

   (a) Christians
   (b) Hindus
   (c) Muslims
   (d) Buddhists

6. Scrotal temperature tends to be _____ body temperature.

   (a) 5 to 6° F higher than
   (b) 5 to 6° F lower than
   (c) the same as
   (d) unpredictable with relation to

7. The scrotum is developed from the same embryonic tissue that becomes the _____ of the female.

   (a) perineum
   (b) uterus
   (c) labia minora
   (d) labia majora

8. _LH_ stimulates secretion of testosterone by interstitial cells.

   (a) Progestin
   (b) Prolactin
   (c) LH
   (d) FSH

9. It would take about _____ sperm laid out head to tail to make up an inch.

   (a) 100
   (b) 500
   (c) 1,000
   (d) 5,000

10. _____ nanograms of PSA per milliliter of blood are considered normal.

    (a) Less than four
    (b) Four to 10
    (c) Ten to 20
    (d) More than 20

11. Both semen and urine pass through the

    (a) vas deferens
    (b) bladder
    (c) urethral meatus
    (d) intestines

12. Ciproflaxin is used to treat

    (a) prostate cancer
    (b) prostatitis
    (c) BPH
    (d) testicular cancer

13. Men have erections every _____ minutes or so while they sleep.

    (a) 30
    (b) 60
    (c) 90
    (d) 120

14. The human penis contains

    (a) corpora cavernosa
    (b) bone
    (c) muscle
    (d) interstitial tissue

15. BPH is caused by

    (a) proliferation of cancer cells
    (b) STIs
    (c) an infection unrelated to sexual activity
    (d) hormonal changes associated with aging

Answers 1. d; 2. a; 3. d; 4. b; 5. c; 6. b; 7. d; 8. c; 9. d; 10. a; 11. c; 12. b; 13. c; 14. a; 15. d

Sexual Arousal and Response

TRUTH fiction?

Which of the following statements are true, and which are fiction? Look for the Truth/Fiction icons on the pages that follow to find the answers.

1 The ancient Romans were so obsessed with offensive odors that they perfumed their horses. T F

2 The menstrual cycles of women who live together tend to become synchronized. T F

3 The primary erogenous zone is the brain. T F

4 "Spanish fly" will not turn your date on, but it may cure his or her warts. T F

5 Electrical stimulation of certain areas in the human brain can yield sensations similar to those of sexual pleasure and gratification. T F

6 Normal men produce estrogen, and normal women produce androgens. T F

7 Written descriptions of men's and women's experiences during orgasm cannot be differentiated. T F

8 Orgasms attained through sexual intercourse are more intense than those attained through masturbation. T F

You have probably heard about the birds and the bees. How about the buds and the bees?

It may be that we should cover our children's eyes when bees are at work in the yard. Researchers at the Australian National University have learned that bees who land on certain flowers are seeking something other than pollen. It turns out that some plants emit chemical secretions that mimic chemical signals secreted by female bees ("Australia scientists," 2000). As a result, male bees try to mate with them. As a side effect, the bees transfer pollen from one plant to another, facilitating fertilization and the survival of these species of plants.

In case you are wondering, there is no evidence that these plants are "trying" to dupe the bees. Plants do not think, after all. It just happens, evolutionarily speaking, that whatever genes contribute to the development of these chemical secretions are likely to be transmitted to the next generation.

The kinds of plants that are "in on" the signal scam are orchids. One type is found in Europe, and nine types are found in Australia, where the bees are apparently especially active. These orchids produce the same hydrocarbon compounds that are found in chemicals secreted by the female bee.

These chemicals are called **pheromones,** and they are odorless chemicals that are nevertheless detected in the same way that animals detect odors—

A Pheromonal Scam. *Australian researchers have discovered that certain orchids emit pheromones that mimic those of female bees. As a result, male bees attempt to mate with them (the flowers, that is). In the process, they pick up pollen and transfer it to other orchids, helping the orchids reproduce.*

by sampling molecules of substances in the air. Lower animals use pheromones to stimulate sexual response, organize food gathering, maintain pecking orders, sound alarms, and mark territories (Cutler, 1999; Wyatt, 2003). Pheromones induce mating behavior in insects such as bees. In the case of the orchids, the power of the pheromones apparently overrides bees' vision. Even so, one of the researchers noted that "the bees will . . . only try mating with the flowers a few times each" ("Australia scientists," 2000). Better to learn late than never.

What turns *you* on? What springs your heart into your mouth, tightens your throat, and opens the floodgates into your genitals? The sight of your lover undressing, a photo of Jake Gyllenhall or Scarlett Johannson, a sniff of musky perfume, a sip of wine?

Many factors contribute to sexual arousal. Some people are aroused by magazines with photographs of nude or seminude models that have been airbrushed to perfection. Some need only to imagine Hollywood's latest sex symbol. Some become aroused by remembrances of past lovers. Some are stimulated by sexual fantasies of flings with strangers.

People vary greatly in the cues that excite them sexually and in the frequency with which they experience sexual thoughts and feelings. Some young people seem perpetually aroused or arousable. Some people rarely or never entertain sexual thoughts or fantasies.

In this chapter we look at factors that contribute to sexual arousal and the processes that relate to sexual response. Because our experience of the world is initi-

Pheromones Chemical substances secreted externally by certain animals that convey information to, or produce specific responses in, other members of the same species; from the Greek *pherien,* meaning "to bear [a message]" and "hormone"

ated by our senses, we begin the chapter by asking: What are the roles of the senses in sexual arousal? In our discussion we explore the possible role of pheromones.

Making Sense of Sex: The Role of the Senses in Sexual Arousal

We come to apprehend the world around us through our senses—vision, hearing, smell, taste, and the skin senses, which include that all-important sense of touch. Each of the senses plays a role in our sexual experience, but some senses play larger roles than others.

Vision: The Better to See You With

Visual cues can be sexual turn-ons. We may be turned on by the sight of a lover in the nude, disrobing, or dressed in evening wear. Lingerie companies hope to convince customers that they will enhance their sex appeal by wearing strategically concealing and revealing nightwear. Some couples find it arousing to observe themselves making love in an overhead mirror or on videotape. Some people find sexually explicit movies arousing; others are bored or offended by them. Although both males and females can be sexually aroused by visually mediated erotica (a technical term for "porn flicks"), men are more interested in them (Hamann et al., 2004).

REFLECT

Do you find nude people to be sexually arousing? Why or why not?

SafeZone

Q *My boyfriend has to watch pornography to get aroused. Is this normal?*

A No and yes. The no is that he should be able to get aroused without watching pornography. It could be that you don't turn him on (ouch) and for some reason he's prolonging a relationship that isn't working for him. Or maybe he's checking to see what you'll put up with. In either case, the situation may not be a good one for you and you may want to evaluate whether you want to remain in it. We're not casting value judgments on porn per se here, unless it's degrading to women, in which case we're completely opposed. But if your boyfriend is selecting stuff that's violent or otherwise degrading to women, there could be lots of messages for you in what he's doing. It's probably not just a question of something to help him get aroused. Now, the "normal" part is that many males and females use sexual fantasies of some kind to heighten arousal. But again, he shouldn't *have* to have porn to get going, even if he might enjoy it.

Smell: Does the Nose Know Best?

Although the sense of smell plays a lesser role in governing sexual arousal in humans than in lower mammals, odors can be sexual turn-ons or turn-offs. Perfume companies, for example, bottle fragrances purported to be sexually arousing.

Most Westerners prefer their lovers to be clean and fresh smelling (Boston Women's Health Book Collective, 2005). People in our society learn to remove or mask odors by the use of soaps, deodorants, and perfumes or colognes. The ancient Egyptians invented scented bathing to rid themselves of offensive odors (Illes, 2000). **Truth or Fiction Revisited:** The ancient Romans of the upper classes also had a passion for perfume. They would bathe in fragrances and even dab perfume on their horses and household pets.

Inclinations to find underarm or genital odors offensive may reflect cultural conditioning and not biological predispositions. In some societies, genital secretions are considered **aphrodisiacs**. And the underarms? Check out the "Human Sexuality, A Closer Look" feature on pheromones for possible answers.

MENSTRUAL SYNCHRONY   Research by several investigators suggests that exposure to other women's sweat can modify a woman's menstrual cycle (Morofushi et al., 2000). *Question: How does exposure to other women's sweat modify the menstrual cycle?* Let us examine some research on the subject and see.

In one study, women exposed to underarm secretions from other women, which contain steroids that may function as pheromones, showed converging shifts in their menstrual cycles (Preti et al., 1986). Similar synchronization of menstrual cycles has also been observed among women who share dormitory rooms. In another study, 80% of the women who dabbed their upper lips with an extract of perspiration from other women began to menstruate in sync with the cycles of the donors after about three menstrual cycles (Cutler, 1999). A control group, consisting of women who dabbed their lips with alcohol, showed no changes in their menstrual cycles. In yet another study from this research group, the length of the cycles of women with unusually short or long cycles began to normalize when they were exposed to an extract of male underarm perspiration (Preti et al., 1986). **Truth or Fiction Revisited:** Therefore, it is true that the menstrual cycles of women who live together tend to become synchronized, as long as the women's cycles are not being regulated by birth control pills.

What Does the Nose Know about Sexual Orientation? *Research by Yolanda Martins, George Preti, Charles Wysocki, and their colleagues (2005) suggests that gay males prefer the body odors of other gay males to those of heterosexuals and lesbians. Heterosexual males, however, seem least likely to prefer the body odors of gay males as compared to heterosexual males and to females, both heterosexual and lesbian.*

TRUTH fiction 1

TRUTH fiction 2

CRITICAL Thinking

Is using perfume or cologne the equivalent of using a pheromone to enhance one's sexual attractiveness?

Aphrodisiac Any drug or other agent that is sexually arousing or increases sexual desire; from *Aphrodite*, the Greek goddess of love and beauty

ATTRACTION TO—OR DISLIKE OF—BODY ODORS OF HETEROSEXUAL MALES AND FEMALES VERSUS GAY MALES AND LESBIANS
There is reason to believe that body odors play a role in the selection of sex partners (Preti et al., 2003; Wyatt, 2003). Yolanda Martins, George Preti, Charles Wysocki, and their colleagues (2005) hypothesized that preferences for axillary (underarm) odors would be related to people's sexual orientation: heterosexual male or female, and gay male or lesbian. They collected samples of axillary odors from 24 volunteers—six exclusively male heterosexual and six exclusively female heterosexual, and six exclusively gay male and six exclusively lesbian, according to the Kinsey heterosexuality–homosexuality scale described in Figure 10.1.

The researchers had a number of interesting findings, as follows:

● Heterosexual males and females, and lesbians, preferred axillary odors taken from heterosexual males over those taken from gay males.

● Gay males preferred axillary odors taken from other gay males.

- Heterosexual males and females and lesbians age 25 years and older preferred axillary odors taken from lesbians to those from gay males.
- When axillary odors of heterosexual females were compared with those of lesbians, all groups except for heterosexual males preferred the odors from heterosexual females.
- Heterosexual males preferred the odor from lesbians over the odor taken from gay male donors.

The researchers suggest that the data show that gay males and lesbians may produce axillary odors that can be distinguished from those of heterosexuals. It would also appear that gay males may perceive these typical odorants differently from the way in which heterosexual males do. We can note that, at least in the few studies that have investigated the relationships between body odor and sexual orientation, gay males are most likely to be attracted to the body odors of other gay males, and that heterosexual males are least likely to prefer the body odors of gay males.

The Skin Senses: Sex as a Touching Experience

Our skin senses enable us to sense pain, changes in temperature, and pressure (or touch). Whatever the roles of vision and smell in sexual attraction and arousal, the sense of touch has the most direct effects on sexual arousal and response. Any region of that sensitive layer we refer to as skin can become eroticized. The touch of your lover's hand upon your cheek, or your lover's gentle massage of your shoulders or back, can be sexually stimulating.

EROGENOUS ZONES **Erogenous zones** are parts of the body that are especially sensitive to tactile sexual stimulation—to strokes and other caresses. **Primary erogenous zones** are erotically sensitive because they are richly endowed with nerve endings.

CRITICAL
Thinking

As critical thinkers read the study by Martins, Preti, Wysocki, and their colleagues (2005), they will recognize the importance of remaining open-minded about the interpretation of the study's results. For example, does the study show that preferences for body odors *causes* sexual attraction or sexual orientation? Could it also be that sexual experiences give rise to preferences for certain body odors? Or is it possible that sexual orientation gives rise both to patterns of sexual attraction and preferences for body odors? Final question: Might the results of the study have any implications for the origins of homophobia?

A Touching Experience. *The sense of touch is intimately connected with sexual experience. The touch of a lover's hand on the cheek, or gentle massage, can be sexually stimulating. Certain parts of the body—called erogenous zones—have special sexual significance because of their response to erotic stimulation.*

Erogenous zones Parts of the body that are especially sensitive to tactile sexual stimulation; derived from roots meaning "giving birth to erotic sensations"

Primary erogenous zones Erogenous zones that are particularly sensitive because they are richly endowed with nerve endings

A Closer Look

THE SEARCH FOR A "MAGIC" LOVE POTION: ON THE THRESHOLD?

For centuries people have searched for a love potion—a magical formula that could make other people fall in love with you or be strongly attracted to you. On the edge of the new millennium, some scientists suggest that such potions may already exist in the form of chemical secretions known as pheromones. Pheromones may enhance people's moods, have effects on fertility, and provide a basis for sexual communication below the level of conscious awareness.

Pheromones are odorless chemicals that in many animals are detected through a "sixth sense"—the *vomeronasal organ (VNO)*. People possess VNOs in the mucous lining of the nose (Rodriguez et al., 2000). During prenatal development, the VNO shuttles sex hormones into the brain, aid-ing in the sexual differentiation of the embryo (Rodriguez et al., 2000). However, before birth, the human VNO shrinks, and some researchers suggest that it stops working (Kouros–Mehr et al., 2001). But if it does continue to work, it might detect pheromones and direct information about them to the hypothalamus, where they might affect sexual response (Wyatt, 2003). Infants apparently use pheromones to recognize their mothers, and adults might respond to them in seeking a mate (Martins et al., 2005). Male rodents such as mice are extremely sensitive to several kinds of pheromones (Leinders–Zufall et al., 2000). Male rodents show less sexual arousal when their sense of smell is blocked, but the role of pheromones in sexual behavior becomes less vital as one moves upward through the ranks of the animal kingdom.

Only a few years ago, most researchers did not believe that pheromones played a role in human behavior, but today the issue has attracted new interest. In a typical study, Winnifred Cutler and her colleagues (1998) had hetero-sexual men wear a suspected male pheromone and a control group wore a placebo. The men using the pheromone increased their frequency of sexual intercourse with their fe-male partners but did not increase the frequency of masturbation. The researchers conclude that the sub-stance increased the sexual attrac-tiveness of the men to their partners, although they do not claim that it di-rectly stimulated sexual behavior.

Experiments that expose men and women to suspected pheromones (*androstadienone* produced by males and *estratetraenol* produced by females) find that they enhance the moods of women, but not of men. The sub-stances also apparently reduce feelings of nervousness and tension in women, but again, not in men (Grosser et al., 2000; Jacob et al., 2001; Jacob & Mc-Clintock, 2000). The findings about estratetraenol are not surprising. This substance is related to estrogen, and

---

Primary erogenous zones include the genitals; the inner thighs, perineum, but-tocks, and anus; the breasts (especially the nipples); the ears (particularly the ear-lobes); the mouth, lips, and tongue; the neck; the navel; and, yes, the armpits. Prefer-ences vary somewhat from person to person, reflecting possible biological, attitudinal, and experiential differences. Areas that are exquisitely sensitive for some people may produce virtually no reaction, or discomfort, in others. Many women, for example, report little sensation when their breasts are stroked or kissed. Many men are uncomfortable when their nipples are caressed. On the other hand (or foot), many people find the areas between their toes sensitive to erotic stimulation and enjoy keeping a toehold on their partners during coitus.

Secondary erogenous zones become eroticized through association with sexual stimulation. For example, a woman might become sexually aroused when her lover gently caresses her shoulders, because such caresses have been incorporated as a reg-ular feature of the couple's lovemaking. A few of the women observed by Masters and Johnson (1966) reached orgasm when the smalls of their backs were rubbed.

Secondary erogenous zones Parts of the body that become erotically sensi-tized through experience.

women tend to function best cognitively and emotionally during the time of the month when estrogen levels are highest (Ross et al., 2000). The fact that the women responded positively to androstadienone is of greater interest. Women may thus generally feel somewhat better when they are around men, even if male chemicals have not been shown to have direct sexual effects. Of course, being in a good mood can indirectly contribute to a woman's interest in sex.

George Preti, Charles Wysocki, and their colleagues (2003) found that male perspiration has beneficial effects on women's moods. It induces feelings of relaxation and helps lessen stress. It even affects the menstrual cycle. The researchers extracted samples from the underarms of men who avoided using deodorant for a month. The samples were blended and applied to the upper lips of 18 women age 25 to 45. The women did not know the source or makeup of the chemicals on the swabs. The women then rated their moods over a six-hour period and reported feeling more relaxed and in better moods. Analysis of their blood revealed a rise in levels of LH, which surges before ovulation. There was no indication that the women were sexually aroused, but it might be that men's perspiration provides "chemical communication" when they meet women, allowing them to coordinate reproductive efforts below the level of awareness. In a more sensual setting, these odors might also give rise to sexual feelings. Researchers suggest that if they can isolate the active agent or agents in male perspiration, studies such as these might lead to new treatments for fertility, by affecting ovulation, and for PMS, by affecting mood. Still, these substances do not directly stimulate behavior, as pheromones do with lower animals.

In a double-blind experiment, 36 university women were randomly assigned to wear a perfume laced with a suspected pheromone extracted from their underarm secretions or a placebo (McCoy & Pitino, 2002). The women recorded their sexual behaviors over three menstrual cycles (12 weeks). Three quarters (74%) of the women who used the suspected pheromone showed significant increases in their frequency of sexual intercourse, sleeping next to a partner, formal dates, and kissing, petting, and other displays of affection compared with one quarter (23%) of the users of the placebo. Perhaps the suspected pheromone increased the women's attractiveness to men.

How Much Sexual Communication Is Occurring below the Level of Conscious Awareness? *Research suggests that underarm secretions may make people more sexually attractive, even when others are unaware of sensing them. Are they drawn to each other's personal traits or to their pheromones?*

People are also highly responsive to images and fantasies. This is why the brain is sometimes referred to as the primary sexual organ or an erogenous zone. Some women report reaching orgasm through fantasy alone (Kinsey et al., 1953). Men regularly experience erection and nocturnal emissions ("wet dreams") without direct stimulation of the genitals.

Truth or Fiction Revisited: The brain is not an erogenous zone, because it is not stimulated directly by touch. The brain processes tactile information from the skin, but it does not have sensory neurons to gather this information directly. However, the brain can certainly pave the path toward erotic sensations through the production of fantasy, erotic memories, and other thoughts.

TRUTH fiction 3

Taste: On Savory Sex

Taste appears to play a minor role in sexual arousal and response. Some people are sexually aroused by the taste of genital secretions, such as vaginal secretions or seminal fluid. We do not know, however, whether these secretions are laced with chemicals that have biologically arousing effects or whether arousal reflects the meaning that these secretions have to the individual. That is, we may learn to become aroused by, or to seek out, flavors or odors that have been associated with sexual pleasure. Others are turned off by them.

Hearing: The Better to Hear You With

The sense of hearing also provides an important medium for sexual arousal and response. Like visual and olfactory cues, sounds can be turn-ons or turn-offs. The sounds of one's lover, whether they be whispers, indications of pleasure, or animated sounds that may attend orgasm, may be arousing during the heat of passion. For some people, key words or vocal intonations may become as arousing as direct stimulation of an erogenous zone. Many people are aroused when their lovers "talk dirty." Spoken vulgarities spur their sexual arousal. Others find vulgar language offensive.

Music can contribute to sexual arousal. Music can relax us and put us "in the mood" or have associations ("They're playing our song!"). Many couples find background music "atmospheric"—a vital accoutrement of lovemaking.

Sounds can also be sexual turnoffs. Most of us would find funeral music a damper on sexual arousal. We may also be inhibited by scratchy, unnerving voices. Heavy metal rock might be a sexual turn-off to many (are your authors showing their age?), but it could help set the right tone for others.

Aphrodisiacs: Of Spanish Flies and Rhino Horns

"The only known aphrodisiac is variety."

—Marc Connolly

An aphrodisiac is a substance that arouses or increases one's capacity for sexual pleasure or response. You may have heard of "Spanish fly," an alleged aphrodisiac once extracted from a Spanish beetle. (The beetle from which it was taken, *Lytta vesicatoria,* is near extinction.) A few drops in a date's drink were believed to make you irresistible. Spanish fly is but one of many purported aphrodisiacs. It is toxic, however, not sexually arousing. Spanish fly is now synthesized—but not as an aphrodisiac.

Truth or Fiction Revisited: It is true that Spanish fly will not turn your date on, but it may cure his or her warts. Spanish fly contains *cantharidin,* a skin irritant that can burn off warts. If it can burn off warts, consider the damage it can do when taken internally. It irritates the urinary tract and can damage tissue or cause death (Sandroni, 2003, as cited in Downs & Nazario, 2003). It inflames the urethra, producing a burning sensation in the penis that is sometimes misinterpreted as sexual feelings.

We should also be concerned about an expectancy, or placebo effect, when evaluating the effectiveness of a purported aphrodisiac (Downs & Nazario, 2003). The belief that a substance has sexually stimulating effects may itself inspire sexual excitement. If a person tries a supposed aphrodisiac and feels sexually aroused, the person may well attribute the turn-on to the effects of the substance, even if the substance had no direct effect on sex drive.

Foods that in some way resemble male genitals have now and then been considered aphrodisiacs. They include oysters, clams, bull's testicles ("prairie oysters"), and tomatoes; "phallic" items such as celery stalks and bananas; and even ground-up rhinoceros, reindeer, and elephant horns (which is one derivation of the slang term *horny*). Even potatoes—both white and sweet—have been held to be aphrodisiacs. None of these foods or substances has been shown to be sexually stimulating, however. Sadly, myths about the sexually arousing properties of substances drawn from rhinoceroses or elephants may be contributing to the rapidly diminishing numbers of these animals (Ascher, 2006).

Other drugs and psychoactive substances may have certain effects on sexual arousal and response. The drug arginine, an amino acid extracted from the African yohimbe tree, does stimulate blood flow to the genitals (Downs & Nazario, 2003). However, its effects are limited and unreliable (Downs & Nazario, 2003). Fortunately, arginine does not appear to be toxic (Finley, 2003).

Amyl nitrate (in the form of "snappers" or "poppers") has been used mostly by gay men (and by some heterosexuals) in the belief that it heightens sensations of arousal and orgasm. Poppers dilate blood vessels in the brain and genitals, producing sensations of warmth in the pelvis and possibly facilitating erection and prolonging orgasm. Amyl nitrate does have some legitimate medical uses, such as helping reduce heart pain (angina) among cardiac patients. It is inhaled from ampules that "pop" open for rapid use when heart pain occurs. Poppers can cause dizziness, fainting, and migraine-type headaches, however. They should be taken only under a doctor's care for a legitimate medical need, not to intensify sexual sensations.

The drug Viagra was originally developed as a treatment for angina (heart pain) because it increases the blood flow to the heart—modestly. However, it also dilates blood vessels in the genital organs, thereby facilitating **vasocongestion** and erection—and, according to some reports, sexual response in women as well (Slovenko, 2001). Viagra and similar drugs—Levitra and Cialis—are a treatment for erectile dysfunction (also termed *impotence*). Is Viagra also an aphrodisiac? It is a matter of definition. Although Viagra facilitates erection, it still takes a sexual turn-on for erection to occur. If an aphrodisiac is directly sexually arousing, Viagra is not an aphrodisiac.

However, certain drugs do appear to have aphrodisiacal effects, apparently because they act on the brain mechanisms controlling the sex drive. For example, drugs that affect brain receptors for the neurotransmitter dopamine, such as the antidepressant drug bupropion (trade name Wellbutrin) and the drug L-dopa, which is used in the treatment of Parkinson disease, can increase the sex drive (Modell et al., 2000).

The most potent chemical "aphrodisiac" may be a naturally occurring substance in the body—the hormone testosterone. It is the basic fuel of sexual desire in both males and females (Apperloo et al., 2003; Davis, 2000).

The safest and perhaps most effective method for increasing the sex drive may not be a drug or substance, but proper diet and exercise. Regular exercise not only enhances general health, it also boosts energy and increases the sex drive in both sexes. Perhaps the strongest aphrodisiac is novelty. Partners can invent new ways of sexually discovering one another. They can make love in novel places, experiment with different techniques, wear provocative clothing, share or enact fantasies, or whatever their imaginations inspire.

Anaphrodisiacs

Aphrodisiacs are thought to stimulate a sexual response. **Anaphrodisiacs** have the opposite effect. These include substances such as potassium nitrate (saltpeter), which has been considered an inhibitor of sexual response. Saltpeter, however, only indirectly dampens sexual arousal. As a diuretic that can increase the need for urination,

Vasocongestion The swelling of the genital tissues with blood, which causes erection of the penis and engorgement of the area surrounding the vaginal opening

Anaphrodisiacs Drugs or other agents with effects that are antagonistic to sexual arousal or sexual desire

it may make the thought of sex unappealing. It does not directly dampen sexual response, however.

Other chemicals do dampen sexual arousal and response. Tranquilizers and central nervous system depressants, such as barbiturates, can lessen sexual desire and impair sexual performance. These drugs may paradoxically enhance sexual arousal in some people, however, by lessening sexual inhibitions or fear of possible repercussions from sexual activity. Antihypertensive drugs, which are used in the treatment of high blood pressure, may produce erectile and ejaculatory difficulties in men and reduction of sexual desire in men and women. Certain antidepressant drugs, such as fluoxetine (brand name Prozac), amitriptyline (brand name Elavil), and imipramine (brand name Tofranil) appear to dampen the sex drive (Ostrager, 2006). Antidepressants may also impair erectile response and delay ejaculation in men and orgasmic responsiveness in women (Ostrager, 2006). (Because they delay ejaculation, some of these drugs are used to treat premature ejaculation.)

Nicotine, the stimulant in tobacco smoke, constricts the blood vessels. Thus, it can impede sexual arousal by reducing the capacity of the genitals to become engorged with blood. Chronic smoking can also reduce the blood levels of testosterone in men, which can in turn lessen sex drive or motivation.

Antiandrogen drugs may have anaphrodisiac effects. They have been used in the treatment of deviant behavior patterns such as sexual violence and sexual interest in children, with some promising results (e.g., Roesler & Witztum, 2000).

Psychoactive Drugs

Psychoactive drugs such as alcohol and cocaine are widely believed to have aphrodisiac effects. Do any psychoactive drugs stimulate a sexual response? Perhaps some do, but their effects may also reflect our expectations of them, or their effects on sexual inhibitions, rather than direct stimulation of sexual response.

ALCOHOL   Small amounts of alcohol are stimulating, but large amounts curb sexual response. This fact should not be surprising, because alcohol is a depressant. Alcohol reduces central nervous system activity. Large amounts of alcohol can severely impair sexual performance in both men and women.

People who drink moderate amounts of alcohol may feel more sexually aroused because of their expectations about alcohol, not because of its chemical properties (George et al., 2000). That is, people who expect alcohol to enhance sexual responsiveness may act the part. Expectations that alcohol serves as an aphrodisiac may lead men with problems achieving erection to turn to alcohol as a cure. The fact is that alcohol *is* a depressant, and a few drinks can reduce sexual potency rather than restore it.

Alcohol may also lower sexual inhibitions, because it allows us to ascribe our behavior to the effects of the alcohol rather than to ourselves. Alcohol is connected with a liberated social role and thus provides an excuse for dubious behavior. "It was the alcohol," people can say, "not me." People may express their sexual desires and do things when drinking that they would not do when sober. For example, a person who feels guilty about sex may become sexually active when drinking because he or she can later blame the alcohol.

Binge drinking—having five or more drinks in a row for a male, or four or more for a female—is connected with high-risk sexual behavior, sexual promiscuity, and sexual assault (Champion et al., 2004; Howard & Wang, 2004; Young et al., 2005). Nevertheless, more than two out of five college students binge at least twice a month,

Antiandrogen A substance that decreases the levels of androgens in the bloodstream

What Are the Effects of Alcohol on Sexual Behavior? *Small doses of alcohol can be stimulating, induce feelings of euphoria, and lower inhibitions, all of which could be connected with sexual interest and could facilitate social and sexual behavior. Alcohol also reduces fear of consequences of engaging in risky behavior—sexual and otherwise. Alcohol also provides an excuse for otherwise unacceptable behavior, such as sexual intercourse on the first date (or upon a casual meeting). That is, drinkers can say, "It was the alcohol, not me." Alcohol is also expected to be sexually liberating, and people often live up to social and cultural expectations. Yet, as a depressant drug, large amounts of alcohol will biochemically dampen sexual response.*

and half this number binge three or more times every two weeks (Johnston et al., 2005; National Institute of Alcohol Abuse and Alcoholism, 2005).

Alcohol can also induce feelings of euphoria. Euphoric feelings may enhance sexual arousal and also wash away qualms about expressing sexual desires. Alcohol also appears to impair the ability to weigh information that might otherwise inhibit sexual impulses (MacDonald et al., 2000; Steele & Josephs, 1990). When people drink, they may be less able to foresee the consequences of misconduct and less likely to ponder their standards of conduct.

HALLUCINOGENICS   There is no evidence that marijuana and other hallucinogenic drugs directly stimulate sexual response. However, fairly to strongly intoxicated marijuana users claim to have more empathy with others, to be more aware of bodily sensations, and to experience time as passing more slowly. These sensations could heighten subjective feelings of sexual response, although some marijuana users report that it inhibits their sexual responsiveness (McCabe et al., 2005; van den Bree & Pickworth, 2005). The effects of the drug on sexual response may depend on prior experiences with it, attitudes toward it, and the amount used.

Other hallucinogenics, such as LSD and mescaline, have also been reported by some users to enhance sexual response. Again, these effects may reflect dosage level, as well as expectations, user experiences, attitudes toward the drugs, and altered perceptions.

STIMULANTS   Stimulants such as amphetamines ("speed," "uppers," "bennies," "dexies") have been reputed to heighten arousal and sensations of orgasm. High

REFLECT

Have you done anything under the influence of alcohol or other drugs that you otherwise would not have done? What role did the drug play? Are you sure?

doses can give rise to irritability, restlessness, hallucinations, paranoid delusions, insomnia, and loss of appetite. These drugs generally activate the central nervous system but are not known to have specific sexual effects. Nevertheless, arousing the nervous system can contribute to sexual arousal (Palace, 1995). The drugs can also elevate mood, and perhaps sexual pleasure is heightened by general elation.

Cocaine is a natural stimulant that is extracted from the leaves of the coca plant—the plant from which the soft drink Coca-Cola obtained its name. In fact, Coke—Coca-Cola, that is—contained cocaine as part of its original formula. Cocaine was removed from the secret formula in 1906 and was replaced with extra caffeine (www.sciencemuseum.org.uk, 2006). Cocaine is ingested in various forms, snorted as a powder, smoked in hardened rock form ("crack" cocaine) or in a freebase form, or injected directly into the bloodstream in liquid form. Cocaine produces a euphoric rush, which tends to ebb quickly. Physically, cocaine constricts blood vessels (reducing the oxygen supply to the heart), elevates blood pressure, and boosts the heart rate. There is also evidence that cocaine enhances sexual arousal in both males and females, in part by increasing levels of the neurotransmitter dopamine (Andersen et al., 2003; Andersen & Tufik, 2005; Festa et al., 2004). In addition, the use of crack cocaine is connected with a higher number of sex partners (Maranda et al., 2004).

CRITICAL
Thinking

Critical thinkers are cautious in their interpretation of research findings. There is evidence that the use of crack is connected with having more sex partners. Does this connection mean that the relationship is causal? Can you think of other possible explanations of the relationship?

Sexual Response and the Brain: Cerebral Sex?

The brain may not be an erogenous zone, but it plays a central role in sexual functioning (Fisher, 2000). Direct genital stimulation may trigger spinal reflexes that produce erection in the male, and vaginal lubrication in the female, without direct involvement of the brain. The same reflexes may also be triggered by sexual stimulation that originates in the brain in the form of erotic memories, fantasies, visual images, and thoughts, however. The brain may also inhibit sexual responsiveness, such as when we experience guilt or anxiety in a sexual situation, or when we suddenly realize in the midst of a sexual encounter that we have left the car lights turned on. Let us explore the brain mechanisms involved in sexual functioning.

Parts of the brain, in particular the cerebral cortex and the limbic system, play key roles in sexual functioning (Figure 5.1). Cells in the cerebral cortex fire (transmit messages) when we experience sexual thoughts, images, wishes, fantasies, and the like. Cells in the cerebral cortex interpret sensory information as sexual turn-ons or turn-offs. The sight of your lover disrobing, the anticipation of a romantic kiss, a passing sexual fantasy, or an erotic photo can trigger the firing of cortical cells. These cells, in turn, transmit messages through the spinal cord that send blood rushing to the genitals, causing erection or vaginal lubrication. The cortex also provides the conscious sense of self. The cortex judges sexual behavior to be proper or improper, moral or immoral, relaxing or anxiety or guilt provoking.

Areas of the brain below the cortex, especially the limbic system, also play roles in sexual processes (Kimble, 1992). For example, when the rear part of a male rat's hypothalamus is stimulated by an electrical probe, the animal mechanically runs through its courting and mounting routine. It nibbles at the ears and the back of the neck of a female rat and mounts her when she responds. People, of course, are influenced by learning, fantasy, and values as well as simple brain (or spinal) stimulation.

The importance of the limbic system in sexual behavior in animals was demonstrated in experiments by Heinrich Klüver and Paul Bucy. Klüver and Bucy (1939) re-

CRITICAL
Thinking

If you electrically stimulate part of the rat's brain, it mechanically runs through a mating routine. Does it seem useful or wise to attempt to apply this research finding to humans?

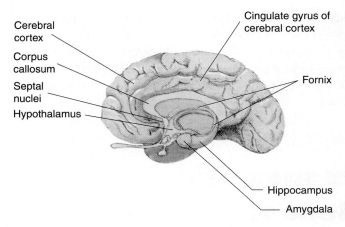

Figure 5.1 **Parts of the Brain Involved in Sexual Functioning.** *A view of the brain, split from top to bottom. Cells in the cerebral cortex transmit messages when we experience sexual thoughts and mental images. Cells in the cortex interpret sensory information as sexual turn-ons or turn-offs. The cerebral cortex may then transmit messages through the spinal cord that send blood coursing to the sex organs, leading to erection or vaginal lubrication. The limbic system lies along the inner edge of the cerebrum. When part of a male rat's hypothalamus is electrically stimulated, the rat engages in its courting and mounting routine. Klüver and Bucy (1939) found that destruction of areas of the limbic system triggered continuous sexual behavior in monkeys. Electrical stimulation of the hippocacampus and septal nuclei produces erections in monkeys.*

ported that destruction of areas of the limbic system triggered persistent sexual behaviors that included masturbation and male–female and male–male mounting attempts. The monkeys even tried to mount the experimenters. For obvious ethical reasons, researchers have not injured or destroyed parts of people's brains to observe the effects on humans.

Electrical stimulation of the hippocampus and septum of the limbic system can produce erections in laboratory monkeys (Ferris et al., 2004). Electrical stimulation of a pathway in the thalamus, moreover, produced a seminal discharge in these monkeys—without erection. Stimulation of certain areas in the thalamus and hypothalamus may induce ejaculation. It remains to be seen how these findings will be useful with humans.

On Pushing the Right Buttons: Are There Pleasure Centers in the Brain?

Research with electrical probes suggests that "pleasure centers" may exist in and near the hypothalamus in other animals and perhaps even in people. Classic research found that when electrodes are implanted in certain parts of the limbic system, investigators find that laboratory animals such as rats (Olds, 1956; Olds & Milner, 1954) will repeatedly press controls to receive bursts of electricity. Of course we cannot know what the rats experience, but people report that stimulation of these so-called pleasure centers led to feelings of sexual arousal and gratification.

Heath (1972) found that electrical stimulation of the septal region of the limbic system resulted in orgasm-like sensations in two people. Delgado (1969) reported that two female epileptic patients who received limbic stimulation as part of a diagnostic evaluation became sexually aroused by the stimulation:

> [One] reported a pleasant tingling sensation in the left side of her body "from my face down to the bottom of my legs." She started giggling and . . . [stated] that she enjoyed the sensation "very much." Repetition of these stimulations made the patient more communicative and flirtatious, and she ended by openly expressing her desire to marry the therapist. [The other patient reported] a pleasant sensation of relaxation and considerably increased her verbal output, which took on a more intimate character. [She] expressed her fondness for the therapist [whom she had just met], kissed his hands, and talked about her immense gratitude. (p. 145)

TRUTH fiction 5

Truth or Fiction Revisited: It is apparently true that electrical stimulation of certain areas in the human brain can yield sensations similar to those of sexual pleasure and gratification. We might wonder whether we would bother to develop sexual relationships if such centers could be stimulated directly. But before you run to the store for electrodes, consider that few researchers suggest that we will someday replace lovers with electronic kits.

Sex Hormones and Sexual Behavior

In a TV situation comedy, a male adolescent was described as a "hormone with feet." Ask parents why teenagers act the way they do, and you are likely to hear a one-word answer: Hormones!

Hormones are chemicals that are secreted by the ductless glands of the endocrine system directly into the bloodstream. The word *hormone* derives from the Greek *horman,* meaning "to stimulate" or "to goad." We could say that they very much goad us into sexual activity. Hormones also regulate various bodily functions, including growth and resistance to stress as well as sexual functions.

The hypothalamus and pituitary gland regulate gonadal secretion of sex hormones, specifically testosterone in males and estrogen and progesterone in females. At puberty a surge of sex hormones causes the blossoming of reproductive maturation: the sperm-producing ability of the testes in males and the maturation of ova and ovulation in females. Sex hormones released at puberty also cause the flowering of **secondary sex characteristics**. In males, the vocal cords lengthen (and the voice consequently lowers), and facial and pubic hair grow. In females, the breasts and hips become rounded with fatty tissue, and pubic hair grows.

Organizing and Activating Influences

Sex hormones have organizing and activating effects on behavior. That is, they exert an influence on the type of behavior that is expressed (an organizing effect) and the frequency or intensity of the drive that motivates the behavior and the ability to perform the behavior (activating effects). For example, sex hormones predispose lower animals and possibly people toward stereotypical masculine or feminine mating behaviors (an organizing effect). They also facilitate sexual response and influence sexual desire (activating effects).

Although sex hormones clearly determine the sex of the partners many lower animals will seek, their roles in human sexual behavior may be relatively more subtle and are not as well understood. Much of our knowledge of the organizing and activating effects of sex hormones comes from research with other species in which hormone levels are manipulated by castration or injection. Ethical standards prohibit such research with human infants, for obvious reasons.

The activating effects of testosterone can be clearly observed among male rats. For example, males who are castrated in adulthood, and thus deprived of testosterone, discontinue sexual behavior. If they are given injections of testosterone, however, they resume stereotypical male sexual behaviors, such as mounting females.

Secondary sex characteristics Physical traits that differentiate males from females but are not directly involved in reproduction

Are Adolescents "Hormones with Feet"? *Research shows that levels of androgens are connected with sexual interest in both male and female adolescents. Hormone levels are more likely to predict sexual behavior in adolescent males, however, perhaps because society places greater restraints on female sexuality.*

In rats, testosterone apparently organizes or differentiates the brain in the masculine direction such that adult male rats display stereotypical masculine behaviors—including sniffing (especially sniffing females) and mounting females—upon activation by testosterone. Male fetuses and newborns normally have sufficient amounts of testosterone in their blood systems to organize their brains in the masculine direction. Female fetuses and newborns normally have lesser amounts of testosterone. Their brains thus become organized in a feminine direction. When female rats are prenatally exposed to large doses of testosterone, their sexual organs became somewhat masculinized, and they are predisposed toward masculine mating behaviors in adulthood (Carlson, 2007).

In rats and other rodents, sexual differentiation of the brain is not complete at birth. Female rodents who are given testosterone injections shortly before or shortly after birth (depending on the species) show typical masculine sexual patterns in adulthood, mounting other females and resisting mounting by males (Ellis & Ames, 1987).

Questions remain about the organizing effects of sex hormones on human sexual behavior. Prenatal sex hormones are known to play a role in the sexual differentiation of the genitalia and of the brain structures, such as the hypothalamus. Their role in patterning sexual behavior in adulthood remains unknown, however. Some researchers have speculated that the brains of **transsexual** individuals may have been prenatally sexually differentiated in one direction, while their genitals were being differentiated in the other (Money, 1994). It has been speculated that prenatal sexual differentiation of the brain may also be connected with sexual orientation (see Chapter 10).

What of the activating effects of sex hormones on human sex drive and behavior? Although the countless attempts to extract or synthesize aphrodisiacs have failed to produce the real thing, men and women normally produce a genuine aphrodisiac—testosterone. Testosterone activates the sex drives of both men and women (Guzick & Hoeger, 2000).

Transsexual A person who feels that he or she is really a member of the other sex and is trapped in a body of the wrong sex

Sex Hormones and Male Sexual Behavior

Male sex hormones are known to influence the sex drive and sexual response in non-human animals and men (Bialy & Sachs, 2002; Cooke et al., 2003). Evidence of the role for hormones in the sex drive is found among men who have declines in testosterone levels as the result of chemical or surgical castration. Surgical castration (removal of the testes) is sometimes performed as a medical treatment for cancer of the prostate or other diseases of the male reproductive tract, such as genital tuberculosis. But some convicted sex offenders have voluntarily undergone castration as a condition of release.

Men who are surgically or chemically castrated usually exhibit a gradual decrease in the incidence of sexual fantasies and loss of sexual desire (Bradford, 1998; Gijs & Gooren, 1996). They also gradually tend to lose their capacity to attain erection and to ejaculate—an indication that testosterone is important in maintaining sexual functioning as well as drive, at least in males. Castrated men show great variation in their sexual interest and functioning, however. Some continue to experience sexual desires and are able to function sexually for years, even decades. Learning appears to play a large role in determining continued sexual response after castration. Males who were sexually experienced before castration show a more gradual decline in sexual activity. Those who were sexually inexperienced at the time show relatively little or no interest in sex. Male sexual motivation and functioning thus involve an interplay of hormonal influences and experience.

Further evidence of the relationship between hormonal levels and male sexuality is found in studies of men with **hypogonadism,** a condition marked by abnormally low levels of testosterone production. Hypogonadal men generally suffer loss of sexual desire and a decline in sexual activity (McElduff & Beange, 2003). Here again, hormones do not tell the whole story. Hypogonadal men are capable of erection, at least for a while, even though their sex drive may wane. The role of testosterone as an activator of sex drive in men is further supported by evidence of the effects of testosterone replacement in hypogonadal men. When such men obtain testosterone injections, their sex drive, fantasies, and activity are often restored to former levels (Seidman, 2003; Tan & Culberson, 2003).

Although minimal levels of androgens are critical to male sexuality, there is no one-to-one correspondence between hormone levels and sex drive or sexual performance in adults. In men who have ample supplies of testosterone, sexual interest and functioning depend more on learning, fantasies, attitudes, memories, and other psychosocial factors than on hormone levels. At puberty, however, hormonal variations may play a more direct role in stimulating sexual interest and activity in males. Udry (2001) found, for example, that testosterone levels predicted sexual interest, masturbation rates, and the likelihood of engaging in sexual intercourse among teenage boys. A positive relationship also has been found between testosterone levels in adult men and frequency of sexual intercourse (Dabbs & Morris, 1990). Moreover, drugs that reduce the levels of androgen in the blood system—antiandrogens—lead to reductions in sex drive and in sexual fantasies (Bradford, 1998).

Truth or Fiction Revisited: Men and women each produce small amounts of the sex hormones of the other sex. Testosterone, the major form of androgen, or male sex hormone, is secreted in small amounts by the adrenal glands (located above the kidneys) in both sexes, but in much larger amounts by the testes. The ovaries produce small amounts of androgens but much larger amounts of the female sex hormones,

TRUTH fiction 6

Hypogonadism An abnormal condition marked by abnormally low levels of testosterone production

estrogen and progesterone. The testes similarly produce small amounts of estrogen and progesterone.

Sex Hormones and Female Sexual Behavior

The female sex hormones estrogen and progesterone play prominent roles in promoting the changes that occur during puberty and in regulating the menstrual cycle. Female sex hormones do not appear to play a direct role in determining sexual motivation or response in human females, however.

In most mammals, females are sexually receptive only during estrus. *Estrus* is a brief period of fertility that corresponds to time of ovulation; and, during estrus, females are said to be "in heat." Estrus occurs once a year in some species; in others, it occurs periodically during the year in mating seasons. Estrogen peaks at the time of ovulation, so there is a close relationship between fertility and sexual receptivity in most female mammals. Human female sexuality is not clearly linked to hormonal fluctuations, however. Unlike females of most other species of mammals, the human female is sexually responsive during all phases of the reproductive (menstrual) cycle—even during menstruation, when ovarian hormone levels are low—and after menopause.

There is some evidence, however, that sexual responsiveness in women is influenced by the presence of circulating androgens, or male sex hormones, in their bodies. The adrenal glands of women produce small amounts of androgens, just as they do in men (Guzick & Hoeger, 2000). The fact that women normally produce smaller amounts of androgens than men does not mean that they necessarily have a weaker sex drive. Rather, women appear to be more sensitive to smaller amounts of androgens. For women, it seems that less is more.

Women who have **ovariectomies**, which are sometimes carried out when a hysterectomy is performed, no longer produce female sex hormones. Nevertheless, they may continue to experience a sex drive and interest in sex as before. Loss of the ovarian hormone estradiol may cause vaginal dryness and make coitus painful, but it does not necessarily reduce sexual desire. (The dryness can be alleviated by a lubricating jelly or by estrogen replacement therapy [ERT].) However, women whose adrenal glands and ovaries have been removed, so that they no longer produce androgens, gradually lose sexual desire (Nappi et al., 2006; Traish et al., 2006). An active and enjoyable sexual history seems to ward off this loss, however, suggestive of the impact of cognitive and experiential factors on human sexual response.

Research provides evidence of the links between testosterone levels and women's sex drives (Williams, 1999). Androgens apparently affect sexual desire in both sexes, but sexual interest may be more likely to be directly translated into sexual activity in men than in women (Peplau, 2003). This sex difference may be explained by society's placement of greater restraints on female sexuality.

Other researchers report that women's sexual activity increases at points in the menstrual cycle when levels of androgens in the bloodstream are high (Guay, 2001; Morley & Perry, 2003). Another study was conducted with women whose ovaries had been surgically removed (*surgical menopause*) as a way of treating disease. The ovaries supply major quantities of estrogen. After surgery, the women in this study were treated either with ERT, with ERT plus androgens, or with a placebo (an inert substance made to resemble an active drug) (Sherwin et al., 1985). This was a double-blind study. Neither the women nor their physicians knew which drug the women

Ovariectomy Surgical removal of the ovaries

REFLECT

Do you know people who have taken testosterone or estrogen for medical or other reasons? What were the reasons for using hormones? What were their effects?

were receiving. The results showed that the combination of androgens and ERT heightened sexual desire and sexual fantasies more than ERT alone or the placebo. The combination also helped women maintain a sense of psychological well-being (Guzick & Hoeger, 2000).

Androgens thus play a more prominent role than ovarian hormones in activating and maintaining women's sex drives. As with men, however, women's sexuality is too complex to be explained fully by hormone levels. For example, an active and enjoyable sexual history seems to ward off the loss of sexual interest that generally follows the surgical removal of the adrenal glands and ovaries.

Sexual Response

Although we may be culturally attuned to focus on sex differences rather than similarities, Masters and Johnson (1966) found that the physiological responses of men and women to sexual stimulation (whether from coitus, masturbation, or other sources) are quite alike. The sequence of changes in the body that takes place as men and women become progressively more aroused is referred to as the **sexual response cycle**.

The Four-Phase Masters and Johnson Sexual Response Cycle

Masters and Johnson (1966) divided the sexual response cycle into four phases: excitement, plateau, orgasm, and resolution. Figure 5.2 suggests the levels of sexual arousal associated with each phase. Both males and females experience vasocongestion and **myotonia** early during the response cycle. Vasocongestion is the swelling of the genital tissues with blood, which causes erection of the penis and engorgement of the area surrounding the vaginal opening. The testes, nipples, and even earlobes become engorged as blood vessels in these areas dilate.

Myotonia refers to muscle tension. Myotonia causes voluntary and involuntary muscle contractions, which produce facial grimaces, spasms in the hands and feet, and eventually, the spasms of orgasm. Let us follow these and the other bodily changes that constitute the sexual response cycle.

EXCITEMENT PHASE In younger men, vasocongestion during the **excitement phase** produces penile erection as early as three to eight seconds after stimulation begins. Erection may occur more slowly in older men, but the response is essentially the same. Erection may subside and return as stimulation varies. The scrotal skin thickens, losing its baggy appearance. The testes increase in size. The testes and scrotum become elevated.

In the female, vaginal lubrication may start 10 to 30 seconds after stimulation begins. Vasocongestion swells the clitoris, flattens the labia majora and spreads them apart, and increases the size of the labia minora. The inner two thirds of the vagina expands. The vaginal walls thicken and, because of the inflow of blood, turn from their normal pink to a deeper hue. The uterus becomes engorged and elevated. The breasts enlarge, and blood vessels near the surface become more prominent.

Sexual response cycle Masters' and Johnson's model of sexual response, which consists of four phases

Myotonia Muscle tension

Excitement phase The first phase of the sexual response cycle; characterized by erection in the male, vaginal lubrication in the female, muscle tension, and an increase in heart rate in both males and females

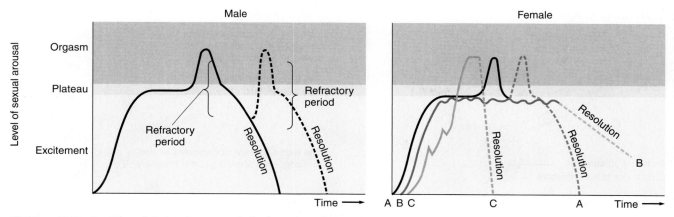

Figure 5.2 Levels of Sexual Arousal during the Phases of the Sexual
Response Cycle. *Masters and Johnson (1966) divide the sexual response cycle into four phases: excitement, plateau, orgasm, and resolution. During the resolution phase, the level of sexual arousal returns to the prearoused state. For men there is a refractory period after orgasm. As shown by the broken line, however, men can become rearoused to orgasm after the refractory period has passed and their level of sexual arousal returns to preplateau levels. Pattern A for women shows a typical response cycle, with the broken line suggesting multiple orgasms. Pattern B shows the cycle of a woman who reaches the plateau phase, but for whom arousal is "resolved" without reaching the orgasmic phase. Pattern C shows the possibility of orgasm in a highly aroused woman who passes quickly through the plateau phase.*

The skin may take on a rosy **sex flush** late during this phase. It varies with intensity of arousal and is more pronounced in women. The nipples may become erect in both sexes, especially in response to direct stimulation. Men and women show some increase in myotonia, heart rate, and blood pressure.

SafeZone

Q *I don't get an erection as quickly as I used to. What is wrong with me?*

A Could be nothing. After the later teens, it's all downhill, physiologically speaking, but it's a very, very long slope—and a very gradual one. Also, in your middle teens you'll have an erection in just a few seconds, so what does it matter if it takes a few more seconds, or a minute or two? Even when you're in your 50s and older, when it can take a few minutes and manual or oral stimulation to become erect, it's the quality of the overall experience that ought to matter and not the stopwatch. So many of our sexual problems are actually problems with our "oughts" and our "shoulds," or with our partner's "oughts" and "shoulds," and not with our bodies. Keep in mind that sex is not a race.

PLATEAU PHASE   A plateau is a level region, and the level of arousal remains somewhat constant during the **plateau phase** of sexual response. Nevertheless, the plateau phase is an <u>advanced state of arousal that precedes orgasm</u>. Men in this phase show a slight increase in the circumference of the coronal ridge of the penis. The penile glans turns a purplish hue, a sign of vasocongestion. The testes are elevated further into position for ejaculation and may reach one and a half times their unaroused size. Cowper's gland secretes a few droplets of fluid that are found at the tip of the penis (Figure 5.3).

Sex flush A reddish rash that appears on the chest or breasts late during the excitement phase of the sexual response cycle

Plateau phase The second phase of the sexual response cycle, which is characterized by increases in vasocongestion, muscle tension, heart rate, and blood pressure in preparation for orgasm

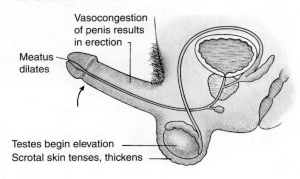

1. EXCITEMENT PHASE

Meatus dilates

Vasocongestion of penis results in erection

Testes begin elevation
Scrotal skin tenses, thickens

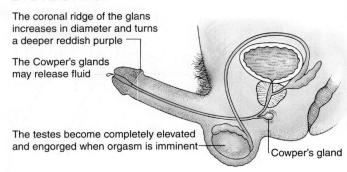

2. PLATEAU PHASE

The coronal ridge of the glans increases in diameter and turns a deeper reddish purple

The Cowper's glands may release fluid

The testes become completely elevated and engorged when orgasm is imminent

Cowper's gland

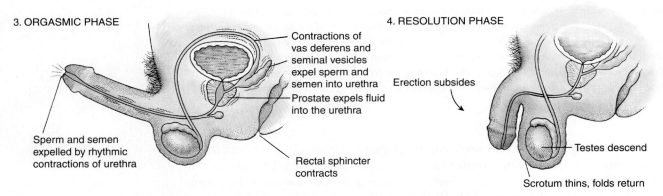

3. ORGASMIC PHASE

Sperm and semen expelled by rhythmic contractions of urethra

Contractions of vas deferens and seminal vesicles expel sperm and semen into urethra

Prostate expels fluid into the urethra

Rectal sphincter contracts

4. RESOLUTION PHASE

Erection subsides

Testes descend

Scrotum thins, folds return

Figure 5.3 The Male Genitals during the Phases of the Sexual Response Cycle

In women, vasocongestion swells the tissues of the outer third of the vagina, contracting the vaginal opening (thus preparing it to "grasp" the penis) and building the **orgasmic platform** (Figure 5.4). The inner part of the vagina expands fully. The uterus becomes fully elevated. The clitoris withdraws beneath the clitoral hood and shortens. Thus, a woman (or her partner) may feel that the clitoris has become lost. This may be mistaken as a sign that the woman's sexual arousal is waning, although it is actually increasing.

Coloration of the labia minora appears, which is referred to as the **sex skin**. The labia minora become a deep wine color in women who have borne children and bright red in women who have not. Further engorgement of the areolas of the breasts may make it seem that the nipples have lost part of their erection (Figure 5.5). Bartholin's glands secrete a fluid that resembles mucus.

About one man in four and about three women in four show a sex flush, which often does not appear until the plateau phase. Myotonia may cause spasmodic contractions in the hands and feet, and facial grimaces. Breathing becomes rapid, like panting, and the heart rate may increase to 100 to 160 beats per minute. Blood pressure continues to rise. The increase in heart rate is usually less dramatic with masturbation than during coitus.

Orgasmic platform The thickening of the walls of the outer third of the vagina, resulting from vasocongestion, that occurs during the plateau phase of the sexual response cycle

Sex skin Reddening of the labia minora that occurs during the plateau phase

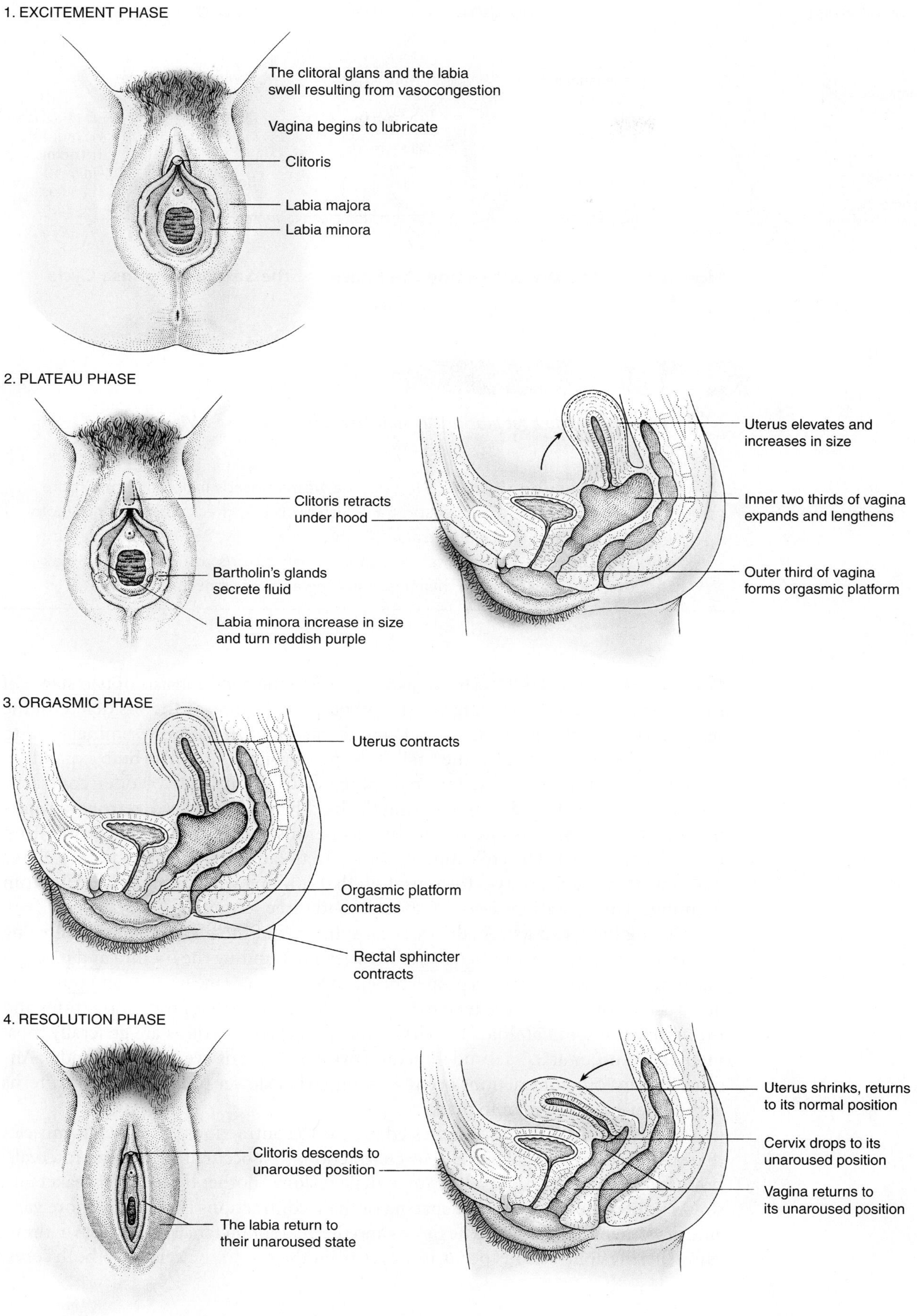

1. EXCITEMENT PHASE

The clitoral glans and the labia swell resulting from vasocongestion

Vagina begins to lubricate

Clitoris

Labia majora

Labia minora

2. PLATEAU PHASE

Clitoris retracts under hood

Bartholin's glands secrete fluid

Labia minora increase in size and turn reddish purple

Uterus elevates and increases in size

Inner two thirds of vagina expands and lengthens

Outer third of vagina forms orgasmic platform

3. ORGASMIC PHASE

Uterus contracts

Orgasmic platform contracts

Rectal sphincter contracts

4. RESOLUTION PHASE

Clitoris descends to unaroused position

The labia return to their unaroused state

Uterus shrinks, returns to its normal position

Cervix drops to its unaroused position

Vagina returns to its unaroused position

Figure 5.4 The Female Genitals during the Phases of the Sexual Response Cycle

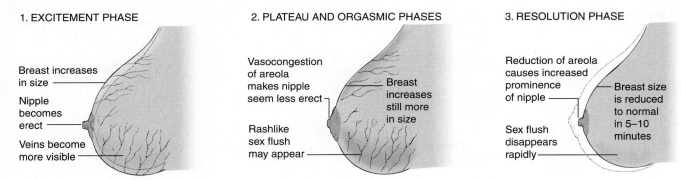

| 1. EXCITEMENT PHASE | 2. PLATEAU AND ORGASMIC PHASES | 3. RESOLUTION PHASE |

Breast increases in size

Nipple becomes erect

Veins become more visible

Vasocongestion of areola makes nipple seem less erect

Breast increases still more in size

Rashlike sex flush may appear

Reduction of areola causes increased prominence of nipple

Breast size is reduced to normal in 5–10 minutes

Sex flush disappears rapidly

Figure 5.5 The Breasts during the Phases of the Sexual Response Cycle

SafeZone

Q *Sometimes I don't get lubricated, and intercourse is painful. Why don't I get lubricated?*

A There are many possibilities. Sometimes a woman needs more time or a more comfortable setting. If you suspect a health problem, check with your gynecologist. You can also try an artificial lubricant, like K-Y jelly. But by and large, simply ask yourself two questions: Do you know what turns you on? Are you making sure you get it? Maybe this means getting a new partner!

ORGASMIC PHASE   The orgasmic phase in the male consists of two stages of muscular contractions. During the first stage, contractions of the vas deferens, the seminal vesicles, the ejaculatory duct, and the prostate gland cause seminal fluid to collect in the urethral bulb at the base of the penis (Figure 5.3). The bulb expands to accommodate the fluid. The internal sphincter of the urinary bladder contracts, preventing seminal fluid from entering the bladder in a backward, retrograde ejaculation. The normal closing off of the bladder also serves to prevent urine from mixing with semen. The collection of semen in the urethral bulb produces feelings of ejaculatory inevitability—the sensation that nothing will stop the ejaculate from "coming." This sensations lasts for about two to three seconds.

During the second stage, the external sphincter of the bladder relaxes, allowing the passage of semen. Contractions of muscles surrounding the urethra and urethral bulb and the base of the penis propel the ejaculate through the urethra and out of the body. Sensations of pleasure tend to be related to the strength of the contractions and the amount of seminal fluid. The first three to four contractions are generally most intense and occur at 0.8-second intervals (five contractions every four seconds). Another two to four contractions occur at a somewhat slower pace. Rates and patterns vary somewhat from man to man.

Orgasm in the female is manifested by 3 to 15 contractions of the pelvic muscles that surround the vaginal barrel. The contractions first occur at 0.8-second intervals, producing, as in the male, a release of sexual tension. Another three to six weaker and slower contractions follow. The spacing of these contractions is generally more variable in women than in men. The uterus and the anal sphincter also contract rhythmically. Uterine contractions occur in waves from the top to the cervix. In both sexes, muscles go into spasm throughout the body. Blood pressure and heart rate reach a peak, with the heart beating up to 180 times per minute. Respiration may increase to 40 breaths per minute.

SafeZone

Q *Is there such thing as a female ejaculation? How does it occur? Where does the fluid come from?*

A This is controversial. Some researchers find evidence of an ejaculate in some women. It could be urine or it might be released by a system called Skene's glands. The only thing we're certain of is that women usually have nothing to worry about if they expel a little liquid during orgasm.

SUBJECTIVE EXPERIENCE OF ORGASM The sensations of orgasm have challenged the descriptive powers of poets. Words like *rush, warmth, explosion,* and *release* do not adequately capture them. We may assume (rightly or wrongly) that others of our sex experience pretty much what we do, but can we understand the sensations of the other sex?

Truth or Fiction Revisited: Several studies suggest that written descriptions of women's and men's orgasms cannot be told apart. The orgasms of both may feel quite similar. In one study, 48 men and women provided written descriptions of orgasms. The researchers (Proctor et al., 1974) modified the language (e.g., changing "penis" to "genitals") so that the authors' sexes would not be apparent. They then asked 70 "experts" (psychologists, gynecologists, and so forth) to indicate the sex of each author. The ratings were no more reliable than guesswork—at least when they were altered to exclude language that gives away exactly which anatomic features are involved. (Thus, this truth-or-fiction item is only qualifiedly "true." Listen: Life is complex. Be tolerant.)

TRUTH fiction **7**

RESOLUTION PHASE The period following orgasm, in which the body returns to its prearoused state, is called the **resolution phase**. After ejaculation, the man loses his erection in two stages. The first occurs in about a minute. Half the volume of the erection is lost as blood from the corpora cavernosa empties into other parts of the body. The second stage occurs during a period of several minutes: The remaining tumescence subsides as the corpus spongiosum empties. The testes and scrotum return to normal size, and the scrotum regains its wrinkled appearance.

In women orgasm also triggers release of blood from engorged areas. In the absence of continued stimulation, swelling of the areolas decreases, then the nipples return to normal size. The sex flush lightens rapidly. In about 5 to 10 seconds, the clitoris descends to its normal position. The clitoris, vaginal barrel, uterus, and labia gradually shrink to their prearoused sizes. The labia minora turn lighter (the "sex skin" disappears) in about 10 to 15 seconds.

Most muscle tension (myotonia) tends to dissipate within five minutes after orgasm in both men and women. Blood pressure, heart rate, and respiration may also return to their prearousal levels within a few minutes. About 30% to 40% of men and women find their palms, the soles of their feet, or their entire bodies covered with a sheen of perspiration. Both men and women may feel relaxed and satiated.

Resolution phase The fourth phase of the sexual response cycle, during which the body gradually returns to its prearoused state

Although the processes by which the body returns to its prearousal state are similar in men and women, there is an important sex difference during the resolution phase. Unlike women, men enter a **refractory period** during which they are physiologically incapable of experiencing another orgasm or ejaculation. The refractory period of adolescent males may last only minutes, whereas that of men age 50 and older may last from several minutes (yes, "it could happen") to a day. Women do not undergo a refractory period and so can become quickly rearoused to the point of repeated **(multiple) orgasms** if they desire and receive continued sexual stimulation (Figure 5.2).

Myotonia and vasocongestion may take an hour or more to dissipate in people who are aroused but who do not reach orgasm. Persistent pelvic vasocongestion may cause "blue balls" in males—the slang term for a throbbing ache. Some men insist that their dates should consent to coitus, because it is unfair to stimulate them to the point at which they have this condition. This condition can be relieved through masturbation as well as coitus, however—or can dissipate naturally. Although it may be uncomfortable, it is not dangerous and should not be an excuse to pressure or coerce another person into any sexual activity. "Blue" sensations are not limited to men. Women, too, may experience unpleasant pelvic throbbing if they have become highly aroused and do not find release. Women, too, can relieve the throbbing through masturbation.

Truth or Fiction Revisited: Masters and Johnson (1966) did find that orgasms experienced during masturbation were generally more physiologically intense than those experienced during intercourse. Perhaps masturbation allows one to focus only on one's own pleasure and ensure that one receives effective stimulation to climax. This does not mean that orgasms during masturbation are more enjoyable or gratifying than those experienced through coitus. Given the sexual attraction and emotional connectedness we may feel toward our lovers, we are unlikely to break off relationships in favor of masturbation. "Physiological intensity" does not directly translate into subjective pleasure or fulfillment.

TRUTH fiction 8

Kaplan's Three Stages of Sexual Response: An Alternative Model

Perhaps the only alternative view of the sexual response cycle that has received continued attention is the one proposed by Helen Singer Kaplan. Kaplan was a prominent sex therapist and author of several professional books (Kaplan, 1974, 1987) on sex therapy. Whereas Masters and Johnson (1966) had proposed a four-stage model of sexual response, Kaplan developed a three-stage model consisting of (1) desire, (2) excitement, and (3) orgasm. Kaplan's model is an outgrowth of her clinical experience in working with people with sexual dysfunctions. She believes that their problems can best be classified according to these three phases. Kaplan's model makes it convenient for clinicians to classify sexual dysfunctions involving desire (low or absent desire), excitement (such as problems with erection in the male or lubrication in the female), and orgasm (such as premature ejaculation in the male or orgasmic dysfunction in the female).

Masters and Johnson (1966) view the sexual response as composed of successive stages; the order is crucial and invariant. Kaplan treats her phases as relatively independent components of sexual response with a sequence that is somewhat variable.

Refractory period The period of time following a response (e.g., orgasm), during which an individual is no longer responsive to stimulation (e.g., sexual stimulation)

Multiple orgasms One or more additional orgasms following the first, which occur within a short period of time and before the body has returned to a preplateau level of arousal

For example, a person may experience sexual excitement and even orgasm, although sexual desire remains low.

Kaplan's model is noteworthy for designating desire as a separate phase of sexual response. Problems in lack of sexual interest or desire are among the most common brought to the attention of sex therapists.

Controversies about Orgasm

Few other topics in human sexuality have aroused more controversies throughout the years than orgasm. We do not have all the answers, but some intriguing research findings have shed light on some continuing controversies. Are women capable of experiencing multiple orgasms? Are men?

MULTIPLE ORGASMS Kinsey and his colleagues (1953) reported that 14% of their female respondents regularly had multiple orgasms, surprising fellow scientists as well as the community at large. Many people were aghast that women could have more than one orgasm at a time. There were comments (mostly by men, of course!) that the women in the Kinsey surveys must be "nymphomaniacs" who were incapable of being satisfied with the "normal" complement of one orgasm per occasion. However, only 13 years later, Masters and Johnson (1966) reported that most if not all women are capable of multiple orgasms. Although all women may have a biological capability for multiple orgasms, not all women report them. A survey of 720 nurses showed that 43% reported experiencing multiple orgasms (Darling et al., 1991). Nearly half of them experienced multiple orgasms when they used a vibrator. They generally applied the vibrator to the clitoris and reported that orgasms experienced with the vibrator were more intense than other kinds. Two thirds of the women, by the way, used the vibrators in conjunction with sexual activity with their husbands.

By Masters' and Johnson's definition (1966), men are not capable of achieving multiple orgasms, because they enter a refractory period after ejaculation. Men who want more than one orgasm during one session may have to pause for a while, yet women can maintain a high level of arousal between multiple orgasms and have them in rapid succession, because women do not have a refractory period. Women can continue to have orgasms if they continue to receive effective stimulation (and, of course, are interested in continuing). Some men thus refrain from reaching orgasm until their partners have had the desired number. The differential capacity for multiple orgasms is one of the major sex differences in sexual response.

Some men have two or more orgasms without ejaculation ("dry orgasms"), preceding a final ejaculatory orgasm. These men may not enter a refractory period after their initial dry orgasms and may therefore be able to maintain their level of stimulation at near-peak levels.

Masters and Johnson (1966) found that some women experienced 20 or more orgasms by masturbating. Still, few women have multiple orgasms during most sexual encounters, and many are satisfied with just one per occasion. Some women who have read or heard about female orgasmic capacity wonder what is "wrong" with them if they are content with just one. Nothing is wrong with them, of course: A biological capacity does not create a behavioral requirement.

HOW MANY KINDS OF ORGASMS DO WOMEN HAVE? ONE, TWO, OR THREE? Until Masters and Johnson (1966) published their laboratory findings, many people believed that there were two types of female orgasm, as

Does the research finding that women, but not men, experience multiple orgasms challenge any prevailing views about female sexuality?

proposed by the psychoanalyst Sigmund Freud: the clitoral orgasm and the vaginal orgasm. Clitoral orgasms were achieved through direct clitoral stimulation, such as by masturbation. Clitoral orgasms were seen by psychoanalysts (mostly male psychoanalysts, naturally) as emblematic of a childhood fixation—a throwback to an erogenous pattern acquired during childhood masturbation.

The term *vaginal orgasm* referred to an orgasm achieved through coitus and was theorized to be a sign of mature sexuality. Freud argued that women achieve sexual maturity when they forsake clitoral stimulation for vaginal stimulation. This view would be little more than an academic footnote, but for the fact that some adult women who continue to require direct clitoral stimulation to reach orgasm, even during coitus, have been led by traditional (generally male) psychoanalysts to believe that they are sexually "fixated" at an immature stage or are sexually inadequate.

Despite Freudian theory, Masters and Johnson (1966) were able to find only one kind of orgasm, physiologically speaking, regardless of the source of stimulation (manual, clitoral or penile, vaginal). By monitoring physiological responses to sexual stimulation, they found that the female orgasm involves the same biological events whether it is reached through masturbation, petting, coitus, or even stimulation of the breasts. In men, it also matters not how orgasm is achieved—through masturbation, petting, oral sex, coitus, or by fantasizing about a fellow student in chem lab. Orgasm still involves the same physiological processes: Involuntary contractions of the pelvic muscles at the base of the penis expel semen and release sexual tension. A woman or a man might prefer one source of orgasm to another—with a lover rather than by masturbation, or with one person rather than another—but the biological events that define orgasm remain the same.

The purported distinction between clitoral and vaginal orgasms also rests on an assumption that the clitoris is not stimulated during coitus. Masters and Johnson (1966) showed this assumption to be false. Penile coital thrusting draws the clitoral hood back and forth against the clitoris. Vaginal pressure also heightens blood flow in the clitoris, helping set the stage for orgasm.

One might think that Masters's and Johnson's research (1966) settled the question of whether there are different types of female orgasm. Other investigators, however, have proposed that there are distinct forms of female orgasm, yet not those suggested by psychoanalytic theory. For example, Singer and Singer (1972) suggested that there are three types of female orgasm: vulval, uterine, and blended. According to the Singers, the vulval orgasm represents the type of orgasm described by Masters and Johnson (1966). It involves vulval contractions—that is, contractions of the vaginal barrel. Consistent with the findings of Masters and Johnson (1966), they accept that a vulval orgasm remains the same regardless of the source of stimulation, clitoral or vaginal.

According to the Singers (1972), the uterine orgasm does not involve vulval contractions. It occurs only in response to deep penile thrusting against the cervix. This thrusting slightly displaces the uterus and stimulates the tissues that cover the abdominal organs. The uterine orgasm is accompanied by a certain pattern of breathing: gasping or gulping of air is followed by an involuntary holding of the breath as orgasm approaches. When orgasm is reached, the breath is explosively exhaled. The uterine orgasm is accompanied by deep feelings of relaxation and sexual satisfaction.

The third type—blended orgasm—combines features of vulval and uterine orgasms. It involves both an involuntary breath-holding response and contractions of the pelvic muscles. The Singers (1972) note that the type of orgasm a woman experiences—vulval, uterine, or blended—depends on factors such as the parts of the body that are stimulated and the duration of stimulation. Each produces its own kind of satisfaction, and no type is necessarily better or preferable to another. The Singers' (1972) hypothesis of three distinct forms of female orgasm remains controversial.

SafeZone

Q *How can you tell if someone is faking an orgasm?*

A Orgasms can be successfully faked, but ask your partner if you suspect this is happening, so you can work through what each of you wants. A male orgasm is hard to fake because it usually involves ejaculation. A female orgasm, like a male orgasm, involves rapid contraction of muscles in the pelvic floor. They can usually be felt with the penis, tongue, or hand, but sometimes they're slight and can be hard to detect. If a woman has orgasms, her partner may be able to detect the muscle contractions.

1. What are the roles of the senses in sexual arousal?

- Each sense plays a role in sexual experience, but some play more of a role than others. Visual information plays a major role in human sexual attraction. Visual cues can be sexual turn-ons or turn-offs. Although the sense of smell plays a lesser role in governing sexual arousal in humans than in lower mammals, particular odors can be sexual turn-ons or turn-offs. The sense of touch has the most direct effects on sexual arousal and response. Taste appears to play only a minor role in sexual arousal and response. Like visual and olfactory cues, sounds can be turn-ons or turn-offs.

- Many organisms are sexually aroused by naturally produced chemicals called pheromones, but their role in human sexual behavior remains somewhat controversial. On the other hand, there is research evidence that underarm secretions may make men and women more sexually attractive and that male underarm secretions have a positive effect on the moods of women.

- Exposure to the odor of other women's sweat appears to cause the menstrual cycles of women who live together to become synchronized.

- Gay males may be drawn to the body odors of other gay males. Heterosexual males prefer the body odors of females—heterosexual and lesbian—and of heterosexual males to those of gay males.

- Erogenous zones are particularly sensitive to the sense of touch. Primary erogenous zones are particularly sensitive because they are richly endowed with nerve endings. Secondary erogenous zones are body parts that become erotically sensitized through experience.

2. What is an aphrodisiac?

- An aphrodisiac is a substance that is sexually arousing or increases sexual desire. Alleged aphrodisiacs such as Spanish fly and foods that in some way resemble the genitals have not been shown to contribute to sexual arousal or response. The male sex hormone testosterone heightens the sex drive in both males and females. Anaphrodisiacs include amyl nitrate and antiandrogen drugs.

- The alleged aphrodisiac effects of psychoactive drugs, such as alcohol and cocaine, may reflect our expectations or their effects on sexual inhibitions, rather than direct stimulation of sexual response. Alcohol is also connected with a liberated social role and thus provides an external excuse for dubious behavior. Some people report initial increased sexual pleasure with cocaine use, but frequent use can lead to sexual dysfunctions. Wellbutrin and L-dopa may have aphrodisiacal properties.

3. What is the role of the brain in sexual response?

- The cerebral cortex interprets sensory information as sexual turn-ons or turn-offs. The cortex transmits messages through the spinal cord that cause vasocongestion. Direct stimulation of parts of the limbic system causes erection and ejaculation in many male animals. Electrical stimulation of certain parts of the limbic system apparently yields sensations similar to those of sexual gratification.

4. How do hormones affect the sex drive and sexual response?

- Sex hormones have organizing and activating effects on behavior. Men and women normally produce one genuine aphrodisiac: testosterone. Female sex hormones do not appear to play a direct role in determining sexual motivation or response in human females, yet levels of testosterone in the bloodstream have been associated with sexual interest in women.

5. How does the body respond to sexual stimulation?

- William Masters and Virginia Johnson found that the physiological responses of men and women to sexual stimulation are quite alike. Both experience vasocongestion and myotonia early during the response cycle. Sexual excitement is characterized by erection in the male and vaginal lubrication in the female. The plateau phase is an advanced state of arousal that precedes orgasm. The third phase of the sexual response cycle is characterized by orgasmic contractions of the pelvic musculature. Orgasm in the male occurs in two stages of muscular contractions. Orgasm in the female is manifested by contractions of the pelvic muscles that surround the vaginal barrel. During the resolution phase, the body returns to its prearoused state.

- Helen Singer Kaplan developed a three-stage model of sexual response consisting of desire, excitement, and orgasm.

- Multiple orgasm is the occurrence of one or more additional orgasms following the first, within a short period of time and before the body has returned to a preplateau level of arousal. Most women, but few if any men, are capable of multiple orgasms.

- Freud theorized two types of female orgasm: clitoral and vaginal. Masters and Johnson found only one kind of orgasm among women. Singer and Singer suggested that there are three types of female orgasm: vulval, uterine, and blended.

1. Heterosexual men are least likely to prefer the body odor of

   (a) heterosexual women

   (b) heterosexual men

   (c) lesbians

   (d) gay men

2. The effects of Spanish fly are the result of _____ in the urinary tract.

   (a) a burning sensation

   (b) moisture

   (c) a burst of cerebral neurons

   (d) ethanol

3. _____ dampens sexual arousal by increasing the need to urinate.

   (a) Saltpeter

   (b) L-Dopa

   (c) Wellbutrin

   (d) Amyl nitrate

4. Alcohol is known to have

   (a) depressing effects only

   (b) stimulating effects only

   (c) both stimulating and depressing effects

   (d) neither stimulating nor depressing effects

5. Cells in the _____ cortex transmit messages when we experience sexual thoughts and fantasies.

   (a) reticular

   (b) avuncular

   (c) sexual

   (d) cerebral

6. When the rear part of a male rat's _____ is stimulated by electricity, the animal runs through its sexual routine mechanically.

   (a) thalamus

   (b) hypothalamus

   (c) occipital lobe

   (d) larynx

7. _____ is/are secreted by the endocrine system.

   (a) Sperm

   (b) Vaginal lubrication

   (c) Sweat

   (d) Hormones

8. According to Masters and Johnson, sexual arousal is characterized by vasocongestion and

   (a) myotonia

   (b) blurry vision

   (c) cramping

   (d) constriction of blood vessels

9. According to Masters and Johnson, erection and lubrication occur during the _____ phase of the sexual response cycle.

   (a) orgasmic

   (b) excitement

   (c) plateau

   (d) resolution

10. Men enter a refractory period after the _____ phase of the sexual response cycle.

   (a) excitement

   (b) plateau

   (c) resolution

   (d) orgasmic

11. Masters and Johnson found _____ kind(s) of orgasm.

   (a) one

   (b) two

   (c) three

   (d) four

12. Which of the following is *not* a type of female orgasm suggested by Singer and Singer?

   (a) blended

   (b) vulval

   (c) clitoral

   (d) uterine

13. The hormone _____ activates the sex drives of both men and women.

   (a) prolactin

   (b) oxytocin

   (c) progesterone

   (d) testosterone

14. Foods such as oysters and bananas have been considered aphrodisiacs because they

   (a) are chemically similar to compounds secreted by the male genitals

   (b) are enjoyed by women

   (c) are popular among the upper classes

   (d) resemble the male genitals

15. In many animals, the VNO detects

   (a) pheromones

   (b) contractions of the orgasmic platform

   (c) pituitary secretions

   (d) cerebral activity

Answers 1. d; 2. a; 3. a; 4. c; 5. d; 6. b; 7. d; 8. a; 9. b; 10. d; 11. a; 12. c; 13. d; 14. d; 15. a

6

Gender Identity and Gender Roles

TRUTH? fiction

Which of the following statements are true, and which are fiction? Look for the Truth/Fiction icons on the pages that follow to find the answers.

1 If male sex hormones were not present during critical stages of prenatal development, we would all develop external female sexual organs.   T   F

2 A woman with Turner syndrome cannot become pregnant, but she can carry and deliver a baby.   T   F

3 Seventeen of 18 boys who appeared to have female external sex organs suddenly developed male sex organs at puberty, when male sex hormones went to work.   T   F

4 The sex of a baby crocodile is determined by the temperature at which the egg develops.   T   F

5 Thousands of people have changed their sexes through sex reassignment surgery.   T   F

6 Men act more aggressively than women.   T   F

7 A two-and-a-half-year-old child may know that he is a boy, but think that he can grow up to be a mommy.   T   F

The following is an excerpt of a letter written by Madeline H. Wyndzen—a male-to-female transsexual woman who also happens to be a psychologist—to her parents.

The Letter

Once I told my parents about my transsexuality, our telephone conversations became an even more difficult experience for me. Every time I called my mom would ask, "Are you happy?" I just couldn't answer her. . . . I stayed up all night trying to write my parents a letter. I had to find a way to focus and express my feelings. I don't know if I suceeded, but this is most of what I wrote that night.

Am I Happy?

Hi Mom and Dad,

Maybe you don't know this, but I think about things we say after we get off the phone. When we leave on bad terms, it bothers me. And, although being overwhelmed by grad school is one reason I don't call often, another reason is that it almost always turns out negatively. Our last conversation was wonderful, but I still think about our other conversations. One question you keeping asking me is, "Does transitioning make you happy?" The question is impossibly difficult for me to answer. . . . It's hard for me to answer because I feel that no matter what my answer is, it's going to hurt you. . . . The more I reveal how bad things were in childhood, the more you seem to feel you did something wrong. I usually just try to say nothing or leave things vague. But that just seems to make you feel like there's no reason behind what I'm doing. I have no idea how to begin expressing something like this to you. . . . I'm going to try to be completely honest about expressing this to you. Please don't feel guilty about anything because I don't, and haven't ever, blamed you for anything. . . .

I guess maybe you look at my transition and think there must be one concrete thing about it that makes me happy. But there just isn't one concrete thing. . . . This isn't about concrete things; it's about abstract feelings.

I spent my childhood in pain, and my adolescence in a desperate attempt not to feel pain. Now I can feel pain. I can feel sadness. But I can also feel happiness. I like myself more today than any other time in my life.

I can relate to people in a positive way unlike ever before. I feel a part of other people's lives. I care about people and I'm passionate about life in a way that's so profoundly different from the way I've lived my life until now. I have more self-confidence today than ever before. . . .

It's hard for me to bring my feelings into focus. Perhaps the answer is that transitioning does not make me happy. Transitioning is what makes it possible for me to find happiness. And I'm still searching and I'm still growing.

I wish you could see me living life everyday. I'm so much more alive than I ever was before. I feel a lot better about myself as I watch myself growing through another adolescence. I truly feel I'm growing into a self-confident, well-balanced, and competent young woman.

And when I think about everything I'm trying to bring into focus for you, I can honestly say that I am happy with making the decision to transition. I am very happy that you are so supportive of me even when you can't understand what I can't say. I love you very much!

Madeline

A Letter from My Dad!

Dear Madeline,

I wanted to drop you a short note to tell you how we enjoyed our visit with you last weekend. It's always nice to see you, but it was exceptionally nice to see you happy. I don't believe I have ever seen you smile as much before, and this, of course, makes me happy. You looked totally comfortable in your new identity, proud of the work you are doing now and your future plans, and also in a loving relationship with someone who is understanding of your situation. . . .

I also wanted to tell you that I am not only glad that you are finally happy with who you are, but that I am also proud of all you have done in the past and present and the courage you are now exhibiting. The changes you are making and planning for the future are difficult for me to imagine. However, I know they are right for you. I only wish the entire process didn't have to take so long.

I don't know how good a job I've done expressing my feelings in this letter. The essence of what I have been trying to say is that I am proud of who you are and proud to be your father and that you will always have my love and understanding.

Dad

SOURCE: Adapted from the Psychology of Gender Identity and Trans-genderism website (www.genderpsychology.org)

This chapter addresses the biological, psychological, and sociological aspects of **gender.** First we define gender as the psychological sense of being female or being male and the roles society ascribes to gender. Anatomic sex is based on, well, anatomy. But gender is a complex concept that is based partly on anatomy, partly on the psychology of the individual, and partly on culture and tradition.

Next we focus on sexual differentiation—the process by which males and females develop distinct reproductive anatomy. We then turn to gender roles—the clusters of behavior that are deemed "masculine" or "feminine" in a particular culture. The chapter examines research findings on sex differences. We next consider **gender typing**—the processes by which boys come to behave in line with what is expected of men (most of the time) and girls with what is expected of women (most of the time). We also explore the concept of psychological androgyny, which applies to people who display characteristics associated with both gender roles in our culture.

Prenatal Sexual Differentiation

Throughout the years, many ideas have been proposed to account for **sexual differentiation.** Aristotle believed that the anatomic difference between males and females was the result of the heat of semen during sexual relations: Hot semen generated

Gender The psychological state of being female or being male, as influenced by cultural concepts of gender-appropriate behavior; compare and contrast the concept of gender with *anatomic sex,* which is based on the physical differences between females and males

Gender typing The process by which children acquire behavior that is deemed appropriate to their sex

Sexual differentiation The process by which males and females develop distinct reproductive anatomy

males, whereas cold semen made females (National Center for Biotechnology Information, 2006). Aristotle may have given in to stereotyping—the stereotypes of "hot-blooded male" and the "frigid female." Others believed that sperm from the right testicle make females, but sperm from the left testicle make males.

When a sperm cell fertilizes an ovum, 23 **chromosomes** from the male parent normally combine with 23 chromosomes from the female parent. The **zygote**, the beginning of a new human being, is only 1/175 of an inch long. Yet, on this tiny stage, one's stamp as a unique individual has already been ensured—whether one will have black or blond hair, grow bald or develop a widow's peak, or become female or male.

The chromosomes from each parent combine to form 23 pairs. The twenty-third pair contains the sex chromosomes. An ovum carries an X sex chromosome, but a sperm cell can carry either an X or a Y sex chromosome. The denotation of X and Y refers to the shapes of the chromosomes. If a sperm cell with an X sex chromosome fertilizes the ovum, the newly conceived individual will have an XX sex chromosomal structure and will normally develop as a female. If the sperm cell carries a Y sex chromosome, the child will normally develop as a male (XY).

After fertilization, the zygote divides repeatedly. After a few short weeks, one cell has become billions of cells. At about three weeks, a primitive heart begins to drive blood through the embryonic bloodstream. At about five to six weeks, when the **embryo** is only one quarter to one half inch long, primitive gonads, ducts, and external genitals—the sex of which cannot yet be distinguished visually—have formed (Figures 6.1 and 6.2). Each embryo possesses primitive external genitals, a pair of sexually undifferentiated gonads, and two sets of primitive duct structures, the Müllerian (female) ducts and the Wolffian (male) ducts.

During the first six weeks or so of prenatal development, embryonic structures of both sexes develop along similar lines and resemble primitive female structures. At about the seventh week after conception, the genetic code (XX or XY) begins to assert itself, causing changes in the gonads, genital ducts, and external genitals. Genetic activity on the Y sex chromosome causes the testes to begin to differentiate (National Center for Biotechnology Information, 2006). Ovaries begin to differentiate if the Y

Chromosome One of the rodlike structures, found in the nucleus of every living cell, that carries the genetic code in the form of genes

Zygote A fertilized ovum (egg cell)

Embryo The stage of prenatal development that begins with implantation of a fertilized ovum in the uterus and concludes with development of the major organ systems at about two months after conception

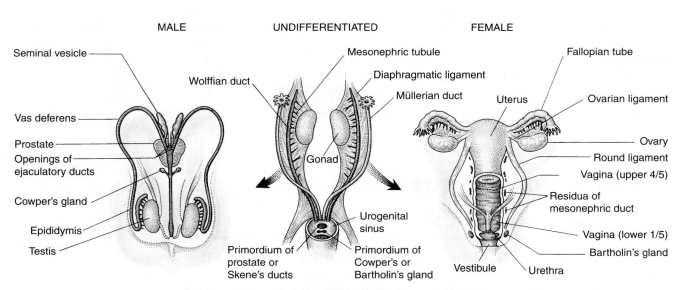

Figure 6.1 **Development of the Internal Sex Organs from an Undifferentiated Stage at about Five or Six Weeks after Conception**

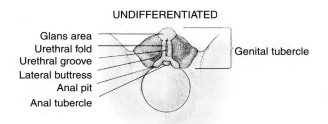

UNDIFFERENTIATED

Glans area
Urethral fold
Urethral groove
Lateral buttress
Anal pit
Anal tubercle

Genital tubercle

45–50 mm

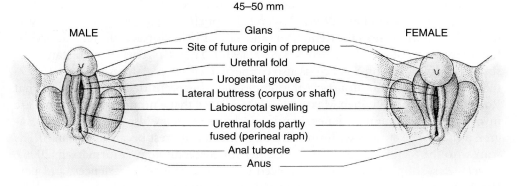

MALE

FEMALE

Glans
Site of future origin of prepuce
Urethral fold
Urogenital groove
Lateral buttress (corpus or shaft)
Labioscrotal swelling
Urethral folds partly
fused (perineal raph)
Anal tubercle
Anus

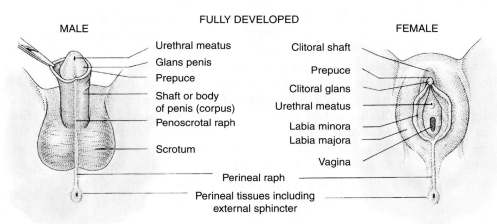

FULLY DEVELOPED

MALE

FEMALE

Urethral meatus
Glans penis
Prepuce
Shaft or body
of penis (corpus)
Penoscrotal raph

Scrotum

Clitoral shaft
Prepuce
Clitoral glans
Urethral meatus
Labia minora
Labia majora
Vagina

Perineal raph
Perineal tissues including
external sphincter

Figure 6.2 **Development of the External Sex Organs from an Undifferentiated Stage at about Five or Six Weeks after Conception**

chromosome is absent. The reproductive organs of some rare individuals who have only one X sex chromosome instead of the typical XY or XX arrangement also become female in appearance, because they too lack the Y sex chromosome. One could thus say that the basic blueprint of the human embryo is female (De Vries et al., 2002; Steinemann & Steinemann, 2005). The genetic instructions in the Y sex chromosome cause the embryo to deviate from the female developmental course.

By about the seventh week of prenatal development, strands of tissue begin to organize into seminiferous tubules. Female gonads begin to develop somewhat later than male gonads. The forerunners of follicles that will bear ova are not found until the fetal stage of development, about 10 weeks after conception. Ovaries begin to form at 11 or 12 weeks.

Genetic Factors in Sexual Differentiation

What roles do genes play in sexual differentiation? Some of the answers to this question are fascinating. Animal studies suggest a role for genes in the determination of mating and other behavior patterns in humans. For example, the interaction of a number of genes has led to the development of three different types of males in a crustacean and quite a complex mating strategy (Shuster & Sassaman, 1997). One sex-determining gene called transformer (*tra*) is needed in the development of female fruit flies. Chromosomal (XX) females with inactive *tra* attempt to mate with other females, but they are attractive to males because they still emit female pheromones (Arthur et al., 1998). Researchers conclude that among fruit flies, sexual differentiation, sexual orientation, and sexual behavior are all determined by the interactions of genes (O'Dell & Kaiser, 1997). The *SRY* gene—which stands for sex-determining region Y gene—is also connected with sexual differentiation (Neerman–Arbez, 2003). In an article that could have been entitled "The Mouse That Roared," researcher Stephen Maxson (1998) reported that a number of genes that are involved in determining maleness in mice, including *SRY,* are also connected with aggressiveness. The studies with mice are of particular interest because human *SRY* is similar to the *SRY* of mice (National Center for Biotechnology Information, 2006). Nevertheless, humans are also influenced by culture, values, experiences, and personal beliefs. In people there is only rarely a direct line between genetics and behavior, especially with regard to social behaviors such as mating and aggression.

SRY is also involved in sex determination in humans (Brodkin et al., 2002; Xu et al., 2002). It binds to DNA, which is a strand of genes—the basic building blocks of heredity—and distorts it. The distortion alters the properties of the DNA and leads to the formation of the testes. Another gene involved in sex determination has also been researched in mice: *Sox 9. Sox 9* appears to regulate the expression of *SRY* (National Center for Biotechnology Information, 2006). Females with an XX sex chromosomal structure normally suppress the action of their own *Sox 9,* which in turn prevents the expression of *SRY.* However, when these XX mice are chemically prevented from turning off *Sox 9,* they develop as males—albeit sterile males. Sperm cells, therefore, are likely to be created by other genes, not *Sox 9* and *SRY.*

The Role of Sex Hormones in Sexual Differentiation

After the genes have done their work and testes develop in the embryo, the testes begin to produce male sex hormones, or **androgens**. Without androgens, we would all develop female external reproductive organs. The most important androgen, **testosterone**, spurs differentiation of the male (Wolffian) duct system (Figure 6.1). Each Wolffian duct develops into an epididymis, vas deferens, and seminal vesicle. The external genitals, including the penis, begin to take shape at about the eighth week of development under the influence of another androgen, dihydrotestosterone (DHT). **Truth or Fiction Revisited:** It is true that without male sex hormones, or androgens, we would all develop female external reproductive organs. However, Müllerian inhibiting substance (MIS), a testicular hormone that is secreted during the fetal stage, prevents the Müllerian ducts from developing into the female duct system.

Small amounts of androgens are produced in female fetuses, but they are not normally sufficient to cause male sexual differentiation. In female fetuses, the relative

Androgens Male sex hormones

Testosterone The male sex hormone that fosters the development of male sex characteristics and is connected with the sex drive

absence of androgens causes degeneration of the Wolffian ducts and prompts development of female sexual organs. The Müllerian ducts evolve into fallopian tubes, the uterus, and the upper two thirds of the vagina. Although female sex hormones are crucial in puberty, they are not involved in fetal sexual differentiation. If a fetus with an XY sex chromosomal structure failed to produce testosterone, it would develop external female sexual organs, but be infertile.

Descent of the Testes and the Ovaries

The testes and ovaries develop from slender structures high in the abdominal cavity. By about 10 weeks after conception, they have descended so that they are almost even with the upper edge of the pelvis. The ovaries remain there for the rest of the prenatal period. Later they rotate and descend farther to their adult position in the pelvis. About four months after conception, the testes normally descend into the scrotal sac via the **inguinal canal**. Then the passageway closes.

In a small percentage of males, one or both testes do not descend and remain in the abdomen at birth. The condition is termed **cryptorchidism**. In most cases of cryptorchidism, the testes migrate to the scrotum during infancy. In still other cases, the testes descend by puberty. Men with undescended testes are usually treated through surgery or hormonal therapy, because they are at higher risk for cancer of the testes. Sperm production is also impaired because the undescended testes are subjected to a higher than optimal body temperature, causing sterility.

Sex Chromosomal Abnormalities

Abnormalities of the sex chromosomes can have profound effects on sexual characteristics, physical health, and psychological development. **Klinefelter syndrome**, a condition that affects about 1 in 500 males, is caused by an extra X sex chromosome, so the man has an XXY rather than an XY pattern. Men with this pattern fail to develop appropriate secondary sex characteristics. They have enlarged breasts, poor muscular development, and, because they fail to produce sperm, they are infertile. They may be mildly retarded.

Turner syndrome occurs in about 1 of every 2,500 females and is a consequence of having one rather than two X sex chromosomes. Individuals with Turner Syndrome are at risk of developing heart disease, short arms and legs, kidney problems, hypothyroidism (producing too little thyroid hormone), and diabetes. Turner syndrome does not cause general cognitive impairment, but women with the syndrome may have specific problems with spatial relationships and math. Females with the syndrome may not naturally undergo puberty, so hormone treatments are usually begun when pubertal changes would start to spur growth of secondary sex characteristics. Nevertheless, nearly all women with the syndrome are infertile. **Truth or Fiction Revisited:** Interestingly, however, if another woman donates an ovum (egg cell), and it is fertilized in a laboratory dish, it can usually be implanted in a woman with Turner syndrome and the embryo can develop normally to term.

The brain, like the genital organs, undergoes prenatal sexual differentiation. Testosterone causes cells in the hypothalamus of male fetuses to become insensitive to the female sex hormone estrogen. In female fetuses the hypothalamus develops a sensitivity to estrogen.

Sensitivity to estrogen is important in the regulation of the menstrual cycle after puberty. The hypothalamus detects low levels of estrogen in the blood at the end of

CRITICAL Thinking

Critical thinkers do not oversimplify or overgeneralize. Consider this statement: In the absence of prenatal male sex hormones, we would all develop as females. Question: Would we all develop as fertile females? Why or why not?

TRUTH fiction 2

Inguinal canal A fetal canal that connects the scrotum and the testes, allowing their descent

Cryptorchidism The condition defined by undescended testes; from roots meaning "hidden testes"

Klinefelter syndrome A sex chromosome disorder caused by an extra X sex chromosome

each cycle and initiates a new cycle by stimulating the pituitary gland to secrete FSH. FSH, in turn, stimulates estrogen production by the ovaries and the ripening of an immature follicle in an ovary.

Gender Identity

Our **gender identity** is our psychological awareness or sense of being male or being female and one of the most obvious and important aspects of our self-concepts. **Sex assignment** (also called *gender assignment*) reflects the child's anatomic sex and usually occurs at birth. A child's sex is so important to parents that they may want to know "Is it a boy or a girl?" before they count fingers and toes.

Most children first become aware of their anatomic sex by about the age of 18 months. By 36 months, most children have acquired a firm sense of gender identity (Rathus, 2006).

Nature and Nurture in Gender Identity

What determines gender identity? Are our brains biologically programmed along masculine or feminine lines by prenatal sex hormones? Does the environment, in the form of postnatal learning experiences, shape our self-concepts as males or females? Or does gender identity reflect an intermingling of biological and environmental influences?

Gender identity is almost always consistent with chromosomal sex, but such consistency does not certify that gender identity is biologically determined. Parents and others also rear us as males or females, according to our anatomic sexes. How, then, might we sort out the roles of nature and nurture, of biology and the environment?

Investigators have found clues in the experiences of rare individuals, **intersexuals,** who possess the gonads of one sex but external genitalia that are ambiguous or typical of the other sex. Intersexuals are sometimes reared as members of the other sex (the sex other than their chromosomal sex). Researchers have wondered whether the gender identity of these children reflects their chromosomal and gonadal sex or the sex to which they were assigned at birth, and according to which they were reared. Before going further, let us distinguish between true **hermaphrodites** and intersexuals.

HERMAPHRODITES AND INTERSEXUALS Hormonal factors during prenatal development produce various congenital outcomes. Some individuals are born with both ovarian and testicular tissue. They are called hermaphrodites, after the Greek myth of the son of Hermes and Aphrodite, whose body became united with that of a nymph while he was bathing. True hermaphrodites may have one gonad of each sex (a testicle and an ovary), or gonads that combine testicular and ovarian tissue.

Regardless of their genetic sex, hermaphrodites often assume the gender identity and gender role of the sex assigned at birth. Figure 6.3 shows a genetic female (XX) with a right testicle and left ovary. This person married and became a stepfather with a firm male identity. The roles of biology and environment remain tangled, however, because true hermaphrodites have gonadal tissue of both sexes.

Gender identity One's belief that one is male or female

Sex assignment The labeling of a newborn as a male or female; also termed *gender assignment*

Intersexual A person who possesses the gonads of one sex but external genitalia that are ambiguous or typical of the other sex; also termed *pseudohermaphrodite*

Hermaphrodite A person who possesses both ovarian and testicular tissue; from the names of the male and female Greek gods *Hermes* and *Aphrodite*

INTERSEXUALISM True hermaphroditism is quite rare (Kuhnle et al., 2003). Less rare is intersexualism, which occurs in perhaps 1 in 5,000 or so infants (Intersex Society of North America, 2006; Sax, 2002). Intersexuals have testes or ovaries, but not both. Unlike hermaphrodites, their gonads (testes or ovaries) match their chromosomal sex. Because of prenatal hormonal factors, however, their external genitals and sometimes their internal reproductive anatomy are ambiguous or resemble those of the other sex. Intersexualism has given scientists an opportunity to examine the roles of nature (biology) and nurture (environmental influences) in the shaping of gender identity.

The most common form of female intersexualism is **congenital adrenal hyperplasia** (CAH), in which a genetic (XX) female has female internal sexual structures (ovaries), but masculinized external genitals (www.congenitaladrenalhyperplasia.org, 2006) (Figure 6.4). The clitoris is enlarged and may resemble a small penis. CAH is caused by high levels of androgens, which are usually produced by the fetus's own adrenal glands. In other cases, mothers may have received synthetic androgens during their pregnancies. In the 1950s and 1960s, before these side effects were known, synthetic androgens were sometimes prescribed to help prevent miscarriages in women with histories of miscarriage.

Swedish investigator Anna Servin and her colleagues (2003) studied gender-type behaviors and interests in 26 girls age 2 to 10 years who had CAH, and in 26 girls without CAH who were matched for age. Girls with CAH showed more interest in masculine-type toys, such as transportation toys, and less interest in feminine-type toys, such as dolls. The girls with CAH were also more likely to have boys as playmates and to desire masculine-type careers. Parents rated the behavior of daughters with CAH as being more "boylike" in their choice of toys and their aggressiveness. The investigators did not find any evidence that the girls' parents influenced their style of play. Servin and her colleagues (2003) interpret the results as supporting a hormonal contribution to styles of play between girls with and without CAH.

There are several varieties of **androgen insensitivity syndrome**, another type of intersexualism. One involves genetic (XY) males who, because of a mutated gene, have lower than normal prenatal sensitivity to androgens (U.S. National Library of Medicine, 2006). As a result, their genitals do not become normally masculinized. At birth their external genitals are feminized, including a small vagina, and their testes are undescended. Because of insensitivity to androgens, the male duct system (epididymis, vas deferens, seminal vesicles, and ejaculatory ducts) fails to develop. Nevertheless, the fetal testes produce MIS, preventing the development of a uterus or fallopian tubes. Genetic males with androgen insensitivity syndrome usually have no or sparse pubic and axillary (underarm) hair, because the development of hair in these locations is dependent on androgens.

Girls with *partial androgen insensitivity syndrome (PAIS)* are also intersexuals. PAIS or *complete androgen insensitivity syndrome (CAIS)* occurs in 1 in 2,000 to 5,000 girls. It occurs in girls with a single X sex chromosome and in girls with an XX chromosomal structure who lose some X sex chromosomal material. Girls with CAIS develop typical external genital organs, but their internal reproductive organs do not develop or function normally. By contrast, girls with PAIS develop masculinized external genitals and are sometimes raised as boys, sometimes as girls. A study by Melissa Hines and her colleagues (2003) compared 22 women with CAIS and a single X sex chromosomal structure with 22 women who had the normal XX sex chromosomal structure. They found no differences between the women with CAIS and control subjects in self-esteem, general psychological well-being, gender identity, sexual orientation, gender-type behavior patterns, marital status, personality traits, or

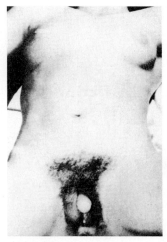

Figure 6.3 A Hermaphrodite. *This genetic (XX) female has one testicle and one ovary and the gender identity of a male.*

Figure 6.4 Intersexualism. *In congenital adrenal hyperplasia, a genetic (XX) female has female internal sexual structures (ovaries) but masculinized external genitals.*

Congenital adrenal hyperplasia A form of intersexualism in which a genetic female has internal female sexual structures but masculinized external genitals

Androgen insensitivity syndrome A form of intersexualism in which a genetic male is prenatally insensitive to androgens such that his genitals are not normally masculinized

Dominican Republic syndrome A form of intersexualism in which a genetic enzyme disorder prevents testosterone from masculinizing the external genitalia

Transsexualism A condition in which people strongly desire to be of the other sex and live as a person of the other sex; referred to as *gender identity disorder* by the American Psychiatric Association

Transgenderism (1) A synonym for transsexualism; (2) an activist movement seeking rights and pride for transgendered individuals (For many in the transgender—or "trans"—movement, the label *transgender* encompasses not only transsexual and transgender people, but also cross-dressers or transvestites, drag queens, drag kings, intersexed individuals, and anyone nonconventionally gendered [i.e., anyone identifying or behaving in a manner that runs counter to expected societal norms concerning the gender assigned them after birth].)

hand preferences. The researchers conclude that two X sex chromosomes and ovaries are not essential to the development of feminine-type behavior patterns in humans.

Dominican Republic syndrome is a form of intersexualism that was first documented in a group of 18 boys in two villages in the Dominican Republic (Imperato–McGinley et al., 1974). Dominican Republic syndrome is a genetic enzyme disorder that prevents testosterone from masculinizing the external genitalia. The boys were born with normal testes and internal male reproductive organs, but their external genitals were malformed. Their penises were stunted and resembled clitorises. Their scrotums were incompletely formed and resembled female labia. They also had partially formed vaginas. Because the boys resembled girls at birth, they were reared as females. At puberty, however, their testes swung into normal testosterone production, causing startling changes: Their testes descended, their voices deepened, their musculature filled out, and their "clitorises" expanded into penises. **Truth or Fiction Revisited:** Of the 18 Dominican Republic boys who were reared as girls, 17 shifted to a male gender identity. Sixteen of the 18 assumed a stereotypical masculine gender role. Of the remaining two, one identified himself as a male but continued to maintain a feminine gender role, including wearing dresses. The eighteenth continued to see herself/himself as female and later sought sex reassignment surgery to counter the pubertal masculinization. Despite being reared as girls, 16 of the 18 made the transition to the male role without problems, suggesting the importance of biology in gender identity (Bailey, 2003).

Many scientists conclude that gender identity is influenced by complex interactions of biological and psychosocial factors. But could the "complex interaction" approach be a way of avoiding the hot-potato issue regarding whether nature (biological factors) or nurture (psychosocial factors) is more important? To place the emphasis on nature is to lessen the role of personal choice and thus has major political consequences. Although some place relatively greater emphasis on psychosocial factors (Bradley et al., 1998; Money, 1994), others emphasize the role of biological factors (Diamond, 1996; Legato, 2000; Servin et al., 2003). However, as noted in the nearby "A Closer Look" feature on "Boys Who Are Reared as Girls," the theory that newborns are psychosexually neutral and that gender identity depends mainly on environmental factors has had rough sledding in recent years.

In case you have had enough discussion of the complex issues surrounding the origins of sex and gender identity in human beings, consider the crocodile. Crocodile eggs do not carry sex chromosomes. **Truth or Fiction Revisited:** The offspring's sex is determined by the temperature at which the eggs develop (Ackerman, 1991). Some (males) like it hot (at least in the mid 90s°F), and some (females) like it not cold perhaps, but colder than the mid 80s°F.

Transsexualism/Transgenderism

In 1953, an ex-GI who journeyed to Denmark for a "sex-change operation" made headlines. She became known as Christine (formerly George) Jorgensen (Michel & Pédinielli, 2005). Since then, thousands of transsexuals (also called *transgendered people*) have undergone sex-reassignment surgery. (This surgery has also been referred to as *gender reassignment surgery*. In this text we use the word *sex* to refer to anatomic sex and the word *gender* to refer to the psychological state of feeling male or female. To be consistent, then, the surgery would be reassigning one's sex, not one's gender.)

In **transsexualism**, the individual wishes to possess the anatomic features of people of the other sex and to live as a person of the other sex. The term **transgenderism** is sometimes used as a synonym for transsexualism. However, transgenderism also refers to an activist movement that seeks rights and pride for various transgendered individuals, including not only transsexuals, but also intersexuals, transvestites (see Chapter 17), and anyone who is unconventionally gendered (i.e., any person who identifies with or behaves in a manner that runs counter to traditional gender roles relevant to their assigned sex).

Many transsexuals undergo hormone treatments and surgery to create the appearance of the external genitals typical of the other sex. This can be done more precisely with male-to-female than female-to-male transsexuals. After surgery people can participate in sexual activity and even attain orgasm. One survey found that 85% of transsexual women attained orgasm during sexual activity (Lawrence, 2005). However, they cannot conceive or bear children.

Truth or Fiction Revisited: Sex reassignment surgery cannot implant the internal reproductive organs of the other sex. Therefore, it is not accurate to say that people have actually changed their sexes through sex reassignment surgery. Instead, surgery creates the appearance of the external genitals typical of the other sex.

Is It a Boy or a Girl? *We haven't checked, but the answer has to do with the temperature at which the egg was incubated. Clue: Some like it hot.*

SafeZone

Q *Can a man who has sex reassignment surgery get pregnant, or is that option futuristic?*

A No. It is also questionable regarding whether his/her getting pregnant is in the future. However—there's often a however in these matters—she could provide sperm prior to the change, use it to fertilize an egg from a donor, and the donor or another woman might carry the embryo to term.

What motivates transsexuals to live as people of the other sex? According to John Money (1994), transsexuals experience **gender dysphoria**. That is, they experience incongruity between their genital anatomy and their gender identity or role. Although they have the anatomic sex of one sex, they feel that they are a member of the other. The discrepancy motivates them to wish to be rid of their own primary sex characteristics (their external genitals and internal sex organs) and to live as a member of the other sex. A male-to-female transsexual perceives himself to be a female who, through some quirk of fate, was born with the wrong genital equipment. A female-to-male transsexual perceives herself as a man trapped in a woman's body.

However, some researchers contend that many men who seek to become women tend to fall into other categories: either men who are extremely feminine or men who are sexually aroused by the idea of becoming a woman. The first category includes **homosexual transsexuals**—men who are extremely feminine gays and not fully satisfied by sexual activity with other males (Blanchard, 1988, 1989). The second

Gender dysphoria A sense of incongruity between one's anatomic sex and one's gender identity

Homosexual transsexuals Extremely feminine gay men who seek sex reassignment

A Closer Look

BOYS WHO ARE REARED AS GIRLS

Are children "psychosexually neutral" at birth? Can you surgically reassign a boy as a female, rear him as a girl, and have him feel that he is truly a girl as the years go on? Will cosmetic surgery, female sex hormone treatments, and laces and ribbons do it? Or will he be maladjusted and his male gender identity sort of "break through"? No one has sought to answer these questions by randomly selecting male babies and reassigning their genders. Evidence on the matter derives from studies of children who have lost their penises or failed to develop them through accidents or unusual medical conditions.

Getting Down to Cases

For example, one of a pair of male twins, David Reimer, lost much of his penis as a result of a circumcision accident. As this case study is related by

Colapinto (2000), the parents wondered what to do. Johns Hopkins sexologist John Money believed that gender identity was sufficiently malleable that the boy could undergo sex reassignment surgery (have his testes removed and an artificial vagina constructed) and female hormone treatments, and be successfully reared as a girl.

For a number of years, the case seemed to supply evidence for the view that children may be psychosexually neutral at birth. The sex-reassigned twin, unlike his brother, seemed to develop like a "real girl," albeit with a number of "tomboyish" traits. But at the age of 14, when "she" was informed about the circumcision accident and the process of sex reassignment, David immediately decided to pursue life as a male. As an adult, he recalled that he had never felt quite comfortable as a girl—a view confirmed

by the recollections of his mother. At the age of 25, he married a woman and adopted her children. He reported being sexually attracted to women only. According to researchers such as Milton Diamond (1996), this outcome would appear to support the view that gender identity may be determined to a considerable extent in the uterus, as the fetal brain is being exposed to androgens.

Reimer committed suicide with a sawed-off shotgun in 2004, at the age of 38. When Colapinto received the news from David's father, he wrote, "I was shocked, but I cannot say I was surprised. Anyone familiar with David's life—as a baby, after a botched circumcision, [after] an operation to change him from boy to girl—would have understood that the real mystery was how he managed to stay alive for 38 years, given the physical and mental torments he suffered in childhood and that haunted him the rest of his life" (Colapinto, 2004).

Another Case Study Susan Bradley and her colleagues (1998) reported the development of another boy who suffered a circumcision accident in infancy. Again, John Money recommended sex reassignment, and the surgery was carried out at the age of 21 months. In this

category refers to males who are **autogynephilic**, or sexually stimulated by fantasies of their own bodies as being female (Bailey, 2003a, 2003b; Lawrence, 2004).

Although the prevalence of transsexualism remains unknown, it is thought to be relatively rare. The number of transsexuals in the United States is estimated to be less than 50,000. Fewer than 20,000 are known to have undergone sex reassignment surgery (Jones & Hill, 2002).

Homosexual transsexuals usually show cross-gender preferences in play and dress during early childhood. Some report that they felt they belonged to the other sex for as long as they can remember (Zucker, 2005a, 2005b). Some male-to-female transsexuals recall that, as children, they preferred playing with dolls, enjoyed wearing frilly dresses, and disliked rough-and-tumble play. They were often perceived by their peers as "sissy boys." Some female-to-male transsexuals report that as children they disliked dresses and acted much like "tomboys." They preferred playing "boys' games" and doing so with boys. Female transsexuals appear to have an easier time adjusting than male transsexuals. Even during adulthood, it may be easier for a female transsexual to don men's clothes and pass as a slightly built man than it is for a brawny man to pass for a tall woman.

Autogynephilic (aw-toe-gone-uh-FEE-lick) Descriptive of transsexuals who are sexually stimulated by fantasies that their own bodies are female; from roots meaning "self," "woman," and "love" or "desire"

case, as Money found out in a follow-up with the child at the age of nine that the individual was also tomboyish in behavior and personality traits, but considered herself to be a girl.

She was interviewed subsequently at the ages of 16 and 26, and her situation had grown more complex. She considered herself to be bisexual and had sexual relationships with both men and women. However, when last interviewed, she had begun living with a woman in what the authors label a "lesbian" relationship. Of course, if one remembers that the individual has an XY sex chromosomal structure, the relationship with the woman is not with a person of the same sex at all. On the other hand, the individual did retain the self-concept of being female.

A Larger Study These celebrated cases are far from the only ones. On May 12, 2000, researchers from the Johns Hopkins Hospital, including William G. Reiner, a psychiatrist and urologist, presented a paper on the subject to the Lawson Wilkins Pediatric Endocrine Society Meeting in Boston. They recounted the development of 27 children who had been born without penises resulting from a rare condition called cloacal exstrophy. However, the children had normal testicles, male sex

chromosomal structure, and male sex hormones.

David Reimer

Nevertheless, the sex of 25 of the 27 children was reassigned shortly after birth. They were surgically castrated and reared as girls by their parents. As the years went on, all 25—now 5 to 16 years old—showed the rough-and-tumble play considered stereotypical of males. Of the 25, 14 declared themselves to be males. Reiner (2000) suggests that "with time and age, children may well know what their gender is, regardless of any and all information and child-rearing to the contrary," he said. "They seem to be quite capable of telling us who they are." Reiner (2000) also noted that 2 of the 27 children who were not sex reassigned fit in with male peers and appeared to be better adjusted than the children who were reassigned.

Marianne J. Legato (2000), a professor of medicine at Columbia University, believes that gender identity tends to be formed during the first trimester of pregnancy, even if children cannot verbally express their identities until a few years afterward. As Legato describes it, "When the brain has been masculinized by exposure to testosterone, it is kind of useless to say to this individual, 'You're a girl.' It is this impact of testosterone that gives males the feelings that they are men."

It should be noted that not all researchers, including Bradley and her colleagues (1998) agree with regard to the prominence of prenatal male sex hormones in the formation of gender identity. However, the view that newborns are psychosexually neutral and that gender identity depends mainly on nurture has become increasingly controversial in recent years.

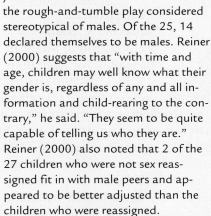

SafeZone

Q *Aren't all male cross-dressers gay?*

A No. Some are—those who have adopted or developed a feminine gender role and are sexually attracted to males. Others, who are not gay, are sexually aroused by the thoughts of themselves in feminine attire. There are other permutations and combinations. Stay tuned for Chapters 10 and 17.

SEX REASSIGNMENT Surgery is one element of sex reassignment. Because the surgery is irreversible, health professionals conduct careful evaluations to determine that people seeking reassignment are competent to make such decisions and have thought through the consequences (Bockting & Fung, 2006). They usually require that the transsexual live openly as a member of the other sex for an extended trial period before surgery.

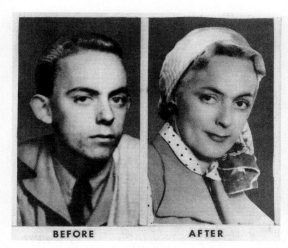

Christine Jorgensen. *The concept of sex reassignment suddenly entered the American lexicon in 1953 when Jorgensen had a sex-change operation.*

After the decision is reached, a lifetime of hormone treatments is begun. Male-to-female transsexuals receive estrogen, which fosters the development of female secondary sex characteristics. It causes fatty deposits to develop in the breasts and hips, softens the skin, and inhibits growth of the beard. Female-to-male transsexuals receive androgens, which promote male secondary sex characteristics. The voice deepens, hair becomes distributed according to the male pattern, muscles enlarge, and the fatty deposits in the breasts and hips are lost. The clitoris may also grow more prominent. In the case of male-to-female transsexuals, *phonosurgery* can raise the pitch of the voice (Bockting & Fung, 2006).

Despite its complexity and intimacy, sex reassignment surgery is largely cosmetic. Medical science cannot construct internal genital organs or gonads. Male-to-female surgery is generally more successful. The penis and testicles are first removed. Tissue from the penis is placed in an artificial vagina so that sensitive nerve endings will provide sexual sensations. A penis-shaped form of plastic or balsa wood is used to keep the vagina distended during healing.

In female-to-male transsexuals, the internal sex organs (ovaries, fallopian tubes, uterus) are removed, along with the fatty tissue in the breasts. Some female-to-male transsexuals engage in a series of operations, termed **phalloplasty**, to construct an artificial penis, but the penises don't work very well and the procedures are costly. Therefore, most female-to-male transsexuals are content to have hysterectomies, mastectomies, and testosterone treatments (Bailey, 2003b).

Some transsexuals hesitate to undertake surgery because they are repulsed by the prospect of extreme medical intervention. Others forgo surgery so as not to jeopardize high-status careers or family relationships. Such people continue to think of themselves as members of the other sex, even without surgery.

SafeZone

Q *Does an artificial penis get an erection? Can it ejaculate?*

A Yes and no. Female-to-male transsexuals who undergo phalloplasty (construction of an artificial penis) can have a pump installed that enables them to get erections, but medical science cannot create the glands that make ejaculation of seminal fluid possible.

OUTCOMES OF SEX REASSIGNMENT SURGERY Most reports of the postoperative adjustment of transsexuals are positive (Smith et al., 2005). A Canadian follow-up study of 116 transsexuals at least one year after surgery found that most were content with the results and were reasonably well adjusted (Blanchard et al., 1985). Positive results for surgery were also reported in a study of 141 Dutch transsexuals (Kuiper & Cohen–Kettenis, 1988).

A study of 326 Dutch candidates for sex reassignment surgery found that about two thirds (222 individuals) began hormone treatment, whereas 103 did not (Smith et al., 2005). Of the 222, about 15% dropped out before surgery. Generally speaking, after surgery the group was no longer gender dysphoric and most individuals functioned well sexually, psychologically, and socially. Only two male-to-female transsexuals regretted their decision. Male-to-female transsexuals outnumbered

Phalloplasty The surgical creation of an artificial penis

Third Gender/Third Sex

The terms *third gender* and *third sex* describe people who are considered to be neither women nor men, along with the social category in societies that recognize three or more sexes. Being neither male nor female has ramifications not only in terms of the person's sex, but also in terms of the person's gender role, gender identity, and sexual orientation. In some cultures or to some individuals, a third sex or gender may represent an intermediate state between men and women, or it may represent a state of being both, as in the case of "the spirit of a man in the body of a woman." It may also represent the state of being neither (neuter), the ability to cross or swap sexes and gender roles, or another category that is independent of being male or being female. This last definition is favored by those who argue for a strict interpretation of the third gender concept.

The term *third gender* has been used to describe the Hijras of India and Pakistan, the Fa'afafine of Polynesia, and the Sworn virgins of the Balkans. In the Western world, lesbian, gay, transgender, and intersex people have also been described as belonging to a third sex or gender, although many object to being so categorized.

Third Sex in Biology

A small number of individuals within a population will not differentiate sexually into typical male or female bodies. They may be called *hermaphrodites* or (especially among humans) *intersexuals*. Biologist and gender theorist Anne Fausto–Sterling proposed that five sexes may be more adequate than just two, for describing human bodies. In addition to the physical morphology of sex, transgender biologist Joan Roughgarden (2004) argues that in some nonhuman animal species, there may be more than two *genders* (understood in terms of behavior and identity). She argues that there might be multiple behavior patterns available to individuals with a given biological sex.

Feminists distinguish between (biological) sex and (social/psychological) gender. Contemporary gender theorists usually argue that that a two-gender system is neither inborn nor universal. A sex/gender system that only recognizes the following two social norms has been labeled *heteronormativity*, and feminists and queer theorists consider it to be too limited to describe the variety of sexual interests and behaviors we find in the real world:

- Female genitalia, female gender identity, feminine behavior, desire male partner

- Male genitalia, male gender identity, masculine behavior, desire female partner

Let's have a look at some *non*heteronormative patterns around the world.

South–Central Asia

The Hijra of India, Pakistan, and Bangladesh are probably the most well-known and populous third sex type in the modern world. The Mumbai-based community health organization, The Humsafar Trust, estimates there are between five and six million hijras in India. In different areas they are known as Aravani/Aruvani or Jo-gappa. British photographer Dayanita Singh writes about her friendship with a hijra, Mona Ahmed, and their two different society's beliefs about gender: "When I once asked her if she would like to go to Singapore for a sex change operation, she told me, 'You really do not understand. I am the third sex, not a man trying to be a woman. It is your society's problem that you only recognize two sexes.'" Hijra social movements have campaigned for recognition as a third sex, and in 2005, Indian passport application forms were updated with three gender options: M, F, and E ("Third sex" finds a place, 2005).

The "Ladyboys" of Thailand

Also commonly referred to as a third sex are the kathoeys (or "ladyboys") of Thailand. However, although a significant number of Thais perceive kathoeys as belonging to a third gender, including many kathoeys themselves, others see them as either a kind of man or a kind of woman. Researcher Sam Winter writes:

> We asked our 190 [kathoeys] to say whether they thought of themselves as men, women, *sao praphet song* ["a second kind of woman"] or *kathoey*. None thought of themselves as male, and only 11% saw themselves as kathoey (i.e., "nonmale"). By contrast 45% thought of themselves as women, with another 36% as *sao praphet song*. . . . Unfortunately we did not include the category *phet tee sam* (third sex/gender); conceivably if we had done so there may have been many respondents who would have chosen that term. . . . Around 50% [of nontransgender Thais] see them as males with the mistaken minds, but the other half see them as either women born into the wrong body (around 15%) or as a third sex/gender (35%).

(Continued)

Thai "Ladyboys"

In 2004, the Chiang Mai Technology School allocated a separate restroom for kathoeys, with an intertwined male and female symbol on the door. The 15 kathoey students are required to wear male clothing at school but are allowed to sport feminine hairdos. The restroom features four stalls, but no urinals.

The Western World

Some writers suggest that a third gender emerged around 1700 CE in England: the male sodomite. According to these writers, this was marked by the emergence of a subculture of effeminate males and meeting places (molly houses), as well as a marked increase in hostility toward effeminate and/or homosexual males. People described themselves as members of a third sex in Europe from at least the 1860s, with the writings of Karl Heinrich Ulrichs, and continuing in the late 19th century with Magnus Hirschfeld, John Addington Symonds, Edward Carpenter, Aimée Duc, and others. These writers described themselves and those like them as being of an "inverted" or "intermediate" sex and experiencing homosexual desire, and

their writing argued for social acceptance of such sexual intermediates.

Throughout much of the 20th century, the term *third sex* was a popular descriptor for homosexuals and gender nonconformists, but after the gay liberation movement of the 1970s and a growing separation of the concepts of sexual orientation and gender identity, the term fell out of favor among LGBT (lesbian–gay–bisexual–transgender) communities and the wider public. With the renewed exploration of gender that feminism, the modern transgender movement, and queer theory has fostered, some in the contemporary West have begun to describe themselves as a third sex again. One well-known social movement of male-bodied people that identify as neither men nor women are the radical faeries. Other modern identities that cover similar ground include pangender, bigender, genderqueer, androgyne, other gender, and differently gendered.

The term *transgender,* which often refers to those who change their gender, is increasingly being used to signify a gendered subjectivity that is neither male nor female—one recent example is on a form for the Harvard Business School, which has three gender options—male, female, and transgender.

Indigenous Cultures of North America: "Two-Spirits"

Native American cultures are also very much associated with multiple genders. They often contain social gender categories that are collectively known as *berdache* or Two-Spirit. Individual examples include the Winkte of Lakota culture, the *ninauposkitzipxpe* (manly-hearted woman) of the North Piegan (Blackfoot) community, and the Zapotec Muxe. Various scholars have debated the nature of such categories, as well as the definition of the term *third gender.* Different researchers may characterize the berdache as a gender-crosser, a mixed gender, an intermediate gender, or distinct third and fourth genders that are

female-to-males, but postoperative adjustment was more favorable for female-to-males. One reason may be that society is more accepting of women who desire to become men (Smith et al., 2005). Female-to-male transsexuals tend to be better adjusted socially before surgery as well, so their superior postoperative adjustment may be nothing more than a selection factor.

Gender Roles and Stereotypes

"Why can't a woman be more like a man?" You may recall this lyric from the song that Professor Henry Higgins sings in the musical *My Fair Lady.* In the song the professor laments that women are emotional and fickle, whereas men are logical

not dependent on male and female as primary categories. Those (such as Will Roscoe) who have argued for the latter interpretation also argue that mixed-, intermediate-, cross- or nongender social roles should not be understood as truly representing a third gender. According to Jean-Guy Goulet (2006):

"Berdache" may signify a category of male human beings who fill an established social status other than that of man or woman; a category of male and female human beings who behave and dress "like a member of the opposite sex"; or categories of male and female human beings who occupy well-established third or fourth genders. Scheffler, however, sees Native American cases of "berdache" and "amazon" as "situations in which some men (less often women) are permitted to act, in some degree, as though they were women (or men), and may be spoken of as though they were women (or men), or as anomalous 'he-she' or 'she-he.'" In Scheffler's view, "ethnographic data . . . provide definitive evidence that such persons were not regarded as having somehow moved from one sex category to the other, but were only metaphorically 'women' (or 'men')." In other words, according to Scheffler, we need not imagine a multiple gender system. Individuals who appeared in the dress and/or occupation of the opposite sex were only metaphorically spoken of as members of that sex or gender.

And More . . .

The following gender categories have also been described as a third gender:

Middle East

- Oman: *xanith* or *khanith*

Asia–Pacific

- Polynesia: Fa'afafine (Samoa), fakaleiti (Tonga), mahu wahine (Hawaii), mahu vahine (Tahiti),

whakawahine (Maori), and akava'ine (Cook Islands)

- Indonesia: Waria. Additionally, the Bugis culture of Sulawesi has been described as having three sexes (male, female, and intersex) as well as five genders with distinct social roles.
- In the Philippines, a number of local sex/gender identities are commonly referred to as a third sex in popular discourse, as well as by some academic studies. Local terms for these identities (which are considered derogatory by some) include *bakla* (Tagalog), *bayot* (Cebuano), *agi* (Ilonggo), *bantut* (Tausug), *binabae, bading*—all of which refer to effeminate "gay" men/transwomen. Gender-variant females may be called *lakin-on* or tomboy.

Europe

- The Balkans: Sworn virgins, females who work and dress as men and inhabit some men-only spaces, but do not marry
- 18th century England: Mollies

Africa

- Southern Ethiopia: *Ashtime* of Maale culture
- Kenya: *Mashoga* of Swahili-speaking areas of the Kenyan coast, particularly Mombasa
- Democratic Republic of the Congo: *Mangaiko* among the Mbo people

SOURCE: This World of Human Sexuality feature is adapted from the Wikipedia entry on third gender and obtains information from Agrawal (1997), Fausto–Sterling (1993), Goulet (2006), Hester (2005), Murray and Roscoe (1997), Roscoe (2000), Roughgarden (2004), Stockett (2005), Totman (2004), and Winter (2003).

and dependable. The "emotional woman" is a stereotype. The "logical man" is also a stereotype—albeit more generous. Even emotions are stereotyped. People assume that women are more likely to experience feelings of fear, sadness, and sympathy, whereas men are more likely to experience anger and pride (Plant et al., 2000). A **stereotype** is a fixed, conventional—and often distorted—idea about a group of people. Sex assignment (our identification of ourselves as female or male) does not determine the roles or behaviors that are deemed masculine or feminine in our culture. Cultures have broad expectations for the personalities and behaviors of men and women that are termed **gender roles**. A survey of 30 countries confirmed that these gender-role stereotypes are widespread (Williams & Best, 1994) (Table 6.1). One of the effects of stereotyping is sexism, as we see in the following section.

Stereotype A fixed, conventional idea about a group of people

Gender roles Complex clusters of behavioral expectations for males and females

TABLE 6.1

Gender Role Stereotypes in 30 Nations

Stereotypes of Males		Stereotypes of Females	
Active	Opinionated	Affectionate	Nervous
Adventurous	Pleasure seeking	Appreciative	Patient
Aggressive	Precise	Cautious	Pleasant
Arrogant	Quick	Changeable	Prudish
Autocratic	Rational	Charming	Self-pitying
Capable	Realistic	Complaining	Sensitive
Coarse	Reckless	Complicated	Sentimental
Conceited	Resourceful	Confused	Sexy
Confident	Rigid	Dependent	Shy
Courageous	Robust	Dreamy	Softhearted
Cruel	Sharp witted	Emotional	Sophisticated
Determined	Show-off	Excitable	Submissive
Disorderly	Steady	Fault finding	Suggestible
Enterprising	Stern	Fearful	Superstitious
Hardheaded	Stingy	Fickle	Talkative
Individualistic	Stolid	Foolish	Timid
Inventive	Tough	Forgiving	Touchy
Loud	Unscrupulous	Frivolous	Unambitious
Obnoxious		Fussy	Understanding
		Gentle	Unstable
		Imaginative	Warm
		Kind	Weak
		Mild	Worrying
		Modest	

Psychologists John Williams and Deborah Best (1994) found that people in 30 countries largely agreed on what constituted masculine and feminine gender-role stereotypes.
SOURCE: Williams, J. E., & Best, D. L. (1994). Cross-cultural views of women and men. In W. J. Lonner & R. Malpass (Eds.), *Psychology and culture* (p. 193, Table 1). Boston: Allyn & Bacon.

CRITICAL Thinking

Why would a researcher bother to study whether traditional gender-role stereotypes are found around the world?

SafeZone

Q *If a boy plays with dolls when he's young, won't he be gay?*

A Complicated question and complicated answer: The politically correct answer is no, suggesting that choices of toys in childhood have no implications for sexual orientation, but the truth is that studies show that they might—as long as it is the child who is doing the choosing. In other words, many gay males report that as children they were drawn to "girls' toys." But there are also layers of values implied by your question, one of which is that it's bad to be gay or bad to give a young boy dolls as toys. We don't buy into either of these assumptions. Children will choose the toys they want, and forcing toys on them won't have much of an effect, except encouraging them to set aside the ones they don't want. Labels, by the way, are also interesting. For example, is not a toy soldier a "doll"?

REFLECT

Do you remember learning that you were a girl or a boy? Did you share stereotypical preferences of toys and playmates? How did your preferences affect your identity and your self-esteem?

Sexism

We have all encountered the effects of **sexism**—the prejudgment that because of her or his sex, a person will possess certain negative traits. These negative traits are assumed to disqualify the person for certain vocations or prevent him or her from performing adequately in these jobs or in some social situations.

Sexism may lead us to interpret the same behavior in prejudicial ways when performed by women or by men. A "sensitive" woman is simply sensitive, but a sensitive man may be seen as a "sissy." We may see a man as "self-assertive," but a woman who behaves in the same way is seen as "pushy."

Children develop stereotypes about the differences between "man's work" and "woman's work" (Rathus, 2006). Women have been historically excluded from "male occupations," and stereotypical expectations concerning "men's work" and "women's work" filter down to the primary grades. For example, according to traditional stereotypes, women are not expected to excel in math. Exposure to such negative expectations may discourage women from careers in science and technology. Even when they choose a career in science or technology, women are often subject to discrimination in hiring, promotions, allocation of facilities for research, and funds to conduct research (Loder, 2000). Similarly, only recently have men begun to enter occupational domains previously restricted largely to women, such as secretarial work, nursing, and teaching in the primary grades.

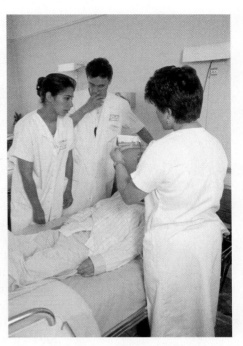

A Nurse. *If you think there is something wrong with this picture, could it be because you have fallen prey to traditional gender-role stereotypes? Tradition has prevented many women from seeking jobs in "male" preserves such as construction work and the military. Tradition has also prevented many men from obtaining work in "female" domains such as secretarial work, nursing, and teaching at the elementary level.*

Sexism is psychologically damaging. One experiment found that women who were led to believe that sexism was pervasive reported lower self-esteem than women who were led to think that sexism was rare (Schmitt et al., 2003). In another experiment, men and women were led to believe that they were rejected from taking a course either because of sexism or personal reasons (Major et al., 2003). Attributing the rejection to prejudice rather than to personal deservingness had the effect of protecting their self-esteem ("It's not me; it's society").

Fortunately, it appears that education can modify sexist attitudes. One study reported the degree to which women's studies courses can help individuals become more aware of sexism and develop more egalitarian attitudes (Stake & Hoffman, 2001). In the study, 548 women's studies students completed questionnaires before and after the courses in areas such as openness to women's studies, egalitarian attitudes toward females and gender issues, and awareness of sexism and discrimination against females. Compared with students who did not take women's studies, the students in the courses reported increased awareness of sexism and other kinds of prejudice, more egalitarian attitudes toward women and other stigmatized groups, and more interest in engaging in activism for social causes.

In the next section, we see that gender-role stereotypes are also connected with sexual behavior.

Gender Roles and Sexual Behavior

Gender roles affect relationships and sexual behavior. Children learn at an early age that men usually approach women and initiate sexual interactions, whereas women usually serve as the "gatekeepers" in romantic relationships (Bailey et al., 2000b). In their traditional role as gatekeepers, women are expected to wait to be approached

REFLECT

Have you ever been guilty of engaging in or been victimized by sexism? What was the effect? How do you view the incident now?

Sexism The prejudgment that, because of her or his sex, a person will possess negative traits

and to screen suitors. Men are expected to make the first (sexual) move and women are to determine how far they will go.

The cultural expectation that men are initiators and women are gatekeepers is embedded within the larger stereotype that men are sexually aggressive and women are sexually passive. Men are expected to have a higher number of sexual partners than women do (Mikach & Bailey, 1999). Men not only initiate sexual encounters, they are expected to dictate all the "moves" thereafter, just as they are expected to take the lead on the dance floor. People who adhere to the masculine gender-role stereotype, whether male or female, are more likely to engage in risky (unprotected) sexual behavior (Belgrave et al., 2000). According to the stereotype, women are supposed to let male partners determine the choice, timing, and sequence of sexual positions and techniques. Unfortunately, the stereotype favors men's sexual preferences, denying women the opportunity to give and receive their preferred kinds of stimulation.

According to another stereotype, men become sexually aroused at puberty and remain at the ready throughout adulthood. Women, however, do not share men's natural interests in sex, and a woman discovers her own sexuality only when a man "ignites her sexual flame." Despite the stereotype, it is not clear that women are biologically less arousable than men; however, they are more likely to desire to limit sexual activity to intimate, committed relationships (Peplau, 2003; Vohs & Baumeister, 2004). On the other hand, researchers (Peplau, 2003; Vohs & Baumeister, 2004) find consistent empirical support for the view that men generally have more sexual desire than women.

Questions remain regarding the extent to which the sex differences associated with gender-role stereotypes reflect nature or the influences of culture and tradition. Sex differences are also vastly more pervasive than those involving sexual behavior, as we see next.

CRITICAL Thinking

Why do you think that some writers suggest that it is "politically correct" to minimize sex differences in cognitive abilities?

Sex Differences in Cognition, Personality, and Behavior

If females and males were not anatomically different, this book would never have been written. But how do females and males differ in cognitive abilities, personality, and social behavior, if at all?

Differences in Cognitive Abilities

The finding of sex differences in cognitive abilities is one of the most controversial issues in human sexuality. On the surface, it is a "political minefield" (Kersting, 2003). But more important, the possible existence of cognitive sex differences has affected the academic and occupational choices of both sexes. What does the research suggest and what can we believe?

Assessments of intelligence do not show overall sex differences in cognitive abilities (Halpern & LaMay, 2000). However, reviews of the research suggest that girls are somewhat superior to boys in verbal abilities, such as verbal fluency, ability to generate words that are similar in meaning to other words, spelling, knowledge of foreign languages, and pronunciation (Halpern, 1997, 2003). Far more boys than girls have reading problems, ranging from reading below grade level to severe disabilities.

Males seem to be somewhat superior in the ability to manipulate visual images in working memory. Males as a group excel in visual-spatial abilities of the sort used in math, science, and reading maps (Collaer & Nelson, 2002; Halpern & LaMay, 2000). They especially excel at mentally rotating geometric figures in space (Figure 6.5). Studies have compared the car navigation strategies of males and females. In giving directions, males more often refer to miles and directional coordinates (north, south, east, and west), whereas women are more likely to refer to landmarks and right or left turns (MacFadden et al., 2003).

Studies in the United States and elsewhere find that males generally obtain higher scores on math tests than females (Benbow et al., 2000; Collaer & Hill, 2006; Leahey & Guo, 2001; Webb et al., 2002). Differences in problem solving are reflected on the mathematics test of the Scholastic Aptitude Test (SAT). The mean score is 500, and about two thirds of the test takers receive scores between 400 and 600. Twice as many boys as girls attain math scores of more than 500.

Despite these reports, investigators and commentators have noted the following:

Are There Sex Differences in Cognitive Abilities? *The physical differences between females and males are well established—and well celebrated! But are there cognitive differences between females and males? If so, what are they? How large are they? Are they the result of nature (heredity) or nurture (environmental influences such as educational experiences and cultural expectations)?*

1. In most cases, sex differences in math and spatial abilities are small and growing smaller (Hyde & Plant, 1995). However, psychologist J. Michael Bailey (2003) and others suggest that these differences are more robust than Hyde and Plant would have us believe. At the same time, psychologist Elizabeth Spelke (2005) reports that there is no reason to believe that sex differences in ability in math and science are inborn. There is ample evidence that male and female infants possess equal ability to achieve in these areas. The small differences that may exist reflect cultural expectations and differences in education (Leahey & Guo, 2001).

2. Such sex differences that may exist are *group* differences. Variation in ability on tests of verbal or math skills is larger *within*, than between, the sexes. Despite possible differences between large groups of boys and girls, millions of boys exceed the "average" girl in writing and spelling skills. Likewise, millions of girls outperform the "average" boy in math and science. The male sex has produced its Shakespeares and the female sex its Madame Curies.

While scholars sit around and debate sex differences in intellectual functioning, women are voting on the issue by flooding fields once populated almost exclusively by men (Cox & Alm, 2005). Table 6.2 and Figure 6.6 show that women are tossing

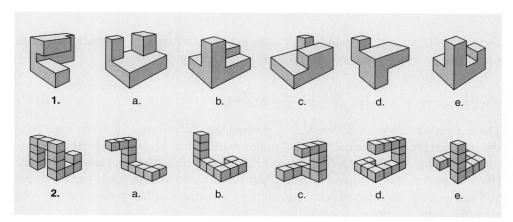

Figure 6.5 Rotating Geometric Figures in Space. *Visual-spatial skills—for example, the ability to rotate geometric figures in space—are considered part of the male gender-role stereotype. But such sex differences are small and can be modified by training.*

TABLE 6.2

Women as a Percentage of College Students Receiving Bachelor's Degrees in the Sciences

Field	Year	
	1971	2002
Biology	29	61
Chemistry	18	48
Computer science	14	28
Engineering	1	19
Geology	11	45
Mathematics	38	47
Physics	7	23

SOURCE: Cox, W. M. & Alm, R. (2005, February 25). Scientists are made, not born. *The New York Times.* [Online].

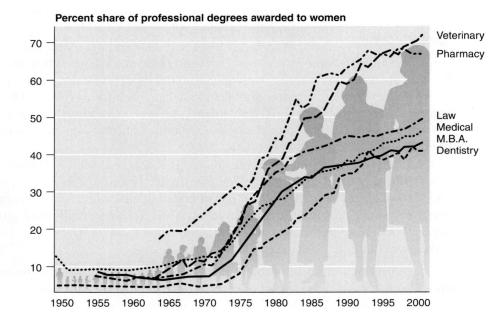

Figure 6.6 Women Flood Professions Once Populated Almost Exclusively by Men.

SOURCE: As appeared in "Scientists are Made, Not Born" by W. Michael Cox and Richard Alm, *The New York Times,* February 28, 2005. Reprinted by permission of Management Design.

these stereotypes out the window by entering the sciences and professional fields, ranging from business to law to medicine, in increasing numbers.

Differences in Personality

There are also many sex differences in personality. According to a meta-analysis of the research literature, females exceed males in extraversion, anxiety, trust, and nurturance (Feingold, 1994). Overall, however, differences in personality tend to be small (Bailey, 2003b). Males do tend to exceed females in assertiveness, tough-mindedness, and self-esteem. Two factors that may largely account for the relatively lower self-esteem of females include the fact that

- parents, on the average, prefer to have boys
- society has created an unlevel playing field in which females have to perform better than males to be seen as doing equally well

Differences in Social Behavior

There are important sex differences in social behavior, particularly in matters concerning sex and aggression. Consider communication styles. Research shows that males dominate classroom discussions (Sadker & Sadker, 1994). As girls mature, it appears that they learn to "take a backseat" to boys and let the boys do most of the talking when they are in mixed-gender groups. Women are more willing than men to disclose their feelings and personal experiences, however (Dindia & Allen, 1992). The stereotype of the "strong and silent" male may not discourage men from hogging the conversation, but it may inhibit them from expressing their personal feelings.

According to almost any measure that is used, men show more interest in sex than women (Peplau, 2003; Vohs & Baumeister, 2004). Women are more likely to want to combine sex with a romantic relationship (Peplau, 2003). Men also report being more interested than women in casual sex and in multiple sex partners (Schmitt, 2003).

DIFFERENCES IN AGGRESSIVENESS **Truth or Fiction Revisited:** It is true that males tend to behave more aggressively than females (Felson, 2002; Hines & Saudino, 2003; Zeichner et al., 2003). In almost all cultures, it is the male who marches off to war and who battles for fame, glory (and shaving cream commercial contracts in stadiums and arenas). As we will see, the key question is why?

DIFFERENCES IN WILLINGNESS TO SEEK HEALTH CARE Men's life expectancies are seven years shorter, on average, than women's. Female and male anatomy and physiology predispose them to different health issues, but part of the difference, according to surveys of physicians and of the general population, is women's greater willingness to seek health care (Courtenay, 2000). Men often let symptoms go until a problem that could have been prevented or readily treated becomes serious or life threatening. Women, for example, are much more likely to check themselves for breast cancer than men are even to recognize the symptoms of prostate cancer. Many men have a "bulletproof mentality." They are too strong to see the doctor in their 20s, too busy in their 30s, and too frightened later on.

REFLECT

Do any of the sex differences in cognition and personality reported in the scientific literature surprise you? Why or why not?

REFLECT

How can you make use of the information in this section to enhance and maintain your health?

On Becoming a Man or a Woman: Gender Typing

We have chronicled the biological processes of sexual differentiation, and we have explored sex differences in cognitive abilities, personality, and social behavior. In this section we consider various explanations of gender typing, beginning with the biological.

Biological Perspectives

Biological views on gender typing tend to focus on the roles of genetics and prenatal influences in predisposing men and women to gender-linked behavior patterns.

The Eye That Roves around the World?

One of the more controversial sex differences is the suggestion that males are naturally polygamous and females are naturally monogamous. If this were so, it would place a greater burden on societies in which men are expected to remain loyal to their mates. If the man strayed, after all, he could have the attitude, "Don't blame me. It's in my genes." Women, moreover, might wonder how realistic it is to expect that their partners will remain faithful.

Evolutionary psychologists have hypothesized the *sexual strategies theory,* which holds that men and women differ in their long-term and short-term mating strategies, with men more interested in sexual variety in the short term (Klusmann, 2002; McBurney et al., 2005). In the long term, both males and females may seek a heavy investment in a relationship, feelings of love, companionship, and a sharing of resources. Even so, men are hypothesized to place more value on signals of fertility and reproductive value, as found in a woman's youth and physical appearance. But women are hypothesized to place relatively more value on a man's social status, maturity, and resources—cues that are relevant to his ability to provide over the long term. The qualities that men and women seek are believed to help solve adaptive problems that humans have faced throughout their evolutionary history.

But in the short term, men are more interested in one-night stands and relatively brief affairs. Women, evolutionarily speaking, would have little to gain from such encounters. Impregnation requires a long-term commitment to child rearing, and evolutionary forces would favor the survival of the children of women who created a long-term nurturing environment. But men would have a greater chance of contributing their genes to future generations by impregnating as many women as possible.

Because a "universal" form of behavior is more likely to be embedded in people's genes, the evolutionary theory of different sexual strategies would find support if males and females from various cultures showed similar sex differences in short-term mating strategies. In seeking just such evidence, David Schmitt (2003) supervised a survey of 16,288 people across 10 major regions of the world, including North America, South America, Western Europe, Eastern Europe, Southern Europe, Middle East, Africa, Oceania, South/Southeast Asia, and East Asia. He found, indeed, that sex differences in the desire for sexual variety were culturally universal.

Table 6.3 and Figure 6.7 reveal some of Schmitt's (2003) key findings regarding the desire for variety in short-term and long-term relationships. When asked whether they would like to have more than one sex partner in the next month, men from all 10 areas of the world were significantly more likely than women to say that they would. For example, 23.1% of North American men would like more than one partner, compared with just 2.9% of North American women (Table 6.3). When asked about the mean (average) number of sex partners they would like to have during the next 30 years, men from every area

Biological perspectives have also focused on the possible role of hormones in sculpting the brain during prenatal development.

THE EVOLUTIONARY PERSPECTIVE: IT'S ONLY NATURAL From the evolutionary perspective, the story of the survival of our ancient ancestors is etched in our genes. Genes that bestow attributes that increase an organism's chances of surviving to produce viable offspring are most likely to be transmitted to future generations. We thus possess the genetic remnants of traits that helped our ancestors survive and reproduce (Buss, 2005; Plomin & Crabbe, 2000). This heritage influences our social and sexual behavior as well as our anatomic features.

According to the evolutionary perspective, men's traditional roles as hunters and warriors, and women's roles as caregivers and gatherers of fruits and vegetables, are bequeathed to us in our genes. Men are better suited to war and the hunt because of physical attributes passed along since ancestral times. Upper body strength, for ex-

CRITICAL
Thinking

According to evolutionary theory, men have inherited a tendency to be interested in having multiple sex partners. Does this mean that it is "unnatural" for society to promote monogamous relationships?

said they would like to have significantly more sex partners than the women (Figure 6.7).

We cannot conclude that these research findings, intriguing as they are, "prove" the validity of the evolutionary approach to understanding sex differences in "sexual strategies." For example, we could point to details such as the fact that Oceanic women reported that they wanted more sex partners in the long term than did African men (Figure 6.7). We can also accept the universality of the finding but consider rival explanations for the data. For example, in a world with common global communication, it might not be surprising that there is worldwide overlap in gender roles. This overlap might affect the ways in which parents and cultural institutions influence children around the world.

Do Men around the World Have Roving Eyes? *A study of 10 different areas of the world found that in every culture surveyed, men were more likely than women to desire multiple sex partners. According to the sexual strategies theory, this sex difference reflects human adaptation to environmental forces. Here's a question for critical thinking: Does this research finding mean that it is "unnatural" to expect men to remain faithful to their partners?*

ample, would have enabled them to throw spears and overpower adversaries. Men also possess perceptual–cognitive advantages, such as superior visual–motor skills that favor aggression. Visual–motor skills would have enabled men to aim spears or bows and arrows.

Women, it is argued, are genetically predisposed to be empathic and nurturing because these traits enabled ancestral women to respond to children's needs and enhance the likelihood that their children would flourish and eventually reproduce, thereby transmitting their own genetic legacy to future generations. Prehistoric women thus tended to stay close to home, cared for the children, and gathered edible plants, whereas men ventured from home to hunt and raid their neighbors' storehouses.

The evolutionary perspective is steeped in controversy. Although scientists do not dispute the importance of evolution in determining physical attributes, many are reluctant to attribute complex social behaviors, such as aggression and gender roles,

CRITICAL Thinking

Why do you think many feminists and queer theorists argue that evolutionary theory is little more than a sophisticated excuse for maintaining the status quo in the centers of power in society?

TABLE 6.3

Sex Differences in the Percentage of Men and Women Who Desire More Than One Sex Partner "in the Next Month" across 10 World Regions

World Region	Percentage of Men Wanting More Than One Sexual Partner	Percentage of Women Wanting More Than One Sexual Partner
North America	23.1	2.9
South America	35.0	6.1
Western Europe	22.6	5.5
Eastern Europe	31.7	7.1
Southern Europe	31.0	6.0
Middle East	33.1	5.9
Africa	18.2	4.2
Oceania	25.3	5.8
South/Southeast Asia	32.4	6.4
East Asia	17.9	2.6

The chances that any sex differences within a given region are the result of chance is less than 1 in 1,000 ($P < 0.001$).

SOURCE: From "Universal sex differences in the desire for sexual variety: Tests from 52 nations, 6 continents, and 13 islands", by David P. Schmitt, *Journal of Personality and Social Psychology,* (2003) 85 (1): 85–104. Copyright © 2003 by the American Psychological Assiciation. Reprinted with permission.

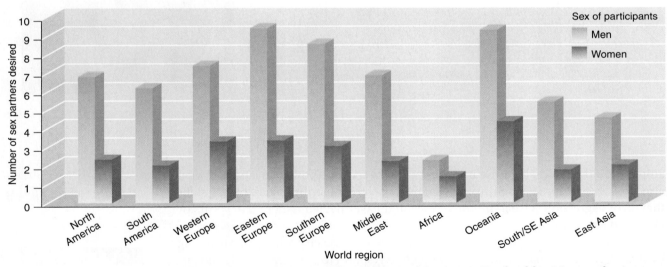

Figure 6.7   **Mean Number of Sexual Partners Desired by Men and Women—in the Next 30 Years—across 10 World Regions**

SOURCE: From "Universal sex differences in the desire for sexual variety: Tests from 52 nations, 6 continents, and 13 islands", by David P. Schmitt, *Journal of Personality and Social Psychology,* (2003) 85 (1): 85–104. Copyright © 2003 by the American Psychological Assiciation. Reprinted with permission.

to heredity. The evolutionary perspective implies that stereotypical gender roles—men as breadwinners and women as homemakers, for example—reflect the natural order of things. Critics contend that, among humans, biology is not destiny, and behavior is not dictated by genes.

SafeZone

Q *Aren't there cultures in which women do the hunting/gathering and men take care of the children?*

A There certainly have been some. In her 1935 book *Sex and Temperament in Three Primitive Societies,* anthropologist Margaret Mead described the Tchambuli of New Guinea as follows: "The men 'primped' and spent their time decorating themselves while the women worked and were the practical ones—the opposite of how it seemed in early 20th century America." But, frankly, what makes this finding notable is its rarity.

PRENATAL BRAIN ORGANIZATION Researchers have sought the origins of gender-type behavior in the organization of the brain. Is it possible that the cornerstone of gender-type behavior is laid in the brain before the first breath is taken?

The hemispheres of the brain are specialized to carry out certain functions (Shaywitz et al., 1995). In most people, the right hemisphere ("right brain") appears to be specialized to perform visual–spatial tasks. The "left brain" appears to be more essential to verbal functions, such as speech, in most people.

We know that sex hormones are responsible for prenatal sexual differentiation of the genitals and for the gender-related structural differences in the hypothalamus of the developing prenatal brain. Sexual differentiation of the brain may also partly explain men's superiority at spatial relations tasks, such as interpreting road maps and visualizing objects in space. Testosterone in the brain of male fetuses spurs greater growth of the right hemisphere and slows the rate of growth of the left hemisphere (Cohen–Bendahan et al., 2005; Siegel–Hinson & McKeever, 2002). This difference may be connected with the ability to accomplish spatial relations tasks, and with preferences for childhood toys.

Might boys' inclinations toward aggression and rough-and-tumble play also be prenatally imprinted in the brain? Some theorists argue that prenatal sex hormones may masculinize or feminize the brain by creating predispositions that are consistent with gender-role stereotypes, such as rough-and-tumble play and aggressive behavior in males (Cohen–Bendahan et al., 2005).

Psychological Perspectives

Developmentally speaking, children acquire awareness of gender-role stereotypes by the tender ages of two and a half to three and a half years old (Rathus, 2006). When asked to describe sex differences, boys and girls generally agree that boys build things, play with transportation toys such as cars and fire trucks, enjoy helping their fathers, and hit other children. Both boys and girls also agree that girls enjoy playing with dolls, help their mothers cook and clean, and are talkative, dependent on others for help, and nonviolent. They perceive the label *cruel* to be a masculine trait, whereas "cries a lot" is perceived as feminine. By the time they are three years old, most children have become aware of the stereotypical ways in which men and women dress and the types of occupations that are considered appropriate for each (Rathus, 2006).

Psychologists have attempted to explain how children acquire such knowledge and adopt stereotypical behavior patterns in terms of psychoanalytic, social–cognitive, and cognitive–developmental theories.

PSYCHOANALYTIC THEORY Sigmund Freud explained gender typing in terms of **identification**. Appropriate gender typing, in Freud's view, requires that boys come to identify with their fathers and girls with their mothers. Identification is completed, in Freud's view, as children resolve the **Oedipus complex** (sometimes called the Electra complex in girls).

According to Freud, the Oedipus complex occurs during the phallic period of psychosexual development, from three to five years old. During this period, the child develops incestuous wishes for the parent of the other sex and comes to perceive the parent of the same sex as a rival. The complex is resolved by the child's forsaking incestuous wishes for the parent of the other sex and identifying with the parent of the same sex. Through identification with the same-sex parent, the child comes to develop preferences and behavior patterns that are typically associated with that sex. However, children display stereotypical gender-typed behaviors earlier than Freud would have predicted. Even during the first year, boys are more independent than girls. Girls are more quiet and restrained. Girls show preferences for dolls and soft toys, and boys for hard transportation toys, by one and a half to three years old (Alexander, 2003). Because of their lack of empirical support, many researchers believe that Freud's views are now of historical interest only.

SOCIAL–COGNITIVE THEORY Social–cognitive theorists explain the development of gender-type behavior in terms of processes such as observational learning, identification, and socialization (Balter & Tamis–LeMonda, 1999; Fagot et al., 2000). Children can learn what is deemed masculine or feminine by observational learning, as suggested by the results of a classic experiment by Perry and Bussey (1979). In that study, eight- and nine-year-olds watched adult role models indicate preferences for each of 16 pairs of items—such as toy cows versus toy horses and oranges versus apples. But the children didn't know that the expressed preferences were made arbitrarily. The children then were asked to indicate their own preferences for the items represented in the pairs. The boys' choices agreed with the adult men's an average of 14 out of 16 times. Girls chose the pair item selected by the men, on the average, only 3 out of 16 times.

In social–cognitive theory, identification is seen as a continuous learning process in which rewards and punishments influence children to imitate adult models of the same sex (Balter & Tamis–LeMonda, 1999; Fagot et al., 2000). In identification, the child not only imitates the behavior of the model, but tries to become broadly like the model.

Socialization also plays a role in gender typing (Balter & Tamis–LeMonda, 1999; Fagot et al., 2000). Almost from the moment a baby comes into the world, it is treated according to its gender. Parents tend to talk more to baby girls, and fathers especially engage in more roughhousing with boys. When children are old enough to speak, parents and other adults—even other children—begin to instruct children in how they are expected to behave. Parents may reward children for behavior they consider gender appropriate and may punish (or fail to reinforce) them for behavior they consider inappropriate for their gender. Girls are encouraged to practice caretaking be-

Identification In psychoanalytic theory, the process of incorporating within ourselves our perceptions of the behaviors, thoughts, and feelings of others

Oedipus complex According to psychoanalytic theory, a conflict of the phallic stage in which the boy wishes to possess his mother sexually and perceives his father as a rival in love

Socialization The process of guiding people into socially acceptable behavior patterns by means of information, rewards, and punishments

Gender Typing through Observational Learning. *According to social–cognitive theory, people learn about the gender roles that are available to them—and expected of them—at an early age. Gender schema theory adds that once children have learned the expected gender roles (i.e., the gender schema of their culture), they blend these roles with their self-concepts. Their self-esteem comes to be dependent on their adherence to the expected gender roles.*

haviors, which are intended to prepare them for traditional feminine adult roles. Boys are handed Legos or doctor sets to help prepare them for traditional masculine adult roles.

Fathers generally encourage their sons to develop assertive, instrumental behavior (i.e., behavior that gets things done or accomplishes something) and their daughters to develop nurturing, cooperative behavior. Fathers are likely to cuddle their daughters gently. They are likely to carry their sons like footballs or toss them into the air. Fathers also tend to use heartier and harsher language with their sons, such as "How're yuh doin', Tiger?" and "Hey, you; get your keester over here." Being a nontraditionalist, your first author made sure to toss his young daughters into the air, which raised immediate objections from the relatives, who chastised him for being too rough. This, of course, led him to modify his behavior. He learned to toss his daughters into the air when the relatives were not around.

Generally speaking, from an early age boys are more likely to receive toy cars, guns, and athletic equipment, and are encouraged to compete aggressively. Even relatively sophisticated college students are likely to select traditionally masculine toys as gifts for boys and traditionally feminine toys for girls. Girls are spoken to more often, whereas boys are handled more frequently and more roughly. Whatever the biological determinants of sex differences in aggressiveness and verbal skills, early socialization experiences clearly play a role.

Parental roles in gender typing are apparently changing. With more mothers working outside the home in our society, daughters are exposed to more women who represent career-minded role models than was the case in earlier generations. More parents today are encouraging their daughters to become career minded and to engage in strenuous physical activities, such as organized sports. Many boys today are exposed to fathers who take a larger role than men used to in child care and household responsibilities.

Social–cognitive theorists believe that aggression is largely influenced by learning. Boys are permitted, even encouraged, to engage in more aggressive behavior than girls.

Social–cognitive theorists have contributed to our understanding of how rewards, punishments, and modeling influences foster gender-typed behavior patterns. How do children integrate gender-role expectations within their self-concepts? And how do their concepts concerning gender influence their development of gender-typed behavior? Let us consider two cognitive approaches to gender typing that shed light on these matters: cognitive–developmental theory and gender schema theory.

COGNITIVE–DEVELOPMENTAL THEORY Psychologist Lawrence Kohlberg (1966) proposed a cognitive–developmental view of gender typing. From this perspective, gender typing is not the product of environmental influences that mechanically "stamp in" gender-appropriate behavior. Rather, children themselves play an active role. They form concepts, or **schemas**, about gender and then conform their behavior to their gender concepts. These developments occur in stages and are entwined with general cognitive development.

According to Kohlberg (1966), gender typing entails the emergence of three concepts: *gender identity, gender stability,* and *gender constancy.* Gender identity is usually acquired by the age of three. By the age of four or five years, most children develop a concept of **gender stability**—the recognition that people retain their genders for a lifetime.

TRUTH **fiction 7**

Truth or Fiction Revisited: Prior to the age of four or five or so, children may not have developed the concept of gender stability. As a result, boys may think that they will become mommies when they grow up, and girls may believe that they can become daddies.

The more sophisticated concept of **gender constancy** develops in most children by the age of seven or eight. They recognize that gender does not change, even if people alter their dress or behavior. So gender remains constant even when appearances change. A woman who wears her hair short (or shaves it off) remains a woman. A man who dons an apron and cooks dinner remains a man.

According to cognitive–developmental theory, children are motivated to behave in gender-appropriate ways after they have established the concepts of gender stability and gender constancy. They then make an active effort to obtain information regarding which behavior patterns are considered "masculine" and which are "feminine" (Perry & Bussey, 1979). After they obtain this information, they imitate the "gender-appropriate" pattern. So boys and girls who come to recognize that their genders will remain a fixed part of their identity will show preferences for "masculine" and "feminine" activities respectively. Researchers find, for instance, that boys who had achieved gender constancy played with an uninteresting gender-typed toy for a longer period of time than did boys who hadn't yet achieved gender constancy (Frey & Ruble, 1992). Both groups of boys played with an interesting gender-typed toy for about an equal length of time.

Cross-cultural studies of the United States, Samoa, Nepal, Belize, and Kenya find that the concepts of gender identity, gender stability, and gender constancy emerge in the order predicted by Kohlberg (1966). However, gender-typed play often emerges at an earlier age than predicted by cognitive–developmental theory. Many children make gender-typed choices of toys by the age of two years. Children as young as 18 months are likely to have developed a sense of gender identity, but gender stability and con-

Schema Concept; a way of interpreting experience or processing information

Gender stability The concept that people retain their genders for a lifetime

Gender constancy The concept that people's genders do not change, even if they alter their dress or behavior

stancy are some years off. Gender identity alone thus seems sufficient to prompt children to assume gender-typed behavior patterns. Psychologist Sandra Bem (1983) also notes that Kohlberg's theory does not explain why the concept of gender plays such a prominent role in children's classification of people and behavior. Another cognitive view, gender schema theory, attempts to address these concerns.

GENDER SCHEMA THEORY Gender schema theory proposes that children develop a **gender schema** as a means of organizing their perceptions of the world (Bem, 1993). A gender schema is a cluster of mental representations about masculine and feminine physical qualities, behaviors, and personality traits. Gender gains prominence as a schema for organizing experience because of society's emphasis on it. Even young children start to mentally group people of the same sex according to the traits they believe represent them.

Children's gender schemas determine how important gender-typed traits are to them. Consider the dimension of *strength–weakness.* Children may learn that strength is connected with maleness and weakness with femaleness. (Other dimensions, such as *light–dark,* are not gender-typed and thus may fall outside children's gender schemas.) Children also gather that some dimensions, such as *strong–weak,* are more important to one sex (in this case, the male) than the other.

After children acquire a gender schema, they begin to judge themselves according to traits considered appropriate to their sex (Fagot et al., 2000). In doing so, they blend their developing self-concepts with the prominent gender schema of their culture. Children with self-concepts that are consistent with the prominent gender schema of their culture are likely to develop higher self-esteem than children whose self-concepts are inconsistent. Jack learns that muscle strength is a characteristic associated with "manliness." He is likely to think more highly of himself if he perceives himself as embodying this attribute than if he does not. Alexis is likely to discover that the dimension of kindness–cruelty is more crucial than strength–weakness to the way in which women are perceived in society.

According to gender schema theory, gender identity itself is sufficient to inspire gender-appropriate behavior. After children develop a concept of gender identity, they begin to seek information concerning gender-type traits and try to live up to them. Jack will retaliate when provoked, because boys are expected to do so. Alexis will be "sugary and sweet," if such is expected of little girls. Thus, gender-typed behavior emerges earlier than would be proposed by cognitive–developmental theory.

In the following section, we see that Sandra Bem and Richard Lippa have also theorized that some people have traits that are stereotypical of both males and females, and that they promote psychological adjustment to a complex society.

REFLECT

How do your recollections of the development of your own gender-typed behavior fit the theories described in this section? For example, do you recall making a conscious effort to behave in ways that are expected of people of your sex?

Psychological Androgyny and the Reconstruction of Masculinity–Femininity: The More Traits, the Merrier?

Gender schema A cluster of mental representations about male and female physical qualities, behaviors, and personality traits

Most people think of masculinity and femininity as opposite ends of one continuum. People tend to assume that the more masculine a person is, the less feminine he or she must be, and vice versa. So a man who exhibits stereotypical feminine traits of nurturance, tenderness, and emotionality is often considered less masculine than other men. Women who compete with men in business are perceived not only as more masculine, but also as less feminine than other women.

Some investigators, such as Sandra Bem (1993), argue that masculinity and femininity comprise separate personality dimensions. A person who is highly masculine, whether male or female, may also possess feminine traits—and vice versa. People who exhibit "masculine" assertiveness and instrumental skills (skills in the sciences and business, for example) along with "feminine" nurturance and cooperation fit both the masculine and feminine gender-role stereotypes. They are said to show **psychological androgyny**. Assertiveness and instrumental skills are consistent with the masculine stereotype. Nurturance and cooperation are consistent with the feminine stereotype. People low in the stereotypical masculine and feminine traits are "undifferentiated," according to gender-role stereotypes.

People who are psychologically androgynous may be capable of summoning a wider range of masculine and feminine traits to meet the demands of various situations and to express their desires and talents. Researchers, for example, have found psychologically androgynous persons of both genders to show "masculine" independence under group pressures to conform and "feminine" nurturance in interactions with a kitten or a baby (Bem, 1975; Bem et al., 1976). Psychologically androgynous adolescents are less likely to stereotype occupations as masculine or feminine (Kulik, 2000).

Many people who oppose the constraints of traditional gender roles may perceive psychological androgyny as a desirable goal. Some feminist writers, however, criticize psychological androgyny on the grounds that the concept is defined in terms of, and thereby perpetuates, belief in the existence of masculine and feminine gender roles.

Other critics suggest that the so-called benefits of psychological androgyny can become confused with those of masculinity. The research evidence does show that psychologically androgynous people tend to have higher self-esteem and to be generally better adjusted psychologically than people who are feminine or undifferentiated (Whitley, 1983; Williams & D'Alessandro, 1994). That is, masculine traits such as assertiveness and independence may be related to psychological well-being, regardless of whether they are combined with feminine traits such as warmth, nurturance, and cooperation.

Psychologist Richard Lippa (2001) of California State University at Fullerton finds the model of psychological androgyny to be somewhat simplified. His research is based on surveys of personality traits and vocational interests. For example, in terms of vocational interests, he finds that traditional measures of "masculinity" tend to be positively related to interest in working with "things," whereas "femininity" is more related to working with people. In terms of personality traits, masculinity is more related to "instrumentality," or making things happen. Femininity is more related to expressiveness, or experiencing and expressing aspects of the emotional life. There are subordinate but interesting findings. For example, masculinity is also related to a heterosexual orientation, social dominance, and prejudice in men. Femininity is connected with behaviors that tend to provide the glue in interpersonal relationships. Keep in mind—again—that not all males are extremely "masculine" and not all females are overwhelmingly "feminine." Lippa, like many other researchers, has been attempting to define the nature and implications of the traditional cultural concepts (also called constructs) of masculinity and femininity. Perhaps it is fortunate that few of us are completely masculine or feminine, despite our anatomic sex.

REFLECT

Why might a woman desire a psychologically androgynous man as a partner?

CRITICAL Thinking

Explain the feminist argument against the concept of psychological androgyny.

Psychological androgyny A state characterized by possession of both stereotypical masculine traits and stereotypical feminine traits

In this chapter we have explored what it means to be female, male, or another sex within a cultural setting such as ours. In the following chapter we consider how feelings of attraction and love develop in females, males, and others.

SafeZone

Q *Are there more similarities or differences between men and women?*

A Here's a shocking answer: It depends on how you look at it. We are used to focusing on the differences, but we'll take a flyer and say there are more similarities. For example, men and women share well over 99% of their genetic material. They both walk upright, use language, think, perform in the sciences and the arts, play tennis and golf, have iPods and cell phones attached to their ears, and on and on. And, sadly, they both pay taxes and carry mortgages.

1. How are males differentiated from females during prenatal development?

- During the first six weeks or so of prenatal development, embryonic structures of both sexes resemble female structures. At about the seventh week after conception, the genetic code (XX or XY) begins to assert itself, causing changes in the gonads, genital ducts, and external genitals.

- Testosterone spurs differentiation of the male (Wolffian) duct system. In the absence of testosterone, the Wolffian ducts degenerate, and female sex organs develop. Testosterone causes cells in the hypothalamus of male fetuses to become insensitive to estrogen.

- The testes and ovaries develop in the abdominal cavity. A few months after conception, the ovaries descend to the pelvic region, and the testes descend into the scrotal sac.

2. What are the determinants of gender identity?

- Gender identity is the psychological sense of being female or being male and is almost always consistent with anatomic sex. However, research with intersexuals suggests that prenatal exposure to androgens may masculinize the brain as well as the sex organs.

- Transsexualism/transgenderism is the desire to have the genital organs of, and to live as, a member of the other sex. There is debate regarding whether transsexuals experience gender dysphoria, whether they are highly and effeminate gays, or are sexually excited by the idea of having the genitals of the other sex.

- What is the third gender/third sex area of study about? The third gender area addresses matters that have to do with people whose anatomy and/or patterns of sexual behavior or sexual desire do not fit heteronormativity. For example, they refer to Thai ladyboys and Native American Two-Spirits.

3. What are gender roles and stereotypes?

- Cultures have broad expectations of men and women that are termed *gender roles.* In our culture the stereotypical female is seen as nurturing, gentle, dependent, kind, helpful, patient, and submissive. The stereotypical male is self-assertive, tough, competitive, gentlemanly, and protective.

- Sexism is the prejudgment that because of gender, a person will possess negative traits. Women have disproportionately suffered the effects of sexism.

- Gender roles have encouraged many males to take the initiative in approaching members of the other sex and in sexual activity itself.

4. How do females and males differ in cognitive abilities, personality, and social behavior?

- Although males tend to perform slightly better in math and science, researchers challenge the notion that cognitive differences may be inborn. Males are more aggressive and more interested in sex than females.

5. How does gender typing occur?

- Biological views on gender typing focus on the roles of evolution, genetics, and prenatal influences in predisposing males and females to stereotypical behavior patterns. Evolutionary theory explains sex differences in terms of adaptation to environmental forces. Testosterone in the brain of male fetuses spurs greater growth of the right hemisphere, which may be connected with spatial relations tasks.

- Psychologists have attempted to explain gender typing in terms of psychodynamic, social cognitive, and cognitive–developmental theories. Freud explained gender typing in terms of identification with the parent of the same sex through resolution of the Oedipus complex. Social–cognitive theorists explain the development of gender-type behavior in terms of processes such as observational learning, identification, and socialization. According to Kohlberg, gender typing entails the emergence of gender identity, gender stability, and gender constancy. Gender schema theory proposes that children blend their developing self-concepts with the prominent gender schema of their culture.

6. What is psychological androgyny?

- Bem and Lippa raise the issue regarding whether masculinity and femininity comprise two independent personality dimensions rather than a single bipolar dimension. According to Bem, people who combine stereotypical masculine and feminine behavior patterns are psychologically androgynous. Lippa finds relationships between masculinity and instrumentality, and between femininity and nurturance.

1. Ovaries begin to form at _____ weeks after conception.

   (a) one or two
   (b) 11 or 12
   (c) 21 or 22
   (d) 31 or 32

2. Müllerian inhibiting substance prevents the Müllerian ducts from developing into

   (a) the female duct system
   (b) the male duct system
   (c) interstitial cells
   (d) external genital organs

3. Klinefelter syndrome is caused by an _____ sex chromosomal pattern.

   (a) X
   (b) XY
   (c) XXY
   (d) XYY

4. Congenital adrenal hyperplasia is caused by excessive levels of

   (a) androgens
   (b) estradiol
   (c) pheromones
   (d) Müllerian inhibiting substance

5. Transsexuals are most likely to have

   (a) an extra X chromosome
   (b) androgen insensitivity syndrome
   (c) aggressive tendencies
   (d) gender dysphoria

6. The masculine gender-role stereotype is seen as all of the following *except*

   (a) sensitive
   (b) tough
   (c) protective
   (d) gentlemanly

7. Which sex difference is supported by evidence?

   (a) Males are better writers.
   (b) Females are better in math and science.
   (c) Females are more aggressive.
   (d) Males have more reading problems.

8. According to sexual strategies theory,

   (a) women choose the best-looking men
   (b) only humans have long-term mates
   (c) men are more interested in short-term sexual variety
   (d) women seek sex without commitment

9. According to Kohlberg, gender _____ develops last.

   (a) stability
   (b) identity
   (c) exclusivity
   (d) constancy

10. Feminists criticize the concept of psychological androgyny on grounds that it

    (a) is based on psychoanalytic theory
    (b) perpetuates belief in the existence of masculine and feminine gender roles
    (c) is supported by cross-species but not cross-cultural evidence
    (d) suggests that there should be no individual differences

11. The concept of the third gender challenges

    (a) feminist theory
    (b) queer theory
    (c) heteronormativity
    (d) transgender activism

12. Females with Turner syndrome are

    (a) fertile
    (b) skilled in spatial relations
    (c) aggressive
    (d) short

13. Research shows that after sex reassignment, most male-to-female transsexuals

    (a) are orgasmic during sexual intercourse
    (b) regret their decision to have the operation
    (c) develop psychological disorders they did not show evidence of previously
    (d) eventually discontinue hormone treatments

14. The most common form of female intersexualism is

    (a) Dominican Republic syndrome
    (b) congenital adrenal hyperplasia
    (c) transsexualism
    (d) gender instability

15. Being _____ is perceived as being part of the feminine gender-role stereotype.

    (a) active
    (b) adventurous
    (c) affectionate
    (d) aggressive

7

Attraction and Love—Binding Forces

TRUTH fiction ?

Which of the following statements are true, and which are fiction? Look for the Truth/Fiction icons on the pages that follow to find the answers.

1 Beauty is in the eye of the beholder.   T   F

2 Women find men with deeper voices to be more attractive.   T   F

3 People are regarded as more attractive when they are smiling.   T   F

4 Women who are randomly assigned names like Kathy and Jennifer are rated as more attractive than women assigned names like Harriet and Gertrude.   T   F

5 Physical appeal is the most important trait we seek in partners for long-term relationships.   T   F

6 "Opposites attract." We are more apt to be attracted to people who disagree with our views and tastes than to people who share them.   T   F

7 It is possible to be in love with someone who is not also a friend.   T   F

8 Committed couples can remain in love even after passion fades.   T   F

Candy and Stretch. A new technique for controlling weight gain? No, these are the names of a couple who have just met at a camera club that doubles as a meeting place for singles.

Candy and Stretch stand above the crowd—literally. She is almost six feet tall, an attractive woman in her early 30s. He is more average looking, but "wholesome." He is in his late 30s and six feet, five inches tall. Stretch has been in the group for some time. Candy is a new member. Let us follow them as they meet during a coffee break. As you will see, there are some differences between what they say and what they think.

They Say	They Think
STRETCH:	
Well, you're certainly a welcome addition to our group.	*(Can't I ever say something clever?)*
CANDY:	
Thank you. It certainly is friendly and interesting.	*(He's cute.)*
STRETCH:	
My friends call me Stretch. It's left over from my basketball days. Silly, but I'm used to it.	*(It's safer than saying my name is David Stein.)*
CANDY:	
My name is Candy.	*(At least my nickname is. He doesn't have to hear Hortense O'Brien.)*
STRETCH:	
What kind of camera is that?	*(Why couldn't a girl named Candy be Jewish? It's only a nickname, isn't it?)*
CANDY:	
Just this old German one of my uncle's. I borrowed it from the office.	*(He could be Irish. And that camera looks expensive.)*
STRETCH:	
May I? (He takes her camera, brushing her hand and then tingling with the touch.) Fine lens. You work for your uncle?	*(Now I've done it. Brought up work.)*
CANDY:	
Ever since college.	*(Okay, so what if I only went for a year?)*
It's more than being just a secretary. I get into sales, too.	*(If he asks what I sell, I'll tell him anything except underwear.)*
STRETCH:	
Sales? That's funny. I'm in sales, too, but mainly as an executive. I run our department.	*(Is there a nice way to say used cars? I'd better change the subject.)*
I started using cameras on trips. Last time I was in the Bahamas, I took—	*(Great legs! And the way her hips move—)*
CANDY:	
Oh! Do you go to the Bahamas, too? I love those islands.	*(So I went just once, and it was for the brassiere manufacturers' convention. At least we're off the subject of jobs.)*
STRETCH:	
I did a little underwater work there last summer.	*(She's probably been around. Well, at least we're off the subject of jobs.)*
Fantastic colors. So rich in life.	*(And lonelier than hell.)*
CANDY:	
I wish I'd had time when I was there.	*(Look at that build. He must swim like a fish. I should learn.)*
I love the water.	*(Well, I do. At the beach, anyway, where I can wade in and not go too deep.)*

Thus begins a relationship. Candy and Stretch have a drink and talk, talk, talk—sharing their likes and dislikes. Amazingly, they seem to agree on everything, from clothing to cars to politics. The attraction they feel is very strong and neither of them is willing to turn the other off by disagreeing.

They fall in love. Weeks later they still agree on everything, even though there is one topic they avoid scrupulously: religion. Their different backgrounds became apparent after they exchanged last names. That doesn't mean they have to talk about it, however.

They delay introductions to their parents. The O'Briens and the Steins are narrow-minded about religion. If the truth be known, so are Candy and Stretch. Candy errs by telling Stretch, "You're not like other Jews I know." Stretch also voices his feelings now and then. After Candy has nursed him through a cold, he remarks, "You know, you're very Jewish." Candy and Stretch play the games required to maintain the relationship. They tell themselves that their remarks were mistakes and, after all, anyone can make mistakes. They were meant as compliments, weren't they? Yet each is becoming isolated from family and friends.

One of the topics they ignore is birth control. As a Catholic, Candy does not take oral contraceptives. (Stretch later claimed that he assumed she did.) Candy becomes pregnant and they get married. Only through professional help do they learn each other's genuine feelings. And on several occasions, the union comes close to dissolving.

How do we explain the goings-on in this tangled web of deception? Candy and Stretch felt strongly attracted to each other. What determines who is at-

tractive? Why did Candy and Stretch pretend to agree on everything? Why did they put off introductions to their parents?

Two possible outcomes of attraction are friendship and love. Candy and Stretch "fell in love." What is love? When the first author was a teenager, the answer was, "Five feet of heaven in a ponytail." However, this answer may lack scientific merit. In this chapter see that there are different forms of love and that our concepts of love are not universal.

Attraction: The Force That Binds?

Investigators define feelings of attraction as psychological forces that draw people together. Many factors enter into personal attraction. The first of these that we consider is physical appearance.

Physical Attractiveness: How Important Is Looking Good?

We might like to think of ourselves as so sophisticated that physical attractiveness does not move us. We might like to claim that sensitivity, warmth, and intelligence are more important to us. However, we may never learn about other people's personalities if they do not meet our minimal standards for physical attractiveness. Research shows that physical attractiveness is a major determinant of interpersonal and sexual attraction (Langlois et al., 2000; Sangrador & Yela, 2000; Strassberg & Holty, 2003). Some researchers, in fact, contend that physical appearance is the key factor in consideration of partners for dates, sex, and long-term relationships (Wilson et al., 2005).

IS BEAUTY IN THE EYE OF THE BEHOLDER? Are our standards fully subjective or is there broad agreement on what is attractive? Cross-cultural studies of preliterate societies have found that people universally want physically appealing partners (Ford & Beach, 1951). However, is that which appeals in one culture repulsive in others?

In certain African tribes, long necks and round, disklike lips are signs of feminine beauty. Women thus stretch their necks and lips to make themselves more appealing. Women of the Nama tribe persistently tug at their labia majora to make them "beautiful"—that is, prominent and elongated (Ford & Beach, 1951). **Truth or Fiction Revisited:** Yet beauty may not be completely in the eye of the beholder. As noted in the nearby "The World of Human Sexuality" feature, some aspects of beauty seem to be largely cross-cultural.

In our culture, taller men are considered to be more attractive by women (Kurzban & Weeden, 2005; Pawlowski & Koziel, 2002). Undergraduate women prefer their dates to be about six inches taller than they are. Undergraduate men, on the average, prefer women who are about four and a half inches shorter (Gillis & Avis, 1980). Tall women are not viewed so positively.

Some women of Candy's stature find that shorter men are discouraged from asking them out. Some walk with a hunch, as if to minimize their height. A neighbor of the first and third authors refers to herself as 5 feet 13 inches tall.

Female plumpness is valued in many, perhaps most, preliterate societies (Frayser, 1985). In our culture, however, "thin is in." Some young women suffer from an eating disorder called **anorexia nervosa,** in which they literally starve themselves to conform to the contemporary ideal. Both females and males find slenderness (although not anorexic thinness) attractive, especially for females (Furnham et al., 2005; Weeden & Sabini, 2005; Wilson et al., 2005).

Our society prefers the hourglass figure. Studies find that women of average weight with a waist-to-hip ratio of 0.7 to 0.8 are rated as most attractive and desirable for relationships (Furnham et al., 2005; Weeden & Sabini, 2005). Neither gaunt nor obese women were found to be as attractive, regardless of their waist-to-hip ratio.

LESBIANS' PREFERENCES CONCERNING WAIST-TO-HIP RATIO
Cohen and Tannenbaum (2001) conducted an Internet study in which they posted various women's body shapes and asked lesbian and bisexual women to indicate which were most sexually attractive to them. Respondents included 209 women self-identified as lesbian and 141 women self-identified as bisexual. The women, like heterosexual men, found women with a 0.7 waist-to-hip body ratio to be the most sexually attractive. How-

TRUTH ? **fiction** 1

Anorexia nervosa A potentially life-threatening eating disorder characterized by refusal to maintain a healthy body weight, an intense fear of being overweight, a distorted body image, and, in females, lack of menstruation (amenorrhea)

Wide Eyed with . . . Beauty

Research suggests that European Americans, African Americans, Asian Americans, and Latino and Latina Americans tend to agree on the facial features they find to be attractive (Cunningham et al., 1995). They all prefer female faces with large eyes; greater distance between the eyes; small noses; narrower faces with smaller chins; high, expressive eyebrows; larger lower lips; and a well-groomed, full head of hair.

Consider the methodology of a study that compared the facial preferences of people in Japan and England. Perrett (1994) created computer composites of the faces of 60 women. Part A of Figure 7.1 is a composite of the 15 women who were rated the most attractive. He then used computer enhancement to exaggerate the differences between the composite of the 60—that is, the average face—and the composite of the 15 most attractive women. He found that both Japanese and British men deemed women with large eyes, high cheekbones, and narrow jaws to be the most attractive (Perret, 1994). Computer enhancement resulted in the image shown in Figure 7.1B. The enhanced composite has still higher cheekbones and a narrower jaw than view A. Figure 7.1B was then rated as the most attractive image. Similar results were found for the image of a Japanese woman.

Cunningham and his colleagues (1995) reported historical anecdotes that suggest that the facial preferences of people as diverse as Europeans, Black Africans, Native Americans, Indians (in India, that is), and Chinese are quite consistent. They quoted from Charles Darwin's 1871 treatise, *The Descent of Man,* and *Selection in Relation to Sex:*

> Mr. Winwood Reade . . . who has had ample opportunities for observation [with Black Africans] who have never associated with Europeans is convinced that their ideas of beauty are, on the whole, the same as ours; and Dr. Rohlfs writes to me the same effect with respect to Borneo and the countries inhabited by the Pullo tribes. . . . Capt. Burton believes that a woman whom we consider beautiful is admired throughout the world.

Darwin believed that our physical preferences were largely inborn and related to survival of our species. What do you think? Do you believe that "their ideas of beauty are, on the whole, the same as ours?" Or do you think that research hasn't yet ferreted out significant cultural or ethnic differences that might exist? If there is ethnic consistency in these preferences, how would you explain them? For example, do you believe

- they are coincidental?
- there has been more exchange of ideas among cultures than has been believed?
- there is something instinctive about them?

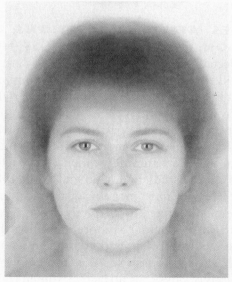

A

B

Figure 7.1 What Features Contribute to Facial Attractiveness?

In both England and Japan, features such as large eyes, high cheekbones, and narrow jaws contribute to perceptions of the attractiveness of women. View A is a computer composite of the faces of 15 women rated as the most attractive of a group of 60. View B is a computer composite that exaggerates the features of these 15 women. That is, they are developed further in the direction that separates them from the average of the full group.

REFLECT

What do you look for in a romantic partner? Why?

ever, they differed from the men in that their first choice was for heavy women with a 0.7 waist-to-hip body ratio and large breasts. Their second choice was for heavy women with the same waist-to-hip body ratio but with small breasts. The authors of the study suggest that lesbians rejected societal emphasis on excessive slenderness.

It is no secret that most men in our society are more attracted to women with ample bustlines (Hill et al., 2005). In one study, men rated a continuum of female figures that differed only in the size of the bust (Thompson & Tantleff, 1992). Men, as predicted, preferred women with larger busts, but not huge busts.

People who are attractive know it. In one study, men and women rated each other for attractiveness and also rated themselves (Marcus & Miller, 2003). By and large, the individuals' self-ratings meshed with those by others, both female and male. Women's judgments were most closely related to how men perceived them, suggesting that they were reflecting men's opinions of them more so than women's.

An experiment manipulated men's voices and asked women to rate them for attractiveness. Heterosexual women at the fertile (late follicular) phase of the menstrual cycle found men with more "masculine"— that is, deeper—voices to be more attractive (Feinberg et al., 2006). The study did not assess possible differences between heterosexual and lesbian women. **Truth or Fiction Revisited:** Thus it is only partly true that women preferred men with deeper voices. First of all, the finding was true for heterosexual women only. Second, it was true for heterosexual women only during the time of the month when they were fertile.

NONPHYSICAL TRAITS AFFECT PERCEPTIONS OF PHYSICAL BEAUTY   Although there are physical standards for beauty in our culture, nonphysical traits also affect our perceptions of beauty. For example, the perceived beauty of a partner is likely to be enhanced by nonphysical traits such as familiarity, liking, respect, and sharing of values and goals (Kniffin & Wilson, 2004).

Truth or Fiction Revisited: Females and males rate the attractiveness of faces higher when they are smiling than when they are not smiling (O'Doherty et al., 2003). So there is reason to "put on a happy face" when you meet people.

CRITICAL Thinking

Do you think that the study that found that heterosexual women find men with deeper voices to be more attractive during the late follicular phase of the menstrual cycle is consistent with evolutionary theory? Explain.

HOW BEHAVIOR AND NAMES AFFECT PERCEPTIONS OF PHYSICAL ATTRACTIVENESS: ON THE IMPORTANCE OF *NOT* BEING EARNEST   Gender-role expectations may affect perceptions of attractiveness. For example, women are more likely to be attracted to socially dominant men than men are to be attracted to socially dominant women (Buunk et al., 2002). Women who viewed videos of prospective dates found men who acted outgoing and self-expressive more appealing than men who were passive (Riggio & Woll, 1984). Another study found that highly feminine women are more likely to be attracted to dominant "macho" men than are less feminine women (Maybach & Gold, 1994). Yet men who viewed videos in the study by Riggio and Woll (1984) were put off by outgoing, self-expressive behavior in women. In yet another study, women rated videos of dominant college men (defined in this study as social control over a troublesome interaction with an instructor) as more appealing than submissive men. Again, male viewers were put off by similarly dominant women (Sadalla et al., 1987). Men are more likely to be jealous of socially dominant men, whereas women are more likely to be jealous of physically attractive women (Dijkstra & Buunk, 2002).

Sex Differences in Preferences in Mates across 37 Cultures

What do men in Nigeria, Japan, Brazil, Canada, and the United States have in common? For one thing, men in these countries report that they prefer mates who are younger than themselves. Buss (1994) reviewed survey evidence on the preferred age difference between oneself and one's mate in 37 cultures (representing 33 countries) in Europe, Africa, Asia, Australia, New Zealand, and North and South America. In every culture men preferred younger mates (the range was from 0.38 to 6.45 years). Women, however, preferred older mates (the range was from 1.82 to 5.1 years).

Sex differences in the preferred age of mates paralleled actual differences in age of men and women at the time of marriage. Men were between two and five years older on the average than their wives at the time of marriage. The smallest average age difference at marriage, 2.1 years, was found in Poland. The largest average difference, 4.92 years, was found in Greece. Men in the mainland United States averaged 2.71 years older than women at the time of marriage. In Canada, men were 2.51 years older than their mates, on average.

Buss (1994) found that in all 37 cultures, men placed greater value on a prospective partner's "good looks" than did women. On the other hand, women in 36 of 37 cultures placed greater value on "good earning capacity" of prospective mates.

The consistency of Buss' findings lends credence to the notion that there are widespread sex differences in preferences with respect to age, physical characteristics, and financial status of prospective mates. Generally speaking, men place greater value on the physical attractiveness and relative youth of prospective mates. Women place relatively greater value on the earning capacity of prospective mates. Buss interpreted women's preferences for relatively older mates as additional evidence that women appraise future mates on the basis of their ability to provide for a wife and family, because age and income tend to be linked among men.

Despite these sex differences in preferences for mates, Buss found that both men and women placed greater weight on personal qualities than on looks or income potential of prospective mates. In all 37 cultures, the characteristics "kind," "understanding," and "intelligent" were rated higher than earning power or physical attractiveness.

Who Is Mr. or Ms. Right? *Are your judgments of attractiveness based on universal standards or on your cultural experiences? Evolutionary psychologist David Buss found some nearly universal standards for beauty in his study of 37 cultures.*

TRUTH or fiction 4

TRUTH or fiction 5

Truth or Fiction Revisited: Names can also affect perceptions of attractiveness. In one study, women who were randomly assigned names like Kathy, Jennifer, and Christine were rated more attractive than women assigned the names Harriet, Gertrude, and Ethel (Garwood et al., 1980). Seems silly, does it not? After all, our parents name us, and there need be no relationship between our names and our physical appeal. On the other hand, we may choose to keep our names or to use nicknames. So if you are unhappy with your name, why not assume a more popular nickname? Beginning college or a new job is an ideal time for doing so. Men, too, can doff their Sylvesters and Ernests, if they prefer. If you have an unusual name and are content with it, be yourself, however.

WHAT DO YOU LOOK FOR IN A LONG-TERM, MEANINGFUL RELATIONSHIP? **Truth or Fiction Revisited:** It is not true that physical appeal is the most important trait we seek in partners for long-term relationships. Women place relatively greater emphasis than men on traits like vocational status, earning potential, expressiveness, kindness, consideration, dependability, and fondness for children (Kniffin & Wilson, 2004). Men give relatively more consideration to youth, physical attractiveness, cooking ability (can't they turn on the microwave by themselves?), and frugality (Kniffin & Wilson, 2004). When it comes to mate selection, females in a sample of students from Germany and the Netherlands also emphasized the financial prospects and status of a potential mate, whereas males emphasized the importance of physical attractiveness (de Raad & Doddema–Winsemius, 1992). A study of some 200 Korean college students found that in mate selection, women placed relatively more emphasis on education, jobs, and family of origin than men did (Brown, 1994). Men placed relatively more emphasis on physical attractiveness and affection. (Yes, men were more "romantic"; women were more pragmatic.)

Susan Sprecher and her colleagues (1994) surveyed a random national sample of 13,017 English- or Spanish-speaking people, age 19 or older, living in households in the United States. In one section of their questionnaire, they asked respondents how willing they would be to marry someone who was older, younger, of a different religion, not likely to hold a steady job, not good looking, and so forth. Each item was followed by a 7-point scale in which 1 point meant "not at all" and 7 points meant "very willing." As shown in Table 7.1, women were more willing than men to marry someone who was not good looking. On the other hand, women were less willing to marry someone not likely to hold a steady job.

SafeZone

Q *I keep attracting the same kind of guy—one that is not good for me. Why do I do this?*

A We don't know you well enough to give you a precise answer, but your complaint sounds familiar enough. Try listing the traits you want in a guy. Seriously—write them down. Then write down how you go about meeting guys and how you decide to get intimate with them, or whether you just let it happen. Should you meet guys in other places, in other ways? Should you get to know them better before getting intimate? Should you end things early on if things aren't going the way you want them to? Just be honest with yourself and figure it out. It's more likely dumb choices, lack of self-confidence, low self-esteem (if you think you're not worth very much, maybe you allow people to treat you as if you aren't), or—gulp—laziness, rather than something like a deep unconscious desire to punish yourself.

204 CHAPTER 7 • Attraction and Love—Binding Forces

TABLE 7.1

Sex Differences in Preferences for Mates

How willing would you be to marry someone who	Men	Women
• was not good looking?	3.41	4.42†
• was older than you by six or more years?	4.15	5.29†
• was younger than you by six or more years?	4.54	2.80†
• was not likely to hold a steady job?	2.73	1.62†
• would earn much less than you?	4.60	3.76†
• would earn much more than you?	5.19	5.93†
• had more education than you?	5.22	5.82†
• had less education than you?	4.67	4.08†
• had been married before?	3.35	3.44†
• already had children?	2.84	3.11*
• was of a different religion?	4.24	4.31
• was of a different race?	3.08	2.84*

*Difference statistically significant at the 0.01 level of confidence.
†Difference statistically significant at the 0.001 level of confidence.
SOURCE: From "Mate Selection Preferences: Gender Differences Examined in a National Sample" by Susan Sprecher, Quintin Sullivan, & Elaine Hatfield, *Journal of Personality and Social Psychology,* 1994, 66(6), 1074–1080. Copyright © 1994 by the American Psychological Association. Reproduced with permission. No further reproduction or distribution is permitted without written permission from the American Psychological Association.

ARE PREFERENCES CONCERNING ATTRACTIVENESS INHERITED? On the surface, sex differences in perceptions of attractiveness seem unbearably sexist—and perhaps they are. Yet some evolutionary psychologists believe that evolutionary forces favor the continuation of sex differences in preferences for mates because certain preferred traits provide reproductive advantages (Buss, 2005). Some physical features, like cleanliness, good complexion, clear eyes, good teeth, good hair, firm muscle tone, and a steady gait, are universally appealing to both females and males. Perhaps they are markers of reproductive potential (Buss, 2005). Age and health may be relatively more important to a woman's appeal, because these characteristics tend to be associated with her reproductive capacity; the "biological clock" limits her reproductive potential. Physical characteristics associated with a woman's youthfulness, such as smooth skin, firm muscle tone, and lustrous hair, may thus have become more closely linked to a woman's appeal (Buss, 2005). A man's reproductive value, however, may depend more on how well he can provide for his family than on his age or physical appeal. The value of men as reproducers, therefore, is more intertwined with factors that contribute to a stable environment for child rearing, such as economic status and reliability. Evolutionary psychologists argue that these sex differences in mate preferences may have been passed down through the generations as part of our genetic heritage (Buss, 2005).

The Attraction–Similarity Hypothesis: Who Is "Right" for You?

Do not despair if you are less than exquisite in appearance, along with most of us mere mortals. You may be saved from permanently blending in with the wallpaper by the effects of the **attraction–similarity hypothesis.**

CRITICAL Thinking

Do your own preferences in a romantic partner appear to support or contradict evolutionary theory? Explain.

Attraction–similarity hypothesis The view that people tend to develop romantic relationships with people who are similar to themselves in factors such as physical attractiveness, cultural background, personality traits, and interests

Who Is Right for You? *Research shows that people tend to pair off with others who are similar in physical characteristics and personality traits.*

The attraction–similarity hypothesis holds that people tend to develop romantic relationships with people who are similar to themselves in physical attractiveness and other traits (Klohnen & Luo, 2003; Morry & Gaines, 2005). Researchers have found that people who are involved in committed relationships are most likely to be similar to their partners in their attitudes and cultural attributes (Amodio & Showers, 2005).

Our partners tend to be like us in race and ethnicity, age, level of education, and religion. Consider some findings of the NHSLS study (Michael et al., 1994):

- The sex partners of nearly 94% of single European American men are European American women.

- About 2% of single European American men are partnered with Latina American women, 2% with Asian American women, and fewer than 1% with African American women.

- The sex partners of nearly 82% of African American men are African American women.

- Nearly 8% of African American men are partnered with European American women. Less than 5% are partnered with Latina American women.

- About 83% of the women and men in the study chose partners within five years of their own age and of the same or a similar religion.

- Of all the women in the study, not one with a graduate college degree had a partner who had not finished high school.

- Men with a college degree almost never had sexual relationships with women with much more or much less education than they had.

Attitudes: Do "Opposites Attract" or Do "Birds of a Feather Flock Together"?

TRUTH **fiction 6**

Truth or Fiction Revisited: Actually, it is not true that "opposites attract." We are actually less apt to be attracted to people who disagree with our views and tastes than to people who share them.

Why do the great majority of us have partners from our own backgrounds? One reason is **propinquity**—that is, relationships are made in the neighborhood and not in heaven. Although mobility has increased in Western societies in recent decades, we tend to live among people who are reasonably similar to us in background and thus come into contact with them. Another is that we are drawn to people who are similar in their attitudes. People similar in background are more likely to be similar in their attitudes. Similarity in attitudes and tastes is a key contributor to attraction, friendships, and love relationships (Brown et al., 2003; Morry & Gaines, 2005).

Let us also note a sex difference. Evidence shows that women place greater weight on attitude similarity as a determinant of attraction to a stranger of the other sex than do men, whereas men place more value on physical attractiveness (Feingold, 1991). We also tend to assume that people we find attractive share our attitudes (Morry & Gaines, 2005). The physical attraction between Candy and Stretch motivated them to pretend that their preferences, tastes, and opinions coincided. They entered into an unspoken agreement not to discuss their religious differences. When sexual attraction is strong, perhaps we want to think that we can iron out all the kinks in the relationship. Although similarity may be important in determining initial attraction, compatibility appears to be a stronger predictor of maintaining an intimate relationship (Amodio & Showers, 2005).

Propinquity Nearness

A Closer Look

"THE (ELECTRONIC) NEARNESS OF YOU"

Physical closeness, or proximity, has always been a factor in interpersonal attraction. People have always been drawn to the boy or girl next door (or next cave?). People tend to form romantic relationships with the people they meet in the neighborhood, in school, in their religious community, or on the job.

In the age of electronics, proximity is closer, yet it can also be farther away. It's as close as the monitor in front of your nose as you surf the 'Net. Yet you can find yourself corresponding with, and finding things in common with, people who are thousands of miles away.

When you meet somebody in person, you immediately observe what they look like, you hear their voice, and perhaps you get something like a sniff of their pheromones. But when you meet somebody in a chatroom or a computer-mediated multiuser dungeon, the cues that might spark interest are different. Mantovani (2001) notes

that in the case of online relationships, the use of the written (keyboarded) language becomes more important, timing and the speed of writing and responding are crucial, and punctuation and those smiley-face emoticons can all make a difference. But frequency of contact in the virtual world, as in the real world, plays a role (Levine, 2000; Montovani, 2001). Visiting the same chatroom repeatedly allows mutual awareness to develop and suggests similarity in interests.

Deb Levine (2000) notes that people are more likely to disclose intimate information about themselves on the Internet, perhaps because the actual—or unknown—distance between the parties provides a sense of security. Similarly, other people are quicker to reciprocate expressions of interest. Levine notes that flirting and erotic activity on the Internet can be extremely exciting, but people can also build unrealistic expectations and disqualify participants for relationships in the

"Surfing Blind?" *What "rules" of interpersonal attraction apply when people meet online? They cannot directly see or hear each other, so what cues do they rely on to determine whether there is a fit? What happens when one person wants to see, hear, or meet the other?*

physical world. (Would you want to have a real-world relationship with someone who quickly enters sexual discussions online?)

Levine and Mantovani both warn that expressions of similarity are easy to feign on the 'Net. Levine (2000) warns against becoming overly wrapped up in people who are reluctant to exchange sound files or pictures. And she adds that it makes sense to meet in the real world within a month or so to check out the accuracy of computer-mediated impressions—preferably in a safe, public place.

Reciprocity: If You Like Me, You Must Have Excellent Judgment

Has anyone told you that you are good looking, brilliant, and emotionally mature to boot? That your taste is elegant? Ah, what superb judgment!

When we feel admired and complimented, we tend to return these feelings and behaviors. This is called **reciprocity**. Reciprocity is a potent determinant of attraction (Levine, 2000; Sprecher, 1998). We tend to be much more warm, helpful, and candid when we are with strangers who we believe like us (Sprecher, 1998). We even tend to welcome positive comments from others when we know them to be inaccurate (Levine, 2000).

Reciprocity Mutual exchange

Perhaps the power of reciprocity has enabled many couples to become happy with one another and reasonably well adjusted. By reciprocating positive words and actions, a person can perhaps stoke neutral or mild feelings into robust, affirmative feelings of attraction.

Attraction can lead to feelings of love. Let us now turn to that most fascinating topic.

Love: "The Morning and the Evening Star?"

For thousands of years, poets have sought to capture love in words. A 17th-century poet wrote that his love was like "a red, red rose." The novelist Sinclair Lewis wrote of love as "the morning and the evening star." Love is beautiful and elusive. It shines, brilliant and heavenly. Passion and romantic love are also earthy and sexy, brimming with sexual desire.

Our culture idealizes the concept of romantic love (Hatfield & Rapson, 2002; Hendrick & Hendrick, 2003). Thus we readily identify with the plight of the "star-crossed" lovers in *Romeo and Juliet* and *West Side Story,* who sacrificed for love. We learn that "love makes the world go round" and that "love is everything." Like other aspects of sexual and social behavior among humans, the concept of love must be understood within a cultural context.

We can trace the concept of love at least as far back as the classical age of Greece. The Greeks distinguished four concepts related to the modern meanings of love:

1. **Storge:** loving attachment, deep friendship, or nonsexual affection
2. **Agape:** selfless giving
3. **Philia:** friendship
4. **Eros:** passion

Storge is the emotion that binds friends and parents and children. Some scholars believe that even romantic love is a form of attachment that is similar to the types of attachments infants have to their mothers (Gonzaga et al., 2006; Moore & Leung, 2002).

Agape is similar to generosity and charity. It implies the wish to share one's bounty and is epitomized by anonymous donations of money. Agape, according to Lee's research, is the kind of love least frequently found between adults in committed relationships.

Philia is based on liking and respect, rather than sexual desire. It involves the desire to do and enjoy things with the other person and to see him or her when one is lonely or bored.

Eros was a character in Greek mythology (transformed in Roman mythology into Cupid) who would shoot the unsuspecting with love arrows, causing them to fall madly in love with whoever was nearby at the time. Erotic love embraces sudden passionate desire: "love at first sight" and "falling head over heels in love." Younger college students are more likely to believe in love at first sight and that "love conquers all" than older (and wiser?) college students (Knox et al., 1999a). Passion can be so gripping that one is convinced that life has been changed forever. This feeling of sudden transformation was captured by the Italian poet Dante Alighieri (1265–1321), who exclaimed upon first beholding his beloved Beatrice, "Incipit vita nuova," which can be translated as "My life begins anew." Unlike the Greeks, we tend to use the word

Storge (STORE-gay) Loving attachment and nonsexual affection; the type of emotion that binds parents to children

Agape (AH-gah-pay) Selfless love; a kind of love that is similar to generosity and charity

Philia (FEEL-yuh) Friendship love, which is based on liking and respect rather than sexual desire

Eros The kind of love that is closest in meaning to the modern-day concept of passion

A Closer Look

WATCHING NEW LOVE AS IT SEARS THE BRAIN

Anthropologist Helen Fisher of Rutgers University. *Dr. Fisher has investigated the biochemical aspects of attraction and love in human sexuality.*

New love can look for all the world like mental illness—a blend of mania, dementia, and obsession—that cuts people off from friends and family, and prompts out-of-character behavior: compulsive phone calling, serenades, yelling from rooftops. It could almost be mistaken for psychosis.

Now neuroscientists have produced brain scan images of this fevered activity, before it settles into the wine and roses phase of romance or the joint holiday card routines of long-term commitment. In an analysis of the images in *The Journal of Neurophysiology,* researchers argue that romantic love is a biological urge distinct from sexual arousal.

It is closer in its neural profile to drives like hunger, thirst, or drug craving, the researchers assert, than to emotional states like excitement or affection. As a relationship deepens, the brain scans suggest that the neural activity associated with romantic love alters slightly, and in some cases primes areas deep in the primitive brain that are involved in long-term attachment.

The research helps explain why love produces such disparate emotions, from euphoria to anger to anxiety, and

why it seems to become even more intense when it is withdrawn. In a separate, continuing experiment, the researchers are analyzing brain images from people who have been rejected by their lovers.

"When you're in the throes of this romantic love it's overwhelming, you're out of control, you're irrational, you're going to the gym at 6 AM every day—why? Because she's there," said Dr. Helen Fisher, an anthropologist at Rutgers University and the co-author of the analysis. "And when rejected, some people contemplate stalking, homicide, suicide. This drive for romantic love can be stronger than the will to live."

Brain imaging technology cannot read people's minds, experts caution, and a phenomenon as many sided and socially influenced as love transcends simple computer graphics, like those produced by the technique used in the study, called functional magnetic resonance imaging (MRI).

"Still," said Dr. Hans Breiter, director of the Motivation and Emotion Neuroscience Collaboration at Massachusetts General Hospital, "I distrust about 95% of the MRI literature and I would give this study an A+; it really

moves the ball in terms of understanding infatuation love."

He added: "The findings fit nicely with a large, growing body of literature describing a generalized reward and aversion system in the brain, and put this intellectual construct of love directly onto the same axis as homeostatic rewards such as food, warmth, craving for drugs."

In the study, Drs. Fisher, Lucy Brown of Albert Einstein College of Medicine, and Arthur Aron of the State University of New York at Stony Brook led a team that analyzed about 2,500 brain images from 17 college students who were in the first weeks or months of new love. The students looked at a picture of their beloved while an MRI machine imaged their brains. The researchers then compared the images

love to describe everything from feelings of affection toward another to romantic ardor to sexual intercourse ("making love"). Still, different types or styles of love are recognized in our own culture, as we will see.

Romantic Love

The experience of romantic love, as opposed to loving attachment or sexual arousal per se, occurs within a cultural context in which the concept is idealized (Berscheid, 2003; Hatfield & Rapson, 2002; Hendrick & Hendrick, 2003). Western culture has a

with others taken while the students looked at picture of an acquaintance.

Functional MRI technology detects increases or decreases of blood flow in the brain, which reflect changes in neural activity. In the study, a computer-generated map of particularly active areas showed hot spots deep in the brain, below conscious awareness, in areas called the caudate nucleus and the ventral tegmental area, which communicate with each other as part of a circuit. These areas are dense with cells that produce or receive a brain chemical called dopamine, which circulates actively when people desire or anticipate a reward. In studies of gamblers, cocaine users, and even people playing computer games for small amounts of money, these dopamine sites become extremely active as people score or win.

Yet falling in love is among the most irrational of human behaviors, not merely a matter of satisfying a simple pleasure or winning a reward. And the researchers found that one particular spot in the MR images, in the caudate nucleus, was especially active in people who scored highly on a questionnaire measuring passionate love. This passion-related region was on the opposite side of the brain from another area that registers physical attractiveness, and it appeared to be involved in longing, desire, and the unexplainable tug that people feel toward one person, among many attractive alternative partners.

This distinction, between finding someone attractive and desiring him or her, between liking and wanting, "is all happening in an area of the mammalian brain that takes care of most

basic functions, like eating, drinking, eye movements, all at an unconscious level, and I don't think anyone expected this part of the brain to be so specialized," Dr. Brown said.

The intoxication of new love mellows with time, of course, and the brain imaging findings reflect some evidence of this change, as noted by Dr. Fisher. The researchers saw individual differences in their group of smitten lovers, based on how long the participants had been in the relationships. Compared with the students who were in the first weeks of a new love, those who had been paired off for a year or more showed significantly more activity in an area of the brain linked to long-term commitment.

And When You've Been Dumped . . .

In a follow-up experiment, Drs. Fisher, Aron, and Brown carried out brain scans on 17 other young men and women who recently were dumped by their lovers. As in the new love study, the researchers compared two sets of images: one taken when the participants were looking at a photo of a friend, the other when looking at a picture of their ex.

The investigators increased activation in an area of the brain related to the region associated with passionate love. "It seems to suggest what the psychological literature, poetry, and people have long noticed: that being dumped actually does heighten romantic love, a phenomenon I call frustration–attraction," Dr. Fisher said.

One volunteer in the study was Suzanna Katz, 22, of New York, who suffered through a breakup with her

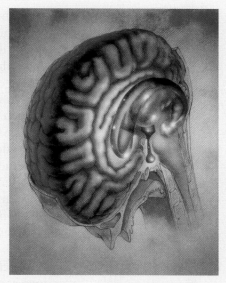

Figure 7.2   The Caudate Nucleus. *A part of the brain that is particularly active when we undergo the throes of a new romantic love.*

boyfriend three years earlier. Ms. Katz said she became hyperactive to distract herself after the split, but said she also had moments of almost physical withdrawal, as if weaning herself from a drug.

"It had little to do with him, but more with the fact that there was something there, inside myself, a hope, a knowledge that there's someone out there for you, and that you're capable of feeling this way, and suddenly I felt like that was being lost," she said.

Source: From "Watching New Love as It Sears the Brain" by Benedict Carey. *The New York Times.* May 31, 2005. Reprinted by permission.

long tradition of idealizing the concept of romantic love, as represented, for instance, by romantic fairy tales that have been passed down through the generations. In fact, our exposure to the concept of romantic love may begin with hearing the fairy tales of Sleeping Beauty, Cinderella, and Snow White—along with their princes charming. Later, perhaps, the concept of romantic love blossoms with exposure to romantic novels, television and film scripts, and the heady tales of friends and relatives.

During adolescence, strong sexual arousal along with an idealized image of the object of our desires leads us to label our feelings as love. We may learn to speak of "love" rather than "lust," because sexual desire in the absence of a committed relationship might be viewed as primitive or animalistic. Being "in love" ennobles attraction and sexual arousal, not only to society but also to oneself. Unlike lust, love can be discussed even at the dinner table. If others think we are too young to experience "the real thing," which presumably includes knowledge of and respect for the other person's personality traits, our feelings may be called "puppy love" or a "crush."

Western society maintains much of the double standard toward sexuality. Thus, women are more often expected to justify sexual experiences as involving someone they love. Young men usually need not attribute sexual urges to love. So men are more apt to deem love a "mushy" concept. The vast majority of people in the United States nonetheless believe romantic love is a prerequisite for marriage or another kind of long-term or permanent relationship. Romantic love is rated by young people as the single most important reason for marriage (Roper Organization, 1985). You can explore your self-perceptions of being a romantic or a realist when it comes to love by completing the Triangular Love Scale Self-Assessment feature (see page 217).

When reciprocated, romantic love is usually a source of deep fulfillment and ecstasy (Hatfield & Rapson, 2002). How wonderful when love meets its match! When love is unrequited, however, it can lead to emptiness, anxiety, or despair. Romantic love can thus teeter between states of ecstasy and misery. Perhaps no other feature of our lives can lift us up as high or plunge us down as low as romantic love.

Infatuation versus "True Love": Will Time Tell?

Perhaps you first noticed each other when your eyes met across a classroom. Or perhaps you met when you were both assigned to the same Bunsen burner in chemistry lab—less romantic, but closer to the flame. However it happened, the meeting triggered such an electric charge through your body that you could not get him (or her) out of your mind. Were you truly in love, however, or was it merely a passing fancy? Was it **infatuation** or the "real thing"— a "true," lasting, and mutual love? How do you tell them apart?

Perhaps you don't, at least not at first. Infatuation is a state of intense absorption in or focusing on another person (Aloni & Bernieri, 2004). It is usually accompanied by sexual desire, elation, and general physiological arousal or excitement. Some refer to passion as infatuation. Others dub it a "crush." Both monikers suggest that it is a passing fancy. With infatuation, your heart may pound whenever the other person draws near or enters your fantasies.

For the first month or two, infatuation and the more enduring forms of romantic love are hard to differentiate. At first, both may be characterized by intense focusing or absorption. Infatuated people may become so absorbed that they cannot sleep, work, or carry out routine chores. Logic and reason are swept aside (Hatfield & Rapson, 2002). Infatuated people hold idealized images of their love objects and overlook their faults. Caution may be cast to the winds. In some cases, couples in the throes of infatuation rush to the altar, only to find a few weeks or months later that they are not well suited.

As time goes on, signs that distinguish infatuation from a lasting romantic love begin to emerge. The partners begin to view each other more realistically and determine whether the relationship should continue. Although the tendency to idealize one's lover is strongest at the outset of a relationship, we should note that a so-called "positive illusion" tends to persist in relationships (Martz et al., 1998). That is, we maintain some tendency to differentiate our partners from the average and also to differentiate the value of our relationships from the average.

Infatuation A state of intense absorption in or focus on another person; usually accompanied by sexual desire, elation, and general physiological arousal or excitement; passion

Infatuation is based on feelings of passion, but not on the deeper feelings of attachment and caring that typify a more lasting, mutual love (Hatfield & Rapson, 2002). Although infatuation may be a passing fancy, it can be supplanted by the deeper feelings of attachment and caring that characterize enduring love relationships.

Note, too, that infatuation is not a necessary first step on the path to a lasting, mutual love. Some couples develop deep feelings of love without ever experiencing the fireworks of infatuation (Barnes & Sternberg, 1997). Or sometimes one partner is infatuated while the other manages to keep his or her head below the clouds.

Contemporary Models of Love: Dare Science Intrude?

Despite the importance of love, scientists have historically paid little attention to it. Some people have believed that love cannot be analyzed scientifically. Love, they maintain, should be left to the poets, philosophers, and theologians. Others have thought that love is sort of a silly topic for the purview of science.

Yet researchers today are applying the scientific method to the study of love. They recognize that love is a complex concept, involving many areas of experience—biological, emotional, cognitive, and motivational (Berscheid, 2003). Let us begin with some biological comments and then move on to some psychological approaches.

Infatuation or "True Love"? *Infatuation is a state of intense absorption in another person. It is characterized by sexual longing and general excitement. Infatuation is often referred to as passion or as a crush. Infatuation is assumed to fade as relationships develop.*

BIOLOGICAL MECHANISMS Some researchers focus on the bodily changes that occur when we experience feelings of romantic love. There are many. Some of the research focuses on the search for distinct neural pathways (road maps in the brain) that define feelings of love (Marazziti, 2005). Others involve chemistry, with a special focus on

- monoamines and neuropeptides, including dopamine and naturally produced opium look-alikes we call endorphins, that are involved in the brain's pleasure system
- the hormones oxytocin and vasopressin

There are always interesting new studies arriving on our desks. For example, we tend to have heightened levels of *nerve growth factor* (Emanuele et al., 2006), which partly explains—at least on a biological level—why new lovers are so acutely aware of everything going on around them and why everything seems so bathed in a luxurious light. (How's that for a sad attempt at poetry in a textbook?)

As we noted in an earlier "A Closer Look" feature, functional MRI research shows heightened activity in a part of the brain called the caudate nucleus. What is perhaps of interest here is that the caudate nucleus is part of the brain's "limbic system," which is intimately connected with emotional arousal.

Let us now consider several psychologically oriented views of love. They may touch indirectly on things that happen in the body, but as we will see, they do so almost apologetically.

LOVE AS APPRAISAL OF AROUSAL Social psychologists Ellen Berscheid and Elaine Hatfield (Berscheid, 2003; Berscheid & Walster, 1978; Hatfield & Rapson,

CRITICAL Thinking

The student of psychology or sociology might wonder what all this biological research *means*. Does it mean, for example, that students of human sexuality must memorize every corner of the brain and every neurological activity? Or does it call, rather, for a more general appreciation that thoughts and emotions are based in the body—and particularly in the brain—and that these scientific facts are not to be ignored when we discuss the nature of human beings? How can you best make use of this information?

2002) defined romantic love in terms of a state of intense physiological arousal and the cognitive appraisal of that arousal as love. The physiological arousal may be experienced as a pounding heart, sweaty palms, and butterflies in the stomach when one is in the presence of or thinking about one's love interest. Cognitive appraisal of the arousal means attributing it to some cause, such as fear or love. The perception that one has fallen in love is thus derived from several simultaneous events: (1) a state of intense physiological arousal that is connected with an appropriate love object (i.e., a person, not an event like a rock concert), (2) a cultural setting that idealizes romantic love, and (3) the attribution of the arousal to feelings of love toward the person.

STYLES OF LOVE Some researchers speak in terms of styles of love. Susan and Clyde Hendrick (2002) and their colleagues (Hendrick et al., 2006) speak of love as a positive emotion that contributes to happiness, feelings of psychological well-being, and optimism about the future. The Hendricks (2003) developed a Love Attitude Scale that suggests the existence of six styles of love. The following is a list of the styles. Each one is exemplified by statements similar to those on the original scale. As you can see, the styles owe a debt to the Greeks:

1. Romantic love (eros): "My lover fits my ideal." "My lover and I were attracted to one another immediately."
2. Game-playing love (ludus): "I keep my lover up in the air about my commitment." "I get over love affairs pretty easily."
3. Friendship (storge, philia): "The best love grows out of an enduring friendship."
4. Logical love (pragma): "I consider a lover's potential in life before committing myself." "I consider whether my lover will be a good parent."
5. Possessive, excited love (mania): "I get so excited about my love that I cannot sleep." "When my lover ignores me, I get sick all over."
6. Selfless love (agape): "I would do anything I can to help my lover." "My lover's needs and wishes are more important than my own."

Most people who are "in love" experience a number of these styles, but the Hendricks (1986) found some interesting sex differences in styles of love. College men are significantly more likely than college women to develop game-playing and romantic love styles. College women are more apt than college men to develop friendly, logical, and possessive love styles. (There were no sex differences in selfless love.) The Hendricks (2003) have also found that romantically involved couples tend to experience the same kinds of love styles. They also found evidence that couples with romantic and selfless styles of love are more likely to remain together. A game-playing love style leads to unhappiness, however, and is one reason that relationships come to an end.

REFLECT

Have you ever practiced a style of love listed by the Hendricks? Have you ever been victimized by one? What was the experience like? Did you learn anything from it?

SafeZone

Q *I am in love with two people at the same time. Can this continue or must I choose?*

A You can probably continue until you want to settle down, one of them gets fed up with it, or you conclude it's immoral. We'll add this to the mix: It's not abnormal to be in love with two people at the same time. There's no reason to think there's just one perfect person for you. But given the realities of life in our culture today, the situation will probably eventually become unstable. In the meantime, we'll be jealous of you.

STERNBERG'S TRIANGULAR THEORY OF LOVE Robert Sternberg (1988) offers a "triangular theory" of love that organizes the relationships among kinds of love discussed by many theorists, including passionate love, romantic love, and companionate love (Hatfield & Rapson, 2002; Hendrick & Hendrick, 2003). The three building blocks, or components, of loving experiences include

1. **intimacy**—The experience of warmth toward another person that arises from feelings of closeness, bondedness, and connectedness to the other. Intimacy also involves the desire to give and receive emotional support and to share one's innermost thoughts with the other.
2. **passion**—An intense romantic or sexual desire for another person, which is accompanied by physiological arousal
3. **commitment**—A component of love that involves commitment to maintain the relationship through good times and bad

Sternberg's model is triangular in that various kinds of love can be conceptualized in terms of a triangle in which each vertex (corner?) represents one of the building blocks (Figure 7.3). The strength of each component can be represented by the shape of the triangle. For example, a love in which all three components were equally balanced—as in consummate love—would be represented by an equilateral triangle, as in Figure 7.3.

The Hendricks (2003) noted that couples who are romantically involved tend to share similar love styles. In terms of Sternberg's model, couples are well matched if

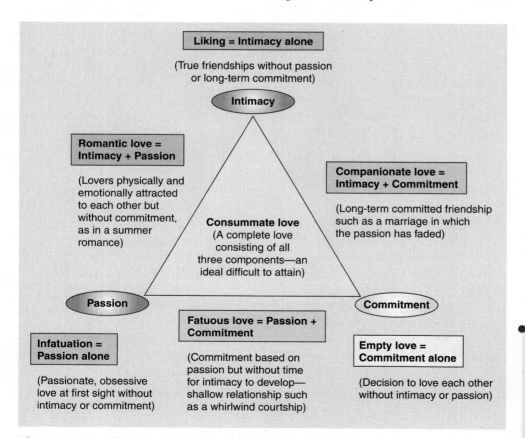

Figure 7.3 **The Triangular Model of Love.** *According to psychologist Robert Sternberg, love consists of three components, as shown by the vertices of this triangle. Various kinds of love consist of different combinations of these components. Romantic love, for example, consists of passion and intimacy. Consummate love—the cultural ideal—consists of all three.*

Intimacy Closeness, characterized by deep knowledge and understanding of another person

Passion A powerful, compelling emotion; in this case, one involving sexual feelings

Commitment A pledge, promise, or decision to maintain a relationship

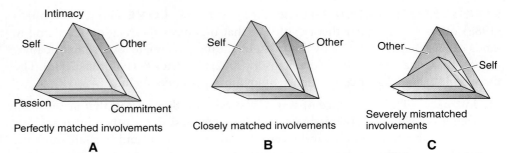

Figure 7.4 **Compatibility and Incompatibility, According to the Triangular Model of Love.** *Compatibility in terms of Sternberg's types of love can be represented as triangles. View A shows a perfect match in which triangles are congruent. View B depicts a good match; the partners are similar according to the three dimensions. View C shows a mismatch; major differences exist between the partners on all three components.*

they possess corresponding levels of passion, intimacy, and commitment (Drigotas et al., 1999; Sternberg, 1988). Compatibility can be represented visually in terms of the congruence (fit?) of the love triangles. Figure 7.4A shows a perfect match, in which the triangles are congruent. Figure 7.4B depicts a good match; the partners are similar in the three building blocks of love. Figure 7.4C shows a mismatch; major differences exist between the partners on all three components. Relationships may run aground when partners are mismatched. A relationship may fizzle, rather than sizzle, when one partner experiences more passion than the other, or when one wants a long-term commitment when the other's idea of commitment is to stay the night.

According to the Sternberg model, various combinations of the three elements of love characterize different types of love relationships (Figure 7.3 and Table 7.2). For example, infatuation (passionate love) is typified by strong sexual desire, but not by intimacy and commitment. The partners may each feel passionate love for the other, or, as in the case of Tom, such feelings may go unrequited:

> Tom sat behind Lisa in physics class. Tom hated physics, but he could not say the same for Lisa. One look at her was enough to change his life. He had fallen madly in love with her. Instead of listening to the teacher or looking at the blackboard, he would gaze at Lisa throughout the class. Lisa was aware of this and was not happy about it. She did not much care for Tom, and when he tried to start a conversation with her, she moved on as quickly as possible. Tom's staring and his awkwardness in talking to her made her feel uncomfortable. Tom, on the other hand, could think of little else besides Lisa, and his grades began to suffer as he spent the time he should have been devoting to his homework thinking about her. He was a man obsessed. The obsession might have gone on for quite some time had not both Tom and Lisa graduated that June and gone to different colleges. Tom never saw Lisa again, and after several unanswered love letters, he finally gave up on her. (Sternberg, 1988, p. 123)

Liking is a basis for friendship. It consists of feelings of closeness and emotional warmth without passion or commitment. Liking is not felt toward passing acquaintances. It is reserved for people to whom one feels close enough to share one's innermost feelings and thoughts. We sometimes develop these intimate relationships without making the commitment to maintaining a long-term relationship that typifies other types of love, however. Liking may develop into a passionate love, however, or into a more committed form of love called companionate love by many

Sternberg's Triangular Love Scale

Which are the strongest components of your love relationship? Intimacy? Passion? Commitment? All three components? Two of them?

DIRECTIONS To complete the following scale, fill in the blank spaces with the name of one person you love or care about deeply. Then rate your agreement with each of the items by using a 9-point scale in which 1 point = "not at all," 5 points = "moderately," and 9 points = "extremely." Use points in between to indicate intermediate levels of agreement between these values.

Intimacy Component

_____ 1. I am actively supportive of _____'s well-being.

_____ 2. I have a warm relationship with _____.

_____ 3. I am able to count on _____ in times of need.

_____ 4. _____ is able to count on me in times of need.

_____ 5. I am willing to share myself and my possessions with _____.

_____ 6. I receive considerable emotional support from _____.

_____ 7. I give considerable emotional support to _____.

_____ 8. I communicate well with _____.

_____ 9. I value _____ greatly in my life.

_____ 10. I feel close to _____.

_____ 11. I have a comfortable relationship with _____.

_____ 12. I feel that I really understand _____.

_____ 13. I feel that _____ really understands me.

_____ 14. I feel that I can really trust _____.

_____ 15. I share deeply personal information about myself with _____.

Passion Component

_____ 16. Just seeing _____ excites me.

_____ 17. I find myself thinking about _____ frequently during the day.

_____ 18. My relationship with _____ is very romantic.

_____ 19. I find _____ to be very personally attractive.

_____ 20. I idealize _____.

_____ 21. I cannot imagine another person making me as happy as _____ does.

_____ 22. I would rather be with _____ than anyone else.

_____ 23. There is nothing more important to me than my relationship with _____.

_____ 24. I especially like physical contact with _____.

_____ 25. There is something almost "magical" about my relationship with _____.

_____ 26. I adore _____.

_____ 27. I cannot imagine life without _____.

_____ 28. My relationship with _____ is passionate.

_____ 29. When I see romantic movies and read romantic books, I think of _____.

_____ 30. I fantasize about _____.

Commitment Component

_____ 31. I know that I care about _____.

_____ 32. I am committed to maintaining my relationship with _____.

_____ 33. Because of my commitment to _____, I would not let other people come between us.

_____ 34. I have confidence in the stability of my relationship with _____.

_____ 35. I could not let anything get in the way of my commitment to _____.

_____ 36. I expect my love for _____ to last for the rest of my life.

_____ 37. I will always feel a strong responsibility for _____.

_____ 38. I view my commitment to _____ as a solid one.

_____ 39. I cannot imagine ending my relationship with _____.

_____ 40. I am certain of my love for _____.

_____ 41. I view my relationship with _____ as permanent.

_____ 42. I view my relationship with _____ as a good decision.

_____ 43. I feel a sense of responsibility toward _____.

_____ 44. I plan to continue my relationship with _____.

_____ 45. Even when _____ is hard to deal with, I remain committed to our relationship.

SOURCE: Sternberg, 1988. Reprinted by permission of Basic Books, Inc., Publishers, New York.

TABLE 7.2

Types of Love, According to Sternberg's Triangular Model

1. Nonlove	A relationship in which all three components of love are absent. Most of our personal relationships are of this type—casual interactions or acquaintances that do not involve any elements of love.
2. Liking	An experience with another person such as a friendship in which intimacy is present, but passion and commitment are lacking.
3. Infatuation	A kind of "love at first sight," in which one experiences a passionate desire for another person in the absence of intimacy and commitment.
4. Empty love	A kind of love characterized by commitment (to maintain the relationship) in the absence of either passion and intimacy. Stagnant relationships that no longer involve the emotional intimacy or physical attraction that once characterized them are of this type.
5. Romantic love	A loving experience characterized by the combination of passion and intimacy but without commitment.
6. Companionate love	A kind of love characterized by intimacy and commitment. It often occurs in long-term relationships in which passionate attraction has waned and has been replaced by a kind of committed friendship.
7. Fatuous love	The type of love associated with whirlwind romances and "quickie marriages" in which passion and commitment are present, but intimacy is not.
8. Consummate love	The full or complete measure of love involving the combination of passion, intimacy, and commitment. Many of us strive for consummate love.

SOURCE: Adapted from Sternberg, 1988.

TRUTH fiction 7

REFLECT

Have you ever been in love? If so, how did you know that you were in love?

CRITICAL Thinking

Why do you think that most people in the United States believe that people should get married only when they experience romantic love?

writers, including Sternberg (1988), Clyde and Susan Hendrick (2003), and Elaine Hatfield (Hatfield & Rapson, 2002). Should lovers also be friends? Or are lovers and friends part of the twain that never meet? Candy and Stretch's relationship lacked the quality most often associated with true friendship: the willingness to share confidences. Despite their physical intimacy, their relationship remained so superficial that they couldn't even share information about their religious backgrounds.

Candy and Stretch were "in love" although they were far from friends. **Truth or Fiction Revisited:** It is indeed possible to be in love with someone who is not also a friend. Being in love can refer to states of passion or infatuation, whereas friendship is usually based on shared interests, liking, and respect. Friendship and passionate love do not necessarily overlap. There is nothing that prevents people in love from becoming good friends, however—perhaps even the best of friends. Sternberg's model recognizes that the intimacy we find in true friendships and the passion we find in love are blended in two forms of love—romantic love and consummate love. These love types differ along the dimension of commitment, however.

Romantic love has both passion and intimacy but lacks commitment. Romantic love may burn brightly and then flicker out. Or it may develop into a more complete love, called consummate love, in which all three components flower. Desire is accompanied by a deeper intimacy and commitment. The flames of passion can be stoked across the years, even if they do not burn quite as brightly as they once did. Consummate love is most special and certainly an ideal toward which many Westerners strive.

With empty love, by contrast, there is naught but commitment. Neither the warm emotional embrace of intimacy nor the flame of passion exists. With empty love, one's lover is a person whom one tolerates and remains with because of a sense of duty.

Sometimes a love relationship has both passion and commitment but lacks intimacy. Sternberg (1988) calls this fatuous (foolish) love. Fatuous love is associated with whirlwind courtships that burn brightly but briefly, as the partners come to the realization that they are not well matched. Intimacy can develop in such relationships, but couples who rush into promises or marriage often find that the realities of their relationship give the lie to their expectations.

Truth or Fiction Revisited: It is true that couples can remain "in love" after passion fades; for example, they can experience companionate love. Companionate love need not be lacking in romance, however. Although passion may have ebbed, sexual pleasure can help strengthen bonds. In companionate love, intimacy and commitment are strong, but passion is lacking. This form of love typifies long-term (so-called platonic) relationships and marriages in which passion has ebbed but a deep and abiding friendship remains for those with whom one's life is entwined (Hatfield & Rapson, 2002; Hendrick & Hendrick, 2003).

Friends. *Respect and intimacy are qualities of friendships. Friends also tend to share common interests.*

TRUTH? fiction 8

The balance among Sternberg's three aspects of love is likely to shift through the course of a relationship. A strong dose of all three components—found in consummate love—typifies, for many of us, an ideal relationship. At the outset of a relationship, passions may be strong, but intimacy may be weak. Couples may only just beginning to know each other's innermost thoughts and feelings. Time alone does not cause intimacy and commitment to grow, however. Some couples are able to peer into each other's deeper selves and form meaningful commitments at relatively early stages during their relationship. Yet some couples who have been together for many years may remain distant or waver in their commitment. Some couples experience only a faint flickering of passion early during the relationship. Then it becomes quickly extinguished. For some, the flames of passion burn ever brightly. Yet many couples find that passion tends to fade while intimacy and commitment grow stronger.

Knowledge of the components of love can help couples avoid pitfalls. Couples who recognize that passion exerts a strong pull early in a relationship may be less likely to let passion rush them into a premature long-term legal commitment. Couples who recognize that it is normal for passion to fade may avoid assuming that their love is at an end when it may, in fact, be changing into a deeper, more intimate and committed form of love. This knowledge may also encourage couples to focus on finding ways of rekindling the embers of romance, rather than looking to escape at the first sign that the fires may be cooling.

SafeZone

Q *What is the secret to a loving relationship?*

A A few secrets: One is honesty; that is, being honest about your likes and dislikes, your feelings, and your values. Another is sharing of interests and values. You can't expect a relationship to endure if you're only pretending to agree with your partner. A third is respect. You probably cannot really love your partner if you do not respect him or her as a person.

1. What factors contribute to attraction?

- Physical attractiveness is a major determinant of sexual attraction. In our culture, slenderness is in style. Females and males both consider smiling faces more attractive. Socially dominant men, but not dominant women, are usually found attractive. Women place relatively greater emphasis on traits like vocational status and earning potential, whereas men give relatively more consideration to physical attractiveness. Some evolutionary psychologists believe that evolutionary forces favor such sex differences in preferred traits because these traits provide reproductive advantages.

- Despite the adage "opposites attract," research tends to support the similarity–attraction hypothesis, which holds that people tend to develop romantic relationships with people who are similar to themselves in attractiveness, cultural background, and interests.

- Our feelings are warmer toward people who appear to like us. Through reciprocation of positive words and actions, neutral or mild feelings may be stoked into strong feelings of attraction.

2. What are the various meanings of love? What is romantic love?

- The ancient Greeks had four concepts related to the modern meanings of love: storge (loving attachment, as between parents and children), agape (generosity and charity), philia (friendship, liking, respect), and eros (passion).

- Western culture has a long tradition of idealizing the concept of romantic love. Most people in the United States see romantic love as a prerequisite to marriage. At first, infatuation and more enduring forms of romantic love may be indistinguishable.

- Berscheid and Hatfield define romantic love in terms of intense physiological arousal and cognitive appraisal of that arousal as love. Cultural belief in romantic love contributes to that labeling of arousal.

- Hendrick and Hendrick suggest that there are six styles of love among college students: romantic love, game-playing love, friendship, logical love, possessive love, and selfless love.

- Sternberg suggests that there are three distinct components of love: intimacy, passion, and commitment. Various combinations of these components typify different kinds of love. Romantic love is characterized by the combination of passion and intimacy. Consummate love—the cultural ideal—is described by all three components. Relationships are more likely to last when the "triangles" that describe each individual's feelings tend to be congruent (to overlap).

1. _____ is found to be universally attractive in women.

   (a) A good complexion
   (b) Slenderness
   (c) Plumpness
   (d) Socially dominant behavior

2. Susan Sprecher and her colleagues found that women are more willing than men to marry someone who is

   (a) six or more years younger than they are
   (b) not good looking
   (c) less well educated than they are
   (d) not likely to hold a steady job

3. Loving attachment, deep friendship, or nonsexual affection describe the ancient Greek concept of

   (a) agape
   (b) storge
   (c) eros
   (d) philia

4. People who say "I keep my lover up in the air about my commitment," or "I get over love affairs pretty easily" appear to be "in" the _____ style of love.

   (a) logical
   (b) romantic
   (c) game-playing
   (d) possessive

5. According to Sternberg, romantic love involves

   (a) passion and intimacy
   (b) passion and commitment
   (c) intimacy and commitment
   (d) passion alone

6. Susan Sprecher and her colleagues found that men are more willing than women to marry someone who

   (a) is better educated
   (b) already has children
   (c) is of a different religion
   (d) earns less than they do

7. According to the NHSLS study, the sex partners of nearly _____% of single European American men are European American women.

   (a) 34
   (b) 54
   (c) 74
   (d) 94

8. In his study on sex differences in preferences for mates across 37 cultures, Buss found that

   (a) men preferred women who earned more money than they did
   (b) women preferred men who were older than they were
   (c) only European men expressed an interest in marriage
   (d) evolutionary forces contributed to preferences in some cultures but not others

9. The Greek word _____ captures what is meant by generosity and charity.

   (a) agape
   (b) eros
   (c) philia
   (d) storge

10. Helen Fisher and her colleagues found that the _____ is highly active when we experience a new romantic love.

    (a) reticular activating system
    (b) prefrontal cortex
    (c) metatarsal–phalangeal joint
    (d) caudate nucleus

11. In his study on sex differences in preferences for mates, Buss found that both men and women placed greatest emphasis on

    (a) intelligence
    (b) income potential
    (c) facial features
    (d) complexion

12. Which is true of weight and physical attractiveness in our culture?

    (a) Only heterosexual males find slenderness attractive in a partner.
    (b) Only females find slenderness attractive in a partner.
    (c) Both females and males find slenderness attractive in a partner.
    (d) Only gay males find slenderness attractive in a partner.

13. The Hendricks found that college men were significantly more likely than college women to develop a _____ love style.

    (a) friendly
    (b) logical
    (c) romantic
    (d) possessive

14. Which of the following is true of infatuation?

    (a) It is responsible for most of the unhappiness in the world.
    (b) It can be supplanted by the deeper feelings of attachment.
    (c) It cannot be distinguished from true love.
    (d) It has no biological components, whereas romantic loves does.

15. According to Sternberg, fatuous love involves

    (a) passion and intimacy
    (b) passion and commitment
    (c) intimacy and commitment
    (d) passion alone

Answers 1. a; 2. b; 3. d; 4. c; 5. a; 6. d; 7. d; 8. d; 9. a; 10. d; 11. a; 12. c; 13. c; 14. b; 15. b

8

Relationships and Communication

TRUTH fiction

Which of the following statements are true, and which are fiction? Look for the Truth/Fiction icons on the pages that follow to find the answers.

1 Small talk is an insincere method of opening a relationship.   T   F

2 Only phonies practice opening lines.   T   F

3 Swift self-disclosure of intimate information is the best way to deepen a new relationship.   T   F

4 People can have intimate relationships without being sexually intimate.   T   F

5 Many people remain lonely because they fear being rejected by others.   T   F

6 Conflict is destructive to a relationship.   T   F

7 "Love is all you need." That is, when partners truly love one another, they instinctively know how to satisfy each other sexually.   T   F

8 If you are criticized, the best course is to retaliate.   T   F

9 Relationships come to an end when the partners cannot resolve their differences.   T   F

Will you, won't you, will you, won't you, will you join the dance?

—Lewis Carroll, *Alice in Wonderland*

No man is an island, entire of itself.

—John Donne, *No Man Is an Island*

"One, two. One, two." A great opening line? In the film *Play It Again, Sam,* Woody Allen plays Allan Felix, a social klutz who has just been divorced. Diane Keaton plays his platonic friend Linda. At a bar one evening with Linda and her husband, Allan Felix spots a young woman on the dance floor who is so attractive that he wishes he could have her children.

The thing to do, Linda prompts him, is to begin dancing, then dance over to her and "say something." With a bit more prodding, Linda convinces Allan to dance. It's so simple, she tells him. He need only keep time—"One, two, one, two."

"One, two," repeats Allan. Linda shoves him off to his dream woman.

Hesitantly, Allan dances up to her. Working up courage, he says, "One, two. One, two, one, two." He is ignored and finds his way back to Linda.

"Allan, try something more meaningful," Linda implores.

Once more, Allan dances nervously back toward the woman of his dreams. He stammers, "Three, four, three, four."

"Speak to her, Allan," Linda insists.

He dances up to her again and tries, "You interested in dancing at all?"

"Get lost, creep," she replies.

Allan dances rapidly back toward Linda. "What'd she say?" Linda asks.

"She'd rather not," he shrugs.

So much for "One, two, one, two" and, for that matter, "Three, four, three, four." Striking up a relationship requires some social skills, and the first few conversational steps can be big ones.

In this chapter we define the stages that lead to intimate relationships. We define intimacy and see that not all relationships—not even all long-term, committed relationships—achieve this level of interrelatedness. Moreover, some of us remain alone, and, perhaps, lonely. There are steps that people can take to overcome loneliness, however, as we illustrate in the pages ahead. Finally, we discuss satisfaction in relationships and enumerate ways of increasing satisfaction by enhancing communication skills.

The ABC(DE)s of Romantic Relationships

Romantic relationships, like people, undergo stages of development. According to **social exchange theory**, the development reflects the unfolding of social exchanges, which involve the rewards and costs of maintaining the relationship as opposed to dissolving it. During each stage, positive factors sway partners toward maintaining and enhancing their relationship. Negative factors incline them toward letting it deteriorate and end.

Numerous investigators have viewed the development of romantic relationships in terms of phases or stages (Berscheid & Reis, 1998; Dindia & Timmerman, 2003; Hendrick & Hendrick, 2000; Honeycutt & Cantrill, 2001; Levinger, 1980). From their work, we can build a five-stage **ABCDE model** of romantic relationships: (1) attraction, (2) building, (3) continuation, (4) deterioration, and (5) termination, or ending.

Attraction occurs when two people become aware of each other and find one another appealing or enticing. We may find ourselves attracted to an enchanting person "across a crowded room," in a nearby office, or in a new class. We may meet others through blind dates, introductions by mutual friends, computer match-ups, or by "accident." According to the NHSLS (Michael et al., 1994), married people are most likely to have met their spouses through mutual friends (35%) or self-introductions (32%; Figure 8.1). Other sources of introductions are family members (15%) and coworkers, classmates, or neighbors (13%). Unmarried couples also most commonly report meeting through mutual friends and self-introductions (Michael et al., 1994).

Being in a good mood apparently heightens feelings of attraction. George Levinger and his colleagues (Forgas et al., 1994) exposed 128 male and female moviegoers to either a happy or a sad film. Those shown the happy film reported more positive feelings about their partners and their relationships. (Think twice about what you take your date to see.)

Factors that motivate us to build relationships include similarity in physical attractiveness, similarity in attitudes, and mutual liking. Factors that deter building of relationships include lack of physical appeal, dissimilar attitudes, and lack of liking.

Many studies show that males tend to be more "romantic" (meaning passionate) than women in choosing whether to build relationships. For example, three German

Social exchange theory The view that the development of a relationship reflects the unfolding of social exchanges—that is, the rewards and costs of maintaining the relationship as opposed to ending it

ABCDE model The view that romantic relationships encompass five stages or phases: attraction, building, continuation, deterioration, and ending

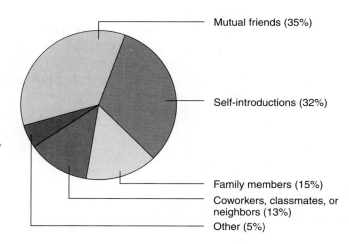

Figure 8.1 How People Met Their Partners. *According to the NHSLS study (Michael et al., 1994), two-thirds of married people met their partners through either mutual friends or self-introductions. Mutual friends and self-introductions were also the main ways of meeting for unmarried couples in committed relationships.*

- Mutual friends (35%)
- Self-introductions (32%)
- Family members (15%)
- Coworkers, classmates, or neighbors (13%)
- Other (5%)

A Closer Look

THEY SAY YOU CAN'T HURRY LOVE . . . BUT HOW ABOUT SPEED DATING?

This is a short story about two cable news network reporters who tried speed dating in the line of duty. But of course they also thought that it wouldn't hurt if they found someone spectacular along the way.

Allie, 25, is a fresh field reporter from the Midwest who is looking for someone who is a professional, is a bit older but not too much older, loves animals, likes traveling, is well-groomed, speaks well, and meets her minimal physical standards. He doesn't have to be Daniel Craig, but he has to take care of himself, Allie says.

Michael is a 24-year-old news editor from Delaware who would like to find someone who knows a good bottle of wine, likes the theater, reads, and is good looking.

Allie and Michael tried speed dating so they could do a story about it. The idea behind speed dating is that singles without a lot of time to spare can meet a whole bunch of people in a short amount of time. Using Hurry-Date, the Manhattan dating service, Allie and Michael talked to potential soul mates for only four minutes each.

They paid HurryDate a fee, signed up for an event, posted their profiles on the HurryDate website, and attended the event at a conveniently located bar where they were matched with other single people who were each assigned a number—no names.

Then the men played musical chairs, with a switch taking place every four minutes, except that no chairs were pulled out of the bunch. A part of the bar was cordoned off and the men sat down across from the women, with just four minutes to chat them up, back and forth. Then a whistle blew—literally—and the men moved over a seat, and the process continued, couple by couple. After each conversation, both parties jot down quick notes on a sheet provided by HurryDate next to their current partner's number so they can remember how they reacted to them later on.

Once the event is over and the participants have returned home, they can log on to the HurryDate website and search for the numbers of the people they met at the event. They can indicate whether they would like to hear from them by entering a "yes" or a "no." Then the yesses are matched and participants can send messages through HurryDate to their matches.

What happened with Allie and Michael? Read on.

Allie

I did this for a story and I didn't expect much from it. To be honest, I got from it what I expected—very little. I thought

---

studies found that men are more likely than women to focus on sex and fun, whereas women are more likely to focus on issues such as communication ability and reciprocity (Hassebrauck, 2003). Thus, in male–male relationships, both partners are likely to entertain sexual behavior relatively early. In female–female relationships, both partners are likely to be relatively cautious, unless they are revolting against female stereotypes. The German findings also fit with the evolutionary view that the male is more likely to be the initiator of sexual activity and that the female is more likely to be contemplating the value of the male as a reliable provider.

Not-So-Small Talk: An Audition for Building a Relationship

Truth or Fiction Revisited: Small talk is not an insincere method of opening a relationship. It is a useful way of seeking common ground. Successful small talk encourages a couple to venture beneath the surface. At a get-together or a club, individuals

it might be amusing, and sometimes it was, but it was also sort of hectic, and if I didn't distance myself from it a bit, I think I would have found it sort of emotionally churning, if you know what I mean. I didn't think for a minute there would be a chance of meeting Mr. Right, and I was right about that. Twenty faces in an hour and a half were sort of tough going if you take this sort of thing too seriously, I guess.

Almost all the guys told me what they did for a living, though I didn't ask. Maybe they thought that was strange, but when I saw them, I guess I really didn't feel like I had to know. Some said they were into finance with some sort of emphasis as if that was supposed to mean millions. There were a couple of teachers, no college professors. No doctors. Oh, yes—"sales," generic. Some said they lived in Manhattan, again emphasizing Manhattan, like to say they could afford it.

They asked me what I did, as if I was supposed to contribute to the rent or the mortgage. They also wanted to know where I lived and what I liked to do in my spare time.

I did ask them if they traveled or liked foreign films.

I wound up with 15 guys saying "yes" on the website. Truth is, I'm going to find Mr. Right another way.

Michael

Allie told me about her experience, and, frankly, I guess mine was a bit better than hers. She's sort of outgoing and guys sort of flock to her, if you know what I mean. I'm outgoing when I know people, but people don't flock to me the way they flock to Allie, so the idea of meeting 20 people in an hour and a half isn't a negative for me. In fact, six of them said "yes," meaning that they're willing to have more contact with me, and of that six, I find two attractive enough in one way or another. Now, you could say that's low odds, right? One in ten. I mean I met 20 women and something could happen with two of them. But that's not bad at all. If I were out with my friends at a bar on the weekend, I might wind up talking with one woman, and the chances of her having an interest in seeing me again might be, what, one in five?

I'll say this about the four minutes. It may sound like very little, but it's more than you think. I mean you say what do you do and what do you like and stuff, and she asks you what do you do and what do you like, and

Allie and Michael, scouting out a location in a park.

a couple of more questions, and if the answers are pretty short, you can be done in pretty much two minutes. Well, let me put it this way: If you're both kind of shy and you're both not long-winded, you might run out of stuff to say fairly quickly. Well, that's one of my problems, looking at someone and wondering what to say next.

Anyhow, and don't ask me how, with one of the women who said yes, my favorite, somehow we wound up talking about Gilbert and Sullivan and all sorts of mutual cultural interests. I guess she's the one who did it. I'm really looking forward to seeing her again!

may flit about from person to person, exchanging small talk, but now and then a couple finds common ground and pairs off.

Small talk enables people to probe one another during the early stages of building a relationship. It helps people find an overlapping of attitudes and interests—and to check out feelings of attraction (Knapp & Vangelista, 2000). Small talk stresses breadth of topic coverage rather than in-depth discussion. Engaging in small talk may have a "phony" ring to it, but it is a legitimate trial balloon for a relationship. Moreover, the ability to make small talk is a valuable social skill.

"Opening Lines": How Do You Get Things Started?

One kind of small talk is the greeting, or opening line. We usually precede greetings with eye contact and decide to try talking if eye contact is reciprocated. Avoidance of eye contact may mean that the person is shy, but it can also signify lack of interest. If

Small talk A superficial kind of conversation that allows exchange of information but stresses breadth of topic coverage, rather than in-depth discussion

you are interested in somebody, try a smile and eye contact. If the eye contact is reciprocated, try an opening line, or greeting. These include

- verbal salutes, such as "Good morning"
- personal inquiries, such as "How are you doing?"
- compliments, such as "I like your outfit"
- references to your mutual surroundings, such as "What do you think of that painting?" or "This is a nice apartment house, isn't it?"
- references to people or events outside the immediate setting, such as "Have you been following the [local athletic team]?"
- references to the other person's behavior, such as "I couldn't help noticing you were sitting alone" or "I see you out on this track every Saturday morning"
- references to your own behavior, or to yourself, such as "Hi, my name is Allan Felix" (feel free to use your own name, if you prefer)

A simple hi or hello is very useful. A friendly glance followed by a cheerful hello ought to give you some idea of whether the attraction is reciprocated. If the hello is returned with a friendly smile and inviting eye contact, follow it up with another greeting, such as a reference to your surroundings, the other person's behavior, or your name.

Truth or Fiction Revisited: It is not true that only phonies practice opening lines. It can be helpful for everyone to practice opening lines.

EXCHANGING "NAME, RANK, AND SERIAL NUMBER" Early exchanges are likely to include name, occupation, marital status, and hometown. This has been likened to exchanging "name, rank, and serial number" with the other person. Each person seeks a sociological profile of the other to discover common ground that may provide a basis for pursuing the conversation. An unspoken rule seems to be at work: "If I provide you with some information about myself, you will reciprocate by giving me an equal amount of information about yourself." Or ... "I'll tell you my hometown if you tell me yours" (Knapp & Vangelista, 2000). If the other person is unresponsive, she or he may not be attracted to you. But you may also be awkward in your approach or perhaps turn the other person off by disclosing too much about yourself at the outset.

Self-Disclosure: You Tell Me and I'll Tell You . . . Carefully

Self-disclosure, or opening up, is central to building intimate relationships (Ben Ze'ev, 2003; Dindia & Timmerman, 2003; Morry, 2005). But what sort of information is it safe to disclose upon meeting someone? If you refuse to go beyond name, rank, and serial number, you may look uninterested or as though you are trying to keep things under wraps. But if you spill out the fact that you have a painful rash on your thigh, you may have disclosed too much, too soon.

Truth or Fiction Revisited: Research suggests that we should refrain from disclosing intimate information too rapidly (Punyanunt–Carter, 2006). In a classic experiment, confederates of the researchers (Wortman et al., 1976) engaged in 10-minute conversations with study participants. Some confederates were "early disclosers," who shared intimate information early. Others, "late disclosers," shared intimate information toward the end of the conversation only. In both cases, the information was identical. Study participants then rated the disclosers. The early dis-

Self-disclosure The revelation of personal, perhaps intimate, information

closers in this study were rated less mature, secure, well adjusted, and genuine than the late disclosers.

SELF-DISCLOSURE IN CYBERSPACE On the other hand, rapid self-disclosure seems to be something of a new norm when people meet in cyberspace (Ben-Ze'ev, 2003; Punyanunt–Carter, 2006). Cyberspace allows for relative anonymity and enables people to control what they want to reveal—to safeguard their privacy even as they increase their emotional closeness and openness. The very nature of privacy changes in cyberspace, because matters that are usually kept under wraps tend to be discussed.

If the **surface contact** provided by small talk and initial self-disclosure has been mutually rewarding, partners in a relationship tend to develop feelings of liking for each other (Abell et al., 2006). Self-disclosure may build through the course of a relationship as partners come to trust each other enough to share intimate feelings.

What Do You Say When You're Meeting Someone New?
Do you make small talk? About what? Do you use an opening line? Which one? Are you genuine? Are you phony? Are you tense? At ease? Small talk actually isn't so small at all. People use it to search for common ground and test possible feelings of attraction.

SEX DIFFERENCES IN SELF-DISCLOSURE A woman complains to a friend, "He never opens up to me. It's like living with a stone wall." Women commonly declare that men are loathe to express their feelings. Researchers find that masculine-type individuals, whether male or female, tend to be less willing to disclose their feelings, perhaps in adherence to the traditional "strong and silent" masculine stereotype (Basow & Rubenfeld, 2003). A study by Susan Basow and Kimberly Rubenfeld (2003) found that feminine-type individuals are more likely to be empathic and to listen to other people's troubles than masculine-type individuals, regardless of their anatomic sex.

Factors that encourage continuation of relationships include seeking ways to introduce variety and maintain interest (such as trying out new sexual practices and social activities), showing evidence of caring and positive evaluation (such as sending birthday or Valentine's Day cards), trusting one's partner, perceiving fairness in the relationship, and experiencing feelings of general satisfaction. One of the developments in a continuing relationship is that of **mutuality,** which leads a couple to regard themselves as "we," not just two "I's" who happen to be in the same place at the same time (Deci et al., 2006; Neff & Harter, 2003). Mutuality favors continuation and further deepening of the relationship. Mutuality implies cognitive interdependence. Planning for the future in both little ways (What will I do this weekend?) and big ways (What will I do about my education and my career?) comes to include consideration of the needs and desires of one's partner. Cognitive interdependence is related to intimacy, as we will see in the following section.

Intimacy: Sharing Innermost Thoughts and Feelings

Intimacy consists of feelings of emotional connectedness with another person and the desire to share one's innermost thoughts and feelings (Yela, 2006). Partners in the throes of romantic love usually want to disclose everything to and know everything

CRITICAL Thinking
You cannot develop a relationship without some self-disclosure, but too much self-disclosure, too soon, can seem somewhat strange—or worse, give the appearance that you are out of control. Can you think of any rules of thumb for controlling the outflow of personal information?

Surface contact A probing phase of building a relationship in which people seek common ground and check out feelings of attraction

Mutuality A phase in building a relationship during which members of a couple come to regard themselves as "we," no longer as two "I's" who happen to be in the same place at the same time

Intimacy Feelings of closeness and connectedness that are marked by sharing of innermost thoughts and feelings

Working on the Relationship. *When one partner works on the relationship, the other partner is more motivated to reciprocate. Why did one partner give this gift? "Just because."*

CRITICAL
Thinking

Do you believe it is possible for a person to maintain complete individuality while at the same time investing in mutuality with another person? Explain.

TRUTH **fiction** 4

about one another (Kito, 2005; Vaculík & Hudecek, 2005). Along with sex, intimacy is one of the key ingredients in passionate relationships (Firestone et al., 2006; Korobov & Thorne, 2006). Feelings of intimacy and affection tend to grow as romantic relationships develop (Nieder & Sieffge–Krenke, 2001). Relationships also develop from being more casual and superficial to being relatively committed (Nieder & Sieffge–Krenke, 2001). As couples age, intimacy becomes one of the most valued—if not *the* most valued—components of the relationship (Villar et al., 2005). Intimate relationships are also characterized by trust, caring, and acceptance.

Sternberg's (2004) triangular theory of love regards intimacy as a basic component of romantic love, but people can be intimate and not in love, at least not in romantic love. Close friends and family members become emotionally intimate when they care deeply for each other and share their feelings and experiences.

Truth or Fiction Revisited: People need not be *sexually* intimate to be emotionally intimate. Nor does sexual intimacy automatically create emotional intimacy. People who are sexually involved may not achieve emotional closeness. People can be more emotionally intimate with friends than with lovers.

Because intimacy involves the sharing of one's innermost thoughts and feelings, honesty is a core feature of intimacy. A person need not be an "open book" to develop and maintain intimacy, however. Some aspects of experience are better kept even from one's most intimate partners, especially when they are embarrassing or threatening (Finkenauer & Hazam, 2000; Korobov & Thorne, 2006). We would not expect partners to disclose every passing sexual fantasy. Nor should we expect intimate partners to divulge the details of past sexual experiences. Honesty means *saying what one means,* not providing hurtful details.

Intimacy is important not only to interpersonal relationships but also to one's health. Researchers have found that intimacy fosters well-being and that its absence can be psychologically and physically harmful (Driver et al., 2003).

Q *When is the best time in a relationship to tell someone you love them? When is it too early? Too late?*

A Wait until you've gotten to know the person—at least a few weeks. Let it be "true love" and not merely infatuation, which you can feel pretty quickly, even immediately. You can say the other person is "wow" or something like that right away, but save the word *love* until you've had a while to show your head is screwed on right. When is it too late? We don't hear that question very often, but it could be too late if your partner has concluded that your feelings are too shallow or that you're not the kind of person who can make the commitment he or she is looking for. But that's not likely to happen out of the blue. You're likely to get lots of hints, like "So where is this relationship going?"

INTIMACY AND SELF-ESTEEM Some social scientists suggest that getting to know and like yourself is an initial step toward intimacy with others. By coming to know and value yourself, you identify your own feelings and needs and develop the security to share them. Research suggests that partners with low self-esteem are more likely to harbor self-doubts that can interfere with the development and maintenance of romantic relationships (Murray & Holmes, 2000). For example, experiments show that when their partner is in a "bad mood," people with low self-esteem tend to feel more responsible for that mood, to feel more rejected, and, consequently, to behave in a more hostile manner (Bellavia & Murray, 2003). Yet people with high self-esteem seem to be more likely to use their partners' acceptance and approval as a way of maintaining their self-esteem when self-doubts arise (Murray et al., 2001). That is, even when we feel rather good about ourselves, we can come to rely on our partner's impressions of us.

Too much self-esteem can also be detrimental to a relationship if it takes the form of narcissism (being wrapped up in oneself). Research shows that narcissists tend to play love games with their partners; they show less commitment and are more likely to have alternatives handy if relationships do not work out (Campbell et al., 2002). The same researchers found that self-esteem, as opposed to narcissism, was positively linked to romantic love.

Two other ingredients of an intimate relationship are trust and caring. Trust enables partners to feel confident that disclosing intimate feelings will not lead to ridicule or rejection. Trust usually builds gradually, as partners learn whether it is safe to share confidences.

A German study of 72 adolescents who were followed from the ages of 14 through 20 found that the quality of their relationships with their parents contributed to their ability to trust romantic partners (Seiffge–Krenke & Kuehnemund, 2001). Research also shows that people come to trust their partners when they see that their partners have made sincere investments in the relationship, as evidenced, for example, by making sacrifices to be with them, such as incurring the disapproval of their family (Rusbult & Van Lange, 2003; Wieselquist et al., 1999). Commitment and trust in a relationship can be seen as developing according to a model of **mutual cyclical growth**:

- Feeling that one needs one's partner promotes commitment to and dependence on the relationship

Mutual cyclical growth
The view that the need for one's partner promotes commitment, and commitment promotes acts that enhance the relationship; these acts build trust, increasing one's partner's commitment to the relationship

- Commitment to the relationship encourages partners to do things that are good for the relationship.
- One's partner perceives the pro-relationship acts.
- Perception of pro-relationship acts enhances the partner's trust in the other partner and in the relationship
- Feelings of trust increase the partner's willingness to depend on the relationship.

Caring is an emotional bond that allows intimacy to develop. Caring means that partners try to satisfy each other's needs, gratify each other's interests, and make sacrifices, if necessary. Research shows that willingness to sacrifice is connected with commitment to the relationship, level of satisfaction in the relationship, and, interestingly, poor alternatives to the relationship (Van Lange et al., 1997). In other words, it may not be easy to find partners if one does not sacrifice for relationships. Is self-sacrifice thus self-serving (Finkenauer & Meeus, 2000)?

MAKING A COMMITMENT   People may open up to strangers on airplanes or trains, or to health care providers and still find it hard to talk openly with people to whom they are closest. Yet we know that we will not see the strangers again, or that the health professionals are required to keep our personal matters confidential. Truly intimate relationships are marked by commitment to maintain the relationship through thick and thin (Sternberg, 2004).

Numerous studies find that men tend to be more reluctant than women to make commitments. David Popenoe, co-director of the National Marriage Project at Rutgers University in New Jersey, conducted a study with 60 unmarried heterosexual men and found that the commonness of cohabitation is one reason why they are reluctant to make a commitment. In cohabitation, sex—traditionally a key reason for men to marry—is readily available. Popenoe notes that "In a sense, with cohabitation he gets a quasi-wife without having to commit" (Hussain, 2002).

In committed relationships, a delicate balance exists between individuality and mutuality. In healthy unions, a strong sense of togetherness does not eradicate individuality. Partners in such relationships remain free to be themselves. Neither seeks to dominate or submerge himself or herself into the personality of the other. Each partner maintains individual interests, likes and dislikes, needs and goals.

Factors that can throw continuing relationships into a downward spiral include boredom, as in falling into a rut in leisure activities or sexual practices. Yet boredom does not always end relationships. Consider a study of 12 men who admitted to experiencing sexual boredom in long-term heterosexual relationships (Tunariu & Reavey, 2003). The men were not happy with sexual boredom, particularly in a culture in which men are viewed as highly sexual, and romantic love is supposed to remain passionate. On the other hand, they viewed their boredom as a normal trade-off for so-called true love and long-term companionship.

Other factors that contribute to the discontinuation of a relationship include evidence of negative evaluation (such as bickering, and forgetting anniversaries and other important dates or pretending that they do not exist), lack

How do we explain feelings of jealousy? What does jealousy do to an intimate relationship?

of fairness in the relationship (such as one partner's always deciding how the couple will spend their free time), jealousy, and general dissatisfaction. *Question:* How does jealousy affect relationships?

Jealousy: Is the World a Real-Life Temptation Island?

> O! beware, my lord, of jealousy;
> It is the green-ey'd monster . . .
>
> —William Shakespeare, *Othello*

Thus was Othello, the Moor of Venice, warned of jealousy in the Shakespearean play that bears his name. Yet Othello could not control his feelings and so he killed his beloved wife, Desdemona. The English poet John Dryden labeled jealousy a "tyrant of the mind." Anthropologists find evidence of jealousy in all cultures, although it may vary in amount and intensity across and within cultures. It appears to be more common and intense among cultures with a stronger machismo tradition, in which men are expected to display their virility. It is also powerful in cultures in which men view a woman's infidelity as a threat to their honor. But jealousy is found among gay males and lesbians as well as among heterosexuals (Hughes et al., 2004; Kim & Hahn, 2006).

Sexual jealousy is aroused when we suspect that an intimate relationship is threatened by a rival. Lovers can become jealous when others show sexual interest in their partners or when their partners show an interest (even a casual or nonsexual interest) in another. Jealousy can lead to loss of feelings of affection, feelings of insecurity and rejection, anxiety and loss of self-esteem, and feelings of mistrust of one's partner and potential rivals. Jealousy is one of the commonly mentioned reasons why relationships fail. Feelings of possessiveness, related to jealousy, also place stress on a relationship. In extreme cases jealousy can cause depression or give rise to spouse abuse, suicide, or, as with Othello, murder (Puente & Cohen, 2003; Vandello & Cohen, 2003). However, milder forms of jealousy are not necessarily destructive to a relationship. They may even serve the positive function of revealing how much one cares for one's partner. For this reason, some investigators distinguish between "normal jealousy," which reflects occasional self-doubts and the belief that one's partner is attractive, and "obsessional jealousy," in which the individual, like Othello, is consumed by his or her fears of interference in the relationship (Marazziti et al., 2003).

What causes jealousy? Experience and personality variables play roles. People may become mistrustful of their partners because former partners had cheated.

People with low self-esteem may experience sexual jealousy because they become overly dependent on their partners. They may fear that they will not be able to find another partner if their current partner leaves.

REFLECT

Would you want a partner to experience feelings of jealousy? Explain.

JEALOUSY AND EVOLUTIONARY THEORY   David Buss, Todd Shackelford, and their colleagues (e.g., Murphy et al., 2006, Shackelford et al., 2002, 2005) note that sex differences in jealousy appear to support evolutionary theory. Males seem to be more upset by sexual infidelity, females by emotional infidelity. That is, males are made more insecure and angry when their partners have sexual relations with someone else. Females are made more insecure and angry when their partners become emotionally attached to someone else. Why? Evolutionary theory hypothesizes that sexual jealousy was shaped by natural selection as a method of ensuring males that their female partner's offspring are their own, and of ensuring females that their male partners will continue to provide resources to facilitate child rearing (Buss, 2003, 2005; Harris, 2003).

LACK OF SEX DIFFERENCES IN RESPONSES TO AFFAIRS AMONG GAY MALES AND LESBIANS   Interestingly, the hypothesized sex differences in reactions to infidelity disappear when one's partner has an affair with someone of his or her own sex (Sagarin et al., 2003). Is it because the affair carries no threat of impregnation (a view that would be consistent with evolutionary theory)? Or is it because the victim consoles himself or herself by thinking that he or she really isn't competing in the same arena with the intruder? Are both explanations and other explanations possible?

A COGNITIVE PERSPECTIVE   In recent years, cognitive theory has gained importance in many areas of the behavioral sciences, and sexual jealousy is no exception. In two studies, Stacie Bauerle and her colleagues (2002) presented 156 college undergraduates and 128 members of the general population with various scenarios in which their partners were unfaithful. By and large, jealousy increased when the individuals attributed their partner's infidelity to internal causes, such as clear personal choice. When they attributed the infidelity to external causes, such as alcohol or social pressure, the individuals in the study reported feeling significantly less jealous. ("Don't blame me; it was the alcohol.")

Many lovers—including many college students—play jealousy games. They let their partners know that they are attracted to other people. They flirt openly or manufacture tales to make their partners pay more attention to them, to test the relationship, to inflict pain, or to take revenge for a partner's disloyalty.

Responses to Deterioration of a Relationship

A relationship begins to fail when it becomes less rewarding than it was. Couples can respond to deterioration in active or passive ways. Active means of response include doing something that may enhance the relationship (such as working on improving communication skills, negotiating differences, or seeking professional help) or deciding to end the relationship. Passive methods of responding include merely waiting for something to happen, doing little or nothing. People can sit back and wait for the relationship to improve on its own (occasionally it does) or for the relationship to deteriorate to the point where it ends. ("Hey, these things happen.")

It is irrational (and damaging to a relationship) to assume that good relationships require no investment of time and effort. No two people are matched perfectly. When problems arise, it is better to work to resolve them than to act as though they don't exist and hope that they will just disappear.

Breaking Up—Breaking Up Is (Often) Hard to Do

According to social exchange theory, relationships draw to a close when the partners find little satisfaction in the affiliation, when the barriers to leaving the relationship are low (i.e., the social, religious, and financial constraints are manageable), and especially when alternative partners are available. Problems with jealousy and communication are common reasons for ending a relationship. The availability of alternatives decreases one's commitment to a relationship (Knox et al., 1997a; Rusbult et al., 1998). This fact has been widely recognized throughout the ages, which is one reason why patriarchal cultures like to keep their women locked up—or, in the Middle East, literally "under wraps"—as much as possible.

Breaking up, as the song goes, can be hard to do—both for the person terminating the relationship and for the other party. For this reason, as noted in the following "A Closer Look" feature, some people break up via e-mail rather than in person or on the telephone.

Some people obviously take breaking up better than others. A study of more than 5,000 people who responded to a survey on the Internet found that anxious people were more likely to be highly preoccupied with the lost partner, to suffer more physical and emotional distress, to attempt to reestablish the relationship, and to be angry and vengeful (Davis et al., 2003). Emotionally secure individuals were most

People Who Have Been Rejected Sometimes Stalk Their Former Partners. *Stalking includes behaviors such as breaking into their e-mail. (Hint: Change your passwords from time to time.)*

A Closer Look

IN MODERN E-MAIL ROMANCE, "TRASH" IS JUST A CLICK AWAY

One summer night, Jason Kellogg, a 24-year-old publishing assistant, left a bar in Brooklyn after spending a good deal of time talking with a woman he had met that evening. When he left the bar, his friends demanded the requisite information: How old is she? Is she from the area? Does she have any good-looking friends? And most important, did you get a phone number?

Mr. Kellogg hesitated on the last question. "Well, not exactly," he said. "She gave me her e-mail."

That was a first for Mr. Kellogg. He sent her an e-mail message a few days later, although nothing came of their correspondence. "I suppose it was better than a flat-out rejection," he said.

"She was probably turned off by my bad spelling."

E-mail, which has long been an indispensable tool in business, is beginning to influence more romantic relationships as well. With more and more Americans in front of [computers] at work and spending time on them at home, e-mail is changing the ways people meet, court, and even break up.

"It's changed every aspect of dating," said Sherry Amatenstein, a dating expert for the iVillage online network (www.ivillage.com) and author of *The Q & A Dating Book* (Adams Media, 2000). "Our new technology is both boon and curse for the modern dater."

One reason for the change in etiquette from requesting a phone number to requesting an e-mail address is comfort, particularly for women. "It's safer than a phone number," said Brenda Ross, dating adviser for About.com and creator of the Dating Advice for Geeks website (www.geekcheck.com) "With a few e-mails you can get some details, find out what a guy is like, and then decide if you want to go out with him. It takes a lot of pressure off."

Some women are now using e-mail as a way to avoid people they have no intention of ever going out with. In many instances, Ms. Ross said, a woman doesn't want to give out her phone number, but she also doesn't want to be pestered all night for it by some libidinous Neanderthal. Solution: Give him your e-mail address and never respond, or give an e-mail address that you never use, an updating of the time-honored dating tradition of giving a wrong phone number. Eventually he will get the idea, and trashing an e-mail message is easier than dodging a phone call.

Many single people have found that e-mail can be a solution to another age-old dating problem—when to call? Ellen Lavery, a 25-year-old from Manhattan, found herself in that situa-

---

likely to seek social support among their friends and their families. Insecure individuals were most likely to turn to alcohol and drugs. A survey of 92 college undergraduates found that many believed they would grow from the experience of breaking up (Tashiro & Frazier, 2003). Individuals' "attributional styles" entered the picture: People who blamed themselves for the breakup experienced more stress than those who blamed external factors, such as the situation.

Breaking up is sometimes followed by **stalking,** or other "unwanted pursuit behaviors," such as unwelcome phone calls or e-mails, asking third parties about the person who dissolved the relationship, and following, threatening, or attacking that person or new partners of that person (Davis et al., 2002; Langhinrichsen–Rohling et al., 2002). Jealousy, abusiveness, and physical violence in relationships are key predictors of unwanted pursuit (Puente & Cohen, 2003). Stalkers and violent individuals also tend to have a strong need to control others (Dye & Davis, 2003). We will see in Chapter 18 that a need to control other people is also connected with the violent crime of rape.

Various factors can save a deteriorating relationship. For example, people who continue to find some sources of satisfaction, who are committed to maintaining the relationship, or who believe that they will eventually be able to overcome their problems are more likely to invest what they must to prevent the collapse.

Stalking Following or observing a person persistently, especially because of obsession with the person; can occur online as well as in person, as when a person breaks into someone else's e-mail

tion a few months ago, the morning after a party where she exchanged phone numbers and e-mail addresses with a man. "The next day, I would have absolutely considered a phone call too soon, too desperate," she said, "a severe violation of the three-day rule. So I shot him off a brief 'We should get together sometime' e-mail. It seemed more acceptable and less threatening, but not overbearing."

Traditionally, the first phone call can be more nerve-racking than transporting nuclear weapons across a rope bridge. You have to be on your toes: funny but not obnoxious, charming yet not hammy, deep but not psychotic, all on the spot. An e-mail message, however, can go through multiple drafts; wording and tone can painstakingly be thought out, reviewed, edited, and, if it's not quite right, sent back to committee. "I always show my e-mails to friends before I send them out," said Drew Brooks, a 25-year-old in Manhattan. "Involving other people is fun."

Single people who follow up on chance encounters with e-mail are finding that the awkward first stages of a relationship can be made easier online.

One reason relationships can move so far so fast over the Internet is the solitary nature of e-mail. "When you're e-mailing, you can be at home, cozy, in your pajamas," Ms. Amatenstein said. "It's so psychologically inviting, people say things they normally would not say."

Increasingly, people are also finding that the distance of e-mail simplifies one of the potentially messier tasks in a relationship: the breakup. "That's one great thing about e-mail," Mr. Brooks said. "There's no ramifications for you in just blowing someone off."

Not everyone sees it that way, though. Brenda Ross, whose former boyfriend broke up with her via e-mail, after they had talked about the possibility of marriage, said it was about the "lamest" thing a person could do. "E-mail is a great way to break up with someone," she said, "if you're a coward."

How Will She Get Rid of Him? *Perhaps she will give him a phony e-mail address. Some women now use e-mail as a method of avoiding seeing people they do not want to go out with. They may give out their actual e-mail addresses but never respond, or they may give out seldom-used or erroneous e-mail addresses. It's like giving out the wrong phone number. (Bye bye.)*

On the other hand, the swan song of a relationship—moving on—can be a sign of healthful decision making, not a sign of failure. When people are highly incompatible, and when genuine attempts to preserve the relationship have failed, ending the relationship can offer each partner a chance for happiness with someone else.

SafeZone

Q *How do you tell someone the relationship is over?*

A It's never easy. Nor should it be. The other person has invested in you, and losing someone a person cares about hurts. A lot. But once you've made up your mind, do it as quickly as possible to give the other person as much time as possible to rebuild his or her life. In the "old days," people would pick public places, so the person who was "dumped" was unlikely to make a scene. Now people often use e-mail. The most decent thing to do is to tell the person face to face in private. Just say that it no longer works for you—not that the other person is somehow bad or a loser. And don't be surprised if the other person has suspected something was wrong. After all, how good an actor can you be?

Loneliness: "All the Lonely People, Where Do They All Come From?"

Many people start relationships because of loneliness. ***Question:*** What is loneliness? Loneliness and solitude (being alone) are not synonymous. Loneliness is a state of painful isolation, of feeling cut off from others (Long et al., 2003). Solitude, however, can be quite positive. Inner-directed solitude can be characterized by self-discovery and inner peace (Long et al., 2003). Outer-directed solitude can refer to spirituality or can allow us to reflect on the world around us. Solitude is usually a matter of choice; loneliness is not.

Lonely people tend to spend a lot of time by themselves, eat dinner alone, spend weekends alone, and participate in few social activities. They are unlikely to date. Some lonely people report having many friends, but a closer look suggests that these "friendships" are shallow. Lonely people are unlikely to share confidences. Loneliness tends to peak during adolescence, when peer relationships begin to supplant family ties. A study of 90 adolescents age 16 to 18 found that feelings of loneliness were connected with low self-confidence, introversion, unhappiness, and emotional instability (Cheng & Furnham, 2002). Loneliness is also often connected with feelings of depression. A study of 101 dating couples with a mean age of 21 found that poor relationships contributed to feelings of loneliness and to depression—even though the individuals had partners (Segrin et al., 2003).

Loneliness or Solitude? *Solitude can be a positive experience, allowing us to think or read or write. But loneliness is painful social isolation that can be detrimental to both our psychological and our physical health.*

Loneliness is connected with physical health problems as well as with psychological problems such as depression. One study, for example, found that lonely people had higher blood pressure than people who were not lonely (Hawkley et al., 2003). Lonely people also found stressful experiences to be more discomfiting, an observation that suggests the value of social support when we are undergoing stress (Hawkley et al., 2003). Social isolation has also been shown to predict cancer, cardiovascular disease, various other diseases, and a higher mortality rate (Hawkley & Cacioppo, 2003). It appears that one causal pathway between loneliness and illness involves stress. Stress impairs the functioning of the immune system, and lonely people perceive stress to be more aversive (Cacioppo et al., 2003).

The causes of loneliness are many and complex. Lonely people tend to have several of the following characteristics:

- Lack of social skills. Lonely people often lack the interpersonal skills to make friends or cope with disagreements.

- Lack of interest in other people

- Lack of empathy. Empathy is a key aspect of satisfaction in romantic relationships (Cramer, 2003).

- Failure to disclose personal information to potential friends (Valkenburg & Peter, 2007)

- Cynicism about human nature (e.g., seeing people as only out for themselves)

- Demanding too much, too soon. The lonely perceive other people as cold and unfriendly during the early stages of a relationship.

- General pessimism. When we expect the worst, we often get . . . you guessed it.

- An external locus of control. That is, lonely people do not see themselves as capable of taking their lives into their own hands and achieving their goals.

Truth or Fiction Revisited: It is true that many people remain lonely because of the fear of rejection. This fear is often connected with self-criticism of social skills and expectations of failure in relating to others (Vorauer et al., 2003).

Coping with Loneliness

Helping professionals encourage lonely people develop more adaptive ways of thinking and behaving. Lonely people often have distorted views of others. They may have one or two unfortunate experiences and jump to the conclusion that people are generally selfish and not worth the effort of getting involved. Yes, some people are basically out for themselves, but the belief that everyone is selfish can perpetuate loneliness by motivating us to avoid others.

What can you do to deal with loneliness in your own life? Here are some suggestions:

1. Challenge your feelings of pessimism. Adopt the attitude that things happen when you make them happen.
2. Challenge your cynicism about human nature. Yes, lots of people are selfish and not worth knowing, but if you assume that all people are like that, you can doom

yourself to a lifetime of loneliness. Your task is to find people who possess the qualities that you value.

3. Challenge the idea that failure in social relationships is unbearable and is thus a valid reason for giving up on them. Sure, social rejection can be painful. We must all learn to live with some rejection, but keep looking for the people who possess the qualities you value and who will find things of equal value in you.

4. Get out among people. Sit down at a table with people in the coffee shop, not off in a corner by yourself. Smile and say hi to people who interest you. Practice opening lines for different occasions—and a few follow-up lines. Try them out while looking in the mirror.

5. Make numerous social contacts. Join committees for student activities. Try intra-mural sports. Join social action groups, such as environmental groups and com-munity betterment groups. Join the photography club or the ski club. Get on the school yearbook or newspaper staff.

6. Be assertive. Express your genuine opinions.

7. Become a good listener. Ask people how they're doing. Ask them for their opinions about classes, politics, or the campus events of the day. Then actually *listen* to what they have to say. Tolerate diverse opinions; remember that no two of us are identi-cal in our outlooks (not even your "perfectly" matched first and third authors). Maintain eye contact. Keep your face friendly. (No, you don't have to remain neu-tral and friendly if someone becomes insulting toward a religious or ethnic group.)

8. Give people the chance to know you. Exchange opinions and talk about your in-terests. Yes, you'll turn some people off—who doesn't?—but how else will you learn whether you and another person share common ground?

9. Fight fair. Friends will inevitably disappoint you, and you'll want to tell them about it. Do so, but fairly. You can start by asking if it's okay to be open about something. Then say, "I feel upset because you . . . ." You can ask your friend whether he or she realized that his or her behavior upset you. Try to work to-gether to find a way to avoid recurrences. Finish by thanking your friend for helping you resolve the problem.

10. Remember that you're worthy of friends. It's true—warts and all. None of us is perfect. We're all unique, but you may connect with more people than you imag-ine. Give people a chance.

11. Use your college counseling center. Many thousands of students are lonely but don't know what to do about it. Others just cannot find the courage to approach others. College counseling centers are very familiar with the problem of loneli-ness, and you should consider them a valuable resource. You might even ask whether there's a group at the center for students seeking to improve their dating or social skills.

Satisfaction in Relationships: Communication as Key

Some relationships work out. Others don't. In Western culture, where people tend to form relationships with more than one partner as they develop, perhaps the major-ity of relationships draw to an end. Termination of a relationship is not always a bad

Working with Lesbians, Gays, and Bisexuals. *Couples therapists who work with LGBs (lesbian, gays, and bisexual couples) will find many problems akin to those of heterosexual couples, but some will reflect the sexual orientations of the members of the couple; for example, LGB identity development, gays as parents, and so on.*

thing. As people spend time together, they learn more about whether they are well matched or poorly matched. Most also learn how to compromise to help build relationships and how to approach resolving conflicts in a constructive way.

Relationships between Heterosexuals, Gay Males, Lesbians, Bisexuals, and Transgendered Individuals

Numerous researchers have studied the factors that predict satisfaction in a relationship or the deterioration and ending of a relationship. Much of this research has sought to determine whether there are differences in the factors that satisfy heterosexual and homosexual couples, and the interesting finding is that we are hardpressed to find differences. One difference is that gay and lesbian couples tend to distribute household chores evenly and not in terms of gender-role sterotypes (Kurdek, 2005, 2006). Now for the similarities: Sexual satisfaction is tied to satisfaction with the relationship in both heterosexual and lesbian women (Mathews et al., 2006; Twist, 2005). Gay, lesbian, and male–female couples are all more satisfied when they receive social support from their partners, there is sharing of power in the relationship, they fight fair, and they perceive their partners to be committed to the relationship. But there are a couple of differences that favor stability in the relationships of male–female couples: They are more likely to have the support of their families and less likely to be stigmatized by society at large.

Couples therapists who work with gays, lesbians, bisexuals, and transgendered individuals and couples will find problems akin to those in heterosexual couples, such as infidelity (Martell & Prince, 2005), and many that need special sensitivity to these commonly stigmatized subpopulations (Pachankis & Goldfried, 2004). Here are a few examples:

- Lesbian–gay–bisexual (LGB) identity development and how it affects the functioning of the couple
- Parenting and its effect on the couple
- LGB individuals as members of families
- The kinds of stressors that affect individuals who are underrepresented in the LGB literature, including older LGB people, LGB individuals who are also members of ethnic minority groups, LGB individuals and religious group membership
- Legal issues and their effect on the couple
- Workplace issues and their effect on the couple

Conflict Resolution

Some researchers, such as John M. Gottman (Driver & Gottman, 2004; Gottman & Driver, 2005; Gottman et al., 1998, 1999; Yoshimoto et al., 2006) and Susan Johnson (2005) have focused on the ways in which couples resolve conflicts. Gottman has videotaped couples as they do so and monitored their physiological responses as well, including their heart rates, sweating, and large motor movement. He found that deterioration of satisfaction in the relationship could be predicted by physiological measures, particularly on the part of the male. The calmer the couple's bodily responses, the more their relationship improved as time went on. On the other hand, couples whose hearts beat more rapidly, who sweated more, and who moved about agitatedly had relationships that deteriorated during the following three years.

Truth or Fiction Revisited: Gottman found that conflict itself is not necessarily destructive to a relationship. The important thing is the way in which the couple attempts to resolve it. Couples who were open and calm during the conflict tended to improve their satisfaction. Couples who were defensive experienced deterioration in the relationship. A notable trait that contributed to deterioration was "stonewalling" by the male. Stonewalling means that there is little movement of the head, few if any nods, and few of the verbal acknowledgments made by listeners who are participating in a discussion. Deterioration of the relationship was also predicted by excessively agreeable, compliant behavior on the part of the female or by her verbalizing feelings of contempt. Facial expressions predicted deterioration, especially facial expressions that suggested disgust on the part of the female, fear on the face of the male, and then miserable smiles by both parties. These nonverbal behaviors were accompanied by more defensiveness, excuses, and denial of responsibility.

Stonewallers suffer not only in terms of their relationships. Stonewalling predicted loneliness after the relationship ended, and loneliness, in turn, was connected with deteriorating health.

Good outcomes for relationships could also be predicted by positive attributes during conflict, such as displays of humor, empathy, and affection; by mutual efforts to solve problems; and by determination to listen to one's partner nondefensively. These positive elements kept physiological responses in check as well.

Other researchers have generally found evidence in support of Gottman's conclusions about couples in conflict. For example, Holman and Jarvis (2003) also found that the ways in which couples communicate to resolve conflicts are the key to the survival or termination of a relationship. Couples who validated each other's feelings in a respectful and helpful manner were most satisfied with their relationships. Couples who were hostile or explosive, or who attempted to avoid conflict, were less satisfied with their relationships.

Communication Skills for Enhancing Relationships and Sexual Relations: How to Do It

Truth or Fiction Revisited: Despite the Beatles' song lyrics, love is not all you need. You also need communication. Couples learn about each other's desires and needs through communication. Otherwise, this knowledge remains a mystery.

Couples therapists and sex therapists might find less work if more couples communicated effectively about their sexual feelings. Unfortunately, when it comes to sex, *talk* may be the most overlooked four-letter word.

Many couples suffer for years because one or both partners are unwilling to speak up. Or problems arise when one partner misinterprets the other. Clear communication can take the guesswork out of relationships, avert misunderstandings, relieve resentments and frustrations, and increase sexual and general satisfaction with the relationship.

Obstacles to Sexual Communication

Why is it so difficult for couples to communicate about sex? There are several reasons.

Some couples believe that talking about sex is vulgar. But vulgarity, like beauty, is, to some degree, in the eye of the beholder. One couple's vulgarity may be another couple's love talk. Some people may maintain a Victorian belief that any talk about sex is not fit for mixed company, even between intimate partners. Sex, that is, is something you may do, but not something to be talked about. Other couples may be willing in principle to talk about sex but may find it difficult to actually do so, because they lack an agreeable, common language.

How, for example, are they to refer to their genitals or to sexual activities? One partner may prefer to use coarse four-letter (or five-letter) words to refer to them. The other might prefer more clinical terms. A partner who prefers slang for the sexual organs might be regarded by the other as vulgar or demeaning. One who uses clinical terms, such as fellatio or coitus, might be regarded as, well, clinical. Some couples try to find a common verbal ground that is not vulgar at one extreme or clinical at the other. They might speak, for example, of "doing it" or "having sex" rather than "engaging in sexual intercourse." (The title of the Eddie Cantor musical of the 1930s suggests that some people once spoke of "making whoopie.") Or they might speak of "kissing me down there" rather than of practicing fellatio or cunnilingus.

A Closer Look

THE ACTIVE-LISTENING CONTROVERSY

For decades, couples have listed communication problems as a prime cause of dissatisfaction in their relationships. Part of the problem, they have complained, is that their partners simply do not listen to them.

For this reason, couples therapists have suggested that couples use a technique that therapists themselves frequently use when listening to clients: active listening. Active listening involves recognizing that when your partner is speaking, it is helpful to do more than sit back passively. Sitting back passively can be confused with stonewalling, which is one of the behavior patterns that can lead to the termination of a relationship (Driver et al., 2003; Gottman & Levenson, 1999; Gottman et al., 1998, 1999; Pasupathi et al., 1999).

In other words, it is not helpful to stare off into space while your partner is talking, or to offer a begrudging "mm-hmm" now and then just to be polite. Instead, you can listen actively by maintaining eye contact and modifying your facial expressions to show that you understand his or her feelings and ideas (Cole & Cole, 1999). For example, nod your head when appropriate.

Listening actively also involves asking helpful questions, such as "Would you please give me an example?" or "Was that good for you?"

An active listener does not simply hear what the other person is saying, but also focuses attentively on the speaker's words and gestures to grasp meaning. Nonverbal cues may reveal more about the speaker's inner feelings than the spoken word. Good listeners do not interrupt, change the topic, or walk away when their partners are speaking.

Paraphrasing is another form of active listening that shows that you understand what your partner is trying to say. When paraphrasing, you recast or restate your partner's words to confirm your comprehension. For example, if your partner says, "You hardly ever say anything when we're making love. I don't want you to scream or make obligatory grunts, or do something silly, but sometimes I wonder if I'm trying to make love to a brick wall." You can paraphrase this by saying something like "So it's sort of hard to know if I'm really enjoying it."

All of this made good common sense and was consistent with what was "known" by therapists for decades, but then John Gottman and his colleagues (1998) published a controversial study that was based on observations of the ways in which 130 newlywed couples

Many couples also harbor irrational beliefs about relationships and sex, such as the notion that people should somehow know what their partners want, without having to ask. The common misconception that people should know what pleases their partners undercuts communication. Men, in particular, seem burdened with the stereotype that they should have a natural expertise at sex. Women may feel it is "unladylike" to talk openly about their sexual needs and feelings. Both partners may hold the idealized romantic notion that "love is all you need" to achieve sexual happiness.

A related irrational belief is that if our partners truly loved us, they would somehow "read our minds" and know what types of sexual stimulation we desire. Unfortunately, or fortunately, others cannot read our minds. We must assume the responsibility for communicating our preferences.

Some people communicate more effectively than others, perhaps because they are more sensitive to others' needs or because their parents served as good models as communicators. However, communication skills can be acquired at any time. Learning takes time and work, but the following guidelines should prove helpful if you want to enhance your communication skills. These skills can also improve communication in areas of intimacy other than the sexual.

went about trying to resolve conflicts. Gottman and his colleagues (1998) found that they could predict which couples would remain together and which would break up on the basis of their bodily responses to "discussing" their differences and what they said and did. The Gottman (1998) group reported that, contrary to popular opinion (among helping professionals), active listening did not help couples resolve conflicts and remain together. Instead, it was often perceived as confrontational and damaging to the relationship. The Gottman group also reported that the expression of anger was not necessarily damaging and—in a suggestion that outraged feminists—that females would be well advised to raise issues gently, so as not, perhaps, to bruise the male ego. On the other hand, the Gottman group did find support for encouraging males to be open to (nonabrasive?) suggestions from females.

The Gottman group received a great deal of criticism. Some of the criticism referred to methodological flaws in their study, such as the fact that couples were not selected at random from the general population and that the investigators drew conclusions about

Is Actively Listening to Your Partner a Good Idea? *It might seem that the obvious answer is yes, because effective communication requires learning the other person's view of things. But be aware that John Gottman and his colleagues found some evidence that the specific form of listening that therapists term* active listening *can appear to be confrontational. Partners can listen actively by maintaining eye contact and modifying their facial expressions to show that they understand their partner's feelings and ideas. They can ask helpful, nonconfrontational questions, such as, "Did I disappoint you when I . . . ?" Tone of voice and sincerity are important.*

cause and effect from correlational data (Stanley et al., 2000 [see Chapter 2]). Other critics noted that active listening, when carried out properly, does not appear to be confrontational, and that couples in therapy might benefit from more careful training in using the method (Cole & Cole, 1999; Hafen & Crane, 2003).

Is it dangerous to express anger when attempting to resolve conflict? When anger leads to stonewalling, character assassination, or physical confrontation, perhaps all therapists would agree that it is destructive. But if discussion can remain civil, it may be useful to recognize emotions—even negative emotions such as anger—for what they are.

GETTING STARTED   How do you broach tough topics? Here are some ideas. You can start by talking about talking. You can inform your partner that it is difficult for you to talk about problems and conflicts: "You know, I've always found it awkward to find a way of bringing things up" or "You know, I think other people have an easier time than I do when it comes to talking about some things." You can allude to troublesome things that happened in the past when you attempted to resolve conflicts. This approach encourages your partner to invite you to proceed.

Broaching the topic of sex can be difficult. Couples who gab endlessly about finances, children, and work, may clam up about sex. So it may be helpful to first agree to talk about talking about sex. You can admit that it is difficult to talk about sex. You can say that your sexual relationship is important to you and that you want to do everything you can to enhance it. Gently probe your partner's willingness to set aside time to talk about sex, preferably when you can dim the lights and avoid interruptions.

The "right time" may be when you are both relaxed, rested, and unpressed for time. The "right place" can be anyplace where you can enjoy privacy and speak undisturbed. Sex talk need not be limited to the bedroom. Couples may feel more comfortable talking about sex over dinner, when cuddling on the sofa, or when just relaxing together.

CRITICAL Thinking

Critical thinkers avoid overgeneralizations and oversimplifications. Think about what actually happens during so-called "active listening." What types of things might the listener do that his or her partner finds to be annoying? Now that you are aware of the possible "dangers" of being too "active" while listening, what can the listener do so that "listening" will be more productive and less annoying?

Another possibility is to request permission to raise an issue. You can say something like this: "There's something on my mind. Do you have a few minutes? Is now a good time to tell you about it?" Or you can say, "There's something that we need to talk about, but I'm not sure how to bring it up. Can you help me with it?"

You can also tell your partner that it is okay to point out ways in which you can become a more effective lover. For example, you can say, "I know that you don't want to hurt my feelings, but I wonder if I'm doing anything that you'd rather I didn't do?"

LISTENING   Effective listening involves such skills as active listening, paraphrasing, the use of reinforcement, and valuing your partner even when the two of you disagree. To listen actively rather than passively, first adopt the attitude that you may actually learn something—or perceive things from another vantage point—by listening. You can learn more about active listening—and the controversy surrounding the procedure!—in the "A Closer Look" feature.

Even when you disagree with what your partner is saying, you can maintain good relations and keep channels of communication open by saying something like, "I really appreciate your taking the time to try to work this out with me" or "I hope you'll think it's okay if I don't see things entirely in the same way, but I'm glad that we had a chance to talk about it."

When you disagree with your partner, do so in a way that shows that you still value your partner as a person. In other words, say something like "I love you very much, but it annoys me when you . . ." rather than "You're really contemptible for doing . . . ." In this manner, you encourage your partner to disclose sensitive material without the risk of attack or of losing your love or support.

LEARNING ABOUT YOUR PARTNER'S NEEDS   Listening is basic to learning about another person's needs, but sometimes it helps to go a few steps further. You can ask open-ended questions that allow for a broader exploration of issues, such as

"What do you like best about the way we make love?"
"Do you think that I do things to bug you?"
"Does it bother you that I go to bed later than you do?"
"Does anything disappoint you about our relationship?"
"Do you think that I do things that are inconsiderate when you're studying for a test?"

Close-ended questions that call for a limited range of responses are most useful when you're looking for a simple yes or no type of response: "Would you rather make love with the stereo off?"

Self-disclosure is essential to developing intimacy. You can also use self-disclosure to learn more about your partner's needs, because communicating your own feelings and ideas invites reciprocation. For example, you might say, "There are times when I feel that I disappoint you when we make love. Should I be doing something differently?"

You can ask your partner to level with you about an irksome issue. You can say that you recognize that it might be awkward to discuss it, but that you will try your best to listen conscientiously and not get too disturbed. You can also limit yourselves to one such difficult issue per conversation. If the entire emotional dam were to burst, the job of mopping up could be overwhelming.

PROVIDING INFORMATION   There are skillful ways of communicating information, including "accentuating the positive" and using verbal and nonverbal cues. It is irrational to expect that your partner can read your mind. He or she can tell when you're wearing a grumpy face, but your expression does not provide much information about your specific feelings. When your partner asks, "What would you like me to do?" don't say, "Well, I think you can figure out what I want" or "Just do whatever you think is best." Only you know what pleases you.

Let your partner know when he or she is doing something right! Speak up or find another way to express your appreciation. Accentuating the positive is rewarding and also informs your partner about what pleases you. In other words, don't just wait around until your partner does something wrong and then seize the opportunity to complain!

Sexual activity provides an excellent opportunity for direct communication. You can say something like, "Oh, that's great" or "Don't stop." Or you can ask for feedback, as in "How does that feel?"

Feedback provides direct guidance about what is pleasing. Partners can also make specific requests and suggestions.

Sexual communication also occurs without words. Facial expressions and body language communicate likes and dislikes. Our partners may lean toward us or away from us when we touch them, or they may relax or tense up. In any case, they speak volumes in silence. The following exercises may help couples use nonverbal cues to communicate their sexual likes and dislikes.

- *Taking turns petting.* Taking turns petting can help partners learn what turns one another on. Each partner takes turns caressing the other, stopping frequently enough to receive feedback by asking questions like, "How does that feel?" The recipient is to provide feedback, which can be expressed verbally ("Yes, that's it—yes, just like that" or "No, a little lighter than that") or nonverbally, as in making appreciative or disapproving sounds. The knowledge gained through this exercise can be incorporated into the couple's regular pattern of lovemaking.

- *Directing your partner's hand.* Gently guiding your partner's hand—to show your partner where and how you like to be touched—is a most direct way of communicating sexual likes. Women might show partners how to caress the breasts or clitoral shaft in this manner. Men might cup their partners' hands to show them how to stroke the penile shaft or caress the testes.

- *Signaling.* Couples can use agreed-upon nonverbal cues to signal sexual pleasure. For example, one partner may rub the other in a certain way, or tap the other, to signal that something is being done right. The recipient of the signal takes mental notes and incorporates the pleasurable stimulation into the couple's lovemaking. This is a sort of "hit-or-miss" technique, but even near misses can be rewarding.

MAKING REQUESTS   A basic part of improving relationships or lovemaking is asking partners to change their behavior—to do something differently or to stop doing something that hurts or is ungratifying. The skill of making requests now comes to the fore.

Be specific in requesting changes. Telling your partner something like, "I'd like you to be nicer to me" may accomplish little. Your partner may not know that his or her behavior is not nice and may not understand how to be "nicer." It is better to say something like "I would appreciate it if you would get coffee for yourself, or at least ask me in a more pleasant way." Or, "I really have a hard time with the way you talk to me in front of your friends. It's as if you're trying to show them that you have control over me or something." Similarly, it may be less effective to say, "I'd like you to be more loving" than to say, "When we make love, I'd like you to kiss me more and tell me how you care about me."

Of course, you can precede your specific requests with openers such as "There's something on my mind. Is this a good time for me to bring it up with you?"

You are more likely to achieve desired results by framing requests in "I" talk than by heaping criticisms on your partner. For example, "*I* would like it if we spent some time cuddling after sex" is superior to "*You* don't seem to care enough about me to want to hold me after we make love." Saying "*I* find it very painful when you use a harsh voice with me" is probably more effective than "Sometimes people's feelings get hurt when their boyfriends [girlfriends] speak to them harshly in front of their friends or families."

You can try out "I" talk in front of a mirror or with a confidante before using it with your partner. In this way, you can see whether your facial expressions and tone of voice are consistent with what you are saying. Friends may provide constructive feedback.

DELIVERING CRITICISM   Delivering criticism effectively is a skill. It requires focusing partners' attention on the problem without inducing resentment or reducing them to trembling masses of guilt or fear.

First, weigh your goals forthrightly. Is your primary intention to punish your partner, or are you more interested in gaining cooperation? If your goal is punishment, you may as well be coarse and disparaging, but expect to invite reprisals. If your goal is to improve the relationship, however, a tactful approach may be in order.

Deliver criticism privately—not in front of friends or family. Your partner has a right to be upset when you make criticism public. Making private matters public prompts indignation and cuts off communication.

Be specific about the behavior that disturbs you so that you bypass the trap of disparaging your partner's personality or motives. For example, you may be more effective by saying. "I could lose this job because you didn't write down the message" than by saying, "You're completely irresponsible" or "You're a flake." Similarly, you may achieve better results by saying, "The bathroom looks and smells dirty when you throw your underwear on the floor" rather than "You're a filthy pig." Complain about specific, modifiable behavior rather than trying to overhaul another individual's whole personality.

Your partner will feel less threatened if you express displeasure in terms of your own feelings rather than by directly attacking his or her personality. Attacks often arouse defensive behavior, and sometimes retaliation. When confronting your partner for failing to be sensitive to your sexual needs when making love, it may be more effective to say, "You know, it really upsets me that you don't seem to care about my feelings when we make love" than to say, "You're so wrapped up in yourself that you never think about anyone else."

Keep criticism and complaints to the present. Think how many times you have been in an argument and heard things like "You never appreciated me!" or "Last summer you did the same thing!" Bringing up the past muddles current issues and heightens resentments. When your partner forgets to jot down a telephone message, it is more useful to note, "This was a vital phone call" than "Three weeks ago you didn't tell me about the phone call from Chris, and as a result I missed out on seeing *Terminator 17*." It's better to leave who did what to whom last year (or even last week) alone.

Avoid blunt criticisms or personal attacks and suggest constructive alternatives. Avoid saying, "You're really a lousy lover." Say instead, "Can I take your hand and show you what I'd like?"

Whenever possible, express criticism positively and combine it with a concrete request. When commenting on your partner's failure to display affection during love-making say, "I love it when you kiss me. Please kiss me more" rather than "You never kiss me when we're in bed and I'm sick of it."

RECEIVING CRITICISM

Honest criticism is hard to take, particularly from a relative, a friend, an acquaintance, or a stranger.

—Franklin P. Jones

Truth or Fiction Revisited: Retaliation is not the best course of action when you are criticized. We suggest that you do not seize the opportunity to strike back by saying, "Who're you to complain about the bathroom? What about your breath and that pigsty you call your closet?" Retaliation is tempting and may make you feel good at the moment, but it can do a relationship more harm than good in the long run.

Delivering criticism can be tricky, especially when you want to inspire cooperation. Receiving criticism can be even trickier. Nevertheless, the following suggestions offer some help.

When you hear, "It's time you did something about . . . ," it is understandable if the hair stands up on the back of your arms. After all, it's a blunt challenge. When we are confronted harshly, we are likely to become defensive and think of retaliating. But if your objective is to enhance the relationship, take a few moments to stop and think. To resolve conflicts, we need to learn about the other person's concerns, keep lines of communication open, and find ways of changing problem behavior.

So when your partner says, "It's about time you did something about the bathroom," stop and think before you summon up your most menacing voice and say, "Just what the hell is that supposed to mean?" Ask yourself what you want to find out.

Just as it's important to be specific when delivering criticism, it helps if you encourage the other person to be specific when you are on the receiving end of criticism. In the example of the complaint about the bathroom, you can help your partner be specific and, perhaps, avert the worst by asking clarifying questions, such as "Can you tell me exactly what you mean?" or "The bathroom?"

Consider a situation in which a lover says something like "You're one of the most irritating people I know." Rather than retaliating and further harming the relationship, you can say something like, "How about forgoing the character assassination and telling me what I did that's bothering you?" This response requests an end to insults and asks your partner to be specific.

Even when you disagree with a criticism, you can keep lines of communication open and show respect for your partner's feelings by acknowledging and paraphrasing the criticism.

On the other hand, if you are at fault, you can admit it. For example, you can say, "You're right. It was my day to clean the bathroom and it totally slipped my mind" or "I was so busy, I just couldn't get to it." Now the two of you should look for a way to work out the problem. When you acknowledge criticism, you cue your partner to back off and look for ways to improve the situation. What if your partner then becomes abusive and says something like, "So you admit you blew it?" You might then try a little education in conflict resolution. You could say, "I admitted that I was at fault. If you're willing to work with me to find a way to handle it, great; but I'm not going to let you pound me into the ground over it."

Now, if you think that you were not at fault, express your feelings. Use "I" talk and be specific. Don't seize the opportunity to angrily point out your partner's short-comings. By doing so, you may shut down lines of communication.

NEGOTIATING DIFFERENCES Negotiate your differences if you feel that there is merit on both sides of the argument. You may want to say something like "Would it help if I . . . ?" And if there's something about your obligation to clean the bathroom that seems totally out of place, perhaps you and your partner can work out an exchange—that is, you get relieved of cleaning the bathroom in exchange for tackling a chore that your partner finds equally odious.

If none of these approaches helps resolve the conflict, perhaps your partner is using the comment about the bathroom to express anger over other issues. You may find out by saying something like, "I've been trying to find a way to resolve this thing, but nothing I say seems to be helping. Is this really about the bathroom or are there other things on your mind?"

WHEN COMMUNICATION IS NOT ENOUGH: HANDLING IMPASSES Communication helps build and maintain relationships, but sometimes partners have profound, substantial disagreements. In fact, it is normal to have disagreements from time to time. Even when their communication skills are superbly tuned, partners now and then reach an impasse. Couples who reach an impasse may find these suggestions helpful.

Research shows that taking one's partner's perspective (i.e., looking at things from one's partner's point of view) during a dispute results in more positive feelings about the relationship and greater effort to respond in a constructive manner (Arriaga & Rusbult, 1998; Driver et al., 2003). Thus, if there is an impasse, ill feeling may be resolved by (honestly) saying something like, "I still disagree with you, but I can understand why you take your position." But if you do not follow your partner's logic, you can say something like, "Please believe me. I'm trying very hard to look at this from your point of view, but I can't follow your reasoning. Would you try to help me understand your point of view?"

Sometimes when you reach a stalemate, it helps to allow the problem to "incubate" for a while. If you and your partner put the issue aside for a time, perhaps a resolution will dawn on one of you later. Although we tend to form relationships with people who share similar attitudes, there is never a perfect overlap. A partner who pretends to be your clone will most likely become a bore. Assuming that your relationship is generally rewarding and pleasurable, you may find it possible to tolerate some differences. Part of respecting other people is allowing them to be who they are. When we have a solid sense of who we are as individuals and what we stand for, we are more apt to tolerate differentness in our partners.

Truth or Fiction Revisited: It is not necessarily true that relationships come to an end when the partners cannot resolve their differences. You and your partner can agree to disagree on various issues. Remember that disagreement itself is not necessarily destructive to a relationship—unless you are convinced that it must be. Two people cannot see everything in the same way. Failure to disagree ever will leave at least one partner feeling frustrated now and then. Conflict is nearly inevitable in a relationship. The key to satisfaction with the relationship is how the couple goes about trying to resolve the conflict.

Q *How do you keep relationships going, long-term?*

A It takes two of you to do that, and the answer may surprise you: *work.* People often get fed up with one another's weak points, but also think about the strong points. Don't only build—also rebuild. Be open about what's wrong and talk about ways to make things right, or more right. If passion fades, try some new things (read that magazine about the 647 things that will drive her/him crazy). Check out some new films, new restaurants. Go somewhere for the weekend. Confide in a friend. Call a therapist. And sometimes the reality is you *don't* keep the relationship going. Add up the pluses and minuses, figure out where you are in life, and make a decision that works for you.

1. How do relationships develop?

- According to the ABCDE model, relationships develop through five stages: attraction, building, continuation, deterioration, and ending.

- Small talk enables individuals to learn whether they share interests, attitudes, and feelings of attraction with another person.

- The opening line—or greeting—enables individuals to begin surface contact with one another so they can test whether they are matched and share feelings of attraction.

- Self-disclosure enables people to get below surface contact to determine whether they have things in common. Too little self-disclosure prevents development of intimacy; too much may appear to be socially inappropriate.

- Intimacy involves feelings of emotional closeness with another person and the desire to share each other's innermost thoughts and feelings. Intimacy involves self-esteem, trust, caring, tenderness, honesty, and commitment.

- Jealousy is fear that a rival will intrude upon an intimate relationship. According to evolutionary theory, males are more concerned when their partners have sexual relations with an outsider, whereas females are more concerned when their partners develop emotional closeness with an outsider. Gay males and lesbians do not fit the patterns predicted by evolutionary theory.

- Partners can take active means either to improve or to terminate the relationship, or they can sit back passively and let what happens happen.

2. What is loneliness? What can people do about it?

- Loneliness is a state of painful isolation, of feeling cut off from others. Solitude, by contrast, can be a positive experience.

- The causes of loneliness include lack of social skills, lack of interest in other people, lack of empathy, fear of rejection, lack of self-disclosure, cynicism about human nature, demanding too much too soon, general pessimism, and an external locus of control.

- People are helped to overcome loneliness by challenging self-defeating attitudes, developing social skills, and placing themselves among others rather than withdrawing socially.

3. What factors are associated with satisfaction in relationships?

- Factors such as caring, lack of excessive jealousy, perceived fairness, mutual respect, and ability to communicate are connected with satisfaction in relationships.

- Lesbians, gay males, bisexuals, and transgendered people have problems in relationships similar to those of heterosexuals. However, they also have problems such as those associated with LGB identity development, LGB parenting, and LGB issues with the law and in the workplace.

4. How can couples enhance their communication skills to maintain and improve their relationships?

- Couples may find it difficult to talk about sex because of the lack of an agreeable common language or because they harbor irrational beliefs about relationships and sex. Therapists help couples develop communication skills, such as getting started in communicating, listening to one's partner, learning about one's partner's needs, providing information, making requests, delivering and receiving criticism, and coping with impasses. Controversy exists regarding whether active listening helps couples communicate.

1. Sexual satisfaction for lesbians is connected with

   (a) their sexual orientation

   (b) their relationship

   (c) social stigmatization

   (d) issues in the workplace

2. Evolutionary theory predicts that _____ will be most jealous about their partner's sexual infidelity.

   (a) heterosexual males

   (b) heterosexual females

   (c) gay males

   (d) lesbians

3. Married people are most likely to have met their spouses through

   (a) church activities

   (b) school activities

   (c) mutual friends

   (d) family activities

4. Self-disclosure in cyberspace tends to be

   (a) slow

   (b) accurate

   (c) one sided

   (d) rapid

5. Which of the following is not part of an intimate relationship?

   (a) narcissism

   (b) trust

   (c) caring

   (d) honesty

6. "Small talk"

   (a) is a phony way to begin a relationship

   (b) is an in-depth discussion of issues

   (c) promotes premature self-disclosure

   (d) stresses breadth of topic coverage

7. It is not true that

   (a) good relationships require no work

   (b) jealousy harms a relationship

   (c) partners need to work to keep relationships strong

   (d) communication skills are important to relationships

8. Which is damaging to a relationship?

   (a) The partners' religious tradition encourages maintaining relationships.

   (b) The partners find the relationship to be satisfying.

   (c) Barriers to leaving the relationship are high.

   (d) Stonewalling

9. Which statement is accurate?

   (a) People need to be sexually intimate to have an emotionally intimate relationship.

   (b) People need not be sexually intimate to have an emotionally intimate relationship.

   (c) Love is necessary for intimacy.

   (d) Intimacy requires total honesty.

10. It is true that

   (a) men should naturally know about sex

   (b) people should know what their partners want without having to communicate

   (c) sexual knowledge is learned

   (d) it is sluttish for women to talk about sex

11. According to the text, _____ are most reluctant to make commitments in relationships.

   (a) men

   (b) heterosexual women

   (c) lesbians

   (d) transgendered individuals

12. Research into the cognitive perspective found that feelings of jealousy increase when people attribute their partners' infidelity to _____ causes.

   (a) unstable

   (b) specific

   (c) external

   (d) internal

13. Research suggests that lonely people tend to have

   (a) social skills

   (b) interest in other people

   (c) cynicism about human nature

   (d) empathy for other people's feelings

14. Kurdek finds that LGB couples tend to differ from heterosexual couples in that they

   (a) distribute household chores more evenly

   (b) avoid conflict at all costs

   (c) do not consider sexual activity per se to be an important aspect of their relationship

   (d) believe that love conquers all and that it is not necessary to work on relationships

15. Gottman's research challenges the view that _____ is a valuable aspect of communication skills.

   (a) knowing how to receive criticism

   (b) active listening

   (c) being specific about complaints

   (d) knowing when to agree to disagree

Answers 1. b; 2. a; 3. c; 4. d; 5. a; 6. d; 7. a; 8. d; 9. b; 10. c; 11. a; 12. d; 13. c; 14. a; 15. b

Sexual Behaviors and Fantasies

TRUTH fiction

Which of the following statements are true, and which are fiction? Look for the Truth/Fiction icons on the pages that follow to find the answers.

1 Married people rarely if ever masturbate. T F

2 European American men are more likely to masturbate than African American men. T F

3 Women who masturbate during adolescence are less likely to find gratification in marital coitus than women who do not. T F

4 Women are more likely to reach orgasm through sexual intercourse than through masturbation. T F

5 Most women masturbate by inserting a finger or other object into the vagina. T F

6 Lesbian couples commonly strap on dildos and engage in sexual intercourse with them. T F

7 Statistically speaking, oral sex is the norm for today's young couples. T F

8 Anal sex is more common among less well educated people. T F

9 Sexual fantasies are abnormal. T F

10 When lovers fantasize about other people, the relationship is in trouble. T F

11 People who have sexual fantasies are likely to have sexual or social problems. T F

Rachel Maines's intentions were innocent enough. She was going to write a book about needlework in the late 19th and early 20th centuries. (Yawn.) But in the course of her research, she noticed advertisements for vibrators—100 years ago! Being a scholar with a free-ranging mind, she turned her attention to the meaning and use of vibrators in U.S. history and wound up writing a book called *The Technology of Orgasm: "Hysteria," the Vibrator, and Women's Sexual Satisfaction*.

It turns out that genital massage to orgasm—often using a vibrator—was once a standard treatment for "hysteria," a health problem considered common in women. (After all, a man would never be hysterical, would he?) The treatment was usually carried out by a physician or a midwife. Genital massage would be used to bring the woman to "hysterical paroxysm" (another name for orgasm, at least in women). The introduction of the vibrator in the 1880s made treatment more efficient.

Hysteria? What's that? In earlier centuries the diagnosis of hysteria would be made on the basis of symptoms such as anxiety, irritability, nervousness, pelvic swelling, heaviness in the abdomen (bloating), and fainting. There were other symptoms as well, including sexual fantasies and vaginal lubrication. The word *hysteria* derives from the Greek word for "uterus." The medical establishment believed that the uterus caused these symptoms by choking the patient because of sexual deprivation. Pregnancy would help; so would coitus. Single women were encouraged to get married, and married women were encouraged to get pregnant. Women without men might try horseback riding, use rocking chairs (yes, rocking chairs), or obtain genital massage. Maines found no evidence that physicians delighted in the task. Rather, they apparently relegated it to midwives whenever they could. Women, by the way, were not encouraged to masturbate as a way of achieving, uh, "hysterical paroxysm." Masturbation was seen as deviant and unhealthful. Use of the vibrator in the

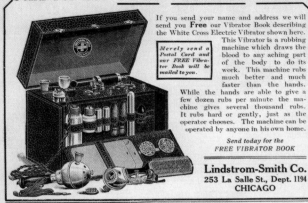

Send For Our Free Vibrator Book

If you send your name and address we will send you **Free** our Vibrator Book describing the White Cross Electric Vibrator shown here.

Merely send a Postal Card and our FREE Vibrator Book will be mailed to you.

This Vibrator is a rubbing machine which draws the blood to any aching part of the body to do its work. This machine rubs much better and much faster than the hands. While the hands are able to give a few dozen rubs per minute the machine gives several thousand rubs. It rubs hard or gently, just as the operator chooses. The machine can be operated by anyone in his own home.

Send today for the
FREE VIBRATOR BOOK

Lindstrom-Smith Co.
253 La Salle St., Dept. 1194
CHICAGO

In the late 19th and early 20th centuries, vibrators came into use as means of helping women with "hysterical" health problems—as they were conceptualized by the health establishment at the time. At most times and in most places, women's sexuality has taken a back seat to that of men.

hands of the physician or midwife was seen as a medical treatment, not a sexual act. An orgasm was a "hysterical crisis," not an orgasm.

It is obvious that the "symptoms of hysteria" are related to menstruation. Today we recognize that menstrual and premenstrual symptoms are associated with the secretion of sex hormones, but even as late as the mid 20th century, health professionals attributed a wide variety of mental disorders to hysteria. Therefore, the behaviors connected with the disorders—such as the development of physical symptoms in response to stress—were expected in women but surprising in men.

Some psychologists believe that the content and the sources cited by Maines deserve further scrutiny by other scholars. It is surprising that this piece of history has remained relatively hidden until now. Yet the book does have a solid list of references, along with illustrations of the vibrators and treatment tables. It would appear that the practice Maines describes did, in fact, occur. How widespread it was is still uncertain.

This is the chapter that presents sexual techniques and statistical breakdowns of "who does what with whom." There is great variety in human sexual expression, and vibrators are still in use, but we do not hear of them resulting in hysterical paroxysms anymore.

Some of us practice few, if any, of the techniques described in the chapter. Some of us practice most or all of them. Some of us practice some of them some of the time. Our best knowledge of the prevalence of these techniques comes mainly from the sex surveys of Kinsey and the University of Chicago group (the NHSLS). But even these surveys are plagued by problems such as sampling that is not fully representative, social desirability, and volunteer bias.

Readers of this textbook are as varied in their sexual values, preferences, and attitudes as society is in general. Some of the techniques discussed may thus strike some readers as indecent. Our aim is to provide information about the diversity of sexual expression. We are not seeking unanimity on what is acceptable, nor do we pass judgment or encourage readers to expand their sexual repertoires.

The human body is sensitive to many forms of sexual stimulation, yet biology is not destiny. A biological capacity does not impose a behavioral requirement. Cultural expectations, personal values, and individual experience—not only our biological capacities—determine our sexual behavior. What is right for you is right for you— and not necessarily for your neighbor.

We begin by reviewing the techniques that people practice on their own to derive sexual pleasure. We then consider techniques that involve a partner.

CRITICAL Thinking

A—shall we say—easily upset male character in the musical comedy *A Funny Thing Happened on the Way to the Forum,* set in ancient Rome, is named "Hysterium." What's funny about that?

Solitary Sexual Behavior

In solitude he pollutes himself, and with his own hand blights all his prospects for both this world and the next. Even after being solemnly warned, he will often continue this worse than beastly practice, deliberately forfeiting his right to health and happiness for a moment's mad sensuality.

—J. H. Kellogg, M.D., *Plain Facts for Old and Young,* 1888

Various forms of sexual expression do not require a partner or are not generally practiced in the presence of a partner. **Masturbation** is one of the principal forms of one-person sexual expression. Masturbation involves direct stimulation of the genitals. Other forms of individual sexual experience, such as sexual fantasy, may or may not be accompanied by genital stimulation.

The word *masturbation* is not simply a descriptive term. It derives from the Latin *masturbari,* from the roots for "hand" and "to defile." The derivation provides clues to historical cultural attitudes toward the practice (Polonsky, 2006). Masturbation may be practiced by manual stimulation of the genitals, perhaps with the aid of artificial stimulation, such as a vibrator. One may use an object, such as a pillow or a **dildo,** that touches the genitals. Even before we conceive of sexual experiences with others, we may learn early during childhood that touching our genitals can produce pleasure.

Pleasure is not the only reason that people masturbate. Table 9.1 lists reasons for masturbation, according to the findings of the NHSLS.

Within the Judeo-Christian tradition, masturbation has been condemned as sinful (Bullough, 2002). Early Judeo-Christian attitudes toward masturbation reflected the censure that was applied toward nonprocreative sex. Masturbation has also been referred to as "onanism" or "onania," names derived from the biblical story of Onan (Gutmann, 2006). According to the Book of Genesis (38:9–11), Onan was the

Masturbation Sexual self-stimulation

Dildo A penis-shaped object used in sexual activity

TABLE 9.1

Reasons for Masturbation (Percentage of Respondents Who Report Reason), According to the NHSLS

Reasons for Masturbation	Men	Women
To relax	26	32
To relieve sexual tension	73	63
Partners are unavailable	32	32
Partner does not want to engage in sexual activity	16	6
Boredom	11	5
To obtain physical pleasure	40	42
To help get to sleep	16	12
Fear of HIV/AIDS and other STIs	7	5
Other reasons	5	5

SOURCE: Adapted by permission from E. O. Laumann, J. H. Gagnon, R. T. Michael, & S. Michaels (1994). *The Social Organization of Sexuality: Sexual Practices in the United States.* Chicago: University of Chicago Press, Table 3.3, p. 86.

second-born son of Judah. Judah's first son, Er, died without an heir. Biblical law required that if a man died without a male heir, his brother must take the widow as his wife and rear their first son as his brother's heir. Judah thus directed Onan to "Go in unto thy brother's wife, and perform the duty of a husband's brother unto her, and raise up seed to thy brother." But Onan "spilled [his seed] upon the ground" during relations with his deceased brother's wife and was struck down by God for his deed.

Although "onanism" has come to be associated with masturbation, scholars have noted that Onan's act was **coitus interruptus**, not masturbation. Both acts, however, involve nonprocreative sex—"spilling the seed." Whatever its biblical origins, masturbation is prohibited under Jewish law. St. Augustine was influenced by ancient Persian beliefs, which condemned all nonprocreative sex as sinful (Bullough, 2002; Gutmann, 2006). Historians suspect that people in ancient times condemned sex that did not lead to pregnancy because of the need for an increase in their numbers. The need for progeny is also linked to the widespread view that marital intercourse is the only morally acceptable avenue of sexual expression.

Historical Medical Views of Masturbation

St. Augustine's views were carried into medicine during the 18th century, and the medical profession "translated" sin into disease (Polansky, 2006). Thus, until recent times, masturbation was thought to be physically and mentally harmful, as well as degrading. The 18th-century physician Benjamin Rush, a signer of the Declaration of Independence, believed that masturbation caused tuberculosis, "nervous diseases," poor eyesight, memory loss, and epilepsy.

Many clergy and medical authorities of the 19th century were persuaded that certain foods had a stimulating effect on the sex organs. They thus advised parents to modify their children's diets to eliminate foods that were believed to excite the sexual organs, notably meat, coffee, tea, and chocolate. Parents should substitute "unstimulating" foods, most notably grain products. In the 1830s the Reverend Sylvester Gra-

Coitus interruptus The practice of withdrawing the penis prior to ejaculation during sexual intercourse; also called the *withdrawal method*

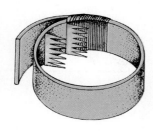

Figure 9.1 Devices Designed to Curb Masturbation.
Because of widespread beliefs that masturbation was harmful, various contraptions were introduced during the 19th century to prevent the practice in children. Some of the devices were barbarous.

ham developed a cracker, since called the graham cracker, to help people control their sexual impulses.

Yet another household name belongs to a man who made his mark by introducing a bland diet that was also intended to help people, especially youngsters, control sexual impulses. One of the more influential medical writers of the 19th century was the superintendent of the Battle Creek Sanatorium in Michigan, Dr. J. H. Kellogg (1852–1943), better known now as the creator of the modern breakfast cereal. Kellogg identified 39 "signs of masturbation," including acne, paleness, heart palpitations, rounded shoulders, weak backs, and convulsions. Kellogg, like Graham, believed that sexual desires could be controlled by a diet of simple foods, especially grains, including the corn flakes that have since borne his name.

Many 19th-century physicians also advised parents to take measures to prevent their children from masturbating. Kellogg suggested that parents bandage or cage their children's genitals, or tie their hands. Some contraptions devised to prevent masturbation were barbarous (Figure 9.1).

Several 19th-century scholars of sexuality joined the crusade against masturbation. Richard von Krafft–Ebing (in *Psychopathia Sexualis,* 1886) and Havelock Ellis (in *Studies in the Psychology of Sex,* 1900) condemned masturbation as psychologically dangerous. Krafft–Ebing linked masturbation to sexual orientation. Male masturbation, or so it was mistakenly believed, arrested the development of normal erotic instincts and led to **impotence** with women. Thus, it encouraged male–male sexual activity.

Despite this history, there is no scientific evidence that masturbation is harmful. It doesn't cause insanity, grow hair on the hands, or cause warts or any of the other ills once ascribed to it, save for rare injuries to the genitals resulting from rough stimulation. Nor is masturbation in itself psychologically harmful, although it may suggest an adjustment problem if people use masturbation as an exclusive sexual outlet when they have opportunities for sexual relationships. Sex therapists have used masturbation as a treatment for individuals with low sexual desire and for women who have difficulty reaching orgasm (Coleman, 2002; Zamboni & Crawford, 2002) (see Chapter 15).

Of course, people who consider masturbation wrong, harmful, or sinful may experience anxiety or guilt about it (Ortega et al., 2005), but these negative reactions are linked to their beliefs about masturbation, not masturbation per se. Nevertheless, feelings of guilt can lower the incidence and frequency of masturbation (Ortega et al., 2005).

Surveys indicate that most people in our society masturbate at some time. However, individuals are now masturbating at earlier ages than in Kinsey's day (Dekker & Schmidt, 2002). The incidence of masturbation is generally greater among men than women. The nearby "The World of Human Sexuality" feature elaborates on masturbation among different demographic groups.

REFLECT

What misinformation, if any, did you receive about masturbation when you were growing up? What was the source of the misinformation?

Impotence Recurrent difficulty in achieving or sustaining an erection sufficient to engage in sexual intercourse successfully (The term has been replaced by the terms *male erectile disorder* and *erectile dysfunction;* see Chapter 15.)

Demographic Factors and Masturbation

Few "forbidden" activities have been as widespread as masturbation. Nearly all the adult men and about two thirds of the adult women in the classic Kinsey studies (Kinsey et al., 1948, 1953) reported that they had masturbated at some time. The NHSLS also found a gender gap in reported frequencies of masturbation (Laumann et al., 1994). Table 9.2 shows how study participants reported the frequency of masturbation "during the past 12 months," according to sex, age, marital status, level of education, religion, and race/ethnicity.

Overall, 37% of the men and 58% of the women sampled reported that they had *not* masturbated during the past year. Within every social category, men reported masturbating more frequently than women. Despite the sexual revolution, women may still find masturbation less acceptable than do men (Dantzker & Eisenman, 2003). Traditional women may still be subject to socialization pressures that teach that sexual activity for pleasure's sake is more of a taboo for women than men (Dantzker & Eisenman, 2003). Then, too, women are more likely to pursue sexual activity within the context of a relationship.

Truth or Fiction Revisited: Married people are less likely to have masturbated during the past 12 months than never-married and formerly married people. Nevertheless, only 43% of the married men and 63% of the married women sampled said that they did not masturbate at all during the past year. Therefore, many married people do masturbate.

People with more education—both female and male—reported more frequent masturbation. Perhaps people with more schooling are more likely to learn that masturbation itself is harmless or are less likely to follow traditional social restrictions. Traditional religious beliefs appear to restrain masturbation. Conservative Protestants are less likely to masturbate than liberal and moderate Protestants.

Truth or Fiction Revisited: African Americans are *less* likely—not more likely— to report masturbating during a 12-month period than other ethnic groups. Perhaps African American men are relatively more likely to adhere to traditional views concerning masturbation.

There appears to be a link between masturbation and orgasm during sex with others (Coleman, 2002). **Truth or Fiction Revisited:** According to the Kinsey studies, women who had masturbated during adolescence were more likely, not less likely, to find gratification in sex with others in adulthood than women who had not.

The evidence does not suggest that adolescents should be encouraged to masturbate to foster sexual fulfillment in adulthood. A selection factor may explain the link (Figure 9.2). That is, people who masturbate early may be more open to exploring their sexuality. These attitudes would carry over into adulthood and increase the likelihood that women would seek the stimulation they need to obtain sexual gratification. Adolescent masturbation may also set the stage for sexual satisfaction in adulthood by providing information about the types of stimulation that lead to sexual gratification. **Truth or Fiction Revisited:** Researchers have found that women achieve orgasm more reliably through masturbation than through sexual intercourse (Masters & Johnson, 1966; Young et al., 1998).

In our efforts to correct misinformation about masturbation, let us not suggest that there is anything wrong with choosing *not* to masturbate. Readers are encouraged to make their own choices on the basis of their own values.

TABLE 9.2

Demographic Factors and Frequency of Masturbation during the Past 12 Months, as Found in the NHSLS

| | Frequency of Masterbation, % | | | |
| | Not at All | | At Least Once a Week | |
Demographic Factors	Men (N = 36.7)	Women (N = 58.3)	Men (N = 26.7)	Women (N = 7.6)
Age, Y				
18–24	41.2	64.4	29.2	9.4
25–29	28.9	58.3	32.7	9.9
30–34	27.6	51.1	34.6	8.6
35–39	38.5	52.3	20.8	6.6
40–44	34.5	49.8	28.7	8.7
45–49	35.2	55.6	27.2	8.6
50–54	52.5	71.8	13.9	2.3
55–59	51.7	77.6	10.3	2.4
Marital status				
Never married (not cohabiting)	31.8	51.8	41.3	12.3
Married	42.6	62.9	16.5	4.7
Formerly married (not cohabiting)	30.2	52.7	34.9	9.6
Education				
Less than high school	54.8	75.1	19.2	7.6
High school graduate	45.1	68.4	20.0	5.6
Some college	33.2	51.3	30.8	6.9
College graduate	24.2	47.7	33.2	10.2
Advanced degree	18.6	41.2	33.6	13.7
Religion				
None	32.6	41.4	37.6	13.8
Liberal or moderate Protestant	28.9	55.1	28.2	7.4
Conservative Protestant	48.4	67.3	19.5	5.8
Catholic	34.0	57.3	24.9	6.6
Race/ethnicity				
European American	33.4	55.7	28.3	7.3
African American	60.3	67.8	16.9	10.7
Latino and Latina American	33.1	65.5	24.4	4.7
Asian American	38.7	—*	31.3	—*
Native American	—*	—*	—*	—*

*Sample sizes too small to report findings.

SOURCE: Adapted by permission from E. O. Laumann, J. H. Gagnon, R. T. Michael, & S. Michaels (1994). *The Social Organization of Sexuality: Sexual Practices in the United States.* Chicago: University of Chicago Press, Table 3.1, p. 82.

Masturbation Techniques Used by Males

> Sex is like bridge—if you don't have a good partner, you'd better have a good hand.
>
> —Bathroom graffiti

Although masturbation techniques vary widely, most men report that they masturbate by manual manipulation of the penis (Figure 9.3). Kinsey and his colleagues

Figure 9.2 What Are the Connections between Masturbation during Adolescence and Sexual Satisfaction during Marriage? *There is a positive correlation between masturbation during adolescence and sexual satisfaction during marriage. What hypotheses can we make about the causal connections? Does experience with masturbation teach people about their sexual needs so that they are more likely to obtain adequate sexual stimulation during marriage? Are people who masturbate early generally more open to exploring their sexuality and learning about the types of stimulation that arouse them? Such attitudes might also increase the likelihood that people would seek the coital stimulation they need to achieve sexual gratification during marriage.*

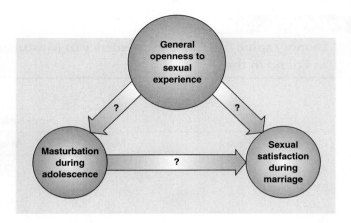

(1948) reported that they typically take one or two minutes to reach orgasm. Men tend to grip the penile shaft with one hand, jerking it up and down in a milking motion. Some men move the whole hand up and down the penis, while others use just two fingers, generally the thumb and index finger. Men usually shift from a gentler rubbing action during the flaccid or semierect state of arousal to a more vigorous milking motion once full erection takes place. Men are also likely to stroke the glans and frenulum lightly at the outset, but their grip tightens and their motions speed up as orgasm nears. At orgasm, the penile shaft may be gripped tightly, but the glans has become sensitive, and contact with it is usually avoided. (Likewise, women usually avoid stimulating the clitoris directly during orgasm because of increased sensitivity.)

Some men use soapsuds (which may become irritating) as a lubricant for masturbation during baths or showers. Other lubricants, such as petroleum jelly or K-Y jelly, are less irritating and also more effective at reducing friction and simulating the moist conditions of coitus.

A few men prefer to masturbate by rubbing the penis and testicles against clothing or bedding. A few men rub their genitals against inflatable dolls sold in sex shops. These dolls may come with artificial mouths or vaginas that can be filled with liquid to mimic the sensations of coitus. Artificial vaginas are also for sale.

Some men strap vibrators to the backs of their hands. Electrical vibrators save labor but do not simulate the type of up-and-down motions of the penis that men favor. Hence, they are not used very often. Most men use fantasy, photos, videos, or the Internet, but not sex shop devices. With the exception of a real-life partner—a notable exception, indeed—the Internet offers one-stop sex shopping for millions.

Masturbation Techniques Used by Females

Techniques of female masturbation also vary widely. In fact, Masters and Johnson reported never observing two women masturbate in precisely the same way. Even when the general technique was similar, women varied in the tempo and style of their self-caresses.

However, some general trends have been noted. Most women masturbate by massaging the mons, labia minora, and clitoral re-

Figure 9.3 Male Masturbation.
Masturbation techniques vary widely, but most men report that they masturbate by manual manipulation of the penis. They tend to grip the penile shaft with one hand and jerk it up and down in a milking motion.

Figure 9.4 **Female Masturbation.** *Techniques of female masturbation vary so widely that Masters and Johnson reported never observing two women masturbating in precisely the same way. Most women masturbate by massaging the mons, labia minora, and clitoral region, however, either with circular or back-and-forth motions.*

gion with circular or back-and-forth motions (Kinsey et al., 1953). They may also straddle the clitoris with their fingers, stroking the shaft rather than the glans (Figure 9.4). The glans may be lightly touched early during arousal, but because of its exquisite sensitivity, it is rarely stroked for any length of time during masturbation. Women typically achieve clitoral stimulation by rubbing or stroking the clitoral shaft or pulling or tugging on the vaginal lips. Some women also massage other sensitive areas, such as their breasts or nipples, with the free hand. Many women, like men, fantasize during masturbation.

Truth or Fiction Revisited: In contrast to the male myth that women usually masturbate by simulating penile thrusting through the insertion of fingers or phallic objects into their vaginas, relatively few women actually do. Kinsey and his colleagues (1953) found that only one in five women inserted objects into the vagina during masturbation. Some women experimented with vaginal insertion, but gave it up as they became more familiar with their sexual anatomy and capabilities. Others practiced the technique because their male partners found it sexually stimulating to watch them. Still, some women reported erotic pleasure from deep vaginal penetration.

When women do use insertion, they usually precede or combine it with clitoral stimulation. Sex shops sell dildos, which women can use to rub their vulvas or insert. Penis-shaped vibrators may be used in the same way. Many women masturbate during baths some spraying their genitals with jets of water.

Handheld electrical vibrators (Figure 9.5) massage the genitals in a way that can be erotic. But some women find this type of stimulation too intense and favor

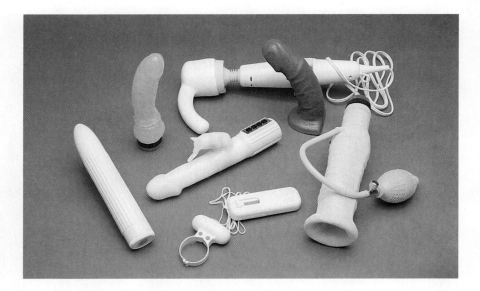

Figure 9.5 Electric Vibrators and Other Sex Toys. *Both females and males use devices like these in the place of real penises, to try to increase the volume of the penis, or for other sexual ends. If they are to be used at all, they should be used with extreme caution.*

vibrators that strap onto the back of the hand, helping the fingers to vibrate during manual stimulation of the genitals. But this type of vibration may numb the hand attached to the vibrator. Women experiment with different vibrators to find one with the shape and intensity of vibration that suits them.

SafeZone

Q *Are vibrators bad for your health in any way?*

A Could be. As a rule of thumb, vibrators that penetrate the body are more potentially harmful than vibrators that simply strap onto the back of the hand (or foot, or whatever). And vibrators that have sharp or pointed edges, even if they're called ticklers, are more potentially dangerous than those that have smooth edges or don't directly touch the body at all.

Sexual Behavior with Others

Partners' feelings for one another, and the quality of their relationship, may be stronger determinants of their sexual arousal and response than the techniques they use (Colson et al., 2006). Partners are most likely to experience mutually enjoyable sexual interactions when they are sensitive to each other's sexual needs and incorporate techniques with which they are both comfortable. As with other aspects of sharing relationships, communication is the most important "sexual" technique. Let us begin our discussion of sex with others as many sexual episodes begin—with a discussion of foreplay.

Foreplay

Foreplay Physical interactions that are sexually stimulating and set the stage for intercourse

Various forms of noncoital sex, such as cuddling, kissing, petting, and oral–genital contact, are used as **foreplay.** The pattern and duration of foreplay vary widely within and across cultures.

There is a general assumption in the United States and Canada that women in heterosexual relationships want more foreplay than men do, which may be more or less the case. But a side effect of this stereotype is that men often wind up receiving less foreplay than they would actually like (Miller & Byers, 2004). Because women usually require a longer period of stimulation during sex with a partner to reach orgasm, increasing the duration of foreplay may increase female coital responsiveness. On the other hand, men have become more aware of this since Kinsey's day, and women sometimes want men to "get on with it" (Miller & Byers, 2004).

A telephone survey of more than 1,000 French subjects in heterosexual relationships found that simultaneous orgasms and feelings of closeness were highly important for about 36% of the respondents (Colson et al., 2006). Foreplay, by contrast, was mentioned as being crucial by only about 13%—which, of course, begs the question as to whether the couple would reach simultaneous orgasm and closeness without it.

We're going to report a finding from a Shanghai study (Guo et al., 2004), not because it illuminates very much, but because it left us scratching our heads and we wanted share our confusion with you. It was sizable—following more than 7,000 married couples over several years. About 4% of wives and 2% of husbands said they used no foreplay at all, but that's not the finding in question. The authors also reported that "Husbands who used breast stroking or talking seemed to have wives with less marital satisfaction" (Guo et al., 2004). Perhaps we should offer a prize for students who can make sense of that one.

Kissing, genital touching, and oral–genital contact may also be experienced as ends in themselves, not as preludes to coitus. Yet some people object to petting for petting's sake, equating it with masturbation as a form of sexual activity without a "product." Many people behave as though all sexual contact must lead to coitus, perhaps because of the importance that our culture places on it.

SafeZone

Q *What is tantric sex?*

A Something like foreplay taken to the outer limits, which could lead some to have a tantrum. (Bad pun.) Practitioners of tantric sex point to Eastern philosophies as their points of inspiration. They speak of releasing body energies and auras and herbs and ritual cleansing baths and massages and aromatics and healing and . . . did we mention herbs? It's yoga, it's Kama Sutra. We'll summarize it like this: We don't know of any scientific or government accrediting agency that trains and supervises tantric sex practitioners. Having said that, it's probably as much fun as an erotic massage in a bubble bath—depending on who's doing what to whom. Light the candles.

Kissing

Kissing is almost universal in our culture, but is unknown in some cultures, such as among the Thonga of Africa and the Siriono of Bolivia. Variations in styles of kissing also exist across cultures (Ford & Beach, 1951). Kissing is now practiced in Japan because of the influence of Western culture, but was previously unknown there. Instead of kissing, the Balinese of the South Pacific bring their faces close enough to each other to smell each other's perfume and feel the warmth of each other's skin.

Kissing. *Kissing is a nearly universal part of lovemaking. Nonerotic kissing may also be used with relatives and friends.*

This practice has been dubbed "rubbing noses" by Europeans. Among some preliterate societies, kissing consists of sucking the partner's lips and tongue and allowing saliva to pass from one mouth to the other.

Couples may kiss for their own enjoyment or as a prelude to intercourse, in which case it is a part of foreplay. In *simple kissing,* the partners keep their mouths closed. Simple kissing may develop into caresses of the lips with the tongue, or into nibbling of the lower lip. In what Kinsey called *deep kissing,* which is also called French or soul kissing, the partners part their lips and insert their tongues into each other's mouths. Some prefer the lips parted slightly. Others open their mouths widely.

Kissing may also be an affectionate gesture without erotic significance, as in kissing someone good night. Some people kiss relatives and close friends affectionately on the lips. Others limit kissing relatives to the cheek. Sustained kissing on the lips and deep kissing are almost always erotic gestures.

Kissing is not limited to the partner's mouth. Kinsey found that more than 9 husbands in 10 kissed their wives' breasts. Women usually prefer several minutes of body contact and gentle caresses before desiring to have their partner kiss their breasts, or suck or lick their nipples. Women also usually do not prefer sucking until they are highly aroused. Many women are reluctant to tell their partners that sucking hurts because they do not want to interfere with their partner's pleasure.

Other parts of the body are also often kissed, including the hands and feet, the neck and earlobes, the insides of the thighs, and the genitals themselves. When we kiss, we touch each other with our lips.

Touching

Touching or caressing erogenous zones with the hands or other parts of the body can be highly arousing. Even simple hand-holding can be sexually stimulating for couples who are sexually attracted to one another. The hands are rich in nerve endings.

Touching is a common form of foreplay. Both men and women generally prefer manual or oral stimulation of the genitals as a prelude to intercourse. Women generally prefer that direct caressing of the genitals be focused around the clitoris, but not directly on the extremely sensitive clitoral glans. Men sometimes assume (often mistakenly) that their partners want them to insert their finger or fingers into the vagina as a form of foreplay. But not all women enjoy this form of stimulation. Some women go along with it because it's what their partners want or something they think their partners want. Ironically, men may do it because they assume that their partners want it. When in doubt, it would not hurt to *ask.* If you are not sure what to say, you can always blame us: "Listen, I read this thing in my human sexuality text, and I was wondering. . . ."

Masters and Johnson (1979) noted sex differences with respect to preferences in foreplay. Men typically prefer direct stroking of their genitals by their partner early during lovemaking. Women, however, tend to prefer that their partners caress their genitals after a period of general body contact that includes holding, hugging, and nongenital massage. This is not a hard-and-fast (or slow) rule, but it concurs with other observations that men tend to be more genitally oriented than women. Women are more likely to view sex within a broader framework of affection and love.

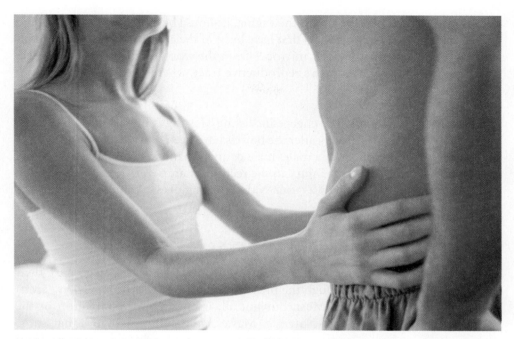

How Touching? *Touching is a common form of foreplay. Most people like manual or oral stimulation of the genital organs as a prelude to sexual intercourse.*

TECHNIQUES OF MANUAL STIMULATION OF THE GENITALS

Here again, variability in technique is the rule, so partners need to communicate their preferences. The man's partner may use two hands to stimulate his genitals. One may be used to fondle the scrotum, by gently squeezing the skin between the fingers (taking care not to apply pressure to the testes themselves). The other hand may circle the coronal ridge and engage in gentle stroking of the penis, followed by more vigorous up-and-down movements as the man becomes more aroused.

The penis may also be gently rolled back and forth between the palms as if one were making a ball of clay into a sausage, increasing pressure as arousal progresses. Note that men who are highly aroused or who have just had an orgasm may find direct stimulation of the penile glans uncomfortable.

The woman may prefer that her partner approach genital stimulation gradually, following stimulation of other body parts. Genital stimulation may begin with light, stroking motions of the inner thighs and move on to the vaginal lips (labia) and the clitoral area. Women may enjoy pressure against the mons pubis from the heel of the hand, or tactile stimulation of the labia, which are sensitive to stroking motions. Clitoral stimulation can focus on the clitoral shaft or the region surrounding the shaft, rather than the clitoris itself, because of the extreme sensitivity of the clitoral glans to touch.

Moreover, the clitoris should not be stroked if it is dry, lest it become irritated. Because it produces no lubrication of its own, a finger may enter the outer portion of the vagina to apply some vaginal lubrication to the clitoral region.

Some, but not all, women enjoy having a finger inserted into the vagina, which can stroke the vaginal walls or simulate thrusting of the penis. Vaginal insertion is usually not preferred, if at all, until the woman has become highly aroused. Many women desire that their partners discontinue stroking motions while they are experiencing orgasm, but others wish stimulation to continue. Men and women woman may physically guide their partners' hands or otherwise express their preferences regarding the types of strokes they find most pleasurable.

If a finger is to be inserted into the vagina, it should be clean. Fingernails should be well trimmed. Inserting fingers that have been in the anus into the vagina is dangerous. The fingers may transfer microbes from the woman's digestive tract, where they do no harm, to the woman's reproductive tract, where they can cause serious infections.

FISTING   Some individuals engage in "fisting." Fisting is the insertion of the fist or hand into the rectum, usually after the bowels have been evacuated with an enema. Fisting is more common among male–male couples than male–female couples, and carries the risk of infection or injury to the rectum or anus. A survey of 75 gay men in Australia found that fisting was usually done with gloves, although fingering was not (Richters et al., 2003).

Stimulation of the Breasts

Heterosexual men are more likely to stimulate women's breasts than to have their own breasts fondled, even though the breasts (and especially the nipples) are erotically sensitive in both sexes. Most, but not all, women enjoy stimulation of the breasts. Masters and Johnson report that some women are capable of achieving orgasm from stimulation of the breasts alone.

The hands and the mouth can be used to stimulate the breasts and the nipples. Because the desired type and intensity of stimulation of the breasts varies from person to person, partners need to communicate their preferences.

GAY MALES AND STIMULATION OF THE BREASTS   Gay men apparently make more use of stimulation of their partner's nipples than heterosexual women do. Gay male couples tend to engage in sexual activities such as kissing, hugging, petting, mutual masturbation, fellatio, and anal intercourse. Laboratory observations of sexual relations between gay males by Masters and Johnson (1979) showed that gay males spent a good deal of time caressing their partners' bodies before approaching the genitals (Figure 9.6). After hugging and kissing, 31 of 42 gay male couples observed by Masters and Johnson (1979) used oral or manual nipple stimulation.

Although some heterosexual men enjoy having their breasts and nipples stimulated by their partners, many, perhaps most, do not. Many men are unaware that their breasts are erotically sensitive. Others may feel uncomfortable receiving a form of stimulation that they have learned to associate with the stereotypical feminine sexual role.

Sexual techniques practiced by lesbians vary. Lesbian couples report kissing, manual and oral breast stimulation, and manual and oral stimulation of the genitals (Kinsey et al., 1953). Manual

Figure 9.6   Gay Males Hugging. *Masters' and Johnson's observations suggest that gay males are likely to spend more time than heterosexual males in hugging their partners. Gay males are also more likely than heterosexual males to want their nipples to be caressed.*

genital stimulation is the most common and frequent sexual activity among lesbian couples (Bell & Weinberg, 1978). Most lesbian couples also engage in genital apposition. That is, they position themselves so as to rub their genitals together rhythmically (Kinsey et al., 1953). Like gay males, lesbians spend a good deal of time holding, kissing, and caressing each other's bodies before they approach the breasts and genitals (Figure 9.7). By contrast, heterosexual males tend to move quickly to stimulate their partners' breasts or start directly with genital stimulation (Masters & Johnson, 1979).

Like heterosexual women, lesbians are less genitally oriented and less fixated on orgasm than men. Lesbians generally begin stimulating their partners with more general genital stimulation rather than direct clitoral stimulation, whereas heterosexual males often begin by stimulating the clitoris (Masters & Johnson, 1979). Nor do lesbian couples generally engage in deep penetration of the vagina with fingers. Rather, they may use more shallow vaginal penetration, focusing stimulation on the vaginal lips and entrance.

Truth or Fiction Revisited: Images of lesbians strapping on dildos for vaginal penetration exist more in the imagination of uninformed heterosexual people than in the sexual repertoire of lesbian couples (Masters & Johnson, 1979). The emotional components of lovemaking—gentle touching, cuddling, and hugging—are important elements of sexual sharing in lesbian relationships.

Figure 9.7 **Lesbians Holding One Another.** *This position enables lesbians to hug one another and to reach one another's genitals. If the couple draws a bit closer, they can rub their genitals against one another's.*

TRUTH?fiction 6

Oral–Genital Stimulation

Oral stimulation of the male genitals is called **fellatio**. Fellatio is referred to by slang terms such as "blow job," "sucking," "sucking off," or "giving head." Oral stimulation of the female genitals is called **cunnilingus**, which is referred to by slang expressions such as "eating" (a woman) or "going down" on her.

The popularity of oral–genital stimulation has increased dramatically since Kinsey's day, especially among young married couples. Kinsey and his colleagues (1948, 1953) found that at least 60% of married, *college-educated* couples had experienced oral–genital contact. Such experiences were reported by only about 20% of couples who only had a high school education and 10% who only had a grade school education. According to the NHSLS, the incidence of oral sex was higher in recent years (Laumann et al., 1994).

About three of four men (77%) and two of three women (68%) reported playing the active role in oral sex during their lifetimes. Nearly four men in five (79%) and three of four women (73%) reported having been the recipients of oral–genital sex during their lifetimes. Among married couples, 80% of the men and 71% of the women have performed oral sex. Eighty percent of the men and 74% of the women have received oral sex.

Truth or Fiction Revisited: Oral sex is, in fact, the norm for today's young couples, statistically speaking. A majority of young couples report participating in this form of sexual expression. These are dramatic increases since Kinsey's day. Among

TRUTH?fiction 7

Fellatio Oral stimulation of the male genitals
Cunnilingus Oral stimulation of the female genitals

Demographic Factors and Oral Sex

What are the roles of education and race/ethnicity in the incidence of oral sex? Some answers reported by people in the NHSLS are suggested in Table 9.3. As with masturbation, the incidence of oral sex correlates with level of education. That is, more highly educated individuals are more likely to have practiced oral sex. Why? Perhaps education encourages experimentation. Perhaps education dispels myths that nontraditional behavior patterns are necessarily harmful. Note also that African American men and women are less likely to have engaged in oral sex than people from other racial/ethnic backgrounds. African American men and women were also less likely than other ethnic groups to report masturbating during the past 12 months. African Americans may adhere more strictly to traditional ideas regarding what kinds of sexual behavior are and are not proper.

Findings from a national survey of more than 3,000 sexually active men between the ages of 20 and 39 conducted by the Battelle Human Affairs Research Center in Seattle are consistent with the NHSLS findings. Seventy-five percent of the men reported performing oral sex. Seventy-nine percent reported receiving oral sex (Billy et al., 1993). Mirroring the racial differences observed by Laumann and his colleagues (1994), African Americans in other surveys are also less likely than European Americans to have performed or received oral sex (Ompad et al., 2006).

young European American women (age 18 to 36) in Kinsey's sample, only about half reported engaging in oral sex.

As with touching, oral–genital stimulation can be used as a prelude to intercourse or as a sexual end in itself. If orgasm is reached through oral–genital stimulation, a partner may be concerned about tasting or swallowing the ejaculate. There is no evidence that swallowing semen is harmful to one's health unless the man has an

TABLE 9.3

Percent of NHSLS Respondents Who Report Experience with Oral Sex

Demographic Factor	Performed Oral Sex		Received Oral Sex	
	Men	Women	Men	Women
Education				
Less than high school	59.2	42.1	60.7	49.6
High school graduate	75.3	59.6	76.6	67.1
Some college	80.0	78.2	84.0	81.6
College graduate	83.7	78.9	84.6	83.1
Advanced college degree	80.5	79.0	81.4	81.9
Race/ethnicity				
European American	81.4	75.3	81.4	78.9
African American	50.5	34.4	66.3	48.9
Latino and Latina American	70.7	59.7	73.2	63.7
Asian American	63.6	—*	72.7	—*

*There were not enough Asian American women in the sample to report meaningful findings.
SOURCE: Adapted by permission from E. O. Laumann, J. H. Gagnon, R. T. Michael, & S. Michaels (1994). *The Social Organization of Sexuality: Sexual Practices in the United States.* Chicago: University of Chicago Press, Table 3.6, p. 98.

infection that can be transmitted via semen. Oral contact with the genitals of an infected partner, even without semen, may transmit harmful organisms. Couples are thus advised to practice "safer sex" techniques (see Chapter 16) unless they know that they are free of STIs.

TECHNIQUES OF FELLATIO   Although the word *fellatio* is derived from a Latin root meaning "to suck," sucking is generally not highly arousing. The up-and-down movements of the penis in the partner's mouth, or the licking of the penis, are generally the most stimulating. Gentle licking of the scrotum may also be highly arousing.

The mouth stimulates the penis because it contains warm, moist mucous membranes, as does the vagina. Muscles of the mouth and jaw can vary pressure and movements. Erection may be stimulated by gently pulling the penis with the mouth (being careful not to touch the penis with the teeth) and simultaneously providing manual stimulation.

Higher levels of sexual arousal or orgasm can be promoted by thrusting the penis in and out of the mouth. The speed of the motions can be varied, and manual stimulation near the base of the penis (firmly encircling the lower portion of the penis or providing pressure behind the scrotum) can also be stimulating.

Some people may gag during fellatio, a reflex that is triggered by pressure of the penis against the back of the tongue or against the throat. Gagging may be avoided if the man's partner grasps the shaft of the penis with one hand and controls the depth of penetration. Gagging is less likely to occur if the partner performing fellatio is on the top, rather than below, or if there is verbal communication about how deep the man may comfortably penetrate. Gagging may also be overcome by allowing gradually deeper penetration of the penis on successive occasions while keeping the throat muscles relaxed.

TECHNIQUES OF CUNNILINGUS   Women can be highly aroused by their partner's tongue because it is soft, warm, and well lubricated. In contrast to a finger, the tongue can almost never be used too harshly. A woman may thus be more receptive to direct clitoral contact by a tongue. Cunnilingus provides such intense stimulation that many women find it to be the best means for achieving orgasm.

In performing cunnilingus, the partner may begin by kissing and licking the woman's abdomen and inner thighs, gradually nearing the vulva. Gentle tugging at or sucking of the labia minora can be stimulating, but the partner should take care not to bite. Many women enjoy licking of the clitoral region, and others desire sucking of the clitoris itself. The tongue may also be inserted into the vagina where it may imitate thrusting.

"69"   The term *sixty-nine* describes simultaneous oral–genital stimulation (Figure 9.8). The numerals 6 and 9 are used because they resemble two partners who are upside down and facing each other.

The "69" position has the psychologically positive feature of allowing couples to experience simultaneous stimulation, but it can be awkward if two people are not similar in size. Some couples avoid "69" because it deprives each partner of the opportunity to focus fully on receiving or providing sexual pleasure.

The "69" technique may be practiced side by side or with one partner on top of the other. There are no strict rules, and couples often alternate positions.

Figure 9.8 **Simultaneous Oral–Genital Contact.** *The "69" position allows partners to engage in simultaneous oral–genital stimulation.*

ABSTAINING FROM ORAL SEX Despite the popularity of oral sex among couples today, many people choose to abstain. Some people object on grounds of cleanliness. They view the genitals as "dirty," because of their proximity to the urinary and anal openings. Concerns about offensive odors or cleanliness may be relieved by thoroughly washing the genitals beforehand. Some abstain because they are concerned or embarrassed about providing (or receiving) a direct view of parts of the body we have been reared to keep private.

Some prefer not to taste or swallow semen because they find it to be "dirty," sinful, or repulsive. Others are put off by the taste or texture. Semen has a salty taste and a texture similar to the white of an egg. The aesthetics of swallowing semen involve the preferences of the individual. If couples are to engage in unprotected oral sex, open discussion of feelings can enhance pleasure and diminish anxiety. For example, a man can be encouraged to warn his partner or remove his penis from her or his mouth when he is nearing ejaculation.

Sexual Intercourse: Positions and Techniques

Sexual intercourse, or *coitus* (from the Latin *coire*, meaning "to go together"), is sexual activity between a man and a woman, in which the penis is inserted into the vagina. Each position of sexual intercourse must allow the genitals to be aligned so that the penis is contained by the vagina. In addition to varying positions, couples also vary the depth and rate of thrusting (in-and-out motions) and additional sexual stimulation.

Although the number of possible coital positions is virtually endless, we will focus on four of the most commonly used positions: the male-superior (man-on-top) position, the female-superior (woman-on-top) position, the lateral-entry (side-entry) position, and the rear-entry position. We discuss anal intercourse as well, a sexual technique used by both male–female and male–male couples.

Figure 9.9 The Male-Superior Coital Position. *In this position, the couple face one another. The man lies above the woman, perhaps supporting himself on his hands and knees rather than allowing his full weight to press against his partner. The position is also referred to as the* missionary position.

THE MALE-SUPERIOR (MAN-ON-TOP) POSITION The male-superior position ("superiority" is used purely in relation to body position, but has sometimes been taken as a symbol of male domination) has also been called the **missionary position.** In this position the partners face one another. The man lies above the woman, perhaps supporting himself on his hands and knees rather than applying his full weight against his partner (Figure 9.9). Still, movement is easier for the man than for the woman, which suggests that he is responsible for directing their activity.

Many students of human sexuality suggest that it is preferable for the woman to guide the penis into the vagina, rather than having the man do so. The idea is that the woman can feel the location of the vaginal opening and determine the proper angle of entry. To accomplish this, the woman must feel comfortable "taking charge" of the couple's lovemaking. With the breaking down of the traditional stereotype of the female as passive, women are feeling more comfortable taking on this role. On the other hand, if the couple prefers that the man guide his penis into his partner's vagina, the slight loss of efficiency need not trouble them, as long as he moves prudently to avoid hurting his partner.

The male-superior position has the advantage of permitting the couple to face one another so that kissing is easier. The woman may run her hands along her partner's body, stroking his buttocks and perhaps cupping a hand beneath his scrotum to increase stimulation as he reaches orgasm.

But the male-superior position makes it difficult for the man to caress his partner while simultaneously supporting himself with his hands. So the position may not be favored by women who enjoy having their partners provide manual clitoral stimulation during coitus. This position can be highly stimulating to the man, which can make it difficult for him to delay ejaculation. The position also limits the opportunity for the woman to control the angle, rate, and depth of penetration. It may thus be more difficult for her to attain the type of stimulation she may need to

Missionary position The coital position in which the man is on top; also termed the *male-superior position*

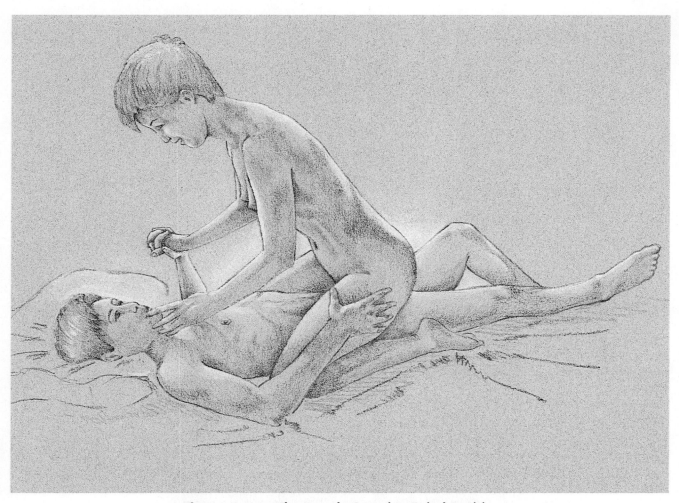

Figure 9.10 The Female-Superior Coital Position. *The woman straddles the male from above, controlling the angle of penile entry and the depth of thrusting. The female-superior position puts the woman psychologically and physically in charge. The woman can ensure that she receives adequate clitoral stimulation from the penis or the hand. The position also tends to be less stimulating for the male and may thus help him to control ejaculation.*

achieve orgasm, especially if she favors combining penile thrusting with manual clitoral stimulation. Finally, this position is not advisable during the late stages of pregnancy. At that time the woman's distended abdomen would force the man to arch severely above her, lest he place undue pressure on her abdomen.

THE FEMALE-SUPERIOR (WOMAN-ON-TOP) POSITION   In the female-superior position, the couple face one another with the woman on top. The woman straddles the male from above, controlling the angle of penile entry and the depth of thrusting (Figure 9.10). Some women maintain a sitting position; others lie on top of their partners. Many women vary their position.

In the female-superior position, the woman is psychologically, and to some degree physically, in charge. She can move as rapidly or as slowly as she wishes with little effort, adjusting her body to vary the angle and depth of penetration. She can reach behind her to stroke her partner's scrotum, or lean down to kiss him.

As in the male-superior position, kissing is relatively easy. This position has additional advantages. The man may readily reach the woman's buttocks or clitoris to

Figure 9.11 **The Lateral-Entry Coital Position.** *In this position, the couple face each other side by side. Each partner has relatively free movement and easy access to the other. Because both partners rest easily on the bedding, it is an excellent position for prolonged coitus or for coitus when couples are fatigued.*

provide manual stimulation. If the woman is shorter than he is, it is rather easy for him to stimulate her breasts orally (a pillow tucked behind his head may help). The woman can, in effect, guarantee that she receives adequate clitoral stimulation, either by the penis or manually by his hand or her own. This position thus facilitates orgasm in the woman. Because it tends to be less stimulating for the male, it may help him to control ejaculation. For these reasons this position is commonly used by couples who are learning to overcome sexual difficulties.

THE LATERAL-ENTRY (SIDE-ENTRY) POSITION   In the lateral-entry position, the man and woman lie side by side, facing one another (Figure 9.11). This position has the advantages of allowing each partner relatively free movement and easy access to the other. The man and woman may kiss freely, and they can stroke each other's bodies with a free arm. The position is not physically taxing, because both partners are resting easily on the bedding. Thus it is an excellent position for prolonged coitus or for coitus when couples are somewhat fatigued.

Let us note some disadvantages to this position. First, inserting the penis into the vagina while lying side by side may be awkward. Many couples thus begin coitus in another position and then change to the lateral-entry position—often because they wish to prolong coitus. Second, one or both partners may have an arm lying beneath the other that will "fall asleep" or become numb because of the constricted blood supply. Third, women may not receive adequate clitoral stimulation from the penis in this position. Of course, such stimulation may be provided manually (by hand) or by switching to another position after a while. Fourth, it may be difficult to achieve deeper penetration. The lateral position is useful during pregnancy (at least until the final stages, when the distension of the woman's abdomen may make lateral entry difficult).

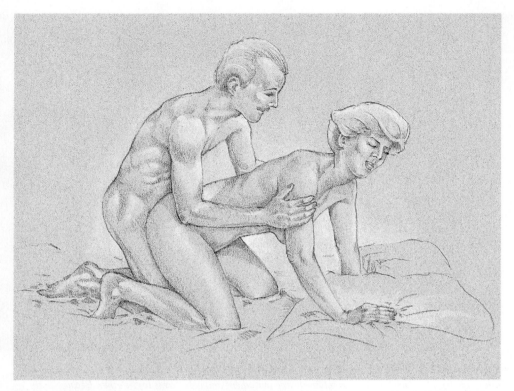

Figure 9.12 **The Rear-Entry Coital Position.** *The rear-entry position is highly erotic for men who enjoy viewing and pressing their abdomens against their partners' buttocks. Some couples feel uncomfortable about the position because of its association with animal mating patterns. The position is also impersonal in that the partners do not face one another. Moreover, some couples dislike the feeling that the man is psychologically in charge because he can see his partner but she cannot readily see him.*

THE REAR-ENTRY POSITION   In the rear-entry position, the man faces the woman's rear. In one variation (Figure 9.12), the woman supports herself on her hands and knees while the man supports himself on his knees, entering her from behind. In another, the couple lie alongside one another and the woman lifts one leg, draping it backward over her partner's thigh. The latter position is particularly useful during the later stages of pregnancy.

The rear-entry position may be highly stimulating for both partners. Men may enjoy viewing and pressing their abdomens against their partner's buttocks. The man can reach around or underneath to provide additional stimulation of the clitoris or breasts, and she may reach behind (if she is on her hands and knees) to stroke or grasp her partner's testicles.

Potential disadvantages to this position include the following: First, this position is the mating position used by most other mammals, which is why it is sometimes referred to as *doggy style.* Some couples may feel uncomfortable about using the position because of its association with animal mating patterns. The position is also impersonal in the sense that the partners do not face one another, which may create a sense of emotional distance. Because the man is at the woman's back, the couple may feel that he is very much in charge; he can see her, but she cannot readily see him. Physically, the penis does not provide adequate stimulation to the clitoris. The penis also tends to pop out of the vagina from time to time. Finally, air tends to enter the vagina during rear-entry coitus. When it is expelled, it can sound as though the woman has passed air through the anus—a possibly embarrassing, although harmless, occurrence.

REFLECT

How do your own attitudes and values affect the kinds of sexual practices with which you feel, or may feel, comfortable?

Q *What is the sexual position that gives both a man and a woman the greatest pleasure?*

A Each position has its pluses and minuses, and the answer may be that variety is the spice of life. Many couples take turns—her favorite, then his, that sort of thing. Nobody should feel compelled to participate in any act he or she finds distasteful. (Yes, we know that the last comment didn't answer the question, but we're the authors and we decided to toss it into the mix.)

ANAL INTERCOURSE Anal intercourse involves insertion of the penis into the rectum and can be practiced by male–female couples and male–male couples. The rectum is richly endowed with nerve endings and highly sensitive to sexual stimulation. Both partners may reach orgasm through anal sex. Anal intercourse is also referred to as "Greek culture," or lovemaking in the "Greek style" because of male bisexuality in ancient Greece. It is also the major act that comes under the legal definition of *sodomy*.

During anal intercourse, the penetrator can situate himself behind his partner, or lie above or below his partner face to face. The receiving partner can supplement anal stimulation with manual stimulation of the clitoral region or penis to reach orgasm. Because the rectum produces no natural lubrication, couples are advised to use an artificial lubricant, such as K-Y jelly.

People often want their partner's fingers in the anus at the height of passion or at the moment of orgasm. A finger in the rectum can heighten sexual sensation because the anal sphincters contract during orgasm.

Many couples are repulsed by the idea of anal intercourse. They view it as unnatural, immoral, or risky. Others find anal sex to be an enjoyable sexual variation, although perhaps not a regular feature of their sexual diet.

The NHSLS found that one man in four (26%) and one woman in five (20%) reported having engaged in anal sex at some time (Laumann et al., 1994). Yet only about 1 person in 10 (10% of the men and 9% of the women) had engaged in anal sex during the past year. Other surveys report numbers in the same ballpark (e.g., Ompad et al., 2006). As with oral sex, there was a higher incidence of anal sex among more highly educated people. Education appears to be a liberating influence on sexual experimentation. About one in five men in one sample reported engaging in anal intercourse (Billy et al., 1993). **Truth or Fiction Revisited:** As in the NHSLS, anal intercourse turned out to be more common among better-educated men.

Religion appears to be a restraint on anal sex. About 34% of the men and 36% of the women in the NHSLS who said they had no religion reported engaging in anal sex at some time. Percentages for male Christians ranged from the lower to upper 20s, and for female Christians, from the mid teens to the lower 20s (Laumann et al., 1994, p. 99).

Many couples kiss or lick the anus in their foreplay. This practice is called **anilingus**. Oral–anal sex carries a health risk because microorganisms causing intestinal diseases and many STIs can be spread through oral–anal contact.

Many couples today hesitate to engage in anal intercourse because of the fear of HIV/AIDS and other STIs (see Chapter 16). HIV and microorganisms causing STIs such as gonorrhea, syphilis, and hepatitis can be spread by anal intercourse (Koblin et al., 2006; Lane et al., 2006). Cells in the rectum are especially susceptible to infection by some organisms, and small tears in the rectal tissues may allow other microbes to

TRUTH?fiction 8

CRITICAL Thinking

What is the relationship between level of education and sexual practices such as oral sex and anal sex? How do you account for the relationship?

Anilingus Oral stimulation of the anus; slang: *rimming, rim job*

enter the recipient's blood system (see Chapter 16). However, partners who are both infection free are at no risk of contracting STIs.

Not all gay males enjoy or practice anal intercourse. Of those who do, most alternate between being the inserter ("the top") and the insertee ("the bottom"). Interviews with 51 gay men suggest that playing the inserter role in anal intercourse is sometimes associated with fantasies of domination, and the insertee role with fantasies of submission (Kippax & Smith, 2001). But some gays who practice anal intercourse deny that sex has to do with power; sex, to them, is about sharing.

The incidence of anal intercourse—especially without using condoms—among gay males declined as gays became aware of the connection between anal sex and transmission of HIV. However, now that highly active antiretroviral therapy (HAART) is prolonging the lives of many people with HIV/AIDS, some gay males are again forgoing use of condoms in anal intercourse (Dilley et al., 2003). Men report that they prefer to forgo condoms because condoms reduce sexual sensations and emotional connectedness with a partner (Bancroft et al., 2005a; Crosby et al., 2005). Moreover, gay men—like heterosexuals—are more likely to forgo condoms with strangers when they are under the influence of alcohol and drugs (Irwin et al., 2006; Semple et al., 2003).

Sexual Fantasies

People may use sexual fantasies either when they are alone or to heighten sexual excitement with a partner. Some couples find it sexually arousing to share fantasies or to enact them. Sexual fantasies may also be experienced without sexual behavior, as in erotic dreams or daydreams. Masturbators often require some form of cognitive stimulation, such as fantasy or viewing erotica, to reach orgasm.

There are many theories about sexual fantasies. One view that apparently has little if any research evidence behind it is that people who fantasize about sex are less likely to have enjoyable sex lives. That is, the fantasy takes the place of real life. But fantasies can also enhance sexual arousal, providing greater pleasure.

Truth or Fiction Revisited: Research suggests that sexual fantasies are normal. Most people have them—even during sex with another person. Fantasies heighten their sexual arousal during activity with their partners (Leitenberg & Henning, 1995). Males seem to engage in sexual fantasies more often than females, but most females do so as well—at least within our culture. A survey of 349 university students and employees, age 18 to 70, who were involved in heterosexual relationships, found that the great majority—98% of the men and 80% of the women—reported sexual fantasies about someone *other* than their sex partner (Hicks & Leitenberg, 2001). These fantasies were more common among people who had been in their relationships longer, perhaps providing sexual novelty. Women were more likely than the men to fantasize about *prior* sex partners, suggesting, perhaps, that they had less need to mentally stray from familiar relationships. According to a *New York Times* poll, men are somewhat more likely than women—52% versus 40%—to think it is acceptable to fantasize about sex with someone other than their partner (Eggers, 2000).

Evolutionary theorists conjecture that women are relatively more likely to fantasize about the images of familiar lovers because female reproductive success in ancestral times was more likely to depend on a protective relationship with a reliable partner (Goleman, 1995). Women can bear and rear relatively few offspring. Thus, they would have a relatively greater genetic investment in each reproductive opportunity.

In keeping with gender-role stereotypes, studies also find that males are more likely to fantasize about forcing women into sexual activity. Women are more likely to fantasize about being victimized (Donnelly & Fraser, 1998; Yost & Zurbriggen, 2006).

Researchers, by the way, use the frequency and variety of sexual fantasies as one measure of the sex drive (Baumeister et al., 2001; Peplau, 2003). The sex drive—and the frequency of sexual fantasizing—is related to testosterone levels in both males and females. One study surveyed the frequency of sexual activity and sexual fantasies among women who had had their ovaries and uteruses surgically removed (Shifren et al., 2000). The women were then administered various doses of testosterone or a placebo via skin patches. Women given higher doses of testosterone doubled or tripled their reported incidence of sexual fantasies, masturbation, and sexual intercourse.

Studies suggest that most of us consider sexual fantasies normal. One study surveyed 178 university students and staff and found that 84% of them reported having sexual fantasies at least occasionally during sexual intercourse (Cado & Leitenberg, 1990). Most of these individuals said that they believed that such fantasies were common, normal, moral, socially acceptable, and more beneficial than harmful. Still, about one quarter of the sample reported feeling guilty about the fantasies. Those who felt most guilty were also most likely to experience sexual dissatisfaction and problems in their actual lives. **Truth or Fiction Revisited:** It is therefore not true that people who have sexual fantasies are likely to have sexual or social problems.

There are also "deviant" sexual fantasies, such as sadistic rape fantasies. Research evidence with the Minnesota Multiphasic Personality Inventory-2 (MMPI-2), a commonly used personality test, suggests that men with frequent deviant sexual fantasies are more likely to be socially isolated and emotionally unstable (Curnoe & Langevin, 2002). Yet the extent to which deviant sexual fantasies contribute to crimes involving sex and aggression remained clouded. Nevertheless, many helping professionals work with men with deviant sexual fantasies in the hope that by changing their fantasies, the men will be less likely to commit crimes of violence (Leitenberg & Henning, 1995). And when it comes to fantasies about being victimized, Nancy Friday (1973) reports the following from a woman she interviewed:

> My fantasies are so personal, and the pleasure I get from them derives so
> much, I think, from the fact that they are private and locked away in my
> imagination, that I wouldn't dream of trying to make them come true. . . .
> But act my fantasies out? Make them come true? No, absolutely not. My
> real life's not what they're about; I don't want those things to really happen

A Closer Look

THE BRODY STUDIES ON THE EFFECTS OF MASTURBATION VERSUS PENILE–VAGINAL INTERCOURSE: TIME FOR SOME CRITICAL THINKING

If you want to talk about real science, recent studies by Stuart Brody and his colleagues would seem to have it all—or at least a lot of it. For example, in one study, Brody and Krüger (2005) studied the biological effects of orgasm resulting from masturbation with those resulting from penile–vaginal intercourse via direct laboratory measurement. Without getting overly technical, we'll summarize by saying that the amount of the hormone prolactin present in the bloodstream after orgasm was taken as a measure of sexual satisfaction. We'll also say that both males and females had four times as much prolactin circulating after intercourse than after masturbating.

In the second study, Brody (2006) measured increases in blood pressure in response to stress. For two weeks, 24 women and 22 men kept diaries to record the incidence of masturbation and penile–vaginal intercourse. The blood pressure of groups that had masturbated or engaged in intercourse was then exposed to stressors including public speaking and solving math problems out loud. Now, normal blood pressure is 120/80 mmHg. Let's say that the group that had had intercourse had a blood pressure response averaging 130/90 when stressed. The group that had masturbated had an average systolic blood pressure (the first number) of 14 points higher—say, 144/90.

Critical thinkers question whether there are rival explanations for results. In the first study, let's grant that prolactin is a good thing. But one group was instructed to masturbate; another was instructed to engage in sexual intercourse. Which activity is more socially acceptable? Might greater social acceptability account for the results? Moreover, participants who engaged in intercourse were "in it" with a partner, whereas masturbators had to go it alone. Might that factor have had an effect?

How about the second study? Can we be certain that participants kept accurate records? Can you think of anything that might have biased them in the direction of reporting penile–vaginal intercourse?

And so it goes. A healthy dose of skepticism is vital in science.

CRITICAL Thinking

These studies sound rather "tight," do they not? And many of us sort of back away when scientists toss in biological factors like prolactin and blood pressure. But let's have a look.

TRUTH fiction 11

to me, I simply want to imagine what it would be like. So that's where they'll stay. (p. 288)

As with masturbation, mental excursions into fantasy during coitus may be used to enhance sexual arousal and response (Bader, 2003; Zubeidat et al., 2004). Fantasies enable couples to inject sexual variety into their sexual activity without being unfaithful. Researchers find that most married people have coital fantasies (Bader, 2003; Boss & Maltz, 2001). In one study, 71% of the men and 72% of the women reported engaging in coital fantasies to enhance their sexual arousal (Zimmer et al., 1983). A survey of a sample of 178 students, faculty, and staff members at a college in Vermont found that 84% reported fantasizing at least occasionally during intercourse (Cado & Leitenberg, 1990). **Truth or Fiction Revisited:** There does not appear to be any connection between sexual dissatisfaction with one's relationship and the use of coital fantasies (Davidson & Hoffman, 1986). Thus, coital fantasies are not a form of compensation for an unrewarding sexual relationship.

Coital fantasies, like masturbation fantasies, run a gamut of themes. They include making love to another partner, group sex, orgies, images of past lovers or special erotic experiences, and making love in fantastic and wonderful places, among others. Heterosexual men are likely to fantasize about women, and gay men are more likely to fantasize about men (Chivers et al., 2004). Heterosexual women and lesbians are more flexible in their selection of the sex of the objects of their fantasies (Chivers et al., 2004).

Partners may be reluctant to share their fantasies, or even to admit to them, especially when the fantasy includes people other than the partner. The fantasizer might fear being accused of disloyalty, or that the partner will interpret fantasies as a sign of rejection: "What's the matter, don't I turn you on anymore?"

Sexual Fantasies of Lesbian, Gay, and Bisexual (LGB) Individuals

If you just change the sex of the person being fantasized about, most fantasies of LGB people would appear to be familiar enough. For example, a survey of 129 women (85 lesbian, 44 bisexual) who were in same-sex relationships that had lasted 5 to 10 years found connections between satisfaction in the relationship and the nature of sexual fantasies (Robinson & Parks, 2003). By and large, the happier the women were with their relationships, the more likely they were to fantasize about common activities with their partners. If their relationships were not going so well, they were relatively more likely to fantasize about things they used to do with their partners or things they did with former partners. In these regards, the patterns were quite similar to those for heterosexual women.

A study in India compared the sexual fantasies of 30 heterosexual males with those of 30 gay males (Bhugra et al., 2006). The heterosexual males appeared to be more limited in the sphere is their fantasies, restricting them to more standard sexual activities with females. The gay males were more open to fantasizing about exploratory techniques, and with partners of both sexes. Fantasy apparently mirrored behavior. The authors suggested that the heterosexual males were more "inhibited" or "restricted" in both their sex lives and their fantasies, but a simpler explanation of the findings might be that both groups—heterosexual and gay—were simply fantasizing about the people and activities that enticed them.

In this chapter we observed many of the variations in human sexual expression. No other species shows such diversity in sexual behavior. People show diversity not only in sexual behavior, but also in sexual orientation—which is the focus of the following chapter.

1. What kinds of solitary sexual activities do people engage in?

- Masturbation is self-stimulation of the genitals for purposes such as relieving sexual tension and obtaining sexual pleasure.

- Within the Judeo-Christian tradition, masturbation has been condemned as sinful, as have many other nonprocreative sexual acts. During the 18th and 19th centuries, many physical and psychological ills were ascribed to masturbation.

- Masturbation itself is rarely, if ever, physically harmful, although people whose values oppose masturbation may experience guilt and anxiety if they masturbate.

- Surveys indicate that most people have masturbated at some point in their lives. Males are more likely than females to masturbate. European American males are more likely than African American males to masturbate.

- Males tend to masturbate by using a manual milking motion. Some males use vibrators.

- Females tend to stroke the mons and the area around the clitoral shaft. They usually do not insert fingers or objects into the vagina. Some females use dildos or vibrators.

2. What kinds of sexual activities do people engage in with others?

- Foreplay involves kissing, touching, and other activities that heighten sexual arousal prior to coitus. Women usually desire longer periods of foreplay than men do.

- Kissing is nearly universal in our culture, but is not as popular around the world. Kissing signals intimacy, and prolonged, deep kissing can be sexually arousing in its own right.

- Touching or caressing erogenous zones can be highly arousing. Men typically prefer stroking of their genitals by their partner early during lovemaking. Women, however, tend to prefer that their genitals be caressed after a period of general body contact.

- Most, but not all, women enjoy stimulation of the breasts by the hands and mouth as foreplay or in its own right.

- Gay males and lesbians both tend to spend more time focusing on their partner's breasts and nipples than do heterosexuals.

- Fellatio is oral stimulation—kissing, licking, sucking, and so on—of the male genitals. Cunnilingus is oral stimulation of the female genitals.

- The popularity of oral–genital stimulation has increased dramatically since Kinsey's day, such that the majority of couples today use it. European Americans are more likely than African Americans to use oral–genital stimulation.

- Couples today use a greater variety of coital positions than in Kinsey's time. Four of the most commonly used coital positions are the male-superior position, the female-superior position, the lateral-entry position, and the rear-entry position. The female-superior position allows the female to obtain better the stimulation needed to reach orgasm.

- Anal intercourse is insertion of the penis into the rectum and may be carried out within heterosexual or gay relationships. Artificial lubrication facilitates anal intercourse.

3. How do people use sexual fantasies?

- Sexual fantasies are often incorporated with masturbation or with sex with another person to heighten sexual response. Sexual fantasies range from the realistic to flights of fancy. Many people fantasize about sexual activities that they would not actually engage in.

- Sexual fantasies are normal in that most people have them and that they are not signs of psychological disorders or troubled relationships. However, some people oppose masturbation on religious grounds.

- Evolutionary theory suggests that the male tendency to fantasize about novel and multiple partners, and the female tendency to fantasize about former lovers, represent mating strategies that helped people survive to reproductive age and rear children.

- Sexual fantasies tend to heighten sexual excitement during coitus.

1. What is the connection between education and masturbation?

   (a) There is no connection.
   (b) More educated people are more likely to masturbate.
   (c) Education causes masturbation.
   (d) Education is a pack of lies that distorts the truth about masturbation.

2. Who supposedly identified 39 "signs of masturbation," including acne, paleness, heart palpitations, rounded shoulders, weak backs, and convulsions?

   (a) Havelock Ellis
   (b) Sylvester Graham
   (c) Richard von Krafft–Ebing
   (d) J. H. Kellogg

3. Brody found that people who have reported having engaged in penile–vaginal intercourse show lower levels of _____ in response to stress.

   (a) systolic blood pressure
   (b) prolactin
   (c) galvanic skin response
   (d) hostility

4. _____ American men are least likely to report masturbating.

   (a) African
   (b) Asian
   (c) European
   (d) Latino

5. According to the NHSLS, the most common reason for masturbating is to

   (a) relax
   (b) get to sleep
   (c) relieve sexual tension
   (d) obtain physical pleasure

6. Research suggests that sexual fantasies are

   (a) sent from evil spirits
   (b) a sign of masturbation
   (c) bad for the health
   (d) normal

7. Onanism refers to

   (a) anal intercourse
   (b) foreplay
   (c) masturbation
   (d) the lateral-entry position

8. _____ are most likely to report having performed oral sex.

   (a) African American men
   (b) African American women
   (c) European American men
   (d) European American women

9. A woman is most likely to reach orgasm in the _____ coital position.

   (a) male-superior
   (b) female-superior
   (c) lateral-entry
   (d) rear-entry

10. Couples are least likely to report engaging in

    (a) fellatio
    (b) cunnilingus
    (c) penile–vaginal intercourse
    (d) anal intercourse

11. According to Kinsey, women who masturbated during adolescence

    (a) grew hair in the palms of their hands
    (b) had difficulty forming social relationships in adulthood
    (c) were more likely to find sexual gratification with others in adulthood
    (d) were less likely to find sexual gratification with others in adulthood

12. Kinsey and his colleagues found that one in _____ women inserted objects into the vagina during masturbation

    (a) two
    (b) three
    (c) five
    (d) ten

13. Kinsey found that about _____% of husbands kissed their wives' breasts.

    (a) 25
    (b) 50
    (c) 75
    (d) 90

14. Bell and Weinberg reported that _____ is the most common and frequent sexual activity among lesbian couples.

    (a) use of a dildo in simulated sexual intercourse
    (b) manual genital stimulation
    (c) oral–genital stimulation
    (d) anal stimulation

15. The _____ position is also referred to as the missionary position.

    (a) male-superior
    (b) female-superior
    (c) lateral-entry
    (d) rear-entry

Answers 1. b; 2. d; 3. a; 4. a; 5. c; 6. d; 7. c; 8. c; 9. b; 10. d; 11. c; 12. c; 13. d; 14. b; 15. a

10

Sexual Orientation

TRUTH?fiction

Which of the following statements are true, and which are fiction? Look for the Truth/Fiction icons on the pages that follow to find the answers.

1 Gay males and lesbians would prefer to be members of the other sex.　T　F

2 Members of ethnic minority groups in the United States are more tolerant of homosexuals than European Americans.　T　F

3 Most Americans would prefer that gay people be allowed to get married to one another.　T　F

4 Most Americans believe that gay people are born gay.　T　F

5 Gay males unconsciously fear women's genitals because they associate them with castration.　T　F

6 Many gay couples have lifestyles similar to those of committed heterosexual couples and are as well adjusted.　T　F

The movie *Brokeback Mountain,* with Heath Ledger as Ennis Del Mar and Jake Gyllenhaal as Jack Twist, won four Golden Globe awards, including the coveted award for best drama. What made the movie remarkable? Not the fact that it was about a love affair between gay men. *Entertainment Weekly* counted nine movies debuting in the same year, including *Capote* and *Rent,* that had gay characters in major roles. Nor was it the fact that some lovemaking appeared on the screen. There are many more sexually explicit movies with gay males, including those produced by the pornography factories.

Nor was it remarkable that the characters got married to women and had children. Many gay people do just that.

Nor was it notable that the film was set in the past. There have been many movies about gay characters in ancient Greece and Rome.

But none, perhaps, about sheepherders in the mountains of Wyoming in 1963. The movie took place in a time and a setting in which gay people had few words—or no words—to describe their emotions or who they were. As social commentator Frank Rich

Brokeback Mountain. *In the film* Brokeback Mountain, *Jake Gyllenhaal and Heath Ledger portray two cowboys who begin a love affair in Wyoming in 1963. Because of the time and the geographic setting of the story, neither understands what it means to have a gay sexual orientation.*

noted, the heroes of Brokeback Mountain are "neither midnight cowboys, drugstore cowboys, nor Village People cowboys." Instead, they're high school dropouts in the country, brought up to work hard for little reward.

This chapter is about **sexual orientation.** Sexual orientation concerns the *direction* of one's romantic interests and erotic attractions—toward members of the same sex, the other sex, or both.

In this chapter we will see that homosexual people, like heterosexual people, struggle to incorporate their sexuality within their personal identity, to find lovers, and to establish satisfying lifestyles. Unlike heterosexual people, gay people in our culture face a backdrop of social intolerance, even if they commit themselves to long-term relationships.

Sexual orientation The directionality of one's sexual interests—toward members of the same sex, the other sex, or both

Heterosexual orientation Erotic attraction to and preference for developing romantic relationships with members of the other sex

Getting Oriented toward Sexual Orientation

Sexual orientation refers to one's erotic attractions toward, and interests in developing romantic relationships with, members of one's own or the other sex. A **heterosexual orientation** refers to an erotic attraction to, and preference for developing romantic relationships with, members of the other sex. (Many homosexual people refer to heterosexual people as *straights,* or as being *straight.*)

A **homosexual orientation** refers to an erotic attraction to, and interest in forming romantic relationships with, members of one's own sex. The term *homosexuality* denotes sexual interest in members of one's own anatomic sex and applies to both men and women. Homosexual men are often referred to as **gay males.** Homosexual women are often called **lesbians.** Gay males and lesbians may also be referred to collectively as *gays* or *gay people.* The term **bisexuality** describes an orientation in which one is sexually attracted to, and interested in forming romantic relationships with, both males and females.

Coming to Terms with Terms

Now that we have defined *homosexuality,* let us note that the term is somewhat controversial. Some gay people object to it because they feel that it draws attention to sexual behavior. Moreover, the term bears a social stigma. It has also been historically associated with concepts of deviance and mental illness. Also, the term is often used to refer to men only. It thus renders lesbians invisible. Thus, many people would prefer terms such as *gay male* or *lesbian sexual orientation.* Then, too, the word *homosexual* is ambiguous in meaning. (Savin–Williams, 2006). Does it refer to sexual behavior or to sexual orientation? In this book, we speak of male–female sexual behavior (not *heterosexual* behavior), male–male sexual behavior, and female–female sexual behavior to help distinguish sexual behavior from sexual orientation.

Sexual Orientation and Gender Identity

Because gay people are attracted to members of their own sex, some people assume that they would prefer to be members of the other sex. **Truth or Fiction Revisited:** Like heterosexuals, most gay people have a gender identity that is consistent with their anatomic sex. J. Michael Bailey (2003) writes that some "extremely gay" people become transsexuals—that is, adopt the lifestyle of people of the other sex within our culture. But feeling "trapped" in the body of the other sex is *not* part of the definition of homosexuality.

When heterosexuals think about homosexuals, they tend to focus almost exclusively on the sexual aspects of male–male and female–female relationships. But the relationships of homosexuals, like those of heterosexuals, involve more than sex. Homosexuals, like heterosexuals, spend only a small amount of time in sexual activity. More basic to a gay male or a lesbian sexual orientation is the formation of romantic attachments with members of one's own sex. These attachments, like male–female attachments, provide a framework for love and intimacy. Sexual orientations are not defined by sexual activity per se, but rather by the *direction* of one's romantic interests and erotic attractions (Mosher et al., 2005).

SafeZone

Q *Are some people so unsuccessful with the opposite sex they become gay?*

A No. Sexual orientation has nothing to do with success or failure with one sex or the other.

CRITICAL
Thinking

Critical thinkers pay close attention to the meanings—and implications—of terms. Why do some writers prefer to use the terms *male–male sexual behavior* or *female–female sexual behavior* rather than *homosexual behavior?*

TRUTH **fiction 1**

Homosexual orientation Erotic attraction to and preference for developing romantic relationships with members of the same sex; from the Greek *homos,* meaning "same," not the Latin *homo,* which means "man"

Gay males Males who are erotically attracted to and desire to form romantic relationships with other males

Lesbians Females who are erotically attracted to and desire to form romantic relationships with other females; after *Lesbos,* the Greek island on which, legend has it, female–female sexual activity was idealized

Bisexuality Erotic attraction to and interest in developing romantic relationships with both males and females

Classification of Sexual Orientation: Is Yes or No Enough?

Determining a person's sexual orientation might seem to be a clear-cut task. Some people are exclusively gay and limit their sexual activities to partners of their own sex. Others are strictly heterosexual and limit their sexual activities to partners of the other sex. Some people fall in between.

It is possible, indeed not unusual, for heterosexual people to have had sexual experiences with people of their own sex (Mosher et al., 2005; Savin–Williams, 2006). In the absence of heterosexual outlets, adolescents and those in isolated populations (such as prison inmates) may have sexual experiences with people of their own sex while they maintain their heterosexual identities.

Gay males and lesbians, too, may engage in male–female sexual activity while maintaining a gay sexual orientation. Some gay males and lesbians marry members of the other sex, but harbor unfulfilled desires for members of their own sex. Then, too, some people are bisexual but may not act on their attraction to members of their own sex (Edser & Shea, 2002).

Sexual orientation is not necessarily expressed in sexual behavior. Many people see themselves as gay or heterosexual long before they ever have sex with members of their own sex (Diamond, 2003b; Savin–Williams & Diamond, 2000). Some people, gay and heterosexual alike, adopt a celibate lifestyle for religious or ascetic reasons.

People's erotic interests and fantasies may also shift over time. Gay males and lesbians may experience sporadic **heteroerotic** interests. Heterosexual people may have occasional **homoerotic** interests. Women's sexual orientations are apparently somewhat more flexible or plastic than men's, with women being somewhat more dependent on social experience (Diamond, 2000, 2002, 2003b; Bailey, personal communication, 2003). A classic survey of homosexuals found that about 50% of lesbians sampled reported that they are sometimes attracted to men (Bell & Weinberg, 1978). Lisa M. Diamond (2003a) conducted a survey of lesbian and bisexual women that involved three interviews over a five-year period. She found that more than 25% of the women relinquished their lesbian or bisexual orientation as time went on. Half of these relabeled themselves as heterosexual, and the other half renounced any effort at self-labeling. Some heterosexual people report fantasies about sexual activity with people of their own sex. In their classic study of homosexuals, Masters and Johnson (1979) found that many gay people reported having fantasies about sexual activity with people of the other sex.

Attraction to people of the other sex and people of one's own sex may thus not always be mutually exclusive. People may have various degrees of sexual interest in, and sexual experience with, people of either sex. Kinsey and his colleagues recognized that the boundaries between gay male and lesbian sexual orientations on the one hand, and a heterosexual orientation on the other, are sometimes blurry. As Kinsey and his colleagues noted,

> The world is not to be divided into sheep and goats. . . . Only the human mind invents categories and tries to force facts into separated pigeonholes. The living world is a continuum in each and every one of its aspects. (1948, p. 639)

Kinsey and his colleagues (1948, 1953) found evidence of a continuum of sexual orientation among the people they surveyed, with bisexuality representing a midpoint between exclusively heterosexual and exclusively homosexual sexual orientations (Figure 10.1). People are located on the continuum according to their patterns

Heteroerotic Of an erotic nature and involving members of the other sex

Homoerotic Of an erotic nature and involving members of one's own sex

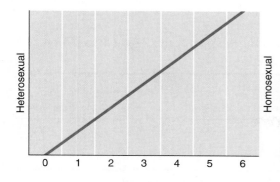

Figure 10.1 The Kinsey Continuum. *Kinsey and his colleagues conceived of a 7-point heterosexual–homosexual continuum that classifies people according to their homosexual behavior and the magnitude of their attraction to members of their own gender. People in category 0, who accounted for most of Kinsey's study participants, were considered exclusively heterosexual. People in category 6 were considered exclusively homosexual.*

of sexual attraction and behavior. People in category 0 are considered exclusively heterosexual. People in category 6 are considered exclusively gay.

Kinsey and his colleagues reported that about 4% of men and 1% to 3% of women in their samples were exclusively gay (6 points on their scale). A larger percentage of people were considered predominantly gay (4 or 5 points) or predominantly heterosexual (1 or 2 points on their scale). All in all, Kinsey's data suggested that close to 10% of the U.S. population was gay or predominantly gay, a number that dramatically exceeds current estimates. Some were classified as equally gay and heterosexual in orientation and could be labeled bisexual (3 points). Most people were classified as exclusively heterosexual (0 point).

Statistics concerning *past* sexual activity with a member of one's own sex can be misleading. They may represent a single episode or a brief period of adolescent experimentation. Half the men who reported male–male sexual activity in Kinsey's sample limited it to the age of 12 to 14. Another third had male–male sexual experience by the age of 18, but not again.

Kinsey's research also showed that sexual behavior patterns can change, sometimes dramatically so. Sexual experiences or feelings involving people of one's own sex are common, especially in adolescence, and do not necessarily mean that one will engage in sexual activity exclusively with people of one's own sex in adulthood (Diamond, 2003a).

The controversy regarding how many people are gay continues. Research in the United States, Britain, France, and Denmark finds that about 3% of men surveyed *identify* themselves as gay (Hamer et al., 1993; Mosher et al., 2005; Savin–Williams, 2006). About 1% to 2% of the U.S. women surveyed *identify* themselves as lesbians (Mosher et al., 2005; Savin–Williams, 2006).

About 6% of the males and 11% of the females in the NSFG said they had engaged in sexual activity with a member of their own sex (Mosher et al., 2005). Yet, as shown in Table 10.1, only 2.3% of the males and 1.3% of the females said they think of themselves as being homosexuals. The same table shows that most respondents considered themselves heterosexual. Some respondents thought of themselves as being bisexual, and a few thought of themselves as "something else." And then some had no response, which is difficult to interpret. However, 90% of the males and the females labeled themselves heterosexual. Overall, it is estimated that anywhere from 2% to 10% of the population is gay male or lesbian (Martins et al., 2005).

Keep in mind that the following factors affect survey results:

- The ways in which the questions are phrased (e.g., do they look into sexual identity, sexual behavior, or sexual attraction—and over what period of time?)
- The social desirability of the professed behavior

TABLE 10.1

Self-Labeling of Sexual Orientation by Respondents Age 18 to 44 to the National Survey of Family Growth

	Heterosexual	Homosexual	Bisexual	"Something else"	No response
Male, %	90	2.3	1.8	3.9	1.8
Female, %	90	1.3	2.8	3.8	1.8

SOURCE: Mosher, W. D., Chandra, A., & Jones, J. (2005). *Sexual behavior and selected health measures: Men and women 15–44 years of age, United States, 2002. Advance data from vital and health statistics, no. 362.* Hyattsville, MD: National Center for Health Statistics.

- The sex of the interviewer
- The manner in which the questions were administered, such as by face-to-face interviews, phone calls, or in written form
- Possible biases of respondents, such as volunteer bias

CHALLENGES TO THE KINSEY CONTINUUM   Alfred Kinsey believed that exclusive heterosexual and gay sexual orientations lay at opposite poles of one continuum. Therefore, the more heterosexual a person is, the less gay that person is, and vice versa. Viewing gay and heterosexual orientations as opposite poles of one continuum is akin to the traditional view of masculinity and femininity as opposite poles of one continuum, such that the more masculine one is, the less feminine, and vice versa.

We may also regard masculinity and femininity as independent personality dimensions. Yet it may be that these sexual orientations are in fact separate dimensions, rather than polar opposites, at least for women.

Using the self-reporting of the content of erotic fantasies as an indication of sexual orientation, Storms (1980) found evidence that there are separate dimensions of responsiveness to male–female sexual stimulation (heteroeroticism) and sexual stimulation that involves someone of the same sex (homoeroticism), as shown in Figure 10.2. According to this model, bisexuals are high in both dimensions, whereas people who are low in both are essentially asexual. According to Kinsey, bisexual individuals would be *less* responsive to stimulation by people of the other sex than heterosexual people, but *more* responsive to stimulation by people of their own sex. But the two-dimensional model allows for people to be as responsive to stimulation by people of the other sex as heterosexual people, and as responsive to stimulation by people of their own sex as gay people.

Researchers find that the two-dimensional model may hold only for women, if it is valid at all. For example, Lippa and Arad (1997) administered tests of personality to 148 male and 246 female college undergraduates with a median age of 18 years. The tests assessed "masculine" instrumentality, "feminine" emotional expressiveness, and other personality traits such as extraversion, agreeableness, conscientiousness, emotional, and openness to new experiences. Students also completed a sexual behavior and attitude questionnaire that asked them about their sexual attraction to men and women, their emotional commitment in sexual relationships, their sex drive, and their interest in sexual fantasies and erotic stimuli. A statistical grouping technique called factor analysis found four factors that characterized men's sexual be-

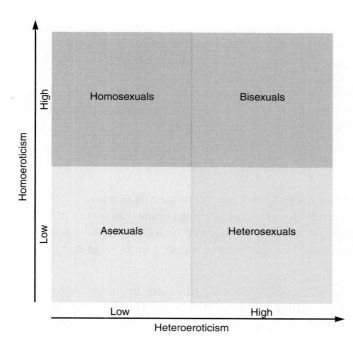

Figure 10.2 **Heterosexuality and Homo-sexuality as Separate Dimensions.** According to this model, homosexuality and heterosexuality are independent dimensions. One can thus be high or low on both dimensions at the same time. Most people are high on one dimension. Bisexuals are high on both dimensions. People who are low on both are considered *asexual.*

haviors and attitudes and four that characterized women's (Table 10.2). They differed in important ways. Perhaps the most telling is that men seemed to largely fit the Kinsey model in that they showed a "bipolar" sexual orientation. That is, the more aroused they were by women, the less they were aroused by men, and vice versa. Women, by contrast, showed factors both for homosexuality and heterosexuality. That is, whether they were aroused by men could be independent of whether they were aroused by other women, and vice versa, but sexual behaviors and attitudes had little to do with the other personality measures.

Chivers and Bailey (2005) took another approach, but their results support those of Lippa and Arad. Chivers and Bailey exposed men and women to visual male and female sexual stimuli. They measured both their genital responses and their self-reports of sexual arousal. Male heterosexuals responded genitally only to the female stimuli, and gay males showed the reverse pattern. Their genital responses bore out their verbal reports. The women, both heterosexual and lesbian, were more likely to be aroused by both male and female sexual stimuli.

Lippa and Arad's and Chivers and Bailey's findings are consistent with research showing that women's sexual orientations are more flexible than men's and apparently

TABLE 10.2

Factors in Males' and Females' Sexual Behaviors and Attitudes

Males	Females
Bipolar sexual orientation	Homosexuality
Emotional commitment	Heterosexuality
Sex drive	Emotional commitment
Sexual fantasy	Sex drive

Source: "The structure of sexual orientation and its relation to masculinity, femininity, and gender diagnosticity: Different for men and women" by Richard Lippa and Sara Arad, *Sex Roles,* 1997, 37(3-4), 187–208, with kind permission from Springer Science and Business Media.

more intertwined with their social experience (Bailey, 2003a; Diamond, 2000, 2002, 2003b). When we discuss *homophobia,* or hatred of homosexuals, we will see that men tend to be more homophobic than women. Homophobia is connected with traditional "tough" masculine attitudes (Davies, 2004). However, it may also be that part of the reason for this sex difference in homophobia is that heterosexual men have a more difficult time than heterosexual women understanding how any man could be attracted to a person of the same sex.

Bisexuality

To me, I never felt like I had a stronger attraction to men or women. I didn't have a problem identifying myself as gay, but I knew that wasn't the whole picture. (A 29-year-old social worker from North Carolina who fell in love with a woman and then had a sexual relationship with his male roommate)

I don't limit myself to a guy or a girl. Whoever comes into my life, if we hit it off, great. That's happened with a lot of people I know. They'll say, "Guess what happened last night." It's very accepted. (A 22-year-old political science major)

She finally came out of the closet and said, "Mom, there's this girl and she's the most gorgeous girl you've ever seen." I said, "You're only for girls?" She said, "No, it's not just the girls. I can see a really good-looking guy, too." (The mother of a 19-year-old woman who uses a computer bulletin board to meet other bisexuals)

—Adapted from Gabriel, 1995

Bisexual people are sexually attracted to both males and females. Bisexual people are sometimes said to "swing both ways," or to be "AC/DC" (as in "alternating current" and "direct current"). Yet many have a somewhat stronger attraction to people of one sex than the other. In fact, Weinrich and Klein (2002) speak of bisexuals as being bi-gay, bi-straight, or bi-bi, meaning that some have a stronger leaning toward people of their own sex (bi-gays), some toward people of the other sex (bi-straights), and still others appear to be equally attracted to people of their own sex and the other sex (bi-bi's). Depending on how one defines bisexuality, perhaps 1% to 4% of the population is bisexual. About 1% of the people (0.8% of the men and 0.9% of the women) surveyed in the NHSLS (Laumann et al., 1994) reported having a bisexual *identity*. However, about 4% said they were sexually attracted to both women and men.

Some gay people (and some heterosexual people) believe that claims to bisexuality are a "cop-out" that people use to deny being gay. Perhaps they fear leaving their spouses or "coming out" (declaring their gay male or lesbian sexual orientation publicly). Others view bisexuality as a form of sexual experimentation with people of one's own sex by people who are mostly heterosexual. Surveys of more than 600 college undergraduates confirm that **biphobia,** or hatred of bisexuals, can be found in both the heterosexual and homosexual populations (Mulick & Wright, 2002).

But many avowed bisexuals and researchers assert that bisexuals can maintain erotic interests in, and romantic relationships with, members of both sexes. They insist that bisexuality is an authentic sexual orientation with its own developmental patterns, and is not just a "cover" for a gay male or lesbian sexual orientation (Brown, 2002; Weinrich & Klein, 2002).

Some bisexual people follow lifestyles that permit them to satisfy their dual inclinations. Others feel pressured by heterosexual and gay people alike to commit them-

Biphobia Negative attitudes and feelings toward bisexual people, including intolerance, hatred, and fear

selves one way or the other (Edser & Shea, 2002). Some gay people also mask their sexual orientation by adopting a bisexual lifestyle. That is, they get married but also enter into clandestine sexual liaisons with members of their own sex.

Still, it appears that many bisexual men remain reasonably comfortable in committed heterosexual relationships, such as marriages. An in-depth study of 20 married men who scored as bisexual on the Kinsey scale found that they encountered some anxiety, some feelings of guilt, and some sense of loss, but not to the point where they experienced high levels of stress (Edser & Shea, 2002). By and large, the men were psychologically stable and most of their marriages were in what the authors call "relatively good condition." The authors conclude that long-term committed relationships with women are a "viable option" for bisexual men. The authors were not moralistic; that is, they were not suggesting that bisexual men *should* seek committed relationships with women. They merely pointed out that such relationships can work.

SafeZone

Q *Why do some homosexuals dislike people who are bisexual?*

A They think bisexuals are straddling the fence and should come out (or should come out "already"). That is, they doubt there is such a thing as true bisexualism. The literature would seem to support the view that some people are truly bisexual, however.

Perspectives on Gay Male and Lesbian Sexual Orientations

Gay male and lesbian sexual orientations have existed throughout history. Attitudes toward them have varied widely. They have been accepted in some societies, openly encouraged in others, but condemned in most. In this section we review historical and other perspectives on gay male and lesbian sexual orientations.

Historical Perspectives

In Western culture, few sexual practices have met with such widespread censure as sexual activities with members of one's own sex. Yet it was not always that way. In ancient Greece, for example, men frequently formed sexual relationships with adolescent males. "How can we know anything about the sex lives of Greeks who lived 2,500 years ago?" quips J. Michael Bailey (2003, p. 126). "It is difficult enough to know about the sex lives of Americans today." Having posed the question, Bailey nevertheless goes on to describe such relationships between established men and adolescents at about the age of first growing a beard. The main sexual activity depicted on Greek vases is of the older male inserting his penis between the boy's thighs (not in the anus) and thrusting until he ejaculates.

A few centuries later, Bailey (2003) continues, the Romans described highly feminine gay men who dressed flamboyantly, had showy hair styles and mannerisms,

Ethnicity and Sexual Orientation: A Matter of Belonging

Lesbians and gay males frequently suffer the slings and arrows of an outraged society. Because of societal prejudices, it is difficult for many young people to come to terms with an emerging lesbian or gay male sexual orientation. You might assume that people who have been subjected to prejudice and discrimination—members of ethnic minority groups in the United States—would be more tolerant of a lesbian or gay male sexual orientation. **Truth or Fiction Revisited:** Members of ethnic minority groups in the United States tend to be less tolerant of homosexuals than European Americans (Greene, 2005; Herek & Gonzalez–Rivera, 2006).

Greene (2005) addresses the experiences of lesbians and gay men from ethnic minority groups. She notes that it is difficult to generalize about ethnic groups in the United States. For example, African Americans may find their cultural origins in the tribes of West Africa, but they have also been influenced by Christianity and the local subcultures of their North American towns and cities. Native Americans represent hundreds of tribal groups, languages, and cultures. By and large, however, a lesbian or gay male sexual orientation is rejected by ethnic minority groups in the United States. Lesbians and gay males are pressured to keep their sexual orientations a secret or to move to communities where they can live openly without sanction.

Within traditional Latino and Latina American culture, the family is the primary social unit. Men are expected to support and defend the family, and women are expected to be submissive, respectable, and deferential to men. Because women are expected to remain virgins until marriage, men sometimes engage in male–male sexual behavior without considering themselves gay (Barrett et al., 2005). Latino and Latina American culture frequently denies the sexuality of women. Thus, women who label themselves lesbians are doubly condemned—because they are lesbians and because they are confronting others with their sexuality. Because lesbians are independent of men, most Latino and Latina American heterosexual people view Latina American lesbians as threats to the tradition of male dominance (Barrett et al., 2005).

Asian American cultures emphasize respect for elders, obedience to parents, and sharp distinctions in gender roles (Kumashiro, 2004). The topic of sex is generally taboo within the family. Asian Americans, like Latino and Latina Americans, tend to assume that sex is unimportant to women. Women are also considered less important than men. Open admission of a lesbian or gay male sexual orientation is seen as a rejection of traditional cultural roles and a threat to the continuity of the family line (Collins, 2004). For all these reasons, it is not surprising that Asian American college students report being more homophobic than their European American counterparts.

and cruised certain neighborhoods, searching for partners. The Apostle Paul commented on this behavior as the key sign of the decadence of Rome, and the Christian Church assumed a strongly negative attitude toward homosexuality.

In the 15th century, Florence, a Christian city, was reputed to house numerous "sodomites." Jews and Christians have traditionally referred to male–male sexual activity as the sin of Sodom. Hence the origins of the term *sodomy,* which generally alludes to anal intercourse, and sometimes to oral–genital contact. According to the Book of Genesis, the city of Sodom was destroyed by God. Yet it is unclear what behavior incurred God's wrath. Pope Gregory III was not ambiguous, however, in his eighth-century account of the city's obliteration as a punishment for sexual activity with members of the same sex. Sodomy was so common in Florence, and (theoretically) so disturbing to the city's governors, that they created "the Office of the Night" in 1432, which enabled the populace to anonymously accuse individuals of sodomy. During the 70 years that the Office was in operation, some 17,000 men were investigated as possible sodomites—nearly half of the male population of Florence throughout this period! Fewer than 3,000 were actually convicted, however, and

Gender roles among African Americans have been more flexible than those found among European Americans and most other ethnic minority groups (Greene, 2000). Nevertheless, the African American community appears to strongly reject gay men and lesbians, pressuring them to remain secretive about their sexual orientations. Greene (2000) hypothesizes a number of factors that influence African Americans to be hostile toward lesbians and gay men. One is allegiance to Christianity and Biblical scripture. Another is internalization of the dominant culture's stereotyping of African Americans as highly sexual beings. That is, many African Americans may feel a need to assert their sexual "normalcy."

Prior to European colonialization, sex may not have been discussed openly by Native Americans, but sex was generally seen as a natural part of life. Individuals who incorporated both traditional feminine and masculine styles were generally accepted and even admired. The influence of the religions of colonists led to greater rejection of lesbians and gay men, and pressure to move off the reservation to the big city (Adams & Phillips, 2006; Balsam et al., 2004). Native American lesbians and gay men, like Asian American lesbians and gay men, thus often feel doubly removed from their families.

If any generalization is possible, it may be that lesbians and gay men find more of a sense of belonging in the gay community than in their ethnic communities.

Ethnicity and Sexual Orientation. *The experiences of lesbians and gay men can differ according to their ethnicity. For example, traditional Latino and Latina American culture supports strong differences in gender roles. Men are expected to support and defend the family. Women are expected to be submissive, respectable, and deferential to men. Latino and Latina American culture also often denies the sexuality of women. Thus, Latina American lesbians are multiply condemned—because they are lesbians, because they confront others with their sexuality, and because their independence from men is perceived as a threat to the tradition of male dominance.*

those who were convicted were required to pay a fine rather than go to prison (Bailey, 2003).

The Book of Leviticus was also clear in its condemnation:

> If a man lies with a man as with a woman, both of them have committed an abomination; they shall be put to death, their blood is upon them. (Leviticus 20:13)

Sexual activity with members of one's own sex was not the only sexual act considered sinful by the early Christians. Any nonprocreative sexual act was considered sinful, even within marriage. With the fall of the Roman Empire, the influence of Christianity spread across Western Europe. Christian beliefs were eventually encoded into secular law. By the late Middle Ages, most civil statutes throughout Western Europe contained penalties for nonprocreative sexual acts involving the discharge of semen, including oral or anal sex, masturbation, male–male sexual behavior, and bestiality. Male–male and female–female sexual practices continue to be condemned by most Christian and Jewish denominations, and by Islam.

Our legal system, grounded in this religious tradition, maintains criminal penalties for sexual practices commonly associated with male–male and female–female sex, such as anal and oral sex. But much of the criminalization of male–male and female–female sex has been directed against men.

Cross-Cultural Perspectives

Male–male sexual behavior has been practiced in many preliterate societies. In their review of the literature on 76 preliterate societies, Ford and Beach (1951) found that in 49 societies (64%), male–male sexual interactions were viewed as normal and deemed socially acceptable for some members of the group. The other 27 societies (36%) had sanctions against male–male sexual behavior. Nevertheless, male–male sexual activity persisted. In another cross-cultural analysis, Broude and Greene (1976) found that male–male sexual behavior was present but uncommon in 41% of a sample of 70 of the world's non-European societies. It was rare or absent in 59% of these societies. Broude and Greene also found evidence of societal disapproval and punishment of male–male sexual activity in 41% of a sample of 42 societies for which information was available.

Sexual activities between males are sometimes limited to rites that mark the young male's initiation into manhood. In some preliterate societies, semen is believed to boost strength and virility. Older males thus transmit semen to younger males through oral or anal sexual activities. Among the Sambian people of New Guinea, 7- to 10-year-old males leave their parents' households and live in a "clubhouse" with other prepubertal and adolescent males. There they undergo sexual rites of passage. To acquire the fierce manhood of the headhunter, they fellate older males and drink semen (Bailey, 2003). They are encouraged to take in as much semen as they can, as if it were mother's milk. Ingestion of semen is believed to give rise to puberty. After puberty, adolescents are fellated by younger males. In their late teens or early 20s, however, young men are expected to take brides and enter into exclusively male–female sexual relationships.

These practices of Sambian culture might seem to suggest that the sexual orientations of males are fluid and malleable. But the practices involve *behavior* and not *sexual orientation*. Male–male sexual behavior among Sambians takes place within a cultural context that bears little resemblance to consensual male–male sexual activity in Western society. The prepubertal Sambian male does not *seek* sexual liaisons with other males. He is removed from his home and thrust into male–male sexual encounters by older males.

Little is known about female–female sexual activity in non-Western cultures. Evidence of female–female sexual behavior was found by Ford and Beach in only 17 of the 76 societies they studied. Perhaps female sexual behavior in general, not just sexual activity with other females, was more likely to be repressed. Perhaps women are less likely than men to develop sexual interests in, or romantic relationships with, members of their own sex. Whatever the reasons, this cross-cultural evidence is consistent with data from our own culture. Here, too, males are more likely than females to develop sexual interests in, or romantic relationships with, members of their own sex.

Cross-Species Perspectives

Biologists have observed male–male and female–female sexual behavior in at least 450 different animal species in every part of the world (Hird, 2006). Rare it's not.

On the other hand, what you see isn't always what you get. A male baboon may present his rear and allow himself to be mounted by another male. This behavior may resemble anal intercourse among gay men. Is the behavior sexually motivated, however? Mounting behavior among male baboons may represent a type of dominance ritual in which lower ranking males adopt a submissive (feminine) posture to ward off attack from dominant males. (Some male–male acts among people also involve themes of dominance, as in the case of a dominant male prisoner forcing a less dominant one to submit to anal intercourse.) In other cases, male baboons may be seeking favors or protection from more dominant males. Among juvenile animals, male–male behaviors may also be a form of play. Females may also attempt to mount other females, but here, too, the motives may not be the same as those of humans.

Sexual motivation appears to play a role in some, but not all, male–male and female–female sexual interactions among animals. Fellatio and anal intercourse to ejaculation among juvenile male orangutans may be a case in point, as may be thrusting by one adult female gorilla against another.

Attitudes toward Sexual Orientation in Contemporary Society

The General Social Survey, done by the University of Chicago, found that the percentage of people saying intercourse between people of the same sex is "always wrong" has dropped by 21 points in the last 10 years, to 56% from 77%, notes Tom W. Smith, director of the survey. Although opposition remains high, Smith said the decline "is as large a social change as any ever." Much survey data suggest that greater acceptance has come from more people knowing someone who is gay.

"It's the same as racial equality," says Smith. "The point is to think of them as individuals, who are also coworkers, neighbors, someone who supports the local charity drive—to see people as people, except in this one little way they're different" (Zernicke, 2003).

But historically speaking, negative attitudes toward gay people have pervaded our society. Male–male and female–female sexual behavior at worst has been viewed as a crime against God or "nature." A national survey of males in their late teens conducted in the early 1990s showed that 9 of 10 felt that sex between men was "disgusting." Three of five could not even see themselves being friends with a gay man (Marsiglio, 1993b). Young males tend to be the harshest group in their judgments of gay people. A national poll conducted in June 1998 found that 59% of American adults believe that homosexuality is morally wrong, compared with 35% who say it is not wrong (Berke, 1998). (The remaining 6% had no answer or said they didn't know.)

Still, there are signs that Americans have grown more accepting of gay people during the past few decades. For example, a poll conducted in June 1977 found that 56% of Americans said that gay people should have equal rights in terms of job opportunities (33% said they should not). By November 1996, 84% of Americans endorsed equal rights for gay people and only 12% were opposed (Berke, 1998).

Civil unions are allowed in several states. Massachusetts legalized gay marriage in 2004, and is currently the only state to do so. However, a *New York Times* poll found that only 28% of Americans agreed that "marriage between two people of the same sex should be legal" (Eggers, 2000). **Truth or Fiction Revisited:** The majority of Americans oppose gay marriages. An Associated Press poll conducted in 2000 found that 34% supported gay marriages (Lester, 2000). However, Americans are becoming more liberal on the issue: Although only 13% of people older than 70 in the article by Eggers (2000) reported that such unions should be legal, 42% of those younger than

REFLECT

What are the attitudes of most people from your background toward gay males and lesbians? Do you share these attitudes? Explain.

TABLE 10.3

Effect of Wording in Poll on Gay Rights

Question	Percentage saying "should"	Percentage saying "should not"	Percentage saying "don't know"	Percentage refusing to answer
In general, do you think gays and lesbians should or should not be allowed to be legally married?	34	51	11	3
In general, do you think gays and lesbians should or should not be allowed to form a domestic partnership that would give the same-sex couple the same rights and benefits as opposite-sex marriage?	41	46	11	3

SOURCE: Lester, W. (2000, May 31). *Poll: Americans back some gay rights.* The Associated Press. [Online].

30 endorsed them. The Associated Press poll showed a similar age discrepancy: Fifty-four percent of respondents age 18 to 34 said gay people should be allowed to get married, compared with 14% of those older than 65 (Lester, 2000).

The word *marriage* seems to be the barrier. The Associated Press poll (Lester, 2000) of a national sample of 1,012 adults in the United States split the sample so that half were asked whether they approved of gay people getting married, whereas the other half we asked whether they approved of "domestic partnerships" that would give gay couples the same rights as married couples. As you can see in Table 10.3, more people approved of domestic partnerships than marriage for gay couples. Despite the fact that a majority of those polled would not allow gay couples to form domestic partnerships that give partners the same rights as married partners, a majority would allow domestic partners specific rights, as shown in Table 10.4. In other words, heterosexuals may be more wary of giving gays marriage certificates than health benefits.

TABLE 10.4

Percentage of Americans Who Would Approve of Certain Rights for Gay People in Domestic Partnerships

Would respondent approve of	Percentage in favor	Percentage opposed	Percentage who say "don't know"	Percentage who refuse to answer
Providing health coverage to gay partners?	53	37	7	3
Providing Social Security benefits to gay partners?	50	41	6	3
Providing inheritance rights to gay partners?	56	32	9	3

SOURCE: Lester, W. (2000, May 31). *Poll: Americans back some gay rights.* The Associated Press. [Online].

Truth or Fiction Revisited: Most Americans assume that gay people choose to be gay, despite the accumulation of research evidence that inborn biological factors play a strong role in the development of sexual orientation. For example, a nationwide poll conducted in 1977 found that only 13% of Americans believed that gay people were "born with" their sexual orientation compared with 56% who favored environmental causes. In 1989, 18% of Americans said that gay people were born with their orientation compared with 48% who favored an environmental explanation. An Associated Press poll, conducted in 2000, found that 30% of Americans believe that gay people are born that way compared with 46% who say they "choose" to be gay. More people are coming to look upon sexual orientation as something that one is born with. Thus, fewer people are likely to believe that young people can be "seduced" into one sexual orientation or another.

SafeZone

Q *I don't understand why people can be supportive of gays/lesbians, but not supportive of marriage for gays/lesbians. Can you explain?*

A Marriage seems to be the trip-word. Many people who are otherwise tolerant see marriage as something defined by scripture to apply only to a man and a woman. We'll toss a question back at you: Can one be truly tolerant of gays and lesbians if one restricts marriage to males and females? We imagine that the answer is a case-by-case thing, but we do know of otherwise tolerant people who would grant gays and lesbians all the civil benefits of marriage but want to reserve marriage per se as a religious contract for males and females. One comedian came out in favor of gay marriage: "Why," he asked, "shouldn't gay people have the right to be as miserable as the rest of us?"

MEXICAN AMERICAN ATTITUDES TOWARD GAY MALES AND LESBIANS A recent survey by Herek and Gonzalez–Rivera (2006) examined attitudes toward gay males and lesbians among a sample of California residents of Mexican origin. It was found that men's attitudes toward homosexual men were significantly more negative than women's. Women expressed relatively more negative attitudes toward lesbians. When compared with respondents reporting positive attitudes, respondents reporting negative attitudes

- endorsed more traditional gender attitudes
- tended to be older and less educated
- had more children
- were more likely to belong to a fundamentalist religious denomination and to attend religious services religiously
- were more conservative politically
- were less likely to have personal contact with gay people

SEXUAL ORIENTATION AND THE LAW During the past generation, gay people have organized effective political groups to fight discrimination and to overturn the sodomy laws that have traditionally targeted them. Despite their success, sodomy laws are still on the books in many states. Sodomy laws prohibit "unnatural" sexual acts, even between consenting adults. Certain sexual acts that many gay

The New Look of *Bride's Magazine*? *Many newspapers and magazines regularly report stories and photos of gay couples who are getting engaged or married.*

people (and heterosexual people) practice, such as anal intercourse and oral–genital contact, fall under the legal definition of sodomy in many states. Although sodomy laws are usually written to apply equally to all adults, the vast majority of prosecutions have been directed against gay people.

A 1986 Supreme Court decision (*Hardwick v. Bowers*) let stand a Georgia sodomy law that makes oral–genital or anal–genital sexual contact crimes punishable by up to 20 years in prison, even when engaged in by consenting adults. The decision was a blow to gay rights organizations, which had looked to the Supreme Court to overturn state sodomy laws.

However, in 2003, by a vote of six to three, the Supreme Court reversed that decision by striking down a Texas law against "deviate sexual intercourse with another individual of the same sex." The Texas law "demeans the lives of homosexual persons," wrote Justice Anthony M. Kennedy, explaining the majority vote. Over the years, the Constitution's right to privacy has been in conflict with laws against same-sex sexual behavior. Gay people "are entitled to respect for their private lives," Kennedy wrote further. In an interview, he added that "The state cannot demean their existence or control their destiny by making their private sexual conduct a crime."

Many other countries, including Mexico, Holland, Italy, Spain, England, France, and the Scandinavian countries have also struck down laws against male–male and female–female sexual activity. A number of countries including the Netherlands, Belgium, and Canada have extended full marriage rights to same-sex couples. Many others have allowed gay males and lesbians to enter into legal partnerships that, in effect, provide the protections and responsibilities of marriage. Nearly all developed countries are debating the issue of gay marriage.

GAY ACTIVISM   Gay activism is the joining together of gay people to achieve political ends. Nowhere in the United States have gay people been more politically effective than in San Francisco. They are well represented on the city police force and in other public agencies. The coming out of many gay people, and their flocking to more tolerant urban centers, has rendered them formidable political forces in these locales.

HIV/AIDS has had a profound effect on the political agenda of gay rights organizations. These organizations combat the HIV/AIDS epidemic on several fronts:

- They lobby for increased funding for HIV/AIDS research and treatment.
- They educate the gay and wider communities of the dangers of high-risk sexual behavior.
- They encourage gay men and others to adopt safer sex practices, including the use of condoms.
- They protect the civil rights of people with HIV/AIDS with respect to employment, housing, and medical and dental treatment.
- They provide counseling and support services for people with HIV/AIDS.

STEREOTYPES AND SEXUAL BEHAVIOR   Among heterosexual people, sexual aggressiveness is linked to the masculine gender role. Sexual passivity is linked to the feminine role. Some heterosexual people assume (often erroneously) that in gay male and lesbian relationships, one partner consistently assumes the masculine role in sexual relations, and the other, the feminine.

Many gay couples vary the active and passive roles, however. Among gay male couples, for example, roles in anal intercourse (*inserter* vs. *insertee*) and in fellatio are often reversed. Contrary to popular assumptions, sexual behavior between lesbians seldom reflects distinct **butch/femme** gender roles. Most lesbians report providing and receiving oral–genital stimulation, alternating roles, or interacting simultaneously. Many gay people claim that the labels of *masculine* and *feminine* only represent the "straight" community's efforts to pigeonhole them in terms heterosexuals can understand.

Biological Perspectives

Biological perspectives focus on the possible roles of evolution, genetics, and hormonal influences in shaping sexual orientation.

THE EVOLUTIONARY PERSPECTIVE It might seem odd that evolutionary theorists have endeavored to explain gay male and lesbian sexual orientations. After all, gay males and lesbians are not motivated to engage in sexual activity with members of the other sex. How, then, can gay and lesbian sexual orientations confer any evolutionary advantage?

To answer the question, we must look to the group or the species, rather than the individual. Kirkpatrick (2000) suggests that male–male and female–female sexual behavior derive from individual selection for reciprocal *altruism*. That is, strong male–male and female–female alliances have advantages for group survival in that they bind group members together emotionally. This hypothesis remains speculative.

GENETICS AND SEXUAL ORIENTATION Considerable evidence exists that gay male and lesbian sexual orientations run in families (Bailey et al., 2000a; Dawood et al., 2000; Mustanski et al., 2005; Rahman & Wilson, 2003). Twin studies shed light on the possible role of heredity (Bailey, 2003). **Monozygotic (MZ) twins,** or identical twins, develop from a single fertilized ovum and share 100% of their heredity. **Dizygotic (DZ) twins,** or fraternal twins, develop from two fertilized ova. Like other brothers and sisters, DZ twins share only 50% of their heredity. Thus, if a gay male or lesbian sexual orientation were transmitted genetically, it should be found about twice as often among identical twins of gay people as among fraternal twins. Because MZ and DZ twins who are reared together share similar environmental influences, differences in the degree of **concordance** for a given trait between the types of twin pairs are further indicative of genetic origins. Several studies have identified gay men who had either identical (MZ) or fraternal (DZ) twin brothers to examine the prevalence of a gay male sexual orientation in their twin brothers. In one of the most carefully conducted twin studies, about 52% of identical (MZ) twin pairs were found to be "concordant" (in agreement) for a gay male sexual orientation compared with 22% of fraternal (DZ) twins and only 11% of adoptive brothers (Bailey, 2003a; Bailey & Pillard, 1991). Bear in mind that MZ twins are more likely to be dressed alike and treated alike than DZ twins. Thus, their greater concordance for a gay sexual orientation may, at least in part, reflect environmental factors (Kendler et al., 2000a).

Researchers have found evidence linking a region on the X sex chromosome to a gay male sexual orientation (Bailey et al., 1999). One group of researchers (Hamer et al., 1993) found that gay males in a sample of 114 gay men were more likely to have gay male relatives on the maternal side of the family than would be expected, based on the prevalence of a gay male sexual orientation in the general population. Yet they did not have a greater than expected number of gay male relatives on the paternal side of the family. This pattern of inheritance is consistent with genetic traits, like hemophilia, that are linked to the X sex chromosome, which men receive from their mothers.

Butch A lesbian who assumes a traditional masculine gender role

Femme A lesbian who assumes a traditional feminine gender role

Monozygotic (MZ) twins Twins who develop from the same fertilized ovum; identical twins

Dizygotic (DZ) twins Twins who develop from different fertilized ova; fraternal twins

Concordance Agreement

The researchers then examined the X sex chromosome in 40 pairs of gay male, nontwin brothers. In 33 of the pairs, the brothers had identical DNA markers on the end tip of the X chromosome. For brothers overall in the general population, about half would be expected to have inherited this chromosomal structure. It is suspected, therefore, that this chromosomal region may hold a gene that predisposes men to a gay male sexual orientation.

The researchers cautioned that they had not found a particular gene linked to sexual orientation, just a general location of where the gene may be found. Nor do scientists know how such a gene, or combination of genes, might account for sexual orientation. Perhaps a particular gene or genes governs the development of proteins that sculpt parts of the brain in ways that favor the development of a gay male sexual orientation. On the other hand, a number of the gay brothers, 7 of the 40 pairs, did *not* share the chromosomal marker.

HORMONAL INFLUENCES AND SEXUAL ORIENTATION Sex hormones strongly influence the mating behavior of other species (Crews, 1994). Researchers have thus looked into possible hormonal factors in determining sexual orientation in humans.

Testosterone is essential to male sexual differentiation. Thus, levels of testosterone and its by-products in the blood and urine have been studied as possible influences on sexual orientation. Research has failed to connect sexual orientation in either sex with differences in the levels of either male or female sex hormones in adulthood (Friedman & Downey, 1994). In adulthood, testosterone appears to have **activating effects.** That is, it affects the intensity of sexual desire, but not the preference for partners of the same or the other sex (van Anders & Watson, 2006).

What of the possible *prenatal* effects of sex hormones? Pregnant rats in experiments were given antiandrogen drugs that block the effects of testosterone. When the drugs were given during critical periods in which the fetuses' brains were becoming sexually differentiated, male offspring were likely to show feminine mating patterns as adults (Ellis & Ames, 1987). The adult males became receptive to mounting attempts by other males and failed to mount females.

Do prenatal sex hormones play a similar role in determining sexual orientation in people? There is suggestive evidence. For example, Meyer–Bahlburg and his colleagues (1995) interviewed groups of women exposed prenatally to diethylstilbestrol (DES), a synthetic estrogen. They found that these women were more likely to be rated as lesbian or bisexual than women who were not exposed to DES. The genitals of gay people differentiate prenatally in accordance with their chromosomal sex. However, it remains possible that imbalances in prenatal sex hormones may cause brain tissue to be sexually differentiated in one direction even though the genitals are differentiated in the other (Collaer & Hines, 1995). Moreover, as we will see later, "butch" lesbians may differ somewhat biologically from "femme" lesbians.

THE STRUCTURE OF THE BRAIN Evidence suggests that there may be structural differences between the brains of heterosexual and gay men. In 1991, Simon LeVay, a neurobiologist at the Salk Institute in La Jolla, California, carried out autopsies on the brains of 35 AIDS victims—19 gay men and 16 (presumably) heterosexual men. He found that a segment of the hypothalamus—specifically, the third interstitial nucleus of the anterior hypothalamus—in the brains of gay men was less than half the size of the same segment in heterosexual men. The same brain segment was larger in the brain tissues of heterosexual men than in brain tissues obtained from a comparison group of six presumably heterosexual women. No significant differences in size were found between the brain tissues of the gay men and the women, however.

CRITICAL Thinking

Some people believe that sexual orientation is inborn; others believe that it represents the choice of the individual. Why are people who believe sexual orientation is inborn more accepting of homosexuals?

Activating effects The effects of sex hormones that influence the level of the sex drive but not sexual orientation

A Closer Look

PHEROMONES AND SEXUAL ORIENTATION

In the film *Scent of a Woman,* Al Pacino plays a blind man who is drawn to women by their odor. Are there odors that are characteristic of the other sex? If so, does one's response to these odors play a role in one's sexual orientation?

Some answers are suggested by a study by Swedish researchers (Savic et al., 2005) who used position emission tomographic (PET) scans to show that gay and heterosexual men respond differently when smelling chemicals that may affect sexual arousal, and that the gay men respond similarly to heterosexual women (Figure 10.3). The Swedish study investigated the effects of two chemicals: a testosterone derivative produced in men's sweat and an estrogenlike compound found in women's urine. Most odors activate neurons in specific regions of the brain, increasing the blood flow to these regions and causing them to "light up" when imaged using PET scanning. The estrogen-like compound activated the usual smell-related areas in women, but it lit up the hypothalamus—a structure involved in sexual behavior—in heterosexual men. The chemical extracted from male sweat, in contrast, did the opposite; it activated the hypothalamus in women and the usual smell-related areas in men. Each chemical seemed to be just another odor with one sex, but a pheromone with the other. However, gay men in the study responded to the chemicals as women did. That is, their hypothalamus was lit up by the chemical drawn from male sweat.

It must be noted that the Swedish study does not reveal cause and effect. A "snapshot" was taken of brain functioning at a point in time. The snapshot did not show how the brain's responses develop. Were the activity patterns in heterosexual and gay men a cause of their sexual orientation or an effect of their sexual orientation? If sexual orientation has a genetic basis, or is influenced by hormones in the womb or at puberty, it might be that the neurons in the hypothalamus become hardwired in a way that shapes sexual orientation. Conversely, the findings could mean that experience leads straight and gay men to respond in different ways. In any event, the study does suggest a role for pheromones in human sexual response and lays the groundwork for further research.

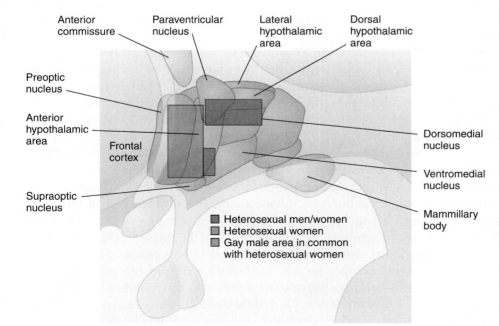

Figure 10.3 **Who Lights Up Your Hypothalamus?**
Certain areas of the hypothalamus "light up" when heterosexual males smell an estrogenlike compound ("estratetraenol") found in women's urine, when heterosexual women smell an androgenlike compound ("androstadienone"), and when gay males smell the androstadienone. The hypothalamus of gay males responds similarly to that of heterosexual women when the person is presented with the odor of androstadienone.

Adapted with permission from I. Savic, H. Berglund and P. Lindström (2005). Brain response to putative pheromones in homosexual men. *Proceedings of the National Academy of Sciences,* Vol. 102, pp. 7356–7361, p. 7539. Copyright © 2005 National Academy of Sciences, U.S.A.

The belief that sexual orientation is innate or inborn has many adherents—both in the scientific and general communities. Support for the possible influences of prenatal hormonal factors in "sculpting" the brain in a masculine or feminine direction is based largely on animal studies, however. Direct evidence with people is lacking. We must also be careful when generalizing results from other species to our own.

Psychological Perspectives

Psychoanalytic theory and learning theory provide two of the major psychological approaches to understanding the origins of sexual orientation.

PSYCHOANALYTIC VIEWS Sigmund Freud, the originator of psychoanalytic theory, believed that children are naturally open to all forms of sexual stimulation. However, through proper resolution of the Oedipus complex, a boy will forsake his incestuous desires for his mother and come to identify with his father. As a result, his erotic attraction to his mother will eventually be transferred to more appropriate *female* partners. A girl, through proper resolution of her Electra complex, will identify with her mother and seek erotic stimulation from men when she becomes sexually mature.

In Freud's view, a gay male or lesbian sexual orientation results from failure to successfully resolve the Oedipus complex by identifying with the parent of the same sex. In men, faulty resolution of the Oedipus complex is most likely to result from the so-called classic pattern of an emotionally "close-binding" mother and a "detached–hostile" father. A boy reared in such a family may come to identify with his mother and even to "transform himself into her" (Freud, 1922/1959, p. 40). He may thus become effeminate and develop sexual interests in men.

Freud believed that unresolved **castration anxiety** plays a role in a gay male sexual orientation. By the time the Oedipus complex takes effect, the boy will have learned from self-stimulation that he can obtain sexual pleasure from his penis. In his youthful fantasies, he associates this pleasure with mental images of his mother. Similarly, he is likely to have learned that females do not possess a penis. Somewhere along the line, the psychoanalyst theorizes that the boy may also have been warned that his penis will be removed if he plays with himself. From all this, the boy may surmise that females—including his mother—once had penises, but that they were removed.

During the throes of the Oedipus complex, the boy unconsciously comes to fear that his father, his rival in love for the mother, will retaliate by removing the organ that the boy has come to associate with sexual pleasure. His fear causes him to repress his sexual desire for his mother and to identify with the potential aggressor—his father. The boy thus overcomes his castration anxiety and is headed along the path of adult heterosexuality.

If the Oedipus complex is not successfully resolved, castration anxiety may persist. When sexually mature, the man will not be able to tolerate sex with women. Their lack of a penis will arouse unconscious castration anxiety within himself.

The Electra complex in little girls follows a somewhat different course. Freud believed that little girls become envious of boys' penises, because they lack their own. Jealousy leads little girls to resent their mothers, whom they blame for their anatomic "deficiency," and to turn from their mothers to their fathers as sexual objects. They now desire to possess the father, because the father's penis provides what they lack. But incestuous desires bring the girl into competition with her mother. Motivated by fear that her mother will withdraw her love if the desires persist, the girl normally represses them and identifies with her mother. She supplants her childhood desire for

Castration anxiety In psychoanalytic theory, a man's fear that his genitals will be removed; an element of the Oedipus complex, implicated in the directionality of erotic interests

a penis with a desire to marry a man and bear children. The baby, emitted from between her legs, serves as the ultimate penis substitute.

A nagging problem for Freudian theory is that many of its concepts, such as castration anxiety and penis envy, are believed to operate at an unconscious level. As such, they lie beyond the scope of scientific observation and measurement. Moreover, as pointed out by Friedman and Downey (2001), viewing childhood sexuality from the vantage point of adulthood, as happens in psychoanalysis, can provide a distorted view of what really took place—especially when the analyst is motivated to find support for his or her theory. **Truth or Fiction Revisited:** Therefore, the idea that castration anxiety in gay males is aroused by knowledge of male–female intercourse has not been scientifically demonstrated.

Research evidence provides another perspective on the issue of family relationships and gay sons. Richard Pillard and his colleagues (Pillard, 1990; Pillard & Weinrich, 1986) found that gay males described themselves as more distant from their fathers during childhood than did heterosexual control subjects or the gay men's own heterosexual brothers. The gay men in their sample also reported greater closeness to their mothers. Still, the father's psychological distance from the son may have reflected the *son's* alienation from him, not the reverse. That is, the son may have been so attached to his mother, or so uninterested in traditional masculine activities, that he rebuffed paternal attempts to engage him in conventional father–son activities.

LEARNING THEORIES   Learning theorists agree with Freud that early experiences play an important role in the development of sexual orientation. They focus on the role of reinforcement of early patterns of sexual behavior, however, rather than on the resolution of unconscious conflicts. People generally repeat pleasurable activities and discontinue painful ones. Thus, people may learn to engage in sexual activity with people of their own sex if childhood sexual experimentation with them is connected with sexual pleasure.

If sexual motivation is high, as it tends to be during adolescence, and the only outlets are with others of one's own sex, adolescents may experiment sexually with them. If these encounters are pleasurable, and heterosexual experiences are unpleasant, a firmer gay male or lesbian sexual orientation may develop (Gagnon & Simon, 1973). Conversely, pain, anxiety, or social disapproval may be connected with early contacts with people of one's own sex. In such cases, the child may learn to inhibit feelings of attraction to people of one's own sex and develop a firmer heterosexual orientation.

Although learning may play a role in the development of a gay male or lesbian sexual orientation, learning theorists have not identified specific learning experiences that would lead to these orientations. Moreover, most adolescent encounters with people of the same sex, even if pleasurable, do not lead to an adult gay male or lesbian sexual orientation. Many heterosexual people have had adolescent encounters with members of their own sex without swaying their adult orientations. This is true even of people whose early sexual interactions with the other sex were fumbling and frustrating. Moreover, the overwhelming majority of gay males and lesbians were aware of sexual interest in people of their own sex *before* they had sexual encounters with them, pleasurable or otherwise (Bell et al., 1981; Savin–Williams & Diamond, 2000).

Gender Nonconformity

Gender nonconformity means not behaving in a way that is consistent with the gender-role stereotype associated with one's anatomic sex in a given culture. On average, gay males tend to be somewhat feminine and lesbians to be somewhat masculine, but there is a good deal of variation within each group (Bailey, 2003; Dawood et al., 2000). Thus it seems that stereotypes of the effeminate gay male and the masculine lesbian are exaggerated. Gender nonconformity begins in childhood. Gay males and lesbians are more likely than heterosexuals to report childhood behavior stereotypical of the other sex (Bailey & Zucker, 1995; Singh et al., 1999). Many gay males and lesbians recall acting and feeling "different" from their childhood peers. Many gay males from a variety of groups, such as prisoners, psychiatric patients, and members of gay rights organizations report that they avoided participating in competitive sports as children, were more fearful of physical injury, and were more likely to avoid getting into fights than heterosexual males (Dawood et al., 2000). Some gay males recall feeling different as young as three or four years of age—a feeling that was related to behavior that is stereotypical of the other sex.

Gay males are also more likely to recall feeling more sensitive than their heterosexual peers during childhood (Isay, 1990). They cried more easily. Their feelings were more readily hurt. They had more artistic interests. They had fewer male buddies but more female playmates. Gay males were more likely than their heterosexual counterparts to have preferred "girls' toys." They preferred playing with girls to playing with trucks or guns, or engaging in rough-and-tumble play (Dawood et al., 2000). Their preferences often led to their being called "sissies." Gay men also recall more crossdressing during childhood. They preferred the company of older women to older men and engaged in childhood sex play with other boys rather than with girls.

SafeZone

Q *Can parents know if their child will be homosexual by a certain age? Are there attributes they should look for?*

A Children who become gay or lesbian often but not always show gender nonconformity. That is, the boy may not be very interested in sports. The girl may not want to play with dolls. A word to the wise parent: Pushing sports and dolls on a child will not affect his or her sexual orientation. It might make him or her miserable if he or she wants something else.

GENDER NONCONFORMITY AND THE BUTCH–FEMME DIMENSION There is also evidence of masculine-type behavior among lesbians as children (Bailey & Zucker, 1995). Lesbians as a group were more likely than heterosexual women to perceive themselves as having been "tomboys." They were more likely to prefer rough-and-tumble games than playing with dolls, and they enjoyed wearing boy's clothing rather than "cutesy" dresses.

A study by Devendra Singh and colleagues (1999) relates gender nonconformity in lesbians to the butch–femme dimension and biological factors. The investigators compared self-identified butch and femme lesbians on various personality, behavioral, and biological measures. They found that butch lesbians were significantly more likely than femme lesbians to recall gender-atypical behavioral preferences during childhood. Butch lesbians also had higher waist-to-hip ratios and higher testosterone levels in their saliva, both of which are more typical of males. The Singh group suggests that their findings support the validity of the butch–femme distinction and that the distinction may be caused by differences in exposure to prenatal androgens (male sex hormones).

CHILDHOOD EFFEMINACY AND A GAY MALE SEXUAL ORIEN-TATION How might extreme childhood effeminacy lead to a gay male sexual orientation? Those who support an environmental view speculate that the social detachment of these boys from male peers and role models (especially fathers) creates strong, unfulfilled cravings for male affection. This craving then leads them to seek males as partners in sex and love relationships in adolescence and adulthood. Alan Bell of the Kinsey Institute believes that self-perceptions of differentness and social distance from other males during childhood lead these boys to develop erotic attractions that differ from those of other boys. These are erotic attractions toward members of their own sex.

Of course, there is another possibility, as suggested by research by J. Michael Bailey and his colleagues (Bailey et al., 2000a; Dawood et al., 2000a): Gender nonconformity appears to be somewhat heritable. Moreover, if a tendency toward homosexuality is inherited, gender nonconformity could also be an expression of that tendency.

All in all, the origins of a gay male or lesbian sexual orientation remain mysterious and complex, just as mysterious as the origins of heterosexuality. In reviewing theories and research, we are left with the impression that sexual orientation is unlikely to have a single cause. Sexual orientation appears to spring from multiple origins, including biological and psychosocial factors. Genetic and biochemical factors (such as hormone levels) may affect the prenatal organization of the brain. These factors may predispose people to a certain sexual orientation, but it may be that early socialization experiences are also required to give rise to a gay male, lesbian, heterosexual, or bisexual sexual orientation. The precise influences and interactions of these factors have so far eluded researchers.

Adjustment of Gay Males and Lesbians

Are homosexuals more likely than heterosexuals to suffer from mental disorders? Recent carefully controlled studies have found that gay males and lesbians are more likely than heterosexuals to experience feelings of anxiety and depression, and they are more prone to suicide (Cochran et al., 2003; de Graaf et al., 2006; Ferguson et al., 2005; Meyer, 2003). Gay males, moreover, are more likely to have eating disorders (anorexia nervosa and bulimia nervosa) than heterosexual males (Ferguson et al., 1999).

Many observers have reviewed the issues surrounding the origins and correlates of adjustment issues and homosexuality, and they all allow for the possibility that societal oppression might cause the greater incidence of depression and suicidality we find among gay males and lesbians. "Surely," writes psychologist J. Michal Bailey (1999), "it must be difficult for young people to come to grips with their homosexuality in a world where homosexual people are often scorned, mocked, mourned, and feared." Even de Graaf and colleagues (2006), who write about gay males in the generally tolerant Dutch population, admit that many gays there *perceive* there to be some social stigmatization.

There are also connections between lifestyle and health—physical and psychological—among gay males and lesbians, and among heterosexual people. Gay men and lesbians occupy all socioeconomic and vocational levels and follow a variety of lifestyles. In their classic research, Bell and Weinberg (1978) found variations in adjustment in the gay community that seem to mirror the variations in the heterosexual community. Gay people who lived with partners in stable, intimate relationships—so-called close couples—were about as well adjusted as married heterosexual couples. Older gay people who lived alone and had few sexual contacts were more poorly adjusted. So, too, are many heterosexual people who have similar lifestyles. All in all, Bell and Weinberg found that differences in adjustment were more likely to reflect the lifestyle of the individual rather than his or her sexual orientation.

Most gay males and lesbians who share close relationships with their partners are satisfied with the quality of their relationships. Researchers have found that heterosexual and gay couples report similar levels of satisfaction with their relationships (Kurdek, 2005). Gay males and lesbians in enduring relationships generally report high levels of love, attachment, closeness, caring, and intimacy.

As with heterosexual people, not all the relationships of gay people are satisfying. Among both groups, satisfaction is higher when both partners feel that the benefits they receive from the relationship outweigh the costs (Veniegas & Peplau, 1997). Like heterosexual people, gay men and lesbians are happier in relationships in which they share power and make joint decisions (Veniegas & Peplau, 1997).

Homophobia

In 2006, Jacob Robida, 18, entered a gay bar in New Bedford, Massachusetts, with a hatchet and a handgun beneath his clothing. He would soon be charged with three counts of assault with intent to murder, assault with a dangerous weapon, and hate crimes.

Robida entered the Puzzles Lounge at midnight and ordered a shot of liquor. Then he asked the bartender whether the lounge was intended for gay or straight patrons. The bartender told Robida that Puzzles was usually patronized by gays. Robida had another shot of liquor and then pulled out the hatchet and struck a patron in the head. He also struck a man who tried to help the first victim. Robida next pulled out the gun out and shot the man who tried to help the first hatchet victim. Before fleeing, he shot another man across the bar.

A bartender at Puzzles Lounge, right, is consoled by a friend after the homophobic assaults by Jacob Robida.

Robida had also aimed the gun at the bartender, but it failed to fire. "I heard a click, and his eyes were just squinted," the bartender told a reporter (Zezima, 2006).

Before it was all over, Robida would shoot a police officer to death at a traffic stop. He is also believed to have killed a woman in West Virginia. He was finally felled during a shootout with Arkansas police officers (Belluck, 2006).

Robida's hatred of gay males was an extreme example of **homophobia**, but certainly not the only one. Homophobia is clearly the greatest challenge to the adjustment of gay males and lesbians. Homophobia takes many forms, including

- use of derogatory names (such as *queer, faggot,* and *dyke*)
- telling disparaging "queer jokes"
- barring gay people from housing, employment, or social opportunities
- taunting (verbal abuse)
- **gay bashing** (physical, sometimes lethal, abuse)

Homophobia derives from root words meaning "fear of homosexuals." Although some psychologists link homophobia to fears of a gay male or lesbian sexual orientation within oneself, homophobic attitudes may also be embedded within a cluster of stereotypical gender-role attitudes toward family life (Cotten–Huston & Waite, 2000). These attitudes support male dominance and the belief that it is natural and appropriate for women to sacrifice for their husbands and children (Cotten–Huston & Waite, 2000). People who have a strong stake in maintaining stereotypical gender roles may feel more readily threatened by homosexuals, because gay people appear to confuse or reverse these roles. Men have more of a stake in maintaining the tradition of male dominance, so perhaps it is not surprising that college men are more intolerant of gay males than college women (Schellenberg et al., 1999).

Homophobic attitudes are more common among males who identify with a traditional male gender role, a conservative political orientation (Cotton–Huston & Waite, 2000), those who hold a fundamentalist religious orientation (Davies, 2004), and those who identify with Nazi beliefs and regalia (Zezima, 2006). But those who actually engage in violence against gay males, and especially those who kill, tend to be criminal psychopaths (Parrot et al., 2006). That is, they are in frequent conflict with the law and feel neither guilt nor shame when they cause others pain (Parrott et al., 2006).

Some homophobic men may have homoerotic impulses of which they are unaware. Denial of these impulses may be connected with their fear and disapproval of gay males. Henry Adams and his colleagues (1996) showed men sexually explicit videotapes of male–female, female–female, and male–male sexual activity and measured their sexual response by means of the penile plethysmograph. The plethysmograph measures size of erection. Subjects were also asked to report how sexually aroused they felt in response to the videos. The men were also evaluated for their attitudes toward gay males. Men who were not homophobic were sexually aroused, according to their penile circumference, only by videos of male–female and female–female sexual activity. The homophobic viewers were also aroused in terms of penile circumference by the video of male–male sexual activity. However, the homophobic men also reported that they did not *feel* aroused by the male–male sexual activity. Were they out of touch with their biological response or was their biological response misleading?

Although strides toward social acceptance of gay people have been made since Kinsey's day, the advent of HIV/AIDS has added fuel to the fire of homophobia (Herek et al., 2005). When HIV/AIDS first appeared, it primarily struck the gay male community. Some homophobes in the larger society believed that the epidemic was

Homophobia A cluster of negative attitudes and feelings toward gay people, including intolerance, hatred, and fear; from Greek roots meaning "fear" [of members of the] "same" [sex]

Gay bashing Violence against homosexuals

a God-sent plague intended to punish gay people for sinful behavior. Perhaps the epidemic serves as a pretext for some people to attack gay males, whom they blame for spreading the disease.

"Treatment" of Gay Male and Lesbian Sexual Orientations

Most gay men and lesbians see their sexual orientation as an integral part of their personal identity. Bell and Weinberg (1978) found only a few gay people who were interested in changing their sexual orientation—even if a "magic pill" were available to bring about the change (Table 10.5). Only a minority of their sample had *ever* considered discontinuing male–male or female–female sexual activity.

A few gay males and lesbians do express an interest in changing their orientations, however, for such reasons as religious beliefs or the desire to create a typical family life (Haldeman, 2002; Rosik, 2003). But because doing so is relatively rare, many helping professionals believe that gay males and lesbians would not wish to change their sexual orientation if it were not for social pressure and prejudice. Green (2003) adds that most gay people who seek to change their sexual orientation are ambivalent. Haldeman (2002) notes that the very existence of "conversion therapy" contributes to the social devaluation of homosexuals and bisexuals. The controversy continues.

Nonetheless, a few therapists have reported changing the sexual orientations of some individuals. Among the best known of these, Masters and Johnson (1979) used methods that treat sexual dysfunctions to "reverse" clients' gay male or lesbian sexual orientations. For example, they involved gay males in a graded series of pleasurable activities with women, such as massage and genital stimulation. Masters and Johnson (1979) reported a failure rate of 20% for the gay men and 23% for the lesbians they treated in their therapy program. At a five-year follow-up, more than 70% of the clients continued to engage in male–female sexual activity (Schwartz & Masters, 1984). For many reasons, however, these patients do not seem to represent the general gay population:

- Most of them were bisexuals. Only about one in five engaged exclusively in male–male or female–female sexual activities.
- More than half were married.
- All were highly motivated to switch their sexual orientations.

TABLE 10.5

Percentages of Gay People Who Wish They Had Received a "Magic Heterosexuality Pill" at Birth or Could Receive One Today

	European American males	African American males	European American females	African American females
Desire magic pill at birth	28	23	16	11
Desire magic pill today	14	13	5	6

Regardless of these people's changes in sexual behavior, remember that sexual behavior is *not* the equivalent of sexual orientation (Bhugra, 2004). There is no evidence that Masters and Johnson changed their clients' sexual *orientation*. On the other hand, psychiatrist Robert Spitzer addressed the American Psychiatric Association in 2001, informing them of interviews with some 200 men and women who said that they had experienced a significant shift from homoerotic to heteroerotic attraction and sustained the change for five years. The issue regarding whether exclusively gay people can change their sexual orientation, rather than their behavior, remains hotly debated.

Coming Out: Coming to Terms with Being Gay

Because of the backdrop of social condemnation and discrimination, gay males and lesbians in our culture often struggle to come to terms with their sexual orientation. Homosexuals usually speak of the process of accepting their sexual orientation as "coming out" or as "coming out of the closet." Coming out is a two-pronged process: coming out to oneself (recognizing one's sexual orientation) and coming out to others (declaring one's orientation to the world). Coming out can create a sense of pride in one's sexual orientation and foster the ability to form emotionally and sexually satisfying relationships with gay male or lesbian partners.

Coming Out to Oneself

Many gay people have a difficult time coming to recognize, let alone accept, their sexual orientation:

> Youths with emerging identities that are gay, lesbian, or bisexual, living in generally hostile climates, face particular dilemmas. They are well aware that in many secondary schools the words "fag" and "dyke" are terms of denigration and that anyone who is openly gay, lesbian, or bisexual is open to social exclusion and psychological and physical persecution. Some of their families too will express negative feelings about people who are gay, lesbian, or bisexual; youths in such families may be victimized if they disclose that they are not heterosexual. (Bagley & D'Augelli, 2000)

According to Ritch Savin–Williams and Lisa Diamond (2000), the development of sexual identity in gay males and lesbians involves four steps or features: attraction to members of the same sex, self-labeling as gay or lesbian, sexual contact with members of the same sex, and disclosure of one's sexual orientation to other people. The researchers by and large found a 10-year gap between initial attraction to members of one's own sex, which tended to occur at about the age of eight or nine, and disclosure of one's orientation to other people, which usually occurred at about age 18. Females were more likely to focus on the emotional or romantic aspects of their budding feelings. Males were more likely to focus on the sexual aspects. Males—who are generally more open than females to sexual experimentation—were likely to become involved in sexual activity with other males before they labeled themselves as being gay. Females, on the other hand, were more likely to label themselves as lesbians before pursuing relationships with other females.

For some people, coming to recognize and accept a gay male or lesbian sexual orientation involves gradually stripping away layers of denial. For others it may be a

4 Steps

Coming out to one's parents can be a scary thing, and many lesbians and gay males avoid it for years, or even for a lifetime. On the other hand, some parents have suspected or known about their children's sexual orientation for quite some time, and even though they may have initially had deep concerns, they may be more accepting than the "children" (who may already be in their thirties or forties) expect.

CRITICAL
Thinking

How do you account for the sex differences in the processes of coming out in males and females?

REFLECT

Do you know anyone who "came out"? Was it a surprise? How did people react? Did you learn anything about people from observing the process?

sudden awakening. Long-standing sexual interests in members of one's own sex may rush into focus on a particular person, as happened with a graduate student named David:

> In college [David's] closest friend was gay. Although this friend had wanted to have sex with David and the attraction was mutual, David still could not associate this attraction with a sexuality that was not acceptable to him. In his first year of graduate school, when he was about 23, he fell in love and then suddenly and with a great sense of relief recognized and acknowledged to himself that he was homosexual. He then had sex for the first time and has subsequently been . . . open about his sexuality. (Isay, 1990, p. 295)

Coming Out to Others

There are different patterns of coming out to others. Coming out occasionally means an open declaration to the world. More often a person may inform only one or a few select people. The person might tell friends but not family members.

Many gay men and lesbians remain reluctant to declare their sexual orientation, even to friends and family. Disclosure is fraught with the risk of loss of jobs, friendships, and social standing (Bagley & D'Augelli, 2000; Griffith & Hebl, 2002). On the other hand, if the organization at which the individual works is generally supportive of gays, coming out can be related to greater job satisfaction and less anxiety (Griffith & Hebl, 2002).

Gay men and lesbians often anticipate negative reactions from informing family members, including denial, anger, and rejection (Bagley & D'Augelli, 2000). Family members and loved ones may refuse to hear or be unwilling to accept reality, as Martha Barron Barrett (1990) notes in her book *Invisible Lives*, which chronicles the lives of a sample of lesbians in the United States:

> Parents, children, neighbors, and friends of lesbians deny, or compartmentalize, or struggle with their knowledge in the same way the women themselves do. "My parents know I've lived with my partner for six years. She goes home with me. We sleep in the same bed there. The word *lesbian* has never been mentioned." "I told my mother and she said, 'Well, now that's over with. We don't need to mention it again.' She never has, and that was ten years ago. I don't know if she ever told my father." A husband may dismiss it as "just a phase," a boyfriend may interpret it as a sexual tease, a straight woman may believe "she's just saying that because she couldn't get a man."
>
> The strong message is, "Keep it quiet." Many lesbians do that by becoming invisible. . . . They [lesbians] leave their lesbian persona at home when they go to work on Monday morning. On Friday they don it again. That weekend at home, the flip side of the double life, is what most of heterosexual society never sees. (Barrett, 1990, p. 52)

Some families are more accepting. They may have had suspicions and prepared themselves for such news (Aveline, 2006). Other families are initially rejecting but eventually come to at least grudging acceptance that a family member is gay.

What Is the Sexual Orientation of These Soldiers? *During Bill Clinton's presidency, a "Don't Ask, Don't Tell" policy was adopted toward gay people in the military. If they divulge their sexual orientation, they may be removed from the military, but superiors are not allowed to ask them about it.*

Gay Lifestyles

There is a tendency to treat gay people as if they were all the same. According to Bell and Weinberg (1978), gay people do not adopt a single, stereotypical lifestyle. Variations in sexual expression exist within and across sexual orientations.

Gay men and lesbians in larger U.S. urban centers can usually look to gay communal structures to provide services and support. These include gay rights organizations and gay-oriented newspapers, magazines, bookstores, housing cooperatives, medical services, and other support services. The gay community provides a sense of acceptance and belonging that gay people usually do not find in society at large.

Restrictions on gay people serving in the armed services has been a continuing controversy. In 1993, President Clinton encountered opposition when he sought to follow through on his campaign pledge to permit gay men and women to serve openly in the military. As a compromise measure, he instituted a "Don't Ask, Don't Tell" policy. It permits gay males and lesbians to serve as long as they do not publicly express or reveal their sexual orientation. Moreover, military officials are prohibited from inquiring about the sexual orientation of recruits.

Gay rights organizations fight for rights for gay people to participate fully in society—to teach in public schools, to adopt children, to live together in sanctioned relationships, and to serve openly and proudly in the military. Cafés and social clubs provide places where gay men and lesbians can socialize and be open about their sexual orientations.

Not all gay people feel a part of the "gay community" or participate in gay rights organizations, however. For many, their sexual orientation is a part of their identity, but not a dominant theme that governs their social and political activities.

Q *Are there studies that show the effects of being raised by homosexual parents?*

A Loads of them, and they do not show that having one or two gay parents affects a child's sexual orientation. Children of gay parents do develop more egalitarian attitudes; that is, they are less fixated on the tunnel vision of traditional gender-role stereotypes.

Lifestyle Differences between Gay Males and Lesbians

Researchers have consistently found that gay males are more likely than lesbians to engage in casual sex with many partners. Lesbians more often confine their sexual activity to a committed, affectionate relationship (LaSala, 2004; Walther & Poston, 2004). In their classic research, Bell and Weinberg (1978) reported that 84% of gay males, compared with about 7% of lesbian women, report having more than 50 partners in their lifetimes. Seventy-nine percent of gay males in their study, compared with only 6% of lesbians, reported that more than half their partners were strangers.

A Lesbian Couple and Their Child. *Many gay couples, such as this one, have children. Sometimes the children derive from earlier marriages. Sometimes they are adopted. Some lesbians are artificially inseminated or else engage in sexual intercourse for the purpose of becoming pregnant. And then again . . . in 2004, as reported in the journal* Nature *(vol. 428, pp. 860–864), Japanese researcher Tomohiro Kono and his colleagues actually created mice from the genetic material of two mothers. The name of the article is a bit bland, considering the subject matter: "Birth of parthenogenetic mice that can develop to adulthood." The article leads to speculation regarding whether a day may come when two dads or two moms can actually have children who share their genetic material.*

Even gay males within committed relationships have more permissive attitudes toward extracurricular sexual activity than lesbians do (Blumstein & Schwartz, 1990; Peplau & Cochran, 1990).

Traditionally, the gay bar was an arena for making sexual contacts. The word *cruising* means searching for a sex partner, principally for casual sex. One can "cruise," and one can "be cruised." Gay males were more likely than lesbians to cruise in public places, like gay bars. Lesbians were more likely to find partners among friends, at work, and at informal social gatherings.

Today, with the threat of being infected with HIV hanging over every casual sexual encounter, many gay bathhouses, long a setting for casual sexual contacts, have closed. In the early days of the HIV/AIDS epidemic, when being infected with HIV was a death sentence, many gay males became more likely to avoid unprotected anal and oral sex, especially with new partners. However, the advent of HAART (see Chapter 16) has apparently led some gays, as some heterosexuals, to throw caution to the winds once more and have unprotected sex with multiple partners (Katz et al., 2002; Ostrow et al., 2002; Poppen et al., 2005).

Research also shows that extracurricular sexual activity is common among gay male couples. One study surveyed 943 gay males and 1,510 married heterosexual males who had been living with a partner for 2 to 10 years. Four of five (79%) of the gay males reported sex with another partner during the preceding year, compared with only 11% of the heterosexual males (Blumstein & Schwartz, 1990). Among couples who had been together for longer than 10 years, 94% of gay men reported extracurricular activity at some time during the relationship. Many gay men who "stray" separate sex from intimacy in their minds (LaSala, 2004).

CRITICAL Thinking

How do you account for the sex differences in the lifestyle preferences of gay males and lesbians?

Variations in Gay Lifestyles

Bell and Weinberg (1978) found that about three out of four gay couples they studied could be classified according to one of five lifestyles: *close couples, open couples, functionals, dysfunctionals,* and *asexuals.* **Truth or Fiction Revisited:** It is true that many gay couples have lifestyles similar to those of married heterosexual couples and are as well adjusted. They are referred to as *close couples* by Bell and Weinberg (1978). Close couples evidenced deep emotional commitment and few outside sexual relationships. Almost three times as many lesbians (28%) as gay males (10%) lived in such committed, intimate relationships. Gay people living in close relationships showed fewer social and psychological problems than those with any other lifestyle.

TRUTH fiction 6

Open couples lived together but engaged in clandestine affairs. Gay people in open couples were not as well adjusted as those in close couples. Nevertheless, their overall adjustment was similar to that of heterosexual people. Still other gay people lived alone and had sexual contacts with numerous partners—a kind of "swinging singles" gay lifestyle. Some of those who lived alone—functionals—appeared to have adapted well to their swinging lifestyle and were sociable and well adjusted. Others—dysfunctionals—had sexual, social, or psychological problems. Dysfunctionals were often anxious, unhappy, and found it difficult to form intimate relationships. Asexuals lived alone and had few sexual contacts. Asexuals tended to be older than other groups.

Homosexuals, like heterosexuals, have many different styles of life. Things are no simpler in the gay world than in the straight world. And the reasons that some people are homosexual remain no clearer than the reasons that most people are heterosexual.

REFLECT

What did you learn about gay males and lesbians from this chapter? What misinformation was corrected? What was completely new to you?

A Closer Look

MANY COUPLES MUST NEGOTIATE TERMS OF "BROKEBACK" MARRIAGES

One hour into *Brokeback Mountain,* Amy Jo Remmele began to cry, and not just for the woman on screen, standing in a doorway in Riverton, Wyoming, watching her husband embrace a man. "When I saw that look in her eyes, I thought, 'Oh, yeah.' Even though I never saw my husband with another man, I knew exactly how that woman would have felt," said Mrs. Remmele, a respiratory therapist in rural Minnesota.

On June 1, 2000, Mrs. Remmele, then 31, discovered her husband's profile on the website www.gay.com. The couple stayed up all that night weeping and talking. Soon afterward, 10 days before she gave birth to her second child, Mrs. Remmele's husband went off to spend a couple of nights with his new boyfriend. "I tried to talk him out of it, and he left anyway," Mrs. Remmele said. "I was devastated." Three months later, the couple divorced.

Mrs. Remmele—now married to a farmer who raises cattle, corn, and soybeans—is one of an estimated 1.7 million to 3.4 million American women who once were or are now married to men who have sex with men. The estimate derives from "The Social Organization of Sexuality," a 1990 study that found that 3.9% of American men who had ever been married had had sex with men in the previous five years. The lead author, Edward O. Laumann, a sociol-

ogist at the University of Chicago, estimated that 2% to 4% of ever-married American women had knowingly or unknowingly been in what are now called mixed-orientation marriages.

Such marriages are not just artifacts of the closeted 1950s. In the 16th century, Queen Anne of Denmark had eight children with King James I of England, known not only for the King James Bible, but also for his devotion to male favorites, one of whom he called "my sweet child and wife."

Other women include Constance Wilde, Phyllis Gates, Linda Porter, Renata Blauel, and Dina Matos McGreevey, wed respectively to Oscar Wilde, Rock Hudson, Cole Porter, Elton John and James E. McGreevey, the former governor of New Jersey. Although precise numbers are impossible to come by, 10,000 to 20,000 such wives have contacted online support groups, and increasing numbers of them are women in their 20s or 30s.

On the whole these are not marriages of convenience or cynical efforts to create cover. Gay and bisexual men continue to marry for complex reasons, many impelled not only by discrimination, but also by wishful thinking, the layered ambiguities of sexual love, and authentic affection. "These men genuinely love their wives," said Joe Kort, a clinical social worker in Royal Oak, Michigan, who has counseled hundreds of gay married men, including a minor-

ity who stay in their marriages. Many, he said, considered themselves heterosexual men with homosexual urges that they hoped to confine to private fantasy life. "They fall in love with their wives, they have children, they're on a chemical, romantic high, and then after about seven years, the high falls away and their gay identity starts emerging," Mr. Kort said. "They don't mean any harm."

Helen Fisher, a research anthropologist at Rutgers University, said in an interview that human partnerships are shaped by three independent neurochemical brain–body systems, responsible respectively for sexual attraction, romantic yearning and long-term attachment. "The three systems are very fickle. They can act together, or they can act separately," Dr. Fisher said. This, she said, helps explain why people can be wildly sexually attracted to those they have no romantic interest in, and be romantically drawn to—or permanently attached to—people who hold no sexual interest. "Once the system is triggered, it's so chemically powerful that you can easily overlook everything about that person that doesn't work for you," Dr. Fisher said. "Even straight people have fallen in love with people they could never make a life with," she said.

This is cold comfort to women who lose not only the men they love, but also their faith in how to parse reality. "A lot of women feel that they were just used as covers, but I know in my heart of hearts he loved me," Mrs. Remmele said. "You can't fake the way he used to look at me. I had no suspicions whatsoever. He's very masculine looking. It's not like he had Barbra Streisand or show tunes on."

In the months after the discovery, Mrs. Remmele said, her husband left her alone with the baby on many evenings as he explored desires he had never dared to acknowledge. "So many of the gay spouses, they've denied themselves for so long, and it's like they're going through teenage-hood,"

Mrs. Remmele said. "I don't know if they really realize how much they're hurting their spouse."

At first, Mrs. Remmele told nobody. "We live in a small rural community, and people just aren't openly gay here," she said. "I didn't want people making fun of him."

About two thirds of the women who contact the International Straight Spouse Network in El Cerrito, California, eventually divorce, said Amity Pierce Buxton, 77, a retired school administrator who founded the group. Despite their shock and their anger, many women, especially those criticized by gay husbands for being too sexually demanding, are relieved to understand what was wrong. The remaining third of those she has studied try to preserve their marriages, Dr. Buxton said. Half of those stay married for three years or more. More than 600 such couples belong to online support groups.

In a 2001 study published in *The Journal of Bisexuality*, of 137 still-married gay and bisexual men and their wives, Dr. Buxton found that most lived in suburbs and medium-size cities and had been married for 11 to 30 years. Only tiny percentages lived in rural areas, where family privacy may be harder to maintain. The survival of even a small minority of these marriages calls into question the conceptual shoe boxes into which human partnerships, affection, attraction, commitment, and sexuality are often jammed. Describing their permutations and combinations turns out to be much more complicated than checking a box on a form labeled "gay," "bisexual" or "straight."

One woman in her 50s, who asked to be identified only as Trillian, out of concern for her husband's privacy, said that she and her husband formally divorced after she discovered his secret sexual life seven years ago, but they quickly decided to stay together. She has a satisfying monogamous sexual relationship with him, although he also has sex with men. "He tried to go back in the closet, but the more research I

Former Governor James McGreevey of New Jersey and His Former Wife and Their Daughter. *When McGreevey resigned from office, he announced that he was a "gay American." However, his suggestion that he was forced to resign because of his sexual orientation was an embarrassment to gays. The fact of the matter is that he was compelled to resign because he had appointed a totally unqualified gay lover to a high government post.*

did on the subject, the more I realized this is an integral part of the person," she said. "You can't just turn it off like a light switch. My husband is the man of my dreams, and I could not face the rest of my life with the man of my dreams being miserable and guilt ridden over being gay."

Paulette Cormack, a teacher who lives in Napa, California, has been married to her husband, Jerry, a retired city planner, for 36 years. For 34 years, Mrs. Cormack said in an interview, she has known that although she and her husband are sexually active together, his erotic desires otherwise focus almost exclusively on men. "It's not easy, but I truly do love him," Mrs. Cormack said. Mr. Cormack is now involved with another married gay man, and Mrs. Cor-

mack has had extramarital relationships. Neither has explicitly discussed this with their son, who is 25.

They remain intensely committed to each other. Last year Mr. Cormack nursed Mrs. Cormack through four months of treatments for cancer of the fallopian tubes. She eventually made a full recovery. "What is intimacy?" pondered Mr. Cormack, as the couple sat in a coffeehouse in Berkeley, California, after watching *Brokeback Mountain* with others in similar situations. He added: "I am totally committed on all levels to Paulette. I felt so intimate with her when I was caring for her during her cancer treatments—to me, that's a stronger expression of love than whether I'm having anonymous sex with a man."

1. What kinds of sexual orientation are there?

- Sexual orientation describes the directionality of one's sexual and romantic interests. Heterosexuals are attracted to members of the other sex. Homosexuals are attracted to members of the same sex. Bisexuals are attracted to both males and females.

- Most homosexuals are content with their anatomic sex. Some extremely feminine gay males may wish to have the body of a woman.

- There are questions regarding whether heteroeroticism and homoeroticism are opposite poles of a single dimension or independent dimensions. Researchers find that men tend to be bipolar in their erotic interests, but for women, heterosexuality and homosexuality may be independent dimensions.

- The best evidence we have suggests that about 3% of American males are exclusively gay, and about 2% of American women are exclusively lesbian.

2. How has homosexuality been viewed historically and scientifically?

- The Judeo-Christian and Islamic traditions frown on homosexuality and other forms of nonprocreative sex. In ancient Greece, men often had sexual relationships with adolescent males.

- Most Americans are growing more tolerant of homosexuals. Most oppose gay marriage but would grant gay people equal rights to jobs and housing.

- Men are more likely than women to be homophobic. The HIV/AIDS epidemic has contributed to homophobia and gay bashing.

- Sodomy laws have been enforced against gay males more often than male–female couples.

- Research with MZ and DZ twins suggests a role for genetic factors in the development of sexual orientation.

Prenatal sex hormones are also believed to play a role; female embryos exposed to androgens tend to develop more masculine behavior patterns. Butch lesbians appear to have higher saliva levels of testosterone than femme lesbians.

- It is unclear whether gay males have distant relationships with their fathers and close-binding mothers. Early sexual experience does not appear to sway sexual orientation.

- Many homosexuals showed gender nonconformity during childhood. Many gay males were effeminate, and many lesbians were tomboys.

3. What do we know about the adjustment of homosexuals?

- Homosexuals are more likely than heterosexuals to encounter anxiety and depression and to have suicidal thoughts, possibly because of social prejudice. Most professionals agree that homosexuals who seek to change their sexual orientation are influenced by social prejudice.

4. What is "coming out"?

- Coming out to oneself is a gradual process during which the individual eventually comes to accept his or her homosexual orientation. Coming out to others is, for many, an anxiety-evoking process characterized by fear of social disapproval, loss of a job, and the like.

5. What kinds of lifestyles are adopted by gay people?

- Gay people adopt a variety of lifestyles. Lesbians tend to form deep romantic attachments and committed relationships; gay males are relatively more likely to seek multiple partners. "Close couples" of either sex form committed, exclusive relationships.

1. _____ are sexually attracted to both males and females.

   (a) Homosexuals
   (b) Heterosexuals
   (c) Bisexuals
   (d) Intersexuals

2. In ancient _____, men frequently formed sexual relationships with adolescent males.

   (a) Egypt
   (b) Greece
   (c) Rome
   (d) Macedonia

3. _____ are most likely to share a homosexual orientation.

   (a) Monozygotic twins
   (b) Dizygotic twins
   (c) Parents and their biological children
   (d) Adoptive parents and their adopted children

4. Psychoanalytic theory ties male homosexuality to faulty resolution of the _____ complex.

   (a) inferiority
   (b) Electra
   (c) whore–madonna
   (d) Oedipus

5. A Swedish study found that the hypothalamus of gay males responds similarly to that of _____ when gay males are presented with the odor of a testosterone derivative.

   (a) heterosexual men
   (b) heterosexual women
   (c) lesbians
   (d) bisexuals

6. Homosexuals differ from transsexuals in that homosexuals

   (a) are generally satisfied with their anatomic sex
   (b) are generally dissatisfied with their anatomic sex
   (c) are confused about their gender identity
   (d) seek therapy to change their sexual orientation

7. Which of the following is true about the lifestyles of gay males and lesbians?

   (a) Gay males are more interested in having children.
   (b) Gay males are more likely to form deep, romantic attachments.
   (c) Only lesbians show gender nonconformity in childhood.
   (d) Gay males are more likely to have multiple sex partners.

8. Bailey suggests that gay males experience more anxiety and depression than heterosexual males because gay males are

   (a) less sensitive to the effects of serotonin
   (b) reluctant to get married
   (c) likely to experience social condemnation
   (d) reluctant to change their sexual orientation

9. According to Savin–Williams and Diamond, the first step in the development of sexual identity in homosexuals is

   (a) sexual contact with members of the same sex
   (b) attraction to members of the same sex
   (c) acceptance of one's sexual orientation
   (d) self-labeling as gay or lesbian

10. _____ attempted to develop methods to "reverse" a homosexual orientation.

    (a) Masters and Johnson
    (b) Laumann
    (c) Freud
    (d) Kinsey

11. Gay marriage is illegal in

    (a) Canada
    (b) Belgium
    (c) the Netherlands
    (d) the United States

12. Bell and Weinberg found that the adjustment of gay people was related to their

    (a) medical coverage
    (b) lifestyles
    (c) income
    (d) relationships with their families of origin

13. Christians and Jews tend to refer to male–male sexual activity as

    (a) onanism
    (b) lust
    (c) sodomy
    (d) pride

14. The oldest of Bell's and Weinberg's groups were

    (a) asexuals
    (b) bixexuals
    (c) close couples
    (d) dysfunctionals

15. The behavior of adolescent Sambian males provides evidence that

    (a) some cultures are superior to others
    (b) heterosexuality and homosexuality are present at birth
    (c) homosexuality is normal
    (d) culture influences sexual practices

11

Conception, Pregnancy, and Childbirth

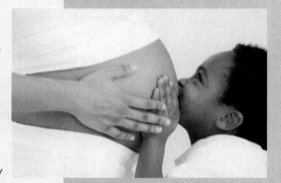

TRUTH?
fiction

Which of the following statements are true, and which are fiction? Look for the Truth/Fiction icons on the pages that follow to find the answers.

1 Prolonged athletic activity may decrease fertility in the male.   T   F

2 A "test-tube baby" is grown in a laboratory dish throughout the nine-month gestation period.   T   F

3 Morning sickness is a sign that a pregnancy is progressing normally.   T   F

4 For the first week after conception, a fertilized egg cell is not attached to its mother's body.   T   F

5 Pregnant women can have one or two alcoholic beverages a day without harming their babies.   T   F

6 The way that the umbilical cord is cut determines whether the baby will have an "inny" or an "outy."   T   F

7 In the United States, nearly 3 births in 10 are by cesarean section.   T   F

8 Couples should abstain from sexual activity for at least six weeks after childbirth.   T   F

On a balmy day in October, Marta and her partner Jorge rush to catch the train to their jobs in the city. Marta's workday is outwardly the same as any other. Within her body, however, a drama is unfolding. Yesterday, hormones had caused an ovarian follicle to rupture, releasing its egg cell, or ovum. Like all women, Marta possessed all the ova she would ever have at birth, each encased in a follicle. How this particular follicle was selected to ripen and release its ovum this month remains a mystery. But for the next day or so, Marta will be capable of conceiving.

The previous morning Marta had used her ovulation timing kit, which showed that she was about to ovulate. So later that night, Marta and Jorge had made love, hoping that Marta would conceive. Jorge ejaculated hundreds of millions of sperm within Marta's vagina. Only a few thousand survived the journey through the cervix and uterus to the fallopian tube that contained the ovum, released just hours earlier. Of these, a few hundred remained to bombard the ovum. One succeeded in penetrating the ovum's covering, resulting in conception. From a single cell formed by the union of sperm and ovum, a new life begins to form. The **zygote** is but 1/175 of an inch across—a tiny beginning for the drama about to take place.

Marta is 37 years old. Four months into her pregnancy, Marta obtains **amniocentesis** to check for the presence of chromosomal abnormalities, such as **Down syndrome.** (Down syndrome is more common among children born to women in their late 30s and older.) Amniocentesis also indicates the

sex of the fetus. Although many parents prefer to know the sex of their baby before it is born, Marta and Jorge ask their doctor not to inform them. "Why ruin the surprise?" Jorge tells his friends. So Marta and Jorge are left to debate boys' names and girls' names for the next few months.

Zygote A fertilized ovum

Amniocentesis A procedure for extracting and examining fetal cells in the amniotic fluid to determine the presence of various disorders in the fetus

Down syndrome A chromosomal abnormality that leads to mental retardation; caused by an extra chromosome on the 21st pair

Conception: Against All Odds

Conception is the union of a sperm cell and an ovum. On the one hand, conception is the beginning of a new human life. On the other, conception is the end of a fantastic voyage, during which a viable ovum, one of only several hundred that will mature and ripen during a woman's lifetime, unites with one of several hundred *million* sperm produced by the man in the average ejaculate.

Ova carry X sex chromosomes. Sperm carry either X or Y sex chromosomes. Girls are conceived from the union of an ovum and an X-bearing sperm, boys from the union of an ovum and a Y-bearing sperm. Sperm that bear Y sex chromosomes appear to be faster swimmers than those bearing X sex chromosomes. This is one of the reasons that between 120 and 150 boys are conceived for every 100 girls. What seem to be natural balancing factors favor the survival of female fetuses, however. Male fetuses are more likely to be lost in a **spontaneous abortion,** which often occurs during the first month of pregnancy. In many cases of early spontaneous abortion, the woman never realizes that she had been pregnant. Despite spontaneous abortions, boys still outnumber girls at birth. Boys suffer from a higher incidence of infant mortality, however. Thus, the numbers of boys and girls in the population are further equalized by the time they mature to the point of pairing off.

The 200 to 400 million sperm in an average ejaculate may seem excessive, because only one can fertilize an egg. Only 1 in 1,000 will ever arrive in the vicinity of an ovum, however. Millions deposited in the vagina simply flow out of the woman's body because of gravity, unless she remains prone for quite some time. Normal vaginal acidity kills many more. Many surviving sperm swim against the current of fluid coming from the cervix, through the os and into the uterus. Surviving sperm may reach the fallopian tubes 60 to 90 minutes after ejaculation. About half the sperm end up in the wrong tube—that is, the one not containing the egg. Perhaps some 2,000 sperm find their way into the right tube. Fewer still manage to swim the final two inches against the currents generated by the cilia that line the tube.

The journey of sperm may be blind but not random. Ova secrete a chemical that attracts sperm. Sperm cells have been shown to have odor receptors (Donner & Babcock, 2003; Spehr et al., 2003). It is thus conceivable (pardon the pun) that sperm are attracted to ova through a variation of the sense of smell.

Fertilization normally occurs in a fallopian tube. Figure 11.1 shows sperm swarming around an egg in a fallopian tube. Ova contain chromosomes, proteins, fats, and nutritious fluid, and are surrounded by a gelatinous layer called the **zona pellucida**. This layer must be penetrated if fertilization is to occur. Sperm that have completed their journey secrete the enzyme **hyaluronidase**, which briefly thins the zona pellucida, enabling one sperm to penetrate. After a sperm has entered, the zona pellucida thickens, locking other sperm out. The corresponding chromosomes in the sperm and ovum line up opposite each other. Conception occurs as the chromosomes from the sperm and ovum combine to form 23 new pairs, which carry a unique set of genetic instructions.

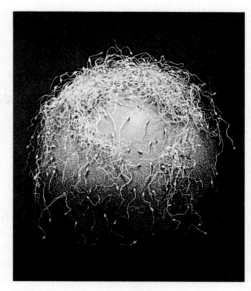

Figure 11.1 Human Sperm Swarming around an Ovum in a Fallopian Tube. *Fertilization normally occurs in a fallopian tube, not in the uterus. Sperm secrete the enzyme* hyaluronidase, *which thins the layer surrounding the ovum, allowing one sperm cell to penetrate.*

Optimizing the Chances of Conception

Couples may wish to optimize their chances of conceiving during a particular month so that birth occurs at a certain time. Others may have trouble conceiving and want to maximize their chances for a few months before seeing a fertility specialist. Fairly simple procedures can increase the chances of conceiving for couples without serious fertility problems.

The ovum can be fertilized for about 4 to 20 hours after ovulation (Wilcox et al., 2000). Sperm are most active within 48 hours after ejaculation, so one way to

Spontaneous abortion The sudden, involuntary expulsion of the embryo or fetus from the uterus before it is capable of independent life

Zona pellucida A gelatinous layer that surrounds an ovum; from roots meaning "zone that light can shine through"

Hyaluronidase An enzyme that briefly thins the zona pellucida, enabling one sperm to penetrate; from roots meaning "substance that breaks down a glasslike fluid"

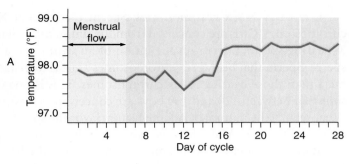

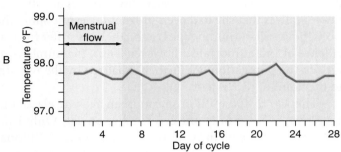

Figure 11.2 A Basal Body Temperature (BBT) Chart. *Because most women have somewhat irregular menstrual cycles, they may not be able to predict ovulation perfectly. The BBT chart helps them to do so. Body temperature is fairly even before ovulation but dips slightly just before ovulation. On the day after ovulation, a woman's body temperature increases about 0.4 to 0.8°F above the level before ovulation.*

optimize the chances of conception is to engage in coitus within a few hours of ovulation. There are several ways to predict ovulation.

USING THE BASAL BODY TEMPERATURE CHART Few women have perfectly regular cycles, so they can only guess when they are ovulating (Wilcox et al., 2000). A basal body temperature (BBT) chart (Figure 11.2) can provide a more reliable estimate.

Body temperature is fairly even before ovulation. Early-morning temperature is usually less than 98.6°F, but just before ovulation, basal temperature dips slightly. Then, on the day after ovulation, temperature tends to increase by about 0.4 to 0.8°F and to remain higher until menstruation. A woman can detect these changes by tracking her temperature after awakening in the morning but before rising from bed. Thermometers that provide finely graded readings, such as electronic digital thermometers, best detect the minor changes. The couple records the woman's temperature and the day of the cycle (as well as the day of the month) and indicate whether they have engaged in coitus. With regular charting for six months, the woman may learn to predict the day of ovulation more accurately, assuming that her cycles are fairly regular.

Opinion is divided regarding whether it is better for couples to have coitus every 24 hours or every 36 to 48 hours for the several-day period during which ovulation is expected. More frequent coitus around the time of ovulation may increase the chances of conception. Relatively less frequent (i.e., every 36 to 48 hours) coitus leads to a higher sperm count during each ejaculation. Most fertility specialists recommend that couples seeking to conceive a baby have intercourse once every day or two during the week in which the woman expects to ovulate. Men with lower than normal sperm counts may be advised to wait 48 hours between ejaculations.

ANALYZING URINE OR SALIVA FOR LUTEINIZING HORMONE Over-the-counter (OTC) kits are more accurate than the BBT method and predict ovulation by analyzing the woman's urine or saliva for the surge in LH that precedes ovulation by about 12 to 24 hours (Peris, 2006).

TRACKING VAGINAL MUCUS   Women can track the thickness of their vaginal mucus during the menstrual cycle by rolling it between their fingers and noting changes in texture. The mucus is thick, white, and cloudy during most phases of the cycle but turns thin, slippery, and clear for a few days before ovulation. A day or so after ovulation the mucus again thickens and becomes opaque.

ADDITIONAL CONSIDERATIONS   Coitus in the male-superior position allows sperm to be deposited deeper in the vagina and minimizes leakage of sperm out of the vagina as a result of gravity. Women may improve their chances of conceiving by lying on their backs and drawing their knees close to their breasts after ejaculation. This position, perhaps aided by use of a pillow to support the buttocks, may prevent sperm from dripping out and may elevate the pool of semen in relation to the cervix. Gravity thus works for, rather than against, conception. Women may lie still for about 30 to 60 minutes after ejaculation.

Women with severely retroverted or "tipped" uteruses may profit from supporting themselves on their elbows and knees and having their partners enter them from behind. Again, this position helps prevent semen from dripping out.

The man should penetrate as deeply as possible just before ejaculation, hold still during ejaculation, then withdraw slowly in a straight line to avoid dispersing the pool of semen.

Selecting the Sex of Your Child

Parents have wished that they could select the sex of their children for thousands of years. In many cultures, one sex—usually male—has been preferred over the other. In other cases, parents who already have girls (or boys) would like to be able to "balance" their family by having a boy (or girl). Then, too, there are sex-linked diseases that show up only in sons. In such cases, parents would feel safer if they could choose to have daughters.

Folklore is replete with methods for choosing the sex of your child. Some cultures advised coitus under the full moon to conceive boys. The Greek philosopher Aristotle suggested that making love during a north wind would beget sons; a south wind would produce daughters. Sour foods were once suggested for parents desirous of having boys. Those who wanted girls were advised to consume sweets. Husbands who yearned to have boys might be advised to wear their boots to bed. It goes without saying that none of these methods worked (but we will say it anyhow).

These methods, or nonmethods, would supposedly lead to the conception of children of the desired sex. However, methods after conception have also been used, such as the abortion of fetuses because of their sex. There are also many cultures in which infanticide has been used. Because boys have usually been considered more desirable than girls, female infanticide has been more common than male infanticide.

Today, there is a reliable method for selecting the sex of your child prior to implantation: preimplantation genetic diagnosis (PGD). PGD was developed to detect genetic disorders, but also allows health professionals to learn of the sex of the embryo (President's Council on Bioethics, 2004). In PGD, ova are fertilized in vitro, leading to the conception of perhaps six to eight embryos. After a few days of cell division, a cell is extracted from each. The sex chromosomal structure of the cell is examined microscopically to determine whether the embryo is female or male.

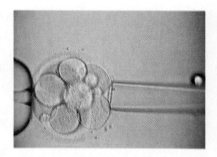
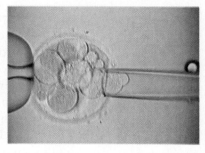
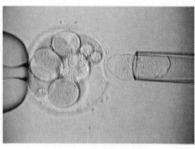

Preimplantation Genetic Diagnosis. *PGD is the only perfectly reliable method for selecting the sex of one's child prior to implantation.*

REFLECT

How can you use the information presented in this section to increase or decrease the chances of pregnancy?

Embryos of the desired sex are implanted in the woman's uterus, where one or more can grow to term. PGD is a foolproof sex selection method, but it is medically invasive, expensive, and implantation cannot be guaranteed. Yet, when implantation occurs, the sex of the embryo is known.

Infertility and Assisted Reproductive Technology

For couples who want children, few problems are more frustrating than the inability to conceive (Clay, 2006). Physicians often recommend that heterosexual couples try to conceive on their own for six months before seeking medical assistance. The term **infertility** is usually not applied until the couple has tried to get pregnant for more than a year, but women older than 35 years are advised to seek help within six months of attempts (American Fertility Association, 2006).

Because the incidence of infertility increases with age, it is partially the result of an increase in couples who postpone childbearing until their 30s and 40s (Shevell et al., 2005). All in all, about 15% of American couples have fertility problems (American Fertility Association, 2006). However, about half of them eventually succeed in conceiving a child. Many treatment options are available, as we will see.

Male Fertility Problems

The fertility problem lies with the man in about 30% of cases. In about 20% of cases, problems are found in both partners (Hatcher et al., 2006; Shevell et al., 2005).

Fertility problems in the male reflect abnormalities such as

- low sperm count
- irregularly shaped sperm (e.g., malformed heads or tails)
- low sperm **motility**
- chronic diseases such as diabetes, as well as infectious diseases such as sexually transmitted diseases
- injury to the testes
- an **autoimmune response,** in which antibodies produced by the man deactivate his own sperm
- a pituitary imbalance and/or thyroid disease

Problems in producing normal, abundant sperm may be caused by genetic factors, advanced age, hormonal problems, diabetes, injuries to the testes, varicose veins in the scrotum, drugs (alcohol, narcotics, marijuana, tobacco), blood pressure medications, environmental toxins, excess heat, and stress. Sperm production gradually declines with age, but normal aging does not necessarily produce infertility. Men in late adulthood have fathered children.

Low sperm count (or no sperm) is the most common problem of infertility in men. Sperm counts of 40 million to 150 million sperm per milliliter of semen are considered normal. A count of less than 20 million is regarded as low. Sperm production may be low among men with undescended testes that were not surgically corrected before puberty. Frequent ejaculation can reduce sperm counts. Sperm production may be impaired in men whose testicles are consistently 1 or 2°F higher than the typical scrotal temperature of 94 to 95°F. Frequent hot baths and tight-fitting

Infertility Inability to conceive a child

Motility Self-propulsion; a measure of the viability of sperm cells

Autoimmune response The production of antibodies that attack naturally occurring substances that are (incorrectly) recognized as being foreign or harmful

underwear can also reduce sperm production, at least temporarily. **Truth or Fiction Revisited:** Some men may encounter fertility problems from prolonged athletic activity, use of electric blankets, or even long, hot baths. In such cases, the problem can be readily corrected. Male runners with fertility problems are often advised to take time off to increase sperm counts.

Sometimes the sperm count is adequate, but prostate, hormonal, or other factors deprive sperm of motility, or deform them. Motility can also be hampered by scar tissue from infections. Scarring may prevent sperm from passing through parts of the male reproductive system, such as the vas deferens. To be considered normal, sperm must be able to swim for at least two hours after coitus and most (60% or more) must be normal in shape.

Sperm counts have been increased by surgical repair of varicose veins in the scrotum. Microsurgery can also open blocked passageways that prevent the outflow of sperm (Schroeder-Printzen et al., 2000). Researchers are also investigating the effects on sperm production of special cooling undergarments. Most men whose infertility is the result of higher than normal scrotal temperatures show increased sperm counts and quality when they wear such undergarments.

ARTIFICIAL INSEMINATION The sperm of men with low sperm counts can be collected and frozen. The sperm from multiple ejaculations can then be injected into a woman's uterus at the time of ovulation. This is one kind of **artificial insemination.** The sperm of men with low sperm motility can also be injected into their partners' uteruses, so that the sperm begin their journey closer to the fallopian tubes. Sperm from a donor can be used to inseminate artificially a woman whose male partner is infertile. The child then bears the genes of one of the parents—the mother. A donor can be chosen who resembles the partner in physical traits and ethnic background.

A variation of artificial insemination has been used with some men with very low (or zero!) sperm counts in the semen, immature sperm, or immotile sperm. Immature sperm can be removed from a testicle by a thin needle and then directly injected into an egg in a laboratory dish. The method has even been successful with a few men who only have tailless spermatids in the testes.

Female Fertility Problems

The major causes of infertility in women include

- irregular ovulation, including failure to ovulate
- obstructions or malfunctions of the reproductive tract, which are often caused by infections or diseases involving the reproductive tract
- endometriosis
- declining hormone levels of estrogen and progesterone that occur with aging and may prevent the ovum from becoming fertilized or remaining implanted in the uterus

Ten percent to 15% of female infertility problems stem from failure to ovulate. Many factors can play a role in failure to ovulate, including hormonal irregularities, malnutrition, genetic factors, stress, and chronic disease. Failure to ovulate may occur in response to low levels of body fat, as seen in some women with eating disorders and in athletes (Frisch, 2002).

Ovulation may often be induced by the use of fertility drugs such as *clomiphene* (Clomid). Clomiphene stimulates the pituitary gland to secrete FSH and LH, which

Artificial insemination
The introduction of sperm in the reproductive tract through means other than sexual intercourse

Endometriosis An abnormal condition in which endometrial tissue is sloughed off into the abdominal cavity rather than out of the body during menstruation; characterized by abdominal pain; may cause infertility

Laparoscopy A medical procedure during which a long, narrow tube (laparoscope) is inserted through an incision in the navel, permitting the visual inspection of organs in the pelvic cavity

Rubin test A test during which carbon dioxide gas is blown through the cervix and its progress through the reproductive tract is tracked to determine whether the fallopian tubes are blocked

Hysterosalpingogram A test during which a dye is injected into the reproductive tract and its progress is tracked by radiography to determine whether the fallopian tubes are blocked; from roots meaning "record of," "uterus," and "fallopian tubes"

In vitro fertilization A method of conception during which mature ova are surgically removed from an ovary and placed in a laboratory dish along with sperm

Gamete intrafallopian transfer (GIFT) A method of conception during which sperm and ova are inserted into a fallopian tube to encourage conception

Zygote intrafallopian transfer (ZIFT) A method of conception during which an ovum is fertilized in a laboratory dish and is then placed in a fallopian tube

in turn stimulates maturation of ova. Clomiphene leads to conception in most cases of infertility that are *solely* the result of irregular or absent ovulation. But because infertility can have multiple causes, only about half the women who use clomiphene become pregnant. Another infertility drug, Pergonal, contains a high concentration of FSH, which directly stimulates maturation of ovarian follicles. Like clomiphene, Pergonal has high success rates with women whose infertility is the result of the lack of ovulation. Clomiphene and Pergonal have been linked to multiple births, including quadruplets and quintuplets (Shevell et al., 2005).

Local infections that scar the fallopian tubes and other organs impede the passage of sperm or ova. Such infections include PID—an inflammation of the woman's internal reproductive tract that can be caused by various infectious agents, such as the bacteria responsible for gonorrhea and chlamydia (see Chapter 16).

In **endometriosis**, cells break away from the uterine lining (the endometrium) and become implanted and grow elsewhere. When they develop on the surface of the ovaries or fallopian tubes, they may block the passage of ova or impair conception. About one case in six of female sterility is believed to be the result of endometriosis. Hormone treatments and surgery sometimes reduce the blockage to the point that women can conceive. A physician may suspect endometriosis during a pelvic exam, but it is diagnosed with certainty by **laparoscopy**. During this procedure, a long, narrow tube is inserted through an incision in the navel, permitting the physician to inspect the organs in the pelvic cavity. (The incision is all but undetectable.)

Suspected blockage of the fallopian tubes may also be checked by a **Rubin test** or a **hysterosalpingogram** (or *hysterogram*). During a Rubin test, carbon dioxide gas is blown through the cervix. Its pressure is then monitored to determine whether it flows freely through the fallopian tubes into the abdomen or is trapped in the uterus. In the common hysterosalpingogram, the movement of an injected dye is monitored by radiography. This procedure may be uncomfortable. Several methods help many couples with problems such as blocked fallopian tubes bear children.

IN VITRO FERTILIZATION   When Louise Brown was born in England after being conceived by the method of **in vitro fertilization** (IVF), the event made headlines around the world. Louise was dubbed the world's first "test-tube baby." **Truth or Fiction Revisited:** With a so-called test-tube baby, conception actually takes place in a laboratory dish (not a test tube), and the embryo is implanted in the mother's uterus, where it develops to term. Before in vitro fertilization, fertility drugs stimulate ripening of ova. Ripe ova are then surgically removed from an ovary and placed in a laboratory dish along with the father's sperm. Fertilized ova are then injected into the mother's uterus to become implanted in the uterine wall.

Laura Schieve and her colleagues (1999) studied nearly 10,000 births from IVF and found that the greatest success rates were achieved when professionals attempted to implant two embryos, 43% among 20- to 29-year-olds and 36% among 30- to 34-year-olds. For each age group, multiple births (of DZ twins) occurred in about half the cases. IVF is associated with some greater risks for mother and child, such as high blood pressure in the mother and spontaneous abortion (Shevell et al., 2005). Discuss the risks and rewards with your gynecologist.

GIFT   In **gamete intrafallopian transfer (GIFT)**, sperm and ova are inserted together into a fallopian tube for fertilization. Unlike IVF, conception occurs in a fallopian tube rather than in a laboratory dish.

ZIFT   Zygote intrafallopian transfer (ZIFT) involves a combination of IVF and GIFT. Sperm and ova are combined in a laboratory dish. After fertilization, the zygote is placed in the mother's fallopian tube to begin its journey to the uterus for implantation. ZIFT has an advantage over GIFT in that fertility specialists can ascertain that fertilization has occurred before insertion is performed.

Intracytoplasmic Sperm Injection. *ICSI is sometimes used when the man has too few sperm for IVF, or when IVF fails. As shown in the photograph, a thin (very thin!) needle injects a single sperm directly into an ovum.*

DONOR IN VITRO FERTILIZATION "I tell her Mommy was having trouble with, I call them ovums, not eggs," says a 50-year-old Los Angeles woman. "I say that I needed these to have a baby, and there was this wonderful woman and she was willing to give me some, and that was how she helped us. I want to be honest that we got pregnant in a special way" (Stolberg, 1998).

The "special way" is termed **donor IVF**. It is a variation of the IVF procedure in which the ovum is taken from another woman, fertilized, and then injected into the uterus or fallopian tube of the intended mother. The procedure is used when the intended mother does not produce ova.

EMBRYONIC TRANSFER **Embryonic transfer** can be used with women who do not produce ova of their own. A woman volunteer is artificially inseminated by the male partner of the infertile woman, or by donor sperm. Five days later, the embryo is removed from the volunteer and inserted within the uterus of the mother-to-be, where it is hoped that it will become implanted.

INTRACYTOPLASMIC SPERM INJECTION **Intracytoplasmic sperm injection** (ICSI) can be used when a man has too few sperm for IVF, or when IVF fails. ICSI injects a sperm cell directly into an ovum. However, these methods may be associated with an increase in birth defects, such as heart, stomach, kidney, and bladder problems; cleft palate; hernia; and, in boys, malformation of the penis (Shevell et al., 2005).

SURROGATE MOTHERHOOD A **surrogate mother** is artificially inseminated with sperm from the male partner of the infertile woman, or by donor sperm, and carries the baby to term. The surrogate signs a contract to turn the baby over to the infertile mother or couple. Such contracts have been invalidated in some states, however, so that surrogate mothers in these states cannot be compelled to hand over the babies.

ADOPTION Adoption is another way for people to obtain children. Despite occasional conflicts that pit adoptive parents against biological parents who change their minds about giving up their children, most adoptions result in the formation of loving new families. Many Americans find it easier to adopt infants from other countries or with special needs.

Pregnancy

Women react to pregnancy in different ways. For those who are psychologically and economically prepared, pregnancy may be greeted with joyous celebration, but an

CRITICAL Thinking

Do some or all methods of overcoming infertility strike you as being "unnatural"? Explain. Would your judgment regarding whether these methods are natural affect your willingness to try one or more of them? Explain.

Donor IVF A variation of in vitro fertilization during which the ovum is taken from one woman, fertilized, and then injected into the uterus or fallopian tube of another woman

Embryonic transfer A method of conception during which a woman volunteer is artificially inseminated by the male partner of the intended mother, after which the embryo is removed from the volunteer and inserted within the uterus of the intended mother

Intracytoplasmic sperm injection A method of conception during which a single sperm is injected directly into an ovum

Surrogate mother A woman who is impregnated through artificial insemination with the sperm of a prospective father, carries the embryo and fetus to term, and then gives the child to the prospective parents

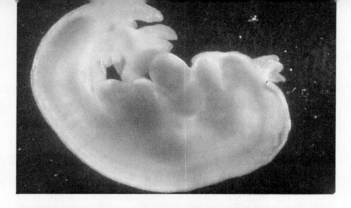

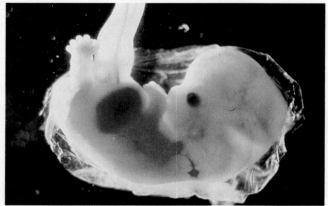

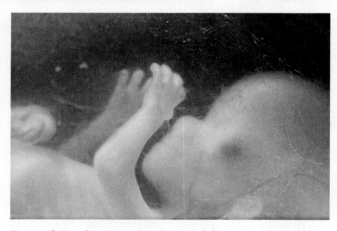

Prenatal Development. *Developmental changes are most rapid and dramatic during prenatal development. Within a few months, a human embryo and then fetus advances from weighing a fraction of an ounce to several pounds, and from one cell to billions of cells. Development is cephalocaudal and proximodistal. Growth of the head takes precedence over the growth of the lower parts of the body.*

Human chorionic gonadotropin (HGC) A hormone produced by women shortly after conception, which stimulates the corpus luteum to continue to produce progesterone, the presence of which in women's urine indicates pregnancy

unwanted pregnancy may evoke feelings of fear and hopelessness. In this section we examine biological and psychological aspects of pregnancy: signs of pregnancy, prenatal development, complications, effects of drugs and sex, and the psychological experiences of pregnant women and fathers.

Early Signs of Pregnancy

For many women the first sign of pregnancy is missing a period. However, some women have irregular menstrual cycles or miss a period because of stress. Missing a period is thus not a fully reliable indicator. Some women experience cyclic bleeding or spotting during pregnancy, although the blood flow is usually lighter than normal. If a woman's BBT remains high for about three weeks after ovulation, there is reason to suspect pregnancy even if she spots two weeks after ovulation.

Pregnancy Tests

You may have heard your parents say that they learned your mother was pregnant by means of the "rabbit test," in which a sample of the woman's urine was injected into a laboratory animal. This procedure, which was once commonly used to confirm pregnancy, relied on the fact that women produce **human chorionic gonadotropin (HCG)** shortly after conception. HCG causes rabbits, mice, or rats to ovulate.

Today, pregnancy can be confirmed in minutes by tests that directly detect HCG in the urine as early as the third week of pregnancy. A blood test—the *beta subunit HCG radioimmunoassay* (RIA)—can detect HCG in the woman's blood as early as the eighth day of pregnancy, about five days preceding her expected period.

Over-the-counter home pregnancy tests are also available. They, too, test the woman's urine for HCG and are intended to be used as early as one day after a missed period. Laboratory-based tests are considered 98% or 99% accurate. Home-based tests performed by laypeople are somewhat less accurate. Women are advised to consult their physicians if they suspect that they are pregnant or wish to confirm a home pregnancy test result.

Early Effects of Pregnancy

Just a few days after conception, a woman may note tenderness of the breasts. Hormonal stimulation of the mammary glands may make the breasts more sensitive and cause sensations of tingling and fullness.

Morning sickness, which can actually occur throughout the day, refers to the nausea, food aversions, and vomiting that many women experience during pregnancy. Women carrying more than one child usually experience more nausea. Although called morning sickness, it is not a "sickness" at all, but rather a perfectly normal part of pregnancy. There is some evidence that the nausea and vomiting experienced by pregnant women reflect bodily changes that promote the development of the placenta (Huxley, 2000). **Truth or Fiction Revisited:** Biologists Samuel Flaxman and Paul Sherman (2000) reviewed records of some 20,000 pregnancies and found that morning sickness was associated with a healthy outcome, including lower incidences of miscarriage and stillbirth. The researchers suggest that the food aversions protect the mother and fetus from likely sources of toxins and disease-causing agents, which are most commonly found in spoiled meat. Although it may have provided an evolutionary advantage, the usefulness of morning sickness has waned over the millennia, especially with the advent of refrigeration to help store foods safely.

All of this may be of little consolation to pregnant women. In some cases, morning sickness is so severe that the woman cannot eat regularly and must be hospitalized to ensure that she and the fetus receive adequate nutrition. In milder cases, having small amounts of food throughout the day is of help. Many woman find that eating a few crackers at bedtime and before getting out of bed in the morning are of help. Other women profit from medication. Women are advised to discuss the situation with their obstetricians rather than assume they have to tough it out. Morning sickness usually—but not always—subsides by about the 12th week of pregnancy.

Pregnant women may experience greater than normal fatigue during the early weeks, so that they sleep longer and fall asleep more readily than usual. Frequent urination, which may also be experienced, is caused by pressure from the swelling uterus on the bladder.

Miscarriage

Miscarriages have many causes, including chromosomal defects in the fetus and abnormalities of the placenta and uterus. Miscarriage is more common among older mothers (Stein & Susser, 2000). About three in four miscarriages occur during the first 16 weeks of pregnancy, and most of these occur during the first seven weeks. Some miscarriages occur so early that the woman does not know she was pregnant.

After a miscarriage, the mother or couple may feel a deep sense of loss and undergo a period of mourning. Emotional support from friends and family often helps the mother or couple cope with the loss. In most cases, women who miscarry can carry subsequent pregnancies to term.

Sex during Pregnancy

Most health professionals agree that coitus is safe throughout pregnancy until the start of labor, provided that the pregnancy is developing normally and the woman has no history of miscarriages. Women who experience bleeding or cramps during pregnancy may be advised by their obstetricians not to engage in coitus.

Masters and Johnson (1966) reported an initial decline in sexual interest among pregnant women during the first trimester. There is increased interest during the second trimester and another decline in interest during the third. Many women show declines in sexual interest and activity during the first trimester because of fatigue,

TRUTH fiction **3**

REFLECT

Do you know any people who adopted a child, or any child who was adopted? How would you describe the experience of adopting a child or knowing one who is adopted?

Morning sickness
Symptoms of pregnancy, including nausea, aversions to specific foods, and vomiting
Miscarriage A spontaneous abortion

nausea, or misguided concerns that coitus will harm the embryo or fetus. Also during the first trimester, vasocongestion may cause tenderness of the breasts, discouraging touch there. One study found that 90% of 570 women were engaging in coitus at five months into their pregnancies (Byrd et al., 1998). Researchers in Israel reported a gradual decline in sexual interest and frequency of intercourse and orgasm during pregnancy among a sample of 219 women. The greatest decline occurred during the third trimester (Hart et al., 1991). Pain during intercourse is also commonly reported, especially during the third trimester.

As the woman's abdominal region swells, the male-superior position becomes unwieldy. For heterosexual couples, the female-superior, lateral-entry, and rear-entry positions are common alternatives. Manual and oral sex can continue as usual. Some women are concerned that the uterine contractions of orgasm may dislodge an embryo, but such concerns are usually unfounded. Still, women and their partners are advised to ask their obstetricians about it.

CRITICAL
Thinking

How would you explain the relationship between a woman's experience of the physical aspects of pregnancy and her desire to have a child? Why might some women consider "morning sickness" to be a blessing and other women consider it a curse?

Psychological Changes during Pregnancy

A woman's psychological response to pregnancy reflects her desire to be pregnant, her physical changes, and her attitudes toward these changes. Women with the financial, social, and psychological resources to meet the needs of pregnancy and child rearing may welcome pregnancy. Some describe it as the most wondrous experience of their lives. Some women question their ability to handle pregnancy and childbirth. Or they fear that pregnancy will impair their careers or their partner's feelings about them. In general, women who choose to become pregnant are better adjusted during their pregnancies.

The first trimester may be difficult for women who are ambivalent about pregnancy. At that stage, symptoms like morning sickness are most pronounced, and women must come to terms with being pregnant. The second trimester is generally smoother. Morning sickness and other symptoms largely vanish. It is not yet difficult to move about, and childbirth remains a while off. Women first note fetal movement during the second trimester, and for many the experience is stirring:

> I was lying on my stomach and felt—something, like someone lightly touching my deep insides. Then I just sat very still and . . . felt the hugeness of having something living growing in me. Then I said, No, it's not possible, it's too early yet, and then I started to cry. . . . That one moment was my first body awareness of another living thing inside me. (Boston Women's Health Book Collective, 2005)

During the third trimester it is normal, especially for first-time mothers, to worry about the mechanics of delivery and whether the child will be normal. The woman becomes increasingly heavy and literally "bent out of shape." It may become difficult to get up from a chair or out of bed. She must sit farther from the steering wheel when driving. Muscle tension from supporting the extra weight in her abdomen may cause backaches. She may feel impatient in the days and weeks just before delivery.

Men, like women, respond to pregnancy according to the degree to which they want the child. Many men are proud and look forward to the child with great anticipation. In such cases, pregnancy may bring parents closer together, but fathers who are financially or emotionally unprepared may consider the pregnancy a "trap."

Q *How often do pregnant women have to go to the doctor during the pregnancy, assuming everything is going okay, and what kinds of things happen during the visits?*

A If you think you're pregnant, arrange for prenatal care as soon as possible. If you're not sure how to do that, check in with your college health center or Planned Parenthood. If you're young, 18 to 35, you'll probably have a low-risk pregnancy and will be asked to see the doctor once a month for the first seven months, then every two to three weeks from the 28th through the 36th weeks, and then every week from the 35th week until delivery. If you're older or at higher risk, your doctor will arrange to see you more often.

The first visit is usually longest. You'll provide a full medical history and have a thorough physical exam, including measurements of height and weight, respiration rate (breathing), blood pressure, and pulse rate. You'll have a breast exam, Pap test, and tests for chlamydia and gonorrhea. Your state might require testing for HIV/AIDS. You may have blood, skin, and urine tests to check for anemia, blood type, cystic fibrosis, Gaucher's disease, hepatitis, rubella, sickle-cell anemia, Tay–Sachs disease, thalassemias, tuberculosis, and diabetes.

At follow-ups the doctor will check your urine, blood pressure, fluid retention (swollen hands, face, feet), check the growth of your uterus, examine your abdomen for the position of the fetus, and listen for the fetal heartbeat. At some point ultrasound may be used to show the size and position of the fetus, check the placenta, confirm the due date, detect multiple pregnancies and certain abnormalities, and even check the sex of the fetus. Between 10 and 18 weeks chorionic villus sampling (CVS), a "triple test," and amniocentesis may be offered to screen for various abnormalities.

During the third trimester the doctor will usually perform a biophysical profile, which combines ultrasound with a fetal monitor to check out the fetal heartbeat and movement more closely.

Prenatal Development

We can date pregnancy from the onset of the last menstrual cycle before conception, which makes the normal gestation period 280 days. We can also date pregnancy from the date at which fertilization was assumed to have taken place, which normally corresponds to two weeks after the beginning of the woman's last menstrual cycle. In this case, the normal gestation period is 266 days.

After pregnancy has been confirmed, the delivery date may be calculated by *Nagele's rule:*

- Jot down the date of the first day of the last menstrual period.
- Add seven days.
- Subtract three months.
- Add one year.

For example, if the last period began on November 12, 2008, adding seven days yields November 19, 2008. Then subtracting three months yields August 19, 2008. Adding one year gives a "due date" of August 19, 2009. Few babies are born exactly when they

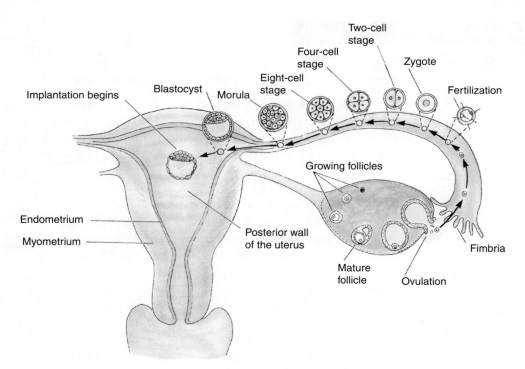

Figure 11.3 The Ovarian Cycle, Conception, and the Early Days of the Germinal Stage. *The zygote first divides about 36 hours after conception. Continuing division creates the hollow sphere of cells termed the* blastocyst. *The blastocyst normally becomes implanted in the wall of the uterus.*

are due,* but the great majority are delivered during a 10-day period that spans the date.

Stages of Prenatal Development

Shortly after conception, the single cell that results from the union of sperm and egg begins to multiply—becoming two cells, then four, then eight, and so on. During the weeks and months that follow, tissues, structures, and organs begin to form, and the fetus gradually takes on the shape of a human being. By the time the fetus is born, it consists of hundreds of billions of cells—more cells than there are stars in the Milky Way. Prenatal development can be divided into three periods: the *germinal stage,* which corresponds to about the first two weeks; the *embryonic stage,* which coincides with the first two months; and the *fetal stage.* We also commonly speak of prenatal development in terms of three trimesters of three months each.

THE GERMINAL STAGE Within 36 hours after conception, the zygote divides into two cells. It then divides repeatedly, becoming 32 cells within another 36 hours as it continues its journey to the uterus. **Truth or Fiction Revisited:** For the first week after conception, a fertilized egg cell is not attached to its mother's body. It takes the zygote perhaps three or four days to reach the uterus. This mass of dividing cells then wanders about the uterus for perhaps another three or four days before it begins to become implanted in the uterine wall. Implantation takes about another week. This period from conception to implantation is termed the **germinal stage,** or the **period of the ovum** (Figure 11.3).

Germinal stage The period of prenatal development before implantation in the uterus

Period of the ovum Germinal stage

---

*The Rathuses wish to boast, however, that their daughters Allyn and Jordan were born precisely on their due dates. At least one of them has been just as compulsive ever since. Nevid adds that he and his wife Judy had their son Michael within one day of the due date. [Close, but no cigar.]

Several days into the germinal stage, the cell mass takes the form of a fluid-filled ball of cells, which is called a **blastocyst.** Already some cell differentiation has begun. Cells begin to separate into groups that will eventually become different structures. Within a thickened mass of cells that is called the **embryonic disk,** two distinct inner layers of cells are beginning to form. These cells will become the embryo and eventually the fetus. The outer part of the blastocyst, called the **trophoblast,** consists of several membranes from which the amniotic sac, placenta, and umbilical cord eventually develop.

Implantation may be accompanied by some bleeding, which results from the usual rupturing of some small blood vessels that line the uterus. Bleeding can also be a sign of a miscarriage, although most women who experience implantation bleeding do not miscarry but go on to have normal pregnancies and deliver healthy babies.

THE EMBRYONIC STAGE The period from implantation to about the eighth week of development is called the **embryonic stage.** The major organ systems of the body begin to differentiate during this stage.

Development of the embryo follows two trends—**cephalocaudal** and **proximodistal** (Figure 11.4). Growth of the head (the cephalic region) takes precedence over the growth of the lower parts of the body. You can also think of the body as containing a central axis that coincides with the spinal cord. The growth of the organ systems that lay close to this axis (i.e., *proximal* to the axis) takes precedence over the growth of those that lay farther away toward the extremities (i.e., *distal* to the axis). Relatively early maturation of the brain and organ systems that lay near the central axis allows these organs to facilitate further development of the embryo and fetus.

As the embryonic stage unfolds, the nervous system, sensory organs, hair, nails, teeth, and the outer layer of skin begin to develop from the outer layer of cells, or **ectoderm,** of the embryonic disk. By about three weeks after conception, two ridges appear in the embryo. The ridges fold together to form the **neural tube.** This tube develops into the nervous system. The inner layer of the embryonic disk is called the **endoderm.** From this layer develop the respiratory and digestive systems, and organs such as the liver and the pancreas. A short time later during the embryonic stage, the middle layer of cells, or **mesoderm,** differentiates and develops into the reproductive, excretory, and circulatory systems, as well as the skeleton, muscles, and the inner layer of the skin.

During the third week of development, the head and blood vessels begin to form. By the fourth week, a primitive heart begins to beat and pump blood in an embryo that measures but a fifth of an inch in length. The heart will normally continue to beat without rest for every minute of every day for the better part of a century. By the end of the first month of development we can see the beginnings of the arms and legs—*arm buds* and *leg buds*. The mouth, eyes, ears, and nose begin to take shape. The brain and other parts of the nervous system begin to develop.

The arms and legs develop in accordance with the proximodistal principle. First the upper arms and legs develop, then the forearms and lower legs, then the hands and feet, followed by webbed fingers and toes by about six to eight weeks into development. The webbing is gone by the end of the second month. By this time the head has become rounded, and the limbs have elongated and separated. Facial features are visible. All this has occurred in an embryo that is about one inch long and weighs 1/30th of an ounce. During the second month, nervous impulses also begin to travel through the developing nervous system.

The embryo—and, later, the fetus—develop within a protective environment in the mother's uterus called the **amniotic sac,** which is surrounded by a clear

Blastocyst A stage within the germinal stage of prenatal development at which the embryo is a sphere of cells surrounding a cavity of fluid

Embryonic disk The platelike inner part of the blastocyst that differentiates into the ectoderm, mesoderm, and endoderm of the embryo

Trophoblast The outer part of the blastocyst from which the amniotic sac, placenta, and umbilical cord develop

Embryonic stage The stage of prenatal development that lasts from implantation through the eighth week and is characterized by the differentiation of the major organ systems

Cephalocaudal From the head downward; from Latin roots meaning "head" and "tail"

Proximodistal From the central axis of the body outward; from Latin roots meaning "near" and "far"

Ectoderm The outermost cell layer of the newly formed embryo from which the skin and nervous system develop

Neural tube A hollow area in the blastocyst from which the nervous system develops

Endoderm The inner layer of the newly formed embryo from which the lungs and digestive system develop

Mesoderm The central layer of the embryo from which the bones and muscles develop

Amniotic sac The sac containing the fetus

Figure 11.4 Human Embryos and Fetuses.

Development is cephalocaudal and proximodistal. Growth of the head takes precedence over the growth of the lower parts of the body.

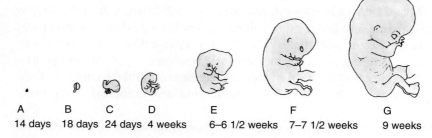

A
14 days

B
18 days

C
24 days

D
4 weeks

E
6–6 1/2 weeks

F
7–7 1/2 weeks

G
9 weeks

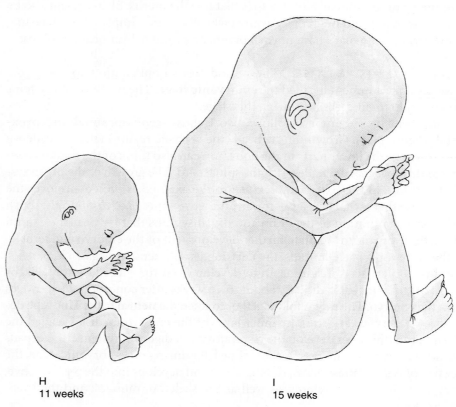

H
11 weeks

I
15 weeks

Amniotic fluid Fluid within the amniotic sac that suspends and protects the fetus

Placenta An organ connected to the fetus by the umbilical cord; serves as a relay station between mother and fetus, allowing the exchange of nutrients and wastes

Umbilical cord A tube that connects the fetus to the placenta

membrane. The embryo and fetus are suspended within the sac in **amniotic fluid.** The amniotic fluid acts like a shock absorber. It cushions the embryo from damage that might result from the mother's movements, and helps maintain a steady temperature.

Nutrients and waste products are exchanged between mother and embryo (or fetus) through a mass of tissue called the **placenta.** The placenta is unique in origin. It develops from material supplied by both mother and embryo. Toward the end of the first trimester, it becomes a flattish, round organ about seven inches in diameter and one inch thick—larger than the fetus itself. The fetus is connected to the placenta by the **umbilical cord.** The mother is connected to the placenta by the system of blood vessels in the uterine wall. The umbilical cord develops about five weeks after conception and reaches 20 inches in length. It contains two arteries through which maternal nutrients reach the embryo. A vein transports waste products back to the mother.

The circulatory systems of mother and embryo do not mix. A membrane in the placenta permits only certain substances to pass through, such as oxygen (from the mother to the fetus), carbon dioxide and other wastes (from the embryo or fetus to the mother, to be eliminated by the mother's lungs and kidneys), nutrients, some microscopic disease-causing organisms, and some drugs, including aspirin, narcotics, alcohol, and tranquilizers.

The placenta is also an endocrine gland. It secretes hormones that preserve the pregnancy, stimulate the uterine contractions that induce childbirth, and help prepare the breasts for breast-feeding. Some of these hormones may also cause the signs of pregnancy. HCG stimulates the corpus luteum to continue to produce progesterone. The placenta itself secretes increasing amounts of estrogen and progesterone. Ultimately, the placenta passes from the woman's body after delivery. For this reason it is also called the afterbirth.

THE FETAL STAGE   The fetal stage begins by the ninth week and continues until birth. By about the 9th or 10th week, the fetus begins to respond to the outside world by turning in the direction of external stimulation. By the end of the first trimester, the major organ systems, the fingers and toes, and the external genitals have been formed. The sex of the fetus can be determined visually. The eyes are clearly distinguishable.

During the second trimester the fetus increases dramatically in size, and its organ systems continue to mature. The brain now contributes to the regulation of basic body functions. The fetus increases in weight from one *ounce* to two *pounds* and grows from about 4 to 14 inches in length. Soft, downy hair grows above the eyes and on the scalp. The skin turns ruddy because of blood vessels that show through the surface. (During the third trimester, layers of fat beneath the skin will give the red a pinkish hue.)

Usually by the middle of the fourth month the mother can feel the first fetal movements. By the end of the second trimester, the fetus moves its limbs so vigorously that the mother may complain of being kicked—often at 4:00 AM. The fetus opens and shuts its eyes, sucks its thumb, alternates between periods of wakefulness and sleep, and perceives lights and sounds. The fetus also does somersaults, which the mother will definitely feel. Fortunately, the umbilical cord will not break or strangle the fetus, no matter what acrobatic feats the fetus performs.

Near the end of the second trimester the fetus approaches the **age of viability.** Still, only a minority of babies born at the end of the second trimester who weigh less than two pounds will survive—even with intense medical efforts.

During the third trimester, the organ systems continue to mature and enlarge. The heart and lungs become increasingly capable of maintaining independent life. Typically, during the seventh month the fetus turns upside down in the uterus so that it will be head first, or in a **cephalic presentation,** for delivery. But some fetuses do not turn during this month. If such a fetus is born prematurely it can have either a **breech presentation** (bottom first) or a shoulder-first presentation, which can complicate problems of prematurity. The closer to term (the full nine months) the baby is born, the more likely it is that the presentation will be cephalic. If birth occurs at the end of the eighth month, the odds are overwhelmingly in favor of survival.

During the final months of pregnancy, the mother may become concerned that the fetus seems to be less active than before. Most of the time the change in activity level is normal. The fetus has grown so large that it is cramped, and its movements are restricted.

Age of viability The age at which a fetus can sustain independent life

Cephalic presentation Emergence of the baby head first from the womb

Breech presentation Emergence of the baby feet first from the womb

Environmental Influences on Prenatal Development

Advances in scientific knowledge have made us more aware of the changes that take place during prenatal development. They have also heightened our awareness of the problems that can occur and what might be done to prevent them. These include the mother's diet, maternal diseases and disorders, and the mother's use of drugs.

THE MOTHER'S DIET   It is a common misconception that the fetus will take what it needs from its mother. Actually, malnutrition in the mother can adversely affect fetal development. Women who are too slender risk preterm deliveries and having babies who are low in birthweight (Cnattingius et al., 1998). Pregnant women who are adequately nourished are more likely to deliver babies of average or above average size. Their infants are also less likely to develop colds and serious respiratory disorders. However, maternal *obesity* is linked with a higher risk of stillbirth (Cnattingius et al., 1998).

A woman can expect to gain at least 20 pounds during pregnancy because of the growth of the placenta, amniotic fluid, and the fetus itself. Most women will gain 25 pounds or so. Overweight women may gain less. Slender women may gain 30 pounds. Regular weight gains are most desirable.

MATERNAL DISEASES AND DISORDERS   Environmental influences or agents that can harm the embryo or fetus are called **teratogens.** These include drugs taken by the mother, such as alcohol and even aspirin, as well as substances produced by the mother's body, such as Rh-positive antibodies. Other teratogens include the metals lead and mercury, radiation, and disease-causing organisms such as viruses and bacteria. Although many disease-causing organisms cannot pass through the placenta to infect the embryo or fetus, some extremely small organisms, such as those causing syphilis, measles, mumps, and chicken pox, can. Some disorders such as toxemia are not transmitted to the embryo or fetus but can adversely affect the environment in which it develops.

CRITICAL PERIODS OF VULNERABILITY   The times at which exposure to particular teratogens can cause the greatest harm are termed **critical periods of vulnerability.** Critical periods correspond to the times at which the structures most affected by the teratogens are developing (Figure 11.5). The heart, for example, develops rapidly from the third to the fifth week after conception. It may be most vulnerable to certain teratogens at this time. The arms and legs, which develop later, are most vulnerable from the fourth through the eighth week of development. Because the major organ systems differentiate during the embryonic stage, the embryo is most vulnerable to the effects of teratogens. Let us now consider some of the most damaging effects of specific maternal diseases and disorders.

RUBELLA (GERMAN MEASLES)   **Rubella** is a viral infection. Women who contract rubella during the first month or two of pregnancy, when rapid differentiation of major organ systems is taking place, may bear children who are deaf or who develop mental retardation, heart disease, or cataracts. Risk of these defects declines as pregnancy progresses.

Nearly 85% of women in the United States had rubella as children and so acquired immunity. Women who do not know whether they have had rubella may be

---

Teratogens Environmental influences or agents that can damage an embryo or fetus; from the Greek *teras,* meaning "monster"

Critical period of vulnerability A period of time during which an embryo or fetus is vulnerable to the effects of a teratogen

Rubella A viral infection that can cause mental retardation and heart disease in an embryo; also called *German measles*

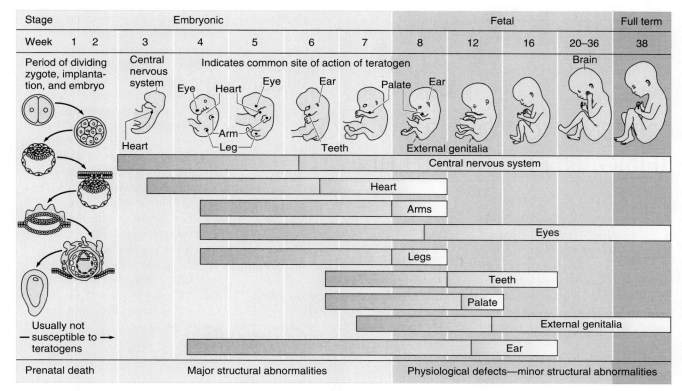

Stage	Embryonic						Fetal				Full term
Week 1 2	3	4	5	6	7	8	12	16	20–36	38

Period of dividing zygote, implantation, and embryo

Central nervous system

Indicates common site of action of teratogen

Eye   Heart   Eye   Ear   Palate   Ear   Brain

Arm
Leg
Heart   Teeth   External genitalia

Usually not susceptible to teratogens

Central nervous system

Heart

Arms

Eyes

Legs

Teeth

Palate

External genitalia

Ear

Prenatal death | Major structural abnormalities | Physiological defects—minor structural abnormalities

Figure 11.5 Critical Periods in Prenatal Development. *The developing embryo is most vulnerable to teratogens when the organ systems are taking shape. The periods of greatest vulnerability of organ systems are shown in gray. Periods of lesser vulnerability are shown in yellow.*

tested. If they are not immune, they can be vaccinated *before pregnancy.* Inoculation during pregnancy is considered risky because the vaccine causes a mild case of the disease in the mother, which can affect the embryo or fetus. Increased awareness of the dangers of rubella during pregnancy and of the protective effects of inoculation has led to a dramatic decline in the number of children born in the United States with defects caused by rubella, from about 20,000 cases in 1964 to 1965 to 28 in the year 2000 (CDC, 2001a).

SYPHILIS   Maternal **syphilis** may cause miscarriage or **stillbirth,** or may be passed along to the child in the form of congenital syphilis. Congenital syphilis can impair vision and hearing, damage the liver, or deform bones and teeth.

Routine blood tests early during pregnancy can diagnose syphilis and other problems. Because the bacteria that cause syphilis do not readily cross the placental membrane during the first months of pregnancy, the fetus will probably not contract syphilis if an infected mother is treated successfully with antibiotics before the fourth month of pregnancy.

HIV/AIDS   **Acquired immunodeficiency syndrome (AIDS)** is caused by the human immunodeficiency virus (HIV). HIV is blood borne and is sometimes transmitted through the placenta to infect the fetus. The rupturing of blood vessels in mother and baby during childbirth provides another opportunity for transmission of HIV. However, the majority of babies born to mothers who are infected with HIV do

Syphilis A sexually transmitted bacterial infection

Stillbirth The birth of a dead fetus

Acquired immunodeficiency syndrome (AIDS) A condition caused by HIV that destroys white blood cells in the immune system, leaving the body vulnerable to various "opportunistic" diseases

PREVENTING YOUR BABY FROM BEING INFECTED WITH HIV

Pregnant women with HIV/AIDS or other STIs should discuss them with their doctors. They can take measures to help protect their babies. For example, the medication zidovudine reduces the amount of HIV in the mother's bloodstream. Infected women who use zidovudine during pregnancy reduce the rate of HIV infection in their neonates by two thirds (Mofenson, 2000). In one study, 8% of the babies born to women who obtained zidovudine became infected with HIV compared with 25% of babies whose mothers did not obtain zidovudine (Connor et al., 1994).

The European Mode of Delivery Collaboration Trial of 400 mothers infected with HIV compared the use of cesarean section (C-section) versus vaginal delivery as a means of decreasing the risk of transmission of HIV to the baby (Ricci et al., 2000). All mothers received zidovudine during pregnancy. Half were randomly assigned to deliver vaginally, and the other half by C-section. The rate of HIV infection among the babies was 10.6% for those delivered vaginally compared with 1.7% for those delivered by C-section. Thus, the combination of zidovudine and C-section cut the chance that an infected mother would transmit HIV to her baby to about 1 in 50.

For up-to-date information on HIV/AIDS, call the National AIDS Hotline at 1-800-342-AIDS. If you want to receive information in Spanish, call 1-800-344-SIDA.

---

not become infected themselves. Using antiviral medication can also minimize the probability of transmission (see the nearby "A Closer Look" feature). HIV can also be transmitted to children by breast-feeding. Research suggests that about half of infected newborns are infected while in the uterus, and half are infected during childbirth (Mofenson, 2000; Wood et al., 2000b).

African American children account for more than half the pediatric cases of HIV/AIDS, and Latino and Latina Americans account for almost one quarter (CDC, 2003). Inner city neighborhoods, where there is widespread intravenous drug use, have been hard hit (CDC, 2003).

TOXEMIA **Toxemia** is a life-threatening condition characterized by high blood pressure. It may afflict women late during the second or early during the third trimester of pregnancy. The first stage is termed _preeclampsia_. It is diagnosed by protein in the urine, swelling from fluid retention, and high blood pressure, and may be mild. As preeclampsia worsens, the mother may have headaches and visual problems from high blood pressure, along with abdominal pain. If left untreated, the disease may progress to the final stage: _eclampsia._ Eclampsia can lead to maternal or fetal death. Babies born to women with toxemia are often undersized or premature.

Toxemia appears to be linked to malnutrition. Ironically, undernourished women may gain weight rapidly through fluid retention, but their swollen appearance may discourage them from eating. Pregnant women who gain weight rapidly but have not increased their food intake should consult their obstetricians.

ECTOPIC PREGNANCY In an **ectopic pregnancy,** the fertilized ovum implants itself someplace other than the uterus. Most ectopic pregnancies occur in a fallopian tube (_tubal pregnancies_) when the ovum is prevented from moving into the uterus because of obstructions caused by infections. Ectopic pregnancies are more common among older women. If ectopic pregnancies do not abort spontaneously,

Toxemia A life-threatening condition that is characterized by high blood pressure

Ectopic pregnancy A pregnancy during which the fertilized ovum becomes implanted someplace other than the uterus

they must be removed by surgery or the use of medicines such as methotrexate, because the fetus cannot develop to term. Delay in removal may cause hemorrhaging and the death of the mother. A woman with a tubal pregnancy will not menstruate, but may notice spotty bleeding and abdominal pain.

RH INCOMPATIBILITY In **Rh incompatibility,** antibodies produced by the mother are transmitted to a fetus or newborn infant. *Rh* is a blood protein found in some people's red blood cells. Rh incompatibility occurs when a woman who does not have this blood factor, and is thus *Rh negative,* is carrying an *Rh-positive* fetus, which can happen if the father is Rh positive. The negative–positive combination is found in about 10% of U.S. marriages. However, it becomes a problem only in a minority of the resulting pregnancies. In such cases the mother's antibodies attack the red blood cells of the fetus, which can cause brain damage or death. Rh incompatibility does not usually adversely affect a first child because women will usually not yet have formed antibodies to the Rh factor.

Because mother and fetus have separate circulatory systems, it is unlikely that Rh-positive fetal red blood cells will enter the Rh-negative mother's body. The probability of an exchange of blood increases during childbirth, however, especially when the placenta becomes detached from the uterine wall. If an exchange of blood occurs, the mother will then produce antibodies to the baby's Rh-positive blood. The mother's antibodies may enter the fetal bloodstream and cause a condition called *fetal erythroblastosis,* which can result in anemia, mental deficiency, or even the death of the fetus or newborn infant.

Fortunately, blood typing of pregnant women significantly decreases the threat of uncontrolled erythroblastosis. If an Rh-negative mother is injected with the vaccine Rhogan within 72 hours after delivery of an Rh-positive baby, she will not develop the dangerous antibodies and thus will not pass them on to the fetus in a subsequent pregnancy. A fetus or newborn child at risk for erythroblastosis may also receive a preventive blood transfusion to remove the mother's Rh-positive antibodies from its blood.

DRUGS TAKEN BY THE MOTHER (OR THE FATHER) Some widely used drugs, including nonprescription drugs, are linked with birth abnormalities. In the 1960s the drug thalidomide was marketed to pregnant women as a presumably safe treatment for nausea and insomnia. However, the drug caused birth deformities, including stunted or missing limbs. Maternal use of illegal drugs such as cocaine and marijuana may also place the fetus at risk.

Paternal use of certain drugs also may endanger the fetus. One question is whether drugs alter the genetic material in the father's sperm. The use of certain substances by those who come into contact with a pregnant woman can harm the fetus. For example, the mother's inhalation of secondhand tobacco or marijuana smoke can hurt the fetus.

Several antibiotics may harm a fetus, especially if they are taken during certain periods of fetal development. Tetracycline may yellow the teeth and deform the bones (Koren et al., 1998). Other antibiotics have been implicated in deafness and jaundice. Acne drugs such as Accutane can cause physical and mental handicaps in the children of women who use them during pregnancy. Antihistamines, used commonly for allergies, may deform the fetus.

If you are pregnant, or suspect that you are, it is advisable to consult your obstetrician before taking any and all drugs, not just prescription drugs. Your obstetrician can usually direct you to a safe and effective substitute for a drug that could harm a fetus.

Rh incompatibility A condition during which antibodies produced by a pregnant woman are transmitted to the fetus and may cause brain damage or death

HORMONES   The hormones progestin and DES have sometimes been used to help women at risk of miscarriage maintain their pregnancies. When taken at about the time that sex organs differentiate, progestin (which is similar in composition to male sex hormones) can masculinize the external sex organs of embryos with female (XX) sex chromosomal structures. Progestin taken during the first trimester has also been linked to increased levels of aggressive behavior during childhood.

   DES (short for *diethylstilbestrol*), a powerful estrogen, was given to many women from the 1940s through the 1960s who were at risk for miscarriage to help maintain their pregnancies. DES is suspected of causing cervical and testicular cancer in some of the children whose mothers used it when pregnant (CDC, 2005b). Other problems have been reported as well. Daughters whose mothers used DES during their pregnancies have a higher than expected rate of miscarriages and premature deliveries. It was once suspected that men who were exposed prenatally to DES had higher than expected rates of infertility. However, research reveals no connection between in utero exposure to DES and male infertility. DES users themselves appear to be at high risk of some serious medical problems, such as breast cancer (CDC, 2005b).

VITAMINS   Many pregnant women are prescribed daily doses of multivitamins to maintain their own health and to promote the development of a healthy pregnancy. "Too much of a good thing" may be hazardous, however. High doses of vitamins such as A, B_6, D, and K have been linked to birth defects. Vitamin A excesses have been linked with cleft palate and eye damage, whereas excesses of vitamin D are linked to mental retardation.

NARCOTICS   Narcotics such as heroin and methadone can readily pass from mother to fetus through the placental membrane. Narcotics are addictive. Fetuses of mothers who use them regularly during their pregnancies can become addicted in utero. At birth, such babies may undergo withdrawal and show muscle tension and agitation. Women who use narcotics are advised to notify their obstetricians so that measures can be taken to aid the infants before and after delivery.

TRANQUILIZERS AND SEDATIVES   The tranquilizers Librium and Valium cross the placental membrane and may cause birth defects such as harelip. Sedatives, such as the barbiturate *phenobarbital,* are suspected of decreasing testosterone production and causing reproductive problems in the sons of women who use them during pregnancy.

MARIJUANA   The active ingredient in marijuana, THC, readily crosses the placenta. Research into the cognitive effects of maternal prenatal use of marijuana suggests that there may be no impairment in global intellectual functioning per se (Fried & Smith, 2001). However, problem solving and decision making may be affected. One study of the behavioral problems of 635 10-year-olds who had been exposed to maternal use of marijuana in utero found that prenatal use of marijuana was significantly related to increased hyperactivity, impulsivity, and problems in paying attention (Goldschmidt et al., 2000).

ALCOHOL   Mothers who drink heavily during pregnancy expose the fetus to greater risk of birth defects, infant mortality, sensory and motor problems, and mental retardation (Connor et al., 2006; Floyd et al., 2005). Nearly 40% of children whose mothers drank heavily during pregnancy develop **fetal alcohol syndrome** (FAS). FAS is

DES Diethylstilbestrol; an estrogen that was once given to women at risk for miscarriage to help maintain pregnancy

Fetal alcohol syndrome A cluster of symptoms caused by maternal drinking in which the child shows developmental lags and characteristic facial features such as an underdeveloped upper jaw, flattened nose, and widely spaced eyes

a cluster of symptoms typified by developmental lags and characteristic facial features, such as an underdeveloped upper jaw, flattened nose, and widely spaced eyes. Infants with FAS are often smaller than average and have smaller than average brains. They may be mentally retarded, lack coordination, and have deformed limbs and heart problems.

Truth or Fiction Revisited: It has *not* been shown that pregnant women can have one or two alcoholic beverages a day without harming their babies. Although research suggests that light drinking is unlikely to harm the fetus in most cases, FAS has been found even among the children of mothers who drank only two ounces of alcohol a day during the first trimester (Astley & Clarren, 2001). Moreover, individual sensitivities to alcohol may vary widely. The critical period for the development of the facial features associated with FAS seems to be the first two months of prenatal development, when the head is taking shape.

A Child with Fetal Alcohol Syndrome

TRUTH?
fiction 5

CIGARETTE SMOKING Cigarette smoke contains chemicals such as carbon monoxide and the stimulant nicotine that are transmitted to the fetus. It also lessens the amount of oxygen received by the fetus. Maternal smoking increases the risk of spontaneous abortion and complications during pregnancy such as premature rupturing of the amniotic sac, stillbirth, premature birth, low birthweight, and early infant mortality (Cnattingius, 2004; Secker–Walker & Vacek, 2003). These risks increase with the amount smoked (Bernstein et al., 2005). Maternal smoking may also impair intellectual development. In one study, women who smoked during pregnancy were 50% more likely than women who did not to have children whose intelligence test scores placed them in the mentally retarded range (i.e., an IQ less than 70) when the children were 10 years old (Drews et al., 1996).

Low birthweight is a common risk factor for infant disease, mortality, and problems in learning in school (O'Keeffe et al., 2003). The combination of smoking and drinking alcohol places the child at greater risk of low birthweight than either practice alone (Spencer, 2006). Maternal smoking affects the fetal heart rate and increases the risk of sudden infant death syndrome (SIDS) (Gordon et al., 2002; Pollack, 2001). Maternal smoking has also been linked to reduced lung function in newborns and asthma in childhood (Sturm et al., 2004). Evidence also points to reduced attention spans, hyperactivity, and lower IQs and achievement test scores in children exposed to maternal smoking during and after pregnancy.

Smoking by the father (or other household members) may be dangerous to a fetus because secondary smoke (smoke exhaled by the smoker or emitted from the tip of a lit cigarette) may be absorbed by the mother and passed along to the fetus. Passive exposure to second-hand smoke during infancy is also linked to increased risk of SIDS (Gordon et al., 2002).

Most American women of reproductive age drink alcohol, at least occasionally. Nearly one in five smokes ("Cigarette smoking

REFLECT

Do you know anyone who smoked or drank heavily during pregnancy? Was she aware of the problems that these behaviors could cause? Did she say anything about them? If so, what? What was your reaction? Explain.

Don't Do It! *Smoking cigarettes and pregnancy do not mix. Maternal smoking has been shown to increase the risk of spontaneous abortion and complications during pregnancy. It is connected with premature rupturing of the amniotic sac, stillbirth, premature birth, low birthweight, infant mortality, and delayed intellectual development in the child.*

among adults," 2005). Many do not suspend drug use until they learn that they are pregnant, which may not occur until weeks into the pregnancy. Some women are unwilling or unable to change their drug use habits even after learning they are pregnant (Cnattingius, 2004).

Our clinical experience suggests that it may be easier for women to quit if they consider quitting as limited to the terms of their pregnancies rather than as permanent. Then, of course, if they should remain abstinent after delivery, perhaps they will not be disappointed.

OTHER AGENTS X-rays increase the risk of malformed organs in the fetus, especially within a month and a half after conception. (Ultrasound has *not* been shown to harm the embryo or fetus.)

SafeZone

Q *What can caffeine do to a baby when it's inside the mom?*

A Make it kick a bit harder. In truth, research suggests that caffeine passes through the placenta and stimulates the fetal heart, but it has not been shown to be connected with any adverse outcomes. On the other hand, the Greek philosopher Aristotle suggested "Moderation in all things." So we wouldn't recommend overdoing the caffeine.

Chromosomal and Genetic Abnormalities

Not all of us have the normal complement of chromosomes. Some of us have genes that threaten our health or our existence (Table 11.1).

DOWN SYNDROME Children with Down syndrome have characteristic round faces; wide, flat noses; and protruding tongues. They often suffer from respiratory problems and heart malformations, problems that tend to claim their lives by middle age—the "prime of life," when most of us are reaching our vocational heights. People with Down syndrome are also moderately mentally retarded, but they usually can learn to read and write. With a little help from family and social agencies, they may hold jobs and lead largely independent lives.

The risk of a child having Down syndrome increases with the mother's age (Brody, 2002; CDC, 2002a) (Table 11.2). Down syndrome is usually caused by an extra chromosome on the 21st pair (trisomy 21). In most cases, Down syndrome is transmitted by the mother. The inner corners of the eyes of people with the syndrome have a downward-sloping crease of skin.

SICKLE-CELL ANEMIA AND TAY–SACHS DISEASE Sickle-cell anemia and Tay–Sachs disease are genetic disorders that are most likely to afflict certain racial and ethnic groups. Sickle-cell anemia is most prevalent in the United States among African Americans. One of every 375 African Americans is affected by the dis-

TABLE 11.1

Some Chromosomal and Genetic Abnormalities

Health Problem	Comments
Cystic fibrosis	A genetic disease in which the pancreas and lungs become clogged with mucus, which impairs the processes of respiration and digestion
Down syndrome	A condition characterized by a third chromosome on the 21st pair. The child with Down syndrome has a characteristic fold of skin over each eye and mental retardation. The risk of having a child with the syndrome increases as parents increase in age.
Hemophilia	A sex-linked disorder in which blood does not clot properly
Huntington disease	A fatal neurological disorder with an onset that occurs in middle adulthood
Neural tube defects	Disorders of the brain or spine, such as *anencephaly,* in which part of the brain is missing, and *spina bifida,* in which part of the spine is exposed or missing. Anencephaly is fatal shortly after birth, but some spina bifida victims survive for a number of years, albeit with severe handicaps.
Phenylketonuria	A disorder in which children cannot metabolize phenylalanine, which builds up in the form of phenylpyruvic acid and causes mental retardation. The disorder can be diagnosed at birth and controlled by diet.
Retinal blastoma	A form of blindness caused by a dominant gene
Sickle-cell anemia	A blood disorder that mostly afflicts African Americans, in which deformed blood cells obstruct small blood vessels, decreasing their capacity to carry oxygen and heightening the risk of occasionally fatal infections
Tay–Sachs disease	A fatal neurological disorder that primarily afflicts Jews of European origin

ease, and 8% are carriers of the sickle-cell trait (Ashley–Koch et al., 2000). In sickle-cell anemia, the red blood cells assume a sickle shape—hence the name—and they form clumps that obstruct narrow blood vessels and diminish the supply of oxygen. As a result, victims can suffer problems ranging from swollen, painful joints to

TABLE 11.2

Risk of Giving Birth to an Infant with Down Syndrome, According to Age of the Mother

Age of Mother	Probability of Down Syndrome in the Child
20	1 in 1,667
30	1 in 953
40	1 in 106
49	1 in 11

Source: American Fertility Association. 2006. [Online]. www.theafa.org.

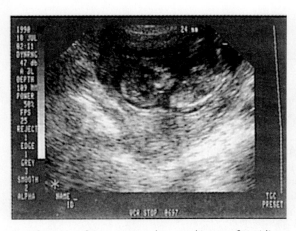

An Ultrasound Image. *An ultrasound image of Nevid's son, Michael, at 12 weeks after conception. The head and upper torso (facing upward) can be seen by those of you willing to look for many hours in the upper middle section of the photo. Michael was handsome even then, his father points out. The first and third author note that they did not insist on including their own boring ultrasound photos in this text.*

CRITICAL Thinking

Why do some women age 35 and older decide to have amniocentesis, and others decide not to do so? Where do you stand on the issue? Explain.

Recessive trait A trait that is not expressed when the gene or genes involved have been paired with dominant genes; transmitted to future generations and expressed if paired with other recessive genes

potentially lethal problems such as pneumonia and heart and kidney failure. Infections are a leading cause of death among those with the disease.

Tay–Sachs disease is a fatal neurological disease of young children. Only 1 in 100,000 people in the United States is affected, but among Jews of Eastern European background, the figure rises steeply to 1 in 3,600 (Khoury et al., 2000). The disease is characterized by degeneration of the central nervous system and gives rise to retardation, loss of muscle control and paralysis, blindness, and deafness. Victims seldom live beyond the age of 5.

SEX-LINKED GENETIC ABNORMALITIES   Some genetic defects, such as hemophilia, are sex linked, in that they are carried only on the X sex chromosome. They are transmitted from generation to generation as **recessive traits.** Females, each of whom has two X sex chromosomes, are less likely than males to be afflicted by sex-linked disorders, because the genes that carry the disorder would have to be present on both of their sex chromosomes for the disorder to be expressed. Sex-linked disorders are more likely to afflict sons of female carriers because they have only one X sex chromosome, which they inherit from their mothers. England's Queen Victoria was a hemophilia carrier and transmitted the condition to many of her children, who in turn carried it into several ruling families of Europe. For this reason hemophilia has been dubbed the "royal disease."

AVERTING CHROMOSOMAL AND GENETIC ABNORMALITIES Based upon information about a couple's medical background and family history of genetic defects, genetic counselors help couples appraise the risks of passing along genetic defects to their children. Some couples facing a high risk of passing along genetic defects to their children decide to adopt. Other couples decide to have an abortion if the fetus is determined to have certain abnormalities.

Various medical procedures are used to detect the presence of these disorders in the fetus. *Amniocentesis* is usually performed about four months into pregnancy but is sometimes done earlier. Fluid is drawn from the amniotic sac (or "bag of waters") with a syringe. Fetal cells in the fluid are grown in a culture and examined under a microscope for the presence of biochemical and chromosomal abnormalities. CVS is performed at about 10 weeks. A narrow tube is used to snip off material from the chorion, which is a membrane that contains the amniotic sac and fetus. The material is analyzed. The risks of amniocentesis and CVS are comparable (Simpson, 2000). The tests detect Down syndrome, sickle-cell anemia, Tay–Sachs disease, spina bifida, muscular dystrophy, Rh incompatibility, and other conditions. The tests also identify the sex of the fetus.

With ultrasound, high-pitched sound waves are bounced off the fetus, like radar, revealing a picture of the fetus on a TV monitor and allowing the obstetrician to detect certain abnormalities. Obstetricians also use ultrasound to locate the fetus during amniocentesis to lower the probability of injuring it with the syringe.

Parental blood tests can suggest the presence of problems such as sickle-cell anemia, Tay–Sachs disease, and neural tube defects. Still other tests examine fetal DNA and can indicate the presence of Huntington chorea, cystic fibrosis, and other disorders. Blood tests also now allow detection of Down syndrome during the first trimester.

Childbirth

Early during the ninth month of pregnancy, the fetus' head settles in the pelvis. This shift is called "dropping" or "lightening." The woman may actually feel lighter because of lessened pressure on the diaphragm. About a day or so before the beginning of labor, the woman may notice blood in her vaginal secretions because fetal pressure on the pelvis may rupture superficial blood vessels in the birth canal. Tissue that had plugged the cervix, possibly preventing entry of infectious agents from the vagina, becomes dislodged. There is a resultant discharge of bloody mucus. At about this time 1 woman in 10 also has a rush of warm "water" from the vagina. The "water" is amniotic fluid, and it means that the amniotic sac has burst. Labor usually begins within a day after rupture of the amniotic sac. For most women the amniotic sac does not burst until the end of the first stage of childbirth. Other signs of impending labor include indigestion, diarrhea, abdominal cramps, and an ache in the small of the back. Labor begins with the onset of regular uterine contractions.

The first uterine contractions are relatively painless and are called **Braxton–Hicks contractions,** or false labor contractions. They are false because they do not widen the cervix or advance the baby through the birth canal. They tend to increase in frequency but are less regular than labor contractions. Real labor contractions, by contrast, become more intense when the woman moves around or walks.

The initiation of labor may involve the secretion of hormones by the fetal adrenal and pituitary glands that stimulate the placenta and mother's uterus to secrete **prostaglandins.** Prostaglandins stimulate the uterine musculature to contract. It would make sense for the fetus to have a mechanism for signaling the mother that it is mature enough to sustain independent life. The mechanisms that initiate and maintain labor are not fully understood, however. Later in labor the pituitary gland releases **oxytocin,** a hormone that stimulates contractions strong enough to expel the baby.

SafeZone

Q *What triggers childbirth? Why does it trigger premature births?*

A It is speculated that hormones secreted by the fetus may stimulate the placenta and the mother's uterus to secrete prostaglandins that, in turn, cause uterine muscles to contract. These contractions may be felt as cramping during PMS. Thus it could be that the fetus has a mechanism for signaling the mother that it is ready to sustain independent life. Other possible triggers include the possible "urge" of the uterus to empty itself when it reaches a certain fullness or aging of the placenta. Later during labor, the mother's pituitary gland releases oxytocin, the hormone that stimulates contractions strong enough to expel the baby. Some common causes of prematurity include infection, inflammation, and maternal smoking.

Braxton–Hicks contractions So-called false labor contractions that are relatively painless

Prostaglandins Uterine hormones that stimulate uterine contractions

Oxytocin A pituitary hormone that stimulates uterine contractions

Efface To become thin

Dilate To open or widen

Stages of Childbirth

Childbirth begins with the onset of labor and has three stages. During the first stage, uterine contractions **efface** and **dilate** the cervix to about four inches in diameter, so that the baby may pass. Stretching of the cervix causes most of the pain of childbirth. A woman may experience little or no pain if her cervix dilates easily and quickly. The

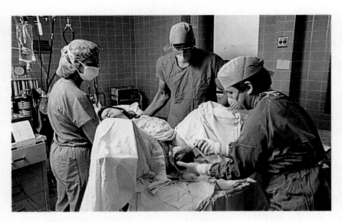

Coming into the World. *Childbirth progresses through three stages. During the first stage, uterine contractions efface and dilate the cervix so that the baby may pass. The second stage lasts from a few minutes to a few hours and ends with the birth of the baby. During the third stage, the placenta is expelled.*

first stage may last from a couple hours to more than a day. Twelve to 24 hours of labor is considered about average for a first pregnancy. During later pregnancies, labor takes about half this time.

The initial contractions are usually mild and spaced widely, at intervals of 10 to 20 minutes. They may last 20 to 40 seconds. As time passes, contractions become more frequent, long, strong, and regular.

Transition is the process that occurs when the cervix becomes nearly fully dilated and the baby's head begins to move into the vagina, or birth canal. Contractions usually come quickly during transition. Transition usually lasts about 30 minutes or less and is often accompanied by feelings of nausea, chills, and intense pain.

The second stage of childbirth follows transition and begins when the cervix has become fully dilated and the baby begins to move into the vagina and first appears at the opening of the birth canal (Figure 11.6). The woman may be taken to a delivery room for the second stage of childbirth. The second stage is shorter than the first stage. It lasts from a few minutes to a few hours and ends with the birth of the baby.

Each contraction of the second stage propels the baby farther along the birth canal (vagina). When the baby's head becomes visible at the vaginal opening, it is said to have *crowned*. The baby typically emerges fully a few minutes after crowning.

An **episiotomy** may be performed on the mother when the baby's head has crowned. The purpose is to prevent random tearing of the **perineum** that can occur if it becomes extremely effaced. Episiotomies are controversial, however. The incision can cause infection and pain, and create discomfort and itching as it heals. In some cases, the discomfort interferes with coitus for months. In some cases, prenatal massage of the perineum can avert the necessity of episiotomy (Eason et al., 2000; Johanson, 2000). For these and other reasons, an article in *Obstetrics & Gynecology* recommends that "Episiotomy should no longer be routine" (Eason & Feldman, 2000). Apparently, it isn't. A national survey reported in *Obstetrics & Gynecology* found that the overall episiotomy rate dropped from nearly 70% to about 19% during the past two decades (Goldberg et al., 2002). Don't hesitate to ask prospective obstetricians about their views on episiotomies.

With or without an episiotomy, the baby's passageway to the external world is a tight fit. As a result, the baby's facial features and the shape of its head may be temporarily distended. The baby may look as if it has been through a prizefight. Its head may be elongated, its nose flattened, and its ears bent. Although parents may be concerned about whether the baby's features will assume a more typical shape, they almost always do.

The third, or placental, stage of childbirth may last from a few minutes to an hour or more. During this stage, the placenta is expelled. Detachment of the placenta from the uterine wall may cause some bleeding. The uterus begins the process of contracting to a smaller size. The attending physician then sews up the episiotomy or any tears in the perineum.

IN THE NEW WORLD As the baby's head emerges, mucus is cleared from its mouth by means of suction aspiration to prevent the breathing passageway from being obstructed. Aspiration is often repeated after the baby is fully delivered. (Newly

Transition The process during which the cervix becomes nearly fully dilated and the head of the fetus begins to move into the birth canal

Episiotomy A surgical incision in the perineum that widens the birth canal, preventing random tearing during childbirth

Perineum The area between the vulva and the anus

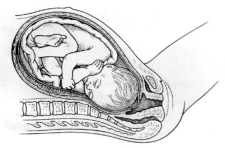

1. The second stage of labor begins

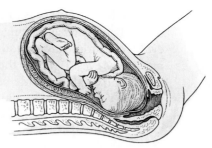

2. Further descent and rotation

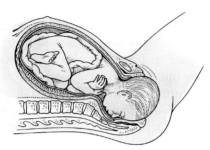

3. The crowning of the head

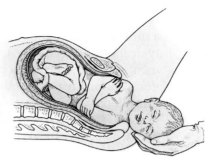

4. Anterior shoulder delivered

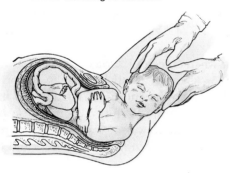

5. Posterior shoulder delivered

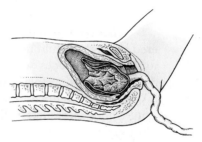

6. The third stage of labor begins with separation of the placenta from the uterine wall

Figure 11.6 The Stages of Childbirth. *During the first stage, uterine contractions efface and dilate the cervix to about four inches so that the baby may pass through. The second stage begins with movement of the baby into the birth canal and ends with birth of the baby. During the third stage, the placenta separates from the uterine wall and is expelled through the birth canal.*

delivered babies are no longer routinely held upside down to help expel mucus. Nor is the baby slapped on the buttocks to stimulate breathing, as in old films.)

When the baby is breathing adequately, the umbilical cord is clamped and severed about three inches from the baby's body. (After the birth of your first and third authors' third child, your first author was invited by the obstetrician to cut the umbilical cord, but the third author seized the scissors and cut the umbilical cord herself, squirting blood on the obstetrician's glasses. "Who gave the obstetrician the right to determine who would cut the umbilical cord!" she wanted to know.) The stump of the umbilical cord dries and falls off in its own time, usually in 7 to 10 days.

Truth or Fiction Revisited: It is *not* true that the cutting of the umbilical cord determines whether the baby will have an "inny" or an "outy." The cord dries and falls off on its own.

While the mother is in the third stage of labor, a nurse may perform procedures on the baby, such as placing drops of silver nitrate or an antibiotic ointment into the eyes. This procedure is required by most states to prevent bacterial infections in the newborn's eyes. Typically the baby is also footprinted and (if the birth has taken place in a hospital) given an identification bracelet. Because neonates do not manufacture vitamin K on their own, the baby may also receive an injection of the vitamin to ensure that her or his blood will clot normally in case of bleeding.

Methods of Childbirth

Until the 20th century, childbirth usually occurred at home and involved the mother, a midwife, family, and friends. These days, women in the United States and Canada typically give birth in hospitals attended by obstetricians, who use surgical instruments and anesthetics to protect mothers and children from infection, complications, and severe pain. Medical procedures save lives but also make childbearing more impersonal. Social critics argue that these procedures have medicalized a natural process. They have usurped control over women's bodies and, through the use of drugs, denied many women the experience of giving birth.

ANESTHETIZED CHILDBIRTH   During the past two centuries, science and medicine have led to the expectation that women should experience minimal discomfort during childbirth. Today only about 10% of American women use no anesthesia (Jameson, 2000).

General anesthesia first became popular when Queen Victoria of England delivered her eighth child under chloroform in 1853. General anesthesia, like the chloroform of old, induces unconsciousness. The drug sodium pentothal, a barbiturate, induces general anesthesia when it is injected into a vein. Barbiturates may also be taken orally to reduce anxiety while the woman remains awake. Women may also receive tranquilizers like Valium or narcotics like Demerol to help them relax and to blunt pain without inducing sleep.

Anesthetic drugs, as well as tranquilizers and narcotics, decrease the strength of uterine contractions during delivery. They may thus delay the process of cervical dilation and prolong labor. They also weaken the woman's ability to push the baby through the birth canal. Because they cross the placental membrane, they also lower the newborn's overall responsiveness.

Regional or **local anesthetics** block pain in parts of the body without generally depressing the mother's alertness or putting her to sleep. With a *pudendal block,* the external genitals are numbed by local injection. With an *epidural block* or a *spinal block,* an anesthetic is injected into the spinal canal, which temporarily numbs the mother's body below the waist. To prevent injury, the needles used for these injections do not come into contact with the spinal cord itself. Although local anesthesia decreases the responsiveness of the newborn baby, there is little evidence that medicated childbirth has serious, long-term consequences on children.

PREPARED CHILDBIRTH: THE LAMAZE METHOD   The French obstetrician Fernand Lamaze visited the Soviet Union in 1951 and found that many Russian women bore babies without anesthetics and without reporting a great deal of pain. Lamaze returned to Western Europe with some of the techniques the women used; they are now termed the **Lamaze method,** or *prepared childbirth.* Lamaze (1981) argued that women can learn to conserve energy during childbirth and reduce the pain of uterine contractions by associating the contractions with other responses,

General anesthesia The use of drugs to put people to sleep and eliminate pain, as during childbirth

Local anesthesia Anesthesia that eliminates pain in a specific area of the body, as during childbirth

Lamaze method A childbirth method during which women learn about childbirth, learn to relax and to breathe in patterns that conserve energy and lessen pain, and have a coach (usually the father) present at childbirth; also termed *prepared childbirth*

such as thinking of pleasant mental images such as beach scenes, or engaging in breathing and relaxation exercises.

A pregnant woman typically attends Lamaze classes with a "coach"— usually the father or partner—who will aid her in the delivery room by timing contractions, offering emotional support, and coaching her in the breathing and relaxation exercises. The woman and her partner also receive general information about childbirth. The partner is integrated into the process, and many couples report that their relationships are strengthened as a result.

The Lamaze method is flexible about the use of anesthetics. Many women report some pain during delivery and obtain anesthetics. However, the Lamaze method appears to help women to gain a greater sense of control over the delivery process.

REFLECT

Do you know people who have used prepared childbirth or C-sections? What were their experiences like?

CESAREAN SECTION During a **cesarean section**, the baby is delivered through surgery rather than through the vagina. The term *section* is derived from the Latin for "to cut." Julius Caesar is said to have been delivered in this way, but health professionals believe this unlikely. During a cesarean section (C-section for short) the woman is anesthetized and incisions are made in the abdomen and uterus so the surgeon can remove the baby. The incisions are then sewn up and the mother can begin walking, often that same day, although generally with some discomfort for a while. Although most C-sections are without complications, some cause urinary tract infections, inflammation of the wall of the uterus, blood clots, or hemorrhaging (ACOG, 2003). All in all, women who have C-sections are four times as likely to experience a pregnancy-related death (35.9 deaths per 100,000 deliveries) as women who deliver vaginally (9.2 deaths per 100,000 deliveries) (ACOG, 2003).

C-sections are most likely to be advised when normal delivery is difficult or threatening to the health of the mother or child. Vaginal deliveries can become difficult if the baby is large, the mother's pelvis is small or misshapen, the mother is tired, weakened, or older. Herpes and HIV infections in the birth canal can be bypassed by C-section. C-sections are also likely to be performed if the baby presents for delivery in the breech position (feet downward) or the **transverse position** (lying crosswise), or if the baby is in distress.

Use of the C-section has mushroomed. **Truth or Fiction Revisited:** Nearly 3 of every 10 births (29%) in the United States are currently by C-section (Bakalar, 2005). Compare this figure with about 1 in 20 births in 1965. Much of the increase in the rate of C-sections reflects advances in medical technology, such as use of fetal monitors that allow doctors to detect fetal distress, concern about malpractice suits, and, simply, current medical practice patterns. Yet some women request C-sections to avoid the discomforts of vaginal delivery or to control the timing of the delivery. Women are also having children at a more advanced age, when there is more risk to the urogenital system from vaginal delivery (Bakalar, 2005).

Medical opinion once held that once a woman had a C-section, subsequent deliveries also had to be by C-section. Otherwise, uterine scars might rupture during labor. Research has shown that rupture is rare, however. In one study, only 10 of 3,249 women who chose to try vaginal delivery after a previous C-section had a uterine rupture (McMahon et al., 1996). Moreover, there were no maternal deaths. In any event, only a small minority of women who have previously had a C-section deliver subsequent babies vaginally (Bakalar, 2005).

Consumer advocates advise pregnant women who would like to deliver vaginally, if possible, to ask about the rates of C-sections when they are choosing a physician and a hospital. Women can try to choose obstetricians who have lower rates or who are open to a second opinion for elective surgery. However, do not forget that

Cesarean section A method of childbirth during which the fetus is delivered through a surgical incision in the abdomen

Transverse position A crosswise birth position

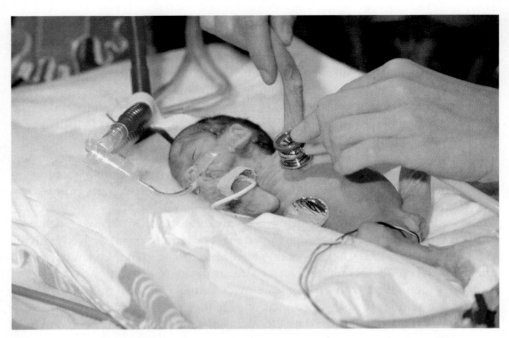

Too Early. *A baby is considered premature if it is born before 37 weeks of gestation. Premature babies are vulnerable to various developmental problems.*

there are excellent reasons for having C-sections. It makes no sense to avoid a C-section if vaginal delivery might put the mother or the baby at risk.

Birth Problems

Most deliveries are uncomplicated, or "unremarkable" in the medical sense—although childbirth is the most remarkable experience of many parents' lives. Problems can and do occur, however. Some of the most common birth problems are anoxia and the birth of preterm and low-birthweight babies.

ANOXIA Prenatal **anoxia** can cause various problems in the neonate and affect later development. It leads to complications such as brain damage and mental retardation. Prolonged anoxia during delivery can also result in cerebral palsy and possibly death.

The baby is supplied with oxygen through the umbilical cord. Passage through the birth canal squeezes the umbilical cord. Temporary squeezing, like holding one's breath for a moment, is unlikely to cause problems. (In fact, slight oxygen deprivation at birth is not unusual because the transition from receiving oxygen through the umbilical cord to breathing on its own may not happen immediately after the baby emerges.) Anoxia can result if constriction of the cord is prolonged, however. Prolonged constriction is more likely to occur with a breech presentation, because the baby's head presses the umbilical cord against the birth canal during delivery. Fetal monitoring can help detect anoxia early, however, before damage occurs. A C-section can be performed if the fetus appears to be in distress.

PRETERM AND LOW-BIRTHWEIGHT CHILDREN A neonate is considered to be premature, or **preterm,** if it is born before 37 weeks of gestation. The

CRITICAL
Thinking

Critical thinkers tackle controversial issues. What are the pros and cons of the following aspects of childbirth: Episiotomy? Use of anesthesia? C-section?

Anoxia Oxygen deprivation
Preterm Born before 37 weeks of gestation

normal period of gestation is 40 weeks. Prematurity is generally linked with low birthweight, because the fetus normally makes dramatic gains in weight during the last weeks of pregnancy.

Regardless of the length of its gestation period, a newborn baby is considered to have a low birthweight if it weighs less than five pounds (about 2,500 grams). Preterm and low-birthweight babies face a heightened risk of infant mortality from causes ranging from asphyxia and infections to SIDS (Berger, 2000; Kramer et al., 2000). Neurological and developmental problems are also common among preterm infants, especially those born at or prior to 25 weeks of gestation (Saigal et al., 2006b; Wood et al., 2000b).

Twins and other multiple birth groupings are more likely to be of low birthweight than individual births (Blickstein et al., 2000). There is also a relationship between prematurity and the spacing of babies. Women who have babies less than 18 months or more than 59 months apart are at the highest risk for premature infants (Fuentes–Afflick & Hessol, 2000). On the other hand, it is common for women carrying more than one child to deliver prematurely, apparently because the babies are running out of space.

Preterm babies are relatively thin because they have not yet formed the layer of fat that accounts for the round, robust appearance of most full-term babies. Their muscles are immature, weakening their sucking and breathing reflexes. Also, during the last weeks of pregnancy fetuses secrete **surfactant**, which prevent the walls of their airways from sticking together. Muscle weakness and incomplete lining of the airways with surfactant can cause a cluster of problems known as **respiratory distress syndrome,** which is responsible for many neonatal deaths. Today, surfactant replacement therapy is extending the possibilities of survival in preterm infants (Cole, 2000). Preterm babies may also suffer from underdeveloped immune systems, which leave them more vulnerable to infections.

Preterm infants usually remain in the hospital for a time. There they can be monitored and placed in incubators that provide a temperature-controlled environment and that offer some protection from disease. If necessary, they may also receive oxygen. Although remarkable advances are being made in our ability to help preterm babies survive, the likelihood of developmental disabilities continues to increase dramatically for babies who are born at 25 weeks of gestation or earlier (Cole, 2000).

STILLBIRTH Stilbirth, in which the baby is born dead, is the gravest of birth problems. Stillbirth is no surprise. The baby is "silent" prior to birth—no heartbeat is heard; there is no kicking (Trulsson & Rådestad, 2004). Stillbith is connected with fetal abnormalities, infection, medical conditions of the mother, and pregnancy complications such as preeclampsia and problems with the placenta (Pasupathy & Smith, 2005). Yet the majority of cases have no clear cause and are considered unexplained. Even so, many "unexplained" deaths are connected with restriction of growth of the fetus. Growth restriction, in turn, may be associated with the mother's age and smoking (Cnattingius, 2004). The risk of stillbirth is also connected with the functioning of the placenta early on during pregnancy, and pregnancies at risk can be more carefully monitored. Sometimes corrective actions can be taken to improve placental circulation.

Stillbirth has a deep psychological impact on parents, leading, in many cases, to posttraumatic stress disorder (PTSD), which is characterized by rumination about the loss, intrusive thoughts, and nightmares (Born et al., 2006). When a baby still within the mother is declared dead, she may need a few hours before labor is induced to adjust to the fact (Trulsson & Rådestad, 2004). During this period, the

Surfactant Substances that prevent the walls of the airways from sticking together

Respiratory distress syndrome A cluster of breathing problems, including weak and irregular breathing, to which preterm babies are especially vulnerable

Maternal and Infant Mortality around the World

Contemporary medicine has made great contributions to the safety of childbirth and infancy, but they are not distributed equally throughout the world. Save the Children, a nonprofit relief and development organization, tracks the likelihood that women will die during pregnancy and childbirth (maternal mortality) and that infants will die during their first year (infant mortality).

Table 11.3 suggests that these mortality rates reflect factors such as the percent of births that are attended by trained people, the literacy rate of women (a measure of women's education), and participation of women in government (a measure of women's empowerment). The safest place for childbirth and infancy is Sweden, where the chances of a woman's dying in childbirth is about 1 in 30,000, and only 3 in 1,000 infants die before their first birthday. Sweden also has close to a 100% adult female literacy rate, provides trained personnel to assist in all births, and has the greatest participation rate (45%) by women in national government. The most dangerous place is Afghanistan, where one woman in six will die during pregnancy or delivery, and 165 children of 1,000 will die before their first birthday. Only 21% of Afghan women can read; 12% are assisted in birth by a professional; and, in this patriarchal society, women have virtually no role in government. There is also little if any prenatal care in Afghanistan.

Americans who see numbers like those shown in Table 11.3 wonder why the United States is not nearer the top of the list. One answer is that the United States is made up of nations within a nation. States with high poverty rates, large rural populations, and low levels of education have the highest mortality rates. Among these states are Texas, Mississippi, Arkansas, Arizona, and New Mexico.

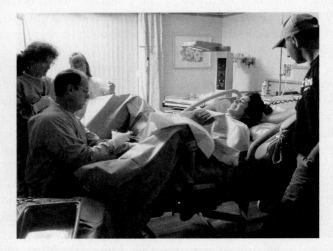

A Mother's Safety Depends on Where She's Having Her Child. *It's not just the medical care. It's the wider issue of whether the culture empowers women. Does your culture empower women? Your subculture? Are all cultures equal? Really?*

woman may seek as much medical information as possible, or be silent herself. Afterward, she may encounter what Brin (2004) refers to as a "grief storm" that can find some outlet through social ritual or speaking with a compassionate therapist.

Subsequent pregnancies are likely to be experienced with extreme anxiety by both parents (Brisch et al., 2005; Turton et al., 2006). In the case of a miscarriage, parents may feel that they have to get safely through the first trimester for the subsequent pregnancy to be valid. In the case of a stillbirth, they are likely to have misgivings for the entire gestational period, and through labor. This is painful, but it is to be expected.

TABLE 11.3

Maternal Mortality and Infant Mortality around the World as Related to Access to Medical Assistance and Empowerment of Women

Country	Lifetime Risk of Maternal Mortality	Percent of Births Attended by Trained Personnel	Adult Female Literacy Rate, %	Participation of Women in National Government, % of Seats Held by Women	Infant Mortality Rate, per 1,000 Live Births
Sweden	1 in 29,800	100	99	45	3
Austria	1 in 16,000	100	99	34	6
Denmark	1 in 9,800	100	99	38	4
United Kingdom	1 in 3,800	99	99	18	5
South Korea	1 in 2,800	100	96	6	5
United States	1 in 2,500	99	99	18	5
Israel	1 in 1,800	99	93	15	6
Russia	1 in 1,000	99	99	8	18
China	1 in 830	76	78	22	31
North Korea	1 in 590	97	96	20	42
Turkey	1 in 480	81	77	4	36
Iran	1 in 370	90	69	4	35
Mexico	1 in 370	86	89	23	24
Egypt	1 in 310	61	44	2	35
Brazil	1 in 140	88	87	9	30
Iraq	1 in 65	72	23	8	102
India	1 in 48	43	45	9	67
Pakistan	1 in 31	20	28	22	83
Zambia	1 in 19	43	72	12	108
Afghanistan	1 in 6	12	21	—	165

Source: Adapted from the Complete Mothers' Index 2004 in *Children Having Children: State of the World's Mothers 2004*. Reprinted by permission of Save the Children USA.

The Postpartum Period

The weeks after delivery are called the **postpartum** period. The first few days postpartum are frequently happy ones. The long wait is over, as are the discomforts of childbirth. However, about 70% of new mothers have periods of tearfulness, sadness, and irritability that the American Psychiatric Association (2000) refers to as "baby blues." Baby blues and other postpartum mood problems are so common that they are statistically normal (Gavin et al., 2005).

These problems include the baby blues and more serious mood disorders (postpartum-onset mood episodes), which occasionally include "psychotic features" (American Psychiatric Association, 2006; Grigoriadis & Romans, 2006). These problems are far-flung; researchers find them in China, Turkey, Guyana, Australia, and South Africa, occurring with similar frequency (Bloch et al., 2006; Cohen et al., 2006).

Postpartum After childbirth

Baby blues affect the majority of women in the weeks after delivery. Researchers believe they are common because they are caused by the hormonal changes that accompany and follow delivery (Bloch et al., 2006; Morris, 2000). They last for about 10 days and are not severe enough to impair the mother's functioning. Don't misunderstand; the baby blues are seriously discomforting and are not to be ignored. Don't say, "Oh, you're just experiencing what most women experience." The point is that most women get by with them even though they're pretty awful at times, partly because they know that they are transient.

As many as 1 in 5 to 10 women encounter a more serious mood disorder called **postpartum depression** (PPD). PPD begins within four weeks after delivery and may linger for weeks or months. PPD is symptomized by serious sadness, feelings of hopelessness and helplessness, feelings of worthlessness, difficulty concentrating, and major changes in appetite (usually loss of appetite) and sleep patterns (frequently insomnia). There can also be severe fluctuations in mood, with women sometimes feeling elated. Some women show obsessive concern with the well-being of their babies at this time.

Some researchers suggest that PPD is caused by the interactions of biological (mainly hormonal), including that precipitous drop-off in estrogen (Johnstone et al., 2001), and psychological factors, such as

- concerns about the life changes that motherhood creates
- concerns about whether one will be a good mother
- marital problems
- having a sick or unwanted baby

But the focus today is on the biological, because there are major changes in body chemistry during and after pregnancy, and because women around the world seem to experience similar disturbances in mood, even when their life experiences and support systems are very different from those we find in the United States (Cohen et al., 2006).

According to the American Psychiatric Association (2000), postpartum mood episodes are accompanied by psychotic features (loss of touch with reality) in 1 woman in 500 to 1,000. Very rarely, women experience delusions that the infant is possessed by the devil or that they must kill the infant.

Women who experience PPD may benefit from psychotherapy or drugs. Drugs that increase estrogen levels or antidepressants may help. Most women get over PPD on their own. At the very least, women need to know that the problem is not unusual and does not necessarily mean that there is something seriously wrong with them or that they are not living up to their obligations.

Breast-feeding versus Bottle Feeding

As one observer puts it, "In today's environment, breast-feeding represents both a medical gold standard for infant feeding and a moral gold standard for mothering" (Knaak, 2005). The majority of mothers in the United States and Canada today breast-feed their children (Figure 11.7). However, the number drops off after six months, and the American Academy of Pediatrics (2006) recommends that women breast-feed for a year or more.

One reason that women bottle feed their babies is that they return to the workforce soon after childbirth. Some choose to share feeding chores with the fa-

Postpartum depression
Persistent and severe mood changes during the postpartum period; involves feelings of despair and apathy, characterized by changes in appetite and sleep, low self-esteem, and difficulty concentrating

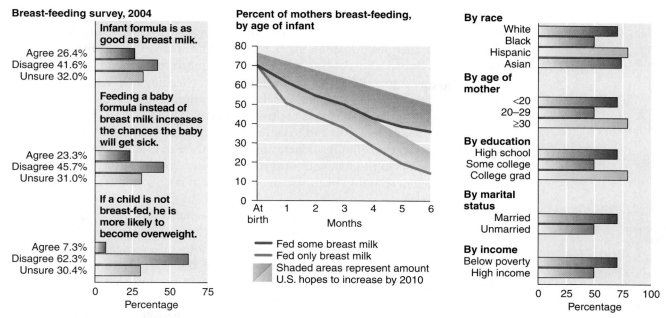

Breast-feeding survey, 2004

Infant formula is as good as breast milk.

Agree 26.4%
Disagree 41.6%
Unsure 32.0%

Feeding a baby formula instead of breast milk increases the chances the baby will get sick.

Agree 23.3%
Disagree 45.7%
Unsure 31.0%

If a child is not breast-fed, he is more likely to become overweight.

Agree 7.3%
Disagree 62.3%
Unsure 30.4%

0   25   50   75
Percentage

Percent of mothers breast-feeding, by age of infant

At birth 1 2 3 4 5 6
Months

—— Fed some breast milk
—— Fed only breast milk
░ Shaded areas represent amount U.S. hopes to increase by 2010

By race
White
Black
Hispanic
Asian

By age of mother
<20
20–29
≥30

By education
High school
Some college
College grad

By marital status
Married
Unmarried

By income
Below poverty
High income

0   25   50   75   100
Percentage

Figure 11.7 Who Breast-Feeds? *Although the majority of mothers breast-feed, many are unsure of its benefits over baby formula.*
SOURCE: CDC, *Health Styles Survey,* 2010.

ther or a partner, who is equally equipped to prepare and hold a bottle. Other women find breast-feeding inconvenient or unpleasant. Long-term comparisons of breast-fed and bottle-fed children show few, if any, significant differences. HIV (the AIDS virus) can be transmitted to infants by breast milk. According to United Nations estimates, one third of the infants with HIV around the world were infected via breast milk (United Nations Special Session on AIDS, 2001). Moreover, when undernourished mothers in developing countries breast-feed, their babies can become malnourished.

Breast-Feeding Seems to Be the "Gold Standard" for Mothers in the United States and Canada Today. *Why? Is it always possible? Under what circumstances should women not breast-feed their children?*

On the other hand, breast-feeding reduces the risk of infectious diseases the baby by transmitting the mother's antibodies to the baby. Breast-feeding also reduces the incidence of allergies in babies, SIDS, diabetes, and many other health problems, both in developed and developing countries (American Academy of Pediatrics, 2006). Uterine contractions that occur during breast-feeding help return the uterus to its typical size. (Breast-feeding also delays resumption of normal menstrual cycles, but is not a perfectly reliable birth control method.)

The hormones prolactin and oxytocin are involved in breast-feeding. **Prolactin** stimulates production of milk, or **lactation,** two to three days after delivery. Oxytocin causes the breasts to produce milk and is secreted in response to suckling. When an infant is weaned, secretion of prolactin and oxytocin is discontinued, and lactation comes to an end.

Should a woman breast-feed her baby? The issue is largely political (Knaak, 2005). Much of the literature on breast-feeding has little to do with the advantages of breast milk or formula, but with occupational and domestic arrangements, child day-care, mother–infant bonding, and the politics of domestic decision making. Although breast-feeding benefits both mother and infant, the outcomes for bottle feeding in the developed world do not show that the relative risks are unacceptable. Each woman is advised to weigh the pluses and minuses for herself.

CRITICAL
Thinking

What are the "political" issues involved in breast-feeding versus bottle feeding?

Resumption of Ovulation and Menstruation

For close to a month after delivery, women experience a reddish vaginal discharge called **lochia.** A nonnursing mother does not resume actual menstrual periods until two to three months postpartum. The first few cycles are likely to be irregular. Many women incorrectly assume that they will resume menstruating after childbirth by having a menstrual period and ovulating two weeks later. In most cases, the opposite is true. Ovulation precedes the first menstrual period after childbirth. Thus, a woman may become pregnant before the menstrual phase of her first postpartum cycle. Some women who suffered PMS before their pregnancies find that their periods give them less discomfort after the birth of their children.

Resumption of Sexual Activity

TRUTH fiction **8**

The resumption of coitus depends on a couple's level of sexual interest, the healing of episiotomies or other injuries, fatigue, the recommendations of obstetricians, and, of course, tradition. Obstetricians usually advise a six-week waiting period for safety and comfort. One study of 570 women found that they actually resumed sexual intercourse an average of seven weeks after childbirth (Byrd et al., 1998).

Truth or Fiction Revisited: It is true that couples should abstain from coitus for at least six weeks after childbirth. However, many other kinds of sexual activities are safe and do not cause discomfort. (Check with your obstetrician.)

Women will typically prefer to delay coitus until it becomes physically comfortable, generally when the episiotomy or other lacerations have healed and the lochia has ended. This may take several weeks. Women who breast-feed may also find they have less vaginal lubrication, and the dryness can cause discomfort during coitus. K-Y jelly or other lubricants may help in such cases.

Prolactin A pituitary hormone that stimulates production of milk; from roots meaning "for milk"

Lactation Production of milk by the mammary glands

Lochia A reddish vaginal discharge that may persist for a month after delivery

The return of sexual interest and resumption of sexual activity may take longer for some couples than for others. Sexual interest depends more on psychological than on physical factors. Many couples encounter declining sexual interest and activity during the first year after childbirth, because child care can sap energy and limit free time. Generally speaking, couples whose sexual relationships were satisfying before the baby arrived tend to show greater sexual interest and to resume sexual activity earlier than those who had less satisfying relationships beforehand. (No surprise.)

1. What happens during conception?

- Conception is the union of a sperm cell and an ovum, which normally occurs in a fallopian tube. More boys than girls are conceived, but male fetuses have a higher rate of miscarriage. Chromosomes from the germs cells align, combining to form 23 new pairs.

- The reliable method for selecting the sex of one's child is PGD.

2. What are the causes of infertility? How are couples helped to have children?

- Male fertility problems mainly involve low sperm count and motility. Female fertility problems include failure to ovulate, infections, endometriosis, and obstructions in the reproductive tract. Fertility drugs regulate ovulation. Artificial insemination may use sperm from donor. IVF may be used when the fallopian tubes are blocked. Some couples adopt.

3. What happens during pregnancy?

- Early signs include a missed period and presence of HCG in the blood or urine. "Morning sickness" is believed to be linked with a healthy pregnancy. Miscarriages have many causes, including chromosomal defects in the fetus. Most health professionals agree that coitus is normally safe until the start of labor.

- Parents respond to pregnancy according to the degree to which they want the child. A woman's response also reflects physical changes and her feelings about these changes.

4. What happens during prenatal development?

- During the germinal stage, the dividing mass of cells travels to the uterus, where it becomes implanted. The embryo and fetus exchange nutrients and wastes with the mother through the placenta and umbilical cord. Major organ systems develop during the embryonic period. The fetal stage is mainly characterized by maturation of organs and gains in size.

- Maternal malnutrition is linked with low birthweight, prematurity, and cognitive problems. Maternal diseases and disorders can harm the embryo and are called teratogens. Women who contract rubella may bear children who suffer from deafness, retardation, heart disease, or cataracts. Syphilis can cause miscarriage or stillbirth. Babies born to HIV-infected mothers may become infected by childbirth. Toxemia, characterized by high blood pressure, is connected with preterm or undersize babies. In Rh incompatibility, antibodies produced by the mother can kill the fetus or cause brain damage. Teratogens are most harmful during periods when certain organs are developing.

Children of women who used DES are at risk for cervical or testicular cancer. Maternal use of alcohol is linked to FAS. Maternal cigarette smoking deprives the fetus of oxygen and is linked to low birthweight, stillbirth, and learning problems.

- Chromosomal abnormalities become more likely as parents age. Down syndrome is caused by an extra chromosome on the 21st pair. Disorders that arise from abnormal numbers of sex chromosomes are sex linked. Sickle-cell anemia is most common among African Americans, and Tay–Sachs disease is common among Jewish children of East European origin.

- Amniocentesis cultures fetal cells found in amniotic fluid to detect genetic abnormalities. CVS is similar to amniocentesis but is conducted earlier. Ultrasound is used to track the growth of the fetus and find structural abnormalities. Parental blood tests can reveal genes and markers for many disorders.

5. What happens during childbirth?

- Before labor begins, blood typically appears in the birth canal. Some women have a rush of amniotic fluid. Oxytocin stimulates contractions strong enough to expel the baby.

- Childbirth begins with the onset of regular contractions of the uterus, which efface and dilate the cervix, causing most of the discomfort of childbirth. The second stage begins when the baby appears and it ends with birth. The third stage expels the placenta.

- General anesthesia puts the woman to sleep. Local anesthetics deaden pain without putting the mother to sleep. The Lamaze method uses breathing and relaxation exercises, along with a "coach." A C-section is a procedure that is used to deliver a baby surgically through the abdomen.

- Prenatal oxygen deprivation can damage the nervous system and kill the baby. Oxygen deprivation can be caused by immaturity of the baby's respiratory system and pressure against the umbilical cord during birth.

6. What are some of the key events during the postpartum period?

- Women may encounter baby blues and more severe PPD. These problems are found around the world and apparently reflect hormonal changes after childbirth.

- Breast-feeding is connected with fewer infections and allergic reactions.

- The first few menstrual cycles after childbirth are likely to be irregular. Obstetricians usually advise a six-week waiting period after childbirth before resuming coitis.

1. The enzyme hyaluronidase

    (a) stimulates production of milk
    (b) passes through the placenta
    (c) stimulates contractions of labor
    (d) thins the zona pellucida

2. The most common cause of male infertility is

    (a) low sperm motility
    (b) low sperm count
    (c) injury to the testes
    (d) higher than normal scrotal temperature

3. The presence of human chorionic gonadotropin is assessed to determine

    (a) blocked fallopian tubes
    (b) sickle-cell anemia
    (c) pregnancy
    (d) Down syndrome

4. If we date pregnancy from the onset of the last menstrual cycle before conception, the normal gestation period is _____ days.

    (a) 266
    (b) 272
    (c) 280
    (d) 288

5. With the method of _____, an ovum is fertilized in a laboratory dish and then placed in a fallopian tube.

    (a) ZIFT
    (b) artificial insemination
    (c) embryonic transfer
    (d) intracytoplasmic injection

6. The umbilical cord contains

    (a) one artery and one vein
    (b) two arteries and two veins
    (c) two arteries and one vein
    (d) one artery and two veins

7. A breech presentation is

    (a) bottom first
    (b) head first
    (c) sideways
    (d) shoulder first

8. Preeclampsia is a stage of

    (a) sickle-cell anemia
    (b) Tay–Sachs disease
    (c) rubella
    (d) toxemia

9. The critical period for the development of the facial features associated with FAS seems to be the first _____ of prenatal development.

    (a) week
    (b) two weeks
    (c) month
    (d) two months

10. The pudendal block is an example of

    (a) general anesthesia
    (b) local anesthesia
    (c) a birth problem
    (d) anoxia

11. _____ is a fatal neurological disorder.

    (a) Huntington disease
    (b) Sickle-cell anemia
    (c) Retinal blastoma
    (d) Down syndrome

12. Which of the following is most likely to attack African Americans?

    (a) Tay–Sachs disease
    (b) Hemophilia
    (c) Sickle-cell anemia
    (d) Retinal blastoma

13. An underdeveloped upper jaw is characteristic of

    (a) children whose mothers smoked during pregnancy
    (b) fetal alcohol syndrome
    (c) prenatal exposure to PCBs
    (d) prenatal exposure to stress

14. Mothers in _____ are most likely to die in childbirth.

    (a) Denmark
    (b) Austria
    (c) Pakistan
    (d) Afghanistan

15. Which of the following aspects of childbirth is not controversial?

    (a) Vaginal delivery
    (b) Cesarean section
    (c) Prepping
    (d) Episiotomy

Answers 1. d; 2. b; 3. c; 4. c; 5. a; 6. c; 7. a; 8. d; 9. d; 10. b; 11. a; 12. c; 13. b; 14. d; 15. a

12

Contraception and Abortion

TRUTH?
fiction

Which of the following statements are true, and which are fiction? Look for the
Truth/Fiction icons on the pages that follow to find the answers.

1 Ancient Egyptians used crocodile dung as a contraceptive.   T   F

2 There is an oral contraceptive that can be taken the morning after unprotected intercourse.   T   F

3 Douching quickly after unprotected intercourse is a reasonably good contraceptive method.   T   F

4 Sterilization operations can be surgically reversed.   T   F

5 Contraceptives not only prevent conception, they also provide protection against sexually transmitted infections.   T   F

6 Abortions were legal in the newly founded United States.   T   F

7 The D&C is the most widely used abortion method in the United States.   T   F

It was a stifling day in July 1912. Margaret Sanger (1883–1966), a nurse practitioner, was summoned to the house of a woman near death from a botched self-induced abortion. Her husband had called a doctor, and the doctor sent for Sanger. Together, doctor and nurse worked feverishly through the days and nights that followed to stem an infection that had taken hold in the woman. Sanger later commented,

> Never had I worked so fast, never so concentratedly. The sultry days and nights were melted into a torpid inferno. It did not seem possible there could be such heat, and every bit of food, ice, and drugs had to be carried up three flights of stairs.

After two interminable weeks, the woman began to recover. Her neighbors, who had feared the worst, came to express their joy. But the woman, who smiled wanly at those who came to see her, appeared more depressed and anxious than would be expected of someone who was recovering from a grave illness. By the end of the third week, when Sanger prepared to leave her patient, the woman, Mrs. Sachs, voiced the fear that was haunting her. Her face registered deep despair as she explained to Sanger that she dreaded becoming pregnant again and facing a choice between attempting another abortion, which she feared might kill her, and bearing a baby whose care it was beyond her means to support. She pleaded for information about contraception but Sanger could offer none. In 1912 it was a crime even for health professionals like Margaret Sanger to dispense information about contraceptives. Abortions, too, were illegal. Sanger tried to comfort her and promised to return to talk again (Reed & Lampe, 2003).

Margaret Sanger Testifying Before a Senate Committee

Three months later she received another urgent call. It was Mr. Sachs. His wife was sick again—from the same cause. Sanger recalled,

> For a wild moment I thought of sending someone else, but actually, of course, I hurried into my uniform, caught up my bag, and started out. All the way I longed for a subway wreck, an explosion, anything to keep me from having to enter that home again. But nothing happened, even to delay me. I turned into the dingy doorway and climbed the familiar stairs once more. The children were there, young little things.
>
> Mrs. Sachs was in a coma and died within ten minutes. I folded her still hands across her breast, remembering how they had pleaded with me, begging so humbly for the knowledge which was her right. I drew a sheet over her pallid face. Jake was sobbing, running his hands through his hair and pulling it out like an insane person. Over and over again he wailed, "My God! My God! My God!" (Sanger, 1938)

Today, partly because of the work of Margaret Sanger, who went on to become a key advocate for birth control, information about contraceptives is disseminated freely throughout the United States.

Methods of birth control include contraception and abortion. The term *contraception* refers to techniques that prevent conception. The term *abortion* refers to the termination of a pregnancy before the embryo or fetus is capable of surviving outside the womb, as we see later in the chapter.

Contraception

People have been devising means of contraception since they became aware of the relationship between coitus and conception. The safest and most effective method of contraception is abstinence. The Bible contains many references to contraceptive techniques, including vaginal sponges and contraceptive concoctions. It also refers to **coitus interruptus,** or withdrawal. The story of Onan, for example, implies knowledge of the withdrawal method.

Ancient Egyptian methods of birth control included douching with wine and garlic after coitus, and soaking crocodile dung in sour milk and stuffing the mixture deep within the vagina. The dung blocked the passage of many—if not all—sperm through the cervix and also soaked up sperm. The dung may also have done its job through a social mechanism. It may have discouraged all but the most ardent suitors. **Truth or Fiction Revisited:** It is true that ancient Egyptians used crocodile dung as a contraceptive. (No comment.)

Ancient Greek and Roman women placed absorbent materials within the vagina to absorb semen. The use of sheaths or coverings for the penis has a long history. Sheaths worn over the penis as decorative covers can be traced to ancient Egypt (1350 BCE). Sheaths of linen were first described in European writings in 1564 by the Italian anatomist Fallopius (from whom the term *fallopian tube* is derived). Linen sheaths were used, without success, as a barrier against syphilis. The term **condom** was not used to describe penile sheaths until the 18th century. At that time, sheaths made of animal intestines became popular as a means of preventing STIs and unwanted pregnancies. Among the early advocates of condoms as a method of contraception was the Italian adventurer and writer Giovanni Casanova (1725–1798). We now associate his name with men who are known for their amorous adventures. James Boswell (1740–1795), the biographer of Samuel Johnson, described his use of "armor," or condoms, in his graphic *London Journal.* On one occasion, however, he was so enamored with a street prostitute that he neglected to use his armor and contracted gonorrhea. Condoms made of rubber (hence the slang "rubbers") were introduced shortly after Charles Goodyear invented vulcanization of rubber in 1843. Many other forms of contraception were also used widely in the 19th century, including withdrawal, vaginal sponges, and douching.

Contraception in the United States: The Legal Battle

As methods of contraception grew more popular in the 19th century, opponents waged a battle to make contraception illegal. One powerful opponent of contraception was Anthony Comstock, who served for a time as the secretary of the New York Society for the Suppression of Vice. Comstock lobbied successfully for passage of a federal law in 1873—the Comstock Law—that prohibited the dissemination of birth control information through the mail on the grounds that it was "obscene and indecent." Many states passed even more restrictive laws. They outlawed passage of information from one person to another, even from physician to patient.

Consider the resistance that Margaret Sanger met when she challenged the laws restricting information about contraception (Reed & Lampe, 2003). In 1914 she established the National Birth Control League, which published the magazine *The Woman Rebel. Rebel* did not publish birth control information, but challenged the view that it was obscene. Nevertheless, charges were brought against Sanger and she

TRUTH **fiction** **1**

CRITICAL Thinking

Critical thinkers pay attention to definitions of terms. The Roman Catholic Church opposes the use of **artificial contraception**. What is meant by artificial contraception?

Coitus interruptus A method of contraception in which the penis is withdrawn from the vagina prior to ejaculation; also referred to as the *withdrawal method*

Artificial contraception A method of contraception that applies a human-made device

Condom A sheath made of animal membrane or latex that covers the penis during coitus and serves as a barrier to sperm after ejaculation.

fled to Europe before her trial. During her self-imposed exile, she visited birth control clinics in the Netherlands. When the charges against her in the United States were dropped in 1916, Sanger returned and established a birth control clinic in Brooklyn, New York. The clinic was closed by the police and Sanger was arrested. Released on bail, she reopened the clinic and was thereupon sentenced to 30 days in jail. She successfully appealed the sentence. In 1918 the courts ruled that physicians must be allowed to disseminate information that might aid in the cure and prevention of disease. Dismantling of the Comstock law had begun. With the financial support of a wealthy friend, Katherine Dexter McCormack, Sanger spurred research into the use of hormones as one approach to contraception. In 1960, only six years before Sanger's death, oral contraception—"the pill"— was finally marketed in the United States. In 1965, the Supreme Court struck down the last impediment to free use of contraception: a law preventing the sale of contraceptives in Connecticut (*Griswold v. Connecticut*, 1965). In 1973, abortion was in effect legalized by the Supreme Court in the case of *Roe v. Wade*, permitting women to terminate unwanted pregnancies.

Today, contraceptives are advertised in popular magazines and sold through vending machines in college dormitories. U.S. history is not a one-way road to unrestricted use of birth control, however. Recent Supreme Court decisions have set aside bits and pieces of *Roe v. Wade*, giving the states more discretion over the regulation of abortion and restricting access to abortions for minors. Use of artificial contraception continues to be opposed by many groups, including the Roman Catholic Church. Yet many individual Catholics, including many priests, are tolerant of artificial contraception.

SafeZone

Q *If my druggist refuses to fill my birth control pills, can I sue?*

A Cases on suits involving pharmacists who refuse to provide patients with prescribed birth control pills, Plan B medications, and RU-486 are currently in courts and legislatures around the country. The answer to your question really depends on where you are and what legislation applies. By and large, a pharmacist is more likely to be compelled to supply birth control pills than abortion pills. There are ways in many states, including California, for pharmacists to "opt out" of supplying abortion pills based on their conscience, or to pass the job to a fellow pharmacist without such objections. Right now the trend is for pharmacists to be fired for refusal to fill certain prescriptions and then to sue to get their jobs back based on the view that their freedom to practice their religion was abridged by their loss of job. Sometimes they succeed; sometimes they don't. The long and short of it is this: Check with a local attorney.

REFLECT

What are some of the problems people experience in discussing contraception with their partners?

Methods of Contraception

There are many methods of contraception, including hormonal methods (the pill, the contraceptive patch, and injectable contraceptives), IUDs, diaphragms, cervical caps, spermicides, condoms, douching, withdrawal (coitus interruptus), and timing of ovulation (rhythm methods).

A Closer Look

TALKING WITH YOUR PARTNER ABOUT CONTRACEPTION

When is the right time to discuss contraception? On a first date? When you are invited to meet your partner's family? When you are lost in amorous embraces? Broaching the topic can be awkward. *Not* broaching it can be disastrous.

Technically speaking, the right time to discuss birth control is *any time* that allows your contraceptive to become effective before you engage in coitus. That can mean weeks or months before, if you decide to use a prescription contraceptive such as the birth control pill, the Intrauterine device (IUD), the diaphragm, or the cervical cap. Or it can mean a few moments before coitus, if you decide to use a condom and have one ready. Despite the obvious advantage to deciding upon contraception before coitus, the issue is often broached, if it is broached at all, only after the partners become sexually intimate. Practically speaking, it is awkward—and perhaps presumptuous!—to discuss contraception when you meet or are on a first date. But at the very least, it is advisable to prepare oneself for the possibility of coitus. Either partner may bring along a condom. The woman may already be on the pill, have an IUD in place, or be using a diaphragm.

Talking about contraception helps many couples make the transition from a casual relationship to an intimate one. Talking enables partners to share the responsibility. As a result, the woman is less likely to be resentful that the responsibility rests on her alone.

Yes, it can be awkward or difficult to raise the topic. Couples may not feel that their relationship is secure enough. They might think, "We'll cross that bridge when we come to it." Not planning ahead, however, prevents the effective use of contraceptives that require advance planning. Couples who choose to discuss contraception before engaging in coitus may benefit from these communication guidelines:

- *Pick a strategic time and place that is private and free of distractions.*

- *Couch your discussion in terms of your feelings about your partner and your relationship.* Talk about your general feelings toward your partner and your general relationship before you narrow in on contraception.

- *Don't apologize for raising the topic.* You may feel embarrassed talking about sensitive topics like birth control, but you need not apologize for bringing up the subject. Apologizing suggests that you think you are doing something wrong.

- *Raise the subject in a way that encourages candid discussion.* Use open-ended questions to explore your partner's attitudes. Say something like, "I think our relationship has reached the point where we need to talk about contraception. I know we're not sleeping together yet, but some forms of contraception require advanced planning. Have you been thinking about it?"

- *Explore options.* Don't make demands of your partner. Don't say, "Since we may start sleeping together, I think you should go on the pill." Rather, say something like, "I know that many different types of contraceptives are available. Why don't we discuss which method might be best for us if we become intimate?" Use the opportunity to explore each other's views about birth control in general and specific techniques in particular.

Oral Contraceptives

An **oral contraceptive** is commonly referred to as a birth control pill or simply "the pill." However, there are many kinds of birth control pills that vary in the type and doses of hormones they contain. Birth control pills fall into two major categories: combination pills and minipills. Available only by prescription, birth control pills are the most popular forms of contraception among single women of reproductive age (Frost & Frohwirth, 2005; Planned Parenthood, 2006).

Combination pills (such as Ortho-Novum, Ovcon, and Loestrin) contain a combination of synthetic forms of the hormones estrogen and progesterone

> **Oral contraceptive** A contraceptive, consisting of sex hormones, which is taken by mouth
>
> **Combination pill** A birth control pill that contains synthetic estrogen and progesterone

Is the use of the minipill or of
the IUD a method of contraception or of abortion? Does
it matter? Explain your views.

(progestin). Most combination pills provide a steady dose of synthetic estrogen and progesterone. Other combination pills, called *multiphasic* pills, vary the dose of these hormones across the menstrual cycle to reduce the overall doses to which the woman is exposed and possible side effects. The **minipill** contains synthetic progesterone (progestin) only.

HOW THEY WORK   Women cannot conceive when they are already pregnant because their bodies suppress maturation of egg follicles and ovulation. The combination pill fools the brain into acting as though the woman is already pregnant, so that no additional ova mature or are released. If ovulation does not take place, a woman cannot become pregnant.

During a normal menstrual cycle, low levels of estrogen during and just after the menstrual phase stimulate the pituitary gland to secrete FSH, which in turn stimulates the maturation of ovarian follicles. The estrogen in the combination pill inhibits FSH production, so follicles do not mature. The progesterone (progestin) inhibits the pituitary's secretion of LH, which would otherwise lead to ovulation. The woman continues to have menstrual periods, but there is no unfertilized ovum to be sloughed off in the menstrual flow.

The combination pill is taken for 21 days of the typical 28-day cycle. Then, for seven days, the woman either takes no pill at all or takes an inert placebo pill to maintain the habit of taking a pill a day. The sudden drop in hormone levels causes the endometrium to disintegrate and menstruation to follow three or four days after the last pill has been taken. Then the cycle is repeated.

The progestin in the combination pill also increases the thickness and acidity of the cervical mucus. The mucus thus becomes a more resistant barrier to sperm and inhibits development of the endometrium. Therefore, even if an egg were somehow to mature and become fertilized in a fallopian tube, sperm would not be likely to survive the passage through the cervix. Even if sperm were somehow to succeed in fertilizing an egg, the failure of the endometrium to develop would mean that the fertilized ovum could not become implanted in the uterus. Progestin may also impede the progress of ova through the fallopian tubes and make it more difficult for sperm to penetrate ova.

The minipill contains progestin but no estrogen. Minipills are taken daily through the menstrual cycle, even during menstruation. They act in two ways. They thicken the cervical mucus to impede the passage of sperm through the cervix, and they render the inner lining of the uterus less receptive to a fertilized egg. Thus, even if the woman does conceive, the fertilized egg will pass from the body, rather than becoming implanted in the uterine wall.

In Chapter 3 we noted that hormonal preparations such as Seasonique and Lybrel provide birth control as well as decrease the number of periods a woman has.

EFFECTIVENESS   The failure rate of the birth control pill associated with perfect use is very low—0.5% or less depending on the type of pill (see Table 12.1 on page 390). The failure rate increases to 3% with typical use. Failures can occur when women forget to take the pill for two days or more, when they do not use backup methods when they first start taking the pill, and when they switch from one brand to another. But forgetting to take the pill for a day or two might allow ovulation—and fertilization.

REVERSIBILITY   Oral contraceptives may temporarily reduce fertility after they are stopped, but they are not associated with permanent infertility. Nearly all women

Minipill A birth control pill that contains synthetic progesterone but no estrogen begin ovulating regularly within three months of suspending use (Hatcher et al., 2006). When a woman appears not to be ovulating after going off the pill, a drug like clomiphene is often used to induce ovulation.

ADVANTAGES AND DISADVANTAGES   The great advantage of oral contraception is that when used properly it is nearly 100% effective. Unlike many other forms of contraception, such as the condom or diaphragm, its use does not interfere with sexual spontaneity or diminish sexual sensations. The sex act need not be interrupted, as it would be by the use of a condom.

Birth control pills may also have some *healthful* side effects. They appear to reduce the risk of pelvic inflammatory disease (PID), benign ovarian cysts, and fibrocystic (benign) breast growths. The pill regularizes menstrual cycles and reduces menstrual cramping and premenstrual discomfort. The pill may also be helpful in the treatment of iron-deficiency anemia and facial acne. The combination pill reduces the risks of ovarian and endometrial cancer, even for a number of years after the woman has stopped taking it (Gnagy et al., 2000; Hatcher et al., 2006).

The pill does have some disadvantages. The pill provides no protection against STIs. Moreover, it may reduce the effectiveness of antibiotics used to treat STIs. Going on the pill requires medical consultation, so a woman must plan to begin using the pill at least several weeks before becoming sexually active or before discontinuing the use of other contraceptives, and must incur the expense of medical visits. Marchbanks and her colleagues (2002) compared 4,575 women with breast cancer with 4,682 control subjects and found no increased risk for breast cancer among women who were using or had used oral contraceptives. Moreover, the pill did not increase the risk of breast cancer in women with a family history of the disorder.

The main drawbacks of birth control pills are potential side effects and possible health risks. Although there is a good deal of research that suggests that the pill is safe for healthy women, the American College of Obstetricians and Gynecologists (2006) suggests caution among women with medical conditions such as hypertension, diabetes, migraine headaches, fibrocystic breast tissue, uterine fibroids, or elevated cholesterol.

The estrogen in combination pills may produce side effects such as nausea and vomiting, fluid retention (feeling bloated), weight gain, increased vaginal discharge, headaches, tenderness in the breasts, and dizziness. Many of these are temporary. When they persist, women may be switched from one pill to another, perhaps to one with lower doses of hormones. Pregnant women produce high estrogen levels in the corpus luteum and placenta. The combination pill artificially raises levels of estrogen, so it is not surprising that some women who use it have side effects that mimic the early signs of pregnancy, such as weight gain or nausea ("morning sickness"). Weight gain can result from estrogen (through fluid retention) or progestin (through increased appetite and development of muscle). Oral contraceptives may also increase blood pressure in some women, but clinically significant elevations are rare in women using the low-dose pills that are available today (Hatcher et al., 2006). Still, it is wise for women who use the pill to have their blood pressure checked regularly. Women who encounter problems with high blood pressure from taking the pill are usually advised to switch to another form of contraception. Many women experience hormone withdrawal symptoms when they discontinue the pill (Sulak et al., 2000). These include headaches, pelvic pain, bloating, and breast tenderness.

Many women have avoided using the pill because of the risk of blood clots. The lower doses of estrogen found in most types of birth control pills today are associated with a much lower risk of blood clots than was the case in the 1960s and 1970s, when higher doses were used (Hatcher et al., 2006). Still, women who are at increased risk for blood clotting, such as women with a history of circulatory problems or stroke, are typically advised not to use the pill.

Women who are considering using the pill need to weigh the benefits and risks with their health care providers. For the great majority of young, healthy women in their 20s and early 30s, the pill is unlikely to cause blood clots or other cardiovascular problems (Hatcher et al., 2006). Although research has found the pill to be safe for most women who do not smoke and are younger than 35, pill users may have a slightly higher chance than nonusers of developing blood clots in the veins and lungs, stroke, and heart attack (Rako, 2003).

Some women should not be on the pill at all: women who have had circulatory problems or blood clots, women who have suffered a heart attack or stroke, or women who have a history of coronary disease, breast or uterine cancer, genital bleeding, liver tumors, or sickle-cell anemia (because of associated blood-clotting problems). Because of their increased risk of cardiovascular problems, caution should be exercised when the combination pill is used with women older than 35 years of age who smoke (Hatcher et al., 2006). Nursing mothers should also avoid using the pill, because the hormones may be passed to the baby in the mother's milk.

Because the risks of cardiovascular complications generally increase with age, many women older than 35 have been encouraged by their gynecologists to use other forms of birth control. However, the American College of Obstetricians and Gynecologists (2006) believes that healthy nonsmokers can use the pill safely at least until the age of 45. This number keeps expanding, with many women now being advised to continue using pills to regulate their periods into their 50s.

The pill may also have psychological effects. Some users report depression or irritability. Switching brands or altering doses may help. Evidence is lacking concerning the effects of lower estrogen pills on sexual desire.

Progestin fosters male secondary sex characteristics, so women who take the minipill may develop acne, facial hair, thinning of scalp hair, reduction in breast size, vaginal dryness, and missed or shorter periods. Irregular bleeding, or so-called breakthrough bleeding, between menstrual periods is a common side effect of the minipill. Irregular bleeding should be brought to the attention of a health professional. Because they can produce vaginal dryness, minipills can hinder vaginal lubrication during intercourse, decreasing sexual sensations and rendering sex painful.

Researchers have also examined suspected links between the use of the pill and certain forms of cancer, especially breast cancer, because breast cancer is sensitive to hormonal changes. Results from several large-scale studies show no overall increase

SafeZone

Q *Are there negative effects from taking birth control pills for too long?*

A Yes and no. To some degree, it depends on the pill. Pills with higher hormone levels are more likely to have side effects. Moreover, the pill seems to have protective effects against some disorders, even though it might elevate the risk of others. Researchers keep lowering the dose of hormones in the pill, and gynecologists keep extending the period of time that women can "safely" use the pill. Many women now use it through perimenopause.

in the rates of breast cancer among pill users, but it remains possible that some subgroups of women who use the pill may be at increased risk (Hatcher et al., 2006). The evidence linking use of the pill with cervical cancer is mixed, with some studies showing a link and others showing none (Hatcher et al., 2006).

Women considering the pill are advised to have a thorough medical evaluation to rule out conditions that might make usage unsafe. The evaluation should include a detailed medical and family history, and a physical exam including a Pap smear, assessment of blood pressure, screening for STIs, urinalysis, breast and pelvic exam, and possibly an EKG (electrocardiogram). Women who begin to use the pill, regardless of their age or risk status, should pay attention to changes in their physical condition, have regular checkups, and promptly report any physical complaints or unusual symptoms to their physicians.

SafeZone

Q *Why is it taking so long for male birth control pills to be available? What are the side effects? How would they work?*

A Actually, many male birth control methods have been "just around the corner" for a number of years, including a pill. Pills would include testosterone and progestin. Test pills are 95% effective in reducing the sperm counts to levels at which impregnation is highly unlikely. Testosterone reduces sperm production as follows. The pituitary gland normally stimulates the testes to produce sperm. Testosterone suppresses the pituitary, in turn suppressing sperm production. Men can also receive long-lasting injections of testosterone or progestin. However, the injections apparently increase the risk of prostate cancer and increase cholesterol levels in the bloodstream, which may heighten the risk of cardiovascular disease. Other methods are also being researched, including use of an extract from the cotton plant (gossypol), production of an immune response to one's own sperm, and application of ultrasound to the testes. There remain serious questions about the safety, effectiveness, and reversibility of these various methods.

The "Morning-After" Pill

Truth or Fiction Revisited: There is a morning-after pill. The so-called morning-after pill, or postcoital contraceptive, refers to several types of pills that have high doses of estrogen and progestin. Because they are not taken regularly, they do not prevent ovulation. Instead, they prevent fertilization or prevent the fertilized egg from implanting in the uterus. In 2006, the Food and Drug Administration (FDA) approved sale of the morning-after pill, Plan B, to women age 18 and older. Younger females may obtain it by prescription.

Morning-after pills are most effective when taken within 72 hours after ovulation. Women who wait to see whether they have missed a period are no longer candidates for the morning-after pill.

Morning-after pills have a higher hormone content than most birth control pills. For this reason, nausea is a common side effect. Nausea is usually mild and passes within a day or two after treatment, it can be treated with antinausea medication.

The morning-after pill is certainly not recommended as a regular form of birth control. They are *one-time* forms of emergency protection (Hatcher et al., 2006), which may be most appropriate to use after a rape or when regular contraceptive

TRUTH
fiction 2

Plan B. *Plan B—the "morning-after pill"—is available over the counter for women 18 and over, and by prescription for those who are younger.*

devices fail (e.g., if a condom breaks or a diaphragm becomes dislodged). The morning-after pill generally prevents implantation of a zygote, but health professionals caution that if it fails, the fetus may be damaged by exposure to the hormones.

The Contraceptive Patch

The contraceptive patch is another method of delivering estrogen and progestin to prevent ovulation and implantation. The patch is thin and measures about two inches by two inches. It is worn on the abdomen, buttocks, upper arm, or upper torso. The patch contains a week's worth of hormones and releases them gradually into the bloodstream.

Like the birth control pill, when used correctly, the patch is more than 99% effective. Women who use the patch need not think about contraception daily. Also like the pill, the patch doesn't interrupt sex. Its side effects and potential hazards are similar to those of the pill.

Injectable Contraceptives

Lunelle and Depo-Provera are injectable hormone preparations available by prescription. Lunelle is similar to the combination pill in that it contains estrogen and progestin. It is injected monthly. Like the minipill, Depo-Provera contains progestin only. It prevents pregnancy for three months. Injectables have become the second most popular contraceptive method after the pill, accounting for 18% of users (Frost & Frohwirth, 2005).

Lunelle prevents ovulation, thickens cervical mucus, preventing the sperm from reaching the egg, and changes the lining of the uterus to prevent implantation. Depo-

Provera prevents ovulation. Lunelle, like oral contraceptives, has a failure rate of less than 1% when used properly. Depo-Provera is as effective as female sterilization, according to the American Academy of Family Physicians (2006).

Injectable contraceptives have the advantages of being highly effective, permitting spontaneous sex, and remaining effective without being taken every day. They have side effects similar to those of other types of hormonal contraceptives, including oral contraceptives, such as vaginal bleeding, headaches, tenderness in the breast, irregular menstrual cycles, weight gain, bloating, nausea, and vomiting. Injectable contraceptives are usually not recommended for women who smoke, have elevated blood pressure, have breast or uterine cancer, have a history of blood clots, have a history of heart attack or stroke, have diabetes, have liver disease, or are allergic to hormones.

The effects of Lunelle and Depo-Provera are reversible, but ovulation may take a few months to return. Neither contraceptive affords protection against STIs.

Intrauterine Devices

Camel drivers setting out on long desert journeys once placed round stones in the uteruses of female camels to prevent them from becoming pregnant and lost to service. The stones may have acted as primitive **intrauterine devices** (IUDs). IUDs are small objects of various shapes that are inserted into the uterus. IUDs have been used by humans since the days of ancient Greece. Today, they are inserted into the uterus by a physician or nurse practitioner and usually left in place for a year or more. Fine plastic threads or strings hang down from the IUD into the vagina, so that the woman can check to see that the IUD remains in place.

IUDs are used by more than 100 million women around the world (Hatcher et al., 2006). Most of them live in China, where nearly one in three married women uses an IUD during her childbearing years. By contrast, IUDs are used by only about 3% of women in committed relationships in the United States (Hatcher et al., 2006).

IUDs achieved their greatest popularity in the United States in the 1960s and 1970s. Then there was a sharp drop in use during the 1980s after use of a popular model, the Dalkon Shield, was linked to a high incidence of pelvic infections and tubal infertility.

There are two IUDs: the Progestasert T, which releases small quantities of progesterone (progestin) daily, and the Copper T 380A (ParaGard), a T-shaped, copper-based device. Because the Progestasert T must be replaced annually, and any insertion carries some risk of infection, health authorities recommend the use of the ParaGard device, which can be used for eight years or more, unless the woman is allergic to copper (Hatcher et al., 2006).

HOW THEY WORK   We do not know exactly how IUDs work. A foreign body, such as the IUD, apparently irritates the uterine lining. This irritation gives rise to mild inflammation and the production of antibodies that may be toxic to sperm or to fertilized ova and/or may prevent fertilized eggs from becoming implanted. Inflammation may also impair proliferation of the endometrium—another impediment to implantation. Progestin released by the Progestasert T also has effects like the progestin-only minipill: It lessens the likelihood of fertilization and implantation. Because action on fertilized ova may be considered an early abortion method, many people who oppose abortion also oppose the IUD.

EFFECTIVENESS   The failure rate associated with typical use of the Progestasert T is about 2% (Table 12.1). Most failures occur within three months of

Intrauterine device A small object that is inserted into the uterus and is left in place to prevent conception

insertion, often because the device shifts position or is expelled. ParaGard is the most effective IUD. The first-year failure rate in typical use of the ParaGard is 0.8%.

The IUD may irritate the muscular layer of the uterine wall, causing contractions that expel it through the vagina. The device is most likely to be expelled during menstruation, so users are advised to check their sanitary napkins or tampons before discarding them. Women who use IUDs are advised to check the string several times a month to ensure that the IUD is in place. Spontaneous expulsions occur in 2% to 10% of users within a year of use (Hatcher et al., 2006). Some family planning clinics advise women to supplement their use of IUDs with other devices for the first three months, when the risks of a shift in position or expulsion are greatest.

REVERSIBILITY   IUDs may be removed readily by professionals. Nine out of 10 former IUD users who try to do so become pregnant within a year (Hatcher et al., 2006).

ADVANTAGES AND DISADVANTAGES   The IUD has the advantages of being highly effective, not diminishing sexual spontaneity or sexual sensations, and, once in place, the woman need not do anything more to prevent pregnancy. The small risk of failure is reduced, in effect, to zero if the couple also use an additional form of birth control, such as the diaphragm or condom.

The IUD also does not interfere with a woman's normal hormonal production. Users continue to produce pituitary hormones that stimulate ovarian follicles to mature and rupture, thereby releasing mature ova and producing female sex hormones.

A disadvantage is that insertion can be painful. Another disadvantage is side effects. The most common side effects are excessive menstrual cramping, irregular bleeding (spotting) between periods, and heavier than usual menstrual bleeding (Hatcher et al., 2006). These side effects usually occur shortly after insertion and are among the primary reasons women ask to have the device removed. A more serious concern is the possible risk of pelvic inflammatory disease (PID)—a serious disease that can become life threatening if left untreated. Women who use the IUD may have an increased risk of PID. The risk of infection is associated more with the insertion of the device (bacteria may enter the woman's reproductive tract during insertion) than with use of the device itself.

PID can produce scar tissue that blocks the fallopian tubes, causing infertility. Women with pelvic infections should not use an IUD. Women who have risk factors for PID may also wish to consider the advisability of an IUD. Risk factors include a recent episode of gonorrhea or chlamydia, recurrent episodes of these STIs, sexual contact with multiple partners, or sexual contact with a partner who has had multiple partners.

Another risk is that the IUD may perforate (tear) the uterine or cervical walls, which can cause bleeding, pain, and adhesions. Perforations are not common, but can be serious when they occur (Hatcher et al., 2006). IUD users are also at greater risk for ectopic pregnancies, both during and after use, and for miscarriage. Ectopic pregnancies occur in about 5% of women who become pregnant while using an IUD (Hatcher et al., 2006). The IUD is not recommended for women with a history of ectopic pregnancy. Women who become pregnant while using the IUD stand about a 50/50 chance of miscarriage (Hatcher et al., 2006).

Another drawback to the IUD is its cost. The typical cost of an IUD insertion in a family planning clinic is a few hundred dollars. Potential expulsion of the IUD presents yet another disadvantage. Moreover, the IUD, like the pill, offers no protection against STIs. Finally, like the pill, IUDs place the burden of contraception entirely on the woman.

The Diaphragm

Diaphragms were once used by about one third of American couples who practiced birth control. When invented in 1882, they were a breakthrough. Their popularity declined only in the 1960s with the advent of the pill and the IUD.

The diaphragm is a shallow cup or dome made of thin latex rubber (Figure 12.1). The rim is a flexible metal ring covered with rubber. Diaphragms come in different sizes to allow a precise fit.

Diaphragms are available by prescription and must be fitted to the contour of the vagina by a health professional. Several sizes and types of diaphragms may be tried during a fitting. Women practice insertion in a health professional's office so they can be guided as needed.

HOW IT WORKS   The diaphragm is inserted and removed by the woman, much like a tampon. It is akin to a condom in that it forms a barrier against sperm when placed snugly over the cervical opening. Yet it is unreliable as a barrier alone. Thus, the diaphragm should be used in conjunction with a spermicidal cream or jelly. The diaphragm's main function is to keep the spermicide in place.

HOW IT IS USED   The diaphragm should be inserted no more than two hours before coitus, because the spermicides that are used may begin to lose effectiveness beyond this time. Some health professionals, however, suggest that the diaphragm may be inserted up to six hours preceding intercourse. (It seems reasonable to err on the side of caution and assume that there is a two-hour time limit.) The woman or her partner places a tablespoonful of spermicidal cream or jelly on the inside of the cup and spreads it inside the rim. (Cream spread outside the rim might cause the diaphragm to slip.) The woman opens the inner lips of the vagina with one hand and folds the diaphragm with the other by squeezing the ring. She inserts the diaphragm against the cervix, with the inner side facing upward (Figure 12.2). Her partner can help insert the diaphragm, but the woman is advised to check its placement. Some women prefer a plastic insertion device, but most find it easier to insert the diaphragm without it. The diaphragm should be left in place *at least six hours* to allow the spermicide to kill sperm remaining in the vagina (Hatcher et al., 2006). It should not be left in place for longer than 24 hours, to guard against toxic shock syndrome (TSS).

After use, the diaphragm should be washed with mild soap and warm water and stored in a dry, cool place. When cared for properly, a diaphragm can last about two years. Women may need to be refitted after pregnancy or a change in weight of about 10 pounds or more.

EFFECTIVENESS   If used consistently and correctly, the failure rate of the diaphragm is estimated to be 6% during a year of use (Table 12.1). In typical use, however, the failure rate is believed to be three times as high—18%. Some women become pregnant because they do not use the diaphragm during every coital experience. Others may insert it too early or not leave it in long enough. The diaphragm may not fit well or it may slip, especially if the couple is acrobatic. A diaphragm may develop tiny holes or cracks. Women are advised to inspect the diaphragm for signs of wear and consult their health professionals when in doubt. Effectiveness also is seriously compromised when the diaphragm is not used along with a correctly applied spermicide.

REVERSIBILITY   The effects of the diaphragm are fully reversible. To become pregnant, the woman simply stops using it. The diaphragm has not been shown to influence subsequent fertility.

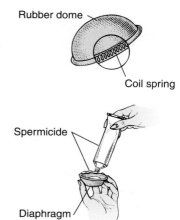

Figure 12.1
A Diaphragm. *The diaphragm is a shallow cup or dome made of latex. Diaphragms must be fitted to the contour of the vagina by a health professional. The diaphragm forms a barrier to sperm but should be used in conjunction with a spermicidal cream or jelly.*

Diaphragm A shallow rubber cup or dome, fitted to the contour of a woman's vagina, that is coated with a spermicide and inserted prior to coitus to prevent conception

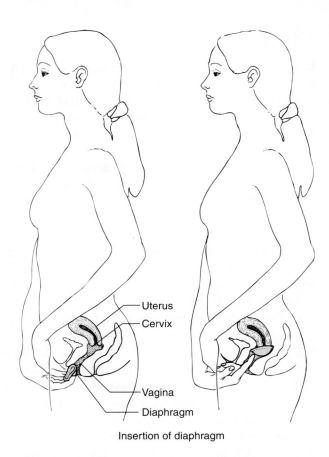

Figure 12.2 Insertion and Checking of the Diaphragm. *Women are instructed in insertion of the diaphragm by a health professional. In practice, a woman and her partner may find joint insertion an erotic experience.*

Uterus
Cervix
Vagina
Diaphragm

Insertion of diaphragm

ADVANTAGES AND DISADVANTAGES The major advantage of the diaphragm is that when used correctly it is a safe and effective means of birth control and does not alter the woman's hormone production or reproductive cycle. The diaphragm can be used as needed, whereas the pill must be used daily and the IUD remains in place regardless of whether the woman engages in coitus. Another advantage is the virtual absence of side effects. The few women who are allergic to the rubber in the diaphragm can switch to a plastic model.

The major disadvantage is the high failure rate of typical users. Nearly one in five typical users (18%), who also use a spermicide, become pregnant during a year of use (Hatcher et al., 2006). Another disadvantage is the need to insert the diaphragm prior to intercourse, which the couple may find disruptive. The woman's partner may find the taste of the spermicide to be unpleasant during oral sex. The pressure exerted by the diaphragm against the vaginal and cervical walls may also irritate the urinary tract and cause urinary or even vaginal infections. Switching to a different-size diaphragm or one with a different type of rim may help alleviate this problem. About 1 woman or man in 20 may develop allergies to the particular spermicide that is used, which can lead to irritation of the genitals. This problem may also be alleviated by switching to another brand.

Spermicides

Spermicides are agents that kill sperm. They coat the cervical opening, blocking the passage of sperm and killing sperm by chemical action. They come in different forms, including jellies and creams, suppositories, aerosol foam, and a contraceptive

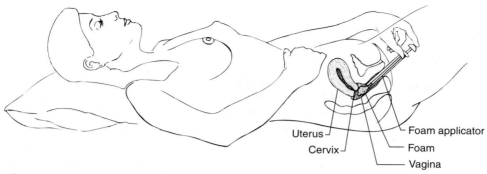

Uterus
Cervix
Foam applicator
Foam
Vagina

Figure 12.3 The Application of Spermicidal Foam. *Spermicidal jellies and creams come in tubes with plastic applicators. Spermicidal foam comes in a pressurized can and is applied with a plastic applicator in much the same way as spermicidal jellies and creams.*

film. Spermicides should be left in place in the vagina (no douching) for several hours after coitus (Hatcher et al., 2006).

Spermicidal jellies, creams, foam, and suppositories should be used no more than 60 minutes preceding coitus to provide for maximum effectiveness (Hatcher et al., 2006). Spermicidal jellies and creams come in tubes with plastic applicators that introduce the spermicide into the vagina (Figure 12.3). Spermicidal foam is a fluffy white cream with the consistency of shaving cream. It is contained in a pressurized can and is introduced with a plastic applicator in much the same way as spermicidal jellies and creams.

Vaginal suppositories are inserted into the upper vagina, near the cervix, where they release spermicide as they dissolve. Unlike spermicidal jellies, creams, and foam, which become effective immediately when applied, suppositories must be inserted no less than 10 to 15 minutes before coitus so that they have sufficient time to dissolve (Hatcher et al., 2006).

Spermicidal film consists of thin, two-inch-square sheets that are saturated with spermicide. When placed in the vagina, they dissolve into a gel and release the spermicide. The spermicidal film should be inserted at least five minutes before intercourse to allow it time to melt and for the spermicide to be dispersed. It remains effective for as long as one hour. One disadvantage of the film that some users have noted is a tendency for it to adhere to the fingertips, which makes it difficult to insert correctly.

In typical use, the yearly failure rate of spermicides used alone is 21% (Hatcher et al., 2006). When used correctly and consistently, the failure rate is estimated to drop to about 6%. Spermicides are more effective when combined with other forms of contraception, such as the condom or diaphragm.

The major advantages of spermicides are that they do not alter the woman's natural biological processes and are applied only as needed. Spermicides have not been linked with any changes in reproductive potential. So couples who wish to become pregnant simply stop using them. Unlike a diaphragm, they do not require a doctor's prescription or a fitting. They can be bought in virtually any drugstore.

The major disadvantage is the high failure rate among typical users. Foam often fails when the can is not shaken enough, when too little is used, when it is not applied deeply enough within the vagina near the cervix, or when it is used after coitus has begun.

Spermicides are generally free of side effects but sometimes irritate the vagina or penis. Irritation is sometimes alleviated by changing brands. Partners may find the taste of spermicides unpleasant. Spermicides may pose a danger to an embryo, so women who suspect they are pregnant are advised to suspend use until they are certain.

It was once thought that spermicides that contain nonoxynol-9 might afford protection against STIs such as HIV/AIDS, genital herpes, trichomoniasis ("trich"), syphilis, and chlamydia, yet an experiment in Africa found that nonoxynol-9 provided no protection against STIs (Roddy et al., 1998). In a study of the effectiveness of the spermicide as a means of preventing HIV infection among African and Thai prostitutes, it turned out that the group using nonoxynol-9 actually had a significantly higher rate of HIV infection (15%) than the group using the placebo (10%) (Stephenson, 2000). Joseph Perriëns (2000), head of the UNAIDS **microbicide** effort, suggested that the local irritation caused by nonoxynol-9 might have made the vaginal tract an easier port of entry for HIV.

The Contraceptive Sponge

The contraceptive sponge was taken off the market because FDA inspectors had found some problems in production, including bacterial contamination. The manufacturer decided that it would be too costly to modify procedures to meet FDA objections, but if you go online, you'll find that contraceptive sponges are available, mainly at Canadian pharmacies, which, of course, will ship them. Before using them, check with your gynecologist.

The contraceptive sponge is a soft, disposable device. Unlike the diaphragm, the sponge does not need to be fitted. Like the diaphragm, it provides a barrier that holds a spermicide, but the spermicide is built in. The sponge can also be inserted into the vagina several hours before coitus and has the additional advantage of absorbing sperm. It is odorless and tasteless, and users found it less drippy than the diaphragm. On the negative side, about 1 user in 20 (male and female) is mildly irritated by the spermicide. There is also a remote chance of TSS: One case arose for every four *million* days of use.

The Cervical Cap

The cervical cap, like the diaphragm, is a dome-shaped cup. It comes in different sizes and must be fitted by a health professional. It is smaller than the diaphragm, however—about the size of a thimble—and is meant to fit snugly over the cervical opening.

Like the diaphragm, the cap is intended to be used with a spermicide applied inside it. When inserting it, the woman (or her partner) fills the cap about a third full of spermicide. Then, squeezing the edges together, the woman inserts the cap high in the vagina, so that it presses firmly against the cervix. The woman can test the fit by running a finger around the cap to ensure that the cervical opening is covered. It should be left in place for at least eight hours after intercourse. The cap provides continuous protection for as long as 48 hours without the need for additional spermicide. To reduce the risk of TSS, the cap should not be left in place longer than 48 hours. Like the diaphragm, the cap should be cleaned after use and checked for wear and tear. When cared for properly, the cap can last as long as three years.

Like the diaphragm, the cervical cap forms a barrier and also holds spermicide in place against the cervix. It prevents sperm from passing into the uterus and fallopian tubes, and kills sperm by chemical action.

The failure rate in typical use is estimated to be high, ranging from 18% in women who have not borne children to 36% in women who have (Hatcher et al.,

Microbicide A chemical substance that kills viruses and bacteria

2006). Failures may be attributed, at least in part, to the cap's becoming dislodged and to changes in the cervix during the menstrual cycle, which can cause the cap to fit less snugly over the cervix.

There is no evidence that the cervical cap affects fertility. Like the diaphragm, the cap is a mechanical device that does not affect the woman's hormonal production or reproductive cycle. The cap may be especially suited to women who cannot support a diaphragm because of lack of vaginal muscle tone. Because of concern that the cap may irritate cervical tissue, however, users are advised to have regular Pap tests.

Some women find the cap uncomfortable. The cap can also become dislodged during sexual activity. Side effects include urinary tract infections and allergic reactions or sensitivities to the rubber or spermicide. Other disadvantages include the expense and inconvenience of being fitted by a health professional. Moreover, some women are shaped so that the cap does not remain in place. For these reasons, and because they may be hard to obtain, cervical caps are not very popular in the United States.

The Condom

Condoms are also called *rubbers, safes,* **prophylactics** (because latex condoms protect against STIs), and *skins* (referring to those that are made from lamb intestines). Condoms lost popularity with the advent of the pill and the IUD. They are less effective than either of them, may disrupt sexual spontaneity, and can lessen sexual sensations because they prevent the penis from touching the vaginal wall.

Condoms have been making a comeback, however, because those made of latex rubber can help prevent the spread of the HIV/AIDS and other STIs and, to a lesser extent, because of concerns about side effects of the pill and the IUD. Largely because of concerns about HIV/AIDS and other STIs, use of condoms among single women has mushroomed.

The renewed popularity of condoms has also been spurred by the increased assertiveness of contemporary women. They make the point that contraception is as much the man's responsibility as the woman's. Condoms alter the psychology of heterosexual relations. By using a condom the man assumes much of the responsibility for contraception. Condoms are the only contraceptive device worn by men, and the only readily reversible method of contraception that is available to men. Condoms are inexpensive and can be obtained without prescription from pharmacies, family planning clinics, and vending machines.

Some condoms are made of latex rubber. Thinner, more expensive condoms (skins) are made from the intestinal membranes of lambs. The latter allow greater sexual sensation but do not protect as well against STIs. Only latex condoms are effective against HIV (the AIDS virus). Condoms made of animal intestines have pores large enough to permit HIV and other viruses, such as the one that causes hepatitis B, to slip through (Hatcher et al., 2006). A few condoms are made from other materials, such as plastic (polyurethane). Questions remain about the effectiveness of polyurethane condoms. Some condoms have plain ends. Others have nipples or reservoirs (Figure 12.4) that catch semen and may help prevent the condom from bursting during ejaculation.

HOW THEY WORK   A condom is a cylindrical sheath that serves as a barrier, preventing the passage of sperm and disease-carrying microorganisms from the man to his partner. It also helps prevent infected vaginal fluids (and microorganisms) from entering the man's urethral opening or from penetrating through small cracks in the skin of the penis.

Prophylactic An agent that protects against disease

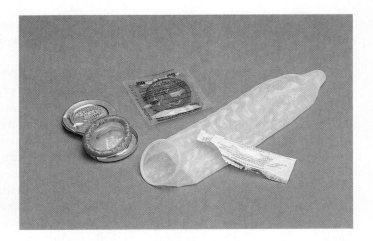

Figure 12.4 **Condoms.** *Some condoms are plain tipped, whereas others have nipples or reservoirs that catch semen and may help prevent the condom from bursting during ejaculation. Latex condoms form effective barriers to HIV (the AIDS virus).*

HOW THEY ARE USED   The condom is rolled onto the penis after erection is achieved and before contact between the penis and the vagina or anus (Figure 12.5). If the condom is *not* used until moments before the point of ejaculation, sperm-carrying fluid from the Cowper's glands or from preorgasmic spasms may already have passed into the vagina. Nor does the condom afford protection against STIs if it is fitted after penetration.

Condoms sometimes fall off or break. Between 1% and 2% of condoms break or fall off during intercourse, or when withdrawing the penis afterward (Hatcher et al., 2006). Condoms also sometimes slip down the shaft of the penis without falling off. To use a condom most effectively and to help prevent it from either breaking or falling off, a couple should observe the following guidelines:*

- Use a condom each and every time you have intercourse. Inexperienced users should also practice putting on a condom before they have the occasion to use one with a partner.

- Handle the condom carefully, making sure not to damage it with your fingernails, teeth, or sharp objects.

- Place the condom on the erect penis before it touches the vulva.

- Uncircumcised men should pull back the foreskin before putting on the condom.

- If you use a spermicide, place some inside the tip of the condom before placing the condom on the penis. You may also wish to use additional spermicide applied by an applicator inside the vagina to provide extra protection, especially in the event of breakage of the condom.

- Do not pull the condom tightly against the tip of the penis.

- For a condom without a reservoir tip, leave a small empty space—about a half inch—at the end of the condom to hold semen, yet do not allow any air to be trapped at the tip. Some condoms come equipped with a reservoir (nipple) tip that will hold semen.

- Unroll the condom all the way to the bottom of the penis.

- Ensure that adequate vaginal lubrication during intercourse is present, possibly using lubricants if necessary. Use only water-based lubricants such as contracep-

*Adapted from the Centers for Disease Control pamphlet, *Condoms and Sexually Transmitted Diseases . . . Especially AIDS* (HHS Publication FDA 90-4329) and other sources.

tive jelly or K-Y jelly. Never use an oil-based lubricant, which can weaken the latex material, such as petroleum jelly (Vaseline), cold cream, baby oil or lotion, mineral oil, massage oil, vegetable oil, Crisco, hand or body lotions, and most skin creams.

- If the condom breaks during intercourse, withdraw the penis immediately and use a spermicide.
- After ejaculation, carefully withdraw the penis while it remains erect.
- Hold the rim of the condom against the base of the penis as the condom is withdrawn to prevent it from slipping off.
- Check the removed condom for tears or cracks. If any are found, use a spermicide. Wrap the used condom in a tissue, and discard it in the garbage. (Condoms can be hard to flush down the toilet.) Wash your hands thoroughly with soap and water.

Because condoms can be eroded by exposure to body heat or other sources of heat, they should not be kept for any length of time in a pocket or the glove compartment of a car. Here are other things you should know about a condom:

- Open the condom package carefully to avoid tearing or puncturing the condom.
- Do not test a condom by inflating it or stretching it.
- Do not use a condom after its expiration date.
- Do not use damaged condoms. Condoms that are sticky, gummy, discolored, brittle, or appear otherwise damaged, or that show signs of deterioration should be considered damaged.
- Do not use a condom if the sealed packet containing the condom is damaged, cracked, or brittle.
- Do not open the sealed packet until you are ready to use the condom. A condom contained in a packet that has been opened can become dry and brittle within a few hours, causing it to tear more easily.
- Use a condom only once.
- If you want to carry a condom with you, place it in a loose jacket pocket or purse, not in your pants pocket or in a wallet held in your pants pocket, where it might be exposed to body heat.
- Do not buy condoms from vending machines that are exposed to heat or direct sunlight.

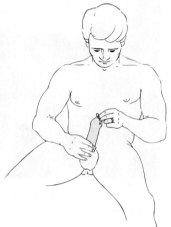

Figure 12.5 Applying a Condom. *First the rolled-up condom is placed on the head of the penis, and then it is rolled down the shaft of the penis. If a condom without a reservoir tip is used, a one-half-inch space should be left at the tip for the ejaculate to accumulate.*

EFFECTIVENESS   With typical use, the failure rate of the male condom is estimated at 12% (Table 12.1). That is, 12 women out of 100 whose male partners rely on condoms alone can expect to become pregnant within a year of use. The rate drops dramatically if the condom is used with a spermicide (Hatcher et al., 2006). The effectiveness of a condom and spermicide combined rivals that of the pill when used correctly.

REVERSIBILITY   The condom is simply a mechanical barrier to sperm and does not compromise fertility. Therefore, a couple who wish to conceive a child may simply discontinue its use.

ADVANTAGES AND DISADVANTAGES   Condoms have the advantage of being readily available. They can be purchased without prescription. They require no fitting and can remain in sealed packages until needed. They are readily discarded

The Condom. *Many single women carry condoms in case their partners are not prepared.*

after use. The combination of condoms and spermicides increases effectiveness. Some condoms contain a spermicide as a lubricant. When in doubt, ask a pharmacist.

Condoms do not affect production of hormones, ova, or sperm. Women whose partners use condoms ovulate normally. Men who use them produce sperm and ejaculate normally. With all these advantages, why are condoms not more popular?

One disadvantage of the condom is that it may render sex less spontaneous. The couple must interrupt lovemaking to apply the condom. Condoms also lessen sexual sensations, especially for the man (Crosby et al., 2005). Latex condoms do so more than animal membrane sheaths. Condoms also sometimes slip off or tear, allowing sperm to leak through.

On the other hand, condoms are almost entirely free of side effects. They offer protection against STIs that is unparalleled among contraceptive devices. They can also be used without prior medical consultation. Both partners can share putting on the condom, which makes it an erotic part of their lovemaking, not an intrusion. The use of textured or ultra-thin condoms may increase sensitivity, especially for the male. Thus, many couples find that the advantages outweigh the disadvantages. Sex in the age of HIV/AIDS has given condoms a new respectability, even a certain trendiness. Note the "designer colors" and styles on display at your local pharmacy. Advertisers now also target women in their ads, suggesting that women, like men, can come prepared with condoms.

It is tempting to claim that the condom has a perfect safety record and no side effects. Let us settle for "close to perfect." Some people have allergic reactions to the spermicides with which some lubricated condoms are coated or that the woman may apply. In such cases the couple may need to use a condom without a spermicidal lubricant or stop using supplemental spermicides. Some people are allergic to latex.

Women have the right to insist that their male sex partners wear latex condoms if their partners are not latex sensitive. STIs such as gonorrhea and chlamydia (Chapter 16) do more damage to a woman's reproductive tract than to a man's. Condoms can help protect women from vaginitis, PID, infections that can harm a fetus or cause infertility, and HIV (Crosby et al., 2005).

SafeZone

Q *If I use two condoms, does it give double protection?*

A You decrease the likelihood of pregnancy resulting from breakage of the surface of a condom, but you complicate the application and removal of the condoms. Also, condoms reduce sexual sensations to some degree. Using two will reduce sensations even further, possibly decreasing motivation to use a condom at all. As an alternative, consider using the condom along with a spermicide. Also, pay close attention to the integrity of the packaging of the condom, and withdraw carefully after you're finished.

Douching

Many couples believe that if a woman **douches** shortly after coitus, she will not become pregnant. Women who douche for contraceptive purposes often use syringes to flush the vagina with water or a spermicidal agent. The water is intended to wash sperm out; the spermicide, to kill them. **Truth or Fiction Revisited:** Douching is ineffective, however, because large numbers of sperm move beyond the range of the douche seconds after ejaculation. In addition, squirting a liquid into the vagina may even propel sperm *toward* the uterus. Regular douching may also alter the natural chemistry of the vagina, increasing the risk of vaginal infection. In short, douching is a "nonmethod" of contraception.

TRUTH fiction 3

The Withdrawal Method

Withdrawal means that the man removes his penis from the vagina before ejaculating. Withdrawal—also referred to as *coitus interruptus*—has a first-year failure rate among typical users of about 20% (Hatcher et al., 2006). There are several reasons for these failures. The man may not withdraw in time. Even if the penis is withdrawn just before ejaculation, some ejaculate may still fall on the vaginal lips, and sperm may find their way to the fallopian tubes. Active sperm may also be present in the *pre*ejaculatory secretions of fluid from the Cowper's glands, the discharge of which the man is usually unaware and cannot control. These sperm are capable of fertilizing an ovum even if the man withdraws before orgasm. Because of its unreliability and high failure rate, withdrawal, like douching, is *not* a method of contraception.

Fertility Awareness Methods

There are several fertility awareness methods, which are also referred to as *rhythm methods.* They all rely on awareness of the occurrence of the fertile segments of the woman's menstrual cycle. You will also hear them referred to as *natural birth control* or *natural family planning.* Each of them aims to avoid coitus on days when conception is likely. Fertility awareness methods are used by a small minority of women, and more so by women in committed relationships. Because the rhythm methods do not use artificial devices, it is acceptable to the Roman Catholic Church.

HOW THEY WORK A number of rhythm methods are used to predict the likelihood of conception. They are the mirror images of the methods that couples use to increase their chances of conceiving (see Chapter 11). Methods for enhancing the chances of conception seek to predict time of ovulation so the couple can arrange to have sperm present in the woman's reproductive tract at about that time. As methods of *birth control,* rhythm methods predict ovulation so that the couple can *abstain* from coitus when the woman is fertile.

THE CALENDAR METHOD The **calendar method** assumes that ovulation occurs 14 days prior to menstruation. The couple abstains from intercourse during the period that begins three days prior to day 13 (because sperm are unlikely to survive for more than 72 hours in the female reproductive tract) and ends two days after day 15 (because an unfertilized ovum is unlikely to remain receptive to fertilization for longer than 48 hours). The period of abstention thus covers days 10 to 17 of the woman's cycle.

When a woman has regular 28-day cycles, predicting the period of abstention is relatively straightforward. Women with irregular cycles are generally advised to chart

Douche To rinse or wash the vaginal canal by inserting a liquid and allowing it to drain out

Calendar method A fertility awareness (rhythm) method of contraception that relies on prediction of ovulation by tracking menstrual cycles, typically for a 10- to 12-month period, and assuming that ovulation occurs 14 days prior to menstruation

their cycles for 10 to 12 months to determine their shortest and longest cycles. The first day of menstruation counts as day one of the cycle. The last day of the cycle is the day preceding the onset of menstruation.

Consider a woman whose cycles vary from 23 to 33 days. In theory she will ovulate 14 days before menstruation begins. (To be safe she should assume that ovulation will take place anywhere from 13 to 15 days before her period.) Applying the rule of "three days before" and "two days after," she should avoid coitus from day five of her cycle, which corresponds to three days before her earliest expected ovulation (computed by subtracting 15 days from the 23 days of her shortest cycle and then subtracting three days), through day 22, which corresponds to two days after her latest expected ovulation (computed by subtracting 13 days from the 33 days of her longest cycle and then adding two days). Another way of determining this period of abstention would be to subtract 18 days from the woman's shortest cycle to determine the start of the "unsafe" period and 11 days from her longest cycle to determine the last "unsafe" day. The woman in the example has irregular cycles. She thus faces an 18-day abstention period each month—quite a burden for a sexually active couple.

Most women who follow the calendar method need to abstain from coitus for at least 10 days during the middle of each cycle. Moreover, the calendar method cannot ensure that the woman's longest or shortest menstrual cycles will occur during the 10- to 12-month period of baseline tracking. Some women, too, have such irregular cycles that the range of "unsafe" days cannot be predicted reliably even if baseline tracking is extended.

THE BASAL BODY TEMPERATURE METHOD With the **basal body temperature (BBT) method,** the woman tracks her body temperature upon awakening each morning to detect the small changes that occur directly before and after ovulation. A woman's BBT sometimes dips slightly just before ovulation and then tends to rise between 0.4 and 0.8°F just before, during, and after ovulation. It remains elevated until the onset of menstruation. (The increase in temperature is caused by the increased production of progesterone by the corpus luteum during the luteal phase of the cycle.) Thermometers that provide finely graded readings, such as electronic thermometers, are best suited for determining minor changes. A major problem with the BBT method is that it does not indicate the several *unsafe* preovulatory days during which sperm deposited in the vagina may remain viable. Rather, the BBT method indicates when a woman *has* ovulated. Thus, many women use the calendar method to predict the number of "safe" days prior to ovulation and the BBT method to determine the number of "unsafe" days after. A woman would avoid coitus during the "unsafe" preovulatory period (as determined by the calendar method) and then for three days when her temperature rises and remains elevated. A drawback of the BBT method is that changes in body temperature may also result from factors unrelated to ovulation, such as infections, sleeplessness, or stress. So some women triple-check themselves by also tracking their cervical mucus.

THE CERVICAL MUCUS (OVULATION) METHOD The **ovulation method** tracks changes in the **viscosity** of the cervical mucus. After menstruation, the vagina feels rather dry. There is also little or no discharge from the cervix. These dry days are relatively safe. Then a mucus discharge appears in the vagina that is first thick and sticky, and white or cloudy in color. Coitus (or unprotected coitus) should be avoided at the first sign of any mucus. As the cycle progresses, the mucus discharge thins and clears, becoming slippery or stringy, like raw egg white. These are the **peak days.** This mucus discharge, called the *ovulatory mucus,* may be accompanied by a feeling of vaginal lubrication or wetness. Ovulation takes place about a day

Basal body temperature (BBT) method A fertility awareness method of contraception that relies on prediction of ovulation by tracking the woman's temperature during the course of the menstrual cycle

Ovulation method A fertility awareness method of contraception that relies on prediction of ovulation by tracking the viscosity of the cervical mucus

Viscosity Stickiness, consistency

Peak days The days during the menstrual cycle during which a woman is most likely to be fertile

after the last peak day (about four days after this ovulatory mucus first appears). Then the mucus becomes cloudy and tacky once more. Intercourse may resume four days after the last peak day. However, many women have difficulty detecting changes in the mucus discharge. Such changes may also result from infections, certain medications, or contraceptive creams, jellies, or foam. Sexual arousal may also induce changes in viscosity.

OVULATION PREDICTION KITS Predicting ovulation is more accurate with an ovulation prediction kit. Kits allow women to test their urine regularly for the presence of LH. LH levels surge about 12 to 24 hours prior to ovulation. Kits can be used to help couples conceive or avoid pregnancy. But, ovulation kits can be costly.

EFFECTIVENESS The estimated first-year failure rate of rhythm methods is 20%, which reminds us of the joke: What do you call people who use the rhythm method? Parents!

Fewer failures occur when these methods are applied conscientiously, when a combination of rhythm methods is used, and when the woman's cycles are regular. Restricting coitus to the postovulatory period can reduce the pregnancy rate to 1% (Hatcher et al., 2006). The trick is to determine when ovulation occurs. The pregnancy rate can be reduced to practically zero if rhythm methods are used with other forms of birth control, such as the condom or diaphragm.

ADVANTAGES AND DISADVANTAGES Because they are a natural form of birth control, rhythm methods appeal to many people who, for religious or other reasons, prefer not to use artificial means. Because no devices or chemicals are used, there are no side effects. Nor do they cause loss of sensation, as condoms do. Nor is there disruption of sex, as with condoms, diaphragms, or foam—although sex could be said to be quite "disrupted" during the period of abstention. Rhythm methods are inexpensive, except for ovulation prediction kits. Both partners may share the responsibility for rhythm methods. The man, for example, can take his partner's temperature or assist with charting. All rhythm methods are fully reversible.

Rhythm methods may be unsuitable for women with irregular cycles. Women with irregular cycles who ovulate as early as a week after their menstrual flows can become pregnant even if they engage in unprotected intercourse only when they are menstruating, because some sperm remaining in a woman's reproductive tract may survive for up to eight days and fertilize an ovum that is released at that time. Moreover, the rhythm methods require abstaining from coitus for many days, perhaps weeks, each month. Rhythm methods also require that records of the menstrual cycle be kept for many months prior to implementation. Rhythm methods cannot be used spontaneously. Finally, rhythm methods do not afford protection against STIs.

Sterilization

Sterilization permanently makes the individual incapable of fertilizing a partner or of conceiving. Many people decide to be sterilized when they plan to have no children or no more children. With the exception of abstinence, sterilization is the most effective form of contraception. Yet the prospect of sterilization arouses strong feelings because a person is transformed all at once, and presumably permanently, from someone who might be capable of bearing children to someone who cannot. This transformation involves a change in self-concept, which may disturb people who link fertility to their self-identity. Still, sterilization is the most widely used form of birth control among couples in committed relationships age 30 and older.

Sterilization Surgical procedures that render people incapable of reproduction without affecting sexual activity

MALE STERILIZATION   The male sterilization procedure used today is the **vasectomy.** About one man in six in the United States has had a vasectomy.

A vasectomy is usually carried out in a doctor's office, under local anesthesia, in 15 to 20 minutes. Small incisions are made in the scrotum. Each vas is cut, a small segment is removed, and the ends are tied off or cauterized to prevent them from growing back together (Figure 12.6). Sperm no longer reach the urethra and are reabsorbed harmlessly by the body.

The man can usually resume sexual relations within a few days. However, health care providers recommend follow-ups to check for the presence of sperm in the ejaculate, because sperm can be found for many weeks and sometimes months even when operations have been successful (Dhar, 2006). And rarely—in about 1 case in 500—the vas "recanalizes," meaning that the severed ends rejoin spontaneously (Lucon et al., 2006).

Vasectomy does not diminish sex drive or result in any change in sexual arousal, erectile or ejaculatory ability, or sensations of ejaculation. No significant differences have been found among men in sexual satisfaction, marital satisfaction, communication, and frequency of sexual intercourse before and after vasectomy (Hofmeyr & Greeff, 2002). Male sex hormones and sperm are still produced by the testes. Without a passageway to the urethra, however, sperm are no longer expelled with the ejaculate. Because sperm account for only about 1% of the ejaculate, the volume of the ejaculate is not noticeably different.

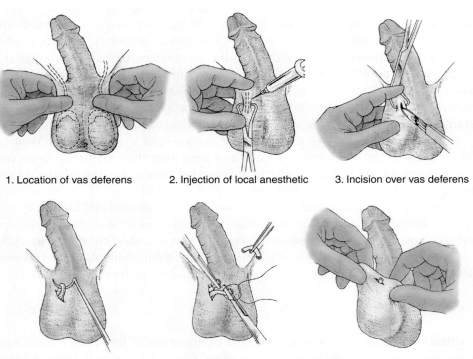

1. Location of vas deferens   2. Injection of local anesthetic   3. Incision over vas deferens

4. Isolation of vas from surrounding tissue   5. Removal of segment of vas; tying of ends   6. Return of vas to position; incision is closed and process is repeated on the other side

Vasectomy The surgical method of male sterilization during which sperm are prevented from reaching the urethra by cutting each vas deferens and tying it off or cauterizing it

Figure 12.6   Vasectomy. *The male sterilization procedure is usually carried out in a doctor's office, using local anesthesia. Small incisions are made in the scrotum. Each vas deferens is cut, and the ends are tied off or cauterized to prevent sperm from reaching the urethra. Sperm are harmlessly reabsorbed by the body after the operation.*

Throughout the years there has been some concern regarding whether vasectomy raises the risk of prostate cancer. If you search for the possible connection online, you will find many commentaries to the effect that connections are "suspected" and that there is a slight "increased risk" of prostate cancer among men who have had vasectomies, but that the evidence is "inconsistent." A New Zealand study comparing the incidence of vasectomy among 923 men who had had prostate cancer and a matched group of 1,224 who had not (Cox et al., 2006) found no connection between the two. In sum, vasectomy appears to be connected with a none-to-slightly increased risk of prostate cancer. Individuals considering vasectomy should discuss the most recent available findings with their physicians.

Reversibility is simple in concept but not in practice. Thus, vasectomies should be considered permanent. During an operation to reverse a vasectomy, called a **vasovasotomy,** the ends of the vas deferens are sewn together, and in a few days they grow together. Estimates of success at reversal, as measured by subsequent pregnancies, are quite variable and range from 16% to 79% (Hatcher et al., 2006). Even so, the man still produces sperm and they are capable of being harvested, albeit with some difficulty, and of fertilizing a partner's ova via methods such as ICSI (Karpman et al., 2006). Becoming a father for a man who changes his mind is anything but hopeless today.

Few serious complications from vasectomies have been reported, but minor complications are not uncommon. They typically involve temporary local inflammation or swelling after the operation. Ice packs and anti-inflammatory drugs such as aspirin may help reduce swelling and discomfort.

FEMALE STERILIZATION   About 21% of American women between the age of 15 and 44 have been surgically sterilized (U.S. Bureau of the Census, 2006). The percentages are higher among older women in committed relationships. **Tubal sterilization,** also called *tubal ligation,* is the most common method of female sterilization. Tubal sterilization prevents ova and sperm from passing through the fallopian tubes.

The two main surgical procedures for tubal sterilization are the **minilaparotomy** and **laparoscopy.** In a **minilaparotomy,** a small incision is made in the abdomen, just above the pubic hairline, to provide access to the fallopian tubes. Each tube is cut and either tied off or clamped with a clip. In a **laparoscopy** (Figure 12.7), sometimes called "belly button surgery," the fallopian tubes are approached through a small incision in the abdomen just below the navel. The surgeon uses a narrow, lighted viewing instrument called a *laparoscope* to locate the tubes. A small section of each of the tubes is cauterized, cut, or clamped. The woman usually returns to her daily routine in a few days and can resume coitus when it becomes comfortable. In an alternative sterilization procedure, a **culpotomy,** the fallopian tubes are approached through an incision in the back wall of the vagina.

None of these methods disrupts sex drive or sexual response. Surgical sterilization does not induce premature menopause or alter the woman's production of sex hormones. The menstrual cycle is undisturbed. The unfertilized egg is simply reabsorbed by the body, rather than being sloughed off in the menstrual flow.

A **hysterectomy** also sterilizes a woman, but a hysterectomy is a major operation that is commonly performed because of cancer or other diseases of the reproductive tract; it is inappropriate as a method of sterilization. Hysterectomy carries the risks of major surgery and, when the ovaries are removed along with the uterus, it induces "surgical menopause" because the woman no longer produces female sex hormones.

Vasovasotomy The surgical method of reversing a vasectomy during which the cut or cauterized ends of the vas deferens are sewn together

Tubal sterilization The most common method of female sterilization, during which the fallopian tubes are surgically blocked to prevent the meeting of sperm and ova; also called *tubal ligation*

Minilaparotomy A kind of tubal sterilization during which a small incision is made in the abdomen to provide access to the fallopian tubes

Laparoscopy Tubal sterilization by means of a *laparoscope,* which is inserted through a small incision just below the navel and is used to cauterize, cut, or clamp the fallopian tubes; sometimes referred to as *belly button surgery*

Culpotomy A kind of tubal sterilization during which the fallopian tubes are approached through an incision in the back wall of the vagina

Hysterectomy Surgical removal of the uterus; *not* appropriate as a method of sterilization

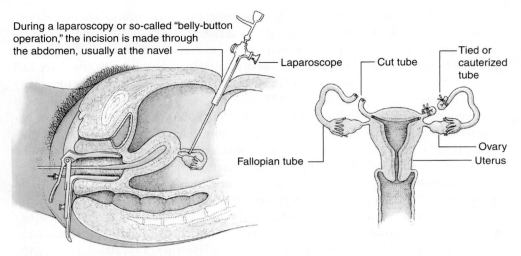

During a laparoscopy or so-called "belly-button operation," the incision is made through the abdomen, usually at the navel

Laparoscope

Cut tube

Tied or cauterized tube

Fallopian tube

Ovary

Uterus

Figure 12.7 Laparoscopy. During this method of female sterilization, the surgeon approaches the fallopian tubes through a small incision in the abdomen just below the navel. A narrow instrument called a *laparoscope* is inserted through the incision, and a small section of each fallopian tube is cauterized, cut, or clamped to prevent ova from joining with sperm.

Female sterilization is highly effective in preventing pregnancy, although slightly less effective than male sterilization. Overall, about 1 women in 200 (0.4%) is likely to become pregnant during the first year after tubal sterilization (Hatcher et al., 2006)—most likely the result of a failed surgical procedure or an undetected pregnancy at the time of the procedure. Like vasectomy, tubal ligation should be considered irreversible. Reversals are successful, as measured by subsequent pregnancies in 43% to 88% of cases (Hatcher et al., 2006). Reversal is difficult and costly, however.

Truth or Fiction Revisited: Not all sterilization operations can be surgically reversed. Therefore, sterilization is not advised for individuals who believe they might later change their minds about becoming pregnant. Nevertheless, the woman continues to ovulate and, even if the tubes cannot be rejoined, it may be possible to harvest the ova, fertilize them in vitro, and insert them into the uterus for implantation. However, these procedures can be invasive and costly, and they are not guaranteed to work.

Some women have medical complications. The most common complications are abdominal infections, excessive bleeding, inadvertent punctures of nearby organs, and scarring. The use of general anesthesia (typical in laparoscopies and in some minilaparotomies) poses additional risks, as in any major operation. (Most of the deaths that are attributed to tubal sterilization actually result from the anesthesia. The overall death rate is quite small, however—2 to 5 deaths per 100,000 operations.)

ADVANTAGES AND DISADVANTAGES OF STERILIZATION The major advantages of sterilization are effectiveness and permanence. Sterilization is nearly 100% effective. After surgery, the couple need not do anything more to prevent conception. The permanence is also its major drawback, however. People sometimes change their minds about wanting to have children.

Sterilization procedures create varying risks of complications after surgery, with women generally incurring more risks than men. Another disadvantage of sterilization is that it affords no protection against STIs. People who are sterilized may still wish to use condoms and spermicides for protection against STIs.

TRUTH fiction 4

REFLECT

What method or methods of birth control do you find to be medically and ethically acceptable? Why?

A Closer Look

SELECTING A METHOD OF CONTRACEPTION

If you believe that you and your partner should use contraception, how will you determine which method is right for you? There is no simple answer. What is right for your peers may be wrong for you. You and your partner will make your own selections, but there are some issues you may want to consider:

1. *Convenience.* Is the method convenient? Does it require a device that must be purchased in advance? If so, is a prescription required? Will the method work at a moment's notice or, as with the birth control pill, will it require time to reach maximum effectiveness?

2. *Moral acceptability.* A method that is morally acceptable to one person may be objectionable to another. For example, those who follow the teachings of the Roman Catholic Church may find any artificial means of contraception to be objectionable.

3. *Cost.* Methods vary in cost. Some more costly methods involve devices (such as the diaphragm, the cervical cap, and the IUD) or hormones that require medical visits in addition to the cost of the devices themselves.

4. *Sharing responsibility.* Most forms of birth control place the burden of responsibility largely, if not entirely, on the woman. The woman must consult with her doctor to obtain birth control pills or other prescriptive devices such as diaphragms, cervical caps, and IUDs. The woman must take birth control pills reliably or check to see that her IUD remains in place.

   Some couples prefer methods that allow for greater sharing of responsibility, such as alternating use of the condom and diaphragm. A man can also share the responsibility for the birth control pill by accompanying his partner on her medical visits and sharing the expense.

5. *Safety.* How safe is the method? What are the side effects?

6. *Reversibility.* In most cases the effects of birth control methods can be fully reversed by discontinuing their use. In other cases reversibility may not occur immediately, as with oral contraceptives. It's most cautious to consider sterilization irreversible.

7. *Protection against STIs.*

   Truth or Fiction Revisited: The truth is that only some contraceptives, like the condom, prevent STIs as well as conception.

8. *Effectiveness.* Techniques and devices vary widely in their effectiveness in actual use. The failure rate for a particular method refers to the percentage of women who become pregnant when using the method for a given period of time, such as during the first year of use. Most contraceptive methods are not used correctly all or even much of the time. Failure rates among typical users are often considerably higher because of incorrect, unreliable, or inconsistent use. Table 12.1 shows the failure rates, reversibility, and degree of protection against STIs associated with various contraceptive methods.

Selecting a Method of Contraception. *Should you and your partner use contraception? If so, how can you determine which method is right for you? Issues you may want to consider include convenience, effectiveness, moral acceptability, safety, reversibility, and cost. Other issues include whether the method allows you and your partner to share the responsibility and whether it also affords protection from STIs.*

TABLE 12.1

Failure Rates, Reversibility, and Protection Provided against STIs by Various Methods of Birth Control in Women Who Become Pregnant within the First Year of Use

| Method | Women Who Have an Unplanned Pregnancy within the First Year of Use, % | | Is It Reversible? | Does It Protect against STIs? |
	Typical use*	Consistent, correct use		
None	85	85	Yes	No
Spermicides	26	6	Yes	No
Rhythm methods	20		Yes	No
Calendar		9		
Ovulation method		3		
Basal body temperature		2		
Postovulation		1		
Withdrawal	19	4	Yes	No
Cervical cap	20–40	10–30	Yes	Some
Diaphragm	20	6	Yes	Some
Condom alone				
Female condom	21	5	Yes	(Scarce information)
Male condom	14	3	Yes	Yes
The Pill	3		Yes	No, but may *reduce* the risk of PID
Progestin Only		0.5		
Combined		0.1		
IUD				
Progestasert	2.0	1.5	Yes, except if fertility is impaired	No, but may *increase* the risk of PID
ParaGard Copper T 380A	0.8	0.6		
Depo-Provera	0.3	0.3	Yes	No
Injectable contraceptives	0.3	0.3	Yes	No
Female sterilization	0.5	0.5	Questionable	No
Male sterilization	0.15	0.10	Questionable	No

*Accidental pregnancies among typical couples.
†With spermicide.
SOURCES: Academy of Family Physicians (2006), Hatcher et al. (2004, 2006), Planned Parenthood (2006).

SafeZone

Q *I was watching* Grey's Anatomy *the other night, and a patient wanted to have her tubes tied without her husband knowing. Is there a law that says that spouses need to talk to each other before a procedure is done?*

A By and large, medical procedures requested by competent adults are protected by patient–physician confidentiality.

Abortion

"When I was young, I felt it myself, that it was wrong to kill a baby," said Maria, a 17-year-old Latina American high school student who lives in Houston. She is waiting to be seen at an abortion clinic. "But when I got to be a teenager and started having sex, things looked different. It's more complicated when it's your own life. I want to go to college and I know that having a baby now, without a husband or anything, would make that very hard" (Lewin, 1998a).

Maria is not all that unusual for young people in the United States today. Abortion has little to do with politics to her. The *Roe v. Wade* decision occurred a decade before Maria was born. Like many adults in the United States, Maria believes that abortion is murder, but like many of those, Maria also believes that abortion is an acceptable solution to a very bad situation.

In common usage, the term *abortion* usually refers to an **induced abortion** (in contrast to a spontaneous abortion, or miscarriage), or the purposeful termination of a pregnancy. Perhaps more than any other contemporary social issue, induced abortion (hereafter referred to simply as *abortion*) has divided neighbors and family members into opposing camps.

Thirty-seven million abortions worldwide are performed each year. In the United States, the abortion rate increased steadily from the early 1970s through 1980, leveled off somewhat in the 1980s, reached a peak in about 1990, when there were about 1.4 million abortions, and has declined to about 1.2 million abortions per year (Frost & Frohwirth, 2005). The great majority of abortions in the United States occur during the first trimester (Figure 12.8). This is when they are safest to the woman and least costly.

About 43% of women in the United States induce an abortion at some time (Davis, 2000a; Frost & Frohwirth, 2005). The great majority of them are single, and about half are mothers who already have family responsibilities. They are young. Nearly three quarters of them are younger than 30. Sixty percent of them are European American. About one in three (35%) is African American. Nearly one in six is Latina American.

Abortion is practiced widely in Canada, Japan, Russia, and many European nations. It is less common in developing nations, largely because of sparse medical facilities. Abortion is rarely used as a primary means of birth control. It usually comes into play when other methods have failed.

There are many reasons why women have abortions, including psychological factors as well as external circumstances, such as rape. Abortion is often motivated by a

Induced abortion The purposeful termination of a pregnancy before the embryo or fetus is capable of sustaining independent life; from the Latin *abortio,* meaning "that which is miscarried"

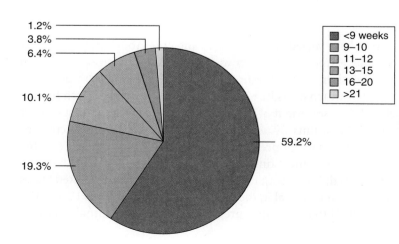

Figure 12.8 **When Women Have Abortions (in Weeks).** *Eighty-eight percent of abortions occur during the first 12 weeks of pregnancy, 2001.*

Source: Guttmacher Institute, Facts on induced abortion in the United States, *In Brief*, New York: Guttmacher Institute, 2006, www.guttmacher.org/pubs/fb_induced_abortion.html, accessed 9/16/06.

desire to reduce the risk of physical, economic, psychological, and social disadvantages that the woman perceives for herself and her present and future children should she take the pregnancy to term.

The national debate over abortion has been played out in recent years against a backdrop of demonstrations, marches, and occasional acts of violence, such as fire-bombing of abortion clinics and even murder. Most in the right-to-life (pro-life) movement assert that human life begins at conception and thus view abortion as the murder of an unborn child. Some in the pro-life movement brook no exception to their opposition to abortion. Others would permit abortion to save the mother's life or when a pregnancy results from rape or incest.

The pro-choice movement contends that abortion is a matter of personal choice and that the government has no right to interfere with a woman's right to terminate a pregnancy. Pro-choice advocates argue that women are free to control what happens within their bodies, including pregnancies.

When Does Human Life Begin?

The question regarding when human life begins is one that you will have to answer for yourself. We can only note that moral concerns about abortion often turn on the question of when human life begins. For some religious individuals, the matter revolves around when they believe the fetus obtains a soul.

In his thesis on *ensoulment*, the 13th-century Christian theologian Saint Thomas Aquinas wrote that a male fetus does not acquire a human soul until 40 days after conception. A female fetus does not acquire a soul until after 80 days. Scientists, too, have attempted to define when human life can be said to begin. Astronomer Carl Sagan, for example, wrote that fetal brain activity can be considered a scientific marker of human life (Sagan & Druyan, 1990). Brain activity is needed for thought, the quality that is considered most "human" by many. Brain wave patterns typical of children do not begin until about the 30th week of pregnancy. Before then, the human fetus lacks the brain architecture to begin thinking (Sagan & Druyan, 1990). But opponents argue that a newly fertilized ovum carries the *potential* for human thought in the same way that the embryonic or fetal brain does. It could even be argued that sperm cells and ova are living things in that they carry out the biological processes characteristic of cellular life. All in all, the question of when *human* life begins is a matter of definition that is apparently not to be resolved by science.

Historical and Legal Perspectives on Abortion

Attitudes toward abortion have varied across cultures and eras. Abortion was permitted in ancient Greece and Rome, but women in ancient Assyria were impaled on stakes for attempting abortion. The Bible does not specifically prohibit abortion (Sagan & Dryan, 1990). For much of its history, the Roman Catholic Church held to Thomas Aquinas' belief that ensoulment of the fetus did not occur for at least 40 days after conception. In 1869, Pope Pius IX declared that human life begins at conception. Thus, an abortion at any stage of pregnancy became murder in the eyes of the church and grounds for excommunication.

Truth or Fiction Revisited: It is true that abortions were legal in the United States prior to the Civil War. Abortion was legal in the United States from 1607 to 1828 (Hitt, 1998). Women were permitted to terminate a pregnancy until "quickening" occurred

TRUTH
fiction 6

Pro-Choice or Pro-Life? Where Do You Stand?

What does it mean to be "pro-life" on the abortion issue? What does it mean to be "pro-choice"? Which position is closer to your own views on abortion?

DIRECTIONS The *Reasoning about Abortion Questionnaire* (Parsons et al., 1990) assesses agreement with pro-life or pro-choice lines of reasoning about abortion. To find out which position is closer to your own, indicate your level of agreement or disagreement with each of the following items by circling the number that most closely represents your feelings. Then refer to the key in the appendix to interpret your score.

5 = strongly agree
4 = agree
3 = mixed feelings
2 = disagree
1 = strongly disagree

1. Abortion is a matter of personal choice.   5 4 3 2 1

2. Abortion is a threat to our society.   5 4 3 2 1

3. A woman should have control over what is happening to her own body by having the option to choose abortion.   5 4 3 2 1

4. Only God, not people, can decide whether a fetus should live.   5 4 3 2 1

5. Even if one believes that there may be some exceptions, abortion is still basically wrong.   5 4 3 2 1

6. Abortion violates an unborn person's fundamental right to life.   5 4 3 2 1

7. A woman should be able to exercise her right to self-determination by choosing to have an abortion.   5 4 3 2 1

8. Outlawing abortion could take away a woman's sense of self and personal autonomy.   5 4 3 2 1

9. Outlawing abortion violates a woman's civil rights.   5 4 3 2 1

10. Abortion is morally unacceptable and unjustified.   5 4 3 2 1

11. In my reasoning, the notion that an unborn fetus may be a human life is not a deciding issue in considering abortion.   5 4 3 2 1

12. Abortion can be described as taking a life unjustly.   5 4 3 2 1

13. A woman should have the right to decide to have an abortion based on her own life circumstances.   5 4 3 2 1

14. If a woman feels that having a child might ruin her life, she should consider an abortion.   5 4 3 2 1

15. Abortion could destroy the sanctity of motherhood.   5 4 3 2 1

16. An unborn fetus is a viable human being with rights.   5 4 3 2 1

17. If a woman feels she can't care for a baby, she should be able to have an abortion.   5 4 3 2 1

18. Abortion is the destruction of one life for the convenience of another.   5 4 3 2 1

19. Abortion is the same as murder.   5 4 3 2 1

20. Even if one believes that there are times when abortion is immoral, it is still basically the woman's own choice.   5 4 3 2 1

A Pro-Life Rally. *Few issues in American life provoke as much emotion as the Pro-Life/Pro-Choice debate.*

(the point at which the woman was first able to feel the fetus stirring within her). More restrictive abortion laws emerged because of a national desire to increase the population and because of concerns voiced by physicians about protecting women from botched abortions (Hitt, 1998). By 1900, virtually all states in the union had enacted legislation banning abortion *at any point* during pregnancy, except when necessary to save the woman's life.

Abortion laws remained essentially unchanged until the late 1960s, when some states liberalized their abortion laws under mounting public pressure. Then, in 1973, the U.S. Supreme Court in effect legalized abortion nationwide in the landmark *Roe v. Wade* decision. *Roe v. Wade* held that a woman's right to an abortion was protected under the right to privacy guaranteed by the Constitution. The decision legalized abortions for any reason during the first trimester. In its ruling, the Court also noted that a fetus is not considered a person and is thus not entitled to constitutional protection. The Court ruled that states may regulate a woman's right to have an abortion during the second trimester to protect her health, as in requiring her to obtain an abortion in a hospital rather than a doctor's office. The Court also held that when a fetus becomes viable, its rights override the mother's right to privacy. Because the fetus may become viable early during the third trimester, states may prohibit third-trimester abortions, except when an abortion is necessary to protect a woman's health.

Since *Roe v. Wade,* most states have also enacted laws requiring parental consent or notification before a minor may have an abortion. According to a CBS News Poll taken in 2005, 80% of adults in the United States say that at least one parent should be notified before minor girls can have abortions (Figure 12.9). Yet, with or without such rules, most girls seeking abortion do consult their parents. On the other hand, a survey reported in the *Journal of the American Medical Association* found that 48% of a sample of 950 girls visiting Planned Parenthood said that they

Question 1*: "In 1973 the *Roe v. Wade* decision established a woman's constitutional right to an abortion, at least in the first three months of pregnancy. Would you like to see the Supreme Court completely overturn its *Roe v. Wade* decision or not?"

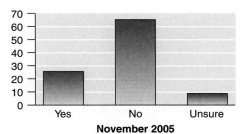

November 2005

Question 2†: "If one of the U.S. Supreme Court justices retired, would you want the new Supreme Court justice to be someone who would vote to overturn *Roe v. Wade*—the decision that legalized abortion—or vote to uphold it?"

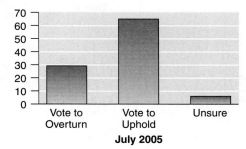

July 2005

Question 3‡: "With respect to the abortion issue, would you consider yourself to be pro-choice or pro-life?"

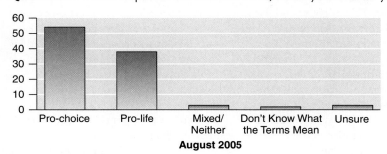

August 2005

Question 4§: "What is your personal feeling about abortion? (1) It should be permitted in all cases. (2) It should be permitted, but subject to greater restrictions than it is now. (3) It should be permitted only in cases such as rape, incest, and to save the woman's life. *Or,* (4) it should only be permitted to save the woman's life."

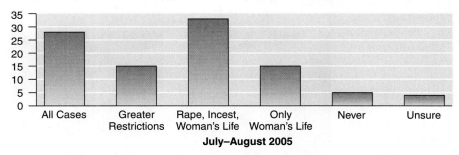

July–August 2005

Question 5¶: "Would you favor or oppose requiring that at least one parent be told before a girl under 18 years of age could have an abortion?"

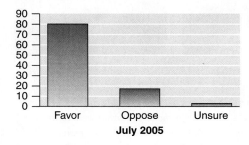

July 2005

Figure 12.9 Americans' Attitudes toward Abortion, 2000s

*Pew Research Center/Pew Forum on Religion & Public Life survey. N = 589 adults nationwide.

†CBS News Poll. N = 632 adults nationwide.

‡CNN/USA Today/Gallup Poll. N = 1,007 adults nationwide.

§CBS News Poll. N = 1,222 adults nationwide.

¶CBS News Poll. N = 632 adults nationwide.

A Closer Look

THE ABORTION BATTLE: A NATION DIVIDED?

Every time a Supreme Court seat becomes available, the president nominates a new judge. And with each nomination, pro-life and pro-choice groups battle for public opinion and the votes of the United States senators who will either confirm or deny the president's choice. A case in point is the nomination of Samuel Alito, who was nominated and confirmed to occupy the seat being vacated by the retiring Sandra Day O'-Connor. O'Connor's vote had been a middle-of-the-road swing vote in an evenly divided Court, and pro-choice advocates feared that the conservative Alito would seek an opportunity to overturn the 1973 *Roe v. Wade* decision, and hence toss abortion decisions back to the states. Under such a scenario, women seeking a legal abortion might have to cross state lines.

Not only is the Court divided when it comes to the issue of abortion, we are a nation divided. However, the majority of Americans do appear to want Supreme Court justices to uphold *Roe v. Wade*. As shown in a Pew Research Center poll (Figure 12.9, question 1), nearly two thirds (65%) of Americans did not want *Roe v. Wade* overturned. When the question was reversed in a CBS News poll (Figure 12.9, question 2), the same percentage (65%) of Americans said they would want a new justice to uphold *Roe v. Wade*.

In responding to a CNN/USA Today/Gallup poll (Figure 12.9, question 3), more than half of Americans

(54%) said they considered themselves to be pro-choice, and nearly two out of five reported that they were pro-choice (38%). This might sound like a landslide victory for being pro-choice, but in responding to another CBS News poll (Figure 12.9, question 4), only about 3 out of 10 Americans (28%) said that abortion should be permitted in *all* cases. That's about half the number (54%) who labeled themselves pro-choice in the CNN/USA Today/Gallup poll. Moreover, only 5% of the sample reported that they would *never* allow abortion. About two thirds of the respondents to question 4, in other words, were somewhere in the middle—willing to allow abortion, but under restricted circumstances.

As shown in the CBS News poll mentioned earlier (Figure 12.9, question 5), the great majority of Americans (80%) would want to know whether their underage daughters were seeking to have an abortion. If you compare the answers to questions 3 and 5, you'll see

that this 80% must include the majority of pro-choice respondents. The answers to this question do not mean, by the way, that the parents would stop the abortion; they do mean that parents at the very least think they have the right to know about their child's behavior.

So, are we a nation divided? As in so many other cases, it depends on how you look at it. Do people divide themselves into two camps: pro-life and pro-choice? Yes. But it seems that a huge majority agree that they should be informed whether their underage daughter is seeking an abortion. A majority also would allow abortion under some, but not all, circumstances. Nevertheless, other divides are suggested by the data. For example, for some respondents, religious teachings are clearly the source of values. For others, the issue revolves around whether a woman has the right to control what happens in her own body.

Are not such divisions what we should be celebrating in a pluralistic society?

When moderate justice Sandra Day O'Connor announced her retirement from the Supreme Court, President Bush nominated the conservative Samuel Alito to replace her. There was a subsequent battle over his confirmation in the Senate. Pro-choice politicians were concerned that he would work to overturn Roe v. Wade. *Pro-life politicians supported his nomination in the hope that he would do precisely that.*

would stop using all the organization's services if their parents were notified of the visits (Reddy et al., 2002).

ATTITUDES TOWARD LEGALIZED ABORTION National public opinion polls taken since *Roe v. Wade* have consistently shown that a majority of people in the United States support the decision legalizing abortion (Figure 12.9). Reduced support for legal abortion is associated with religious commitment, conservative attitudes on premarital sex, and belief in having large families.

Although most people in the United States favor legalized abortion, they do not do so under all circumstances (Figure 10.9). Elizabeth Cook (1998), author of a book about abortion entitled *Between Two Absolutes,* suggests that a consensus about abortion may be emerging—that abortion should be allowed under some circumstances, but is not to be taken lightly. Most Americans seem to want the individual to have the right to an abortion, even if they disapprove of it.

Many people in the pro-choice movement argue that if abortions were to be made illegal again, thousands of women, especially poor women, would die or suffer serious physical consequences from botched or nonsterile abortions. People in the pro-life movement counter that alternatives to abortion such as adoption are available. Pro-choice advocates argue that the debate about abortion should be framed not only by notions of the mother's right to privacy but also by the issue of the quality of life of an unwanted child. They argue that minority and physically or mentally disabled children are often hard to place for adoption. These children often spend their childhoods being shuffled from one foster home to another. Pro-life advocates counter that killing a fetus eliminates any potential that it might have, despite hardships, of living a fruitful and meaningful life.

Roe v. Wade is not in the personal memories of most individual women who choose to have abortions in the United States today. Many of them have a hard time recognizing that abortion was ever illegal, and cannot imagine what it would mean if abortion were to be made illegal again.

Says a 19-year-old woman from Chicago who is waiting in an abortion clinic: "I've never heard anything about *Roe v. Wade.* I know there is tension between different groups and that there are people who are really, really against abortion. My mom is totally against it. If she knew I was here, Wow! I can't even imagine what it was like when abortion was illegal. I just opened up the phone book. People definitely take it for granted today. I think of the movie *Dirty Dancing.* I never understood why she was so sick, but it was because she got an illegal abortion" (Lewin, 1998a).

Says Sirena, a 24-year-old woman from Brooklyn who has two young children and has had three abortions: "I don't think there could ever be a time when abortion would be illegal. No one would let that happen. There would be too many girls throwing babies in the garbage or abusing their kids. But there's always going to be people who are against abortion, like my sister, and people who are pro-choice, like me. It's always been the same and it's always going to be" (Lewin, 1998a).

Methods of Abortion

Regardless of the moral, legal, and political issues that surround abortion, there are many abortion methods.

VACUUM ASPIRATION **Vacuum aspiration,** or suction curettage, is the safest and most common method of abortion. **Truth or Fiction Revisited:** It is not

Vacuum aspiration
Removal of the uterine contents by suction; an abortion method used early during a pregnancy; from the Latin *aspirare,* meaning "to breathe upon"

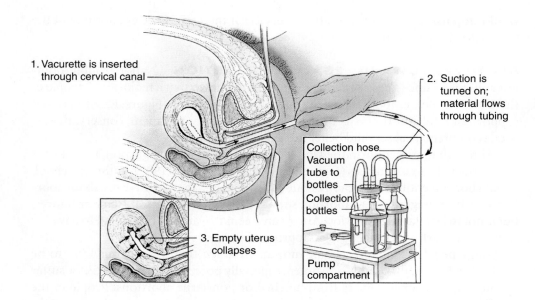

1. Vacurette is inserted through cervical canal

2. Suction is turned on; material flows through tubing

Collection hose
Vacuum tube to bottles
Collection bottles

3. Empty uterus collapses

Pump compartment

Figure 12.10 **Vacuum Aspiration.** *This is the safest and most common method of abortion, but it can be performed only during the first trimester. An angled tube is inserted through the cervix into the uterus, and the uterine contents are then evacuated (emptied) by suction.*

true that the D&C is the most widely used type of abortion method; vacuum aspiration accounts for more than 90% of abortions in the United States. It is relatively painless and inexpensive. It can be done with little or no anesthesia in a medical office or clinic, but only during the first trimester. Later, thinning of the uterine walls increases the risks of perforation and bleeding.

During the procedure the cervix is usually dilated first by insertion of progressively larger curved metal rods, or "dilators," or by insertion, hours earlier, of a stick of seaweed called *Laminaria digitata*. *Laminaria* expands as it absorbs cervical moisture, providing a gentler means of opening the os. Then an angled tube connected to an aspirator (suction machine) is inserted through the cervix into the uterus. The uterine contents are then evacuated (emptied) by suction (Figure 12.10). Possible complications include perforation of the uterus, infection, cervical lacerations, and hemorrhaging, but these are rare.

DILATION AND CURETTAGE (D&C)

The **D&C** was once the customary method of performing abortions. It now accounts for only a small number of abortions in the United States. It is usually performed 8 to 20 weeks after the last menstrual period. After the cervix has been dilated, the uterine contents are scraped from the uterine lining with a blunt scraping tool.

D&Cs are carried out in a hospital, usually under general anesthesia. The scraping increases the chances of hemorrhaging, infection, and perforation. Because of these risks, D&Cs have largely been replaced by the vacuum aspiration method. D&Cs are still used to treat various gynecological problems, however, such as abnormally heavy menstrual bleeding.

DILATION AND EVACUATION (D&E)

The **D&E** is used most commonly during the second trimester, when vacuum aspiration alone would be too risky.

D&C Abbreviation for *dilation and curettage;* an operation during which the cervix is dilated and uterine contents are then gently scraped away

D&E Abbreviation for *dilation and evacuation;* an abortion method during which the cervix is dilated prior to vacuum aspiration

The D&E combines suction and the D&C. First, the cervix is dilated. The cervix must also be dilated more fully than with vacuum aspiration to allow for passage of the larger fetus. Then a suction tube is inserted to remove some of the contents of the uterus. However, suction alone cannot safely remove all uterine contents, so the remaining contents are removed with forceps. A blunt scraper may also be used to scrape the uterine wall to make sure that the lining has been removed fully. Like the D&C, the D&E is usually performed in the hospital under general anesthesia. Most women recover quickly and relatively painlessly. In rare instances, however, complications such as excessive bleeding, infection, and perforation of the uterine lining can arise.

INDUCING LABOR BY INTRAAMNIOTIC INFUSION Second-trimester abortions are sometimes performed by chemically inducing premature labor and delivery. The procedure, which must be performed in a hospital, is called instillation, or **intraamniotic infusion**. It is usually performed when fetal development has progressed beyond the point at which other methods are deemed safe. A saline (salt) solution or a solution of prostaglandins (hormones that stimulate uterine contractions during labor) is injected into the amniotic sac. Prostaglandins may also be administered by vaginal suppository. Uterine contractions (labor) begin within a few hours after infusion. The fetus and placenta are expelled from the uterus within the next 24 or 48 hours.

Intraamniotic infusion accounts for only a small number of abortions. Medical complications, risks, and costs are greater with this procedure than with other methods of abortion. Overly rapid labor can tear the cervix, but previous dilation of the cervix with *Laminaria* lessens the risk. Perforation, infection, and hemorrhaging are rare if prostaglandins are used, but about half the recipients experience nausea and vomiting, diarrhea, or headaches. Saline infusion can cause shock and even death if the solution is carelessly introduced into the bloodstream.

SafeZone

Q *Will having an abortion make it difficult for me to get pregnant again?*

A There is usually no connection between having an abortion and getting pregnant again, as long as the abortion is carried out competently by a licensed health care provider.

HYSTEROTOMY The **hysterotomy** is, in effect, a cesarean section. Incisions are made in the abdomen and uterus, and the fetus and uterine contents are removed. Hysterotomy may be performed during the late second trimester, between the 16th and 24th weeks after the last menstrual period. It is performed very rarely, usually only when intraamniotic infusion is not advised. A hysterotomy is major surgery that must be carried out under general anesthesia in a hospital. Hysterotomy involves risks of complications from the anesthesia and the surgery itself.

ABORTION DRUGS RU-486 (mifepristone) was approved by the U.S. FDA in 2000, 12 years after its debut in France. The chemical mifepristone induces early abortion by blocking the effects of progesterone. Progesterone is the hormone that stimulates proliferation of the endometrium, allowing implantation of the fertilized ovum and, subsequently, development of the placenta.

Intraamniotic infusion An abortion method during which a substance is injected into the amniotic sac to induce premature labor; also called *instillation*

Hysterotomy An abortion method during which the fetus is removed by cesarean section

RU-486 can only be used within 49 days of the beginning of the woman's last menstrual period. The typical course is for the woman to take three mifepristone pills. Two days later, she is given a second oral drug, misoprostol, that causes uterine contractions to expel the embryo. There is also usually a follow-up visit within two weeks to make sure that the abortion is complete and the woman is well.

Supporters of RU-486 argue that it offers a safe, noninvasive substitute for more costly and unpleasant abortion procedures (Christin–Maitre et al., 2000). Supporters also note that RU-486 may reduce the numbers of women who die each year from complications from self-induced abortions. Such women are usually too poor to avail themselves of legally sanctioned abortion facilities, or else they live in countries that lack adequate medical services. On the other hand, an 18-year-old died in the United States after using RU-486, apparently from an infection caused by fragments of the fetus left inside the uterus (2003).

As the abortion debate continues, so does research into the use of other drugs (Christin–Maitre et al., 2000). A combination of the cancer drug methotrexate and misoprostol can also be used to terminate early pregnancy (Ngai et al., 2000). Methotrexate is toxic to the trophoblastic tissue of the embryo, and—as in combination with RU-486—misoprostol causes the uterus to expel the embryo.

SafeZone

Q *Can you buy that abortion pill online or over the counter?*

A RU-486 is a prescription drug. You can buy almost anything online these days, but we strongly advise against using RU-486 without medical supervision. We're not being alarmists, but there are side effects, and something could go wrong. Plan B—the emergency contraception pill—is available to adults without prescription.

Psychological Consequences of Abortion

The woman who faces an unwanted pregnancy may experience a range of negative emotions, including fear, anger directed inward ("How could I let this happen?"), guilt ("What would my parents think if they knew I was having an abortion?"), and ambivalence ("Will I regret it if I have an abortion? Will I regret it more if I don't?").

Consider the comments of Yardena, a 22-year-old woman who is the mother of a 3-year-old. Yardena had an abortion at the age of 16 and was waiting to be seen at the Planned Parenthood clinic when she learned that she was pregnant again: "I'm not pro-choice; I'm antiabortion. I still have negative feelings about abortion, and I love children, but this is something I have to do at this point in my life" (Lewin, 1998a).

A 19-year-old college student says: "I don't like the idea of abortion being used as birth control. This is my first time [at the clinic] and my last. If I get pregnant again, which I won't, I'm having the child. That will mean I was stupid twice. Once is all right, but not the same mistake twice."

Whether to have an abortion is typically a painful decision—perhaps the most difficult decision a woman will ever make. Even women who apparently make the decision without hesitation may regret it later. Although the woman's partner is often overlooked in the research on abortion, he may encounter similar feelings.

A Closer Look

THE BATTLE OVER PARTIAL-BIRTH ABORTION

Most Americans believe that early abortions should be permitted, but there is great concern over the late-term surgical abortion method generally known as "partial-birth abortion" and referred to, medically, as an "intact dilation and extraction," or "intact D and X." In this method, the cervix is dilated and a fetus that may be 10 inches long is extracted through the birth canal. Brain tissue is destroyed to rapidly terminate any life functions in the fetus.

Support of abortion rights drops off rapidly as the stages of pregnancy progress. Most people who support early first-trimester abortions oppose partial-birth abortion because of its timing. Others oppose it because of the nature of the disposal of the fetus. However, many pro-choice people argue in favor of partial-birth abortions for at least two reasons. One is that they are relatively rare and are usually performed when the health of the mother is at stake. Another is the "slippery-slope" argument, or fear that surrendering a woman's right to have a partial-birth abortion could eventually lead to surrendering other rights to her own body.

The general attitudes of the medical profession toward the partial-birth abortion may be expressed in the fact that the procedure is rarely found in medical books. Many states have passed bills to outlaw partial-birth abortion, and a number of them have been struck down by the courts on the grounds that the bans do not provide for a health exception—that is, an exception in the case when the mother's life is at stake. The battle will likely continue.

In the year 2000, the U.S. Supreme Court struck down a Nebraska statute (*Stenberg v. Carhart*) that banned partial-birth abortion on two grounds. One was that the definition of partial-birth abortion was too vague. The second was that the law did not make an exception for the case in which the procedure was necessary to protect the mother's health.

But in 2007, in a split (5 to 4) decision, the U.S. Supreme Court upheld a law against partial birth abortion passed by Congress in 2003. The majority decision held that the law does not violate the Constitution by imposing an undue burden on a woman's right to end a pregnancy and the law also reflects the government's "legitimate, substantial interest in preserving and promoting fetal life." The one exception allowed by the Court is to save a woman's life. Justice Ruth Bader Ginsburg, speaking for the minority, labeled the 2007 majority decision "alarming." She wrote that "It tolerates, indeed applauds, federal intervention to ban nationwide, a procedure found necessary and proper in certain cases by the American College of Obstetricians and Gynecologists (Toner, 2007)."

Women's reactions depend on various factors, including the support they receive from others (or the lack thereof) and the strength of their relationships with their partners (Ring-Cassidy & Gentles, 2002; Williams, 2001). Women with greater support from their male partners or parents tend to show a more positive emotional reaction after an abortion. Generally speaking, the sooner the abortion occurs, the less stressful it is. Women who have a difficult time reaching an abortion decision, who blame the pregnancy on their character, who have lower coping ability, and who have less social support experience more distress after having an abortion.

Many male partners are very concerned and supportive; others detach themselves from the situation. And of course there are some cases in which the identity of the father is unknown. Some men consider pregnancy the woman's responsibility: "She's the one who let herself get pregnant." No wonder feminists insist that men should share full responsibility for pregnancies.

We know that people on both sides of the abortion issue cite moral and social reasons regarding why their views are correct. But what of the experiences of women who have abortions? How do they react? We reported a couple of anecdotes at the

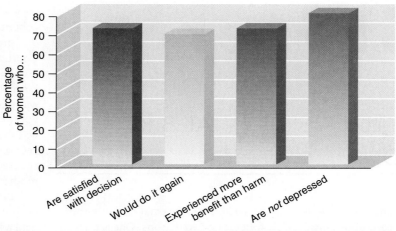

Figure 12.12 **Women's Psychological Adjustment Two Years after Having Had an Abortion.** Of several hundred respondents to an *Archives of General Psychiatry* survey (Major et al., 2000), 72% of those who had had an abortion reported being satisfied with their decision two years after the fact. How do you interpret this finding? Do you focus on the fact that the great majority of women are satisfied with their choice or do you focus on the fact that a significant number of women (28%) is not?

beginning of this section, but let's forget about anecdotes. We can all point to people who are well adjusted after having an abortion and to others who are "a mess." What do the carefully conducted surveys tell us?

Frankly, their results are less than crystal clear. Consider one survey of several hundred women reported in *Archives of General Psychiatry* (Major et al., 2000) who showed up at one of three sites for a first-trimester abortion. More than 1,000 women were approached at random as they arrived at the clinic, and 882 (85%) agreed to be monitored for two years so that their responses could be assessed at various times. Of these 882, 442 were actually monitored for the two years. As you can see in Figure 12.11, the majority (72%) said they were satisfied with their decision to have the abortion. A majority said they would make the same decision if they had it to do it again (69%) and that they had experienced more benefit than harm from having the abortion (72%). Moreover, four out of five women (80%) were *not* depressed.

Note that you can interpret these findings in any way that you like. Pro-choice advocates can say that the great majority of women appear to be psychologically well adjusted two years after having an abortion. But pro-life advocates can say that a significant number are not. To see what we mean, assume that the percentages reported in this study are accurate predictors of the adjustment of all women in the United States who have had abortions. Also assume that there are one million abortions per year (which is a slight underestimate). We'll keep the math straightforward. With these assumptions in place, 720,000 women (72%) every year will say they are satisfied with their decision two years later, but 280,000 women will *not* say they are satisfied with their decision. Similarly, 310,000 women (31%) each year will *not* be able to say they would do it again, and 280,000 women each year will *not* be able to say that they found the effects of the abortion to be more beneficial than harmful.

Our conclusion is that both sides are correct. The great majority of women appear to be psychologically well-adjusted a couple of years after having an abortion. It is also true that hundreds of thousands of women per year cannot say that they are satisfied with their decision to have an abortion. In other words, numbers alone do not tell this tale. There is no simple answer to the question regarding the nature of the psychological effects of having an abortion.

However, neither side is entitled to make overgeneralized, extreme claims. Pro-choice advocates cannot claim that women who have abortions suffer no ill psychological effects. (Some women do.) Nor can pro-life advocates argue that the psychological effects of having an abortion are devastating to women. (Most women who have abortions are well adjusted.)

SafeZone

Q *I had an abortion. Should I tell the father—even if we are not seeing each other?*

A Complicated question. What would be your motive? To show him what he lost? To punish him? We are doubtful that he would fully understand the extent of *your* loss. So if your motive is to make him understand, you might be headed down a blind alley. Looking at it from another point of view, we can't think of any reason you would be *obligated* to tell him. After all, it was, and is, your body. Have an honest talk with yourself about your motives, and maybe your answer will develop from that.

1. What is contraception?

- Contraception refers to any technique that prevents a sperm cell and ovum from uniting. In the United States, Anthony Comstock lobbied for passage of a federal law in 1873 that prohibited the dissemination of birth control information through the mail on the grounds that it was obscene and indecent. In 1918 the courts ruled that physicians must be allowed to disseminate information that might aid in the cure and prevention of diseases. Dismantling of the Comstock law had begun.

2. What methods of contraception are there?

- Hormone methods supply estrogen and progestin, or just the latter. Birth control pills include combination pills (both hormones) and minipills (progestin). Combination pills contain estrogen and progestin and fool the brain into acting as though the woman is already pregnant, so that no additional ova mature or are released. Minipills contain progestin, thicken the cervical mucus to impede the passage of sperm through the cervix, and render the inner lining of the uterus less receptive to a fertilized egg. Other methods of supplying these hormones include skin patches and injections. Oral contraception is nearly 100% effective. The main drawbacks are side effects and potential health risks.

- "Morning-after" pills have a high hormone content that prevents fertilization or implantation of a fertilized ovum.

- The IUD apparently irritates the uterine lining, causing inflammation and the production of antibodies that may be toxic to sperm or fertilized ova and/or may prevent fertilized eggs from becoming implanted.

- The diaphragm covers the cervix and should be used with a spermicide. Spermicides block the passage of sperm and kill sperm. The contraceptive sponge absorbs sperm and also contains a spermicide. Like the diaphragm, the cervical cap covers the cervix and is most effective when used with a spermicide.

- Latex condoms afford protection against STIs as well as conception. Condoms are the only contraceptive device worn by men and the only readily reversible method of contraception that is available to men.

- Two "nonmethods" are douching and withdrawal. Douching is ineffective because sperm may pass beyond the range of the douche within seconds after ejaculation. Withdrawal has a high failure rate.

- There are several rhythm methods, each of which relies on awareness of the occurrence of fertile segments of the woman's menstrual cycle. Rhythm methods include the calendar method, the BBT method, and the cervical mucus method.

- Sterilization is to be considered a permanent method of contraception, although it may be reversed in many cases. The male vasectomy cuts the vas deferens. Female sterilization methods—tubal sterilization or ligation—prevent ova and sperm from passing through the fallopian tubes.

3. What is the abortion controversy about?

- The abortion controversy is largely about when human life begins. Some argue that it begins at conception; others, when the fetus becomes viable; and still others, sometime in between, as, for example, when neural activity begins in the fetal brain.

- In 1973, the U.S. Supreme Court in effect legalized abortion nationwide in the landmark *Roe v. Wade* decision. Some pro-life activists have been challenging the extent of the *Roe v. Wade* decision; some would like it completely overturned.

4. What abortion methods are in use?

- Abortion methods in use today include vacuum aspiration, D&C, D&E, induction of labor by intraamniotic infusion, hysterotomy, and drugs such as RU-486. Partial-birth abortion (intact D&X) is the most controversial method.

1. Birth control pills appear to reduce the risk of

   (a) pelvic inflammatory disease
   (b) sexually transmitted infections
   (c) blood clots
   (d) nausea and vomiting

2. Which of the following is termed a "nonmethod" of birth control in the text?

   (a) Sterilization
   (b) The condom
   (c) Withdrawal
   (d) Fertility awareness techniques

3. Which of the following is the most effective method of birth control?

   (a) The female condom
   (b) Oral contraceptives
   (c) The contraceptive sponge
   (d) Douching

4. Which of the following methods of birth control has the most side effects?

   (a) The IUD
   (b) The male condom
   (c) The diaphragm
   (d) The minilaparotomy

5. The male sterilization procedure used today is the

   (a) vasovasotomy
   (b) culpotomy
   (c) laparoscopy
   (d) vasectomy

6. Which is true of attitudes toward abortion in the United States?

   (a) Most people would allow abortion under some circumstances.
   (b) Most people would allow abortion for women who cannot afford children.
   (c) All Roman Catholics oppose abortion under all circumstances.
   (d) Few parents want to be notified if an underage daughter is seeking an abortion.

7. The most common method of abortion practiced in the United States today is

   (a) the D&C
   (b) the D&E
   (c) vacuum aspiration
   (d) ectopic pregnancy

8. _____ is/are the most widely used contraceptive.

   (a) Injectable contraceptives
   (b) The contraceptive sponge
   (c) The diaphragm
   (d) The pill

9. The most controversial abortion method is the

   (a) minipill
   (b) D&C
   (c) hysterotomy
   (d) intact D&X

10. About _____% of Americans report that they are pro-choice.

    (a) 86
    (b) 54
    (c) 38
    (d) 15

11. Rhythm methods rely on

    (a) fertility awareness
    (b) hormonal preparations
    (c) barriers
    (d) spermicides

12. Research with African and Thai prostitutes shows that nonoxynol-9 _____ the chances of being infected with HIV.

    (a) decreases
    (b) increases
    (c) has no measurable effect on
    (d) has mixed effects on

13. The Supreme Court struck down a Nebraska statute (*Stenberg v. Carhart*) that banned partial-birth abortion because

    (a) partial-birth abortion was politically popular
    (b) partial-birth abortion was a medical issue and not a legal issue
    (c) the court was conservative
    (d) the law did not make an exception when the procedure was necessary to protect the mother's health

14. Polls suggest that about _____ % of Americans believe that abortion should never be allowed under any circumstances.

    (a) 5
    (b) 20
    (c) 35
    (d) 50

15. The percentages of women who are sterilized are higher among those who

    (a) have seven or more children
    (b) are religious fundamentalists
    (c) are in committed relationships
    (d) are younger

Answers 1. a; 2. c; 3. b; 4. a; 5. d; 6. a; 7. c; 8. d; 9. d; 10. b; 11. a; 12. b; 13. d; 14. a; 15. c

13

Sexuality in Childhood and Adolescence

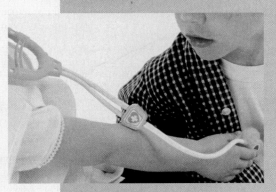

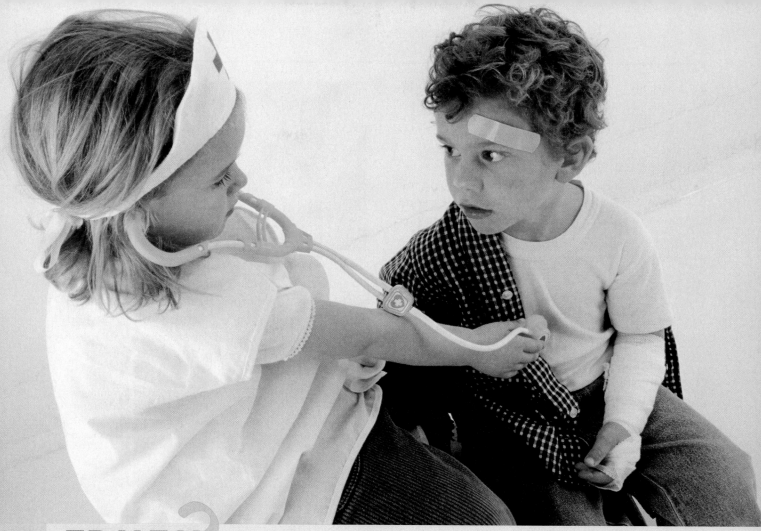

TRUTH? fiction

Which of the following statements are true, and which are fiction? Look for the Truth/Fiction icons on the pages that follow to find the answers.

1 Many boys are born with erections.   T   F

2 Infants often engage in pelvic thrusting at 8 to 10 months of age.   T   F

3 Most children learn the facts of life from parents or from school sex education programs.   T   F

4 Sex education encourages sexual activity among children and adolescents.   T   F

5 The Islamic fundamentalist country of Iran is more explicit and detailed in its sex education programs than the United States.   T   F

6 Nocturnal emissions in boys accompany erotic dreams.   T   F

7 Petting is practically universal among adolescents in the United States.   T   F

8 About 800,000 adolescent girls in the United States become pregnant each year.   T   F

Let's listen in on a woman describing her memories when she was on the cusp of preadolescence:

> When I was 8 and had just learned about menstruation, I fashioned a small sanitary napkin for [my Barbie doll] out of neatly folded tissues. Rubber bands held it in place. "Look," said my bemused mother, "Barbie's got her little period. Now she can have a baby."* I was disappointed, but my girlfriends snickered in a way that satisfied me. You see, we all wanted Barbie to be, well. Dirty.
>
> Our Barbies had sex, at least our childish version of it. They hugged and kissed the few available boy dolls we had—clean-cut and oh-so-square Ken, the more relaxed and sexy Allan. Our Barbies also danced, pranced, and strutted, but mostly they stripped. An adult friend tells me how she used to put her Barbie's low-backed bathing suit on backward, so the doll's breasts were exposed. I dressed mine in her candy-

> striped babysitter's apron—and nothing else. Girls respond intuitively to the doll's sexuality, and it lets them play out those roles in an endlessly compelling and yet ultimately safe manner. (McDonough, 1998, p. 70)

*Yes, we know that most girls cannot get pregnant during the early cycles after the onset of menstruation, but we are recounting what someone *said*. So far as we know, it is difficult for Barbie dolls to get pregnant under the best of circumstances.

The "childish version" of things has a way of shaping a lifetime of sexual experiences. As we see in the saga of the Barbie dolls, children tend to play at sex for many years before they are ready for "real" sex. In this chapter we chronicle sexual behavior during childhood and adolescence. Within children's and adults' reactions to them lay the seeds of adult sexual competence and self-esteem—or the seeds of incompetence, guilt, and shame. We begin long before children are capable of understanding anything about menstruation.

Infancy (0 to 2 Years): The Search for the Origins of Human Sexuality

Infants—and fetuses!—engage in a variety of "sexual" behaviors, although the "meaning" of these behaviors, if there is one, is a matter for speculation. Imaging techniques such as ultrasound have shown, for example, that male fetuses have erections. Fetuses of both sexes suck their fingers. The sucking reflex allows babies to obtain nourishment, but infants also appear to reap pleasure from sucking fingers, pacifiers, nipples, or whatever else fits into the mouth. None of this is surprising, given the sensitivity of the mouth's mucous lining.

Stimulation of the genitals in infancy can also produce pleasure. Parents who touch their infants' genitals while changing or washing them may discover the infants smiling or becoming excited. Infants discover the pleasure of self-stimulation (*masturbation*) for themselves when they gain the ability to manipulate their genitals with their hands.

[handwritten note: babies have erections and experience pleasure when their genitals are touched.]

The Infant's Capacity for Sexual Response

Boys not only have erections in utero. **Truth or Fiction Revisited:** Many boys are, in fact, born with erections. Erection is a reflex that begins to operate early in life. Most boys have erections during the first few weeks. Signs of sexual arousal in infant girls, such as vaginal lubrication, are less readily detected. Yet evidence of lubrication and genital swelling has been reported (Mazur, 2006).

But do not interpret children's reflexes according to adult concepts of sexuality. The reflexes of lubrication and erection do not necessarily signify "interest" in sex. We cannot say what, if anything, infants' sexual reflexes "mean" to them.

TRUTH fiction 1

[handwritten note: these reflexes are not sexual.]

PELVIC THRUSTING   Pelvic thrusting is observed in infant monkeys, apes, and humans. These observations led ethologist John Bowlby (1969) to suggest that infantile sexual behavior may be the rule in mammals, not the exception. **Truth or Fiction Revisited:** Thrusting has been observed in humans at 8 to 10 months of age and may be an expression of affection. Typically, the infant clings to the parent, then nuzzles, thrusts, and rotates the pelvis for several seconds.

TRUTH fiction 2

ORGASM   At least some infants seem capable of involuntary muscular contractions that closely resemble orgasm. Kinsey and his colleagues (1953) noted that baby boys show behaviors that resemble orgasm as early as 5 months, baby girls as early as 4 months. Orgasms in boys are similar to those in men, but lack ejaculation. Ejaculation occurs only after puberty.

Masturbation

Masturbation is typical for infants and young children and may start as early as 5 months of age (Health24.com, 2006; Narchi, 2003). Infants may masturbate by rubbing their genitals against a soft object, such as a towel, bedding, or doll. As they mature and develop sensorimotor coordination, infants may prefer manual stimulation of the genitals.

Masturbation to orgasm is rare until the second year (Reinisch, 1990). Some children begin masturbating to orgasm later. Some never do. All in all, however, orgasm from masturbation is found frequently among children, as among adults (Reinisch, 1990).

[handwritten note: young children masturbate but they don't orgasm until they are older.]

Sexual Curiosity

Children frequently develop sexual curiosity as early as 12 to 15 months of age. They play "doctor" and show their curiosity about the sexual anatomy of other people in

> **CRITICAL Thinking**
>
> What are the scientific problems in attempting to explain or interpret the meaning of pelvic thrusting in infants? Is it possible that pelvic thrusting in infants can have no meaning? (What does *meaning* mean?)

> **REFLECT**
>
> How would you respond if you observed your infant masturbating? Why?

other ways, such as wanting to watch a parent take a shower or bath (Health24.com, 2006; Pike, 2005).

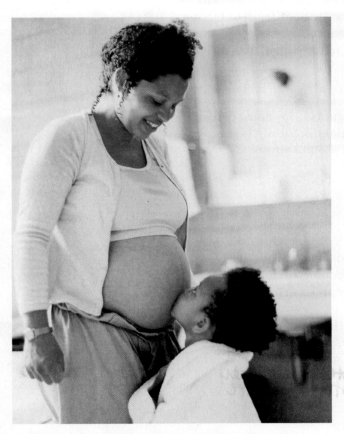

At What Age Does Curiosity about Sex Develop? *Children are naturally inquisitive about sexual anatomy and sexual behavior. Much curiosity is triggered when they become aware that males and females differ in anatomy.*

Genital Play

Children in the United States typically do not engage in genital play with others until about the age of 2. Then, as an expression of their curiosity about their environment and other people, they may investigate other children's genitals or may hug, cuddle, kiss, or climb on top of them. None of this need cause concern. Spiro (1965) describes two-year-olds at play in an Israeli kibbutz:

> Ofer [a boy] and Pnina [a girl] sit side by side on chamber pots. . . . Ofer puts his foot on Pnina's foot, she then does the same—this happens several times. . . . Finally, Pnina shifts her pot away, then moves back, then away . . . they laugh. . . . Pnina stands up, lies on the table on her stomach, . . . Ofer pats her buttocks. . . . Ofer kicks Pnina gently, and they laugh . . . Pnina touches and caresses Ofer's leg with her foot . . . says "more more." . . . Ofer stands, then Pnina stands, both bounce up and down . . . both children are excited, bounce, laugh together . . . Pnina grabs Ofer's penis, and he pushes her away . . . she repeats, he pushes her away, and turns around. . . . Pnina touches his buttocks. (p. 225)

There is no reason to infer that Ofer and Pnina were seeking sexual gratification. Rough-and-tumble play, including touching the genitals, is common among children.

Co-Sleeping

An issue that causes concern among many parents is whether it is "safe" for infants to share their beds. Parents have several motives for doing so, including the fact that infants are more likely to get back to sleep in their parents' beds when they awaken during the night. It also simplifies breast-feeding at odd hours. However, there is also the fear that allowing infants to spend the night with parents may have adverse effects on their sexual development.

Research does not reveal harmful effects in co-sleeping. For example, an Austrian study found no significant connections between children's sleeping arrangements and their social development (Rothrauff et al., 2004). Another research group followed the development of children in 205 families from infancy to 18 years of age (Okami et al., 2002). They found that the children who shared beds with their parents during infancy showed superior intellectual development at the age of 6, compared with children who did not co-sleep. The advantage of bed sharing essentially disappeared by the age of 18. Most instructive is the finding that no sexual problems were connected with bed sharing, at any age.

Sexual Orientation of Parents

Questions have been raised about the effects—if any—of being reared by gay parents on the sexual orientation of their children. A Scandinavian research group supported the findings of most studies of the issue. The group analyzed the findings of 23 studies of 615 children reared from infancy by gay and lesbian parents and 387 control children reared by heterosexual parents (Anderssen et al., 2002). Outcome measures included emotional stability, sexual orientation, gender-type behavior, adjustment, gender identity, and intellectual functioning. The children reared by homosexual parents did not differ from control parents on any of the variables, including sexual orientation and gender-type behavior patterns.

Early Childhood (3 to 8 Years)

Susan: Once my younger sister and I were over at a girlfriend's house playing in her bedroom. For some reason she pulled her pants down and exposed her rear to us. We were amazed to see she had an extra opening down there we didn't know about. My sister reciprocated by pulling her pants down so we could see if she had the same extra opening. We were amazed at our discovery, our mothers not having mentioned to us that we had a vagina!

Christopher: Nancy was a willing playmate, and we spent many hours together examining each other's bodies as doctor and nurse. We even once figured out a pact that we would continue these examinations and watch each other develop. That was before we had started school. (Morrison et al., 1980, p. 19)

These recollections from early childhood illustrate children's interest in sexual anatomy and behavior. Children in early childhood often show each other their bodies (Pike, 2005). The unwritten rule seems to be, "I'll show you mine if you'll show me yours."

REFLECT

Have you "caught" or observed children playing "Doctor"? What was your reaction? Why?

at such a young age, it is hard to determine of their actions are sexual. They are too young to understand

CRITICAL Thinking

Why is it difficult to obtain accurate information about sexual behavior in childhood?

Masturbation

Kim: I began to masturbate when I was 3 years old. My parents . . . tried long and hard to discourage me. They told me it wasn't nice for a young lady to have her hand between her legs.

When I was five I remember my mother discovering that I masturbated with a rag doll I slept with. She was upset, but she didn't make a big deal about it. She just told me in a matter-of-fact way, "Do you know that what you're doing is called masturbating?" That didn't make much sense to me, except I got the impression she didn't want me to do it. (Morrison et al., 1980, pp. 4–5)

Because of the difficulties in conducting research into childhood sexuality, statistics on masturbation and other sexual activities are largely speculative (Bancroft, 2003). Parents may not wish to answer questions about their children's sexual behavior. Or they may want to present their children as little "gentlemen" and "ladies" by underreporting their sexual activity. Their biases may lead them not to perceive genital touching as masturbation. Many parents will not even allow their adolescents to be interviewed about sex (Kaiser Family Foundation et al., 2003), let alone younger children. And when we try to look back as adults, our memories may be cloudy.

A study by William Friedrich (1998) of the Mayo Institute relied on interviews with the mothers of more than 1,100 children. The goal of the study was to establish what kinds of sexual behaviors can normally be expected in childhood to help educators and other professionals determine when sexual behavior might be suggestive of childhood sexual abuse. The study did not provide data about masturbation per se, but, as shown in Table 13.1, it offered some insight into how many children touch their "private parts." Friedrich (1998) suggests that behavior that occurs in at least 20% of children is normal from a statistical point of view.

SafeZone

Q *Will masturbating earlier make you develop sooner?*

A Physically? No. Emotionally or mentally? Let's simply say it will help one get in touch with one's sexuality—with what feels good and what happens when it feels good—at whatever age one masturbates.

Male–Female Sexual Behavior

Alicia: On my birthday when I was in the second grade, I remember a classmate, Tim, walked home with a friend and me. He kept chasing me to give me kisses all over my face, and I acted like I didn't want him to do it, yet I knew I liked it a lot; when he would stop, I thought he didn't like me anymore. (Morrison et al., 1980, pp. 21, 29)

Three- and four-year-olds commonly express affection through kissing. Curiosity about the genitals increases in this stage. Sex games like "show" and playing "doctor" may begin earlier, but they become common between the ages of 6 and 10 (Pike, 2005). Much of this sexual activity takes place in same-sex groups, although mixed-sex sex games are not uncommon. Children may show their genitals to each other, touch each other's genitals, or masturbate together.

TABLE 13.1

Some Common Sexual Behaviors during Childhood

	Boys	Girls
Ages 2–5		
Touches or tries to touch mother's or other women's breasts	42.4%	43.7%
Touches private parts when at home	60.2%	43.8%
Tries to look at people when they are nude or undressing	26.8%	26.9%
Ages 6–9		
Touches private parts when at home	39.8%	20.7%
Tries to look at people when they are nude or undressing	20.2%	20.5%
Ages 10–12		
Is very interested in the opposite sex	24.1%	28.7%

SOURCE: Friedrich, W. M., Fisher, J., Broughton, D., Houston, M., & Shafran, C. R. (1998). Normative sexual behavior in children: A contemporary sample. *Pediatrics, 101*(4) e9 [electronic article].

Male–Male and Female–Female Sexual Behavior

Arnold: When I was about 5, my cousin and I . . . went into the basement and dropped our pants. We touched each other's penises, and that was it. I guess I didn't realize the total significance of the secrecy in which we carried out this act. For later . . . my parents questioned me . . . and I told them exactly what we had done. They were horrified and told me that that was definitely forbidden. (Morrison et al., 1980, p. 24)

Despite Arnold's parents' "horror," same-sex sexual play in childhood does not foreshadow adult sexual orientation (Reinisch, 1990). It may, in fact, be more common than heterosexual play. It typically involves handling the other child's genitals, although it may include oral or anal contact. It may also include an outdoor variation of the game of "show" in which boys urinate together and see who can reach farthest or highest.

SafeZone

Q *How can you tell the difference between normal childhood sex play or exploration and signs of sexual abuse?*

A It's not always easy. Children often know or suspect when something is wrong. Abuse most often comes from someone older and close to the child—not a stranger—so parents need to be open to listening to the child, even when they implicate a family member or close friend. Children who are abused often act depressed—withdrawn, listless—or, at the other extreme, aggressively. They may not have the concept of abuse or the words to talk about it. Or they may fear *they* have done something wrong. Children need to be taught the difference between "good touching" and "bad touching." They need to know they can tell you what's on their mind without being judged or scolded. By and large, a good deal of abuse can be avoided simply by having children play with children who are pretty much their own age. They may play "doctor" or "show," but such games are usually not abusive.

A Closer Look

HOW SHOULD PARENTS REACT WHEN CHILDREN MASTURBATE?

Few parents today believe that childhood masturbation sets the stage for physical and mental maladies. Still, some parents react to childhood masturbation with concern, disgust, or shock.

Parents who are unaware that masturbation is commonplace among children may erroneously think that children who masturbate are oversexed or abnormal. They may pull a child's hands away and scold her or him. Some may slap the child's hand. Once the child is capable of understanding speech, the parent may say things like, "Don't touch down there! That's a bad thing to do. Stop doing that." Parents may use threats and punishments. Or parents may "ignore" the behavior openly, but move the child's hands away from the genitals or pick up the child whenever he or she is found masturbating.

Sex educators argue that punishment may cause children to become secretive and guilty about masturbation (Health24.com, 2006). Sex guilt tends to persist and may impede sexual pleasure in marriage. June Reinisch (1990) of the Kinsey Institute noted:

Parents who scowl, scold, or punish in response to a child's exploring his or her genitals may be teaching the child that this kind of pleasure is wrong and that the *child* is "bad" for engaging in this kind of behavior. This message may hinder the ability to give and receive erotic pleasures as an adult and ultimately interfere with the ability to establish a loving and intimate relationship. (p. 248)

But most sex educators agree that children need to learn that public masturbation is not acceptable in our culture. Pike (2005) suggests that the child who masturbates publicly can be told something like this by the age of 4: "It's okay in your room, but not in the grocery store."

Not all authorities, and certainly not all parents, endorse tolerance. Some object to masturbation on religious or moral grounds. Others feel uncomfortable or conflicted about masturbation themselves. We must also recognize that some religious leaders sincerely believe that it does a child—and a parent—little good to be relaxed about bodily pleasures if the payoff is going to hell. From their point of view, there is nothing new about the body's capacity to respond to sexual stimulation with pleasure, and certainly nothing new about the necessity to make sometimes painful and self-denying choices. Parents must examine their own values and decide for themselves how to react when they discover their children masturbating.

Preadolescence (9 to 13 Years)

Preadolescence:

Some preadolescent behaviors are sexually related rather than sexual per se. For example, preadolescents typically form relationships with a "best friend" of the same sex that enable them to share secrets and confidences. Preadolescents also tend to socialize with larger networks of friends in sex-segregated groups. At this stage, boys are likely to think that girls are "dorks." To girls at this stage, "dork" is too nice an epithet to apply to most boys.

Preadolescents grow increasingly preoccupied with and self-conscious about their bodies. Peers pressure preadolescents to conform to dress codes, the "proper" slang, and group norms concerning sex and drugs. Peer disapproval can be an intense punishment.

Sexual urges are experienced by many preadolescents but may not emerge until adolescence (O'Sullivan, 2003). Sigmund Freud had theorized that sexual impulses are hidden ("latent") during preadolescence, but many preadolescents are quite active sexually.

Masturbation

Paul: When I was about 10, stories about masturbation got me worried. A friend and I went to a friend's older brother whom we respected and asked, "Is it really bad?" His reply stuck in my mind for years. "Well, it's like a bottle of olives—every time you take one out, there is one less in there." We were very worried because we thought we'd run out before we got to girls. (Morrison et al., 1980, pp. 6–8)

Kinsey and his colleagues (1948, 1953) reported that masturbation is the primary means of achieving orgasm during preadolescence for both boys and girls. They found that 45% of males and 15% of females masturbated by age 13. Although the frequencies of masturbation reported by Kinsey and his colleagues are suspect, other studies agree that adolescent males are more likely to masturbate than adolescent females (Pinkerton et al., 2002). As noted by Steven Pinkerton and his colleagues (2002), the frequency of masturbation is connected with social norms that appear to hold that masturbation is more acceptable or normal for males than for females.

[handwritten note: adolescent males masturbate more frequently than females.]

Male–Female Sexual Behavior

Preadolescent sex play often involves mutual display of the genitals, with or without touching. Such sexual experiences are quite common and do not appear to affect future sexual adjustment (www.guttmacher.org, 2006; Health24.com, 2006).

Although preadolescents tend to socialize in same-sex groups, interest in the other sex among heterosexuals tends to increase gradually as they approach puberty. Group activities and mixed-sex parties often provide preadolescents with their first exposure to heterosexual activities (Connolly et al., 2004). However, couples may not begin to pair off until middle adolescence.

[handwritten note: display genitals. no touch. — no affect on on future sexual adjustment]

Male–Male and Female–Female Sexual Behavior

Much preadolescent sexual behavior among members of the same sex is simply exploration. Some incidents reflect lack of availability of partners of the other sex. As with younger children, preadolescent experiences with children of the same sex may be more common than heterosexual experiences (www.guttmacher.org, 2006; Health24.com, 2006). These activities are usually limited to touching each other's genitals or mutual masturbation. Because preadolescents generally socialize with peers of their own sex, their sexual explorations are also often with peers of their own sex. Most same-sex sexual experiences involve single episodes or short-lived relationships and do not always reflect one's sexual orientation.

[handwritten note: exploration. — no affect on future sexual orientation.]

Sex Education and Miseducation: More Than "Don't"

Imagine teaching driving the same way sex education is taught. You'd be told never to drive or ride as a passenger because you could be injured and go to the hospital. No one would ever take a car out. (Mark Miller, 1998)

Preadolescents and adolescents usually learn about sex through a combination of education and miseducation. Scholars of human sexuality lament the approaches of most sex education programs. Psychiatrist Anke Ehrhardt (1998) notes, "In other

A Closer Look

TALKING WITH YOUR CHILDREN ABOUT SEX

Talking with Children about Sex. *Answer the questions truthfully. Use language the child will understand, but don't make it silly child language. In other words, don't talk about pee-pees and wee-wees and Mommy's tummy. Try penis, vagina, and uterus. Get a book with drawings or pictures.*

"Daddy, where do babies come from?"

"What are you asking me for? Go ask your mother."

Most children do not find it easy to talk to their parents about sex. Only about one quarter of the children in a national survey had done so (National Campaign to Prevent Teen Pregnancy, 2003). Children and adolescents usually find it easier to approach their mothers than their fathers. Many receive *mis*information from their friends, and misinformed teenagers run a higher risk of unwanted pregnancies and STIs (Ben-Zur, 2003).

Yet most young children are curious about where babies come from, about how girls and boys differ, and so on (Pike, 2005). Parents who avoid discussing these matters convey their own uneasiness about sex and may teach children that sex is something to be ashamed of.

Parents need not be sex experts to talk to their children about sex. Parents can turn to books or surf the 'Net to fill gaps in knowledge, or turn to books written for parents to read to children. They can admit they do not know all the answers. Children often respect such honesty.

In answering children's questions, parents need to think about what children can understand (Pike, 2005). The 4-year-old who wants to know where babies come from is probably not interested in sexual details. It may be enough to say, "From Mommy's uterus" and then point to the abdominal region. Why say "tummy"? "Tummy" is wrong and confusing.

Sex researchers offer pointers about discussing sex with children:

- **Be "askable."** Be willing to answer questions about sex.

- **Use appropriate language.** Children need to learn the correct names of their sex organs and that the "dirty words" others use to refer to the sex organs are not acceptable in most social settings. Nor should parents use silly words like "pee pee" or "privates" to describe sex organs.

- **Give advice in the form of information that the child can use to make sound decisions, not as an imperial edict.** Parents who "lay down the law" may be less effective than parents who provide information and encourage discussion.

- **Share information in small doses.** Pick a time and place that feels natural for these discussions, such as when the child is preparing for bed or when you are in the car.

- **Encourage the child to talk about sex.** Children may feel embarrassed about talking about sex, especially with family members. Children's books about sex can left around or given to the child with a suggestion such as "I thought you might be interested in this book about sex. If you want to read it, we can talk about it."

- **Respect privacy rights.** Most of us, parents and children alike, value privacy at times. A parent who feels uncomfortable sharing a bathroom with a child can tell the child. The parent might explain, "I like privacy when my door is closed. If you knock, I'll tell you whether you may come in. I'll knock when your door is closed too." Fair is fair.

TABLE 13.2

Percentage of Adolescents and Young Adults (Ages 13 to 24) Who Say They Have Learned "A Lot" or "Some" from the Following Sources

Friends	76%
Media sources (movies, magazine, Internet)	72%
Sex education classes	68%
Parents	68%
Boyfriends, girlfriends, or partners	65%
Doctors or other health care providers	58%
Brothers and sisters	39%

SOURCE: From *National Survey of Adolescents and Young Adults: Sexual Health Knowledge, Attitudes and Experiences,* (#3218), The Henry J. Kaiser Family Foundation, 2003. This information was reprinted with permission from the Henry J. Kaiser Family Foundation. The Kaiser Family Foundation, based in Menlo Park, California, is a nonprofit, private operating foundation focusing on the major health care issues facing the nation and is not associated with Kaiser Permanente or Kaiser Industries.

countries, sex education is put in a positive context of loving relationships, but here we spread fear. And it hasn't worked. We have a much higher rate of teen pregnancy."

As noted in Table 13.2, adolescents and young adults in the study conducted by the Kaiser Family Foundation and others (2003), the researchers reported that they were somewhat more likely to receive information about sex from friends and the media—TV shows, films, magazines, and the Internet—than from sex education classes or parents. **Truth or Fiction Revisited:** It is not true that most children learn the facts of life from parents or from school sex education programs. Most children learn about sex from peers.

Nearly all states mandate or recommend sex education, although the content varies widely. Most programs emphasize biological aspects of puberty, reproduction, and STIs. Few deal with controversial topics such as abortion, masturbation, sexual orientation, or even sexual pleasure.

Some people argue that sex education ought to be left to parents and religious authorities (Woog, 2005), but the data suggest that the real alternatives to the schools are peers, the Internet, and the corner newsstand, which sells more copies of "adult" magazines than textbooks. Many parents worry that teaching about sexual techniques and contraception encourages sexual activity, but research does not support this concern (Blake et al., 2003; Kirchheimer & Smith, 2003; Woog, 2005). **Truth or Fiction Revisited:** There is no evidence that sex education encourages sexual activity among children and adolescents.

Obtaining accurate information during preadolescence might prevent sexual mishaps. Many teens, for example, erroneously believe that a female cannot get pregnant from her first coital experience. Others believe that douching prevents pregnancy and disease. Wrong and wrong. Table 13.3 on the next page shows the topics parents want covered in sex education.

Sex Education. *Despite the availability of sex education in most schools, many young people still learn about sex from their peers. Survey data show that most parents want sex education to cover abstinence, avoiding pregnancy, sexually transmitted infections, abortion, and sexual orientation. However, we may do a poorer job of teaching our children about sex than most European nations do, and even Iran!*

TABLE 13.3

What American Parents Want from Sex Education

Percent of parents who say sex education should cover . . .

HIV/AIDS and other STIs	98%
abstinence, what to do in cases of rape or sexual assault, and how to talk with parents about sex	97%
how to deal with pressure to have sex and the emotional consequences of sex	94%
how to be tested for HIV and other STIs	92%
the basics of reproduction and birth control	90%
how to talk with a partner about birth control and STIs	88%
how to use condoms	85%
how to use and where to get other birth control	84%
abortion	79%
sexual orientation and homosexuality	76%

SOURCE: From "Survey Finds Parents Favor More Detailed Sex Education" by Dianna Jean Schemo, *The New York Times,* October 4, 2000, pp. A1, A27. Copyright © 2000 by The New York Times Co. Reprinted by permission.

Adolescence

Adolescence is bounded by the onset of puberty at the lower end and the capacity to take on adult responsibilities at the upper end. In our society, adolescents are "neither fish nor fowl," as the saying goes—neither children nor adults. Adolescents may be able to reproduce and be taller than their parents, but they may not be allowed to get a driver's license or attend R-rated films. They are prevented from working long hours and must usually stay in school until age 16. They cannot marry until they reach the "age of consent." The message is clear: Adults see adolescents as impulsive, and needing to be restricted for "their own good." Given these restrictions, a sex drive that is heightened by surges of sex hormones, and media inundation with sexual themes, it is not surprising that many adolescents are in conflict with their families about going around with certain friends, sex, and using the family car (McGue et al., 2005; Renk et al., 2005).

Puberty

Puberty begins with the appearance of **secondary sex characteristics** and ends when the long bones make no further gains in length (Table 13.4, on page 422). The appearance of pubic hair is often the first visible sign of puberty. Puberty also involves changes in **primary sex characteristics.** Most major changes occur within three years in girls and within four years in boys.

Reproduction becomes possible toward the end of puberty. The two principal markers of reproductive potential are **menarche** in the girl and the first ejaculation in the boy. However, these events may not signify immediate fertility.

Girls typically experience menarche between the age of 10 and 18. In the mid 1800s, European girls typically achieved menarche by about age 17 (Figure 13.1). The age of menarche has declined sharply since then among girls in Western nations, most likely because of improved nutrition and health care. In the United States, the

Puberty The biological stage of development during which reproduction first becomes possible; begins with the appearance of secondary sex characteristics and ends when the long bones make no further gains in length; from the Latin *puber,* meaning "of ripe age"

Secondary sex characteristics Physical characteristics that differentiate males and females and that usually appear at puberty but are not directly involved in reproduction, such as the bodily distribution of hair and fat, development of muscle mass, and deepening of the voice

Primary sex characteristics Physical characteristics that differentiate males and females and are directly involved in reproduction, such as the sex organs

Menarche The onset of menstruation; first menstruation; from the Greek roots *men,* meaning "month," and *arche,* meaning "beginning"

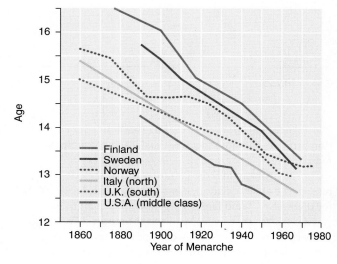

Figure 13.1 **Age at Menarche.** *The age at menarche has been declining since the mid-1800s among girls in Western nations, apparently because of improved nutrition and health care. Menarche may be triggered by the accumulation of a critical percentage of body fat.*

average age of menarche by the 2000s had dropped to about 12.1 years for African American girls and 12.6 years for European American girls (Anderson et al., 2003).

The **critical fat hypothesis** suggests that girls must reach a certain body weight (perhaps 103 to 109 pounds) to trigger pubertal changes such as menarche, and children today grow faster (Frisch, 2002). Body fat would play a key role because fat cells secrete a chemical called leptin that signals the body to secrete hormones that increase estrogen levels in the body. Higher body weight is associated with earlier menarche (Anderson, 2003). Menarche also comes later to athletes, who have a lower percentage of body fat (Frisch, 2002).

PUBERTAL CHANGES IN THE FEMALE Menarche is the most obvious sign of puberty in girls. Yet other, less obvious changes have already occurred that set the stage for menstruation. Between 8 and 14 years of age, the release of FSH by the pituitary gland causes the ovaries to begin to secrete estrogen. Estrogen stimulates the growth of breast tissue (*breast buds*), perhaps as early as age 8 or 9. The breasts usually begin to enlarge during the 10th year.

Estrogen also promotes the growth of the uterus and the thickening of the vaginal lining. It stimulates growth of fatty and supporting tissue in the hips and buttocks. This tissue and the widening of the pelvis round the hips and permit childbearing, but growth of fatty deposits and connective tissue varies considerably. Some women may have pronounced breasts; others may have relatively large hips.

Small amounts of androgens produced by the female's adrenal glands, along with estrogen, stimulate development of pubic and underarm hair, beginning at about age 11. Excessive androgen production can darken or thicken facial hair.

Estrogen causes the labia to grow during puberty, but androgens cause the clitoris to develop. Estrogen stimulates growth of the vagina and uterus. Estrogen typically stops the female growth spurt some years before that of the male. Girls who reach menarche late may grow taller than their peers because of lower estrogen levels.

Estrogen production becomes cyclical in puberty and regulates the menstrual cycle. A girl's initial menstrual cycles are typically **anovulatory.** Girls cannot become pregnant until ovulation occurs, which may lag menarche by a year or two. However, some teenagers are highly fertile soon after menarche (Frisch, 2002).

PUBERTAL CHANGES IN THE MALE At puberty, the hypothalamus signals the pituitary to increase production of FSH and LH. These hormones

Critical fat hypothesis
The view that girls must reach a certain body weight to trigger pubertal changes such as menarche

Anovulatory Without ovulation

U.S. Falls Behind in Sex Education

Iran may let nine-year-old girls get married, but it could still teach the United States something about sex education, Population Action International said in a report issued in 2002. Well-meaning adults trying to protect children and teenagers from sexual activity are actually keeping vital knowledge from them, and this is true around the world, the report from the nonprofit family-planning advocacy group says.

Only the Netherlands has an exemplary policy, the group said, citing statistics that show the Dutch reap benefits from their policies that include exceptionally low rates of teenage pregnancy, HIV infection in youth, and STIs.

TRUTH fiction 5 **Truth or Fiction Revisited:** It is true that the Islamic fundamentalist country of Iran is more explicit and detailed than the United States in its sex education programs. "Iran has a relatively strong public health system through which family planning and maternal health services are widely delivered," Margaret Greene, who helped write the report, told a news conference. "In the United States we are increasingly headed toward a politicized content with no guarantee of medical accuracy . . . whereas Iran has developed age-appropriate sex materials that are very accurate and explicit," Greene said. "I'd say there is far less hypocrisy in this area."

The group cited moves in Congress, where a House of Representatives panel endorsed funding "abstinence-only" sex education, defeating opponents who called for a broader sex education curriculum providing information on birth control and STIs. The panel also dropped wording in the bill that would require sex education programs to be backed by scientific research.

Blocked Moves

The group also points out, however, that Iran's religious leaders recently blocked moves to raise the legal age of marriage for girls from 9 to 15, and that Iran's sex education programs assume that all sexually active couples are married.

"The problem in most countries is that they do not respect the ability of adolescents to make wise decisions for themselves," said James Waggoner, president of Advocates for Youth, which supported the report. "Too many policymakers subscribe to the caricature of adolescents as mere hormone-driven accidents waiting to happen," Waggoner said.

The groups especially attacked abstinence-only education programs, which teach only that sex before marriage is wrong and do not offer any information to teens who may be having sex anyway. The result can be deadly, Waggoner said: "Our HIV rate for young men is 3 times higher than in the Netherlands. Our rate for teen births is 11 times higher than in the Netherlands. Our teen gonorrhea rate is 74 times higher than in the Netherlands."

Many studies have shown that open sex education that includes information about contraception and that also attempts to build self-esteem can lower sexual activity rates and result in fewer pregnancies and cases of disease, the report says.

"We have over 87 percent of Americans who believe there should be comprehensive sex education in schools (Table 13.3), and we have a Congress that does not support this in their legislation," Population Action International president Amy Coen said. "It is a battle between religious conservatives and the rest of the country and the rest of the world."

SOURCE: Adapted from *U.S. falls behind in sex education, study finds* (2002, April 26). Washington, DC: Reuters.

stimulate the testes to increase their output of testosterone. Testosterone prompts growth of the male genitals: the testes, scrotum, and penis. It fosters differentiation of male secondary sex characteristics: the growth of facial, body, and pubic hair, and the deepening of the voice. Testicle growth, in turn, accelerates testosterone production and pubertal changes. The testes continue to grow, and the scrotal sac becomes larger and hangs loosely from the body. The penis widens and lengthens, and pubic hair appears.

By age 13 or 14, erections become common. Many middle school boys dread that they may be caught between classes with erections, or asked to stand before the

Adolescence. *Adolescence begins with puberty. Many adults see adolescents as impulsive, as needing to be controlled for "their own good." However, adolescents have a sex drive that is heightened by surges of sex hormones, and they are flooded with sexual themes in the media. Therefore, it is not surprising that many of them are in conflict with their families about issues of autonomy and sexual behavior.*

class. Testosterone causes the prostate and seminal vesicles—the organs that produce semen—to grow and produce semen. Boys typically experience their first ejaculation by age 13 or 14, often through masturbation. However, there is much variation. Mature sperm are not usually found in the ejaculate until about a year after the first ejaculation, at age 14 on average, but sperm may be present in the first ejaculate, so pubertal boys should not assume that they have an infertile "grace period" after their first ejaculation. About a year after their first ejaculation, boys may also begin to experience **nocturnal emissions,** which are also called "wet dreams" because of the belief that nocturnal emissions accompany erotic dreams, which need not be so. **Truth or Fiction Revisited:** Despite the term *wet dreams,* nocturnal emissions need not accompany boys' erotic dreams.

Underarm hair appears at about age 15. Facial hair is at first a fuzz on the upper lip. A beard does not appear for another two or three years. Only half of U.S. boys shave (of necessity) by age 17. The beard and chest hair continue to develop past the age of 20. At age 14 or 15, the voice deepens because of the growth of the voice box, or **larynx,** and the lengthening of the vocal cords. Development is gradual, and the voices of adolescent boys sometimes crack embarrassingly.

Boys and girls undergo general growth spurts during puberty. Girls usually shoot up before boys. Individuals differ, however, and some boys spurt before some girls.

Increases in muscle mass increase body weight. The shoulders and the circumference of the chest widen. At the age of 18 or so, men stop growing taller because estrogen prevents the long bones from making further gains in length. (Males normally produce some estrogen in the adrenal glands and testes.) Nearly one in two

TRUTH ? fiction 6

TABLE 13.4

Stages of Pubertal Development

In Females

Beginning sometime between age 8 and 11	Pituitary hormones stimulate ovaries to increase production of estrogen. Internal reproductive organs begin to grow.
Beginning sometime between age 9 and 15	First the areolas (the darker area around the nipple) and then the breasts increase in size and become more rounded. Pubic hair becomes darker and coarser. Growth in height continues. Body fat continues to round body contours. A normal vaginal discharge becomes noticeable. Sweat and oil glands increase in activity, and acne may appear. Internal and external reproductive organs and genitals grow, making the vagina longer and the labia more pronounced
Beginning sometime between age 10 and 16	Areolas and nipples grow, often forming a second mound that sticks out from the rounded breast mound. Pubic hair begins to grow in a triangular shape and to cover the center of the mons. Underarm hair appears. Menarche occurs. Internal reproductive organs continue to develop. Ovaries may begin to release mature eggs capable of being fertilized. Growth in height slows.
Beginning sometime between age 12 and 19	Breasts near adult size and shape. Public hair fully covers the mons and spreads to the top of the thighs. The voice may deepen slightly (but not as much as in males). Menstrual cycles gradually become more regular. Further changes in body shape may occur into the early 20s.

boys experiences temporary enlargement of the breasts, or **gynecomastia,** during puberty, which is also caused by estrogen.

In both females and males, sex hormones course through the bloodstream in copious amounts, giving rise to a relatively strong sex drive. Thus, many adolescents seek sexual outlets, such as masturbation.

Masturbation

Gynecomastia
Overdevelopment of a male's breasts; from the Greek roots *gyne,* meaning "woman," and *mastos,* meaning "breast"

Masturbation is a major sexual outlet during adolescence. Surveys consistently show that boys are more likely than girls to masturbate (Larsson & Svedin, 2002). Boys who masturbate may do so several times a week, on average, many times more often than girls who masturbate. It is unclear whether this sex difference reflects a stronger sex drive in boys (Peplau, 2003), greater social constraints on girls (Pinkerton et al.,

TABLE 13.4

(Continued)

In Males

Beginning sometime between age 9 and 15	The testicles begin to grow.
	The skin of the scrotum becomes redder and coarser.
	A few straight pubic hairs appear at the base of the penis.
	Muscle mass develops, and the boy begins to grow taller.
	The areolas grow larger and darker.
Beginning sometime between age 11 and 16	The penis begins to grow longer.
	The testicles and scrotum continue to grow.
	Pubic hair becomes coarser and more curled, and spreads to cover the area between the legs.
	The body gains in height.
	The shoulders broaden.
	The hips narrow.
	The larynx enlarges, resulting in a deepening of the voice.
	Sparse facial and underarm hair appears.
Beginning sometime between age 11 and 17	The penis begins to increase in circumference as well as in length (although more slowly).
	The testicles continue to increase in size.
	The texture of the pubic hair is more like an adult's.
	Growth of facial and underarm hair increases.
	Shaving may begin.
	First ejaculation occurs.
	In nearly half of all boys, gynecomastia (breast enlargement) occurs, which then decreases within a year or two.
	Increased skin oils may produce acne.
Beginning sometime between age 14 and 18	The body nears final adult height, and the genitals achieve adult shape and size, with pubic hair spreading to the thighs and slightly upward toward the belly.
	Chest hair appears.
	Facial hair reaches full growth.
	Shaving becomes more frequent.
	For some young men, further increases in height, body hair, and muscle growth and strength continue into their early 20s.

This table is a general guideline. Changes may appear sooner or later than shown and do not always appear in the indicated sequence.

SOURCE: From *The Kinsey Institute New Report on Sex*, 1990, pp. 264–265, 272–273. Reprinted by permission of The Kinsey Institute for Research in Sex, Gender, and Reproduction, Inc.

2002), or both. Researchers find no links between adolescent masturbation and sexual adjustment in adulthood (Leitenberg et al., 1993).

Male–Female Sexual Behavior

Young people today start dating and going out earlier than past generations. Teens who date earlier are more likely to engage in sexual relations during high school (www.guttmacher.org, 2006). Teens who initiate sexual intercourse earlier are also less likely to use contraception and are more likely to incur an unwanted pregnancy. If the girl decides to keep her baby, she is also more likely to have to leave school and

Teen Sex Is Common Worldwide

In a new analysis of data from 30 countries, Guttmacher Institute researchers (Singh et al., 2005) report that large proportions of 15- to 19-year-olds are sexually active, but many lack critical knowledge, such as the fact that a healthy-looking person can have HIV, or where to get a condom. The study highlights the need for programs that provide young people with accurate, complete information about sex, STIs, and contraception.

The authors studied 24 countries in sub-Saharan Africa and six in Latin America. The majority of females age 15 to 19 in 16 of the countries had had sex, as had the majority of males in the same age group in 14 of the countries. (Similarly, in the United States and Europe, 50% to 60% of teenagers have had sex.) Large percentages of the female teenagers who were sexually active, and almost all the males, were single.

Many teenagers in developing countries receive little or no sex education before they initiate sex. As a result, many are unaware of modern methods of preventing STIs and pregnancy.

"Our work in the United States and Europe has shown that being open and honest with teenagers does not encourage them to have sex earlier, but it does enable them to act responsibly when they become sexually active," says Sharon Camp of the Guttmacher Institute. "This new analysis suggests that the same is true for developing countries—teens are already having sex, but in the absence of information that would protect them from pregnancy and disease. Adults worldwide need to do more to keep young people safe."

Guttmacher Institute research has indicated that adolescents in countries that provide them with comprehensive sex education have low rates of STIs and childbearing. Similarly, program evaluations in the United States show that sex education does not promote sexual activity among adolescents, but may actually delay sex, reduce the number of sex partners, and increase the use of contraception.

By contrast, sound research on abstinence-only programs shows little positive impact. Nevertheless, the U.S. government in the 2000s spends heavily on abstinence-only-until-marriage programs that prevent teachers from promoting the use of contraception and prevention of STIs contraceptives, and similarly promotes the same approach overseas.

"The abstinence-only movement, which already puts young Americans at risk, is now endangering adolescents in poor countries," says Dr. Camp. "Restrictions on the use of U.S. HIV/AIDS funding and the growing reach of the U.S.-based "religious right" will only make it harder for young people in Africa and Latin America to get the information they so desperately need. Policymakers should take note of this new study and recognize that to help teenagers avoid disease and unwanted pregnancies, we need realistic prevention efforts aimed at sexually active adolescents."

SOURCE: J. Nadeau, abridgement of *Teen sex is common worldwide.* News Release media/nr/2005/11/08/index.html. accessed September 2006.

---

scuttle educational and vocational plans. Early dating does not always lead to early coitus, however. Nor does early coitus always lead to unwanted pregnancies. Still, some young women find their options in adulthood restricted by a chain of events that began in early adolescence.

TRUTH fiction 7

alternative to sex (handwritten annotation)

PETTING   Truth or Fiction Revisited: It is true that petting is practically universal among adolescents in the United States, and has been for many generations. Many adolescents use petting to express affection, satisfy their curiosities, heighten their sexual arousal, and reach orgasm while avoiding pregnancy and maintaining virginity. Many teens believe that they are not really engaging in sexual relations if they stop short of sexual intercourse. Girls are more likely than boys to be pushed into petting and to feel guilty about it (Larsson & Svedin, 2002).

ORAL SEX   The incidence of oral sex increases with age. According to a survey by the CDC, 42% of girls age 15 to 17 reported engaging in oral sex compared with

72% of girls age 18 to 19 (Mosher et al., 2005). Overall, 54% of adolescent girls and 55% of adolescent boys have engaged in oral sex. Among adolescents who have not engaged in sexual intercourse, the lowest rates of oral sex—about 19%—were for adolescents who cited moral or religious reasons for abstaining from sexual intercourse (Mosher et al., 2005). Some adolescent couples use oral sex as a means of preventing pregnancy.

PREMARITAL INTERCOURSE

Mark: As we had no place to go, we went out into the woods with several blankets and made love. It was like something out of a Woody Allen movie. I couldn't get my pants off because I was shaking from nerves and from the cold. The nerves and cold made it all but impossible for me to get an erection and then after I had and we made love I couldn't find the car keys.

Aimee: My first sexual experience occurred after the Junior Prom in high school in a car at the drive-in. We were both virgins, very uncertain, but very much in love. We had been going together since eighth grade. The experience was somewhat painful. I remember wondering if I would look different to my mother the next day. I guess I didn't because nothing was said.

For those who do not remain celibate, there must be a first time. Given the inexperience and awkwardness of at least one member of the couple, and frequent feelings of guilt and fear, it is not surprising that most people, like Mark and Amy, don't get it quite right the first time. Adolescent boys and girls often report different concerns about first intercourse. The girl is more likely to be concerned about whether she is doing the right thing. The boy is more likely to be concerned about whether he is doing the thing right. Women are more likely than men to be physically and psychologically disappointed with the experience and to feel guilty afterward (Sprecher et al., 1995).

Surveys find that about half the high school students in the United States are sexually active. According to the NSFG (Mosher et al., 2005), the percentages of adolescents who have had vaginal intercourse increases each year between age 15 and 19 (Figure 13.2). African American males (78%) are more likely than Latino Americans (58%) and European American males (50%) to have engaged in sexual intercourse (Table 13.5).

african americans more likely to participate in premarital sex.

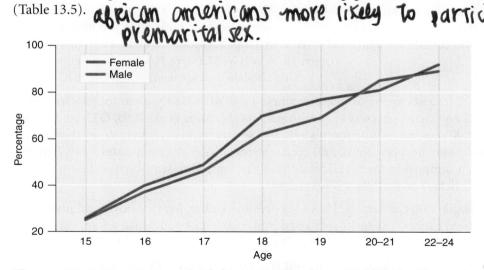

Figure 13.2 Percentage of Adolescents Who Have Had Vaginal Intercourse, According to the National Survey of Family Growth.

SOURCE: Mosher, William D., Chandra, A., & Jones, J. (2005). *Sexual behavior and selected health measures: Men and women 15–44 years of age, United States, 2002. Advance data from vital and health statistics.* Centers for Disease Control and Prevention. National Center for Health Statistics. N. 362, Figures 2 and 3.

TABLE 13.5

Percentage of Never-Married European American, African American, and Latino American Males Age 15 to 19 Who Report Having Ever Engaged in Various Sexual Activities

	N	Masturbated by a female	Received oral sex from female	Gave oral sex to female	Had anal intercourse	Had vaginal intercourse
European American	474	53%	51%	42%	9%	50%
African American	360	52	47	21	16	78
Latino American	426	48	44	37	16	58

SOURCE: From "Heterosexual Genital Sexual Activity Among Adolescent Males" by Gary J. Gates and Freya L. Sonenstein. *Family Planning Perspectives,* 32(6), 295–297, 304, (2000). Copyright © 2000. Reprinted by permission of The Alan Guttmacher Institute.

MOTIVES FOR INTERCOURSE Premarital intercourse is motivated by a number of factors. The pubertal surge of sex hormones directly activates sexual arousal, at least among boys (Peplau, 2003). However, about half the men (51%) and one quarter of the women (24%) in the NHSLS reported that the main reason for their first experience was curiosity, or "readiness for sex" (Michael et al., 1994, p. 93). Hormonal changes stoke the development of secondary sex characteristics. Some early maturers are pressured into dating or sex—ready or not.

Motives including love, desire for pleasure, conformity to peer norms, peer recognition, and even the desire to dominate someone are involved in sexual activity (Browning et al., 2000; O'Donnell et al., 2003). The NHSLS found that affection for the partner was the primary reason for first intercourse among nearly half (48%) of the women and one quarter (25%) of the men sampled (Michael et al., 1994). Betsy believed she was in love:

> I was 17 when I had my first sexual experience. I had been going out with my boyfriend for about five months, during which time he had been continually pressuring me to have sex. He made it seem as though I had to comply or he would end the relationship. Because I was deeply in love with him (or so I thought), I allowed it to happen. (McIntyre et al., 1991, p. 64)
>
> (Copyright © 1991 by McIntyre, Formichella, Osterhout, and Gresh by arrangement with AVON BOOKS)

Adolescents may consider intercourse a sign of maturity, a way for girls to reward a loyal boyfriend, or a way to punish parents (McBride et al., 2003; O'Donnell et al., 2003). Adolescents whose friends have had sex are more likely to have sex themselves. Sometimes the pressure comes from partners. About one quarter (24%) of the women sampled in the NHSLS said that they agreed to sex only for their partner's sake (Michael et al., 1994):

> *Megan* (18, California): I have felt pressure before. My first boyfriend pressured me because he knew I loved him and that he could take advantage of my feelings. I was blinded by my feelings and I had sex with him. I hated it.

> *Amy* (18, Washington, DC): I was sexually pressured by my second boyfriend. He didn't love me, but he did want to have sex. I helped him sneak into my room in the middle of the night. Just before we were about to have sex, I realized that it wasn't something I wanted to do. I wanted my first time to be with someone I loved and who loved me. I stopped him,

although he tried everything to get me to say yes. The next day we broke up, and I couldn't have been happier. (McIntyre et al., 1991, pp. 4–6)

About 8% of the men in the NHSLS study say they went along with intercourse for the sake of their partners (Michael et al., 1994). As one young man describes it:

Matt (18, New York): My girlfriend pressured me and I didn't handle it very well. I submitted so she wouldn't be mad or disappointed. (McIntyre et al., 1991, p. 65)

Many young people abstain from premarital coitus for religious or moral reasons (Mosher et al., 2005). Family values and relationships deter some adolescents. Other reasons for abstention include fear—fear of being caught, of pregnancy, of disease. Studies of African American and European American adolescent females have found that girls who are not sexually active, or who engage in less risky sexual activities, tend to be younger and more career oriented, to live in two-parent households, to hold more conservative values, and to be more influenced by family values and religion (Belgrave et al., 2000; Langille & Curtis, 2002). Teens who have higher educational goals and do better in school are less likely to engage in coitus than their less scholarly peers (Belgrave et al., 2000).

The relationship between teens and their parents is a factor (Belgrave et al., 2000; Langille & Curtis, 2002). Adolescents whose parents are permissive are more likely to have premarital intercourse (Mundy, 2000). Parents who show interest in their children's behavior and communicate their expectations with understanding and respect often influence their children to show sexual restraint (National Campaign to Prevent Teen Pregnancy, 2003).

Male–Male and Female–Female Sexual Behavior

About 4.5% of the male adolescents and 10.6% of the female adolescents in the SFG (Mosher et al., 2005) reported ever having "same-sex sexual contact." Among all respondents age 15 to 44, the percentages grow to 6% for males and 11.2% for females. But again, among all respondents, the percentages drop to 2.9% for males and 4.4% for females when asked about the incidence of same-sex sexual activity during the past year. Same-sex sexual activity in adolescence can reflect limited availability of partners, not sexual orientation. Seduction of adolescents by gay male and lesbian adults is relatively rare.

Many gay males and lesbians, of course, develop a firm sense of being gay during adolescence. Coming to terms with adolescence is often a struggle in itself, but it is usually more intense for gay people (see Chapter 10). Adolescents can be particularly cruel in their stigmatization, referring to gay peers as "homos," "queers," "faggots," and so on. Many adolescent gays therefore feel isolated and cloak their sexual orientation.

Teenage Pregnancy

The title of this section is ironic in a way. It suggests there is a problem with teenage pregnancy. Actually, throughout most of history, even most of the history of developed nations, girls were first becoming pregnant in their teens. Second, throughout

A Closer Look

KEEPING TEENAGERS IN LINE ONLINE

A mother of teenagers in an affluent New York suburb finally got it that her 15-year-old son's online behavior called for drastic action. For months he had been glued to the family computer. His grades were plummeting, and letters from the Internet service provider (ISP) cited violations of its language policy in its forums.

The mother tried parental control programs, but he got around them in minutes. She closed the ISP account a number of times, but her son pretended to be an adult on the telephone and reopened it. She required that a password be entered to boot up the computer; he circumvented it.

A Battle for Control

Parents' Tactics

- Enforcing time limits by installing software like ContentProtect, CYBERsitter, NetNanny, and Cyber Patrol.

- Recording the keystrokes their children have typed in by using software like Child Safe.

- Using AOL's parental controls or installing filtering software (e.g., FilterPak).

- Setting up parent-only passwords.

- Checking the temporary Internet files, the Web browser history log, or the Recycle Bin.

Adolescents' Tactics

- Switching screens or minimizing windows when Mom enters the room.

- Forgoing the family's service provider account in favor of free e-mail sources like Hotmail and g-mail.

- Arguing that homework requires more time online.

- Complaining that filtering software blocks too many educational sites.

- Deleting temporary Internet files, the history log, and emptying the Recycle Bin before logging off.

The Information Age has led many parents to use parental controls and computer curfews, but some parents pay no attention to their teenagers' online antics. Many parents who do care about their children's online behavior try reading their children's e-mail and listen for the difference between typing patterns that suggest that their children are doing homework or I-Ming friends.

Parents who exercise control say they are concerned about online pornography and sexual predators. Others simply fear that their teens are wasting valuable time they could be applying to academic pursuits.

Inspired by Lisa Guernsey. Guernsey, L. (2001, July 19). Looking for clues in junior's keystrokes. *The New York Times,* pp. G1, G9.

Where Is This Adolescent Going (Online) Today? *Because the sex sites are all but countless, that's the question many parents would like to have answered. Many parents have developed strategies for snooping, and many adolescents have developed strategies for evading detection.*

most cultures in the world today, girls first become pregnant in their teens (Save the Children, 2004). Why, then, have a section on this topic? The answer is that in the United States today, 9 in 10 adolescents who become pregnant do so accidentally and without committed partners (www.guttmacher.org, 2006). Most young women in developed nations defer pregnancy until after they have completed some or all of their education. Many defer pregnancy until they are well into their careers—in their late 20s, their 30s, even their 40s. So it is in our place and time that we have a topic called "teenage pregnancy."

About one in five sexually active American girls age 15 to 19 become pregnant each year (www.guttmacher.org, 2006). **Truth or Fiction Revisited:** This percentage amounts to nearly 800,000 pregnancies a year, resulting in about half a million births and a quarter of a million abortions (Figure 13.3).

The consequences of unplanned teenage pregnancies can devastate young mothers, their children, and society at large. Poverty, dropping out of school, joblessness, and lack of hope for the future are recurrent themes in such pregnancies (www.guttmacher.org, 2006). Working teenage mothers earn half as much as those who have children in their 20s. Barely able to cope with one baby, many mothers who give birth at age 15 or 16 have at least one more baby by the age of 20. Among teenage girls who become pregnant, nearly one in five will become pregnant again within a year.

The children of teenage mothers are at greater risk of physical, emotional, and intellectual problems during their preschool years as a result of poor nutrition and health care, family instability, and inadequate parenting. They are more aggressive and impulsive as preschoolers than children of older mothers. They do more poorly in school. They are also more likely to suffer maternal abuse or neglect.

Many factors contribute to the incidence of teenage pregnancy. They include a loosening of traditional taboos on adolescent sexuality, impaired relationships with parents, academic problems, misunderstandings about reproduction, and lack of contraception (www.guttmacher.org, 2006). Some adolescent girls believe that a baby will elicit a commitment from their partners or will fill an emotional void. Some become pregnant as a way of rebelling against parents. Some poor teenagers view childbearing as the best of the limited options they perceive for their future. However, the largest number of girls become pregnant because of misunderstandings about reproduction or miscalculation of the odds of conception. Many teens who know about contraception fail to use it consistently.

More attention has been focused on teenage mothers, but young fathers bear equal responsibility for teenage pregnancies. Teenage mothers apparently fare better when they have the support of the father of the child (Bunting & McAuley, 2004), but most teenage fathers cannot support themselves, let alone a family. Teenage fathers

TRUTH fiction 8

REFLECT

Do you know any teenagers who were surprised by becoming pregnant? Why were they surprised? Do you think they should have known better? Explain.

Nearly one-third of all teen pregnancies end up in abortion.

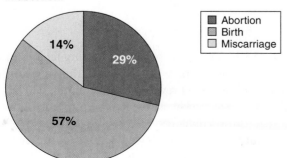

- Abortion
- Birth
- Miscarriage

14%
29%
57%

Figure 13.3 Teen Pregnancy Outcomes, September 2006

tend to have lower grades in school than their peers, and they enter the workforce at an earlier age.

CONTRACEPTIVE USE AMONG SEXUALLY ACTIVE TEENS Sexually active teenagers use contraception inconsistently, if at all (www.guttmacher.org, 2006; Mundy, 2000). Contraception is most likely to be used by teens in stable, monogamous relationships, but even teens in monogamous relationships tend to use ineffective methods of contraception or to use effective methods inconsistently.

Various factors influence the use of contraceptives. Teens whose peers use contraceptives are more likely to use them themselves (O'Donnell et al., 2003). Older teenagers are more likely than younger ones to use contraception (O'Donnell et al., 2003). Younger teens who are sexually active may be less likely to use contraception because they lack information about contraception and because they do not always perceive the repercussions of their actions (O'Donnell et al., 2003). Younger teens may also have less access to contraceptives.

Poor family relationships and communication with parents are associated with inconsistent contraceptive use (McBride et al., 2003; National Campaign to Prevent Teen Pregnancy, 2003). Poor performance in school and low educational ambitions predict irregular contraceptive use and early sexual initiation.

When asked to explain why they don't use contraceptives, sexually active teens often cite factors such as not having intercourse often enough to use it and the fact that it gets in the way of sexual spontaneity (Mosher et al., 2005). Some teenagers just get "carried away."

Myths also decrease the likelihood of using birth control. Some adolescents believe they are too young to become pregnant. Others believe that pregnancy results only from repeated coitus, or will not occur if they are standing up. Still other adolescents simply do not admit to themselves that they are "going all the way."

Preventing Teenage Pregnancy. *Even with the recent decline in the rate of pregnancy among teenagers, hundreds of thousands of girls in the United States age 15 to 19 become pregnant each year. Teenage mothers are more likely to live in poverty and to receive welfare than other girls their age. Half of them quit school and rely on public assistance. Few receive meaningful help from the fathers.*

Teenagers who focus on the long-term consequences of their actions are more likely to use contraceptives. The quality of the relationship is also a factor. Satisfaction with the relationship is associated with more frequent intercourse *and* more consistent use of contraception. More consistent contraceptive use is found in relationships in which the young woman takes the initiative in making decisions and resolving conflicts.

COMBATING TEENAGE PREGNANCY One of the interesting factors in teenage pregnancy is that parents tend to underestimate the influence they have on their teenagers. According to a National Campaign to Prevent Teen Pregnancy (2003) poll of several thousand teenagers, 88% said it would be easier for them to postpone sex and avoid pregnancy if they could have more open discussions with their parents! Yet nearly one teen in four (23%) said that they had never discussed sex, contraception, or pregnancy with their parents. Parents: Talk to your kids.

Other means for combating teenage pregnancy include sex education and free contraceptive services. Given the effects of sex education in other industrialized countries, many helping professionals believe that the rate of teenage pregnancy and the spread of STIs in the United States could be curtailed through education and provision of contraceptives.

Pregnancy prevention programs in the schools range from encouraging teens to delay sex ("just say no") to providing information about contraception to distributing condoms or referring students to contraceptive clinics (Santelli et al., 2003). Most sex educators recommend abstinence as the best way to prevent pregnancy and HIV/AIDS, but three out of four large school districts in the United States also provide instruction about methods of contraception and prevention of STIs.

Blake and her colleagues (2003) surveyed more than 4,000 high school students in Massachusetts. About 20% of Massachusetts schools made condoms available to students. Distributing condoms did not increase the percentage of students who were sexually active; however, it led to more consistent use of condoms among students who were already sexually active. In sum:

> Studies consistently show that making condoms available to students does not increase any measure of their sexual behavior—whether the teens have sex, how frequently they have it, or the number of partners they have. And some studies, including one that I conducted involving thousands of Seattle high school students show . . . that the percentage of teens having sex declined after condoms were made available to them. (Kirchheimer & Smith, 2003)

CRITICAL Thinking

Where do you stand on the issue of whether school districts should make contraceptive devices available to students? On what do you base your views? Moral values? Research findings? Explain. As an intellectual exercise, can you argue a point of view opposed to your own?

1. **What sexual behaviors do we find among fetuses and newborns?**

   - Male fetuses have erections; male and female fetuses suck their fingers. Stimulation of the genitals in infancy may produce sensations of pleasure. Pelvic thrusting has been observed as early as 8 months of age. Masturbation may begin at 6 to 12 months. Some infants seem capable of sexual responses that resemble orgasm. Co-sleeping has no effect on sexual development. Gay and lesbian parents are no more likely than heterosexuals to have gay or lesbian children.

2. **What types of sexual behaviors do we find during early childhood?**

   - Statistics concerning the incidence of masturbation at age 3 to 8 is speculative. During early childhood, children show curiosity about the genitals and may play "doctor." Same-sex sexual activity play may be more common than heterosexual play and does not foreshadow sexual orientation.

3. **What types of sexual behaviors do we find in preadolescence?**

   - Preadolescents tend to socialize with same-sex peers and to become self-conscious about their bodies. Masturbation is the primary means of achieving orgasm during preadolescence for both sexes. Preadolescent sex play often involves mutual display of the genitals, with or without touching. Much preadolescent same-sex sexual behavior involves sexual exploration and is short-lived.

   - Despite the increased availability of sex education programs, friends remain a major source of sexual information.

4. **What is adolescence?**

   - Adolescence is bounded at its beginning by the advent of puberty and at its end by the capacity to take on adult responsibilities.

   - Pubertal changes are ushered in by sex hormones. Puberty begins with the appearance of secondary sex characteristics and ends when the long bones make no further gains in length. After puberty begins, most major changes in primary sex characteristics occur within three years in girls and within four years in boys.

5. **What types of sexual behaviors do we find in adolescence?**

   - Masturbation is a major sexual outlet during adolescence. Adolescents today date and "go steady" earlier than in past generations—a change that has apparently increased the incidence of teenage pregnancy. Many adolescents use petting as a way of achieving sexual gratification without becoming pregnant or ending their virginity. The incidence of premarital intercourse, especially for females, has increased dramatically since Kinsey's day.

   - A minority of adolescents report sexual experience with people of the same sex—in 9 of 10 cases, with age-mates. Most of these sexual encounters are transitory. Coming to terms with adolescence is often more intense for gay males and lesbians, largely because of stigmatization.

   - About 800,000 adolescent girls in the United States become pregnant each year. Factors in teenage pregnancy include lack of closeness with parents, low interest and achievement in academics, and inconsistent use of contraceptives.

   - Prevention may involve better communication with parents and, for sexually active teenagers, reliable use of contraceptives.

1. According to Kinsey, children first engage in behaviors that resemble orgasm

    (a) in infancy
    (b) between the ages of 2 and 5
    (c) between the ages of 5 and 8
    (d) between the ages of 8 and adolescence

2. It is *not* true that

    (a) about 1 in 5 sexually active teenage girls gets pregnant each year
    (b) pregnant teenagers obtain a good deal of support from their partner
    (c) most teenage pregnancies are by choice
    (d) babies of teenage mothers are healthier than babies of mothers in their 20s

3. Parental co-sleeping with infants

    (a) has not been shown to be harmful
    (b) leads to sexual problems in adulthood
    (c) causes infants to have sexual fantasies
    (d) leads to parent–child conflict

4. Puberty ends

    (a) with the appearance of primary sex characteristics
    (b) with the appearance of secondary sex characteristics
    (c) when people assume adult responsibilities
    (d) when the long bones make no further gains in length

5. Estrogen does *not* cause

    (a) growth of the uterus
    (b) growth of fatty and supporting tissue in the breasts
    (c) growth of underarm and pubic hair
    (d) thickening of the vaginal lining

6. _____ encourages teenagers to abstain from premarital sexual intercourse.

    (a) Curiosity about sex
    (b) High educational goals
    (c) Peer pressure
    (d) Poor communication with parents

7. According to the Guttmacher Institute, about _____% of teenage pregnancies in the United States end in abortion.

    (a) 10
    (b) 30
    (c) 50
    (d) 70

8. American male adolescents age 15 to 19 are most likely to have

    (a) received oral sex from a female
    (b) given oral sex to a female
    (c) been "masturbated" by a female
    (d) had anal intercourse

9. Sex games like "show" and "playing doctor" become common between the ages of

    (a) one and two
    (b) three and five
    (c) 6 and 10
    (d) 11 and 15

10. According to the Kaiser Family Foundation and others, about _____ % of American parents want sex education to cover the topic of abortion.

    (a) 20
    (b) 40
    (c) 60
    (d) 80

11. Research shows that sex education is

    (a) more detailed in Iran than in the United States
    (b) largely responsible for the high incidence of teenage pregnancy in the United States
    (c) immoral
    (d) being shoved down the throats of American teenagers against the will of American taxpayers

12. According to the CDC National Center for Health Statistics' National Survey of Family Growth, more than half of Americans have *first* engaged in vaginal sexual sexual intercourse by the age of

    (a) 14
    (b) 16
    (c) 18
    (d) 20

13. Which of the following is *not* true of adolescent masturbation?

    (a) It is a major sexual outlet in adolescence.
    (b) It has a harmful effects on sexual relationships in adulthood.
    (c) The incidence of masturbation is higher among boys than girls.
    (d) Boys who masturbate do so more frequently than girls who masturbate.

14. Which of the following is *not* a reason it is difficult to obtain information about childhood sexual activity?

    (a) There is no childhood sexual activity.
    (b) Adults may not accurately recall childhood sexual activity.
    (c) Adults may not wish to talk about the sexual activity of their children.
    (d) Children may hide sexual activities.

15. Young people report they are *least* likely to have acquired sexual information from

    (a) parents
    (b) sex education courses
    (c) brothers and sisters
    (d) friends

14

Sexuality in Adulthood

TRUTH?
fiction

Which of the following statements are true, and which are fiction? Look for the Truth/Fiction icons on the pages that follow to find the answers.

1 Being single has become a more common U.S. lifestyle during the past few decades. T F

2 Divorced people are more likely than never-married people to cohabit. T F

3 Most of today's sophisticated young people see nothing wrong with an occasional extramarital fling. T F

4 Few women can reach orgasm after the age of 70. T F

5 People who are paralyzed because of spinal cord injuries cannot become sexually aroused or engage in sexual intercourse. T F

At a time when marriage may be in trouble, a new HBO series with too much marriage for some is creating a stir. It's called *Big Love,* and *The New York Times,* which sometimes likes to make its own news, recruited some women to watch the show in a hotel room in Salt Lake City, Utah, and then comment on it.

What were their qualifications? Each of the women was in, or had been in, a polygamous marriage—that is, a marriage of one man to two or more women.

As told by Felicia Lee (2006), this particular show began with a sex scene. The fictitious Bill Henrickson, played by Bill Paxton, was getting it on with the youngest of his three wives, Margene, played by Ginnifer Goodwin. As if to demonstrate that having a harem is a job rather than a blast, Henrickson pops Viagra to meet the demands of the women—the older who are played by the wise and calm Jeanne Tripplehorn and Chloë Sevigny, a shopaholic. The husband and wives have a total of seven children and share a rather wide backyard. Bill works and tries to cope in a Salt Lake City suburb. They're religious; in fact, they're religious fundamentalists who believe that their polygamy is required by God. But they're not Mormons, as the show points out

Big Love. *The HBO series* Big Love *is about a fundamentalist family in Utah consisting of one husband and three wives.*

briefly each week. The Mormon Church abandoned polygamy many years ago.

In case you haven't caught on yet, the family is irretrievably middle class and middle America.

Despite turning away from the sex scenes, one of the group said, "This is a glimpse of a family that is mainstream."

"This guy is just trying to support his family, and the family is just trying to make it," chimed in another.

Americans entering adulthood today face a wider range of sexual choices and lifestyles than those available to earlier generations—although polygamy is not one of them, at least not within the law. The sexual revolution loosened traditional constraints on sexual choices, especially for women. Couples experiment with lifestyles that would have been unthinkable in earlier generations. An increasing number of young people choose to remain single as a way of life, not merely as a way station preceding the arrival of Mr. or Ms. Right.

In this chapter we discuss diverse forms of adult sexuality in the United States today, including being single, marriage, and alternative lifestyles such as cohabitation, **open marriage**, and **group marriage**. Let us begin as people begin—with being single.

Open marriage A marriage that is characterized by the personal privacy of the spouses and the agreed-upon liberty of each spouse to form intimate relationships, which may include sexual relationships, with people other than the spouse

Group marriage A social arrangement in which three or more people share an intimate relationship; illegal in the United States

Being Single

Truth or Fiction Revisited: Recent years have seen a sharp increase in the numbers of single young people in our society. Being single, not married, is now the most common lifestyle among people in their early 20s. Marriages may be made in heaven, but many Americans are saying heaven can wait. By 2000, one woman in four and three men in ten in the United States 15 years of age and older had never married. Half a century earlier, in 1950, one woman in five and about one man in four age 15 and older had never been married. The rate of marriages had also fallen off. More than four men in five (84%) in the 20- to 24-year age range were unmarried, up from 55% in 1970 (U.S. Bureau of the Census, 2006). By 2000, the number of single women in this age group had doubled to 73%, from 36% in 1970 (U.S. Bureau of the Census, 2006).

Several factors contribute to the increased proportion of singles. For one thing, more people are postponing marriage to pursue educational and career goals. Many young people are deciding to "live together" (cohabit), at least for a while, rather than get married. Also, as you can see in Table 14.1, people are getting married later. The typical man in the United States gets married at about age 27 today, compared with age 23 just 50 years earlier (U.S. Bureau of the Census, 2006). The typical woman gets married today at about age 25; 50 years earlier, the typical woman married at age 20.

Single-mother family groups have doubled to more than one quarter of all families compared with three decades ago (U.S. Bureau of the Census, 2005). Some of these women started their families as single mothers, but the increased prevalence of divorce also swells the ranks of single mothers.

Single people encounter less social stigma today. Although they are less likely today to be perceived as socially inadequate or as failures, some unmarried people still encounter stereotypes. Men who have never married may be suspected of being gay. Single women may feel that men perceive them as "loose" or lesbians. See the findings of a *Time Magazine*/CNN poll in Figure 14.1.

Many single people do not choose to be single. Some remain single because they have not yet found Mr. or Ms. Right. Yet many young people see being single as an

Singles. *There is no single "singles scene." Although some singles meet in singles' bars, many meet in more casual settings, such as the neighborhood laundromat. Some singles advertise online or in newspapers or magazines.*

CRITICAL Thinking

People face a variety of sources of pressure to get married. Which arguments for getting married or remaining single make sense to you? Why?

TABLE 14.1

Estimated Median Age at First Marriage, by Sex: 1950 to the Present

Year	Males	Females
2005	27.1	25.3
2000	26.8	25.1
1990	26.1	23.9
1980	24.7	22.0
1970	23.2	20.8
1960	22.8	20.3
1950	22.8	20.3

SOURCE: U.S. Bureau of the Census. (2006). *U.S. Bureau of the census, current population reports, estimated median age at first marriage, by sex: 1890–to present.* [Online]. Table MS-2. www.census.gov/population/socdemo/hh-fam/ms2pdf.

- In 1963, 83% of American women age 25 to 55 were married, compared with about 65% today.
- When asked what they missed most because of being single, 75% of women said companionship, and only 4% said sex.
- Even as the birthrate has been falling among teenagers, it has been climbing among single adult women—up 15% since 1990 among women in their 30s.
- When single women were asked whether they would consider rearing a child on their own, 61% of those age 18 to 49 said yes.
- Single women are an economic force. About a fifth of all home sales were to unmarried women, up from 10% in 1985.
- Only 34% of single women said they would settle for less than a perfect mate if they couldn't find one, as compared with 41% of men.

Figure 14.1 Some Results of a *Time*/CNN Poll, Year 2000. *Single adult women in the United States are more self-confident and selective than ever before. They are assuming many of the social, economic, and sexual freedoms that had formerly been reserved for single men.* SOURCE: From "Single by Choice" by Tamala Edwards, *Time Magazine Online,* 156(9), August 28, 2000 © 2000 Time Inc. Reprinted by permission.

alternative, open-ended way of life—not a temporary stage that precedes marriage. As career options for women have expanded, they are not as financially dependent on men as their mothers and grandmothers. A number of career women, like career-oriented men, choose to remain single (at least for a time) to focus on their careers.

Being single is not without its problems. Many single people are lonely. Some singles express concerns about a lack of a steady, meaningful social relationship. Others, usually women, worry about their physical safety. Some people living alone find it difficult to satisfy their needs for intimacy, companionship, sex, and emotional support. Despite these concerns, most singles are well adjusted and content. Singles who have a greater number of friends and a supportive social network tend to be more satisfied with their lifestyles.

There is no single "singles scene." Single people differ in their sexual interests and lifestyles. Many achieve emotional and psychological security through a network of intimate relationships with friends. Most are sexually active and practice **serial monogamy**. Other singles have a primary sexual relationship with one steady partner but occasional brief flings. A few, even in this age of AIDS, are "swinging singles." That is, they pursue casual sexual encounters, or "one-night stands."

Some singles remain celibate, either by choice or for lack of opportunity. People choose **celibacy** for a number of reasons. Nuns and priests do so for religious reasons. Others believe that celibacy allows them to focus their energies and attention on work or to commit themselves to an important cause. They see celibacy as a temporary accommodation to other pursuits. Others remain celibate because they view sex outside of marriage as immoral. Still others remain celibate because they find the prospects of sexual activity aversive or unalluring, or because of fears of STIs.

Dating—Hooking Up? Having "Friends with Benefits"?

People are single prior to getting married, after divorce, and when widowed. Some do remain single for a lifetime. Throughout those years, many of them date, although

Serial monogamy A pattern of involvement in one exclusive relationship after another, as opposed to engaging in multiple sexual relationships at the same time

Celibacy Complete sexual abstinence; sometimes used to describe the state of being unmarried, especially in the case of people who take vows to remain single

A Closer Look

"HOOKING UP"

Only yesterday [we] spoke of embracing and kissing (necking) as getting to first base. Second base was deep kissing, plus groping and fondling this and that." No longer; first base is today deep kissing, also known as *tonsil hockey.* The writer of this article then speeds up to date in orally touching second and rounding third base, which is now "going all the way."

To *hook up* has for a century . . . meant "to marry," a synonym of "to get hitched," as a horse is to a wagon. But not until the 1980s did the meaning change to a less formal sexual involvement. It was first defined as "to pick someone up at a party" and then pro-gressed to "become sexually involved with; to make out."

The swinging sense mainstreamed in the 1990s. "A few women insist," wrote *USA Today,* "they never go out with the intention of *'hooking up'* or having sex," whereas a CNN commentator noted, [young people] "see shacking up and *hooking up* as the equivalent of marriage." The *Cleveland Plain Dealer* quoted a Brown University student as saying, "In a normal Brown relationship, you meet, get drunk, *hook up,* and then either avoid eye contact the next day or find yourself in a relationship." The scholarly reporter noted, "Depending on the context, a *hook-up* can mean anything from 20 minutes of strenuous

kissing to spending the night together fully clothed to sexual intercourse."

To be *hooked,* taken from the fishing vocabulary, is to be addicted to drugs; however, with the addition of *up* to make the compound, the term has no sinister narcotics meaning. In current usage, which may not last long and is probably already fading, it most often means "have a sexual relationship." Nor is the "linking" verb limited to American English. An exasperated Liz Jones, editor of *Marie Claire,* wrote in *The Sunday Times* of London about men who are habitual sexual deceivers (*Lotharios*), "Are all men like this or is it just the ones I *hook up* with?"

Although *hooking up* seems a mediumistic metaphor for what used to be euphemized as "sleeping together," it is more romantic than another phrase heard on college campuses: *parallel parking.*

SOURCE: From "Hooking Up" by William Safire, *The New York Times Magazine Online,* June 18, 2000. © 2000 The New York Times. Reprinted by permission.

---

the term *dating* is not usually heard among people of high school or college age these days. We are more likely to hear of young people *hooking up* (see the nearby "A Closer Look" feature). They meet in class, on campus, at sporting events, at parties, in cafeterias—wherever—and "hook up." Going out on a date is likely to be something their parents did, or something you do if you hook up with somebody online.

Single people sometimes engage in serial monogamy, a series of relationships that may or may not be long-term relationships, which may have the potential to turn into marriages. Some have casual relationships with **friends with benefits** (FWBs), that might coexist with other relationships. Also known as *friends with privileges* or *cut friends,* these are people for casual sexual relationships. FWBs are usually intended to meet singles' sexual needs rather than their romantic needs. Sometimes cut friends engage in sexual intercourse; sometimes they stay at second or third base, with mutual masturbation or oral sex. Relationships with FWBs are usually intended to be temporary and to end when either partner wishes it to, as when she or he finds "Mr. or Ms. Right."

Divorced or widowed singles may be somewhat more formal in their dating practices for a number of reasons. One is that they come from an older cohort, perhaps one that was not as current with contemporary values (although many of them were a part of the sexual revolution!). They are likely to be concerned that they cannot make small talk about current pop stars and trends. (Neither can their peers, of course.) Another is that many of them have children for whom they are responsible, serious jobs, and mortgages, and cannot afford to be as playful and adventurous as

Friends with benefits
Friends with whom a person has a sexual but not a romantic relationship

younger, less burdened singles. They may also be more concerned about their bodies—more desirous of making love with the lights off, if a relationship develops to that point. Then, too, those who have been divorced may have been painfully "burned" by a former relationship, or former relationships, and not be ready to jump quickly into the fray. In these cases, dinner, nice clothing, a movie, even flowers—all the classic trappings—may be in order.

Cohabitation: "Darling, Would You Be My POSSLQ?"

There is nothing I would not do
If you would be my POSSLQ

—Charles Osgood

Cohabitation Living together as though married, but without legal sanction

POSSLQ? POSSLQ is the unromantic abbreviation introduced by the U.S. Bureau of the Census to refer to **cohabitation**. It stands for *people of opposite sex sharing living quarters* and applies to unmarried couples who live together.

Some social scientists believe that cohabitation has become accepted within the social mainstream. Whether this is so, society in general has become more tolerant. We seldom hear cohabitation referred to as "living in sin" or "shacking up" as we once did. People today are more likely to refer to cohabitation with value-free expressions such as "living together." Perhaps the current tolerance reflects society's adjustment to the increase in the numbers of cohabiting couples. Or perhaps the numbers of cohabiting couples have increased as a consequence of tolerance.

The numbers of households consisting of an unmarried adult male and female couple living together in the United States has increased more than tenfold since 1960, from fewer than half a million couples to nearly five million couples today (Whitehead & Popenoe, 2006). Another half million households consist of same-sex partners (Whitehead & Popenoe, 2006). Although much attention is focused on college students living together, cohabitation is actually more prevalent among less well-educated and less-affluent people (Bramlett & Mosher, 2002). The cohabitation rate is about twice as high among African American couples as European American couples.

More than half (56%) the marriages that took place in the 1990s were preceded by living together (Bramlett & Mosher, 2002). There is a 75% probability that a cohabiting European American woman will marry her partner if the couple cohabit for five years (Bramlett & Mosher, 2002). The probabilities drop to 61% for Latina women and to 48% for African American women. Some social scientists suggest that cohabitation is a new stage of courtship for many couples. As you can see in Table 14.2, more than half of today's high school seniors believe that it is a good idea for couples to live together before getting married to test their compatibility. Even so, about 40% of these couples get divorced later on, so "trial marriage" may not provide couples with the information they are seeking.

Children are about as common in cohabiting households as among married couples (Marquis, 2003). Nearly half the

Cohabitation. *Cohabitation was once referred to as "living in sin," but it has become an increasingly common lifestyle. Some sociologists predict that cohabitation will replace marriage as the nation's most popular lifestyle sometime during the first century of the new millennium.*

TABLE 14.2

Percentage of High School Seniors Who Agreed or Mostly Agreed with the Statement: "It Is Usually a Good Idea for a Couple to Live Together before Getting Married in Order to Find Out Whether They Really Get Along," by Five-Year Period, United States

Year	Boys	Girls
1976–1980	44.9	32.3
1981–1985	47.4	36.5
1986–1990	57.8	45.2
1991–1995	60.5	51.3
1996–2000	65.7	59.1
2001–2004	64.1	57.0

Number of respondents for each sex for each period is about 6,000, except for 2001 to 2004, for which it is about 4,500. The overall trend is significantly upward for both girls and boys.
SOURCE: From "Life Without Children" by Barbara Dafoe Whitehead and David Popenoe, *The State of Our Unions: The Social Health of Marriage in America,* 2006, Figure 18. Reprinted by permission of The National Marriage Project at Rutgers University.

divorced people who are cohabiting with new partners have children in the household (Bramlett & Mosher, 2002). At least one in three households with never-married cohabiting couples also have children living with them.

People cohabit for many reasons. Cohabitation, like marriage, is an alternative to living alone. Romantic partners may have deep feelings for each other but may not be ready to get married. Some couples prefer cohabitation because it provides an abiding relationship without the legal entanglements of marriage (Hussain, 2002; Marquis, 2003).

Willingness to cohabit is related to more liberal attitudes toward sexual behavior, less traditional views of marriage, and less traditional views of gender roles (Hussain, 2002; Marquis, 2003). **Truth or Fiction Revisited:** For example, divorced people are more likely than people who have never been married to cohabit. (Does the experience of divorce make some people more willing to share their lives than their bank accounts?) Cohabitants are less likely than noncohabitants to say that religion is very important to them (Bramlett & Mosher, 2002).

Many cohabitants are less committed to their relationships than married people (Hussain, 2002; Marquis, 2003). It is more often the man who is unwilling to make a marital commitment (Peplau, 2003). Mark, a 44-year-old computer consultant, lives with Nancy and their 7-year-old daughter, Janet. Mark says, "We feel we are not primarily a couple, but, rather, primarily individuals who happen to be in a couple. It allows me to be a little more at arm's length. Men don't like committing, so maybe this is just some sort of excuse." David Popenoe of Rutgers University notes that many men cohabit because they get a "quasi-wife" without having to make a commitment (Hussain, 2002).

Economic factors also come into play. Partners may decide to cohabit because of the economic advantages of sharing household expenses. Cohabiting individuals who receive public assistance risk losing support if they get married (Hussain, 2002; Marquis, 2003). Some older couples cohabit rather than marry because of resistance from adult children. Some children fear that a parent will be victimized by a needy

TRUTH fiction **2**

REFLECT

Do you know people who are living together without being married? What is their motivation for doing so? How do most people from your sociocultural background feel about cohabitation? Why?

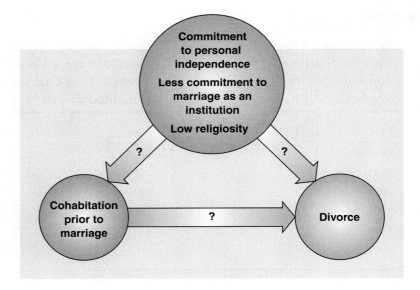

Figure 14.2 Does Cohabitation Prior to Marriage Increase the Risk of Eventual Divorce? *There is a correlational relationship between cohabitation prior to marriage and the risk of divorce later on. Does cohabitation increase the risk of divorce, or do other factors—such as a commitment to personal independence—contribute to both the likelihood of cohabitation and eventual divorce?*

REFLECT

What are your own views on the importance of marriage? How do they appear to fit with trends in modern-day America?

CRITICAL Thinking

Why might cohabiting couples run a greater risk of divorce than couples who did not cohabit prior to marriage? Do not assume that cohabitation causes divorce. We must always be cautious about drawing causal conclusions from correlational data. Note that none of the couples in such studies were randomly assigned to cohabitation or noncohabitation. Therefore, selection factors such as those shown in Figure 14.2 may lead some couples to cohabit and others not to cohabit.

senior citizen. Others may not want their inheritances to come into question or may not want to decide where to bury the remaining parent. Younger couples may cohabit secretly to maintain parental support that they might lose if they were to get married or reveal their living arrangements.

Cohabitation and Later Marriage: Benefit or Risk?

Cohabiting couples may believe that cohabitation will strengthen eventual marriage by helping them iron out the kinks in their relationship. Yet cohabitors who later marry also run a serious risk of getting divorced. According to Pamela Smock's survey (2000) at the Institute for Social Research at the University of Michigan, 40% of couples who cohabited before tying the knot got divorced later on. Cohabitors who marry may run a greater—not lesser—risk of divorce than noncohabitors. Some studies suggest that the likelihood of divorce within 10 years of marriage is nearly twice as great among married couples who cohabited before marriage (Smock, 2000).

Marriage: Tying the Knot

Despite all the challenges to marriage, marriage remains our most common lifestyle. Table 14.4 on page 444 shows the marital status of 35- to 44-year-olds in 2005, as compiled by the U.S. Bureau of the Census (Whitehead & Popenoe, 2006). This is the group of Americans who is mature enough to have completed graduate school or to have established themselves in careers. This is also a group that is young enough not to have generally suffered being widowed.

The overall percentage of Americans households made up of married couples has been decreasing, most recently from 52% in 2000 to 49.7% in 2005 (Roberts, 2006). On the other hand, two-thirds of American men and women age 35 to 44 are married.

Marriage has a long and varied history. The ancient Hebrews, Greeks, and Romans lived in patriarchies in which men dominated most aspects of life. The wife was

A Closer Look

IS MARRIAGE IN TROUBLE?

So, who needs to be married? And why? After all, can't you just live together if you want to?

In the Western world, the answer would appear to be yes. You can do pretty much what you want to do. Even the bottom-line reasons for marriage are no longer as compelling as they once were. Many corporations and government agencies, for example, are extending employment benefits to unmarried partners and the civil partners of gay males and lesbians.

And opinion polls are reflecting the more voluntary nature of marriage in modern times. For example, it was once a given that if a couple were going to have a child, they should get married. Marriage would provide the socially sanctioned, psychologically nurturant nest for rearing a secure child.

However, a 2006 Gallup Poll (Jayson, 2006) of a nationally representative sample or more than 1,000 adults age 18 and older asked the question: *How important is it to marry when a couple have a child together?*

The answers?

- 37% said "very important"
- 34% said "somewhat important"
- 27% said "not too important" or "not at all important"

The majority of respondents saw no clear necessity for the presence of the traditional two-parent family. And where is the trend headed? Fifty-eight percent of respondents age 65 and older said it was "very important" for a couple to be married when they have a child together compared with only 30% of respondents age 18 to 39.

Another survey asked high school seniors whether it was acceptable to have a child outside of marriage. As you can see in Table 14.3, more seniors have said yes as we have drawn closer to contemporary times, and now a majority would agree.

The poll also asked: *How important is it to marry when a couple plan to spend their lives together?*

The answers?

- 65% said "very important"
- 20% said "somewhat important"
- 14% said "not too important" or "not at all important"

considered the husband's property—chattel, whose responsibilities consisted of child rearing and homemaking. Marriages were usually arranged by men, sometimes for financial or political gain. In classical Greece, men would turn to high-class prostitutes for sensual sex and sophisticated conversation.

TABLE 14.3

Percentage of High School Seniors Who Said Having a Child without Being Married Is Experimenting with a Worthwhile Lifestyle or Not Affecting Anyone Else, by Five-Year Period, United States

Year	Boys	Girls
1976–1980	41.2	33.3
1981–1985	43.2	40.3
1986–1990	46.6	47.8
1991–1995	49.1	53.3
1996–2000	49.1	54.3
2001–2004	55.9	55.8

Number of respondents for each sex for each period is about 6,000 except for 2001 to 2004, for which it is about 4,500. The trend for both boys and girls is statistically significant.
SOURCE: From "Life Without Children" by Barbara Dafoe Whitehead and David Popenoe, *The State of Our Unions: The Social Health of Marriage in America,* 2006, Figure 18. Reprinted by permission of The National Marriage Project at Rutgers University.

CRITICAL Thinking

Would you conclude that the institution of marriage is "in trouble"? What might be the results for society if marriage were done away with or simply became a rarity?

TABLE 14.4

Percentage of Persons Age 35 through 44 Who Were Married, by Sex, 1960–2005, United States

Year	Males	Females
1960	88.0	87.4
1970	89.3	86.9
1980	84.2	81.4
1990	74.1	73.0
2000	69.0	71.6
2005	66.2	67.2

SOURCE: From "Life Without Children" by Barbara Dafoe Whitehead and David Popenoe, *The State of Our Unions: The Social Health of Marriage in America,* 2006, Figure 4. Reprinted by permission of the National Marriage Project at Rutgers University.

The Christian tradition also has a patriarchal foundation. Male dominance was legitimized by biblical scripture, as we can see in this passage from the New Testament: "Wives, submit to your own husbands, as unto the Lord. For the husband is the head of the wife, as Christ is the head of the church" (Ephesians 5:23–24).

Over time, women came to be viewed as loving companions rather than chattel. They became recognized as being capable of profiting from education. However, the notion that a married woman might seek fulfillment through a career unrelated to her husband's needs is a recent development. The idea that women have a right to sexual fulfillment is also new. American couples today are more likely to share or even reverse marital roles than in the past.

Why Do People Marry?

Even in this era of serial monogamy and cohabitation, people still get married. Why? Marriage meets a number of personal and cultural needs. For traditionalists—even the "traditional" polygamists we met at the beginning of the chapter—it legitimizes sexual relations. Even though the majority of young people in the United States today no longer think of marriage as very important when a couple are going to have a child (Jayson, 2006), it still provides an institution in which children can be supported and socialized. Marriage (theoretically) restricts sexual relations so that a man can be assured—or at least assume—that his wife's children are his. Unless one has signed a prenuptial agreement to the contrary, marriage permits the orderly transmission of wealth from one family to another and from one generation to another. Notions such as romantic love, equality, and the radical concept that men as well as women would do well to aspire to the ideal of faithfulness are recent additions to the structure of marriage in Western society. Not until the 19th century did the notion of love as a basis for marriage become widespread in Western culture.

Today, because more people believe that premarital sex is acceptable between two people who feel affectionate toward each other, the desire for sex is less likely to motivate marriage. But marriage provides a sense of security and opportunities to share feelings, experiences, and ideas with someone with whom one forms a special attachment. Even younger people still buy into the notion that marriage is important for people who plan to spend the rest of their lives together (Jayson, 2006).

Broadly speaking, many people in the United States today want to get married because they believe they will be happier. A University of Chicago poll (Table 14.5) suggests that the majority of them may well be correct, even if the percentages have deteriorated somewhat during the past few decades.

Types of Marriage

There are several types of marriage. Among male and female couples, we have two types: monogamy and polygamy. In **monogamy,** a husband and wife are wed only to each other. But let us not confuse monogamy, which is a form of matrimony, with sexual exclusivity. People who are monogamously wed often do have extramarital affairs, as we shall see, but they are married to one person at a time. In **polygamy,** a person has more than one spouse (of the other sex) and is permitted sexual access to each of them. In **gay marriage,** an individual is married to someone of the same sex.

Polygyny has been the most prevalent form of polygamy among the world's preliterate societies (Ford & Beach, 1951; Frayser, 1985). **Polyandry** is relatively rare. In polygynous societies, including many Islamic societies, men are permitted to have multiple wives. Practically speaking, in many cases, only wealthy men can afford to support multiple wives and the children of these unions. But few societies have enough women to allow most men to have multiple wives.

"Tradition." *The popular song from* Fiddler on the Roof *is of a time when arranged marriage was the means of mating of the day. Much of the conflict in the musical derives from the fact that the father's daughters each fall in love with men whom the father would rather not see them marry.*

Arranged Marriage

Traditional societies such as those of modern-day India (Myers et al., 2005) and Pakistan (Zaidi & Shuraydi, 2002), and olden Europe (Seward, 2005), frequently use arranged marriages in which the families of the bride and groom more or less arrange for the union. Arranged marriage by Jewish families was one of the main themes of the Broadway musical *Fiddler on the Roof.*

As in *Fiddler,* one of the purposes of arranged marriage is to make certain that the bride and groom come from similar backgrounds so they will carry on their

---

TABLE 14.5

Percentage of Married Persons Age 18 and Older Who Said Their Marriages Were "Very Happy," by Five-Year Period, United States

Period	Men	Women
1973–1976	69.6	68.6
1977–1981	68.3	64.2
1982–1986	62.9	61.7
1987–1991	66.4	59.6
1993–1996	63.2	59.7
1998–2004	64.4	60.4

SOURCE: From "Life Without Children" by Barbara Dafoe Whitehead and David Popenoe, *The State of Our Unions: The Social Health of Marriage in America,* 2006, Figure 4. Reprinted by permission of the National Marriage Project at Rutgers University.

Monogamy Marriage to one person

Polygamy Simultaneous marriage to more than one person

Gay marriage Marriage to a person of the same sex

Polygyny A form of marriage in which a man is married to more than one woman at the same time

Polyandry A form of marriage in which a woman is married to more than one man at the same time

families' religious and cultural traditions. Supporters of arranged marriage argue that it is wiser to follow family wisdom than one's own heart, especially because the attraction couples feel is often infatuation and not a deep, abiding love. Couples also begin arranged marriages with low expectations and are then pleasantly surprised when things go reasonably well. Proponents also claim a lower divorce rate for arranged marriages than for "self-arranged marriages," but it must be noted that couples who enter arranged marriages are also more traditional.

Gay Marriage

Mike and Sue Weinberg were out to dinner when their 6-year-old son, Jack, declared, "Mommy, I'm going to marry you." When Ms. Weinberg explained that she was already married, Jack persisted, "Then I'll marry Daddy."

"You can't marry Daddy," Ms. Weinberg said patiently, "He's a boy."

"But Mark and Kevin are boys," replied Jack, logic that his mother could not refute.

Mark Demich and Kevin Hengst, the couple across the street, are not actually married. Still, in the seven years they have lived in this Chicago suburb they have become like the Buckinghams, the Therrons, the Siconolfis—just another young family in the neighborhood, socializing porch to porch on summer evenings.

Choosing the suburbs over the city, Mr. Demich and Mr. Hengst feared they would be The Gay Couple. But even in Wheaton—the home of an evangelical Christian college that until last year prohibited drinking and dancing, and the seat of a reliably Republican county—they have found plenty of company. Sixty gay men and lesbians turned out for a wine tasting a few weeks earlier. About 30 played softball at a local park on a recent Saturday.

Thirty miles away, in the Chicago area known as Boystown, which officials say is the nation's first city-designated gay business district, business owners and residents

Gay Marriage. *The state of Massachusetts and a number of countries around the world are allowing gay males and lesbians to get married or to enter civil unions that provide many of the benefits of marriage. Gay and lesbian couples are fitting into mainstream life in many locales across the United States.*

say the influx of young heterosexual families has rendered the neighborhood's name an anachronism. The gay bookstore now sells more children's books than gay books.

In churches and in politics, the debate about homosexuality has focused recently on whether gays should be allowed to marry or whether gay sex should be legal. But in places like Wheaton and Boystown, people are sorting out more fundamental questions about everyday life. As gays live openly with straights, they are confronting stereotypes about one another and testing comfort zones, with varying degrees of conflict and cooperation.

And in many places today, gay and lesbian couples are getting married. In many other places, where gay marriage is not allowed, they are entering civil unions, which provide all or most of the advantages of married life.

You may also hear gay marriage referred to as *same-sex marriage,* as *lesbian marriage,* as *gender-neutral marriage,* as *equal marriage,* as *homosexual marriage,* or as *same-gender marriage.*

The Netherlands, Belgium, Spain, Canada, and the state of Massachusetts have extended full marriage rights to same-sex couples. By the time you hold this book in your hands, South Africa is expected to have joined the group.

Committed gay and lesbian couples who cannot get legally married may enter into civil unions, domestic partnerships, or registered partnerships in various places. These offer varying degrees of the benefits of marriage and are available in the countries of Andorra, Argentina, Brazil, Croatia, the Czech Republic, Denmark, Finland, France, Germany, Iceland, Israel, Luxembourg, New Zealand, Norway, Portugal, Slovenia, Sweden, Switzerland, and the United Kingdom; the Australian state of Tasmania; and in the United States, the states of California, Connecticut, Hawaii, Maine, New Jersey, Vermont, and the District of Columbia (Washington, DC). In Scandinavia, registered partnerships are about equal to marriage, and provide legal adoption rights in Sweden and Iceland. However, these partnerships are not legally identical to marriage, even though couples in the partnerships commonly refer to themselves as being married. Figure 14.3 shows the current status of gay marriage in civil unions in Europe; however, Scandinavian countries (Sweden, Denmark, Norway, and Iceland) may soon be allowing gay marriage.

Polls of the opinions of Americans about allowing gay marriage are "all over the map." A recent poll in California found that the public opposed gay marriage by about 50% to 42% of the population (Half in California, 2003). In the same year, residents of Massachusetts supported gay marriage by 50% to 44% of those sampled (Phillips, 2003). But there are two important trends worth nothing: First, younger people, especially college students, are more supportive of gay marriage than older and less well educated people. Second, majorities in most areas polled would allow gays to enter into civil contracts that are similar to marriage, even if they define the term *marriage* to exclude gay unions.

CRITICAL
Thinking
Some have suggested that the term *marriage* should be restricted to a religious ceremony and status, and that the term *civil union* should be restricted to a civil union and status. However, the religious status would also include the civil benefits. What do you think?

Other Wrinkles in Marriage

Marriages are generally based on the expectation of sexual exclusivity. Alternative or nontraditional lifestyles, however, such as open marriages and group marriages, permit intimate relationships with people outside the marriage. Such alternative lifestyles attracted a flurry of attention during the heyday of the sexual revolution in the 1960s and 1970s, but even then they were more often talked about than practiced (Bozell, 2005; Gates, 2001). Today, they find still fewer adherents.

Although the ideal of the traditional marriage remains strong in our culture, men are somewhat more likely than women to express an interest in sexual freedom

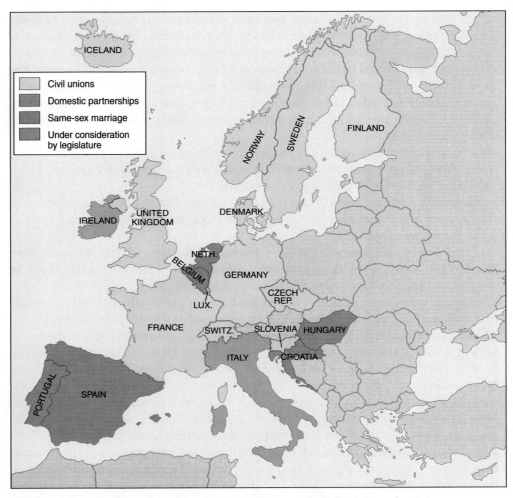

Figure 14.3 Status of Same-Sex Marriage and Civil Unions in Europe

(Knox & Schacht, 2002). However, even most of those who have tried lifestyles such as cohabitation, open marriage, or group marriage enter into traditional marriages at some time.

Whom Do We Marry? Are Marriages Made in Heaven or in the Neighborhood?

Most preliterate societies regulate the selection of spouses in some way. The universal incest taboo proscribes mating of close relatives. Societal rules and customs also determine which people are desirable mates and which are not.

In contemporary Western culture, mate selection is presumably free. Parents seldom arrange marriages, although they may still encourage their child to date that wonderful son or daughter of the solid churchgoing couple who live down the street. Nevertheless, factors such as race, social class, and religion often determine the categories of people within which we seek mates (Carey, 2005). People in our culture tend to marry others from the same geographical area and social class. Because neighborhoods are often made up of people from a similar social class, storybook marriages like Cinderella's are the exception to the rule.

Because we make choices, we tend to marry people who are similar to us in physical attractiveness and attitudes. As relationships progress through stages such as meeting, dating, perhaps cohabiting, and marriage, we tend to become more selective—that is, to narrow our choices to people yet more similar to us in background, attitudes, and interests (Blackwell & Lichter, 2004). We are more often than not similar to our mates in height, weight, personality traits, and intelligence, even on apparently minute matters such as use of alcohol and tobacco (Reynolds et al., 2006). We also tend to think about whether potential mates are likely to meet our material, sexual, and psychological needs.

The concept of "like marrying like" is termed **homogamy.** Most of the time, we also marry people of the same racial and ethnic background, educational level, and religion. And research tends to show that marriages between people from similar backgrounds tend to be more stable (Myers, 2006; Willetts, 2006). Yet more than one-third of Asian Americans and Latino and Latina Americans marry outside their racial/ethnic groups, along with about 13% of African Americans and 7% of European Americans (Carey, 2005). Individuals who are alike in background may be more likely to remain together because they are more likely to share values and attitudes (Willetts, 2006). Still, more and more Americans are intermarrying because of love (Kennedy, 2003).

We also tend to follow *age homogamy*—to select a partner who falls in one's own age range (Michael et al., 1994). Age homogamy may reflect the tendency to marry early during adulthood. Persons who marry late or who remarry tend not to select partners so close in age. Bridegrooms tend to be two to five years older than their wives, on average, in European, North American, and South American countries (Buss, 1994).

Some marriages also show a mating gradient. The stereotype has been that an economically established older man would take an attractive, younger woman as his wife. But by and large, we are attracted to and marry the boy or girl (almost) next door or in the same office. Most marriages seem to be made, not in heaven, but in the neighborhood.

Marital Sex

Patterns of marital sexuality vary across cultures, yet anthropologists note common threads. Privacy for sexual relations is valued in almost all cultures. Most cultures also place restrictions on sex during menstruation, during some stages of pregnancy, and for a while after childbirth.

Until the sexual revolution of the 1960s and 1970s, Western culture could have been characterized as restrictive, even toward marital sex. We usually think of the sexual revolution in terms of the changes in sexual behaviors and attitudes that occurred among young, unmarried people. It also ushered in profound changes in marital sexuality, however. Compared with Kinsey's "prerevolution" samples from the late 1930s and 1940s, married couples today engage in coitus more frequently, with greater variety, and for longer periods of time. They report greater sexual satisfaction. The sexual revolution helped dislodge the view that sexual pleasure is meant for men and that it is the duty of women to satisfy their husbands' sexual needs. Cable TV and Internet downloads bring sexually explicit movies into suburban homes and cellphones.

Scientific findings were also liberalizing influences. Kinsey's and Masters and Johnson's findings that normal women were capable not only of orgasm, but also of multiple orgasms, punctured traditional beliefs that sexual gratification was the birthright of men alone. TV shows, films, and radio talk shows began to portray

Homogamy The practice of marrying people who are similar in social background and standing; from the Greek roots *homos,* meaning "same," and *gamos,* meaning "marriage"

women as sexual initiators who enjoy sex. The affluence of the post–World War II years also encouraged more young people to pursue a college education and live away from home. College liberates not only through exposure to great books and scientific knowledge, but also through interaction with students from different backgrounds.

The development of effective contraceptives separated sex from reproduction. Motives for sexual pleasure became more open. All these liberalizing forces have led to changes in the frequency of marital sex and in techniques of foreplay and coitus since Kinsey's day (Mosher et al., 2005).

CHANGES IN FOREPLAY   Married women in Kinsey's sample reported an average (median) length of foreplay of about 12 minutes. Kinsey found that men at lower educational levels engaged in briefer foreplay, generally lasting but a minute or two before penetration. The length of foreplay rose to 5 to 15 minutes among college-educated men. Marital foreplay has gained in duration and variety since Kinsey's day. Couples in more recent surveys report using a wider variety of foreplay techniques, including oral stimulation of the breasts and oral–genital contact (Laumann et al., 1994).

CHANGES IN FREQUENCY OF MARITAL COITUS   How frequently do married couples engage in coitus? Table 14.6 summarizes results from the Kinsey surveys. The frequency of coitus was negatively related to age. That is, older couples engaged in coitus less frequently.

As shown in Table 14.7, most married men and women in the NHSLS engaged in sexual relations either a few times per month or two to three times a week (Laumann et al., 1994). The average is seven times a month (Michael et al., 1994, p. 136). These figures are not notably different from Kinsey's.

The frequency of sexual relations declines with age, however (Call et al., 1995; Laumann et al., 1994). At the age of 50 to 59, for example, people reported an average of four to five times per month (Laumann et al., 1994). Regardless of a couple's age, sexual frequency also appears to decline with years of marriage. There would thus appear to be a novelty effect.

CHANGES IN COITUS   In coitus, as in foreplay, the marital bed since Kinsey's day has become a stage on which the players act more varied roles. Today's couples use greater variety in positions.

TABLE 14.6

Median Weekly Frequency of Marital Sexual Relations, Male and Female Estimates Combined, According to the Kinsey Surveys

Age	Frequency
16–25	2.45
26–35	1.95
36–45	1.40
46–55	0.85
55–60	0.50

SOURCES: Kinsey, A. C., Pomeroy, W. B., & Martin, C. E. (1948). *Sexual behavior in the human male.* Philadelphia: W. B. Saunders. Kinsey, A. C., Pomeroy, W. B., Martin, C. E., & Gebhard, P. H. (1953). *Sexual behavior in the human female.* Philadelphia: W. B. Saunders.

TABLE 14.7

Frequency of Marital Sexual Relations during the Past Year, according to the NHSLS

Frequency of Sexual Relations	Men, %	Women, %
Not at all	1.3	3.0
A few times per year	12.8	11.9
A few times per month	42.5	46.5
Two to three times a week	36.1	31.9
Four or more times a week	7.3	6.6

SOURCE: Adapted by permission from E. O. Laumann, J. H. Gagnon, R. T. Michael, and S. Michaels (1994). *The Social Organization of Sexuality: Sexual Practices in the United States.* Chicago: University of Chicago Press, Table 3.4, pp. 88–89.

As many as 70% of Kinsey's males used the male-superior position only (Kinsey et al., 1948). Perhaps 3 couples in 10 used the female-superior position frequently. One in four or five used the lateral-entry position frequently, and about 1 in 10 used the rear-entry position. Younger and more highly educated men showed greater variety, however.

An important difference between Kinsey's and current samples involves the length of intercourse. In Kinsey's time it was widely believed that the "virile" man ejaculated rapidly during intercourse. Kinsey estimated that most men reached orgasm within two minutes after penetration, many within 10 or 20 seconds. Yet some clinicians at the time were already asserting that a man's ejaculation was "premature" unless he delayed it until his partner was ready to reach orgasm. According to the NHSLS, men now spend more time on their partner's needs: The "duration of the last sexual event" in three out of four married couples was 15 minutes to an hour (Michael et al., 1994).

SEXUAL SATISFACTION   One index of sexual satisfaction is orgasmic consistency. Men tend to reach orgasm more consistently than women do. The NHSLS found that more than 90% of the men and about 70% of women reported reaching orgasm "always" or "usually" with their primary partner during the 12 months prior to the survey (Laumann et al., 1994; Michael et al., 1994) (Table 14.8). Three of four men (75%) and nearly three women in ten (28.6%) reported reaching orgasm every time (not shown). Only 2% of the married women reported never reaching orgasm with their husbands during the past year (not shown).

Women in their 40s were somewhat more likely to reach orgasm than younger and older women. Women in their 40s have presumably had time to learn about their sexuality and are more secure in their relationships than younger women are. The falloff for older women and men may be biologically related. Married women were most likely to reach orgasm consistently, followed by cohabiting women, then noncohabiting women. Security apparently promotes orgasmic consistency. There do not seem to be notable racial or ethnic differences.

Orgasm is not the only way of measuring sexual satisfaction. The NHSLS asked participants whether they had been extremely physically satisfied with their primary partners during the past year. It is apparent, from Table 14.8, that men's and women's general physical satisfaction is comparable—about 47% and 41% respectively. Orgasm, then, is not a guarantee of satisfaction. And lack of orgasm is not necessarily a

TABLE 14.8

A World of Diversity: Demographic Factors and Sexual Satisfaction in Primary Relationship during the Past Year

Demographic Characteristics	Always or Usually Had an Orgasm with Partner		Has Been Extremely Physically Satisfied with Partner		Has Been Extremely Emotionally Satisfied with Partner	
	Men	Women	Men	Women	Men	Women
Age, years						
18–24	92%	61%	44%	44%	41%	39%
25–29	94	71	50	39	46	40
30–39	97	70	45	41	39	38
40–49	97	78	44	42	38	42
50–59	91	73	53	32	52	32
Marital status						
Noncohabiting	94	62	39	40	32	31
Cohabiting	95	68	44	46	35	44
Married	95	75	52	41	49	42
Race/ethnicity*						
European American	96	70	47	40	43	38
African American	90	72	43	44	43	38
Latino and Latina American	96	68	51	39	43	39

*The numbers of Asian Americans and Native Americans were too small to report reliable statistics.
SOURCES: Combined from Laumann, E. O., Gagnon, J. H., Michael, R. T., & Michaels, S. (1994). *The social organization of sexuality: Sexual practices in the United States.* Chicago: University of Chicago Press, Table 3.7, pp. 116–117, and Michael, R. T., Gagnon, J. H., Laumann, E. O., & Kolata, G. (1994). *Sex in America: A definitive survey.* Boston: Little, Brown, Table 9, pp. 128–129.

CRITICAL Thinking

Agree or disagree with the following statement, and support your answer: Marriage is an old-fashioned, outdated lifestyle that has become irrelevant for today's sophisticated young people.

sign of dissatisfaction. But emotional satisfaction is linked with sexual satisfaction. Table 14.8 shows that about 40% of men and women report being extremely emotionally satisfied with their primary partners. Closer relationships are connected with more consistent orgasm.

SafeZone

Q *How can I keep my partner interested in sex? We have been together for five years.*

A Do you have any "barriers" to sex? Like kids running into the room? Like incredibly stressful jobs? Like impossibly long commutes? Like fatigue? Like (too much) alcohol? If so, you may want to consider reengineering your life in general. But if you've just got a little sexual boredom going, you may want to remember that the greatest known aphrodisiac, to quote from an earlier chapter, is variety. How about a new perfume or cologne? How about a change in hairstyle? Nightclothes or lingerie? How about a weekend away from things? How about trying something new sexually? A 75-year-old endocrinologist said he and his wife watched pornography while they were having sex. He said it was pretty much a yawner for her, but she appreciated what it did for him. In sum: Remove barriers. Create novelty. And if you happen to be a 75-year-old endocrinologist . . .

Extramarital Sex

Some people engage in extramarital sex for variety (Lamanna & Riedman, 2005). Some have affairs to break the routine of a confining marriage (Allen & Atkins, 2005; Markman, 2005). Others enter affairs for reasons similar to the nonsexual reasons adolescents often have for sex: as a way of expressing hostility toward a spouse or retaliating for injustice. Husbands and wives who engage in affairs often report that they are not satisfied with, or fulfilled by, their marital relationships. Curiosity and desire for personal growth are often more prominent motives than marital dissatisfaction. Middle-age people may have affairs to boost their self-esteem or to prove that they are still attractive.

Many times the sexual motive is less pressing than the desire for emotional closeness. Some women say they are seeking someone whom they can talk to or communicate with (Lamanna & Riedmann, 2005). There is a sex difference here (Peplau, 2003). According to Janis Abrahms Spring, author of *After the Affair,* women are usually seeking "soul mates," while men are seeking "playmates." Women tend to justify affairs when they are for love, but men do so when the affair is *not* for love (Smart, 2006).

As noted throughout this text, and as "traditional" as it may sound, women are less accepting of sex without emotional involvement (Peplau, 2003). Men are more likely than women to distinguish between sex and love, whereas women see love and sex as going together so that falling in love justifies sex (Peplau, 2003). But these are *group* differences. Many individual men are interested primarily in the extramarital relationship rather than the sex per se. Similarly, some women are out for the sex and not the relationship.

PATTERNS OF EXTRAMARITAL SEX   Let us begin with a few definitions. **Extramarital sex** is usually conducted without the spouse's knowledge or approval. Secret affairs are referred to as **conventional adultery,** infidelity, or simply "cheating." Conventional adultery runs the gamut from the "one-night stand" to the affair that persists for years. (Bill Clinton's affair with Gennifer Flowers allegedly persisted for a dozen years.) In **consensual adultery,** extramarital relationships are conducted openly—that is, with the knowledge and consent of the partner. In what is called **swinging**, or *mate swapping,* the partner participates.

How many people "cheat" on their spouses? Viewers of TV talk shows may get the impression that everyone cheats, but reliable surveys paint a different picture. More than 90% of the married women and 75% of the married men in the NHSLS reported remaining loyal to their spouses (Laumann et al., 1994). The vast majority of people who were cohabiting also reported that they were sexually faithful to their partners (Laumann et al., 1994). Similarly, the overwhelming majority—86%—of respondents to a *New York Times* poll reported that they were "absolutely certain" that their partners were faithful to them (Eggers, 2000). What can we conclude? Perhaps two things: One is that men are about twice as likely as women to admit to affairs. The other is that only a minority of married people admit to affairs.

Those are the conclusions, but note that we said "*admit* to affairs." Having presented the percentages of reported extramarital sex, we point out that these reports cannot be verified. People may be reluctant to reveal they have "cheated," even when they are assured of anonymity.

ATTITUDES TOWARD EXTRAMARITAL SEX   Although Americans, especially younger Americans, may no longer see marriage as "very important,"

Extramarital sex Sexual relations between a married person and someone other than his or her spouse

Conventional adultery Extramarital sex that is kept hidden from one's spouse

Consensual adultery Extramarital sex that is engaged in openly with the knowledge and consent of one's spouse

Swinging A form of consensual adultery in which both spouses share extramarital sexual experiences; also referred to as *mate swapping*

A Closer Look

FROM TINSELTOWN TO SPLITSVILLE: JUST DO THE MATH

By John Tierney, The New York Times

Please don't take this the wrong way.

I wish no ill to Brangelina or TomKat. Like any mortal, I revere the romances on Olympus. I thrilled to hear of Pam's secret wedding and agonized at reports of Angelina's reluctance to marry (or is Brad dragging his feet?). When I finished poring over *Vanity Fair*'s photo spread of Tom Cruise and Katie Holmes with their daughter, my only bitter thought was: Why just 22 pages?

But we inquiring minds must be realistic. Remember your crazy joy at past celebrity marriages—Jessica and Nick, Julia and Lyle, Uma and Ethan? You made space on your mantle for the smiling couple's picture. You rushed them a set of monogrammed towels. You ignored the rumors of fights and the photos with people they weren't married to (it was just a friendly dinner!).

No, you were sure this one was for the ages—until the day their publicist put out the statement about an "amicable" decision to pursue "separate lives." Amicable! How could the couple of the century bear to be apart? You felt deceived, used, discarded. You stared at their photo and thought: I don't even know you anymore.

I can't bear any more of these breakups, so I have turned to science to steel my heart. I went to Garth Sundem, the wickedly ingenious author of *Geek Logik*, a new book of mathematical formulas for deciding questions like whether you should sleep with a coworker, whether you should join a gym or see a therapist, and whether you can wear a Speedo without frightening small children.

I asked Sundem to set his sights even higher. The result of our labors (well, mostly his labors, but I want a piece of this scientific breakthrough) is the Sundem/Tierney Unified Celebrity Theory, an equation for predicting the odds that a celebrity marriage will last.

By comparing the many failed marriages with the few successes (like Johnny Cash and June Carter, or Paul Newman and Joanne Woodward), Sundem identified telltale factors like celebrities' ages, marital track records, and levels of fame.

Younger couples have worse prospects than older couples do, particularly if they rush to the altar before getting to know each other. Britney Spears and Kevin Federline (now FedEx) had only a 1% chance of making it to their fifth anniversary, according to our equation, and the most famously impetuous young couple of all, Romeo and Juliet, would have had zero chance of lasting five years.

Fame, as measured by Google hits, is no good for a marriage. The odds get even worse when the woman's Google hits outnumber the man's, as when Jennifer Lopez fell for a waiter named Ojani Noa. Our equation gave their marriage a less than 1% chance of surviving five years; it actually lasted 13 months.

A crucial predictor is the sex-symbol factor, determined by looking at the woman's first five Google hits and counting how many show her in sexy attire (or no attire). The skimpier the outfits, the skimpier the marriage, as illustrated in the short unions of Jessica Simpson (three years to Nick) and Marilyn Monroe (274 days to Joe DiMaggio).

This factor bodes ill for Brangelina. Our equation gave Brad Pitt's marriage to Jennifer Anniston a fighting 34% chance of lasting five years (thanks to the divorce proceedings, they barely made it). But Angelina Jolie's sex-symbol factor is much higher than Jen's. If Brangelina get married, their chance of lasting five years is less than 5%, in the same ballpark as the odds for Pamela Anderson and Kid Rock were. (Bye, bye Kid.)

The good news is that a few celebrity couples have roughly an even chance of lasting five years: Will Smith and Jada Pinkett, Matt Damon and Luciana Barroso, Ben Affleck and Jennifer Garner.

But not Tom and Katie. They have so many Google hits and so many other factors against them—a whirlwind courtship, a big age gap, his two failed marriages—that their odds of celebrating a fifth anniversary are only 8%.

Maybe you can't stop yourself from rooting for them. Don't let me discourage you. But if you must send towels, skip the monograms.

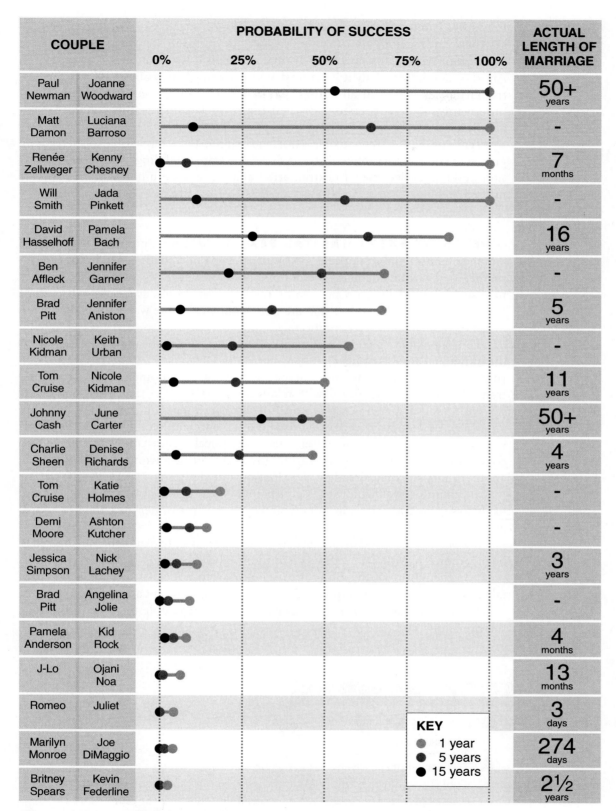

COUPLE		PROBABILITY OF SUCCESS					ACTUAL LENGTH OF MARRIAGE
		0%	25%	50%	75%	100%	
Paul Newman	Joanne Woodward						50+ years
Matt Damon	Luciana Barroso						-
Renée Zellweger	Kenny Chesney						7 months
Will Smith	Jada Pinkett						-
David Hasselhoff	Pamela Bach						16 years
Ben Affleck	Jennifer Garner						-
Brad Pitt	Jennifer Aniston						5 years
Nicole Kidman	Keith Urban						-
Tom Cruise	Nicole Kidman						11 years
Johnny Cash	June Carter						50+ years
Charlie Sheen	Denise Richards						4 years
Tom Cruise	Katie Holmes						-
Demi Moore	Ashton Kutcher						-
Jessica Simpson	Nick Lachey						3 years
Brad Pitt	Angelina Jolie						-
Pamela Anderson	Kid Rock						4 months
J-Lo	Ojani Noa						13 months
Romeo	Juliet						3 days
Marilyn Monroe	Joe DiMaggio						274 days
Britney Spears	Kevin Federline						2½ years

KEY
● 1 year
● 5 years
● 15 years

Figure 14.4 Predicting Celebrity Marriages. *Predicting the length of celebrity marriages is not yet an exact science, but Garth Sundem, the author of* Geek Logik, *has come up with a formula. It's based on variables including the celebrities' ages, the length of their courtship, their previous marital history, and their fame (as measured by their name). As this chart shows, the odds are against the stars, but a few manage to stick together anyway.*

SOURCE: Chart created from an equation by Garth Sundem.

they still seem to value keeping one's promises. About nine out of ten Americans say that extramarital affairs are "always wrong" or "almost always wrong." Three out of four Americans say that extramarital sex is "always wrong" (Berke, 1997). Another one in seven say it is "almost always wrong." Only about 1% say that extramarital sex is "not at all wrong." Most married couples embrace the value of monogamy as the cornerstone of their marital relationship (Silva, 2005; Smart, 2006).

TRUTH fiction 3

Truth or Fiction Revisited: It is not true that most of today's sophisticated young people see nothing wrong with an occasional extramarital fling. The sexual revolution never extended itself to extramarital affairs—at least among the majority of married people.

EFFECTS OF EXTRAMARITAL SEX   The discovery of infidelity can evoke a range of emotional responses. The spouse may be filled with anger, jealousy, even shame. Feelings of inadequacy and doubts about one's attractiveness and desirability may surface. Infidelity may be seen by the betrayed spouse as a serious breach of trust and intimacy. Marriages that are not terminated in the wake of the disclosure may survive in a damaged condition.

The harm an affair does to a marriage may reflect the meaning of the affair to the individual and his or her spouse (Smart, 2006). Deborah Lamberti, director of a counseling and psychotherapy center in New York City, points again to women's traditional intertwining of sex with relationships and argues that "Men don't view sex with another person as a reason to leave a primary relationship" (1997, pp. 131–132). Women may recognize this and be able to tell themselves that their husbands are sleeping with someone else just for physical reasons. But women are more concerned about remaining monogamous. Therefore, if a woman is sleeping with another man, she may already have a foot out the door, so to speak. A wife's affair may be an unforgivable blow to the husband's ego or pride. A woman may be more likely to see the transgression as a threat to the structure of her life (Allen & Atkins, 2005; Silva, 2005).

If a person has an affair because the marriage is deeply troubled, the affair may be one more factor that speeds its dissolution. The effects on the marriage may depend on the nature of the affair. It may be easier to understand that a spouse has fallen prey to an isolated, unplanned encounter than to accept an extended affair. In some cases, the discovery of infidelity stimulates the couple to work to improve their relationship.

SafeZone

Q *Is there any credibility to the "seven-year itch" idea—that partners will tend to stray every seven years?*

A The notion of the seven-year itch is presumably related to the fact that wool is one of the traditional seventh-year anniversary gifts. (The other is copper.) Hence, itchy. But the only credibility to the seven-year notion is that as time goes by, people become more accustomed to one another, and men especially may become more interested in looking for some sexual novelty.

Should They Remain Together "for the Sake of the Children?" *The research seems to suggest that children may fare better when parents who are in regular conflict separate. The key issue appears to be how the parents interact in the presence of the children, not whether they get a divorce.*

Divorce: Breaking Bonds

My wife and I were considering a divorce, but after pricing lawyers we decided to buy a new car instead.

—Henny Youngman

Whenever I date a guy, I think, is this the man I want my children to spend their weekends with?

—Rita Rudner

Some 40% to 50% of the marriages in the United States end in divorce (Whitehead & Popenoe, 2006). The divorce rate in the United States rose steadily through much of the 20th century before leveling off in the 1980s. Divorced women outnumber divorced men, in part because men are more likely to remarry.

Why the increase in divorce? Until the mid-1960s, adultery was the only legal grounds for divorce in most states. But no-fault divorce laws have been enacted in nearly every state, allowing a divorce to be granted without a finding of marital misconduct. The increased economic independence of women has also contributed to the divorce rate. More women today have the economic means of breaking away from a troubled marriage. Today, more people consider marriage an alterable condition than in prior generations.

People today also hold higher expectations of marriage than did their parents or grandparents. They expect marriage to be personally fulfilling as well as an institution for family life and rearing children. Most people want to be happy in marriage. The most common reasons given for a divorce today are problems in communication and a lack of understanding. Key predictors of divorce today include a husband's criticism, defensiveness, contempt, and stonewalling—not lack of financial support (Carrère et al., 2000; Gottman et al., 1998).

THE COST OF DIVORCE Divorce is usually connected with financial and emotional problems. When a household splits, the resources often cannot maintain the earlier standard of living for each partner. Divorce hits women in the pocketbook harder than men. According to a Population Reference Bureau report, a woman's household income drops by about 24% (Bianchi & Spain, 1997). A man's declines by about 6%. Women who have not pursued a career may have to struggle to compete with younger, more experienced workers. Divorced mothers often face the combined stress of the sole responsibility for child rearing and the need to increase their incomes. Divorced fathers may find it difficult to pay alimony and child support while establishing a new lifestyle.

Divorce can also prompt feelings of failure as a spouse and parent, loneliness and uncertainty about the future, and depression. Married people appear to be better able to cope with the stresses and strains of life, perhaps because they can lend each other emotional support. Divorced and separated people have the highest rates of physical and mental illness (Carrère et al., 2000; Lorenz et al., 2006). They also have high rates of suicide (Donald et al., 2006; Lorant et al., 2005). On the other hand, divorce may permit personal growth and renewal—an opportunity to take stock of oneself and establish a new, more rewarding life.

Children are often the biggest losers when parents get a divorce, Yet chronic marital conflict is also connected with psychological distress in children (Amato, 2006; Troxel & Matthews, 2004). Boys have greater problems adjusting to conflict or divorce, such as conduct problems at school and increased anxiety and dependence. The children of divorce are more likely to have psychological problems and conduct disorders, have lower self-esteem, abuse drugs and alcohol, and do more poorly in school (Amato, 2006; Chao et al., 2001). There are individual differences in all of this, and boys tend to fare worse than girls (Grych et al., 2000); but, by and large, the fallout for children is worst during the first year after the breakup. Children tend to rebound within a year or two.

Researchers attribute children's problems after divorce not only to the divorce itself, but also to a consequent decline in the quality of parenting. Children's adjustment is enhanced when both parents maintain parenting responsibilities and set aside their differences long enough to agree on child-rearing practices (Hetherington, 2006). Children of divorce also benefit when their parents avoid saying negative things about each other in the children's presence (Amato & Afifi, 2006; Hetherington, 2006).

Despite the difficulties in adjustment, most divorced people eventually bounce back. Most remarry. Among older people, divorced men are more likely than divorced women to remarry—in part because men usually die earlier than women (and so fewer prospective husbands are available), in part because older men tend to remarry younger women (Whitehead & Popenoe, 2006).

"ALL RIGHT, WE FIGHT—SHOULD WE REMAIN MARRIED FOR THE SAKE OF THE CHILDREN?" Let's have it out at once. We are going to address this issue from a scientific perspective only. Many readers believe—for moral reasons—that marriage must be permanent, no matter what. Readers will consider the moral aspects of divorce in the light of their own value systems.

So—from a purely scientific perspective—what should bickering parents do? The answer seems to depend largely on how they behave in front of the children.

Research shows that parental bickering—especially severe fighting—is linked to the same kinds of problems that children experience when their parents get separated or divorced (Furstenberg & Kiernan, 2001; Troxel & Matthews, 2004). Moreover, when children are exposed to marital conflict, they display a biological "alarm reaction": their heart rate, blood pressure, and sweating rise sharply (El-Sheikh & Harger, 2001). The bodily response is stronger yet when children blame themselves for parental conflict, as is common among younger children. These symptoms of stress also weaken the immune system and leave children more vulnerable to stress-related health problems.

One study analyzed data from 727 children age 4 to 9 years from intact families and followed them six years later, when many of the families had undergone separation or divorce (Morrison & Coiro, 1999). Both separation and divorce were associated with increases in behavior problems in children, regardless of the amount of conflict between the parents. However, in the marriages that remained intact, high levels of marital conflict were associated with yet more behavior problems in the children. Message? Although separation and divorce are connected with adjustment problems in children, the outcome can be even worse for children when conflicted parents stay together. The problems caused by parents in conflict are further highlighted by studies that show that many psychological problems seen in the children of divorce were present prior to the breakup (Furstenberg & Kiernan, 2001; Kelly, 2000; Troxel & Matthews, 2004). Because of the stresses experienced by children caught up in marital conflict, child psychologists E. Mavis Hetherington and John Kelly (2003) suggest that divorce can be a positive response to destructive family functioning.

SafeZone

Q *Is it possible to stay in an unhappy marriage and not have it affect children in the family?*

A The research strongly suggests that the answer depends on how the parents behave in front of the children. If the parents fight viciously in front of the children, the children may be better off with the parents living separately. For those of you whose religious views forbid divorce, we note that our conclusion is based on psychological research and not strict moral values.

Life in Blended Families: His, Hers, Theirs, and . . .

Because of the high incidence of divorce and remarriage, the stepfamily is becoming a more common family unit in the United States. Although many stepfamilies disband, often because of conflict over stepchildren, such as parental favoritism for their own (Golish, 2003; Hofferth & Anderson, 2003), levels of happiness in others can be as high as they were in original marriages (Braithwaite et al., 2001). In any event, more than one in three American children will spend part of his or her childhood in a stepfamily (U.S. Bureau of the Census, 2005).

The rule of thumb about the effects of living in stepfamilies is that there is no rule of thumb. Living in a stepfamily may have no measurable psychological effects

(Coleman et al., 2000). Stepparents may claim stepchildren as their own (Marsiglio, 2004). One study of the effects of stepparenting on middle schoolers found that good stepmother–stepchild relationships were linked with less aggressive behavior in both boys and girls, and with higher self-esteem among stepdaughters (Anderson et al., 1999). But not everything comes up roses in stepfamilies. There are some risks. Infanticide (killing infants) is a rarity in the United States, but the crime occurs much more often in stepfamilies than in families with biological kinship (Daly & Wilson, 2003, 2005). There is also a significantly higher incidence of sexual abuse by stepparents than by natural parents.

Why do we find these risks in stepfamilies? According to evolutionary psychologists, people often behave as if they want their genes to flourish in the next generation. Thus it could be that stepparents are less devoted to rearing the children of other people than their own. They may even see "foreign" children as competitors for resources with their own children. Or a stepfather may see a woman's possession of children by another man as lessening her capacity to bear and rear his children (Daly & Wilson, 2003, 2005).

Sex in the Later Years

What is the fastest growing segment of the U.S. population? People age 65 and older. The "graying" of the United States may have a profound effect on our views of the sexuality of older people. Many people think of sex as appropriate only for the young. This belief falls within a constellation of unfounded cultural myths about older people, which includes the notions that older people are sexless, older people with sexual urges are abnormal, and older men with sexual interests are "dirty old men" (Walz, 2002).

Researchers find that sexual daydreaming, sex drive, and sexual activity tend to decline with age, whereas negative sexual attitudes tend to increase (Barnett & Dunning, 2003). However, research does not support the belief that people lose their sexuality as they age (Laumann et al., 2006). Most older people report that they like sex, and a majority report that orgasm is important to their sexual fulfillment. Sexual activity among older people, as among other groups, is influenced not only by physical structures and changes, but also by psychological well-being, feelings of intimacy, and cultural expectations (Laumann et al., 2006).

Physical Changes

Although many older people retain the capacity to respond sexually, physical changes do occur as the years pass (Table 14.9). If we are aware of them, we will not view them as abnormal or find ourselves unprepared to cope with them. Many potential problems can be averted by changing our expectations or making behavioral changes to accommodate aging.

Let's not start this section with a deeply biological focus on changes in cells, hormones, and the like. Let's talk, first, about what happens when we look in the mirror. Many of us are dismayed by visible changes that occur as we age. We develop wrinkles. Our hair turns gray. Our muscle tone decreases. We tend to put on weight, especially if we do not exercise regularly. All in all, we are likely to feel less attractive than we did. And the fact is that our partners may find us to be less attractive. Neverthe-

Sexuality in Late Adulthood. *Are older people sexually active? If they are, are they abnormal or deviant? Although young people frequently find it difficult to imagine older people engaging in sexual activity, it is normal to retain sexual interest and activity for a lifetime.*

less, in enduring intimate relationships, feelings of love, intimacy, and sharing life can outweigh those changes and feelings. However, if we are single in our later years, perhaps because of divorce or becoming widowed, the future, including the sexual future, may look more bleak.

Yet, older people can also lead sexually fulfilling lives. If they fine-tune their expectations, they may find themselves leading some of the most sexually fulfilling years of their lives (Trudel et al., 2000).

TABLE 14.9

Changes in Sexual Response Connected with Aging

Changes in the Female	Changes in the Male
Reduced muscle tension (myotonia)	Longer time to achieve erection and orgasm
Reduced lubrication	Need for more direct stimulation to achieve erection and orgasm
Reduced elasticity in the vaginal walls	
Smaller increases in breast size during sexual arousal	Less semen emitted during ejaculation
Reduced intensity of spasms of orgasm	Softer erections
	Testicles may not elevate as high prior to ejaculation
	Reduced intensity of spasms of orgasm
	Less need to ejaculate
	Longer refractory period

SOURCE: From *The Kinsey Institute New Report on Sex,* 1990, pp. 227. Reprinted by permission of The Kinsey Institute for Research in Sex, Gender, and Reproduction, Inc.

CHANGES IN THE FEMALE   Many of the physical changes in older women stem from a decline in the production of estrogen. The vaginal walls lose much elasticity and the thick, corrugated texture of the childbearing years. They grow paler and thinner. Thus, coitus may become irritating. The thinning of the walls may also place greater pressure against the bladder and urethra during sex, leading now and then to urinary urgency and burning urination. The condition may persist for days.

The vagina also shrinks. The labia majora lose much of their fatty deposits and thin. The introitus constricts, and penile entry may become difficult. On the other hand, increased friction between the penis and vaginal walls may heighten sexual sensations. After menopause, women also produce less vaginal lubrication, and lubrication may take minutes, not seconds, to appear. Lack of adequate lubrication is a key reason for painful coitus.

Many of these changes may be slowed or reversed through ERT, although estrogen replacement has its hazards (see Chapter 3). Natural lubrication may be increased through more elaborate foreplay. Older men, too, will likely need more time to become aroused. An artificial lubricant can also ease problems in penile entry and thrusting.

Women's breasts show smaller increases in size with sexual arousal as they age, but the nipples still become erect. Because the muscle tone of the urethra and anal sphincters decreases, the spasms of orgasm become less powerful and fewer in number. Thus orgasms may feel less intense, but the subjective experience of orgasm may remain satisfying. **Truth or Fiction Revisited:** Despite these changes, women can retain their ability to reach orgasm well into their advanced years. Nevertheless, the uterine contractions that occur during orgasm may become discouragingly painful for some older women.

CHANGES IN THE MALE   Age-related changes tend to occur more gradually in men than in women and are not clearly connected with any one biological event (Barnett & Dunning, 2003). Male adolescents may achieve erection in seconds through sexual fantasy alone. After about age 50, men take progressively longer to achieve erection. Erections become less firm, perhaps because of lowered testosterone levels (Laumann et al., 2006). Older men may require prolonged direct stimulation of the penis to obtain an erection. Couples can adjust to these changes by extending the length and variety of foreplay.

Most men remain capable of erection throughout their lives. Erectile dysfunction is not inevitable with aging. Men generally require more time to reach orgasm as they age, however, which may again reflect lowered testosterone levels.

Testosterone production usually declines gradually from about age 40 to 60, and then begins to level off. However, the decline is not inevitable and may be related to the man's general health. Sperm production tends to decline as the seminiferous tubules degenerate, but viable sperm may be produced by men in their 70s, 80s, and 90s.

Nocturnal erections tend to diminish in intensity, duration, and frequency as men age, but they do not normally disappear in healthy men (Perry et al., 2001). The refractory period tends to lengthen with age. An adolescent may require but a few minutes to regain erection and ejaculate again after a first orgasm, whereas a man in his 30s may require half an hour. Past age 50, the refractory period may increase to several hours.

Older men produce less ejaculate, and it may seep out rather than shoot out. The contractions of orgasm become weaker and fewer. Still, an older male may enjoy orgasm as thoroughly as he did at a younger age. After orgasm, erection subsides more rapidly than in a younger man.

Patterns of Sexual Activity

Despite decline in physical functions, older people can continue to lead a fulfilling sex life. Years of sexual experience may more than compensate for any diminution of physical response (Barnett & Dunning, 2003; Laumann et al., 2006). Coital frequency tends to decline with age (Laumann et al., 2006). Several factors play a role in declining activity, including physical problems, boredom, and cultural attitudes. Despite general trends, sexuality among older people is variable (Knox & Schacht, 2002). Many older people engage in intercourse, oral sex, and masturbation as or more often as when younger; some become disgusted by sex; others simply lose interest.

Couples may accommodate the physical changes of aging by broadening their sexual repertoire to include more diverse forms of stimulation. Many older people report using oral–genital stimulation, sexual fantasy, pornography, anal stimulation, vibrators, and other techniques to offset problems in achieving lubrication or erection. Sexual satisfaction may be derived from manual or oral stimulation, cuddling, caressing, and tenderness, as well as intercourse to orgasm. The availability of a sexually interested and supportive partner may be the most important determinant of continued sexual activity (Laumann et al., 2006).

SafeZone

Q *I caught my grandparents having sex. Now they will not talk to me, and they act differently toward me. What can I do?*

A Lesson for everyone: You gotta knock. Or you have to say "Anyone home?" or whatever when entering. They're not talking to you? They're embarrassed, and for a number of reasons. One is that they were likely brought up in more traditional times. There is also the stereotype that sex is for young people. Why not drop them a hand-written note (without a return address so that they'll open it). Say you're sorry you didn't knock or whatever. Ask them to forgive you. And say something humorous like you wish your love life was as good as theirs. If you do that and they don't get over it, you tried. End of story.

Sex and Disability

Like older people, people with disabilities (especially those whose physical disabilities render them dependent on others) are often seen as sexless and childlike. Such views are based on misconceptions about the sexual functioning of people with disabilities. Some of these myths and stereotypes may be eroding, however, in part because of the success of the civil and social rights movements, and in part because of the attention focused on the sexuality of people with disabilities in films such as *Born on the Fourth of July* and *My Left Foot*.

A person may have been born with or acquire a bodily impairment or may suffer a loss of function or a disfiguring change in appearance. Although the disability may require the person to make adjustments to perform sexually, most people with disabilities have the same sexual needs, feelings, and desires as people without disabilities. Their ability to express their sexual feelings and needs depends on the physical limitations imposed by their disabilities, their adjustment to their disabilities, and the availability of partners. The establishment of mature sexual relationships generally demands some distance from one's parents. Therefore, people with disabilities who are physically dependent on their parents may find it especially difficult to develop sexual relationships. Parents who acknowledge their children's sexual development can be helpful by facilitating dating. Far too often, parents become overprotective.

Physical Disabilities

According to Margaret A. Nosek and her colleagues (Nosek, 2005; Nosek et al., 2004), sexual wellness, among the disabled, as among the population at large, involves five factors:

1. Positive sexual self-concept; seeing oneself as valuable sexually and as a person
2. Knowledge about sexuality
3. Positive, productive relationships
4. Coping with barriers to sexuality (social, environmental, physical, and emotional)
5. Maintaining the best possible general and sexual health, given one's limitations

Cerebral palsy A muscular disorder that is caused by damage to the central nervous system (usually prior to or during birth) and characterized by spastic paralysis

This model applies to all of us, of course. Let us now consider aspects of specific physical disabilities and human sexuality.

MULTIPLE SCLEROSIS Multiple sclerosis (MS) is a chronic, unpredictable disease that affects the nervous system. The tissue called myelin, which surrounds and protects nerve cells, disintegrates, leaving scar tissue in its place. MS impairs sexual functioning, and people with MS report more sexual problems than people without the disorder (Forbes et al., 2006; McCabe, 2004). However, there is a good deal of individual variation, and the progression of the disorder, and its effects, do not follow a straight line. Many people with MS in good relationships enjoy fine sex lives for many years.

CEREBRAL PALSY **Cerebral palsy** and related disorders of the nervous system do not necessarily impair sexual interest, capacity for orgasm, or fertility. Depending on the nature and degree of muscle spasticity or lack of voluntary muscle control, however, afflicted people may be limited to certain types of sexual activities and coital positions (Cho et al., 2004).

People with disabilities such as cerebral palsy often suffer social rejection during adolescence and perceive themselves as unfit for or unworthy of intimate sexual relationships, especially with people who are not disabled. They are often socialized into an asexual role. Counseling can help them understand and accept their sexuality, promote a more positive body image, and provide the social skills to establish intimate relationships.

Many spinal cord–injured men can obtain erections and many spinal cord–injured women can lubricate. Their ability to become sexually aroused—biologically—depends on the nature and extent of their injury. They may not be able to sense their own arousal or orgasm, but they can observe their partner's response and take psychological pleasure in it.

SPINAL CORD INJURIES People who suffer physical disabilities as the result of traumatic injuries or physical illness must not only learn to cope with their physical limitations but also adjust to a world designed for nondisabled people. The majority of persons who suffer disabling spinal cord injuries are young, active males. Automobile or pedestrian accidents account for about half these cases. Other common causes include stabbing or bullet wounds, sports injuries, and falls. Depending on the location of the injury to the spinal cord, a loss of voluntary control (*paralysis*) can occur in either the legs (*paraplegia*) or all four limbs (*quadriplegia*). A loss of sensation may also occur in parts of the body that lie beneath the site of injury.

Truth or Fiction Revisited: Many people who are paralyzed as a result of spinal cord injuries usually can become sexually aroused and engage in coitus. The effect of spinal cord injuries on sexual response depends on the site and severity of the injury. Men have two erection centers in the spinal cord: a higher center in the lumbar region that controls psychogenic erections and a lower one in the sacral region that controls reflexive erections. When damage occurs at or above the level of the lumbar center, men lose the capacity for psychogenic erections, the kinds of erections that occur in response to mental stimulation alone, such as when viewing erotic films or fantasizing. They may still be able to achieve reflexive erections from direct stimulation of the penis, because these erections are controlled by the sacral erection center located in a lower portion of the spinal cord. However, they cannot feel any genital sensations because the nerve connections to the brain are severed. Men with damage to the sacral erection center lose the capacity for reflexive erections but can still achieve psychogenic erections as long as their upper spinal cord remains intact. Overall, researchers find that about three of four men with spinal cord injuries are able to achieve erections, but only about one in ten continues to ejaculate naturally. Others can ejaculate with a vibrator. Their brains may help to fill in some of the missing sensations associated with coitus and even orgasm.

Although the frequency of sexual activity among spinal cord–injured men tends to decline after the injury, about one-third continue to engage in sexual intercourse (Hyde, 2005; Komisaruk & Whipple, 2005). Such men typically report increased interest in alternative sexual activities, especially those involving areas above the level of the spinal injury, such as those involving the mouth, lips, neck and ears.

Retention of sexual response in women depends on the site and severity of the spinal cord injury. Women may lose the ability to experience genital sensations or to lubricate normally during sexual stimulation (Hyde, 2005; Komisaruk & Whipple, 2005). However, sensations in the breasts may not be affected, making the breasts more erotogenic. Most women with spinal cord injuries can engage in coitus, become impregnated, and deliver vaginally. A survey of 68 spinal cord–injured women showed that about half were able to achieve orgasm as a result of audiovisual erotic material combined with manual genital stimulation (Sipski et al., 2001). Spinal cord–injured women can heighten their sexual pleasure by using sexual imagery and manual stimulation (Sipski et al., 2001).

Couples facing the challenge of spinal cord injury may expand their sexual repertoire to focus less on genital stimulation (except to attain the reflexes of erection and lubrication) and more on the parts of the body that retain sensation. Stimulation of some areas of the body, such as the ears, the neck, and the breasts (in both men and women) can yield pleasurable erotic sensations.

SENSORY DISABILITIES   Sensory disabilities, such as blindness and deafness, do not directly affect genital responsiveness. Still, sexuality may be affected in many ways. A person who has been blind since birth or early childhood may have difficulty understanding a partner's anatomy. Sex education curricula have been designed specifically to enable visually impaired people to learn about sexual anatomy via models. Anatomically correct dolls may be used to simulate positions of intercourse.

People who are deaf often lack knowledge about sex. Their ability to comprehend the social cues involved in forming and maintaining intimate relationships may also

TRUTH *fiction* **5**

be impaired. Sex education programs based on sign language are helping many people with hearing impairments become more socially perceptive as well as more knowledgeable about the physical aspects of sex. People with visual and hearing impairments often lack self-esteem and self-confidence—problems that make it difficult for them to establish intimate relationships. Counseling may help them become more aware of their sexuality and develop social skills.

OTHER PHYSICAL DISABILITIES AND IMPAIRMENTS Specific disabilities pose particular challenges to, and impose particular limitations on, sexual functioning. **Arthritis** may make it difficult or painful for affected individuals to bend their arms, knees, and hips during sexual activity. Coital positions that minimize discomfort and the application of moist heat to the joints before sexual relations may be helpful.

A male amputee may find that he is better balanced in the lateral-entry or female-superior position than in the male-superior position. A woman with limited hand function may find it difficult or impossible to insert a diaphragm and may need to request assistance from her partner or switch to another contraceptive. Sensitivity to each other's needs is as vital to couples in which one member has a disability as it is to nondisabled couples.

Speaking of sensitivity, let us turn to psychological issues.

Psychological Disabilities

People with psychological disabilities, such as mental retardation, are often stereotyped as incapable of understanding or controlling their sexual impulses. Retarded people are sometimes assumed to maintain childlike innocence through their lives or to be devoid of sexuality. On the other hand, it is widely acknowledged that individuals with limited mental capacities are vulnerable to sexual abuse and may not be able to provide consent to sexual activity with others (Levy & Packman, 2004; Plaut, 2006; Servais, 2006).

Some stereotype retarded people in the opposite direction: as having stronger-than-normal sex drives and being incapable of controlling them. Some mentally retarded people do act inappropriately—by masturbating publicly, for example. The stereotypes are exaggerated, however, and many mentally retarded people who act inappropriately can be trained to follow social rules.

Parents and caretakers often discourage retarded people from learning about their sexuality or teach them to deny or suppress their sexual feelings (Gross, 2006). Although the physical changes of puberty may be delayed in some mentally retarded people, most develop normal sexual needs. Most are capable of learning about their sexuality and can be guided into rewarding and responsible intimate relationships (Gross, 2006).

One of the greatest impediments to sexual fulfillment among people with disabilities is difficulty in finding a loving and supportive partner. Some people engage in sexual relations with people with disabilities out of sympathy. By and large, however, the partners are other people with disabilities or nondisabled people who have overcome stereotypes that portray disabled people as undesirable. Many partners have had some prior positive relationship with a person with a disability, usually during childhood. Experience facilitates acceptance of the idea that a disabled person can be desirable. Depending on the nature of the disability, the nondisabled partner may need to be open to assuming a more active sexual role to compensate for the limitations of the partner with the disability. Two partners with disabilities need to be sen-

Arthritis A progressive disease that is characterized by inflammation and pain in the joints

sitive to each other's needs and physical limitations. People with disabilities and their partners may also need to expand their sexual repertoires to incorporate ways of pleasuring each other that are not fixated on genital stimulation.

The message of this chapter is simple: Sexuality can enrich the lives of nearly all adults at virtually any age and in most physical and mental conditions.

SafeZone

Q *How do individuals who are mentally retarded ever truly consent to sexual activity?*

A Most mentally retarded individuals are mildly retarded, and of these, the great majority understand the concept of consenting to sexual activity. Many live in committed long-term relationships; some are married. But many mentally retarded people cannot provide consent, and laws in almost all states have been enacted to prevent others from sexually exploiting them.

1. What are the trends in the numbers of people remaining single?

- Recent years have seen an increase the numbers of single young people in our society. Reasons include increased permissiveness toward premarital sex and, particularly for women, the desire to become established in a career. Some people remain single or celibate for religious reasons. No one lifestyle characterizes single people.

2. Who cohabits?

- Cohabitation is more prevalent among less well educated and less affluent people. Some couples prefer cohabitation because it provides a consistent intimate relationship without the legal and economic entanglements of marriage. Some emotionally committed couples cohabit because of the economic advantages of sharing household expenses.

- Cohabitors who later marry may run a greater risk of divorce than noncohabitors, perhaps because of a selection factor; that is, cohabitors tend to be more liberal than people who do not live together before getting married.

3. Why do people get married?

- Marriage is found in all human societies and may still be our most common lifestyle. Throughout Western history, marriages have legitimized sexual relations, sanctioned the permanence of a deeply committed relationship, provided for the orderly transmission of wealth, and facilitated child rearing. In Western society today, romantic love is seen as an essential aspect of marriage.

- The major types of marriages between men and women are monogamy and polygamy. Polygamy includes polygyny and polyandry. Gay marriages are now recognized in several Western nations. Open marriages permit each partner open companionship and personal privacy, which may allow sexual intimacy with others. In a group marriage, three or more people share an intimate relationship.

- People in the United States tend to practice homogamy. They marry within their geographic area and social class. They tend to marry people who are similar in physical attractiveness, who share similar attitudes, and who seem likely to meet their material, sexual, and psychological needs.

- Married couples today engage in coitus more frequently and for longer durations of time than in Kinsey's day. They report higher levels of sexual satisfaction and engage in a greater variety of sexual activities.

- American women today are more likely to reach orgasm through marital sex than in Kinsey's day. Wives take more active sexual roles than in Kinsey's day.

- People may have affairs for sexual variety, to punish their spouses, to achieve emotional closeness with someone, or to prove that they are attractive.

- Extramarital sex is usually conducted without the spouse's knowledge or approval. Secret affairs are termed *conventional adultery, infidelity,* or simply *cheating.* Conventional adultery runs the gamut from "one-night stands" to affairs that persist for years. In consensual adultery, extramarital relationships are conducted with the knowledge and consent of the partner. In swinging, or mate swapping, the partner participates. The incidence of extramarital sex remains unknown, but it appears that men are more likely than women to have affairs.

- Extramarital sex continues to be viewed negatively by the majority of married people in our society.

- The discovery of infidelity can evoke anger, jealousy, shame, and divorce. Affairs typically damage marriages.

- About half the marriages in the United States end in divorce. Reasons for divorce include relaxed restrictions on divorce, greater financial independence among women, and the idea that marriages should be happy.

- Divorce is often associated with financial and emotional problems, however. Divorce can give rise to feelings of failure and depression, and can make it difficult to rear children. Yet divorce can be preferable to remaining married, even for the sake of the children, if conflict persists.

4. What sex-related changes take place during the later years?

- As the years go on and bodies change, partners may become less attractive to one another. It becomes more difficult for males to attain and maintain erections, and for females to lubricate. Many potential problems can be averted by changing expectations and making changes to accommodate aging.

5. How do disabilities affect sexual functioning?

- Cerebral palsy does not usually impair sexual interest, capacity for orgasm, or fertility, but afflicted people may be limited to certain types of sexual activities and coital positions. People with spinal cord injuries may be paralyzed and lose sensation below the waist. They often respond reflexively to direct genital stimulation. Sensory disabilities do not directly affect sexual response but may impair sexual knowledge and social skills.

- Most mentally retarded people can learn the basics of their own sexuality and develop responsible intimate relationships.

1. All of the following are connected with getting married at later ages today *except*

   (a) living together first to test compatibility
   (b) the desire of many women to focus on careers during their 20s
   (c) social pressure to remain single
   (d) advanced education

2. About _____% of European Americans marry outside their racial group.

   (a) 1
   (b) 7
   (c) 13
   (d) 37

3. All of the following have contributed to the divorce rate in the United States *except*

   (a) higher expectations from marriage
   (b) relaxation of legal restrictions on divorce
   (c) increased economic independence of women
   (d) sexual problems

4. During late adulthood

   (a) men's testes increase slightly in size
   (b) most men cannot obtain an erection
   (c) most men still like sex
   (d) testosterone production increases

5. In the 2006 Gallup poll, _____% of Americans said it was very important for a couple to get married if they were having a child together.

   (a) 17
   (b) 37
   (c) 57
   (d) 77

6. In the 2006 Gallup poll, _____% of Americans said it was very important for a couple to get married if they were going to spend their lives together.

   (a) 25
   (b) 45
   (c) 65
   (d) 85

7. A Gallup poll finds that a higher percentage of married people report that they are happier than unmarried people. The text suggests that we regard these results with skepticism because

   (a) of the selection factor
   (b) they did not include gay marriages
   (c) the definition of happiness was unclear
   (d) the statistics were applied carelessly

8. Polyandry is a form of marriage in which

   (a) one wife has more than one husband
   (b) one husband has more than one wife
   (c) there are multiple wives and husbands
   (d) there is rapid divorce and remarriage

9. Marriages between people from similar backgrounds

   (a) are prejudiced
   (b) bear more children
   (c) lead to strife among in-laws
   (d) are more stable

10. About _____% of American marriages end in divorce.

    (a) 10
    (b) 25
    (c) 50
    (d) 60

11. The TV series *Big Love* is about

    (a) serial monogamy
    (b) polygamy
    (c) divorce
    (d) extramarital sex

12. The term *homogamy* refers to

    (a) like marrying like
    (b) gay marriage
    (c) polygyny
    (d) polyandry

13. According to the NHSLS, couples are most likely to report engaging in sexual intercourse

    (a) a few times per year
    (b) a few times per month
    (c) two to three times a week
    (d) four or more times a week

14. Secret affairs are referred to as

    (a) conventional adultery
    (b) consensual adultery
    (c) swinging
    (d) mate swapping

15. After divorce, a woman's household income drops by about _____%.

    (a) 4
    (b) 14
    (c) 24
    (d) 34

Answers 1. c; 2. b; 3. d; 4. c; 5. b; 6. c; 7. a; 8. a; 9. d; 10. c; 11. b; 12. a; 13. b; 14. a; 15. c

15

Sexual Dysfunctions

TRUTH? fiction

Which of the following statements are true, and which are fiction? Look for the Truth/Fiction icons on the pages that follow to find the answers.

1 Sexual dysfunctions are rare.   T F

2 Only men can reach orgasm too early.   T F

3 The most common cause of painful intercourse in women is vaginal infection. T F

4 Sex therapy teaches a man with erectile disorder how to will an erection.   T F

5 A doctor made a somewhat unusual presentation to a medical convention by dropping his pants to reveal an erection.   T F

6 Many sex therapists recommend masturbation as the treatment for women who have never been able to reach orgasm.   T F

7 A man can be prevented from ejaculating by squeezing his penis when he feels that he is about to ejaculate.   T F

Derek, 39, and his wife Pam, 37, had not attempted sexual intercourse for five years. Sexual relations had been limited to fondling, caressing, and occasional oral–genital contact. They had given up attempting intercourse because of Derek's difficulty in attaining and sustaining erections. But recently they had begun trying again. Some nights Derek would have an erection that enabled him to penetrate, only to find that he quickly lost the erection. Many nights he was unable to perform at all. Each failure was another blow to his self-esteem. Pam worried that he could not perform because he was no longer attracted to her.

Terry, 24, has decided she is built differently from friends and women she reads about. They all reach orgasm, it seems, at the drop of a hat. But she has never managed "one of those things." Her husband David, also 24, is considerate, but Terry knows that he, too, is frustrated and feels guilty with every ejaculation. Why should he enjoy sex if Terry cannot? Terry and David anticipate sex with fear rather than pleasure, and David has been having difficulty at-

(Models for illustrative purposes.)

taining erection. Terry wonders whether she should try to fake orgasm to hold on to him. But she fears she would not know how.

—Authors' Files

CRITICAL Thinking

When does a sexual problem become a sexual dysfunction? Where do you draw the line? How can concern about a sexual problem make it into a dysfunction?

Sexual dysfunctions Persistent or recurrent difficulties in becoming sexually aroused or reaching orgasm

Derek and Terry have sexual dysfunctions. **Sexual dysfunctions** are persistent or recurrent problems in becoming sexually aroused or reaching orgasm. Many of us have sexual problems from time to time. Men occasionally have difficulty obtaining an erection or they ejaculate more quickly than they would like. Women occasionally have difficulty lubricating or reaching orgasm. But sexual dysfunctions, per se, are persistent and cause significant distress.

People with sexual dysfunctions may avoid sexual opportunities for fear of failure. They may anticipate that sex will result in frustration or pain rather than pleasure and gratification. Because our culture emphasizes sexual competence, people with sexual dysfunctions may feel inadequate or incompetent—feelings that diminish their self-esteem (Fishman & Mamo, 2001). They may also experience guilt, shame, frustration, depression, and anxiety.

Many people with sexual dysfunctions find it difficult to talk about them, even with spouses or helping professionals. A woman who cannot reach orgasm with her husband may not want to "make a fuss." A man may find it difficult to admit erectile problems to his physician during a physical exam. Many physicians are also uncomfortable talking about sex and may never ask about it.

We do not have precise figures on the occurrence of sexual dysfunctions. The most accurate information may be based on the NHSLS (Laumann et al., 1994) (Table 15.1). The NHSLS group asked respondents whether there had been a period of several months during the past year when they were disinterested in sex, could not reach orgasm, reached orgasm too rapidly, had pain during sex, did not enjoy sex,

TABLE 15.1

Sexual Dysfunctions Reported within the Past Year, According to the NHSLS

	Men	Women
Pain during sex	3.0%	14.4%
Sex not pleasurable	8.1	21.2
Unable to reach orgasm	8.3	24.1
Lack of interest in sex	15.8	33.4
Anxiety about performance*	17.0	11.5
Reaching climax too early	28.5	10.3
Unable to keep an erection†	10.4	—
Having trouble lubricating	—	18.8

*Anxiety about performance is not itself a sexual dysfunction. However, it figures prominently in many sexual dysfunctions.

† Incidence increases with age, and the NHSLS figures may be an underestimate.

SOURCE: Adapted by permission from E. O. Laumann, J. H. Gagnon, R. T. Michael, and S. Michaels (1994). *The Social Organization of Sexuality: Sexual Practices in the United States.* Chicago: University of Chicago Press, Tables 10.8A and 10.8B, pp. 370 & 371.

were anxious about their sexual performance, had trouble obtaining or maintaining an erection (for men), or had trouble lubricating (for women). Women more often reported painful sex, lack of pleasure, inability to reach orgasm, and lack of desire. Men were more likely to report reaching orgasm too soon and anxiety about their performance. **Truth or Fiction Revisited:** It is not true that sexual dysfunctions are rare. A national telephone survey found that perhaps one woman in four is seriously distressed about her sexuality or her sexual relationship (Bancroft et al., 2003). However, the NHSLS estimated that 43% of women had a sexual dysfunction (Laumann et al., 1994). Moreover, Rosen and Laumann (2003) argue that the telephone survey was inferior in methodology to the face-to-face interviews of the NHSLS.

TRUTH fiction **1**

Types of Sexual Dysfunctions

The most widely used system of classification of sexual dysfunctions is based upon the American Psychiatric Association's (2000) *Diagnostic and Statistical Manual of Mental Disorders.* The DSM proposes four categories of sexual dysfunctions:

1. **Sexual desire disorders.** These involve lack of interest in sex or aversion to sexual contact.

2. **Sexual arousal disorders.** Sexual arousal is mainly characterized by erection in the male and vaginal lubrication and swelling of the external genitalia in the female. In men, sexual arousal disorders involve difficulty in obtaining or sustaining erections sufficient to engage in sexual intercourse. In women, they typically involve insufficient lubrication.

3. **Orgasmic disorders.** Men or women may have difficulty reaching orgasm or reach orgasm more quickly than they would like. Women are more likely to

Sexual desire disorders Sexual dysfunctions in which people have persistent or recurrent lack of sexual desire or aversion to sexual contact

Sexual arousal disorders Sexual dysfunctions in which people persistently or recurrently fail to become adequately sexually aroused to engage in or sustain sexual intercourse

Orgasmic disorders Sexual dysfunctions in which people persistently or recurrently have difficulty reaching orgasm or reach orgasm more rapidly than they would like, despite attaining a level of sexual stimulation of sufficient intensity that normally results in orgasm encounter difficulties reaching orgasm. Men are more likely to reach orgasm too quickly (have premature ejaculation).

4. **Sexual pain disorders.** Both men and women may suffer from **dyspareunia** (painful intercourse). Women may experience **vaginismus,** or involuntary contraction of muscles that surround the vaginal barrel, preventing penetration by the penis or making penetration painful.

Sexual dysfunctions are classified as lifelong or acquired. (Acquired dysfunctions follow a period of normal functioning.) Dysfunctions are also classified as generalized or situational. *Generalized* dysfunctions occur in all situations. *Situational* dysfunctions affect sexual functioning only in some situations, as during intercourse but not masturbation, or with one partner but not another. If a man has never been able to obtain an erection during sexual relations with a partner but can do so during masturbation, his dysfunction is lifelong and situational.

SafeZone

Q *I do not feel sexual during times when I have a lot of schoolwork. Is that normal?*

A If "a lot of schoolwork" translates into stress, it is absolutely normal. Some people turn to sex as a way of trying to escape feelings of stress, but it is just as normal—and perhaps more common—for stress to have a dampening effect on sexual desire.

Sexual Desire Disorders

Sexual desire disorders involve lack of sexual desire or aversion to genital sexual activity. People with little or no sexual interest or desire are said to have *hypoactive sexual desire disorder.* They often report an absence of sexual fantasies. Lack of desire is more common among women than men (Goldstein et al., 2006). Nevertheless, the belief that men are always eager for sex is a myth.

Lack of sexual desire does not imply that a person is unable to achieve erection, lubricate adequately, or reach orgasm. Some people with low sexual desire can become sexually aroused and reach orgasm when stimulated adequately. Many enjoy sexual activity, even if they are unlikely to initiate it. Many appreciate the affection and closeness of physical intimacy, but have no interest in genital stimulation.

Hypoactive sexual desire is one of the most commonly diagnosed sexual dysfunctions, yet there is no clear consensus among clinicians and researchers concerning the definition of low sexual desire (McCarthy et al., 2006). How much sexual interest or desire is "normal?" There is no standard level of sexual desire—no 98.6°F reading on the "sexual thermometer." Lack of desire is usually considered a problem when couples recognize that their level of sexual interest has gotten so low that little remains. The lack of desire is often limited to one partner. When one member of a couple is more interested in sex than the other, sex therapists often recommend that couples try to compromise. They also try to resolve problems in the relationship that may dampen sexual ardor (Moore & Heiman, 2006).

When is lack of sexual desire among women a dysfunction (Goldstein et al., 2006)? The literature on sex differences strongly suggests that women, in general, are less interested in sex than men (Peplau, 2003). This is not to suggest that there is anything wrong with women who experience strong, regular sexual urges. Keep in mind that lack of desire usually does not come to the health care provider's attention unless one partner is more desirous of sex than the other.

Sexual pain disorders Sexual dysfunctions in which people persistently or recurrently experience pain during coitus

Dyspareunia A sexual dysfunction characterized by persistent or recurrent pain during sexual intercourse; from roots meaning "badly paired"

Vaginismus A sexual dysfunction characterized by involuntary contraction of the muscles surrounding the vaginal barrel, preventing penile penetration or rendering penetration painful

Q *What does "prude" mean? Is this considered a sexual dysfunction?*

A The word *prude* has the same origin as the word *proud,* and it refers to being highly or evenly excessively proper or modest in one's own speech, behavior, and dress. In other words, prudes prefer not to curse, engage in behaviors such as serious kissing in public, or dress seductively. They also typically disapprove of such displays by others. What they do privately in a committed relationship might be quite different. In fact, they might enjoy sex a great deal, so there is no necessary connection between public prudery and sexual functioning or dysfunctioning. The origins of prudery are uncertain. Being reared strictly may have something to do with it, although many young people rebel, especially in open societies. And there might just be a genetic component.

SEXUAL AVERSION DISORDER   People with low sexual desire may have little or no interest in sex, but they are not repelled by genital contact. Some people, however, find sex disgusting or aversive and avoid genital contact.

A history of erectile problems can cause sexual aversion in men (Bancroft et al., 2005b, c). Men with such histories may be anxious in sexual situations because they trigger feelings of failure and shame. Their partners may also develop an aversion to sexual contact because of their own frustration. A history of sexual trauma such as rape, childhood sexual abuse, or incest often figures prominently in cases of sexual aversion, especially in women (Firestone et al., 2006a; Najman et al., 2005).

Sexual Arousal Disorders

When we are sexually stimulated, our bodies normally respond with **vasocongestion,** which produces erection in the male and vaginal lubrication in the female. People with sexual arousal disorders fail to achieve or sustain the lubrication or erection necessary to enable sexual activity. Or they lack the feelings of sexual pleasure or excitement that normally accompany sexual arousal.

Problems of sexual arousal have sometimes been labeled *impotence* in the male and *frigidity* in the female. But these terms are pejorative, so many professionals prefer to use less threatening, more descriptive labels.

MALE ERECTILE DISORDER   Sexual arousal disorder in the male is called **male erectile disorder** or *erectile dysfunction.* It is characterized by persistent difficulty in achieving or maintaining an erection sufficient to allow the completion of sexual activity. In most cases, the failure is limited to sexual activity with partners, or with some partners and not others. It can thus be classified as *situational.* In rare cases the dysfunction is found during any sexual activity, including masturbation. In such cases, it is considered *generalized.* Some men with erectile disorder are unable to attain an erection with their partners. Others can achieve erection but not sustain it (or recover it) long enough for penetration and ejaculation (Bancroft et al., 2005b).

As many as 30 million men in the United States experience some degree of erectile dysfunction (Goldstein, as cited in Kolata, 1998). The incidence of erectile disorder increases with age, although there is great disagreement at to how many men are affected. The NHSLS reported that difficulty keeping an erection increases from about 6% in the 18- to 24-year-old age group to about 20% in the 55- to 59-year-old age group. Another study reported that about 3% of men in their 50s had difficulty

Vasocongestion
Engorgement of blood vessels with blood, which swells the genitals and breasts during sexual arousal

Male erectile disorder
Persistent difficulty achieving or maintaining an erection sufficient to allow the man to engage in or complete sexual intercourse; also termed *erectile dysfunction*

The Emotional Toll of Erectile Dysfunction. *Male erectile disorder or erectile dysfunction is characterized by persistent difficulty in achieving or maintaining an erection sufficient to allow the completion of sexual activity. As many as 30 million men in the United States experience some degree of erectile dysfunction, and the incidence increases with age. Occasional erectile problems are common and may be caused by fatigue, alcohol, or anxiety about a new partner. However, fear of recurrence can create a vicious cycle, in which anxiety leads to failure, and failure heightens anxiety.*

obtaining or maintaining erections, and that this figure rose to about 35% for men in their 70s (Blanker et al., 2001). But urologist Irwin Goldstein (as cited in Kolata, 1998) found that nearly *half* the men age 40 to 70 in a Massachusetts survey reported problems in obtaining and maintaining erections—at least now and then. We cannot account for these discrepancies between studies. We can only suggest that the incidence of erectile disorder may be more frequent than is commonly believed. Drugs used to treat the disorder sell quite briskly, although it is not know how many men with erectile disorder use them.

Erectile disorder usually develops after a period of normal functioning. Many men engage in years of successful coitus before the problem begins. Occasional problems in achieving or maintaining erection are quite common. Fatigue, alcohol, anxiety over impressing a new partner, and other factors may account for a transient episode. Even an isolated occurrence can lead to a persistent problem if the man fears recurrence, however. The more anxious and concerned the man becomes about his sexual ability, the more likely he is to suffer **performance anxiety.** This anxiety can contribute to repeated failure, and a vicious cycle of anxiety and failure may develop (Bancroft et al., 2005c).

A man with erectile problems may try to "will" an erection, which can compound the problem. Each failure may further demoralize and defeat him. He may ruminate about his sexual inadequacy, setting the stage for yet more anxiety. His partner may try to comfort and support him by saying things like "It can happen to anyone," "Don't worry about it," or "It will get better in time." But attempts at reassurance may be to no avail. As one client put it,

Performance anxiety
Anxiety concerning one's ability to perform behaviors, especially behaviors that may be evaluated by other people

I always felt inferior, like I was on probation, having to prove myself. I felt like I was up against the wall. You can't imagine how embarrassing this [erectile failure] was. It's like you walk out in front of an audience that you think is a nudist convention and it turns out to be a tuxedo convention.

—Authors' Files

The vicious cycle of anxiety and erectile failure may be interrupted if the man recognizes that occasional problems are normal and he does not overreact. The emphasis in our culture on men's sexual prowess may spur them to view occasional failures as catastrophes rather than transient disappointments, however. Viewing occasional problems as an inconvenience, rather than a tragedy, may help avert the development of persistent erectile difficulties.

SafeZone

Q *I was molested as a child, and the thought of sex does not interest me. What can I do about this?*

A We will offer you some generalizations, but we will also admit, right at the beginning, that we do not know enough about your situation and suggest that you might want to talk it over with a helping professional. Having said that, you might begin by allowing a good relationship to develop with a decent, caring person. If you are comfortable in the relationship, and are engaging in some cuddling and so on, you might find some interest in sex developing. Even if such a relationship seems available to you, it would not hurt to discuss the situation with a professional.

FEMALE SEXUAL AROUSAL DISORDER Women may encounter persistent difficulties becoming sexually excited or sufficiently lubricated in response to sexual stimulation. In some cases these difficulties are lifelong. In others they develop after a period of normal functioning. In some cases difficulties are pervasive and occur during both masturbation and sex with a partner. More often they occur in certain situations. For example, they occur with some partners and not with others, or during intercourse but not during oral sex or masturbation (Goldstein et al., 2006).

Female sexual arousal disorder often accompanies other sexual disorders such as hypoactive sexual desire disorder and orgasmic disorders. Despite problems in becoming sexually aroused, women with sexual arousal disorders can often engage in coitus. Vaginal dryness may produce discomfort, however.

Female sexual arousal disorder, like its male counterpart, may have physical causes. A thorough evaluation by a medical specialist is recommended. Any neurological, vascular, or hormonal problem that interferes with the lubrication or swelling response of the vagina to sexual stimulation may contribute to female sexual arousal disorder. For example, *diabetes mellitus* may damage the nerves and blood vessels servicing the clitoral region. Reduced estrogen production can result in vaginal dryness.

Another interesting line of research suggests that the skin of some women with sexual arousal problems is not as sensitive to touch as the skin of women who do not have such problems (Frohlich & Meston, 2005). In such cases, the woman might seek to increase sexual stimulation—psychological as well as physical.

Female sexual arousal disorder more commonly has psychological causes, however. In some cases women harbor deep-seated anger and resentment toward their partners (Moore & Heiman, 2006). They thus find it difficult to turn off these feelings when they go to bed. In other cases, sexual trauma is implicated. Survivors of sexual abuse often find it difficult to respond sexually to their partners. Childhood sexual abuse is especially prevalent in cases of female sexual arousal disorder (Bean, 2002; Fishman & Mamo, 2001; Najman et al., 2005). Feelings of helplessness, anger, or guilt, or even flashbacks of the abuse, may surface when the woman begins sexual activity, dampening her ability to become aroused. Other psychosocial causes include anxiety or guilt about sex and ineffective stimulation by the partner (Goldstein et al., 2006).

Orgasmic Disorders

Orgasmic disorders include (1) female orgasmic disorder, (2) male orgasmic disorder, and (3) premature or rapid ejaculation. In female or male orgasmic disorder, the woman or man is persistently delayed in reaching orgasm or does not reach orgasm at all, despite achieving sexual stimulation of sufficient intensity that normally results in orgasm. The problem is more common among women than men. In some cases a person can reach orgasm without difficulty while engaging in sexual relations with one partner, but not with another.

FEMALE ORGASMIC DISORDER   Women with female orgasmic disorder are unable to reach orgasm or have difficulty reaching orgasm after what would usually be an adequate amount of sexual stimulation. Women who have never achieved orgasm through any means are sometimes labeled **anorgasmic** or *pre*orgasmic.

A woman who reaches orgasm through masturbation or oral sex may not necessarily reach orgasm during coitus with her partner. Penile thrusting during coitus may not provide sufficient clitoral stimulation to facilitate orgasm. An orgasmic disorder may be diagnosed, however, if orgasm during coitus was impaired by factors such as sexual guilt or performance anxiety. Women who try to force an orgasm may also find themselves unable to do so. They may assume a **spectator role** and observe, rather than fully participate in, their sexual encounters. "Spectatoring" may further decrease the likelihood of orgasm.

MALE ORGASMIC DISORDER   Male orgasmic disorder has also been termed *delayed ejaculation, retarded ejaculation,* or *ejaculatory incompetence.* The problem may be lifelong or acquired, generalized or situational. There are very few cases of men who have never ejaculated. In most cases the disorder is limited to coitus. The man may be capable of ejaculating during masturbation or oral sex, but find it difficult, if not impossible—despite high levels of sexual excitement—to ejaculate during intercourse. One might think that partners might enjoy such a dysfunction because it would enable a man to last longer, but the experience can be frustrating for both partners (Richardson et al., 2006a). Male orgasmic disorder is relatively infrequent in the general population and in clinical practice, where it is among the least frequently diagnosed disorders.

Male orgasmic disorder may be caused by physical problems such as MS or neurological damage that interferes with neural control of ejaculation. It may also be a side effect of certain drugs. Various psychological factors may also play a role, including performance anxiety, sexual guilt, and hostility toward one's partner. Fear that one's partner might get pregnant can also play a role.

Anorgasmic Never having reached orgasm; literally, "without orgasm"

Spectator role A role, usually taken on because of performance anxiety, in which people observe, rather than fully participate in, their sexual encounters

As with other sexual dysfunctions, men with orgasmic disorder and their partners may "try harder," but trying harder may worsen rather than help sexual problems. Sexual relations become a job to get done—a chore—rather than an opportunity for pleasure and gratification.

PREMATURE OR RAPID EJACULATION   A second type of male orgasmic disorder, premature (or rapid) ejaculation, is the most common male sexual dysfunction (Patrick et al., 2005; Table 15.1). Men with **premature (rapid) ejaculation** ejaculate too rapidly to permit their partners or themselves to enjoy sexual relations fully. The degree of prematurity or rapidity varies. Some men ejaculate during foreplay, even at the sight of their partner disrobing. However, most ejaculate either just prior to or immediately upon penetration, or following a few coital thrusts (Byers & Grenier, 2003). The point is that his partner—and he—would rather wait a while. In determining what is too rapid, some scholars argue that the focus should be on whether the couple is satisfied with the duration of coitus rather than on a specific time period (Byers & Grenier, 2003).

Helen Singer Kaplan (1974) suggested that the label "premature" should be applied to cases in which men persistently or recurrently lack voluntary control over their ejaculations. This may sound like a contradiction in terms, because ejaculation is a reflex, and reflexes need not involve thought or conscious control. Kaplan meant, however, that a man may control ejaculation by regulating the amount of sexual stimulation he experiences so that it remains low enough not to trigger the ejaculation reflex until the partners are ready.

SafeZone

Q *Do women find a man ejaculating disgusting? Is that a dysfunction?*

A Some women find ejaculation disgusting. Others are turned on by it. Still others have no particular feelings about it. The reasons for these variations are unclear. Finding ejaculating disgusting is not in itself a sexual dysfunction. If it gives rise to a sexual aversion, it might be.

RAPID FEMALE ORGASM: CAN WOMEN REACH ORGASM TOO QUICKLY?   The female counterpart to premature ejaculation, *rapid orgasm,* is so rarely recognized as a problem that it is generally ignored by clinicians and is not classified as a sexual dysfunction in the *DSM*. **Truth or Fiction Revisited:** Still, some women experience orgasm rapidly and may show little interest in continuing sexual activity so that their partners can achieve gratification. Many women who reach orgasm rapidly are open to continued sexual stimulation and capable of experiencing successive orgasms, however.

Sexual Pain Disorders

For most of us, coitus is a source of pleasure. For some of us, however, coitus gives rise to pain and discomfort.

DYSPAREUNIA   One sexual pain disorder, dyspareunia, or painful coitus, afflicts both men and women. Dyspareunia is a common sexual dysfunction and a common complaint of women seeking gynecological services.

Premature ejaculation
A sexual dysfunction in which ejaculation occurs with minimal sexual stimulation and before the partners desire it

Pain is usually a sign that something is physically wrong (Binik, 2005; Schultz et al., 2005). Dyspareunia may result from physical causes, emotional factors, or an interaction of the two (Goldstein et al., 2006). However, it should be noted that it is widely disputed whether dyspareunia should be listed in the *DSM* of the American Psychiatric Association (2000), because its inclusion suggests that it is a mental disorder (Binik, 2005; Spitzer, 2005).

TRUTH fiction 3

Truth or Fiction Revisited: The most common cause of painful intercourse—or dyspareunia—in women is not vaginal infection. It is lack of adequate lubrication. In such a case, additional foreplay or artificial lubrication may help. The normal changes of aging may play a role among perimenopausal and postmenopausal women (Goldstein & Alexander, 2005; Hayes & Dennerstein, 2005). Vaginal infections or STIs may also produce painful sex, however. Allergic reactions to spermicides, even the latex material in condoms, can give rise to painful sex. Pain during deep thrusting may indicate endometriosis, PID, or structural disorders of the reproductive organs.

Psychological factors such as unresolved guilt or anxiety about sex, or the lingering effects of sexual trauma may also be involved. These factors may inhibit lubrication and cause involuntary contractions of the vaginal musculature, making penetration painful or uncomfortable.

Painful intercourse is less common in men and is generally associated with genital infections that cause burning or painful ejaculation. Smegma under the penile foreskin of uncircumcised men may also irritate the penile glans during sexual contact.

VAGINISMUS   Another sexual pain disorder, vaginismus, involves involuntary contraction of the pelvic muscles that surround the outer third of the vaginal barrel. Vaginismus occurs reflexively during attempts at vaginal penetration, making entry by the penis painful or impossible. The muscle contractions are accompanied by fear of penetration. Some women with vaginismus are unable to tolerate penetration by any object, including a finger, tampon, or a physician's speculum. The prevalence of vaginismus is unknown.

The woman with vaginismus usually is not aware that she is contracting her vaginal muscles. In some cases, male partners of women with vaginismus develop erectile disorder after repeated failures at penetration.

Vaginismus is considered to be caused by psychological fear of penetration rather than physical injury or defect (Leiblum & Rosen, 2000). Women with vaginismus often have histories of sexual trauma, rape, or botched abortions that resulted in vaginal injuries. They may desire sexual relations. They may be capable of becoming sexually aroused and achieving orgasm. However, fear of penetration triggers an involuntary spasm of the vaginal musculature at the point of penile insertion. Vaginismus can also be a cause or an effect of dyspareunia. Women who experience painful coitus may develop a fear of penetration. Fear then leads to the development of involuntary vaginal contractions. Vaginismus and dyspareunia may also give rise to, or result from, erectile disorder in men. Feelings of failure and anxiety can overwhelm both partners.

Table 15.2 shows differences in the incidences of current sexual dysfunctions and other problems between European Americans and African Americans, according to the NHSLS (Laumann et al., 1994). African American men report a higher incidence than European American men of sexual dysfunctions. African American women report a higher incidence of most sexual dysfunctions, with the exceptions of painful sex and trouble lubricating.

TABLE 15.2

A World of Diversity: Differences between European Americans and African Americans in the Incidence of Current Sexual Problems (Respondents Reporting the Problem within the Past Year)

	European American Men	African American Men	European American Women	African American Women
Pain during sex	3.0%	3.3%	14.7%	12.5%
Sex not pleasurable	7.0	15.2	19.7	30.0
Unable to reach orgasm	7.4	9.9	23.2	29.2
Lack of interest in sex	14.7	20.0	30.9	44.5
Anxiety about performance	16.8	23.7	10.5	14.5
Reaching climax too early	27.7	33.8	7.5	20.4
Unable to keep an erection	9.9	14.5	—	—
Having trouble lubricating	—	—	20.7	13.0

SOURCE: Adapted by permission from E. O. Laumann, J. H. Gagnon, R. T. Michael, and S. Michaels (1994). *The Social Organization of Sexuality: Sexual Practices in the United States.* Chicago: University of Chicago Press, Tables 10.8A and 10.8B, pp. 370 & 371.

VULVODYNIA

The pain has lasted for months. You're so uncomfortable you can hardly sit. Having sex is unthinkable. Nothing alleviates the pain, burning, and irritation, at least not for long.

—Mayo Clinic, 2006

This is a description of vulvodynia, posted by the Mayo Clinic (2006). Vulvodynia is a gynecological condition characterized by vulval pain, particularly chronic burning sensations, irritation, and soreness (Lotery et al., 2004; Masheb et al., 2004). Although vulvodynia and related conditions, such as vestibulitis, can give rise to painful intercourse, they are not in themselves considered sexual dysfunctions (Kaler, 2005). Their causes are unknown, although a history of local infections, damage to local nerves, and allergies are among the suspects. Cold compresses, local anesthetics, and topical creams with estrogen or cortisone may provide relief (Mayo Clinic, 2006). Consult your gynecologist about other possible treatments.

Origins of Sexual Dysfunctions: A Biopsychosocial Approach

Human beings are complex, with complex bodies as well as complex mental processes. We are also reared in families within cultural settings. For these reasons, we need to consider possible biological, psychological, and social factors in sexual dysfunctions (Brown & Haaser, 2005). For example, biological and psychosocial factors—

hormonal deficiencies, depression, dissatisfaction with one's relationship, and so on—contribute to lack of desire. Moreover, these factors can interact in a number of ways. Researchers refer to such an approach as a **biopsychosocial model.**

Biological Causes

Among the medical conditions that diminish sexual desire are testosterone deficiencies, thyroid overactivity or underactivity, and temporal lobe epilepsy. Sexual desire is stoked by testosterone, which is produced by men in the testes and both men and women in the adrenal glands (Tuiten et al., 2000). Women may experience less sexual desire when their adrenal glands are surgically removed. Low sexual interest, along with erectile difficulties, are also common among men with **hypogonadism,** which is treated with testosterone (Lue, 2000).

The reduction in testosterone levels that occurs in middle and later life may in part explain a gradual decline in sexual desire among men (Janssen, 2006; Janssen et al., 2006). However, women's sexual desire may also decline with age, because of physical and psychological changes, as we will see (Goldstein et al., 2006). Some medications, especially those used to control anxiety or hypertension, may also reduce desire. Changing medications or doses may increase the person's level of desire.

Fatigue may lead to erectile disorder and orgasmic disorder in men, and to inadequate lubrication and orgasmic disorder in women, but these will be isolated incidents unless the person attaches too much meaning to them and becomes concerned about future performance. Painful sex, however, often reflects underlying infections (Binik, 2005; Schultz et al., 2005). Medical conditions that affect sexual response include heart disease (Thompson et al., 2005), diabetes mellitus, MS, spinal cord injuries, complications from surgery (such as removal of the prostate in men), hormonal problems, and use of some medicines, such as those used to treat hypertension and psychiatric disorders (Byerly et al., 2006; Olfson et al., 2005; Taylor et al., 2005).

A SPECIAL WARNING ABOUT SSRIs AND SEXUAL RESPONSE

People and physicians need to be aware of the sexual side effects of some drugs used to treat depression. So-called selective serotonin reuptake inhibitors—SSRIs for short—are widely prescribed not only for depression, but also for panic disorder, obsessive–compulsive disorder, anorexia nervosa, and other ills. Most physicians are aware that these drugs have "some" sexual side effects in "some" patients. However, the fact of the matter is that they almost completely impair sexual arousal in many patients, especially older patients (Clayton et al., 2006; Williams et al., 2006). Moreover, even when the patients discontinue the drugs, sexual functioning does *not* necessarily bounce back (Bolton et al., 2006; Csoka & Shipko, 2006).

The "good" news is that some drugs that are helpful with depression are less likely to impair sexual functioning. Wellbutrin, as a matter of fact, can have a positive effect on sexual functioning and is sometimes prescribed along with an SSRI to help prevent sexual side effects. Ask your physician.

Researchers find that health problems can contribute to all kinds of sexual dysfunctions in men, but mostly to sexual pain in women (Barsky et al., 2006; Binik, 2005; Schultz et al., 2005). Even when biological factors are involved in sexual dysfunctions, psychological factors such as anger and depression can prolong or worsen them (Goldstein & Alexander, 2005; Mohan & Bhugra, 2005).

Cardiovascular problems can lead to erectile disorder by affecting the flow of blood to and through the penis, a problem that becomes more common as men age. Damage to the nerves involved in erection can also play a role (Goldstein, as cited in Kolata, 1998; Goldstein, as cited in Norton, 2000). Erectile problems can arise when

Biopsychosocial model An approach to explaining dysfunctions that refers to the interactions of biological, psychological, and social/ cultural factors

Hypogonadism An endocrine disorder that reduces the output of testosterone

clogged or narrow arteries leading to the penis deprive the penis of oxygen (Thompson et al., 2005). For example, erectile disorder is common among men with diabetes mellitus, a disease that can damage blood vessels and nerves. Eric Rimm (2000) of the Harvard School of Public Health studied 2,000 men and found that erectile dysfunction was connected with a large waist, physical inactivity, and drinking too much alcohol (or not having any alcohol!). The common condition among these men may be high cholesterol levels. Cholesterol can impede the flow of blood to the penis just as it impedes the flow of blood to the heart. Another study connects erectile dysfunction with heart disease and hypertension (Johannes et al., 2000). Exercise, weight loss, and eating fewer animal fats help lower cholesterol levels.

Similarly, aging can affect the sexual response of women. Perimenopausal and postmenopausal women usually produce less vaginal lubrication than younger women, and the vaginal walls thin—changes that can render sex painful (Dennerstein & Goldstein, 2005; Dennerstein & Hayes, 2005; Hayes & Dennerstein, 2005). These physical changes, along with negative stereotypes of older women and men, can create performance anxiety and fumbling performances, and discourage both partners from attempting sexual activity (McCabe, 2005; McCarthy & Fucito, 2005; Schultz et al., 2005). In such cases, artificial lubrication can supplement the woman's own production, and estrogen replacement may halt or reverse some of the sexual changes of aging (Goldstein & Alexander, 2005). However, partners also need to have realistic expectations and consider enjoyable sexual activities they can engage in without discomfort or high demands (McCarthy & Fucito, 2005; Mohan & Bhugra, 2005).

Middle-age and older men might try weight control and regular exercise. The findings of the Massachusetts Male Aging Study suggest that men who exercise regularly seem to ward off erectile dysfunction (Derby, 2000). Men who burned 200 calories or more a day in physical activity, an amount that be achieved by walking briskly for two miles, cut their risk of erectile dysfunction almost in half. Exercise seems to prevent clogging of arteries, keeping them clear for the flow of blood into the penis.

Nerve damage resulting from prostate surgery may impair erectile response. Erectile disorder may also result from MS, a disease in which nerve cells lose the protective coatings that facilitate transmission of neural messages. MS has also been implicated in male orgasmic disorder.

The bacteria that cause syphilis, an STI, can invade the spinal cord and affect the cells that control erection, resulting in erectile dysfunction. Chronic kidney disease, hypertension, cancer, emphysema, and heart disease can all impair erectile response. So can endocrine disorders that impair testosterone production (Ralph & McNicholas, 2000).

Women also develop vascular or nervous disorders that impair genital blood flow, reducing lubrication and sexual excitement, rendering intercourse painful, and reducing their ability to reach orgasm. As with men, these problems become more likely as women age.

People with sexual dysfunctions are generally advised to undergo a physical examination to determine whether their problems are biologically based. Men with erectile disorder may be evaluated in a sleep center to determine whether they attain erections while asleep. The technique is termed *nocturnal penile* **tumescence** (NPT). Healthy men usually have erections during REM sleep, which occurs every 90 to 100 minutes. Men with biologically based erectile disorder often do not have nocturnal erections.

Prescription drugs and illicit drugs account for many cases of erectile disorder. Antidepressant medication and antipsychotic drugs may impair erectile functioning and cause orgasmic disorders (Olfson et al., 2005; Taylor et al., 2005). Tranquilizers

Tumescence Swelling; erection; from the Latin *tumere*, meaning "to swell" (*Tumor* has the same root.)

like Valium and Xanax may cause orgasmic disorder in either sex. Some drugs used to treat high blood pressure can impair erectile response (Ralph & McNicholas, 2000). Switching to other blood pressure drugs or adjusting dosages may help. Other drugs that can lead to erectile disorder include adrenergic blockers, diuretics, cholesterol-lowering drugs ("statins"), anticonvulsants, anti-Parkinsonian drugs, and dyspepsia and ulcer-healing drugs (Ralph & McNicholas, 2000).

Central nervous system depressants such as alcohol, heroin, and methadone can reduce sexual desire and impair sexual arousal (Brown et al., 2005). Narcotics also depress testosterone production, thereby reducing sexual desire and leading to erectile failure. Marijuana use has been associated with reduced sexual desire and performance (Wilson et al., 2000).

Regular use of cocaine can cause erectile disorder or male orgasmic disorder and may reduce sexual desire in both women and men (Rawson et al., 2002). Some people report increased sexual pleasure from the initial use of cocaine, but repeated use can lead to dependency on the drug for sexual arousal. Long-term use may compromise the ability to experience sexual pleasure. Despite the fact that alcohol can impair sexual arousal on a given occasion, Edward Laumann and his colleagues (1999) found no general relationship between alcohol consumption and sexual dysfunctions.

HIV AND SEXUAL DYSFUNCTIONS   There is little doubt that HIV/AIDS is associated with sexual dysfunction in both men and women. Men with HIV are also more likely to have hypogonadism and erectile dysfunction, which are apparently worsened by antiretroviral therapy (Crum et al., 2005). Antiretroviral therapy increases levels of estrogen in men (Lamba et al., 2004). A study of 78 seropositive gay males found a host of sexual dysfunctions, ranging from loss of interest in sex to delayed ejaculation and erectile disorder (Cove & Petrak, 2004). Because the men were more capable of obtaining and maintaining erections without condoms than with condoms, many of them used condoms inconsistently.

HIV-seropositive women, too, show various sexual dysfunctions, from lack of interest to sexual arousal disorders to orgasmic dysfunction (Florence et al., 2004). Researchers attribute the dysfunctions to psychological factors—anxiety, irritability, and depression—and to the effects of HIV.

Psychosocial Causes

Abrupt changes in sexual desire are more often explained by psychological and interpersonal factors such as depression, stress, and problems in the relationship (Bodenmann et al., 2006; Moore & Heiman, 2006). Psychological problems can contribute to low sexual desire (Bancroft et al., 2005b, c). Anxiety is the most commonly reported factor. Anxiety may dampen sexual desire, including performance anxiety (anxiety over being evaluated negatively), anxiety involving fears of pleasure or loss of control, and deeper sources of anxiety relating to fears of injury (Janssen & Bancroft, 2006). Depression is also a common cause of lack of desire (Frohlich & Meston, 2002; Kuffel & Heiman, 2006; Lykins et al., 2006). A history of sexual assault has also been linked to low sexual desire (McCarthy et al., 2006).

Psychosocial factors connected with sexual dysfunctions include cultural influences, economic problems, psychosexual trauma, being gay within a heterosexual marriage, dissatisfaction with one's relationship, lack of sexual skills, irrational beliefs, and performance anxiety (Bancroft et al., 2005b; McCabe, 2005).

CULTURAL INFLUENCES   Children reared in sexually repressive cultural or home environments may learn to respond to sex with feelings of anxiety and shame, rather than anticipation and pleasure (Nobre & Pinto–Gouveia, 2006). People whose parents instilled in them a sense of guilt over touching their genitals may find it difficult to accept their sex organs as sources of pleasure (McCarthy et al., 2006).

In most cultures, sexual pleasure has traditionally been a male preserve. Young women may be reared to believe that sex is a duty to be performed for their husbands, not a source of personal pleasure. Although the traditional double standard has diminished in developed countries (Fugl–Meyer et al., 2006), some girls are still exposed to repressive attitudes. Women are more likely than men to be taught to suppress sexual desires (Nobre & Pinto–Gouveia, 2006). Self-control and vigilance— not sexual awareness and acceptance—become identified as feminine virtues. Women reared with such attitudes may not learn about their sexual potentials or express their erotic desires to their partners.

Many women who are exposed to negative attitudes about sex during childhood and adolescence find it difficult to suddenly view sex as a source of pleasure and satisfaction as adults. A lifetime of learning to turn themselves off sexually may impair sexual arousal and enjoyment when an acceptable opportunity arises (Bean, 2002; Fishman & Mamo, 2001).

PSYCHOSEXUAL TRAUMA   Women and men who were sexually victimized in childhood are more likely to experience difficulty in becoming sexually aroused (Matthews et al., 2006; McCarthy et al., 2006; Mosher et al., 2005). Some learning theorists speak of conditioned anxiety in explaining sexual dysfunctions. Sexual stimuli come to elicit anxiety when they have been paired with traumatic experiences, such as rape, incest, or sexual molestation. Unresolved anger, misplaced guilt, and feelings of disgust also make it difficult for victims of sexual trauma to respond sexually, even years later and with loving partners.

SEXUAL ORIENTATION   Some gay males and lesbians test their sexual orientation by developing heterosexual relationships, even by entering "Brokeback marriages," in which they rear children with partners of the other sex. Others may wish to maintain the appearance of heterosexuality to avoid the social stigma attached to a gay sexual orientation. In such cases, problems with heterosexual partners can signify lack of heteroerotic interest (McCarthy et al., 2006).

INEFFECTIVE SEXUAL TECHNIQUES   In some relationships, couples fall into a narrow sexual routine because one partner controls the timing and sequence of sexual techniques. A woman who remains unknowledgeable about the erotic importance of her clitoris may be unlikely to seek direct clitoral stimulation. A man who responds to one erectile failure by trying to force an erection may be unintentionally setting himself up for repeated failure. The couple who fail to communicate their sexual preferences or to experiment with new techniques may find themselves losing interest. Brevity of foreplay and coitus may contribute to female orgasmic disorder.

EMOTIONAL FACTORS   Orgasm involves a sudden loss of voluntary control. Fear of losing control or "letting go" may block sexual arousal. Other emotional factors, especially depression, are often implicated in sexual dysfunctions (Ralph & McNicholas, 2000). Depression can contribute to lack of sexual desire (Frohlich & Meston, 2002). Stress can also interfere with sexual interest and response.

PROBLEMS IN THE RELATIONSHIP   Problems in the relationship are not easily left at the bedroom door (McCarthy et al., 2006; Moore & Heiman, 2006). Heterosexual and homosexual couples alike usually find that sex is no better than

REFLECT

Are there any sexual attitudes common to people of your demographic background that can give rise to sexual problems or dysfunctions? What are the attitudes? Do you share these attitudes? Explain.

CRITICAL Thinking

Given our cultural values, why might it lead to a problem in a relationship if a woman were to exhibit sexual competence?

A Vicious Cycle? Conflict in the Relationship and Lack of Sexual Desire. *Conflicts in a relationship may dampen sexual interest. Lack of sexual interest may then further strain the relationship.*

other facets of their relationship (Matthews et al., 2006). Partners who have general trouble communicating may also be unable to communicate their sexual desires. Couples who harbor resentments may make sex their combat arena. They may fail to become aroused by their partners or "withhold" orgasm to make their partners feel guilty or inadequate (Firestone et al., 2006b).

The following case highlights how sexual dysfunctions can develop against the backdrop of a troubled relationship:

> After living together for six months, Paul and Petula are contemplating marriage. But a problem has brought them to a **sex therapy** clinic. As Petula puts it, "For the last two months he hasn't been able to keep his erection after he enters me." Paul is 26, a lawyer; Petula, 24, is a buyer for a large department store. They both grew up in middle-class, suburban families, were introduced through mutual friends and began having intercourse, without difficulty, a few months into their relationship. At Petula's urging, Paul moved into her apartment, although he wasn't sure he was ready for such a step. A week later he began to have difficulty maintaining his erection during intercourse, although he felt strong desires for his partner. When his erection waned, he would try again, but would lose his desire and be unable to achieve another erection. After a few times like this, Petula would become so angry that she began striking Paul in the chest and screaming at him. Paul, who at 200 pounds weighed more than twice as much as Petula, would just walk away, which angered Petula even more.
>
> It became clear that sex was not the only trouble spot in their relationship. Petula complained that he preferred to be with his friends and go to baseball games than to spend time with her. When they were together at home, he would become absorbed in watching sports events on television, and showed no interest in activities she enjoyed—attending the theater, visiting museums, etc. Since there was no evidence that the sexual difficulty

was due to either organic problems or depression, a diagnosis of male erectile disorder was given. Neither Paul or Petula were willing to discuss their nonsexual problems with a therapist. While the sexual problem was treated successfully with a form of sex therapy modeled after techniques developed by Masters and Johnson [see discussion later in the chapter] and the couple later married, Paul's ambivalence continued well into their marriage, and there were future recurrences of sexual problems as well. (Adapted from Spitzer et al., 1989, pp. 149–150)

LACK OF SEXUAL SKILLS   Sexual competency involves sexual knowledge and skills that are acquired through learning. We generally learn what makes us and others feel good through trial and error, and by talking and reading about sex. Some people may not develop sexual competency because of a lack of opportunity to acquire knowledge and experience—even within a committed relationship. People with sexual dysfunctions may have been reared in families in which discussions of sexuality were off limits, and early sexual experimentation was harshly punished.

IRRATIONAL BELIEFS   Irrational beliefs and attitudes may contribute to sexual dysfunctions. We cannot expect our partners to read our minds. We cannot assume that if they truly cared for us, they would know what we need, or want. Communication is one of the keys to sexual satisfaction.

PERFORMANCE ANXIETY   Anxiety—especially performance anxiety—plays an important role in sexual dysfunctions (Bancroft et al., 2005b; McCabe, 2005). Performance anxiety occurs when a person becomes overly concerned with how well he or she performs a certain act or task. Performance anxiety may place a dysfunctional individual in a spectator role rather than a performer role. Rather than focusing on erotic sensations and allowing reflexes like erection, lubrication, and orgasm to occur naturally, he or she focuses on self-doubts and thinks, "Will I be able to do it this time? Will this be another failure?"

In men, performance anxiety can inhibit erection and trigger a premature ejaculation as well (Bancroft et al., 2005b; Hellstrom et al., 2006; Janssen & Bancroft, 2006). Erection, mediated by the parasympathetic nervous system, can be blocked by activation of the sympathetic nervous system in the form of anxiety. Because ejaculation, like anxiety, is mediated by the sympathetic nervous system, arousal of this system in the form of anxiety can increase the level of stimulation and thereby heighten the potential for premature ejaculation.

In women, performance anxiety can reduce vaginal lubrication and contribute to orgasmic disorder (Goldstein et al., 2006). Women with performance anxieties may try to force an orgasm, only to find that the harder they try, the more elusive it becomes.

Treatment of Sexual Dysfunctions

When Kinsey conducted his surveys in the 1930s and 1940s, there was no effective treatment for sexual dysfunctions. At the time, the predominant model of therapy for sexual dysfunctions was long-term psychoanalysis. Psychoanalysts believed that the sexual problem would abate only if the presumed unconscious conflicts that lay at the root of the problem were resolved through long-term therapy. Evidence of the effectiveness of psychoanalysis in treating sexual dysfunctions is still lacking, however.

Since that time, cognitive and behavioral models of short-term treatment, collectively called sex therapy, have emerged. Sex therapy aims to modify dysfunctional cognitions (beliefs and attitudes) and behavior as directly as possible. Sex therapists also recognize the roles of childhood conflicts and the quality of the partners' relationship. Therefore, they draw upon various forms of therapy, as needed (Adams, 2006; Kleinplatz, 2003; Corty, 2006).

Although the particular approaches vary, sex therapies aim to

- change self-defeating beliefs and attitudes
- teach sexual skills
- enhance sexual knowledge
- improve sexual communication
- reduce performance anxiety

Sex therapy usually involves both partners, although individual therapy is preferred in some cases. Therapists find that granting people "permission" to sexually experiment or to discuss negative attitudes about sex helps many people overcome sexual problems without the need for more intensive therapy.

Today, biological treatments have also been emerging for various sexual dysfunctions. Most public attention has been focused on Viagra, a drug that is helpful in most cases of erectile dysfunction. But competitors of Viagra and biological treatments for premature ejaculation, female orgasmic dysfunction, and lack of sexual desire are also emerging.

In this section we explore psychological and behavioral approaches to the treatment of sexual dysfunctions. Let us begin with the pioneering work of Masters and Johnson.

The Masters-and-Johnson Approach

Masters and Johnson (1970) pioneered the use of direct cognitive–behavioral approaches to treating sexual dysfunctions. A female–male therapy team focuses on the married couple as the unit of treatment during a two-week residential program. Masters and Johnson consider the couple, not the individual, dysfunctional. A couple may describe the husband's erectile disorder as the problem, but this problem is likely to have led to problems in the couple by the time they seek therapy. Similarly, a man whose wife has an orgasmic disorder is likely to be anxious about his ability to provide effective sexual stimulation.

The dual-therapist team permits each partner to discuss problems with someone of his or her own gender. It reduces the chance of therapist bias in favor of the female or male partner. It allows each partner to hear concerns expressed by another member of the other gender. Anxieties and resentments are aired, but the focus of treatment is behavioral change. Couples perform daily sexual homework assignments, such as **sensate focus exercises,** in the privacy of their own rooms.

Sensate focus sessions are carried out in the nude. Partners take turns giving and receiving stimulation in nongenital areas of the body. Without touching the breasts or genitals, the giver massages or fondles the receiving partner to provide pleasure under relaxing and nondemanding conditions. Because genital activity is restricted, there is no pressure to "perform." The giving partner is freed to engage in trial-and-error learning about the receiving partner's sensate preferences. The receiving partner is also freed to enjoy the experience without feeling rushed to reciprocate or

Sensate focus exercises
Exercises during which sex partners take turns giving and receiving pleasurable stimulation in nongenital areas of the body

obliged to perform by becoming sexually aroused. The receiving partner's only responsibility is to direct the giving partner as needed. In addition to these general sensate focus exercises, Masters and Johnson used specific assignments designed to help couples overcome particular sexual dysfunctions.

Masters and Johnson were pioneers in the development of sex therapy. Yet many sex therapists today depart from the Masters-and-Johnson format. For example, many do not treat clients in an intensive residential program. Many question the necessity of female–male therapist teams. Researchers find that one therapist is about as effective as two, regardless of her or his sex. Nor does it seem to matter whether sessions are conducted within a short period of time, as in the Masters-and-Johnson approach, or spaced over time.

Integration of Sex Therapy and Psychotherapy

Sex therapy, as noted, has cognitive components, for example, addressing self-defeating attitudes and expectations, and sex education. Because sexual activity is so often embedded in relationships, many therapists (e.g., Coyle, 2006; McCarthy et al., 2004, 2006) use psychotherapy and couples therapy to help couples learn how to share the power in relationships, how to improve sexual communication, and how to negotiate differences. The combination of sex therapy and couples therapy appears to be a powerful tool for enhancing relationships as well as sex lives.

Helen Singer Kaplan (1974) combined sex therapy with psychoanalytic methods. She saw sexual dysfunctions as having *immediate* causes and *remote* causes (conflicts that date to childhood). As a sex therapist, Kaplan focused on improving the couple's sexual communication, eliminating performance anxiety, and fostering sexual skills and knowledge. As a psychoanalyst, she used insight-oriented therapy when it appeared that remote causes impaired response to sex therapy. By so doing, she aimed to bring to awareness unconscious conflicts that might have stifled the person's sexual desire or response.

Let us next consider some of the specific techniques that sex therapists have introduced in treating several of the major types of sexual dysfunction.

Treatment of Sexual Desire Disorders

Some therapists help kindle the sexual appetites of people with hypoactive sexual desire by prescribing self-stimulation exercises combined with erotic fantasies (Leiblum & Rosen, 2000; McCarthy et al., 2006). Sex therapists may also assist dysfunctional couples by prescribing sensate focus exercises, enhancing communication, and expanding the couple's repertoire of sexual skills. Sex therapists recognize that hypoactive sexual desire is often a complex problem that requires more intensive treatment than problems of the arousal or orgasmic phases. Counseling or psychotherapy may be helpful in the treatment of hypoactive sexual desire and sexual aversion to uncover and resolve psychological conflicts (McCarthy et al., 2006).

Some cases of hypoactive sexual desire in men involve hormonal deficiencies, especially deficiencies in testosterone. Testosterone replacement therapy works for about half of men who have low testosterone levels (Rakic et al., 1997). Among women, as among men, lack of sexual desire can be connected with low levels of androgens, and testosterone shows promise in heightening desire (Brown & Haaser, 2005).

If lack of desire is connected with depression, sexual interest may rebound when the depression lifts. Treatment in such cases may involve psychotherapy or medi-

REFLECT

If you had a sexual dysfunction, do you think that you would be willing to participate in sex therapy? Explain.

A Closer
LOOK

HOW DO YOU FIND A QUALIFIED SEX THERAPIST?

How would you find a qualified sex therapist if you had a sexual dysfunction? You might find advertisements for "sex therapists" in the Yellow Pages, but beware. Most states do not restrict usage of the term *sex therapist* to recognized professionals. In these states, anyone who wants to use the label may do so, including quacks and prostitutes.

Thus, it is essential to determine that a sex therapist is a member of a recognized profession (such as psychology, social work, medicine, or marriage and family counseling) with training and supervision in sex therapy. Professionals are usually licensed or certified by their states. All states require licensing of psychologists and physicians, but some states do not license social workers or couples therapists. If you have questions about the license laws in your state, contact your state's professional licensing board. The ethical standards of these professions prohibit practitioners from claiming expertise in sex therapy without suitable training.

If you are uncertain with regard to how to locate a qualified sex therapist in your area, you may obtain names of local practitioners from various sources, such as your university or college psychology department, health department, or counseling center; a local medical or psychological association; a family physician; or your instructor. You may also seek services from a sex therapy clinic affiliated with a local medical center or medical school in your area, many of which charge for services on a sliding scale, depending on your income level. You may also contact the American Association of Sex Educators, Counselors, and Therapists (AASECT), a professional organization that certifies sex therapists. They can provide you with the names of certified sex therapists in your area. They are located at 11 Dupont Circle, N.W., Washington, DC.

Ethical professionals are not annoyed or embarrassed if you ask them (1) what their profession is, (2) where they earned their advanced degree, (3) whether they are licensed or certified by the state, (4) what their fees are, (5) what their plans for treatment are, and (6) the nature of their training in human sexuality and sex therapy. If the therapist hems and haws, asks why you are asking such questions, or fails to provide a direct answer, beware.

Professionals are also restricted by the ethical principles of their professions from engaging in unethical practices, such as sexual relations with their clients. Clients may be vulnerable because the nature of therapy creates an unequal power relationship between the therapist and the client.

cures, not sex therapy per se. When problems in the relationship are involved, couple therapy may be indicated. After interpersonal problems are ironed out, sexual interest may return.

Treatment of sexual aversion disorder may involve a multifaceted approach, including biological treatments, such as the use of medications to reduce anxiety, and psychological treatments designed to help the individual overcome the underlying sexual phobia. Couples therapy may be used in cases in which sexual aversions arise from problems in relationships. Sensate focus exercises may be used to lessen anxiety about sexual contact. Fears may also need to be overcome through cognitive–behavioral exercises during which the client learns to manage the stimuli that evoke fears of sexual contact:

> Bridget, 26, and Bryan, 30, were married for four years but had never consummated their relationship because Bridget would panic whenever Bryan attempted coitus with her. While she enjoyed foreplay and was capable of achieving orgasm with clitoral stimulation, her fears of sexual contact were triggered by Bryan's attempts at vaginal penetration. The therapist employed a program of gradual exposure to the feared stimuli to allow Bridget

the opportunity to overcome her fears in small, graduated steps. First she was instructed to view her genitals in a mirror when she was alone—this in order to violate her long-standing prohibition against looking at and enjoying her body. While this exercise initially made her feel anxious, with repeated exposure she became comfortable performing it and then progressed to touching her genitals directly. When she became comfortable with this step, and reported experiencing pleasurable erotic sensations, she was instructed to insert a finger into the vagina. She encountered intense anxiety at this step and required daily practice for two weeks before she could tolerate inserting her finger into her vagina without discomfort. Her husband was then brought into the treatment process. The couple was instructed to have Bridget insert her own finger in her vagina while Bryan watched. When she was comfortable with this exercise, she then guided his finger into her vagina. Later he placed one and then two fingers into her vagina, while she controlled the depth, speed, and duration of penetration. When she felt ready, they proceeded to attempt penile penetration in the female-superior position, which allowed her to maintain control over penetration. Over time, Bridget became more comfortable with penetration to the point that the couple developed a normal sexual relationship. (Adapted from Kaplan, 1987, pp. 102–103)

Treatment of Sexual Arousal Disorders

Sex therapists treat both male and female sexual arousal disorders.

ERECTILE DISORDER   Male sexual arousal disorder is also known as erectile disorder. Men with erectile disorder may ask their therapists to "teach" them or "show them" how to obtain an erection. Some of our clients have asked us to tell them what fantasies they should entertain to obtain an erection, or how they should touch their partners or be touched. Erection is a reflex, however, not a skill. A man need not learn how to have an erection any more than he need learn how to breathe.

In sex therapy, women who have trouble becoming lubricated and men with erectile problems learn that they need not "do" anything to become sexually aroused. As long as their problems are psychologically and not organically based, they need only receive sexual stimulation under relaxed circumstances, so that anxiety does not inhibit natural reflexes.

Truth or Fiction Revisited: It is not true that sex therapy teaches a man with erectile disorder how to "will" an erection. Men with erectile disorder are actually taught that it is not possible to will an erection. One can only set the stage for erection (or vaginal lubrication) to occur and then allow it to happen reflexively.

To reduce performance anxiety, the partners engage in nondemanding sexual contacts—contacts that do not demand lubrication or erection. They may start with nongenital sensate focus exercises in the style of Masters and Johnson. After a couple of sessions, sensate focus extends to the genitals. The position shown in Figure 15.1 allows a woman easy access to her male partner's genitals. She repeatedly "teases" him to erection and allows the erection to subside. Thus she avoids creating performance anxiety that could lead to loss of erection. By repeatedly regaining his erection, the man loses the fear that loss of erection means it will not return. He learns also to focus on erotic sensations for their own sake. He experiences no demand to perform, because the couple is instructed to refrain from coitus.

Figure 15.1 **The Training Position Recommended by Masters and Johnson for Treatment of Erectile Disorder and Premature Ejaculation.** *By lying in front of her partner, who has his legs spread, the woman has ready access to his genitals. In one part of a program designed to overcome erectile disorder, she repeatedly "teases" him to erection and allows the erection to subside. Thus she avoids creating performance anxiety that could lead to loss of erection. Through repeated regaining of erection, the man loses the fear that loss of erection means it will not return.*

When the partner with the dysfunction can reliably achieve sexual excitement (denoted by erection in the male and lubrication in the female), the couple does not immediately attempt coitus, because this might rekindle performance anxiety. Rather, the couple engages in a series of nondemanding, pleasurable sexual activities, eventually culminating in coitus.

In Masters's and Johnson's approach, the couple begin coitus after about 10 days of treatment. The woman teases the man to erection while she is sitting above him, straddling his thighs. When he is erect, she inserts the penis—to avoid fumbling attempts at entry—and moves slowly back and forth in a *nondemanding way*. Neither attempts to reach orgasm. If erection is lost, teasing and coitus are repeated. When the couple become confident that erection can be retained—or reinstated if lost—they may increase coital thrusting gradually to reach orgasm.

BIOLOGICAL APPROACHES TO TREATMENT OF ERECTILE DISORDER

It takes women authors to write articles about Viagra with titles such as

- *The Rise of Viagra* (Plante, 2006)— our runaway favorite
- *The New Virility* (Marshall, 2006)
- *Sex for Life?* (Potts et al., 2006)

Of course, none of them can top the performance of a urologist at a medical convention some years ago. He sounded the opening shot (wrong metaphor) in the biological war against erectile disorder through a somewhat unusual presentation. **Truth or Fiction Revisited:** He dropped his pants to reveal an erection. He was demonstrating the effects of a chemical compound called alprostadil. The erection was not the result of sexual stimulation or sexual fantasies, but of an injection of *alprostadil* directly into his penis. Alprostadil is a vasodilator; it relaxes the muscles surrounding the arteries in the penis, allowing more blood to flow in, increasing vasocongestion and causing erection. The speaker was giving a "live" demonstration of a biological method of treating erectile disorder.

Biological or biomedical approaches are helpful in treating erectile disorder, especially when organic factors are involved. Treatments include surgery, medication, and vacuum pumps (Table 15.3).

TRUTH fiction 5

TABLE 15.3

Biological Treatments of Erectile Problems

Surgery	
Vascular surgery	Helps when blood vessels that supply the penis are blocked.
Penile implants	May be used when other treatments fail because of biological problems.
Medication	
Hormone therapy	Helps men (and women) with abnormally low levels of male sex hormones.
Injections	Muscle relaxants such as *alprostadil* and *phentolamine* are injected into the corpus cavernosum of the penis, relaxing the muscles that surround the arteries in the penis, allowing the vessels to dilate and blood to flow more freely.
Suppository	Alprostadil is inserted into the tip of the penis in gel form.
Oral medication	Oral forms of several compounds—sildenafil (Viagra), vardenafil (Levitra), and tadalafil (Cialis)—relax the muscles that surround the small blood vessels in the penis, allowing them to dilate so that blood can flow into them more freely. Apomorphine increases brain levels of the neurotransmitter dopamine. Called "Uprima," the drug is in clinical trials. Bremelanotide apparently acts directly on the central nervous system and, as the book goes to press, is also in clinical trials.
Vacuum Pump	
Vacuum pump	A *vacuum constriction device* creates a vacuum when it is held over the penis. The vacuum induces erection by increasing the flow of blood into the penis. Rubber bands around the base of the penis maintain the erection.

SafeZone

Q *I know that Viagra helps put more blood into the penis—but how does it do that? How does it actually work?*

A The answer is chemical and applies to Levitra and Cialis as well as Viagra. The end point is to allow the arteries in the penis to dilate and fill up with blood to produce an erection. Chemically, what has to happen for arteries to dilate is that the brain sends a signal along a nerve fiber ending in a nonadrenergic-noncholinergic (NANC) cell in an artery; the NANC cell produces nitric oxide and injects it into the bloodstream and nearby cells. The nitric oxide causes a chemical called cyclic guanosine monophosphate (cGMP) to be produced, which relaxes the muscles that line an artery, increasing the flow of blood. However, a chemical called phosphodiesterase (PDE) deactivates cGMP. The specific type of PDE found in the penis is called PDE5.

Viagra, Levitra, and Cialis are all PDE5 inhibitors. That is, they work by deactivating PDE5. Step by step:

1. A man takes Viagra, Levitra, or Cialis.
2. The chemical in the pill circulates throughout his bloodstream.
3. The chemical attaches to PDE5 in his penis and deactivates most of it.
4. When he is sexually aroused, his brain sends the usual message to the cells in his penis, resulting in the output of nitric oxide.
5. In turn, the nitric oxide produces cGMP.
6. Because most PDE5 has been deactivated, cGMP builds up, allowing the arteries in the penis to dilate and produce a fuller erection.

Note: Although Viagra and its chemical cousins are marketed as PDE5 inhibitors, their effects are somewhat broader, which is why they sometimes produce migraines.

SURGERY   There are two main types of surgery: vascular surgery and the installation of penile implants. *Vascular surgery* can help in cases when the blood vessels that supply the penis are blocked, or when structural defects in the penis restrict blood flow. Arterial bypass surgery reroutes vessels around the blockage.

A *penile implant* may be used when other treatments fail. Implants are either malleable (semirigid) or inflatable (Figure 15.2). The semirigid implant is made of rods that remain in a *permanent* semirigid position. It is rigid enough for intercourse but permits the penis to hang reasonably close to the body at other times. The inflatable type requires that cylinders be implanted in the penis. A fluid reservoir is placed near the bladder, and a tiny pump is inserted in the scrotum. To attain erection, the man squeezes the pump, releasing fluid into the cylinders. When the erection is no longer needed, a release valve returns the fluid to the reservoir, deflating the penis. The inflatable implant more closely duplicates the normal processes of tumescence and detumescence. Some adverse side effects of penile implants have been reported, including destruction of erectile tissue, which impairs the man's ability to have normal erections. Penile implants do not affect sex drive, sexual sensations, or ejaculation.

Implant surgery is irreversible. Therefore, the National Institutes of Health recommend that penile implants be used only when less invasive techniques, such as sex therapy and medication, are unsuccessful.

MEDICATION   There are several ways in which medication can be used to help men with erectile problems. For example, hormone (testosterone) treatments help restore the sex drive and erectile ability in many men with abnormally low levels of testosterone (Lue, 2000; Rakic et al., 1997). Hormone therapy does not appear to help men with normal hormone levels.

The muscle relaxants *alprostadil* (brand names Caverject and Edex) and *phentolamine* (Invicorp) can be injected into the corpus cavernosum of the penis. These chemicals relax the muscles that surround the small blood vessels in the penis. The vessels dilate and allow blood to flow more freely. Alprostadil erections last for an hour or more and occur regardless of whether there is sexual stimulation. A physician teaches the man how to inject himself. If phentolamine is used along with the protein VIP, erection only occurs when sexual stimulation is applied.

Penile injections may have side effects, including pain from the injection itself and prolonged, painful erections (*priapism*) (Ralph & McNicholas, 2000). Many men find the idea of penile injections distasteful (the "wince factor") and refuse them.

Alprostadil is also available as a suppository in gel form (brand name MUSE). It is inserted into the tip of the penis by an applicator. The suppository helps men get around the "wince" factor that many experience with injections. "Putting a needle in your penis is not everybody's idea of foreplay," notes Dr. John Seely (Kolata, 2000).

Other medications are taken orally or by nasal spray. For example, the oral form of sildenafil is sold as Viagra, and the oral form of vardenafil is sold as Levitra. The oral form of talafadil (Cialis) becomes effective in about half an hour and lasts up to 36 hours. Users in France dubbed it "the weekend pill." There is ample evidence that these oral medications are effective with most men (e.g., Fisher et al., 2005; Hatzichristou et al., 2000, 2005).

The drug apomorphine (Uprima) heightens brain levels of dopamine, a **neurotransmitter** involved in erection. Uprima is available in the United Kingdom and without prescription online, but it is advisable to consult your physician before using it. Bremelanotide was developed as a drug to promote tanning, but its effects were found to be more than skin deep. Many male laboratory rats given the drug had spontaneous erections. The drug would probably be taken by nasal spray and appears to act on the central nervous system. It may produce erections with fewer side effects than Viagra, Levitra, and Cialis.

VACUUM PUMPS   Sounding like something from the "what will they think of next" category, a *vacuum constriction device* helps men achieve erections through vacuum pressure. The device (brand name ErecAid) consists of a cylinder that is connected to a hand-operated vacuum pump. It creates a vacuum when it is held over the limp penis. The vacuum induces erection by increasing the flow of blood into the penis. Rubber bands around the base of the penis can maintain the erection for as long as 30 minutes.

The device has been used successfully by men with both organically and psychologically based erectile failure. However, side effects such as pain and black-and-blue marks are common. The rubber bands prevent normal ejaculation, so semen remains trapped in the urethra until the bands are released. The quality of the erections produced by the device is also considered inferior to spontaneous erections.

WHERE DO WE GO FROM HERE?   It would appear that oral medications (pills) will be the most popular biological treatment of erectile problems. They are helpful with most men and avoid the "wince factor." Viagra and Levitra have side effects, though, such as migraine headaches and flushing. The migraines are not surprising because they are related to increased blood flow, and these drugs are not precise enough to direct blood to the genitals only. Soon after Viagra was approved by the FDA, there were scattered reports of men with cardiovascular problems experiencing heart attacks. A carefully conducted study of the effects of Viagra on 14 older men with at least one severely constricted coronary artery suggests that Viagra by

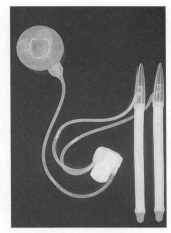

Figure 15.2   A Penile Implant. *Penile implants provide erection when the man's cardiovascular system does not do the job. This implant consists of cylinders that are implanted in the penis. A fluid reservoir (top left) is placed near the bladder. A pump (lower middle) is typically inserted in the scrotum. Squeezing the pump forces fluid into the cylinders, inflating the penis. A release valve returns the fluid to the reservoir, deflating the penis.*

Neurotransmitter A chemical that transmits messages from one brain cell to another

A Closer Look

THINKING CRITICALLY ABOUT BUYING VIAGRA AND OTHER DRUGS ONLINE

Viagra, Levitra, and Cialis are prescription drugs. Many men who might otherwise use them are reluctant to discuss erectile dysfunction with their physicians. The anonymity of doing things on the 'Net is a lure—you don't have to admit your personal worries to your doctor face to face. Some men, unfortunately, do not even have a regular physician. What to do?

Many have discovered that by searching "Viagra" on the 'Net, they can find many websites where they can "consult" with online physicians, obtain a prescription, and order the drug for home delivery. Easy! A few questions and a fee, and they've got it. But is it wise? Perhaps; perhaps not.

Prescriptions are needed for various drugs because physicians are better equipped than most laypeople to diagnose an individual's health problems, understand the chemical nature and side effects of the drugs that are available for treatment, and predict how the drugs will affect the individual patient. Physicians are also usually prepared to deal with the unexpected effects of the drugs, and there can be many.

So ask yourself what kind of physician would prescribe drugs online, without personally knowing the patient. Is it possible that some of them would have difficulty establishing private practices or getting jobs in hospitals? If you have a question about the drug after you use it, will you be able to get back to the prescriber easily for an answer? Or will you wind up with an embarrassed call to your own physician or a trip to the emergency room?

You will find that many of the sites are online pharmacies that also advertise Propecia for treatment of hair loss, drugs that reverse the loss of pubic hair (yes, pubic hair), weight control drugs that prevent the absorption of some of the fat in food (e.g., Xenical), herbal supplements, and so on. What you will tend to hit in your search are chemical armories of weapons that sound as if

they can stop you from aging, or even reverse the aging process. It may sound as if they will help you remain (or return you to status as) a studmuffin. But the fact is that medical science isn't there yet.

While surfing the 'Net, you will also come across sites that claim to have "natural" preparations, including a variety of herbs that are as effective as Viagra, but without the side effects, and without the need to get a prescription. Use some critical thinking: Are you convinced of the effectiveness and safety of these preparations? Because they are foods (sort of) rather than drugs, they escape the scrutiny of the Food and Drug Administration. That is, the government is not watching over them. Be warned.

In sum, even if it is convenient to buy a drug online, you are well advised to get your prescription face to face—from a doctor you know and trust.

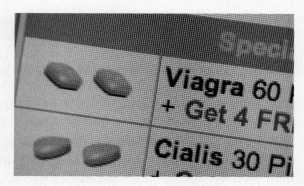

Should You Buy Viagra Online? *Many websites enable men to consult with physicians and order Viagra online. Is it wise to purchase Viagra—or other prescription drugs—online? Prescriptions are needed for drugs when the person's diagnosis is in question and when the drugs have side effects. Physicians are better equipped than most laypeople to diagnose health problems, understand the chemical composition and effects of drugs, and predict how drugs will affect the individual.*

itself is not the problem (Herrmann et al., 2000). In that study, reported in the prestigious *New England Journal of Medicine,* Viagra was not shown to have adverse effects on the blood supply to the heart. As a matter of fact, Viagra, which dilates blood vessels, is now being considered by some for use as a heart *medicine.*

FEMALE SEXUAL AROUSAL DISORDER   Psychological treatments for female sexual arousal disorder parallel those for orgasmic disorder and are discussed in the following pages. They involve sex education (labeling the parts, discussing their functions, and explaining how to arouse them), searching out and coping with possible cognitive interference (such as negative sexual attitudes), creating nondemanding situations during which sexual arousal may occur, and—when appropriate—working on problems in the relationship.

Yet many cases of female sexual arousal disorder reflect impaired blood flow to the genitals, just as in erectile disorder. Female sexual arousal involves vaginal lubrication, which permits sexual intercourse without a great deal of pain-causing friction. Lubrication is made possible by vasocongestion (the flow of blood into the genitals). Lack of lubrication can reflect the physical effects of aging, menopause, and surgically induced menopause, as through surgery.

Sometimes all that is necessary to deal with lack of lubrication is an artificial lubricant such as K-Y jelly. However, lessened blood flow to the genitals can also sap sexual pleasure and, as a consequence, lessen a woman's desire for sex.

The development of treatments for women has lagged the development of treatments for men. Ironically, the treatments that are emerging are highly similar to those that help men with erectile disorder.

For example, drugs identical or similar to those used for men are being investigated for use with women (Leland, 2000). Many trials have been undertaken with Viagra for women. Researchers are also developing alprostadil (the vasodilator) for use with women, largely in the form of creams that are inserted into the vagina to enhance the flow of blood and hence lubrication. (See Table 15.4)

Figure 15.3 A Clitoral Device That Stimulates Genital Vasocongestion in Women by Creating (Gentle) Suction over the Clitoris

TABLE 15.4

Various Biological Treatments in Use or under Investigation to Help Women with Sexual Dysfunctions

Method	How Used	Effect	Current Status
Alprostadil	Gel, cream	May improve blood flow to the clitoris, enhancing arousal	Studies under way
DHEA	Pill	May boost libido by increasing testosterone levels	Available by prescription; available as a dietary supplement, although experts caution against unsupervised use; studies under way
Eros (Figure 15.3)	Hand-held device that applies gentle suction to the clitoris	Promotes blood flow to the clitoris, enhancing arousal	Available by prescription
Estrogen	Pill, patch, gel, cream	Counters vaginal dryness	Available by prescription
PDE5 inhibitors	Pill	May improve blood flow to the clitoris, enhancing arousal	Viagra and Levitra available by prescription; studies under way for treating women's sexual problems
Testosterone	Pill, patch, gel, cream	May boost libido	Available by prescription; studies under way for treating women's sexual problems
VasoFem, Alista, FemProx	Viagra-like drugs	May improve blood flow to the clitoris, enhancing arousal	Studies under way for treating women's sexual problems
Yohimbine with nitric oxide	Pill	May improve blood flow to the clitoris enhancing arousal	Studies under way

There is a perfect parallel in the area of lack of sexual desire for women who are low in sexual desire because of low levels of "male" sex hormones. As an aside, we might begin to wonder out loud whether we should stop referring to estrogen as a female sex hormone and testosterone as a male sex hormone because they are produced by women and men—although in different quantities—and are both intricately involved with women's and men's health, sexual functioning, and other kinds of behavior. In any event, testosterone skin patches can be used by women who lack sexual desire because they lack adequate quantities of testosterone.

There is even a device—*Eros*—that is a parallel to the vacuum pump that is used by some men with erectile disorder. It is a clitoral device that is available by prescription. The clitoris swells during sexual arousal because of vasocongestion, and vasocongestion increases clitoral sexual sensations, thus moving somewhat in step with sexual interest and lubrication. The device creates gentle suction over the clitoris, increasing vasocongestion and sexual sensations (refer back to Figure 15.3).

Treatment of Orgasmic Disorders

Because orgasmic disorders among men are relatively rare, our response will focus mainly on women. Women who have never experienced orgasm often harbor negative sexual attitudes that cause anxiety and inhibit sexual response. Treatment in such cases may first address these attitudes.

Figure 15.4 The Training Position for Nondemanding Stimulation of the Female Genitals. *This position gives the man access to his partner's breasts and genitals. She can guide his hands to show him the types of stimulation she enjoys.*

Masters and Johnson use a couples-oriented approach in treating anorgasmic women. They begin with sensate focus exercises. Then, during genital massage and later, during coitus, the woman guides her partner in the caresses and movements that she finds sexually exciting. Taking charge helps free the woman from the traditional role of the passive, subordinate female.

Masters and Johnson, recommend a training position (Figure 15.4) that gives a partner access to his or her partner's breasts and genitals. She can guide her partner's hands to show the types of stimulation she enjoys. The genital play is *nondemanding*. The goals are to learn to provide and enjoy effective sexual stimulation, not to reach orgasm. The clitoris is not stimulated early, because doing so may produce a high level of stimulation, even pain, before the woman is prepared.

After a number of occasions of genital play, the heterosexual couple undertake coitus in the female–superior position (Figure 15.5). This position allows the woman freedom of movement and control over her genital sensations. The couple engage in several sessions of deliberately slow thrusting to sensitize the woman to sensations produced by the penis and to break the common counterproductive pattern of desperate, rapid thrusting.

Orgasm cannot be willed or forced. When a woman receives effective stimulation, feels free to focus on erotic sensations, and feels that nothing is being demanded of her, she will generally reach orgasm. After the woman is able to attain orgasm in the female-superior position, the couple may extend their sexual repertoire to other positions.

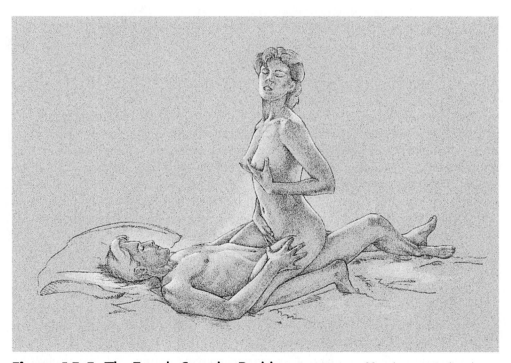

Figure 15.5 The Female-Superior Position. *In treatment of female orgasmic disorder, the couple undertake coitus in the female-superior position after a number of occasions of genital play. This position allows the woman freedom of movement and control over her genital sensations. She is told to regard the penis as her "toy." The couple engages in several sessions of deliberately slow thrusting to sensitize the woman to sensations produced by the penis and to break the common counterproductive pattern of desperate, rapid thrusting.*

A Closer Look

THE SEARCH FOR THE FEMALE EQUIVALENT OF VIAGRA

By Natalie Angier, The New York Times

Even in the most sexually liberated and self-satisfied of nations, many people still yearn to burn more, to feel ready for bedding no matter what the clock says and to desire their partner of 23 years as much as they did when their love was brand new.

The market is saturated with books on how to revive a flagging libido or spice up monotonous sex, and sex therapists say "lack of desire" is one of the most common complaints they hear from patients, particularly women.

And though there may be legitimate sociological or personal underpinnings to that diminished desire—chronic overwork and stress, a hostile workplace, a slovenly or unsupportive spouse—still the age-old search continues for a simple chemical fix, Cupid encapsulated, a thrill in a pill.

Since the spectacular success of Viagra and similar drugs, the pharmaceutical industry has been searching for the female equivalent of Viagra—a treatment that would do for women's most common sexual complaint, lack of desire, what sildenafil did for men's, erectile dysfunction.

Initial trials of Viagra in women proved highly disappointing. True, the drug enhanced engorgement of vaginal tissue, just as it had of the penis, but that extra bit of pelvic swelling did nothing to amplify women's desire for or enjoyment of sex.

What is needed for the treatment of so-called female hypoactive sexual desire disorder, researchers decided, is a reasonably safe and effective drug that acts on the central nervous system, on the pleasure centers of the brain or the sensory circuitry that serves them.

For a while, many sex therapists and doctors were optimistic about Procter & Gamble's Intrinsa, a testosterone patch that delivers small transdermal pulses of the sex hormone thought to play a crucial if poorly understood role in male and female libido alike. But in 2005, the Food and Drug Administration refused to approve

Masters and Johnson prefer working with the couple in cases of anorgasmia, but other sex therapists prefer to work with the woman individually through masturbation. **Truth or Fiction Revisited:** Many sex therapists do recommend masturbation as a treatment for women who have never been able to reach orgasm (Leiblum & Rosen, 2000). Masturbation allows people to get in touch with their sexual responses at their own pace. The sexual pleasure they experience helps counter lingering sexual anxieties. Although there is some variation among therapists, the following elements are commonly found in directed masturbation programs:

1. *Education.* The woman and her partner (if she has one) are educated about female sexuality.
2. *Self-exploration.* Self-exploration is encouraged as a way of increasing the woman's sense of body awareness. She may hold a mirror between her legs to locate her sexual anatomic features.
3. *Self-massage.* The woman creates a private, relaxing setting for self-massage. She begins to explore the sensitivity of her body to touch, discovering and repeating the caresses she finds pleasurable. Nonalcohol-based oils and lotions may be used to enhance the sensuous quality of the massage and to provide lubrication for the external genitalia. To prevent performance anxiety, the woman does not attempt to reach orgasm during the first few occasions.

Intrinsa, declaring that its medical risks outweighed whatever modest and spotty benefits it might offer.

More recently, another potentially promising treatment for hypoactive desire has been making its way through clinical trials. The compound, called bremelanotide, is a synthetic version of a hormone involved in skin pigmentation, and it was initially developed by Palatin Technologies of New Jersey as a potential tanning agent to help prevent skin cancer. But when male college students participating in early safety tests began reporting that the drug sometimes gave them erections, the company began exploring bremelanotide's utility as a treatment for sexual disorders.

Studies in rodents demonstrated that the drug not only gave male rats spontaneous erections, but also fomented sexual excitement in female rats, prompting them to wiggle their ears, hop excitedly, rub noses with males and otherwise display unmistakable hallmarks of rodent arousal.

Importantly, the females responded to the drug only under laboratory conditions where they could maintain a sense of control over the mating game. Take away the female's opportunity to escape or proceed at her preferred pace, and no amount of bremelanotide would get those ears to wiggle. In other words, Annette M. Shadiack, director of biological research of Palatin, said, "this doesn't look like a potential date-rape drug."

Inspired by the rodent work, the company decided to give the drug a whirl on women. Results from a pilot study of 26 postmenopausal women with diagnoses of sexual arousal disorder suggest that bremelanotide may well have some mild aphrodisiacal properties.

Responding to questionnaires after taking either the drug or a dummy pill, 73 percent of the women on bremelanotide reported feeling genitally aroused, compared with 23 percent given the placebo; and 43 percent of the bremelanotide group said the treatment augmented their sexual desire, against

only 19 percent of those on dummy pills.

Women in the treatment group also were slightly more likely to have sex with their partners during the course of the trial than were those in the control group, although who initiated the romps was not specified.

Larger trials of the drug at some 20 clinical centers around the United States are now under way. Among other things, the researchers will try adjusting the dosage to see if more bremelanotide may provoke a more robust response with a minimum of unpleasant or embarrassing side effects.

For example, researchers are as yet unsure whether sustained use of bremelanotide will end up doing what the drug was meant to do in the first place, and bestow on its beaming clients a truly healthy tan.

SOURCE: From "The Search for the Female Equivalent of Viagra" by Natalie Angier, *The New York Times*, April 10, 2007. Copyright © 2007 by The New York Times Co. Reprinted by permission.

4. *Giving oneself permission.* The woman may be advised to challenge lingering guilt and anxiety about sex. For example, she might repeat to herself, "This is my body. I have a right to learn about my body and receive pleasure from it."

5. *Use of fantasy.* Arousal is heightened through the use of sexual images, fantasies, and fantasy aids, such as erotic written or visual materials.

6. *Use of a vibrator.* A vibrator may provide more intense stimulation.

7. *Involvement of the partner.* After the woman is capable of regularly achieving orgasm through masturbation, the focus may shift to her sexual relationship with her partner. Nondemanding sensate focus exercises may be followed by nondemanding coitus. The female-superior position is often used so that the woman can control the depth, angle, and rate of thrusting. She thus ensures that she receives the kinds of stimulation she needs to reach orgasm.

Our focus has been on sexual techniques, but it is worth noting that a combination of approaches that focus on sexual techniques and underlying interpersonal problems may be more effective than focusing on sexual techniques alone, at least for couples whose relationships are troubled (Firestone et al., 2006a).

MALE ORGASMIC DISORDER Treatment of male orgasmic disorder generally focuses on increasing sexual stimulation and reducing performance anxiety

(Leiblum & Rosen, 2000). Masters and Johnson instruct the couple to practice sensate focus exercises for several days, during which the man makes no attempt to ejaculate. The couple is then instructed to bring the man to orgasm in any way they can, usually manually. After the man can ejaculate in his partner's presence, she brings him to the point at which he is about to ejaculate. Then, in the female-superior position, she inserts the penis and thrusts vigorously to bring him to orgasm.

PREMATURE EJACULATION   In the Masters-and-Johnson approach, sensate focus exercises are followed by practice in the training position shown in Figure 15.1. The woman teases her partner to erection and uses the **squeeze technique** when he indicates that he is about to ejaculate. She squeezes the tip of the penis, which temporarily prevents ejaculation. This process is repeated three or four times in a 15- to 20-minute session before the man purposely ejaculates.

Truth or Fiction Revisited: It is true that a man can be prevented from ejaculating by squeezing his penis when he feels that he is about to ejaculate. In using the squeeze technique, the partner holds the penis between the thumb and first two fingers of the same hand. The thumb presses against the frenulum. The fingers straddle the coronal ridge on the other side of the penis. Squeezing the thumb and forefingers together fairly hard for about 20 seconds (or until the man's urge to ejaculate passes) prevents ejaculation. The erect penis can withstand fairly strong pressure without discomfort, but erection may be partially lost.

After two or three days of these sessions, Masters and Johnson have the couple begin coitus in the female-superior position because it creates less pressure to ejaculate. The woman inserts the penis. At first she contains it without thrusting, allowing the man to get used to intravaginal sensations. If he signals that he is about to ejaculate, she lifts off and squeezes the penis. After some repetitions, she begins slowly to move backward and forward, lifting off and squeezing as needed. The man learns gradually to tolerate higher levels of sexual stimulation without ejaculating.

The "stop–start" method for treating premature ejaculation was introduced by urologist James Semans (1956). The method can be applied to manual stimulation or coitus. For example, the man's partner can manually stimulate him until he is about to ejaculate. He then signals her/him to suspend sexual stimulation and allows his arousal to subside before stimulation is resumed. This process enables the man to recognize the cues that precede his point of ejaculatory inevitability, or "point of no return," and to tolerate longer periods of sexual stimulation. When the stop–start technique is applied to coitus, the couple begins with simple vaginal containment with no pelvic thrusting, preferably in the female-superior position. The man withdraws if he feels he is about to ejaculate. As the man's sense of control increases, thrusting can begin, along with variations in coital positions. The couple again stop when the man signals that he is approaching ejaculatory inevitability.

BIOLOGICAL TREATMENT OF PREMATURE EJACULATION   Some drugs that are usually used to treat psychological problems have been helpful in treating premature ejaculation (Bancroft et al., 2005b, c). Clomipramine, which is used to treat people with obsessive–compulsive disorder or schizophrenia, can impair erectile response at high doses. But in a study with 15 couples, low doses helped men engage in coitus five times longer than usual without ejaculating (Althof, 1994). Antidepressant drugs have also been helpful in the treatment of premature ejaculation (Meston & Frohlich, 2000; Waldinger et al., 2001, 2002).

Why do drugs used to treat psychological problems help with premature ejaculation? The psychological problems are frequently connected with imbalances in

TRUTH **fiction 7**

Squeeze technique A method for treating premature ejaculation whereby the tip of the penis is squeezed temporarily to prevent ejaculation

body chemistry, such as neurotransmitters—the chemical messengers of the brain. Neurotransmitters are also involved in other bodily functions, including ejaculation. "Antidepressant" drugs all work by increasing the action of the neurotransmitter serotonin. Serotonin inhibits the ejaculatory reflex (Meston & Frohlich, 2000; Shipko, 2000). (But note the cautions about using SSRIs expressed earlier in the chapter!)

Treatment of Sexual Pain Disorders

There are two major sexual pain disorders: dyspareunia and vaginismus. Both of these disorders are described in the following subsections.

DYSPAREUNIA   Dyspareunia, or painful intercourse, generally calls for medical intervention to ascertain and treat any underlying physical problems, such as urinary tract infections, that might give rise to pain (Brown & Haaser, 2005; Goldstein & Alexander, 2005). When dyspareunia is caused by vaginismus, treatment of vaginismus through a cognitive–behavioral approach, described next, may reduce pain.

VAGINISMUS   Vaginismus is generally treated with the insertion of plastic vaginal dilators of increasing size to help relax vaginal muscles. A gynecologist may first demonstrate insertion of the narrowest dilator. Later the woman practices insertion of wider dilators at home. The woman increases the size of the dilator as she becomes capable of tolerating insertion and containment (for 10 or 15 minutes) without discomfort or pain (Crowley et al., 2006). The woman's or her partner's fingers (first the littlest finger, then two fingers, and so on) may be used in place of the plastic dilators, with the woman controlling the speed and depth of penetration (Crowley et al., 2006). When the woman is able to tolerate dilators (or fingers) equivalent in thickness to the penis, the couple may try coitus, but the woman should control insertion. Circumstances should be relaxed and nondemanding. The idea is to avoid resensitizing her to fears of penetration. Because vaginismus often occurs among women with a history of sexual trauma, such as rape or incest, treatment for the psychological effects of these experiences may also be in order (Crowley et al., 2006).

CRITICAL Thinking

One researcher writes that the treatment of sexual dysfunctions is becoming "medicalized." What does that mean? Do you agree or disagree? Explain.

1. What kinds of sexual dysfunctions are there?

- Sexual dysfunctions are persistent or recurrent difficulties in becoming sexually aroused or reaching orgasm. They appear to be somewhat more common among women than men. Men are more likely to experience rapid orgasm, and women are more likely to experience lack of desire, difficulty reaching orgasm, and painful sex.

- In sexual desire disorders, the person experiences a lack of sexual desire or an aversion to genital sexual contact.

- In men, sexual arousal disorders involve recurrent difficulty in achieving or sustaining erections sufficient to engage in sexual intercourse successfully. In women, they typically involve failure to become sufficiently lubricated.

- Orgasmic disorders involve difficulty reaching orgasm or reaching orgasm too soon. Women are more likely to have difficulty reaching orgasm.

- Sexual pain disorders include dyspareunia, or painful sex, and vaginismus, which is characterized by involuntary contraction of vaginal muscles, making penetration painful.

2. What are the causes of sexual dysfunctions?

- Fatigue may lead to erectile disorder in men, and to orgasmic disorder and dyspareunia in women. Dyspareunia may reflect vaginal infections and STIs. Biological factors are believed to be involved in more than half the cases of erectile disorder. Medications for various health problems may impair sexual functioning. Aging can also impair sexual functioning.

- Psychosocial factors connected with sexual dysfunctions include cultural influences, psychosexual trauma, problems in the relationship, lack of sexual skills, irrational beliefs, and performance anxiety. Children reared in sexually repressive environments may learn to respond to sex with feelings of anxiety and shame rather than pleasure. Some people do not acquire sexual competencies because of lack of opportunity to acquire knowledge and experience. Excessive need for approval and perfection can contribute to sexual problems. Performance anxiety may place dysfunctional partners in a spectator role rather than a performer role.

3. How are sexual dysfunctions treated?

- Sex therapy directly modifies dysfunctional behavior by changing self-defeating beliefs and attitudes, fostering sexual skills and knowledge, enhancing sexual communication, and providing exercises that enhance sexual stimulation while reducing performance anxiety.

- Masters and Johnson pioneered the direct approach to treating sexual dysfunctions. They used a male-and-female therapy team during an in-residence program that focused on the couple as the unit of treatment. Sensate focus exercises were used to enable the partners to give each other pleasure in a nondemanding situation and then allow sexual response to proceed "naturally." Other therapists combine sex therapy with couples therapy or, in the case of Helen Singer Kaplan, psychoanalytic therapy.

- Some sex therapists kindle the sexual appetites of people lacking sexual desire through prescribing self-stimulation exercises combined with erotic fantasies. Androgens also heighten the sex drive in people with androgen deficiencies.

- Men and women with impaired sexual arousal receive sexual stimulation from their partners under relaxed circumstances, so that anxiety does not inhibit their natural reflexes. Noninvasive biological treatments are available for both men and women. They facilitate blood flow to the genitals or affect levels of neurotransmitters.

- Masters and Johnson used a couples approach in treating anorgasmic women. Other therapists prefer directed masturbation to enable women to learn about their own body at their own pace and to free them of the need to rely on partners. Premature ejaculation is usually treated with the squeeze or stop–start methods. Biological treatment methods for female orgasmic disorder and premature ejaculation are under development.

- Dyspareunia, or painful intercourse, may be treated by tackling health problems, ensuring that the female is adequately lubricated, or, among older women, using estrogen replacement. Vaginismus is generally treated with a series of dilators.

1. According to the NHSHS, the most common male sexual dysfunction is
   (a) male orgasmic disorder
   (b) erectile disorder
   (c) premature ejaculation
   (d) performance anxiety

2. Which of the following is most likely to have biological causes?
   (a) dyspareunia
   (b) vaginismus
   (c) female orgasmic disorder
   (d) performance anxiety

3. According to the NHSLS, the most common female sexual dysfunction is
   (a) dyspareunia
   (b) lack of interest in sex
   (c) reaching climax too early
   (d) having trouble lubricating

4. Masters and Johnson used all of the following treatment methods except
   (a) sensate focus exercises
   (b) a male-and-female therapy team
   (c) a two-week residential program
   (d) guided masturbation

5. _____ is most likely to be connected with a history of sexual trauma.
   (a) Dyspareunia
   (b) Rapid ejaculation
   (c) Performance anxiety
   (d) Vaginismus

6. Alprostadil is used in the treatment of
   (a) premature ejaculation
   (b) male erectile disorder
   (c) female orgasmic disorder
   (d) hypoactive sexual desire

7. According to the text, a low level of _____ can lessen sexual desire.
   (a) testosterone
   (b) sildenafil
   (c) Depo-Provera
   (d) alprostadil

8. _____ deal(s) with unconscious conflicts that might impair response to sex therapy.
   (a) Barry McCarthy
   (b) Masters and Johnson
   (c) Irwin Goldstein
   (d) Helen Singer Kaplan

9. All of the following are sex therapy methods, with the exception of
   (a) penile implants
   (b) improving sexual communication
   (c) reducing performance anxiety
   (d) sensate focus exercises

10. _____ does *not* contribute to male erectile disorder.
    (a) Antidepressant medication
    (b) Blood pressure medication
    (c) Alprostadil
    (d) Clomipramine

11. _____ is sometimes treated with a series of plastic dilators.
    (a) Dyspareunia
    (b) Female sexual arousal disorder
    (c) Vaginismus
    (d) Erectile disorder

12. Irwin Goldstein found that about _____% of men age 40 to 70 in a Massachusetts survey reported at least intermittent problems in obtaining and maintaining erections.
    (a) 10%
    (b) 25%
    (c) 35%
    (d) 50%

13. Cialis is used to treat
    (a) erectile disorder
    (b) female sexual arousal disorder
    (c) dyspareunia
    (d) premature ejaculation

14. Selective serotonin reuptake inhibitors have been used to treat
    (a) erectile disorder
    (b) female sexual arousal disorder
    (c) dyspareunia
    (d) premature ejaculation

15. Sex therapists are most likely to recommend masturbation as a treatment for
    (a) premature ejaculation
    (b) female orgasmic disorder
    (c) vaginismus
    (d) retarded ejaculation

Answers 1. c; 2. a; 3. b; 4. d; 5. d; 6. b; 7. a; 8. d; 9. a; 10. c; 11. c; 12. d; 13. a; 14. d; 15. b

16

Sexually Transmitted Infections

TRUTH? fiction

Which of the following statements are true, and which are fiction? Look for the Truth/Fiction icons on the pages that follow to find the answers.

1 Most women who contract gonorrhea do not develop symptoms.   T F

2 Christopher Columbus brought more than beads, blankets, and tobacco back to Europe from the New World. He also brought syphilis.   T F

3 Gonorrhea and syphilis can be contracted from toilet seats in public rest-rooms.   T F

4 If a syphilitic sore goes away by itself, the infection does not require medical treatment.   T F

5 Men can develop vaginal infections.   T F

6 As you are reading this page, you are engaged in search-and-destroy missions against foreign agents within your body.   T F

7 Most people who are infected by HIV remain symptom free and appear healthy for years.   T F

8 Genital herpes can be transmitted only during flare-ups of the infection.   T F

9 Pubic lice belong to the biological crab family.   T F

Harold and Carin, both 20, have been dating for several months. They feel a strong sexual attraction toward each other but have hesitated to become sexually intimate because of fears about AIDS. Harold believes that using condoms is no guarantee against infection and wants the two of them to be tested for HIV, the virus that causes AIDS. Carin has resisted undergoing an HIV test, partly because she feels insulted that Harold fears that she may be infected, and frankly, partly in fear of the test results. She has heard that symptoms may not develop for years after infection. She wonders whether she might have been infected by one of the men with whom she slept in the past.

Keisha has genital herpes. A 19-year-old prelaw student, she has had no recurrences since the initial outbreak two years earlier, but she knows that herpes is a lifelong infection and may recur periodically from time to time. She also knows that she may inadvertently pass the herpes virus along to her sex partners, even to the man she eventually marries. She has begun thinking seriously about Steve, a man she has been dating for the past month. She would like to tell him that she has herpes before they become sexually intimate, yet she fears that telling him might scare him off.

José, 21, a math and computer science major, is planning a career in computer operations, hoping

one day to run the computer systems for a large corporation. He lives off-campus with several of his buddies in a run-down house they've dubbed the "Nuclear Dumpsite." He has been dating Maria, a theater major, for several months. They have begun having sexual relations and have practiced "safer sex"—at least most of the time. During the past week he noticed a burning sensation while urinating. It seems to have passed now, so he figures that it was probably nothing to worry about. But he's not sure and wonders whether he should see a doctor.

Harold, Carin, Keisha, and José express some of the fears and concerns of a generation of young people who are becoming sexually active at a time when the threat of human immunodeficiency virus (HIV)/acquired immune deficiency syndrome (AIDS) and other **sexually transmitted infections (STIs)** hangs over every sexual decision.

Sexually transmitted infections (STIs) Infections that are communicated through sexual contact, although some can also be transmitted in other ways

An Epidemic

STIs are rampant. HIV/AIDS is indeed a scary thing. But HIV/AIDS is only one of many STIs, and other STIs actually pose wider threats. There are about 40,000 new cases of HIV/AIDS in the United States each year, compared with more than seven million new cases of trichomoniasis and nearly three million cases of chlamydia

(CDC, 2006). *Human papilloma virus* (or HPV), the organism that causes genital warts, is estimated to be present in at least 20% of Americans older than the age of 12, and in more than 50% of some populations of college women (Guttmacher, 2006).

College students have become reasonably well versed about HIV/AIDS. However, many are unaware that chlamydia can go undetected for years. Moreover, if it is left untreated, it can cause pelvic inflammation and infertility. Most college students appear to be ignorant about HPV and its links to genital warts and cervical cancer (www.guttmacher.org, 2006). Yet the CDC estimates that as many as one million new cases of HPV infection occur each year in the United States—more than syphilis, genital herpes, and HIV/AIDS combined. Although nearly one million Americans are thought to be infected with HIV, an estimated 50 to 60 million are infected with other STI-causing viruses, such as those causing genital warts, herpes, and hepatitis.

STIs are transmitted through sexual means, such as vaginal or anal intercourse or oral sex. They were formerly called *sexually transmitted diseases,* and before that *venereal diseases*—after Venus, the Roman goddess of love.

Some STIs can be spread through nonsexual contact as well. For example, HIV/AIDS and viral hepatitis may be spread by sharing contaminated hypodermic syringes such as those used by people "shooting up" drugs. And a few STIs (such as "crabs") may be picked up from bedding or other objects, such as moist towels, that harbor the infectious organisms that cause these STIs.

The World Health Organization (WHO) estimates that at least 333 million people around the world are stricken with curable STIs each year (UNAIDS, 2006). The United States is believed to have the highest rate of infection by STIs in the industrialized world. In a recent year, for example, 150 cases of gonorrhea were reported per 100,000 people in the United States compared with 18.6 per 100,000 in Canada and three per 100,000 in Sweden.

In the United States, 10 to 15 million new cases of STIs are reported to the CDC each year, including 2.5 million adolescents (about one in six). At least one in four

Who Is at Risk? *Evidence suggests that young people are more sexually active than ever before. Thus, it is as important as ever that they be aware of the risks involved and take responsibility for their sexual health.*

A Closer Look

TALKING WITH YOUR PARTNER ABOUT STIs

Many people find it hard to talk about STIs with their partners. As one young woman explained:

It's one thing to talk about being responsible . . . and a much harder thing to do it at the very moment. It's just plain hard to say to someone I am feeling very erotic with, "Oh, yes, before we go any further, can we have a conversation about STI?" It's hard to imagine murmuring into someone's ear at a time of passion, "Would you mind slipping on this condom or using this cream just in case one of us has [an STI]?" Yet it seems awkward to bring it up any sooner if it's not clear between us that we want to make love. (Boston Women's Health Book Collective, 2005)

Because talking about STIs with sex partners can be awkward, many people wing it (Montano et al., 2001). They assume that their partners are free of STIs and hope for the best. Some people act as if not talking about HIV/AIDS and other STIs will cause them to go away. But the microbes that cause AIDS, herpes, chlamydia, genital warts, and other STIs will not simply go away by ignoring them.

Imagine yourself in this situation: You've gone out with Chris a few times and you're keenly attracted. Chris is attractive, bright, witty, shares some of your attitudes, and, all in all, is a powerful turn-on. Now the evening is winding down. You've been cuddling, and you think you know where things are heading.

Something clicks in your mind! You realize that as wonderful as Chris is, you don't know every place Chris has "been." As healthy as Chris looks and acts, you don't know what's swimming around in Chris' bloodstream. Chris may not know either. In a moment of pent-up desire, Chris may also (how should we put this delicately?) lie about not being infected or about past sexual experiences.

What do you say now? How do you protect yourself without turning Chris off? Ah, the clumsiness! If you ask about condoms or STIs, it is sort of making a verbal commitment to have sexual relations, and perhaps you're not exactly sure that's what your partner intends. Even if it's clear that's where you're heading, will you seem too straightforward? Will you kill the romance? The spontaneity of the moment? Sure you might—life has its risks. But which is riskier: an awkward moment or being infected with a fatal illness? Let's put it another way: Are you *really* willing to die for sex? Given that few responses are perfect, here are some things you can try:

1. You might say something like this: "I've brought something and I'd like to use it . . ." (referring to a condom).

2. Or you can say, "I know this is a bit clumsy," [you are assertively expressing a feeling and asking permission to pursue a clumsy topic; Chris is likely to respond with "That's okay," or "Don't worry; what is it?"] "but the world isn't as safe as it used to be and I think we should talk about what we're going to do."

Your partner hasn't been living in a cave. Your partner is also aware of the dangers of STIs and ought to be working with you to make things safe and unpressured. If your partner is pressing for unsafe sex and is inconsiderate of your feelings and concerns, you need to reassess whether you want to be with this person. Perhaps you can do better.

REFLECT

What problems would you expect to encounter when discussing STIs with a partner? How could you handle them?

Americans is likely to contract an STI at some time. Two cases in three occur in people younger than the age of 25.

Some readers have STIs and do not realize it. But ignorance is not bliss. Some STIs may not produce noticeable symptoms, but they can be harmful if left untreated. STIs can also be painful and—in the case of HIV/AIDS, advanced syphilis, and the cervical cancer that can follow infection with HPV—lethal. Hundreds of thousands of women become infertile each year because of STIs that are spreading through their reproductive system. Overall, STIs are believed to account for 15% to 30% of cases of infertility among women. In addition to their biological effects, STIs exact an emotional toll and strain relationships to the breaking point.

Why the surge in the incidence of STIs? One is the increased numbers of young people who have sex. Many of them fail to use latex condoms consistently, if at all (www.guttmacher.org, 2006). Some people do not use condoms because the woman is on the pill. Although birth control pills are reliable methods of contraception, they do not prevent STIs. Another reason is that some infections, like chlamydia, may have no symptoms. Therefore, some infected individuals unwittingly pass them on to others. Other risk factors include early sexual involvement and sex with multiple partners. Drug use is also associated with an increased risk of STIs (Abbey et al., 2006; Appel et al., 2006; Bernstein et al., 2006). People who abuse drugs are more likely than others to engage in risky sexual practices. Moreover, certain forms of drug use, such as needle sharing, can directly transmit infectious organisms like HIV. Another risk factor, ironically, is the success of new drugs in treating HIV/AIDS. As a result, many individuals who had become more cautious in their sexual behavior have once again thrown caution to the wind (Crepaz et al., 2004; Dilley et al., 2003).

Education is critical to curtailing the epidemic among young people (Collins et al., 2006; Shoveller et al., 2006). The goals are to promote responsible sexual decision making and to alter risky behavior. However, education may not be enough. Young people must also want to practice prevention and risk reduction strategies if education is to change their behavior (Benotsch & Kalichman, 2002; Shoveller et al., 2006).

CRITICAL Thinking

Why do you think the United States has the largest incidence of STIs in the industrialized world?

Bacterial Infections

Bacteria are one-celled microorganisms, some of which are essential to human life and some of which are harmful. Bacteria play vital roles in our body's digestive systems. Bacteria are essential to fermentation. Without bacteria, there would be no wine. Unfortunately, bacteria also cause many diseases such as pneumonia, tuberculosis, and meningitis—along with the common STIs gonorrhea, syphilis, and chlamydia.

Gonorrhea

Gonorrhea, also known as "the clap" or "the drip," was once the most widespread bacterial STI in the United States, but it has been replaced by chlamydia. The rate of infection declined substantially from the mid 1980s through the mid 1990s, apparently because of safer sexual practices. However, the rate surged by about 9% in the late 1990s, possibly because of the advances in the treatment of HIV/AIDS. As HIV/AIDS becomes less frightening, people may engage in more spontaneous sexual behavior and increase the rate of STIs. About 800,000 to 900,000 new cases of gonorrhea are now reported each year. Most new cases are contracted by people between the age of 20 and 24.

Gonorrhea is caused by the gonococcus bacterium (Table 16.1). A penile discharge that was probably gonorrhea is described in ancient Egyptian and Chinese writings, and is mentioned in the Old Testament (*Leviticus* 15). Ancient Jews and Greeks assumed that the discharge was an involuntary loss of seminal fluid. In about 400 BCE, the Greek physician Hippocrates suggested that the loss stemmed from excessive sex or "worship" of Aphrodite (whom the Romans would later rename *Venus*). The term *gonorrhea* is credited to the Greek physician Galen, who lived during the second century CE. Albert L. S. Neisser identified the gonococcus bacterium that bears his name in 1879: *Neisseria gonorrhoeae*.

Bacteria Plural of *bacterium;* a class of one-celled microorganisms that have no chlorophyll and can give rise to many illnesses

Gonorrhea An STI caused by the bacterium *Neisseria gonorrhoeae* and characterized by a discharge and burning during urination; left untreated, gonorrhea can give rise to PID and infertility

STI Attitude Scale

Do your attitudes toward STIs lead you to take risks that increase the chances of contracting one? The STI Attitude Scale (Yarber et al., 1989) was constructed to measure the attitudes of young adults toward STIs and provide insight into these questions.

DIRECTIONS To complete the self-assessment, read each statement carefully. Record your reactions by circling the letters according to this code:

SA = Strongly Agree
A = Agree
U = Undecided
D = Disagree
SD = Strongly Disagree

Interpret your responses by referring to the scoring key in the appendix.

1. How one uses her or his sexuality has nothing to do with STIs.   SA A U D SD

2. It is easy to use the prevention methods that reduce one's chances of getting an STI.   SA A U D SD

3. Responsible sex is one of the best ways of reducing the risk of STIs.   SA A U D SD

4. Getting early medical care is the main key to preventing harmful effects of STIs.   SA A U D SD

5. Choosing the right sex partner is important in reducing the risk of getting an STI.   SA A U D SD

6. A high rate of STIs should be a concern for all people.   SA A U D SD

7. People with an STI have a duty to get their sex partners to medical care.   SA A U D SD

8. The best way to get a sex partner to STI treatment is to take him or her to the doctor with you.   SA A U D SD

9. Changing one's sex habits is necessary once the presence of an STI is known.   SA A U D SD

10. I would dislike having to follow the medical steps for treating an STI.   SA A U D SD

11. If I were sexually active, I would feel uneasy doing things before and after sex to prevent getting an STI.   SA A U D SD

12. If I were sexually active, it would be insulting if a sex partner suggested we use a condom to avoid an STI.   SA A U D SD

13. I dislike talking about STIs with my peers.   SA A U D SD

14. I would be uncertain about going to the doctor unless I was sure I really had an STI.   SA A U D SD

15. I would feel that I should take my sex partner with me to a clinic if I thought I had an STI.   SA A U D SD

16. It would be embarrassing to discuss STIs with one's partner if one were sexually active.   SA A U D SD

17. If I were to have sex, the chance of getting an STI makes me uneasy about having sex with more than one person.   SA A U D SD

18. I like the idea of sexual abstinence (not having sex) as the best way of avoiding STIs.   SA A U D SD

19. If I had an STI, I would cooperate with public health persons to find the sources of the STI.   SA A U D SD

20. If I had an STI, I would avoid exposing others while I was being treated.   SA A U D SD

21. I would have regular STI checkups if I were having sex with more than one partner.   SA A U D SD

22. I intend to look for STI signs before deciding to have sex with anyone.   SA A U D SD

23. I will limit my sex activity to just one partner because of the chances I might get an STI.   SA A U D SD

24. I will avoid sexual contact any time I think there is even a slight chance of getting an STI.   SA A U D SD

25. The chance of getting an STI would not stop me from having sex.   SA A U D SD

26. If I had a chance, I would support community efforts toward controlling STIs.   SA A U D SD

27. I would be willing to work with others to make people aware of STI problems in my town.   SA A U D SD

SOURCE: From "Development of a three-component sexually transmitted disease scale", W. L. Yarber, et al., *Journal of Sex Education & Therapy*, 1989, 15, 36–49. Reprinted by permission of William L. Yarber.

TABLE 16.1

Causes, Modes of Transmission, Symptoms, Diagnosis, and Treatment of Major STIs

STI and Pathogen	Modes of Transmission	Symptoms	Diagnosis	Treatment
Bacterial Diseases				
Gonorrhea ("clap," "drip"): Gonococcus bacterium (*Neisseria gonorrhoeae*)	Transmitted by vaginal, oral, or anal sexual activity, or from mother to newborn during delivery	In men, yellowish, thick penile discharge, burning urination In women, increased vaginal discharge, burning urination, irregular menstrual bleeding (most women show no early symptoms)	Clinical inspection, culture of sample discharge	Antibiotics: ceftriaxone, ceftriaxone, ciprofloaxin, cefixime, ofloxacin
Syphilis: *Treponema pallidum*	Transmitted by vaginal, oral, or anal sexual activity, or by touching an infectious chancre	In primary stage, a hard, round painless chancre or sore appears at site of infection within two to four weeks; may progress through secondary, latent, and tertiary stages if left untreated	Primary-stage syphilis is diagnosed by clinical examination and by examination of fluid from a chancre in a dark-field test; secondary-stage syphilis is diagnosed by blood test (the VDRL)	Penicillin, or doxycycline, tetracycline, or erythromycin for nonpregnant penicillin-allergic patients
Chlamydia and nongonococcal urethritis (NGU): *Chlamydia trachomatous* bacterium; NGU in men may also be caused by *Ureaplasma urealycticum* bacterium and other pathogens	Transmitted by vaginal, oral, or anal sexual activity; to the eye by touching one's eyes after touching the genitals of an infected partner, or to newborns passing through the birth canal of an infected mother	In women, frequent and painful urination, lower abdominal pain and inflammation, and vaginal discharge (but most women are symptom free) In men, symptoms are similar to but milder than those of gonorrhea: burning or painful urination, slight penile discharge (most men are also symptom free) Sore throat may indicate infection from oral–genital contact	The Abbott Testpack analyzes a cervical smear in women; in men, an extract of fluid from the penis is analyzed	Antibiotics: azithromycin, doxycycline, ofloxacin, amoxicillin
Vaginal Infections				
Bacterial vaginosis: *Gardnerella vaginalis* bacterium and others	Can arise by overgrowth of organisms in vagina, allergic reactions, etc.; also transmitted by sexual contact	In women, thin, foul-smelling vaginal discharge; irritation of genitals and mild pain during urination	Culture and examination of bacterium	Metronidazole, clindamycin

(Continued)

TABLE 16.1

(Continued)

STI and Pathogen	Modes of Transmission	Symptoms	Diagnosis	Treatment
		In men, inflammation of penile foreskin and glans, urethritis, and cystitis.		
		May be symptom-free in both sexes		
Candidiasis (moniliasis, thrush, "yeast infection"): *Candida albicans*—a yeastlike fungus	Can arise by overgrowth of fungus in vagina; may also be transmitted by sexual contact or by sharing a washcloth with an infected person	In women, vulval itching; white, cheesy, foul-smelling discharge; soreness or swelling of vaginal and vulval tissues	Diagnosis usually made on basis of symptoms	Single-dose oral fluconazole, or suppositories of miconazole, clotrimazole, or butaconazole; modification of use of other medicines and chemical agents; keep infected area dry
		In men, itching and burning on urination, or a reddening of the penis		
Trichomoniasis ("trich"): *Trichomonas vaginalis*—a protozoan (one-celled animal)	Almost always transmitted sexually	In women, foamy, yellowish, odorous vaginal discharge; itching or burning sensation in vulva; many women are symptom free	Microscopic examination of a smear of vaginal secretions or of culture of the sample (latter method preferred)	Metronidazole
		In men, usually symptom free, but mild urethritis is possible		

Viral Infections

STI and Pathogen	Modes of Transmission	Symptoms	Diagnosis	Treatment
Oral herpes: *herpes simplex virus type 1 (or HSV-1)*	Touching, kissing, sexual contact with sores or blisters; sharing cups, towels, toilet seats	Cold sores or fever blisters on the lips, mouth, or throat; herpetic sores on the genitals	Usually, clinical inspection	OTC lip balms, cold sore medications; check with your physician, however
Genital herpes: *herpes simplex virus type 2 (or HSV-2)*	Almost always by means of vaginal, oral, or anal sexual activity; most contagious during active outbreaks of the disease	Painful, reddish bumps around the genitals, thigh, or buttocks; in women, may also be in the vagina or on the cervix; bumps become blisters or sores that fill with pus and break, shedding viral particles; other possible symptoms:	Clinical inspection of sores; culture and examination of fluid drawn from the base of a genital sore	No cure, but the antiviral drugs acyclovir, famciclovir, and valacyclovir may provide relief and prompt healing; people with herpes often profit from counseling and group support

TABLE 16.1

(Continued)

STI and Pathogen	Modes of Transmission	Symptoms	Diagnosis	Treatment
		burning urination, fever, aches and pains, swollen glands; in women, vaginal discharge		
Viral hepatitis: hepatitis A, B, C, and D type viruses	Sexual contact, especially involving the anus (especially hepatitis A); contact with infected fecal matter; transfusion of contaminated blood (especially hepatitis B and C)	Ranges from being symptom free to mild flulike symptoms and more severe symptoms, including fever, abdominal pain, vomiting, and "jaundiced" (yellowish) skin and eyes	Examination of blood for hepatitis antibodies; liver biopsy	Treatment usually involves bed rest, intake of fluids, and, sometimes, antibiotics to ward off bacterial infections that might take hold because of lowered resistance; alpha interferon is sometimes used in treating hepatitis C
AIDS/HIV	HIV is transmitted by sexual contact, by infusion with contaminated blood, from mother to fetus during pregnancy, or through childbirth or breast-feeding	Infected people may initially have no symptoms or develop mild flulike symptoms that may then disappear for many years prior to the development of "full-blown" AIDS; full-blown AIDS symptomized by fever, weight loss, fatigue, diarrhea, and opportunistic infections such as rare forms of cancer (Kaposi's sarcoma) and pneumonia	Blood, saliva, or urine tests detect HIV antibodies; more expensive tests confirm the presence of the HIV virus itself; the diagnosis of HIV/AIDS is usually made on the basis of antibodies, a low count of CD4 cells, and/or the presence of indicator diseases	There is no cure for HIV infection or AIDS; treatment (HAART) is a "cocktail" of antiviral drugs including a protease inhibitor and nucleoside analogues such as zidovudine; new drugs such as fusion inhibitors are also coming online
HPV/genital warts (venereal warts)	Transmission is by sexual and other forms of contact, such as with infected towels or clothing	Appearance of painless warts, often resembling cauliflowers, on the penis, foreskin, scrotum, or internal urethra in men; or on the vulva, labia, wall of the vagina, or cervix in women; may occur around the anus and in the rectum of both males and females	Clinical inspection	Methods include cryotherapy (freezing), podophyllin, trichloroacetic acid or bichloroacetic acid, burning, surgical removal; a vaccine can protect most women from being infected with HPV

(Continued)

TABLE 16.1

(Continued)

STI and Pathogen	Modes of Transmission	Symptoms	Diagnosis	Treatment
Ectoparasitic Infestations				
Pediculosis ("crabs"): *Pthirus pubis (pubic lice)*	Transmission by sexual contact or by contact with an infested towel, sheet, or toilet seat	Intense itching in pubic area and other hairy regions to which lice can attach	Clinical examination	Lindane (brand name Kwell)—a prescription shampoo; nonprescription medications containing pyrethrins or piperonal butoxide (brand names RID, Triple X)
Scabies: *Sarcoptes scabiei*	Transmission by sexual contact or by contact with infested clothing or bed linen, towels, and other fabrics	Intense itching; reddish lines on skin where mites have burrowed in; welts and pus-filled blisters in affected areas	Clinical inspection	Lindane (Kwell)

REFLECT

Why should people *not* be relieved when the symptoms of an STI "disappear"?

Pharyngeal gonorrhea A gonorrheal infection that is characterized by a sore throat

Ophthalmia neonatorum A gonorrheal infection of the eyes of newborn children who contract the disease by passing through an infected birth canal

TRANSMISSION Gonococcal bacteria require a warm, moist environment, like that found along the mucous membranes of the urinary tract in both genders or the cervix in women. Outside the body, these bacteria die in about a minute. There is no evidence that gonorrhea can be picked up from public toilet seats or by touching dry objects. In rare cases, gonorrhea is contracted by contact with a moist, warm towel or sheet used immediately beforehand by an infected person. Gonorrhea is almost always transmitted by unprotected vaginal, oral, or anal sexual activity, or from mother to newborn during delivery.

A person who performs fellatio on an infected man may develop **pharyngeal gonorrhea**, which produces a throat infection. Mouth-to-mouth kissing and cunnilingus are less likely to spread gonorrhea. The eyes provide a good environment for the bacterium. Thus, a person whose hands come into contact with infected genitals and who inadvertently touches his or her eyes afterward may infect them. Babies have contracted gonorrhea of the eyes (**ophthalmia neonatorum**) when passing through the birth canals of infected mothers. This disorder may cause blindness, but has become rare because the eyes of newborns are treated routinely with silver nitrate or penicillin ointment, which are toxic to gonococcal bacteria.

A gonorrheal infection may be spread from the penis to the partner's rectum during anal intercourse. A cervical gonorrheal infection can be spread to the rectum if an infected woman and her partner follow vaginal intercourse with anal intercourse. Gonorrhea is less likely to be spread by vaginal discharge than by penile discharge.

Gonorrhea is highly contagious. Women stand nearly a 50% chance of contracting gonorrhea after one exposure. Men have a 25% risk of infection (Hatcher et al., 2006). The risks to heterosexual women are apparently greater because they retain infected semen in the vagina. The risk of infection increases with repeated exposure.

SYMPTOMS Most men experience symptoms within two to five days after infection. Symptoms include a penile discharge that is clear at first (Figure 16.1). Within a day it turns yellow to yellow–green, thickens, and becomes puslike. The urethra becomes inflamed, and urination is accompanied by a burning sensation. Thirty percent to 40% of males have swelling and tenderness in the lymph glands of the groin. Inflammation and other symptoms may become chronic if left untreated.

The initial symptoms of gonorrhea usually abate within a few weeks without treatment, leading people to think of gonorrhea as being no worse than a bad cold. However, the *gonococcus* bacterium will usually continue to damage the body internally.

The primary site of infection in women is the cervix, where it causes **cervicitis**. Cervicitis may cause a yellowish to yellow–green puslike discharge that irritates the vulva. If the infection spreads to the urethra, women may also note burning urination. **Truth or Fiction Revisited:** It is true that most women who contract gonorrhea do not have noticeable symptoms. *About 80% of the women who contract gonorrhea have no symptoms during the early stages of the infection.* Because many infected women do not seek treatment until symptoms develop, they may innocently infect another sex partner.

When gonorrhea is not treated early, it may spread through the urogenital systems in both genders and strike the internal reproductive organs. In men, it can lead to **epididymitis**, which can cause fertility problems. Swelling and feelings of tenderness or pain in the scrotum are the principal symptoms of epididymitis. Fever may also be present. Occasionally the kidneys are affected.

In women, the bacterium can spread through the cervix to the uterus, fallopian tubes, ovaries, and other parts of the abdominal cavity, causing **pelvic inflammatory disease (PID)**. Symptoms of PID include cramps, abdominal pain and tenderness, cervical tenderness and discharge, irregular menstrual cycles, coital pain, fever, nausea, and vomiting. PID may also occur without symptoms. Regardless of symptoms, PID can cause scarring that blocks the fallopian tubes, leading to infertility. PID is a serious illness that requires aggressive treatment with antibiotics. Surgery may be needed to remove infected tissue. Unfortunately, many women become aware of a gonococcal infection only when they develop PID. These consequences are all the more unfortunate because gonorrhea, when diagnosed and treated early, clears up rapidly in more than 90% of cases.

DIAGNOSIS AND TREATMENT Diagnosis of gonorrhea involves clinical inspection of the genitals by a physician (e.g., a family practitioner, urologist, or gynecologist) and the culturing and examination of a sample of genital discharge.

Antibiotics are the standard treatment for gonorrhea. Penicillin was once the favored antibiotic, but the rise of penicillin-resistant strains of *N. gonorrhoeae* has required that alternative antibiotics be used (Hatcher et al., 2006). An injection of the antibiotic ceftriaxone is often recommended. Other antibiotics that are used to treat gonorrhea include ciprofloaxin and ofloxacin. Because gonorrhea and chlamydia often occur together, people who are infected with gonorrhea are usually also treated for chlamydia through the use of another antibiotic (Hatcher et al., 2006). Sex partners of people with gonorrhea should also be examined.

Syphilis

Nobody wanted to be associated with **syphilis.** In Naples they called it "the French disease." In France it was "the Neapolitan disease." Many Italians called it "the Spanish disease," but in Spain they called it "the disease of Española" (modern Haiti).

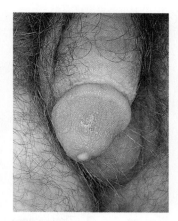

Figure 16.1
Gonorrheal Discharge.
Gonorrhea in the male often causes a thick, yellowish, puslike discharge from the penis.

TRUTH
fiction 1

CRITICAL
Thinking

How do penicillin-resistant strains of a bacterial agent "evolve"?

Cervicitis Inflammation of the cervix

Epididymitis Inflammation of the epididymis

Pelvic inflammatory disease (PID) Inflammation of the pelvic region that can be caused by some STIs; symptoms include abdominal pain, tenderness, nausea, fever, and irregular menstrual cycles; PID may lead to infertility

Syphilis An STI that is caused by the *Treponema pallidum* bacterium, which may progress through several stages of development—often from a chancre to a rash—to damage to vital body systems

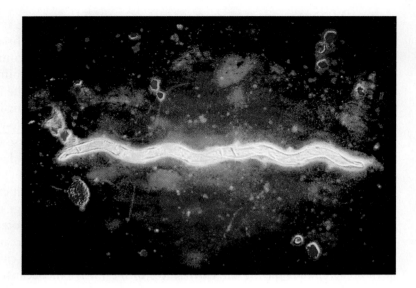

Figure 16.2 *Treponema pallidum.*
Treponema pallidum is the bacterium that causes syphilis. Because of the spiral shape, *T. pallidum* is also called a spirochete.

In 1530 the Italian physician Girolamo Fracastoro wrote a poem about Syphilus, a shepherd boy. Syphilus was afflicted with the disease as retribution for insulting the sun god Apollo.

Syphilis is caused by a bacterium isolated in 1905 by the German scientist Fritz Schaudinn: *Treponema pallidum* (*T. pallidum,* for short; Figure 16.2). The name contains roots meaning a "faintly colored (pallid) turning thread," describing the corkscrewlike shape of the microscopic organism. Because of the spiral shape, *T. pallidum* is also called a *spirochete,* from Greek roots meaning "spiral" and "hair."

THE ORIGINS OF SYPHILIS   The origins of syphilis are controversial. The Columbian theory holds that Christopher Columbus returned to Spain from his first voyage to the West Indies (1492–1493) with more than beads, blankets, and tobacco. Then, from Spain, Spanish mercenaries may have carried the disease to Naples when they were hired to protect that city from French invaders. Then the French army may have contracted syphilis from prostitutes, who also practiced their profession with the Spaniards and Neapolitans. Sailors may have eventually spread syphilis to the East.

It is generally accepted that Columbus exhibited symptoms of advanced syphilis when he died in 1506. **Truth or Fiction Revisited:** But it is apparently not true that Columbus brought syphilis back to Europe from the New World. Syphilis existed in Europe prior to the voyages of Columbus.

The incidence of syphilis decreased in the United States with the introduction of penicillin. But despite the availability of penicillin, there has been a recent resurgence in rates of syphilis to about 10,000 cases per year, because the advent of effective drugs for HIV/AIDS has contributed to a new wave of risky sexual behavior among many individuals (Dilley et al., 2003). Although syphilis is less widespread than it once was, its effects can be extremely harmful. They include heart disease, blindness, confusion, and death. Syphilis killed the painter Paul Gauguin.

TRANSMISSION   **Truth or Fiction Revisited:** It is not true that gonorrhea and syphilis can be contracted from toilet seats in public restrooms. Syphilis, like gonorrhea, is most often transmitted by vaginal or anal intercourse, or oral–genital or oral–anal contact with an infected person. The spirochete is usually transmitted

TRUTH fiction **2**

TRUTH fiction **3**

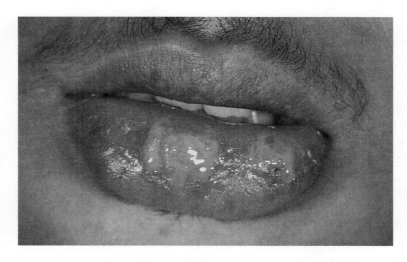

Figure 16.3 Syphilis Chancre. *The first stage, or primary stage, of a syphilis infection is marked by the appearance of a painless sore or chancre at the site of the infection.*

when open lesions on an infected person come in contact with the mucous membranes or skin abrasions of the partner's body during sexual activity. Syphilis may also be contracted by touching an infectious **chancre,** but not from using the same toilet seat as an infected person.

Pregnant women may transmit syphilis to their fetuses, because the spirochete can cross the placental membrane. Miscarriage, stillbirth, or **congenital syphilis** may result. Congenital syphilis may impair vision and hearing or deform bones and teeth. Blood tests are administered routinely during pregnancy to diagnose syphilis in the mother so that congenital problems in the baby may be averted. The fetus will probably not be harmed if an infected mother is treated before the fourth month of pregnancy.

SYMPTOMS AND COURSE OF ILLNESS Syphilis develops through several stages. In the first or *primary stage* of syphilis, a painless chancre (a hard, round, ulcerlike lesion with raised edges) appears at the site of infection two to four weeks after contact. When women are infected, the chancre usually forms on the vaginal walls or the cervix. It may also form on the external genitalia, most often on the labia. When men are infected, the chancre usually forms on the penile glans. It may also form on the scrotum or penile shaft. If the mode of transmission is oral sex, the chancre may appear on the lips or tongue (Figure 16.3). If the infection is spread by anal sex, the rectum may serve as the site of the chancre. The chancre disappears within a few weeks, but if the infection remains untreated, syphilis will continue to work within the body.

The *secondary stage* begins a few weeks to a few months later. A skin rash develops, consisting of painless, reddish, raised bumps that darken after a while and burst, oozing a discharge. Other symptoms include sores in the mouth, painful swelling of the joints, a sore throat, headaches, and fever. A person with syphilis may thus wrongly assume that he or she has the flu.

These symptoms also disappear. Syphilis then enters the *latent stage* and may lie dormant for 1 to 40 years. However, spirochetes continue to multiply and burrow into the circulatory system, central nervous system (brain and spinal cord), and bones. The person may no longer be contagious to sex partners after several years in the latent stage, but a pregnant woman may pass along the infection to her newborn at any time.

In many cases the disease eventually progresses to the *late or tertiary stage.* A large ulcer may form on the skin, muscle tissue, digestive organs, lungs, liver, or other

Chancre A sore or ulcer
Congenital syphilis A syphilis infection that is present at birth

organs. This destructive ulcer can often be successfully treated, but still more serious damage can occur as the infection attacks the central nervous system or the cardiovascular system (the heart and the major blood vessels). Either outcome can be fatal. **Neurosyphilis** can cause brain damage, resulting in paralysis or the mental illness called **general paresis.**

The primary and secondary symptoms of syphilis inevitably disappear. **Truth or Fiction Revisited:** But it is not true that the infection does not require medical treatment if a syphilitic chancre (sore) goes away by itself. The belief that medical treatment is unnecessary if the symptoms of an STI disappear by themselves is unfounded. Gonorrhea and syphilis, for example, both can damage the body even when their early symptoms have abated.

DIAGNOSIS AND TREATMENT Primary-stage syphilis is diagnosed by clinical examination. If a chancre is found, fluid drawn from it can be examined under a microscope. The spirochetes are usually quite visible. Blood tests are not definitive until the secondary stage begins. The most frequently used blood test is the **VDRL.** The VDRL tests for the presence of **antibodies** to *T. pallidum* in the blood.

Penicillin is the treatment of choice for syphilis, although for people allergic to penicillin, doxycycline and some other antibiotics can be used (Hatcher et al., 2006). Sex partners of persons infected with syphilis should also be evaluated by a physician.

Chlamydia

Chlamydia, another bacterial STI, is more common than gonorrhea and syphilis in the United States (Hatcher et al., 2006). Chlamydial infections are caused by the bacterium *Chlamydia trachomatis,* a parasitic organism that can survive only within cells. The bacterium can cause several different types of infection, including *nongonococcal urethritis (NGU)* in men and women, *epididymitis* (infection of the epididymis) in men, and *cervicitis* (infection of the cervix), *endometritis* (infection of the endometrium), and PID in women (Hatcher et al., 2006).

About 2.8 million new chlamydial infections occur each year (CDC, 2006). The incidence of chlamydial infections is especially high among teenagers and college students (CDC, 2006).

TRANSMISSION *C. trachomatis* is usually transmitted through vaginal or anal sexual intercourse. *C. trachomatis* may also cause an eye infection if a person touches his or her eyes after handling the genitals of an infected partner. Oral sex with an infected partner can infect the throat. Newborns can acquire potentially serious chlamydial eye infections as they pass through the cervix of an infected mother during birth. Even newborns delivered by cesarean section may be infected if the amniotic sac breaks before delivery.

SYMPTOMS Chlamydial infections usually produce symptoms that are similar to but milder than those of gonorrhea. In men, *C. trachomatis* can lead to NGU. *Urethritis* is an inflammation of the urethra. NGU refers to forms of urethritis that are not caused by the gonococcal bacterium. (NGU is generally diagnosed only in men. In women, an inflammation of the urethra caused by *C. trachomatis* is called a chlamydial infection or, simply, chlamydia.) NGU was formerly called nonspecific urethritis or NSU. Many organisms can cause NGU. *C. trachomatis* accounts for about half the cases among men (Hatcher et al., 2006).

NGU in men may give rise to a thin, whitish discharge from the penis and some burning or other pain during urination. These symptoms contrast with the

TRUTH fiction **4**

Neurosyphilis Syphilitic infection of the central nervous system, which can cause brain damage and death

General paresis A progressive form of mental illness caused by neurosyphilis and characterized by gross confusion

VDRL Named after the Venereal Disease Research Laboratory, a test for the presence of antibodies to *Treponema pallidum* in the blood

Antibodies Specialized proteins produced by the white blood cells of the immune system in response to disease organisms and other toxic substances; functions are to recognize and attack the invading organisms or substances

yellow–green discharge and more intense pain produced by gonorrhea. There may be soreness in the scrotum and a feeling of heaviness in the testes. NGU is about two to three times as prevalent among American men as gonorrhea (Hatcher et al., 2006). Young male adults are at the highest risk of contracting gonorrhea and NGU, presumably because of their high levels of sexual activity (CDC, 2006).

In women, chlamydial infections usually give rise to infections of the urethra or cervix (CDC, 2006). Women, like men, may experience burning when they urinate, genital irritation, and a mild (vaginal) discharge. Women are also likely to encounter pelvic pain and irregular menstrual cycles. The cervix may look swollen and inflamed. However, as many as 25% of men and 70% of women infected with chlamydia have no noticeable symptoms (Hatcher et al., 2006). For this reason, chlamydia has been dubbed the "silent disease." Symptom-free people may go untreated and unknowingly pass their infections to new partners. In women, an untreated chlamydial infection can spread throughout the reproductive system, leading to PID and scarring of the fallopian tubes, resulting in infertility. About half of the more than one million annual cases of PID are attributed to chlamydia (Hatcher et al., 2006). Women exposed to *C. trachomatis* also stand a greater chance of incurring an ectopic (tubal) pregnancy.

Untreated chlamydial infections can also damage the internal reproductive organs of men. About 50% of cases of epididymitis are caused by chlamydial infections (Hatcher et al., 2006). Yet only about 1% or 2% of men with untreated NGU caused by *C. trachomatis* go on to develop epididymitis. The long-term effects of untreated chlamydial infections in men remain undetermined.

Chlamydial infections also frequently occur together with other STIs, most often gonorrhea. Nearly half the cases of gonorrhea involve coexisting chlamydial infections (Hatcher et al., 2006).

DIAGNOSIS AND TREATMENT Various tests are used in the laboratory or the physician's office to verify a diagnosis of chlamydia in women (CDC, 2006). The tests analyze a cervical smear and are highly reliable. In men, a swab may be inserted through the penile opening to extract fluid that is analyzed for the presence of *C. trachomatis*.

Antibiotics other than penicillin are highly effective in eradicating chlamydial infections. These include azithromycin, doxycycline, ofloxacin, and amoxicillin (CDC, 2006). Sex partners are treated when possible to prevent the infection from bouncing back and forth (CDC, 2006). Both partners may be unaware that they are infected and may be oblivious to the internal damage the infection is causing. Because of the risks posed by untreated chlamydial infections, especially to women, and the high rate of symptom-free infections, many physicians screen young women for chlamydia during regular checkups. More information is available at the website for the CDC (www.cdc.gov/std/treatment/2006/summary.htm).

Other Bacterial Infections

Several other bacterial STIs occur in the United States and Canada, but less frequently. These include chancroid, shigellosis, granuloma inguinale, and lymphogranuloma venereum (LGV).

CHANCROID **Chancroid,** or "soft chancre," is caused by the bacterium *Hemophilus ducreyi*. It is more commonly found in the tropics and Eastern nations than in Western countries. The chancroid sore consists of a cluster of small bumps or pimples on the genitals, perineum (the area of skin that lies between the genitals and

Chancroid An STI caused by the bacterium *Hemophilus ducreyi*; also called *soft chancre*

the anus), or the anus itself. These lesions usually appear within seven days of infection. Within a few days the lesion ruptures, producing an open sore or ulcer. Several ulcers may merge with other ulcers, forming giant ulcers. There is usually an accompanying swelling of a nearby lymph node. In contrast to the syphilis chancre, the chancroid ulcer has a soft rim (hence the name) and is painful in men. Women frequently do not experience any pain and may be unaware of being infected (CDC, 2006). The bacterium is typically transmitted through sexual or bodily contact with the lesion or its discharge. Diagnosis is usually confirmed by culturing the bacterium, which is found in pus from the sore, and examining it under a microscope. Antibiotics are usually effective in treating the disease (Hatcher et al., 2006).

SHIGELLOSIS **Shigellosis** is caused by the *Shigella* bacterium and is characterized by fever and severe abdominal symptoms, including diarrhea and inflammation of the large intestine. About 25,000 cases of shigellosis are reported each year in the United States. Shigellosis can result from food poisoning, but it is also often contracted by oral contact with infected fecal material, which may stem from oral–anal sex. Shigellosis often resolves itself, but people with the disease may become severely dehydrated from the diarrhea. Severe cases are usually treated with antibiotics.

GRANULOMA INGUINALE Rare in the United States, **granuloma inguinale,** like chancroid, is more common in tropical regions. It is caused by the bacterium *Calymmatobacterium granulomatous* and is not as contagious as many other STIs. Primary symptoms are painless red bumps or sores in the groin area that ulcerate and spread. Like chancroid, it is usually spread by intimate bodily or sexual contact with a lesion or its discharge. Diagnosis is confirmed by microscopic examination of tissue of the rim of the sore. Numerous antibiotics are effective in treating this disease (Hatcher et al., 2006). If left untreated, however, it may lead to the development of fistulas (holes) in the rectum or bladder, destruction of infected tissues or organs, or scarring of skin tissue that results in a condition called **elephantiasis,** a condition that afflicted the so-called Elephant Man in the 19th century.

LYMPHOGRANULOMA VENEREUM **Lymphogranuloma venereum** (LGV) is another tropical STI that occurs only rarely in the United States and Canada. Some U.S. soldiers returned home from the Vietnam War with cases of LGV. It is caused by several strains of the bacterium *C. trachomatis*. LGV usually enters the body through the penis, vulva, or cervix, where a small, painless sore may form. The sore may go unnoticed, but a nearby lymph gland in the groin swells and grows tender. Other symptoms mimic those of flu: chills, fever, and headache. Other possible symptoms include backache (especially in women) and arthritic complaints (painful joints). If LGV is untreated, growths and fistulas in the genitals and elephantiasis of the legs and genitals may occur. Diagnosis is made by skin tests and blood tests. Antibiotics are the usual treatment (Hatcher et al., 2006).

Vaginal Infections

A vaginal infection or inflammation is technically termed **vaginitis.** Vaginitis is typically symptomized by genital irritation or itching and burning during urination, but the most common symptom is an odious discharge.

Shigellosis An STI caused by the bacterium *Shigella*

Granuloma inguinale A tropical STI caused by bacterium *Calymmatobacterium granulomatous*

Elephantiasis A disease characterized by enlargement of parts of the body, especially the legs and genitals, and by hardening and ulceration of the surrounding skin

Lymphogranuloma venereum A tropical STI caused by the bacterium *Chlamydia trachomatis*

Vaginitis Any type of vaginal infection or inflammation

Most cases of vaginitis are caused by organisms that reside in the vagina or by sexually transmitted organisms. Organisms that reside in the vagina may overgrow when the environmental balance of the vagina is upset by factors such as birth control pills, antibiotics, dietary changes, excessive douching, nylon underwear or pantyhose, or stress. (See Chapter 3 for ways to reduce the risk of vaginitis.) Still other cases are caused by sensitivities or allergic reactions to various chemicals.

The great majority of vaginal infections involve bacterial vaginosis (BV), candidiasis (commonly called a "yeast" infection), or trichomoniasis ("trich"). BV is the most common form of vaginitis, followed by candidiasis, then by trichomoniasis, but some cases involve combinations of the three (CDC, 2006).

For heterosexual couples, the microbes causing vaginal infections in women can also infect a man's urethral tract. A "vaginal infection" can be passed back and forth between sex partners.

Truth or Fiction Revisited: Men cannot literally develop vaginal infections. Only women have vaginas. However, the microbes that cause these infections in women may also cause problems for men.

CRITICAL
Thinking
Critical thinkers pay attention to definitions of terms. What does it mean to say that men "have" a vaginal infection?

TRUTH?fiction 5

Bacterial Vaginosis

Bacterial vaginosis (BV, formerly called *nonspecific vaginitis*) is most often caused by overgrowth of the bacterium *Gardnerella vaginalis* (CDC, 2006). The bacterium is mainly transmitted sexually. The most characteristic symptom in women is a thin, foul-smelling vaginal discharge, but infected women often have no symptoms. Diagnosis requires culturing the bacterium in the laboratory. Besides causing troublesome symptoms in some cases, BV may increase the risk of various gynecological problems, including infections of the reproductive tract (CDC, 2006). Oral treatment with metronidazole (brand name Flagyl) is recommended and is effective in most cases. Topical treatments with metronidazole or clindamycin are also effective. However, recurrences are common.

Questions remain regarding whether a male partner should also be treated. The bacterium can usually be found in the urethra of a symptom-free male (CDC, 2006). Being symptom free, the male may unknowingly pass the bacterium on to others.

Candidiasis

Candidiasis is caused by a yeastlike fungus, *Candida albicans.* It is also known as *moniliasis, thrush,* or, more simply, a yeast infection. Candidiasis commonly produces soreness, inflammation, and intense (sometimes maddening!) itching around the vulva that is accompanied by a white, thick, curdlike vaginal discharge (Figure 16.4). Yeast generally produces no symptoms when the vaginal environment is normal. Yeast infections can also occur in the mouth in both men and women, and in the penis in men.

Infections most often arise from changes in the vaginal environment that allow the fungus to overgrow. Factors such as the use of antibiotics, birth control pills, IUDs, pregnancy, and diabetes may alter the vaginal balance, allowing the fungus that causes yeast infections to grow to infectious levels. Wearing nylon underwear and tight, restrictive, poorly ventilated clothing may also set the stage for a yeast infection.

Diet may play a role in recurrent yeast infections. Reducing intake of substances that produce excessive excretion of urinary sugars (such as dairy products, sugar,

Bacterial vaginosis A form of vaginitis usually caused by the bacterium *Gardnerella vaginalis*

Candidiasis A form of vaginitis caused by a yeastlike fungus, *Candida albicans*

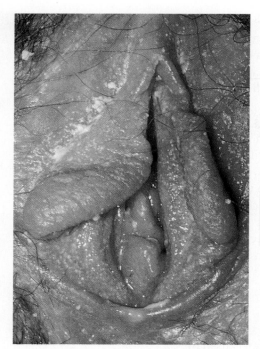

Figure 16.4 Candidiasis. A "yeast infection" is caused by the *Candida albicans* fungus and causes soreness, inflammation, and itching around the vulva, accompanied by a thick, white vaginal discharge.

and artificial sweeteners) apparently reduces the frequency of recurrent yeast infections. Eating a pint of yogurt containing active bacterial (*Lactobacillus acidophilus*) cultures daily may reduce the rate of recurrent infections.

Candidiasis can be passed back and forth between sex partners through vaginal intercourse. It may also be passed back and forth between the mouth and the genitals through oral–genital contact and may infect the anus through anal intercourse. However, most infections in women are believed to be caused by an overgrowth of "yeast" normally found in the vagina, not by sexual transmission. Still, it is advisable to evaluate partners simultaneously. Although most men with *Candida* have no symptoms, some may develop NGU or a genital thrush that is accompanied by itching and burning during urination or by reddening of the penis. Candidiasis may also be transmitted nonsexually, such as between women who share a washcloth.

At least half of adult women will experience at least one episode of candidiasis by their mid 20s (Marrazzo, 2003). About 25% of these will have recurrent infections. A single dose of oral fluconazole, or vaginal suppositories or creams containing miconazole, clotrimazole, or butaconazole are recommended for treatment (CDC, 2006; Hatcher et al., 2006). Many of these treatments are sold OTC. Ask the pharmacist which preparations contain these medicines (or read the labels). We advise women with vaginal complaints to consult their physicians before using any of these medications to ensure that they receive the proper diagnosis and treatment.

Trichomoniasis

Trichomoniasis ("trich") is the most common STI. It is caused by *Trichomonas vaginalis,* a one-celled parasite. There are more than seven million new cases a year among women (and men) in the United States (CDC, 2006). Symptoms include burning or itching in the vulva, mild pain during urination or coitus, and an odorous, foamy whitish to yellowish green discharge. Lower abdominal pain is reported by some infected women. Many women notice symptoms appearing or worsening during, or just after, their menstrual periods. Trichomoniasis facilitates the transmission of HIV and is linked to the development of tubal adhesions that can result in infertility. As with many other STIs, many infected women have no symptoms.

Candidiasis often reflects the overgrowth of organisms normally found in the vagina, but trich is almost always sexually transmitted. Because the parasite can survive for several hours on moist surfaces outside the body, trich can be communicated from contact with infected semen or vaginal discharges on towels, washcloths, and bedclothes. This parasite is one of the few disease agents that can be picked up from a toilet seat, but it would have to come into contact with the penis or vulva.

T. vaginalis can cause NGU in the male, which can be symptom free or cause a slight penile discharge that is usually noticeable prior to first urination in the morning. There may be tingling, itching, and other irritating sensations in the urethral tract. However, most infected men are symptom free and can unwittingly transfer the organism to other sex partners. Diagnosis is frequently made by microscopic examination of a smear of a woman's vaginal fluids.

Except during the first three months of pregnancy, trichomoniasis is usually treated in both women and men with metronidazole (Flagyl). If both partners are treated, the success rate approaches 100% (CDC, 2006; Hatcher et al., 2006).

Trichomoniasis A form of vaginitis caused by the protozoan *Trichomonas vaginalis*

Viral Infections

Viruses are tiny particles of DNA coated with a protein. They cannot reproduce on their own. When they invade a body cell, however, they can direct the cell's own reproductive machinery to spin off new viral particles that spread to other cells, causing infection. Our immune systems defeat many viruses, and many others are not lethal. In this section we discuss viral STIs, some of which are indeed deadly: HIV/AIDS, herpes, viral hepatitis, genital warts, and molluscum contagiosum.

HIV/AIDS

HIV stands for **human immunodeficiency virus**, the virus that causes AIDS. AIDS stands for **acquired immunodeficiency syndrome**. HIV attacks and disables the immune system, the body's natural line of defense, stripping it of its ability to fend off disease-causing organisms. AIDS is considered fatal, although many people currently live with HIV/AIDS as a result of the development of powerful antiviral medications. For people in industrialized nations like the United States and Canada, Western European nations, Japan, and the like, HIV/AIDS may become a chronic but manageable condition, like diabetes. But for many millions in developing nations, where medications are too expensive or difficult to deliver, HIV/AIDS may remain a death sentence.

PREVALENCE OF HIV/AIDS Nearly one million Americans are living with HIV/AIDS (CDC, 2006). More than half a million Americans have died from it (CDC, 2006). The incidence of HIV/AIDS is increasing most rapidly among women, people of color (Table 16.2), people who share needles when they inject drugs, and people who engage in unprotected male–female sex. Here are some facts about HIV/AIDS around the world (UNAIDS, 2006):

- About 39.5 million people around the world are estimated to be living with HIV/AIDS, split nearly evenly between males and females (Figure 16.5). About three million are children.

- An estimated 70 million people will die of HIV/AIDS-related diseases during the next two decades, unless effective antiretroviral drugs are distributed in undeveloped nations.

- An estimated 4.3 million people were infected with HIV in 2006.

- During 2006, AIDS caused the deaths of approximately 2.9 million people, including about 380,000 children.

TABLE 16.2

U.S. AIDS Cases by Race or Ethnicity

Race or Ethnicity	No. of Cases	Percentage
European American (not Latino or Latina American)	375,155	39.9
African American (not Latino or Latina American)	379,278	40.2
Latino and Latina American	177,164	18.8
Asian/Pacific Islander	7,317	0.7
American Indian/Alaska Native	3,084	0.3

SOURCE: Centers for Disease Control and Prevention. (2005a). *HIV/AIDS Surveillance Report, 2004, vol. 16.* U.S. Department of Health and Human Services, Centers for Disease Control and Prevention.

Human immunodeficiency virus (HIV) A sexually transmitted virus that destroys white blood cells in the immune system, leaving the body vulnerable to life-threatening diseases

Acquired immunedeficiency syndrome (AIDS) A condition caused by HIV and characterized by destruction of the immune system so that the body is stripped of its ability to fend off life-threatening diseases

Global Summary of the HIV/AIDS Epidemic, 2006

Number of people living with HIV in 2006 (estimate)	Totals	**39.5 million**
	Adults	37.2 million
	Women	17.7 million
	Children under 15 years	2.3 million
People newly infected with HIV in 2006 (estimate)	**Total**	**4.3 million**
	Adults	3.8 million
	Children under 15 years	530,000
AIDS deaths in 2006 (estimate)	**Total**	**2.9 million**
	Adults	2.6 million
	Children under 15 years	380,000

Adults and Children Estimated to Be Living with HIV, 2006

North America 1.4 million
Western & Central Europe 740,000
Eastern Europe & Central Asia 1.7 million
East Asia 750,000
Caribbean 250,000
Middle East & North Africa 460,000
South & South-East Asia 7.8 million
Latin America 1.7 million
Sub-Saharan Africa 24.7 million
Oceania 81,000

Total: 39.5 million

Figure 16.5 Global Summary of the HIV/AIDS Epidemic, 2006

SOURCE: Reproduced with kind permission from UNAIDS (2006) and the World Health Organization. WHO logo courtesy of the World Health Organization.

Although half of those infected with HIV around the world are female, in the United States, HIV/AIDS is predominantly found among men who engage in sexual activity with other men or who share needles when injecting drugs (CDC, 2005b; Table 16.3). But male–female sex is the fastest-growing exposure category in the United States. Among women, male–female sexual contact now accounts for more than half of cases (CDC, 2005; Table 16.3 on page 529).

THE IMMUNE SYSTEM AND HIV/AIDS AIDS is caused by a virus that attacks the body's **immune system**—the body's natural line of defense against disease-causing organisms. The immune system combats disease in several ways. It produces white blood cells that envelop and kill **pathogens** such as bacteria, viruses, and funguses; worn out body cells; and cancer cells. White blood cells are called **leukocytes.** Leukocytes engage in microscopic search-and-destroy missions. They identify and eradicate foreign agents and debilitated cells.

Immune system The body's complex of mechanisms for protecting itself from disease-causing agents such as pathogens

Pathogen An agent, especially a microorganism, that can cause a disease

Leukocytes White blood cells, which are essential to the body's defenses against infection

Estimated Adult and Child Deaths from AIDS, 2006

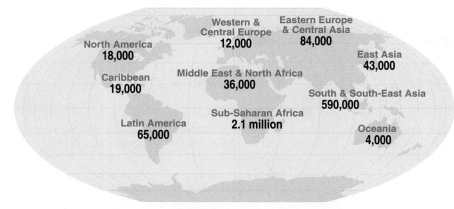

North America
18,000

Western & Central Europe
12,000

Eastern Europe & Central Asia
84,000

East Asia
43,000

Caribbean
19,000

Middle East & North Africa
36,000

South & South-East Asia
590,000

Latin America
65,000

Sub-Saharan Africa
2.1 million

Oceania
4,000

Total: 2.9 million

Estimated Number of Adults and Children Newly Infected with HIV, 2006

North America
43,000

Western & Central Europe
22,000

Eastern Europe & Central Asia
270,000

East Asia
100,000

Caribbean
27,000

Middle East & North Africa
68,000

South & South-East Asia
860,000

Latin America
140,000

Sub-Saharan Africa
2.8 million

Oceania
7,100

Total: 4.3 million

Truth or Fiction Revisited: It is true that as you read this page, you are engaged in search-and-destroy missions against foreign agents within your body. The white cells in your immune system continuously seek and destroy foreign pathogens within your body.

TRUTH fiction 6

Leukocytes recognize foreign agents by their surface fragments. The surface fragments are termed **antigens**, because the body reacts to their presence by developing specialized proteins, or antibodies. Antibodies attach themselves to the foreign bodies, inactivate them, and mark them for destruction. (Infection by HIV may be determined by examining the blood, saliva, or urine for the presence of antibodies.)

Rather than mark pathogens for destruction or war against them, special "memory lymphocytes" are held in reserve. Memory lymphocytes can remain in the bloodstream for years, and they form the basis for a quick immune response to an invader the second time around.

Another function of the immune system is to promote **inflammation.** When you sustain an injury, blood vessels in the region initially contract to check bleeding. Then they dilate. Dilation expands blood flow to the injured region, causing the redness and warmth that identify inflammation. The elevated blood supply also brings

Antigen A protein, toxin, or other substance to which the body reacts by producing antibodies; combined word formed from *anti*body *gen*erator

Inflammation Redness and warmth that develop at the site of an injury, reflecting dilation of blood vessels that permits the expanded flow of leukocytes to the region

Killer of Dreams

By Nicholas D. Kristof, The New York Times

KwaMhlanga, South Africa—One of the great mysteries to me about AIDS in Africa has been this: Why do people not take precautions during sex even when they see friends and relatives dying?

It's easy for Westerners to say that widespread promiscuity is the root of the AIDS problem in Africa, where the virus is transmitted mainly by heterosexual contact. And there's definitely something to that. But the reasons for reckless promiscuity go beyond hormones, and I came to understood them better near this town of KwaMhlanga in the northeastern part of South Africa, in the tin shack where Gertrude Tobela frets about her teenage daughter.

Ms. Tobela, 34, slim and quick to smile—and now to cry—is the first in her family to graduate from elementary school, high school, or college. Two years ago, she was at the top of her world, preparing to graduate from the university, have her second child, and join the middle class.

Now she is another African widow, poor, dying, and heartbroken because she cannot protect her children from the same fate. She is but one of 30 million Africans with HIV/AIDS (24 will die of it while you're reading this column), but her tale underscores how HIV in Africa is not just a virus but also a self-replicating cycle of AIDS, poverty, and hopelessness.

Ms. Tobela's world began to collapse when her husband, Simon, an electrician, was found to have AIDS. Then she tested positive for HIV, apparently after getting it from him. And her newborn son, Victor, turned out to have caught the virus from her.

Her husband died last year, and she is now too sick to hold a job. She survives on $22.50 a month in government child support and spends her time wondering about who should raise Victor after her death.

"I think maybe if I die first, before him, then maybe my mother can take Victor," she says, her voice catching.

Ms. Tobela seems typical of Africa's AIDS victims. In Africa, 58% of HIV carriers are female, and among teenagers with HIV, more than 75% are girls. This is largely because of an explosion in quasi prostitution between young girls and older men.

"It's not just promiscuity," said Blanche Pitt, director of the South Africa office of the African Medical and Research Foundation. "It's poverty. It's desperation."

As young women become infected, so do their babies. One fifth of pregnant women in southern Africa have HIV, and worldwide, 800,000 babies a year get HIV from their mothers.

Ms. Tobela managed to talk in a composed way about her death and Victor's. But she broke down when I asked about her 14-year-old daughter, Thabang (she has a different surname, which I'll keep to myself).

"My daughter left me because she wants liberty," Ms. Tobela said, weeping. "She is so sexually active, and she stays in bars and rental rooms."

It began in June, when Thabang began coming home late. Ms. Tobela screamed at her and then beat her, but it did no good. The girl ran off to live with her grandmother, but then stayed away for days at a time. After the grandmother beat Thabang as well, she ran away again.

I searched the town for Thabang, and finally found her at a relative's house. She is very pretty, with a fondness for makeup, well spoken and smart. I told her that her mom scolded her only because she loved her. Thabang began to cry.

"She doesn't love me," she said fiercely. "If she did, she would talk to me instead of beating me. She wouldn't say these things about me. She would accept my friends." Thabang insisted that while her friends slept with men for cash or gifts, she did not.

Why would girls who have seen what AIDS can do commit suicide by sex?

Part of the answer is that the disease carries a mechanism for perpetuating itself: It first devastates families financially and emotionally, then leaves adults unable to mind their children, and finally breeds crippling despair. Death, poverty, and hopelessness so suffuse Ms. Tobela's tin shack that I can imagine them impelling a mixed-up 14-year-old girl into the arms of older men for a few coins.

When a girl's mother and brother are dying, when a family's middle-class dreams collapse in a ramshackle hut, when there isn't enough money to pay for Victor's visits to the doctor—when a girl's world is shattering in slow motion—she doesn't know what to live for.

And so AIDS insinuates itself into the next generation.

TABLE 16.3

U.S. Adolescents and Adults with AIDS—Number of Cases by Exposure Category

Exposure Category	Male	Female	Total
Men who have sex with men	441,380	—	441,380
Injecting drug users	176,162	72,651	248,813
Men who have sex with men and inject drugs	64,833	—	64,833
Male–female sex	59,939	99,175	159,114
Other	14,085	6,636	20,721
Total	756,399	178,463	934,862

SOURCE: Centers for Disease Control and Prevention. (2005a). *HIV/AIDS Surveillance Report, 2004, vol. 16.* U.S. Department of Health and Human Services, Centers for Disease Control and Prevention.

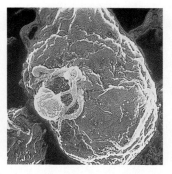

Figure 16.6 HIV (the AIDS Virus) Attacks a White Blood Cell.

HIV progressively weakens the immune system, leaving the body vulnerable to infections and diseases that would otherwise be fended off.

in an army of leukocytes to combat invading microscopic life forms, such as bacteria, that might otherwise use the local injury to establish a beachhead into the body.

EFFECTS OF HIV ON THE IMMUNE SYSTEM Spikes on the surface of HIV allow it to bind to sites on cells in the immune system. Like other viruses, HIV uses the cells it invades to spin off copies of itself. HIV uses the enzyme *reverse transcriptase* to cause the genes in the cells it attacks to make proteins that the virus needs to reproduce.

HIV attacks the immune system by destroying a type of lymphocyte called the CD4 cell (also known as T4 cells or helper T cells; Figure 16.6). The CD4 cell is the "quarterback" of the immune system. CD4 cells "recognize" invading pathogens and signal B lymphocytes or B cells—another kind of white blood cell—to produce antibodies that inactivate pathogens and mark them for annihilation. CD4 cells also signal another class of T cells, called killer T cells, to destroy infected cells. By attacking and destroying helper T cells, HIV disables the very cells on which the body relies to fend off diseases. As HIV cripples the body's defenses, the individual develops infections that would not otherwise take hold. Cancer cells might also proliferate. Although the CD4 cells appear to be its main target, HIV also attacks other types of white blood cells.

The blood normally contains about 1,000 CD4 cells/mm^3. The numbers of CD4 cells may remain at about this level for years after HIV infection. Many people show no symptoms and appear healthy while CD4 cells remain at this level. Then, for reasons that are not clearly understood, the levels of CD4 cells begin to drop off, although symptoms may not appear for a decade or more. As the numbers of CD4 cells decline, symptoms generally increase, and people fall prey to diseases that their weakened immune systems are unable to fight. People become most vulnerable to opportunistic infections when the level of CD4 cells decreases to less than 200 cells/mm^3.

PROGRESSION OF HIV/AIDS HIV follows a complex course after it enters the body. Shortly after infection, the person may experience mild flulike symptoms—fatigue, fever, headaches, muscle pain, lack of appetite, nausea, swollen glands, and possibly a rash. Such symptoms usually disappear within a few weeks, and people may dismiss them as a case of flu. People who enter this symptom-free or carrier state generally look and act well and do not realize that they are infectious. Thus, they can unwittingly pass the virus on to others.

Truth or Fiction Revisited: Most people who are infected with HIV remain symptom free for years. Others enter a symptomatic state that is typically denoted by symptoms such as chronically swollen lymph nodes and intermittent weight loss, fever, fatigue, and diarrhea. This symptomatic state does not constitute full-blown AIDS, but shows that HIV is undermining the integrity of the immune system.

Even during the years when HIV appears to be dormant, billions of viral particles are being spun off. In a seesaw battle, the great majority of them are wiped out by the immune system. Eventually, in almost all cases, the balance tips in favor of HIV. Then the virus' numbers swell. Perhaps a decade or more after the person is infected with HIV, the virus begins to overtake the immune system. It obliterates the cells that house it and spreads to other immune system cells. About half the people with HIV develop AIDS within 10 years of initial infection. For this reason, people who know that they are infected with HIV may feel that they are carrying a time bomb within them.

AIDS is called a *syndrome* because it is characterized by a variety of different symptoms. The beginnings of full-blown cases of AIDS are often marked by symptoms such as swollen lymph nodes, fatigue, fever, night sweats, diarrhea, and weight loss (a "wasting syndrome") that cannot be attributed to dieting or exercise. AIDS is connected with the appearance of diseases such as *Pneumocystis carinii* pneumonia (PCP), Kaposi's sarcoma (a form of cancer), toxoplasmosis of the brain (an infection of parasites), or *herpes simplex* with chronic ulcers. These are termed **opportunistic diseases** because they are not likely to emerge unless a weakened immune system grants the opportunity.

About 10% of people with AIDS have the wasting syndrome. Wasting is the unintentional loss of more than 10% of a person's body weight and is connected with HIV/AIDS, some other infections, and cancer. As HIV/AIDS progresses, the individual grows thinner and more fatigued. He or she becomes unable to perform ordinary life functions and falls prey to opportunistic infections. If left untreated, AIDS almost always results in death within a few years.

TRANSMISSION   HIV can be transmitted by certain contaminated bodily fluids—blood, semen, vaginal secretions, or breast milk. The first three of these may enter the body through vaginal, anal, or oral–genital intercourse with an infected partner. An African study that monitored seropositive mothers and their babies for two years found that the probability of transmission of HIV via breast milk was about 16.2% (one in six) (Nduati et al., 2000). Other avenues of infection include sharing a hypodermic needle with an infected person (as do many people who inject drugs), transfusion with contaminated blood, transplants of organs and tissues that have been infected with HIV, artificial insemination with infected semen, or being stuck by a needle used previously on an infected person. HIV may enter the body through tiny cuts or sores in the mucous lining of the vagina, the rectum, and even the mouth. These cuts or sores can be so tiny that you are not aware of them.

Transmission of HIV through kissing, even prolonged kissing or "French" kissing, is considered unlikely. When a person injects drugs, a small amount of his or her blood remains inside the needle and syringe. If the person is infected with HIV, the virus may be found in the blood remaining in the needle or syringe. Others who use the needle inject the infected blood into their bloodstream. HIV can also be spread by sharing needles used for other purposes, such as injecting steroids, ear piercing, or tattooing.

HIV can also be transmitted from mother to fetus during pregnancy or from mother to child through childbirth or breast-feeding (Becquet et al., 2005; Bulterys et al., 2004). Transmission is most likely during childbirth.

Opportunistic diseases
Diseases that take hold only when the immune system is weakened and unable to fend them off; examples include Kaposi's sarcoma and *Pneumocystis carinii* pneumonia (or PCP) and are found in people with AIDS

Male-to-female transmission through vaginal intercourse is about twice as likely as female-to-male transmission (CDC, 2005a; Table 16.2), partly because more of the virus is found in the ejaculate than in vaginal secretions. A man's ejaculate may also remain for many days in the vagina, providing greater opportunity for infection to occur. Male–female or male–male anal intercourse is especially risky, because it often tears or abrades rectal tissue, facilitating entry of the virus into the bloodstream (UNAIDS, 2006).

Male–female transmission via sexual intercourse is the primary route of HIV infection in Africa, Latin America, and Asia. Worldwide, male–female sexual intercourse accounts for the majority of cases of HIV/AIDS (UNAIDS, 2006). In the United States, many cases of male–female transmission occur among people who inject drugs, and their sex partners.

In the early years of the AIDS epidemic, HIV spread rapidly among hemophiliacs who had unknowingly been transfused with contaminated blood. However, blood supplies are now routinely screened for HIV.

HIV may also be spread by donor semen, such as that used in artificial insemination. Cases have also been reported of women who have become infected with hepatitis B, gonorrhea, trichomoniasis (trich), and chlamydia by donor semen.

Can Kissing Transmit HIV? *HIV is a blood-borne virus that is transmitted via various bodily fluids, including blood, semen, and vaginal fluids. However, the Centers for Disease Control and Prevention (CDC) have not found that HIV occurs in infectious quantities in saliva.*

Factors Affecting the Risk of Sexual Transmission Some people seem more likely to communicate HIV, and others seem to be especially vulnerable to infection. Several factors appear to affect the risk of HIV infection and development of AIDS:

- The probability of transmission increases with the number of sexual contacts with an infected partner.

- The probability of transmission is affected by the type of sexual activity. Anal intercourse provides a convenient port of entry for HIV because it abrades the rectal lining, and rectal cells are particularly vulnerable.

- The amount of virus (viral load) in semen peaks shortly after initial infection and when full-blown AIDS develops.

- STIs such as genital warts, gonorrhea, trichomoniasis, and chlamydia inflame the genital region, which heightens the risk of sexual transmission of other STIs. STIs that produce genital ulcers, such as syphilis and genital herpes, heighten vulnerability to HIV infection.

- Circumcision has been found to cut the risk of infection by HIV in half (Bailey et al., 2007; Gray et al., 2007). Uncircumcised men may be more vulnerable to HIV for two reasons. First, the underside of the foreskin has many Langerhans cells, to which HIV readily attaches. Second, the foreskin frequently suffers small tears during sexual intercourse, providing a convenient port of entry for HIV.

- Genetic factors may also be at work. About 1% of people of Western European descent inherited a gene from both parents that prevents HIV from entering cells in the immune system and are therefore apparently immune to HIV infection. Perhaps 20% of individuals of Western European descent have inherited the gene from one parent; HIV disease appears to progress more slowly in them. Some prostitutes in Thailand and Africa, where HIV infection has been running rampant, also appear to be immune to HIV infection (Royce et al., 1997).

How HIV Is *Not* Transmitted There is much misinformation about the transmission of HIV. Let us consider some of the ways in which HIV is not transmitted:

- HIV is not transmitted from donating blood. AIDS cannot be contracted by donating blood, because needles are discarded after a single use.
- HIV is not transmitted through casual, everyday contact. There is no evidence of transmission of HIV through hugging someone, shaking hands, bumping into strangers on buses and trains; handling money, doorknobs, or other objects that have been touched by infected people; sharing drinking fountains, public telephones, public toilets, or swimming pools; or by trying on clothing that has been worn by an infected person.
- HIV is not transmitted by insect bites or bites from other animals.
- HIV is not transmitted by airborne germs or contact with contaminated food.
- HIV is not transmitted through sharing work or home environments. No cases of HIV transmission have been documented based on nonsexual contact in schools or in the workplace.
- HIV is apparently not transmitted by kissing, but check out the nearby "Closer Look" feature.

DIAGNOSIS OF HIV INFECTION AND AIDS The enzyme-linked immunosorbent assay (ELISA for short) is one widely used test for HIV. ELISA does not directly detect HIV. Instead, it reveals HIV antibodies. Rapid tests such as OraQuick indicate the presence of HIV antibodies within 20 minutes. People may show an antibody response to HIV long before they develop symptoms of infection. A positive (**seropositive**) test result means that HIV antibodies were found. A negative (**seronegative**) outcome means that antibodies to HIV were not detected.

ELISA can be performed on samples of blood, saliva, or urine. OraQuick is based on a blood sample from pricking the finger with a needle. A saliva test is not quite as accurate as a blood test, but it is less expensive, accurate enough, and might encourage people who avoid blood tests to be tested. Although HIV antibodies can be detected in saliva, HIV itself is not found in measurable quantities. This is why kissing is not considered an avenue of transmission of HIV. Saliva is absorbed by a cotton pad on a stick that is placed between the lower gum and the cheek. The saliva undergoes analysis in a laboratory. When people show evidence of the presence of HIV antibodies, the presence of the virus itself can be confirmed by more expensive tests, such as the Western blot test or an immunofluorescence assay.

TREATMENT OF HIV/AIDS For many years, researchers were frustrated by failure in the effort to develop effective vaccines and treatments for HIV/AIDS. Potential HIV/AIDS vaccines are being tested on people and animals, but optimism seems to grow and then wane. There is still no safe, effective vaccine, but recent developments in drug therapy have raised hopes in the area of treatment. Today many drugs are used to combat HIV/AIDS. They offer a good deal of hope to people with HIV/AIDS, including pregnant women who are infected with HIV.

Zidovudine (AZT) has been the most widely used HIV/AIDS drug. Zidovudine is one of a number of so-called nucleoside analogues that inhibit replication (reproduction) of HIV by targeting the enzyme called reverse transcriptase. HIV-infected pregnant women who use zidovudine reduce the rate of HIV infection in their newborns by two thirds (Connor et al., 1994). Zidovudine helps prevent transmission during childbirth by reducing the amount of the virus in the mother's bloodstream. Only 8% of the babies born to the zidovudine-treated women became infected with

Seropositive Having a pathogen or antibodies to that pathogen in the bloodstream

Seronegative Lacking a pathogen or antibodies to that pathogen in the bloodstream

A Closer Look

IS KISSING SAFE?

In a presentation on the safety of kissing that leaves us less than happy, the CDC looks as though it comes close to speaking out of two sides of its mouth. But actually it doesn't. The following two quotations were downloaded on September 30, 2006 (www.cdc.gov/hiv/resources/factsheets/transmission.htm). Read them carefully. Then see our commentary later.

Kissing

Casual contact through closed-mouth or social kissing is not a risk for transmission of HIV. Because of the potential for contact with blood during French or open-mouth kissing, the CDC recommends against engaging in this activity with a person known to be infected. However, the risk of acquiring HIV during open-mouth kissing is believed to be very low. The CDC has investigated only one case of HIV infection that may be attributed to contact with blood during open-mouth kissing.

Saliva, Tears, and Sweat

HIV has been found in saliva and tears in very low quantities from some AIDS patients. It is important to understand that finding a small amount of HIV in a body fluid does not necessarily mean that HIV can be transmitted by that body fluid. HIV has not been recovered from the sweat of HIV-infected persons. Contact with saliva, tears, or sweat has never been shown to result in transmission of HIV.

Here's the skinny. If you engage in deep kissing—also known as open-mouth kissing, tongue kissing, or French kissing—with a person who is infected with HIV, there is no evidence whatsoever that you will catch HIV from that person's *saliva*.

However, there is a remote chance you could be infected by sharing blood. How might that happen? One possibility is that the two of you might have brushed your teeth recently, creating tiny abrasions or cuts in your gums. Some blood from your kissing partner might make its way into your mouth and into one of those temporary ports of entry. It's an extremely slight risk, but that extremely slight risk does exist.

Here's our bottom-line recommendation: If you really don't know your partner, don't engage in deep kissing. (Why would you deep kiss a stranger anyway?) If you have gotten to know your partner for a while and you have no reason to be suspicious that his or her sexual or injecting drug history places him or her at high risk of being infected with HIV, kiss away. (That does *not* mean you should also risk unprotected sex!)

HIV compared with 25% of babies whose mothers are untreated. Zidovudine is usually used for 26 weeks prior to childbirth. However, using zidovudine for even the final few weeks cuts the transmission rate of HIV from mother to child by half (Meyer, 1998). Because zidovudine is expensive, briefer treatment may be of most help in developing nations or when the mother has not sought prenatal treatment early during pregnancy.

The results of the European Mode of Delivery Collaboration Trial on the efficacy of elective C-section versus vaginal delivery show that C-section further decreases the risk of maternal transmission of HIV to the baby (Ricci et al., 2000). The study enlisted about 400 seropositive mothers. All mothers received zidovudine during pregnancy. Half the mothers were assigned at random to deliver vaginally, and half by C-section. The HIV infection rate was 10.6% for babies delivered vaginally (similar to the 8% reported by Meyer [1998]) and 1.7% for babies delivered by C-section. Thus, the combination of zidovudine during pregnancy and C-section cuts the chance that a seropositive mother will transmit HIV to her baby to about 1 in 50.

Other drugs that block the replication of HIV include *protease inhibitors.* Protease inhibitors target the protease enzyme. Fusion inhibitors attack HIV during yet another phase in its reproductive cycle (Lalezari et al., 2003; Tashima & Carpenter, 2003).

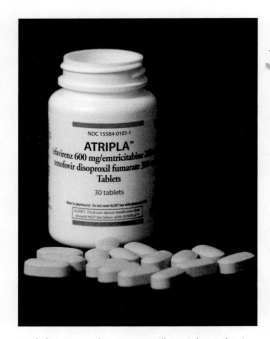

Atripla. *A new three-in-one pill, Atripla, makes it easy to manage the regimen of HAART ("highly active antiretroviral therapy"), even if it doesn't reduce the expense. Atripla contains a "cocktail" of antiviral drugs that have become the standard treatment of HIV/AIDS in developed countries. People in less developed nations make do, or not, on less expensive medications or on no medication. Even though HAART has saved lives in developed nations, it is expensive, there are side effects, and it does not work for everyone.*

A combination or "cocktail" of antiviral drugs has become the standard treatment of HIV/AIDS. This combination—referred to as **HAART** (which stands for *highly active antiretroviral therapy*)—decreases the likelihood that HIV will develop resistance to treatment. It has created hope that AIDS will become increasingly manageable—a chronic health problem as opposed to a terminal illness. However, HAART is expensive, and many people who could benefit from it cannot afford it. The side effects of these medicines can be unpleasant, including nausea and, in the case of protease inhibitors, unusual accumulations of fat, such as "buffalo humps" in the neck.

It is now possible to get the benefits of HAART by taking a three-in-one pill, Atripla, with "sandwiched" ingredients that are released at different rates. However, the expense of treatment has not diminished. As this book went to press, Atripla was priced at $1,150 for a 30-day supply (Bridges, 2006).

HAART has worked wonders to date (Bridges, 2006). It has cut the U.S. death rate from HIV/AIDS-related causes by about 75% since the mid to late 1990s (CDC, 2005a). Yet even when HIV has been reduced to undetectable levels by common tests, scientists have been able to locate it in "resting" (nonreplicating) CD4 cells (Lederman & Valdez, 2000). Therefore, HAART is not a cure. In fact, HAART-resistant strains of HIV may evolve as HAART is being used. For this and other reasons, many HIV-infected people go on drug "vacations" after using HAART for a number of months or years. Promising results are also reported in treating opportunistic infections such as PCP and fungal infections that take hold in people with weakened immune systems.

Despite the advent of HAART, nearly 10,000 people in the United States still die of HIV/AIDS each year (CDC, 2005). The CDC (2005a) attributes these deaths to lack of early testing and treatment for some people, failure of some people with HIV/AIDS to follow HAART treatment regimens, and, in some cases, treatment failure. People who assume that HIV/AIDS is no longer a deadly syndrome need to recognize that HAART does not help everyone with HIV/AIDS. Ironically, however, the advent of HAART has increased the frequency of risky sexual behavior by some people (Dilley et al., 2003).

Unfortunately, the advances in treatment in the United States do not extend to everyone in the world, not even to everyone in the United States. Among women in the United States today, the risks of HIV/AIDS fall most heavily on poor women, mostly African American or Latina American, who live in urban areas. African American and Latina American women account for nearly three quarters of women with HIV/AIDS in the United States, although they make up only about one quarter of the female population (CDC, 2005a) (Table 16.3).

PREVENTION What can we do to curb the spread of HIV/AIDS? Given the lack of a vaccine or cure, prevention is our best hope. Our discussion of prevention will focus on sexual transmission, but other efforts have been made to prevent transmission of HIV from mother to child, through injection of drugs, and through blood transfusions. For example, HIV-infected women are advised to avoid breast-feeding. Zidovudine given to the mother and other measures, such as C-section (as mentioned earlier), decrease the probability of transmission through childbirth (Ricci et al., 2000). Zidovudine and other drugs given to newborn babies further lessen their risk of being infected during childbirth (Taha et al., 2003). The screening of blood

HAART (pronounced *hart*) The acronym for "highly active antiretroviral therapy; the combination or "cocktail" of drugs used to treat HIV/AIDS

donors and sperm donors has reduced the probability of transmission by transfusion and artificial insemination. We have been less successful in reducing the risk of infection through unsafe sexual contact.

Most prevention efforts focus on education. Sexually active people have been advised to alter their sexual behavior either by practicing abstinence, by limiting their sexual experiences to a lifelong monogamous relationship, or by practicing "safe sex," which—as we shall see—could be more accurately dubbed "safer sex."

Genital Herpes

Genital herpes is an STI caused by the herpes simplex virus. The hysteria that surrounded the rapid spread of genital herpes in the 1970s and 1980s died down with the advent of AIDS. Nevertheless, there are 200,000 to 500,000 new cases of genital herpes each year. The CDC (2001b) estimates that as many as 45 million Americans age 12 and older may be infected with genital herpes.

Once you get herpes, it's yours for life. After the initial attack, it remains an unwelcome guest in your body. It finds a cozy place to lay low until it stirs up trouble again. It causes recurrent outbreaks that often happen at the worst times, such as around final exams. This is because stress can depress the functioning of the immune system and heighten the likelihood of outbreaks.

You can also pass the infection along to sex partners for the rest of your life. Flare-ups may continue to recur, sometimes with annoying frequency. On the other hand, some people have no recurrences. Still others have mild, brief recurrences that become less frequent over time.

Different types of herpes are caused by variants of the *herpes simplex* virus. The most common type, **_herpes simplex_ virus type 1 (HSV-1)** causes oral herpes. Oral herpes is characterized by cold sores or fever blisters on the lips or mouth. It can also be transferred to the genitals by the hands or by oral–genital contact. **Genital herpes** is caused by a related but distinct virus, the **_herpes simplex_ virus type 2 (HSV-2)**. This virus produces painful, shallow sores and blisters on the genitals. HSV-2 can also be transferred to the mouth through oral–genital contact. Both types of herpes can be transmitted sexually.

TRANSMISSION Herpes can be transmitted through oral, anal, or vaginal sexual activity with an infected person. The herpes viruses can also survive for several hours on toilet seats or other objects, where they can be picked up by direct contact. Oral herpes is easily contracted by drinking from the same cup as an infected person, by kissing, even by sharing towels. But genital herpes is generally spread by coitus or by oral or anal sex.

One problem is that many people do not realize that they are infected. They can thus unknowingly transmit the virus through sexual contact. And many of the people who know they are infected don't realize that they can pass along the virus even when they have no noticeable outbreak. Although genital herpes is most contagious during active flare-ups, it can also be transmitted when an infected partner has no symptoms (genital sores or feelings of burning or itching in the genitals). Any intimate contact with an infected person carries some risk of transmission of the virus, even if the infected person never has another outbreak. People may also be infected with the virus and have no outbreaks, yet may pass the virus along to others.

Truth or Fiction Revisited: It is not true that genital herpes can be transmitted only during flare-ups of the infection. Although people are most contagious during flare-ups, genital herpes can also be transmitted between them.

REFLECT

Do you favor distribution of condoms in the public schools as a means of attempting to prevent transmission of HIV/AIDS? Do you support the distribution of free hypodermic needles to people who inject drugs? Explain.

TRUTH fiction **8**

Herpes simplex virus type 1 (HSV-1) The virus that causes oral herpes, which is characterized by cold sores or fever blisters on the lips or mouth

Genital herpes An STI caused by *herpes simplex* virus type 2, characterized by painful shallow sores and blisters on the genitals

Herpes simplex virus type 2 (HSV-2) The virus that causes genital herpes

Herpes can also be spread from one part of the body to another by touching the infected area and then touching another body part. One potentially serious result is a herpes infection of the eye: **ocular herpes**. Thorough washing with soap and water after touching an infected area may reduce the risk of spreading the infection to other parts of the body. Still, it is best to avoid touching the infected area altogether, especially if there are active sores.

Women with genital herpes are more likely than the general population to have miscarriages. Passage through the birth canal of an infected mother can infect babies with genital herpes, damaging or killing baby. Obstetricians thus often perform cesarean sections if the mother has active lesions or **prodromal symptoms** at the time of delivery. Herpes can also place women at greater risk of genital cancers, such as cervical cancer. (All women, not just women with herpes, are advised to have regular pelvic examinations, including Pap tests for early detection of cervical cancer.)

SafeZone

Q *If you have a cold sore on your lips or mouth (oral herpes), can you give your partner genital herpes through oral sex?*

A No, but you can give your partner "oral herpes" (that is, HSV-1) on the genitals.

SYMPTOMS Genital lesions or sores appear about six to eight days after infection with genital herpes. At first they appear as reddish, painful bumps, or papules, along the penis or the vulva (Figure 16.7). They may also appear on the thighs or buttocks, in the vagina, or on the cervix. These papules turn into groups of small blisters that are filled with fluid containing infectious viral particles. The blisters are attacked by the body's immune system (white blood cells). They fill with pus, burst, and become extremely painful, shallow sores or ulcers that are surrounded by a red ring. People are especially infectious during such outbreaks, because the ulcers shed millions of viral particles. Other symptoms may include headaches and muscle aches, swollen lymph glands, fever, burning during urination, and a vaginal discharge. The blisters crust over and heal in one to three weeks. Internal sores in the vagina or on the cervix may take 10 days longer than external (labial) sores to heal. Physicians thus advise infected women to avoid unprotected intercourse for at least 10 days after the healing of external sores.

Although the symptoms disappear, the disease does not. The virus remains in the body, burrowing into nerve cells in the base of the spine, where it may lie dormant for years or a lifetime. The infected person is least contagious during this dormant stage. For reasons that remain unclear, the virus becomes reactivated and gives rise to recurrences in most cases.

Recurrences may be related to factors such as infections (as in a cold), stress, fatigue, depression, exposure to the sun, and hormonal changes, such as those that occur during pregnancy or menstruation. Recurrences tend to occur within 3 to 12 months of the initial episode and to affect the same part of the body.

Symptoms of oral herpes include sores or blisters on the lips, the inside of the mouth, the tongue, or the throat. Fever and feelings of sickness may occur. The gums may swell and redden. The sores heal over in about two weeks, and the virus retreats into nerve cells at the base of the neck, where it lies dormant between flare-ups. Most people with oral herpes experience recurrences.

Ocular herpes A herpes infection of the eye, usually caused by touching an infected area of the body and then touching the eye

Prodromal symptoms Warning symptoms that signal the onset of a disease

DIAGNOSIS AND TREATMENT Genital herpes is first diagnosed by clinical inspection of herpetic sores or ulcers in the mouth or on the genitals. A sample of fluid may be taken from the base of a genital sore and cultured in the laboratory to detect the growth of the virus.

There is encouraging news about the development of a vaccine against genital herpes, called Simplirix, which will probably be available in 2007 (Cunningham et al., 2006). In pilot studies, the vaccine is reported to have prevented herpes outbreaks in more than 70% of women who had not previously had cold sores or genital herpes. The herpes virus that causes cold sores ironically confers some protection against genital herpes, but the vaccine does not help women who have already contracted genital herpes. It remains unclear why the vaccine has been ineffective with men.

Viruses, unlike the bacteria that cause gonorrhea or syphilis, do not respond to antibiotics. Antiviral drugs such as acyclovir (brand name Zovirax), famciclovir, and valacyclovir can relieve pain, speed healing, and reduce the duration of viral shedding (Hatcher et al., 2006). Acyclovir can be applied directly to the sores in ointment form, but must be taken orally, in pill form, to help combat internal lesions in the vagina or on the cervix. Oral administration of antiviral drugs may reduce the severity of the initial episode and, if taken regularly, the frequency and duration of recurrent outbreaks (Hatcher et al., 2006). On the other hand, users may develop a tolerance for these drugs, meaning that larger doses must be used to maintain effectiveness.

Warm baths, loose-fitting clothing, aspirin, and cold, wet compresses may relieve pain during flare-ups. People with herpes are advised to maintain regular sleeping habits and to learn to manage stress.

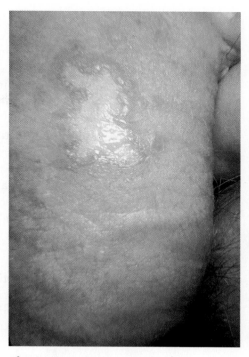

Figure 16.7 Herpes Lesions on the Male Genitals. *Herpes lesions or sores can appear on the genitals in both men and women. In contrast to the syphilis chancre, they can be quite painful. Herpes is most likely to be transmitted during outbreaks of the disease (when the sores are present, that is), but it can be transmitted at other times as well. Stress increases the likelihood of outbreaks. Antiviral drugs tend to decrease the frequency, duration, and discomfort of outbreaks.*

COPING WITH GENITAL HERPES The psychological problems connected with herpes can be more distressing than the physical effects of the illness. The prospect of a lifetime of recurrences and concerns about infecting one's sex partners exacerbate the emotional impact of herpes. People with herpes often feel angry, especially toward those who transmitted the disease to them. They may feel anxious about making a long-term commitment or bearing children:

> After the first big episode of herpes, I felt distant from my body. When we began lovemaking again, I had a hard time having orgasms or trusting the rhythm of my responses. I shed some tears over that. I felt my body had been invaded. My body feels riddled with it; I'm somehow contaminated. And there is always that lingering anxiety: Is my baby okay? It's unjust that the birth of my child may be affected. (Boston Women's Health Book Collective, 2005)

Most people with herpes learn to cope. Some are helped by support groups that share ways of living with the disease. A caring and trusting partner is important. Joanne, a 26-year-old securities analyst, kept her herpes a secret from Jonathan during the first month they were dating. But when they approached the point of becoming sexually intimate, she felt obligated to tell him that she carried the virus:

> "I feared that telling him would scare him off. After all, who wants to have a relationship with someone who can give them herpes? After the first few dates I felt that this was the person I could spend the rest of my life with. I knew he also felt the same way. I had to tell him before things became too

intense between us. Believe me, it wasn't easy blurting it out. He wasn't shocked or anything, although he did ask me all kinds of questions about it. I remember telling him that I got recurrences about once a year or so for about a week at a time. I told him that there was always the potential that I could infect him but that we would play it safe and avoid having sex whenever I had an outbreak. I also told him that even at other times I couldn't guarantee that it would be perfectly safe. He said at first that he needed some time to think about it. But later, that very night in fact, he called to tell me that he didn't want this to come between us and that we should try to make our relationship work."

Joanne and Jonathan were married about six months later. A year after that their daughter Andrea was born. Jonathan remains uninfected. Joanne's occasional outbreaks are treated with acyclovir ointment and pass within a week or so.

—Authors' Files

The attitudes of people with herpes also play a role in adjusting. People who view herpes as a manageable illness or problem, and not as a medical disaster or character deficit, seem to find it easier to cope.

Viral Hepatitis

Viral hepatitis refers to various types of liver infections (**hepatitis** is an inflammation of the liver) that are caused by viruses. The major types are *hepatitis A* (formerly called infectious hepatitis), *hepatitis B* (formerly called serum hepatitis), *hepatitis C* (formerly called hepatitis non-A, non-B), and *hepatitis D.*

Most people with hepatitis have no symptoms. When symptoms do appear, they often include **jaundice, feelings of weakness and nausea, loss of appetite, abdominal discomfort, whitish bowel movements, and brownish or tea-colored urine**. The symptoms of hepatitis B tend to be more severe and long-lasting than those of hepatitis A or C. In about 10% of cases, hepatitis B can lead to chronic liver disease. Hepatitis C tends to have milder symptoms but often leads to chronic liver disease such as cirrhosis or cancer of the liver. Hepatitis D—also called *delta hepatitis* or type D hepatitis—occurs only in the presence of hepatitis B. Hepatitis D, which has symptoms similar to those of hepatitis B, can produce severe liver damage and often leads to death.

The hepatitis A virus is transmitted through contact with infected fecal matter found in contaminated food or water, and by oral contact with fecal matter, as through oral–anal sexual activity (licking or mouthing the partner's anus). (It is largely because of the risk of hepatitis A that restaurant employees are required to wash their hands after using the toilet.) Eating raw, infested shellfish is also a common means of transmitting hepatitis A.

Hepatitis B can be transmitted sexually through anal, vaginal, or oral intercourse with an infected partner; through transfusion with contaminated blood supplies; by the sharing of contaminated needles or syringes; and by contact with contaminated saliva, menstrual blood, nasal mucus, or semen. Sharing razors, toothbrushes, or other personal articles with an infected person can also transmit hepatitis B. Hepatitis C and hepatitis D can also be transmitted sexually or through contact with contaminated blood. A person can transmit the viruses that cause hepatitis even if he or she is unaware of having any symptoms of the disease.

Hepatitis is usually diagnosed by testing blood samples for the presence of hepatitis antigens and antibodies. There is no cure for viral hepatitis. Bed rest and

Hepatitis An inflammation of the liver

Jaundice A yellowish discoloration of the skin and the whites of the eyes fluids are usually recommended until the acute stage of the infection subsides, generally in a few weeks. Full recovery may take months. A vaccine provides protection against hepatitis B and also against hepatitis D, because hepatitis D can occur only if hepatitis B is present (Hatcher et al., 2006). A hepatitis B vaccine, Dynavax, may be available in 2007.

Human Papilloma Virus

Genital warts are a symptom of infection by HPV. HPV is the world's most common STI, with signs of infection found in nearly half the adult women in some countries (Wald, 2005). Half or more of the sexually active college women in the United States are infected with HPV. Although the warts may appear in visible areas of the skin, in most cases they appear in areas that cannot be seen, such as on the cervix in women or in the urethra in men. They occur most commonly among people in the 20- to 24-year-old age range (Wald, 2005). Within a few months after infection, the warts are usually found in the genital and anal regions. Women are more susceptible to HPV infection because cells in the cervix divide swiftly, facilitating the multiplication of HPV. Women who initiate coitus prior to the age of 18 and who have many sex partners are particularly susceptible to infection. It is estimated that nearly half the sexually active teenage women in some American cities are infected with HPV (Wald, 2005).

But let's pause for some good news about HPV!

- First, a vaccine is now available that can make most women immune to HPV, if they are vaccinated before they are infected.

- Second, although it is true that HPV infections are pandemic, most healthy women clear most HPV infections on their own.

Genital warts are similar to common plantar warts—itchy bumps that vary in size and shape. Genital warts are hard and yellow–gray when they form on dry skin. They take on pink, soft, cauliflower shapes in moist areas such as the lower vagina (Figure 16.8). In men they appear on the penis, foreskin, and scrotum, and in the urethra. They appear on the vulva, along the vaginal wall, and on the cervix in women. They can also occur outside the genital area—for example, in the mouth; on the lips, eyelids, or nipples; around the anus; or in the rectum.

Genital warts may not cause any symptoms, but those that form on the urethra can cause bleeding or painful discharges. HPV has been implicated in cancers of the genital organs, particularly cervical cancer and penile cancer (American Cancer Society, 2006). Nearly all cases of cervical cancer are linked to HPV (American Cancer Society, 2006). Men who have been circumcised are significantly less likely to carry HPV than men who have not been circumcised (American Cancer Society, 2006). All in all, it would seem wise for women to safeguard themselves from HPV-related cervical cancer by limiting their number of sex partners (to reduce their risk of exposure to HPV), thinking about the extracurricular sexual activities of their mates, and having regular Pap smears.

HPV can be transmitted sexually through skin-to-skin contact during vaginal, anal, or oral sex. It can also be transmitted by other forms of contact, such as touching infected towels or clothing. The incubation period may vary from a few weeks to a couple of years.

Freezing the wart (*cryotherapy*) with liquid nitrogen is a preferred treatment. One alternative treatment involves painting or coating the warts over several days with podofilox solution or gel, imiquimod cream, trichloroacetic acid, or bichloroacetic

Figure 16.8 Genital Warts. *Genital warts are caused by HPV and may have a cauliflowerlike appearance. Many—perhaps most—cases occur where they can go visually undetected. HPV is implicated in cervical cancer, and women should be checked regularly for genital warts and other possibly "silent" STIs.*

Genital warts An STI that is caused by HPV and takes the form of warts that appear around the genitals and anus

acid (Hatcher et al., 2006). An alcohol-based podophyllin solution causes the warts to dry up and fall off. Although the warts may be removed, treatment does not rid the body of the virus (Hatcher et al., 2006). There may thus be recurrences. Podophyllin is not recommended for use with pregnant women or for treatment of warts that form on the cervix. The warts can also be treated by a doctor with electrodes (burning) or surgery (by laser or surgical removal).

SafeZone

Q *Do some infections just naturally go away?*

A Absolutely. Your immune system does clear some of them, and, fortunately, HPV can be one of those. Unfortunately, some of the worst ones, including HIV/AIDS, do not just disappear permanently on their own, even if they lie dormant for many years.

Molluscum Contagiosum

Molluscum contagiosum is an STI that is characterized by painless, raised lesions that appear on the genitals, buttocks, thighs, or lower abdomen and are caused by a pox virus. Pinkish in appearance with a waxy or pearly top, the lesions usually appear within two or three months of infection. Most infected people have between 10 and 20 lesions, although the number of lesions can range from 1 to 100 or more. The lesions are generally not associated with serious complications and often disappear on their own within six months. Or they can be treated by squeezing them (like "popping" a blackhead) to exude the whitish center plug. Solutions of podophyllin, trichloroacetic acid, or silver nitrate are also used. Freezing with liquid nitrogen (*cryotherapy*) can also be used to remove the lesions. However, do not try to treat any lesions on your own. See your doctor.

TRUTH **fiction 9**

Molluscum contagiosum An STI caused by a pox virus that causes painless, raised lesions to appear on the genitals, buttocks, thighs, or lower abdomen

Ectoparasites Parasites that live on the outside of the host's body; in contrast to *endo*parasites, which live within the body

Pediculosis A parasitic infestation by pubic lice (*Pthirus pubis*) that causes itching

Ectoparasitic Infestations

Ectoparasites, as opposed to *endoparasites,* live on the outer surfaces of animals (*ecto-* means "outer"). *T. vaginalis* is an endoparasite (*endo-* means "inner"). Ectoparasites are larger than the agents that cause other STIs. In this section we consider two types of STIs caused by ectoparasites: pediculosis and scabies.

Pediculosis

Pediculosis is the name given to an infestation of a parasite whose proper Latin name, *Pthirus pubis* (pubic lice), sounds rather too dignified for these bothersome (dare we say ugly?) creatures that are better known as "crabs." **Truth or Fiction Revisited:** It is not true that pubic lice are of the same family of animals as crabs, but when viewed under a microscope, they look similar to crabs (Figure 16.9). They belong to a family of insects called "biting lice." Another member of the family, the human head louse, is an annoying insect that clings to hair on the scalp and often spreads among schoolchildren.

In the adult stage, pubic lice are large enough to be seen with the naked eye. They are spread sexually but can also be transmitted by contact with an infested towel, sheet, or—yes—toilet seat. They can survive for only about 24 hours without a human host, but they may deposit eggs that can take up to seven days to hatch in bedding or towels. Therefore, all bedding, towels, and clothes that have been used by an infested person must be washed in hot water and dried on the hot cycle, or dry-cleaned to ensure they are free of lice. Fingers may also transmit the lice from the genitals to other hair-covered parts of the body, including the scalp and armpits. Sexual contact should be avoided until the infestation is eradicated.

Itching, ranging from the mildly irritating to the intolerable, is the most prominent symptom of a pubic lice infestation. The itching is caused by the "crabs" attaching themselves to the pubic hair and piercing the skin to feed on the blood of their hosts. The life span of these insects is only about one month, but they are prolific egg layers and may spawn several generations before they die. An infestation can be treated effectively with a prescription medication, a 1% solution of lindane (brand name Kwell), which is available as a cream, lotion, or shampoo. Nonprescription medications containing pyrethrins or piperonyl butoxide (brand names RID, Triple X, and others) will also do the job. Kwell is not recommended for use by pregnant or lactating women. A careful reexamination of the body is necessary after several days of treatment to ensure that all lice and eggs were killed.

Figure 16.9 Pubic Lice. Pediculosis is an infestation by public lice (*Phthirus pubis*). Pubic lice are commonly called "crabs" because of their appearance under a microscope.

REFLECT

If pubic lice can be transmitted by contact with an infested toilet seat, why is it referred to as an STI?

SafeZone

Q *Can you get crabs if you are shaved?*

A Probably not. They attach to the base of pubic hairs (or other hairs) and bite through the skin from there so they can feed on blood.

CRITICAL Thinking

Do you believe that it is a good idea that medications for ectoparasites are available without prescription? Discuss the pros and cons.

Scabies

Scabies (short for *Sarcoptes scabiei*) is a parasitic infestation caused by a tiny mite that may be transmitted through sexual contact or contact with infested clothing, bed linen, towels, and other fabrics. The mites attach themselves to the base of pubic hair and burrow into the skin, where they lay eggs and subsist for the duration of their 30-day life span. Like pubic lice, scabies are often found in the genital region and cause itching and discomfort. They are also responsible for reddish lines (created by burrowing) and sores, welts, or blisters on the skin. Unlike lice, they are too tiny to be seen by the naked eye. Diagnosis is made by detecting the mite or its by-products on microscopic examination of scrapings from suspicious-looking areas of skin. Scabies are most often found on the hands and wrists, but they may also appear on the genitals, buttocks, armpits, and feet. They do not appear above the neck—thankfully!

Scabies, like pubic lice, may be treated effectively with 1% lindane (Kwell). The entire body from the neck down must be coated with a thin layer of the medication, which should not be washed off for eight hours. But lindane should not be used by women who are pregnant or lactating. To avoid reinfection, sex partners and others in close bodily contact with infected individuals should also be treated. Clothing and bed linen that the infected person has used must be washed and dried on the hot

Scabies A parasitic infestation caused by a tiny mite (*Sarcoptes scabiei*) that causes itching cycle or dry-cleaned. As with "crabs," sexual contact should be avoided until the infestation is eliminated.

SafeZone

Q *Isn't it true that if you get treated for an STI once, you have immunity to it?*

A No. (Unless the "treatment" is a vaccination.)

Prevention of STIs: More Than Safer Sex

Prevention is the best way to control the spread of STIs, especially those for which there is no cure or vaccine. Prevention of even one case of an STI can prevent its spread to others—perhaps eventually to you.

There are many things that you can do to lower the risk of contracting STIs. As you will see, "safer sex" is only one aspect of prevention.

Practice Abstinence or Monogamy

> "I don't even masturbate anymore. I'm so afraid I'll give myself something. I just want to be friends with myself."
>
> —Richard Lewis

The only fully effective strategies to prevent the sexual transmission of STIs are abstinence or maintaining a monogamous sexual relationship with an uninfected partner. If you are celibate, or if you and your sex partner are not infected and neither of you engages in sexual activity with anyone else, you have little to be concerned about. Many people are sexually active and have not committed themselves to a monogamous relationship, however. Even for those who seek monogamous relationships, there must always be that "first time."

Be Knowledgeable about the Risks

Be aware of the risks of STIs. Many of us try to put the dangers of STIs out of our minds, especially in moments of passion. Make a pact with yourself to refuse to play the dangerous game of pretending that the dangers of STIs do not exist or that you are somehow immune.

Knowledge about HIV transmission does not always translate into behavioral change, such as increased use of latex condoms (which can block the transmission of HIV) and other safer sex practices. In fact, knowledge about the transmission of HIV and other STIs is not reliably related to condom use (www.guttmacher.org, 2006; Lin & Wang, 2003; Mansergh et al., 2002; Pinkerton et al., 2003a). Despite widespread efforts to educate the public about the dangers of unprotected sex, negative attitudes toward using condoms persist, especially among males. Consider the litany of complaints we come across: "They reduce sexual pleasure." "They're a nuisance to put on." "They cost too much." "They interrupt sex." And on and on.

Talking about Preventing Transmission of HIV/AIDS and other STIs. *Most people do not find it easy to talk frankly about preventing STIs, but what is the alternative?*

If virtually all young people in the United States are aware of the sexual transmission of HIV, why do so many continue to engage in risky sexual behavior? For one thing, teenagers do not perceive risky behavior to be as dangerous as adults do. This generalization extends to drinking, smoking, failure to use seat belts, and drag racing, as well as sexual behavior. Young people also profit from being taught specific skills to protect themselves from engaging in risky behaviors, such as communication skills for discussing safer sex options with their partners, assertiveness skills for ensuring that their needs and interests are respected by their partners, social skills to resist peer pressures, and correct use of condoms.

Researchers have identified several factors that underlie risky sexual behavior among young people:

1. *Perceived low risk of infection.* One of the major stumbling blocks in promoting safer sex practices is that many young heterosexuals perceive a low risk of contracting HIV. Given the current low rate of known infections among heterosexuals who do not inject drugs, many heterosexuals may dismiss HIV/AIDS as a problem that affects other types of people. Even gay men may operate under the "I'm not the type" fallacy and underestimate their personal risk.

2. *Negative attitudes toward condom use.* For some, the risk of being infected with HIV seems to fly out of the mind when the opportunity for sex arises. Some claim that a condom dampens romantic ardor in moments of passion and decreases sexual sensations. Some people consider them too much of a fuss.

3. *Myth of personal invulnerability.* Some people subscribe to a myth of personal invulnerability and believe they are somehow immune to HIV/AIDS and other diseases. Even students who are generally well informed about STIs may think of themselves as personally immune. One junior at the University of Miami (Ohio) explained to an interviewer why she did not insist that her partners use a condom: "I have an attitude—it may be wrong—that any guy I would sleep with

REFLECT

Why doesn't knowledge of methods of transmission and the effects of STIs reliably result in behavioral change?

would not have AIDS." The adventurous spirit that we often associate with youth may confer a dangerous sense of immortality and a greater willingness to take risks. Perceptions of personal invulnerability help to explain why AIDS education does not always translate into behavioral change.

Remain Sober

Alcohol—especially binge drinking—and other drugs increase the likelihood of engaging in risky sexual behavior.

Inspect Yourself and Your Partner

Inspect yourself for a discharge, bumps, rashes, warts, blisters, chancres, sores, lice, or foul odors. Do not expect to find telltale signs of an HIV infection, but infected people often have other STIs. Check out any unusual feature with a physician before you engage in sexual activity.

You may be able to work an inspection of your partner into foreplay—a reason for making love the first time with the lights on. In particular, a partner may hold his or her male partner's penis firmly, pulling the loose skin up and down, as if "milking" it. Then he or she can check for a discharge at the penile opening. A partner may use his or her fingers to detect any sign of a vaginal discharge. Other visible features of STIs include herpes blisters, genital warts, syphilitic chancres or rashes, and pubic lice.

If you find anything that doesn't look, feel, or smell right, bring it to your partner's attention. Treat any unpleasant odor as a warning sign. Your partner may not be aware of the symptom and may be carrying an infection. If you notice any suspicious signs, refrain from further sexual contact until your partner has the chance to seek a medical evaluation. It is advisable to be informed about the common signs and symptoms of STIs, but you need not become a medical expert. Even if your concerns prove groundless, you can resume sexual relations without the uncertainty that you would have had if you had ignored them.

Of course, your partner may become defensive or hostile if you express a concern that he or she may be carrying an STI. Try to be empathetic. The social stigma attached to people with STIs makes it difficult to accept the possibility of infection. It may be appropriate to point out that STIs are quite common (among college students, bank officers, military personnel, or . . . fill in the blank) and that many people are unaware they carry them.

But for your sake as well as your partner's, if you are not sure that sex is safe, stop. Think carefully about the risks, and seek expert advice.

Use Latex Condoms

Latex condoms are effective in blocking nearly all sexually transmissible organisms. Improper use or inconsistent use is a common reason for failures in using condoms to prevent STI transmission (Hatcher et al., 2006). Yet even when used properly, condoms may be of limited or no value against disease-causing organisms that are transmitted externally, such as those causing herpes and genital warts, and ectoparasitic infestations.

Condoms made from animal membranes ("skins") are less effective barriers against STIs because they contain pores that allow tiny microbes, including HIV, to penetrate. Even latex condoms are not 100% effective in preventing the transmission of HIV and other STIs. Condoms (and the people who use them) are fallible. Condoms can break or slip off.

Use Barrier Devices When Practicing Oral Sex (Fellatio or Cunnilingus)

If you decide to practice oral sex, use a condom before practicing fellatio and a dental dam (a square piece of latex rubber used by dentists during oral surgery) to cover the vagina before engaging in cunnilingus.

Avoid High-Risk Sexual Behaviors

Avoid unprotected vaginal intercourse (intercourse without the use of a latex condom). Unprotected anal intercourse is one of riskiest practices. Other high-risk behaviors include unprotected oral–genital activity, oral–anal activity, insertion of a hand or fist ("fisting") into someone's rectum or vagina, or any activity in which you or your partner would come into contact with the other's blood, semen, or vaginal secretions. If you do engage in anal–genital sex and are uncertain whether you or your partner is infected, use a latex condom. Oral–anal sex, or anilingus (sometimes called *rimming*), should be avoided because of the potential of transmitting microbes between the mouth and the anus. Also avoid sexual contact with people with STIs, people who practice high-risk sexual behaviors, people who inject drugs, and prostitutes or people who frequent prostitutes.

Wash the Genitals before and after Sex

Washing the genitals before and after sex removes a quantity of potentially harmful agents. Washing together may be incorporated into erotic foreplay. Right after intercourse, washing with soap and water may help reduce the risk of infection. Do not, however, deceive yourself into believing that washing your genitals is an effective substitute for safer sex. Most STIs are transmitted internally. Washing is useless against them. Douching right after coitus might have some limited benefits for women, but frequent douching should be avoided, because it may change the vaginal flora and encourage the growth of infectious organisms.

Have Regular Medical Checkups

A sexually active person should have health examinations regularly, at least once a year. Many community clinics and family planning centers scale their charges to one's ability to pay. Checkups are a small investment to make in one's own health. Many people are symptomless carriers of STIs, especially of chlamydial infections. Medical checkups enable them to learn about and receive treatment for disorders that might otherwise go unnoticed. Many physicians advise routine testing of **asymptomatic** young women for chlamydial infections to prevent the hidden damage that can occur if the infection goes untreated.

Asymptomatic Without symptoms

Discuss Whether You and Your Partner Should Undergo Testing before Initiating Sexual Relations

Some couples reach a mutual agreement to be tested for HIV and other STIs before they initiate sexual relations. (Some people simply insist that their prospective partners be tested before they initiate sexual relations.) However, many people resist testing or feel insulted when their partners raise the issue. People usually assume that they are free of STIs if they are symptom free and have been reasonably selective in their choice of partners. But STIs happen to the "nicest people," and the absence of symptoms is no guarantee of freedom from infection. Unless you have been celibate or involved in a monogamous relationship with an uninfected partner, you should consider yourself at risk of carrying or contracting an infectious STI.

Engage in Noncoital Sexual Activities

Other forms of sexual expression, such as hugging, massage, caressing, mutual masturbation, or rubbing bodies together without vaginal, anal, or oral contact, are low-risk ways of finding sexual pleasure, as long as semen or vaginal fluids do not come into contact with mucous membranes or breaks in the skin. Many sexologists refer to such activities as **outercourse** to distinguish them from sexual intercourse. Sharing sexual fantasies can be very titillating, as can taking a bath or shower together. Vibrators, dildos, and other "sex toys" may also be erotically stimulating and carry a low risk of infection, if they are washed thoroughly with soap and water before use and between uses by two people.

CRITICAL
Thinking

What is the difference between being *exposed* to HIV and being *infected* with HIV? Why does the difference matter?

Consult Your Physician If You Suspect That You Have Been Exposed to an STI

If you think that you may have been exposed to an STI, such as HIV, see a doctor as soon as possible. Many STIs are detectable in the early stages of development and can be successfully treated. If HIV is in your bloodstream, there is some chance that it may be eradicated before it infects cells in the immune system. If you are infected with HIV, early treatment may keep virus levels low and prevent you from developing AIDS. Early intervention may also prevent the damage of STIs spreading to vital body organs. Be sensitive to any physical changes that may be symptomatic of STIs. Talk to a health professional when in doubt.

However, research suggests that many people at risk of being exposed to STIs, including HIV, do not follow through on treatment regimens. Elyse Olshen and her colleagues (2006) followed up on more than 100 adolescents given postexposure antiviral medication after sexual assault. Most of them did not complete the recommended 28-day course.

Outercourse Forms of sexual expression, such as massage, hugging, caressing, mutual masturbation, and rubbing bodies together that do not involve the exchange of body fluids; contrast with *intercourse*

Get to Know Your Partner before Initiating Sexual Relations

Be selective in your choice of sex partners. Having sex with multiple partners—especially "one-night stands"—increases your risk of sexual contact with an infected person. It also lessens the opportunity to get to know your partner well enough to know whether he or she has participated in high-risk sexual practices or has had sex partners in the past who practiced high-risk behaviors.

Avoid Other High-Risk Behaviors

Avoid contact with bodily substances (blood, semen, vaginal secretions, fecal matter) from other people. Do not share hypodermic needles, razors, cuticle scissors, or other implements that could contain another person's blood. Be careful when handling wet towels, bed linen, or other material that might contain bodily substances.

Sources of Help

Do you have questions about the signs and symptoms of STIs? Do you need assistance in coping with an STI? A number of organizations have established telephone hotlines that provide anonymous callers with information. Some organizations publish newsletters and other material to help people with particular diseases cope more effectively.

The following national toll-free hotlines provide information about AIDS and other STIs, as well as referral sources. You needn't identify yourself to get information.

AIDS hotline for teens: 800-234-TEEN

AIDS hotline for the hearing impaired: 800-243-7889

Canadian toll-free hotline (toll free in Canada), AIDS Committee of Toronto: 800-267-6600

National AIDS hotline, Centers for Disease Control AIDS hotline: 800-342-AIDS: information and referral resources nationwide, 24 hours a day

National STI hotline: 800-227-8922 (in California, 800-982-5883): a hotline sponsored by the American Social Health Association that dispenses information about STI symptoms and refers callers to local STI clinics that provide confidential, minimal, or no-cost treatment

Spanish AIDS/SIDA hotline: 800-344-7432

For information on where to obtain help about herpes, contact the following:

National herpes hotline: 919-361-8488

National STI hotline: 800-227-8922

Herpes Resource Center, Box 100, Palo Alto, CA 94302

1. **How common are STIs?**

   - More than 13 million people in the United States contract an STI each year. Although public attention has been riveted on HIV/AIDS, other STIs such as chlamydia and HPV pose wider threats.

2. **What kinds of bacterial STIs are there?**

   - Gonorrhea is caused by the during bacterium *gonococcus*. For men, symptoms include a penile discharge and burning urination. Most women are asymptomatic, but if left untreated, it can lend to PID. Gonorrhea is treated with antibiotics.

   - Syphilis is caused by the bacterium *Treponema pallidum*. Syphilis undergoes several stages of development, beginning with a chancre. Although it can lay dormant for many years, it may eventually be lethal. Syphilis is treated with antibiotics.

   - Chlamydial infections are the most common bacterial STIs and are caused by *Chlamydia trachomatous*. Symptoms resemble those of gonorrhea but tend to be milder. They respond to antibiotics.

   - Other bacterial infections include chancroid, shigellosis, granuloma inguinale, and lymphogranuloma venereum.

3. **What kinds of vaginal infections are there?**

   - Vaginitis is usually known by a foul-smelling discharge, genital irritation, and burning during urination. Most cases of vaginitis involve BV, candidiasis (caused by a fungus), or trichomoniasis (caused by a protozoan). These microbes are normally found in the body but can "overgrow" under certain conditions.

4. **What kinds of viral STIs are there?**

   - HIV causes AIDS by attacking the body's immune system. As HIV disables the body's natural defenses, the person becomes vulnerable to opportunistic diseases—such as serious infections and cancers—that are normally held in check. HIV is found in blood, semen, vaginal secretions, and breast milk. Common avenues of transmission include vaginal and anal intercourse, hypodermic needles, childbirth, and breast-feeding. HIV infection can be diagnosed through tests of blood, saliva, or urine. There is no cure or vaccine for HIV. The most effective form of treatment is HAART, which uses a "cocktail" of antiviral agents.

   - Oral herpes is caused by HSV-1. Genital herpes is caused by HSV-2, which produces painful, shallow sores and blisters on the genitals. A vaccine helps prevent women from contracting genital herpes but is ineffective with men. Antiviral drugs can relieve pain and speed healing during flare-ups.

   - The several types of hepatitis are caused by different viruses. Most cases are transmitted sexually or by contact with contaminated blood or fecal matter.

   - HPV causes genital warts and has been linked to cervical cancer. Most cases clear on their own.

   - Molluscum contagiosum causes an outbreak of painless, raised lesions on the genitals, buttocks, thighs, or lower abdomen. Most cases disappear on their own.

5. **What kinds of parasitic STIs are there?**

   - Pediculosis ("crabs") is caused by pubic lice (*Pthirus pubis*). Pubic lice attach themselves to pubic hair and feed on the blood of their hosts, which often causes itching. Infestations can be treated with lindane.

   - Scabies (*Sarcoptes scabiei*) is a parasitic infestation caused by a tiny mite that causes itching and can be treated with lindane.

6. **How can we prevent STIs?**

   - Strategies for preventing STIs include abstinence, monogamy, using latex condoms, washing the genitals before and after sex, having regular medical checkups, and getting to know one's partner before having sex.

1. Which of the following is the most widespread STI?

   (a) Scabies
   (b) HIV/AIDS
   (c) Genital herpes
   (d) HPV

2. Silver nitrate is used to prevent

   (a) PCP
   (b) ophthalmia neonatorum
   (c) general paresis
   (d) hepatitis C

3. _____ is also known as "the drip" or "the clap."

   (a) Gonorrhea
   (b) Genital herpes
   (c) Bacterial vaginosis
   (d) Candidiasis

4. *Treponema pallidum* is the organism that causes

   (a) gonorrhea
   (b) syphilis
   (c) chlamydia
   (d) genital herpes

5. The Abbott Testpack is used to diagnose _____.

   (a) trichomoniasis
   (b) HIV infection
   (c) chlamydia
   (d) candidiasis

6. Miconazole is used to treat

   (a) candidiasis
   (b) hepatitis
   (c) pediculosis
   (d) syphilis

7. HAART is used to treat

   (a) herpes simplex virus type 1
   (b) HPV
   (c) *Pthirus pubis*
   (d) HIV/AIDS

8. Which of the following is an antiviral drug?

   (a) Acyclovir
   (b) Podophyllin
   (c) Lindane
   (d) Penicillin

9. General paresis may develop during the _____ stage of syphilis.

   (a) primary
   (b) secondary
   (c) tertiary
   (d) all of the above

10. As many as half of some populations of college women are infected with

    (a) gonorrhea
    (b) genital herpes
    (c) HPV
    (d) HIV/AIDS

11. Simplirix is a vaccine under development for

    (a) genital herpes
    (b) HPV
    (c) hepatitis B
    (d) trichomoniasis

12. HIV is *not* found in

    (a) breast milk
    (b) saliva
    (c) blood
    (d) semen

13. Which of the following is an opportunistic disease that occurs because of a weakened immune system?

    (a) Syphilis
    (b) Lymphogranuloma venereum
    (c) Pediculosis
    (d) Toxoplasmosis of the brain

14. _____ often reflects the overgrowth of organisms normally found in the vagina.

    (a) Gonorrhea
    (b) Candidiasis
    (c) Molluscum contagiosum
    (d) Chlamydia

15. Women infected with _____ are likely to encounter pelvic pain and irregular menstrual cycles.

    (a) *Hemophilus ducreyi*
    (b) *Herpes simplex* virus type 2
    (c) HPV
    (d) Chlamydia trachomatis

Answers 1. d; 2. b; 3. a; 4. b; 5. c; 6. a; 7. d; 8. a; 9. c; 10. c; 11. a; 12. b; 13. d; 14. b; 15. d

17

Atypical Sexual Variations

TRUTH? fiction

Which of the following statements are true, and which are fiction? Look for the Truth/Fiction icons on the pages that follow to find the answers.

1 King Henry III of France insisted on being considered a woman and addressed as "Her Majesty."   T   F

2 Female strippers are exhibitionists.   T   F

3 People who enjoy watching their partners undress are voyeurs.   T   F

4 Exhibitionists and voyeurs are never violent.   T   F

5 It is considered normal to enjoy some mild forms of pain during sexual activity.   T   F

6 Some people cannot become sexually aroused unless they are bound, flogged, or humiliated by their sex partners.   T   F

7 There is a subculture in the United States in which sexual sadists and sexual masochists form liaisons to inflict and receive pain and humiliation during sexual activity.   T   F

Jenna Caccaro, 22, a fashion student who lives in Brooklyn, said she was first flashed on the subway when she was 15. She thought it might have been because she was wearing her Catholic school uniform. "I thought that maybe I'd done something to attract him," she said, "but my family reassured me he was just a sleaze."

Sara Payne, 25, of Manhattan, who takes the No. 1 train to work for a jewelry company in the Bronx, said she has been flashed about six times on the subway in the eight years she has lived in New York. She said it happened more when she was a freshman in college than it does now.

"Maybe I'm a little more confident now," she said, "so people are less prone to try and intimidate me."

Vivian Lynch, 68, used to take the F train home to Queens. She shivered at the memory. "It happened to me in the '70s," she said. "Men used to touch women on the train and stand close to them and ruin their clothes."

In some ways, groping seems almost an accepted part of subway culture. Stephanie Vullo, 43, said she has dealt many times with men rubbing up against her or trying to touch her on crowded No. 4 or 5 trains in the morning when she takes her daugh-

ter to school. "It's worse in the summer months when everyone is wearing less clothing," she said. "The first time I turned around and yelled at the guy, but with my daughter, I don't want to get her upset."

—Hartocollis, 2006

The trials of these women on the New York subway system—and on subway systems around the world (Hartcollis, 2006)—raise a number of questions. For example, why is it that almost all perpetrators of crimes such as *exhibitionism* and *mashing* are male? Are the causes of such behavior psychological? Sociological? Could there be biological differences between people who engage in such deviant behavior and those who do not? What sort of satisfaction does a male obtain from exposing his genitals to a female stranger? How should a female victim respond? Why? If a perpetrator is apprehended by the law, how should he be treated?

Males who expose themselves to females usually seek sexual release by masturbating afterward, or, in the subways, by rubbing against females. Obtaining sexual satisfaction through exposing oneself or rubbing against a female stranger is considered abnormal. Just what is "normal" in sexual behavior and what is abnormal or deviant? In this chapter we explore a number of sexual and sexually related behaviors that deviate from the norm in one sense or another. Let us begin by exploring the question of normal versus deviant sexual behavior more deeply.

Normal versus Deviant Sexual Behavior

One common approach to defining *normality* is based on a statistical norm. From this perspective, rare or unusual sexual behaviors are considered abnormal or deviant. The statistical approach may seem value free, because the yardstick of normality is based on the frequency of behavior, not on judgment of its social acceptability. But having sex while standing, or more than seven times a week, might be considered deviant by this yardstick.

Moreover, the choice of behaviors we subject to statistical comparison is not divorced from our underlying values. We tend to consider sexual behaviors abnormal or deviant, for example, when they run counter to our religious values, when they make most of us wince (as in sadism or masochism), or when they seem inexplicable (as in being turned on more by a woman's shoe than the woman herself) (Fedoroff, 2003). Behaviors that run against someone's religious values may be common enough, but that individual might label them deviant because they deviate from what the person has been led to believe is normal (or "proper").

What is considered normal in one culture or at a particular time may be considered abnormal in other cultures and at other times. What is "normal" behavior for the female adolescent Trobriand islander (see Chapter 1) might be considered deviant—even *nymphomaniacal*—by Western cultural standards.

In our own culture, sexual practices such as oral sex and masturbation were once considered to be deviant or abnormal. Today, however, they are practiced so widely that few people would label them as deviant. Concepts of "normalcy" and "deviance," then, reflect the mores and customs of a particular culture at a given time.

Another basis for determining sexual deviance is to classify sexual practices as deviant when they involve the persistent preference for nongenital sexual outlets (Fedoroff, 2003; Seligman & Hardenburg, 2000). If a man prefers fondling a woman's panties to engaging in sexual relations with her, or prefers to masturbate against her foot rather than engage in coitus, his behavior is likely to be labeled deviant.

Because of the confusing array of meanings of the terms *deviant* and *abnormal,* some professionals speak about unusual patterns of sexual arousal or behavior as "atypical variations" in sexual behavior rather than as "sexual deviations." Atypical patterns of sexual arousal or behavior that become problematic in the eyes of the individual or society are labeled *paraphilias* by the *DSM* (American Psychiatric Association, 2000). Clinicians consider paraphilias to be mental disorders. However, milder forms of these behaviors may be practiced by many people and fall within the normal spectrum of human sexuality.

REFLECT

Do you consider sexual practices such as oral sex and masturbation to be deviant or abnormal? Why or why not?

CRITICAL Thinking

Why is statistical rarity an inadequate standard for considering a sexual practice to be normal or abnormal?

SafeZone

Q *Is having sex underwater considered atypical? Can it cause infection?*

A It's not a paraphilia, and we hate to burst your bubble (pardon the pun), but it's not really all that unusual. You're unlikely to get anyone infected with salt water, although there can be some irritation. The same goes for the chlorine in a pool, but irritation is no fun, and the water is no lubricant. Remember to hold your breath or get scuba gear.

The Paraphilias

Paraphilias involve sexual arousal in response to unusual stimuli such as children or other nonconsenting persons (such as unsuspecting people whom one watches or to whom one exposes one's genitals), nonhuman objects (such as shoes, leather, rubber, or undergarments), or pain or humiliation (Fedoroff, 2003; Seligman & Hardenburg, 2000). The psychiatric diagnosis of paraphilia requires that the person has acted on the urges or is distinctly distressed by them.

People with paraphilias usually feel their urges are insistent, demanding, or compulsory (Fedoroff, 2003; Seligman & Hardenburg, 2000). They may describe themselves as overcome by them now and then. People with paraphilias tend to experience their urges as beyond their control, just as drug addicts or compulsive gamblers see themselves as helpless to avert irresistible urges. For these reasons, theorists have speculated that paraphilias may represent a type of sexual compulsion or an addiction.

Paraphilias vary in severity. In some cases the person can function sexually in the absence of the unusual stimuli and seldom if ever acts upon his or her deviant urges. In other cases the person resorts to paraphilic behavior only in times of stress. In more extreme forms, the person repeatedly engages in paraphilic behavior and may become preoccupied with thoughts and fantasies about these experiences. In such cases the person may not be able to become sexually aroused without either fantasizing about the paraphilic stimulus or having it present. For some people, paraphilic behavior is the only means of attaining sexual gratification.

The person with a paraphilia typically replays the paraphilic act in sexual fantasies to stimulate arousal during masturbation or sexual relations. It is as if he or she is mentally replaying a videotape of the paraphilic scene. But the scene grows stale after a while, and the individual feels the urge to perform another paraphilic act to make a new "video."

Some paraphilias are mostly harmless and victimless, such as *fetishism* and cross-dressing to achieve sexual arousal (*transvestic fetishism*). Even being humiliated by one's partner may be relatively harmless if the partner consents. Other paraphilic behaviors, such as exposing oneself in public or enticing children into sexual relations, do have victims and may cause harm, sometimes severe physical or psychological harm. They are also against the law. Sexual sadism, in which sexual arousal is connected to hurting or humiliating another person, can be a most harmful paraphilia when it is forced upon a nonconsenting person. Some brutal rapes involve sexual sadism.

Except in the case of sexual masochism, paraphilias are believed to occur almost exclusively among men (Seligman & Hardenburg, 2000). The prevalence of paraphilias in the general population remains unknown, because people are generally unwilling to talk about them. Much of what we have learned about paraphilias derives from the reported experiences of people who have been apprehended for performing illegal acts (such as exposing themselves in public) and the few who have voluntarily sought help. The characteristics of people who have not been identified or studied remain virtually unknown.

We discuss the major types of paraphilia in this chapter, beginning with fetishism. The one exception is *pedophilia*. In pedophilia, children become the objects of sexual arousal. Pedophilia often takes the form of sexual coercion of children, as in incest or sexual molestation (Lalumière et al., 2005b). It is discussed in Chapter 18 as a form of sexual coercion.

Paraphilia An atypical pattern of sexual arousal or behavior that become problematic in the eyes of the individual or society, such as fetishism or exhibitionism; urges are recurrent and are either acted on or are distressing to the individual; from Greek roots meaning "to the side of" (*para-*) and "loving" (*philos*)

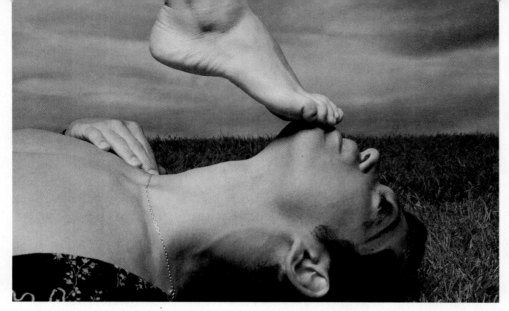

Fetishism. *In fetishism, inanimate objects such as leather shoes or boots, or parts of the body such as feet, elicit sexual arousal. Many fetishists cannot achieve sexual arousal without contact with the desired objects or without fantasizing about them. Women's undergarments and objects made of rubber, leather, silk, or fur are common fetishistic objects. Why is it that some men are more aroused by women's feet than by women's genitals?*

Fetishism

The roots of the word *fetish* come from the French *fétiche,* which is thought to derive from the Portuguese *feitico,* meaning "magic charm." The "magic" in this case lies in an object's ability to arouse a person sexually. In **fetishism,** an inanimate object elicits sexual arousal. Articles of clothing (e.g., women's panties, bras, lingerie, stockings, gloves, shoes, or boots) and materials made of rubber, leather, silk, or fur are among the more common fetishistic objects. Leather boots and high-heeled shoes are popular. There is a reported case of a diaper fetishist (Oguz & Uygur, 2005).

The fetishist may act on the urges to engage in fetishistic behavior, such as by masturbating by stroking an object or while fantasizing about it, or he may be distressed about such urges or fantasies and not act upon them. In a related paraphilia, **partialism,** people are excessively aroused by a particular body part, such as the feet, breasts, or buttocks.

Most fetishes and partialisms are harmless. Fetishistic practices are almost always private and involve masturbation or are incorporated into coitus with a willing partner. Only rarely have fetishists coerced others into paraphilic activities. Yet some partialists have touched parts of women's bodies in public. And some fetishists commit burglaries to acquire the fetishistic objects. Now and then we hear of someone who has stolen hundreds of pairs of women's shoes, for example.

Fetishism A paraphilia in which an inanimate object such as an article of clothing or items made of rubber, leather, or silk elicit sexual arousal

Partialism A paraphilia related to fetishism in which sexual arousal is exaggeratedly associated with a particular body part, such as feet, breasts, or buttocks

SafeZone

Q *At what point does a sexual interest become a fetish?*

A If your interest in an object or a body part makes it difficult or impossible for you to enjoy genital sex with another person without it, you likely have a fetish.

Transvestism. *Transvestites cross-dress for purposes of obtaining sexual arousal and gratification. Are women who wear blue jeans engaging in transvestic activity? (The answer is no. But, as a critical thinker, explain why.)*

Transvestism

Fetishism appears to include **transvestism**. Although other fetishists become sexually aroused by handling the fetishistic object while they masturbate, transvestites become excited by wearing articles of clothing—the fetishistic objects—of the other gender. A fetishist may find the object or sex involving the object to be erotically stimulating. For the transvestite, the object is sexually alluring only when it is worn. Transvestites are mostly males (Långström & Zucker, 2005). Transvestism has been described among both heterosexual and gay males (Taylor & Rupp, 2004). Many are in committed male–female relationships and otherwise stereotypically masculine in behavior.

Truth or Fiction Revisited: It is true that King Henry III of France insisted on being considered a woman and addressed as "Her Majesty." But cross-dressing may occur in other cultures for reasons other than sexual arousal. In the case of Henry III, it appears that transsexualism, and not transvestism, was involved.

Transvestism differs markedly from transsexualism. It is true that some transvestites and some transsexuals appear to be motived by *autogynephilia*—a condition in which the individual is sexually stimulated by fantasies that their own bodies are female (Bailey, 2003; Lawrence, 2004). However, transvestites are usually sexually gratified by cross-dressing and masturbating or having sex with others while cross-dressing. They may also find it gratifying to masturbate while fantasizing about cross-dressing. However, many transvestites have masculine gender identities and do not seek to change their anatomic sex. Transsexuals usually cross-dress because they are uncomfortable with the attire associated with their anatomic sex and truly wish to be members of the other sex. For this reason, many transsexuals seek sex reassignment.

Like fetishism in general, the origins of transvestism remain obscure. Evidence of biological hormonal and neurological abnormalities in transvestism is mixed (Bailey, 2003). Långström and Zucker (2005) surveyed 2,450 Swedes and found transvestism in about 2.8% of men and 0.4% of women. A history of transvestism was associated with separation from parents, same-sex sexual experiences, use of pornography, high rates of masturbation, and other paraphilias—namely, sexual masochism, exhibitionism, and voyeurism.

Some men cross-dress for reasons other than sexual arousal and so are not "true transvestites." Some men make a living by impersonating women like Marilyn Monroe and Madonna on stage and are not motivated by sexual arousal. Among some segments of the gay male community, it is fashionable to masquerade as women. Gay men do not usually cross-dress to become sexually stimulated, however.

Transvestic behaviors may range from wearing a single female garment when alone to sporting dresses, wigs, makeup, and feminine mannerisms at a transvestite club. Some transvestites become sexually aroused by masquerading as women and attracting the interest of unsuspecting males. They sometimes entice these men or string them along until they find some excuse to back out before their anatomic sex

A Closer Look

ARCHIE: A CASE OF TRANSVESTISM

Many transvestites are in long-term, committed, male–female relationships and engage in sexual activity with their regular partners. Yet they seek additional sexual gratification through dressing as women, as in the case of Archie.

Archie, a 55-year-old plumber, had been cross-dressing for many years. There was a time when he would go out in public as a woman, but as his prominence in the community grew, he became more afraid of being discovered in public. His wife, Myrna, knew of his "peccadillo," especially since he borrowed many of her clothes. She urged him to stay at home, offering to help him with his "weirdness." For many years his paraphilia had been restricted to the home.

The couple went to the clinic at the urging of the wife. Myrna described how Archie had imposed his will on her for 20 years. Archie would wear her undergarments and masturbate while she told him how disgusting he was. (The couple also regularly engaged in "normal" sexual intercourse, which Myrna enjoyed.) The cross-dressing had come to a head because their teenage daughter had almost walked into the couple's bedroom while they were acting out Archie's fantasies.

With Myrna out of the consulting room, Archie explained how he grew up in a family with several older sisters. He described how underwear had been perpetually hanging to dry in the one bathroom. As an adolescent Archie experimented with rubbing against articles of underwear, then with trying them on. On one occasion a sister walked in while he was modeling panties before the mirror. She told him he was a "dredge to society," and he straightaway experienced unparalleled sexual excitement. He masturbated when she left the room, and his orgasm was the strongest of his young life.

Archie did not think that there was anything wrong with wearing women's undergarments and masturbating. He was not about to give it up, regardless of whether it destroyed his marriage. Myrna's main concern was finally separating herself from Archie's "sickness." She didn't care what he did anymore, as long as he did it by himself. "Enough is enough," she said.

That was the compromise the couple worked out. Archie would engage in his fantasies by himself. He would do so when Myrna was not at home, and she would not be told of his activities. He would also be very, very careful to choose times when the children would not be around.

Six months later the couple were together and content. Archie had replaced Myrna's input into his fantasies with transvestic–sadomasochistic magazines. Myrna said, "I see no evil, hear no evil, smell no evil." They continued to have sexual intercourse. After a while, Myrna forgot to check to see which underwear had been used.

---

is revealed. The great majority of transvestites do not engage in antisocial or illegal behavior. Most practice their sexual predilection in private and would be horrified or embarrassed to be discovered by associates while dressed in female attire.

A study of male heterosexual cross-dressers in New England found that most of their wives were tolerant, but many who found out about their husbands' cross-dressing years into the marriage felt betrayed and angry (Reynolds & Caron, 2000). A common worry of the wives was that outsiders would learn about their husbands' behavior.

Exhibitionism

If fetishism is often victimless, the same cannot be said for exhibitionism. **Exhibitionism** ("flashing") involves persistent, powerful urges and sexual fantasies involving exposing one's genitals to unsuspecting strangers for the purpose of achieving sexual arousal or gratification. (The urges are either acted upon or are disturbing to the individual.) Exhibitionists are almost always males, but there are some cases of female exhibitionists (Hugh-Jones et al., 2005a).

Exhibitionism A paraphilia characterized by persistent, powerful urges and sexual fantasies involving exposing one's genitals to unsuspecting strangers for the purpose of achieving sexual arousal or gratification

An Exhibitionist. *What are the motives of the exhibitionist? Sexual? Aggressive? These and more?*

What we know of exhibitionists, as with most other people with paraphilias, is almost entirely derived from studies of men who have been apprehended or treated by mental health professionals (Langevin et al., 2004). Such knowledge may yield a biased picture because relatively few incidents result in apprehension and conviction. The characteristics of most perpetrators may thus differ from those of people who have been made available for study.

The prevalence of exhibitionism in the general population is unknown, but a survey of 846 college women at nine randomly selected American universities found exposure to exhibitionism to be widespread. A third of the women reported that they had run into a "flasher" (Cox, 1988). A majority of the women had been approached for the first time (some had been approached more than once) by 16 years of age. Only 15 of the women had reported these incidents to the police. The clinical definition of exhibitionism involves exposure to a stranger, but about a third (36%) of the incidents among the college women were committed by acquaintances, relatives, or "good friends."

The typical exhibitionist is young, either lonely or in an unhappy male–female relationship, and sexually repressed. An exhibitionist may claim that sex with his regular partner is reasonably satisfactory, but that he also experiences the compulsion to expose himself to strangers. Many exhibitionists are single, however. They typically have difficulties relating to women and have been unable to establish meaningful heterosexual relationships (Leue et al., 2004).

Exhibitionism usually begins before age 18 (American Psychiatric Association, 2000). The urge to exhibit oneself, if not the actual act, usually begins in early adolescence, generally between the ages of 13 and 16. The frequency of exhibitionism declines markedly after the age of 40 (American Psychiatric Association, 2000). The typical exhibitionist does not attempt further sexual contact with the victim. Thus, he does not usually pose a physical threat (American Psychiatric Association, 2000).

The police sometimes trivialize exhibitionism as a "nuisance crime," but the psychological consequences among victims, especially young children, indicate that exhibitionism is not victimless. Victims may feel violated and may be bothered by recurrent images or nightmares. They may harbor misplaced guilt that they had unwittingly enticed the exhibitionist. They may blame themselves for reacting excessively or for failing to apprehend the perpetrator. They may develop fears of venturing out on their own. Moreover, exhibitionists are highly likely to repeat their crimes, even if they spend time in prison for them (Langevin et al., 2004).

Some writers see exhibitionism as a means of expressing hostility toward women. Exposure may be an attempt by the exhibitionist to strike back at women because of a belief that women have wronged him or damaged his self-esteem by failing to notice him or take him seriously. The direct expression of anger may be perceived as too risky, so the exhibitionist vents his rage by humiliating a defenseless stranger. The urge to expose oneself often occurs when the exhibitionist feels that his masculinity has been insulted. Some evidence suggests that exhibitionists may be attempting to assert their masculinity by evoking a response from victims.

Other studies show exhibitionists to be shy, dependent, passive, lacking in sexual and social skills, even inhibited (Leue et al., 2004). They tend to have doubts about their masculinity, and to suffer from feelings of inadequacy and inferiority. Exhibitionists who are socially shy or inadequate may be using exhibitionism as a substitute for intimate relationships.

A Closer Look

MICHAEL: A CASE OF EXHIBITIONISM

Michael was a 26-year-old, handsome, boyish-looking married man with a three-year-old daughter. He had spent about one quarter of his life in reform schools and in prison. As an adolescent he had been a fire setter. As a young adult, he had begun to expose himself. He came to the clinic without his wife's knowledge because he was exposing himself more and more often—up to three times a day—and he was afraid that he would eventually be arrested and thrown into prison again.

Michael said he liked sex with his wife, but it wasn't as exciting as exposing himself. He couldn't prevent his exhibitionism, especially now, when he was between jobs and worried about where the family's next month's rent was coming from. He loved his daughter more than anything and couldn't stand the thought of being separated from her.

Michael's method of operation was as follows: He would look for slender adolescent females, usually near the junior high school and the senior high school. He would take his penis out of his pants and play with it while he drove up to a girl or a small group of girls. He would lower the car window,

continuing to play with himself, and ask them for directions. Sometimes the girls didn't see his penis. That was okay. Sometimes they saw it and didn't react. That was okay, too. When they saw it and became flustered and afraid, that was best of all. He would start to masturbate harder, and now and then he managed to ejaculate before the girls had departed.

Michael's history was unsettled. His father had left home before he was born, and his mother had drunk heavily. He was in and out of foster homes throughout his childhood, "all over" the capital district area of New York state. Before he was 10 years old he was involved in sexual activities with neighborhood boys. Now and then the boys also forced neighborhood girls into petting, and Michael had mixed feelings when the girls got upset. He felt bad for them, but he also enjoyed it. A couple of times girls seemed horrified at the sight of his penis, and it made him "really feel like a man. To see that look, you know, with a girl, not a woman, but a girl—a slender girl; that's what I'm after."

The preferred victims are typically girls or young women. The typical exhibitionist drives up to, or walks in front of, a stranger and exposes his penis. In one sample of 130 exhibitionists, about half reported that they always or nearly always had erections when they exposed themselves (Langevin et al., 1979). After his victim has registered fear, disgust, confusion, or surprise, an exhibitionist will typically cover himself and flee. He usually masturbates, either while exposing himself or shortly afterward while thinking about the act and the victim's response (American Psychiatric Association, 2000). Some exhibitionists ejaculate during the act. Most of the 238 exhibitionists in a Canadian study reported masturbating to orgasm while exposing themselves or afterward while fantasizing about it (Freund et al., 1988).

Exhibitionists and some other people with paraphilias may find the risk of being caught to heighten their erotic response because it causes a rush of stress hormones that are chemically similar to testosterone (Haake et al., 2003). The exhibitionist may even purposefully increase the risk, as by exposing himself in the same location in his own easily identifiable car.

Courts tend to be hard on exhibitionists, partly because of evidence that shows that some exhibitionists progress to more serious crimes of sexual aggression (Price et al., 2002). Still, most exhibitionists do not appear to become rapists or child molesters.

Definitions of exhibitionism also bring into focus the boundaries between normal and abnormal behavior (Hugh–Jones et al., 2005b). For example, people in

TRUTH **fiction 2**

CRITICAL
Thinking

Critical thinkers pay closer attention to definitions. Why are (most) stripteasers and nude sunbathers *not* exhibitionists?

intimate relationships may enjoy showing their bodies to their partners to arouse them sexually. That is normal. And we might ask, are exotic dancers (stripteasers) exhibitionists? After all, aren't they exposing themselves to strangers? **Truth or Fiction Revisited:** Yes they are, but it is not true that strippers are exhibitionists. They are more successful at their work if they sexually excite their audiences, but their audiences are not unsuspecting victims. They pay for the privilege of watching them. Strippers' main motive is (usually) to earn a living (Philaretou, 2006).

It is also normal to become sexually excited while stripping before one's sex partner. Such stripping is done to sexually excite a willing partner, not to surprise or shock a stranger.

How to Respond to an Exhibitionist

It is understandable that an unsuspecting woman who is exposed to an exhibitionist may react with shock, surprise, or fear. Unfortunately, her display of shock or fear may reinforce the flasher's tendencies to expose himself. She may fear that the flasher, who has already broken at least one social code, is likely to assault her physically as well. Fortunately, most exhibitionists do not seek actual sexual contact with their victims and run away before they can be apprehended by the police or passersby.

Some women respond with anger, insults, even arguments that the offender should feel ashamed. A display of anger may reinforce exhibitionism. We do not recommend that the victim insult the flasher, lest it provoke a violent response. Although most exhibitionists are not violent, some have considered or attempted rape (Langevin, 2003; Price et al., 2002).

When possible, showing no reaction or simply continuing on one's way may be the best response. If women do desire to respond to the flasher, they might calmly say something like "You really need professional help. You should see a professional to help you with this problem." They should promptly report the incident to police, so that authorities can apprehend the offender.

Obscene Telephone Calling and Chat Scatophilia

Like exhibitionists, obscene phone callers (almost all of whom are male) seek to become sexually aroused by shocking their victims (Briken et al., 2005; Pakhomou, 2006). Although an exhibitionist exposes his genitals to produce the desired response, the obscene phone caller "exposes" himself verbally by uttering obscenities and sexual provocations to a nonconsenting person. The *DSM* (American Psychiatric Association, 2000) labels this type of paraphilia **telephone scatologia.** People practicing "chat scatophilia" are sexually aroused by sending obscene e-mail, instant messages, and chatroom messages (Abal et al., 2003). These behaviors are sometimes considered a form of exhibitionism.

Relatively few obscene callers are women (Price et al., 2002). Women who are charged with such offenses are generally motivated by rage for some actual or fantasized rejection rather than the desire for sexual arousal. They use the phone to hurl sexual invectives against men whom they feel have wronged them. By contrast, male obscene phone callers are generally motivated by a desire for sexual excitement and usually choose their victims randomly from the phone book or by chance dialing. They typically masturbate during the phone call or shortly afterward. Most obscene telephone callers also engage in other paraphilic acts, especially voyeurism and exhibitionism (Price et al., 2001, 2002).

Telephone scatologia
A paraphilia characterized by the making of obscene telephone calls

There are many patterns of obscene phone calling. Some callers limit themselves to obscenities. Others make sexual overtures. Some just breathe heavily into the receiver. Others describe their masturbatory activity to their victims. Some profess to have previously met the victim at a social gathering or through a mutual acquaintance. Some even present themselves as "taking a sex survey" and ask a series of personally revealing questions.

The typical obscene phone caller is a socially inadequate heterosexual male who has had difficulty forming intimate relationships with women (Leue et al., 2004). The relative safety and anonymity of the telephone may shield him from the risk of rejection (Leue et al., 2004). A reaction of shock or fright from his victims may fill him with feelings of power and control that are lacking in his life, especially in his relationships with women. The obscenities may vent rage that he holds against women who have rejected him.

Obscene phone calls are illegal, but it has been difficult for authorities to track down perpetrators. Call tracing can help police track obscene or offending phone callers. Call tracing works in different ways in different locales. Caller ID shows the caller's telephone number on a display panel on the receiving party's telephone. In some locales, people can program their telephone service so that a caller who calls from a private number or one without caller ID receives a message stating that the recipient only accepts calls from people who identify their phone numbers or names. These services may deter some obscene callers, but others may use public phones instead of their home phones. Check with your local telephone company if you are interested in these services.

What should a woman do if she receives an obscene phone call? Advice generally parallels that given to women who are victimized by exhibitionists. Above all, women are advised to remain calm and not reveal shock or fright, because such reactions tend to reinforce the caller and increase the probability of repeat calls. Women may be best advised to say nothing at all and gently hang up the receiver. A woman might alternatively offer a brief response that alludes to the caller's problems before hanging up. She might say in a calm but strong voice, "It's unfortunate you have this problem. I think you should seek professional help." If she should receive repeated calls, the woman might request an unlisted number or contact the police. Many women list themselves only by their initials in the phone directory to disguise their sex, but because this practice is so widespread, obscene callers may surmise that people listed by initials are women living alone.

Voyeurism

Voyeurism could be considered the "flip side of the coin" of exhibitionism. It involves strong, repetitive urges to observe unsuspecting strangers who are nude, undressing, or involved in sexual relations (American Psychiatric Associations, 2000). The voyeur becomes sexually aroused by watching and typically does not seek sexual relations with the "victim." Like fetishism and exhibitionism, voyeurism is found almost exclusively among males. It usually begins before age 15 (American Psychiatric Association, 2000).

The voyeur may masturbate while peeping or afterward while replaying the incident in his mind. The voyeur may fantasize about sex with the observed person but have no intention of actually seeking sexual relations with her.

Are people voyeurs who become sexually aroused by the sight of their lovers undressing? What about people who enjoy watching pornographic films or stripteasers? No, no, and no. The people being observed are not unsuspecting strangers. The lover knows that his or her partner is watching. Porn actors and strippers know that

Voyeurism A paraphilia characterized by strong, repetitive urges and related sexual fantasies of observing unsuspecting strangers who are naked, disrobing, or engaged in sexual relations

others will be viewing them. They would not be performing if they did not expect or have an audience.

Truth or Fiction Revisited: It is not true that people who enjoy watching their mates undress are voyeurs. In such cases the person who is disrobing is knowingly and willingly observed, and the observer's enjoyment is normal (Montemurro et al., 2003). But true voyeurs want to peep on *unsuspecting* strangers. Women who attend male strip clubs also enjoy "bonding" with their friends and other women at the clubs (Montemurro et al., 2003).

Voyeurs are also known as *peepers,* or *peeping Toms.* Why "peeping Toms"? According to an old English legend, Lady Godiva asked the townspeople not to look upon her while she rode horseback in the nude to protest the oppressive tax that her husband, a landowner, had imposed on them. A tailor named Tom of Coventry was the only townsperson not to grant her request.

Voyeurs often put themselves in risky situations in which they face the prospect of being caught. They may risk injury by perching themselves in trees or otherwise assume precarious positions to catch a preferred view of their target. They will occupy rooftops and fire escapes in brutal winter weather. Peepers can be exceedingly patient. They may wait hour after hour, night after night, for a furtive glimpse of the target. Part of the sexual excitement seems to stem from the risks voyeurs run. The need for risk may explain why voyeurs are not known to frequent nude beaches or nudist camps, where it is acceptable to look (although not to stare) at nude people.

Truth or Fiction Revisited: It is fiction that exhibitionists and voyeurs are *never* violent. Exhibitionism and voyeurism per se are not violent in themselves, but some exhibitionists and voyeurs have been known to be violent. Moreover, if provoked or angered, they react violently (Lalumière et al., 2005b; Langevin, 2003). Voyeurs who break into and enter homes or buildings, or who tap at windows to gain the attention of victims, are among the more dangerous.

Compared with other types of sex offenders, voyeurs tend to be less sexually experienced and are less likely to be married (Gebhard et al., 1965). Like many exhibitionists, voyeurs tend to harbor feelings of inadequacy and to lack social and sexual skills (Leue et al., 2004). They may thus have difficulty forming romantic relationships with women. For this shy and socially inadequate type of voyeur, "peeping" affords sexual gratification without risk of rejection. Yet not all voyeurs are socially awkward and inept with women.

Sexual Masochism

Truth or Fiction Revisited: It is considered normal if you enjoy some mild forms of pain during sexual activity. Love bites, hair pulls, and minor scratches are examples of sources of pain that are considered to fall within normal limits.

However, people who prefer or require having pain or humiliation inflicted on them by their sex partners are sexual masochists. A sexual masochist either acts upon or is distressed by persistent urges and sexual fantasies involving the desire to be bound, flogged, humiliated, or made to suffer in some way by a sexual partner to achieve sexual excitement. **Truth or Fiction Revisited:** In some cases, the sexual masochist cannot become sexually aroused unless they are bound, flogged, or humiliated by their sex partners.

Sexual masochism is the only paraphilia that is found among women with some frequency (American Psychiatric Association, 2000). Even sexual masochism is much more prevalent among men than women, however. Male masochists may outnumber females by a margin of 20 to 1 (American Psychiatric Association, 2000).

Sexual masochism A paraphilia characterized by the desire or need for pain or humiliation to enhance sexual arousal so that gratification may be attained

A Closer Look

SHOOTING PRIVATE PARTS IN PUBLIC PLACES

Police have this warning for Washington, DC, women: Beware of geeks bearing tiny cameras.

In what they describe as a growing trend, police are beginning to catch video voyeurs trying to shoot private parts in public places. These men are aiming the latest compact camcorders up women's skirts in crowded stores and shopping malls, parks and fairs—and often posting the pictures on the Internet.

Fairfax County, Va., police arrested a 21-year-old man who was holding a palm-sized video camera under a woman's dress at a Tower Records store. At a Hecht's department store, Alexandria, Va., police nabbed a 19-year-old man toting a bulky VHS video camera. He was angling for similar shots in the china department, they said. At the Fairfax Fair, a man was arrested for videotaping from a camera bag dangling on a long strap down to his ankles.

"I had one guy who was doing it on Metro trains," said Alexandria De-tective Harold Duquette, who tracked the suspect's movements across the region by watching days' worth of his videotapes. "I mean, he was in DC [District of Columbia]. He was in tunnels. He was sitting on benches. He had one lady reading the newspaper."

"Upskirt Sites"

What began as a small photo gallery on the Internet a couple of years ago has rapidly expanded to a multitude of "up-skirt" sites, including one devoted entirely to shots taken up skirts in Maryland, said Duquette.

Through the Internet, many of these video peepers learn about new techniques and exchange stories, Duquette said. The most popular method, he said, is concealing a small video camera in a shoulder bag, with the lens pointing out of the top. The bag is either dangled under a woman's skirt or set on the ground next to her.

"Next time I go to the mall," said Kim Chinn, a Prince William County

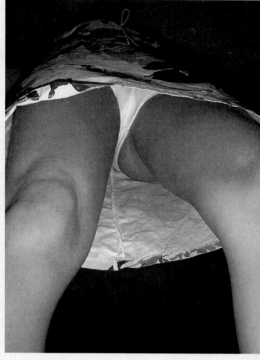

Shooting Private Parts in Public Places. *In places like suburban malls, police are beginning to catch people who are trying to shoot private parts in public places. They aim compact camcorders up women's skirts in crowded stores and shopping malls, parks, and fairs. Sometimes they post the pictures on the Internet. Often the pictures or videos wind up for sale on sex sites.*

police spokeswoman. "I'm wearing jeans."

The word *masochism* is derived from the name of the Austrian storyteller Leopold von Sacher–Masoch (1835–895). He wrote tales of men who derived sexual satisfaction from having a female partner inflict pain on them, typically by flagellation (beating or whipping).

Sexual masochists may derive pleasure from various types of punishing experiences, including being restrained (a practice known as **bondage**), blindfolded (sensory bondage), spanked, whipped, or made to perform humiliating acts, such as walking around on all fours and licking the boots or shoes of the partner, or being subjected to vulgar insults. Some masochists have their partners urinate or defecate

Bondage Ritual restraint, as by shackles, as practiced by many sexual masochists

on them. Some masochists prefer a particular source of pain. Others seek an assortment. But we should not think that sexual masochists enjoy types of pain that do not involve sex. Sexual masochists are no more likely than anyone else to derive pleasure from the pain they experience when they stub their toes or touch a hot stove. Pain must be part of an elaborate sexual ritual to provide erotic gratification.

Sexual masochists and **sexual sadists** often form sexual relationships to meet each other's needs. Some sexual masochists enlist the services of prostitutes or obtain the cooperation of their regular sexual partners to enact their masochistic fantasies.

It may seem contradictory for pain to become connected with sexual pleasure. The association of sexual arousal with mildly painful stimuli is actually quite common, however. Kinsey and his colleagues (1953) reported that perhaps as many as one person in four has experienced erotic sensations from being bitten during lovemaking. The eroticization of mild forms of pain (love bites, hair pulls, minor scratches) may fall within the normal range of sexual variation. Pain from these sources increases overall bodily arousal, which may enhance sexual excitement. Some of us become sexually excited when our partners "talk dirty" to us or call us vulgar names. When the urge for pain for purposes of sexual arousal becomes so persistent or strong that it overshadows other sources of sexual stimulation, or when the masochistic experience causes physical or psychological harm, we may say that the boundary between normality and abnormality has been breached.

Baumeister (1988a) proposes that independent and responsible selfhood become burdensome or stressful at times. Sexual masochism provides a temporary reprieve from the responsibilities of independent selfhood. It is a blunting of one's ordinary level of self-awareness that is achieved by "focusing on immediate sensations (both painful and pleasant) and on being a sexual object" (Baumeister, 1988b, p. 54).

Sexual masochism can range from relatively benign to potentially lethal practices, like **hypoxyphilia.** Hypoxyphiliacs put plastic bags over their heads, nooses around their necks, or pressure on their chests to deprive themselves temporarily of oxygen and to enhance their sexual arousal. They usually fantasize that they are being strangled by a lover. They try to discontinue oxygen deprivation before they lose consciousness, but some miscalculations result in death by suffocation or strangulation (Behrendt et al., 2002; Santtila et al., 2002).

SafeZone

Q *Do people get genital piercings for sexual pleasure?*

A Some do, but the results are iffy at best and body piercings can carry dangers. Please check with your doctor before having any piercings. You will be surprised to hear that some are actually fine, but others are not fine. In any event, the kinds of piercings usually recommended for women who are looking to enhance their sexual pleasure are clitoral hood piercings, clitoral piercings, and labial piercings. Of these, clitoral piercings are the most dangerous since they pass through the most nerves and blood vessels. Piercings of nipples, male sex organs, and navels are usually for aesthetic purposes and have a subcultural message or appeal more than an aphrodisiacal effect. The really frightening thing here is how some people will allow anyone with a storefront to pierce their bodies—anywhere. Don't be one of them. Use a reputable piercing studio that employs only trained and licensed employees.

Sexual sadists People who become sexually aroused by inflicting pain or humiliation on others

Hypoxyphilia A practice in which a person seeks to enhance sexual arousal, usually during masturbation, by becoming deprived of oxygen

Sexual Sadism

Sexual sadism seems to be the flip side of the coin of sexual masochism. Sadism is named after the infamous Marquis de Sade (1774–1814), a Frenchman who wrote tales of becoming sexually aroused by inflicting pain or humiliation on others. The virtuous Justine, the heroine of his best-known novel of the same name, endures terrible suffering at the hands of fiendish men.

Sexual sadism is characterized by persistent, powerful urges and sexual fantasies involving the inflicting of pain and suffering on others to achieve sexual excitement or gratification. The urges are acted on or are disturbing enough to cause personal distress. Some sexual sadists cannot become sexually aroused unless they make their sex partners suffer. Others can become sexually excited without such acts.

Some sadists hurt or humiliate willing partners, such as prostitutes or masochists. Others—a small minority—stalk and attack nonconsenting victims (Berner et al., 2003).

SADOMASOCHISM Sadomasochism (S&M) involves *mutually gratifying sexual interactions* between *consenting partners.* Occasional S&M is quite common among the general population. Couples may incorporate mild or light forms of S&M in their lovemaking now and then, such as mild dominance and submission games or gentle physical restraint. It is also not uncommon for lovers to scratch or bite their partners to heighten their mutual arousal during coitus. They generally do not inflict severe pain or damage, however.

Twenty-two percent of the men and 12% of the women surveyed by Kinsey and his colleagues (1953) reported at least some sexual response to sadomasochistic stories. Although mild sadomasochism may fall within the boundaries of normal sexual variation, sadomasochism becomes pathological when such fantasies are acted upon in ways that become destructive, dangerous, or distressing to oneself or others, as we find in the following case example:

> A 25-year-old female graduate student described a range of masochistic experiences. She reported feelings of sexual excitement during arguments with her husband when he would scream at her or hit her in a rage. She would sometimes taunt him to make love to her in a brutal fashion, as though she were being raped. She found the brutality and sense of being punished to be sexually stimulating. She had also begun having sex with strange men and enjoyed being physically punished by them during sex more than any other type of sexual stimulus. Being beaten or whipped produced the most intense sexual experiences she had ever had. Although she recognized the dangers posed by her sexual behavior, and felt somewhat ashamed about it, she was not sure that she wanted treatment for "it" because of the pleasure that it provided her. (Adapted from Spitzer et al., 1989, pp. 87–88)

Truth or Fiction Revisited: There is a subculture in the United States in which sexual sadists and sexual masochists form liaisons to inflict and receive pain and humiliation during sexual activity. It is called the *S&M subculture* and is catered to by sex shops that sell S&M paraphernalia and magazines. Paraphernalia includes leather restraints and leather face masks that resemble the ancient masks of executioners. People in the subculture seek one another out through mutual contacts, S&M social organizations, or personal ads in S&M magazines.

Participants in sadomasochism often engage in highly elaborate rituals involving dominance and submission. Rituals are staged, as if they were scenes in a play (Gross, 2006). In the "master-and-slave" game, the sadist leads the masochist around by a

Sexual sadism A paraphilia characterized by the desire or need to inflict pain or humiliation on others to enhance sexual arousal so that gratification is attained

Sadomasochism (S&M) A mutually gratifying sexual interaction between consenting sex partners in which sexual arousal is associated with the infliction and receipt of pain or humiliation

S&M. *An S&M club goer pays a small fortune for the services of a dominatrix.*

leash. The masochist performs degrading or menial acts. In bondage and discipline (B&D), the dominant partner restrains the submissive partner and flagellates (spanks or whips) or sexually stimulates the submissive partner. The erotic appeal of bondage seems connected with controlling or being controlled.

Various sources of pain may be used during S&M encounters, but pain is not always used. When it is, it is usually mild or moderate. Psychological pain, or humiliation, may be as common. Pain may also be symbolic, as in the case of a sadist who uses a harmless, soft rubber paddle to spank the masochist. Thus, the erotic appeal of pain for some S&M participants may derive from the ritual of control rather than pain itself. Extreme forms of pain, such as torture or severe beatings, are rarely reported by sadomasochists. Masochists may seek pain, but they usually avoid serious injury and dangerous partners (Gross, 2006).

S&M participants may be heterosexual, gay, or bisexual (Gross, 2006). They may assume either the masochistic or the sadistic role, or may alternate roles depending on the sexual script. People who seek sexual excitement by enacting both sadistic and masochistic roles are known as *sadomasochists*. In heterosexual relationships the partners may reverse traditional gender roles. The man may assume the submissive or masochistic role, and the woman may take the dominant or sadistic role (Gross, 2006). The majority of S&M participants are male, but a sizable minority are female (American Psychiatric Association, 2000). Most are in committed relationships.

The causes of sexual masochism and sadism, as of other paraphilias, are unclear, but pain might have biological links to pleasure. Natural chemicals called *endorphins*, similar to opiates, are released in the brain in response to pain and produce feelings of euphoria and general well-being. Perhaps, then, pleasure is derived from pain because of the release or augmentation of endorphins. But this theory fails to explain the erotic appeal of sadomasochistic encounters that involve minimal or symbolic pain. Nor does it explain the erotic appeal to the sadist of inflicting pain.

Whatever their causes, the roots of sexual masochism and sadism apparently date to childhood. Sadomasochistic behavior commonly begins during early adulthood, but sadomasochistic fantasies are likely to have been present during childhood (American Psychiatric Association, 2000).

Frotteurism

Some people who use the subway run into pickpockets. Some women who use the subway find themselves victimized by frotteurs. **Frotteurism** (also known as "mashing" or "groping") is rubbing against or touching a nonconsenting person. As with other paraphilias, a diagnosis of frotteurism requires either acting upon these urges or being distressed by them. Mashing has been reported exclusively among males (American Psychiatric Association, 2000).

Most mashing takes place in crowded places, such as buses, subway cars, or elevators. The man finds the rubbing or the touching, not the coercive nature of the act, to be sexually stimulating. While rubbing against a woman, he may fantasize a consensual, affectionate sexual relationship with her. Typically the man incorporates images of his mashing within his masturbation fantasies. Mashing also incorporates a related practice, **toucherism:** fondling nonconsenting strangers.

Mashing may be so fleeting and furtive that the woman may not realize what has happened. Mashers thus stand little chance of being caught. Consider the case of a man who victimized a thousand or so women within a decade but was arrested only twice:

Frotteurism A paraphilia characterized by recurrent, powerful sexual urges and related fantasies involving rubbing against or touching a nonconsenting person

Toucherism A practice related to frotteurism and characterized by the persistent urge to fondle nonconsenting strangers

Charles, 45, was seen by a psychiatrist following his second arrest for rubbing against a woman in the subway. He would select as his target a woman in her 20s as she entered the subway station. He would then position himself behind her on the platform and wait for the train to arrive. He would then follow her into the subway car and when the doors closed would begin bumping his penis against her buttocks, while fantasizing that they were enjoying having intercourse in a loving and consensual manner. About half of the time he would ejaculate into a plastic bag that he had wrapped around his penis to prevent staining his pants. He would then continue on his way to work. Sometimes when he hadn't ejaculated he would change trains and seek another victim. While he felt guilty for a time after each episode, he would soon become preoccupied with thoughts about his next encounter. He never gave any thought to the feelings his victims might have about what he had done to them. While he was married to the same woman for 25 years, he appears to be rather socially inept and unassertive, especially with women. (Adapted from Spitzer et al., 1989, pp. 106–107)

Although this masher was married, many mashers have difficulties forming relationships with women and are handicapped by fears of rejection. Mashing provides sexual contact in a relatively nonthreatening context.

Other Paraphilias

The paraphilias we have been discussing, fetishism through frotteurism, are the most common. But there are others, such as zoophilia.

ZOOPHILIA   Zoophilia is one of the rarest paraphilias and is often associated with other disorders (Dittert et al., 2005; Lesjak et al., 2004). A person with **zoophilia** experiences repeated, intense urges and related fantasies involving sexual contact with animals. As with other paraphilias, the urges may be acted upon or cause personal distress. A child or adolescent who shows some sexual response to an occasional episode of rough-and-tumble play with the family pet is not displaying zoophilia.

The term *bestiality* applies to actual sexual contact with an animal. Human sexual contact with animals, mythical and real, has a long history. Michelangelo's painting *Leda and the Swan* depicts the Greek god Zeus taking the form of a swan to mate with a woman, Leda. Zeus was also portrayed as taking the form of a bull or serpent to mate with humans. In the Old Testament, God is said to have put to death people who had sexual relations with animals. The Greek historian Herodotus notes that goats at the Egyptian temple at Mendes were trained to copulate with people.

Although the prevalence of zoophilia in the general population is unknown, Kinsey and his colleagues (1948, 1953) found that about 8% of the men and 3% to 4% of the women interviewed admitted to sexual contact with animals. Men more often had sexual contact with farm animals, such as calves and sheep. Women more often reported sexual contact with household pets. Men were more likely to masturbate or copulate with the animals. Women more often reported general body contact. People of both sexes reported encouraging the animals to lick their genitals. A few women reported that they had trained a dog to have sex with them. Urban–rural differences also emerged. Rates of bestiality were higher among boys reared on farms. Compared with only a few city boys, 17% of farm boys had reached orgasm at some time through sexual contact with dogs, cows, and goats. These contacts were generally restricted to adolescence, when human outlets were not available. Still, adults some-

Zoophilia A paraphilia involving persistent or repeated sexual urges and related fantasies involving sexual contact with animals

A Closer Look

SAY CHEESE, YOU SLEAZE! CAM-PHONE GALS SNAP SUBWAY GROPERS

Picture This. *Some self-defense experts recommend that women use camera-equipped cellphones to expose and humiliate subway-riding exhibitionists and frotteurs. Others are not so sure.*

Camera phones are becoming one means of defense for women to combat exhibitionists and frotteurs in the subway.

Some self-defense pros argue that the power to humiliate flashers and gropers by exposing their overexposure with a snapshot is an even more powerful weapon for women than a can of Mace or a kick in the groin.

"The simplest thing that someone can actually do with zero training is to employ public humiliation," said Rudy Zadwarny, 50, who teaches martial arts and women's self-defense. "These guys try to do it when they think no one knows it." The snapshots would be turned over to police or posted on a "wall of shame" at subway stops along lines frequented by the offenders.

Some Responses to the Article

- Posted online: "Hmmm. I was born in and grew up in New York until a couple of years after graduate school. If I were a woman I think Mace might be a better defense than a camera phone photo! Or maybe an Uzi."

- A 23-year-old Manhattanite waiting for a train says, "Why do that? Just punch them like a true New Yorker would."

Our recommendation: Whatever you do, make sure you don't get hurt. You and your safety are the most important things.

SOURCE: From "'Say Cheese, You Sleaze' Cam-Phone Gals Snap Subway Gropers" by Jennifer Fermino and Jeremy Olshan, *New York Post*, June 24, 2006. © NYP Holdings, Inc. Reprinted by permission. Responses posted at www.wirelessmoment.com/2006/06/index.html.

times engage in sexual contacts with animals, generally because of curiosity or novelty or for a sexual release when human partners are unavailable. Whether such contacts constitute zoophilia depends upon their frequency and intensity, or whether they cause the person distress. True zoophilia is often associated with problems such as alcoholism and intellectual deficiency (Lesjak et al., 2004).

SafeZone

Q *Are there cultures that allow sex with animals/pets?*

A No modern cultures do, but ancient cave paintings and other artifacts suggest that sex with animals might have been allowed and sometimes incorporated into magical rituals before the advent of the so-called "Abrahamic" religions of Judaism, Christianity, and Islam. Many Egyptian gods were depicted as part animal, suggesting that sex with animals might have been included in some rituals. Goats and baboons might have been occasional sex partners in ancient Egypt.

NECROPHILIA In **necrophilia,** a rare paraphilia, a person desires sex with corpses. Three types of necrophilia have been identified (Holmes & Holmes, 2002). In *regular necrophilia,* the person has sex with a deceased person. In *necrophilic homicide,* the person commits murder to obtain a corpse for sexual purposes. In *necrophilic fantasy,* the person fantasizes about sex with a corpse but does not actually carry out necrophilic acts. Necrophiles often obtain jobs that provide them with access to corpses, such as working in cemeteries, morgues, or funeral homes. The primary motivation for necrophilia appears to be the desire to sexually possess a completely unresisting and nonrejecting partner (Holmes & Holmes, 2002). Many necrophiles have serious psychological disorders.

LESS COMMON PARAPHILIAS In **klismaphilia,** sexual arousal is derived from the use of enemas. Klismaphiles generally prefer the receiving role to the giving role. Klismaphiles may have derived sexual pleasure in childhood from the anal stimulation provided by parents giving them enemas.

In **coprophilia,** sexual arousal is connected with feces. The person may desire to be defecated on or to defecate on a sex partner. The association of feces with sexual arousal may also be a throwback to childhood. Many children appear to obtain anal sexual pleasure by holding in and then purposefully expelling feces. It may also be that the incidental connection between erections or sexual arousal and soiled diapers during infancy eroticizes feces.

In **urophilia,** sexual arousal is associated with urine. As with coprophilia, the person may desire to be urinated upon or to urinate upon a sexual partner. Also like coprophilia, urophilia may have childhood origins. Stimulation of the urethral canal during urination may become associated with sexual pleasure. Or urine may have become eroticized by experiences in which erections occurred while the infant was clothed in a wet diaper.

Theoretical Perspectives

The paraphilias are fascinating and perplexing variations in sexual behavior. We may find it difficult to understand how people can become sexually excited by fondling an article of clothing or by cross-dressing. It may also be difficult to identify with people who feel compelled to exhibit their genitals or to rub their genitals against unsuspecting victims in crowded places. Perhaps we can recognize some voyeuristic tendencies in ourselves, but we cannot imagine peeping through binoculars while perched in a nearby tree or, for that matter, risking the social and legal consequences of being discovered in the act. Nor might we understand how people can become sexually turned on by inflicting or receiving pain. Let us consider explanations that have been advanced from various theoretical perspectives.

Biological Perspectives

Researchers are investigating whether there are biological factors in paraphilic behavior. The biological perspective looks into factors such as the endocrine system (hormones) and the nervous system in paraphilic behavior.

Studies appear to confirm that many paraphilics have higher than normal sex drives (Haake et al., 2003; Kafka, 2003). A German study, for example, found that people with paraphilias had shorter refractory periods after orgasm by masturbation than most men and experienced a higher frequency of sexual fantasies and urges

Necrophilia A paraphilia characterized by the desire for sexual activity with corpses

Klismaphilia A paraphilia in which sexual arousal is derived from the use of enemas

Coprophilia A paraphilia in which sexual arousal is attained in connection with feces

Urophilia A paraphilia in which sexual arousal is associated with urine

(Haake et al., 2003). Kafka (2003) refers to this heightened sex drive as *hypersexual desire*—the opposite of hypoactive sexual desire disorder (see Chapter 15).

But these studies address the strength of the sex drive, not the direction it takes. More recent studies have used the electroencephalograph (EEG) to investigate electrical responses in the brain among paraphilics and control subjects (e.g., Kirenskaya–Berus & Tkachenko, 2003). They measure what is termed *evoked electrical potentials* to erotic stimuli in a sample of 62 right-handed men, half of whom were considered to be normal in terms of their sexual fantasies and behaviors (the control subjects), and half of whom had been diagnosed as paraphilic (fetishistic and sadomasochistic) (Waismann et al., 2003). The men were shown three sets of 57 slides each in random order—57 paraphilic slides that portrayed depicting fetishistic and sadomasochistic themes; 57 "normal" slides that depicted nude women, coitus, and oral sex; and 57 neutral slides of landscapes, street scenes, and the like. An electrical response labeled "P600" was determined to be the best indicator of sexual arousal in men. It was found that the main site for evoking the P600 response to "normal" sexual stimuli was on the right side of the brain. The main site for paraphilic stimuli was the left frontal part of the brain. Paraphilic men showed a significantly greater response than the control subjects in the P600 response in the left frontal part of the brain. Moreover, control subjects were more likely to differentiate between paraphilic and normal stimuli on the right side of the brain.

Another neurological study may offer some insight into masochism. A research team from Massachusetts General Hospital found that the same neural circuits in the brain are often activated either by painful or by pleasurable stimuli (Becerra et al., 2001). The researchers discovered that a painfully hot (115°F) stimulus to the hand activated areas of the brain believed to involve "reward" circuitry. The researchers had set out to find ways to help chronic pain patients and not to investigate sexual masochism, but their findings certainly have implications for masochism.

As time goes on, we may learn more about potential biological foundations of paraphilic behavior. A better understanding of these atypical patterns of sexual behavior may lead to the development of more effective treatments.

Psychoanalytic Perspectives

Psychoanalytic theory suggests that paraphilias are psychological defenses, usually against unresolved castration anxiety dating to the Oedipus complex (Friedman & Downey, 2001; Horne, 2003). Perhaps the sight of a woman's vagina threatens to arouse castration anxiety in the transvestite, reminding him that women do not have penises and that he might suffer the same fate. Sequestering his penis beneath women's clothing symbolically asserts that women do have penises, which provides unconscious reassurance against his own fears of castration. By exposing his genitals, perhaps the exhibitionist unconsciously seeks reassurance that his penis is secure. It is as if he were asserting, "Look! I have a penis!" Shock or surprise on the victim's face confirms that his penis exists, temporarily relieving castration anxiety. Perhaps masturbation with an object such as a shoe allows the fetishist to gratify his sexual desires while keeping a safe distance from the dangers that he unconsciously associates with sexual contact with women. Or the fetishistic object itself—the shoe, in this case—may unconsciously symbolize the penis. Are sadists attempting to defend themselves against unconscious feelings of impotence by inflicting pain on others?

One psychoanalyst associates a type of male sexual masochism with a history of suppressed or repressed feelings of sexual guilt and shame (Schrut, 2005). As an adult, the male wants to be punished for feelings of wrongdoing at the same time he experiences sexual arousal. The pain or humiliation makes the experience "okay."

The paraphilias have provided a fertile ground for psycho-analytic theories. However, whatever evidence there is consists of case studies and anecdotes, which are open to interpretation.

Cognitive–Behavioral Perspectives

Cognitive–behavioral theorists generally believe that fetishes and other paraphilias are learned through experience. An object may acquire sexually arousing properties through association with sexual arousal or orgasm. Alfred Kinsey and his colleagues (1953) wrote:

> Even some of the most extremely variant types of human sexual behavior may need no more explanation than is provided by our understanding of the processes of learning and conditioning. Behavior which may appear bizarre, perverse, or unthinkably unacceptable to some persons, and even to most persons, may have significance for other individuals because of the way in which they have been conditioned. (pp. 645–646)

For example, a boy who glimpses his mother's stockings hanging on the towel rack while he is masturbating may develop a fetish for stockings. Orgasm in the presence of the object reinforces the erotic connection, especially if it is repeated.

Friedrich and Gerber (1994) studied five adolescent boys who practiced hypoxyphilia and found extensive early histories of choking in combination with physical or sexual abuse. The combination seems to have encouraged each of the boys to associate choking with sexual arousal.

Cognitive–behavioral explanations of sexual masochism focus on the pairing of sexual excitement with punishment. For example, a child may be punished when discovered masturbating. Or a boy may reflexively experience an erection if his penis accidentally rubs against the parent's body as he is being spanked. With repeated encounters like these, pain and pleasure may become linked.

Many exhibitionists, voyeurs, frotteurs, and other people with paraphilias have few interpersonal skills relating to women and may avoid "normal" social interactions with them for fear of rejection (Leue et al., 2004). Their furtive, paraphilic behaviors may provide sexual release without the risk of rejection.

Observational learning may also play a role. Parents, for example, may inadvertently model exhibitionistic behavior to young sons, which can lead the sons to eroticize the act of exposing themselves. Young people may also read books or magazines, or view films or TV programs with paraphilic content. Media may give them the idea of trying paraphilic behavior, and they may find it exciting, especially if acts such as exhibitionism or voyeurism provide a rush or adrenaline.

Sociological Perspectives

Sociological perspectives focus on the effects of the group and of society on individual and group behavior. For example, although most people indulge paraphilias privately, sexual masochists and sadists require a partner. Most sadomasochists learn S&M rituals, make sexual contacts, acquire sexual paraphernalia, and confirm their

Do People Become Addicted to Cybersex? *According to Dr. Mark Schwartz of the Masters and Johnson Institute, "Sex on the Net is like heroin," for some people. "It grabs them and takes over their lives." Some people spend hours each day masturbating to pornographic images they find online, or engaging in "mutual" online sex with someone they contact through a chat room. Is becoming hooked on cybersex a safe kind of "addiction"? What do you think?*

CRITICAL Thinking

If people with paraphilias have powerful urges to engage in deviant behavior because of biological forces or unconscious fears, can they be expected to control their behavior?

sadomasochistic self-identities within what is termed an *S&M subculture*—a loosely connected network of S&M clubs, specialty shops, organizations, magazines, and so on. But the S&M subculture exists in the context of the larger society, and its rituals mirror widely based social and gender roles.

Martin Weinberg (1987) proposes a sociological model that focuses on the social context of sadomasochism. S&M rituals generally involve some form of dominance and submission. Weinberg (1987) attributes their erotic appeal to the opportunity to reverse the customary power relationships that exist between males and females and between social classes. Within the confines of the carefully scripted S&M encounter, the meek can be powerful and the powerful, meek. People from lower social classes or in menial jobs may be drawn to S&M so they can enact a dominant role. Dominance and submission games allow people to accentuate or reverse the gender stereotypes that identify masculinity with dominance and femininity with submissiveness. Interviews with, and observations of, sadomasochists suggest that most often dominance–submission relationships tend to be consistent with traditional masculine and feminine gender roles in society (Damon, 2002; Santtila et al., 2002). Although there are many exceptions, men more often tend to be dominant and women to be submissive in S&M rituals.

An Integrated Perspective: The "Lovemap"

Paraphilias may have complex biopsychosocial origins (Seligman & Hardenburg, 2000). Might our understanding of them thus be best approached from a theoretical framework that incorporates multiple perspectives? John Money (2003), for example, traces the origins of paraphilias to childhood. He believes that childhood experiences etch a pattern in the brain, called a **lovemap.** This lovemap determines the types of stimuli and activities that become sexually arousing to the individual. In the case of paraphilias, lovemaps become distorted by early traumatic experiences such as incest, antisexual upbringing, and abuse or neglect.

Research suggests that voyeurs and exhibitionists were often the victims of childhood sexual abuse (Lee et al., 2002). Not all children exposed to such influences develop paraphilic compulsions, however. For reasons that remain unknown, some children exposed to such influences appear to be more vulnerable to developing distorted lovemaps than others. A genetic predisposition, hormonal factors, brain abnormalities, or a combination of these and other factors may play a role in determining one's vulnerability to vandalized lovemaps.

Treatment of the Paraphilias

The treatment of paraphilias raises a number of issues. First, many people with paraphilias do not want or seek treatment, at least not voluntarily. The Canadian criminologist Ron Langevin (2006), for example, followed nearly 800 sex offenders from the 1960s through the 2000s and found that only about half desired treatment and completed a course of treatment. But many offenders are seen by health care providers only when they come into conflict with the law or at the urging of their family members or partners.

Second, health care providers may encounter ethical problems when they are asked to contribute to a judicial process by trying to persuade a sex offender that he

Lovemap A representation in the mind and in the brain of the idealized lover, and the idealized erotic activity with the lover (virtually all are male) *ought* to change his behavior. Health care providers traditionally help clients clarify or meet their own goals; it is not their role to impose societal goals on the individual. Many health care providers believe that the criminal justice system, not they, ought to enforce social standards.

The third issue is a treatment problem. Health care providers realize they are generally less successful with resistant or recalcitrant clients.

The fourth problem is the issue of perceived responsibility. Sex offenders typically claim they cannot control their impulses, and accepting personal responsibility for one's actions is a prelude to change.

Despite these issues, many offenders are referred for treatment by the courts. Some seek therapy themselves because they have come to see how their behavior harms themselves or others (Langevin, 2006). We shall consider psychological and biological approaches to the treatment of people with paraphilias. Most sexual offender treatment programs use a combination of psychoanalytic psychotherapy, cognitive–behavioral treatment, and medication (Marvasti, 2004).

Is Her Behavior Appropriate or Inappropriate? *Many theorists suggest that early learning experiences contribute to the development of paraphilias. Is this woman's interaction with her young child of the sort that can lead to sexual problems as the child matures?*

Psychoanalytic Psychotherapy

Psychoanalysis focuses on resolving the unconscious conflicts that are believed to originate in childhood and to give rise in adulthood to pathological problems such as paraphilias. The aim of therapy is to help bring unconscious conflicts, principally oedipal conflicts, into conscious awareness so that they might be worked through in the light of the individual's adult personality (Laws & Marshall, 2003).

Although some favorable case results have been reported, psychoanalytic therapy of the paraphilias is rarely subjected to experimental analysis. We thus know little about whether successes are the result of the psychoanalytic treatment itself or other factors, such as spontaneous improvement or a client's willingness to change.

REFLECT

Is it ethical for mental health professionals to work with clients who do not want treatment?

Cognitive–Behavioral Therapy

Although traditional psychoanalysis tends to entail a lengthy process of exploration of the childhood origins of problem behaviors, **cognitive–behavioral therapy** is relatively briefer and focuses directly on changing behavior. Cognitive–behavioral therapy has spawned a number of techniques to help eliminate paraphilic behaviors and strengthen appropriate sexual behaviors: **systematic desensitization,** relapse prevention training, **aversion therapy,** empathy training, **social skills training,** anger management, **covert sensitization,** and **orgasmic reconditioning,** to name a few (Krueger & Kaplan, 2002; Marvasti, 2004).

Systematic desensitization attempts to break the link between the sexual stimulus (such as a fetishistic stimulus) and the inappropriate response (sexual arousal). The client is first taught to relax selected muscle groups in the body. Muscle relaxation is then paired repeatedly with a series of progressively more arousing paraphilic images or fantasies. Relaxation comes to replace sexual arousal in response to each of these stimuli, even the most provocative. In one case study, a fetishistic transvestite who had become attracted to his mother's lingerie at age 13

Cognitive–behavioral therapy Therapy that attempts to change directly the ways in which people view events and respond to them, relying frequently on principles of learning

Systematic desensitization A method that uses muscle relaxation to break the connection between a stimulus (such as a fetishistic object) and an inappropriate response (sexual arousal)

was taught to relax when presented with audiotaped scenes representing transvestite or fetishistic themes (Fensterheim & Kantor, 1980). He played such tapes daily while remaining relaxed. He later reported a complete absence of transvestite thoughts or activities.

In **aversion therapy,** the undesirable sexual behavior (e.g., masturbation to fetishistic fantasies) is paired repeatedly with an aversive stimulus (such as a harmless but painful electric shock or a nausea-inducing chemical) in the hope that the client will develop a conditioned aversion toward the paraphilic behavior.

Covert sensitization is a variation of aversion therapy in which paraphilic fantasies are paired with an aversive stimulus in imagination. In one study of 38 **pedophiles** and 62 exhibitionists, more than half of whom were court referred, subjects were treated by pairing imagined aversive odors with fantasies of the problem behavior (Maletzky, 1980). They were instructed to fantasize pedophiliac or exhibitionistic scenes. Then,

> [a]t a point . . . when sexual pleasure is aroused, aversive images are presented. . . . Examples might include a pedophiliac fellating a child, but discovering a festering sore on the boy's penis, an exhibitionist exposing to a woman but suddenly being discovered by his wife or the police, or a pedophiliac laying a young boy down in a field, only to lie next to him in a pile of dog feces. (Maletzky, 1980, p. 308)

Maletzky (1980) used this treatment weekly for six months, then followed it with booster sessions every three months for a three-year period. The procedure resulted in at least a 75% reduction of the deviant activities and fantasies for more than 80% of the study participants at follow-up periods of up to 36 months. At a 25-year follow-up of 7,275 sex offenders who received similar treatment, Maletzky and Steinhauser (2002) found that benefits were maintained for many of the exhibitionists, but for fewer of the pedophiles. But fewer than 50% of the original participants could be contacted after this amount of time elapsed.

Social skills training focuses on helping the individual improve his ability to relate to the other gender. The therapist might first model a desired behavior, such as how to ask a woman out on a date or how to handle a rejection. The client might then role-play the behavior, with the therapist playing the part of the woman. Following the role-playing enactment, the therapist would provide feedback and additional guidance and modeling to help the client improve his skills. This process would be repeated until the client mastered the skill.

Orgasmic reconditioning aims to increase sexual arousal to socially appropriate sexual stimuli by pairing culturally appropriate imagery with orgasmic pleasure. The person is instructed to become sexually aroused by masturbating to paraphilic images or fantasies. But as he approaches the point of orgasm, he switches to appropriate imagery and focuses on it during orgasm. In a case example, Davison (1977) reports reduction of sadistic fantasies in a 21-year-old college man. The client was instructed to attain an erection in any way he could, even through the use of the sadistic fantasies he wished to eliminate. However, when erection was achieved, he was to masturbate while looking at photos of *Playboy* models. Orgasm was thus paired with nonsadistic images. These images and fantasies eventually acquire the capacity to elicit sexual arousal. Orgasmic reconditioning is often combined with other techniques, such as social skills training, so that more desirable social behaviors can be strengthened as well (Marvasti, 2004).

As we see next, in many ways the treatment of sexual problems is becoming more "medicalized" (Kleinplatz, 2003).

Aversion therapy A method for terminating undesirable sexual behavior in which the behavior is repeatedly paired with an aversive stimulus, such as electric shock, to condition an aversion

Covert sensitization A form of aversion therapy in which thoughts of engaging in undesirable behavior are paired repeatedly with imagined aversive stimuli

Pedophiles Persons with a paraphilia involving sexual interest in children

Social skills training Cognitive–behavioral therapy methods for building social skills that rely on a therapist's coaching and practice

Orgasmic reconditioning A method for strengthening the connection between sexual arousal and appropriate sexual stimuli (such as fantasies about an adult of the other sex) by repeatedly pairing the desired stimuli with orgasm

Medical Approaches

There may be no medical "cure" for the paraphilias. No drug or surgical technique eliminates paraphilic ideas. Yet some progress has recently been reported in using SSRIs, which are mainly used as antidepressants, in treating exhibitionism, voyeurism, and fetishism (Bradford, 2001; Roesler & Witztum, 2000). Why SSRIs? For one thing, SSRIs often depress erectile response (Dunsieth et al., 2004). SSRIs are also often used to treat obsessive–compulsive disorder, a psychological disorder involving recurrent obsessions (intrusive ideas) and/or compulsions (urges to repeat a certain behavior or thought). People with paraphilias often experience intrusive, repetitive fantasies and urges.

People who experience such intense urges that they are at risk of committing sexual offenses may be helped by drugs that reduce the level of testosterone in the bloodstream (Briken et al., 2003). Testosterone is closely linked to sex drive and interest. *Medroxyprogesterone acetate* (brand name Depo-Provera), which is administered in weekly injections, is the antiandrogen that has been used most extensively in the treatment of sex offenders. In men, antiandrogen drugs reduce testosterone to a level that is typical of a prepubertal boy (Bradford, 2001). This treatment consequently reduces sexual desire and the frequency of erections and ejaculations (Bradford, 2001).

Depo-Provera suppresses sexual appetite in men. It can lower the intensity of one's sex drive and erotic fantasies and urges so that the man may feel less compelled to act upon them (Roesler & Witztum, 2000). Antiandrogens do not, however, eliminate all paraphilic urges or completely change a person's sexual behavior.

The use of antiandrogens is sometimes incorrectly referred to as *chemical castration*. Surgical castration, the surgical removal of the testes, has sometimes been performed on convicted rapists and violent sex offenders (Roesler & Witztum, 2000). Surgical castration eliminates testicular sources of testosterone. Antiandrogens suppress, but do not eliminate, testicular production of testosterone. Also, unlike surgical castration, the effects of antiandrogens can be reversed when the treatment is terminated.

Evidence suggests that antiandrogens help some people when they are used in conjunction with psychological treatment (Roesler & Witztum, 2000). The value of antiandrogens has been limited by high refusal and dropout rates, however (Roesler & Witztum, 2000). Questions also remain concerning side effects.

Although we have amassed a great deal of research on atypical variations in sexual behavior, our understanding of them and our treatment approaches to them remain less than satisfactory.

CRITICAL Thinking

Which methods of therapy aim to work by reducing the sex drive in general, and which aim to replace sexual response to socially inappropriate stimuli with sexual response to appropriate stimuli?

SafeZone

Q *Do you think it's unhealthy to try and fulfill wild, way out, socially unacceptable fantasies, such as group sex?*

A Group sex is actually not all that "way out," especially threesomes. In terms of socially unacceptable fantasies, when you get into the healthy-unhealthy distinction, we think you have to deal with the realities of contemporary society as it is and not as you would like to fantasize it to be. Way out fantasies are fine; way out behavior may backfire. We would suggest that you distinguish between the two and consider all the consequences of your behavior—for others and yourself.

1. How do we determine what behavior is normal and what behavior is deviant or abnormal?

- Sexual behaviors have been labeled deviant when they are statistically rare, run counter to our values, or—as in the case of the paraphilias—show a persistent preference for nongenital outlets.

2. What are paraphilias?

- Paraphilias involve sexual arousal in response to unusual stimuli such as children or other nonconsenting persons, certain objects, or pain or humiliation. The psychiatric diagnosis of paraphilia requires that the person has acted on these persistent urges or is distinctly distressed by them. The great majority of paraphilias occur among men.

3. What kinds of paraphilias are there?

- In fetishism, an inanimate object elicits sexual arousal. In partialism, people are inordinately aroused by a particular body part, such as the feet. Although other fetishists become sexually aroused by handling the fetishistic object while they masturbate, transvestites become excited by wearing articles of clothing—the fetishistic objects—of the other sex.

- An exhibitionist experiences the compulsion to expose himself to strangers. Most exhibitionists do not attempt further sexual contact with the victim, but some do pose a physical threat.

- Voyeurs become sexually aroused by watching, and usually do not seek sexual relations with the target. The voyeur may masturbate while peeping or afterward while engaging in voyeuristic fantasies. Some exhibitionists and voyeurs harbor feelings of inadequacy and lack social skills.

- The obscene phone caller is motivated to become sexually aroused by shocking his victim. Such callers typically masturbate during the phone call or shortly afterward.

- Sexual masochists associate the receipt of pain or humiliation with sexual arousal. Sexual masochists and sexual sadists sometimes form liaisons to meet each other's needs. Sexual sadism is characterized by persistent, powerful urges and sexual fantasies involving the inflicting of pain and suffering on others to achieve sexual excitement or gratification. Sexual sadists may be quite dangerous, especially when they seek nonconsenting "partners." An S&M subculture enlists sadists and masochists.

- Most frotteuristic acts—rubbing against nonconsenting persons, also known as mashing—take place in crowded places, such as buses, subway cars, or elevators.

- Zoophiles desire sexual contact with animals. Necrophiles desire sexual contact with dead bodies.

4. How do we explain paraphilias?

- The biological perspective has to date determined that many people with paraphilias have higher than normal sex drives. Their brains may also respond differently to paraphilic and "normal" sexual stimuli.

- Classic psychoanalytic theory suggests that paraphilias in males are psychological defenses against castration anxiety.

- Some cognitive–behavioral theorists suggest that unusual stimuli may acquire sexually arousing properties through association with sexual arousal or orgasm. Unusual stimuli may gradually acquire sexually arousing properties through incorporation in masturbatory fantasies.

- According to Weinberg's sociological model, the erotic appeal of S&M rituals may result from the opportunity to reverse the customary power relationships that exist between men and women, and between the social classes in society.

- Money theorizes that childhood experiences etch a pattern in the brain—a lovemap—that determines the types of stimuli and activities that become sexually arousing. In the case of paraphilias, these lovemaps become distorted by early traumatic experiences.

5. How do we treat paraphilias?

- Psychoanalysis aims to bring unconscious conflicts that prompt paraphilic behavior into awareness so that they can be worked through in adulthood.

- Cognitive–behavioral therapy attempts to eliminate paraphilic behaviors through techniques such as systematic desensitization, aversion therapy, social skills training, covert sensitization, and orgasmic reconditioning.

- SSRIs, which are usually used as antidepressants, tend to curb compulsive behavior and depress sexual response, and have been used with some paraphilic individuals.

1. A subculture has sprung up around
   - (a) exhibitionism
   - (b) frotteurism
   - (c) distortion of the "lovemap'
   - (d) sexual sadism and masochism

2. People who are excessively aroused by a particular body part, such as the feet, breasts, or buttocks are said to have
   - (a) voyeurism
   - (b) frotteurism
   - (c) partialism
   - (d) transvestism

3. Hypoxyphilia is an activity related to
   - (a) sexual sadism
   - (b) sexual masochism
   - (c) fetishism
   - (d) zoophilia

4. When cognitive–behavioral therapists work with people with paraphilias, they may use all of the following methods *except*
   - (a) covert sensitization
   - (b) orgasmic reconditioning
   - (c) systematic desensitization
   - (d) antidepressant drugs

5. According to psychoanalytic theory, the _____ is declaring "Look, I have a penis!"
   - (a) exhibitionist
   - (b) voyeur
   - (c) masher
   - (d) sexual sadist

6. A "lovemap" is most likely to become distorted or "vandalized" by
   - (a) alcohol
   - (b) physical abuse or neglect
   - (c) unconscious conflicts from the oedipal period
   - (d) the sadomasochistic subculture

7. Transvestism is considered to be most closely related to
   - (a) fetishism
   - (b) exhibitionism
   - (c) mashing
   - (d) sadomasochism

8. Telephone scatalogia is considered to be most closely related to
   - (a) coprophilia
   - (b) sexual sadism
   - (c) voyeurism
   - (d) exhibitionism

9. Which of the following are most likely to need to risk capture to heighten their sexual arousal?
   - (a) Sadomasochists
   - (b) Coprophiliacs
   - (c) Exhibitionists
   - (d) Mashers

10. Waismann and colleagues showed men sets of slides and found that the main site for evoking the _____ response to "normal" sexual stimuli was on the right side of the brain.
    - (a) P100
    - (b) P300
    - (c) P400
    - (d) P600

11. Paraphilias are defined by
    - (a) preference for deviant stimuli over genital contact
    - (b) statistical rarity of the sexual interest
    - (c) sexual interests that deviate from the core values of a society
    - (d) a high sex drive

12. About _____% of the men in the Kinsey studies reported some sexual response to sadomasochistic stories.
    - (a) 12
    - (b) 22
    - (c) 44
    - (d) 84

13. A finding that is true for all paraphilias is that they
    - (a) pose a physical threat to the victims
    - (b) are evidence that the perpetrator is out of touch with reality
    - (c) are more common among males
    - (d) can be treated by psychoanalytic psychotherapy

14. The legend of Lady Godiva is connected with a slang term for
    - (a) exhibitionists
    - (b) voyeurs
    - (c) sexual sadists
    - (d) sexual masochists

15. The text states that it is normal to
    - (a) expose oneself to a stranger to shock the stranger
    - (b) hurt sex partners
    - (c) enjoy exposing one's body to an intimate partner
    - (d) fantasize about having sex with corpses

Answers 1. d; 2. c; 3. b; 4. d; 5. a; 6. b; 7. a; 8. d; 9. c; 10. d; 11. a; 12. b; 13. c; 14. b; 15. c

18

Sexual Coercion

TRUTH? fiction

Which of the following statements are true, and which are fiction? Look for the Truth/Fiction icons on the pages that follow to find the answers.

1 A woman is raped every 10 minutes in the United States.   T   F

2 The majority of rapes are committed by strangers in deserted neighborhoods or darkened alleyways.   T   F

3 One in ten rape survivors in the United States is a man.   T   F

4 Men who rape other men are gay.   T   F

5 Many women say no when they mean yes.   T   F

6 Most rapists are mentally ill.   T   F

7 Women who encounter a rapist should attempt to fight him off.   T   F

8 Father–daughter incest is the most common type of incest.   T   F

The 13-year-old boy sat in his California home, eyes fixed on a computer screen. He had never run with the popular crowd and long ago had turned to the Internet for the friends he craved. But on this day, Justin Berry's fascination with cyberspace would change his life.

Weeks before, Justin had hooked up a Web camera to his computer, hoping to use it to meet other teenagers online. Instead, he heard only from men who chatted with him by instant message as they watched his image on the Internet. To Justin, they seemed just like friends, ready with compliments and always offering gifts.

Now, on an afternoon in 2000, one member of his audience sent a proposal: He would pay Justin $50 to sit bare-chested in front of his webcam for three minutes. The man explained that Justin could receive the money instantly and helped him open an account on PayPal.com, an online payment system.

"I figured, I took off my shirt at the pool for nothing," he said recently. "So, I was kind of like, what's the difference?" Justin removed his T-shirt. The men watching him oozed compliments.

So began the secret life of a teenager who was lured into selling images of his body on the Internet over the course of five years. From the seduction that began that day, this soccer-playing honor roll student was drawn into performing in front of the webcam—undressing, showering, masturbating, and even having sex—for an audience of more than 1,500 people who paid him, over the years, hundreds of thousands of dollars.

Justin's dark coming-of-age story is a collateral effect of recent technological advances. Minors, often under the online tutelage of adults, are opening for-pay pornography sites featuring their own images sent onto the Internet by inexpensive webcams. And they perform from the privacy of home, while parents are nearby, beyond their children's closed bedroom doors.

Justin Berry, now of age, is one of many victims of sexual child abuse who testified on Capitol Hill.

The business has created youthful Internet pornography stars—with nicknames like Riotboyy, Miss Honey, and Gigglez—whose images are traded online long after their sites have vanished. In this world, adolescents announce schedules of their next masturbation for customers who pay fees for the performance or monthly subscription charges. Eager customers can even buy "private shows," in which teenagers sexually perform while following real-time instructions. A six-month investigation by *The New York Times* into this corner of the Internet found that such sites had emerged largely without attracting the attention of law enforcement or youth protection organizations. While experts with these groups said they had witnessed a recent deluge of illicit, self-generated webcam images, they had not known of the evolution of sites where minors sold images of themselves for money.

SOURCE: From "Through His Webcam, a Boy Joins a Sordid Online World" by Kurt Eichenwald, *The New York Times,* December 19, 2005 by The New York Times Co. Reprinted with permission.

The media are in a continuous feeding frenzy over sexual offenses involving minors, celebrities, highly placed politicians, and members of the armed services. In the 1990s, the spotlight was on the rape trial of boxer Mike Tyson and then on an affair between Bill Clinton and a young White House intern named Monica Lewinsky. Many argued that their relationship comprised sexual harassment because of the disparity in their power, even though Lewinsky was a willing partner.

In the 2000s there came the stories of American priests who sexually abused children. The Boston Archdiocese alone was reported to have received more than 1,000 complaints of child sexual abuse during the past several decades and to have turned a blind eye to the charges (Finkelhor, 2003; Sex Abuse Victims, 2003). Some wondered aloud whether the church's requirement that priests remain celibate has contributed to the problem (Adams, 2003).

At about the same time, it was charged that the Air Force Academy had "traditions" that encouraged or legitimized the sexual assault of female cadets. A number of women cadets left the academy, officers resigned, and policies were changed (Janofsky & Schemo, 2003).

Then there were the cases of Mary Kay LeTourneau, Pamela Rogers, and Debra LaFave—women who were prosecuted for having sex with minor boys. Although some men wondered whether these boys just "got lucky," David Finkelhor (as cited in Zerwike, 2005), director of the Crimes Against Children Research Center at the University of New Hampshire, notes that the bringing of these cases to court reflects a decline in the double standard that is applied to men and women. Finkelhor suggests that increasing numbers of female police and prosecutors are less likely to buy into the traditional idea that boys who have sex with older women have something to be thankful for (Zerwicke, 2005).

A Pair of Sex Offenders? *What do boxer Mike Tyson and teacher Debra LaFave have in common? Both were both found guilty of sexual offenses. Tyson was convicted of the forcible rape of a woman who accompanied him to his hotel room. LaFave pleaded guilty to having sex with a minor boy. Tyson's crime was violent; LaFave's case involved statutory rape. In LaFave's case, although the boy was not forced into sex, at the age of 14 he was legally too young to provide consent.*

All in all, a team of professional writers could not have developed more scandalous material, but the plots and the characters in these media series are very real. Many observers wince as they see aspects of themselves—either as aggressors or victims—laid bare before the public.

This chapter is about sexual coercion. Our topics include rape and other forms of sexual pressure, including sexual harassment. As we see in the cases involving minors, sexual coercion also includes *any* sexual activity between an adult and a child. Even when children cooperate, sexual relations with children are coercive because children are younger than the legal age of consent.

Rape: The Most Intimate Crime of Violence

During the school year, you talk to people it has happened to, even upper-classmen, and they all say the same thing. They tell you to expect getting raped, and if it doesn't happen to you, you're one of the rare ones. They say if you want a chance to stay [at the Air Force Academy], if you want to graduate, you don't tell. You just deal with it. (Sharon Fullilove, cited in Janofsky & Schemo, 2003)

The women at the Air Force Academy, like another half a million American women each year, were victimized by a most common crime of violence: rape. **Rape** has its sexual aspects—ugly and grossly sexual aspects, indeed—but it is also the subjugation of women or men by force or threat of force (Malamuth et al., 2005; Rozee & Koss, 2001).

For the first few thousand years of history, the only rapes that were punished were those that defiled virgins. These rapes were considered crimes against property (virgins being the property of their fathers)—not crimes against persons. In ancient Babylonia, rape laws applied to married women as well. Babylonian law required the assailant *and his victim* to be bound and thrown into a river. As the injured party (after all, *his* property had been damaged), the husband could choose to let his wife drown or save her. Blaming the victim of rape is thus an age-old tradition. The ancient Hebrews stoned to death a married woman who was raped, along with her assailant. In the ancient Babylonian and Hebrew cultures, the wife was seen as guilty of adultery. Virgins who were raped within the protection of the city gates would also be stoned by the Hebrews. It was thought that they could have maintained their purity by crying out.

The current definition of rape varies from state to state. **Forcible rape** is usually defined as sex with a nonconsenting person by the use of force or the threat of force. **Statutory rape** refers to sex with a person who is younger than the age of consent, even if the person cooperates.

Traditionally, a man could not be convicted for raping his wife, although he might have forced her to submit to sexual activity by physical power or threats. This marital exclusion was derived from the English common law that held that a woman "gives herself over" to her husband when she becomes his wife and cannot retract her consent. Today, however, most states permit the prosecution of husbands who rape their wives.

Rape laws are now also applied to men who rape men and to women who coerce men into sexual activity or assist men in raping other women. Forcible rape is a form of **sexual assault.**

Rape Sexual activity that takes place without consent; see *forcible rape* and *statutory rape*

Forcible rape Sexual activity obtained by the use of force or the threat of force

Statutory rape Sexual activity with a person younger than the age of consent, even when the victim cooperates

Sexual assault Any sexual activity that involves the use of force or the threat of force

Pakistan's War of Terror on Rape Victims

Pakistan's Hudood Ordinances make no distinction between rape and adultery, and have created a war of terror against women. Particularly when there are few witnesses, a rape victim often ends up in prison when she "admits" to illicit intercourse or *zina,* forced or not. *Zina* is male–female sexual intercourse between an unmarried couple (Western Resistance, 2006).

The law allows men or women who are found guilty of *zina* to be subjected to *Hadd,* which is carried out in the form of public stoning to death if the perpetrator is a Muslim. If the perpetrator is not a Muslim, then the perpetrator of *zina* can be given a public flogging of 100 lashes.

A March 2006 report published by The Human Rights Commission of Pakistan (HRCP) stated that of the 6,000 women and children being held in prison in Pakistan, 80% were imprisoned because of the Hudood Ordinances.

The sin of rape is regarded as *zina-bil-jabr* and the sentence is the same, except that a non-Muslim can be sentenced to death as well as receiving 100 lashes. If a perpetrator (or victim) of *zina-bil-jabr* is a minor, the person can be given a sentence of five years, along with 30 lashes and a fine.

A man can only be found guilty of rape if he makes a confession or at least four Muslim adult male eyewitnesses, held to be in good religious standing by the court, provide testimony against him. Testimony by women, including the victim, is not admissible. Thus, if a woman reports a rape, she is therefore confessing to *zina* and is liable to stoning. Fortunately, nobody has thus far been stoned to death under these rulings. The sentence of stoning to death has been given out, but so far, appeals to superior courts have reversed them.

HRCP states the fear of stoning prevents women from reporting rape. For example, five women from Larkana were gang-raped. They withdrew their accusations when threatened with being charged with Hudood. A woman called Majeeda Mujid was kidnapped by a gang of men and repeatedly raped over two months. When she went to the police, she was imprisoned and her rapists were set free.

HRCP states that the way most Hudood trials work, it is assumed that women are guilty until proven innocent.

SafeZone

Q *What is the statute of limitations on pressing rape charges?*

A A friend who is a professor of criminal justice informs us that there is no standard. Some states such as New York do not have a statute of limitations for rape, but most do. Each state that does is different and, to make it more complicated, they usually distinguish by age and evidence. So for example, the statute might be seven years for adults but 12 for kids. There are also exemptions for DNA evidence. For example, for a statute of 10 years, if new DNA techniques identify someone, it can be extended to 15.

Incidence of Rape

The government's National Crime Victimization Survey (U.S. Department of Justice, 2006) estimates that 191,000 women were sexually assaulted in 2004. This figure included some 72,000 rapes and another 40,000 attempted rapes. **Truth or Fiction Revisited:** This means that a woman was reported to be raped about every seven minutes on the average—more often than every 10 minutes. About 10% of rape victims are men.

TRUTH or fiction 1

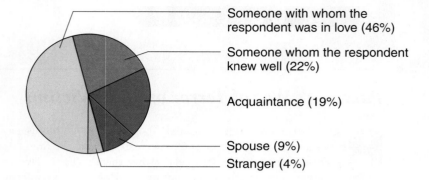

Figure 18.1 Women's Relationships with Men Who Forced Them to Do Something Sexual They Did Not Want to Do. *Only 4% of the sexual assaults reported in the NHSLS study were perpetrated by strangers.*

SOURCE: Adapted by permission from E. O. Laumann, J. H. Gagnon, R. T. Michael and S. Michaels (1994). *The Social Organization of Sexuality: Sexual Practices in the United States.* Chicago: University of Chicago Press, Figure 9.3, p. 338.

Someone with whom the respondent was in love (46%)

Someone whom the respondent knew well (22%)

Acquaintance (19%)

Spouse (9%)

Stranger (4%)

But these numbers tend to underreport the incidence of rape. They largely rely on crime statistics. About two thirds of rapes are not reported to the police or prosecuted (Fisher et al., 2003; U.S. Department of Justice, 2006). Many women choose not to report assaults because of concern that they will be humiliated by the criminal justice system. Others fear reprisal from their families or the rapist. Some simply assume that the offender will not be apprehended or prosecuted. Because they live in a culture in which women are often expected to "suffer in silence," Mexican American women are even more likely to remain quite about rape and sexual abuse than European American women (Lira et al., 1999).

There are two reasons that even the National Crime Victimization Survey underestimates the incidence of rape in the United States (Watts & Zimmerman, 2002). First, many women mistakenly believe that coercive sex is rape only when the rapist is a stranger (Ullman et al., 2006). Second, many women mistakenly assume that only forced vaginal penetration is defined as rape. However, many states define rape more broadly. All in all, the weight of the evidence suggests that about one in four women in the United States are raped during their lifetimes (Campbell & Wasco, 2005).

Women of all ages, races, and social classes are raped, but young women are at greater risk (Burgess & Morgenbesser, 2005). Women age 16 to 24 are two to three times more likely to be raped than older women, but many offenders rape children and young and older adults (Quinsey et al., 2006; U.S. Department of Justice, 2006).

Types of Rape

TRUTH fiction **2**

Truth or Fiction Revisited: It is not true that the majority of rapes are committed by strangers in deserted neighborhoods or darkened alleyways. Actually, most women are raped by men they know—often by men they have come to trust. Figure 18.1 shows that only 4% of the women in the NHSLS were "forced to do something sexual that they did not want to do" by a stranger. According to the U.S. Department of Justice (2006), about 83% of rapes are committed by acquaintances of the victim. The types of rape include stranger rape, acquaintance rape, gang rape, partner rape, male rape, and rape by females.

STRANGER RAPE **Stranger rape** refers to rape committed by an assailant (or assailants) who is not previously known to the person attacked. The stranger rapist often selects targets who seem vulnerable—women who live alone, who are older or retarded, who are walking down deserted streets, or who are asleep or intoxicated. After choosing a target, the rapist may search for a safe time and place to commit the crime—a deserted, run-down part of town; a darkened street; a second-floor apartment without window bars or locks.

Stranger rape Rape that is committed by an assailant previously unknown to the victim

A Closer Look

ANATOMY OF A DATE RAPE: ANN AND JIM

Ann

I first met him at a party. He was really good looking and he had a great smile. I wanted to meet him but I wasn't sure how. I didn't want to appear too forward. Then he came over and introduced himself. We talked and found we had a lot in common. I really liked him. When he asked me over to his place for a drink, I thought it would be okay. He was such a good listener, and I wanted him to ask me out again.

When we got to his room, the only place to sit was on the bed. I didn't want him to get the wrong idea, but what else could I do? We talked for awhile and then he made his move. I was so startled. He started by kissing. I really liked him so the kissing was nice. But then he pushed me down on the bed. I tried to get up and I told him to stop. He was so much bigger and stronger. I got scared and I started to cry. I froze and he raped me.

It took only a couple of minutes and it was terrible, he was so rough. When it was over he kept asking me what was wrong, like he didn't know. He had just forced himself on me and he thought that was OK. He drove me home and said he wanted to see me again. I'm so afraid to see him. I never thought it would happen to me.

Jim

I first met her at a party. She looked really hot, wearing a sexy dress that showed off her great body. We started talking right away. I knew that she liked me by the way she kept smiling and touching my arm while she was speaking. She seemed pretty relaxed so I asked her back to my place for a drink. . . . When she said yes, I knew that I was going to be lucky!

When we got to my place, we sat on the bed kissing. At first, everything was great. Then, when I started to lay her down on the bed, she started twisting and saying she didn't want to. Most women don't like to appear too easy, so I knew that she was just going through the motions. When she stopped struggling, I knew that she would have to throw in some tears before we did it.

She was still very upset afterward, and I just don't understand it! If she didn't want to have sex, why did she come back to the room with me? You could tell by the way she dressed and acted that she was no virgin, so why she had to put up such a big struggle I don't know.

ACQUAINTANCE RAPE Women are more likely to be raped by men they know, such as classmates, fellow office workers, and even their brothers' friends, than by strangers. **Acquaintance rapes** are less likely than stranger rapes to be reported to the police (Fisher et al., 2003). One reason is that rape survivors may not perceive sexual assaults by acquaintances as rapes. Only about one quarter of the women in a national college survey who had been sexually assaulted saw themselves as rape victims (Koss & Kilkpatrick, 2001; Koss et al., 1987; Rozee & Koss, 2001). Despite increased public awareness of acquaintance rape, many still think of rapists as strangers lurking in shadows and that a woman should be able to resist a sexual advance unless the man uses a weapon. Acquaintance rapists tend to rationalize their behavior by believing in myths such as the traditional view that men are expected to assume a sexually aggressive role in dating and the belief that rapists are strangers (Bletzner & Koss, 2006). Even when acquaintance rapes are reported to police, they may be treated as "misunderstandings" or lovers' quarrels rather than violent crimes (Campbell, 2006; Logan et al., 2006).

DATE RAPE Date rape is a form of acquaintance rape. Studies of college women show a consistent trend: 10% to 20% of women report being forced into sexual intercourse by dates (Koss & Kilpatrick, 2001). Date rape is more likely to occur when the

Acquaintance rape Rape by an acquaintance of the victim

couple has too much to drink and then parks in the man's car or goes back to his residence (Cole, 2006; Locke & Mahalik, 2005). The man tends to perceive his partner's willingness to return home with him as a signal of sexual interest, even if she resists his advances.

Date rapists may believe that acceptance of a date indicates willingness to have sexual relations. They may think that women should reciprocate with sex if they are taken to dinner. Other men assume that women who frequent places like singles bars are expressing tacit agreement to sex with men who show interest in them. Some date rapists believe that a woman who resists advances is just "protesting too much" so that she will not look "easy." They interpret resistance as coyness—a ploy in the cat-and-mouse game that typifies the "battle of the sexes." They may believe that when a woman says no, she means yes, especially when a sexual relationship has already been established (Lalumière et al., 2005c; Monson et al., 2000; Osman, 2003).

According to Roy Baumeister and his colleagues (2001) perpetrators and victims view sexual assaults in very different ways. Women see themselves as overpowered and deeply hurt. Men often focus on their own feelings, ignoring those of the victim, and act on their sexual frustration when the woman says it's time to call it quits. The more the man focuses on his own wants and ignores those of the woman, the more likely he is to commit rape (Bushman et al., 2003). In these cases, the motive may be largely sexual, but the man remains a violent criminal who refuses to take no for an answer.

The issue of consent lies at heart of determining whether a sexual act is rape. Unlike cases of stranger rape, date rape occurs within a context in which sexual relations could occur voluntarily. Thus, the issue of consent can become murky. Juries and judges are often faced with a woman plaintiff who alleges that the male defendant, who may appear neatly dressed and looking like the boy next door, forced her into sexual relations against her will. As in the Mike Tyson court appearances, the defendant may admit that sexual intercourse took place but claim that it was consensual. Judges and juries then have to distinguish shadings in meaning regarding "consent."

Cases of date rape often come down to his word against hers. Her word often becomes less persuasive in the eyes of the jury if it was clear that she had consented to consensual acts beforehand, such as sharing dinner, attending the movies together, accompanying him to his home, sharing a drink alone, and perhaps kissing or petting (Maxwell et al., 2003; Osman, 2003). The issue becomes further clouded because some survivors of date rape continue their relationships, and even marry, the perpetrators.

The problem of date rape has been brought within closer public scrutiny in recent years. "Take Back the Night" marches have become a common form of student protest on college campuses against the sexual misconduct of men. Many colleges have mandated date rape seminars and workshops.

GANG RAPE Consider the story of Kurt, a 23-year-old European American, married father of three who was involved in a number of rapes with a friend, Pete:

> I always looked up to Pete and felt second-class to him. I felt I owed him and couldn't chicken out on the rapes. I worshiped him. He was the best fighter, lover, water-skier, motorcyclist I knew. Taking part in the sexual assaults made me feel equal to him. . . . I didn't have any friends and felt like a nobody. . . . He brought me into his bike club. He made me a somebody.
>
> I'd go to a shopping center and find a victim. I'd approach her with a knife or a gun and then bring her to him. He'd rape her first and then I would. . . . We raped about eight girls together over a four-month period. (Groth & Birnbaum, 1979, p. 113)

REFLECT

Have you ever been involved in a discussion regarding when sexual activity becomes rape? If a woman pets with a man in the nude and then says no when he attempts intercourse, is he guilty of rape if he forces her? Explain.

Taking Back the Night. *Whose fault is it if a woman is raped when she goes out alone at night? Many women—and men who care about women—have marched to demonstrate their disgust for the men who might assault them if they were out walking by themselves, and toward a society that too often blames the victim for what happens to her.*

By participating in gang rape, the follower, like Kurt, is attempting to conform to the stereotype of the tough, competent, "masculine" he-man. Followers, however, may fortify the courage of the instigator of the act. Another rapist says, "Having a partner is like having something to drink. I felt braver. I felt stronger. This gave me the courage to do something I might not have done on my own" (Groth & Birnbaum, 1979, p. 112).

Exercise of power is a major motive behind gang rapes, although some attackers may also be expressing anger against women. Gang members often believe that after women engage in coitus they are "whores." Thus, each offending gang member may become more aggressive as he takes his turn. The Koss college survey showed that sexual assaults involving a group of assailants tend to be more vicious than individual assaults (Gidycz & Koss, 1990).

MALE RAPE The prevalence of male rape is unknown because most assaults are not reported. **Truth or Fiction Revisited:** The U.S. Department of Justice (2006) estimates that 1 in 10 rape survivors is a man. **Truth or Fiction Revisited:** It is *not* true that men who rape other men are gay. Most are heterosexual. Their motives tend to include domination and control, revenge and retaliation, sadism and degradation, and (when the rape is carried out by a gang member) status and affiliation (Krahe et al., 2003).

Most male rapes occur in prison settings, but some occur outside prison walls. Males are more often attacked by multiple assailants, are held captive longer, and are more often reluctant to report the assault. After all, victimization does not fit the male stereotype of toughness. Men are expected to be not only strong but silent. But male rape survivors may suffer traumatic effects similar to those suffered by female survivors (Bogin, 2006; Krahe et al., 2003; Walker et al., 2005).

PARTNER RAPE Partner rapes are probably more common than date rapes because a sexual relationship has already been established (Monson et al., 2000; Osman, 2003). A "traditional" man may believe that it is his partner's duty to satisfy his sexual needs even when she or he is uninterested. However, men who are better educated and less rigid about stereotypes about sexual relationships are less likely to rape their partners (Basile, 2002).

Partner rape has been largely unreported and often unrecognized by survivors as actually being rape (Monson et al., 2000). Women may also fail to report partner rape because of fear that no one will believe them.

Motives for partner rape vary. Sex is a motive, but some people use sex to dominate their partners. Others degrade their partners through sex, especially after arguments. Sexual coercion often occurs within a context of a pattern of violence and physical intimidation (Johnson, 2003). In some cases, though, violence is limited to the sexual relationship. Some men see sex as the solution to disputes. They think if they can force their partners into sex, "Everything will be OK."

Survivors of partner rape may be as fearful as survivors of stranger rape of serious injury or death. The long-term effects of partner rape on survivors are also similar to those experienced by survivors of stranger rape, including fear, depression, and sexual dysfunctions (Kaczmarek et al., 2006; Polusny & Arbisi, 2006). Moreover, the woman who is raped by her partner or husband usually continues to live with her assailant and may fear repeated attacks.

RAPE BY WOMEN Rape by women is rare. When it does occur, it often involves aiding or abetting men who are attacking another woman. Rape by women may occur during gang rape in which women follow male leaders to gain their approval. In such cases, a woman may be used to lure another woman to a reasonably safe place for the rape. Or the woman may hold the other woman down while she is assaulted.

But some men have been raped by women (Sarrel & Masters, 1982; Walker et al., 2005). Sarrel and Masters (1982) reported 11 such cases, including a 37-year-old man who was coerced into sexual intercourse by two women at gunpoint. In another case, a 27-year-old man fell asleep in his hotel room with a woman he had just met in a bar and then awakened to find that he was bound to his bed, gagged, and blindfolded. He was then forced into sexual intercourse with four different women, who threatened him with castration if he did not perform satisfactorily.

Social Attitudes, Myths, and Cultural Factors That Encourage Rape

Many people believe a number of myths about rape, such as "women say no when they mean yes," "all women like a man who is pushy and forceful," "the way women dress, they are just asking to be raped," and "rapists are crazed by sexual desire" (Maxwell et al., 2003; Osman, 2003). Yet another myth is that deep down inside, women want to be overpowered and forced into sex by men. **Truth or Fiction Revisited:** But it is not true that women say no when they mean yes. This myth has the effect of encouraging rape.

Rape myths create a social climate that legitimizes rape. Although both men and women are susceptible to rape myths, researchers find that college men show greater acceptance of rape myths than college women (Maxwell et al., 2003; Van

TRUTH fiction 5

Wie & Gross, 2001). Men also cling more stubbornly to myths about date rape than women, even after attending date rape education classes designed to challenge these views (Maxwell et al., 2003). Such myths do not occur in a social vacuum. They are related to other social attitudes, including gender-role stereotyping, perception of sex as adversarial, and acceptance of violence in relationships. The nearby "Self-Assessment" will afford you insight regarding whether you harbor myths that legitimize rape.

CRITICAL Thinking

Agree or disagree with the following statement and support your answer: A woman who walks in a dangerous neighborhood or talks to a stranger deserves what she gets.

SafeZone

Q *Can a prostitute be raped?*

A Absolutely. Sex workers consider it one of the hazards of the job. It causes physical harm, psychological disturbance, and, in the case of sex workers, job burnout.

Many observers note that our society pushes males into socially and sexually dominant roles (Davis & Liddell, 2002; Holcomb et al., 2002; Malamuth et al., 2005). Males are often reinforced from childhood for aggressive and competitive behavior. Gender typing may lead men to reject "feminine" traits such as tenderness and empathy that might restrain aggression (Davis & Liddell, 2002; Shultz et al., 2000).

Research with college students supports the connection between stereotypical masculine identification and tendencies to rape or condone rape. Studies have compared students who believed strictly in traditional gender roles with students holding less rigid attitudes. The "traditionalists" express a greater likelihood of committing rape, are more accepting of violence against women, are more likely to blame rape survivors, and are more aroused by depictions of rape (Malamuth et al., 2000; Raichle & Lambert, 2000). College men who identify with the traditional masculine gender role more often report pushing women verbally and by force (Shultz et al., 2000; Yost & Zurbriggen, 2006).

Do the lessons learned in competitive sports predispose young American males to sexual violence (Holcomb et al., 2002; Locke & Mahalik, 2005)? Boys are often exposed to coaches who emphasize winning at all costs. They are taught to be dominant and to vanquish their opponents, even if winning means injuring or "taking out" the opposition. Does this philosophy carry over from the playing field into relationships with women?

Sexual behavior and sports in our culture are linked through common idioms. A young man may be taunted by his friends after a date with a woman with such questions as "Did you score?" or more bluntly, "Did you get in?" Consider, for example, the aggressive competitiveness with which this male college student views dating relationships between men and women:

A man is supposed to view a date with a woman as a premeditated scheme for getting the most sex out of her. Everything he does, he judges in terms of one criterion—"getting laid." He's supposed to constantly pressure her to see how far he can get. She is his adversary, his opponent in a battle, and he begins to view her as a prize, an object, not a person. While she's dreaming about love, he's thinking about how to conquer her. (Powell, 1991, p. 55)

Cultural Myths That Create a Climate That Supports Rape

DIRECTIONS The following statements are based on a questionnaire by Martha Burt (1980). Read each statement and indicate whether you believe it to be true or false by circling the T or the F. Then turn to the key in the appendix to learn about the implications of your answers.

T F 1. A woman who goes to the home or apartment of a man on their first date implies that she is willing to have sex.

T F 2. Any female can get raped.

T F 3. One reason why women falsely report a rape is because they need to call attention to themselves.

T F 4. Any healthy woman can successfully resist a rapist if she really wants to.

T F 5. When women go around braless or wearing short skirts and tight tops, they are just asking for trouble.

T F 6. In the majority of rapes, the victim is promiscuous or has a bad reputation.

T F 7. If a girl engages in necking or petting and she lets things get out of hand, it is her own fault if her partner forces sex on her.

T F 8. Women who get raped while hitchhiking get what they deserve.

T F 9. A woman who is stuck-up and thinks she is too good to talk to guys on the street deserves to be taught a lesson.

T F 10. Many women have an unconscious wish to be raped and may then unconsciously set up a situation in which they are likely to be attacked.

T F 11. If a woman gets drunk at a party and has intercourse with a man she's just met there, she should be considered "fair game" to other males at the party who want to have sex with her too, whether she wants to or not.

T F 12. Many women who report a rape are lying because they are angry and want to get back at the man they accuse.

T F 13. Many, if not most, rapes are merely invented by women who discovered they were pregnant and wanted to protect their reputation.

A Closer Look

"ROPHIES"—THE DATE RAPE DRUG

Rophies, roofies, R2, roofenol, roachies, la rocha, rope, or whatever you call it is dubbed the "date rape" drug because it has been slipped into the drinks of unsuspecting women, lowers their inhibitions, lessens their ability to resist a sexual assault, and, when mixed with alcohol, often causes blackouts that prevent victims from remembering what happened to them. For this reason, Rohypnol has also been called the "forget pill," "trip-and-fall," and "mind erasers." The drug has no taste or odor, so the victims don't realize what is happening when an assailant slips it into a drink. About 10 minutes after taking it, the woman may feel dizzy and disoriented, simultaneously too hot and too cold, or nauseated. She may have difficulty speaking and moving, and then pass out. She may "black out" for 8 to 24 hours, having little or no memory of what happened.

Rohypnol is not manufactured or sold legally in the United States, but it is prescribed as a treatment for insomnia and as a sedative hypnotic in other countries. It is in the same class of drugs as the tranquilizer Valium, but about 10 times stronger.

Rohypnol is often used with other drugs, such as alcohol, to create a dramatic "high." Rohypnol intoxication is generally associated with impaired judgment, memory, and motor skills, and can make a victim unable to resist or recall a sexual attack. Effects begin within 30 minutes, peak within two hours, and can persist for eight hours or more.

Here are some ideas for avoiding problems with Rohypnol:

- Be wary about accepting drinks from anyone you don't know well or long enough to trust.

- Don't put your drink down and leave it unattended, even to go to the bathroom.

- If you think that you have been a victim, notify authorities immediately.

SOURCE: U.S. Department of Health and Human Services. Fact sheets prepared by the National Institute on Drug Abuse (Rohypnol and GHB): www.drugabuse.gov/Infofacts/RohypnolGHB.html.

SafeZone

Q *Isn't there a dye you can put into your drink so you know if someone has given you a date-rape drug?*

A Rophynol, as manufactured by Hoffman–La Roche, now contains a blue-tinted dye to make it visible if it is slipped into a drink. However, generic versions of the drug will not contain the dye, and if the drink itself is dark, you're unlikely to see the dye if it is present. You increase your odds of being safe by drinking light-color drinks and getting to know your drinking buddies before drinking.

Psychological Characteristics of Rapists: Who Are They?

Although sexual aggressiveness may be embedded within our social fabric, not all men are equally vulnerable to these cultural influences. Personal factors are thus also involved. Are rapists mentally disturbed? Intellectually deficient? Driven by insatiable sexual urges?

Although most researchers acknowledge that sexual motivation plays a key role in rape (Bushman et al., 2003; Malamuth et al., 2005), a generation ago some social scientists focused more on emotional and social factors. Perhaps by deemphasizing the role of sex in rape, they sought to bring more attention to its character as a crime of violence (Groth & Birnbaum, 1979). Based on their clinical work with more than 1,000 rapists, Groth and Birnbaum (1979) inferred that rape was typically motivated by anger, striving toward power, sadism, or some combination of the three. Anger usually motivates the rapist to use more force than needed to obtain compliance and to force the victim into degrading and humiliating acts. Typically, the anger rapist reports that he had suffered humiliations at the hands of women and uses the rape as a means of revenge. Those who are motivated by power, seek to control and dominate the victim (Mardorossian, 2002). Sadistic rapists are most vicious; some torture or murder their victims.

Much of our knowledge of the psychological characteristics of rapists derives from studies of samples of incarcerated rapists. One conclusion that emerges is that there is no single type of rapist. Rapists vary in their psychological characteristics, family backgrounds, mental health, and criminal histories (Lalumière et al., 2005b). **Truth or Fiction Revisited:** It is not true that most rapists are mentally ill, even though their crimes might strike observers as being "sick." Generally speaking, rapists are no less intelligent or more mentally ill than other people. But although many rapists do not show a deep psychological disturbance, they do have an antisocial personality that enables them to violate their victims without guilt, shame, anxiety, or empathy (Lalumière et al., 2005b). Some antisocial rapists have long histories of violent behavior (Lalumière et al., 2005a, b). The use of alcohol may also dampen self-restraint and spur sexual aggressiveness.

For some rapists, violence and sexual arousal become enmeshed. Thus, they seek to combine sex and violence to enhance their sexual arousal (Lalumière et al., 2005b). Some rapists are more sexually aroused (as measured by the size of erections) by verbal descriptions, films, or audiotapes that portray themes of rape than are other people (Lalumière et al., 2005a, 2005b, 2005c). Other researchers, however, have failed to find deviant patterns of arousal in rapists (Hall et al., 2000; Lalumière et al., 2005a, b, c).

Studies of incarcerated rapists may be criticized on grounds that the samples may not represent the total population of rapists. To offset this methodological concern, researchers have turned to the survey method to study men who anonymously report they have engaged in sexually coercive behaviors, including rape, but have not been identified by the criminal justice system (Locke & Mahalik, 2005; Yost & Zurbriggen, 2006). Sexually coercive men are more likely than other men to

- condone rape and violence against women
- hold traditional gender-role attitudes
- be sexually experienced
- be hostile toward women
- engage in sexual activity to express social dominance
- be sexually aroused by depictions of rape
- be irresponsible and lack a social conscience
- have peer groups, such as fraternities, that pressure them into sexual activity

Adjustment of Rape Survivors

Many survivors of stranger rape fear for their lives during the attack (Polusny & Arbisi, 2006). Regardless of whether weapons or threats are used, the experience of

A Closer Look

THE (HIGHLY CONTROVERSIAL!) EVOLUTIONARY VIEW OF RAPE

According to evolutionary theory, those traits that help an individual reach sexual maturity and reproduce are more likely to be passed on to future generations. Could such a trait in males be sexual aggressiveness? Could sexual aggressiveness be somehow embedded in the human genetic code?

According to evolutionary psychologists, it might just be true. One argument is that rape is a common—even "normal"—way of mating in many species (Archer & Vaughan, 2001; Lalumière et al., 2005a, 2005b). Evolu-

tionary psychologists tend to agree that sexually aggressive prehistoric males were more likely to transmit their genes to future generations (Fisher, 2000; Koss, 2003; Malamuth et al., 2005; Thornhill & Palmer, 2000). Modern-day society may value personal qualities such as intelligence and reliability and social behaviors such as maintaining lasting relationships as being more important than brute strength. Modern society has also outlawed sexual aggression—viewing it as a crime against the woman who is victimized, rather than as a crime against the "property" of some other

man. But modern society and the legal system are "new" things on the planet, and the human genetic code has evolved over millions of years. There might thus remain a "natural" tendency for males to be more sexually aggressive than females and to try to take what they want (Lalumière et al., 2005a, 2005b).

Although the evolutionary perspective may view sexual coerciveness in men as "natural," many or most psychologists agree that rape is inexcusable and criminal, and that males can *choose* not to be aggressive (Koss, 2003). Perhaps men carry genes that now and then give rise to aggressive impulses, some of which involve sex, but men also carry other genes that enable them to picture themselves in the place of the victim and choose *not* to behave aggressively. Empathy—that is, experiencing the feelings of another person—may be more common in women than in men, but it is not absent in men and can be cultivated in men, as has been shown by rape prevention programs (Foubert & Newberry, 2006; Klaw et al., 2005; O'Donohue et al., 2003).

being dominated by an unpredictable and threatening assailant is terrifying. The woman does not know whether she will survive and may feel helpless to do anything about it.

Many survivors are in crisis in the days and weeks after the rape (Campbell, 2006; Macy et al., 2006). They have insomnia and cry frequently. They tend to report eating problems, cystitis, headaches, irritability, mood changes, anxiety and depression, and menstrual irregularity (Kaczmarek et al., 2006). They may become withdrawn, sullen, and mistrustful. People in the United States tend to believe that women who are raped are at least partly to blame for the assault (Boros et al., 2005); therefore, some survivors experience feelings of guilt and shame. Emotional distress tends to peak in severity by about three weeks after the assault and generally remains high, before beginning to abate about a month or two later (Koss et al., 2002, 2003). Many survivors encounter more lasting problems. Victims' feelings of being powerless to affect their own fate can endure and change their personality (McEwan et al., 2005). A study of women in the military who had survived rape and physical abuse revealed health problems a decade afterward (Sadler et al., 2000). Some survivors suffer physical injuries and STIs.

Survivors may also encounter problems at work, such as problems relating to coworkers or bosses, or difficulties in concentrating. Relationships with spouses or partners may also be impaired. Disturbances in sexual functioning are common and

CRITICAL Thinking

We do not "accept" the natural aggressiveness of predators such as snakes, large cats, and poisonous insects by walking unarmed into the jungle. Why should we accept aggressiveness in other people, regardless of whether it is "natural"?

may last for years or a lifetime. Survivors often report a lack of sexual desire, fears of sex, and difficulty becoming sexually aroused (Koss et al., 2002, 2003).

Most women fail to report sexual assaults to police. Why? Reasons include fears of retaliation, the social stigma attached to the survivors of rape, doubts that others will believe them, feelings that it would be hopeless to try to bring charges against the perpetrator, concerns about negative publicity, and fears about the emotional distress to which they would be subjected if the case were to go to trial (Campbell, 2006; Logan et al., 2006).

RAPE AND PSYCHOLOGICAL DISORDERS Rape survivors are at higher than average risk of developing anxiety disorders and depression, and of abusing alcohol and other substances (Koss et al., 2002, 2003). One anxiety disorder common among rape survivors is **posttraumatic stress disorder** (or **PTSD**) (Koss et al., 2003). PTSD is brought on by exposure to a traumatic event and is also often seen in soldiers who were in combat (American Psychiatric Association, 2000). People with PTSD may have flashbacks to the traumatic experience, disturbing dreams, emotional numbing, and nervousness. PTSD may persist for years. The person may also develop fears of situations connected with the traumatic event. For example, a woman who was raped on an elevator may develop a fear of riding elevators by herself. Researchers also report that women who blame themselves for the rape tend to suffer more severe depression and adjustment problems, including sexual problems (Kaczmarek et al., 2006; Koss et al., 2002).

IF YOU ARE RAPED . . . Here are some suggestions on what to do if you are raped:

- Don't change anything about your body—don't wash, don't even comb your hair. Leave your clothes as they are. Otherwise, you could destroy evidence.

- Strongly consider reporting the incident to police. You may prevent another woman from being assaulted, and you will be taking charge, starting on the path from victim to survivor.

- Ask a relative or friend to take you to a hospital, if you can't get an ambulance or a police car. If you call the hospital, tell them why you're requesting an ambulance, in case they are able to send someone trained to deal with rape cases.

- Seek help in an assertive way. Seek medical help. Injuries you are unaware of may be detected. Insist that a written or photographic record be made to document your condition. If you decide to file charges, the prosecutor may need this evidence to obtain a conviction.

- Question health professionals. Ask about your biological risks. Ask about prophylactic treatment against HIV infection. Ask what treatments are available. Ask for whatever will help make you comfortable. Call the shots. Demand confidentiality if that's what you want. Refuse what you don't want.

You may also wish to call a rape hotline or rape crisis center for advice, if one is available in your area. A rape crisis volunteer may be available to accompany you to the hospital and help see you through the medical evaluation and police investigation if you report the attack. It is not unusual for rape survivors to try to erase the details of the rape from their mind. However, trying to remember details clearly will permit you to provide an accurate description of the rapist to the police, including his clothing, type of car, and so on. This information may help police apprehend the rapist and assist in the prosecution.

Posttraumatic stress disorder (PTSD) A type of stress reaction brought on by a traumatic event and characterized by flashbacks of the experience in the form of disturbing dreams or intrusive recollections, a sense of emotional numbing or restricted range of feelings, and heightened body arousal

Q *A friend of mine was raped at a party last semester. I took her to the hospital, but she refused to report it to the police. How can I convince her?*

A Good question. When one is at a party, and perhaps drinking and making out, one may not be sure where permission ended and rape began. There is also such a history of blaming the victim for sexual assault, or at least trotting out in public the victim's sexual history, that it is no surprise that your friend is reluctant to contact the criminal justice system. Perhaps she would talk it over first with a private attorney. But that takes money. She can also call the National Sexual Assault Hotline at 1-800-656-HOPE (4673). The call can be made 24/7. It's free, and all info will be kept confidential. But ultimately, your friend will have to decide for herself.

Treatment of Rape Survivors

The treatment of survivors typically involves helping the woman (the vast majority are female) through the crisis after the attack and then helping to foster long-term adjustment (Hensley, 2002). Crisis intervention typically provides the survivor with support and information to help her express her feelings and develop strategies for coping with the trauma. Psychotherapy, involving group or individual approaches, can help the survivor cope with the emotional consequences of rape, avoid self-blame, improve self-esteem, validate the welter of feelings surrounding the experience, and help her establish or maintain loving relationships. Therapists also recognize the importance of helping the rape survivor mobilize social support. Family, friends, religious leaders, and health care specialists are all potential sources of help. However, women often find that those from whom they seek support, including family and clergy, blame them for the attack (Macy et al., 2006; Sheldon & Parent, 2002). In major cities and many towns, concerned men and women have formed rape crisis centers and hotlines, peer counseling groups, and referral agencies geared to assessing and treating survivors' needs after the assault. Some counselors are specially trained to mediate between survivors of rape and their loved ones—husbands, lovers, and so forth. These counselors help people to discuss and work through the often complex emotional legacy of rape. Phone numbers for these services can be obtained from feminist groups (e.g., your local office of the National Organization for Women [NOW]), the police department, or the telephone directory.

Of course, if we prevent rape, we may not need to help as many survivors adjust.

Rape Prevention

The elimination of rape will require massive changes in cultural attitudes and socialization processes. Educational intervention on a smaller scale may reduce its incidence, however. Many colleges and universities offer coeducational programs about date rape that have apparently reduced the incidence of date rape (Foubert & Newberry, 2006; O'Donohue et al., 2003; Shultz et al., 2000). These programs aim to develop empathy for the victim by explaining the damage done by rape, exposing traditional cultural myths that endorse rape, and explaining the borders between encouraging a date to have sex and rape.

Until the basic cultural attitudes that support rape change, however, "rape prevention" means that women take a number of precautions. Why should women be advised to take measures to avoid rape? Is not the very listing of such measures a subtle way of blaming the woman if she should fall prey to an attacker? No, providing the information does not blame the person who is attacked. The rapist is *always* responsible for the assault.

Women can take precautions to protect themselves (Boston Women's Health Book Collective, 2005):

- Establish a set of signals with other women in the building or neighborhood.
- List yourself in the phone directory and on the mailbox by your first initials only.
- Use dead bolts on your doors.
- Lock windows, and install iron grids on first-floor windows.
- Keep doorways and entries well lit.
- Keep your keys handy when approaching the car or the front door.
- Do not walk by yourself after dark.
- Avoid deserted areas.
- Do not allow strange men into your house or apartment without first checking their credentials.
- Keep your car doors locked and the windows up.
- Check out the backseat of your car before entering.
- Don't live in a risky building. (We realize that this suggestion may be of little use to poor women who have relatively little choice regarding where they live.)
- Don't give rides to hitchhikers (including women hitchhikers).
- Don't converse with strange men on the street.
- Shout "Fire!" not "Rape!" People are likely to flock to fires but to avoid scenes of violence.

Here are some suggestions for avoiding date rape:

- Tell your partner how far you would like to go so that he will know what the limits are. For example, if your partner starts fondling you in ways that make you uncomfortable, you might say, "I'd prefer if you didn't touch me there. I really like you, but I prefer not getting so intimate at this point in our relationship."
- Meet new dates in public places, and avoid driving with a stranger or a group of people you've just met. When meeting a new date, drive in your own car and meet your date at a public place. Don't offer rides to strangers or groups of people.
- Be firm in refusing a sexual overture. Look your partner straight in the eye. The more definite you are, the less likely your partner will misinterpret your wishes.
- Become aware of your fears. Take notice of any fears of displeasing your partner that might stifle your assertiveness. If your partner is respectful of you, you need not fear an angry or demeaning response. If your partner is not respectful, end the relationship right there.
- Listen to your "vibes." Trust your gut-level feelings. Many victims of acquaintance rape say they had had a strange feeling about the man but failed to act to it.
- Be especially cautious if you are in a new environment, such as college or a foreign country. You are more vulnerable to exploitation when you are becoming acquainted with a new environment, different people, and different customs.

- If you have broken off a relationship with someone you don't really like or feel good about, don't let him into your place. Many acquaintance rapes are committed by ex-boyfriends.

CONFRONTING A RAPIST: SHOULD YOU FIGHT, FLEE, OR PLEAD? What if you are accosted by a rapist? Should you try to fight him off, flee, or try to plead with him to stop? Some women have thwarted attacks by pleading or crying. Screaming may help ward off some attacks. Running away sometimes works (Gidycz et al., 2006). No single suggestion is likely to work in all cases.

Self-defense training may help women become better prepared to fend off an assailant (Gidycz et al., 2006). **Truth or Fiction Revisited:** Yet, physical resistance may spur some rapists to become more aggressive (Gidycz et al., 2006). Women who resist increase their chances of preventing the completion of a rape, but resistance also increases the odds of being injured.

It may be difficult, if not impossible, for people to think through their options clearly and calmly when they are attacked. Rape experts recommend that women practice alternative responses to a rape attack. Effective self-defense may be built upon the use of multiple strategies, ranging from attempts to avoid potential rape situations (such as by installing home security systems or by walking only in well-lit areas), to acquiescence when active resistance would seem too risky, to the use of more active verbal or physical forms of resistance in apparently low-risk situations (Gidycz et al., 2006).

Sexual Abuse of Children

Many view the sexual abuse of children as among the most heinous of crimes. Children who are sexually assaulted often suffer social and emotional problems that impair their development and persist into adulthood, affecting their self-esteem and their ability to form intimate relationships.

No one knows how many children are sexually abused (Finkelhor et al., 2005a, 2005b). Although most sexually abused children are girls, one quarter to one third are boys (Edwards et al., 2003). Interviews with 8,667 adult members of a health maintenance organization suggest that the prevalence of sexual abuse among boys is about 18% and among girls, 25% (Edwards et al., 2003). These estimates may underrepresent the actual prevalence, because people may fail to report incidents because of faulty memory, shame, or embarrassment.

Sexual abuse of children ranges from exhibitionism, kissing, fondling, and sexual touching to oral sex and anal intercourse and, with girls, vaginal intercourse. Acts such as touching children's sexual organs while changing or bathing them, sleeping with children, or appearing nude before them are open to interpretation and are often innocent (Haugaard, 2000). Sexual contact between an adult and a child is abusive, even if the child is willing, because children are legally incapable of consenting. Although the age of consent varies among states, sexual relations between adults and children younger than the age of consent is a criminal offense in every state.

Sexual abuse also occurs over the Internet, as in the case of Justin Berry. Most parents of adolescent children are aware that there is filtering software that may protect their children, but most of those who know about it do not use it (Bross, 2005; Mitchell et al., 2005). And most of those who tried it stopped using it.

Voluntary sexual activity *between children* of similar ages is not sexual abuse. Children often engage in consensual sex play with peers or siblings, as in "playing

CRITICAL Thinking

Why do you think that most cases of child sexual abuse are not reported to the authorities?

The Monster in the Bedroom. *Not all monsters are make-believe. Some, like the perpetrators of incest, are members of the family.*

doctor" or in mutual masturbation. Although such experiences may be recalled in adulthood with feelings of shame or guilt, they are not typically as harmful as experiences with adults. When the experience involves coercion, or when the other child is significantly older or in a position of power over the younger child, the sexual contact may be considered sexual abuse.

Patterns of Abuse

Children from stable, middle-class families appear to be generally at lower risk of encountering sexual abuse than children from poorer, single-parent, or stepfamilies (Amodeo et al., 2006; Turner et al., 2006). In most cases, children who are sexually abused are not accosted by the proverbial stranger lurking in the schoolyard. Most molesters are close to them: relatives, steprelatives, family friends, and neighbors (Turner et al., 2006).

Parents who discover that their child has been abused by a family member are often reluctant to notify authorities (Zerubavel, 2006). Some may feel that such problems are "family matters" that are best kept private. Others may be reluctant to notify authorities for fear that it may shame the family or that they may be held accountable for failing to protect the child. The decision to report abuse to the police depends largely on the relationship between the abuser and the person who discovers the abuse (Finkelhor et al., 2005a). In one survey, none of the parents whose children were abused by family members notified authorities. By contrast, most parents whose children have been abused by strangers did so.

Typically, the child initially trusts the abuser. Physical force is seldom needed to gain compliance, largely because of the child's helplessness, gullibility, and submission to adult authority. Although most sexually abused children are abused once, those who are abused by family members are more likely to suffer repeated abuse.

Genital fondling is the most common type of abuse (Edwards et al., 2003). In one sample of women who had been molested during childhood, most contacts involved genital fondling (38% of cases) or exhibitionism (20% of cases). Intercourse is rare. Repeated abuse by a family member, however, commonly follows a pattern that begins with fondling during preschool, progresses to oral sex or mutual masturbation during the early school years, and then to penetration (vaginal or anal intercourse) in preadolescence or adolescence.

Abused children rarely report the abuse, often because of fear of retaliation from the abuser or because they believe they will be blamed for it. Adults may suspect abuse if a child shows sudden personality changes or develops fears, problems in school, or eating or sleeping problems. A pediatrician may discover physical signs of abuse during a medical exam. The average age at which most children are first sexually abused ranges from 6 to 12 years for girls and 7 to 10 years for boys (Finkelhor et al., 2005b).

TYPES OF ABUSERS The overwhelming majority of people who sexually abuse children (both boys and girls) are males (Turner et al., 2006). Although most child abusers are adults, some are adolescents. Male adolescent sex offenders are more likely than other adolescents to have been molested themselves as boys. Some adolescent sex offenders may be imitating their own victimization. Adolescent child molesters also tend to feel socially inadequate and to be fearful of social interactions with agemates of the other gender.

Although the great majority of sexual abusers are male, the number of female sexual abusers may be greater than has been generally believed (Zernicke, 2005). Many female sexual abusers may go undetected because society accords women a

A Closer Look

DESPERATE HOUSEWIVES' STAR TERI HATCHER REVEALS HISTORY OF CHILDHOOD SEXUAL ABUSE

Teri Hatcher. *In a* Vanity Fair *interview, Teri Hatcher revealed a history of sexual child abuse at the hands of an uncle, beginning at the age of 5.*

Desperate Housewives' star Teri Hatcher revealed that she was sexually abused by an uncle as a child but kept it secret until he was arrested years later for molesting a girl who ultimately committed suicide.

In an interview appearing in *Vanity Fair* magazine, Hatcher said she told prosecutors about her abuse in 2002 because she was haunted by thoughts of the 14-year-old girl who shot herself and feared that her uncle might escape conviction.

"I was just blown over by this girl's pain," the 41-year-old television star told *Vanity Fair,* recalling she learned about the case from newspaper clippings.

"I thought, 'Boy, that's really close to being me.' Any day of the week, I could feel that sort of pain. I haven't tried to kill myself, but I've certainly thought about it, and then I feel guilty about thinking about it, because what's so terrible about my life?"

Santa Clara County Deputy District Attorney Chuck Gillingham credits Hatcher for putting her uncle, Richard Hayes Stone, who was then 64, behind bars.

"Without Teri, this case would have been dismissed," he told the magazine, explaining that Hatcher's account provided key corroborating evidence to establish a pattern of behavior.

Stone, who was married to Hatcher's mother's sister when she was a girl, pleaded guilty to four counts of child molestation in December 2002 and was sentenced to 14 years in prison after Hatcher agreed to testify against him.

"He pleaded guilty, and even though it wasn't to my crime, it was because of my crime, and that made me feel validated," the television star told the magazine.

"That's a victim thing; you ask yourself, 'Am I just crazy? Did I make all this up?' Somehow it might be easier to accept that you're crazy and you made it all up than to admit that it happened, and how awful it was," she said.

Hatcher initially kept her involvement in the case, which never went to trial, a closely guarded secret, declining to include the experience in her upcoming book *Burned Toast,* in part because she worried it might harm her career.

"But I'm 41 years old, and it's time for me to stop hiding," she said.

Hatcher is best known for her TV role as the disaster-prone Susan Mayer on ABC's *Desperate Housewives.* She previously co-starred as Lois Lane in *Lois & Clark: The New Adventures of Superman.*

Hatcher recalled in chilling detail how she was sexually molested by Stone starting at age 5, when she and her parents lived in Sunnyvale, California, and the conflicted emotions of feeling both special and ashamed.

"The most horrible thing, that has stuck with me all my life, is that he was touching me and doing things to me,

and he said, 'Doesn't that feel good?' [And] I said, 'No, it doesn't.' He said, 'Well, someday you'll know what I'm talking about.' "

Hatcher said that before going to prosecutors four years ago, she had never told anyone of her own ordeal, not even her parents. She said she last saw Stone when she was 8 or 9.

SOURCE: "'Housewives' star Hatcher reveals sex abuse" by Steve Gorman, March 7, 2006. Copyright 2006 Reuters. Reprinted with permission from Reuters. Reuters content is the intellectual property of Reuters or its third party content providers. Any copying, republication or redistribution of Reuters content is expressly prohivited without the prior consent of Reuters. Reuters shall not be liable for any errors or delays in content, or for any actions taken in reliance thereon. Reuters and the Reuters Sphere Logo are registered trademarks of Reuters group of companies around the world. For additional information about Reuters content and services, please visit Reuters website at www.reuters.com. License #REU-GS8952.

A Closer Look

THE SIREN SONG OF SEX WITH BOYS

When Sandra Beth Geisel, a former Catholic schoolteacher, was sentenced to six months in jail last month for having sex with a 16-year-old student, she received sympathy from a surprising source.

The judge, Stephen Herrick of Albany County Court in New York, told her she had "crossed the line" into "totally unacceptable" behavior. But, he added, the teenager was a victim in only the strictly legal sense. "He was certainly not victimized by you in any other sense of the word," the judge said. The prosecutor and a lawyer for the boy's family called the judge's comments outrageous. But is it possible that the 16-year-old wasn't really harmed?

The last few months have produced a spate of cases where women are prosecuted for having sex with boys: Debra LaFave of Florida, another teacher, faces trial for sleeping with a 14-year-old student; Lisa Lynette Clark of Georgia was impregnated by her son's 15-year-old friend, whom she married a day before she was arrested; Silvia Johnson of Colorado was sentenced to 30 years for having sex with teenagers and providing drugs and alcohol.

Certainly no one doubts that a teacher who has sex with her students should lose her job. Or that a 37-year-old mother should not find herself pregnant by her son's 15-year-old friend. Or that a 41-year-old mother who provides sex, drugs, and alcohol to teenagers so she can be cool among her daughter's friends is troubled.

But when the women face prison, questions are raised about where to set the age of consent. And because many of those named as victims refused to testify against the women in what they said were consensual relationships, not everyone agrees that the cases involve child abuse.

"We need to untangle the moral issues from the psychological issues from the legal issues," said Carol Tavris, the author of *The Mismeasure of Women* and a social psychologist. "That's the knot." She added: "You may not like something, but does that mean it should be illegal? If we have laws that are based on moral notions and developmental notions that are outdated, do we need to change the laws?"

Though it might seem that way from the headlines, women having sex with teenage boys is not new. A federal Department of Education study called "Educator Sexual Misconduct," released last year, found that 40% of the educators who had been reported for sexual misconduct with students were women.

Charol Shakeshaft, the author of the study and a professor of education at Hofstra University, said that even when the woman is not a teacher, the relationships are not healthy. "A 16-year-old is just not fully developed," she said. "Male brains tend to develop the part that can make decisions about whether it is a wise thing to do later."

Prosecutions of women have been rising slightly in the last several years, said David Finkelhor, director of the Crimes against Children Research Center at the University of New Hampshire. Mr. Finkelhor says he believes that the scandal involving sexual abuse by priests called more attention to cases with teachers and other authority figures. But the cases also reflect a decline in the double standard applied to men and women, brought on, he said, by increasing numbers of female prosecutors and police officers who may not buy into the traditional notion that a much freer range of physical contact with children than it does men. A woman who fondles a child might be seen as affectionate, or at worst seductive, whereas a man would be more likely to be perceived as a child molester.

What motivates a woman to sexually abuse children, even her own children? Some female abusers have histories of becoming dependent on, or rejected by, abusive males. Some appear to have been manipulated into engaging in sexual abuse by their husbands. Others appear to have unmet emotional needs and low self-esteem, and may have been seeking acceptance, closeness, and attention through sexual acts with children (Zerwicke, 2005). Some, motivated by unresolved feelings of anger, revenge, powerlessness, or jealousy, may view their own and others' children as safe targets for venting these feelings. Some view their crimes as expressions of love.

boy who has sex with an older woman just got lucky.

But several studies have raised questions about whether the recent cases should be filed under child sex abuse.

The most controversial study was published in 1998 in *Psychological Bulletin*. The article, a statistical reanalysis of 59 studies of college students who said they were sexually abused in childhood, concluded that the effects of such abuse "were neither pervasive nor typically intense, and that men reacted much less negatively than women."

The researchers questioned the practice, common in many studies, of lumping all sexual abuse together. They contended that treating all types equally presented problems that, they wrote, "are perhaps most apparent when contrasting cases such as the repeated rape of a five-year-old girl by her father and the willing sexual involvement of a mature 15-year-old adolescent boy with an unrelated adult."

In the first case, serious harm may result, the article said, but the second case "may represent only a violation of social norms with no implication for personal harm."

They suggested substituting the term *adult–adolescent sex* for child abuse in some cases where the sex was consensual.

"Abuse implies harm in a scientific usage, and the term should not be in use if there is consent and no evidence of harm," said Bruce Rind, an author of the study and a psychology professor at Temple University.

This view could prove a hard sell, politically and legally. The article in *Psychological Bulletin* was roundly criticized by prominent conservatives and denounced in Congress, as was the judge in Ms. Geisel's case. In 2003, Bruce Gaeta, a New Jersey judge, was reprimanded by the state's highest court for characterizing an encounter between a 43-year-old female teacher and a 13-year-old boy who had been a student as "just something between two people that clicked beyond the teacher–student relationship."

Pamela Rogers Turner, a Tennessee teacher, was sentenced in August to nine months in jail for sex with a 13-year-old boy.

Thirteen? Professor Rind and others agree that that is too low to set the age of consent, making 12 truly out of bounds—the age of Vili Fualaau when he began having sex with Mary Kay Letourneau. (The fact that a decade later the two are married and even registered for china at Macy's has not changed anyone's mind.)

But Professor Rind and others point out that Canada and about half of Europe have set the age of consent at 14 after recommendations by national commissions. To set it much higher, as most states do, they say, ignores the research, and the hormones.

Even those who argue for more protection of children agree that the laws in this country can be arbitrary. In Ms. Geisel's case, she was caught first with a 17-year-old student, but because he was of legal age, she was charged

Pamela Rogers Turner. *Pamela Rogers Turner was sentenced to nine months for having sex with a minor boy.*

only after his 16-year-old friend came forward and said they had taken turns having sex. Can a few months make such a difference?

"I'm torn. I don't know," Professor Shakeshaft said. "Teachers are always wrong. And it would be my belief that people aren't formed by 16. On the other hand, my mother married my father at 16 and they were married 65 years."

Professor Finkelhor agrees that there is variability among cases and teenagers, but says it's better to err on the side of safety.

Sexual interest in children may also be motivated by unusual patterns of sexual arousal. This brings us to pedophilia.

Pedophilia

In 2006, Florida representative Mark Foley abruptly resigned from the House of Representatives when it became known that he had been pursuing congressional pages—predominantly boys age 16 or so—for several years via e-mail and instant messages. His lawyer came out and stated Foley was gay and a closet alcoholic. After resigning, Foley admitted himself somewhere for alcohol rehabilitation. Alcoholics protested

Mark Foley. *Foley abruptly resigned from the House of Representatives when it became known that he had sent seductive e-mails and instant messages to underage boys who served as pages in Congress.*

that Foley had given alcoholism a bad name, and gay males protested that the great majority of gay males did not seek relationships with underage boys. (We have not yet heard protests from closets.) In any event, Foley had admittedly pedophilic interests, although his lawyer protested he had never actually engaged in a pedophilic *act*.

Pedophilia is a paraphilia in which an adult finds children to be the preferred and sometimes exclusive objects of sexual desire. The prevalence of pedophilia in the general population is unknown. Some pedophiles are so distressed by their urges that they never act on them. However, many molest young children and adolescents, often repeatedly.

Although pedophiles are sometimes called child molesters, not all child molesters are pedophiles. Pedophilia involves persistent or recurrent sexual attraction to children. Some molesters, however, may seek sexual contact only with children when they are under unusual stress or lack other sexual outlets. Thus, they do not meet the clinical definition of pedophilia.

Pedophiles are almost exclusively male (Finkelhor, 2005a, 2005b), although some female pedophiles have been reported. Some pedophiles are sexually attracted only to children. Others are sexually attracted to adults as well. Some pedophiles limit their sexual interest in children to incestuous relationships with family members. Others abuse children to whom they are unrelated. Some pedophiles limit their sexual interest in children to looking at them or undressing them. Others fondle them or masturbate in their presence. Some manipulate children into penetration.

Children tend not to be worldly-wise. They can often be "taken in" by pedophiles who tell them that they would like to "show them something," "teach them something," or do something with them that they would "like." Some pedophiles seek to gain the child's affection and discourage the child from disclosing the sexual activity by showering the child with attention and gifts. Others threaten the child or the child's family to prevent disclosure.

Although most pedophiles may not wear trench coats and hang around schoolyards, there is research evidence that many of them have personality disorders (Madsen et al., 2006). Research finds them to be emotionally unstable, disagreeable, angry, impulsive, and mistrustful.

Some pedophiles who are lacking in social skills may turn to children after failing to establish gratifying relationships with adult women. Yet psychological investigation has found that many pedophiles distort reality in ways that enable them to pursue sexual activity with children (Marziano et al., 2006). Pedophiles often

- see children as sexual beings who want to have sex with adults
- believe that sex does not harm children and may be beneficial
- think of themselves as being so important that they are entitled to have sex with whomever they want
- see others as dangerous and controlling, and think they must fight to gain control of their lives
- believe they cannot control their impulses

Pedophilia A paraphilia that is defined by sexual attraction to children

Incest Marriage or sexual relations between people who are so closely related (by "blood") that sexual relations are prohibited and punishable by law

Incest: Breaking Taboos

Incest involves people who are related by blood, or *consanguineous*. Although a few societies have permitted incestuous pairings among royalty, most known cultures have an incest taboo (Argentieri, 2005).

PERSPECTIVES ON THE INCEST TABOO   Speculations about the origin of incest taboos abound. One explanation holds that the incest taboo developed because it was adaptive for ancient humans to prevent the harmful effects of inbreeding that may result when genetic defects or diseases are carried within family bloodlines (Ellis & Bjorklund, 2005). Our ancient ancestors lacked knowledge of genetics, but they may have observed that certain health problems tended to run in families. Evidence suggests that the offspring of close relatives bear an increased rate of genetic diseases, mental retardation, and other physical abnormalities. Inbreeding may also be counterproductive to survival because it reduces genetic variation in the gene pool. Therefore, it can reduce the ability of the population to adapt to changes in the environment.

The incest taboo may also play a role in maintaining stability in the family and establishing kinship ties within the larger group (Argentieri, 2005). The anthropologist Bronislaw Malinowski (1927), for example, argued that the incest taboo reduces sexual competition within the family. If left uncontrolled, competition would create rivalry and hostility such that the family might be unable to function as a unit. Because the family unit fosters survival of a society, the incest taboo may have developed as a means of keeping the family intact.

TYPES OF INCEST   Most of our knowledge of incestuous relationships concerns father–daughter incest. Why? Most identified cases involve fathers who were eventually incarcerated. **Truth or Fiction Revisited:** But brother–sister incest, not parent–child incest, is the most common type of incest (Caffaro & Conn–Caffaro, 2005). Brother–sister incest is also believed to be greatly underreported, possibly because it tends to be transient and is apparently less harmful than parent–child incest. Mother–daughter incest is the least common form of incest, but it does occur (Bartolo, 2005; Turton, 2005).

Let us further consider the two most common incest patterns: father–daughter incest and brother–sister incest.

Father–Daughter Incest   Father–daughter incest often begins with affectionate cuddling or embraces and then progresses to teasing sexual play, lengthy caresses, hugs, kisses, and genital contact, even penetration. In some cases genital contact occurs more abruptly, usually when the father has been drinking, or arguing with his wife. Force is not typically used to gain compliance, but daughters are sometimes physically overcome and injured by their fathers.

Brother–Sister Incest   In sibling incest, the brother usually initiates sexual activity and assumes the dominant role. Some younger brothers and sisters may view their sexual activity as natural experimentation or play and not realize it is taboo.

Evidence on the effects of incest between brothers and sisters is mixed. In a study of college undergraduates, those who reported childhood incest with siblings did not reveal greater evidence of sexual adjustment problems than other undergraduates (Greenwald & Leitenberg, 1989). Sibling incest is most likely to be harmful when it is forced, or when parental response is harsh.

Family Factors in Incest   Incest frequently occurs within the context of general family disruption, as in families in which there is spousal abuse, a dysfunctional marriage, or alcoholic or physically abusive parents (Welldon, 2005). Stressful events in the father's life, such as the loss of a job or problems at work, often precede the initiation of incest.

Fathers who abuse older daughters tend to be domineering and authoritarian with their families (Waterman, 1986). Fathers who abuse younger, preschool daughters are more likely to be passive, dependent, and low in self-esteem. As Waterman (1986) notes:

> [The fathers] may need soothing and comforting, and may feel especially safe with preschool children: "I felt safe with her. . . . I didn't have to perform. She was so little that I knew she wouldn't and couldn't hurt me."
> (p. 215)

Marriages in incestuous families tend to be characterized by an uneven power relationship between the spouses. The abusive father is usually dominant. Another thread that frequently runs through incestuous families is a troubled sexual relationship between the spouses. The wife often rejects the husband sexually (Waterman, 1986).

In their classic research, Gebhard and his colleagues (1965) found that many fathers who committed incest with their daughters were religiously devout, fundamentalist, and moralistic. Perhaps such men, when sexually frustrated, are less likely to seek extramarital and extrafamilial sexual outlets or to turn to masturbation as a sexual release. In many cases the father is under stress but does not find adequate emotional and sexual support from his wife (Gagnon, 1977). He turns to a daughter as a wife surrogate, often when he has been drinking alcohol (Gebhard et al., 1965). The daughter may become, in her father's fantasies, the "woman of the house." This fantasy may become his justification for continuing the incestuous relationship. In some incestuous families, a role reversal occurs. The abused daughter assumes many of the mother's responsibilities for managing the household and caring for the younger children.

Incestuous abuse is often repeated from generation to generation. One study found that in 154 cases of children who were sexually abused within the family, more than a third of the male offenders and about half of the mothers had either been abused themselves or were exposed to abuse as children (Faller, 1989b).

Effects of Sexual Abuse on Children

The effects of sexual abuse are variable and there is no single identifiable syndrome that emerges from sexual abuse (Resick, 2003; Saywitz et al., 2000). Nevertheless, sexual abuse often inflicts great psychological harm on the child, whether perpetrated by a family member, acquaintance, or stranger. Children who are sexually abused may suffer from a litany of short- and long-term psychological complaints, including anger, depression, anxiety, eating disorders, inappropriate sexual behavior, aggressive behavior, self-destructive behavior, sexual promiscuity, drug abuse, suicide attempts, PTSD, low self-esteem, sexual dysfunction, mistrust of others, and feelings of detachment (Edwards et al., 2003). Sexual abuse may also have physical effects such as genital injuries and may cause psychosomatic problems such as stomachaches and headaches.

Abused children commonly "act out." Younger children have tantrums or display aggressive or antisocial behavior. Older children turn to substance abuse (Herrera & McCloskey, 2003; Kendler et al., 2000a). Some abused children become withdrawn and retreat into fantasy or refuse to leave the house. Regressive behaviors, such as thumb sucking, fear of the dark, and fear of strangers, are also common among sexually abused children. On the heels of the assault and in the ensuing years, many survivors of childhood sexual abuse—like many rape survivors—show signs of PTSD. They have flashbacks, nightmares, numbing of emotions, and feelings of estrangement from others (Herrera & McCloskey, 2003).

Sexual development of abused children may also become shaped in dysfunctional ways. The survivor may become prematurely sexually active or promiscuous in adolescence and adulthood (Browning, 2002; Herrera & McCloskey, 2003; Kendler et al., 2000a). Researchers find that adolescent girls who are sexually abused tend to have consensual sex at earlier ages than nonabused peers (Browning, 2002; Herrera & McCloskey, 2003).

Researchers generally find more similarities than differences between the sexes with respect to the effects of sexual abuse in childhood (Edwards et al., 2003). For example, both boys and girls tend to suffer fears and sleep disturbance. There are some sex differences, however. The most consistent sex difference appears to be that boys more often "externalize" their problems, perhaps by becoming more physically aggressive. Girls more often "internalize" their difficulties, such as by becoming depressed (Edwards et al., 2003).

Late adolescence and early adulthood seem to pose especially difficult periods for survivors of childhood sexual abuse. Studies of women in these age groups reveal more psychological and social problems in abused women (Herrera & McCloskey, 2003; Kendler et al., 2000a). Women who blame themselves for the abuse apparently have relatively lower self-esteem and more depression than those who do not (Edwards et al., 2003b).

Sexual abuse of children is a devastating crime. How do we prevent it?

Prevention of Sexual Abuse of Children

Many of us were taught by our parents never to accept a ride or an offer of candy from a stranger. However, many instances of sexual abuse are perpetrated by familiar adults, often a family member or friend (Zielbauer, 2000). Prevention programs help children understand what sexual abuse is and how they can avoid it. In addition to learning to avoid strangers, children need to recognize the differences between acceptable touching, as in an affectionate embrace or pat on the head, and unacceptable or "bad" touching. Even elementary school-age children can learn the distinction between "good touching and bad touching." School-based programs can help prepare children to handle an actual encounter with a molester. Children who receive training are more likely to use strategies such as running away, yelling, or saying no when they are threatened by an abuser. They are also more likely to report incidents to adults.

Researchers recognize that children can easily be intimidated or overpowered by adults or older children (Miller, 2005). Children may be unable to say no in a sexually abusive situation, even though they want to and know it is the right thing to do. Although children may not always be able to prevent abuse, they can be encouraged to tell someone about it. Most prevention programs emphasize teaching children messages such as "It's not your fault," "Never keep a bad or scary secret," and "Always tell your parents about this, especially if someone says you shouldn't tell them."

Children also need to be alerted to the types of threats they might receive for disclosing the abuse. They are more likely to resist threats if they are reassured that they will be believed if they disclose the abuse, that their parents will continue to love them, and that they and their families will be protected from the molester.

REFLECT

How would you attempt to teach a child the difference between "good touching" and "bad touching"?

School-based prevention programs focus on protecting the child. In most states, teachers and helping professionals are required to report suspected abuse to authorities. Tighter controls and better screening are needed to monitor the hiring of daycare employees. Administrators and teachers in preschool and daycare facilities also need to be educated to recognize the signs of sexual abuse and to report suspected cases. Treatment programs to help people who are sexually attracted to children *before* they commit abusive acts would also be of use.

SafeZone

Q *Does being sexually abused as a child mean someone will sexually abuse their children?*

A It puts a person in a higher risk category for abusing his or her own children. However, when one is an adult, child abuse is a choice and not a necessity based on one's history. Anyone who feels in danger of harming a child can call 1-800-4-A-CHILD or another child abuse hotline for nonjudgmental help and support.

Treatment of Survivors of Sexual Abuse

Because the majority of cases of sexual abuse go unreported during childhood, psychotherapy in adulthood can be the first opportunity for survivors to confront left-over feelings of pain, anger, and misplaced guilt (Finkelhor, 2005). Group or individual therapy can help improve survivors' self-esteem and ability to develop intimate relationships. Social support is an important factor in helping survivors of childhood sexual abuse maintain their self-esteem and minimize the stress they experience (Hyman et al., 2003).

Many therapists recommend a comprehensive approach: individual therapy for the child, mother, and father; group therapy for the adolescent or even preadolescent survivor; art therapy or play therapy for the younger child (e.g., using drawings or puppets to express feelings); marital counseling for the parents; and family therapy for the entire family.

Treatment of Rapists and Child Molesters

Treating offenders? Just what does *treatment* mean? When a helping professional treats someone, the goal is usually to help that individual. When we speak of treating a sex offender, the goal is as likely, or more likely, to be to help society by eliminating the problem behavior.

Rapists and child molesters are criminals, not patients. Most convicted rapists and child molesters are incarcerated as a form of punishment, not treatment. They may receive psychological treatment or rehabilitation in prison to help prepare them for release and reentry into society, however. The most common form of treatment is group therapy, which is based on the belief that although offenders may fool counselors, they do not easily fool one another. Yet most incarcerated sex offenders receive little or no treatment (Ward & Gannon, 2006).

The results of prison-based treatment programs are mixed at best. Treatment programs fail to curb recidivism among a majority of child molesters (Prentky et al., 2006; Yates & Kingston, 2006).

More promising findings may result from programs incorporating cognitive–behavioral techniques such as empathy training and covert sensitization (Ward & Gannon, 2006). Empathy training is intended to increase the offender's sensitivity to his victims. One empathy exercise had offenders write about their crimes from the perspective of the victim. Covert sensitization can be used to help offenders resist deviant sex fantasies, which often lead to deviant behavior. The offender would pair, in his imagination, scenes involving rape and molestation with aversive consequences. A child molester might fantasize about sexually approaching a child, only to find himself confronted by police officers.

Another approach uses medical interventions such as castration to reduce testosterone levels and, consequently, offenders' sex drives. Experts do not agree on whether castration helps sex offenders control their sexual urges (Roesler & Witztum, 2000). Many castrated rapists report lowered sex drives, as might be expected from the reductions in testosterone production that result from the removal of the testes. They may retain sexual interest and remain capable of erection, however. And some do repeat their crimes. Other researchers report lower recidivism rates among castrated offenders than among other offenders.

Surgical castration is an extreme measure. It raises ethical concerns because of its invasive character and irreversibility. Antiandrogen drugs such as Depo-Provera chemically reduce testosterone levels (Roesler & Witztum, 2000). Unlike surgical castration, "chemical castration"—via antiandrogen drugs—is reversible (Roesler & Witztum, 2000). One study showed that antiandrogen drugs decreased pedophilic fantasies and masturbation to pedophilic fantasies in a group of incarcerated offenders (Schober et al., 2005). However, the hard truth was that there was no reason to believe that subjects would voluntarily use such drugs upon release.

Sexual Harassment

Sexual harassment occurs everywhere: in schools and colleges, in the workplace, in the military, and, of course, online (Barak, 2005; Foote & Goodman–Delahunty, 2005; Langhout et al., 2005; Sullivan, 2006). It even occurs between landlords and tenants, especially when the tenants are poor (Reed et al., 2005). Even so, sexual harassment can be difficult to define. For example, President Bill Clinton was accused of sexually touching or "groping" a resistant White House volunteer Kathleen Willey. Such behavior would clearly constitute sexual harassment. But Clinton also engaged in fellatio with a young White House intern, Monica Lewinsky. Although Lewinsky participated voluntarily, the White House is a workplace, and Clinton's power over the intern caused their interaction to constitute sexual harassment.

For legal purposes, **sexual harassment** in the workplace is usually defined as deliberate or repeated unwanted comments, gestures, or physical contact (Craig, 2005; Finkelman, 2005). Sexual harassment makes the workplace or other setting a hostile place. Examples range from unwelcome sexual jokes, overtures, suggestive comments, and sexual innuendos to outright sexual assault, and may include behaviors such as the ones that follow.

CRITICAL
Thinking
Agree or disagree with the following statement and support your answer: We should punish sex offenders and not worry about "treating" them.

Sexual harassment
Deliberate or repeated unsolicited verbal comments, gestures, or physical contact of a sexual nature that is considered to be unwelcome by the recipient

Sexual Harassment **607**

- Verbal harassment or abuse
- Subtle pressure for sexual activity
- Remarks about a person's clothing, body, or sexual activities
- Leering at or ogling a person's body
- Unwelcome touching, patting, or pinching
- Brushing against a person's body
- Demands for sexual favors accompanied by implied or overt threats concerning one's job or student status
- Physical assault

Men or women can both commit, and be subjected to, sexual harassment. However, about 99% of harassers are men (Table 18.1) (American Psychological Association, 1998).

Charges of sexual harassment are often ignored or trivialized by coworkers and employers. The victim may hear, "Why make a big deal out of it? It's not like you were attacked in the street." Evidence shows, however, that persons subjected to sexual harassment do suffer from it. Some become physically ill (Rospenda et al., 2005). Others report anxiety, irritability, lowered self-esteem, and anger. Some find harassment on the job so unbearable that they resign (Sims et al., 2005). College women's grades suffer (Huerta et al., 2006). College women have dropped courses, and switched majors and even medical residency programs to avoid sexual harassment (Huerta et al., 2006; Stratton et al., 2005).

One reason that sexual harassment is so stressful is that, as with so many other forms of sexual exploitation or coercion, the blame tends to fall on the victim. Some harassers seem to believe that charges of harassment were exaggerated or that the victim "overreacted" or "took me too seriously." In some segments of our society, women are expected to be "nice"—to be passive and not "make a scene." The woman who assertively protects her rights may be seen as "strange" and disturbing, or a "troublemaker." "Women are damned if they assert themselves and victimized if they don't" (Bowes-Sperry & O'Leary-Kelly, 2005; Cortina & Wasti, 2005; Witkowska & Gådin, 2005).

Sexual harassment sometimes has more to do with the abuse of power than sexual desire (Craig, 2005; Finkelman, 2005). Relatively few cases of sexual harassment involve outright requests for sexual favors. Most involve the expression of power as a tactic to control or frighten someone, usually a woman. The harasser is usually in a dominant position and abuses that position by exploiting the victim's vulnerability. Sexual harassment may be used as a tactic of social control. It may be a means of keeping women "in their place." This is especially so in work settings that are traditional male preserves, such as the firehouse, the construction site, or the military academy—even in certain areas of medical practice, such as surgery (Stratton et al., 2005). Sexual harassment can be a way of expressing resentment and hostility toward women who venture beyond the boundaries of the traditional feminine role.

Sexual harassment is not confined to the workplace or the university. It may also occur between patients and doctors, and between therapists and clients. Therapists may use their power and influence to pressure clients into sexual relations. The harassment may be disguised, expressed in terms of the "therapeutic benefits" of sexual activity.

TABLE 18.1

Sexual Harassment: Myths and Realities

Myths	Realities
Sexual harassment is rare.	Sexual harassment is extremely widespread. It touches the lives of 40% to 60% of working women, and similar proportions of female students in colleges and universities.
The seriousness of sexual harassment has been exaggerated; most so-called harassment is really trivial and harmless flirtation.	Sexual harassment can be devastating. Studies indicate that most harassment has nothing to do with "flirtation" or sincere sexual or social interest. Rather, it is offensive, often frightening, and insulting to women. Research shows that women are often forced to leave school or jobs to avoid harassment; many experience serious psychological and health-related problems.
Many women make up and report stories of sexual harassment to get back at their employers or others who have angered them.	Research shows that fewer than 1% of complaints are false. Women rarely file false complaints. Women rarely file complaints even when they are justified in doing so.
Women who are sexually harassed generally provoke harassment by the way they look, dress, and behave.	Harassment does not occur because women dress provocatively or initiate sexual activity in the hope of getting promoted and advancing their careers. Studies have found that victims of sexual harassment vary in physical appearance, type of dress, age, and behavior. The only thing they have in common is that more than 99% of them are female.
If you ignore harassment, it will go away.	Harassment does not go away if it is ignored. Research has shown that simply ignoring the behavior is ineffective; harassers generally will not stop on their own. Ignoring such behavior may even be seen as agreement or encouragement.

SOURCE: American Psychological Association.

Sexual Harassment with Victims from Minority Groups

A Canadian study shed light on different wrinkles and experiences of harassment (Berdahl & Moore, 2006). It compared the experiences of white women, black women, and Filipina women. White women with full rights as citizens felt freest to report the harassment to authorities. Black women and Filipinas felt that the term *sexual harassment* did not fully capture their experience—that their treatment also had to do with the power that white men could exercise over blacks and, especially, live-in Filipina caregivers. It also found that women experienced more sexual harassment than men, and in what the authors call "double jeopardy," minority women encountered more harassment than white women.

CRITICAL Thinking

Agree or disagree with the following statement and support your answer: Because of all the publicity, people who are intolerant of normal sexual advances, or who want to punish their supervisors, are now crying sexual harassment.

Sexual Harassment in the Workplace

Harassers in the workplace can be employers, supervisors, coworkers, or clients of a company. In some cases clients make unwelcome sexual advances to employees who are ignored or approved of by the boss. If a worker asks a coworker for a date and is refused, it is not sexual harassment. If the coworker persists with unwelcome advances and does not take no for an answer, however, the behavior crosses the line and becomes harassment.

Perhaps the most severe form of sexual harassment, short of an outright assault, involves an employer or supervisor who demands sexual favors as a condition of employment or advancement. The definition of sexual harassment in the workplace includes any behavior of a sexual nature that interferes with an individual's work performance or creates a hostile, intimidating, or offensive work environment.

The U.S. Supreme Court has recognized sexual harassment as a form of sex discrimination under Title VII of the Civil Rights Act of 1964. It holds that employers can be held accountable if such behavior was deemed to create a hostile or abusive work environment or to interfere with an employee's work performance. A unanimous 1993 Supreme Court ruling held that a person need not suffer psychological damage to sue an employer on grounds of sexual harassment. Moreover, employers can be held responsible not only for their own actions, but also for sexual harassment by their employees when they either knew *or should have known* that harassment was taking place and failed to eliminate it promptly (Craig, 2005; Finkelman, 2005) To protect themselves, many companies and universities have developed programs to educate workers about sexual harassment, have established mechanisms for dealing with complaints, and have imposed sanctions against harassers.

Under the law, persons subjected to sexual harassment can obtain a court order to have the harassment stopped, have their jobs reinstated (when they have lost them by resisting sexual advances), receive back pay and lost benefits, and obtain monetary awards for the emotional strain imposed by the harassment. However, proving charges of sexual harassment is generally difficult because there are usually no corroborating witnesses or evidence (Bowes-Sperry & O'Leary-Kelly, 2005; Craig, 2005). As a result, relatively few persons who encounter sexual harassment in the workplace file formal complaints or seek legal remedies. Like people subjected to other forms of sexual coercion, persons experiencing sexual harassment often do not report the offense for fear that they will not be believed or will be subjected to retaliation. Some fear that they will be branded as "troublemakers" or that they will lose their jobs.

Sexual Harassment on Campus

Estimates of the frequency of sexual harassment of college students vary widely across studies. Overall, 25% to 30% of students report at least one incident of sexual harassment in college, and males are about twice as likely as females to commit sexual harassment (Menard et al., 2003). The federal law prohibiting sex discrimination in academic institutions permits students to sue their schools for monetary damages for sexual harassment.

Sexual harassment on campus usually involves the less severe forms of harassment, such as sexist comments and sexual remarks, as well as come-ons, suggestive looks, propositions, and light touching (Menard et al., 2003). Relatively few acts involve the use of direct pressure for sexual intercourse. Most students who encounter sexual harassment do not report the incident. If they do, it is usually to a confidant and not a person in authority.

Most forms of harassment involve unequal power relationships between the harasser and the person harassed (Huerta et al., 2006). *Peer harassment* involves cases between people who are equal in power, as in the cases of repeated sexual taunts from fellow employees, students, or colleagues. In some cases, the harasser may even have less formal power than the person harassed. Women professors have been sexually harassed by male students, but the traditional social dominance of the male may override the academic position of the woman—at least in the mind of the offender.

One common form of harassment by students, reported by nearly one third of the female professors polled in one survey, involves sexist remarks (Champion, 2006). Other common forms of harassment include obscene phone calls, undue attention, and sexual remarks.

Sexual harassment also occurs long before students get to college. Surveys of high school and junior high school students find that many boys and girls have encountered harassment in the form of others grabbing or groping them or subjecting them to sexually explicit putdowns when walking through school hallways (Witkowska & Gådin, 2005). Sexual taunts and advances have become part of an unwelcome ritual for many students, especially girls, in trying to make their way through the hallways and stairwells of high schools. Many harassers and victims view harassment as "just part of school life" and "no big deal." Many girls who experience sexual harassment at school report that it made them feel that they didn't want to go to school. Some say it makes it more difficult to pay attention in class and lowers their grades.

REFLECT

Imagine that you are sexually harassed and want to report it, but a friend advises, "Why make such a fuss? Is it really worth it? After all, complaining could backfire." How would you respond?

How to Resist Sexual Harassment

What would you do if you were sexually harassed by an employer or a professor? How would you handle it? Would you try to ignore it and hope that it would stop? Here are some suggestions that may be helpful. Recognize, however, that responsibility for sexual harassment always lies with the perpetrator and the organization that permits sexual harassment to take place, not with the victim.

- *Convey a professional attitude.* Harassment may be stopped cold by responding to the harasser with a businesslike, professional attitude.
- *Discourage harassing behavior, and encourage appropriate behavior.* Harassment may also be stopped by shaping the harasser's behavior. Your reactions to the harasser may encourage businesslike behavior and discourage flirtatious or suggestive behavior. If a harassing professor suggests that you come back after school to review your term paper so that the two of you will be undisturbed, set limits assertively. Tell the professor that you'd feel more comfortable discussing the paper during regular office hours. Remain task oriented. Stick to business. The harasser should quickly get the message that you wish to maintain a strictly professional relationship. If the harasser persists, do not blame yourself. You are responsible only for your own actions. When the harasser persists, a more direct response may be appropriate: "Professor Jones, I'd like to keep our relationship on a purely professional basis, okay?"
- *Avoid being alone with the harasser.* If you are being harassed by your professor but need some advice about preparing your term paper, approach him or her after class when other students are milling about, not privately during office hours. Or bring a friend to wait outside the office while you consult the professor.

- *Maintain a record.* Keep a record of all incidents of harassment as documentation in the event you decide to lodge an official complaint. The record should include (1) where the incident took place; (2) the date and time; (3) what happened, including the exact words that were used, if you can recall them; (4) how you felt; and (5) the names of witnesses. Some people who have been subjected to sexual harassment have carried a hidden tape recorder during contacts with the harasser. Such recordings may not be admissible in a court of law, but they are persuasive in organizational grievance procedures. A hidden tape recorder may be illegal in your state, however. It is thus advisable to check the law.

- *Talk with the harasser.* It may be uncomfortable to address the issue directly with a harasser, but doing so puts the offender on notice that you are aware of the harassment and want it to stop. It may be helpful to frame your approach in terms of a description of the specific offending actions (e.g., "When we were alone in the office, you repeatedly attempted to touch me or brush up against me"), your feelings about the offending behavior ("It made me feel like my privacy was being violated. I'm very upset about this and haven't been sleeping well"); and what you would like the offender to do ("So I'd like you to agree never to attempt to touch me again, okay?"). Having a talk with the harasser may stop the harassment. If the harasser denies the accusations, it may be necessary to take further action.

- *Write a letter to the harasser.* Set down on paper a record of the offending behavior, and put the harasser on notice that the harassment must stop. Your letter might (1) describe what happened ("Several times you have made sexist comments about my body"), (2) describe how you feel ("It made me feel like a sexual object when you talked to me that way"), and (3) describe what you would like the harasser to do ("I want you to stop making sexist comments to me").

- *Seek support.* Support from people you trust can help you through the often trying process of resisting sexual harassment. Talking with others allows you to express your feelings and receive emotional support, encouragement, and advice. In addition, it may strengthen your case if you have the opportunity to identify and talk with other people who have been harassed by the offender.

- *File a complaint.* Companies and organizations are required by law to respond reasonably to complaints of sexual harassment. In large organizations, a designated official (sometimes an ombudsman, affirmative action officer, or sexual harassment advisor) is usually charged to handle such complaints. Set up an appointment with this official to discuss your experiences. Ask about the grievance procedures in the organization and your right to confidentiality. Have available a record of the dates of the incidents, what happened, how you felt about it, and so on. The two major government agencies that handle charges of sexual harassment are the Equal Employment Opportunity Commission (look under the government section of your phone book for the telephone number of the nearest office) and your state's Human Rights Commission (listed in your phone book under state or municipal government). These agencies may offer advice on how you can protect your legal rights and proceed with a formal complaint.

- *Seek legal remedies.* Sexual harassment is illegal and actionable. If you are considering legal action, consult an attorney familiar with this area of law. You may be entitled to back pay (if you were fired for reasons arising from the sexual harassment), job reinstatement, and punitive damages.

In closing, we ask not only what persons who suffer rape, incest, and sexual harassment will do to redress the harm that has been done to them. We ask what all of us will do to reshape our society so that sex is no longer used as an instrument of power, coercion, and violence.

SafeZone

Q *Isn't S&M the same thing as sexual coercion? How does one know the difference?*

A The term *S&M* usually refers to a subculture in which all acts are voluntary. Sometimes, prostitutes called dominatrixes are hired for the purpose of imposing punishments (usually in the form of humiliation or mild physical punishments) on the customer, and there is a voluntary business transaction. In those extremely ugly cases in which a sadistic rapist attacks a victim, there is no reason to assume that the victim is a masochist.

1. What do we know about rape?

- The perpetrator of forcible rape coerces a nonconsenting person into sex. Statutory rape involves sex with a willing person who is unable to provide consent, as in being too young.

- Types of rapes include stranger rape, acquaintance rape, marital rape, gang rape, male rape, and rape by females. Women are more likely to be raped by men they know than by strangers. Most male rapes occur in prison settings.

- Social attitudes such as gender-role stereotyping, seeing sex as adversarial, and acceptance of violence in interpersonal relationships help create a climate that encourages rape. Social critics argue that our society breeds rapists by encouraging males to play socially dominant roles.

- Sexually aggressive men are more likely than other men to condone rape and violence against women, have traditional gender-role attitudes, be hostile toward women, use sex as a way of expressing social dominance, lack empathy, and have peers that pressure them into sexual activity.

- Rape survivors often experience crisis and stress disorders. Treatment of survivors typically involves supporting them through the crisis and then helping foster long-term adjustment.

- Rape prevention involves education of society at large and the taking of precautions. Regardless of whether women take precautions to prevent rape, however, the rapist is responsible for the assault.

2. What do we know about sexual abuse of children?

- Any sexual contact between an adult and a child is abusive, because children are legally incapable of providing consent. Sexual abuse of children cuts across all socioeconomic classes. In most cases, the molesters are close to the children they abuse—relatives, steprelatives, family friends, and neighbors. Genital fondling is the most common type of abuse. Sexual abuse of children is underreported.

- Pedophilia is a paraphilia in which adults are sexually attracted to children. Pedophiles are almost exclusively male.

- Incest is marriage or sex between people who are so closely related that sex is prohibited by virtue of the kinship tie. Theories expounded to explain the development of the incest taboo include recognition of the dangers of inbreeding and the role of the taboo in maintaining stability in the family. Father–daughter incest is most likely to be reported and prosecuted, but brother–sister incest is the most common type.

- Children who are sexually abused often suffer social and emotional problems that impair their development and persist into adulthood, affecting their self-esteem and their formation of intimate relationships.

- In addition to learning to avoid strangers, children need to learn the difference between acceptable touching and unacceptable or "bad" touching. Psychotherapy may help adult survivors of sexual abuse improve their self-esteem and ability to develop intimate relationships.

3. How shall we treat rapists and child molesters?

- Methods include prison-based rehabilitation programs, often in the form of group therapy, and chemical (via antiandrogen drugs) or surgical castration.

4. What do we know about sexual harassment?

- Sexual harassment involves unwanted sexual comments, gestures, or contact.

- Sexual harassment is often an expression of unequal power relationships. It may be used as a weapon to keep women "in their place," especially in work settings that are traditional male preserves. About 25% to 30% of college students report at least one incident of sexual harassment. Sexual harassment below the college level has become an unwelcome ritual that victimizes many middle and high school students.

- There is no guaranteed way to end sexual harassment, but some suggestions include: convey a professional attitude, avoid being alone with the harasser, keep a record of incidents, and seek legal remedies.

1. All forms of sexual activity between adults and children are coercive because

   (a) children resist
   (b) adults need to dominate the children
   (c) children are hurt by sexual activity
   (d) children are younger than the age of consent

2. Which of the following is *not* a reason why the incidence of rape is underreported?

   (a) Some women fear that they will be humiliated by the criminal justice system.
   (b) Some women fear reprisal from their families or the rapist.
   (c) Some women assume that the offender will not be caught or prosecuted.
   (d) Some women are raped by strangers.

3. The most common type of rape is

   (a) rape by an acquaintance
   (b) rape by a stranger
   (c) marital rape
   (d) rape by females

4. Most men who rape other men are

   (a) heterosexual
   (b) gay
   (c) pedophiles
   (d) insane

5. Which one of the following is *not* a cultural myth that encourages rape?

   (a) Women say no when they mean yes.
   (b) The way women dress, they are asking to be raped.
   (c) Women do not wish to forced into sexual activity.
   (d) Women want a truly masculine, sexually aggressive man.

6. Pedophiles often

   (a) rape adult victims
   (b) seek treatment on their own
   (c) deny that sex is harmful to the child
   (d) come from liberal backgrounds

7. Sexual harassment

   (a) has never been defined
   (b) makes a workplace hostile
   (c) always involves physical contact
   (d) occurs among adults only

8. The most common type of incest is

   (a) father–daughter incest
   (b) father–son incest
   (c) mother–son incest
   (d) brother–sister incest

9. Which of the following is the most common form of child sexual abuse?

   (a) Exhibitionism
   (b) Genital fondling
   (c) Oral–genital sex
   (d) Sexual intercourse

10. Which of the following has been used to induce "chemical castration" in sex offenders?

    (a) Testosterone
    (b) Estrogen
    (c) Depo-Provera
    (d) Progesterone

11. Pakistan's Hudood laws

    (a) require male rapists to be excommunicated from the Islamic religion
    (b) consider female rape victims guilty of sex outside of marriage
    (c) allow only Islamic women to testify in court
    (d) consider the testimony of four women to be equal to the testimony of one man

12. Rohypnol functions as a "date rape" drug because it

    (a) can cause forgetfulness
    (b) is an aphrodisiac
    (c) multiplies the effects of testosterone
    (d) encourages women to recall consensual sex as an assault

13. On-campus rape prevention programs focus on increasing male students'

    (a) academic interests
    (b) competitiveness
    (c) interest in sports
    (d) empathy

14. Many pedophiles have been found to have

    (a) long criminal records as rapists
    (b) interest in victims of both sexes and at all ages
    (c) personality disorders
    (d) gender identity disorders

15. Which of the following is *not* child sexual abuse?

    (a) Voluntary sexual contact between a female teacher and an underage high school student
    (b) Voluntary sexual contact between children of similar ages
    (c) Voluntary sexual contact between a parent and an underage child
    (d) Involuntary sexual contact between an adult and an underage child

Answers 1. d; 2. d; 3. a; 4. a; 5. c; 6. c; 7. b; 8. d; 9. b; 10. c; 11. b; 12. a; 13. d; 14. c; 15. b

19

The World of Commercial Sex

A Disneyland for Adults?

TRUTH? fiction

Which of the following statements are true, and which are fiction? Look for the Truth/Fiction icons on the pages that follow to find the answers.

1 Prostitution is illegal throughout the United States. T F

2 The massage and escort services advertised in the Yellow Pages are fronts for prostitution. T F

3 Most female prostitutes were sexually abused as children. T F

4 Typical customers of prostitutes have difficulty forming sexual relationships with other women. T F

5 Only males are sexually aroused by pornography. T F

6 One quarter of Internet surfing is surfing for sex. T F

7 Pornography causes violence against women. T F

A few years ago, England's floppy-haired actor Hugh Grant was caught with a prostitute in a BMW on Hollywood's Sunset Boulevard. Why? His girlfriend was supermodel Elizabeth Hurley, who at the time was promoting the perfume called "Pleasures." Grant exemplified good looks, charm, innocence, and success. Still, he sought the sexual services of a woman for hire.

Why, indeed. Why have millions of men (and some women) paid for sex through the ages? In the caverns of Wall Street, brokers and traders sell stocks and other financial instruments that drive the nation's commercial enterprises. On the floor of Chicago's Board of Trade, brokers trade commodities—soybeans, corn, wheat, and other goods. Prices go up, prices go down, responding to the law of supply and demand. On street corners a few short blocks from these financial institutions another sort of commerce takes place. In New York City and Chicago, as in Hollywood and the nation's smaller towns and villages, prostitutes exchange sex for money or for goods such as drugs.

Sex as commerce runs the gamut from adult bookshops to strip clubs, sex toy shops, erotic hotels and motels, escort/outcall services, streetwalkers, "massage parlors," some "tanning salons," "900" telephone services, cybersex (e.g., sex over the Inter-

British Actor Hugh Grant in L.A.? *Why would the handsome and popular actor Hugh Grant seek the services of a streetwalker? Especially when his significant other at the time was supermodel Elizabeth Hurley? As we will see in this chapter, there are many reasons.*

net), and the use of sex appeal in advertisements for products. The "world of commercial sex is a kind of X-rated amusement park—Disneyland for Adults" (Edgley, 1989, p. 372).

Prostitution: Sex on the Run

Hugh Grant ran afoul of the law because **prostitution**—the sale of sex for money—is illegal in California. **Truth or Fiction Revisited:** Prostitution is illegal everywhere in the United States except for some rural counties in Nevada, where it is restricted to state-licensed brothels. Although prostitutes and their clients can be male or female, most prostitutes are female and virtually all customers are male.

Soliciting a prostitute is also illegal in many states, but police rarely crack down on customers or "johns." Hugh Grant came to their attention because he was engaging in a "lewd act" in a car parked on a public street. The few who are arrested are usually penalized with a small fine. On occasion, the names of convicted johns are published in local newspapers to deter men who fear publicity. On the other hand, some believe that Hugh Grant's indiscretion *boosted* receipts for his upcoming film.

Prostitution is often called "the world's oldest profession"— for good reason. It can be traced at least to ancient Mesopotamia, where temple prostitution flourished. The Greek historian Herodotus noted that all women in the city were expected to put

Prostitution The sale of sexual activity for money or goods of value, such as drugs; also termed *sex work*

in some time at the temple. They would offer their bodies to passersby who would make a "religious" donation.

Prostitution flourished in medieval Europe and during the sexually repressive Victorian era. Then, as now, the major motive for prostitutes was economic. Many poor women were—and are—drawn to prostitution as a means of survival. In Victorian England, it was widely held that women did not enjoy sex. Therefore, it was better for a man to visit a prostitute than to "soil" his wife with his carnal passions.

In the 19th-century United States, married and unmarried men frequented prostitutes regularly. Use of prostitution cut across all economic and social boundaries. Prostitution most often occurred within two contexts: sexual initiation for males and regular brothel visitation.

As we see in the nearby "A Closer Look" feature, many prostitutes, along with many researchers, have redefined prostitution as *sex work* (Lucas, 2005). Conventional work has been widely studied, but "crime as work" has received less attention—especially when it involves women and sexual labor. Elite prostitutes—call girls and escorts—analyze their markets and their relationships with their customers and make career choices.

Incidence of Prostitution in the United States Today

There are hundreds of thousands of prostitutes or sex workers in the United States, but no one has an exact number. Sex workers are found in the streets, in brothels, in adult films, on the Internet, and in the phone book and classified ads.

Almost two thirds of the European American males in Kinsey's sample (Kinsey et al., 1948) reported visiting a prostitute at least once. About 15% to 20% visited them regularly. The use of prostitutes varied with educational level, however. By the age of 20, about half of Kinsey's noncollege-educated single males, but only one in five of his college-educated males, had visited a prostitute.

Kinsey's data foreshadowed a falling off of experience with prostitutes that seems linked to the decay of the sexual double standard. Young men in recent generations appear to be less likely to visit prostitutes because they are more likely to become sexually initiated with their girlfriends. As Edgley (1989) put it, "An old and hallowed economic principle was at work; those who charge for a service cannot compete with those who give it away" (p. 392). Increased concern about STIs, especially HIV/AIDS, has also limited the clientele of sex workers. Nevertheless, prostitution continues to flourish.

Types of Female Prostitutes

Female prostitutes—commonly called *hookers, whores, working girls,* or *escorts*—are usually classified according to the settings in which they work. The major types of prostitutes today are streetwalkers; brothel or "house" prostitutes, many of whom work in massage parlors; and "escorts" or call girls (many prostitutes today have their customers "let their fingers do the walking" through the Yellow Pages).

STREETWALKERS Part of the mystery about Hugh Grant was why he would seek the services of any prostitute. Another part of it was why he would seek out a **streetwalker.**

Although most prostitutes are streetwalkers, streetwalkers occupy the bottom rung in the hierarchy of prostitutes. They earn the lowest incomes and are usually the

Streetwalkers Prostitutes who solicit customers on the streets

A Closer Look

"PROSTITUTION" OR "SEX WORK"? WHAT'S IN A NAME?

Many prostitutes have redefined themselves as *sex workers,* and prostitution as *sex work* (Lucas, 2005). The new terms underscore the economic aspects of the work and are less laden with a history of lewdness and depravity. They have also caught on in the research literature. The Commercial Sex Information Service (CSIS) of Vancouver, Canada explains the shift as follows:

> Sex workers, usually referred to as prostitutes, have occupied an anomalous position in societies throughout history. Prostitutes are generally regarded as a social category, as women who do not adhere to sexual and other behavioral norms; pitied or despised, they are excluded from mainstream society, their lowly and marginal position analogous to that of a low caste or minority ethnic group. Outcast status denies them whatever international, national or customary protection from abuse is available to others as citizens, women, or workers. This social exclusion renders the prostitute vulnerable to exploitation. . . .
>
> The terms *sex work* and *sex worker* have been coined by sex workers themselves to redefine commercial sex, not as the social or psychological characteristic of a class of women, but as an income-generating activity or form of employment for women and men. As such it can be considered along with other forms of economic activity. An employment or labor perspective is a necessary, if not sufficient, condition for making sex work a part of the mainstream debate on human, women's, and workers' rights at local, national, and international levels.
>
> The lack of international and local protection renders sex workers vulnerable to exploitation in the workplace, and to harassment or violence at the hands of employers, law enforcement officials, clients, and the public. The need for worker protection, including occupational health and safety provisions, is of particular relevance in the current context of HIV/AIDS. Sex workers without rights in their place of work are uniquely vulnerable to infection with HIV and other [STIs], as they routinely lack the information, materials, or authority to protect themselves and their clients.

SOURCE: From *Redefining Prostitution as Sex Work on the International Agenda* by Jo Bindman, Network of Sex Work Projects, 1997. Reprinted by kind permission Anti-Slavery International 2006.

---

least desirable. They also incur the greatest risk of abuse by customers and **pimps.** Streetwalkers tend to come from poverty and to have had unhappy childhoods (Carter & Dalla, 2006; Farley et al., 2005; Rubenson et al., 2005). Many are survivors of rape, sexual abuse, or incest (Brown, 2005; Medrano et al., 2003). Many are teenage runaways who turn to drugs and sex work to survive (Sterk & Elifson, 2006).

Streetwalkers operate in the open. They are thus more likely than other prostitutes to draw attention to themselves and risk arrest (McKeganey, 2006). To avoid arrest, streetwalkers may be indirect about their services. They may ask passersby if they are interested in a "good time" or some "fun" rather than sex per se. In many cities, streetwalkers dress in revealing or provocative fashions. Many cities throughout the United States and Europe have "tolerance zones," where streetwalkers ply their trade with relatively little interference from police (McKeganey, 2006).

In most locales, penalties for prostitution involve small fines or short jail terms. Many police departments, besieged by crimes such as drug peddling and violent crimes, consider prostitution a "minor" or "nuisance" crime. Many prostitutes find the criminal justice system a revolving door. They pay the fine. They spend a night or two in jail. They return to the streets.

Pimps Men who serve as agents for prostitutes and live off their earnings

620 CHAPTER 19 • The World of Commercial Sex

A bar prostitute is a variation of the streetwalker. She approaches men in a bar she frequents, rather than on the streets. Payoffs to bar owners or managers secure their cooperation, although the women are sometimes tolerated because they draw customers. Some streetwalkers work X-rated, or "adult," movie houses and may service their patrons in their seats with manual or oral sex. Payoffs may secure the cooperation of the management.

About 40% of streetwalkers support a pimp (Norton-Hawk, 2004; Williamson & Cluse-Tolar, 2002). A pimp acts as lover–father–companion–master. He provides streetwalkers with protection, bail, and sometimes room and board, in exchange for a high percentage of their earnings. Still, prostitutes are often physically abused by their pimps, who may use threats and beatings as means of control (Norton-Hawk, 2004). Pimp-controlled prostitutes are more likely than their peers to come from dysfunctional families, to be poorly educated, to have never held legitimate jobs, and to come from racial minority groups (Norton-Hawk, 2004).

For many streetwalkers, "the life" is a round of sex, violence, disease, and drugs, including cocaine and heroin (Degenhardt et al., 2006; Gilchrist et al., 2005; Romero-Daza et al., 2005; Surratt et al., 2005). Many street prostitutes feel powerless to control their own fates, and are often talked into oral or vaginal sex without protection. Given these realities, streetwalkers do not stay in "the life" very long. Some make the transition to a more traditional life or get married. Others die young from drug abuse, disease, suicide, or physical abuse from pimps or customers. Those who survive become less marketable with age.

Streetwalkers in Mexico City

Researchers also find a high level of psychological disturbance among prostitutes, especially female street sex workers (Brown, 2005; Raphael & Shapiro, 2005). Melissa Farley and her colleagues (2005) interviewed 100 prostitutes in Canada. They found that

- 82% had a history of childhood sexual abuse
- 72% had a history of childhood physical abuse
- 90% had been physically assaulted on the job
- 78% had been raped on the job
- 72% could be diagnosed with **posttraumatic stress disorder** (or **PTSD**).

Only 5% of the general population have PTSD, and only 20% to 30% of combat veterans. The prostitutes also developed many health problems (other than STIs). Ninety to 95% said that they wanted to get out of "the life" (Farley et al., 2005). However, many who exit the life find themselves back in for financial and social reasons (Dalla, 2006).

Streetwalkers who work hotels and conventions generally have higher status than those that work the streets or bars. Clients are typically traveling conventioneers or businessmen. The hotel prostitute must be skilled in conveying subtle messages to potential clients without drawing the attention of hotel management or security. They usually provide sexual services in the client's hotel room. Some hotel managers will tolerate known prostitutes (usually for a payoff under the table), as long as the woman conducts herself discreetly.

Posttraumatic stress disorder (PTSD) A stress reaction brought on by a traumatic event and characterized by flashbacks in the form of disturbing dreams or intrusive recollections, emotional numbing or restricted range of feelings, and heightened vigilance

BROTHEL PROSTITUTION   Many brothel prostitutes occupy a middle status in the hierarchy of prostitutes, between streetwalkers on one end and call girls on the other. They work in a brothel or in a massage parlor (Parent & Bruckert, 2005).

The life of the brothel (or "house") prostitute is usually neither as lucrative as that of the call girl nor as degrading as that of the streetwalker. Some prostitutes in massage parlors or working for escort services may not consider themselves to be "real prostitutes," because they do not walk the streets and because they work for businesses that present a legitimate front. *Cathouse, bordello, cat wagon, parlor house, whorehouse, joy house, sport house, house of ill repute*—these are but a handful of the names given to houses in which prostitutes work. The heyday of the brothel is all but over in the United States. Formal brothels are rare, except in Nevada, where they are legal but regulated. Brothel prostitutes split their fees with management. In addition to their "split," they receive free room and board. They are on duty three weeks a month and on call 24 hours a day during that time. When a customer arrives, they step into the living room "lineup." After one has been chosen, they wait again, resting, reading, or watching television.

Some brothel prostitutes lead lives of degradation. Many poor Asian and East European women are lured to the big city or to the West by promises of the good life (Rubenson et al., 2005). Upon arrival, they find themselves enslaved in brothels—working for tips and not allowed to leave. *The New York Times* columnist Nicholas Kristof (2004, 2006) has written many articles on sexual slavery, including cases in which families sells their daughters into slavery. "The World of Human Sexuality" feature on page 624 describes the case of a Pakistani woman who was abducted and placed in a brothel.

THE MASSAGE PARLOR   Nature abhors a vacuum. "Massage parlors" have sprung up from coast to coast to fill the vacuum left by the departure of the brothels. Many massage parlors are legitimate establishments that provide massage, and only massage. Masseuses and masseurs are licensed in many states, and laws prohibit them from offering sexual services. Many localities require that the masseuse keep certain parts of her or his body clothed (some masseuses in suburban Detroit wear a scarf or a garter to comply) and not touch the client's genitals.

Many massage parlors serve as fronts for prostitution, however (Lewis et al., 2005; Nemoto et al., 2004). They are often found in malls in middle-class suburbs, where there is ample parking. In these establishments, clients typically pay fees for a standard massage and then tip the workers for sexual extras.

Massage parlor prostitutes generally offer manual stimulation of the penis ("a local"), oral sex, or less frequently, coitus ("full service"). Some massage parlor prostitutes are better educated than streetwalkers and brothel workers and would not work in those other venues. But many massage parlor workers are Asians who are spirited from parlor to parlor, from city to city, and then back to Asia (Nemoto et al., 2004).

STRIP CLUBS   Many sex workers in strip clubs limit their activity to dancing and doffing their clothes. Others do "lap dances" or "table dances" during which they contact customers as they dance. Customers may buy the dance from the club and then also be expected to tip the stripper (Frank, 2002, 2003). Some strip clubs have private shows, "VIP rooms," and the like, where strippers may be alone with their customers. What happens in these private shows may be tightly regulated by the club or may depend on the size of the tip.

SafeZone

Q   *I worked as a dancer and sometimes had sex for money. Should I tell my present boyfriend (who I might marry), who does not know my past?*

A   Our advice is that your past is your own and that your future belongs to the two of you, if you decide that you will in fact be a committed couple. Your boyfriend might not be able to live with the details of your past, and if you promise yourself to him, you are promising your future, not your history.

ESCORT SERVICES   If Hugh Grant had hired an "escort," we probably would never have learned of it. Conventioneers and businessmen are more likely to turn to the listings for "massage" and "escort services" in the telephone directory or under the personal ads in local newspapers than to seek hotel prostitutes. Services that provide "outcall" send masseuses (or masseurs) or escorts to the hotel room.

TRUTH?fiction 2

Truth or Fiction Revisited: Massage and escort services advertised in the Yellow Pages are typically, but not always, fronts for prostitution. Legitimate masseuses and masseurs often advertise that they are licensed by their states.

Escort services are found in every major American city and present themselves as legitimate business providing escorts for men. Indeed, one will find female companionship for corporate functions and for unattached men traveling away from home under "escort services." Many escort services provide only prostitution, however, and clients of other escort services sometimes negotiate sexual services after formal escort duties are completed—or in their stead.

Prostitutes who work for escort services often come from middle-class backgrounds and are well educated—so much the better to help prepare them to hold their own in social conversation. Escort services may establish arrangements with legitimate companies to provide "escorts" for visiting customers or potential clients. Escort services also provide female escorts to "entertain" at conventions. Because of her high-society background, Sidney Biddle Barrow, the so-called Mayflower Madam, attracted a great deal of publicity when it was discovered that she ran an exclusive "escort service" in New York City in the 1980s.

CALL GIRLS   **Call girls** occupy the highest status on the social ladder of female prostitution. Many of them overlap with escorts. Call girls tend to be the most attractive and well-educated prostitutes and tend to charge more for their services. Many come from middle-class backgrounds. Unlike other types of prostitutes, call girls usually work on their own. Thus, they need not split their income with a pimp, escort

Call girls Prostitutes who arrange for their sexual contacts by telephone; *call* refers both to telephone calls and to being "on call"

A Woman without Importance: Sex Slavery in Pakistan

By Nicholas Kristof, The New York Times

KHANPUR, PAKISTAN: Aisha Parveen doesn't matter. She's simply one more impoverished girl from the countryside, and if her brothel's owner goes ahead and kills her, almost no one will care.

Ms. Parveen, an outspoken 20-year-old woman with flashing eyes, is steeling herself for a state-administered horror. Just two months after she escaped from the brothel in which she was tortured and imprisoned for six years, the courts are poised to hand her back to the brothel owner.

Sex trafficking, nurtured by globalization and increased mobility, is becoming worse. The [United Nations] estimates that one million children are held in conditions of slavery in Asia alone. Yet it never gets much attention, because the victims tend to be the least powerful people in these societies: poor and uneducated rural girls.

Ms. Parveen was a 14-year-old Pashtun living in the northwest of Pakistan when she was hit on the head while walking to school. She says she awoke to find herself imprisoned in a brothel hundreds of miles away, in this remote southeastern Pakistani town of Khanpur.

A person of unbelievable strength, Ms. Parveen fought back and refused to sleep with customers. So, she says, the brothel owner—Mian Sher, the violent sadist who had kidnapped her—beat and sexually tortured her, and regularly drugged her so that she would fall unconscious and customers could do with her as they liked.

This went on for six years, during which she says she was beaten every day. The girls in the brothel were forced to sleep naked at night, so that they would be too embarrassed to try to escape. Ms. Parveen says she believes that two of them, Malo Jan and Suwa Tai, were killed after they repeatedly refused to sleep with customers. In any case, condoms were never available, so all the girls may eventually die of AIDS.

I wanted to look into the eyes of a man who could do these things. So I barged into Mian Sher's brothel, identified myself and interviewed him.

He warily offered me tea, pleasantries, and flashes of violent temper. He denied kidnapping Ms. Parveen, saying that he had married her six years earlier. He also denied that he pimped the girls—a claim undermined by a customer who was walking out of his brothel as I arrived. Others working in the area said that Mian Sher unquestionably ran a brothel, and that Ms. Parveen had been imprisoned in it.

In January, Ms. Parveen got a break. A metalworker, Mohamed Akram, had been doing work in the brothel, and he pitied her. "She laid her scarf down on my feet and begged me, in the name of the Holy Koran, to rescue her," he remembers, and soon he felt not only pity but also love.

So on Jan. 5, 2006, Ms. Parveen stealthily arose in the middle of the night, crept past Mian Sher and pad-

---

service, or massage parlor. Consequently, they can afford to lead a luxurious lifestyle when business is good, living in expensive neighborhoods and wearing stylish clothes, and to be more selective about the customers they will accept. Yet they incur expenses for answering services and laundry services, and for payoffs to landlords, doormen, and sometimes to police to maintain their livelihood and avoid arrest.

Call girls often escort their clients to dinner and social functions, and are expected not only to provide sex, but also charming and gracious company and conversation. Call girls often give clients the feeling that they are important and attractive (Sanders, 2005). They may effectively simulate pleasure and orgasm, and can create the illusion that time does not matter. It does, of course. To the call girl, as to other entrepreneurs, time is money.

Call girls may receive clients in their apartments ("incalls") or make "outcalls" to clients' homes and hotels. Some call girls trade or sell "black books" that list clients and their sexual preferences. To protect themselves from police and abusive clients, call girls may insist on reviewing a client's business card or learning his home tele-

locked the door with him inside. Then she ran to a car that Mr. Akram had sent. The next day, they were married.

Then the judicial nightmare began. Mian Sher brought charges against the couple, claiming that Ms. Parveen is his wife and must return to him.

"The police have taken money from him," Ms. Parveen said. "They say, 'You're married to him, so you should go back to him.' Well, I would rather die than go back to the brothel."

The police are now prosecuting Ms. Parveen for adultery. She is free on bail, but thugs have attacked her home and tried to kidnap her.

Mian Sher told me his plan: If Ms. Parveen is jailed for adultery, then as her supposed husband he will bail her out and take her away. Ms. Parveen says she believes he will then rape and torture her, and finally kill her.

So the judicial system, while ignoring the sex trafficking of children, may now, in the name of morality, hand a young woman over to a brothel owner to do with her as he wants.

The new abolitionism, against sex trafficking, is being pushed in America by an unlikely coalition of religious conservatives and liberal feminists; leaders include the Coalition Against Trafficking in Women, Ecpat, Equality Now and International Justice Mission. But progress is slow because the victims tend to be voiceless young people like Ms. Parveen.

Whether Ms. Parveen is returned to her brothel owner and killed may be, in terms of global issues, a small matter. But after spending a couple of days with this smart and lovely young woman, after seeing her in moments of giddy laughter and terrified weeping, I can't help thinking that slavery should be just as outrageous in the 21st century as it was in the 19th.

In a court appearance the following day, a court found Aisha Parveen guilty of adultery (*zina*), but she was released because of the publicity from Kristof's story. Nevertheless, she and her husband haven't lived happily ever after.

Her husband, Akram, told Kristof that he received a message from his brother-in-law, who wrote, "Unless you divorce [Aisha], I will divorce your sister." Akram explained that his sister had two children and her husband was beating her because of Akram's marriage to a girl who was not a virgin, who had been in a brothel. The couple are also unwelcome in Aisha's family's home because Pashtun parents kill daughters accused of *zina* to defend the family's honor, regardless of whether they were raped.

phone number before personal contact is made. They may investigate whether the customer is who he claims to be.

Getting into "The Life"

No single factor explains entry into female prostitution. **Truth or Fiction Revisited:** Yet, poverty and sexual and/or physical abuse figure prominently in the backgrounds of the majority of female prostitutes (Carter & Dalla, 2006; Farley et al., 2005; Inciardi et al., 2006). They often come from conflict-ridden or single-parent homes in poor urban areas or rural farming communities.

For young women of impoverished backgrounds and marginal skills, sex work may seem alluring. It is an alternative to the menial and dismal work that is otherwise available. Poverty accounts for the entry of young women into prostitution in many countries. In some Third World nations, such as Thailand, many rural, impoverished parents in effect sell daughters to recruiters who place them in brothels in cities (Bamgbose, 2002; Gomes do Espirito & Etheredge, 2003; Kristof, 2006). Many of the women send home whatever money they can and also work hard to try to pay off the procurers and break free of their financial bonds.

In the United States and Canada, many initiates into prostitution are teenage runaways. The family backgrounds of teenage runaways vary in socioeconomic status. Some come from middle-class or affluent homes, whereas others are reared in poverty. However, family discord and dysfunction frequently set the stage for entry into street life and prostitution (Carter & Dalla, 2006; Medrano et al., 2003). Many teenage runaways perceive life on the street to be the only possible escape from family strife and conflict, or from the physical, emotional, or sexual abuse they suffer at home. Despite its dangers, life on the streets appears more attractive than remaining in the troubled family environment.

Some teenagers who have endured sexual abuse or incest learn how to detach themselves emotionally from sex to survive unwanted sexual experiences (Sanders, 2005). The transition to sex work may represent an extension of this unfortunate learning experience.

REFLECT

Have any people you know used the services of prostitutes? What were their motives?

"Johns"—The Customers of Female Prostitutes

Many prostitutes refer to their customers as "johns" or "tricks." Terms such as *patron, meatball, sucker,* and *beefbuyer* are also heard.

Men who use female prostitutes come from all walks of life and represent all socioeconomic and racial groups. Many, perhaps most, are married men of middle-class background (Klusman, 2002; Schmitt, 2003).

Most patrons are "occasional johns." Examples include traveling salesmen or military personnel who are stopping over in town without their regular sex partners. Men are more interested than women in sexual novelty or variety (Barash & Lipton, 2001; Peplau, 2003), and the quest for variety may motivate occasional johns with regular sex partners.

"Habitual johns" use prostitutes as their major or exclusive sexual outlet. Some habitual johns have never established an intimate sexual relationship. Some wealthy men who wish to avoid intimate relationships habitually patronize call girls.

"Compulsive johns" feel driven to prostitutes to meet some psychological or sexual need. They may repeatedly resolve to stop using prostitutes but feel unable to control their compulsions. Some compulsive johns engage in acts of fetishism or transvestism with prostitutes but would not inform their wives or girlfriends of their variant interests. Some men who are compulsive users of prostitutes suffer from a **whore–Madonna complex**. They see women as either sinners or saints. They can permit themselves to enjoy sex only with prostitutes or would ask only prostitutes to engage in acts such as fellatio. They see marital coitus as a duty or obligation.

MOTIVES FOR HIRING PROSTITUTES   There appear to be six common motives for using prostitutes:

1. *Sex without negotiation.* The research on sex differences suggests strongly that men have a stronger sex drive than women (Peplau, 2003). Sex work evens things up, making women available at the whim of the man. By turning to prostitutes, men need not spend the time, effort, and money involved in dating and getting to know someone for the sake of sexual activity. Hugh Grant might have wanted

Whore–Madonna complex The rigid stereotyping of women as either sinners or saints

sex, and his girlfriend was a continent and an ocean away. The streetwalker was willing to supply sex without a relationship.

2. *Sex without commitment.* Research on sex differences also shows that men are more willing to enter into sexual activity in the absence of a commitment (Peplau, 2003). Sex workers require no commitment from the customer other than payment for services rendered.

3. *Sex for eroticism and variety.* Many sex workers offer "something extra" in the way of novel or kinky sex—for example, oral sex, use of costumes (e.g., leather attire), and S&M rituals (such as bondage and discipline or B&D). Men may desire such activity but not obtain it with their regular partners. They may even be afraid to mention the idea. Men are also more interested than women in sexual variety (Klusman, 2002; Peplau, 2003; Schmitt, 2003), and sex workers provide variety in partners.

4. *Prostitution as a social outlet.* In the 19th and early 20th centuries, the brothel served not only as a place to obtain sex, but also as a kind of "stopping off" place between home and work. Sex was secondary to the companionship and amiable conversation that men would find in brothels, especially in the days of the "bawdy houses" of the pioneer West. (Similarly, women who attend male strip clubs enjoy "bonding" with their friends at the clubs as well as the stripping itself [Montemurro et al., 2003].)

5. *Sex away from home.* The greatest contemporary use of prostitution occurs among male "road warriors"— traveling businessmen. It is also common among sports fans at out-of-town events. In these typical all-male preserves, peer pressure may encourage sexual adventures.

   Truth or Fiction Revisited: It is not true that typical customers of prostitutes have difficulty forming sexual relationships with other women. Many men often turn to prostitutes for sexual variety or because they seek sexual activity when they are away from home.

6. *Problematical sex.* People who have physical disabilities or disfiguring conditions sometimes seek the services of prostitutes because of difficulty attracting other partners or because of fear of rejection. (One prostitute at a Nevada brothel said that she was a favorite of the management because she accepted johns with cerebral palsy.) Although some prostitutes are selective about their clients, others will accept anyone who will pay. Men with sexual dysfunctions may also turn to prostitutes who do not "demand" a certain quality of performance. Some men who lack partners may seek sex workers as substitutes.

Male Prostitution

The prostitutes we have been discussing are female, but males also work as prostitutes. Some—especially those who work at strip clubs—have female clients, but most have male clients. Male prostitutes who service female clients—*gigolos*—are rare. Gigolos' clients are typically older, wealthy, unattached women. Gigolos may serve as escorts or as surrogate sons for the women, and may or may not offer sexual services. Many gigolos are struggling actors or models.

The overwhelming majority of male sex workers service gay men and are called **hustlers**. Their patrons are typically called **scores**. Hustlers average 17 to 18 years of age and become initiated into prostitution at an average age of 14 or so. They typically have less than eleventh-grade educations and few, if any, marketable skills. The majority come from working-class and lower-class backgrounds. Many male prosti-

Hustlers Males who engage in prostitution with male customers

Scores Customers of hustlers

tutes, like many female prostitutes, come from families troubled by conflict, alcoholism, or physical or sexual abuse (Minichiello et al., 2001).

Hustlers may be gay, bisexual, or heterosexual. In a large-scale Australian study, half the male prostitutes surveyed described themselves as gay (Minichiello et al., 2001). About one third (31%) said they were bisexual, and 5.5% characterized themselves as "straight."

A Norwegian study surveyed all adolescents age 14 to 17 in public and private schools in Oslo, the capital of the country (Pedersen & Hegna, 2003). The response rate was 94%, or 10,828 students. About 1.4% of the sample had sold sexual favors, including three times as many boys as girls. Of these, half had done so more than 10 times. Prostitution was found to be connected with initiation of sexual intercourse at an early age, conduct problems, abuse of alcohol and other drugs (including heroin), and physical and sexual abuse. The male prostitutes reported that many of their clients were gay or bisexual. The adolescents did not reliably use condoms, which placed them at risk of contracting HIV/AIDS and other STIs.

The major motive for male sex work, like female sex work, is money (Minichiello et al., 2001; Zhou et al., 2002). Running away from home typically serves as an entry point. Some males run away because of family problems; others, because of a desire for adventure or independence. Some gay sex workers are literally thrown out because their families cannot accept their sexual orientation.

Most hustlers are part-timers who continue some form of educational or vocational activity as they support themselves through prostitution. Drug dealing and drug use are also common among hustlers (Minichiello et al., 2001).

Hustlers typically are not attached to a pimp. They generally make contacts with clients in gay bars and social clubs, or by working the streets in areas frequented by gay men. They typically learn to hustle from watching other hustlers ply their trade. Various kinds of male sex workers have been identified (Minichiello et al., 2001):

- Strippers dance and strip. Patrons—female and male—may fondle them or sometimes have sex with them.

- Kept boys have relationships with older, economically secure men who keep them in an affluent lifestyle. The older male, or "sugar daddy," may assume a parental role.

- Call boys, like call girls, may work on their own or through an agency or escort service.

- Punks are prison inmates who service other inmates for protection or goods like cigarettes or drugs.

- Drag prostitutes are transvestites or presurgical male-to-female transsexuals who impersonate females and have sex with men who may be unaware of their sex. Some of them conceal their sex and limit themselves to fellatio. Others take the passive role in anal sex.

- Brothel prostitutes are rarer than their female counterparts, but as you see in the nearby The World of Human Sexuality feature, a new wrinkle in male sex work is being added in Nevada.

- Bar hustlers and street hustlers, like their female counterparts, occupy the lowest status and ply their trade in gay bars or on streets frequented by gay passersby. Street hustlers are the most common and typically the youngest subtype. They are also the most visible and consequently the ones most likely to draw the attention of the police.

By and large, hustling is an adolescent enterprise. The younger the hustler, the higher the fee he can command, the more tricks he can turn. By the time he reaches his mid 20s, he may be forced to engage in sexual activities he might have rejected when younger or to seek clients in sleazier places.

SafeZone

Q *Do women use male prostitutes at all? Do they use female prostitutes?*

A The best answer is sometimes, but certainly not as frequently as men do. When women visit strip clubs and toy with male dancers, they are in effect paying for sex. They may pay for sex (male strippers) at bachelorette parties. And now and then a woman uses a gigolo. As you see in the nearby feature, Heidi Fleiss is betting that women will pay for sex in a Nevada brothel. It remains to be seen whether there will be enough customers for her to stay in business. As to whether women use female prostitutes, the best evidence we have is that heterosexual women sometimes get talked into using a female prostitute by their male companions—as a couple.

Sexually Transmitted Infections and Prostitution

Concerns about the spread of STIs by prostitution is nothing new. In the 1960s, two of three prostitutes surveyed by Gebhard (1969) had contracted gonorrhea or syphilis. Although prostitutes are still exposed to a heightened risk of contracting or spreading these and other STIs such as chlamydia, the risk of HIV/AIDS poses a more deadly threat. The risk of HIV/AIDS has been linked to both male and female prostitution (Gomes do Espirito & Etheredge, 2003; Medrano et al., 2003; Pedersen & Hegna, 2003; Zhou et al., 2002).

Criminologist James Inciardi and his colleagues (2006) interviewed 586 prostitutes in low-income sections of Miami, Florida. Their median age was 38 and they had been in "the life" for a median of 14 years. All women in the sample were heavily involved in alcohol and substance abuse, 42% were homeless, and half (51%) had engaged in unprotected vaginal sex with a customer in the past month. Their blood was tested for various STIs and it was found that

- 22.4% tested positive for HIV
- 53.4% tested positive for the hepatitis B virus
- 29.7% tested positive for the hepatitis C virus

Sex with prostitutes is the most important factor in the male–female transmission of HIV in Africa, where HIV is spread mainly by male–female sexual intercourse. Prostitutes incur a greater risk of HIV transmission because they have sexual relations with many partners, often without protection (Gomes do Espirito & Etheredge, 2003; Surratt et al., 2005). Moreover, many prostitutes and their clients and other sex partners inject drugs and share contaminated needles (Miniciello et al., 2001; Romero-Daza et al., 2005). HIV/AIDS may be spread by unprotected sex from prostitutes to customers, then to the customers' wives or lovers.

SHOULD PROSTITUTION BE LEGALIZED? As a counterpoint to the transmission of HIV and other STIs by many street prostitutes, it can be noted that in the Netherlands and parts of Nevada, where prostitution is legal and carefully regulated by the state, transmission of STIs is extremely low (Wagenaar, 2006). In Nevada,

The West Gets Wilder—A Brothel for Women

By Mireya Navarro, The New York Times Online

Picture a pleasure oasis in the Nevada desert, a collection of luxurious bungalows featuring bedrooms with fireplaces where sexual fantasies and desires are catered to. Starting at $250 an hour.

But at this house, Heidi's Stud Farm, the prostitutes will be hunky men and the patrons women.

Heidi Fleiss, former Hollywood madam, is planning the all-male brothel on 60 acres in Nevada, where prostitution is often legal and there are more than two dozen brothels of the conventional sort. Lawyers for Ms. Fleiss, who served time in prison in the late 1990s on federal charges related to a high-end call girl business, plan to apply for a license this month. Ms. Fleiss said she expects to have her house of ill repute up and running later in the year.

"The times have changed so much, with women in control," Ms. Fleiss, 40, said in a telephone interview from Nevada on Thursday. "Women make more money. They are more powerful. And it's a lonely world. People are tired of Internet dating. It's easier to go to a place where you know you'll have your dream man."

Is that possible? Are American women really ready for what will be among the first brothels of its kind? Will they pay for sex as a no-fuss transaction?

A Niche in the Business

Researchers and groups that study or work with prostitutes say that American women already do pay under certain circumstances. Women as well as men can be "sex tourists," for example. While on vacation in spots like Jamaica or the Dominican Republic, women pay for sex and the companionship of usually younger men. Back home, while male escorts overwhelmingly cater to gay clients, groups that study prostitution say there is a niche in the business for those who cater to women.

More often, however, women pay for sex outside of the established sex industry, in the more informal, grayer area of a relationship with somebody they trust: a personal trainer, say, a tennis coach or, yes, a pool boy.

"Women prefer referrals, somebody safe, more intimate contact," said the director of Hook, an advocacy and educational group for men in the sex industry, who goes by the name Hawk Kinkaid.

Women have become major consumers of pornographic films and websites in recent years, largely because of the privacy afforded by the Internet. But women are also openly displaying interest in all things sexual, from the groups that gather for sex toy parties in private homes to the ritual of celebrating birthdays, bachelorette parties, and even divorces at male strip clubs.

Though some of these sexual outlets are just erotic entertainment, some women seek more.

"We get offered all the time, 'How much for this guy?'" said Dan Remington, an owner of *Hollywood Men,* a show of male strippers in Hollywood. "We don't do that."

On a recent Saturday night more than 100 women screamed, hollered, and gawked at a performance of *Hollywood Men,* as well-toned guys peeled down to their G-strings. The crowd included both young and older women. Would they drive or fly to Heidi's Stud Farm in Crystal, Nevada, near Pahrump, about 88 miles northwest of Las Vegas, to indulge their wild side in a brothel?

"I would do it just for the experience," said Mayra Barreras, 20, a customer service representative for a mortgage company who came to the club with three friends.

"Let's face it," said Bianca Nichole, 19, a college student majoring in computer science, "there's a lot of unhappy women out there. If I were in a bad relationship, and I felt I needed something, I would go too."

Gina Pinon, a college student who was celebrating her birthday at the strip club, said she did not believe she would ever pay for sex "because I could go out and get it for free." Then she added: "But some women would pay for it, women who are in unhappy situations or who are into fantasies. I'd say: 'Go for it. Have your fun.' If men can do it, women can do it too."

Some sex experts and psychologists said a brothel for women is overdue. Many more women would avail themselves of a professional if it were legal, some experts argue, for reasons not unlike those of the men who frequent prostitutes.

A regulated business that does criminal and medical screening of its workers would find a market in women, said Patti Britton, the president-elect of the American Association of Sexuality Educators, Counselors and Therapists. The clients would be women who are adverse to hiring escorts or to seeking men in bars because of the risk of violence and disease. "The cultural expectation," Ms. Britton said, "is that any woman can have sex any time she wants it. All she has to do is show up in a public place. But many women are shy socially. And when it comes to sex, women feel more vulnerable and at risk than men."

But some researchers say it takes more than feeling safe for women to shop for sex. Amalia Cabezas, an assistant professor of women's studies at the University of California, Riverside, who has studied sex tourism in the Caribbean, said that female tourists interested in sex tend to shy away from straightforward cash-for-sex transactions.

Instead, she said, they look for a holiday romance, for a companion who not only provides sex but affection, who will wine and dine them. If the woman is footing the bill and the man is a hustler, that fact is obscured by the ambiguous nature of their alliance.

"It doesn't normally come off as a commercial transaction," Ms. Cabezas said. "It's more about friendship and developing relationships, so there's multiple possibilities for these relationships. Women don't want to see themselves as prostitute users."

Mr. Kinkaid said that a brothel for women would need to incorporate an element of seduction to draw customers. "Women wouldn't feel an immediate connection with the men they'll be hiring," he said. "They want someone who's charming and attentive. It would require significantly more time."

He added: "Would it feel cheaper to you if you know 20 other women have hired him? Men, when they hire women, don't pretend to have emotional sensibility."

If some women seem ready for a male brothel, many others are not. Among those voicing opposition to Ms. Fleiss's plans is the Nevada Brothel Association, which represents about 26 bordellos for men and fears that the publicity the ex-Hollywood madam may give to the business would stir up controversy that could shut all the brothels down.

"We believe that in order for brothels to survive in Nevada, we've got to keep a low profile," said George Flint, a lobbyist for the group. "We don't believe Heidi is capable of being low key. The association is terrified of her."

The Rev. Keith Markley, the pastor of New Hope Fellowship in Pahrump, doesn't seem all that afraid of Ms. Fleiss. He said that he and other opponents of prostitution are adopting a wait-and-see attitude "instead of getting worked up" while the business is still just a gleam in Ms. Fleiss' eye.

Mr. Markley said he doubted that a brothel for women would attract much trade, but added that he found it "equally objectionable" as a bordello for men.

"All these things are a bad idea, in a nutshell," he said. "It's bad for marriages and relationships. It's bad for husbands and wives and commitment."

Nevada already has brothels. Heidi Fleiss plans to add another, although hers would not be of the conventional sort.

An On-Site Beauty Salon

Ms. Fleiss, who has struck a deal with HBO for a documentary about her venture, promises that her brothel will be like no other in opulence and in its treatment of workers and customers. She plans to start with 20 men and to offer clients services like an on-site beauty salon.

"Everybody who walks in will feel special and comfortable," she said. She called the project "challenging"—so far, she is the only investor in the house she plans to build from scratch—but said she has received hundreds of e-mail messages from job applicants.

She has already lined up her first "stud," Lester James Brandt, 37, a Los Angeles actor and clothing designer who said he does not have anything on his resumé that would remotely qualify him for the job. During an interview over sushi in December, Mr. Brandt, who is 5 foot 10 and weighs 170 pounds, said he is intrigued by the idea of the brothel and hopes that the attention it is receiving will help him further his acting career, which has included roles in soap operas and television shows.

Though he has not hashed out his employment terms with Ms. Fleiss, who is telling job applicants that they would be able to keep all tips but must split the $250 hourly fee with the house, he said he expected to make good money.

He's a novice "when it comes to the sex trade," Mr. Brandt said. "I have no clue. What I have personal experience with is that when a woman needs love, understanding, attention, and passion, she will look for it."

Amsterdam's Red-Light District. *Amsterdam's red-light district is one of the city's tourist attractions. Prostitution is legal there and regulated. Condoms are a must. Tourists and locals stroll there by the canals and "window shop." Prim grandmothers sometimes join the audiences at the live sex shows.*

condoms have been required since 1986, and prostitutes are tested regularly. Not one case of HIV has been reported to have been transmitted in a Nevada brothel (Caporaletti, 2006).

Legalization of prostitution has benefits beyond ensuring regular testing for STIs in licensed brothels. It also turns prostitutes, other brothel employees, and brothel owners into taxpayers, and provides safer venues for prostitution—both for prostitutes and their customers. Safer settings might help sever some of the links between prostitution and drug abuse. Moreover, brothel owners would be required to obtain proof of age of sex workers.

Opponents of legalization argue both on moral and practical grounds (Grenz, 2006; Munro, 2006). Many traditionalists and feminists alike find it morally reprehensible that civilized societies would legalize practices that degrade women and the value of the family. Moreover, given prostitutes' frequent histories of abuse and sexual exploitation, they wonder whether it can be claimed that prostitutes—even as adults—are ever truly making "free" decisions to enter the world's oldest profession.

On a more practical level, many writers (e.g., Munro, 2006) note that globalization and sex trafficking is likely to create a category of sex slaves regardless of whether prostitution is legalized or tolerated within a given country. Moreover, social class differences and prejudices are likely to remain such that less attractive prostitutes drawn from minority groups will remain on the streets, and unregulated, rather than finding their ways into the safer brothels.

Pornography and Obscenity

Sexually explicit materials are found nearly everywhere. In addition to the adult magazines and the DVD rentals, millions of people use Google or Yahoo to search for pornography on the Internet or to rent pornographic films via cable or satellite dish. People are also downloading pornography onto their camera cellphones and video MP3 players.

Pornography is indeed popular, but also highly controversial. Many are opposed to pornography on moral grounds. Some feminists oppose pornography on the grounds that it portrays women in degrading and dehumanizing roles, as sex objects who are subservient to men's wishes, as sexually insatiable nymphomaniacs, or as sexual masochists who enjoy being raped and violated. Moreover, some feminists hold that depictions of women in sexually subordinate roles may encourage men to treat them as sex objects and increase the potential for rape (Itzin, 2002). On the other hand, many civil libertarians believe that the importance of freedom of speech overrides concerns about pornography.

Art or Obscenity? *Eric Fischl is a mainstream artist, yet some of his subject matter has been labeled obscene by some critics.*

What Is Pornographic?

Webster's Deluxe Unabridged Dictionary defines **pornography** as "writing, pictures, etc., intended to arouse sexual desire." The inclusion of the word *intended* places the determination of what is pornographic in the mind of the person composing the work. Applying this definition makes it all but impossible to determine what is pornographic. If a filmmaker admits that he or she wanted to arouse the audience sexually, may we judge the work to be pornographic, even if no nudity or explicit sex scenes are shown? On the other hand, explicit representations of people engaged in sexual activity would not be pornographic if the work was intended as an artistic expression, rather than created for its **prurient** value. Many works that were once prohibited in this country because of explicit sexual content, such as the novels *Tropic of Cancer* by Henry Miller, *Lady Chatterley's Lover* by D. H. Lawrence, and *Ulysses* by James Joyce, are now generally considered literary works rather than excursions into pornography. Even Mark Twain's *Huckleberry Finn*, John Steinbeck's *The Grapes of Wrath*, and Ernest Hemingway's *For Whom the Bell Tolls* have been banned from place to place because local citizens found them to be offensive, obscene, or morally objectionable.

There is thus a subjective element in the definition of pornography. An erotic statue that sexually arouses viewers may not be considered pornographic if the sculptor's intent was artistic. A grainy photograph of a naked body that was intended to excite sexually may be pornographic. One alternative definition finds material pornographic when it is judged to be offensive by others. This definition, too, relies on the subjective judgment of the person exposed to the material. In other words, one person's pornography is another person's work of art. On the other hand, most people have no difficulty distinguishing between nudity that is art, nudity that is presented for information (such as illustrations presented in this textbook), and nudity that coincides with pornography (Eck, 2001).

Legislative bodies usually write laws about **obscenity** rather than pornography. In the case of *Miller v. California* (1973), Supreme Court Justice William Brennan wrote that obscenity is "incapable of definition with sufficient clarity to withstand attack on vagueness grounds." On the other hand, Justice Potter Stewart quipped that although he could not define obscenity, he knew it when he saw it. But even the Supreme Court has had trouble defining obscenity and determining where, if any-

Pornography Sexually explicit material produced for purposes of eliciting or enhancing sexual arousal

Prurient Tending to excite lust; lewd

Obscenity That which offends people's feelings or goes beyond prevailing standards of decency or modesty

where, laws against obscenity do not run afoul of the Bill of Rights' guarantee of free speech. Recall that *Huckleberry Finn* was once considered obscene.

Pornography is often classified as either *hard-core* (X-rated) or *soft-core* (R-rated). Hard-core pornography includes graphic and sexually explicit depictions of sex organs and sexual acts. Soft-core porn, as represented by R-rated films and *Playboy* photo spreads, features more stylized nude photos and suggested (or simulated) rather than explicit sexual acts.

SafeZone

Q *How much do "porn stars" get paid? And prostitutes? How many times in a day do they need to "perform?" Does sex become just a job for them?*

A It depends on the porn star. Most get paid by the film, and not all that much—perhaps $1,000 to $3,000. Big stars like Jenna Jameson and Ron Jeremy will produce films and get a percentage of the gross receipts. They'll also receive revenues from licensing their names for adult products, but they are the exception. Streetwalkers may earn anywhere from $5 to $100 for a trick and may—as you put it— "perform" 20 or more times a day or night. Some trade sex for drugs. A top-of-the-line escort or call girl may bring in anywhere from $400 to $1,000 an hour, and have one or two appointments per evening, or spend the night for $2,000 or $3,000.

SNUFF FILMS   One rumored twist on the pornographic film is the so-called **snuff film**, in which a person would be killed while engaging in a sex act, perhaps while being raped. The word *snuff* apparently derives from the idea of snuffing out a life—as one snuffs out a candle—and the theoretical existence of snuff films has been one of the arguments occasionally used to convince people of the hidden terrors of the adult film industry.

To be sure, there have been films and videos of real people dying. The documentary of a Rolling Stones tour, *Gimme Shelter,* ends with a fatal stabbing. A 2006 documentary, *The Bridge,* simply placed cameras at various spots along San Francisco's Golden Gate Bridge and, over time, captured images of people jumping to their deaths. But in neither film were the deaths premeditated by the directors. The deaths of a number of prison inmates with death sentences have been recorded, but these records certainly contained no sexual content.

Dennis Lim (2006), a writer for *The New York Times,* sums it up: "There has been no generally accepted verification of the existence of a snuff film as it is strictly defined: a movie in which a premeditated killing takes place for the benefit of the camera, and by implication the viewer."

Pornography and the Law

Laws against obscenity provide the legal framework for outlawing the dissemination of pornography. Because the definition of obscenity relies on offending people or running afoul of community standards, that which is deemed obscene may vary from person to person and from culture to culture. Going topless on a public beach may be deemed obscene in some locales, but not along beaches on the French Riviera or Rio de Janeiro, where this style of (un)dress is customary. The word *obscene* extends be-

Snuff film A film with the premeditated killing of a person during a sex act

A Closer Look

PORN IN YOUR POCKET?

By Gary Strauss, *USA Today*

Porn star Ron Jeremy licensed his name to RJ Mobile, which offers adult content in Britain and Holland.

Quickly developing into big business overseas, cellphone pornography is a step closer to taking off in the USA. Cingular Wireless, the nation's largest cellphone service provider, has quietly launched filtering devices and password-enabled blockers that help thwart underage consumers from buying adult content. The absence of V-chip-style parental controls largely has kept U.S. consumers from using cellphones to access porn, but Cingular, along with rivals, could launch a huge new porn platform.

The evolution of video-capable wireless devices has made mobile porn an emerging cultural phenomenon and booming enterprise. Global 2005 sales will hit $1 billion, up 175% from 2004, says Juniper Research. U.S. sales are just $30 million, mostly because carriers, fearful of a backlash, haven't provided easy access to X-rated theater.

Web-enabled phones can download porn from the Internet, but access is cumbersome, and carriers don't share fees with content providers. By offering "on deck" portals, carriers can reap fat user fees.

The Cellular Telecommunications Industry Association recently issued content ratings standards, prompting Cingular's move.

"Certainly, this is going to make it easier to view porn in more places than ever," says Pamela Paul, author of *Pornified: How Pornography Is Transforming Our Lives, Our Relationships and Our Families.*

Antiporn crusaders say content ratings and parental controls aside, mobile porn will be problematic. "Some parents don't monitor what kids download. And they can't monitor what other kids do," says Charmaine Yoest of the Family Research Council.

Balancing business interests, free-speech rights, and protecting kids "is tricky," says Cingular's Mark Siegel. "But we feel parents should decide what [kids] access. We're giving them the ability to control what they experience."

Notes Yankee Group analyst Linda Barrabee: "Carriers don't want to be known as adult-content purveyors. But they understand the opportunity to make money."

Scores of marketers are lining up to tap the U.S. market. Xobile, a content provider for Web-capable wireless devices, will offer 50,000 video clips, says operations chief Harvey Kaplan. Porn star Ron Jeremy licensed his name to RJ Mobile, which offers adult content in Britain and Holland. He's not sure of the U.S. appetite for mobile porn, though. "Who wants to watch this stuff on a tiny screen?" he says.

Kathee Brewer, an editor for *Adult Video News,* says consumers will be lured by portability. Steve Hirsch, co-CEO of adult film giant Vivid Entertainment, expects mobile porn to eventually account for 30% of sales. "This is going to explode. People will want porn in their pocket," he says.

SOURCE: From "Cellphone technology rings in pornography in USA" by Gary Strauss, *USA Today,* December 12, 2005. Reprinted with permission.

---

yond sexual matters. One could judge TV violence or beer commercials to be obscene because they are personally offensive or are offensive to women, even if such depictions do not meet legal standards of obscenity.

In the United States, legal prohibition of pornography as a form of obscenity dates to the nineteenth century. In 1873, an antiobscenity bill, the Comstock Act, was passed by Congress. One effect of the bill was to outlaw the dissemination of information about birth control. The Comstock Act and similar laws made it a felony to mail obscene books, pamphlets, photographs, drawings, or letters. But what is obscene?

A landmark case in 1957 helped establish the legal basis of obscenity in the United States. In *Roth v. United States,* the U.S. Supreme Court ruled that portrayal of sexual activity was protected under the First Amendment to the Constitution unless its dominant theme dealt with "sex in a manner appealing to prurient interest" (*Roth v. United States,* 1957, p. 487). In a 1973 case, *Miller v. California,* the U.S. Supreme Court held that obscenity is based upon a determination of

(a) Whether the average person, applying contemporary community standards, would find that the work, taken as a whole, appeals to the prurient interest . . . ; (b) whether the work depicts or describes, in a patently offensive way, sexual conduct specifically defined by the applicable state law; and (c) whether the work, taken as a whole, lacks serious literary, artistic, political, or scientific value. (*Miller v. California,* 1973, p. 24)

Courts have since had to grapple with the *Miller* standard in judging whether material is obscene. *Miller* recognizes that judgments of obscenity may vary with "community standards." As a result, the same material may be considered obscene in one community but not in another. The *Miller* standard raises some questions. For example, who is the "average person" who can speak for a community? Many of us live in ethnically, racially, and religiously diverse communities. Can one viewpoint in *any* community truly represent the community? Even in relatively homogeneous communities, a diversity of opinion may exist on particular issues. Moreover, what is a *community*? Is it one's neighborhood, police precinct, municipality, county, or a larger political unit? What does "patently" offensive mean? Who judges "serious" literary, artistic, political, or scientific value? An attempt to clarify this last question was made in a 1987 case, *Pope v. Illinois,* in which the Supreme Court held that

The proper inquiry is not whether an ordinary member of any given community would find serious literary, artistic, political, or scientific value in allegedly obscene material, but whether a reasonable person would find such value in the material, taken as a whole. (p. 445)

In this ruling, the court held that sexually explicit material could not be declared obscene if many or most people in a particular community held it to lack serious literary, artistic, political, or scientific value, unless a "reasonable" person were to reach the same judgment. Whether the concept of a "reasonable" person will provide the courts with a clearer standard than that of an "average" or "ordinary" person for adjudicating obscenity cases remains to be seen.

Child pornography and violent, degrading, or dehumanizing pornography complicate matters further. People who do not find explicit depictions of consensual sex between adults to be obscene may regard child pornography or violent pornography to be obscene. Child pornography is clearly psychologically harmful to the juveniles in the films (McCabe, 2000; Quayle & Taylor, 2002, 2003). Many people also object to sexually explicit material that portrays women as "sex objects" or subordinate to men—gratifying men's sexual appetites.

Some footnotes: The U.S. Supreme Court ruled (in *Stanley v. Georgia,* 1969) that the possession of obscene material in one's home is not a criminal act. However, states can criminalize the downloading and possession of child pornography, and many have done so (McCabe, 2000; Quayle & Taylor, 2002, 2003). It is not unusual today for police to seize suspects' computers and check them for the presence of child pornography.

Many individuals and communities have sought to ban pornography on the grounds that it discriminates against women (noted in Duggan, 2006a). Pornography, that is, damages women's opportunities for equal rights by perpetuating stereotypes of women as subservient to men.

THE REGULATION OF PORNOGRAPHY If the First Amendment has protected people's rights to produce, act in, and possess pornography—with the exception of child pornography—it has not prevented various governing bodies from imposing some regulations on the industry. In sum, actors in adult films must be, in fact, adults, and, in many jurisdictions, they must be certified as free of certain STIs. As you can see in Figure 19.1, actors in southern California, where there are more than 200 adult movie studios, are required to receive monthly tests for HIV, chlamydia, and gonorrhea, and to be tested for other infections on other schedules (AIM Health Care Foundation, 2006). To avoid liability, most studios keep careful records of actors' proof of age and testing.

One might ask why actors are not required to wear condoms, as is common in the Brazilian adult film industry (Clendenning, 2004). The simple answer is that au-

---

IF YOU'RE NEW TO THE ADULT FILM INDUSTRY THIS IS WHAT YOU NEED TO DO BEFORE YOU START WORKING:

1. *Get your blood tested for:
   - HIV (by "PCR DNA")
   - syphilis (an "RPR" test)

2. *Get your urine tested for:
   - gonorrhea (by "ultra-sensitive DNA amplification")
   - chlamydia (by "ultra-sensitive DNA amplification")

3. *View the "PORN 101" video which is available to take home and is also displayed in a condensed version at AIM Healthcare. Also pick up a copy of the "Responsibilities of Performers" list to help make your job easier.

4. *Every month get retested for gonorrhea, chlamydia, and HIV.

5. Get a genital exam:

   If you're a woman: Get a pelvic exam that includes an evaluation for herpes, genital warts, and the following tests:
   - PAP smear ("thin-prep with reflex HPV")
   - vaginal culture for bacterial vaginosis
   - vaginal culture for trichomonas

   If you're a man: Get a genital exam that includes an evaluation for herpes and genital warts.

6. Get your blood tested for Hepatitis A, B, and C.

   (If your test comes back negative, it is highly recommended that you get vaccinated for Hepatitis A and B. There is no vaccine for Hepatitis C.)

7. Get a skin test for tuberculosis.

8. Every six months:
   - women should have a genital exam with a PAP smear
   - men should have a genital exam
   - both men and women should be retested for syphilis

Figure 19.1 *AIM Health Care Foundation helps actors in the adult film industry, especially "new talent," maintain their health and meet government legislated testing requirements.*
*These items are recommended mandatory industry requirements to be done before your first shoot.
SOURCE: Reprinted by permission of AIM Foundation/Dr. Sharon Mitchell.

diences prefer male actors to be "bareback." Very few American studios require actors to use condoms.

Prevalence and Use of Erotica and Pornography

Nearly all of us have been exposed to sexually explicit materials, whether in the form of a novel, a photo spread in *Penthouse* or *Club*, an X-rated film, or an adult website. In perhaps the only credible survey results we have on the issue, the NHSLS found that about one man in four (23%) and 1 woman in 10 (11%) had bought an X-rated movie or video within the past year (Michael et al., 1994). Sixteen percent of the men and 4% of the women had bought sexually explicit magazines or books. Adult websites have proliferated to the point where men's magazines hover over the brink of bankruptcy.

People in the United States are typically introduced to pornography by their high school years, often by peers. Females are more likely to have been exposed to pornography by boyfriends than the reverse.

Pornography is typically used to elicit or enhance sexual arousal, often as a masturbation aid (Boies, 2002; Strager, 2003). Pornographic materials may also be used by couples to enhance sexual arousal during lovemaking. Some physicians recommend that couples with erectile dysfunction use pornography to help become aroused. Many couples find that a sexy video, DVD, or cable TV movie enlivens their sexual appetite or suggests novel techniques.

Researchers have found that both men and women are physiologically sexually aroused by pornographic pictures, movies, or audiotaped passages (Peplau, 2003). That is, both men and women respond to pornographic stimuli with vasocongestion of the genitals and myotonia (muscle tension). However, there is a difference between physiological response and subjective feelings of arousal in women. Despite what is happening within their bodies, women tend to rate romantic scenes as more sexually arousing than sexually explicit scenes. Women are less accepting than men of sex without emotional involvement (Peplau, 2003). Most women want sex to be related to an emotional connection. It is romance that encourages most women to follow the lead of genital arousal, when they do so. Even in the choice of erotic materials, women are much more likely than men to want the element of romance to be included (Hardy, 2001).

Repeated exposure to the same pornographic materials progressively lessens the sexual response to them. People may become aroused by the familiar materials again if some time is allowed to go by. Novel materials are also likely to reactivate a sexual response (Goodson et al., 2001; Stein et al., 2001).

SafeZone

Q *How do you know if you are addicted to pornography?*

A An addiction is usually defined in terms of the role the problem behavior plays in one's life. If you organize your life around obtaining the desired substance or thing (porn); if you find yourself putting aside your academic, vocational, and social responsibilities in favor of experiencing the desired substance or thing, then you're probably addicted. If having the desired substance or thing—in this case, porn—is the normal state of affairs, so that you crave it when you're without it, you are, in that sense, addicted.

Feminists and Antipornography Campaigns

The sexual revolution liberated many in society from sexual inhibitions and prompted sexual exploration. As of the late 1960s, pornography became widespread. But many feminists found the proliferation of sexual imagery to be anything but liberating. Instead, it portrayed women as sex objects intended to be subservient to men.

During the 1980s, some feminists joined with conservative Christian groups such as the Moral Majority to try to ban pornography, thereby aligning themselves with what amounted to a moral crusade (Duggan, 2006a). Their efforts ultimately failed, but it did spark conflict within the feminist movement and from some sexual minorities. Some groups claimed that banning pornography not only intrudes upon First Amendment rights, but also, by legislating what kinds of sexual themes may be portrayed, marginalizes people who derive sexual pleasure from pornography.

In 1980 Andrea Dworkin and Catherine MacKinnon proposed legislation to the city of Minneapolis that would define pornography as

> [t]he graphic, sexually explicit subordination of women whether in pictures or in words that also includes one or more of the following: women are presented dehumanized as sexual objects, . . . or women are presented as sexual objects who enjoy pain or humiliation; or women who experience pleasure in being raped—or women's body parts are exhibited, such that women are reduced to those parts; or women are presented in scenarios of degradation, . . . shown as filthy or inferior, bleeding, bruised or hurt in a context that makes these conditions sexual.

The proposed law included civil rather than criminal remedies for women affected by pornography. Women could sue makers, distributors, and sellers of pornography. The courts could also, in effect, remove pornography from the public, such that publishers and booksellers could be under scrutiny and surveillance.

Reactions against Antipornography Feminists

Lisa Duggan (2006b) notes that feminist historians have criticized efforts to ban pornography and the political movements underlying it. One reason is the very fact that it leads to alliances with groups, such as the Moral Majority, whose agendas are otherwise opposed to "women's liberation." Another reason is the confusion over sexual explicitness, mistreatment of women, and violence. Pornography, per se, need not portray women as victims of men's lust. Nor, as discussed elsewhere in this chapter, has it been shown that pornography per se causes violence against women. Thus the battle against pornography misdirects resources that would be better directed against abuse of women and depictions of violence in the media.

Moreover, ordinances such as those offered by MacKinnon and Dworkin may be presented as ordinances to prevent sex discrimination, as seen recently in Indianapolis (Duggan, 2006a). However, they are clear censorship laws that would counter First Amendment rights (Duggan et al., 2006). The MacKinnon–Dworkin ordinance could have allowed for censorship of art, novels, plays, movies, and other media that refer to sexuality and the female body. The price is unacceptable.

SEX DIFFERENCES IN RESPONSE TO PORNOGRAPHY   **Truth or Fiction Revisited:** Both males and females can become physiologically aroused by erotic materials. Yet males and females do not necessarily share the same subjective response to them or level of interest in them. Visual pornography (sexually explicit pictures or films) is largely a male preserve (Boies, 2002; Goodson et al., 2001). Most erotic visual materials are produced by men for men. Attempts to market visual materials to females have been largely unsuccessful (Hardy, 2001). Women may read erotic romance novels, but they show little interest in erotic pictures, films, or websites (Hardy, 2001). Women may find **erotica** a "turn-off" or disgusting, especially when it portrays women in unflattering roles, as "whorish," subservient to men, and aroused by male domination.

TRUTH fiction 5

Erotica Materials that depict sexual love (Many contemporary writers use the term *erotica* to refer to sexual material that is artistically produced or motivated by artistic intent.)

From the evolutionary perspective, could a basic evolutionary process be at work? Did ancestral men who were more sexually aroused by the sight of a passing female have reproductive advantages over their less arousable peers? Women, however, have fewer mating opportunities than men and must make the most of any reproductive opportunity by selecting the best possible mate and provider. To be sexually aroused by the sight of male genitalia might encourage random couplings, which would undermine their reproductive success.

Cybersex Addiction: For Some, Sex Is Nothing but 'Net

> Sex on the 'Net is like heroin. It grabs [people] and takes over their lives. And it's very difficult to treat because the people affected don't want to give it up.
>
> —Mark Schwartz, Masters and Johnson Institute

Truth or Fiction Revisited: It appears that at least one third of Internet visits are directed to sexually oriented websites, chatrooms, and newsgroups (Cooper et al., 2000, 2004). For most people these ventures into cybersex are harmless enough, but the accessibility and anonymity of sex on the Internet are fueling what many health professionals have labeled a new form of addiction—cybersex addiction—that is spreading rapidly and bringing turmoil into the lives of those afflicted with it (Gerevich et al., 2005; Philaretou et al., 2005).

Surveys show that many people, mostly men, now spend dozens of hours each week surfing pornographic and other sex-related websites (Cooper et al., 2000, 2004; Daneback et al., 2006). Nevertheless, they typically deny that they have a problem and refuse help unless their real relationships or jobs are in jeopardy. Those most strongly hooked on online sex may spend hours a day masturbating to pornographic images or—less commonly—having "online sex" with someone contacted via a chatroom or webcam (Daneback et al., 2005, 2006).

Based on a survey of 9,265 men and women who admitted surfing the 'Net for sex, Cooper and his colleagues (1999a, 2000) concluded that the 'Net is "the crack cocaine of sexual compulsivity," with at least 1% of respondents deeply addicted to online sex.

Cybersex compulsives are like drug addicts (Cooper et al., 2004; Schneider, 2005). They "use the Internet as an important part of their sexual acting out, much like a drug addict who has a drug of choice. [Especially vulnerable are those] whose sexuality may have been suppressed and limited all their lives [who] suddenly find an infinite supply of sexual opportunities" online (Cooper, cited in Brody, 2000). Although some studies find men who become addicted to online sex to have ample sexual opportunities in the real world, other studies find them to be lonelier than men with those opportunities (Yoder et al., 2005).

Physician Jennifer Schneider (2003, 2004) conducted a survey of 94 family members affected by cybersex addiction and found that it can arise even among people in good relationships and who have an abundance of sexual opportunities. "Sex on the 'Net is just so seductive and it's so easy to stumble upon it [that] people who are vulnerable can get hooked before they know it" (cited in Brody, 2000).

Schneider (2005) defends the view that cybersex addiction is a true addiction, characterized by "loss of control, continuation of the behavior despite significant adverse consequences and preoccupation or obsession with obtaining the drug or pursuing the behavior." Although behavioral addictions do not involve taking drugs, they may cause changes in the brain, such as releasing endorphins—brain chemicals with actions that mimic those of the narcotic morphine—that maintain the behavior (Plant & Plant, 2003).

Sexual arousal and orgasm also reinforce the behavior. Mark Schwartz wrote: "Intense orgasms from the minimal investment of a few keystrokes are powerfully reinforcing. Cybersex affords easy, inexpensive access to a myriad of ritualized encounters with idealized partners" (cited in Brody, 2000).

As with other addictions, tolerance to cybersex stimulation can develop, prompting the addict to take more and more risks to recapture the initial high. Online viewing that began as a harmless recreation can become all-consuming and even lead to real sexual encounters with people met online. Cybersex compulsives sometimes ignore their partners and children, and risk their jobs. Many companies monitor employees' online activities, and visits to sexual sites can cost employees their jobs. Schneider (2005) reports other adverse consequences, including broken relationships. Partners often report feeling betrayed, ignored, and unable to compete with the online fantasies.

A 34-year-old woman married 14 years to a minister told Schneider, "How can I compete with hundreds of anonymous others who are now in our bed, in his head? Our bed is crowded with countless faceless strangers, where once we were intimate" (cited in Brody, 2000).

Pornography and Sexual Coercion

Is pornography a harmless diversion or a cause of sexual violence or other antisocial acts? Let us consider several sources of evidence in examining this highly charged question, beginning with history—the findings of a 1970 government commission impaneled to review the evidence that was available at the time.

THE COMMISSION ON OBSCENITY AND PORNOGRAPHY In the 1960s, Congress created the Commission on Obscenity and Pornography to study the effects of pornography. Upon reviewing the existing research, the commission (Abelson et al., 1970) concluded that there was no evidence that pornography led to crimes of violence or sexual offenses such as exhibitionism, voyeurism, or child molestation. Some people were sexually aroused by pornography and increased the frequency of their usual sexual activity, such as masturbation or coitus with regular partners, after exposure. They did not engage in antisocial behavior, however. These results have been replicated many times.

Finding pornography basically harmless, the commission recommended that "federal, state, and local legislation should not seek to interfere with the right of adults who wish to read, obtain, or view explicit sexual materials" (Abelson et al., 1970, p. 58). Congress and then-president Richard Nixon rejected the commission's findings and recommendation, however, on moral and political—not scientific— grounds.

THE MEESE COMMISSION REPORT In 1985, President Ronald Reagan appointed a committee headed by Attorney General Edwin Meese to reexamine the effects of pornography. In 1986, the U.S. Attorney General's Commission on

Pornography, known as the Meese Commission, issued a report that reached very different conclusions from the 1970 commission. The Meese Commission claimed to find a causal link between sexual violence and exposure to violent pornography (U.S. Department of Justice, 1986). The commission asserted that a substantial increase in the proliferation of violent pornography had occurred since the earlier commission had been convened. Moreover, the report concluded that exposure to pornography that portrayed women in degrading or subservient roles increased acceptability of rape in the minds of viewers. The commission found no evidence linking exposure to nonviolent, nondegrading pornography (consensual sexual activity between partners in equal roles) and sexual violence, but noted that only a small fraction of the pornographic materials on the market was of this type.

The commission's findings are controversial. Critics claim that although the Meese Commission did not blatantly falsify the data, its conclusions reflected an overgeneralization of laboratory-based findings (Wilcox, 1987). Two researchers in the area, Edward Donnerstein and Daniel Linz (1987), contended that the Meese Commission failed to distinguish between the effects of sexually explicit materials per se and the effects of violent materials. Evidence of links between exposure to sexually explicit materials (without violent content) and sexual aggression is lacking. Donnerstein and Linz (1987) concluded that violence, not sex, is the obscenity.

If nothing else, the Meese Commission raised awareness about different types of pornography and their potential effects on viewers' behaviors and attitudes. Let us take a look at the scientific evidence on the effects of violent and nonviolent pornography.

PORNOGRAPHY AND SEX OFFENDERS Another approach to examining the role of pornography in crimes of sexual violence involves comparing the experience of sex offenders and nonoffenders with pornographic materials. A review of the research literature found little or no difference in the level of exposure to pornography between incarcerated sex offenders and comparison groups of felons who were incarcerated for nonsexual crimes (Marshall, 1989).

Yet evidence also shows that as many as one in three rapists and child molesters use pornography to become sexually aroused before they commit their crimes (Marshall, 1989). These findings suggest that pornography may stimulate sexually deviant urges in certain subgroups of men who are predisposed to commit crimes of sexual violence (Marshall, 1989).

VIOLENT PORNOGRAPHY Laboratory-based studies have shown that men exposed to violent pornography are more likely to become aggressive against females and to show less sensitivity toward women who have been sexually assaulted. In one classic study (Donnerstein, 1980), 120 college men interacted with a male or female confederate (accomplice) of the experimenter, who treated them in either a neutral or hostile manner. The subjects were then shown neutral, nonviolent pornographic films, or violent pornographic films. In the latter, a man forced himself into a woman's home and raped her. Subjects were then given the opportunity to deliver electric shock to the male or female confederate, presumably to assist the confederate in learning a task. The measure of aggression was the intensity of the shock chosen. No shock was actually delivered, but subjects did not know that the shock apparatus was fake. Unprovoked men who viewed violent pornographic films showed greater aggression toward the women than did unprovoked men who viewed nonviolent films, however. Provoked men who were shown violent pornography selected the highest shock levels of all. The film may have served as a model for retaliation.

In another study, aggression by males against female confederates following exposure to violent pornography (a rape scene) was increased by depictions of the woman being raped as either enjoying the experience or becoming sexually aroused during the rape (Donnerstein & Berkowitz, 1981). These findings suggest that depictions of women enjoying or becoming aroused by their victimization may legitimize violence against women in the viewer's mind, reinforcing the cultural myth that some women need to be dominated and are sexually aroused by an overpowering male.

Some research suggests that it is the violence in violent pornography, and not sexual explicitness, that hardens men's attitudes toward rape survivors. In one study (Donnerstein & Linz, 1987), college men were exposed to films consisting of either violent pornography, nonviolent pornography (a couple having consensual intercourse), or violence that was not sexually explicit. The violent pornographic and nonpornographic films both showed a woman being tied up and slapped at gunpoint, but the nonpornographic version contained no nudity or explicit sexual activity. The men had first been either angered or treated in a neutral manner by a female confederate of the experimenter. The results showed that, in comparison with nonviolent pornography, both violent pornographic films and violent *non*pornographic films produced greater acceptance of rape myths, increased reported willingness to force a woman into sexual activity, and greater reported likelihood of engaging in rape (if the man also knew that he could get away with it). These effects occurred regardless of whether the man was angered by the woman.

Research on the effects of pornography should be interpreted with caution, however (Seto et al., 2001). Most of it has employed college students, whose behavior may or may not be typical of people in general or of people with propensities toward sexual violence. Another issue is that most studies in this area are laboratory-based experiments that involve simulated aggression or judgments of sympathy toward hypothetical women who have been portrayed as rape victims. None measured *actual* violence against women outside the lab. We still lack conclusive evidence that normal men have been, or would be, spurred to rape or to violate women sexually because of exposure to violent pornography.

In their comprehensive review of the research literature on pornography and sexual aggression, Neil Malamuth and his colleagues (2000) analyzed data from studies that found no reliable links between pornography and aggression, integrated the findings of multiple summaries of the experimental and naturalistic research literature, and analyzed questionnaire date obtained from a representative sample of 2,972 college men who were an average of 21 years old. Each method of analysis supported the existence of some reliable connections between the frequent use of pornography and sexually aggressive behavior; particularly in the cases of violent pornography and for men who were likely to engage in sexual aggression.

Truth or Fiction Revisited: Malamuth and his colleagues (2000) conclude not that pornography causes violence, but that relatively aggressive men react differently from nonviolent men to the same pornography. Put it this way: It is not so much that pornography makes men violent; instead, it seems to be more likely that pornography makes violent men more violent.

NONVIOLENT PORNOGRAPHY   Nonviolent pornography may not contain scenes of sexual violence, but it typically portrays women in degrading or dehumanizing roles—as sexually promiscuous, insatiable, and subservient (Itzin, 2002).

TRUTH ? fiction 7

CRITICAL Thinking

Which do you consider to be the greater danger—the danger of widely available pornography or the danger of censorship? Why?

Might such portrayals of women reinforce traditional stereotypes of women as sex objects? Might they lead viewers to condone acts of rape by suggesting that women are essentially promiscuous? Might the depiction of women as readily sexually accessible inspire men to refuse to "take no for an answer" on dates?

In classic research, Zillmann and Bryant (1984) exposed male and female subjects to six sessions of pornography for six consecutive weeks. Subjects were exposed either to a massive dose of pornography, consisting of six nonviolent pornographic films during each session; to an intermediate dose, consisting of three pornographic and three neutral films each session; or to a no-dose control, consisting of six nonsexual films. When surveyed later, both males and females who received extended exposure to pornography, especially those receiving the massive dose, gave more lenient punishments to a rapist who was depicted in a newspaper article. Moreover, males became more callous in their attitudes toward women.

In a more recent study, 71 men watched one of three films: a film that was sexually explicit and degrading of women, a film that was sexually explicit but *not* degrading of women, and a nonsexual (control) film (Mulac et al., 2002). The men then worked in couples with women to solve problems. Men who watched the sexually explicit films behaved more dominantly toward their problem-solving partners than men who watched the control film. Moreover, men who watched the sexually explicit *and* degrading film showed more dominance than those who watched the sexually explicit but not the degrading film.

Overall, it would appear that, at least for some men, exposure to pornography can render attitudes toward women more negative and callous. Some men who view pornography may come to regard women as sexual playthings who are to be valued for their physical attributes and role in providing sexual release, and not as individuals.

Another concern is the possible effect of nonviolent pornography on the viewer's sexual and family values. Nonviolent pornography typically features impromptu sexual encounters between new acquaintances. Might repeated exposure to such material alter viewers' attitudes toward traditional sexual and family values? There is intriguing evidence that repeated exposure to this type of nonviolent pornography loosens traditional sexual and family values (Brown, 2003; Zillmann, 1989). When compared with people who viewed nonsexual films, men and women who were exposed to weekly, hour-long sessions involving scenes of explicit sexual encounters between new acquaintances for a six-week period showed attitudinal changes including greater acceptance, in comparison with control subjects who viewed nonsexual films of premarital and extramarital sex and of simultaneous sexual relationships with multiple partners. Men and women who viewed such pornography also reported desiring fewer children than people in the control groups and were relatively less committed to marriage as an "essential institution."

Nonviolent pornography may loosen traditional family values by projecting an image of sexual enjoyment without responsibility or obligations (Brown, 2003). Prolonged exposure to such pornography may also foster dissatisfaction with the physical appearance and sexual performance of one's intimate partners (Brown, 2003). Society is now adjusting to the fact that pornography is available to almost anyone of any age who can go online. For some, it may well become a psychological disorder, akin to the obsessive–compulsive disorders in which people have difficulty preventing themselves from washing their hands. And more and more students burning the midnight oil in their dorm rooms are surfing for sex rather than research findings. It's available, it's free, it's right in students' rooms; the lure is tremendous and the potential harm is yet to be disclosed.

1. **What are the effects of prostitution on prostitutes, clients, and society at large?**

   - Prostitution—also called sex work—is the sale of sex. Prostitution is illegal everywhere in the United States except rural counties in Nevada.

   - Fewer young men in the United States use prostitutes than in Kinsey's day, apparently because of the liberalizing trends of the sexual revolution. Nevertheless, there are hundreds of thousands of sex workers, including those on adult websites.

   - The major types of female prostitutes are streetwalkers, brothel prostitutes, "masseuses," "escorts," and call girls. Many prostitutes work in adult films and on adult websites.

   - Poverty and child abuse figure prominently in the backgrounds of many prostitutes. Teenage runaways with limited means of support are vulnerable to being drawn into prostitution.

   - Most patrons of prostitutes are occasional johns with regular sex partners, but some people use prostitutes regularly.

   - Most male prostitutes are hustlers who service male clients, but some male sex workers have female customers.

   - Prostitutes are at greater risk of transmission of HIV because they have sexual relations with many partners, often without protection. HIV may be spread by prostitutes to customers, then to the customers' regular partners.

2. **What are the legal status and effects of pornography and obscenity?**

   - Pornography is "writing, pictures, etc., intended to arouse sexual desire." The judgment regarding what is pornographic or obscene varies from person to person and culture to culture.

   - Obscenity refers to statements or materials that offend people or go beyond prevailing standards of decency or modesty. The label "obscenity" has a subjective element.

   - In *Miller v. California,* the U.S. Supreme Court held that obscenity is based on determination of "whether the average person, applying contemporary community standards, would find that the work . . . appeals to the prurient interest . . . ; whether the work depicts [sexual behavior] in a patently offensive way, [and] whether the work, taken as a whole, lacks serious literary, artistic, political, or scientific value." The downloading or possession of child pornography has been criminalized throughout the United States.

   - People in the United States are typically introduced to pornography by their high school years. Although females and males can both be physiologically aroused by pornography, men are relatively more interested. Pornography is frequently used as a masturbation aid.

   - A 1970 government commission found no harmful effects of pornographic material on normal people. A 1986 government commission reported that exposure to violent pornography is linked with sexual aggression, and exposure to degrading but nonviolent pornography with increased acceptability of rape in the minds of viewers. Scientific experiments suggest that exposure to pornography may stimulate sexually deviant urges in men who are predisposed to commit crimes of sexual violence. Experiments also suggest that violent pornography may stimulate college men to act more aggressively toward women. Some researchers argue that it is the violence in violent pornography, and not the sexual explicitness, that contributes to violence against women. The effects of nonviolent pornography on normal populations remain unclear.

1. _____ occupy the bottom rung in the hierarchy of prostitutes.

   (a) Streetwalkers
   (b) Brothel prostitutes
   (c) Massage parlor prostitutes
   (d) Call girls

2. Most patrons of prostitutes are "_____ johns."

   (a) habitual
   (b) gay
   (c) occasional
   (d) atypical

3. Males who engage in male prostitution are called _____.

   (a) pimps
   (b) strippers
   (c) playboys
   (d) hustlers

4. Female prostitutes differ from most women in that they do not require _____ from sex partners.

   (a) money
   (b) commitment
   (c) condoms
   (d) sexual activity

5. Sex with prostitutes is an important factor in the _____ transmission of HIV/AIDS in Africa.

   (a) male–male
   (b) female–female
   (c) male–female
   (d) oral

6. _____ are physiologically sexually aroused by pornography.

   (a) Men and women
   (b) Only men
   (c) Only women
   (d) Only gay males and lesbians

7. The Supreme Court decision in *Miller v. California* stated that _____ standards must be considered in defining obscenity.

   (a) Biblical
   (b) community
   (c) educational
   (d) universal

8. The 1970 Commission on Obscenity and Pornography concluded that pornography

   (a) destroys family life
   (b) leads people to be bored with sex
   (c) stimulates crimes of violence
   (d) has not been shown to cause harm

9. Research appears to show that _____ pornography is connected with sexual aggression.

   (a) explicit
   (b) gay
   (c) violent
   (d) online

10. U.S. courts have held that the _____ Amendment to the Constitution guarantees freedom to use pornography.

   (a) First
   (b) Second
   (c) Fifth
   (d) Twenty-third

11. Research suggests that about _____% of streetwalkers have pimps.

   (a) 20
   (b) 40
   (c) 60
   (d) 80

12. A study of 586 streetwalkers in Miami found that about _____% tested positive for HIV.

   (a) 22
   (b) 42
   (c) 62
   (d) 82

13. One reason Lisa Duggan opposed Catherine MacKinnon's proposed antipornography ordinance was that

   (a) it would have been a city ordinance and not a state law
   (b) the ordinance did not go far enough in censoring pornography
   (c) Duggan produced pornographic materials
   (d) MacKinnon aligned herself with the Moral Majority

14. Farley and her colleagues interviewed 100 Canadian prostitutes and found that _____% reported a history of childhood sexual abuse.

   (a) 22
   (b) 42
   (c) 62
   (d) 82

15. What is true of the sexual orientation of hustlers?

   (a) They are straight
   (b) They are gay
   (c) They are bisexual
   (d) They may be of any sexual orientation

Answers 1. a; 2. c; 3. d; 4. b; 5. c; 6. a; 7. b; 8. d; 9. c; 10. a; 11. b; 12. a; 13. a; 14. d; 15. d

APPENDIX

Scoring Keys for Self-Assessments

"Would You Tell an Interviewer the Truth on a Survey about Your Sexual Behavior? The Social-Desirability Scale" (Chapter 2, p. 48)

Place a check mark on the appropriate line of the scoring key each time your answer agrees with the one listed in the scoring key. Add the check marks and record the total number of check marks here.

1. T_____	12. F_____	23. F_____
2. T_____	13. T_____	24. T_____
3. F_____	14. F_____	25. T_____
4. T_____	15. F_____	26. T_____
5. F_____	16. T_____	27. T_____
6. F_____	17. T_____	28. F_____
7. T_____	18. T_____	29. T_____
8. T_____	19. F_____	30. F_____
9. F_____	20. T_____	31. T_____
10. F_____	21. T_____	32. F_____
11. F_____	22. F_____	33. T_____

Interpreting Your Score

LOW SCORERS (0–8 POINTS) About one respondent in six earns a score between 0 and 8 points. Such respondents answered in a socially *undesirable* direction much of the time. It may be that they are more willing than most people to respond to tests truthfully, even when their answers might meet with social disapproval.

AVERAGE SCORERS (9–19 POINTS) About two respondents in three earn a score from 9 to 19 points. They tend to show an average degree of concern for the social desirability of their responses, and it may be that their general behavior represents an average degree of conformity to social rules and conventions.

HIGH SCORERS (20–33 POINTS) About one respondent in six earns a score between 20 and 33 points. These respondents may be highly concerned about social approval, and respond to test items in such as way as to avoid the disapproval of people who may read their responses. Their general behavior may show high conformity to social rules and conventions.

"Do You Experience PMS?" (Chapter 3, p. 98)

There are no numerical answers to this self-assessment. Ask yourself, rather, whether you are experiencing any moderate to disabling psychological or physical symptoms of PMS. We advise you to discuss any symptoms that are moderate or more severe with your physician, preferably a gynecologist. It is important for your health that you discuss any disabling symptoms at all with your gynecologist. Even if you have some mild symptoms, you may want to check them off and bring them to the attention of your gynecologist. Nothing is to be gained by suffering in silence.

"Sternberg's Triangular Love Scale" (Chapter 7, p. 217)

First add your scores for the items on each of the three components-intimacy, passion, and commitment-and divide each total by 15. This procedure will yield an average rating for each subscale. An average rating of 5 points on a particular subscale indicates a moderate level of the component represented by the subscale. A higher rating indicates a greater level. A lower rating indicates a lower level. Examining your ratings on these components will give you an idea of the degree to which you perceive your love relationship to be characterized by these three components of love. For example, you might find that passion is stronger than commitment, a pattern that is common during the early stages of an intense romantic relationship. You might find it interesting to complete the questionnaire a few months or perhaps a year or so from now to see how your feelings about your relationship change over time. You might also ask your partner to complete the scale so that the two of you can compare your respective scores. Comparing your ratings for each component with those of your partner will give you an idea of the degree to which you and your partner see your relationship in a similar way.

Sternberg (1988) reports the results of administering the scale to a sample of 50 men and 51 women (average age, 31 years) from the New Haven, Connecticut, area who were either married or currently involved in a close relationship. Average scores for the three components were 7.39 points for intimacy, 6.51 points for passion, and 7.20 points for commitment. High scores (scores representing approximately the top 15% of scores) were 8.6 points for intimacy, 8.2 points for passion, and 8.7 points for commitment. Low scores, representing the bottom 15% of scores, were 6.2 points, 4.9 points, and 5.7 points for the three components, respectively. Because romantic ardor may be more difficult to maintain over time, the lower average scores for passion may reflect the length of the relationships in which the people in the sample were involved, which averaged 6.3 years. Although you may want to compare your scores with those from this sample, we caution that the Sternberg sample was small and most likely does not accurately represent the general population.

"Pro-Choice or Pro-Life? Where Do You Stand?" (Chapter 12, p. 393)

First tally your scores for items 1, 3, 7, 8, 9, 11, 13, 14, 17, and 20. This score represents your support for a *pro-choice* point of view: _____.

Now tally your scores for items 2, 4, 5, 6, 10, 12, 15, 16, 18, and 19. This score represents your support for a *pro-life* point of view: _____.

Now subtract your pro-choice score from your pro-life score. Write the difference, including the sign ±, here: _____. A positive score indicates agreement with a pro-life philosophy. A negative score indicates agreement with a pro-choice philosophy. The higher your score, the more strongly you agree with the philosophy you endorsed. Scores may range from −40 to +40 points.

One sample of 230 undergraduate students (115 of each gender) obtained a mean score of −7.48 points and a median score of −13.33 points (Parsons et al., 1990). This indicates that the students tended to be pro-choice in their attitudes. Another sample of 38 graduate students (31 women and 7 men) obtained mean scores of −11 to −12 points and median scores of −17 to −18 points on two separate occasions. Scores for other samples may vary.

"STI Attitude Scale" (Chapter 16, p. 512)

Scores on this scale are interpreted in terms of a predisposition to high-risk sexual behavior. The scale is composed of three subscales, that measure your predisposition to high-risk behavior on the basis of your beliefs about STIs (items 1–9), your feelings about STIs (items 10–18), and your intentions to act (items 19–27). Calculate a total for each subscale and for the total scale by using the following point values.

For items 1, 10 through 14, 16, and 25:

Strongly Agree = 5 points
Agree = 4 points
Undecided = 3 points
Disagree = 2 points
Strongly Disagree = 1 point

For items 2 through −9, 15, 17 through −24, 26, and 27:

Strongly Agree = 1 point
Agree = 2 points
Undecided = 3 points
Disagree = 4 points
Strongly Disagree = 5 points

Subtotal for Beliefs subscale (items 1–9): _____
Subtotal for Feelings subscale (items 10–18): _____
Subtotal for Intentions to Act subscale (items 19–27): _____
Total score (based on all items): _____

The higher your subscale and total scores, the greater the likelihood that your attitudes, feelings, and intentions put you at risk of contracting an STI. The lower your scores, the less risk you are likely to incur. Although we currently have no norms, we suggest that subscale scores higher than 27 points and total scores higher than 81 points indicate that your responses are weighted more toward risky than safe behavior. We suggest that you weigh your particular risk by examining not only your scores, but your responses to the individual scale items as well. Ask yourself, "How do my responses to these items increase or decrease my risk of contracting an STI?" Then ask yourself, "How might I change my attitudes to reduce my chances of contracting an STI?"

"Cultural Myths That Create a Climate That Supports Rape" (Chapter 18, p. 590)

Actually, each item, with the exception of item 2, represents a cultural myth that supports rape. These myths tend to view sex as an adversarial game, stereotype women as flirtatious and deceitful, and blame the victim.

References

Abal, Y. N., Maríín, J. A. L., & Sánchez, S. R. (2003). A new paraphilia of the XXI century: Chat-scatophilia. *Archivos Hispanoamericanos de Sexologíía, 9*(1), 81–104.

Abbey, A., Saenz, C., Buck, P. O., Parkhill, M. R., & Hayman, L. W., Jr. (2006). The effects of acute alcohol consumption, cognitive reserve, partner risk, and gender on sexual decision making. *Journal of Studies on Alcohol, 67*(1), 113–121.

Abell, J., Locke, A., Condor, S., Gibson, S., & Stevenson, C. (2006). Trying similarity, doing difference: The role of interviewer self-disclosure in interview talk with young people. *Qualitative Research, 6*(2), 221–244.

Abelson, H., et al. (1970). Public attitudes toward and experience with erotic materials. In *Technical reports of the commission on obscenity and pornography.* Vol. 6. Washington, DC: U.S. Government Printing Office.

Ackerman, D. (1991). *The moon by whale light.* New York: Random House.

ACOG (The American College of Obstetricians and Gynecologists). (2003, July 31). *Weighing the pros and cons of cesarean delivery.* ACOG news release. [Online]. www.acog.com/from_home/publications/press_releases/nr07-31-03-3.cfm.

Adams, H. E., Wright, L. W., Jr., & Lohr, B. A. (1996). Is homophobia associated with homosexual arousal? *Journal of Abnormal Psychology, 105,* 440–445.

Adams, H., & Phillips, L. (2006). Experiences of two-spirit lesbian and gay Native Americans: An argument for standpoint theory in identity research. *Identity, 6*(3), 273–291.

Adams, K. M. (2003). Clergy sex abuse: A commentary on celibacy. *Sexual Addiction & Compulsivity: The Journal of Treatment and Prevention, 10*(2–3), 91–92.

Adams, N. (2006). Systemic therapy techniques for sexual difficulties. In Hiller, J., et al. (Eds.). *Sex, mind, and emotion: Innovation in psychological theory and practice* (pp. 209–227). London, UK: Karnac Books.

A flock with changing views. (1993, August 1). *The New York Times,* p. A26.

Agrawal, A. (1997). Gendered bodies: The case of the "third gender" in India. *Contributions to Indian Sociology, 31,* 273–97.

Alexander, G. M. (2003). An evolutionary perspective of sex-typed toy preferences: Pink, blue, and the brain. *Archives of Sexual Behavior, 32*(1), 7–14.

Alexander, J. (2006). A critical introduction to queer theory. *Sexualities, 9*(1), 115–117.

Allen, E. S., & Atkins, D. C. (2005). The multidimensional and developmental nature of infidelity: Practical applications. *Journal of Clinical Psychology, 61*(11), 1371–1382.

Allen, P. L. (2000). *The wages of sin: Sex and disease, past and present.* Chicago: University of Chicago Press.

Allyn, D. (2001). *Make love, not war: The sexual revolution: An unfettered history.* London: Routledge.

Aloni, M., & Bernieri, F. J. (2004). Is love blind? The effects of experience and infatuation on the perception of love. *Journal of Nonverbal Behavior, 28*(4), 287–295.

Althof, S. E. (1994). Paper presented at the annual meeting of the American Urological Association, San Francisco, CA.

Altman, L. K. (2000, July 11). Mystery factor is pondered at AIDS talk: Circumcision. *The New York Times.* [Online].

Alzate, H., & Hoch, Z. (1986). The "G spot" and "female ejaculation": A current appraisal. *Journal of Sex and Marital Therapy, 12*(3), 211–220.

Alzate, H., & Londono, M. L. (1984). Vaginal erotic sensitivity. *Journal of Sex and Marital Therapy, 10,* 49–56.

Amato, P. R. (2006). Marital discord, divorce, and children's well-being: Results from a 20-year longitudinal study of two generations. In Clarke–Stewart, A., & Dunn, J. (Eds.). *Families count: Effects on child and adolescent development* (pp. 179–202). The Jacobs Foundation series on adolescence. New York: Cambridge University Press.

Amato, P. R., & Afifi, T. D. (2006). Feeling caught between parents: Adult children's relations with parents and subjective well-being. *Journal of Marriage and Family, 68*(1), 222–235.

American Academy of Family Physicians. (2006). *Depo-Provera: An injectable contraceptive.* [Online]. http://familydoctor.org/043.xml?printxml.

American Academy of Pediatrics. (2005). *Breastfeeding and the use of human milk. Pediatrics, 115,* 496–506. [Online].

American Cancer Society. (2006). *Cancer facts & figures 2006.* [Online]. www.cancer.org/downloads/STT/CAFF2006f4PWSecured.pdf.

American Fertility Association. (2006, February). [Online]. www.theafa.org.

American Psychiatric Association. (2000). *Diagnostic and statistical manual of mental disorders. 4th ed. DSM-IV-TR.* Washington, DC: Author.

American Psychological Association (1998, March 16). Sexual harassment: Myths and realities. APA public information home page. [Online]. www.apa.org.

Amodeo, M., Griffin, M. K., Fassler, I. R., Clay, C. M., & Ellis, M. A. (2006). Childhood sexual abuse among black women and white women from two-parent families. *Child Maltreatment, 11*(3), 237–246.

Amodio, D. M., & Showers, C. J. (2005). "Similarity breeds liking" revisited: The moderating role of commitment. *Journal of Social and Personal Relationships, 22*(6), 817–836.

Andersen, M. L., Bignotto, M., & Tufik, S. (2003). The effect of apomorphine on genital reflexes in male rats deprived of paradoxical sleep. *Physiology & Behavior, 80*(2–3), 211–215.

Andersen, M. L., & Tufik, S. (2005). Effects of progesterone blockade over cocaine-induced genital reflexes of paradoxical sleep-deprived male rats. *Hormones and Behavior, 47*(4), 477–484.

Anderson, E. R., Greene, S. M., Hetherington, E. M., & Clingempeel, W. G. (1999). Dynamics of parental remarriage: Adolescent, parent, and sibling influences. In Hetherington, E. M. (Ed.). *Coping with divorce, single parenting, and remarriage: A risk and resiliency perspective* (pp. 295–319). Hillsdale, NJ: Lawrence Erlbaum Associates.

Anderson, J. K., et al. (2002). Andropause: Knowledge and perceptions among the general public and health care professionals. *Journals of Gerontology: Series A: Biological Sciences & Medical Sciences, 57A*(12).

Anderson, S. E., et al. (2003). Relative weight and race influence average age at menarche: Results from two nationally representative surveys of U.S. girls studied 25 years apart. *Pediatrics, 111,* 844–850.

Anderssen, N., Amlie, C., & Ytteroy, E. A. (2002). Outcomes for children with lesbian or gay parents: A review of studies from 1978 to 2000. *Scandinavian Journal of Psychology, 43*(4), 335–351.

Appel, P. W., Piculell, R., Jansky, H. K., & Griffy, K. (2006). Assessing alcohol and other drug problems (AOD) among sexually transmitted disease (STD) clinic patients with a modified CAGE-A: Implications for AOD intervention services and STD prevention. *American Journal of Drug and Alcohol Abuse, 32*(2), 225–236.

Apperloo, M. J. A., et al. (2003). In the mood for sex: The value of androgens. *Journal of Sex & Marital Therapy, 29*(2), 87–102.

Archer, J., & Vaughan, A. E. (2001). Evolutionary theories of rape. *Psychology, Evolution & Gender, 3*(1), 95–101.

Argentieri, S. (2005). Incest yesterday and today: From conflict to ambiguity. In Ambrosio, G. (Ed.). *On incest: Psychoanalytic perspectives* (pp. 17–49). London: Karnac Books.

Arriaga, X. B., & Rusbult, C. E. (1998). Standing in my partner's shoes: Partner perspective taking and reactions to accommodative dilemmas. *Personality & Social Psychology Bulletin, 24*(9), 927–948.

Arthur, B. I., Jr., et al. (1998). Sexual behaviour in *Drosophila* is irreversibly programmed during critical period. *Current Biology, 8*(21), 1187–1190.

Ascher, N. (2006, July 10.) *Fight ignorance before it's too late.* [Online]. www.classicalvalues.com/archives/003848.html.

Ashley–Koch, A., Yang, Q., & Olney, R. S. (2000). Sickle hemoglobin (Hb S) allele and sickle cell disease. *American Journal of Epidemiology, 151*(9), 839–845.

Astley, S. J., & Clarren, S. K. (2001). Measuring the facial phenotype of individuals with prenatal alcohol exposure: Correlations with brain dysfunction. *Alcohol & Alcoholism, 36*(2), 147–159.

Aveline, D. (2006). "Did I have blinders on or what?": Retrospective sense making by parents of gay sons recalling their sons' earlier years. *Journal of Family Issues, 27*(6), 777–802.

Avis, N. E. (2003). Depression during the menopausal transition. *Psychology of Women Quarterly, 27*(2), 91–100.

Bäckström T., et al. (2003). The role of hormones and hormonal treatments in premenstrual syndrome. *CNS Drugs, 17*(5), 325–342.

Bader, M. (2003). *Arousal: The secret logic of sexual fantasies.* New York: Griffin Trade Paperback.

Bagley, C., & D'Augelli, A. R. (2000). Suicidal behaviour in gay, lesbian, and bisexual youth. *British Medical Journal, 320,* 1617–1618.

Bailes, E., et al. (2003). Hybrid origin of SIV in chimpanzees. *Science, 300*(5626), 1713.

Bailey, J. M. (1999). Homosexuality and mental illness. *Archives of General Psychiatry, 56*(10), 883–884.

Bailey, J. M. (2003a). Personal communication.

Bailey, J. M. (2003b). *The man who would be queen: The science of gender-bending and transsexualism.* Washington, DC: Joseph Henry Press.

Bailey, J. M., & Pillard, R. C. (1991). A genetic study of male sexual orientation. *Archives of General Psychiatry, 48,* 1089–1096.

Bailey, J. M., & Zucker, K. J. (1995). Childhood sex-typed behavior and sexual orientation: A conceptual analysis and quantitative review. *Developmental Psychology, 31,* 43–55.

Bailey, J. M., Dunne, M. P., & Martin, N. G. (2000a). Genetic and environmental influences on sexual orientation and its correlates in an Australian twin sample. *Journal of Personality & Social Psychology, 78*(3), 524–536.

Bailey, J. M., et al. (1999). A family history study of male sexual orientation using three independent samples. *Behavior Genetics, 29*(2), 79–86.

Bailey, R. C. (2000). A study in rural Uganda of heterosexual transmission of human immunodeficiency virus. *New England Journal of Medicine, 343*(5).

Bailey, R. C., et al. (2007). Male circumcision for HIV prevention in young men in Kisumu, Kenya: A randomised controlled trial. *Lancet, 369,* 643–656.

Bakalar, N. (2005, November 22). Premature births increase along with C-sections. *The New York Times,* p. F8.

Ball, H. N. (2005). Sexual offending on elderly women: A review. *Journal of Forensic Psychiatry and Psychology, 16*(1), 127–138.

Balsam, K. F., et al. (2004). Culture, trauma, and wellness: A comparison of heterosexual and lesbian, gay, bisexual, and two-spirit Native Americans. *Cultural Diversity & Ethnic Minority Psychology, 10*(3), 287–301.

Balter, L., & Tamis–LeMonda, C. S. (Eds.). (1999). *Child psychology: A handbook of contemporary issues.* Philadelphia, PA: Psychology Press.

Bamgbose, O. (2002). Teenage prostitution and the future of the female adolescent in Nigeria. *International Journal of Offender Therapy & Comparative Criminology, 46*(5), 569–585.

Bancroft, J. (Ed.). (2003). *Sexual development in childhood.* Bloomington: Indiana University Press.

Bancroft, J., Carnes, L., & Janssen, E. (2005a). Unprotected anal intercourse in HIV-positive and HIV-negative gay men: The relevance of sexual arousability, mood, sensation seeking, and erectile problems. *Archives of Sexual Behavior, 34,* 299–305.

Bancroft, J., Carnes, L., Janssen, E., Goodrich, D., & Long, J. S. (2005b). Erectile and ejaculatory problems in gay and heterosexual men. *Archives of Sexual Behavior, 34*(3), 285–297.

Bancroft, J., et al. (2005c). The relevance of the dual control model to male sexual dysfunction: The Kinsey Institute/BASRT collaborative project. *Sexual & Relationship Therapy, 20,* 13–30.

Bancroft, J., Loftus, J., & Long, J. S. (2003). Distress about sex: A national survey of women in heterosexual relationships. *Archives of Sexual Behavior, 32*(3), 193–208.

Barak, A. (2005). Sexual harassment on the Internet. *Social Science Computer Review, 23*(1), 77–92.

Barash, D. P., & Lipton, J. E. (2001). *The myth of monogamy.* New York: Freeman.

Barnard, N. D., Scialli, A. R., Hurlock, D., & Bertron, P. (2000). Diet and sex-hormone binding globulin, dysmenorrhea, and premenstrual symptoms. *Obstetrics & Gynecology, 95,* 245–250.

Barnes, M. L., & Sternberg, R. J. (1997). A hierarchical model of love and its prediction of satisfaction in close relationships. In Sternberg, R. J., & Hojjat, M. (Eds.). *Satisfaction in close relationships* (pp. 79–101). New York: Guilford Press.

Barnett, J. E., & Dunning, C. (2003). Clinical perspectives on elderly sexuality. *Archives of Sexual Behavior, 32*(3), 295–296.

Barney, D., & Feenberg, A. (Eds.). (2004). *Community in the digital age: Philosophy and practice.* Lanham, MD: Rowman & Littlefield.

Barrett, M. B. (1990). *Invisible lives: The truth about millions of women-loving women.* New York: Harper & Row (Perennial Library).

Barrett, S. E., Chin, J. L., Comas–Diaz, L., Espin, O., Greene, B., & McGoldrick, M. (2005). Multicultural feminist therapy: Theory in context. *Women & Therapy, 28*(3–4), 27–61.

Barsky, J. L., Friedman, M. A., & Rosen, R. C. (2006). Sexual dysfunction and chronic illness: The role of flexibility in coping. *Journal of Sex & Marital Therapy, 32*(3), 235–253.

Barth, R. P., et al. (2002). Methodological lessons from the National Survey of Child and Adolescent Well-Being: The first three years of the USA's first national probability study of children and families investigated for abuse and neglect. *Children & Youth Services Review, 24*(6–7), 513–541.

Bartolo, K. C. (2005). Mother–daughter incest: A guide for helping professionals. *Journal of Family Studies, 11*(2), 328–329.

Basile, K. C. (2002). Attitudes toward wife rape: Effects of social background and victim status. *Violence & Victims, 17*(3), 341–354.

Basow, S. A., & Rubenfeld, K. (2003). "Troubles talk": Effects of gender and gender-typing. *Sex Roles, 48*(3–4), 183–187.

Basson, R. (2000, May). Paper presented at the annual meeting of the American College of Obstetricians and Gynecologists, San Francisco, CA.

Bastian, L. A., Smith, C. M., & Nanda, K. (2003). Is this woman perimenopausal? *Journal of the American Medical Association, 289,* 895–902.

Bauerle, S. Y., Amirkhan, J. H., & Hupka, R. B. (2002). An attribution theory analysis of romantic jealousy. *Motivation & Emotion, 26*(4), 297–319.

Baumeister, R. F., Catanese, K. R., & Vohs, K. D. (2001). Is there a gender difference in strength of sex drive? Theoretical views, conceptual distinctions, and a review of relevant evidence. *Personality & Social Psychology Review, 5*(3), 242–273.

Bean, J. L. (2002). Expressions of female sexuality. *Journal of Sex & Marital Therapy, 28*(Suppl. 1), 29–38.

Bearak, B. (2006, July 9). The bride price. *The New York Times Magazine.* [Online].

Becerra, L., Breiter, H. C., Wise, R., Gonzalez, R. G., & Borsook, D. (2001). Reward circuitry activation by noxious thermal stimuli. *Neuron, 32*(5), 927–946.

Becquet, R., et al. (2005). Acceptability of exclusive breast-feeding with early cessation to prevent HIV transmission through breast milk. *Journal of Acquired Immune Deficiency Syndromes, 40*(5), 600–608.

Behrendt, N., Buhl, N., & Seidl, S. (2002). The lethal paraphiliac syndrome: Accidental autoerotic deaths in four women and a review of the literature. *International Journal of Legal Medicine, 116*(3), 148–152.

Belgrave, F. Z., van Oss Marian, B., & Chambers, D. B. (2000). Cultural, contextual, and intrapersonal predictors of risky sexual attitudes among urban African American girls in early adolescence. *Cultural Diversity and Ethnic Minority Psychology, 6*(3), 309–322.

Bell, A. P., & Weinberg, M. S. (1978). *Homosexualities: A study of diversity among men and women.* New York: Simon & Schuster.

Bell, A. P., Weinberg, M. S., & Hammersmith, S. K. (1981). *Sexual preference: Its development in men and women.* Bloomington, IN: University of Indiana Press.

Bellavia, G., & Murray, S. (2003). Did I do that? Self esteem-related differences in reactions to romantic partner's mood. *Personal Relationships, 10*(1), 77–95.

Belluck, P. (2006, February 6). Fugitive in gay bar attacks dies after shootout with Arkansas police. *The New York Times.* [Online].

Bem, S. L. (1975). Sex role adaptability: One consequence of psychological androgyny. *Journal of Personality and Social Psychology, 31,* 634–643.

Bem, S. L. (1983). Gender schema theory and its implications for child development: Raising gender-aschematic children in a gender-schematic society. *Signs, 8,* 598–616.

Bem, S. L. (1993). *The lenses of gender.* New Haven: Yale University Press.

Bem, S. L., Martyna, W., & Watson, C. (1976). Sex typing and androgyny: Further explorations of the expressive domain. *Journal of Personality and Social Psychology, 34,* 1016–1023.

Benbow, C. P., Lubinski, D., Shea, D. L., & Eftekhari–Sanjani, H. (2000). Sex differences in mathematical reasoning ability at age 13: Their status 20 years later. *Psychological Science, 11,* 474–480.

Benotsch, E. G., & Kalichman, S. C. (2002). Preventing HIV and AIDS. In Jason, L. A., & Glenwick, D. S. (Eds.), *Innovative strategies for promoting health and mental health across the life span* (pp. 205–226). New York: Springer Publishing.

Ben-Ze'ev, A. (2003). Privacy, emotional closeness, and openness in cyberspace. *Computers in Human Behavior, 19*(4), 451–467.

Ben-Zur, H. (2003). Peer risk behavior and denial of HIV/AIDS among adolescents. *Sex Education, 3*(1), 75–85.

Berdahl, J. L., & Moore, C. (2006). Workplace harassment: Double jeopardy for minority women. *Journal of Applied Psychology, 91*(2), 426–436.

Berger, L. (2002, December 10). After long hiatus, new contraceptives emerge. *The New York Times.*

Berke, R. L. (1997, June 15). Suddenly, the new politics of morality. *The New York Times,* p. E3.

Berke, R. L. (1998, August 2). Chasing the polls on gay rights. *The New York Times,* p. WK3.

Berman, J. R., & Berman, L. A., et al. (2001). Effect of sildenafil on subjective and physiologic parameters of the female sexual response in women with sexual arousal disorder. *Journal of Sex & Marital Therapy, 27*(5), 411–420.

Berman, L. A. (2000). Paper presented at the annual meeting of the American Urological Association, Atlanta, GA.

Berner, W., Berger, P., & Hill, A. (2003). Sexual sadism. *International Journal of Offender Therapy and Comparative Criminology, 47*(4), 383–395.

Bernstein, I. M., et al. (2005). Maternal smoking and its association with birth weight. *Obstetrics & Gynecology, 106,* 986–991.

Bernstein, J., et al. (2006). Racial and ethnic differences in health and health care: Lessons from an inner-city patient population actively using heroin and cocaine. *Journal of Ethnicity in Substance Abuse, 5*(2), 35–50.

Berry, D. A., et al. (2005). Effect of screening and adjuvant therapy on mortality from breast cancer. *The New England Journal of Medicine, 353,* 1784–1792.

Berscheid, E. (2003). On stepping on land mines. In Sternberg, R. J. (Ed.). *Psychologists defying the crowd: Stories of those who battled the establishment and won* (pp. 33–44). Washington, DC: American Psychological Association.

Berscheid, E., & Reis, H. T. (1998). Attraction and close relationships. In Gilbert, D. T., Fiske, S. T., et al. (Eds.). *The handbook of social psychology* (pp. 193–281). Vol. 2, 4th ed. New York: McGraw-Hill.

Berscheid, E., & Walster, E. (1978). *Interpersonal attraction.* Reading, MA: Addison-Wesley.

Bhugra, D. (2004). Literature update: A critical review. *Sexual and Relationship Therapy, 19*(2), 201–208.

Bhugra, D. (2005). Queer theory. *Sexual and Relationship Therapy, 20*(4), 476.

Bhugra, D., Rahman, Q., & Bhintade, R. (2006). Sexual fantasy in gay men in India: A comparison with heterosexual men. *Sexual and Relationship Therapy, 21*(2), 197–207.

Bialy, M., & Sachs, B. D. (2002). Androgen implants in medial amygdala briefly maintain noncontact erection in castrated male rats. *Hormones & Behavior, 42*(3), 345–355.

Bianchi, S. M., & Spain, D. (1997). *Women, work and family in America.* Population Reference Bureau.

Billy, J. O. G., et al. (1993). The sexual behavior of men in the United States. *Family Planning Perspectives, 25,* 52–60.

Binik, Y. M. (2005). Should dyspareunia be retained as a sexual dysfunction in *DSM-V*? A painful classification decision. *Archives of Sexual Behavior, 34*(1), 11–21.

Blackwell, D. L., & Lichter, D. T. (2004). Homogamy among dating, cohabiting, and married couples. *Sociological Quarterly, 45*(4), 719–737.

Blake, S. M., et al. (2003). Condom availability programs in Massachusetts high schools: Relationships with condom use and sexual behav-ior. *American Journal of Public Health, 93,* 955–962.

Blanchard, R. (1988). Nonhomosexual gender dysphoria. *Journal of Sex Research, 24,* 188–193.

Blanchard, R. (1989). The concept of autogynephilia and the typology of male gender dysphoria. *Journal of Nervous & Mental Disease, 177*(10), 616–623.

Blanchard, R., Steiner, B. W., & Clemmensen, L. H. (1985). Gender dysphoria, gender reorientation, and the clinical management of transsexualism. *Journal of Consulting and Clinical Psychology, 53,* 295–304.

Blanker, M. H., et al. (2001). Erectile and ejaculatory dysfunction in a community-based sample of men 50 to 78 years old: Prevalence, concern, and relation to sexual activity. *Urology, 57*(4), 763–768.

Bletzner, K. V., & Koss, M. P. (2006). After rape among three populations in the southwest: A time of mourning, a time for recovery. *Violence Against Women, 12*(1), 5–29.

Blickstein, I., Goldman, R. D., & Mazkereth, R. (2000). Risk for one or two very low birth weight twins: A population study. *Obstetrics & Gynecology, 96*(3), 400–402.

Bloch, M., Rotenberg, N., Koren, D., & Ehud, K. (2006). Risk factors for early postpartum depressive symptoms. *General Hospital Psychiatry, 28*(1), 3–8.

Blumstein, P., & Schwartz, P. (1990). Intimate relationships and the creation of sexuality. In McWhirter, D. P., Sanders, S. A., & Reinisch, J. M. (Eds.). *Homosexuality/heterosexuality: Concepts of sexual orientation* (pp. 307–320). New York: Oxford University Press.

Bockting, W. O., & Fung, L. C. T. (2006). Genital reconstruction and gender identity disorders. In Sarwer, D. B., et al. (Eds.). *Psychological aspects of reconstructive and cosmetic plastic surgery: Clinical, empirical, and ethical perspectives* (pp. 207–319). New York: Lippincott Williams & Wilkins.

Bodenmann, G., Ledermann, T., Blattner, D., & Galluzzo, C. (2006). Associations among everyday stress, critical life events, and sexual problems. *Journal of Nervous and Mental Disease, 194*(7), 494–501.

Bogin, G. Y. (2006). Out of the darkness: Male adolescents and the experience of sexual victimization. *School Social Work Journal, 30*(2), 1–21.

Boies, S. C. (2002). University students' uses of and reactions to online sexual information and entertainment: Links to online and offline sexual behavior. *Canadian Journal of Human Sexuality, 11*(3), 77–89.

Boland, E. (2000, October 19). In modern e-mail romance "trash" is just a click away. *The New York Times.* [Online].

Bolton, J. M., Sareen, J., & Reiss, J. P. (2006). Genital anaesthesia persisting six years after sertraline discontinuation. *Journal of Sex & Marital Therapy, 32*(4), 327–330.

Born, L., Soares, C. N., Phillips, S., Jung, M., & Steiner, M. (2006). Women and reproductive-related trauma. In Yehuda, R. (Ed.). (2006). *Psychobiology of posttraumatic stress disorders: A decade of progress* (pp. 491–494). Vol. 1071. New York: Blackwell Publishing.

Boros, S., Mateuca, A., & Matus, M. (2005). The role of social identity in attributions—evaluating the guilt in rape assault. *Cognitie Creier Comportament, 9*(1), 35–57.

Boss, S., & Maltz, W. (2001). *Private thoughts: Exploring the power of women's sexual fantasies.* New York: New World Library.

Boston Women's Health Book Collective. (2005). *Our bodies, ourselves: A new edition for a new era.* New York: Touchstone.

Bowes-Sperry, L., & O'Leary–Kelly, A. M. (2005). To act or not to act: The dilemma faced by sexual harassment observers. *Academy of Management Review, 30*(2), 288–306.

Bowlby, J. (1969). *Attachment and loss.* Vol. 1. New York: Basic Books.

Boxer, S. (2000, July 22). Truth or lies? In sex surveys, you never know. *The New York Times.* [Online].

Boy to sue city over tryst with teacher. (2000, April 14). Reuters News Agency.

Bozell, B. (2005, December 30). Coming in 2006: Group marriage TV? [Online]. www.townhall .com/opinion/columns/brentbozell/2005/12/ 30/180704.html.

Bradford, J. M. W. (1998). Treatment of men with paraphilia. *New England Journal of Medicine, 338,* 464–465.

Bradford, J. M. W. (2001). The neurobiology, neuropharmacology, and pharmacological treatment of the paraphilias and compulsive sexual behaviour. *Canadian Journal of Psychiatry, 46*(1), 26–34.

Bradley, S. J., Oliver, G. D., Chernick, A. B., & Zucker, K. J. (1998). Experiment of nurture: Ablatio penis at 2 months, sex reassignment at 7 months, and a psychosexual follow-up in young adulthood. *Pediatrics, 102*(1), e9.

Braithwaite, D. O., Olson, L. N., Golish, T. D., Soukup, C., & Turman, P. (2001). "Becoming a family": Developmental processes represented in blended family discourse. *Journal of Applied Communication Research, 29*(3), 221–247.

Bramlett, M. D., & Mosher, W. D. (2002). *Cohabitation, marriage, divorce, and remarriage.* National Center for Health Statistics, Vital Health Statistics, 23(22). www.cdc.gov/ nchs/data/series/sr_23/sr23_022.pdf.

Bridges, A. (2006, August 9). HIV patients get first once-a-day pill. www.msnbc.msn.com/id/ 13830719/#StoryContinued.

Briken, P., Hill, A., & Berner, W. (2003). Pharmacotherapy of paraphilias with long-acting agonists of luteinizing hormone–releasing hormone: A systematic review. *Journal of Clinical Psychiatry, 64*(8), 890–897.

Briken, P., Hill, A., Nika, E., & Berner, W. (2005). Obscene telephone calls—Relations to paraphilias, paraphilia related disorders and stalking. *Psychiatrische Praxis, 32*(6), 304–307.

Brin, D. J. (2004). The use of rituals in grieving for a miscarriage or stillbirth. *Women & Therapy, 27*(3–4), 123–132.

Brisch, K. H., et al. (2005). Effects of previous pregnancy loss on level of maternal anxiety after prenatal ultrasound screening for fetal malformation. *Journal of Loss & Trauma, 10*(2), 131–153.

Broder, M. S., Kanouse, D. E., Mittman, B. S., & Bernstein, S. J. (2000). The appropriateness of recommendations for hysterectomy. *Obstetrics & Gynecology, 95,* 199–206.

Brodkin, E. S., et al. (2002). Identification of quantitative trait loci that affect aggressive behavior in mice. *The Journal of Neuroscience, 22*(3), 1165–1170.

Brody, J. E. (1994, March 21). Notions of beauty transcend culture, new study suggests. *The New York Times,* p. A14.

Brody, J. E. (1997, February 12). Abortion doesn't affect well-being, study says. *The New York Times.* [Online].

Brody, J. E. (2000, May 16). Cybersex gives birth to a psychological disorder. *The New York Times,* pp. F7, F12.

Brody, J. E. (2000, May 16). Cybersex gives birth to a psychological disorder. *The New York Times,* pp. F7, F12.

Brody, S. (2006). Blood pressure reactivity to stress is better for people who recently had penile–vaginal intercourse than for people who had other or no sexual activity. *Biological Psychology, 71*(2), 214–222.

Brody, S., & Krüger, T. H. C. (2005). The post-orgasmic prolactin increase following intercourse is greater than following masturbation and suggests greater satiety. *Biological Psychology, 71*(3), 312–315.

Bronner, E. (1998, February 1). "Just say maybe. No sexology, please. We're Americans." *The New York Times,* p. WK6.

Bross, D. C. (2005). Invited commentary: Minimizing risks to children when they access the World Wide Web. *Child Abuse & Neglect, 29*(7), 749–752.

Broude, G. J., & Greene, S. J. (1976). Cross-cultural codes on twenty sexual attitudes and practices. *Ethnology, 15,* 409–429.

Brown, D. (2003). Pornography and erotica. In Bryant, J., Roskos–Ewoldsen, D., & Cantor, J. (Eds.). *Communication and emotion: Essays in honor of Dolf Zillmann* (pp. 221–253). LEA's communication series. Hillsdale, NJ: Lawrence Erlbaum Associates.

Brown, G. R., & Haaser, R. C. (2005). Sexual disorders. In Levenson, J. L. (Ed.). *The American psychiatric publishing textbook of psychosomatic medicine* (pp. 359–386). Washington, DC: American Psychiatric Publishing.

Brown, L. M., McNatt, P. S., & Cooper, G. D. (2003). Ingroup romantic preferences among Jewish and non-Jewish white undergraduates. *International Journal of Intercultural Relations, 27*(3), 335–354.

Brown, L. S. (2005). Prostitution, trafficking and traumatic stress. *Journal of Trauma & Dissociation, 6*(3), 143–145.

Brown, R. A. (1994). Romantic love and the spouse selection criteria of male and female Korean college students. *The Journal of Social Psychology, 134*(2), 183–189.

Brown, R., Balousek, S., Mundt, M., & Fleming, M. (2005). Methadone maintenance and male sexual dysfunction. *Journal of Addictive Diseases, 24*(2), 91–106.

Brown, T. (2002). A proposed model of bisexual identity development that elaborates on experiential differences of women and men. *Journal of Bisexuality, 2*(4), 67–91.

Browning, C. R. (2002). Trauma or transition: A life-course perspective on the link between childhood sexual experiences and men's adult well-being. *Social Science Research, 31*(4), 473–510.

Browning, J. R., Hatfield, E., Kessler, D., & Levine, T. (2000). Sexual motives, gender, and sexual behavior. *Archives of Sexual Behavior, 29*(2), 135–153.

Bullough, V. L. (2002). Masturbation: A historical overview. *Journal of Psychology & Human Sexuality, 14*(2–3), 17–33.

Bulterys, M., et al. (2004). Rapid HIV-1 testing during labor: A multicenter study. *Journal of the American Medical Association, 292*(2), 219–223.

Bunting, L., & McAuley, C. (2004). Teenage pregnancy and motherhood: The contribution of support. *Child & Family Social Work, 9*(2), 207–215.

Burgess, A. W., & Morgenbesser, L. I. (2005). Sexual violence and seniors. *Brief Treatment and Crisis Intervention, 5*(2), 193–202.

Burt, M. R. (1980). Cultural myths and supports for rape. *Journal of Personality and Social Psychology, 38,* 217–230.

Bushman, B. J., Bonacci, A. M., van Dijk, M., & Baumeister, R. F. (2003). Narcissism, sexual refusal, and aggression: Testing a narcissistic reactance model of sexual coercion. *Journal of Personality and Social Psychology, 84*(5), 1027–1040.

Buss, D. M. (1994). *The evolution of desire: Strategies of human mating.* New York: Basic Books.

Buss, D. M. (2003). The dangerous passion: Why jealousy is as necessary as love and sex. *Archives of Sexual Behavior, 32*(1), 79–80.

Buss, D. M. (Ed.). (2005). *The handbook of evolutionary psychology.* Hoboken, NJ: John Wiley & Sons.

Butler, J. (1993). *Bodies that matter: On the discursive limits of sex.* New York: Routledge.

Butler, J. (2003). *Kritik der ethischen Gewalt.* Adorno lectures, 2002. Frankfurt am Main: Institut fur Sozialforschung an der Johann Wolfgang Goethe-Universitat.

Byerly, M. J., et al. (2006). Sexual dysfunction associated with second-generation antipsychotics in outpatients with schizophrenia or schizoaffective disorder: An empirical evaluation of olanzapine, risperidone, and quetiapine. *Schizophrenia Research, 86*(1–3), 244–250.

Byers, E. S., & Grenier, G. (2003). Premature or rapid ejaculation: Heterosexual couples' perceptions of men's ejaculatory behavior. *Archives of Sexual Behavior, 32*(3), 261–270.

Byrd, J., Hyde, J. S., DeLamater, J. D., & Plant, E. A. (1998). Sexuality during pregnancy and the year postpartum. *Journal of Family Practice, 47*(4), 305–308.

Cacioppo, J. T., Hawkley, L. C., & Bernston, G. G. (2003). The anatomy of loneliness. *Current Directions in Psychological Science, 12*(3), 71–74.

Cado, S., & Leitenberg, H. (1990). Guilt reactions to sexual fantasies during intercourse. *Archives of Sexual Behavior, 19,* 49–64.

Caffaro, J. V., & Conn– Caffaro, A. (2005). Treating sibling abuse families. *Aggression and Violent Behavior, 10*(5), 604–623.

Call, V., Sprecher, S., & Schwartz, P. (1995). The incidence and frequency of marital sex in a national sample. *Journal of Marriage and the Family, 57,* 639–652.

Campbell, R. (2006). Rape survivors' experiences with the legal and medical systems: Do rape victim advocates make a difference? *Violence Against Women, 12*(1), 30–45.

Campbell, R., & Wasco, S. M. (2005). Understanding rape and sexual assault: 20 years of progress and future directions. *Journal of Interpersonal Violence, 20*(1), 127–131.

Campbell, W. K., Foster, C. A., & Finkel, E. J. (2002). Does self-love lead to love for others?: A story of narcissistic game playing. *Journal of Personality & Social Psychology, 83*(2), 340–354.

Caporaletti, J. (2006, September 20). Prostitution is a world-wide problem. [Online]. www.collegiatetimes.com.

Carey, L. A., et al. (2006). Race, breast cancer subtypes, and survival in the Carolina Breast Cancer Study. *Journal of the American Medical Association, 295,* 2492–2502.

Carlson, N. (2007). *Physiology of behavior.* 9th ed. Boston: Allyn & Bacon.

Carrère, S., Buehlman, K. T., Gottman, J. M., Coan, J. A., & Ruckstuhl, L. (2000). Predicting marital stability and divorce in newlywed couples. *Journal of Family Psychology, 14*(1), 42–58.

Carrns, A. (2000, July 13). Levels of HIV infection, AIDS fail to decline in the U.S., data show. *The Wall Street Journal Interactive Edition.*

Carter, D. J., & Dalla, R. L. (2006). Transactional analysis case report: Street-level prostituted women as mental health care clients. *Sexual Addiction & Compulsivity, 13*(1), 95–119.

Castellsague, X. et al. (2002). Male circumcision, penile human papillomavirus infection, and cervical cancer in female partners. *New England Journal of Medicine, 346*(15), 1105–1112.

Centers for Disease Control and Prevention (CDC). (2006). Sexually transmitted diseases. Various fact sheets.

Centers for Disease Control and Prevention. (2001b, June). *Genital herpes.* National Center for HIV, STD and TB Prevention. Division of Sexually Transmitted Diseases. [Online]. www.cdc.gov/nchstp/dstd/Fact_Sheets/facts_Genital_Herpes.htm.

Centers for Disease Control and Prevention. (2003). *HIV/AIDS surveillance report: U.S. HIV and AIDS cases reported through December 2002, 14*(2).

Centers for Disease Control and Prevention. (2005a). *STD surveillance 2005.* [Online]. www.cdc.gov/std/stats/toc2004.htm.

Centers for Disease Control and Prevention. (2005b). *DES Update: For Consumers.* [Online]. www.cdc.gov/DES/consumers/index.html.

Centers for Disease Control and Prevention. (2002a). *Oral alternatives to cefixime for the treatment of uncomplicated* Neisseria gonorrhoeae *urogenital infections.* National Center for HIV, STD and TB Prevention. Division of Sexually Transmitted Diseases. [Online]. www.cdc.gov/STD/treatment/Cefixime.htm.

Centers for Disease Control and Prevention. (2002b). *Laboratory guidelines screening tests to detect* Chlamydia trachomatis *and* Neisseria gonorrhoeae *infections.* National Center for HIV, STD and TB Prevention. Division of Sexually Transmitted Diseases. [Online]. www.cdc.gov/STD/LabGuidelines/default.htm.

Champion, D. R. (2006). Sexual harassment: Criminal justice and academia. *Criminal Justice Studies: A Critical Journal of Crime, Law & Society, 19*(2), 101–109.

Champion, H. L. O., et al. (2004). Adolescent sexual victimization, use of alcohol and other substances, and other health risk behaviors. *Journal of Adolescent Health, 35*(4), 321–328.

Chance, S. E., Brown, R. T., Dabbs, J. M., Jr., & Casey, R. (2000). Testosterone, intelligence and behavior disorders in young boys. *Personality & Individual Differences, 28*(3) 437–445.

Chao, Q., Wang, P., & He, N. (2001). Comparative research on self-concept of middle school students from complete and divorced families. *Chinese Journal of Clinical Psychology, 9*(2), 143.

Chavez, M. L., & Spitzer, M. F. (2002). Herbals

and other dietary supplements for premenstrual syndrome and menopause. *Psychiatric Annals, 32*(1), 61–71.

Cheng, H., & Furnham, A. (2002). Personality, peer relations, and self-confidence as predictors of happiness and loneliness. *Journal of Adolescence, 25*(3), 327–339.

Chesler, P. (2006, February 24). The failure of feminism. *Chronicle of Higher Education, 52*(25).

China develops electronic contraceptive for men. (1998, March 15). Reuters News Agency. [Online].

Chivers, M. L., & Bailey, J. M. (2000). Sexual orientation of female-to-male transsexuals: A comparison of homosexual and nonhomosexual types. *Archives of Sexual Behavior, 29*(3), 259–278.

Chivers, M. L., Rieger, G., Latty, E., & Bailey, J. M. (2004). A sex difference in the specificity of sexual arousal. *Psychological Science, 15*(11), 736–744.

Chivers, M., & Bailey, J. M. (2005). A sex difference in features that elicit genital response. *Biological Psychology, 70*(2), 115–120.

Chlebowski, R. T., et al. (2003). Influence of estrogen plus progestin on breast cancer and mammography in healthy postmenopausal women: The Women's Health Initiative Randomized Trial. *Journal of the American Medical Association, 289*, 3243–3253.

Cho, S., Park, E. S., Park, C. I., & Na, S. (2004). Characteristics of psychosexual functioning in adults with cerebral palsy. *Clinical Rehabilitation, 18*(4), 423–429.

Chowdhury, A. N. (2004, November 4). The definition and classification of Koro. *Culture, Medicine, and Psychiatry, 20*(1), 41–65.

Christin–Maitre, S., Bouchard, P., & Spitz, I. M. (2000). Drug therapy: Medical termination of pregnancy. *The New England Journal of Medicine, 342*(13).

Cigarette smoking among adults—United States, 2003. *Morbidity and Mortality Weekly Report, 54*(20), 509–513.

Clay, R. A. (1996). Older men are more involved fathers, studies show. *APA Monitor, 27*(2), 37.

Clay, R. A. (2006). Battling the self-blame of infertility. *Monitor on Psychology, 37*(8), 44–45.

Clayton, A., Keller, A., & McGarvey, E. L. (2006). Burden of phase-specific sexual dysfunction with SSRIs. *Journal of Affective Disorders, 91*(1), 27–32.

Clendenning, A. (2004, April 29). *Yale global online.* [Online]. www.yaleglobal.yale.edu.

Cnattingius, S. (2004). The epidemiology of smoking during pregnancy: Smoking prevalence, maternal characteristics, and pregnancy outcomes. *Nicotine & Tobacco Research, 6*(Suppl. 2), S125–S140.

Cnattingius, S., Bergstrom, R., Lipworth, L., & Kramer, M. S. (1998). Pre-pregnancy weight and the risk of adverse pregnancy outcomes. *New England Journal of Medicine, 338*, 147–152.

Cochran, S. D., Sullivan, J. G., & Mays, V. M. (2003). Prevalence of mental disorders, psychological distress, and mental health services use among lesbian, gay, and bisexual adults in the United States. *Journal of Consulting and Clinical Psychology, 71*(1), 53–61.

Cohen, A. B., & Tannenbaum, I. J. (2001). Lesbian and bisexual women's judgments of the attractiveness of different body types. *Journal of Sex Research, 38*(3), 226–232.

Cohen, L. S., et al. (2006). Relapse of major depression during pregnancy in women who maintain or discontinue antidepressant treatment. *Journal of the American Medical Association, 295*(5), 499–507.

Cohen, M. S. (2000). Preventing sexual transmission of HIV: New ideas from sub-Saharan Africa. *The New England Journal of Medicine, 342*(13), 970–973.

Cohen–Bendahan, C. C. C., van de Beek, C., & Berenbaum, S. A. (2005). Prenatal sex hormone effects on child and adult sex-typed behavior: Methods and findings. *Neuroscience & Biobehavioral Reviews, 29*(2), 353–384.

Colapinto, J. (2000). *As nature made him: The boy who was raised as a girl.* New York: HarperCollins.

Colapinto, J. (2004, June 3). Gender gap: What were the real reasons behind David Reimer's suicide? [Online]. www.slate.com/id/2101678.

Colditz, G. A., & Rosner, B. A. (2000). Cumulative risk for breast cancer to age 70 years according to risk factor status. Data from the Nurses' Health Study. *American Journal of Epidemiology, 152*(10), 950–964.

Colditz, G. A., et al. (2004). Risk factors for breast cancer according to estrogen and progesterone receptor status. *Journal of the National Cancer Institute, 96*, 218–228.

Cole, C. L., & Cole, A. L. (1999). Marriage enrichment and prevention really works: Interpersonal competence training to maintain and enhance relationships. *Family Relations: Interdisciplinary Journal of Applied Family Studies, 48*(3), 273–275.

Cole, F. S. (2000). Extremely preterm birth—Defining the limits of hope. *The New England Journal of Medicine, 343*(6).

Cole, T. B. (2006). Rape at US colleges often fueled by alcohol. *Journal of the American Medical Association, 296*(5), 504–505.

Coleman, E. (2002). Masturbation as a means of achieving sexual health. *Journal of Psychology & Human Sexuality, 14*(2–3), 5–16.

Coleman, M., Ganong, L. H., & Fine, M. (2000). Reinvestigating remarriage: Another decade of progress. *Journal of Marriage & the Family, 62*(4), 1288–1307.

Collaer, M. L., & Hill, E. M. (2006). Large sex difference in adolescents on a timed line judgment task: Attentional contributors and task relationship to mathematics. *Perception, 35*(4), 561–572.

Collaer, M. L., & Nelson, J. D. (2002). Large visuospatial sex difference in line judgment: Possible role of attentional factors. *Brain & Cognition, 49*(1), 1–12.

Collins, C., Harshbarger, C., Sawyer, R., & Hamdallah, M. (2006). The diffusion of effective behavioral interventions project: Development, implementation, and lessons learned. *AIDS Education and Prevention, 18*(Suppl. A), 5–20.

Collins, L. (2004). We are not gay. In Kumashiro, K. K. (Ed.). *Restoried selves: Autobiographies of Queer Asian/Pacific American activists* (pp. 13–17). New York: Harrington Park Press/The Haworth Press.

Colson, M.-H., Lemaire, A., Pinton, P., Hamidi, K., & Klein, P. (2006). Sexual behaviors and mental perception, satisfaction and expectations of sex life in men and women in France. *Journal of Sexual Medicine, 3*(1), 121–131.

Connolly, J., Craig, W., Goldberg, A., & Pepler, D. (2004). Mixed-gender groups, dating, and romantic relationships in early adolescence. *Journal of Research on Adolescence, 14*(2), 185–207.

Connor, E. M., et al. (1994). Reduction of maternal–infant transmission of human immunodeficiency virus type 1 with zidovudine treatment. *New England Journal of Medicine, 331*, 1173–1180.

Connor, P. D., Sampson, P. D., Streissguth, A. P., Bookstein, F. L., & Barr, H. M. (2006). Effects of prenatal alcohol exposure on fine motor coordination and balance: A study of two adult samples. *Neuropsychologia, 44*(5), 744–751.

Cooke, B. M., Breedlove, S. M., & Jordan, C. L. (2003). Both estrogen receptors and androgen receptors contribute to testosterone-induced changes in the morphology of the medial amygdala and sexual arousal in male rats. *Hormones & Behavior, 43*(2), 336–346.

Cooper, A. J., Galbreath, N., & Becker, M. A. (2004). Sex on the Internet: Furthering our understanding of men with online sexual problems. *Psychology of Addictive Behaviors, 18*(3), 223–230.

Cooper, A., Delmonico, D. L., & Burg, R. (2000). Cybersex users, abusers, and compulsives: New findings and implications. *Sexual Addiction & Compulsivity, 7*(1–2), 5–29.

Cooper, A., Delmonico, D. L., Griffin–Shelley, E., & Mathy, R. M. (2004). Online sexual activity: An examination of potentially problematic behaviors. *Sexual Addiction & Compulsivity, 11*(3), 129–143.

Cortina, L. M., & Wasti, S. A. (2005). Profiles in coping: Responses to sexual harassment across persons, organizations, and cultures. *Journal of Applied Psychology, 90*(1), 182–192.

Corty, E. W. (2006). Sexual dysfunction. In Andrasik, F. (Ed.). (2006). *Comprehensive handbook of personality and psychopathology. Vol. 2: Adult psychopathology* (pp. 423–435). John Wiley & Sons.

Cotten–Huston, A. L., & Waite, B. M. (2000). Anti-homosexual attitudes in college students: Predictors and classroom interventions. *Journal of Homosexuality, 38*(3), 117–133.

Courtenay, W. H. (2000). Engendering health: A social constructionist examination of men's health beliefs and behaviors. *Psychology of Men & Masculinity, 1*(1), 4–15.

Cove, J., & Petrak, J. (2004). Factors associated with sexual problems in HIV-positive gay men. *International Journal of STD & AIDS, 15*(11), 732–736.

Cox, B., Sneyd, M. J., Paul, C., & Skegg, D. C. G. (2006). Risk factors for prostate cancer: A national case-control study. *International Journal of Cancer, 119*(7), 1690–1694.

Cox, D. J. (1988). Incidence and nature of male genital exposure behavior as reported by college women. *Journal of Sex Research, 24*, 227–234.

Cox, W. M., & Alm, R. (2005, February 25). Scientists are made, not born. *The New York Times.* [Online].

Coyle, J. P. (2006). Treating difficult couples: Helping clients with coexisting mental and relationship disorders. *Family Relations: Interdisciplinary Journal of Applied Family Studies, 55*(1), 146–147.

Craig, R. J. (2005). Harassment. In Craig, R. J. (Ed.). *Personality-guided forensic psychology. Personality-guided psychology* (pp. 155–167). Washington, DC: American Psychological Association.

Cramer, D. (2003). Facilitativeness, conflict, demand for approval, self-esteem, and satisfaction with romantic relationships. *Journal of Psychology, 137*(1), 85–98.

Crepaz, N., Hart, T. A., & Marks, G. (2004). Highly active antiretroviral therapy and sexual risk behavior: A meta-analytic review. *Journal of the American Medical Association, 292*(2), 224–236.

Crews, D. (1994). Animal sexuality. *Scientific American, 270*(1), 108–114.

Crosby, R., Yarber, W., Sanders, S., & Graham, C. (2005). Condom discomfort and associated problems with their use among university students. *Journal of American College Health 54*(3) 143–147.

Crowley, T., Richardson, D., Goldmeier, D., & BASHH Special Interest Group for Sexual Dysfunction. (2006). Recommendations for the management of vaginismus: BASHH Special Interest Group for Sexual Dysfunction. *International Journal of STD & AIDS, 17*(1), 14–18.

Crum, N. F., Furtek, K. J., Olson, P. E., Amling, C. L., & Wallace, M. R. (2005). A review of hypogonadism and erectile dysfunction among HIV-infected men during the pre- and post-HAART eras: Diagnosis, pathogenesis, and management. *AIDS Patient Care and STDs, 19*(10), 869–885.

Csoka, A. B., & Shipko, S. (2006). Persistent sexual side effects after SSRI discontinuation. *Psychotherapy and Psychosomatics, 75*(3), 187–188.

Cummings, S. R., et al. (1999). The effect of raloxifene on risk of breast cancer in postmenopausal women: Results from the MORE randomized trial. *Journal of the American Medical Association, 281*, 2189–2197.

Cunningham, A. L., et al. (2006). Prevalence of infection with herpes simplex virus types 1 and 2 in Australia: A nationwide population based survey. *Sexually Transmitted Infections, 82*, 164–168.

Cunningham, M. R., et al. (1995). "Their ideas of beauty are, on the whole, the same as ours": Consistency and variability in the cross-cultural perception of female physical attractiveness. *Journal of Personality and Social Psychology, 68*(2), 261–279.

Curnoe, S., & Langevin, R. (2002). Personality and deviant sexual fantasies: An examination of the MMPIs. *Journal of Clinical Psychology, 58*(7), 803–815.

Cutler, W. B. (1999). Human sex-attractant hormones: Discovery, research, development, and application in sex therapy. *Psychiatric Annals, 29*(1), 54–59.

Cutler, W. B., Friedmann, E., & McCoy, N. L. (1998). Pheromonal influences on sociosexual behavior in men. *Archives of Sexual Behavior, 27*(1), 1–13.

Dabbs, J. M., Jr., Hargrove, M. F., & Heusel, C. (1996). Testosterone differences among college fraternities: Well-behaved vs rambunctious. *Personality & Individual Differences, 20*(2), 157–161.

Dabbs, J. M., Jr., & Morris, R. (1990). Testosterone, social class, and antisocial behavior in a sample of 4,462 men. *Psychological Science, 1*, 1–3.

Dalla, R. L. (2006). "You can't hustle all your life": An exploratory investigation of the exit process among street-level prostituted women.

Psychology of Women Quarterly, 30(3), 276–290.

Daly, M., & Wilson, M. (2003). Evolutionary psychology of lethal interpersonal violence. In Heitmeyer, W., & Hagan, J. (Eds.). *Handbook of research on violence* (pp. 709–734). New York: Westview.

Daly, M., & Wilson, M. (2005). Human behavior as animal behavior. In Bolhuis, J. J., & Giraldeau, L. A. (Eds.). *The behavior of animals. Mechanisms, function, and evolution* (pp. 393–408). Oxford: Blackwell Publishing.

Damon, W. (2002). Dominance, sexism, and inadequacy: Testing a compensatory conceptualization in a sample of heterosexual men involved in SM. *Journal of Psychology & Human Sexuality, 14*(4), 25–45.

Daneback, K., Cooper, A., Månsoon, S. (2005). An Internet study of cybersex participants. *Archives of Sexual Behavior, 34*(3), 321–328.

Daneback, K., Ross, M. W., & Månsson, S. (2006). Characteristics and behaviors of sexual compulsives who use the Internet for sexual purposes. *Sexual Addition & Compulsivity, 13*(1), 53–67.

Daneback, K., Ross, M. W., & Månsson, S. (2006). Characteristics and behaviors of sexual compulsives who use the Internet for sexual purposes. *Sexual Addiction & Compulsivity, 13*(1), 53–67.

Dantzker, M. L., & Eisenman, R. (2003). Sexual attitudes among Hispanic college students: Differences between males and females. *International Journal of Adolescence & Youth, 11*(1), 79–89.

Darling, C. A., Davidson, J. K., & Jennings, D. A. (1991). The female sexual response revisited: Understanding the multiorgasmic experience in women. *Archives of Sexual Behavior, 20*, 527–540.

D'Augelli, A. R. (1992a). Lesbian and gay male undergraduates' experiences of harassment and fear on campus. *Journal of Interpersonal Violence, 7*, 383–395.

D'Augelli, A. R. (1992b). Sexual behavior patterns of gay university men: Implications for preventing HIV infection. *Journal of American College Health, 41*, 25–29.

Davidson, J. K., & Hoffman, L. E. (1986). Sexual fantasies and sexual satisfaction: An empirical analysis of erotic thought. *Journal of Sex Research, 22*(2), 184–205.

Davies, M. (2004). Correlates of negative attitudes toward gay men: Sexism, male role norms, and male sexuality. *Journal of Sex Research, 41*(3), 259–266.

Davis, D., Shaver, P. R., & Vernon, M. L. (2003). Physical, emotional, and behavioral reactions to breaking up: The roles of gender, age, emotional involvement, and attachment style. *Personality & Social Psychology Bulletin, 29*(7), 871–884.

Davis, K. E., & Frieze, I. H., & Maiuro, R. D. (Eds.). (2002). *Stalking: Perspectives on victims and perpetrators* (pp. 212–236). New York: Springer.

Davis, P. (1998, June 9). Peeping Toms with videocams plague malls. *The Washington Post.* [Online].

Davis, S. (2000). Testosterone and sexual desire in women. *Journal of Sex Education & Therapy, 25*(1), 25–32.

Davis, T. L., & Liddell, D. L. (2002). Getting inside the house: The effectiveness of a rape prevention program for college fraternity

men. *Journal of College Student Development, 43*(1), 35–50.

Davison, G. C. (1977). Elimination of a sadistic fantasy by a client-controlled counterconditioning technique. In Fischer, J., & Gochios, H. (Eds.). *Handbook of behavior therapy with sexual problems.* New York: Pergamon Press.

Dawood, K., Pillard, R. C., Horvath, C., Revelle, W., & Bailey, J. M. (2000). Familial aspects of male homosexuality. *Archives of Sexual Behavior, 29*(2), 155–163.

de Graaf, R., Sandfort, T. G. M., & ten Have, M. (2006). Suicidality and sexual orientation: Differences between men and women in a general population-based sample from the Netherlands. *Archives of Sexual Behavior, 35*(3), 253–262.

De Vries, G. J., et al. (2002). A model system for study of sex chromosome effects on sexually dimorphic neural and behavioral traits. *Journal of Neuroscience, 22*(20), 9005–9014.

Deci, E. L., La Guardia, J. G., Moller, A. C., Scheiner, M. J., & Ryan, R. M. (2006). On the benefits of giving as well as receiving autonomy support: Mutuality in close friendships. *Personality and Social Psychology Bulletin, 32*(3), 313–327.

Degenhardt, L., Day, C., Conroy, E., & Gilmour, S. (2006). Examining links between cocaine use and street-based sex work in New South Wales, Australia. *Journal of Sex Research, 43*(2), 107–114.

Dekker, A., & Schmidt, G. (2002). Patterns of masturbatory behaviour: Changes between the sixties and the nineties. *Journal of Psychology & Human Sexuality, 14*(2–3), 35–48.

Delgado, J. (1969). *Physical control of the mind.* New York: Harper & Row.

den Tonkelaar, I., & Oddens, B. J. (2000). Determinants of long-term hormone replacement therapy and reasons for early discontinuation. *Obstetrics & Gynecology, 95*(4), 507–512.

Dennerstein, L., Dudley, E. C., Hopper, J. L., Guthrie, J. R., & Burger, H. G. (2000). A prospective population-based study of menopausal symptoms. *Obstetrics & Gynecology, 96*(3), 351–358.

Dennerstein, L., & Goldstein, I. (2005). Postmenopausal female sexual dysfunction: At a crossroads. *Journal of Sexual Medicine, 2*(Suppl. 3), 116–117.

Dennerstein, L., & Hayes, R. D. (2005). Confronting the challenges: Epidemiological study of female sexual dysfunction and the menopause. *Journal of Sexual Medicine, 2*(Suppl. 3), 118–132.

Derby, C. A. (2000, October 2). Cited in Study finds exercise reduces the risk of impotence. The Associated Press.

Dhar, N. B. (2006). Vasectomy men pose pregnancy risk. *British Journal of Urology International, 97*, 773–776.

Diamond, L. M. (2000). Sexual identity, attractions, and behavior among young sexual-minority women over a 2-year period. *Developmental Psychology, 36*(2), 241–250.

Diamond, L. M. (2002). "Having a girlfriend without knowing it": Intimate friendships among adolescent sexual-minority women. *Journal of Lesbian Studies, 6*(1) 5–16.

Diamond, L. M. (2003a). Was it a phase? Young women's relinquishment of lesbian/bisexual identities over a 5-year period. *Journal of Personality & Social Psychology, 84*(2), 352–364.

Diamond, L. M. (2003b). What does sexual orientation orient? A biobehavioral model distinguishing romantic love and sexual desire. *Psychological Review, 110*(1), 173–192.

Diamond, M. (1996). Prenatal predisposition and the clinical management of some pediatric conditions. *Journal of Sex & Marital Therapy, 22*(3), 139–147.

Dijkstra, P., & Buunk, B. P. (2002). Sex differences in the jealousy-evoking effect of rival characteristics. *European Journal of Social Psychology, 32*(6), 829–852.

Dilley, J. W., et al. (2003). Availability of combination therapy for HIV: Effects on sexual risk taking in a sample of high-risk gay and bisexual men. *AIDS Care, 15*(1), 27–37.

Dindia, K., & Allen, M. (1992). Sex differences in self-disclosure: A meta-analysis. *Psychological Bulletin, 112,* 106–124.

Dindia, K., & Timmerman, L. (2003). Accomplishing romantic relationships. In Greene, J. O., & Burleson, B. R. (Eds.). *Handbook of communication and social interaction skills* (pp. 685–721). Mahwah, NJ: Lawrence Erlbaum Associates.

Dittert, S., Seidl, O., & Soyka, M. (2005). Zoophilia as a special case of paraphilia. Presentation of three case reports and an Internet survey. *Nervenarzt, 76*(1), 61–67.

Donald, M., Dower, J., Correa–Velez, I., & Jones, M. (2006). Risk and protective factors for medically serious suicide attempts: A comparison of hospital-based with population-based samples of young adults. *Australian and New Zealand Journal of Psychiatry, 40*(1), 87–96.

Donnelly, D., & Fraser, J. (1998). Gender differences in sado-masochistic arousal among college students. *Sex Roles, 39*(5–6), 391–407.

Donnerstein, E. (1980). Aggressive erotica and violence against women. *Journal of Personality and Social Psychology, 39,* 269–277.

Donnerstein, E. I., & Linz, D. G. (1987). *The question of pornography.* New York: The Free Press.

Donnerstein, E., & Berkowitz, L. (1981). Victim reactions in aggressive erotic films as a factor in violence against women. *Journal of Personality and Social Psychology, 41,* 710–724.

Downs, M., & Nazario, B. (2003, February 11). *Aphrodisiacs through the ages.* WebMD Features. [Online].

Dreifus, C. (2000, July 11). A conversation with Dr. Nawal M. Nour: A life devoted to stopping the suffering of mutilation. *The New York Times.* [Online].

Drews, C. D., et al. (April 1996). *Pediatrics.*

Drigotas, S. M., Rusbult, C. E., & Verette, J. (1999). Level of commitment, mutuality of commitment, and couple well-being. *Personal Relationships, 6*(3) 389–409.

Driver, J. L., & Gottman, J. M. (2004). Daily marital interactions and positive affect during marital conflict among newlywed couples. *Family Process, 43*(3), 301–314.

Driver, J., Tabares, A., Shapiro, A., Nahm, E. Y., & Gottman, J. M. (2003). Interactional patterns in marital success and failure: Gottman laboratory studies. In Walsh, F. (Ed.). *Normal family processes: Growing diversity and complexity* (3rd ed.) (pp. 493–513). New York: Guilford Press.

Duenwald, M. (2002, July 16). Hormone therapy: One size, clearly, no longer fits all. *The New York Times.*

Duggan, L. (2006a). Censorship in the name of feminism. In Duggan, L., & Hunter, N. D. (Eds.). *Sex wars: Sexual dissent and political culture* (pp. 29–39). (10th ed.). Oxford, UK: Routledge/Taylor & Francis Group.

Duggan, L. (2006b). Feminist historians and antipornography campaigns: An overview. In Duggan, L., & Hunter, N. D. (Eds.). *Sex wars: Sexual dissent and political culture* (pp. 65–69). (10th ed.). Oxford, UK: Routledge/Taylor & Francis Group.

Duggan, L., Hunter, N. D., & Vance, C. S. (2006). False promises: Feminist antipornography legislation. In Duggan, L., & Hunter, N. D. (Eds.). *Sex wars: Sexual dissent and political culture* (pp. 43–64). (10th ed.). Oxford, UK: Routledge/Taylor & Francis Group.

Duggirala, M. K., et al. (2003). A human papillomavirus type 16 vaccine. *New England Journal of Medicine, 348,* 1402–1405.

Dunsieth, N. W., Jr., et al. (2004). Psychiatric and legal features of 113 men convicted of sexual offenses. *Journal of Clinical Psychiatry, 65*(3), 293–300.

Dye, M. L., & Davis, K. E. (2003). Stalking and psychological abuse: Common factors and relationship-specific characteristics. *Violence & Victims, 18*(2), 163–180.

Dzokoto, V. A., & Adams, G. (2005). Understanding genital-shrinking epidemics in West Africa: Koro, juju, or mass psychogenic illness? *Culture, Medicine and Psychiatry, 29*(1), 53–78.

Early prostate surgery is found very effective. (1996, August 28). *The New York Times,* p. C9.

Eason, E., & Feldman, P. (2000). Much ado about a little cut: Is episiotomy worthwhile? *Obstetrics & Gynecology, 95*(4), 616–618.

Eason, E., Labrecque, M., Wells, G., & Feldman, P. (2000). Preventing perineal trauma during childbirth: A systematic review. *Obstetrics & Gynecology, 95,* 464–471.

Eck, B. A. (2001). Nudity and framing: Classifying art, pornography, information, and ambiguity. *Sociological Forum, 16*(4), 603–632.

Edgley, C. (1989). Commercial sex: Pornography, prostitution, and advertising. In McKinney, K., & Sprecher, S. (Eds.). *Human sexuality: The societal and interpersonal context* (pp. 370–424). Norwood, NJ: Ablex Publishing.

Edser, S. J., & Shea, J. D. (2002). An exploratory investigation of bisexual men in monogamous, heterosexual marriages. *Journal of Bisexuality, 2*(4), 5–29.

Edwards, T. M. (2000, August 28). Single by choice. *Time Magazine, 156*(9).

Edwards, V. J., Holden, G. W., Felitti, V. J., & Anda, R. F. (2003). Relationship between multiple forms of childhood maltreatment and adult mental health in community respondents: Results from the Adverse Childhood Experiences Study. *American Journal of Psychiatry, 160*(8), 1453–1460.

Eggers, D. (2000, May 7). Intimacies. *The New York Times Magazine,* 76–77.

Eichenwald, K. (2005, December 19). Through his webcam, a boy joins a sordid online world. *The New York Times.*

El-Defrawi, M. H., Lotfy, G., Dandash, K. F., Refaat, A. H., & Eyada, M. (2001). Female genital mutilation and its psychosexual impact. *Journal of Sex & Marital Therapy, 27*(5), 465–473.

El-Gibaly, O., Ibrahim, B., Mensch, B. S., & Clark, W. H. (2002). The decline of female circumcision in Egypt: Evidence and interpretation. *Social Science & Medicine, 54*(2), 205–220.

Elia, J. P., Swanson, C., & Goldberg, A. R. (2003). More queer: Resources on queer theory. *Journal of Homosexuality, 45*(2–4), 391–400.

Ellis, B. J., & Bjorklund, D. F. (Eds.). (2005). *Origins of the social mind: Evolutionary psychology and child development.* New York: Guilford Press.

Ellis, L., & Ames, M. A. (1987). Neurohormonal functioning and sexual orientation: A theory of homosexuality–heterosexuality. *Psychological Bulletin, 101,* 233–258.

El-Sheikh, M. & Harger, J. (2001). Appraisals of marital conflict and children's adjustment, health, and physiological reactivity. *Developmental Psychology, 37*(6), 875–885.

Eltahawy, M. (2003, January 9). *Young Africans reject female genital mutilation.* [Online]. www.feminist.com/news/news141.html.

Emanuele, E., et al. (2006). Raised plasma nerve growth factor levels associated with early-stage romantic love. *Psychoneuroendocrinology, 31*(3), 288–294.

Fagot, B. I., Rodgers, C. S., & Leinbach, M. D. (2000). Theories of gender socialization. In Eckes, T., & Trautner, H. M. (Eds.). *The developmental social psychology of gender* (pp. 65–89). Mahwah, NJ: Lawrence Erlbaum Associates.

Faller, K. C. (1989). Why sexual abuse? An exploration of the intergenerational hypothesis. *Child Abuse and Neglect, 13,* 543–548.

Farley, M., Lynne, J., & Cotton, A. J. (2005). Prostitution in Vancouver: Violence and the colonization of First Nations Women. *Transcultural Psychiatry, 42*(2), 242–271.

Fausto–Sterling, A. (May/April 1993). The five sexes: Why male and female are not enough. *The Sciences,* 20–25.

FDA approves abortion pill. (2000, September 28). Associated Press. [Online].

Fedoroff, J. P. (2003). The paraphilic world. In Levine, S. B., Risen, C. B., & Althof, S. E. (Eds.). *Handbook of clinical sexuality for mental health professionals* (pp. 333–356). London: Brunner-Routledge.

Feinberg, D. R., et al. (2006). Menstrual cycle, trait estrogen level, and masculinity preferences in the human voice. *Hormones and Behavior, 49*(2), 215–222.

Feingold, A. (1991). Sex differences in the effects of similarity and physical attractiveness on opposite-sex attraction. *Basic and Applied Social Psychology, 12,* 357–367.

Feingold, A. (1994). Gender differences in personality: A meta-analysis. *Psychological Bulletin, 116,* 429–456.

Felson, R. B. (2002). *Violence and gender reexamined.* Washington, DC: American Psychological Association.

Fensterheim, H., & Kantor, J. S. (1980). Behavioral approach to sexual disorders. In Wolman, B., & Money, J. (Eds.). *Handbook of human sexuality.* Englewood Cliffs, NJ: Prentice-Hall.

Ferguson, D. M., Horwood, L. J., & Beautrais, A. L. (1999). Is sexual orientation related to mental health problems and suicidality in young people? *Archives of General Psychiatry, 56*(10), 876–880.

Ferguson, D. M., Horwood, L. J., Ridder, E. M., & Beautrais, A. L. (2005). Sexual orientation and mental health in a birth cohort of young adults. *Psychological Medicine, 35*(7), 971–981.

Fermino, J., & Olshan, J. (2006, June 24). *Say cheese, you sleaze! Cam-phone gals snap subway gropers.* [Online]. www.wirelessmoment.com/2006/-06/index.html.

Ferraro, G. (2004). *Cultural anthropology—An applied perspective.* 5th ed. Belmont, CA: Wadsworth.

Ferris, C. F., et al. (2004). Activation of neural pathways associated with sexual arousal in non-human primates. *Journal of Magnetic Resonance Imaging, 19*(2), 168–175.

Festa, E. D., et al. (2004). Sex differences in cocaine-induced behavioral responses, pharmacokinetics, and monoamine levels. *Neuropharmacology, 46*(5), 672–687.

Fichner–Rathus, L. (2007). *Understanding art.* 8th ed. Belmont, CA: Thomson Learning/Wadsworth.

Finkelhor, D. (1990). Early and long-term effects of child sexual abuse: An update. *Professional Psychology: Research and Practice, 21,* 325–330.

Finkelhor, D. (2003). The legacy of the clergy abuse scandal. *Child Abuse & Neglect, 27*(11), 1225–1229.

Finkelhor, D., Cross, T. P., & Cantor, E. N. (2005a). The justice system for juvenile victims: A comprehensive model of case flow. *Trauma, Violence, & Abuse, 6*(2), 83–102.

Finkelhor, D., Ormrod, R., Turner, H., & Hamby, S. L. (2005b). The victimization of children and youth: A comprehensive, national survey. *Child Maltreatment: Journal of the American Professional Society on the Abuse of Children, 10*(1), 5–25.

Finkelman, J. M. (2005). Sexual harassment: The organizational perspective. In Barnes, A. (Ed.). *The handbook of women, psychology, and the law* (pp. 64–78). New York: John Wiley & Sons.

Finkenauer, C., & Hazam, H. (2000). Disclosure and secrecy in marriage: Do both contribute to marital satisfaction? *Journal of Social & Personal Relationships, 17*(2), 245–263.

Finkenauer, C., & Meeus, W. (2000). How (pro)social is the caring motive? *Psychological Inquiry, 11*(2), 100–103.

Firestone, R. W., Firestone, L. A., & Catlett, J. (2006a). *Sex and love in intimate relationships.* Washington, DC: American Psychological Association.

Firestone, R. W., Firestone, L. A., & Catlett, J. (2006b). Sexual withholding. In Firestone, R. W., Firestone, L. A., & Catlett, J. (Eds.). *Sex and love in intimate relationships* (pp. 171–195). Washington, DC: American Psychological Association.

Fisher, B. S., Daigle, L. E., Cullen, F. T., & Turner, M. G. (2003). Reporting sexual victimization to the police and others: Results from a national-level study of college women. *Criminal Justice & Behavior, 30*(1), 6–38.

Fisher, H. E. (2000). Brains do it: Lust, attraction and attachment. *Cerebrum, 2,* 23–42.

Fisher, W. A., et al. (2005). Improving the sexual quality of life of couples affected by erectile dysfunction: A double-blind, randomized, placebo-controlled trial of vardenafil. *Journal of Sexual Medicine, 2*(5), 699–708.

Fishman, J. R., & Mamo, L. (2001). What's in a disorder: A cultural analysis of medical and pharmaceutical constructions of male and female sexual dysfunction. *Women & Therapy, 24*(1–2), 179–193.

Flaxman, S. M., & Sherman, P. W. (2000). Morning sickness: A mechanism for protecting mother and embryo. *The Quarterly Review of Biology, 75*(2), 113–148.

Fletcher, J. (1966). *Situation ethics.* Philadelphia: Westminster Press.

Fletcher, J. (1967). *Moral responsibility: Situation ethics at work.* Philadelphia: Westminster Press.

Fletcher, S. W., & Colditz, G. A. (2002). Failure of estrogen plus progestin therapy for prevention. *Journal of the American Medical Association, 288*(3).

Florence, E., et al. (2004). Prevalence and factors associated with sexual dysfunction among HIV-positive women in Europe. *AIDS Care, 16*(5), 550–557.

Floyd, R. L., O'Connor, M. J., Sokol, R. J., Bertrand, J., & Cordero, F. F. (2005). Recognition and prevention of fetal alcohol syndrome. *Obstetrics & Gynecology, 106,* 1059–1064.

Foote, W. E., & Goodman-Delahunty, J. (2005). Harassers, harassment contexts, same-sex harassment, workplace romance, and harassment theories. In Foote, W. E., & Goodman-Delahunty, J. (Eds.). *Evaluating sexual harassment: Psychological, social, and legal considerations in forensic examinations* (pp. 27–45). Washington, DC: American Psychological Association.

Forbes, A., While, A., Mathes, L., & Griffiths, P. (2006). Health problems and health-related quality of life in people with multiple sclerosis. *Clinical Rehabilitation, 20*(1), 67–78.

Ford, C. S., & Beach, F. A. (1951). *Patterns of sexual behavior.* New York: Harper & Row.

Forgas, J. P., Levinger, G., & Moylan, S. J. (1994). Feeling good and feeling close: Affective influences on the perception of intimate relationships. *Personal Relationships, 1*(2), 165–184.

Foubert, J. D., & Newberry, J. T. (2006). Effects of two versions of an empathy-based rape prevention program on fraternity men's survivor empathy, attitudes, and behavioral intent to commit rape or sexual assault. *Journal of College Student Development, 47*(2), 133–148.

Frank, K. (2002). *G-strings and sympathy: Strip club regulars and male desire.* Raleigh, NC: Duke University Press.

Frank, K. (2003). Just trying to relax: Masculinity, masculinizing practices, and strip club regulars. *The Journal of Sex Research, 40*(1), 61–75.

Frayser, S. (1985). *Varieties of sexual experience: An anthropological perspective on human sexuality.* New Haven, CT: Human Relations Area Files Press.

Frazier, L. (2000, July 16). The new face of HIV is young, black. *The Washington Post,* p. C1.

Freud, S. (1922/1959). Analysis of a phobia in a 5-year-old boy. In Strachey, A. J. (Ed., Trans.). *Collected papers.* Vol. 3. New York: Basic Books. [Original work published 1909].

Freudenmann, R. W., & Schönfeldt–Lecuona, C. (2005). The syndrome of genital retraction from a transcultural psychiatric point of view. Chinese suo yang, Indonesian koro and non-Asian forms (koro-like symptoms). *Nervenarzt, 76*(5), 569–580.

Freund, K., Watson, R., & Rienzo, D. (1988). The value of self-reports in the study of voyeurism and exhibitionism. *Annals of Sex Research, 1,* 243–262.

Frey, K. S., & Ruble, D. N. (1992). Gender constancy and the "cost" of sex-typed behavior: A test of the conflict hypothesis. *Developmental Psychology, 28,* 714–721.

Friday, N. (1973). *My secret garden.* New York: Trident.

Fried, P. A., & Smith, A. M. (2001) A literature review of the consequences of prenatal marihuana exposure: An emerging theme of a deficiency in aspects of executive function. *Neurotoxicology & Teratology, 23*(1), 1–11.

Friedman, R. C., & Downey, J. I. (2001). The Oedipus complex and male homosexuality. In Hartocollis, P. (Ed). *Mankind's Oedipal destiny: Libidinal and aggressive aspects of sexuality* (pp. 113–138). Madison, CT: International Universities Press.

Friedrich, W. M., Fisher, J., Broughton, D., Houston, M., & Shafran, C. R. (1998). Normative sexual behavior in children: A contemporary sample. *Pediatrics, 101*(4), e9. [Electronic article].

Friedrich, W. N., & Gerber, P. N. (1994). Autoerotic asphyxia: The development of a paraphilia. *Journal of the American Academy of Child and Adolescent Psychiatry, 33*(7), 970–974.

Frisch, R. E. (2002). *Female fertility and the body fat connection.* Chicago: University of Chicago Press.

Frohlich, P. F., & Meston, C. M. (2005). Tactile sensitivity in women with sexual arousal disorder. *Archives of Sexual Behavior, 34*(2), 207–217.

Frohlich, P., & Meston, C. (2002). Sexual functioning and self-reported depressive symptoms among college women. *Journal of Sex Research, 39*(4), 321–325.

Frost, J. J., & Frohwirth, L. A. (2005, July). *Family planning annual report: 2004 Summary.* The Alan Guttmacher Institute.

Fuentes–Afflick, E., & Hessol, N. A. (2000). Interpregnancy interval and the risk or premature infants. *Obstetrics & Gynecology, 95,* 383–390.

Fugl–Meyer, K. S., Öberg, K., Lundberg, P. O., Lewin, B., & Fugl–Meyer, A. (2006). On orgasm, sexual techniques, and erotic perceptions in 18- to 74-year-old Swedish women. *Journal of Sexual Medicine, 3*(1), 56–68.

Furnham, A., Petrides, K. V., & Constantinides, A. (2005). The effects of body mass index and waist-to-hip ratio on ratings of female attractiveness, fecundity, and health. *Personality and Individual Differences, 38*(8), 1823–1834.

Furstenberg, F. F., & Kiernan, K. E. (2001). Delayed parental divorce: How much do children benefit? *Journal of Marriage & the Family, 63*(2), 446–457.

Gabriel, T. (1995, June 12). A new generation seems ready to give bisexuality a place in the spectrum. *The New York Times,* p. A12.

Gagnon, J. H. (1977). *Human sexualities.* Glenview, IL: Scott, Foresman.

Gagnon, J. H., & Simon, W. (1973). *Sexual conduct: The social origins of human sexuality.* Chicago: Aldine.

Garwood, S. G., et al. (1980). Beauty is only "name deep": The effect of first name in ratings of physical attraction. *Journal of Applied Social Psychology, 10,* 431–435.

Gates, G. J., & Sonenstein, F. L. (2000). Heterosexual genital sexual activity among adolescent males: 1988 and 1995. *Family Planning Perspectives, 32*(6), 295–297, 304.

Gates, J. (2001). *Survivors of an open marriage.* KiwE Publishing.

Gavin, N. I., et al. (2005). Perinatal depression: A systematic review of prevalence and incidence. *Obstetrics & Gynecology, 106,* 1071–1083.

Gebhard, P. H. (1969). Misconceptions about

female prostitutes. *Medical Aspects of Human Sexuality, 3*, 24–26.

Gebhard, P. H., et al. (1965). *Sex offenders: An analysis of types*. New York: Harper & Row.

George, W. H., Stoner, S. A., Norris, J., Lopez, P. A., & Lehman, G. L. (2000). Alcohol expectancies and sexuality: A self-fulfilling prophecy analysis of dyadic perceptions and behavior. *Journal of Studies on Alcohol, 61*(1), 168–176.

Gerevich, J., Treuer, T., Danics, Z., & Herr, J. (2005). Diagnostic and psychodynamic aspects of sexual addiction appearing as a non-paraphiliac form of compulsive sexual behaviour. *Journal of Substance Use, 10*(4), 253–259.

Gidycz, C. A., & Koss, M. P. (1990). A comparison of group and individual sexual assault victims. *Psychology of Women Quarterly, 14*, 325–342.

Gidycz, C. A., Rich, C. L., Orchowski, L., King, C., & Miller, A. K. (2006). The evaluation of a sexual assault self-defense and risk-reduction program for college women: A prospective study. *Psychology of Women Quarterly, 30*(2), 173–186.

Gijs, L., & Gooren, L. (1996). Hormonal and psychopharmacological interventions in the treatment of paraphilias: An update. *Journal of Sex Research, 33*, 273–290.

Gilbert, S. (1997, April 2). Study adds to doubts about benefits of circumcision. *The New York Times*. [Online].

Gilchrist, G., Cameron, J., & Scoular, J. (2005). Crack and cocaine use among female prostitutes in Glasgow: Risky business. *Drugs: Education, Prevention & Policy, 12*(5), 381–391.

Gillis, J. S., & Avis, W. E. (1980). The male-taller norm in mate selection. *Personality and Social Psychology Bulletin, 6*, 396–401.

Giotakos, O., Markianos, M., & Vaidakis, N. (2005). Aggression, impulsivity, and plasma sex hormone levels in a group of rapists, in relation to their history of childhood attention-deficit/hyperactivity disorder symptoms. *Journal of Forensic Psychiatry & Psychology, 16*(2), 423–433.

Global plague of AIDS. (2000, April 23). *The New York Times*. [Online].

Gnagy, S., Ming, E. E., Devesa, S. S., Hartge, P., & Whittemore, A. S. (2000). Declining ovarian cancer rates in U.S. women in relation to parity and oral contraceptive use. *Epidemiology, 11*(2), 102–105.

Goldberg, J., Holtz, D., Hyslop, T., & Tolosa, J. E. (2002). Has the use of routine episiotomy decreased? Examination of episiotomy rates from 1983 to 2000. *Obstetrics & Gynecology, 99*(3), 395–400.

Goldschmidt, L., Day, N. L., & Richardson, G. A. (2000). Effects of prenatal marijuana exposure on child behavior problems at age 10. *Neurotoxicology & Teratology, 22*(3), 325–336.

Goldstein, I., & Alexander, J. L. (2005). Practical aspects in the management of vaginal atrophy and sexual dysfunction in perimenopausal and postmenopausal women. *Journal of Sexual Medicine, 2*(Suppl. 3), 154–165.

Goldstein, I., et al. (1998). Oral sildenafil in the treatment of erectile dysfunction. *New England Journal of Medicine, 338*, 1397–1404.

Goldstein, I., Meston, C., Davis, S., & Traish, A. (Eds.). (2006). *Female sexual dysfunction*. New York: Parthenon.

Goleman, D. (1995, June 14). Sex fantasy research said to neglect women. *The New York Times*, p. C14.

Golish, T. D. (2003). Stepfamily communication strengths: Understanding the ties that bind. *Human Communication Research, 29*(1), 41–80.

Gomes do Espirito, M. E., & Etheredge, G. D. (2003). HIV prevalence and sexual behaviour of male clients of brothels' prostitutes in Dakar, Senegal. *AIDS Care, 15*(1), 53–62.

Gonzaga, G. C., Turner, R. A., Keltner, D., Campos, B., & Altemus, M. (2006). Romantic love and sexual desire in close relationships. *Emotion, 6*(2), 63–179.

Goodson, P., McCormick, D., & Evans, A. (2001). Searching for sexually explicit materials on the Internet: An exploratory study of college students' behavior and attitudes. *Archives of Sexual Behavior, 30*(2), 101–118.

Gordon, A. E., et al. (2002). Why is smoking a risk factor for sudden infant death syndrome? *Child: Care, Health & Development, 28*(Suppl. 1), 23–25.

Gordon, A. R. (2005). Queer theory, gender theory: An instant primer. *Culture, Health & Sexuality, 7*(6), 642–644.

Gottman, J. M., & Driver, J. L. (2005). Dysfunctional marital conflict and everyday marital interaction. *Journal of Divorce & Remarriage, 43*(3–4), 63–78.

Gottman, J. M., & Levenson, R. W. (1999). What predicts change in marital interaction over time? A study of alternative medicine. *Family Process, 38*(2), 143–158.

Gottman, J. M., Coan, J., Carrère, S., & Swanson, C. (1998). Predicting marital happiness and stability from newlywed interactions. *Journal of Marriage and the Family, 60*, 5–22.

Gottman, J. M., Swanson, C., & Murray, J. (1999). The mathematics of marital conflict: Dynamic mathematical nonlinear modeling of newlywed marital interaction. *Journal of Family Psychology, 13*(1), 3–19.

Goulet, J. (2006). The "berdache"/"two-spirit": A comparison of anthropological and native constructions of gendered identities among the Northern Athapaskans. *Journal of the Royal Anthropological Institute, 683*(19).

Grady, D. (2003a). Postmenopausal hormones—Therapy for symptoms only. *New England Journal of Medicine, 348*(19), 1835–1837.

Grady, D. (2003b, June 25). Study finds new risks in hormone therapy. *The New York Times*.

Grady, D. (2005, October 7). Vaccine prevents most cervical cancer. *The New York Times*. [Online].

Gray, R. H., et al. (2007). Male circumcision for HIV prevention in men in Rakai, Uganda: A randomised trial. *Lancet, 369*, 657–666.

Green, R. (2003). When therapists do not want their clients to be homosexual: A response to Rosik's article. *Journal of Marital & Family Therapy, 29*(1), 29–38.

Greene, B. (2000). African American lesbian and bisexual women. *Journal of Social Issues, 56*(2), 239–249.

Greene, B. (2005). Psychology, diversity and social justice: Beyond heterosexism and across the cultural divide. *Counselling Psychology Quarterly, 18*(4), 295–306.

Greenwald, E., & Leitenberg, H. (1989). Long-term effects of sexual experiences with siblings and non-siblings during childhood. *Archives of Sexual Behavior, 18*, 389–399.

Grenz, S. (2006). Review of *The Politics of Prostitution. Women's Movements, Democratic States and the Globalisation of Sex Commerce* and *Not for Sale: Feminists Resisting Prostitution and Pornography. Sexualities, 9*(2), 256–259.

Griffith, K. H., & Hebl, M. R. (2002). The disclosure dilemma for gay men and lesbians: "Coming out" at work. *Journal of Applied Psychology, 87*(6), 1191–1199.

Grigoriadis, S., & Romans, S. (2006). Postpartum psychiatric disorders: What do we know and where do we go? *Current Psychiatry Reviews, 2*(1), 151–158.

Grodstein, F., Manson, J. E., & Stampfer, M. J. (2006). Hormone therapy and coronary heart disease: The role of time since menopause and age at hormone initiation. *The Journal of Women's Health, 15*(1), 35–44.

Gross, B. (2006). The pleasure of pain. *Forensic Examiner, 15*(1), 57–61.

Gross, J. (2006, April 20). Learning to savor a full life, love life included. *The New York Times*.

Grosser, B. I., Monti–Bloch, L., Jennings-White, C., & Berliner, D. L. (2000). Behavioral and electrophysiological effects of androstadienone, a human pheromone. *Psychoneuroendocrinology, 25*(3), 289–300.

Groth, A. N., & Birnbaum, H. J. (1979). *Men who rape: The psychology of the offender*. New York: Plenum Press.

Grych, J. H., Fincham, F. D., Jouriles, E. N., & McDonald, R. (2000). Interparental conflict and child adjustment: Testing the mediational role of appraisals in the cognitive–contextual framework. *Child Development, 71*(6), 1648–1661.

Guay, A. T. (2001). Decreased testosterone in regularly menstruating women with decreased libido: A clinical observation. *Journal of Sex & Marital Therapy, 27*(5), 513–519.

Guernsey, L. (2001, July 19). Looking for clues in Junior's keystrokes. *The New York Times*, pp. G1, G9.

Guo, Y. N., Ng, E. M. L., & Chan, K. (2004). Foreplay, orgasm and after-play among Shanghai couples and its integrative relation with their marital satisfaction. *Sexual and Relationship Therapy, 19*(1), 65–78.

Gupta, M. (1994). Sexuality in the Indian subcontinent. *Sexual and Marital Therapy, 9*(1), 57–69.

Gutmann, P. (2006). About confusions of the mind due to abnormal conditions of the sexual organs. *History of Psychiatry, 17*(1), 107–111.

Guzick, D. S., & Hoeger, K. (2000). Sex, hormones, and hysterectomies. *The New England Journal of Medicine, 343*(10).

Haake, P., et al. (2003). Acute neuroendocrine response to sexual stimulation in sexual offenders. *Canadian Journal of Psychiatry, 48*(4), 265–271.

Hafen, M., Jr., & Crane, D. R. (2003). When marital interaction and intervention researchers arrive at different points of view: The active listening controversy. *Journal of Family Therapy, 25*(1), 4–14.

Haldeman, D. C. (2002). Gay rights, patient rights: The implications of sexual orientation conversion therapy. *Professional Psychology: Research & Practice, 33*(3), 260–264.

Half in California oppose gay marriage. (2003, August 29). [Online]. www.euroseek.com/news/21323.html.

Hall, G. C. N., Sue, S., Narang, D. S., & Lilly, R. S. (2000). Culture-specific models of men's sexual aggression: Intra- and interpersonal determinants. *Cultural Diversity & Ethnic Minority Psychology, 6*(3), 252–267.

Hall, G., Collins, A., Csemiczky, G., & Landgren, B. (2002). Lipoproteins and BMI: A comparison between women during transition to menopause and regularly menstruating healthy women. *Maturitas, 41*(3), 177–185.

Halpern, D. F. (1997). Sex differences in intelligence: Implications for education. *American Psychologist, 52,* 1091–1102.

Halpern, D. F. (2003). Sex differences in cognitive abilities. *Applied Cognitive Psychology, 17*(3), 375–376.

Halpern, D. F., & LaMay, M. L. (2000). The smarter sex: A critical review of sex differences in intelligence. *Educational Psychology Review, 12*(2), 229–246.

Hamann, S., Herman, R. A., Nolan, C. L., & Wallen, K. (2004). Men and women differ in amygdala response to visual sexual stimuli. *Nature Neuroscience, 7*(4), 411–416.

Hamer, D. H., et al. (1993, July 16). A linkage between DNA markers on the X chromosome and male sexual orientation. *Science, 261,* 321–327.

Hardy, S. (2001). More black lace: Women, eroticism and subjecthood. *Sexualities, 4*(4), 435–453.

Harris, C. R. (2003). A review of sex differences in sexual jealousy, including self-report data, psychophysiological responses, interpersonal violence, and morbid jealousy. *Personality & Social Psychology Review, 7*(2), 102–128.

Hart, J., et al. (1991). Sexual behavior in pregnancy: A study of 219 women. *Journal of Sex Education and Therapy, 17,* 86–90.

Hartley, H. (2006). The "pinking" of Viagra culture: Drug industry efforts to create and repackage sex drugs for women. *Sexualities, 9*(3), 363–378.

Hartocollis, A. (2006, June 24). Women have seen it all on subway, unwillingly. *The New York Times.*

Hassebrauck, M. (2003). Romantische Männer und realistische Frauen: Geschlechtsunterschiede in Beziehungskognitionen. *Zeitschrift für Sozialpsychologie, 34*(1), 25–35.

Hatcher, R. A. (2004). *Contraceptive technologies.* 18th rev. ed. London: British Medical Association.

Hatcher, R. A., et al. (Eds.) (2006). *Contraceptive technologies.* 18th rev. ed. New York: Ardent Media.

Hatfield, E., & Rapson, R. L. (2002). Passionate love and sexual desire: Cultural and historical perspectives. In Vangelisti, A. L., Reis, H. T., et al. (Eds.). *Stability and change in relationships. Advances in personal relationships* (pp. 306–324). New York: Cambridge University Press.

Hatzichristou, D. G., et al. (2000). Sildenafil versus intracavernous injection therapy: Efficacy and preference in patients on intracavernous injection for more than 1 year. *The Journal of Urology, 164,* 1197–1200.

Hatzichristou, D. G., et al. (2005). Vardenafil improves satisfaction rates, depressive symptomatology, and self-confidence in a broad population of men with erectile dysfunction. *Journal of Sexual Medicine, 2*(1), 109–116.

Haugaard, J. J. (2000). The challenge of defining child sexual abuse. *American Psychologist, 55*(9), 1036–1039.

Hawkley, L. C., & Cacioppo, J. T. (2003). Loneli-

ness and pathways to disease. *Brain, Behavior & Immunity, 17*(Suppl. 1), S98–S105.

Hawkley, L. C., Burleson, M. H., Berntson, G. G., & Cacioppo, J. T. (2003). Loneliness in everyday life: Cardiovascular activity, psychosocial context, and health behaviors. *Journal of Personality & Social Psychology, 85*(1), 105–120.

Hayes, R., & Dennerstein, L. (2005). The impact of aging on sexual function and sexual dysfunction in women: A review of population-based studies. *Journal of Sexual Medicine, 2*(3), 317–330.

Health officials alarmed by syphilis outbreak. (2002, September 28). The Associated Press.

Health24.com. *The girl child.* (2006, February 10). [Online]. www.health24.com/sex/sexuality_throughout_life.

Heath, R. (1972). Pleasure and brain activity in man. *Journal of Nervous and Mental Disease, 154,* 3–18.

Hellstrom, W. J. G., Nehra, A., Shabsigh, R., & Sharlip, I. D. (2006). Premature ejaculation: The most common male sexual dysfunction. *Journal of Sexual Medicine, 3*(Suppl. 1), 1–3.

Hendrick, C., & Hendrick, S. S. (2003). Romantic love: Measuring Cupid's arrow. In Lopez, S., & Snyder, C. R. (Eds.). *Positive psychological assessment: A handbook of models and measures* (pp. 235–249). Washington, DC: American Psychological Association.

Hendrick, C., & Hendrick, S. S. (Eds.). (2000). *Close relationships: A sourcebook.* Thousand Oaks, CA: Sage Publications.

Hendrick, C., Hendrick, S. S., & Reich, D. A. (2006). The Brief Sexual Attitudes Scale. *Journal of Sex Research, 43*(1), 76–86.

Hendrick, S. S., & Hendrick, C. (2002). Love. In Snyder, C. R., & Lopez, S. J. (Ed.) *Handbook of positive psychology* (pp. 472–484). London: Oxford University Press.

Henshaw, S. K. (2003, May 1). U.S. teenage pregnancy statistics with comparative statistics for women aged 20–24. [Online]. www.guttmacher.org/pubs/teen_stats.html.

Hensley, L. G. (2002). Treatment for survivors of rape: Issues and interventions. *Journal of Mental Health Counseling, 24*(4), 330–347.

Henslin, J. H. (2007). *Sociology: A down-to-earth approach.* 8th ed. Boston: Allyn & Bacon.

Herek, G. M., & Gonzalez–Rivera, M. (2006). Attitudes toward homosexuality among U.S. residents of Mexican descent. *Journal of Sex Research, 43*(2), 122–135.

Herek, G. M., Widaman, K. F., & Capitanio, J. P. (2005). When sex equals AIDS: Symbolic stigma and heterosexual adults' inaccurate beliefs about sexual transmission of AIDS. *Social Problems, 52*(1), 15–37.

Herrera, V. M., & McCloskey, L. A. (2003). Sexual abuse, family violence, and female delinquency: Findings from a longitudinal study. *Violence & Victims, 18*(3), 319–334.

Herrington, D. M., et al. (2000). Effects of estrogen replacement on the progression of coronary artery atherosclerosis. *The New England Journal of Medicine, 343*(8).

Herrmann, H. C., Chang, G., Klugherz, B. D., Mahoney, P. D. (2000). Hemodynamic effects of sildenafil in men with severe coronary artery disease. *The New England Journal of Medicine, 342*(22), 1622–1626.

Hester, J. D. (2005). Eunuchs and the postgender Jesus: Matthew 19:12 and transgressive sexualities. *Journal for the Study of the New Testament, 28*(1), 13–40.

Hetherington, E. M. (2006). The influence of conflict, marital problem solving and parenting on children's adjustment in nondivorced, divorced and remarried families. In Clarke–Stewart, A., & Dunn, J. (Eds.). *Families count: Effects on child and adolescent development* (pp. 203–237). The Jacobs Foundation series on adolescence. New York: Cambridge University Press.

Hetherington, E. M., & Kelly, J. (2003). For better or for worse: Divorce reconsidered. *American Journal of Psychiatry, 160*(3), 601–602.

Hicks, T. V., & Leitenberg, H. (2001). Sexual fantasies about one's partner versus someone else: Gender differences in incidence and frequency. *Journal of Sex Research, 38*(1), 43–50.

Hill, R. A., Donovan, S., & Koyama, N. F. (2005). Female sexual advertisement reflects resource availability in twentieth-century UK society. *Human Nature, 16*(3), 266–277.

Hines, D. A., & Saudino, K. J. (2003). Gender differences in psychological, physical, and sexual aggression among college students using the Revised Conflict Tactics Scales. *Violence & Victims, 18*(2), 197–217.

Hines, M., Ahmed, S. F., & Hughes, I. A. (2003). Psychological outcomes and gender-related development in complete androgen insensitivity syndrome. *Archives of Sexual Behavior, 32*(2), 93–101.

Hines, T. M. (2001). The G-spot: A modern gynecological myth. *American Journal of Obstetrics and Gynecology, 185*(2), 359–362.

Hird, M. J. (2004). Naturally queer. *Feminist Theory, 5*(1), 85–89.

Hird, M. J. (2006). Sex diversity and evolutionary psychology. *The Psychologist, 19*(1), 30–32.

Hitt, J. (1998, January 18). Who will do abortions here? *The New York Times Magazine,* 20–27, 42, 45–46, 54–55.

Hofferth, S. L., & Anderson, K. G. (2003). Are all dads equal? Biology versus marriage as a basis for paternal investment. *Journal of Marriage & Family, 65*(1), 213–232.

Hofmeyr, D. G., & Greeff, A. P. (2002). The influence of a vasectomy on the marital relationship and sexual satisfaction of the married man. *Journal of Sex & Marital Therapy, 28*(4), 339–352.

Holcomb, D. R., Savage, M. P., Seehafer, R., & Waalkes, D. M. (2002). A mixed-gender date rape prevention intervention targeting freshman college athletes. *College Student Journal, 36*(2), 165–179.

Holman, T. B., & Jarvis, M. O. (2003). Hostile, volatile, avoiding, and validating couple-conflict types: An investigation of Gottman's couple-conflict types. *Personal Relationships, 10*(2), 267–282.

Holmes, S. T., & Holmes, R. M. (2002). *Sex crimes.* Thousand Oaks, CA: Sage Publications.

Honeycutt, J. M., & Cantrill, J. G. (2001). *Cognition, communication, and romantic relationships.* Mahwah, NJ: Lawrence Erlbaum Associates.

Horne, A. (2003). Oedipal aspirations and phallic fears: On fetishism in childhood and young adulthood. *Journal of Child Psychotherapy, 29*(1), 37–52.

Horowitz, H. L. (2002). *Rereading sex: Battles over sexual knowledge and suppression in nineteenth-century America.* New York: Knopf.

Hsiao, M., Liu, C., Chen, K., & Hsieh, T. (2002). Characteristics of women seeking treatment for premenstrual syndrome in Taiwan. *Acta Psychiatrica Scandinavica, 106*(2), 150–155.

Huerta, M., Cortina, L. M., Pang, J. S., Torges, C. M., & Magley, V. J. (2006). Sex and power in the academy: Modeling sexual harassment in the lives of college women. *Personality and Social Psychology Bulletin, 32*(5), 616–628.

Hughes, S. M., Harrison, M. A., & Gallup, G. G. Jr. (2004). Sex differences in mating strategies: Mate guarding, infidelity and multiple concurrent sex partners. *Sexualities, Evolution & Gender, 6*(1), 3–13.

Hugh–Jones, S., Gough, B., & Littlewood, A. (2005a). A critique of psycho-medical discourse from the perspectives of women who exhibit. *Sexualities, 8*(3), 259–281.

Hugh–Jones, S., Gough, B., & Littlewood, A. (2005b). Sexual exhibitionism as "sexuality and individuality": A critique of psychomedical discourse from the perspectives of women who exhibit. *Sexualities, 8*(3), 259–281.

Hunt, M. (1974). *Sexual behavior in the 1970's.* New York: Dell Books.

Hunter, M. S., et al. (2002). Medical (fluoxetine) and psychological (cognitive–behavioural therapy) treatment for premenstrual dysphoric disorder: A study of treatment processes. *Journal of Psychosomatic Research, 53*(3), 811–817.

Hunter, M., & O'Dea, I. (2001). Cognitive appraisal of the menopause: The Menopause Representations Questionnaire (MRQ). *Psychology, Health & Medicine, 6*(1), 65–76.

Hussain, A. (2002, June 26) It's official. Men really are afraid of commitment.

Huxley, R. R. (2000). Nausea and vomiting in early pregnancy: Its role in placental development. *Obstetrics & Gynecology, 95,* 779–782.

Hyde, J. S. (Ed.). (2005). *Biological substrates of human sexuality.* Washington, DC: American Psychological Association.

Hyde, J. S., & Plant, E. A. (1995). Magnitude of psychological gender differences: Another side to the story. *American Psychologist, 50,* 159–161.

Hyman, S. M., Gold, S. N., & Cott, M. A. (2003). Forms of social support that moderate PTSD in childhood sexual abuse survivors. *Journal of Family Violence, 18*(5), 295–300.

Illes, J. (October 2000). Beauty secrets of ancient Egypt: Nefertem, Ancient Lord of Perfume. *Tour Egypt Monthly, 5*(1).

Imperato–McGinley, J., et al. (1974). Steroid 5 reductase deficiency in man: An inherited form of male pseudohermaphroditism. *Science, 186,* 1213–1215.

Inciardi, J. A., Surratt, H. L., & Kurtz, S. P. (2006). HIV, HBV, and HCV infections among drug-involved, inner-city, street sex workers in Miami, Florida. *AIDS and Behavior, 10*(2), 139–147.

Intersex Society of North America. Accessed August 22, 2006. [Online]. www.isna.org.

Irwin, T. W., Morgenstern, J., Parsons, J. T., Wainberg, M., & Labouvie, E. (2006). Alcohol and sexual HIV risk behavior among problem drinking men who have sex with men: An event level analysis of timeline followback data. *AIDS and Behavior, 10*(3), 299–307.

Isay, R. A. (1990). Psychoanalytic theory and the therapy of gay men. In McWhirter, D. P., Sanders, S. A., & Reinisch, J. M. (Eds.). *Homosexuality/heterosexuality: Concepts of sexual orientation* (pp. 283–303). New York: Oxford University Press.

Itzin, C. (2002). Pornography and the construction of misogyny. *Journal of Sexual Aggression, 8*(3), 4–42.

Jacob, S., & McClintock, M. K. (2000). Psychological state and mood effects of steroidal chemosignals in women and men. *Hormones and Behavior, 37*(1), 57–78.

Jacob, S., Hayreh, D. J. S., & McClintock, M. K. (2001). Context-dependent effects of steroid chemosignals on human physiology and mood. *Physiology & Behavior, 74*(1–2), 15–27.

Jameson, M. (2000, June 12). Childbirth that's not so labor-intensive. *Los Angeles Times.*

Janofsky, M., & Schemo, D. J. (2003, March 16). Women recount cadet life: Forced sex and fear. *The New York Times.* [Online].

Janssen, E. (Ed.). (2006). *The psychophysiology of sex.* Bloomington, IN: Indiana University Press.

Janssen, E., & Bancroft, J. (2006). The dual-control model: The role of sexual inhibition & excitation in sexual arousal and behavior. In Janssen, E. (Ed.). *The psychophysiology of sex.* Bloomington, IN: Indiana University Press. [In press].

Janssen, E., Prause, N., & Geer, J. (2006). The sexual response. In Cacioppo, J. T., Tassinary, L. G., & Berntson, G. G. (Eds.). *Handbook of psychophysiology.* 3rd ed. New York: Cambridge University Press.

Jayson, S. (2006, May 29). Poll: Boomers go easy on marriage. *USA Today.*

Johannes, C. B., et al. (2000). Incidence of erectile dysfunction in men 40 to 69 years old: Longitudinal results from the Massachusetts male aging study. *The Journal of Urology, 163,* 460.

Johanson, R. (2000). Perineal massage for prevention of perineal trauma in childbirth. *The Lancet, 355*(9200), 250–251.

Johnson, H. (2003). The cessation of assaults on wives. *Journal of Comparative Family Studies, 34*(1), 75–91.

Johnson, S. (2005). The evolution of couple therapy. *The Psychologist, 18*(9), 538–540.

Johnston, L. D., O'Malley, P. M., Bachman, J. G., & Schulenberg, J. E. (2005). *Monitoring the future national results on adolescent drug use: Overview of key findings, 2004.* NIH publication no. 05-5726. Bethesda, MD: National Institute on Drug Abuse.

Johnstone, S. J., et al. (2001). Obstetric risk factors for postnatal depression in urban and rural community samples. *Australian & New Zealand Journal of Psychiatry, 35*(1), 69–74.

Jones, B. E., & Hill, M. J. (2002). *Mental health issues in lesbian, gay, bisexual, and transgender communities: Review of Psychiatry, Volume 21.* Washington, DC: American Psychiatric Publishing.

Kaczmarek, P., LeVine, E., & Segal, A. F. (2006). Section 6. Civil and criminal trial matters. In Kaczmarek, P., LeVine, E., & Segal, A. F. (Eds.). *Law & mental health professionals: New Mexico* (pp. 269–296). Washington, DC: American Psychological Association.

Kafka, M. P. (2003). Sex offending and sexual appetite: The clinical and theoretical relevance of hypersexual desire. *International Journal of Offender Therapy & Comparative Criminology, 47*(4), 439–451.

Kaiser Family Foundation, Holt, T., Greene, L., & Davis, J. (2003). *National Survey of Adolescents and Young Adults: Sexual health knowledge, attitudes and experiences.* Menlo Park, CA: Henry J. Kaiser Family Foundation.

Kaler, A. (2005). Peer commentaries on Binik (2005): Classifying pain: What's at stake for women with dyspareunia. *Archives of Sexual Behavior, 34*(1), 34–36.

Kamen, P. (2002). *Her way: Young women remake the sexual revolution.* New York: Broadway Books.

Kaplan, H. S. (1974). *The new sex therapy: Active treatment of sexual dysfunctions.* New York: Brunner/Mazel.

Kaplan, H. S. (1987). *Sexual aversion, sexual phobias, and panic disorder.* New York: Brunner/Mazel.

Karpman, E., Williams, D. H., & Lipshultz, L. I. (2006). Vasectomy reversal: New techniques and role in the era of intracytoplasmic sperm injection. *Canadian Journal of Urology, 13*(Suppl. 1), 22–27.

Katz, M. H., et al. (2002). Impact of highly active antiretroviral treatment on HIV seroincidence among men who have sex with men: San Francisco. *American Journal of Public Health, 92*(3), 388–394.

Kelly, J. B. (2000). Children's adjustment in conflicted marriage and divorce: A decade review of research. *Journal of the American Academy of Child & Adolescent Psychiatry, 39*(8), 963–973.

Kendler, K. S., et al. (2000a). Childhood sexual abuse and adult psychiatric and substance use disorders in women: An epidemiological and Cotwin control analysis. *Archives of General Psychiatry, 57*(10), 953–959.

Kennedy, N., & McDonough, M. (2002). Koro: A case in an eastern European asylum seeker in Ireland. *Irish Journal of Psychological Medicine, 19*(4), 130–131.

Kennedy, R. (2003). *Interracial intimacies: Sex, marriage, identity, and adoption.* New York: Knopf.

Kersting, K. (2003). Cognitive sex differences: A "political minefield." *Monitor on Psychology, 34*(5).

Kessler, R. C. (2003). Epidemiology of women and depression. *Journal of Affective Disorders, 74*(1), 5–13.

Khoury, M. J., Burke, W., & Thomson, E. J. (Eds.). (2000). *Genetics and public health in the 21st century: Using genetic information to improve health and prevent disease.* New York: Oxford University Press.

Kim, A. A., Kent, C. K., & Klausner, J. D. (2002). Increased risk of HIV and sexually transmitted disease transmission among gay or bisexual men who use Viagra, San Francisco 2000–2001. *AIDS, 16*(10), 1425–1428.

Kim, Y., & Hahn, S. (2006). Homosexuality in ancient and modern Korea. *Culture, Health & Sexuality, 8*(1), 59–65.

Kimble, D. P. (1992). *Biological psychology.* 2nd ed. Fort Worth, TX: Harcourt Brace Jovanovich.

King, J. A., De Oliveira, W. L., & Patel, N. (2005). Deficits in testosterone facilitate enhanced fear response. *Psychoneuroendocrinology, 30*(4), 333–340.

Kinsey, A. C., Pomeroy, W. B., & Martin, C. E. (1948). *Sexual behavior in the human male.* Philadelphia: W. B. Saunders.

Kinsey, A. C., Pomeroy, W. B., Martin, C. E., & Gebhard, P. H. (1953). *Sexual behavior in the human female.* Philadelphia: W. B. Saunders.

Kippax, S., & Smith, G. (2001). Anal intercourse and power in sex between men. *Sexualities, 4*(4), 413–434.

Kirby, D. (2000, October 3). More options, and decisions, for men with prostate cancer. *The New York Times.* [Online].

Kirchheimer, S., & Smith, M. (2003, May 28). Condoms in schools don't boost teen sex: Key is making condom programs part of overall sex education, says one expert. *WebMD Medical News.* [Online].

Kirenskaya–Berus, A. V., & Tkachenko, A. A. (2003). Characteristic features of EEG spectral characteristics in persons with deviant sexual behavior. *Human Physiology, 29*(3), 278–287.

Kirkpatrick, R. C. (2000). The evolution of human homosexual behavior. *Current Anthropology, 41*(3), 385–413.

Kito, M. (2005). Self-disclosure in romantic relationships and friendships among American and Japanese college students. *Journal of Social Psychology, 145*(2), 127–140.

Kjerulff, K. H., et al. (2000). Effectiveness of hysterectomy. *Obstetrics & Gynecology, 95,* 319–326.

Klaw, E. L., et al. (2005). Challenging rape culture: Awareness, emotion and action through campus acquaintance rape education. *Women & Therapy, 28*(2), 47–63.

Kleinplatz, P. J. (2003). What's new in sex therapy? From stagnation to fragmentation. *Sexual & Relationship Therapy, 18*(1), 95–106.

Klohnen, E. C., & Luo, S. (2003). Interpersonal attraction and personality: What is attractive: self similarity, ideal similarity, complementarity or attachment security? *Journal of Personality and Social Psychology, 85*(4), 709–722.

Klusmann, D. (2002). Sexual motivation and the duration of partnership. *Archives of Sexual Behavior, 31,* 275–287.

Klüver, H., & Bucy, P. C. (1939). Preliminary analysis of functions of the temporal lobes in monkeys. *Archives of Neurology and Psychiatry, 42,* 979.

Knaak, S. (2005). Breast-feeding, bottle-feeding and Dr. Spock: The shifting context of choice. *Canadian Review of Sociology and Anthropology, 42*(2), 197–216.

Knapp, M. L., & Vangelista, A. L. (2000). *Interpersonal communication and human relationships.* 4th ed. Boston: Allyn & Bacon.

Kniffin, K. M., & Wilson, D. S. (2004). The effect of nonphysical traits on the perception of physical attractiveness: Three naturalistic studies. *Evolution and Human Behavior, 25*(2), 88–101.

Knox, D., & Schacht, C. (2002). *Choices in relationships—An introduction to marriage and the family.* 7th ed. Belmont, CA: Wadsworth Publishing.

Knox, D., Gibson, L., Zusman, M., & Gallmeier, C. (1997a). Why college students end relationships. *College Student Journal, 31*(4), 449–452.

Knox, D., Schacht, C., & Zusman, M. E. (1999a). Love relationships among college students. *College Student Journal, 33*(1), 149–151.

Koblin, B. A., et al. (2006). Risk factors for HIV infection among men who have sex with men. *AIDS, 20*(5), 731–739.

Kohlberg, L. (1966). A cognitive–developmental analysis of children's sex-role concepts and attitudes. In Maccoby, E. E. (Ed.). *The development of sex differences.* Stanford, CA: Stanford University Press.

Kolata G. (1998, September 9). Researchers report success in method to pick baby's sex. *The New York Times.* [Online].

Kolata, G. (1998, April 4). Impotence pill: Would it also help women? *The New York Times.* pp. A1, A6.

Kolata, G. (2000, April 18). New name for impotence, and new drugs. *The New York Times,* pp. F6, F14.

Kolata, G. (2000, April 5). Estrogen tied to slight rise in heart attack. *The New York Times,* pp. A1, A20.

Kolata, G. (2002, December 22). Chasing youth, many gamble on hormones. *The New York Times.* [Online].

Kolata, G. (2004, February 26). Cell protein gives monkeys innate immunity to H.I.V. *The New York Times.* [Online].

Kolata, G. (2005, October 27). Screening proves itself in breast cancer fight. *The New York Times.* [Online].

Komisaruk, B. R., & Whipple, B. (2005). Brain activity imaging during sexual response in women with spinal cord injury. In Hyde, J. S. (Ed.). *Biological substrates of human sexuality* (pp. 109–145). Washington, DC: American Psychological Association.

Koren, G., Pastuszak, A., & Ito, S. (1998). Drug therapy: Drugs in pregnancy. *New England Journal of Medicine, 338,* 1128–1137.

Korobov, N., & Thorne, A. (2006). Intimacy and distancing: Young men's conversations about romantic relationships. *Journal of Adolescent Research, 21*(1), 27–55.

Koss, M. P. (1993). Rape: Scope, impact, interventions, and public policy responses. *American Psychologist, 48,* 1062–1069.

Koss, M. P. (2003). Evolutionary models of why men rape: Acknowledging the complexities. In Travis, C. B. (Ed.). *Evolution, gender, and rape* (pp. 191–205). Cambridge, MA: MIT Press.

Koss, M. P., & Kilpatrick, D. G. (2001). Rape and sexual assault. In Gerrity, E., et al. (Eds.). *The mental health consequences of torture. Plenum series on stress and coping* (pp. 177–193). Dordrecht, the Netherlands: Kluwer Academic Publishers.

Koss, M. P., Bailey, J. A., Yuan, N. P., Herrera, V. M., & Lichter, E. L. (2003). Depression and PTSD in survivors of male violence: Research and training initiatives to facilitate recovery. *Psychology of Women Quarterly, 27*(2), 130–142.

Koss, M. P., Figueredo, A. J., & Prince, R. J. (2002). Cognitive mediation of rape's mental, physical and social health impact: Tests of four models in cross-sectional data. *Journal of Consulting & Clinical Psychology, 70*(4), 926–941.

Koss, M. P., Gidycz, C. A., & Wisniewski, N. (1987). The scope of rape: Incidence and prevalence of sexual aggression and victimization in a national sample of higher education students. *Journal of Consulting and Clinical Psychology, 55,* 162–170.

Kouros–Mehr, H., et al. (2001). Identification of non-functional human VNO receptor genes provides evidence for vestigiality of the human VNO. *Chemical Sciences, 26*(9), 1167–1174.

Krahe, B., Waizenhofer, E., & Moller, I. (2003). Women's sexual aggression against men: Prevalence and predictors. *Sex Roles, 49*(5–6), 219–232.

Kramer, M. S., et al. (2000). The contribution of mild and moderate preterm birth to infant mortality. *Journal of the American Medical Association, 284,* 843–849.

Kristof, N. D. (2003, October 4). Killer of dreams. *The New York Times.*

Kristof, N. D. (2004, January 24). Going home, with hope. *The New York Times,* p. A15.

Kristof, N. D. (2006, January 22). Slavery in our time. *The New York Times,* Section 4, p. 17.

Krueger, R. B., & Kaplan, M. S. (2002). Behavioral and psychopharmacological treatment of the paraphilic and hypersexual disorders. *Journal of Psychiatric Practice, 8*(1), 21–32.

Kuffel, S. W., & Heiman, J. R. (2006). Effects of depressive symptoms and experimentally adopted schemas on sexual arousal and affect in sexually healthy women. *Archives of Sexual Behavior, 35*(2), 163–177.

Kuhnle, U., Krob, G., & Maier, E. (2003). True hermaphroditism: Presentation, management, outcomes. *Endocrinologist, 13*(3), 214–218.

Kuiper, B., & Cohen–Kettenis, P. (1988). Sex reassignment surgery: A study of 141 Dutch transsexuals. *Archives of Sexual Behavior, 17,* 439–457.

Kulik, L. (2000). Gender identity, sex typing of occupations, and gender role ideology among adolescents: Are they related? *International Journal for the Advancement of Counselling, 22*(1), 43–56.

Kumashiro, K. K. (Ed.). (2004). *Restoried selves: Autobiographies of Queer Asian/Pacific American activists.* New York: Harrington Park Press/The Haworth Press.

Kurdek, L. A. (2005). What do we know about gay and lesbian couples? *Current Directions in Psychological Science, 14*(5), 251.

Kurdek, L. A. (2005). What do we know about gay and lesbian couples? *Current Directions in Psychological Science, 14*(5), 251–254.

Kurdek, L. A. (2006). Differences between partners from heterosexual, gay, and lesbian cohabiting couples. *Journal of Marriage and Family, 68*(2), 509–528.

Kurzban, R., & Weeden, J. (2005). HurryDate: Mate preferences in action. *Evolution and Human Behavior, 26*(3), 227–244.

Lackluster Latin lovers surf for seduction. (2000, June 1). Reuters News Agency. [Online].

Ladas, A. K., Whipple, B., & Perry, J. D. (1982). *The G spot and other recent discoveries about human sexuality.* New York: Holt, Rinehart & Winston.

Lalezari, J. P., et al. (2003). Enfuvirtide, an HIV-1 fusion inhibitor, for drug-resistant HIV infection in North and South America. *New England Journal of Medicine, 348*(22), 2175–2185.

Lalumière, M. L., Harris, G. T., Quinsey, V. L., & Rice, M. E. (2005a). Introduction. In Lalumière, M. L., Harris, G. T., Quinsey, V. L., & Rice, M. E. (Eds.). *The causes of rape: Understanding individual differences in male propensity for sexual aggression* (pp. 3–6). Washington, DC: American Psychological Association.

Lalumière, M. L., Harris, G. T., Quinsey, V. L., & Rice, M. E. (2005b). Antisociality and mating effort. In Lalumière, M. L., Harris, G. T., Quinsey, V. L., & Rice, M. E. (Eds.). *The causes of rape: Understanding individual differences in male propensity for sexual aggression* (pp. 61–103). Washington, DC: American Psychological Association.

Lalumière, M. L., Harris, G. T., Quinsey, V. L., & Rice, M. E. (2005c). Sexual interest in rape. In Lalumière, M. L., Harris, G. T., Quinsey, V. L., & Rice, M. E. (Eds.). *The causes of rape: Under-*

standing individual differences in male propensity for sexual aggression (pp. 105–128). Washington, DC: American Psychological Association.

Lamanna, M. A., & Riedmann, A. (2005). *Marriages and families.* 8th ed. Belmont, CA: Wadsworth.

Lamaze, F. (1981). *Painless childbirth.* New York: Simon & Schuster.

Lamba, H., Goldmeier, D., Mackie, N. E., & Scullard, G. (2004). Antiretroviral therapy is associated with sexual dysfunction and with increased serum oestradiol levels in men. *International Journal of STD & AIDS, 15*(4), 234–237.

Lane, T., Pettifor, A., Pascoe, S., Fiamma, A., & Rees, H. (2006). Heterosexual anal intercourse increases risk of HIV infection among young South African men. *AIDS, 20*(1), 123–125.

Langevin, R. (2003). A study of the psychosexual characteristics of sex killers: Can we identify them before it is too late? *International Journal of Offender Therapy & Comparative Criminology, 47*(4), 366–382.

Langevin, R. (2006). Acceptance and completion of treatment among sex offenders. *International Journal of Offender Therapy and Comparative Criminology, 50*(4), 402–417.

Langevin, R., et al. (1979). Experimental studies of the etiology of genital exhibitionism. *Archives of Sexual Behavior, 8,* 307–332.

Langevin, R., et al. (2004). Lifetime sex offender recidivism: A 25-year follow-up study. *Canadian Journal of Criminology and Criminal Justice, 46*(5), 531–552.

Langhinrichsen–Rohling, J., Palarea, R. E., Cohen, J., & Rohlin, M. L. (2002). Breaking up is hard to do: Unwanted pursuit behaviors following the dissolution of a romantic relationship. In Davis, K. E., & Frieze, I. H., et al. (Eds.). *Stalking: Perspectives on victims and perpetrators* (pp. 212–236). New York: Springer.

Langhout, R. D., et al. (2005). Sexual harassment severity: Assessing situational and personal determinants and outcomes. *Journal of Applied Social Psychology, 35*(5), 975–1007.

Langille, D. B., & Curtis, L. (2002). Factors associated with sexual intercourse before age 15 among female adolescents in Nova Scotia. *Canadian Journal of Human Sexuality, 11*(3), 91–99.

Langlois, J. H., et al. (2000). Maxims or myths of beauty? A meta-analytic and theoretical review. *Psychological Bulletin, 126*(3), 390–423.

Långström, N., & Zucker, K. J. (2005). Transvestic fetishism in the general population: Prevalence and correlates. *Journal of Sex & Marital Therapy, 31*(2), 87–95.

Laqueur, T. W. (2003). *Solitary sex: A cultural history of masturbation.* Zone Books. www .newzonebooks.com.

Larsson, I., & Svedin, C. (2002). Experiences in childhood: Young adults' recollections. *Archives of Sexual Behavior, 31*(3), 263–273.

LaSala, M. C. (2004). Monogamy of the heart: Extradyadic sex and gay male couples. *Journal of Gay & Lesbian Social Services: Issues in Practice, Policy & Research, 17*(3), 1–24.

Lau, J. T. F., Siah, P. C., & Tsui, H. Y. (2002). A study of the STD/AIDS related attitudes and behaviors of men who have sex with men in Hong Kong. *Archives of Sexual Behavior, 31*(4), 367–373.

Laumann, E. O., et al. (2006). A cross-national study of subjective sexual well-being among older women and men: Findings from the global study of sexual attitudes and behaviors. *Archives of Sexual Behavior, 35*(2), 145–161.

Laumann, E. O., Gagnon, J. H., Michael, R. T., & Michaels, S. (1994). *The social organization of sexuality: Sexual practices in the United States.* Chicago: University of Chicago Press.

Laumann, E. O., Masi, C. M., & Zuckerman, E. W., et al. (1997, April 2). Circumcision in the United States: Prevalence, prophylactic effects, and sexual practice. *The Journal of the American Medical Association, 277,* 1052–1057.

Laumann, E. O., Paik, A., & Rosen, R. C. (1999). Sexual dysfunction in the United States. Prevalence and predictors. *Journal of the American Medical Association, 281*(6), 537–544.

Lawrence, A. A. (2004). Autogynephilia: A paraphilic model of gender identity disorder. *Journal of Gay & Lesbian Psychotherapy, 8*(1–2), 69–87.

Lawrence, A. A. (2005). Sexuality before and after male-to-female sex reassignment surgery. *Archives of Sexual Behavior, 34*(2), 147–166.

Laws, D. R., & Marshall, W. L. (2003). A brief history of behavioral and cognitive behavioral approaches to sexual offenders: Part 1. Early developments. *Sexual Abuse: Journal of Research & Treatment, 15*(2), 75–92.

Leahey, E., & Guo, G. (2001). Gender differences in mathematical trajectories. *Social Forces, 80*(2), 713–732.

Lederman, M. M., & Valdez, H. (2000). Immune restoration with antiretroviral therapies: Implications for clinical management. *Journal of the American Medical Association, 284,* 223–228.

Lee, F. R. (2006, March 28). "Big love": Real polygamists look at HBO polygamists and find sex. *The New York Times.*

Lee, J. K. P., Jackson, H. J., Pattison, P., & Ward, T. (2002). Developmental risk factors for sexual offending. *Child Abuse & Neglect, 26*(1), 73–92.

Leiblum, S. R., & Rosen, R. C. (Ed.). (2000). *Principles and practice of sex therapy.* 3rd ed. New York: Guilford Press.

Leinders–Zufall, T., et al. (2000). Ultrasensitive pheromone detection by mammalian vomeronasal neurons. *Nature, 405,* 792–796.

Leitenberg, H., & Henning, K. (1995). Sexual fantasy. *Psychological Bulletin, 117,* 469–496.

Leitenberg, H., Detzer, M. J., & Srebnik, D. (1993). Gender differences in masturbation and the relation of masturbation experience in preadolescence and/or early adolescence to sexual behavior and sexual adjustment in young adulthood. *Archives of Sexual Behavior, 22,* 87–98.

Leland, J. (2000, May 29). The science of women & sex. *Newsweek,* 48–54.

Lesjak, B., Bogadi, M., & Tošic, G. (2004). Zoophilia in comorbidity with other psychiatric disorders. *Socijalna Psihijatrija, 32*(4), 160–164.

Lester, W. (2000, May 31). *Poll: Americans back some gay rights.* The Associated Press. [Online].

Leue, A., Borchard, B., & Hoyer, J. (2004). Mental disorders in a forensic sample of sexual offenders. *European Psychiatry, 19*(3), 123–130.

LeVay, S. (1991). A difference in hypothalamic structure between heterosexual and homosexual men. *Science, 253,* 1034–1037.

Lever, J., Frederick, D. A., & Peplau, L. A. (2006). Does size matter? Men's and women's views on penis size across the lifespan. *Psychology of Men & Masculinity, 7*(3), 129–143.

Levin, R. J. (2003a). The G-spot: Reality or illusion? *Sexual and Relationship Therapy, 18*(1), 117–119.

Levin, R. J. (2003b). Is prolactin the biological "off switch" for human sexual arousal? *Sexual and Relationship Therapy, 18*(2), 237–243.

Levin, R. J. (2003c). The ins and outs of vaginal lubrication. *Sexual and Relationship Therapy, 18*(4), 509–513.

Levin, R. J. (2005a). The mechanisms of human ejaculation—A critical analysis. *Sexual and Relationship Therapy, 20*(1), 123–131.

Levin, R. J. (2005b). The involvement of the human cervix in reproduction and sex. *Sexual and Relationship Therapy, 20*(2), 251–260.

Levin, R. J. (2006). The breast/nipple/areola complex and human sexuality. *Sexual and Relationship Therapy, 21*(2), 237–249.

Levine, D. (2000). Virtual attraction: What rocks your boat. *CyberPsychology & Behavior, 3*(4), 565–573.

Levinger, G. (1980). Toward the analysis of close relationships. *Journal of Experimental Social Psychology, 16,* 510–544.

Levy, H., & Packman, W. (2004). Sexual abuse prevention for individuals with mental retardation: Considerations for genetic counselors. *Journal of Genetic Counseling, 13*(3), 189–205.

Lewin, T. (1998a, January 17). Debate distant for many having abortions. *The New York Times,* pp. A1, A9.

Lewin, T. (1998b, March 23). Debate centers on definition of harassment. *The New York Times,* pp. A1, A28.

Lewis, J., Maticka–Tyndale, E., Shaver, F., & Schramm, H. (2005). Managing risk and safety on the job: The experiences of Canadian sex workers. *Journal of Psychology & Human Sexuality, 17*(1–2), 147–167.

Lim, D. (2006, October 22). Mondo multiplex: The snuff film turns respectable. *The New York Times.*

Lin, G., & Wang, Q. (2003). Predictors of non-use of condoms among drug users in China: Implications for HIV harm reduction. *Drugs: Education, Prevention & Policy, 10*(2), 141–146.

Ling, F. W. (2000). Recognizing and treating premenstrual dysphoric disorder in the obstetric, gynecologic, and primary care practices. *Journal of Clinical Psychiatry, 61*(Suppl. 12), 9–16.

Lippa, R. (2001). On deconstructing and reconstructing masculinity–femininity. *Journal of Research in Personality, 35*(2), 168–207.

Lippa, R., & Arad, S. (1997). The structure of sexual orientation and its relation to masculinity, femininity, and gender diagnosticity: Different for men and women. *Sex Roles, 37*(3–4), 187–208.

Liptak, A. (2003, January 23). Circumcision opponents use the legal system and legislatures. *The New York Times.* [Online].

Lira, L. R., Koss, M. P., & Russo, N. F. (1999). Mexican American women's definitions of rape and sexual abuse. *Hispanic Journal of Behavioral Sciences, 21*(3), 236–265.

Locke, B. D., & Mahalik, J. R. (2005). Examining masculinity norms, problem drinking, and athletic involvement as predictors of sexual aggression in college men. *Journal of Counseling Psychology, 52*(3), 279–283.

Loder, N. (2000). US science shocked by revelations of sexual discrimination. *Nature, 405,* 713–714.

Logan, T. K., Walker, R., Jordan, C. E., & Leukefeld, C. G. (2006). Justice system options and responses. In Logan, T. K., Walker, R., Jordan, C. E., & Leukefeld, C. G. (Eds.). *Women and victimization: Contributing factors, interventions, and implications* (pp. 161–194). Washington, DC: American Psychological Association.

Long, C. R., Seburn, M., Averill, J. R., & More, T. A. (2003). Solitude experiences: Varieties, settings, and individual differences. *Personality & Social Psychology Bulletin, 29*(5), 578–583.

Lorant, V., et al. (2005). A European comparative study of marital status and socio-economic inequalities in suicide. *Social Science & Medicine, 60*(11), 2431–2441.

Lorenz, F. O., Wickrama, K. A. S., Conger, R. D., & Elder, G. H., Jr. (2006). The short-term and decade-long effects of divorce on women's midlife health. *Journal of Health and Social Behavior, 47*(2), 111–125.

Lotery, H. E., McClure, N., & Galask, R. P. (2004). Vulvodynia. *Lancet, 363*(9414), 1058–1060.

Lucas, A. M. (2005). The work of sex work: Elite prostitutes' vocational orientations and experiences. *Deviant Behavior, 26*(6), 513–546.

Lucon, A. M., et al. (2006). Spontaneous recanalization after vasectomy. *TSW Urology, 1,* 71–74.

Lue, T. F. (2000). Drug therapy: Erectile dysfunction. *The New England Journal of Medicine, 342*(24).

Lykins, A. D., Janssen, E., & Graham, C. A. (2006). The relationship between negative mood and sexuality in heterosexual college women and men. *Journal of Sex Research, 43*(2), 136–143.

Maaita, M. J., Bhaumik, J., & Davies, A. E. (2002). Sexual function after using tension-free vaginal tape for the surgical treatment of genuine stress incontinence. *British Journal of Urology International, 90*(6), 540.

Maartens, L. W. F., Knottnerus, J. A., & Pop, V. J. (2002). Menopausal transition and increased depressive symptomatology: A community based prospective study. *Maturitas, 42*(3), 195–200.

MacDonald, T. K., MacDonald, G., Zanna, M. P., & Fong, G. T. (2000). Alcohol, sexual arousal, and intentions to use condoms in young men: Applying alcohol myopia theory to risky sexual behavior. *Health Psychology, 19,* 290–298.

MacFadden, A., Elias, L., & Saucier, D. (2003). Males and females scan maps similarly, but give directions differently. *Brain and Cognition, 53*(2), 297–300.

MacNeil, S., & Byers, E. S. (2005). Dyadic assessment of sexual self-disclosure and sexual satisfaction in heterosexual dating couples. *Journal of Social and Personal Relationships, 22*(2), 169–181.

Macy, R. J., Nurius, P. S., & Norris, J. (2006). Responding in their best interests: Contextualizing women's coping with acquaintance sexual aggression. *Violence Against Women, 12*(5), 478–500.

Madsen, L., Parsons, S., & Grubin, D. (2006). The relationship between the five-factor model

and *DSM* personality disorder in a sample of child molesters. *Personality and Individual Differences, 40*(2), 227–236.

Major, B., et al. (2000). Psychological responses of women after first-trimester abortion. *Archives of General Psychiatry, 57,* 777–784.

Major, B., Kaiser, C. R., & McCoy, S. K. (2003). It's not my fault: When and why attributions to prejudice protect self-esteem. *Personality & Social Psychology Bulletin, 29*(6), 772–781.

Malamuth, N. M., Addison, T., & Koss, M. (2000). Pornography and sexual aggression: Are there reliable effects and can we understand them? *Annual Review of Sex Research, 11,* 26–91.

Malamuth, N. M., Huppin, M., & Paul, B. (2005). Sexual coercion. In Buss, D. M. (Ed.). *The handbook of evolutionary psychology* (pp. 394–418). Hoboken, NJ: John Wiley & Sons.

Malec, K. (Summer 2003). The abortion–breast cancer link: How politics trumped science and informed consent. *Journal of American Physicians and Surgeons, 8*(2). [Online]. www.abortionbreastcancer.com/jpands.pdf.

Maletzky, B. M., & Steinhauser, C. (2002). A 25-year follow-up of cognitive/behavioral therapy with 7,275 sexual offenders. *Behavior Modification, 26*(2), 123–147.

Malinowski, B. (1927). *Sex and repression in savage society.* London: Kegan Paul, Trench, Trubner & Co.

Malinowski, B. (1929). *The sexual life of savages in north-western Melanesia.* New York: Eugenics.

Man pays victim's husband in fondling case. (2000, June 2). Reuters News Agency. [Online].

Mansergh, G., et al. (2002). "Barebacking" in a diverse sample of men who have sex with men. *AIDS, 16*(4), 653–659.

Mantovani, F. (2001). Networked seduction: A test-bed for the study of strategic communication on the Internet. *CyberPsychology & Behavior, 4*(1), 147–154.

Maranda, M. J., Han, C., & Rainone, G. A. (2004). Crack cocaine and sex. *Journal of Psychoactive Drugs, 36*(3), 315–322.

Maravilla, K. R., et al. (2005). Noncontrast dynamic magnetic resonance imaging for quantitative assessment of female sexual arousal, *Journal of Urology, 172,* 162–166.

Marazziti, D. (2005). The neurobiology of love. *Current Psychiatry Reviews, 1*(3), 331–335.

Marazziti, D., et al. (2003). Normal and obsessional jealousy: A study of a population of young adults. *European Psychiatry, 18*(3), 106–111.

Marchbanks, P. A., et al. (2002). Oral contraceptives and the risk of breast cancer. *New England Journal of Medicine, 346,* 2025–2032.

Marcus, D. K., & Miller, R. S. (2003). Sex differences in judgments of physical attractiveness: A social relations analysis. *Personality & Social Psychology Bulletin, 29*(3), 325–335.

Mardorossian, C. M. (2002). Toward a new feminist theory of rape. *Signs, 27*(3), 743–775.

Markman, H. J. (2005). The prevention of extramarital involvement: Steps toward "affair proofing" marriage. *Clinical Psychology: Science and Practice, 12*(2), 134–138.

Marquis, C. (2003, March 16). Living in sin. *The New York Times,* p. WK2.

Marrazzo, J. (2003). Vulvovaginal candidiasis: Over the counter treatment doesn't seem to

lead to resistance. *British Medical Journal, 326,* 993–994.

Marshall, B. L. (2006). The new virility: Viagra, male aging and sexual function. *Sexualities, 9*(3), 345–362.

Marshall, D. (1971). Sexual behavior on Mangaia. In Marshall, D., & Suggs, R. (Eds.). *Human sexual behavior: Variations in the ethnographic spectrum* (pp. 103–162). New York: Basic Books.

Marshall, W. L. (1989). Pornography and sex offenders. In Zillmann, D., & Bryant, J. (Eds.). *Pornography: Research advances and policy considerations* (pp. 185–214). Hillsdale, NJ: Lawrence Erlbaum Associates.

Marsiglio, W. (2004). When stepfathers claim stepchildren: A conceptual analysis. *Journal of Marriage & Family, 66*(1), 22–39.

Martell, C. R., & Prince, S. E. (2005). Treating infidelity in same-sex couples. *Journal of Clinical Psychology, 61*(11), 1429–1438.

Martino, S. C., et al. (2006). Exposure to degrading versus nondegrading music lyrics and sexual behavior among youth. *Pediatrics, 118,* e430–e441.

Martins, Y., Preti, G., Crabtree, C. R., Runyan, T., Vainius, A. A., & Wysocki, C. J. (2005). Preference for human body odors is influenced by gender and sexual orientation. *Psychological Science, 16*(9), 694.

Martz, J. M., et al. (1998). Positive illusion in close relationships. *Personal Relationships, 5*(2), 159–181.

Marvasti, J. A. (2004). Pharmacotherapy and surgical treatment of paraphiliacs and sexual offenders. In Marvasti, J A. (Ed.). *Psychiatric treatment of sexual offenders: Treating the past traumas in traumatizers. A bio-psycho-social perspective. American series in behavioral science and law* (pp. 97–115). Springfield, IL: Charles C. Thomas.

Marwick, C. (2000). Consensus panel considers osteoporosis. *Journal of the American Medical Association, 283*(16).

Marziano, V., Ward, T., Beech, A. R., & Pattison, P. (2006). Identification of five fundamental implicit theories underlying cognitive distortions in child abusers: A preliminary study. *Psychology, Crime & Law, 12*(1), 97–105.

Masheb, R. M., Lozano–Blanco, C., Kohorn, E. I., Minkin, M J., & Kerns, R. D. (2004). Assessing sexual function and dyspareunia with the female sexual function index (FSFI) in women with vulvodynia. *Journal of Sex & Marital Therapy, 30*(5), 315–324.

Masters, W. H., & Johnson, V. E. (1966). *Human sexual response.* Boston: Little, Brown.

Masters, W. H., & Johnson, V. E. (1970). *Human sexual inadequacy.* Boston: Little, Brown.

Masters, W. H., & Johnson, V. E. (1979). *Homosexuality in perspective.* Boston: Little, Brown.

Matthews, A. K., Hughes, T. L., & Tartaro, J. (2006). Sexual behavior and sexual dysfunction in a community sample of lesbian and heterosexual women. In Omoto, A. M., & Kurtzman, H. S. (Eds.). *Sexual orientation and mental health: Examining identity and development in lesbian, gay, and bisexual people, Contemporary perspectives on lesbian, gay, and bisexual psychology* (pp. 185–205). Washington, DC: American Psychological Association.

Matthews, A. K., Hughes, T. L., Tartaro, J., Omoto, A. M., & Kurtzman, H. S. (Eds.). (2006). *Sexual orientation and mental health:*

Examining identity and development in lesbian, gay, and bisexual people. Contemporary perspectives on lesbian, gay, and bisexual psychology. Washington, DC: American Psychological Association.

Mattson, C. L., Bailey, R. C., Muga, R., Poulussen, R., & Onyango, T. (2005). Acceptability of male circumcision and predictors of circumcision preference among men and women in Nyanza Province, Kenya. *AIDS Care, 17*(2), 182–194.

Maxson, S. C. (1998). Homologous genes, aggression, and animal models. *Developmental Neuropsychology, 14*(1), 143–156.

Maxwell, C. D., Robinson, A. L., & Post, L. A. (2003). The nature and predictors of sexual victimization and offending among adolescents. *Journal of Youth & Adolescence, 32*(6), 465–477.

Maybach, K. L., & Gold, S. R. (1994). Hyperfemininity and attraction to macho and non-macho men. *Journal of Sex Research, 31*(2), 91–98.

Mayo Clinic. (2006, October 10). Vulvodynia. [Online]. www.mayoclinic.com/health/vulvodynia/DS00159.

Mazur, T. *The infant's developing sexuality.* Accessed February 10, 2006. [Online]. www2.hu-berlin.de/sexology/GESUND/ARCHIV/SEN/CH07.HTM#b11-CHILDREN%20AND%20SEX.

McAndrew, S. (2000). Sexual health through leadership and "sanuk" in Thailand. *British Medical Journal, 321*(7253), 114.

McBride, C. K., Paikoff, R. L., & Holmbeck, G. N. (2003). Individual and familial influences on the onset of sexual intercourse among urban African American adolescents. *Journal of Consulting and Clinical Psychology, 71*(1), 159–167.

McBurney, D. H., Zapp, D. J., & Streeter, S. A. (2005). Preferred number of sexual partners: Tails of distributions and tales of mating systems. *Evolution and Human Behavior, 26*(3), 271–278.

McCabe, K. A. (2000). Child pornography and the Internet. *Social Science Computer Review, 18*(1), 73–76.

McCabe, M. P. (2004). Exacerbation of symptoms among people with multiple sclerosis: Impact on sexuality and relationships over time. *Archives of Sexual Behavior, 33*(6), 593–601.

McCabe, M. P. (2005). The role of performance anxiety in the development and maintenance of sexual dysfunction in men and women. *International Journal of Stress Management, 12*(4), 379–388.

McCabe, S. E., et al. (2005). Selection and socialization effects of fraternities and sororities on US college student substance use: A multicohort national longitudinal study. *Addiction, 100*(4), 512–524.

McCarthy, B. W., Bodnar, L. E., & Handal, M. (2004). Integrating sex therapy and couple therapy. In Harvey, J. H., Wenzel, A., & Sprecher, S. (Eds.). *The handbook of sexuality in close relationships* (pp. 573–593). Lawrence Erlbaum Associates.

McCarthy, B. W., & Fucito, L. M. (2005). Integrating medication, realistic expectations, and therapeutic interventions in the treatment of male sexual dysfunction. *Journal of Sex & Marital Therapy, 31*(4), 319–328.

McCarthy, B. W., Ginsberg, R. L., & Fucito, L. M.

(2006). Resilient sexual desire in heterosexual couples. *Family Journal: Counseling and Therapy for Couples and Families, 14*(1), 59–64.

McCoy, N. L., & Pitino, L. (2002). Pheromonal influences on sociosexual behavior in young women. *Physiology & Behavior, 75*(3), 367–375.

McDonough, Y. Z. (1998, January 24). What Barbie really taught me. *The New York Times Magazine,* 70.

McElduff, A., & Beange, H. (2003). Men's health and well-being: Testosterone deficiency. *Journal of Intellectual & Developmental Disability, 28*(2), 211–213.

McEwan, S. L., de Man, A. F., & Simpson–Housley, P. (2005). Acquaintance rape, ego-identity achievement, and locus of control. *Social Behavior and Personality, 33*(6), 587–592.

McGue, M., Elkins, I., Walden, B., & Iacono, W. G. (2005). Perceptions of the parent–adolescent relationship: A longitudinal investigation. *Developmental Psychology, 41*(6), 971–984.

McIntyre, S., Formichella, A., Osterhout, M. B., & Gresh, S. (1991). *Tell it like it is: Straight talk about sex.* New York: Avon Books (a division of HarperCollins).

McKeganey, N. (2006). Street prostitution in Scotland: The views of working women. *Drugs: Education, Prevention & Policy, 13*(2), 151–166.

McNeil, D. G., Jr. (2006, December 14). Circumcision halves HIV risk, U.S. agency finds. *The New York Times.* [Online].

Mead, M. (1935). *Sex and temperament in three primitive societies.* New York: Dell.

Medrano, M. A., Hatch, J. P., Zule, W. A., & Desmond, D. P. (2003). Childhood trauma and adult prostitution behavior in a multi-ethnic heterosexual drug-using population. *American Journal of Drug & Alcohol Abuse, 29*(2), 463–486.

Menard, K. S., et al. (2003). Gender differences in sexual harassment and coercion in college students: Developmental, individual, and situational determinants. *Journal of Interpersonal Violence, 18*(10), 1222–1239.

Messenger, J. C. (1971). Sex and repression in an Irish folk community. In Marshall, D. S., & Suggs, R. C. (Eds.). *Human sexual behavior: Variations in the ethnographic spectrum* (pp. 3–37). New York: Basic Books.

Meston, C. M., & Frohlich, P. F. (2000). The neurobiology of sexual function. *Archives of General Psychiatry, 57*(11), 1012–1030.

Meyer, I. H. (2003). Prejudice, social stress, and mental health in lesbian, gay, and bisexual populations: Conceptual issues and research evidence. *Psychological Bulletin, 129*(5), 674–697.

Meyer, I. H., Rossano, L., Ellis, J. M., & Bradford, J. (2002). A brief telephone interview to identify lesbian and bisexual women in random digit sampling. *Journal of Sex Research, 39*(2), 139–144.

Meyer, T. (1998, February 18). *AZT short treatment works.* The Associated Press. [Online].

Meyer–Bahlburg, H. F. L., et al. (1995). Prenatal estrogens and the development of homosexual orientation. *Developmental Psychology, 31*(1), 12–21.

Michael, R. T., Gagnon, J. H., Laumann, E. O., & Kolata, G. (1994). *Sex in America: A definitive survey.* Boston: Little, Brown.

Michel, A., & Pédinielli, J.-L. (2005). Vers une conceptualisation du transsexualisme. *Annales Médico-Psychologiques, 163*(5), 379–386.

Mikach, S. M., & Bailey, J. M. (1999). What distinguishes women with unusually high numbers of sex partners? *Evolution & Human Behavior, 20*(3) 141–150.

Miller, M. (1998, cited in Bronner, February 1). Just say maybe. No sexology, please. We're Americans. *The New York Times,* p. WK6.

Miller, R. (2005). Overcoming violence against women and girls: The international campaign to eradicate a worldwide problem. *Culture, Health & Sexuality, 7*(5), 519–521.

Miller, S. A., & Byers, E. S. (2004). Actual and desired duration of foreplay and intercourse: Discordance and misperceptions within heterosexual couples. *Journal of Sex Research, 41*(3), 301–309.

Minichiello, V., et al. (2001). Male sex workers in three Australian cities: Socio-demographic and sex work characteristics. *Journal of Homosexuality, 42*(1), 29–51.

Missailidis, K., & Gebre–Medhin, M. (2000). Female genital mutilation in eastern Ethiopia. *The Lancet, 356,* 137–138.

Mitchell, K. J., Finkelhor, D., & Wolak, J. (2005). Protecting youth online: Family use of filtering and blocking software. *Child Abuse & Neglect, 29*(7), 753–765.

Modell, J. G., May, R. S., & Katholi, C. R. (2000). Effect of bupropion-SR on orgasmic dysfunction in nondepressed subjects: A pilot study. *Journal of Sex & Marital Therapy, 26*(3), 231–240.

Mofenson, L. M. (2000). Perinatal exposure to zidovudine—Benefits and risks. *The New England Journal of Medicine, 343*(11).

Mohan, R., & Bhugra, D. (2005). Literature update: A critical review. *Sexual and Relationship Therapy, 20*(1), 115–122.

Money, J. (1994). The concept of gender identity disorder in childhood and adolescence after 39 years. *Journal of Sex and Marital Therapy, 20*(3), 163–177.

Money, J. (2003). History, causality, and sexology. *Journal of Sex Research, 40*(3), 237–239.

Monson, C. M., Langhinrichsen–Rohling, J., & Binderup, T. (2000). Does "no" really mean "no" after you say "yes"? Attributions about date and marital rape. *Journal of Interpersonal Violence, 15*(11), 1156–1174.

Montano, D., Kasprzyk, D., von Haeften, I., & Fishbein, M. (2001). Toward an understanding of condom use behaviours: A theoretical and methodological overview of Project SAFER. *Psychology, Health & Medicine, 6*(2), 139–150.

Montemurro, B., Bloom, C., & Madell, K. (2003). Ladies night out: A typology of women patrons of a male strip club. *Deviant Behavior, 24*(4), 333–352.

Moore, D. R., & Heiman, J. R. (2006). Women's sexuality in context: Relationship factors and female sexual functioning. In Goldstein, I., Meston, C., Davis, S., & Traish, A. (Eds.). *Female sexual dysfunction.* New York: Parthenon.

Moore, S., & Leung, C. (2002). Young people's romantic attachment styles and their association with well-being. *Journal of Adolescence, 25*(2), 243–255.

Morley, J. E., & Perry, H. M., III. (2003). Androgens and women at the menopause and beyond. *Journals of Gerontology: Series A: Bio-*

logical Sciences & Medical Sciences, 58A(5), 409–416.

Morofushi, M., Shinohara, K., Funabashi, T., & Kimura, F. (2000). Positive relationship between menstrual synchrony and ability to smell 5alpha-androst-16-en-3alpha-ol. Chemical Senses, 25(4), 407–411.

Morris, L. B. (2000, June 25). For the partum blues, a question of whether to medicate. The New York Times. [Online].

Morrison, D. R., & Coiro, M. J. (1999). Parental conflict and marital disruption: Do children benefit when high-conflict marriages are dissolved? Journal of Marriage & the Family, 61(3), 626–637.

Morrison, E. S., et al. (1980). Growing up sexual. New York: Van Nostrand Reinhold.

Morry, M. M. (2005). Allocentrism and friendship satisfaction: The mediating roles of disclosure and closeness. Canadian Journal of Behavioural Science, 37(3), 211–222.

Morry, M. M., & Gaines, S. O. (2005). Relationship satisfaction as a predictor of similarity ratings: A test of the attraction–similarity hypothesis. Journal of Social and Personal Relationships, 22(4), 561–584.

Mortola, J. F. (1998). Premenstrual syndrome—Pathophysiologic considerations. New England Journal of Medicine, 338, 256–257.

Mosher, W. D., Chandra, A., & Jones, J. (2005). Sexual behavior and selected health measures: Men and women 15–44 years of age, United States, 2002. Advance data from vital and health statistics. Centers for Disease Control and Prevention. National Center for Health Statistics, No. 362.

Mulac, A., Jansma, L. L., & Linz, D. G. (2002). Men's behavior toward women after viewing sexually-explicit films: Degradation makes a difference. Communication Monographs, 69(4), 311–328.

Mulick, P. S., & Wright, L. W., Jr. (2002). Examining the existence of biphobia in the heterosexual and homosexual populations. Journal of Bisexuality, 2(4), 45–64.

Munarriz, R., et al. (2002). Androgen replacement therapy with dehydroepiandrosterone for androgen insufficiency and female sexual dysfunction: Androgen and questionnaire results. Journal of Sex & Marital Therapy, 28(Suppl. 1), 165–173.

Mundy, L. (2000, July 16). Sex and sensibility. The Washington Post. [Online].

Munro, V. E. (2006). Stopping traffic? A comparative study of responses to the trafficking in women for prostitution. British Journal of Criminology, 46(2), 318–333.

Murphy, S. M., Vallacher, R. R., Shackelford, T. K., Bjorklund, D. F., & Yunger, J. L. (2006). Relationship experience as a predictor of romantic jealousy. Personality and Individual Differences, 40(4), 761–769.

Murray, S. L., & Holmes, J. G. (2000). Seeing the self through a partner's eyes: Why self-doubts turn into relationship insecurities. In Tesser, A., Felson, R. B., et al. (Eds.). Psychological perspectives on self and identity (pp. 173–197). Washington, DC: American Psychological Association.

Murray, S. L., Bellavia, G., Feeney, B., Holmes, J. G., & Rose, P. (2001). The contingencies of interpersonal acceptance: When romantic relationships function as a self-affirmational resource. Motivation & Emotion, 25(2), 163–189.

Murray, S. O., & Roscoe, W. (1997). Islamic homosexualities: Culture, history, and literature. New York: New York University Press.

Mustanski, B. S., Dupree, M. G., Nievergelt, C. M., Bocklandt, S., Schork, N. J., & Hamer, D. H. (2005). A genomewide scan of male sexual orientation. Human Genetics, 116, 272–278.

Myers, J. E., Madathil, J., & Tingle, L. R. (2005). Marriage satisfaction and wellness in India and the United States: A preliminary comparison of arranged marriages and marriages of choice. Journal of Counseling & Development, 83(2), 183–190.

Myers, S. M. (2006). Religious homogamy and marital quality: Historical and generational patterns, 1980–1997. Journal of Marriage and the Family, 68(2), 292–304.

Nadeau, J. (2005). Teen sex is common worldwide. [Online]. www.guttmacher.org/media.

Nagourney, E. (2000, February 15). Study finds families bypassing marriage. The New York Times. p. F8.

Naimi, T. S., et al. (2003). Binge drinking among US adults. Journal of the American Medical Association, 289(1), 70–75.

Najman, J. M., Dunne, M. P., Purdie, D. M., Boyle, F. M., & Coxeter, P. D. (2005). Sexual abuse in childhood and sexual dysfunction in adulthood: An Australian population-based study. Archives of Sexual Behavior, 34(5), 517–526.

Nakaya, M. (2002). Fluvoxamine treatment of a Japanese patient with Koro. Journal of Clinical Psychiatry, 63(12), 1182–1183.

Nanda, S., & Warms, R. L. (2004). Cultural anthropology. 8th ed. Belmont, CA: Wadsworth.

Nappi, R. E., Wawra, K., & Schmitt, S. (2006). Hypoactive sexual desire disorder in postmenopausal women. Gynecological Endocrinology, 22(6), 318–323.

Narchi, H. (2003). Infantile masturbation mimicking paroxysmal disorders. Journal of Pediatric Neurology, 1(1), 43–45.

National Campaign to Prevent Teen Pregnancy. (2003, September 30). Teens say parents most influence their sexual decisions: New polling data and "Tips for Parents" released. [Online]. www.teenpregnancy.org/about/announcements/pr/2003/release9_30_03.asp.

National Cancer Institute. (2006). [Online]. www.nci.nih.gov/.

National Center for Biotechnology Information (NCBI). (2006, February 1). National Institute of Health. [Online]. www.ncbi.nlm.nih.gov/entrez/query.fcgi?-CMD=Search&db=homologene&term=SRY.

National Institute of Alcohol Abuse and Alcoholism. (2005). Apparent per capita ethanol consumption for the United States, 1850–2002. [Gallons of ethanol, based on population age 15 and older prior to 1970 and on population age 14 and older thereafter]. [Online]. www.niaaa.nih.gov/databases/consum01.htm.

Navarro, M. (2006, January 8). The West gets wilder. The New York Times. [Online].

Nduati, R., et al. (2000). Effect of breastfeeding and formula feeding on transmission of HIV-1. Journal of the American Medical Association, 283, 1167–1174.

Neerman–Arbez, M. (2003, June 4). Genes implicated in sexual differentiation. Geneva Foundation for Medical Education and Research.

[Online]. www.gfmer.ch/Endo/Lectures_10/Sexualdi.htm.

Neff, K. D., & Harter, S. (2003). Relationship styles of self-focused autonomy, other-focused connectedness, and mutuality across multiple relationship contexts. Journal of Social & Personal Relationships, 20(1), 81–99.

Nemoto, T., Iwamoto, M., Wong, S., Le, M. N., & Operario, D. (2004). Social factors related to risk for violence and sexually transmitted infections/HIV among Asian massage parlor workers in San Francisco. AIDS and Behavior, 8(4), 475–483.

Nevid, J. S., Rathus, S. A., & Greene, B. A. (2006). Abnormal psychology in a changing world 6th ed. Upper Saddle River, NJ: Prentice Hall.

Ngai, S. W., Tang, O. S., Chan, Y. M., & Ho, P. C. (2000). Vaginal misoprostol alone for medical abortion up to 9 weeks of gestation: Efficacy and acceptability. Human Reproduction, 15(5), 1159–1162.

Nieder, T., & Sieffge–Krenke, I. (2001). Coping with stress in different phases of romantic development. Journal of Adolescence, 24(3), 297–311.

Nieto, J. J., Cogswell, D., Jesinger, D., & Hardiman, P. (2000). Lipid effects of hormone replacement therapy with sequential transdermal 17-beta-estradiol and oral dydrogesterone. Obstetrics & Gynecology, 95, 111–114.

Nobre, P. J., & Pinto-Gouveia, J. (2006). Dysfunctional sexual beliefs as vulnerability factors for sexual dysfunction. Journal of Sex Research, 43(1), 68–75.

Norton, A. (2000, September 1). Exercise helps men avoid impotence. Reuters News Agency. [Online].

Norton–Hawk, M. (2004). A comparison of pimp- and non-pimp-controlled women. Violence Against Women, 10(2), 189–194.

Nosek, M. A. (2005). Wellness in the context of disability. In Myers, J. E., & Sweeney, T. J. (Eds.). Counseling for wellness: Theory, research, and practice (pp. 139–150). Alexandria, VA: American Counseling Association.

Nosek, M. A., et al. (2004). The meaning of health for women with physical disabilities: A qualitative analysis. Family & Community Health, 27(1), 6–21.

O'Dell, K. M. C., & Kaiser, K. (1997). Sexual behaviour: Secrets and flies. Current Biology, 7(6), R345–R347.

O'Doherty, J., et al. (2003). Beauty in a smile: The role of medial orbitofrontal cortex in facial attractiveness. Neuropsychologia, 41(2), 147–155.

O'Donnell, L., et al., (2003). Long-term influence of sexual norms and attitudes on timing of sexual initiation among urban minority youth. Journal of School Health, 23(2), 68–75.

O'Donohue, W., Yeater, E. A., & Fanetti, M. (2003). Rape prevention with college males: The roles of rape myth acceptance, victim empathy, and outcome expectancies. Journal of Interpersonal Violence, 18(5), 513–531.

Ofer, D., & Weitzman, L. (Eds.). (1998). Women in the Holocaust. New Haven, CT: Yale University Press.

Ogletree, S. M., & Ginsburg, H. J. (2000). Kept under the hood: Neglect of the clitoris in common vernacular. Sex Roles, 43(11–12), 917–926.

Oguz, N., & Uygur, N. (2005). A case of diaper fetishism. Türk Psikiyatri Dergisi, 16(2), 133–138.

Okami, P., Weisner, T., & Olmstead, R. (2002). Outcome correlates of parent–child bedsharing: An eighteen-year longitudinal study. *Journal of Developmental & Behavioral Pediatrics, 23*(4), 244–253.

O'Keeffe, M. J., et al. (2003). Learning, cognitive, and attentional problems in adolescents born small for gestational age. *Pediatrics, 112*(2), 301–307.

Olds, J. (1956). Pleasure centers in the brain. *Scientific American, 193*, 105–116.

Olds, J., & Milner, P. (1954). Positive reinforcement produced by electrical stimulation of the septal area and other regions of the rat brain. *Journal of Comparative and Physiological Psychology, 47*, 419–427.

Olfson, M., Uttaro, T., Carson, W. H., & Tafesse, E. (2005). Male sexual dysfunction and quality of life in schizophrenia. *Journal of Clinical Psychiatry, 66*(3), 331–338.

Olshen, E., et al. (2006). Use of human immunodeficiency virus postexposure prophylaxis in adolescent sexual assault victims. *Archives of Pediatric Adolescent Medicine, 160*, 674–680.

Ompad, D.C., et al. (2006). Predictors of early initiation of vaginal and oral sex among urban young adults in Baltimore, Maryland. *Archives of Sexual Behavior, 35*(1), 53–65.

Ortega, V., Ojeda, P., Sutil, F., & Sierra, J. C. (2005). Culpabilidad sexual en adolescentes: Estudio de algunos factores relacionados. *Anales de Psicología, 21*(2), 268–275.

Osman, S. L. (2003). Predicting men's rape perceptions based on the belief that "no" really means "yes." *Journal of Applied Social Psychology, 33*(4), 683–692.

Ostrow, D. E., et al. (2002). Attitudes towards highly active antiretroviral therapy are associated with sexual risk taking among HIV-infected and uninfected homosexual men. *AIDS, 16*(5), 775–780.

O'Sullivan, L. F. (2003). The development of romantic relationships in adolescence. *Archives of Sexual Behavior, 32*(3), 292–294.

Pachankis, J. E., & Goldfried, M. R. (2004). Clinical issues in working with lesbian, gay, and bisexual clients. *Psychotherapy: Theory, Research, Practice, Training, 41*(3), 227–246.

Pakhomou, S. M. (2006). Methodological aspects of telephone scatologia: A case study. *International Journal of Law and Psychiatry, 29*(3), 178–185.

Palace, E. M. (1995). Modification of dysfunctional patterns of sexual arousal through autonomic arousal and false physiological feedback. *Journal of Consulting and Clinical Psychology, 63*, 604–615.

Paraskevis, D., et al. (2003). Analysis of the evolutionary relationships of HIV-1 and SIVcpz sequences using Bayesian inference: Implications for the origin of HIV-1. *Molecular Biology and Evolution, 20*, 1986–1996.

Parent, C., & Bruckert, C. (2005). Sex work in establishments offering erotic services: A form of marginalised work. *Déviance et Societé, 29*(1), 33–53.

Parrott, D., Zeichner, A., & Hoover, R. (2006). Sexual prejudice and anger network activation: Mediating role of negative affect. *Aggressive Behavior, 32*(1), 7–16.

Parsons, N. K., Richards, H. C., & Kanter, G. D. (1990). Validation of a scale to measure reasoning about abortion. *Journal of Counseling Psychology, 37*, 107–112.

Pasupathi, M., Carstensen, L. L., Levenson, R. W., & Gottman, J. M. (1999). Responsive listening in long-married couples: A psycholinguistic perspective. *Journal of Nonverbal Behavior, 23*(2), 173–193.

Pasupathy, D., & Smith, G. C. (2005). The analysis of factors predicting antepartum stillbirth. *Minerva Ginecology, 57*(4), 397–410.

Patrick, D. L., et al. (2005). Premature ejaculation: An observational study of men and their partners. *Journal of Sexual Medicine, 2*(3), 358–367.

Pawlowski, B., & Koziel, S. (2002). The impact of traits offered in personal advertisements on response rates. *Evolution & Human Behavior, 23*(2), 139–149.

Pearlstein, T., & Steiner, M. (2000). Nonantidepressant treatment of premenstrual syndrome. *Journal of Clinical Psychiatry, 61*(Suppl. 12), 22–27.

Pedersen, W., & Hegna, K. (2003). Children and adolescents who sell sex: A community study. *Social Science & Medicine, 56*(1), 135–147.

Peplau, L. A. (2003). Human sexuality: How do men and women differ? *Current Directions in Psychological Science, 12*(2), 37–40.

Peplau, L. A., & Cochran, S. D. (1990). A relationship perspective on homosexuality. In McWhirter, D. P., Sanders, S. A., & Reinisch, J. M. (Eds.). *Homosexuality/heterosexuality: Concepts of sexual orientation* (pp. 321–349). New York: Oxford University Press.

Peris, A. (2006, February 8). *Fertilitext: At the pharmacy: OTC.* [Online]. www.fertilitext.org/p3_pharmacy/OTCproducts.html.

Perrett, D. I. (1994, cited in Brody, March 24). *Nature.* Notions of beauty transcend culture, new study suggests. *The New York Times*, p. A14.

Perry, D. G., & Bussey, K. (1979). The social learning theory of sex differences: Imitation is alive and well. *Journal of Personality and Social Psychology, 37*, 1699–1712.

Perry, J. D., & Whipple, B. (1981). Pelvic muscle strength of female ejaculation: Evidence in support of a new theory of orgasm. *Journal of Sex Research, 17*, 22–39.

Perry, P. J., et al. (2001). Bioavailable testosterone as a correlate of cognition, psychological status, quality of life, and sexual function in aging males: Implications for testosterone replacement therapy. *Annals of Clinical Psychiatry, 13*(2), 75–80.

Philaretou, A. G. (2005). Sexuality and the Internet. *Journal of Sex Research, 42*(2), 180–181.

Philaretou, A. G. (2006). Female exotic dancers: Intrapersonal and interpersonal perspectives. *Sexual Addiction & Compulsivity, 13*(1), 41–52.

Philaretou, A. G., Mahfouz, A. Y., & Allen, K. R. (2005). Use of Internet pornography and men's well-being. *International Journal of Men's Health, 4*(2), 149–169.

Phillips, F. (2003, April 8). Support for gay marriage. *Boston Globe.*

Pike, L. B. (2005, July 1). *Sexuality and your child.* MU Extension, University of Missouri–Columbia.

Pillard, R. C. (1990). The Kinsey Scale: Is it familial? In McWhirter, D. P., Sanders, S. A., & Reinisch, J. M. (Eds.). *Homosexuality/heterosexuality: Concepts of sexual orientation* (pp. 88–100). New York: Oxford University Press.

Pillard, R. C., & Weinrich, J. D. (1986). Evidence of familial nature of male homosexuality. *Archives of Sexual Behavior, 43*, 808–812.

Pinkerton, S. D., Bogart, L. M., Cecil, H., & Abramson, P. R. (2002). Factors associated with masturbation in collegiate sample. *Journal of Psychology & Human Sexuality, 14*(2–3), 103–121.

Pinkerton, S. D., et al. (2003a). HIV/AIDS knowledge and attitudes of STD clinic attendees in St. Petersburg, Russia. *AIDS & Behavior, 7*(3), 221–228.

Pinkerton, S. D., Cecil, H., Bogart, L. M., & Abramson, P. R. (2003b). The pleasures of sex: An empirical investigation. *Cognition & Emotion, 17*(2), 341–353.

Planned Parenthood Federation of America. (2006). [Online]. www.plannedparenthood.org/pp2/portal.

Plant, E. A., Hyde, J. S., Keltner, D., & Devine, P. G. (2000). The gender stereotyping of emotions. *Psychology of Women Quarterly, 24*(1), 81–92.

Plant, M., & Plant, M. (2003). Sex addiction: A comparison with dependence on psychoactive drugs. *Journal of Substance Use, 8*(4), 260–266.

Plant, M., & Plant, M. (2003). Sex addiction: A comparison with dependence on psychoactive drugs. *Journal of Substance Use, 8*(4), 260–266.

Plante, R. F. (2006). The rise of Viagra: How the little blue pill changed sex in America. *Sexualities, 9*(3), 379–380.

Plaut, S. M. (2006). Consent to sexual relations. *Archives of Sexual Behavior, 35*(1), 101–103.

Plomin, R., & Asbury, K. (2005). Nature and nurture: Genetic and environmental influences on behavior. *Annals of the American Academy of Political and Social Science, 600*, 86–98.

Plomin, R., & Crabbe, J. (2000). DNA. *Psychological Bulletin, 126*(6), 806–828.

Poll shows decline in sex by high school students. (1998, September 18). *The New York Times*, p. A26.

Pollack, H. A. (2001). Sudden infant death syndrome, maternal smoking during pregnancy, and the cost-effectiveness of smoking cessation intervention. *American Journal of Public Health, 91*(3), 432–436.

Polonsky, D. C. (2006). The big book of masturbation: From angst to zeal. *Journal of Sex & Marital Therapy, 32*(1), 75–78.

Polusny, M. A., & Arbisi, P. A. (2006). Assessment of psychological distress and disability after sexual assault in adults. In Young, G., et al. (Eds.). *Psychological knowledge in court: PTSD, pain, and TBI* (pp. 97–125). Springer Science + Business Media.

Poppen, P. J., et al. (2005). Serostatus disclosure, seroconcordance, partner relationship, and unprotected anal intercourse among HIV-positive Latino men who have sex with men. *AIDS Education and Prevention, 17*(3), 227–237.

Potosky, A. L., et al. (2000). Health outcomes after prostatectomy or radiotherapy for prostate cancer: Results from the Prostate Cancer Outcomes Study. *Journal of the National Cancer Institute, 92*, 1582–1592.

Potts, A., Grace, V. M., Vares, T., & Gavey, N. (2006). "Sex for life?" Men's counter-stories on "erectile dysfunction," male sexuality and ageing. *Sociology of Health & Illness, 28*(3), 306–329.

Powell, E. (1991). *Talking back to sexual pressure.* Minneapolis: CompCare Publishers.

Prause, N., & Janssen, E. (2006). Blood flow: Vaginal photoplethysmography. In Goldstein, I., Meston, C., Davis, S., & Traish, A. (Eds.).

Female sexual dysfunction. New York: Parthenon.

Prause, N., Cerny, J., & Janssen, E. (2005). The labial photoplethysmograph: A new instrument for assessing genital hemodynamic changes in women. *Journal of Sexual Medicine, 2,* 58–65.

Prentky, R. A., Knight, R. A., & Lee, A. F. S. (2005). Child sexual molestation: Research issues. In Bartol, C. R., & Bartol, A. M. (Eds.). (2006). *Current perspectives in forensic psychology and criminal justice* (pp. 119–129). New York: Sage.

President's Council on Bioethics. (2004, March). *Screening and selection for genetic conditions and traits. Reproduction and responsibility: The regulation of new biotechnologies.* [Online]. www.bioethics.gov/reports/reproduction-andresponsibility/chapter3.html.

Preti, G., et al. (1986). Human axillary secretions influence women's menstrual cycles: The role of donor extract of females. *Hormones and Behavior, 20,* 474–482.

Preti, G., Wysocki, C. J., Barnhart, K. T., Sondheimer, S. J., & Leyden, J. J. (2003). Male axillary extracts contain pheromones that affect pulsatile secretion of luteinizing hormone and mood in women recipients. *Biology of Reproduction, 68*(6), 2107–2113.

Price, M., Gutheil, T. G., Commons, M. L., Kafka, M. P., & Dodd–Kimmey, S. (2001). Telephone scatologia: Comorbidity and theories of etiology. *Psychiatric Annals, 31*(4), 226–232.

Price, M., Kafka, M. P., Commons, M. L., Gutheil, T. G., & Simpson, W. (2002). Telephone scatologia: Comorbidity with other paraphilias and paraphilia-related disorders. *International Journal of Law & Psychiatry, 25*(1), 37–49.

Proctor, F., Wagner, N., & Butler, J. (1974). The differentiation of male and female orgasm: An experimental study. In Wagner, N. (Ed.). *Perspectives on human sexuality.* New York: Behavioral Publications.

Psychology Today. (2006, July 25.) [Online]. www.psychologytoday.com/images/PT_MediaKit_Health_2006.pdf.

Puente, S., & Cohen, D. (2003). Jealousy and the meaning (or nonmeaning) of violence. *Personality & Social Psychology Bulletin, 29*(4), 449–460.

Punyanunt–Carter, N. M. (2006). An analysis of college students' self-disclosure behaviors on the Internet. *College Student Journal, 40*(2), 329–331.

Quartaro, G. K., & Spier, T. E. (2002). We'd like to ask you some questions, but we have to find you first: Internet-based study of lesbian clients in therapy with lesbian feminist therapists. *Journal of Technology in Human Services, 19*(2–3), 109–118.

Quayle, E., & Taylor, M. (2002). Child pornography and the Internet: Perpetuating a cycle of abuse. *Deviant Behavior, 23*(4), 331–362.

Quayle, E., & Taylor, M. (2003). Model of problematic Internet use in people with sexual interest in children. *CyberPsychology & Behavior, 6*(1), 93–106.

Quereshi, B. (2003). [Online]. www.familymedicine.co.uk/features/circum3.htm.

Quinsey, V. L., Harris, G. T., Rice, M. E., & Cormier, C. A. (2006). Sex offenders. In Quinsey, V. L., Harris, G. T., Rice, M. E., & Cormier, C. A. (Eds.). *Violent offenders: Appraising and managing risk. The law and public policy,* 2nd

ed. (pp. 131–151). Washington, DC: American Psychological Association.

Rabin, R. (2006, January 31). Rethinking hormones, again. *The New York Times.* [Online].

Rahman, Q., & Wilson, G. D. (2003). Born gay? The psychobiology of human sexual orientation. *Personality & Individual Differences, 34*(8), 1337–1382.

Raichle, K., & Lambert, A. J. (2000). The role of political ideology in mediating judgments of blame in rape victims and their assailants: A test of the just world, personal responsibility, and legitimization hypotheses. *Personality & Social Psychology Bulletin, 26*(7), 853–863.

Rakic, Z., Starcevic, V., Starcevic, V. P., & Marinkovic, J. (1997). Testosterone treatment in men with erectile disorder and low levels of total testosterone in serum. *Archives of Sexual Behavior, 26*(5), 495–504.

Rako, S. (2003). *No more periods? The risks of menstrual suppression and other cutting-edge issues about hormones and women's health.* New York: Crown.

Ralph, D., & McNicholas, T. (2000). UK management guidelines for erectile dysfunction. *British Medical Journal, 321,* 499–503.

Raphael, J., & Shapiro, D. L. (2005). Reply to Weitzer. *Violence Against Women, 11*(7), 965–970.

Rathus, S. A. (2006). *Childhood and adolescence: Voyages in development.* 2nd ed. Belmont, CA: Thomson Learning/Wadsworth.

Rawson, R. A., Washton, A., Domier, C. P., & Reiber, C. (2002). Drugs and sexual effects: Role of drug type and gender. *Journal of Substance Abuse Treatment, 22*(2), 103–108.

Reddy, D. M., et al. (2002). Effect of mandatory parental notification on adolescent girls' use of sexual health care services. *Journal of the American Medical Association, 288,* 710–714.

Reed, M. E., Collinsworth, L. L., & Fitzgerald, L. F. (2005). There's no place like home: Sexual harassment of low income women in housing. *Psychology, Public Policy, and Law, 11*(3), 439–462.

Reed, M., & Lampe, M. S. (2003). *Margaret Sanger: Her life in her words.* Barricade Books.

Refaat, A., Dandash, K. F., El-Defrawi, M. H., & Eyada, M. (2001). Female genital mutilation and domestic violence among Egyptian women. *Journal of Sex & Marital Therapy, 27*(5), 593–598.

Regan, P. C. (2004). Sex and the attraction process: Lessons from science (and Shakespeare) on lust, love, chastity, and fidelity. In Harvey, J. H., Wenzel, A., & Sprecher, S. (Eds.). *The handbook of sexuality in close relationships* (pp. 115–133). Hillsdale, NJ: Lawrence Erlbaum Associates.

Reiner, W. G. (2000). Cited in Study of children born without penises finds nature determines gender. Associated Press [online].

Reinisch, J. M. (1990). *The Kinsey Institute new report on sex: What you must know to be sexually literate.* New York: St. Martin's Press.

Renk, K., Liljequist, L., Simpson, J. E., & Phares, V. (2005). Gender and age differences in the topics of parent–adolescent conflict. *Family Journal: Counseling and Therapy for Couples and Families, 13*(2), 139–149.

Resick, P. A. (2003). Post hoc reasoning in possible cases of child sexual abuse: Just say no. *Clinical Psychology: Science & Practice, 10*(3), 349–351.

Reyes, J. R., et al. (2006). Assessment of deviant

arousal in adult male sex offenders with developmental disabilities. *Journal of Applied Behavior Analysis, 39*(2), 173–188.

Reynolds, A., & Caron, S. L. (2000). How intimate relationships are impacted when heterosexual men crossdress. *Journal of Psychology & Human Sexuality, 12*(3), 63–77.

Reynolds, C. A., Barlow, T., & Pedersen, N. L. (2006). Alcohol, tobacco and caffeine use: Spouse similarity processes. *Behavior Genetics, 36*(2), 201–215.

Reynolds, S. J., et al. (2004). Male circumcision and risk of HIV-1 and other sexually transmitted infections in India. *The Lancet, 363*(9414), 1039.

Ricci, E., Parazzini, F., & Pardi, G. (2000). Caesarean section and antiretroviral treatment. *The Lancet, 355*(9202), 496–502.

Rice, M. E., Harris, G. T., & Quinsey, V. L. (1990). A follow-up of rapists assessed in a maximum-security psychiatric facility. *Journal of Interpersonal Violence, 5,* 435–448.

Rice, M. E., Quinsey, V. L., & Harris, G. T. (1991). Sexual recidivism among child molesters released from a maximum security psychiatric institution. *Journal of Consulting and Clinical Psychology, 59,* 381–386.

Rich, F. (2005, December 18). Two gay cowboys hit a home run. *The New York Times.* [Online].

Richardson, D., & BASHH Special Interest Group for Sexual Dysfunction. (2006a). Recommendations for the management of premature ejaculation: BASHH Special Interest Group for Sexual Dysfunction. *International Journal of STD & AIDS, 17*(1), 1–6.

Richardson, D., Goldmeier, D., & BASHH Special Interest Group for Sexual Dysfunction. (2006b). Recommendations for the management of retarded ejaculation: BASHH Special Interest Group for Sexual Dysfunction. *International Journal of STD & AIDS, 17*(1), 7–13.

Richters, J., Hendry, O., & Kippax, S. (2003). When safe sex isn't safe. *Culture, Health & Sexuality, 5*(1), 37–52.

Rickwood, A. M. K., Kenny, S. E., & Donnell, S. C. (2000). Towards evidence based circumcision of English boys: Survey of trends in practice. *British Medical Journal, 321,* 792–793.

Riggio, R. E., & Woll, S. B. (1984). The role of nonverbal cues and physical attractiveness in the selection of dating partners. *Journal of Social and Personal Relationships, 1,* 347–357.

Rimm, E. (May 2000). *Lifestyle may play role in potential for impotence.* Presented at the annual meeting of the American Urological Association, Atlanta, GA.

Ring–Cassidy, E., & Gentles, I. (2002). *Women's health after abortion: The medical and psychological evidence.* Toronto, Ontario: The deVeber Institute.

Ritner, C., & Roth, J. (1993). *Different voices: Women and the Holocaust.* New York: Paragon House.

Ritter, C., Hobfoll, S. E., Lavin, J., Cameron, R. P., & Hulsizer, M. R. (2000). Stress, psychosocial resources, and depressive symptomatology during pregnancy in low-income, inner-city women. *Health Psychology, 19*(6), 576–585.

Roan, S. (2006, July 22). Newer contraceptives put an end to "the period." *Los Angeles Times.* [Online].

Roberts, J. M. (2000). Recent advances: Obstetrics. *British Medical Journal, 321*(7252), 33–35.

Roberts, S. (2006, October 15). It's official: To be

married means to be outnumbered. *The New York Times.* [Online].

Robinson, B. B. E., Bockting, W. O., & Harrell, T. (2002). Masturbation and sexual health: An exploratory study of low income African American women. *Journal of Psychology & Human Sexuality, 14*(2–3), 85–102.

Robinson, J. D., & Parks, C. W. (2003). Lesbian and bisexual women's sexual fantasies, psychological adjustment, and close relationship functioning. *Journal of Psychology & Human Sexuality, 15*(4), 185–203.

Robinson, J. N., Norwitz, E. R., Cohen, A. P., & Lieberman, E. (2000). Predictors of episiotomy use at first spontaneous vaginal delivery. *Obstetrics & Gynecology, 96*(2), 214–218.

Roddy, R. E., et al. (1998). A controlled trial of nonoxynol 9 film to reduce male-to-female transmission of sexually transmitted diseases. *New England Journal of Medicine, 339,* 504–510.

Rodriguez, I., Greer, C. A., Mok, M. Y., & Mombaerts, P. (2000). A putative pheromone receptor gene expressed in human olfactory mucosa. *Nature Genetics, 26*(1), 18–19.

Roesler, A., & Witztum, E. (2000). Pharmacotherapy of paraphilias in the next millennium. *Behavioral Sciences & the Law, 18*(1), 43–56.

Romero–Daza, N., Weeks, M., & Singer, M. (2005). Conceptualizing the impact of indirect violence on HIV risk among women involved in street-level prostitution. *Aggression and Violent Behavior, 10*(2), 153–170.

Roscoe, W. (2000). *Changing ones: Third and fourth genders in native North America.* Palgrave Macmillan.

Rosen, R. C., Laumann, E. O. (2003). The prevalence of sexual problems in women: How valid are comparisons across studies? Commentary on Bancroft, Loftus, and Long's (2003) "Distress about sex: A national survey of women in heterosexual relationships." *Archives of Sexual Behavior, 32*(3), 209–211.

Rosenbaum, J. E. (2006). Reborn a virgin: Adolescents' retracting of virginity pledges and sexual histories. *American Journal of Public Health, 96,* 1098–1103.

Rosik, C. H. (2003). Motivational, ethical, and epistemological foundations in the treatment of unwanted homoerotic attraction. *Journal of Marital & Family Therapy, 29*(1), 13–28.

Rospenda, K. M., Richman, J. A., Ehmke, J. L. Z., & Zlatoper, K. W. (2005). Is workplace harassment hazardous to your health? *Journal of Business and Psychology, 20*(1), 95–110.

Ross, J. L., Roeltgen, D., Feuillan, P., Kushner, H., & Cutler, W. B. (2000). Use of estrogen in young girls with Turner syndrome: Effects on memory. *Neurology, 54*(1), 164–170.

Rothrauff, T., Middlemiss, W., & Jacobson, L. (2004). Comparison of American and Austrian infants' and toddlers' sleep habits: A retrospective, exploratory study. *North American Journal of Psychology, 6*(1), 125–144.

Roughgarden, J. (2004). *Evolution's rainbow: Diversity, gender, and sexuality in nature and people.* University of California Press.

Royce, R. A., Seña, A., Cates, W., Jr., & Cohen, M. S. (1997). Sexual transmission of HIV. *New England Journal of Medicine, 336,* 1072–1078.

Rozee, P. D., Koss, M. P. (2001). Rape: A century of resistance. *Psychology of Women Quarterly, 25*(4), 295–311.

Rubenson, B., Hanh, L. T., Höjer, B., & Johanson, E. (2005). Young sex-workers in Ho Chi Minh City telling their life stories. *Childhood: A Global Journal of Child Research, 12*(3), 391–411.

Rusbult, C. E., & Van Lange, P. A. M. (2003). Interdependence, interaction and relationships. *Annual Review of Psychology, 54,* 351–375.

Rusbult, C. E., Martz, J. M., & Agnew, C. R. (1998). The Investment Model Scale: Measuring commitment level, satisfaction level, quality of alternatives, and investment size. *Personal Relationships, 5*(4), 357–391.

Russo, J. (2003). *A new form of birth control pills.* Accessed June 26, 2003. [Online]. www.ivillagehealth.com.

Sachar, E. (2003). Is cyberporn coming between you? *Ladies' Home Journal.* [Online].

Sadalla, E. K., Kenrick, D. T., & Vershure, B. (1987). Dominance and heterosexual attraction. *Journal of Personality and Social Psychology, 52,* 730–738.

Sadker, M., & Sadker, D. (1994). *How America's schools cheat girls.* New York: Scribners.

Sadler, A. G., Booth, B. M., Nielson, D., & Doebbeling, B. N. (2000). Health-related consequences of physical and sexual violence: Women in the military. *Obstetrics & Gynecology, 96*(3), 473–480.

Safire, W. (2000, June 18). Hooking up. *The New York Times Magazine.* [Online].

Sagan, C., & Dryan, A. (1990, April 22). The question of abortion: A search for answers. *Parade Magazine,* 4–8.

Sagarin, B. J., Becker, D. V., Guadagno, R. E., Nicastle, L. D., & Millevoi, A. (2003). Sex differences (and similarities) in jealousy. The moderating influence of infidelity experience and sexual orientation of the infidelity. *Evolution & Human Behavior, 24*(1), 17–23.

Saigal, S., et al. (2006). Transition of extremely low-birth-weight infants from adolescence to young adulthood. *Journal of the American Medical Association, 295,* 667–675.

Sanders, T. (2005). "It's just acting": Sex workers' strategies for capitalizing on sexuality. *Gender, Work & Organization, 12*(4), 319–342.

Sanger, M. (1938). *Margaret Sanger: An autobiography.* New York: Norton.

Sangrador, J. L., & Yela, C. (2000). "What is beautiful is loved": Physical attractiveness in love relationships in a representative sample. *Social Behavior & Personality, 28*(3) 207–218.

Santelli, J. S., et al. (2003). Reproductive health in school-based health centers: Findings from the 1998–99 census of school-based health centers. *Journal of Adolescent Health, 32*(6), 443–451.

Santtila, P., Sandnabba, N. K., Alison, L., & Nordling, N. (2002). Investigating the underlying structure in sadomasochistically oriented behavior. *Archives of Sexual Behavior, 31*(2), 185–196.

Sarrel, P., & Masters, W. (1982). Sexual molestation of men by women. *Archives of Sexual Behavior, 11,* 117–131.

Saul, J. M. (2003). *Feminism: Issues & arguments.* Oxford: Oxford University Press.

Save the Children. (2004). *State of the world's mothers 2004.* Accessed September 2006. [Online]. www.savethechildren.org/mothers/report_2004/index.asp.

Savic, I., Berglund, H., & Lindström, P. (2005). Brain response to putative pheromones in homosexual men. *Proceedings of the National Association of Sciences, 102,* 7356–7361.

Savin–Williams, R. C. (2006). Who's gay? Does it matter? *Current Directions in Psychological Science, 15*(1), 40–44.

Savin–Williams, R. C., & Diamond, L. M. (2000). Sexual identity trajectories among sexual-minority youths: Gender comparisons. *Archives of Sexual Behavior, 29*(6), 607–627.

Sax, L. (2002). How common is intersex? A response to Anne Fausto–Sterling. *Journal of Sex Research, 39,* 174–179.

Saywitz, K. J., Mannarino, A. P., Berliner, L., & Cohen, J. A. (2000). Treatment for sexually abused children and adolescents. *American Psychologist, 55*(9), 1040–1049.

Sbraga, T. P. (2004). Sexual deviance and forensic psychology: A primer. In O'Donohue, W. T., & Levensky, E. R. (Eds.). *Handbook of forensic psychology: Resource for mental health and legal professionals* (pp. 429–470). London: Elsevier Science.

Schellenberg, E. G., Hirt, J., & Sears, A. (1999). Attitudes toward homosexuals among students at a Canadian university. *Sex Roles, 40*(1–2), 139–152.

Schemo, D. J. (2000, October 4). Survey finds parents favor more detailed sex education. *The New York Times,* pp. A1, A27.

Schieve, L. A., et al. (1999). Live-birth rates and multiple-birth risk using in vitro fertilization. *Journal of the American Medical Association, 282,* 1832–1838.

Schlichter, A. (2004). *Contesting "straights," "lesbians," "queer heterosexuals," and the critique of heteronormativity.* Binghamton, NY: The Haworth Press.

Schmidt, P. J., et al. (1998). Differential behavioral effects of gonadal steroids in women with and in those without premenstrual syndrome. *New England Journal of Medicine, 338,* 209–216.

Schmitt, D. P. (2003). Universal sex differences in the desire for sexual variety: Tests from 52 nations, 6 continents, and 13 islands. *Journal of Personality and Social Psychology, 85*(1), 85–104.

Schmitt, D. P., Shackelford, T. K., Duntley, J., Tooke, W., & Buss, D. M. (2001). The desire for sexual variety as a key to understanding basic human mating strategies. *Personal Relationships, 8*(4), 425–455.

Schmitt, M. T., Branscombe, N. R., & Postmes, T. (2003). Women's emotional responses to the pervasiveness of gender discrimination. *European Journal of Social Psychology, 33*(3), 297–312.

Schneider, J. P. (2003). The impact of compulsive cybersex behaviours on the family. *Sexual and Relationship Therapy, 18*(3), 329–354.

Schneider, J. P. (2004). Editorial: Sexual addiction & compulsivity: Twenty years of the field, ten years of the journal. *Sexual Addiction & Compulsivity, 11*(1–2), 3–5.

Schneider, J. P. (2005). Addiction is addiction is addiction. *Sexual Addiction & Compulsivity, 12*(2/3), 75–77.

Schneider, J. P. (2005). Addiction is addiction is addiction. *Sexual Addiction & Compulsivity, 12*(2–3), 75–77.

Schober, J. M., et al. (2005). Leuprolide acetate suppresses pedophilic urges and arousability. *Archives of Sexual Behavior, 34*(6), 691–705.

Schroeder–Printzen, I., et al. (2000). Surgical therapy in infertile men with ejaculatory duct obstruction: Technique and outcome of a standardized surgical approach. *Human Reproduction, 15,* 1364–1368.

Schrut, A. (2005). A psychodynamic (nonoedipal) and brain function hypothesis regarding a type of male sexual masochism. *Journal of the American Academy of Psychoanalysis and Dynamic Psychiatry, 33*(2), 333–349.

Schuhrke, B. (2000). Young children's curiosity about other people's genitals. *Journal of Psychology & Human Sexuality, 12*(1–2), 27–48.

Schultz, W. W., et al. (2005). Women's sexual pain and its management. *Journal of Sexual Medicine, 2*(3), 301–316.

Schwartz, M. F., & Masters, W. H. (1984). The Masters and Johnson treatment program for dissatisfied homosexual men. *American Journal of Psychiatry, 141,* 173–181.

Scott, B. E., Weiss, H. A., & Viljoen, J. I. (2005). The acceptability of male circumcision as an HIV intervention among a rural Zulu population, KwaZulu-Natal, South Africa. *AIDS Care, 17*(3), 304–313.

Secker–Walker, R. H., & Vacek, P. M. (2003). Relationships between cigarette smoking during pregnancy, gestational age, maternal weight gain, and infant birthweight. *Addictive Behaviors, 28*(1), 55–66.

Segrin, C., Powell, H. L., Givertz, M., & Brackin, A. (2003). Symptoms of depression, relational quality, and loneliness in dating relationships. *Personal Relationships, 10*(1), 25–36.

Seidman, S. M. (2003). The aging male: Androgens, erectile dysfunction, and depression. *Journal of Clinical Psychiatry, 64*(Suppl. 10), 31–37.

Seifert–Klauss V., et al. (2005). Bone metabolism, bone density and estrogen levels in perimenopause: A prospective 2-year study. *Zentralbl Gynakol., 127*(3), 132–139.

Seiffge–Krenke, I., & Kuehnemund, M. (2001). Relationship experiences during adolescence: How important are they for predicting romantic outcomes in young adulthood? *Zeitschrift für Entwicklungspsychologie und Paedagogische Psychologie, 33*(2), 112–123.

Seligman, L., & Hardenburg, S. A. (2000). Assessment and treatment of paraphilias. *Journal of Counseling & Development, 78*(1), 107–113.

Semans, J. (1956). Premature ejaculation: A new approach. *Southern Medical Journal, 49,* 353–358.

Semple, S. J., Patterson, T. L., & Grant, I. (2003). HIV-positive gay and bisexual men: Predictors of unsafe sex. *AIDS Care, 15*(1), 3–15.

Servais, L. (2006). Sexual health care in persons with intellectual disabilities. *Mental Retardation and Developmental Disabilities Research Reviews, 12*(1), 48–56.

Servin, A., Nordenström, A., Larsson, A., & Bohlin, G. (2003). Prenatal androgens and gender-typed behavior: A study of girls with mild and severe forms of congenital adrenal hyperplasia. *Developmental Psychology, 39*(3), 440–450.

Seto, M. C., Maric, A., & Barbaree, H. E. (2001). The role of pornography in the etiology of sexual aggression. *Aggression and Violent Behavior, 6,* 35–53.

Seward, R. R. (2005). Family and community in Ireland. *Journal of Comparative Family Studies, 36*(2), 343–344.

Sex abuse victims in Boston Church estimated at over 1,000. (2003). *The New York Times.* [Online].

Shackelford, T. K., Buss, D. M., & Bennett, K.

(2002). Forgiveness or breakup: Sex differences in responses to a partner's infidelity. *Cognition & Emotion, 16*(2), 299–307.

Shackelford, T. K., Goetz, A. T., Buss, D. M., Euler, H. A., & Hoier, S. (2005). When we hurt the ones we love: Predicting violence against women from men's mate retention. *Personal Relationships, 12*(4), 447–463.

Sharp, D. (2002). Telling the truth about sex. *Lancet, 359*(9312), 1084.

Shaywitz, B. A., et al. (1995). Sex differences in the functional organization of the brain for language. *Nature, 373,* 607–609.

Sheffield, J. S., & Cunningham, F. G. (2005). Urinary tract infection in women. *Obstetrics & Gynecology, 106,* 1085–1092.

Sheldon, J. P., & Parent, S. L. (2002). Clergy's attitudes and attributions of blame toward female rape victims. *Violence Against Women, 8*(2), 233–256.

Sherwin, B. B., Gelfand, M. M., & Brender, W. (1985). Androgen enhances sexual motivation in females: A prospective, crossover study of sex steroid administration in the surgical menopause. *Psychosomatic Medicine, 47,* 339–351.

Shevell, T., et al. (2005). Assisted reproductive technology and pregnancy outcome. *Obstetrics & Gynecology, 106,* 1039–1045.

Shifren, J. L., et al. (2000). Transdermal testosterone treatment in women with impaired sexual function after oophorectomy. *The New England Journal of Medicine, 343*(10), 682–688.

Shipko, S. (2000, February 7). *Antidepressants linked to sexual side effects.* WebMD/Healtheon. [Online].

Shlipak, M. G., et al. (2000). Estrogen and progestin, lipoprotein(a), and the risk of recurrent coronary heart disease events after menopause. *Journal of the American Medical Association, 283,* 1845–1852.

Shoveller, J. A., Johnson, J. L., & Savoy, D. M. (2006). Preventing sexually transmitted infections among adolescents: An assessment of ecological approaches and study methods. *Sex Education, 6*(2), 163–183.

Shultz, S. K., Scherman, A., & Marshall, L. J. (2000). Evaluation of a university-based date rape prevention program: Effect on attitudes and behavior related to rape. *Journal of College Student Development, 41*(2), 193–201.

Shuster, S. M., & Sassaman, C. (1997). Genetic interaction between male mating strategy and sex ratio in a marine isopod. *Nature, 388*(6640), 373–377.

Siegel–Hinson, R. I., & McKeever, W. F. (2002). Hemispheric specialisation, spatial activity experience, and sex differences on tests of mental rotation ability. *Laterality: Asymmetries of Body, Brain and Cognition, 7*(1), 59–74.

Silva, P. (2005). The state of affairs. *Sexual and Relationship Therapy, 20*(2), 261–262.

Simonsen, G., Blazina, C., & Watkins, C. E., Jr. (2000). Gender role conflict and psychological well-being among gay men. *Journal of Counseling Psychology, 47*(1), 85–89.

Simpson, J. L. (2000, June 1). Invasive diagnostic procedures for prenatal genetic diagnosis. *Journal Watch Women's Health.*

Sims, C. S., Drasgow, F., & Fitzgerald, L. F. (2005). The effects of sexual harassment on turnover in the military: Time-dependent modeling. *Journal of Applied Psychology, 90*(6), 1141–1152.

Singer, J., & Singer, I. (1972). Types of female orgasm. *Journal of Sex Research, 8,* 255–267.

Singh, D., & Ahmed, M. (2001). *Dyanita Singh: Myself, Mona Ahmed.* Zurich, New York: Scalo Publishers.

Singh, D., Vidaurri, M., Zambarano, R. J., & Dabbs, J. M., Jr. (1999). Lesbian erotic role identification: Behavioral, morphological, and hormonal correlates. *Journal of Personality & Social Psychology, 76*(6), 1035–1049.

Singh, S., Bankole, A., & Woog, V. (2005). Evaluating the need for sex education in developing countries: Sexual behavior, knowledge of preventing sexually transmitted infections/HIV, and unplanned pregnancy. *Sex Education, 5*(4), 307–331.

Singletary, K. W., & Gapstur, S. M. (2001). Alcohol and breast cancer: Review of epidemiologic and experimental evidence and potential mechanisms. *Journal of the American Medical Association, 286,* 2143–2151.

Sipski, M. L., Alexander, C. J., & Rosen, R. (2001). Sexual arousal and orgasm in women. *Annals of Neurology, 49*(1), 35–44.

Slovenko, R. (2001). Aphrodisiacs—then and now. *Journal of Psychiatry & Law, 29*(1), 103–116.

Smart, C. (2006). The state of affairs: Explorations in infidelity and commitment. *Sexualities, 9*(2), 259–262.

Smith, M. J., Schmidt, P. J., & Rubinow, D. R. (2003). Operationalizing *DSM-IV* criteria for PMDD: Selecting symptomatic and asymptomatic cycles for research. *Journal of Psychiatric Research, 37*(1), 75–83.

Smith, Y. L. S., Van Goozen, S. H. M., Kuiper, A. J., & Cohen–Kettenis, P. T. (2005). Sex reassignment: Outcomes and predictors of treatment for adolescent and adult transsexuals. *Psychological Medicine, 35*(1), 89–99.

Smock, P. J. (2000, Cited in Nagourney, E., February 15). *Annual Review of Sociology.* Study finds families bypassing marriage. *The New York Times,* p. F8.

Solomon, C. G., & Dluhy, R. G. (2003). Rethinking postmenopausal hormone therapy. *New England Journal of Medicine, 348*(7), 579–580.

Sommerfeld, J. (2000, April 18). *Lifting the curse: Should monthly periods be optional?* MSNBC. [Online].

Spehr, M., et al. (2003). Identification of a testicular odorant receptor mediating human sperm chemotaxis. *Science, 299*(5615).

Spelke, E. (2005). Sex differences in intrinsic aptitude for mathematics and science?: A critical review. *American Psychologist, 60*(9), 950–958.

Spencer, N. (2006). Explaining the social gradient in smoking in pregnancy: Early life course accumulation and cross-sectional clustering of social risk exposures in the 1958 British national cohort. *Social Science & Medicine, 62*(5), 1250–1259.

Spiegel, D. (2001). Breast cancer: Society shapes and epidemic. *New England Journal of Medicine, 334,* 1337–1338.

Spiro, M. E. (1965). *Children of the kibbutz.* New York: Schocken Books.

Spitzer, R. L. (2005). Peer commentaries on Binik: A more radical proposal: Dyspareunia is not a mental disorder. *Archives of Sexual Behavior, 34*(1), 48.

Spitzer, R. L., et al. (1989). *DSM-III-R casebook.* Washington, DC: American Psychiatric Press.

Sprecher, S. (1998). Insiders' perspectives on reasons for attraction to a close other. *Social Psychology Quarterly, 61*(4), 287–300.

Sprecher, S., Barbee, A., & Schwartz, P. (1995). "Was it good for you, too?" Gender differences in first sexual intercourse experiences. *The Journal of Sex Research, 32,* 3–15.

Sprecher, S., Sullivan, Q., & Hatfield, E. (1994). Mate selection preferences: Gender differences examined in a national sample. *Journal of Personality and Social Psychology, 66*(6), 1074–1080.

Squier, S., & Littlefield, M. M. (Eds.). (2004). Feminist theory and/of science: Feminist Theory special issue. *Feminist Theory, 5*(2), 123–126.

Stake, J. E., & Hoffman, F. L. (2001). Changes in student social attitudes, activism, and personal confidence in higher education: The role of women's studies. *American Educational Research Journal, 38*(2), 411–436.

Stamback, A., & Miriam, D. (2005). Feminist theory and educational policy: How gender has been "involved" in family school choice debates. *Signs, 30*(2), 1633–1658.

Stanley, S. M., Bradbury, T. N., & Markman, H. J. (2000). Structural flaws in the bridge from basic research on marriage to interventions for couples. *Journal of Marriage & the Family, 62*(1), 256–264.

Stearns, V., Beebe, K. L., Iyengar, M., & Dube, E. (2003). Paroxetine controlled release in the treatment of menopausal hot flashes. *Journal of the American Medical Association, 289,* 2827–2834.

Steele, C. M., & Josephs, R. A. (1990). Alcohol myopia: Its prized and dangerous effects. *American Psychologist, 45,* 921–933.

Stefanick, M. L., et al. (2006). Effects of conjugated equine estrogens on breast cancer and mammography screening in postmenopausal women with hysterectomy. *Journal of the American Medical Association, 295,* 1647–1657.

Stein, C. J., & Colditz, G. A. (2004). Modifiable risk factors for cancer. *Journal of Breast Cancer, 90*(2), 299–303.

Stein, D. J., Black, D. W., Shapira, N. A., & Spitzer, R. L. (2001). Hypersexual disorder and preoccupation with Internet pornography. *American Journal of Psychiatry, 158*(10), 1590–1594.

Stein, Z., & Susser, M. (2000). The risks of having children in later life. *British Medical Journal, 320*(7251), 1681–1682.

Steinberg, D. (2004, September 8). Lap victory. *San Francisco Weekly.*

Steinemann, S., & Steinemann, M. (2005). Retroelements: Tools for sex chromosome evolution. *Cytogenetic and Genome Research, 110,* 134–143.

Stengers, J., Van Neck, A., & Hoffmann, K. (2001). *Masturbation: The history of a great terror.* New York: St. Martin's Press.

Stephenson, J. (2000). Widely used spermicide may increase, not decrease, risk of HIV transmission. *Journal of the American Medical Association* [online], *284*(8).

Sterk, C. E., & Elifson, K. W. (2006). Exploring sexual behaviors and sexual orientation: An ethnographic study of African American female crack cocaine users. In Omoto, A. M., & Kurtzman, H. S. (Eds.). (2006). *Sexual orientation and mental health: Examining identity and development in lesbian, gay, and bisexual people. Contemporary perspectives on lesbian, gay, and bisexual psychology* (pp. 269–280).

Washington, DC: American Psychological Association.

Sternberg, R. J. (1988). *The triangle of love: Intimacy, passion, commitment.* New York: Basic Books.

Sternberg, R. J. (2004). A triangular theory of love. In Reis, H. T., & Rusbult, C. E. (Eds.). *Close relationships: Key readings* (pp. 213–227). London: Taylor & Francis.

Stockett, M. K. (2005). On the importance of difference: Re-envisioning sex and gender in ancient Mesoamerica, *World Archaeology. 37*(4), 566–578.

Stolberg, S. G. (1998, January 18). Quandary on donor eggs: What to tell the children. *The New York Times,* pp. 1, 20.

Storms, M. D. (1980). Theories of sexual orientation. *Journal of Personality and Social Psychology, 38,* 783–792.

Strager, S. (2003). What men watch when they watch pornography. *Sexuality & Culture: An Interdisciplinary Quarterly, 7*(1), 50–61.

Strassberg, D. S., & Holty, S. (2003). An experimental study of women's Internet personal ads. *Archives of Sexual Behavior, 32*(3), 253–260.

Stratton, T. D., McLaughlin, M. A., Witte, F. M., Fosson, S. E., & Nora, L. M. (2005). Does students' exposure to gender discrimination and sexual harassment in medical school affect specialty choice and residency program selection? *Academic Medicine, 80*(4), 400–408.

Streeter, S. A., & McBurney, D. H. (2003). Waist–hip ratio and attractiveness: New evidence and a critique of a "critical test." *Evolution & Human Behavior, 24*(2), 88–98.

Stulhofer, A. (2006). How (un)important is penis size for women with heterosexual experience? *Archives of Sexual Behavior, 35*(1), 5–6.

Šturm, J. J., Yeatts, K., & Loomis, D. (2004). Effects of tobacco smoke exposure on asthma prevalence and medical care use in North Carolina middle school children. *American Journal of Public Health. 94*(2), 308–313.

Sulak, P. J., et al., (2000). Hormone withdrawal symptoms in oral contraceptive users. *Obstetrics & Gynecology, 95,* 261–266.

Sullivan, C. (2006). Women and men in management. *Gender, Work & Organization, 13*(1), 96–98.

Sullivan, N. (2003). *A critical introduction to queer theory.* Edinburgh: Edinburgh University Press.

Surratt, H. L., Kurtz, S. P., Weaver, J. C., & Inciardi, J. A. (2005). The connections of mental health problems, violent life experiences, and the social milieu of the "stroll" with the HIV risk behaviors of female street sex workers. *Journal of Psychology & Human Sexuality, 17*(1–2), 23–44.

Symons, D. (1995, Cited in Goleman, D., June 14). Sex fantasy research said to neglect women. *The New York Times,* p. C14.

Szabo, R., & Short, R. V. (2000). How does male circumcision protect against HIV infection? *British Medical Journal, 320,* 1592–1594.

Taha, E. T., et al. (2003). Short postexposure prophylaxis in newborn babies to reduce mother-to-child transmission of HIV-1: NVAZ randomised clinical trial. *The Lancet, 362*(9391), 1171–1177.

Tan, R. S. (2001). *The andropause mystery: Unraveling truths about the male menopause.* Houston: Amred Publishing.

Tan, R. S. (2002). Managing the andropause in

aging men. *Clinical Geriatrics.* [Online]. www .mmhc.com/cg/articles/CG9907/Tan.html.

Tan, R. S., & Culberson, J. W. (2003). An integrative review on current evidence of testosterone replacement therapy for the andropause. *Maturitas, 45*(1), 15–27.

Tanfer, K., Grady, W. R., Klepinger, D. H., & Billy, J. O. G. (1993). Condom use among U.S. men, 1991. *Family Planning Perspectives, 25,* 61–66.

Tang, M. C., Weiss, N. S., & Malone, K. E. (2000). Induced abortion in relation to breast cancer among parous women: A birth certificate registry study. *Epidemiology, 11*(2), 177–180.

Tashima, K. T., & Carpenter, C. C. J. (2003). Fusion inhibition: A major but costly step forward in the treatment of HIV-1. *New England Journal of Medicine, 348*(22), 2249–2250.

Tashiro, T., & Frazier, P. (2003). "I'll never be in a relationship like that again": Personal growth following romantic relationship breakups. *Personal Relationships, 10*(1), 113–128.

Taylor, M. J., Rudkin, L., & Hawton, K. (2005). Strategies for managing antidepressant-induced sexual dysfunction: Systematic review of randomised controlled trials. *Journal of Affective Disorders, 88*(3), 241–254.

Taylor, S. E., et al. (2000). Biobehavioral responses to stress in females: Tend-and-befriend, not fight-or-flight. *Psychological Review, 107*(3), 411–429.

Taylor, V., & Rupp, L. J. (2004). Chicks with dicks, men in dresses: What it means to be a drag queen. *Journal of Homosexuality, 46*(3–4), 113–133.

Teen dies after complications from abortion pill. (2003, September 22). Associated Press.

Thachil, A., & Bhugra, D. (2006). Literature update: A critical review. *Sexual and Relationship Therapy, 21*(2), 229–235.

"Third sex" finds a place on Indian passport forms. (2005, March 10). *The Telegraph.*

Thomas, N. L., & Coughtrie, M. W. H. (2003). Sulfation of apomorphine by human sulfotransferases: Evidence of a major role for the polymorphic phenol sulfotransferase, SULT1A1. *Xenobiotica, 33*(11), 1139–1148.

Thompson, I. M., et al. (2005). Erectile dysfunction and subsequent cardiovascular disease. *Journal of the American Medical Association, 294*(23), 2996–3002.

Thompson, J. K., & Tantleff, S. (1992). Female and male ratings of upper torso: Actual, ideal, and stereotypical conceptions. *Journal of Social Behavior and Personality, 7,* 345–354.

Thornhill, R., & Palmer, C. (2000). *A natural history of rape: Biological bases of sexual coercion.* Cambridge, MA: MIT Press.

Tierney, J. (2006, September 19). From Tinseltown to Splitsville: Just do the math. *The New York Times.*

Toner, R. (2007, April 18). Court ruling catapults abortion back into '08 race. *The New York Times,* p. A1.

Torpy, J. M., Lynm, C., & Glass, R. M. (2003). Perimenopause: Beginning of menopause. *Journal of the American Medical Association, 289,* 940.

Totman, R. (2004). *The third sex: Kathoey: Thailand's ladyboys.* London: Souvenir Press.

Traish, A. M., Goldstein, I., Munarriz, R., & Guay, A. (2006). Roles of androgens in women's sexual function & dysfunction: What have we learned in sex decades? *Current Women's Health Reviews, 2*(1), 75–86.

Transvestites get their own school bathroom. (2004, June 22). Associated Press.

Troxel, W. M., & Matthews, K. A. (2004). What are the costs of marital conflict and dissolution to children's physical health? *Clinical Child & Family Psychology Review, 7*(1), 29–57.

Trudel, G., Turgeon, L., & Piche, L. (2000). Marital and sexual aspects of old age. *Sexual & Relationship Therapy, 15*(4), 381–406.

Trulsson, O., & Rådestad, I. (2004). The silent child—Mothers' experiences before, during, and after stillbirth. *Birth: Issues in Perinatal Care, 31*(3), 189–195.

Tuiten, A., et al. (2000). Time course of effects of testosterone administration on sexual arousal in women. *Archives of General Psychiatry, 57,* 149–153.

Tunariu, A. D., & Reavey, P. (2003). Men in love: Living with sexual boredom. *Sexual & Relationship Therapy, 18*(1), 63–94.

Turner, H. A., Finkelhor, D., & Ormrod, R. (2006). The effect of lifetime victimization on the mental health of children and adolescents. *Social Science & Medicine, 62*(1), 13–27.

Turton, J. (2005). Perspectives on female sex offending: A culture of denial. *Sexualities, 8*(5), 632–633.

Turton, P., et al. (2006). Psychological impact of stillbirth on fathers in the subsequent pregnancy and puerperium. *British Journal of Psychiatry, 188*(2), 165–172.

Twist, M. (2005). Relationship therapy with same-sex couples. *Journal of Marital & Family Therapy, 31*(4), 413.

U.S. Bureau of the Census. (2005). *Statistical abstract of the United States.* 125th ed. Washington, DC: U.S. Government Printing Office.

U.S. Bureau of the Census. (2006). U.S. Bureau of the Census, current population reports, estimated median age at first marriage, by sex: 1890–present. [Online]. www.census.gov/population/socdemo/hh-fam/ms2.pdf.

U.S. Department of Justice. (1986). *Attorney general's commission on pornography: Final report.* Washington, DC: U.S. Government Printing Office.

U.S. Department of Justice. *Criminal victimization in the United States. Statistical tables, 2003.* Office of Justice Programs. Bureau of Justice Statistics. Accessed February 15, 2006. [Online]. www.ojp.usdoj.gov/bjs/abstract/cvus/rape_sexual_assault.htm.

U.S. National Library of Medicine. (2006). *Androgen insensitivity syndrome.* National Institutes of Health. [Online]. http://ghr.nlm.nih.gov/condition-androgeninsensitivitysyndrome.

Udry, J. R. (2001). Feminist critics uncover determinism, positivism, and antiquated theory. *American Sociological Review, 66*(4), 611–618.

Ullman, S. E., Filipas, H. H., Townsend, S. M., & Starzynski, L. L. (2006). The role of victim-offender relationship in women's sexual assault experiences. *Journal of Interpersonal Violence, 21*(6), 798–819.

UNAIDS. (2000a, June 5). *Gender is crucial issue in fight against AIDS, says head of UNAIDS.* New York: UNAIDS.

UNAIDS. (2000b, July 12). UNAIDS calls for continued commitment to microbicides.

UNAIDS. (2006). *Report on the global AIDS epidemic: Executive summary.* Joint United Nations Programme on HIV/AIDS (UNAIDS). Geneva: UNAIDS.

Understanding prostate problems. (2007, May 2). www.prostatecare.com/understanding_prostate_problems/understanding_prostate_problems.html

United Nations Special Session on AIDS. (2001, June 25–27). *Preventing HIV/AIDS among young people.* New York: United Nations.

Vaculík, M., & Hudecek, T. (2005). Development of close relationships in the Internet environment. *Ceskoslovenská Psychologie, 49*(2), 157–174.

Valkenburg, P. M., & Peter, J. (2007). Preadolescents' and adolescents' online communication and their closeness to friends. *Developmental Psychology, 43*(2), 267–277.

Valocchi, S. (2005). Not yet queer enough: The lessons of queer theory for the sociology of gender and sexuality. *Gender & Society, 19*(6), 750–770.

van Anders, S. M., Watson, N. V. (2006). Relationship status and testosterone in North American heterosexual and non-heterosexual men and women: Cross-sectional and longitudinal data. *Psychoneuroendocrinology, 31*(6), 715–723.

van den Bree, M. B. M., & Pickworth, W. B. (2005). Risk factors predicting changes in marijuana involvement in teenagers. *Archives of General Psychiatry, 62*(3), 311–319.

Van Lange, P. A. M., et al. (1997). Willingness to sacrifice in close relationships. *Journal of Personality & Social Psychology, 72*(6), 1373–1395.

Van Minnen, A., & Kampman, M. (2000). The interaction between anxiety and sexual functioning: A controlled study of sexual functioning in women with anxiety disorders. *Sexual & Relationship Therapy, 15*(1), 47–57.

Van Wie, V. E., & Gross, A. M. (2001). The role of woman's explanations for refusal on men's ability to discriminate unwanted sexual behavior in a date rape scenario. *Journal of Family Violence, 16*(4), 331–344.

Vandello, J. A., & Cohen, D. (2003). Male honor and female fidelity: Implicit cultural scripts that perpetuate domestic violence. *Journal of Personality & Social Psychology, 84*(5), 997–1010.

Vastag, B. (2003). Many questions, few answers for testosterone replacement therapy. *Journal of the American Medical Association, 289,* 971–972.

Veniegas, R. C., Peplau, L. A. (1997). Power and the quality of same-sex friendships. *Psychology of Women Quarterly, 21*(2), 279–297.

Villar, F., Villamizar, D. J., & López–Chivrall, S. (2005). Components of loving experience in old age: Older people and long-term relationships. *Revista Espanola de Geriatria y Gerontologia, 40*(3), 166–177.

Vohs, K. D., & Baumeister, R. F. (2004). Sexual passion, intimacy, and gender. In Mashek, D. J., Aron, A. P. (Eds.). *Handbook of closeness and intimacy* (pp. 189–199). Hillsdale, NJ: Lawrence Erlbaum Associates.

von Krafft–Ebbing, R. (1886/1978). *Psychopathia sexualis.* Philadelphia: F. A. Davis. [Original work published 1886].

Vorauer, J. D., Cameron, J. J., Holmes, J. G., & Pearce, D. G. (2003). Invisible overtures: Fears of rejection and the signal amplification bias. *Journal of Personality & Social Psychology, 84*(4), 793–812.

Wagenaar, H. (2006). Democracy and prostitution: Deliberating the legalization of brothels in the Netherlands. *Administration & Society, 38*(2), 98–235.

Waismann, R., Fenwick, P. B. C., Wilson, G. D., Hewett, T. D., & Lumsden, J. (2003). EEG responses to visual erotic stimuli in men with normal and paraphilic interests. *Archives of Sexual Behavior, 32*(2), 135–144.

Wald, A. (2005, November 22). Investigational HPV vaccine shows 100% efficacy. *Journal Watch Women's Health.*

Waldinger, M. D., et al. (2002). The selective serotonin re-uptake inhibitors fluvoxamine and paroxetine differ in sexual inhibitory effects after chronic treatment. *Psychopharmacology, 160*(3), 283–289.

Waldinger, M. D., Zwinderman, A. H., & Olivier, B. (2001). Antidepressants and ejaculation: A double-blind, randomized, placebo-controlled, fixed-dose study with paroxetine, sertraline and nefazodone. *Journal of Clinical Psychopharmacology, 21*(3), 293–297.

Walker, E. M. (2005). The inevitability of idealization. *Contemporary Psychoanalysis, 41*(3), 567–572.

Walker, J., Archer, J., & Davies, M. (2005). Effects of rape on men: A descriptive analysis. *Archives of Sexual Behavior, 34*(1), 69–80.

Walther, C. S., & Poston, D. L., Jr. (2004). Patterns of gay and lesbian partnering in the larger metropolitan areas of the United States. *Journal of Sex Research, 41*(2), 201–214.

Walz, T. (2002). Crones, dirty old men, sexy seniors: Representations of sexuality of older persons. *Journal of Aging & Identity, 7*(2), 99–112.

Wang, S., Fuh, J., Lu, S., Juang, K., & Wang, P. (2003). Migraine prevalence during menopausal transition. *Headache: The Journal of Head and Face Pain, 43*(5), 470–478.

Ward, T., & Gannon, T. A. (2006). Rehabilitation, etiology, and self-regulation: The comprehensive good lives model of treatment for sexual offenders. *Aggression and Violent Behavior, 11*(1), 77–94.

Waterman, J. (1986). Overview of treatment issues. In MacFarlane, K., et al. (Eds.). *Sexual abuse of young children: Evaluation and treatment* (pp. 197–203). New York: Guilford.

Watts, C., & Zimmerman, C. (2002). Violence against women: Global scope and magnitude. *Lancet, 359*(9313), 1232–1237.

Wayment, H. A., Wyatt, G. E., et al. (2003). Predictors of risky and precautionary sexual behaviors among single and married white women. *Journal of Applied Social Psychology, 33*(4), 791–816.

Webb, R. M., Lubinski, D., & Benbow, C. P. (2002). Mathematically facile adolescents with math/science aspirations: New perspectives on their educational and vocational development. *Journal of Educational Psychology, 94,* 785–794.

Weeden, J., & Sabini, J. (2005). Physical attractiveness and health in Western societies: A review. *Psychological Bulletin, 131*(5), 635–653.

Weinberg, T. S. (1987). Sadomasochism in the United States: A review of recent sociological literature. *Journal of Sex Research, 23,* 50–69.

Weinrich, J. D., & Klein, F. (2002). Bi-gay, bi-straight, and bi-bi: Three bisexual subgroups identified using cluster analysis of the Klein Sexual Orientation Grid. *Journal of Bisexuality, 2*(4), 109–139.

Welldon, E. V. (2005). Incest: A therapeutic challenge. In Ambrosio, G. (Ed.). *On incest: Psychoanalytic perspectives* (pp. 81–100). London: Karnac Books.

Welsh, S., Carr, J., Macquarrie, B., & Huntley, A. (2006). "I'm not thinking of it as sexual harassment": Understanding harassment across race and citizenship. *Gender & Society, 20*(1), 87–107.

Western Resistance. (2006, May 25). *Pakistan: "Hudood" ordinances (Islamic rape/adultery laws) may be repealed.* [Online]. www.western-resistance.com/blog/archives/002215.html.

Whipple, B., & Komisaruk, B. R. (1988). Analgesia produced in women by genital self-stimulation. *Journal of Sex Research, 24,* 130–140.

Whitehead, B. D., & Popenoe, D. (2006). The state of our unions: The social health of marriage in America 2006. New Brunswick, NJ: Rutgers University.

Whitley, B. E., Jr. (1983). Sex role orientation and self-esteem: A critical meta-analysis. *Journal of Personality and Social Psychology, 44,* 765–788.

Wieselquist, J., Rusbult, C. E., Foster, C. A., & Agnew, C. R. (1999). Commitment, pro-relationship behavior, and trust in close relationships. *Journal of Personality & Social Psychology, 77*(5), 942–966.

Wilcox, A. J., Dunson, D., & Baird, D. D. (2000). The timing of the "fertile window" in the menstrual cycle: Day specific estimates from a prospective study. *British Medical Journal, 321,* 1259–1262.

Wilcox, B. L. (1987). Pornography, social science and politics: When research and ideology collide. *American Psychologist, 42,* 941–943.

Wilkinson, S. (2003, March 31). Odor receptors may attract sperm to eggs. *CENEAR, 81*(13), 10.

Willetts, M. C. (2006). Union quality comparisons between long-term heterosexual cohabitation and legal marriage. *Journal of Family Issues, 27*(1), 110–127.

Williams, D. E., & D'Alessandro, J. D. (1994). A comparison of three measures of androgyny and their relationship to psychological adjustment. *Journal of Social Behavior and Personality, 9*(3), 469–480.

Williams, J. E., & Best, D. L. (1994). Cross-cultural views of women and men. In Lonner, W. J., & Malpass, R. (Eds.). *Psychology and culture.* Boston: Allyn & Bacon.

Williams, M. E. (Ed.). (2001). *Abortion: Opposing viewpoints.* Greenhaven Press.

Williams, V. S. L., et al. (2006). Estimating the prevalence and impact of antidepressant-induced sexual dysfunction in 2 European countries: A cross-sectional patient survey. *Journal of Clinical Psychiatry, 67*(2), 204–210.

Williamson, C., & Cluse–Tolar, T. (2002). Pimp-controlled prostitution: Still an integral part of street life. *Violence Against Women, 8*(9), 1074–1092.

Wilson, G. D., & Cousins, J. M. (2003). Partner similarity and relationship satisfaction: Development of a compatibility quotient. *Sexual and Relationship Therapy, 18*(2), 161–170.

Wilson, J. M. B., Tripp, D. A., & Boland, F. J. (2005). The relative contributions of waist-to-hip ratio and body mass index to judgments of attractiveness. *Sexualities, Evolution & Gender, 7*(3), 245–267.

Wilson, W., et al. (2000). Brain morphological changes and early marijuana use: A magnetic resonance and positron emission tomography study. *Journal of Addictive Diseases, 19*(1), 1–22.

Winter, S. (2003). *Research and discussion paper: Language and identity in transgender: Gender wars and the case of the Thai kathoey.* Paper presented at the Hawaii conference on Social Sciences. Waikiki, HI.

Witkowska, E., & Gådin, K. G. (2005). Have you been sexually harassed in school? What female high school students regard as harassment. *International Journal of Adolescent Medicine and Health, 17*(4), 391–406.

Wood, J. T. (2005). *Gendered lives: Communication, gender, and culture.* 6th ed. Belmont, CA: Wadsworth.

Wood, N. S., et al. (2000). Neurologic and developmental disability after extremely preterm birth. *The New England Journal of Medicine, 343*(6).

Woog, V. (2005). Talk about sex: The battles over sex education in the United States. *Health & Sexuality, 7*(1), 78–80.

Wooster, R., & Weber, B. L. (2003). Genomic medicine: Breast and ovarian cancer. *New England Journal of Medicine, 348,* 2339–2347.

Wortman, C. B., et al. (1976). Self-disclosure: An attributional perspective. *Journal of Personality and Social Psychology, 33,* 184–191.

Wyatt, G. E. (1985). The sexual abuse of Afro-American and white American women in childhood. *Child Abuse and Neglect, 9,* 507–519.

Wyatt, G. E. (1989). Reexamining factors predicting Afro-American and white American women's age at first coitus. *Archives of Sexual Behavior, 18,* 271–298.

Wyatt, G. E., Carmona, J. V., Loeb, T. B., & Williams, J. K. (2005). HIV-positive black women with histories of childhood sexual abuse: Patterns of substance use and barriers to health care. *Journal of Health Care for the Poor and Underserved, 16*(Suppl. B), 9–23.

Wyatt, G. E., et al. (2004a). The efficacy of an integrated risk reduction intervention for HIV-positive women with child sexual abuse histories. *AIDS and Behavior, 8*(4), 453–462.

Wyatt, G. E., Myers, H. F., & Loeb, T. B. (2004b). Women, trauma, and HIV: An overview. *AIDS and Behavior, 8*(4), 401–403.

Wyatt, G. E., Peters, S. D., & Guthrie, D. (1988a). Kinsey revisited, part I: Comparisons of the sexual socialization and sexual behavior of white women over 33 years. *Archives of Sexual Behavior, 17*(3), 201–209.

Wyatt, G. E., Peters, S. D., & Guthrie, D. (1988b). Kinsey revisited, part II: Comparisons of the sexual socialization and sexual behavior of black women over 33 years. *Archives of Sexual Behavior, 17*(4), 289–332.

Wyatt, T. (2003). *Pheromones and animal behaviour: Communication by smell and taste.* Cambridge, UK: Cambridge University Press.

Xu, J., Burgoyne, P. S., & Arnold, A. P. (2002). Sex differences in sex chromosome gene expression in mouse brain. *Human Molecular Genetics, 11*(12), 1409–1419.

Yaffe, K., Haan, M., Byers, A., Tangen, C., & Kuller, L. (2000). Estrogen use, APOE, and cognitive decline: Evidence of gene-environment interaction. *Neurology, 54*(10), 1949–1953.

Yarber, W. L., Torabi, M. R., & Veenker, C. H. (1989). Development of a three-component sexually transmitted diseases attitude scale. *Journal of Sex Education & Therapy, 15,* 36–49.

Yates, P. M., & Kingston, D. A. (2006). The self-regulation model of sexual offending: The relationship between offence pathways and static and dynamic sexual offence risk. *Sexual Abuse: Journal of Research and Treatment, 18*(3), 259–270.

Yela, C. (2000). Predictors of and factors related to loving and sexual satisfaction for men and women. *European Review of Applied Psychology, 50*(1), 235–243.

Yela, C. (2006). The evaluation of love: Simplified version of the scales for Yela's tetrangular model based on Sternberg's model. *European Journal of Psychological Assessment, 22*(1), 21–27.

Yoder, V. C., Virden, T. B., III, & Amin, K. (2005). Internet pornography and loneliness: An association? *Sexual Addiction & Compulsivity, 12*(1), 19–44.

Yoshimoto, D., et al. (2006). Nonverbal communication coding systems of committed couples. In *The new handbook of methods in nonverbal behavior research* (pp. 369–397). New York: Oxford University Press.

Yost, M. R., & Zurbriggen, E. L. (2006). Gender differences in the enactment of sociosexuality: An examination of implicit social motives, sexual fantasies, coercive sexual attitudes, and aggressive sexual behavior. *Journal of Sex Research, 43*(2), 163–173.

Young, A. M., et al. (2005). Drinking like a guy: Frequent binge drinking among undergraduate women. *Substance Use & Misuse, 40*(2), 241–267.

Young, M., Denny, G., Luquis, R., & Young, T. (1998). Correlates of sexual satisfaction in marriage. *Canadian Journal of Human Sexuality, 7*(2), 115–127.

Zaidi, A. U., & Shuraydi, M. (2002). Perceptions of arranged marriages by young Pakistani Muslim women living in a Western society. *Journal of Comparative Family Studies, 33*(4), 495–514.

Zalar, R. W. (2000). Domestic violence. *The New England Journal of Medicine, 342*(19).

Zamboni, B. D., & Crawford, I. (2002). Using masturbation in sex therapy: Relationships between masturbation, sexual desire, and sexual fantasy. *Journal of Psychology & Human Sexuality, 14*(2–3), 123–141.

Zaviacic, M., et al. (1988a). Concentrations of fructose in female ejaculate and urine: A comparative biochemical study. *Journal of Sex Research, 24,* 319–325.

Zaviacic, M., et al. (1988b). Female urethral expulsions evoked by local digital stimulation of the G-spot: Differences in the response patterns. *Journal of Sex Research, 24,* 311–318.

Zaviacic, M., & Whipple, B. (1993). Update on the female prostate and the phenomenon of female ejaculation. *Journal of Sex Research, 30,* 148–151.

Zeichner, A., Parrott, D. J., & Frey, F. C. (2003). Gender differences in laboratory aggression under response choice conditions. *Aggressive Behavior, 29*(2), 95–106.

Zelenski, J. M., Rusting, C. L., & Larsen, R. J. (2003). Consistency in the time of experimental participation and personality correlates. *Personality & Individual Differences, 34*(4), 547–558.

Zernike, K. (2003, August 24). The new couples next door. *The New York Times.* [Online].

Zernike, K. (2005, December 11). The siren song of sex with boys. *The New York Times.* [Online].

Zerubavel, E. (2006). *The elephant in the room: Silence and denial in everyday life.* New York: Oxford University Press.

Zezima, K. (2006, February 3). Teenager attacks

three men at gay bar in Massachusetts. *The New York Times.* [Online].

Zhou, Q., Zhang, K., Li, Z., Liu, D., & Zhou, X. (2002). Personality of 133 male commercial sex service providers and acceptors. *Chinese Mental Health Journal, 16*(1), 48.

Zielbauer, P. (2000, May 22). Sex offender listings on Web set off debate. *The New York Times.* [Online].

Zilbergeld, B. (1999). *The new male sexuality.* Rev. ed. New York: Bantam Doubleday Dell.

Zillmann, D. (1989). Effects of prolonged consumption of pornography. In Zillmann, D., & Bryant, J. (Eds.). *Pornography: Research advances and policy considerations* (pp. 127–157). Hillsdale, NJ: Lawrence Erlbaum Associates.

Zillmann, D., & Bryant, J. (1984). Effects of massive exposure to pornography. In Malamuth, N. M., & Donnerstein, E. (Eds.). *Pornography and sexual aggression* (pp. 115–138). New York: Academic Press.

Zimmer, D., Borchardt, E., & Fischle, C. (1983). Sexual fantasies of sexually distressed and nondistressed men and women: An empirical investigation. *Journal of Sex and Marital Therapy, 9,* 38–50.

Zubeidat, l., Ortega, V., & Sierra, J. C. (2004). Assessment of some determinant factors of sexual desire: Emotional state, sexual attitudes and sexual fantasies. *Análisis y Modificación de Conducta, 30*(129), 105–128.

Zucker, K. J. (2005a). Gender identity disorder in children and adolescents. *Annual Review of Clinical Psychology, 1*(1), 467–492.

Zucker, K. J. (2005b). Gender identity disorder in girls. In Bell, D. J., Foster, S. L., & Mash, E. J. (Eds.). *Handbook of behavioral and emotional problems in girls. Issues in clinical child psychology* (pp. 285–319). Kluwer Academic/Plenum Publishers.

Name Index

Gates, G. J., 426, 447
Gavey, N., 493
Gavin, N. I., 355
Gebhard, P. H., 19, 41–42, 137, 155, 263, 268, 269, 288, 409, 562, 564, 565, 571, 604, 629
Gebre-Medhin, M., 66
Geer, J., 122
Gelfand, M. M., 147
Gentles, I., 401
George, W. H., 140
Gerber, P. N., 571
Gerevich, J., 640
Gibson, L., 235
Gibson, S., 229
Gidycz, C. A., 585, 587, 597
Gijs, L., 146
Gilchrist, G., 621
Gillis, J., 200
Gilmour, S., 621
Ginsberg, R. L., 474, 484, 485, 489
Ginsburg, H. J., 65
Giotakos, O., 112
Givertz, M., 238
Glass, R. M., 91
Gnagy, S., 369
Goetz, A. T., 234
Gold, S. N., 606
Gold, S. R., 202
Goldberg, A., 415
Goldberg, A. R., 31
Goldberg, J., 348
Goldfried, M. R., 242
Goldman, R. D., 353
Goldmeier, D., 478, 484, 503
Goldschmidt, L., 342
Goldstein, I., 474, 477, 478, 480, 482, 483, 487, 500, 503
Goldtein, I., 147
Goleman, D., 279
Golish, T. D., 459
Gomes do Espirito, M. E., 626, 629
Gonzaga, G. C., 209
Gonzalez, R. G., 570
Gonzalez-Rivera, M., 294, 299
Goodman-Delahunty, J., 607
Goodrich, D., 475, 476, 484, 487, 502
Goodson, P., 638, 639
Gooren, L., 146
Gordon, A. E., 343, 344
Gordon, A. R., 31
Gorman, S., 599
Gottman, J., 244
Gottman, J. M., 230, 242, 244, 250, 458
Gough, B., 557, 559
Goulet, J., 177
Grace, V. M., 493
Grady, D., 92
Grady, W. R., 46
Graham, C., 278, 382
Graham, C. A., 484
Greeff, A. P., 386
Green, R., 310
Greene, B., 294, 295
Greene, L., 44, 412, 417, 418
Greene, S. J., 296
Greene, S. M., 92
Greenwald, E., 603
Greer, C. A., 136
Grenier, G., 479
Grenz, S., 632
Gresh, S., 426, 427
Griffin, M. K., 598
Griffin-Shelley, E., 640

Griffith, K. H., 312
Griffiths, P., 464
Griffy, K., 511
Grigoriadis, S., 355
Grodstein, F., 94
Gross, A. M., 588–589
Gross, B., 565, 566
Gross, J., 466
Grosser, B. I., 136
Groth, A. N., 586, 587, 592
Grubin, D., 602
Grych, J. H., 458
Guadagno, R. E., 234
Guay, A., 147
Guay, A. T., 147
Guernsey, L., 428
Guo, G., 181
Guo, Y. N., 265
Gutheil, T. G., 559, 560
Guthrie, D., 46
Guthrie, J. R., 91
Gutmann, P., 257
Guttmacher, 509
Guzick, D. S., 93, 145, 147, 148

H

Haake, P., 559, 569, 570
Haan, M., 92
Haasser, R. C., 503
Hafen, M., Jr., 245
Hahn, S., 233
Haldeman, D. C., 310
Hall, G., 93
Hall, G. C. N., 592
Halpern, D. F., 31, 180, 181
Hamann, S., 133
Hamby, S. L., 598, 602
Hamdallah, M., 511
Hamer, D. H., 301
Hamidi, K., 264, 265
Hammersmith, S. K., 46, 305
Han, C., 142
Handal, M., 489
Hanh, L. T., 620, 622
Hardenburg, S. A., 553, 554, 572
Hardiman, P., 93
Hardy, S., 638, 639
Harger, J., 459
Hargrove, M. F., 112
Harris, C. R., 234
Harris, G. T., 554, 562, 584, 586, 592, 593
Harrison, M. A., 233
Harshbarger, C., 511
Hart, J., 332
Hart, T. A., 511
Harter, S., 229
Hartge, P., 369
Hartocollis, A., 552
Hassebrauck, M., 226
Hatch, J. P., 629
Hatcher, R. A., 369, 370, 371, 373, 375, 377, 379, 380, 381, 383, 387, 388, 390, 516, 517, 520, 521, 522, 524, 537, 539
Hatfield, E., 204, 205, 209, 210, 212, 213, 215, 218, 219
Hatzichristou, D. G., 495
Haugaard, J. J., 597
Hawkley, L. C., 239
Hawton, K., 482, 483
Hayes, R. D., 483
Hayman, L. W., Jr., 511
Hayreh, D. J. S., 136
Hazam, H., 230

He, N., 458
Health24.com, 409, 410, 414, 415
Heath, R., 143
Hebl, M. R., 312
Hegna, K., 628, 629
Heiman, J. R., 474, 478, 484, 485
Hellstrom, W. J. G., 487
Hendrick, C., 209, 210, 214, 215, 218, 219, 225
Hendrick, S. S., 209, 210, 214, 215, 218, 219, 225
Hendry, O., 268
Henning, K., 278, 279
Henshaw, S. K., 20
Hensley, L. G., 595
Henslin, J. H., 25
Herek, G. M., 294, 299
Herman, R. A., 133
Herr, J., 640
Herrera, V. M., 593, 594, 605
Herrington, D. M., 93
Herrmann, H. C., 496
Hessol, N. A., 353
Hester, J. D., 177
Hetherington, E. M., 92, 458, 459
Heusel, C., 112
Hewett, T. D., 570
Hicks, T. V., 279
Hill, M. J., 172
Hill, A., 560, 565, 575
Hill, E. M., 181
Hill, R. A., 202
Hines, D. A., 183
Hines, M., 169
Hines, T. M., 72
Hird, M. J., 31, 296
Hirt, J., 309
Hitt, J., 392, 394
Hoch, Z., 73
Hoeger, K., 93, 145, 147, 148
Hofferth, S. L., 459
Hoffman, F. L., 179
Hoffman, L. E., 280
Hoffmann, K., 16, 18
Hofmeyr, D. G., 386
Hoier, S., 234
Höjer, B., 620, 622
Holcomb, D. R., 589
Holden, G. W., 597, 598, 605
Holman, T. B., 242
Holmbeck, G. N., 426, 430
Holmes, J. G., 231, 239
Holmes, R. M., 569
Holmes, S. T., 569
Holt, T., 44, 412, 417, 418
Holty, S., 200
Holtz, D., 348
Honeycutt, J. M., 225
Hoover, R., 309
Hopper, J. L., 91
Horowitz, H. L., 18
Horvath, C., 301, 306, 307
Horwood, L. J., 307
Houston, M., 413
Howard, D. E., 140
Hoyer, J., 558, 561, 562, 571
Hsiao, M., 96
Hsieh, T., 96
Hudecek, T., 230
Huerta, M., 608, 611
Hugh-Jones, S., 557, 559
Hughes, I. A., 169
Hughes, S. M., 233
Hughes, T. L., 241, 485, 486
Hunter, M., 93

Hunter, M. S., 97, 99
Hunter, N. D., 639
Hupka, R. B., 234
Huppin, M., 589, 591, 593
Hurlock, D., 99
Hussain, A., 232, 441
Huxley, R. R., 331
Hyde, J. S., 177, 181, 332, 358, 465
Hyman, S. M., 606
Hyslop, T., 348

I

Iacono, W. G., 418
Ibrahim, B., 62
Illes, J., 134
Imperato-McGinley, J., 170
Inciardi, J. A., 621, 629
Intersex Society of North America, 169
Irwin, T. W., 278
Isay, R. A., 306, 312
Ito, S., 341
Itzin, C., 633, 643
Iwamoto, M., 622, 623
Iyengar, M., 94, 99

J

Jackson, H. J., 572
Jacob, S., 136
Jacobson, L., 411
Jameson, M., 350
Janofsky, M., 581, 582
Jansky, H. K., 511
Jansma, L. L., 44, 287, 288, 289, 425, 427, 430, 450, 485, 644
Janssen, E., 122, 475, 476, 482, 484, 487, 502
Jarvis, M. O., 242
Jayson, S., 443, 444, 445
Jennings, D. A., 155
Jennings-White, C., 136
Jesinger, D., 93
Johannes, C. B., 483
Johanson, R., 348
Johansson, E., 620, 622
Johnson, H., 588
Johnson, J. L., 511
Johnson, S., 242
Johnson, V. E., 50, 90, 95, 109, 136, 148, 149, 154, 155, 156, 260, 266, 268, 269, 288, 310, 331, 488
Johnston, L. D., 141
Johnstone, S. J., 356
Jones, B. E., 172
Jones, J., 44, 287, 288, 289, 425, 427, 430, 450, 485
Jones, M., 458
Jordan, C. E., 585, 594
Josephs, R. A., 141
Jouriles, E. N., 458
Juang, K., 92
Jung, M., 353

K

Kaczmarek, P., 588, 593, 594
Kafka, M. P., 559, 560, 569, 570
Kaiser Family Foundation, 44, 412, 417, 418
Kaiser, C. R., 179, 402
Kaiser, K., 166
Kaler, A., 481
Kalichman, S. C., 511
Kamen, P., 19
Kampman, M., 53
Kanouse, D. E., 76
Kaplan, H. S., 154, 479, 489, 491

Kaplan, M. S., 573
Kasprzyk, D., 510
Katholi, C. R., 139
Katz, M. H., 315
Keller, A., 482
Kelly, J. B., 459
Keltner, D., 177, 209
Kendler, K. S., 301, 605
Kennedy, N., 104
Kenny, S. E., 108
Kenrick, D. T., 202
Kent, C. K., 52
Kerns, R. D., 481
Kersting, K., 180
Kessler, R. C., 93
Khoury, M. J., 346
Kiernan, K. E., 459
Kilpatrick, D. G., 585
Kim, A. A., 52
Kim, Y., 233
Kimble, D. P., 142
Kimura, F., 134
King, C., 597
King, J. A., 112
Kingston, D. A., 607
Kinsey, A. C., 19, 41–42, 137, 155, 260, 261–262, 263, 268, 269, 288, 409, 415, 450, 451, 564, 565, 567, 571, 619
Kippax, S., 268, 278
Kirby, D., 121
Kirchheimer, S., 417, 431
Kirenskaya-Berus, A. V., 570
Kirkpatrick, R. C., 301
Kito, M., 230
Kjerulff, K. H., 76
Klausner, J. D., 52
Klaw, E. L., 593
Klein, F., 292
Klein, P., 264, 265
Kleinplatz, P. J., 488, 500, 574
Klepinger, D. H., 46
Klohnen, E. C., 206
Klugherz, B. D., 496
Klusmann, D., 184, 626, 627
Klüver, H., 143
Knaak, S., 356, 358
Knapp, M. L., 227, 228
Kniffin, K. M., 202, 204
Knight, R. A., 607
Knottnerus, J. A., 93
Knox, D., 209, 235, 447, 463
Koblin, B. A., 277
Kohlberg, L., 190
Kohorn, E. I., 481
Kolata, G., 112, 206, 225, 426, 427, 449, 450, 451, 452, 476, 482, 495, 637
Komisaruk, B. R., 72, 465
Koren, D., 355, 356
Koren, G., 341
Korobov, N., 230
Koss, M., 589, 643
Koss, M. P., 582, 584, 585, 587, 593, 594
Kouros-Mehr, H., 136
Koyama, N. F., 202
Koziel, S., 200
Krahe, B., 587
Kramer, M. S., 338, 343, 344, 353
Kristof, N. D., 528, 622, 625, 626
Krob, G., 169
Krueger, R. B., 573
Krüger, T. H. C., 280
Kuehnemund, M., 231
Kuffel, S. W., 484

Kuhnle, U., 169
Kuiper, A. J., 174, 176
Kuiper, B., 174
Kulik, L., 192
Kuller, L., 92
Kumashiro, K. K., 294
Kurdek, L. A., 241, 308
Kurtz, S. P., 621, 629
Kurtzman, H. S., 241
Kurzban, R., 200
Kushner, H., 75, 92, 137

L

La Guardia, J. G., 229
Labouvie, E., 278
Labrecque, M., 348
Ladas, A. K., 72
Lalezari, J. P., 533
Lalumiére, M. L., 554, 562, 586, 592, 593
Lamanna, M. A., 453
LaMay, M. L., 180, 181
Lamaze, F., 350
Lamba, H., 484
Lambert, A. J., 589
Lampe, M. S., 365
Landgren, B., 93
Lane, T., 277
Langevin, R., 558, 559, 560, 562, 572, 573
Langhinrichsen-Rohling, J., 236, 586, 588
Langhout, R. D., 607
Langille, D. B., 427
Langlois, J. H., 200
Langstrom, N., 556
Laqueur, T. W., 15, 16, 18
Larsen, R. J., 40
Larsson, A., 169, 170
Larsson, I., 422, 424
LaSala, M. C., 314, 315
Latty, E., 281
Lau, J. T. F., 40
Laumann, E. O., 23, 24, 42, 107, 206, 225, 260, 261, 269, 270, 277, 292, 316, 426, 427, 449, 450, 451, 452, 453, 460, 462, 463, 472, 473, 480, 481, 489, 584, 637
Lawrence, A. A., 171, 172, 556
Laws, D. R., 573
Le, M. N., 622, 623
Leahey, E., 181
Ledermann, T., 484
Lee, A. F. S., 607
Lee, F. R., 436
Lee, J. K. P., 572
Legato, M. J., 170, 173
Lehman, G. L., 140
Leiblum, S. R., 480, 489, 500, 502
Leinbach, M. D. J., 188, 191
Leinders-Zufall, T., 136
Leitenberg, H., 278, 279, 280, 423, 603
Leland, J., 423, 497
Lemaire, A., 264, 265
Lesjak, B., 567, 568
Lester, W., 297, 298
Leue, A., 558, 561, 562, 571
Leukefeld, C. G., 585, 594
Leung, C., 209
Levenson, R. W., 244
Lever, J., 109
Levin, R. J., 73, 78, 126
Levine, D., 208
LeVine, E., 588, 593, 594
Levinger, G., 225
Levy, H., 446
Lewin, B., 484

91, 397, 400
2
, 134, 137
Li, Z., 628, 629
Lichter, D. T., 449
Lichter, E. L., 593, 594
Liddell, D. L., 589
Liljequist, L., 418
Lilly, R. S., 592
Lim, D., 634
Lin, G., 99, 542
Lindström, P., 303
Linz, D. G., 44, 287, 288, 289, 425, 427, 430, 450,
 485, 642, 643, 644
Lippa, R., 192
Lippa, R., 290, 291
Liptak, A., 107, 108
Lipton, J. E., 626
Lipworth, L., 338, 343, 344, 353
Lira, L. R., 584
Littlefield, M. M., 30
Littlewood, A., 557, 559
Liu, C., 96
Liu, D., 628, 629
Locke, A., 229
Locke, B. D., 586, 589, 592
Loder, N., 179
Loftus, J., 473
Logan, T. K., 585, 594
Lohr, B. A., 309
Long, C. R., 238
Long, J. S., 473, 475, 476, 484, 487, 502
Loomis, D., 343
Lopez, P. A., 140
López-Chivrall, S., 230
Lorant, V., 458
Lorenz, F. O., 458
Lotery, H. E., 481
Lotfy, G., 53, 66
Lozano-Blanco, C., 481
Lu, S., 92
Lubinski, D., 181
Lucon, A. M., 386
Lue, T. F., 482
Lumsden, J., 570
Lundberg, P. O., 484
Luo, S., 206
Luquis, R., 140, 260
Lykins, A. D., 484
Lynm, C., 91
Lynne, J., 620, 621, 625

M

Maaita, M. J., 73
Maartens, L. W. F., 93
MacDonald, G., 141
MacDonald, T. K., 141
MacFadden, A., 181
Mackie, N. E., 484
Macy, R. J., 593, 595
Madathil, J., 445
Madell, K., 562, 627
Madsen, L., 602
Magley, V. J., 608, 611
Mahalik, J. R., 586, 589, 592
Mahfouz, A. Y., 640
Mahoney, P. D., 496
Maier, E., 169
Maiuro, R. D., 236
Major, B., 179, 402
Malamuth, N. M., 589, 591, 593, 643
Malec, K., 81
Malezky, B. M., 574

Malinowski, B., 49, 603
Malone, K. E., 81
Maltz, W., 280
Mamo, L., 472, 478, 485
Mannarino, A. P., 604
Mansergh, G., 542
Manson, J. E., 94
Månsoon, S., 640
Mantovani, F., 208
Maranda, M. J., 142
Marazziti, D., 213, 233
Marchbanks, P. A., 369
Marcus, D. K., 202
Mardorossian, C. M., 592
Maric, A., 643
Marín, J. A.L., 560
Marinkovic, J., 489
Markianos, M., 112
Markman, H. J., 453
Marks, G., 511
Marlowe, D.A., 48
Marquis, C., 441
Marrazzo, J., 524
Marshall, B. L., 493
Marshall, L. J., 589
Marshall, W. L., 573, 642
Marsiglio, W., 297, 460
Martell, C. R., 242
Martin, C. E., 19, 41–42, 137, 155, 260, 261–262,
 263, 268, 269, 288, 409, 415, 450, 451, 564,
 565, 567, 571, 619
Martin, N. G., 307
Martino, S. C., 10
Martins, Y., 134, 135, 136, 289
Martyna, W., 192
Martz, J. M., 212, 235
Marvasti, J. A., 573, 574
Marwick, C., 92
Marziano, V., 602
Masheb, R. M., 481
Masi, C. M., 107
Masters, W., 588
Masters, W. H., 50, 90, 95, 109, 136, 148, 149,
 154, 155, 156, 260, 266, 268, 269, 288, 310,
 331, 488
Mateuca, A., 593
Mathes, L., 464
Mathy, R. M., 640
Maticka-Tyndale, E., 622
Matthews, A. K., 241, 485, 486
Matthews, K. A., 458, 459
Matus, M., 593
Maxson, S. C., 166
Maxwell, C. D., 586, 588, 589
May, R. S., 139
Maybach, K. L., 202
Mayo Clinic, 481
Mays, V. M., 307
Mazkereth, R., 353
Mazur, T., 409
McAuley, C., 429
McBride, C. K., 426, 430
McBurney, D. H., 22, 184
McCabe, K. A., 636
McCabe, M. P., 464, 483, 484, 487
McCabe, S. E., 141
McCarthy, B. W., 474, 483, 484, 485, 489
McClintock, M. K., 136
McCloskey, L. A., 605
McClure, N., 481
McCormick, D., 637, 639
McCoy, N. L., 136, 137
McCoy, S. K., 179, 402

McDonald, R., 458
McDonough, M., 104
McDonough, Y. Z., 408
McElduff, A., 112, 146
McEwan, S. L., 593
McGarvey, E. L., 482
McGoldrick, M., 294
McGue, M., 418
McIntyre, S., 426, 427
McKeever, W. F., 187
McKeganey, N., 620
McLaughlin, M. A., 608, 609
McNatt, P. S., 207
McNeil, D. G., Jr., 531
McNicholas, T., 483, 484, 485, 495
Mead, M., 25, 49
Medrano, M. A., 629
Meeus, W., 232
Menard, K. S., 610
Mensch, B. S., 62
Meston, C., 474, 477, 478, 480, 482, 484, 485,
 487
Meston, C. M., 502, 503
Meyer, I. H., 40, 307
Meyer, T., 533
Meyer-Bahlburg, H. F. L., 302
Michael, R. T., 206, 225, 426, 427, 449, 450, 451,
 452, 638
Michaels, S., 23, 24, 42, 260, 261, 269, 270, 277,
 292, 450, 451, 452, 453, 472, 473, 480, 481,
 584
Michel, A., 170
Middlemiss, W., 411
Mikach, S. M., 180
Miller, A. K., 597
Miller, M., 415
Miller, R., 605
Miller, R. S., 202
Miller, S. A., 265
Millevoi, A., 234
Milner, P., 143
Ming, E. E., 369
Minichiello, V., 628, 629
Minkin, M J., 481
Miriam, D., 31
Missailidis, K., 66
Mitchell, K. J., 597
Mittman, B. S., 76
Modell, J. G., 139
Mofenson, L. M., 339, 340
Mohan, R., 482, 483
Mok, M. Y., 136
Moller, A. C., 229
Moller, I., 587
Mombaerts, P., 136
Money, J., 143, 170, 171, 572
Monson, C. M., 586, 588
Montano, D., 510
Montemurro, B., 562, 627
Monti-Bloch, L., 136
Moore, C., 610
Moore, D. R., 474, 478, 484, 485
Moore, S., 209
More, T. A., 238
Morgenbesser, L. I., 584
Morgenstern, J., 278
Morley, J. E., 147
Morofushi, M., 134
Morris, L. B., 356
Morris, R., 146
Morrison, D. R., 411, 412, 415, 459
Morrison, E. S., 68, 78, 413
Morry, M. M., 206, 207, 228

Subject Index

Aversion therapy, for paraphilias, 574
AZT (zidovudine), 532–533

B

"Baby blues," 355–356
Bacteria, 511
Bacterial infections, sexually transmitted, 511–522
Bacterial vaginosis (nonspecific vaginitis), 513t–514t, 523
Bar prostitute, 621
Barbiturates, sex drive and, 140
Barrier devices, for oral sex, 545
Bartholin's glands, 69, 70, 150
Basal body temperature method (BBT), 88, 324, 384, 390t
B&D (bondage and discipline), 565–566
Behaviorists, 29
"Belly button surgery" (laparoscopy), 328, 387, 388f
Benign, 82
Benign prostatic hyperplasia (BPH), 117–118
"Bennies" (amphetamines), 141–142
Bestiality, 6, 19, 567
Beta subunit HCG radioimmunoassay, 330
Bias, 40
Bible
    Hebrew Old Testament, 12
    sexual decision making and, 6
    sexual orientation and, 294–295
Big Love, 436
"Bikini waxing," 64
Binge drinking, 140–141
Biological perspectives
    on gender typing, 183–184
    on love, 213
    on paraphilias, 569–570
    on sexual orientation, 301–304
    on sexuality, 21
Biology, third sex in, 175
Biopsychosocial model, 481
Biphobia, 292, 293
Birth control. *See* Contraception
Birth control pills. *See* Oral contraceptives
Birthweight, low, 343
Bisexuals (bisexuality), 292–293
    definition of, 14, 287
    relationship satisfaction, 241–242
    sexual fantasies of, 281
    women, relabeling as heterosexuals, 288
Bladder, urinary, during orgasm, 152
Blastocyst, 335
Blended orgasm, 156
Blood clots, risk of, oral contraceptives and, 369–370
Blood pressure, after intercourse *vs.* masturbation, 280
"Blue balls," 154
Body odor
    axillary, sexual orientation and, 134–135
    sexual arousal and, 133–134
Body piercings, for sexual pleasure, 564
Bondage, 563
Bondage and discipline (B&D), 565–566
Boredom, sexual, 232
Bottle feeding, *vs.* breast-feeding, 356–358, 357f
BPH (benign prostatic hyperplasia), 117–118
Brain
    caudate nucleus, 211, 211f
    electrical stimulation of, 143–144
    organization, prenatal, 187
    prenatal sexual differentiation and, 167–168
    sexual response and, 142–144, 143f
    spinal sexual response and, 123–124

structure, in heterosexual *vs.* gay men, 302, 303f, 304
Brain imaging, of emotions, 210–211
Braxton-Hicks contractions, 347
BRCA1 gene mutations, 80
BRCA2 gene mutations, 80
Breast buds, 420
Breast cancer, 79–82
    African American women and, 81
    detection, 82
    risk factors, 80–81
        hormone replacement therapy, 92
        oral contraceptives, 369, 370
    survival rates, 80
    treatment, 80, 82
Breast cysts, 82
Breast implants, 82
Breast reconstruction, 80
Breast self-examination (BSE), 82, 84–85, 85f
Breast tumors, benign, 82
Breast-feeding, *vs.* bottle feeding, 356–358, 357f
Breasts
    female, 77–82, 78f
        age-related changes in, 462
        heterosexual stimulation of, 268, 269
        homosexual stimulation of, 268–269, 269f
        sensitivity of, 78
        during sexual response cycle, 148, 150, 152f
        size/shape variations in, 78–79, 79f
    gay male, stimulation of, 268, 268f
Breech presentation, 337
Bremelanotide, 500–501
"Brokeback marriages," 485
Brokeback Mountain, 286, 316–317
Brothel for women, 630–631
Brothel prostitution, 622
Brother-sister incest, 604
Brown, Louise, 328
BSE (breast self-examination), 82, 84–85, 85f
Bulbourethral glands, 115
Bupropion (Wellbutrin), 139
Butch lesbians, 301, 302, 306

C

Caffeine, maternal usage during pregnancy and, 344
CAIS (complete androgen insensitivity), 169–170
Calcium supplements, 94
Calendar method, failure rates of, 390t
Calendar methods, 383–384
Call girls, 623–625
Calvin, John, 17
Camera phones, in combating exhibitionists and frotteurs, 568
Cancer
    breast. *See* Breast cancer
    cervical. *See* Cervical cancer
    endometrial, 74
    ovarian, 75–76
    prostate. *See* Prostate cancer
    testicular, 116–117
Candidiasis, 514t, 523–524, 524f
Cantharidin, 138
Cardiovascular problems
    oral contraceptives and, 370
    sexual response and, 482–483
Case study, 41
Castration anxiety, 304, 305
Catholic priests, sexual abuse of boys and, 581
Caudate nucleus, 211, 211f
"Cavernous bodies" (corpora cavernosa), 65, 107, 122
CBE (clinical breast examination), 82

CD4 cell, 529
Celebrities, sexual abuse and, 581
Celebrity marriages, probability of success, 454, 455t
Celibacy, 438
Celibate lifestyle, 288
Cell-phone pornography, 635
Cephalic presentation, 337
Cephalocaudal, 335–336
Cerebral cortex, sexual response and, 142
Cerebral palsy, sex and, 464
Cervical cancer
    mortality rates, 73
    oral contraceptives and, 370
    Pap test and, 74
Cervical cap, 378–379, 390t
Cervical mucus or ovulation method, 384–385
Cervicitis, 517, 520
Cervix, 72–73
Cesarean section (C-section), 351–352, 533
cGMP, 494
Chancre, 519
Chancroid, 521–522
Chastity, vow of, 7
"Chat" scatophilia, 560–561
Chemical castration, 575, 607
Child pornography, 636
Childbirth, 347–359
    methods, 350–352
        anesthetized, 350
        cesarean section, 351–352
        prepared or Lamaze, 350–351
    problems, 352–354, 355t
        infant mortality, 354, 355t
        maternal mortality, 354, 355t
    stages of, 347–350, 349f
    triggers for, 347
Childhood
    early, sexual behavior during, 411–414
    effeminacy, gay males and, 307
    normal sex play, *vs.* sexual abuse, 413
Children
    co-sleeping and, 411
    divorce and, 458
    effects of viewing parental sexual behavior, 410
    genital play and, 410
    "good" *vs.* "bad" touching, 413
    of homosexual parents, 314
    masturbation by, parental reaction to, 414
    parental discussions about sex, 416
    sex selection during conception, 325–326, 325f
    sexual abuse of. *See* Sexual abuse of children
    sexual curiosity of, 410
Chinese culture
    Koro syndrome and, 104, 109
    sexuality in, 16–17
Chlamydia, 513t, 520–521
Chlamydia trachomatis, 520–521
Cholesterol, erectile dysfunction and, 483
Christians, early, sexuality and, 15–17
Chromosomal abnormalities
    averting, 346
    pregnancy and, 344–346, 345t, 346f
    prenatal blood tests for, 346
Chromosomes
    definition of, 21, 164
    X. *See* X chromosomes
    Y, 164–165
Cialis (tadalafil), 139, 493t, 494, 496
Cigarette smoking, during pregnancy, 343–344
Cilia, 75, 114
Circulation system, of mother, during pregnancy, 337

Circumcision
    female, 53
    male, 107–108, 108f, 531
Civil Rights Act of 1964, Title VII, 610
Civil unions, 297–298, 298t
"The clap." See Gonorrhea
Classmates, meeting people through, 225, 225f
Climacteric, 91–92
Clinical breast examination (CBE), 82
Clitoral device, 497f, 497–498
Clitoral orgasm, 155–156
Clitoridectomy, 62, 65–66
Clitoris
    anatomy, 63f, 65
    manual stimulation of, 267
    in organic plateau, 150
Cloacal extropohy, 173
Clomiphene (Clomid), 88, 327–328
Clomipramine, 502
Close couples, 315
Coca-Cola, 142
Cocaine, 142
Cognitive abilities, sex differences in, 180–182,
    181f, 182f, 182t
Cognitive psychologists, views on sexuality, 30
Cognitive-behavioral perspectives, on
    paraphilias, 571
Cognitive-behavioral therapy, for paraphilias,
    573–574
Cognitive-developmental theory, gender typing
    and, 190–191
Cohabitation, 440–442
    attitudes toward, 441, 441t
    decision to move in with partner, 233
    effect on college students, 54
    with later marriage, 442
    prior to marriage, divorce rates and, 440, 442
    reasons for, 441
Cohort effects, 23
Coitus, 4. See also Sexual intercourse
Coitus interruptus or withdrawal, 258, 365
College campus, sexual harassment on, 611
Combination pills, 367–368
Commission on obscenity and pornography,
    641
Commitment, 215
Communication skills, for relationship
    enhancement, 243–251
Companionate love, 218t, 219
Compatibility, Sternberg's triangular theory of
    love and, 215–216, 216f
Complete androgen insensitivity (CAIS),
    169–170
Complete hysterectomy, 76
Computer usage, by children, parental controls
    for, 428
Comstock Law, 365–366, 635
Conception
    definition of, 322
    optimizing changes for, 323–325
    selecting sex of child, 325–326, 325f
Conclusions
    in critical thinking, 10
    drawing. See Inferences
Concordance, 301
Concubines, 13
Condoms, 379–382
    advantages/disadvantages of, 381–382
    breakage of, 380
    definition of, 365
    effectiveness of, 381, 390t
    failure rates of, 390t
    how to use, 380–381, 380f, 381f
    negative attitudes toward using, 543
    reversibility of, 381

for STI prevention, 544–545
    using two, 382
Confidentiality, 55–56
Conflict resolution, 242–243
Congenital adrenal hyperplasia (CAH), 169,
    169f
Congenital syphilis, 519
Consensual adultery, 453
Consent, date rape and, 586
Consummate love, 218t
Contraception
    among sexually active teenagers, 430
    definition of, 364
    historical methods of, 365
    legal aspects, in United States, 365–366
    methods, 366–392
        cervical cap, 378–379
        condoms, 379–382, 380f–383f
        contraceptive patch, 372
        contraceptive sponge, 378
        diaphragm, 375–376, 375f, 376f
        douching, 383
        failure rates of, 390t
        fertility awareness, 383–385
        injectable contraceptives, 372–373
        intrauterine devices, 373–374
        male, 371
        "morning-after" pill, 371–372
        separation of sex from reproduction, 450
        spermicides, 376–378, 377f
        sterilization, 385–390
        withdrawal method, 383
    selection of method, 389, 390t
    talking with partner about, 367
Contraceptive patch, 372
Contraceptive sponge, 378
Control groups, 54
Controlling, human behavior, 38–39
Conventional adultery, 453
Copper T 380A (ParaGard), 373
Coprophilia, 569
Copulation, 11
Corona, 107
Corpora cavernosa ("cavernous bodies"), 65,
    107, 122
Corpus luteum, 83, 88
Corpus spongiosum, 107
Correlation, of research, 51–53
Correlation coefficient, 51
Co-sleeping, infants and, 411
Courtesans, 15
Covert sensitization, for paraphilias, 573, 574
Coworkers, meeting people through, 225,
    225f
Cowper's glands, 115, 149
"Crabs" (pediculosis), 516t, 540–541, 541f
"Crack" cocaine, 142
Cremaster muscle, 109
Cribriform hymen, 68f
Critical fat hypothesis, 419
Critical thinking
    about human sexuality, 8–10
    principles of, 9–10
Criticism
    delivering, 248–249
    receiving, 249–250
Cross-cultural perspectives
    on menstruation, 91
    on physical attractiveness, 200
    sexual orientation, 296
Cross-dressing, 173, 556
Cross-species perspectives
    on sexual orientation, 296–297
    on sexuality, 22–24
Crowning, 348

"Cruising," 315
Crura, 69, 107
Cryotherapy, 539
Cryptorchidism, 116, 167
C-section (Cesarean section), 351–352, 533
Culpotomy, 387
Cultural relativism, 7
Culture
    facial preferences and, 201, 201f
    female hunter/gatherers and, 187
    kissing and, 265–266
    myths supporting rape, 590
    sexual behavior and, 553
    sexual dysfunction causes and, 484–487
"Culture wars," 25
Cunnilingus, 15, 269, 271
Cybersex, 640–641
Cyberspace, self-disclosure in, 229
Cystic fibrosis, 345t
Cystitis, 67
Cysts, 82

D

Dartos muscle, 109
Darwin, Charles, 21
Date rape, 584f, 585–586
Date rape drug, 591
Dating, 438–440
D&C (dilation and curettage), 398
D&E (dilation and evacuation), 398–399
Deception, in research, 56–57
Defense mechanisms, 28
Definition of terms, in critical thinking, 9–10
Delayed ejaculation, 478–479
Demographic, 38
Deodorant, sexual arousal and, 133–134
Deoxyribonucleic acid (DNA), 21–22
Dependent variable, 53–54
Depo-Provera (medroxyprogesterone acetate),
    372–373, 390t, 575
Depression
    homosexuals and, 307
    loneliness and, 238
    postmenopausal, 93
    postpartum, 356
    sexual dysfunction and, 485
    sexual response and, 482
DES (diethylstilbestrol), 302, 342
Deterioration of relationship
    active response to, 234–235
    breaking up, 235–237
    excessive agreeability and, 242
    passive response to, 234–235
"Dexies" (amphetamines), 141–142
DHEA, for female sexual dysfunction, 497t
DHT (dihydrotestosterone), 166
Diabetes mellitus, sexual dysfunction and, 477
Diagnostic and Statistical Manual of Mental
    Disorders, sexual dysfunction categories,
    473–474
Diaphragm
    advantages/disadvantages, 375–376
    effectiveness of, 375
    failure rates of, 390t
    reversibility, 375
    use of, 375, 375f, 376f
Diethylstilbestrol (DES), 302, 342
Digital rectal examination (DRE), 118–119,
    119f
Dihydrotestosterone (DHT), 166
Dilate, 347
Dilation and curettage (D&C), 398
Dilation and evacuation (D&E), 398–399
Dildo, 257
Disability, sex and, 463–467

Growth spurts, during puberty, 419–422
Gynecomastia, 422

H

HAART (highly active antiretroviral therapy), 278, 315, 534
Hallucinogenics, 141
Hardwick v. Bowers, 300
Harm, research ethics and, 55
Hatcher, Teri, 599
HCG (human chorionic gonadotropin), 330
HDL (high-density lipoprotein), 93–94
Headaches, during menstruation, 95
Healthcare seeking, sex differences in, 183
Hearing, sexual arousal and, 138
Hedonism, 7, 9t
Hemophilia, 345t, 346
Hemophilus ducreyi, 521
Hepatitis, viral, 515t, 538, 629
Hepatitis A virus, 538
Hepatitis B virus, 538, 629
Hepatitis C virus, 538, 629
Hepatitis D virus, 538
Hermaphrodites, 168
Hermaphroditism, true, 169, 169f
Heroin usage, during pregnancy, 342
Herpes simplex virus type 1 (HSV-1), 514t, 535
Herpes simplex virus type 2 (HSV-2). *See* Genital herpes
Heteroerotic interests, 288
Heteronormativity, 175
Heterosexual men, brain structure in, 302, 303f, 304
Heterosexual orientation, 286
Heterosexual relationships, satisfaction in, 241–242
Heterosexuality
    queer theory and, 31
    as separate dimension from homosexuality, 290–291, 291f
High-density lipoprotein (HDL), 93–94
Highly active antiretroviral therapy (HAART), 278, 315, 534
Hijra, 175
Hindu sexual practices and, 16
Hippocampus, sexual response and, 143
Historical perspective
    on human sexuality, 11–21
    on menstruation, 91
HIV/AIDS, 525–535
    in Africa, 528
    anal intercourse and, 277–278
    cesarean section and, 351
    coping with, 508
    diagnosis, 515t, 532
    epidemic, global summary of, 526f–527f
    exposure categories, 529t
    funding for research, 300, 424
    gay males and, 315
    gay rights political agenda and, 300
    homophobia and, 309–310
    immune system and, 526–529
    infants/children with, 339–340
    male circumcision and, 108
    prevalence of, 509, 525–526, 525t
    prevention of, 534–535
    progression of, 529–530
    prostitution and, 629
    resources, 547
    sexual dysfunction and, 484
    sexual transmission, factors affecting risk of, 531
    spermicides and, 378
    symptoms, 515t
    as syndrome, 530

testing
    seronegative, 532
    seropositive, 532
    transmission, 339, 509, 515t, 530–531
        from kissing, 533
        misinformation about, 532
        from saliva, tears and sweat, 533
        via breast milk, 356–357
    treatment, 515t, 532–534
Homoerotic interests, 288
Homogamy, 449
Homologous, 65
Homophobia, 31, 292, 308–310
Homosexual marriage. *See* Same-sex marriage
Homosexual orientation, 287
Homosexual transsexuals, 171–172
Homosexuality
    genetics and, 307
    learning theories and, 305
    queer theory and, 31
    as separate dimension from heterosexuality, 290–291, 291f
    terminology, 287
Homosexuals
    adjustment issues for, 307–311
    children of, 314
    "coming out"
        to oneself, 311–312
        to others, 312
    hatred of, 292
    lifestyles of, 313–315
        variations in, 315
    Mexican American attitudes toward, 299
Honesty, intimacy and, 230
Honor crimes, 27
Hookers. *See* Female prostitutes
"Hooking up," 439
Hormone, 83
Hormone replacement therapy (HRT), 92–94
    endometrial cancer risk and, 74
    for prostate cancer, 120
Hormones. *See also specific hormones*
    effects on fetus, 341–342
    for erectile disorder, 493t, 495
    influence on sexual orientation, 302
    menstrual cycle regulation and, 83–84
    terminology, 144
    for transsexualism, 171, 174
Hot flashes, 91
HPV (human papilloma virus), 73, 509, 515t, 539–540
HRT. *See* Hormone replacement therapy
HSV-1 (herpes simplex virus type 1), 535
HSV-2 (herpes simplex virus type 2). *See* Genital herpes
Human chorionic gonadotropin (HCG), 330
Human immunodeficiency virus (HIV). *See* HIV/AIDS
Human life, beginning of, 392
Human papilloma virus (HPV), 73, 509, 539–540
Human Sexual Response (Masters & Johnson), 49–50
Human sexuality. *See also specific aspects of human sexuality*
    definition of, 3, 4
    family discussions on, 3
    perspectives on, 10
        biological, 21
        cross-species, 22–24
        evolutionary, 21–22
        historical, 11–21
        multiple, 31–32
        psychological, 28–30, 29t
        sociological, 25

recent trends, 20–21
scientific study, foundations for, 18–19
study of, 4–5
thinking critically about, 8–10
values and, 5–8
Huntington disease, 345t
Hustlers, 627–628
Hyaluronidase, 323
Hymen, 68, 68f
Hypersexual desire, 570
Hypogonadism, 482
Hypothalamus
    definition of, 83
    in gay *vs.* heterosexual men, 302, 303f, 304
    gonadal sex hormone secretion, 144
    during puberty, 419
    sexual response and, 136
Hypothesis, 37
Hypothesis testing, 37
Hypoxyphilia, 564
Hysterectomy, 76, 93, 387
"Hysterical paroxysm," 256
Hysterosalpingogram, 328
Hysterotomy, 399

I

Ice Age, sexuality in, 11
ICSH (interstitial cell stimulating hormone), 110–111
ICSI (intracytoplasmic sperm injection), 329
Identification, 188
Imipramine (Tofranil), 140
Immune system
    HIV/AIDS and, 526, 529
    HIV/AIDS effect on, 529
Imperforate hymen, 68, 68f
Impiramine (Tofranil), 140
Implantation, 335
Impotence, 139, 259
In vitro fertilization (IVF), 328–329
Incest, 603–604
Incest taboo, 11
Incidence, 42
Incompatibility, Sternberg's triangular theory of love and, 215–216, 216f
Independent variable, 53
India
    Hijra of, 175
    Hindu sexual practices and, 16
Induced abortion, 391
Ineffective sexual techniques, sexual dysfunction and, 485
Infant mortality, 354, 355t
Infants
    capacity for sexual response, 409
    masturbation and, 409
    sexual behaviors in, 408–411
    sucking reflex, 408–409
Infatuation, 212–213, 218t
Inferences, 37–38
Infertility, 326
Infidelity, sex differences in, 234
Inflammation, 527
Informed consent, 55, 56
Infundibulum, 75
Inguinal canal, 167
Inis Beag, 2
Injectable contraceptives, 372–373, 390t
Internal sex organs, prenatal development of, 164–165, 164f
Internet
    relationships on, 208
    sexual abuse of children and, 597
    sexual advice on, 12–13
Intersexuals, 168–170

Interstitial cell stimulating hormone (ICSH), 110–111
Interstitial cells, 110
Intimacy
    definition of, 229–230
    honesty and, 230
    love and, 215
    making commitments and, 232–233
    self-esteem and, 231–232
Intraamniotic infusion, 399
Intracytoplasmic sperm injection (ICSI), 329
Intrauterine devices (IUDs)
    advantages/disadvantages of, 374
    ectopic pregnancy risk and, 75
    effectiveness of, 373–374
    failure rates of, 390t
    reversibility, 374
    selection of, 367
    usage, 373
Introitus, 68, 68f
Invicorp (phentolamine), 495
Irrational beliefs
    as obstacle to sexual communication, 245
    sexual dysfunction and, 487
Islam, 16
Isthmus, 75
IUDs. See Intrauterine devices
IVF (in vitro fertilization), 328–329

J

Jaundice, 538
Jealousy
    evolutionary theory and, 234
    normal vs. obsessional, 233–234
Jeremy, Ron, 635
"Johns," 618, 626–627

K

Kama Sutra, 16
Kathoeys ("ladyboys"), of Thailand, 175–176
Kellogg, Dr. J. H., 259
Kinsey, Alfred, 19
Kinsey continuum of sexual orientation, 288–292, 289f
Kinsey Institute (Indiana University Institute for Sex Research), 46
Kinsey Reports, 42–43
Kissing
    cultural differences in, 265–266
    HIV transmission risk and, 530, 533
    simple vs. deep, 266
Kissing gouramis, 38
Klinefelter syndrome, 167
Klismaphilia, 569
Koro syndrome, 104, 109
Kwell (lindane), 541

L

Labia majora, 63, 64
Labia minora, 63, 65, 150
Laboratory observation method, 49–51
Lactation, 358
Lactobacillus acidophilus, 524
"Ladyboys," of Thailand, 175–176
Lamaze method of childbirth, 350–351
Laminaria digitata, 398, 398f
Language, as obstacle to sexual communication, 243
"Lap dances," 623
Laparoscopy ("belly button surgery"), 328, 387, 388f
Larynx, 421
Lateral-entry position, for sexual intercourse, 275, 275f

Latino/Latina Americans
    children with HIV/AIDS, 339
    sexual orientation and, 294
LDL (low-density lipoprotein), 93–94
L-Dopa, 139
Learning theories, 29
Leg buds, 335
Legalism, 6, 9t
Leptin, 419
Lesbian-gay-bisexual-transgender (LGBT), 176
Lesbians
    butch, 302, 306
    definition of, 287
    femme, 302, 306
    gender nonconformity and, 306
    genital apposition, 269, 269f
    lifestyles of, 313–315
        variations in, 315
        vs. gay males, 314–315
    male-female sexual activity and, 288
    marriage and, 446–447
    parents, children of, 314
    relabeling as heterosexuals, 288
    relationship satisfaction, 241–242
    sexual fantasies of, 281
    stimulation of breasts, 268–269
    waist-to-hip ratio preferences, 202
Leukocytes, 526, 527
Levitra (vardenafil), 139, 493t, 494, 496
Leydig's cells, 110
LGBT (lesbian-gay-bisexual-transgender), 176
LGV (lymphogranuloma venereum), 522
LH. See Luteinizing hormone
LH-releasing hormone, control of testes and, 110, 110f
"Lightening," 347
Liking, 218t
Limbic system, 142, 143
Lindane (Kwell), 541
Listening, sexual communication and, 246
Local anesthesia, for childbirth, 350
Lochia, 358
Logical love (pragma), 214
Loneliness
    coping with, 239–240
    stress and, 239
    vs. solitude, 238
Love, 209–219
    as appraisal of arousal, 213–214
    brain imaging of, 210–211
    contemporary models of, 213–219
        biological mechanisms, 213
    disclosure of, 231
    romantic. See Romantic love
    Sternberg's triangular theory of, 215–219, 215f, 216f, 218t
    styles of, 214
    with two people at same time, 214
    vs. infatuation, 212–213
Lovemap, 572
Low-birthweight infants, 352–353
Low-density lipoprotein (LDL), 93–94
LSD, 141
Lumpectomy, 80
Lunelle, 372–373
Luteal phase, of menstrual cycle, 88
Luteinizing hormone (LH)
    control of testes and, 110, 110f
    definition of, 84, 85
    functions of, 88
    ovulation and, 137
    during puberty, 419–420
    in urine or saliva, 324
Luther, Martin, 17
Lymphogranuloma venereum (LGV), 522

M

Magazine surveys, 45
Magnetic resonance imaging (MRI), of emotions, 210–211
Maidenhead, 68
Maines, Rachel, 256
Male birth control pills, 371
Male erectile disorder. See Erectile dysfunction
Male orgasmic disorder, 478–479, 501–502
Male rape, 587
Male sexual arousal disorder. See Erectile dysfunction
Male sexual response, brain and, 123–124
Male sodomite, 176
Male sterilization, 386–387, 386f, 390t
Male-female sexual behavior
    during adolescence, 423–427, 425f, 426t
    during early childhood, 412, 413t
    during preadolescence, 415
Male-male sexual behavior
    during adolescence, 427
    in Ancient Greece, 14–15
    in Ancient Rome, 15
    during preadolescence, 415
Males
    age-related physical changes, sex and, 461t, 462
    double standard for, 581
    erectile dysfunction. See Erectile dysfunction
    fertility problems, 326–327
    genitals, during sexual response cycle, 148–150, 150f, 152–154
    heterosexual, brain structure of, 302, 303f, 304
    homosexual. See Gay males
    masturbation techniques for, 261–262, 262f
    number of sex partners and, 23, 24t
    puberty, developmental stages in, 419–422, 422–423t
    secondary sex characteristics, 144
    sex organs
        external, 105–109, 106f–108f
        internal, 110–115, 110f, 113f, 114f
    sexual behavior, sex hormones and, 146–147
    sexual functions of, 122–126
    sexual response, spinal reflexes and, 122–125, 123f
    socially dominant, 202
    urogenital system health problems, 116–121, 119f
Male-superior position, for sexual intercourse, 273–274, 273f
Mammary glands, 78
Mammogram, 79
Mammography, 80, 82
Mangaia, 2
Mania (possessive excited love), 214
Manopause, 112
Marijuana
    sexual inhibition and, 141
    usage during pregnancy, 342
Marital satisfaction, 445t
Marital sex, 449–452
    changes in coitus, 450–451
    foreplay, 450
    frequency of coitus, 450, 450t, 451t
    keeping interest in, 452
Marital status
    masturbation and, 260, 261t
    number of sex partners and, 23, 24t
Marriage, 442–466
    age and, 444t
    age at first, 437, 437t
    alternative or nontraditional, 447–448
    arranged, 445–446

Nurses Health Study, 94
Nymphomaniacs, 155

O

Obscene telephone calling, 560–561
Obscenity, 633–634, 636
Observation methods, in research, 41–51
 case study, 41
 ethnographic, 49
 laboratory, 49–51
 naturalistic observation or field studies, 47, 49
 participant, 49
 surveys, 41–48
Ocular herpes, 536
Odor
 body. *See* Body odor
 gay *vs.* heterosexual male response to, 303
 vaginal, 70–72
Oedipus complex, 29, 188, 304
Onan, 257–258
Open couples, 315
Open marriage, 436
Opening lines, for starting relationships, 227–228
Ophthalmia neonatorum, 516
Opportunistic diseases, 530
Oral contraceptives (birth control pills), 367–371
 advantages of, 369
 disadvantages of, 369–371
 duration of exposure to, 371
 effectiveness of, 368
 failure rates of, 390*t*
 pharmacist refusal to provide, 366
 reversibility of, 368–369
Oral herpes, 514*t*
Oral sex
 abstaining from, 272
 during adolescence, 425
 barrier devices for, 545
 cunnilingus, 269, 271
 education and, 269, 270*t*
 fellatio, 269, 271
 incidence/prevalence of, 269, 270*t*
 race/ethnicity and, 270*t*
 "69" position, 271, 272*f*
Oral-genital stimulation, 269–272, 270*t*, 272*f*
Orgasmic disorders
 definition of, 473–474
 female, 478
 male, 478–479
 treatment of, 499–503, 498*f*, 499*f*
Orgasmic platform, 150
Orgasmic reconditioning, for paraphilias, 573, 574
Orgasms
 controversies about, 155–157
 faking, 157
 female, 155–157
 during infancy, 409
 male, 125–126
 marital sexual satisfaction and, 451–452, 452*t*
 multiple, 154, 155
 rapid female, 479
 subjective experience of, 153
Ortho-Novum, 367
Os, 73
Osteoporosis, 92
Outercourse, 546
Ova
 definition of, 62, 63
 fertilization of, 323–324
 X chromosomes on, 323
Ovarian cancer, 75–76
Ovarian cycle, 334, 334*f*

Ovarian follicle, maturation and decomposition of, 88–89, 89*f*
Ovariectomy, 147
Ovaries
 androgen production, 146
 definition of, 75
 descent of, 167
Ovcon, 367
Overgeneralization, 10
Oversimplification, 10
Ovulation, 323–324
 basal body temperature and, 324
 definition of, 83
 induction of, 327–328
 LH surge and, 324
 resumption during postpartum period, 358
 tracking vaginal mucus and, 325
Ovulation method of contraception, 384–385, 390*t*
Ovulation prediction kits, 385
Ovulatory mucus, 384
Ovulatory phase, of menstrual cycle, 88
Oxytocin, 84, 347

P

PAIS (partial androgen insensitivity), 169
Pakistan
 Hudood Ordinances, 583
 sex slavery in, 624–625
Pap smear (Pap test), 74, 76
Pap test, 74
ParaGard (Copper T 380A), 373
Paralysis, 465
Paraphilias, 554–569
 biological perspectives, 569–570
 cognitive-behavioral perspectives, 571
 combating, camera phones for, 568
 coprophilia, 569
 definition of, 553, 554
 exhibitionism, 557–560
 fetishism, 554, 555
 frotteurism, 566–567
 integrated perspective, 572
 klismaphilia, 569
 necrophilia, 569
 obscene telephone calling, 560–561
 psychoanalytic perspectives, 570–571
 severity of, 554
 sexual masochism, 562–564
 sexual sadism, 565–566
 sociological perspectives, 571–572
 telephone or "chat" scatophilia, 560–561
 transvestism, 556–557
 treatment, 572–575
  cognitive-behavioral therapy, 573–574
  medical approaches, 575
  psychoanalytic psychotherapy, 573
 urophilia, 569
 voyeurism, 561–562
 zoophilia, 567–568
Paraphrasing, in active listening, 244
Paraplegia, 125–126, 465
Parasympathetic nervous system, 124–125
Parents. *See also* Fathers; Mothers
 discussing sex with children, 416
 reaction to childhood masturbation, 414
 roles, in gender typing, 188–190
 sex education concerns of, 415–417, 418*t*
 sexual orientation of, effects on children, 411
Parkinson disease, 493*t*, 495
Parous introitus, 68, 68*f*
Partial androgen insensitivity (PAIS), 169
Partial hysterectomy, 76
Partialism, 555
Participant observation, 49

Partner rape, 588
Passion, 215
Pathogens, 526
PDE5, 494
PDE5 inhibitors, 494, 497*t*
Peak days, of menstrual cycle, 384
Pederasty, 14–15
Pediculosis ("crabs"), 516*t*, 540–541, 541*f*
Pedophiles, 574
Pedophilia, 554, 601–603
"Peeping toms" or "peepers" (voyeurs), 561–562
Pelvic examination, 76–77, 77*f*
Pelvic inflammatory disease (PID)
 definition of, 517
 ectopic pregnancy risk and, 75
 intrauterine devices and, 374
 risk, oral contraceptives and, 369
Pelvic pressure/bloating, during menstruation, 95
Pelvic thrusting, during infancy, 409
Penile erection. *See* Erection
Penile implants, 493*t*, 494, 495*f*
Penile strain gauges, 50
Penis
 anatomy, 105–107, 106*f*, 107*f*
 artificial, 174
 circumcision, 107–108, 108*f*, 531
 curvature of, 111, 125
 male obsession with, 105
 manual stimulation of, 267
 size, 108–109
 tactile stimulation of, 123, 124
Penis envy, 304–305
Performance anxiety, 122, 477, 487
Perfume
 sexual arousal and, 133–134
 with suspected pheromone, 137
Pergonal, 328
Perimenopause, 90–91
Perimetrium, 74
Perineum, 69, 348
Period of the ovum, 334–335, 334*f*
Personal invulnerability, myth of, 543–544
Personal names, physical beauty perceptions and, 204
Personality, sex differences in, 182–183
Perspiration
 male, effect on female mood, 137
 synchronization of menstrual cycles and, 134
Petting, 247, 424
Peyronie's disease, 125
PGD (preimplantation genetic diagnosis), 325–326, 325*f*
Phallic symbols, 11, 105
Phallic worship, 11
Phalloplasty, 174
Pharyngeal gonorrhea, 516
Phentolamine (Invicorp), 495
Phenylketonuria, 345*t*
Pheromones, 303
 androstadienone, 136, 137
 definition of, 132
 estratetraenol, 136–137
 sexual attractiveness and, 136
 sexual intercourse frequency and, 136, 137
Philia, 209
Phimosis, 108
Phonosurgery, 174
Photographing, of private parts in public places, 563
Physical attractiveness. *See* Attractiveness
Physical beauty, perceptions of
 behavior and, 202
 names, 204
 nonphysical traits and, 202

marrying outside your group, 449
masturbation and, 260, 261*t*
number of sex partners and, 23, 24*t*
oral sex and, 270*t*
Radioactive seed implants, for prostate cancer, 121
Radiotherapy, 74
Raloxifene, 82
Random sampling, 40
Rape, 582–597
acquaintance, 584*f*, 585
blaming victim for, 582
charges, statute of limitations on, 583
date, 584*f*, 585–586
definition of, 582
evolutionary view of, 593
forcible, 582
gang, 586–587
hotlines, 594, 595
incidence of, 583–584, 584*f*
male, 587
partner, 588
prevention, 595–597
reporting, 595
social attitudes toward, 588–590
statutory, 582
stranger, 584, 584*f*
survivors
adjustment problems of, 592–594
advice for, 594
psychological disorders and, 594
treatment of, 595
of wife, 582
by women, 588
Rapists
confronting, 597
psychological characteristics of, 591–592
Rationalism, 8, 9*t*
Rear-entry position, for sexual intercourse, 276, 276*f*
Recessive traits, 346
Reciprocity, 208–209
Refractory period, 154
Relationships. *See also specific types of relationships*
building, 226–227
end of, 237
long-term
keeping them going, 251
meaningful, preferences for, 204
problems, sexual dysfunction and, 485–487
satisfaction in, 240–243
Religion
anal intercourse and, 277
masturbation and, 261*t*
number of sex partners and, 23, 24*t*
sexual decision making and, 6
Remarriage, 459–460
Repression, 18
Reproduction, potential, pubertal markers for, 418
Reproductive system, male, 106
Research
correlation, 51–53
current, 20
ethics in, 55–57
evidence, considering alternative interpretations, 10
experimental method, 53–55
informed consent for, 55
observation methods, 41–51
sampling methods, 40–41
Research questions
formulation of, 37
framing, hypothesis for, 37

Resolution phase, 153–154
Respiratory distress syndrome, 353
Retarded ejaculation, 478–479
Retinal blastoma, 345*t*
Retrograde ejaculation, 126–127
Reverse transcriptase, 529
Rh incompatibility, 341
Rhythm methods, 383, 390*t*
Rites of passage, 296
Roe v. Wade, 366, 394, 396, 397
Romantic love
contemporary models of, 213–219, 218*t*
cultural aspects of, 210–212
vs. infatuation, 212–213
Romantic relationships
ABCDE model of, 225–226
starting
exchanging personal information, 228
opening lines for, 227–228
self-disclosure and, 228–229
small talk and, 226–227
Root, 107
"Rophies" (Rohypnol), 591
Roth v. United States, 636
RU-486 (mifepristone), 366, 399–400
Rubbers. *See* Condoms
Rubella (German measles), 338
Rush, Benjamin, 258

S

Sacral erection center, 123
Sacrum, 123
Sadism, 15
Sadomasochism (S&M), 565–566, 613
Sadomasochists, 566
Safes. *See* Condoms
Saliva, HIV/AIDS transmission risk from, 533
Sambian culture, 296
Same gender marriage (same-sex marriage), 446–447
Same-sex marriage, 297–300, 298*t*, 445–447
Same-sex sexual behavior
during adolescence, 427
during preadolescence, 415
Samples, 39–41
Sampling methods, 40–41
Sanger, Margaret, 364, 365
Scabies (*Sarcoptes scabiei*), 516*t*, 541–542
Scent of a Woman, 303
Schemas, 190
School, pregnancy prevention programs, 430–431
Science of human sexuality, goals of, 38–39
Sciences, women college graduates, 182*t*
Scientific method, 37–38
Scores, 627–628
Scrotum, 109
Secondary amenorrhea, 95
Secondary dysmenorrhea, 95
Secondary erogenous zones, 136–137
Secondary sex characteristics, 78, 110, 144, 418
Sedatives, usage during pregnancy, 342
Selection factor, 54
Selective serotonin reuptake inhibitors (SSRIs), 94, 482–484
Self-assessments, scoring keys for, 647–649
Self-disclosure, 228–229
in cyberspace, 229
intimacy and, 246
sex differences in, 229
Self-esteem
females and, 182–183
intimacy and, 231–232
Self-exploration, 500

Self-introductions, meeting people through, 225, 225*f*
Selfless love (agape), 214
Self-massage, 500
Semen, 106, 115, 152
Seminal vesicles, 114
Seminiferous tubules, 111
Sensate focus exercises, 488
Sensory disabilities, sex and, 465–466
Separation, marital, 459
Septate hymen, 68*f*
Serial monogamy, 438
Seronegative, 532
Seropositive, 532
Sex
as commerce, 618
disability and, 463–467
in later years, physical changes and, 460–463, 461*t*
during menstruation, 90
nonprocreative, 258
Sex and Temperament in Three Primitive Societies (Mead), 25
Sex assignment, 168
Sex chromosomes. *See also* X chromosomes; Y chromosomes
abnormalities of, 167–168
definition of, 164
Sex differences
in attraction, attitude similarity and, 207
in cognitive abilities, 180–182, 181*f*
in mate preferences, 203, 204, 205*t*
in personality, 182–183
in prenatal brain organization, 187
in social behavior, 183
Sex drive
age and, 460
male, 146
sexual fantasies and, 279
Sex education
during preadolescence, 415–417, 417*t*, 418*t*
in United States *vs.* other countries, 420
Sex flush, 149
Sex hormones. *See also specific hormones*
female sexual behavior, 147–148
male sexual behavior and, 146–147
organizing and activating effects on behavior, 144–145
prenatal, sexual differentiation and, 145
sexual behavior and, 144–148
Sex offenders, pornography and, 642
Sex organs
female
external, 63–70, 63*f*, 64*f*, 67*f*–69*f*
internal, 70–77
male
external, 105–109, 106*f*–108*f*
internal, 110–115, 110*f*, 113*f*, 114*f*
terminology, 4
Sex partners, number of
age and, 23, 24*t*
ethnicity and, 23, 24*t*
level of education and, 23
marital status and, 23
religion and, 23
sex differences in, 22, 23
Sex play, with peers/siblings, 597–598
Sex reassignment surgery, 171, 172–173
Sex research. *See* Research
Sex skin, 150
Sex slavery, in Pakistan, 624–625
Sex therapy, 486–487
integration with psychotherapy, 489
purpose of, 488
Sex trafficking, 624–625

Sickle-cell anemia, 344–345, 345*t*
Side-entry position, for sexual intercourse, 275, 275*f*
SIDS (sudden infant death syndrome), 343
Sildenafil. *See* Viagra
Simplirix, 537
Singlehood, 436–440
    problems with, 438
    reasons for, 436–437, 438*t*
Situational ethics, sexual decision making and, 7, 9*t*
"69" position, 271, 272*f*
Skene's glands, 153
Skepticism, critical thinking and, 9
Skin sensation, sexual arousal and, 135
Skinner, B.F., 29
Sleeping arrangements, for children, 411
S&M (sadomasochism), 565–566, 613
S&M subculture, 572
Small talk, for relationship building, 226–227
Smegma, 107
Smoking, chronic, sex drive and, 140
"Snappers" (amyl nitrate), 139
Snuff films, 634
Soap, sexual arousal and, 133–134
Social attitudes, toward rape, 588–590
Social behavior, sex differences in, 183
Social desirability, 47
Social exchange theory, 225, 235
The Social Organization of Sexuality: Sexual Practices in the United States (Gagnon, Michael and Michaels), 43
Social skills training, for paraphilias, 573, 574
Social-cognitive theory, 30, 188–190
Social-desirability scale, 48
Socialization, 188
Sociological perspective, of human sexuality, 25
Sociological perspectives, paraphilias, 571–572
Sodomy, 277–278, 294, 300
"Soft chancre," 521
Solitude, *vs.* loneliness, 238
Sox9 gene, 166
"Spanish fly," 138
Spatial abilities, sex differences in, 180–181, 181*f*
Spectator role, 478
Speculum pelvic examination, 76–77, 77*f*
"Speed" (amphetamines), 141–142
Speed dating, 226–227
Sperm
    abnormalities, 326
    anal intercourse and, 278
    artificial insemination of, 327
    definition of, 110
    fertilization, 323, 323*f*
    intracytoplasmic injection of, 329
    production, problems with, 326
    receptors on, 111–112
Sperm count, low, 326–327
Spermatic cord, 109
Spermatids, 111
Spermatocytes, 111
Spermatozoa. *See also* Sperm
    definition of, 111
    passage, 114*f*
Spermicides, 376–378, 377*f*, 390*t*
Spinal block, 350
Spinal cord injuries, sex and, 464–465
Spinal reflexes, male sexual response and, 122–123, 123*f*
Spontaneous abortion, 323
SRY gene, 166
SSRIs (selective serotonin reuptake inhibitors), 94, 482–484

Stalemates, handling, 251
Stalking, 236
Stanley v. Georgia, 636
Staphylococcus aureus, 89
Statutory rape, 582
Stenberg v. Carhart, 401
Stepbrother, attraction to, 207
Stepfamilies, 459–460
Stepsister, attraction to, 207
Stereotypes
    definition of, 177
    gender role, 178*t*
    sexual behavor and, 300–301
Sterilization
    definition of, 385–386
    failure rates, 390*t*
    female, 387–388, 388*f*
    male, 386–387, 386*f*
Sternberg's triangular theory of love, 215–219, 215*f*, 216*f*, 218*t*
    compatibility and, 215–216, 216*f*
    self-assessment, 217
    type of love in, 218*t*
Stillbirth, 339, 353–354
Stimulants, 141–142
Stone Age, sexuality in, 11
Stonewalling, 242, 244
"Stop-start" method, for treating premature ejaculation, 502
Storge, 209
Stranger rape, 584, 584*f*
Stratified random sample, 40
Streetwalkers, 619–621
Stress, loneliness and, 239
Strip parlors, 623
Sudden infant death syndrome (SIDS), 343
Suicidality, homosexuals and, 307
Surface contact, 229
Surfactant, 353
Surgical menopause, 147–148
Surrogate mother, 329
Surucu, Hatun, 26–27
Survey, National Survey of Adolescents and Young Adults, 44–45
Surveys, 41–47
    advantages of, 41–42
    Kinsey Reports, 42–43
    limitations of, 46–47
    magazine, 45
    National Health and Social Life Survey, 43–44
    National Survey on Family Growth, 44
    Playboy Foundation survey, 45
    of specific populations, 45–46
Sweat, HIV/AIDS transmission risk from, 533
Swinging lifestyle, 315
Swinging or mate swapping, 453
Sympathetic nervous system, 124
Syphilis
    congenital, 519
    course of illness, 519–520
    diagnosis of, 339, 513*t*, 520
    historical aspects of, 517–518
    origins of, 518
    stillbirth and, 339
    symptoms of, 513*t*, 519–520, 519*f*
    transmission of, 513*t*, 518–519
    treatment of, 513*t*, 520
    Treponema pallidum, 518, 518*f*
    Tuskegee Syphilis Study, 56–57
Systematic desensitization, of paraphilias, 573–574

T

T4 cells, 529
Tadalafil (Cialis), 139, 493*t*, 494, 496

"Take Back the Night," 586
"Talking dirty," 564
Tamoxifen, 82
Tampons, 89, 90
Tantric sex, 265
Taoism, sexuality in, 16–17
Tay-Sachs disease, 344, 345*t*, 346
Teachers, female, sexual abuse of boys, 600–601
Tears, HIV/AIDS transmission risk from, 533
The Technology of Orgasm: "Hysteria," the Vibrator, and Women's Sexual Satisfaction, 256
Teen sex, worldwide, 424
Teenage pregnancy, 427, 429–430, 429*f*
Telephone scatophilia, 560–561
Teratogens, 338
Testes (testicles)
    cancer of, 116–117
    definition of, 83
    descent of, 167
    growth during puberty, 420
    self-examination, 117, 117*f*
Testosterone
    activating effects, 144–145
    as aphrodisiac, 139
    definition of, 83
    female sex drive and, 147
    for female sexual dysfunction, 497*t*
    for hypoactive sexual desire, 489
    male sexual behavior and, 146
    prenatal sexual differentiation and, 167–168
    during puberty, 420
    reduction, low sexual desire and, 482
    replacement therapy, 112
    sexual differentiation and, 166
    sexual orientation and, 302
    testicular control and, 110–111, 110*f*
    for women, 500
"Test-tube baby," 328
Tetracycline, 341
Theories, purpose of, 38
Third gender (third sex), 175–177
Thrush, 514*t*
Title VII, 610
Tofranil (imipramine), 140
Tottentot women, in Africa, 65
Touch, sexual arousal and, 135
Toucherism, 566–567
Touching, of erogenous zones, 266–268
Toxemia, 340
Toxic shock syndrome (TSS), 89, 375
Toys, gender identity and, 178
Tranquilizers
    for childbirth, 350
    sex drive and, 140
    usage during pregnancy, 342
Transgenderism, 170–176
    relationship satisfaction and, 241–242
Transition, 348
Transsexualism, 170–176
    personal experience, 162–163
    prenatal sexual differentiation and, 145
Transverse position, 351
Transvestic fetishism, 554
Transvestism, 556–557
Treatment, definition of, 53
Treponema pallidum, 513*t*, 520
Triangular theory of love, 230
Trichomoniasis, 514*t*, 523, 524
Trobrianders, sexuality and, 25
Trophoblast, 335
Trust, in intimate relationships, 231
TSS (toxic shock syndrome), 89, 375
Tubal pregnancies, 340
Tubal sterilization (tubal ligation), 387

Photo Credits

p. 317, © Courtesy NJ Governor Office/ZUMA/CORBIS. **Chapter 11:** p. 320, 321, © Mango Productions/CORBIS; p. 322, © ThinkStock LLC/Index Stock Imagery; p. 323, © Francis Leroy/Photo Researchers, Inc.; p. 325, Courtesy of Dr. Denny Sakkas and the Yale Fertility Center; p. 329, © M. Kulyk/Photo Researchers, Inc.; p. 330 top, © Claude Edelmann/Photo Researchers, Inc.; p. 330 center and bottom, © Petit Format/Photo Researchers, Inc.; p. 343 top, © David H. Wells/CORBIS; p. 343 bottom, © plainpicture GmbH & Co. KG/Alamy; p. 348, © SIU/Photo Researchers, Inc.; p. 352, © Susan Leavines/ Photo Researchers, Inc.; p. 354 top, © 2007 D. G. Arnold/Custom Medical Stock Photo, All rights reserved; p. 354 bottom, © Sean Sprague/The Image Works; p. 357, © Mary Kate Denny/PhotoEdit. **Chapter 12:** p. 362, 363, Neil Setchfield © Rough Guides/Dorling Kindersley; p. 364, © AP Images; p. 372, © UPI/Landov; p. 382, © ThinkStock LLC/Index Stock Imagery; p. 389, © Joel Gordon; p. 394, © Greg Smith/CORBIS; p. 396 both, © AP Images. **Chapter 13:** p. 406, 407, © age fotostock/SuperStock; p. *408*, © Robert Brenner/ PhotoEdit; p. 410, © Ericka McConnell/Getty Images; p. 416, © Frank Siteman/PhotoEdit; p. 417, © Bob Daemmrich/The Image Works; p. 421, © Little Blue Wolf Productions/ CORBIS; p. 428, © Image100/CORBIS; p. 430, © David Young-Wolff/PhotoEdit. **Chapter 14:** p. 434, 435, © Photodisc/Getty Images; p. 436, Ron Batzdorff/© HBO/ Courtesy Everett Collection; p. 437, © Frank Herholdt/Getty Images; p. 440, © Frank Siteman/Getty Images; p. 445, © AP Images/Kathy Willens; p. 446, © Rick Friedman/ CORBIS; p. 457, © Bob Daemmrich/The Image Works; p. 461, © Laurence Monneret/Getty Images; p. 464, © Esbin-Anderson/The Image Works. **Chapter 15:** p. 470, 471, © Noel Hendrickson/Getty Images; p. 472, © Ryan McVay/Getty Images; p. 476, © Michael Newman/PhotoEdit; p. 486, © BananaStock/Jupiter Images; p. 495, © 2007 G. Thomas Bishop/Custom Medical Stock Photo, All rights reserved; p. 496, © Phanie/Photo Researchers, Inc.; p. 497, Courtesy of NuGyn Inc. **Chapter 16:** p. 506, 507, © Marcus Gyger/Reuters/CORBIS; p. 508, © Reed Kaestner/CORBIS; p. 509, © David Young-Wolff/ PhotoEdit; p. 517, © and Courtesy of Dr. Nicholas J. Fiumara; p. 518, © Dr. David Chase/ Phototake—All rights reserved; p. 519, © 2007 Custom Medical Stock Photo, All rights reserved; p. 524, © 2007 NMSB/Custom Medical Stock Photo, All rights reserved; p. 529, © Bill Longcore/Photo Researchers, Inc.; p. 531, © C. Lyttle/zefa/CORBIS; p. 534, © AP Images/Haraz N. Ghanbari; p. 537, © Dr. John Wilson/Photo Researchers, Inc.; p. 539, © Biophoto Associates/Photo Researchers, Inc.; p. 541, © E. Gray/SPL/Photo Researchers, Inc.; p. 543, © Richard Lord/PhotoEdit. **Chapter 17:** p. 550, 551, © Walter Lockwood/ CORBIS; p. 552, © Digital Vision/Getty Images; p. 555, © Templer/zefa/CORBIS; p. 556, © Luis Enrique Ascui/Reuters/Landov; p. 558, © Jutta Klee/CORBIS; p. 563, Courtesy of Upskirtsniper.com; p. 566, © Claire Artman/zefa/CORBIS; p. 568, © Brigitte Stelzer; p. 571, © Bill Aron/PhotoEdit; p. 573, © Bob Daemmrich/The Image Works. **Chapter 18:** p. 578, 579, © image100/CORIBS; p. 580, © AP Images/Lauren Victoria Burke; p. 581 left, © Franz Chavaroche/MAXPPP/Landov; p. 581 right, © Tim Boyles/Getty Images; p. 587, © Sean Cayton/The Image Works; p. 598, Courtesy of LaPorte County Child Abuse Center; p. 599, © Mario Anzuoni/Reuters/Landov; p. 601, © AP Images/Mark Humphrey; p. 602, © Richard Patterson/Getty Images. **Chapter 19:** p. 616, 617, © Randy Faris/CORBIS; p. 618, © CORBIS; p. 621, © AP Images/Marco Ugarte; p. 631, © John Van Hasselt/CORBIS; p. 632, © Floris Leeuwenberg/The Cover Story/CORBIS; p. 633, *Bad Boy,* 1981, oil on canvas, 66 x 96 inches 1981, © Eric Fischl; p. 635, © David Westing/Getty Images.